SMITH AND THOMAS
A CASEBOOK ON CONTRACT

AUSTRALIA
LBC Information Services
Sydney

CANADA and USA
Carswell
Toronto : Ontario

NEW ZEALAND
Brooker's
Auckland

SINGAPORE AND MALAYSIA
Thomson Information (S.E. Asia)
Singapore

SMITH AND THOMAS

A CASEBOOK ON

CONTRACT

TENTH EDITION

By

SIR JOHN SMITH, C.B.E., Q.C., LL.D., F.B.A.
Honorary Bencher of Lincoln's Inn;
Honorary fellow of Downing College, Cambridge;
Emeritus Professor of Law,
University of Nottingham

LONDON
SWEET & MAXWELL
1996

First Edition 1957
Second Impression 1959
Second Edition 1961
Second Impression 1963
Third Edition 1966
Fourth Edition 1969
Fifth Edition 1973
Second Impression 1974
Third Impression 1976
Sixth Edition 1977
Second Impression 1980
Seventh Edition 1982
Eighth Edition 1987
Second Impression 1990
International Student Edition 1990
Third Impression 1991
Ninth Edition 1992
International Student Edition 1992
Second Impression 1994
Tenth Edition 1996

Published in 1996 by
Sweet & Maxwell Limited of
100 Avenue Road, Swiss Cottage, London NW3 3PF
Phototypeset by LBJ Enterprises Ltd., of Aldermaston and Chilcompton
Printed in England by Clays Ltd., St. Ives plc

A CIP catalogue for this book is available from the British Library

ISBN 0 421 53950 X

PREFACE

The most important statutory development affecting the law of contract since the last edition has been the enactment of the Unfair Terms in Consumer Contract Regulations 1994, implementing a directive of the Council of the European Communities. It is not a happy example of the adoption of Community law, being enacted on top of the Unfair Contract Terms Act with no attempt at rationalisation so that the two enactments overlap in a most untidy way. In the chapter on exemption clauses I have attempted to explain the relationship between the two enactments, both of which are reproduced in the Appendix; and attention is drawn to them at various points in the book. Another significant statutory development is the amendment by the Sale and Supply of Goods Act 1994 of certain sections of the Sale of Goods Act 1979, particularly those relating to implied terms, which we have always used as illustrations of this branch of the law.

Contract is, however, essentially a case-law subject and *Smith and Thomas* is essentially a casebook. Since the last edition there has been no shortage of thoughtful and illuminating judgments providing excellent material for the study of the principles of contract law. Their virtues do not always include brevity and, while appreciating that judgments are not written for the benefit of authors of casebooks, one could wish that more judges, in the interests of both clarity and economy, might cultivate that conciseness which characterised the decisions of the great judges of the nineteenth century and, recently, of Lord Denning. I have tried to find room for what I judged to be the most instructive and, if possible, provocative, passages of all the more important recent cases.

More emphasis is given in this edition to the relationship between contract and tort, particularly in the introduction and through the inclusion of *Barclays Bank plc v. Fairclough Building Ltd* stating the principles governing the application of the Contributory Negligence Act 1945. New cases provoke questions as to some fundamental matters, notably the status of *Foakes v. Beer*, following the distinguishing of *Williams v. Roffey Bros Ltd* by *Re Selectmove*, and of *Solle v. Butcher* in the light of *William Sindall plc v. Cambridgeshire County Council*. Privity of contract continues to stimulate lively debate and *The Pioneer Container* has led me to reinstate (with much pleasure) the splendid dissenting judgment of Lord Denning in *Scruttons Ltd v. Midland Silicones Ltd*. Damages is another area with several interesting new cases, particularly *Ruxley Electronics and Construction Ltd v. Forsyth*. For some time I had been looking for a good, modern case on specific performance and, at the very last minute, I was fortunate to be able to include *Co-operative Insurance Society Ltd v. Argyll Stores (Holdings Ltd)* which, as it includes a powerful dissent, has the advantage of presenting to the reader the conflicting opinions to consider and discuss.

Once again I am greatly indebted to my colleague Professor Michael Bridge and to Professor W. V. Horton Rogers who have made many valuable suggestions. My thanks are also due, for the tenth time to the publishers who, forty years ago through the initiative of Peter Allsop, took the book on at a time when it was regarded by some as an eccentric innovation and seemed unlikely to progress beyond the cyclostyled edition on the desks of students at the University of Nottingham.

John Smith

CONTENTS

III   OBLIGATIONS ARISING FROM THE CONTRACT AND ITS FORMATION

ACKNOWLEDGMENTS

The Publishers and Authors wish to thank the following bodies for permission to reprint material from the books and periodicals indicated:

Atiyah, P.S., "Consideration in Contract" (2nd ed., 1971; 4th ed., 1989): Extracts reprinted with permission of Oxford University Press, Walton. Street, Oxford OX2 6DP.

Butterworth Law Publishers Ltd: *The All England Law Reports; The Law Journal Reports; The Law Times Reports;* Cheshire Fifoot and Furmston, *The Law of Contract* (12th ed.), pp. 107–108.

Butterworth (Telepublishing) Ltd: Lexis report of *Controvincial Estates plc v. Merchant Investors Assurance Company Ltd.*

Canada Law Book Inc.: *Tilden Rent-a-Car v. Clendenning* (1978) D.L.R. (3d) 400: Reproduced with the permission of Canada Law Book Inc., 240 Edward Street, Aurora, Ontario L4G 3S9.

The Controller of Her Majesty's Stationery Office: Extracts from Law Revision Committee, Sixth Interim Report, Law Reform Committee, Twelfth Report, Law Commission Working Papers Nos. 61, 65 and 73.

Cornell University: Professor Merton L. Ferson and Fred B. Rothman & Co., Littleton, Colorado. Ferson, "The Formation of Simple Contracts," 9 *Cornell Law Review 402.* (Copyright 1924 by Cornell University. All rights reserved.)

The Incorporated Council of Law Reporting for England and Wales: *The Law Reports; The Weekly Law Reports.*

Lawyers Cooperative Publishing: *Shuey v. United States* 23 L.Ed. 697.

LBC Information Services, Australia: *Commonwealth Law Reports* (40 C.L.R. 227; 84 C.L.R. 377; 119 C.L.R. 460).

LLP Limited: *Lloyd's Law Reports.*

The Modern Law Review (4 M.L.R. 247 and 254; 17 M.L.R. 154).

Sweet & Maxwell Ltd: *The Law Quarterly Review* (20 L.Q.R. 4; 38 L.Q.R. 201; 54 L.Q.R. 233; 55 L.Q.R. 416; 55 L.Q.R. 499; 61 L.Q.R. 401; 102 L.Q.R. 368); *Benjamin on Sale* (8th ed., 1950), pp. 622–623.

Times Newspapers Ltd: (c) *The Times Law Reports.* Extract from report of *King's Norton Metal Co. Ltd v. Edridge, Merret & Co. Ltd* (1897) 14 T.L.R. 98., and *Hoenig v. Isaacs* (1952).

The Yale Law Journal Company: reprinted by permission of the Yale Law Journal Company and Fred B. Rothman & Company from *The Yale Law Journal* Vol. 26, pp. 136–142; Vol. 27, pp. 362, 376.

TABLE OF CASES

TABLE OF STATUTES

PART I

THE FORMATION OF A CONTRACT

CHAPTER 1

INTRODUCTION

Contract and tort. This book is about contractual obligations. The distinguishing feature of these obligations is that they are not imposed by the law but voluntarily undertaken by the contracting parties. The name of the old common law form of action for breach of contract was *Assumpsit*—"he undertook." The plaintiff alleged that the defendant undertook to do something and did not do it or did it badly; or that he undertook that something was so (*e.g.* the horse was sound) and it was not so. The law of tort, on the other hand, imposes duties on us whether we like it or not. If I drive my car on the road I owe an inescapable duty of care to all other road users and if, in breach of that duty, I negligently cause injury to one of them, he may recover damages for the tort of negligence. But the only reason why I have an obligation to go to work in the morning is that I have given an undertaking to my employer to do so; and his undertaking to pay me is the only reason why I am entitled to my salary at the end of the month.

Contractual and tortious duties may exist concurrently. A carrier of passengers in a vehicle owes them the same duty of care which he owes to other road users. If they are fare-paying passengers, it will usually be a term of the contract that he will exercise reasonable care. If the carrier negligently causes injury to the fare payers, they may recover damages for breach of contract. Non-contracting passengers, riding free, can sue in tort. The content of the duty to take care is the same. The question sometimes arises whether a contracting party can sue in tort, relying on the duty imposed by the general law. At one time, it was thought that the existence of the contractual duty excluded the general duty and the right to sue in tort. If so, in our example the fare payer could sue only in contract. The matter has arisen particularly in the context of negligent advice (see below, p. 340) and was considered by the House of Lords in *Henderson v. Merrett Syndicates* [1994] 3 All E. R. 506. The question was whether Lloyd's "names" could sue their agent for negligence in exercising reasonable care. This was important because the limitation period (the period within which an action must be brought) was more favourable to the names in tort than in contract.

LORD GOFF OF CHIEVELEY, responding to an argument that no term should be implied in a contract if it would be co-extensive with a duty in tort: It is however my understanding that by the law in this country contracts for services do contain an implied promise to exercise reasonable care (and skill) in the performance of the relevant services; indeed, as Mr Weir has pointed out (XI Int Enc Comp Law ch 12, para 67), in the nineteenth century the field of concurrent liabilities was expanded "since it was impossible for the judges to deny that contracts contained an implied promise to take reasonable care, at the least, not to injure the other party". My own belief is that, in the present context, the common law is not antipathetic to concurrent liability, and that there is no sound basis for a rule which automatically restricts the claimant to either a tortious or a contractual remedy. The result may be untidy; but, given that the tortious duty is imposed by the general law, and the contractual duty is attributable to the will of the parties, I do not find it objectionable that the claimant may be entitled to take advantage of the remedy which is most advantageous to him, subject only to ascertaining whether the tortious duty is so inconsistent with the applicable contract that, in accordance with ordinary principle, the parties must be taken to have agreed that the tortious remedy is to be limited or excluded. . . .

. . . In the present case liability can, and in my opinion should, be founded squarely on the principle established in *Hedley Byrne* itself, (see below, p. 340) from which it follows that an assumption of responsibility coupled with the concomitant reliance may give rise to a tortious duty of care irrespective of whether there is a contractual relationship between the parties, and in consequence, unless his contract precludes him from doing so, the plaintiff, who has available to him concurrent remedies in contract and tort, may choose that remedy which appears to him to be the most advantageous.

In the above case (and in *Barclays Bank plc. v. Fairclough Building Ltd,* below, p. 615) the contractual and tortious duties to take care were assumed to be co-extensive; but the duty in tort imposed by *Hedley Byrne* on a party to a contract may sometimes be wider than his contractual obligation: *Holt v. Payne Skillington (a Firm)*, The Times, December 22, 1995, C.A. In such a case the other contracting party might succeed in tort when he would fail in contract.

Strict contractual duties. So far we have been discussing duties to take reasonable care—duties not to behave negligently. This is usually the limit of tortious liability, but contractual duties are often stricter. If the defendant has undertaken that something is so, and it is not so, he is in breach of contract, however much care he may have taken to be sure that it is so, or to make it so. A restaurateur impliedly contracts that the food he supplies is reasonably fit for eating. (See below, p. 401) If it is not fit and poisons the buyer he can recover damages from the restaurateur for breach of contract. But a guest, who is not a party to the contract of sale of the food, has no claim against the restaurateur who has not been negligent. He may perhaps have a claim in tort against the restaurateur's supplier if the latter has been negligent in supplying unfit food. See the exploding bottle cases, summarised below, p. 19.

Promises and undertakings. The law of contract is that branch of the law which determines whether a promise is binding and, if it is, what are the consequences of breaking it. A contract is, in Sir Frederick Pollock's words, "a promise or set of promises which the law will enforce." A contractual obligation is a binding promise. So the first essential of a contract is that there should be a promise or promises.

Deeds. It would be impracticable to enforce all promises and the law does not seek to do so. A promise is binding in law only if it is made in "a deed" or is given "for consideration." A person may make any lawful promise binding in law by executing a deed. At common law a deed was a document which was "signed sealed and delivered" but, under the Law of Property (Miscellaneous Provisions) Act 1989, s.1, which came into force on September 27, 1989, the execution of a deed by an individual, as distinct from a corporation, no longer requires a seal. It is sufficient that—

  (i) it makes it clear on its face that it is intended to be a deed (by describing itself as a deed or expressing itself to be executed and signed as a deed or otherwise);
 (ii) it is signed (and "signed" includes making one's mark) either (a) by the maker in the presence of a witness who attests the signature or (b) at the maker's direction and in his presence and the presence of two witnesses who each attest the signature; and

(iii) it is "delivered" as a deed by him or his agent. "Delivery" includes any act done by the maker which indicates that he considers the deed to be binding.

Consideration. The vast majority of contracts are not made by deed. A promise which is not contained in a deed is binding only if it is given "for consideration." This means that the promisor must have asked for and received something in return for his promise. The law does not enforce a purely gratuitous promise unless it is made in a deed. A promise not in a deed is binding only if the promisee has "bought" it by paying the "price"—the consideration—requested by the promisor. The consideration may be the payment of money or (with a few exceptions) it may be any other lawful act—whatever the promisor has required as the price for his promise. If the promisor has asked for nothing in return, then he is promising to make a gift which is not binding, and the promisee cannot make it binding by promising or giving something in return.

Bilateral and Unilateral Contracts. Sometimes the promisor wants a promise from the other party. A offers B a job at a salary of £10,000 a year to commence on January 1 next year. When B accepts there is a binding exchange of promises. A has received consideration in the shape of B's promise to do the work specified in the job description. B has received consideration in the shape of A's promise to pay his salary and fulfil the other obligations of an employer. This is called a "bilateral" contract because there are two promisors and two promisees.

On other occasions the promisor asks not for a promise but for an act in return for his promise. The typical example is that of an offer of a reward—£50 to anyone who returns my lost dog. A, the offeror, is not asking for promises but for action. If B finds the dog and returns it, the promise is binding. B has supplied the consideration by returning the dog—that act was the price of the promise. This is called a "unilateral" contract because, though there are two parties, only one has made a promise. In the case of the bilateral contract we say that the consideration on both sides is "executory" because it is to be performed in the future. In the case of the unilateral contract we say that the consideration supplied by B is "executed"—it is already performed at the moment the contract to pay the reward is made—that is, when the dog is returned.

Oral and written contracts. Newcomers to the law of contract are often surprised to learn that the general rule is that contracts, however important, may be made without any writing. A contract for the sale of diamonds worth a million pounds may be made by word of mouth or by other conduct signifying an intention to contract. There are exceptions to the general rule and it is desirable for the reader of a casebook to be aware of their existence (or former existence) at the outset. The exceptions are of two types. The first allows the contract to be made orally or by conduct but provides that it cannot be enforced in the courts unless there is written evidence of it. The second requires the contract to be made in writing.

Contracts unenforceable for lack of writing. This once large topic requiring a separate chapter may now be adequately dealt with in this introduction. The origin of the unenforceable contract is the Statute of Frauds 1677, ss.4 and 17. The purpose of the statute was to prevent fraud by requiring written evidence of certain types of promise which were then considered to be particularly vulnerable to dishonest claims. Throughout its history the statute was heavily criticised both for its drafting and its substance. It produced a large amount of case law. Some thought that it assisted rather than prevented fraud but it was not until 1954 that the Law Reform (Enforcement of Contracts) Act repealed important parts of it. From 1677 to 1954 the statute applied to—

(a) A promise by an executor or administrator of a deceased person's estate to pay damages out of his own property.

(b) A promise made in consideration of marriage. This referred not to the mutual promises of the engaged couple (which constituted an enforceable contract until the Law Reform (Miscellaneous Provisions) Act 1970, s.1(1) but to marriage settlements and ancillary agreements.

(c) A promise not be performed within one year of its making.

(d) A contract for the sale of any goods of the value of £10 or upwards. This provision had been re-enacted in the Sale of Goods Act 1893, s.4.

For contracts made after 1954 these provisions are of no significance but the student needs to be aware of them for the proper understanding of cases such as *Warlow v. Harrison* below, p. 21; *Felthouse v. Bindley*, below, p. 48 *Shadwell v. Shadwell*, below, p. 225; and *Jorden v. Money*, below, p. 252 The 1954 Act left unrepealed the requirement of written evidence in respect of two classes of contract. The most important was "Any contract for the sale or other disposition of land or an interest in land."

These words of section 40 of the Law of Property Act 1925 replaced section 4 of the 1677 Act. They too have now been repealed by the Law of Property (Miscellaneous Provisions) Act 1989 which replaced the requirement of written evidence with a requirement, considered below, that the contract be in writing.

Guarantees. The only survivor of the 1677 Act is "a special promise to answer for the debt, default or miscarriage of another person."

The antique language of section 4 of the 1677 Act is still in force but it has been heavily overlaid with case law which has restricted its operation within narrow limits. It applies only where three persons, A, B and C, are involved. A is, or may become, liable in contract or tort to B. C promises B for consideration supplied by B that, if A does not discharge his liability, he, C, will do so. C "guarantees" the performance of A's obligation. (A good example of such a guarantee may be seen in *Bradbury v. Morgan* below, p. 84.) C's promise is not enforceable unless evidenced in writing. But a promise made by C to A, the person primarily answerable for the "debt, default or miscarriage," is not within the statute and is enforceable (if A has given consideration to C) without evidence in writing. Another restriction is that the statute does not apply where C promises to meet A's liability in any event, that is, whether A fails to do so or not. Such an unconditional promise is called "an indemnity" as distinct from a guarantee and does not require written evidence. There are other limitations which need not be considered here.

Contracts required to be in writing. Much the most important, and the only contract in this class which need be considered here, is a contract for the sale or other disposition of an interest in land. Section 2 of the Law of Property (Miscellaneous Provisions) Act 1989 provides:

2.—(1) A contract for the sale or other disposition of an interest in land can only be made in writing and only by incorporating all the terms which the parties have expressly agreed in one document or, where contracts are exchanged, in each.

(2) The terms may be incorporated in a document either by being set out in it or by reference to some other document.

(3) The document incorporating the terms or, where contracts are exchanged, one of the documents incorporating them (but not necessarily the same one) must be signed by or on behalf of each party to the contract.

The section does not apply to contracts made before September 29, 1989. They are still governed by section 40 of the Law of Property Act 1925 and are valid though made orally but can be enforced only if there is written evidence as required by that section (s.2(7)). Section 2 does not apply to three classes of contract referred to in section 2(5), the most important of which for the purposes of this book is "(b) a contract made in the course of public auction." A contract for the sale of land at a public auction need not be in writing and there is no longer even any need for written evidence, as there was until September 27, 1989. A binding contract is concluded as soon as the auctioneer's hammer falls if that is what the parties intend.

Section 1. Promises and Offers

We return to the requirement of a promise. In a famous case, *Harvey v. Facey* [1893] A.C. 552 Harvey sent a telegram to Facey: "Will you sell us Bumper Hall Pen (a property in Jamaica)? Telegraph lowest cash price—answer paid." Facey replied: "Lowest price for Bumper Hall Pen £900" whereupon Harvey telegraphed "We agree to buy Bumper Hall Pen for the sum of £900 asked by you . . ." Facey declined to sell and the Privy Council held that he was not bound. Harvey's first telegram asked two questions and Facey answered only the second. He had made no promise, express or implied, to sell. The decision may be criticised on the ground that, truly, a promise was implicit in Facey's reply—if he was not willing to sell why did he answer the second question and not the first? "Bumper Hall Pen not for sale" would have been the natural reply. Why state a price unless he was willing to sell? It is a question of the interpretation of the telegrams, on which opinions differ.

Harvey v. Facey concerned a contract for the sale of land. In 1893 the telegrams (if they had been interpreted to imply a promise to sell) would have been a sufficient memorandum to satisfy the Statute of Frauds. But, if the facts recurred in England today, a written contract would be required. A valid contract for the sale of land can no longer be made by an exchange of letters, telex or faxed messages. But the great majority of contracts may be so made and *Harvey v. Facey* remains a good (though controversial) authority on the general principles of the formation of contracts. An equally good and uncontroversial authority is *Gibson v. Manchester City Council*.

GIBSON v. MANCHESTER CITY COUNCIL

House of Lords [1979] 1 W.L.R. 294; [1979] 1 All E.R. 972; (1979) 77 L.G.R. 405; [1979] J.P.L. 532

In November 1970 the council sent to council tenants details of a scheme for the sale of council houses, giving favourable terms as to prices and mortgages. G immediately replied. He paid £3 administration fee and forwarded his application on the printed form. The city treasurer replied saying: "*The corporation may be prepared to sell the house to you at the purchase price of £2,725 less 20 per cent. £2,180 (freehold).*" The letter gave details about a mortgage and went on "This letter should not be regarded as a firm offer of a mortgage. *If you would like to make a formal application to buy your council house, please complete the enclosed application form and return it to me as soon as possible.*"

G filled in and returned the form but left the purchase price blank, saying in a covering letter that repairs needed to be done and asking the corporation to lower the price or repair the premises. The corporation replied that they had taken into account the state of the property in fixing the price and they could not undertake to do the repairs. On March 18 G replied: "In view of your remarks I would be obliged if you will carry on with the purchase as per my application already in your possession."

In May Labour took control of the council from the Conservatives and instructed their officers not to sell council houses unless they were legally bound to do so. The council declined to sell to G and 350 other tenants in a similar situation.

The Court of Appeal (Denning M.R. and Ormrod L.J., Geoffrey Lane L.J. dissenting) affirmed the judgment of Judge Bailey ordering the council specifically to perform (see below, p. 570) the contract. The council appealed.

LORD DIPLOCK: Lord Denning M.R. rejected what I have described as the conventional approach of looking to see whether on the true construction of the documents relied on there can be discerned an offer and acceptance. One ought, he said, to "look at the correspondence as a whole and at the conduct of the parties and see therefrom whether the parties have come to an agreement on everything that was material." . . .

My Lords, there may be certain types of contract, though I think they are exceptional, which do not fit easily into the normal analysis of a contract as being constituted by offer and acceptance, but a contract alleged to have been made by an exchange of correspondence between the parties in which the successive communications other than the first are in reply to one another is not one of these. I can see no reason in the instant case for departing from the conventional approach of looking at the handful of documents relied on as constituting the contract sued on and seeing whether on their true construction there is to be found in them a contractual offer by the council to sell the house to Mr Gibson and an acceptance of that offer by Mr Gibson. I venture to think that it was by departing from this conventional approach that the majority of the Court of Appeal was led into error. . . .

My Lords, the words I have italicised, (see italicised words in statement of facts, above, p. 7) seem to me, as they seemed to Geoffrey Lane L.J., to make it quite impossible to construe this letter as a contractual offer capable of being converted into a legally enforceable open contract for the sale of land by Mr Gibson's written acceptance of it. The words "may be prepared to sell" are fatal to this; so is the invitation, not, it is to be noted, to accept the offer, but "to make formal application to buy" on the enclosed application form. It is, to quote Geoffrey Lane L.J., a letter setting out the financial terms on which it may be the council would be prepared to consider a sale and purchase in due course.

My Lords, the application form and letter of March 18, 1971 were relied on by Mr Gibson as an unconditional acceptance of the council's offer to sell the house; but this cannot be so unless there was a contractual offer by the council available for acceptance, and, for the reason already given I am of opinion that there was none. It is unnecessary to consider whether the application form and Mr Gibson's letters of March 5 and 18, 1971 are capable of amounting to a contractual offer by him to purchase the freehold interest in the house at a price of £2,180 on the terms of an open contract, for there is no suggestion that, even if it were, it was ever accepted by the council. Nor would it ever have been even if there had been no change in the political control of the council, as the policy of the council before the change required the incorporation in all agreements for sale of council houses to tenants of the conditions referred by Lord Denning M.R. in his judgment and other conditions inconsistent with an open contract. . . .

LORD EDMUND-DAVIES and LORD RUSSELL made speeches allowing the Appeal and LORDS FRASER and KEITH agreed with LORD DIPLOCK.

Appeal Allowed.

Question

1. Might the result have been different if the city treasurer had written: "The corporation *is* prepared to sell the house to you. . . .?"

2. Lord Denning said that the parties had agreed on everything that was material. But *is* agreeing on the terms necessarily the same as agreeing to be bound by them? Was the Council saying, "*If* we agree to sell you the house, these are the terms on which we will do so"? *Cf. A-G of Hong Kong v. Humphreys Estate*, below, p. 90

SPENCER v. HARDING

Common Pleas (1870) L.R. 5 C.P. 561; 39 L.J.C.P. 332; 23 L.T. 237; 19 W.R. 48

The defendants sent out a circular as follows:

"We are instructed to offer to the wholesale trade for sale by tender the stock-in-trade of Messrs. G. Eilbeck & Co. amounting as per stock-book to £2,503 13s. 1d. and which will be sold at a discount in one lot. Payment to be made in cash. The stock may be viewed on the premises . . . up to Thursday, the 20th instant, on which day, at 12 o'clock, noon precisely, the tenders will be received and opened at our offices. . . ."

The plaintiffs alleged that the circular amounted to an offer and undertaking to sell the stock to the highest bidder for cash; and that they, the plaintiffs, had submitted the highest tender; and the defendants refused to accept it and sell the goods to them.

Demurrer on the ground that the declaration showed no promise to accept the plaintiffs' tender or sell them the goods.

Holl in support of the demurrer: Although the declaration is somewhat ambiguous, it is evidently intended to raise the question whether one who advertises for tenders for the purchase of goods thereby engages to sell them to the highest bidder. The nearest analogous case is that of an advertisement for tenders for building. It has never been held or suggested that the advertiser is bound to accept the lowest tender. Suppose here there had been only one tender, would the defendants have been bound to accept that? The advertisement clearly does not amount to a contract; it only invites offers.

Morgan Lloyd, contra: The words of the circular and the averments in the declaration taken together, disclose a contract on the part of the defendants to sell the goods to whoever should make the highest tender. This is not like the case of tenders for a building. There, the acceptance of the lowest tender is always subject to the architect's judgment as to the character and capacity of the builder. Here, the offer is to sell for cash. The allegation in the count may be sustained either by evidence of a direct promise, or by evidence of the custom of the trade.

The nearest analogy is that of advertisements offering rewards for the discovery and conviction of an offender, of which one of the leading instances is the case of *Williams v. Carwardine* (below, p. 36) where Littledale J. says: "The advertisement amounts to a general promise to give a sum of money to any person who shall give information which might lead to the discovery of the offender."

WILLES J.: I am of opinion that the defendants are entitled to judgment. The action is brought against persons who issued a circular offering a stock for sale by tender, to be sold at a discount in one lot. The plaintiffs sent in a tender which turned out to be the highest, but was not accepted. They now insist that the circular amounts to a contract or promise to sell the goods to the highest bidder, that is, in this case, to the person who should tender for them at the smallest rate of discount; and reliance is placed on the cases as to rewards offered for the discovery of an offender. In those cases, however, there never was any doubt that the advertisement amounted to a promise to pay the money to the person who first gave information. The difficulty suggested was that it was a contract with all the world. But that, of course, was soon overruled. It was an offer to become liable to any person who before the offer should be retracted should happen to be the person to fulfil the contract of which the advertisement was an offer or tender. That is not the sort of difficulty which presents itself here. If the circular had gone on, "and we undertake to sell to the highest bidder," the reward cases would have applied, and there would have been a good contract in respect of the persons. But the question is, whether there is here any offer to enter into a contract at all, or whether the circular amounts to anything more than a mere proclamation that the defendants are ready to chaffer for the sale of the goods, and to receive offers for the purchase of them. In advertisements for tenders for buildings, it is not usual to say that the contract will be given to the lowest bidder, and it is not always that the contract is made with the lowest bidder. Here there is a total absence of any words to intimate that the highest bidder is to be the purchaser. It is a mere attempt to ascertain whether an offer can be obtained within such a margin as the sellers are willing to adopt.

KEATING and MONTAGUE SMITH J.J. concurred.

Judgment for the defendants.

Questions
1. Would a reasonable reader of the circular have supposed that the defendants intended to make any binding promise? Was it reasonable to suppose that the defendants intended to bind themselves to sell to the highest bidder, however low the bid might be?
2. In *Rooke v. Dawson* [1895] 1 Ch. 480 trustees announced an examination for an endowed scholarship. The plaintiff and one other candidate presented themselves for the examination. The plaintiff obtained 570 marks and the other candidate 496 marks.
CHITTY J., following *Spencer v. Harding*, dismissed the plaintiff's action for a declaration that he was entitled to the scholarship: the announcement did not state that the scholarship would be awarded to the candidate who obtained the highest marks.
Was the plaintiff reasonably entitled to believe that the defendants were promising to give the scholarship to that candidate, however low his marks might be?
3. Would the plaintiffs in *Spencer v. Harding* and *Rooke v. Dawson* have had any redress if the goods had been sold to the second highest bidder, or the scholarship given to the second candidate? Would that have been a breach of any promise, express or implied, by the defendants in either case? For example, "*If* we sell [award the scholarship] it will be to the highest bidder [candidate with the highest marks]".

Acceptance of tenders and standing offers. An invitation to tender is an offer if it contains a promise to contract with the highest or, as the case may be, lowest, tenderer. If the invitation contains no promise and is, therefore, not an offer, then the tender is an offer. So it looks as if acceptance of the tender would conclude the contract. But this is not necessarily the case. It depends on the nature of the invitation. X may invite tenders for—

   (a) "50,000 bricks to be supplied between June 1 and December 31, as and when ordered by the Jerrybuilder Company."

X's acceptance of a tender by Y will then conclude a contract for the sale of bricks. Y has promised to supply 50,000 bricks as ordered and X has promised to order them during the specified period. Alternatively, X may invite tenders for—

(b) "Such bricks, not exceeding 50,000, as X may see fit to order between June 1 and December 31."

X's acceptance of a tender by Y wil not conclude a contract of sale. X has not promised to order any bricks and may never do so. Y has made an offer to sell bricks but, as an offer to sell, it has not yet been accepted because there is no promise to buy. X's "acceptance" of the tender signifies only that he is agreeable to Y's price and that, if he orders bricks, he intends to order them from Y at Y's price. If, on June 1, he orders 10,000 bricks his order is an acceptance of Y's offer to sell and will conclude a contract for the sale of 10,000 bricks. If, on July 1, he orders a further 10,000, that will conclude a second contract of sale. This was decided in *Great Northern Railway v. Witham* (1873) L.R. 9 C.P. 16 where the facts (though concerned with railway stores, not bricks) were essentially the same as in example (b). Y's tender is an example of a "standing offer" because it is to stand for a specified period and, as the example shows, is capable of repeated acceptance during that time, giving rise to a series of contracts.

Witham's case left open the question whether Y could have absolved himself from further performance by giving notice during the six months of the standing offer. Generally offers can be revoked before they are accepted. X was not obliged to order any more bricks so why should Y be obliged to keep his offer open? Cf. *Offord v. Davies*, below, p. 78. Should Y, as a reasonable man, be entitled to believe that X's acceptance of his tender included an implied promise: "If I order any bricks, I will order them from you"—so that, if he had ordered bricks from Z, he would have been in breach of contract with Y? If Y had received such an implied promise for his offer to sell, should he be allowed to revoke that offer? Had he received consideration for his promise to supply when called on to do so?

BLACKPOOL AND FYLDE AEROCLUB LTD v. BLACKPOOL BOROUGH COUNCIL

Court of Appeal [1990] 1 W.L.R. 1195; [1990] 3 All E.R. 25

From time to time the council granted a concession to an operator to provide pleasure flights from the airport which the council owned. The plaintiff obtained the concession in 1975, 1978 and 1980. As the last concession was reaching its end, the council invited the club and six other parties to tender. The invitations stated that tenders were to be submitted in the envelope provided, which was not to bear any name or mark to identify the sender and that tenders received after the time specified, 12 noon on March 17, 1983 would not be considered. The club and two other invitees responded. The club's tender was delivered by hand and put in the Town Hall letter box at 11 a.m. on March 17, but the letter box was not cleared by council staff at 12 noon as it should have been. The club's tender was recorded as having been received late and was not considered. The club sued for breach of an alleged warranty that a tender received by the deadline would be considered. The judge awarded damages for breach of contract and negligence. The council appealed.

BINGHAM L.J., having considered the arguments of both sides, continued: A tendering procedure of this kind is, in many respects, heavily weighted in favour of the invitor. He can invite tenders from as many or as few parties as he chooses. He need not tell any of them who else, or how many others, he has invited. The invitee may often, although not here, be put to considerable labour and expense in preparing a tender, ordinarily without recompense if he is unsuccessful. The invitation to tender may itself, in a complex case, although again not here, involve time and expense to prepare, but the invitor does not commit himself to proceed with the project, whatever it is; he need not accept the highest tender; he need to accept any tender; he need not give reasons to justify his acceptance or rejection of any tender received. The risk to which the tenderer is exposed does not end with the risk that his tender may not be the highest (or, as the case may be, lowest). But where, as here, tenders are solicited from selected parties all of them known to the invitor, and where a local authority's invitation prescribes a clear, orderly and familiar procedure (draft contract conditions available for inspection and plainly not open to negotiation, a prescribed common form of tender, the supply of envelopes designed to preserve the absolute anonymity of tenderers and clearly to identify the tender in question and an absolute deadline) the invitee is in my judgment protected at least to this extent: if he submits a conforming tender before the deadline he is entitled, not as a matter of mere expectation but of contractual right, to be sure that his tender will after the deadline be opened and considered in conjunction with all other conforming tenders or at least that his tender will be considered if others are. Had the club, before tendering, inquired of the council whether it could rely on any timely and conforming tender being considered along with others, I feel quite sure that the answer would have been "of course." The law would, I think, be defective if it did not give effect to that.

It is of course true that the invitation to tender does not explicitly state that the council will consider timely and conforming tenders. That is why one is concerned with implication. But the council does not either say that it does not bind itself to do so, and in the context of a reasonable invitee would understand the invitation to be saying, quite clearly, that if he submitted a timely and conforming tender it would be considered, at least if any other such tender were considered.

I readily accept that contracts are not to be lightly implied. Having examined what the parties said and did, the court must be able to conclude with confidence both that the parties intended to create contractual relations and that the agreement was to the effect contended for. It must also, in most cases, be able to answer the question posed by Mustill L.J. in *Hispanica de Petroleos SA v. Vencedora Oceanica Navegacion SA, The Kapetan Markos NL (No. 2)* [1987] 2 Lloyd's Rep. 321 at 331: "What was the mechanism for offer and acceptance?" In all the circumstances of this case (and I say nothing about any other) I have no doubt that the parties did intend to create contractual relations to the limited extent contended for. Since it has never been the law that a person is only entitled to enforce his contractual rights in a reasonable way (*White & Carter (Councils) Ltd v. McGregor* [1962] A.C. 413 at 430 per Lord Reid, below, p. 559), counsel for the club was in my view right to contend for no more than a contractual duty to consider. I think it plain that the council's invitation to tender was, to this limited extent, an offer, and the club's submission of a timely and conforming tender an acceptance. . . .

I accordingly agree with the judge's conclusion on the contractual issue, essentially for the reasons which he more briefly gave.

STOCKER L.J. delivered judgment dismissing the appeal and FARQUHAR-SON L.J. agreed.

Appeal dismissed

Questions
1. Was the club reasonably entitled to suppose that the council was promising: "If you submit a timely tender, we will consider it?"
2. How can damages be assessed for loss of an opportunity to be considered? (The court did not have to discuss that question.) *Cf. Chaplin v. Hicks* [1911] 2 K.B. 786, below, p. 595, (plaintiff, in breach of contract, denied opportunity of taking part in a beauty contest). What of the case where the tenderer has been put to considerable trouble and expense?
3. Would the timely tenderers have had any redress (a) if the concession had not been awarded at all? (b) if it had been awarded to one who submitted a late tender?

HARVELA INVESTMENTS LTD v. ROYAL TRUST CO. OF CANADA LTD

House of Lords [1986] A.C. 207; [1985] 3 W.L.R. 276; [1985] 2 All E.R. 966

The Royal Trust Co., by telex, invited Harvela and the second defendant, Sir Leonard Outerbridge, to make offers by sealed tender for shares in a company and undertook to accept the highest offer. Harvela's offer was $2,175,000 and Sir Leonard's was "$2,100,000 or $101,000 in excess of any other offer . . . expressed as a fixed monetary amount, whichever is higher." The vendors thought they were bound to accept, and so did accept, Sir Leonard's bid.

Harvela obtained an injunction preventing Royal Trust from accepting Sir Leonard's "referential bid" of $2,276,000 and claimed a right to enforce a contract for the sale of the shares to it for $2,175,000. Peter Gibson J., following *Liverpool City Council v. Irwin* (below, p. 394), held that there was an implied term in Royal Trust's invitation excluding referential bids and gave judgment for Harvela. The Court of Appeal allowed Sir Leonard's appeal. Harvela appealed to the House of Lords.

LORD DIPLOCK made a speech allowing the appeal (see below, pp. 15–16).

LORDS FRASER and EDMUND-DAVIES said they agreed with LORDS DIPLOCK and TEMPLEMAN.

LORD BRIDGE OF HARWICH: My Lords, on the main issue I agree that, for all the reasons given in the speeches of my noble and learned friends Lord Diplock and Lord Templeman, Sir Leonard's referential bid was not, on the true construction of the invitation, a valid offer. Without intending to derogate in any way from the cogency of the other grounds for reaching that conclusion, there seems to me to be one that is decisive. The invitation embodied an undertaking not to disclose the details of any offer to any party before the deadline of 3 p.m. on Wednesday, September 16, 1981. Sir Leonard's referential bid could not be quantified without reading into it the amount of Harvela's fixed bid. To do this before the deadline would have been, in my opinion, a breach of the undertaking. To do it after the deadline would have been too late.

LORD TEMPLEMAN: A fixed bidding sale met all the requirements of the vendors deducible from the terms of the invitation. A fixed bidding sale was bound to result in a sale of shares save in the unlikely event of both Harvela and Sir Leonard failing to respond to the invitation. A fixed bidding sale gave an equal opportunity to Harvela and Sir Leonard to acquire the shares. A fixed bidding sale provoked the best price, or at any rate something approximate to the best price, which the purchaser was prepared to pay to secure the shares and to ensure that the rival bidder did not acquire the shares. On the other hand, if the invitation is construed so as to create an auction sale by means of referential bids, the requirements of the vendors deducible from the terms of the invitation could not be met.

First, if referential bids were permissible, there was a danger, far from negligible, that the sale might be abortive and the shares remain unsold. The shares would only be sold if at least one bidder submitted a fixed bid and the other bidder based his referential offer on that fixed bid. In the events which happened, Harvela put forward a fixed bid of $2,175,000 and Sir Leonard made a referential bid of $101,000 more than Harvela's fixed bid, thus enabling Sir Leonard's referential bid to be quantified at $2,276,000. But if Sir Leonard's referential bid had not been expressed to be based on Harvela's fixed bid, or if Harvela had not not made a fixed bid but only a referential bid, then Sir Leonard's bid could not have been quantified. Similarly, if Harvela had made a referential bid not expressed to be tied to Sir Leonard's fixed bid, or if Sir Leonard had not made a fixed bid but only a referential bid, then Harvela's bid could not have been quantified. The sale would have been abortive although both bidders were anxious to purchase and submitted offers.

Secondly, if referential bids were permissible, there was also a possibility, which in fact occurred, that one bidder would never have an opportunity to buy. In the present case Harvela, by putting forward a fixed bid, could never succeed in buying the shares although the invitation had been extended to them. Harvela's only part in the sale was unwittingly to determine the price at which Sir Leonard was entitled and bound to purchase the shares. Harvela could not win and Sir Leonard could not lose. There was nothing in the invitation to warn Harvela that they must submit a referential bid if they wished to make sure of being able to compete with Sir Leonard. There was nothing in the invitation which indicated to Sir Leonard that he was entitled to submit a referential bid. But no one has argued that the invitation did not invite fixed bids; indeed, Sir Leonard submitted a fixed bid, albeit as an unsuccessful alternative to his referential bid.

Thirdly, if referential bids were permissible, the vendors' object of provoking the best price that Harvela and Sir Leonard were each prepared to offer in ignorance of the rival bid was frustrated. Harvela put forward the fixed bid of $2,175,000 which represented the amount which Harvela hoped would exceed Sir Leonard's bid and which, because Harvela were bidding in ignorance of Sir Leonard's bid, must be or approximate to the best price which Harvela were prepared to pay to secure the shares and to ensure that Sir Leonard did not acquire the shares. Sir Leonard did not put forward his best price; Sir Leonard put forward his worst price, $2,100,000, but declared that he would pay $101,000 more than Harvela. Sir Leonard could have achieved the same purpose by offering five dollars or one dollar more than Harvela. If Sir Leonard had appreciated that he was taking part in a fixed bidding sale, then, judging by his minimum fixed bid of $2,100,000 and his unlimited referential bid, he might have been prepared to offer as his best price more than the sum of $2,276,000 which he now claims to be the purchase price of the shares. We shall never know because Sir Leonard did not reveal his best price.

Finally, if referential bids were permissible by implication, without express provision in the invitation for that purpose, and without any indication in the invitation of the nature of the referential bids which would be acceptable, the results could have been bizarre. In the present case, Sir Leonard bid $2,100,000 or $101,000 in excess of Harvela's fixed bid. If Harvela had bid $2,000,000 or one dollar more than Sir Leonard's fixed bid, then Sir Leonard would have become the purchaser with his referential bid of $2,101,000 as against Harvela's referential bid of $2,100,001. But if Harvela had offered $1,900,000 or one dollar more than Sir Leonard's fixed bid, then Harvela would have been the purchaser at their referential bid of $2,100,001 as against Sir Leonard's referential bid of $2,001,000. Sir Leonard's bid in the second example is the same as his bid in the first example but he loses. Harvela's bid in the second example is lower than Harvela's bid in the first example but Harvela wins. The vendors are worse off by $999 in the second example.

It would have been possible for the vendors to conduct an auction sale through the medium of confidential referential bids but only by making express provision in the invitation for the purpose. It would not have been sufficient for the invitation expressly to authorise "referential bids" without more. For such an authorisation would have rendered the result of the sale uncertain and random in view of the illustrations and examples I have already given. It would have been necessary for the invitation to require each bidder who made a referential bid to specify a maximum sum he was prepared to bid. That requirement would ensure that the sale was not abortive and that both bidders had a genuine chance of winning. A maximum bid requirement would ensure a sale at a price in excess of the maximum bid of the unsuccessful bidder, but it would not necessarily procure a sale at the maximum price of the successful bidder. The sale would in effect be an auction sale and produce the consequences of an auction sale because the vendors would have made express provision for bids to be adjusted and finalised by reference to the maximum bid of the unsuccessful bidder. But without such express provisions the invitation is not consistent with an auction sale.

To constitute a fixed bidding sale all that was necessary was that the vendors should invite confidential offers and should undertake to accept the highest offer. Such was the form of the invitation. It follows that the invitation upon its true construction created a fixed bidding sale and that Sir Leonard was not entitled to submit and the vendors were not entitled to accept a referential bid.

Appeal Allowed.

Note

The vendors thought they were bound to accept (and did accept) Sir Leonard's referential bid. But an offer means what the reasonable offeree would think it means—*i.e.* what, in the last resort, the court thinks the reasonable offeree would think it means—which is not necessarily what the offeror intends it to mean or thinks it means.

What does the judge mean when he says that referential bids are not "permissible?" Are they illegal? What if the invitor says, "referential bids welcome?" May he not make himself liable to an "uncertain and random" result if he chooses?

Analysis of Harvela. It is instructive to analyse the *Harvela* case apart from the complexity caused by the submission of a referential bid. The Royal Trust's telex to

Harvela and Sir Leonard was an offer to each of them which could be accepted only by one—the one who made the higher valid bid. The telex was an offer of a unilateral contract, like an offer to give a prize to the one of two entrants for a race who comes first. The "prize" was a contract for the sale of the shares—the Trust was bound to accept the higher bidder's offer to buy them.

Until that bid was made, no one was under any obligation. The Trust could have withdrawn its offer and the two offerees were under no obligation to bid. While the offer stood, the Trust was, of course, liable to become bound to one of the offerees through the acceptance of its offer, but that is the position of all offerors, so long as their offer remains open to acceptance. When the higher bid was ascertained, the Trust was bound to accept it. At that moment there was just one contract—a contract by the Trust to accept the higher bidder's offer—a unilateral contract. The bidder was free to withdraw his bid until the Trust accepted it, but when they did he became bound to buy the shares. This was the construction favoured by Peter Gibson J. [1984] 2 All E.R. at 78, *e-c*.

The point is made here because the diligent student who reads Lord Diplock's speech in the full report of the case will find that his Lordship considered that the telex messages, when received by Harvela and Sir Leonard, amounted not merely to offers but to unilateral contracts with each of them; and that, on receipt of the bids, that of the higher bidder would be converted into a bilateral contract to buy and to sell whereas that of the unsuccessful bidder would be terminated. This analysis seems not only unnecessarily complex but also inaccurate in two respects.

(i) The telexes were not contracts but offers. It might be argued that the telexes were "conditional contracts" because the Trust would be bound if the condition (that is, making the higher bid) were satisfied; but the answer is that this is true of all offers; the offeror will become bound if the condition (the act of acceptance) is fulfilled. If the argument were right, all offers would be contracts which is absurd.

(ii) A bilateral contract did not come into existence on receipt of the higher bid. The Trust had invited *offers* and it had received offers. Offers are revocable until accepted. The Trust was bound to accept the offer but, until it did so, the bidder could have revoked his offer.

Harvela made the only valid bid so the Trust was bound to accept that. However the Trust thought (excusably, because the Court of Appeal were of the same opinion) that Sir Leonard's was a higher and valid bid so they accepted that. So they had contracted (i) to accept Harvela's offer to buy the shares and (ii) to sell the shares to Sir Leonard. Peter Gibson J. ([1984] 2 All E.R. at 78–79) held that the second contract was not invalid but Harvela's prior contract prevailed and Harvela was entitled to specific performance of it. He awarded Sir Leonard nominal damages of £2. Lord Templeman, however, held that the contract with Sir Leonard was a nullity because both parties were under the mistaken impression that the Trust was bound to make it. On this, see below, p. 497.

ESSO PETROLEUM LTD v. COMMISSIONERS OF CUSTOMS AND EXCISE

House of Lords [1976] 1 W.L.R. 1; [1976] 1 All E.R. 117

Under a sales promotion scheme devised by Esso, petrol station proprietors displayed posters supplied by Esso stating: "The World Cup Coins," "One coin given with every four gallons of petrol." Millions of coins were distributed. The Commissioners claimed that the coins were chargeable to purchase tax under section 2(1) of the Purchase Tax Act 1963 on the ground that they had been "produced in quantity for general sale." Esso argued that the coins were the subject of a gift not a sale. Pennycuick V.-C. held that the transaction constituted a sale. The poster was an invitation to treat which became a contract. The Court of Appeal allowed Esso's appeal, holding ("as a matter of common sense," *per* Lord Denning M.R.) that the coins were not sold but were distributed as free gifts. The Commissioners' appeal to the House of Lords was dismissed, Lord Fraser dissenting. Lord Simon, with whom Lord Wilberforce agreed, held that there was a contract to supply the coins but it was not a contract of sale. The poster was an offer to supply a coin which the motorist accepted by offering to buy four gallons of petrol. The consideration for the promise to supply a coin was not money (and therefore it was not a sale) but the offer to buy petrol. Viscount Dilhorne and Lord Russell held that Esso did not intend to enter into legal relations (see below, p. 190); it was like an advertisement offering "free air"; and the coins were free gifts; but, if there was a contract, they agreed that it was not a contract of sale. Lord Fraser agreed with Pennycuick V.-C. that the motorist contracted to buy four gallons of petrol and a coin: it was like the case of a baker offering an extra bun "free of charge" to anyone who bought a dozen buns.

Questions
1. LORD SIMON: "The law happily matches the reality. The garage proprietor is saying, 'If you will buy four gallons of my petrol, I will give you one of these coins'." Professor Atiyah (39 M.L.R., 335) writes, "Contrary to Lord Simon's assertion, the reality of the matter surely was that the buyer, having paid for the four gallons of petrol, was entitled by *virtue of that payment* to a coin." Who is right?
2. Bobby, whose petrol tank is low, keeps going under pressure from his children until he comes to an Esso station owned by Nobby. He orders 12 gallons. When one gallon has been delivered, the pump runs dry. Is Nobby in breach of contract (i) to supply petrol (ii) to supply coins?

Problem
The following news item appeared in *The Times*, December 7, 1973: "The Crisis and the Law"—A motorist queued up for half an hour at a Harpenden, Hertfordshire, garage yesterday, then filled up his tank with 2p worth of petrol. But the driver got an unpleasant shock when he was charged £1 for the few drops.
The garage owner said: "We have put up a notice saying '£1 worth. No more, no less.' We checked with the police and we are perfectly within our rights to keep his money."
Were the police right? Was it a contract *to pay £1 for £1 worth of petrol or such less amount as the tank would hold?* Or was it a contract for the *sale of £1 worth of petrol?* If the latter, was the motorist in breach because of his inability to take delivery? If he was in breach, was the garage owner entitled to the price (see s.49(1) and (2) of the Sale of Goods Act, 1979 or only to damages? If he was entitled only to damages, what damage had he suffered? (See Note below, p. 590).

PHARMACEUTICAL SOCIETY OF GREAT BRITAIN v. BOOTS

Court of Appeal [1953] 1 Q.B. 401; [1953] 2 W.L.R. 427; 117 J.P. 132; 97 S.J. 149; [1953] 1 All E.R. 482

Appeal from Lord Goddard C.J.
The defendants' branch shop at Edgware was adapted to the "self-service" system. On entering the shop each customer passed a barrier where he obtained a wire basket. Beyond the barrier, in the principal part of the shop, shelves were fitted around the walls and on a fixture in the centre. On certain of these shelves were displayed various drugs and proprietary medicines. One section of the shelves was devoted exclusively to drugs which were included in, or which contained substances which were included in, Part I of the Poisons List referred to in section 17(1) of the Pharmacy and Poisons Act 1933.
The staff employed included a registered pharmacist, who was stationed near the poisons section whenever the shop was open for the sale of drugs. A customer,

having selected articles which he wished to buy, and placed them in a wire basket, had to pass by one of the two exits, at each of which was a cash desk where a cashier was stationed who scrutinised the articles selected by the customer, assessed the value and accepted payment. In every case involving the sale of a drug the pharmacist supervised that part of the transaction which took place at the cash desk and was authorised by the defendants to prevent, if he thought fit, any customer from removing any drug from the premises. No steps were taken by the defendants to inform the customers, before they selected any article which they wished to purchase, of the pharmacist's authorisation.

Two customers, following the procedure outlined above, purchased medicines containing substances which are included in Part I of the Poisons List. The question for the court was whether the sales were effected by or under the supervision of a registered pharmacist in accordance with section 18(1) of the Pharmacy and Poisons Act 1933.

The Lord Chief Justice answered the question in the affirmative. The Pharmaceutical Society appealed.

SOMERVELL L.J.: This is an appeal from a decision of the Lord Chief Justice on an agreed statement of facts raising a question under section 18(1)(a)(iii) of the Pharmacy and Poisons Act 1933. The plaintiffs are the Pharmaceutical Society, incorporated by Royal Charter. One of their duties is to take all reasonable steps to enforce the provisions of the Act. The provision in question is contained in section 18. [His Lordship read the section and stated the facts, and continued:] It is not disputed that in a chemist's shop where this self-service system does not prevail a customer may go in and ask a young woman assistant, who will not herself be a registered pharmacist, for one of these articles on the list, and the transaction may be completed and the article paid for, although the registered pharmicist, who will no doubt be on the premises, will not know anything himself of the transaction, unless the assistant serving the customer, or the customer, requires to put a question to him. It is right that I should emphasise, as did the Lord Chief Justice, that these are not dangerous drugs. They are substances which contain very small proportions of poison, and I imagine that many of them are the type of drug which has a warning as to what doses are to be taken. They are drugs which can be obtained, under the law, without a doctor's prescription.

The point taken by the plaintiffs is this: it is said that the purchase is complete if and when a customer going round the shelves takes an article and puts it in the receptacle which he or she is carrying, and that therefore, if that is right, when the customer comes to the pay desk, having completed the tour of the premises, the registered pharmacist, if so minded, has no power to say: "This drug ought not to be sold to this customer." Whether and in what circumstances he would have that power we need not inquire, but one can, of course, see that there is a difference if supervision can only be exercised at a time when the contract is completed.

I agree with the Lord Chief Justice in everything that he said, but I will put the matter shortly in my own words. Whether the view contended for by the plaintiffs is a right view depends on what are the legal implications of this layout—the invitation to the customer. Is a contract to be regarded as being completed when the article is put into the receptacle, or is this to be regarded as a more organised way of doing what is done already in many types of shops—and a bookseller is perhaps the best example—namely, enabling customers to have free access to what is in the shop, to look at the different articles, and then, ultimately, having got the ones which they wish to buy, to come up to the assistant saying "I want this"? The assistant in 999 times out of 1,000 says: "That is all right," and the money passes and the transaction is completed. I agree with what the Lord Chief Justice has said, and with the reasons which he has given for his conclusion, that in the case of an ordinary shop, although goods are displayed and it is intended that customers should go and choose what they want, the contract is not completed until, the customer having indicated the articles which he needs, the shopkeeper, or someone on his behalf, accepts that offer. Then the contract is completed. I can see no reason at all, that being clearly the normal position, for drawing any different implication as a result of this layout.

The Lord Chief Justice, I think, expressed one of the most formidable difficulties in the way of the plaintiffs' contention when he pointed out that, if the plaintiffs are right, once an article has been placed in the receptable, the customer himself is bound and would have no right, without paying for the first article, to substitute an article which he saw later of a similar kind and which he perhaps preferred. I can see no reason for implying from this self-service arrangement any implication other than that which the Lord Chief Justice found in it, namely, that it is a convenient method of enabling customers to see what there is and choose, and possibly put back and substitute, articles which they wish to have and then to go up to the cashier and offer to buy what they have so far chosen. On that conclusion the case fails, because it is admitted that there was supervision in the sense required by the Act and at the appropriate moment of time. For these reasons, in my opinion, the appeal should be dismissed.

The concurring judgments of BIRKETT and ROMER L.JJ. are omitted.

Question
  Do you agree that, if the display of goods in a self-service shop amounts to an offer, and a customer picks up an article, it necessarily follows that he is unable to change his mind and put it back?

Notes
  1. The *Boots* case decides who makes the offer in a supermarket. It does not decide what constitutes acceptance. Is the contract concluded (i) when the seller demands the price, thereby accepting the offer to buy? or (ii) when the buyer pays the price, thereby accepting a counter-offer from the seller? See Bernard S. Jackson, "Offer and Acceptance in the Supermarket" (1979) 129 New L.J. 775.
  2. In *Lasky v. Economy Grocery Stores* (1946) 65 N.E. (2d) 305; 163 A.L.R. 235, the plaintiff picked up a bottle of "tonic" in a self-service grocery shop owned by the defendant. As she was about to place it in the carrier basket provided the bottle exploded and severely injured her. She brought an action for breach of an implied warranty under a contract of sale. The Massachusetts Supreme Judicial Court held that the action failed as there was neither a sale nor an agreement to sell at the time the bottle exploded. The Court said that the display of goods constituted an offer which could not be accepted before the goods reached the cashier. Until then the customer was free to return an article to the shelf even though she had put it in the basket.
  In *Sancho-Lopez v. Fedor Food Corpn.* (1961) 211 N.Y.S. (2d) 953 the plaintiff succeeded in the City Court of New York in circumstances similar to those in *Lasky's* case except that he was removing the bottle from the carrier basket and handing it to the cashier when it exploded. *Cf.* 108 S.J. 207.
  In cases of this kind the shopkeeper may have been in no way negligent. It may have been impossible to detect that there was anything wrong with the bottle. So he could not be made liable in the tort of negligence. But contractual liability is strict. If the seller has promised that the bottle is fit for its purpose and it is not, his promise is broken and he is liable in damages.

Of course the manufacturer may have been negligent and, if so, he is liable to the injured customer in tort. But it may be impracticable to sue the manufacturer—perhaps the goods are imported—and, anyway, negligence may be difficult to prove. So the simplest and most convenient course is to sue the shopkeeper in contract; and this is possible only if a contract has been concluded before the explosion. Since 1985, a person injured by a defective product is likely to have an alternative remedy under the wide-ranging provisions of the Consumer Protection Act 1985.

Problem
Ada picks up a chicken marked "£1.50" in a self-service shop and tenders it to the cashier who says that the price tag is erroneous and the true price is £2.50. Advise Ada. What would be the position under the Massachusetts or New York rule?

Winfield, Some Aspects of Offer and Acceptance (1939) 55 L.Q.R. 499, 517

. . . surely a more natural interpretation of the display of goods in a shop with a marked price on them would be that the shopkeeper impliedly reserves to himself a right of selecting his customer. A shop is a place for bargaining, not for compulsory sales. Presumptively, the importance of the personality of the customer cannot be eliminated. If the display of such goods were an offer, then the shopkeeper might be forced to contract with his worst enemy, his greatest trade rival, a reeling drunkard, or a raggard and verminous tramp. That would be a result scarcely likely to be countenanced by the law. Even in a business like that of the innkeeper or the common carrier, where there is by law a duty to render services to such persons as may apply for them, the personal element is never entirely excluded. An innkeeper is not bound to accommodate a common prostitute, a railway company is not bound to find transport for one who is not in a fit condition to travel. Of course, a tradesman may frame his proposal in such way as to abrogate any choice in his selection of a customer. But it is not easy to imagine a case in which he would be likely to do so, and some instances, which might at first sight appear to amount to such abrogation, are more likely to be construed as retaining it. Thus even if the ticket on a clock in a jeweller's window were "For sale for £1, cash down, to first comer," we still think that it is only an invitation to do business and that the first comer must be one of whom the jeweller approves.

SALE OF GOODS ACT 1979

Auction sales
57.—(1) Where goods are put up for sale by auction in lots, each lot is prima facie deemed to be the subject of a separate contract of sale.

(2) A sale by auction is complete when the auctioneer announces its completion by the fall of the hammer, or in other customary manner; and until the announcement is made any bidder may retract his bid.

(3) A sale by auction may be notified to be subject to a reserve or upset price, and a right to bid may also be reserved expressly by or on behalf of the seller.

(4) Where a sale by auction is not notified to be subject to a right to bid by or on behalf of the seller, it is not lawful for the seller to bid himself or to employ any person to bid at the sale, or for the auctioneer knowingly to take any bid from the seller or any such person.

(5) A sale contravening subsection (4) above may be treated as fraudulent by the buyer.

(6) Where, in respect of a sale by auction, a right to bid is expressly reserved (but not otherwise) the seller or any one person on his behalf may bid at the auction.

Note

Section 57(2) codifies the common law rule laid down in *Payne v. Cave* (1789) 3 Term. Rep. 148; 100 E.R. 502. The plaintiff alleged that the defendant had bought the plaintiff's goods at an auction sale. The defendant had made the highest bid but had withdrawn it before the hammer fell. Lord Kenyon nonsuited the plaintiff and it was held that the nonsuit was very proper. The court said: "The auctioneer is the agent of the vendor, and the assent of both parties is necessary to make the contract binding; that is signified on the part of the seller by knocking down the hammer, which was not done here till the defendant had retracted. An auction is not unaptly called *locus poenitentiae*. Every bidding is nothing more than an offer on one side, which is not binding on either side till it is assented to. But according to what is now contended for, one party would be bound by the offer, and the other not, which can never be allowed."

The conditions under which a sale takes place may allow it to be reopened after the fall of the hammer. The National Conditions of Sale provide that if any dispute arises respecting a bid, "the auctioneer may determine the dispute, or the property may, at the vendor's option, either be put up again at the last undisputed bid or be withdrawn." See *Richards v. Phillips* [1969] 1 Ch. 39.

Questions

1. The conditions of sale at an auction sometimes provide "No person shall retract his bidding." What is the effect of this? *Cf. Routledge v. Grant* below, p. 77.

2. Who makes the offer in a Dutch auction? (". . . the offer of articles to be bid for at successively decreasing prices . . ."—Mock Auctions Act 1961, s.3).

WARLOW v. HARRISON

Exchequer Chamber (1859) 1 E. & E. 309; 29 L.J.Q.B. 14; 1 L.T. 211; 6 Jur.(N.S.) 66; 8 W.R. 95; 120 E.R. 925

The defendant was an auctioneer in Birmingham, where he had a repository for the sale of horses. In June 1858, he advertised a sale by auction at the repository. The items for sale included: "the three following horses, the property of a gentleman, without reserve." One of these was a mare called Janet Pride. The plaintiff attended the sale and bid 60 guineas for her. Mr Henderson, the owner of the mare, then bid 61 guineas. The plaintiff was informed that the last bidder was the owner and declined to bid further. The defendant knocked the mare down to Mr Henderson and entered his name in the sale book as purchaser. The plaintiff went at once to the auctioneer's office and claimed the mare as the highest bona fide bidder. Mr Henderson said "I bought her in; and you shall not have her; I gave £130 for the mare; and it is not likely I am going to sell her for £63." On the same day the plaintiff tendered to the defendant £63 in sovereigns as the price of the mare and demanded her. The defendant refused to receive the money or to deliver the mare.

The plaintiff alleged in his declaration that the defendant became and was the agent of the plaintiff to complete the contract on behalf of the plaintiff for the purchase of the said mare, but wholly omitted and refused to do so; whereby the plaintiff was deprived of the benefit of the said contract, and unable to obtain the said mare, as he otherwise would have done, and was put to and incurred divers expenses.

The defendant pleaded: 1. Not guilty. 2. That the plaintiff was not the highest bidder at the sale as alleged. 3. That the defendant did not become the plaintiff's agent as alleged.

The Court of Queen's Bench entered a nonsuit on the ground that the relationship of principal and agent between the plaintiff and the defendant had never come in to existence.

The plaintiff appealed.

In the Exchequer Chamber, MARTIN B. delivered the judgment of the court.

After stating the facts, he went on:

Upon the pleadings as they stand, we think the judgment of the Court of Queen's Bench is right, and that the defendant is entitled to the verdict upon the issue on the third plea: but there is power given to the court to amend; and it has been held that this power extends to the Court of Appeal; and we think we ought to exercise it largely in order to carry out the object of the Common Law Procedure Acts, 1852 and 1854, *viz.*, to determine the real question in controversy between the parties in the existing suit. Upon the facts of the case, it seems to us that the plaintiff is entitled to recover. In a sale by auction there are three parties, *viz.*, the owner of the property to be sold, the auctioneer, and the portion of the public who attend to bid, which of course includes the highest bidder. In this, as in most cases of sales by auction, the owner's name was not disclosed: he was a concealed principal. The name of the auctioneers, of whom the defendant was one, alone was published; and the sale was announced by them to be "without reserve." This, according to all the cases both at law and equity, means that neither the vendor nor any person in his behalf shall bid at the auction, and that the property shall be sold to the highest bidder, whether the sum bid be equivalent to the real value or not: *Thornett v. Haines* (15M. & W. 367). We cannot distinguish the case of an auctioneer putting up property for sale upon such a condition from the case of the loser of property offering a reward, or that of a railway company publishing a time-table stating the times when, and the places to which, the trains run. It has been decided that the person giving the information advertised for, or a passenger taking a ticket, may sue as upon a contract with him: *Denton v. Great Northern Rly.* (5E. & B. 860).[1] Upon the same principle, it seems to us that the highest bona fide bidder at an auction may sue the auctioneer as upon a contract that the sale shall be without reserve. We think the auctioneer who puts the property up for sale upon such a condition pledges himself that the sale shall be without reserve; or in other words, contracts that it shall be so; and that this contract is made with the highest bona fide bidder; and, in case of a breach of it, that he has a right of action against the auctioneer. The case is not at all affected by the 17th section of the Statute of Frauds,[2] which relates only to direct sales, and not to contracts relating to or connected with them. Neither does it seem to us material whether the owner, or person on his behalf, bid with the knowledge or privity of the auctioneer. We think the auctioneer has contracted that the sale shall be without reserve; and that the contract is broken upon a bid being made by or on behalf of the owner, whether it be during the time when the property is under the hammer, or it be the last bid upon which the article is knocked down; in either case, the sale is not "without reserve," and the contract of the auctioneer is broken. We

---

[1] Railway companies have since taken care to exclude any such liability.
[2] See above, p. 5.

entertain no doubt that the owner may, at any time before the contract is legally complete, interfere and revoke the auctioneer's authority: but he does so at his peril; and, if the auctioneer has contracted any liability in consequence of his employment and the subsequent revocation or conduct of the owner, he is entitled to be indemnified.

We do not think the conditions of sale stated in the case (assuming the plaintiff to be taken to have had notice of them) affect it. As to the first, Mr Henderson could not be the buyer: he was the owner; and, if it were material, there is ample evidence that the defendant knew him to be so: indeed, we think he ought not to have taken his bid, but to have refused it; stating, as his reason, that the sale was "without reserve." We feel inclined to differ with the view of the Court of Queen's Bench in this, that we rather think the bid of Mr Henderson was not a revocation of the defendant's authority as auctioneer. The third condition has nothing to do with the case; and the eighth only provides that, if, upon a sale without reserve, the owner act contrary to the conditions, he must pay the usual commission to the auctioneer. For these reasons, if the plaintiff think fit to amend his declaration, he, in our opinion, is entitled to the judgment of the court.

WILLES J.: My brother Bramwell and myself do not dissent from the judgment which has been pronounced. But we prefer to rest our decision, as to the amendment, upon the ground that the defendant undertook to have, and yet there was evidence that he had not, authority to sell without reserve.[1] The result is the same.

Judgment of the Court of Queen's Bench to be affirmed; unless the parties elect to enter a *stet processus*, or the plaintiff amend his declaration, in which latter case, a new trial to be had.

Questions

1. What was the significance of the reference to the Statute of Frauds? Was the contract, in the opinion of the majority or the minority, one of sale? See *Daulia Ltd. v. Four Millbank Nominees*, below, p. 44.

Was it a contract by the auctioneer that, after the highest bona fide bid, he would not withdraw the horse? Is that different in substance from a contract to sell it? The auctioneer may, after the highest bid, have been bound to sell but the "buyer" was not bound to buy until the auctioneer brought down the hammer. Is that a contract for the sale of goods— defined by the Sale of Goods Act 1979, s.2(1) as "a contract by which the seller transfers or agrees to transfer the property in goods to the buyer for a money consideration called the price?" Does "buyer" mean a person who is bound to buy? *Cf. Spiro's* case, below, p. 104.

2. What is the difference between the view expressed by Willes J. and Bramwell B. on the one hand, and the rest of the Court on the other?

3. Can you reconcile the law as stated by Martin B. with *Payne v. Cave?*

4. How can a contract with the highest bidder be broken by the owner's bidding during the auction since the highest bidder is not yet known? Is the answer that there is a contract with every bidder in turn? For example, "If you will come to the sale and bid, I promise that I will not bid (or withdraw the property); provided that, if someone makes a higher bid, this promise is to lapse."? *Cf.* the *Harvela* case, above p. 13.

Note

See C. Slade, 68 L.Q.R. 238 and L.C.B. Gower, 68 L.Q.R. 457. For a modern case in which a bid was held to be an acceptance of a collateral offer of a different kind (as well, of course, as an offer to buy), see *Couchman v. Hill*, below, p. 378.

---

[1] Under a doctrine of the law of agency. A, who purports to make a contract as agent for P with T, is taken to promise T that if T will enter into the contract with P, he, (A) has P's authority to contract. If A does not have P's authority he has committed a breach of warranty of authority.

Note that, although conduct such as that of the seller in *Warlow v. Harrison* is now made unlawful by s.57(4) of the Sale of Goods Act (above, p. 20, the case is still very relevant on the question whether the auctioneer can withdraw the property.

HARRIS v. NICKERSON

Queen's Bench (1873) L.R. 8 Q.B. 286; 42 L.J.Q.B. 171; 28 L.T. 410; 37 J.P. 536; 21 W.R. 635

The defendant, an auctioneer, advertised in the London papers and distributed catalogues to the effect that certain brewing materials, plant and office furniture would be sold to him at Bury St. Edmunds on a certain day. The conditions were the usual conditions, the first being: "The highest bidder to be the buyer." The plaintiff, a commission broker in London, had a commission to purchase at the sale the "office furniture" advertised to be sold. He went to Bury St. Edmunds, attended the sale, and purchased certain lots. Those described as "office furniture" were not put up for sale, but were withdrawn.

The plaintiff brought an action to recover £2 12s. 6d. for two days loss of time, and, on these facts, the judge gave judgement for the plaintiff, but, at the request of the defendant, gave him leave to appeal.

BLACKBURN J.: I am of the opinion that the judge was wrong.

The facts were that the defendant advertised bona fide that certain things would be sold by auction on the days named, and on the third day a certain class of things, *viz.*, office furniture, without any previous notice of their withdrawal, were not put up. The plaintiff says, inasmuch as I confided in the defendant's advertisement, and came down to the auction to buy furniture (which it is found as a fact he was commissioned to buy) and have had no opportunity of buying, I am entitled to recover damages from the defendant, on the ground that the advertisement amounted to a contract by the defendant with anybody that should act upon it, that all the things advertised would be actually put up for sale, and that he would have an opportunity of bidding for them and buying. This is certainly a startling proposition, and would be excessively inconvenient if carried out. It amounts to saying that anyone who advertises a sale by publishing an advertisement becomes responsible to everybody who attends the sale for his cab hire or travelling expenses. As to the cases cited: in the case of *Warlow v. Harrison* (above, p. 21), the opinion of the majority of the judges in the Exchequer Chamber appears to have been that an action would lie for not knocking down the lot to the highest bona fide bidder when the sale was advertised as without reserve; in such a case it may be that there is a contract to sell to the highest bidder, and that if the owner bids there is a breach of the contract; there is very plausible ground at all events for saying, as the minority of the court thought, that the auctioneer warrants that he has power to sell without reserve. In the present case, unless every declaration of intention to do a thing creates a binding contract with those who act upon it, and in all cases after advertising a sale the auctioneer must give notice of any articles that are withdrawn, or be liable to an action, we cannot hold the defendant liable.

QUAIN J.: I am of the same opinion. To uphold the judge's decision it is necessary to go to the extent of saying that when an auctioneer issues an advertisement of the sale of goods, if he withdraws any part of them without notice, the persons attending may all maintain actions against him. In the present case, it is to be observed that the plaintiff bought some other lots; but it is said that he had a commission to buy the furniture, either in whole or in part, and that therefore he has a right of action against the defendant. Such a proposition seems to be destitute of all authority; and it would be introducing an extremely inconvenient rule of law to say that an auctioneer is bound to give notice of withdrawal or to be held liable to everybody attending the sale. The case is certainly of the first impression. When a sale is advertised as without reserve, and a lot is put up and bid for, there is ground for saying, as was said in *Warlow v. Harrison* (above, p. 21), that a contract is entered into between the auctioneer and the highest bona fide bidder, but that has no application to the present case; here the lots were never put up and no offer was made by the plaintiff nor promise made by the defendant, except by his advertisement that certain goods would be sold. It is impossible to say that that is a contract with everybody attending the sale, and that the auctioneer is to be liable for their expenses if any single article is withdrawn. *Spencer v. Harding* (above, p. 9), which was cited by the plaintiff's counsel, as far as it goes, is a direct authority against his proposition.

ARCHIBALD J.: I am of the same opinion. This is an attempt on the part of the plaintiff to make a mere declaration of intention a binding contract. He has utterly failed to show authority or reason for his proposition. If a false and fraudulent representation had been made out, it would have been quite another matter. But to say that a mere advertisement that certain articles will be sold by auction amounts to a contract to indemnify all who attend, if the sale of any part of the articles does not take place, is a proposition without authority or ground for supporting it.

Judgment for the defendant.

Section 2. Promises and Bargains

We have seen (above, p. 4) that a promise which is not in a deed is potentially binding on the promisor only if he has asked for something in return. Virtually all offers to contract can be reduced to the form, "I promise this if you will do, or promise, that." Contract then is a bargain between the parties and the natural way to make a bargain is for one side to propose the terms and the other to agree to them. So, in practice, contracts are almost invariably made by a process of offer and acceptance. The law looks for an offer and acceptance, not for some technical reason but because this is the way in which contracts are in fact made. See Mustill L.J.'s dictum, quoted by Bingham L.J., above, p. 12. Consider all the cases so far discussed. Though judges sometimes speak of offer and acceptance as if it were an essential process, a contract might be made without it if the necessary bargain can be discerned from the facts in some other way.

Problems

Is there (i) an offer and acceptance, (ii) a contract, in the following cases?:

1. A and B, wishing to enter into a partnership, instruct C to draw up a contract. C does so and the document is signed, first by A and then by B.

2. A and B are unable to reach agreement as to the terms of a sale. C, a bystander, proposes the terms of a compromise. A and B say, simultaneously, "I agree."

3. A writes to B offering to sell certain property at a stated price. B writes to A offering to buy the same property at the same price. The letters cross in the post.

Note

Problem 3 was discussed, *obiter*, by the Court of Exchequer Chamber in *Tinn v. Hoffman* (1873) 29 L.T. 271. Blackburn, Keating, Brett, Grove and Archibald JJ. said that cross-offers do not make a binding contract. Honyman J. said they do.

HONYMAN J.: I cannot see why the fact of the letters crossing each other should not make a good contract. If I say I am willing to buy a man's house on certain terms and he at the same moment says he is willing to sell it, and these two letters are posted so that they are irrevocable with respect to the writers, why should that not constitute a good contract? The parties are *ad idem* at one and the same moment.

GROVE J.: Numberless inconveniences might result from our holding that [cross-offers may amount to a contract]. A letter may be put into the post or may be sent out by private messenger, and then the writer may repent of wh... he has written, and may dispatch a telegram or send a special messenger on horseback, saying, "I have posted or sent to you a letter making you a certain offer, I cannot fulfil it, consider it cancelled." This second message or telegram may arrive before the letter itself, which may have been miscarried, and yet in a few days or a week, the parties having meanwhile considered there was no contract, the letter might come to hand. Is it then to become a contract? . . . there must be an offer which the person accepting has had an opportunity of considering, and which when he accepts he knows will form a binding contract. Unless that is done, where each of them is, so to speak, making an offer or a cross-offer, they are, so to speak, *in fieri*, and do not constitute a contract.

BRETT J.: . . . cross-offers are not an acceptance of each other, therefore there will be no offer of either party accepted by the other . . . where the contract is to be made by the letters themselves, you cannot make it by cross-offers, and say that the contract was made by one party accepting the offer which was made to him.

BLACKBURN J.: When a contract is made between two parties there is a promise by one in consideration of the promise made by the other; there are two assenting minds, the parties agreeing in opinion, and one having promised in consideration of the promise of the other— there is an exchange of promises; but I do not think exchanging offers would, upon principle, be at all the same thing. . . . The promise or offer being made on each side in ignorance of the promise or offer made on the other side neither of them can be construed as an acceptance of the other. Either of the parties may write and say "I accept your offer, and, as you perceive, I have already made a similar offer to you," and then people would know what they were about, I think either side might revoke. Such grave inconvenience would arise in mercantile business if people could doubt whether there was an acceptance or not, that it is desirable to keep to the rule that an offer that has been made should be accepted by an acceptance such as would leave no doubt on the matter.

CLARKE v. DUNRAVEN

House of Lords [1897] A.C. 59; 66 L.J.Adm. 1; 75 L.T. 337; 8 Asp.M.C. 190

The Mudhook Yacht Club having advertised a regatta to be held on the Clyde in July 1894, the appellant entered his yacht the *Satanita* and the respondent entered his yacht the *Valkyrie*, for a first class race in the regatta, each owner signing a letter to the secretary of the club undertaking that while sailing under the entry he would obey and be bound by the sailing rules of the Yacht Club Association. Those rules contained a number of regulations to be observed in races, and among them rule 18, which corresponded to article 14 of the Regulations for Preventing Collisions at Sea. By rule 24: ". . . If a yacht, in consequence of her neglect of any of these rules, shall foul another yacht, or compel other yachts to foul, she shall forfeit all claim to the prize, and shall pay all damages." By rule 32: "Any yacht disobeying or infringing any of these rules, which shall apply to all yachts whether sailing in the same or different races, shall be disqualified from receiving any prize she would otherwise have won, and her owner shall be liable for all damages arising therefrom."

While sailing under the entry the *Satanita*, without the actual fault or privity of the owner, broke the 18th rule and ran into and sank the *Valkyrie*. The respondent and the master and crew of the latter vessel brought an action in the Admiralty Division against the appellant claiming damages.

The appellant paid into court the limited sum for which he was liable[1] in the absence of a contract between him and the respondent (£8 per ton on the registered tonnage of the *Satanita*). The respondent alleged that by the terms of the entry and in consideration that the owner of the Valkyrie would race with the appellant under these rules, the appellant had agreed to be liable for *all damages* arising from a breach of the rules. Bruce J. held that even if there was a contract it was not so express as to override the statutory limitation. The Court of Appeal reversed this decision, holding that there was a contract under which the defendant was liable for all damages. Lord Esher M.R. said, [1895] P. 248, 255, that it was clear that the defendant had entered into a contractual obligation with the plaintiff "and the way that he has undertaken that obligation is this. A certain number of gentlemen formed themselves into a committee and proposed to give prizes for matches sailed between yachts at a certain place on a certain day, and they promulgated certain rules, and said: 'If you want to sail in any of our matches for our prize, you cannot do so unless you submit yourselves to the conditions which we have thus laid down. And one of the conditions is, that if you do sail for one of such prizes you must enter into an obligation with the owners of the yachts who are competing, which they at the same time enter into similarly with you, that if by a breach of any of our rules you do damage or injury to the owner of a competing yacht, you shall be liable to make good the damage you have so done.' If that is so, then when they do sail, and not till then, that relation is immediately formed between the yacht owners. There are other conditions with regard to these matches which constitute a relation between each of the yacht owners who enters his yacht and sails it and the committee; but that does not in the least do away with what the yacht owner has undertaken, namely, to enter into a relation with the other yacht owners, that relation containing an obligation."

The defendant appealed to the House of Lords.

LORD HERSCHELL.: I cannot entertain any doubt that there was a contractual relation between the parties to this litigation. The effect of their entering for the race, and undertaking to be bound by these rules to the knowledge of each other, is sufficient, I think, where those rules indicate a liability on the part of the one to the other, to create a contractual obligation to discharge that liability. That being so, the parties must be taken to have contracted that a breach of any of these rules would render the party guilty of that breach liable, in the language of rule 24, to "pay all damages," in the language of rule 32, to be "liable for all damages arising therefrom." The language is somewhat different in the two rules; but I do not think they were intended to have, with regard to payment or liability to damages, any different effect. It is admitted that the appellant broke one of those rules, and, having broken or disobeyed that rule, it is quite clear, on the assumption of a contract such as I have described, that there arose the liability to "pay all damages," or "to be liable for all damages arising therefrom."

Question

How and when did the contract come into existence in this case? Was there an offer and acceptance?

---

[1] Under the Merchant Shipping Act Amendment Act 1862, s.54(1).

Consider the solution offered by Salmond and Williams, *Contracts*, p. 71:

The first competitor to enter must be taken to be offering, to all other persons who may subsequently enter, an undertaking to observe the rules, if they will for their part give similar undertakings. The second competitor to enter, by so doing, accepts this offer, and himself makes a similar offer to all persons who may subsequently enter; and so on.

Treitel, *The Law of Contract* (8th ed.), p. 47, critises this solution as "artificial and unworkable even in theory unless each competitor knew of the existence of the previous ones. It would also lead to the conclusion that entries which were put in the post together were cross-offers and thus not binding on each other." Do you agree?

Note

Where A takes shares in a company, the memorandum and articles of association of the company constitute a contract between A and the company. Do they also constitute a contract between A and B, another shareholder of the company? It was held by Vaisey J. that they do in *Rayfield v. Hands* [1960] Ch. 1, relying, *inter alia*, on *Clarke v. Dunraven*. See Gower, 21 M.L.R. 401 and 657. See also Jeremy Phillips discussing *Moorgate Mercantile Co. Ltd v. Twitchings* [1977] A.C. 890, (1976) 92 L.Q.R. 499.

Section 3. Fairness in the Law of Contract

At common law the courts have always regarded it as their function to enforce whatever contract the parties have made, however bad a bargain it might be for one of them. The courts might refuse to enforce the contract where there had been fraud or misrepresentation, or, where the parties were in one of a number of special relationships, undue influence had been exercised. These matters are all considered below. Where none of these factors was present, the court was not concerned with the question whether there had been unfairness in formation of the contract, or in its terms. The principle of freedom of contract required that it be left to the parties to make whatever bargain they chose. Having made the contract, they must perform it or face the prospect of being ordered to pay damages for not doing so. This is still the general principle though it is now much qualified by legislation relating to particular types of contract. For example, certain promises by the seller are implied in contracts for the sale of goods whether he likes it or not. An employer who exercises his contractual right to dismiss an employee must do so "fairly" or the employee can claim damages for unfair dismissal.

In addition to provisions relating to particular contracts there are two important more general provisions: the Unfair Contract Terms Act 1977 and the Unfair Terms in Consumer Contracts Regulations 1994. But these enactments are not as wide-ranging as they sound. The 1977 Act is not concerned with all contract terms which might be thought "unfair" but only with two types of term, exclusion clauses and indemnity clauses; and the 1994 Regulations, though not restricted to these types of term, apply only to "a term in a contract concluded between a seller or supplier and a consumer where the said term has not been individually negotiated." Even in respect of these contracts the Regulations provide (reg. 3(2)) that

"In so far as it is in plain and intelligible language, no assessment shall be made of any term which—

(a) defines the subject-matter of the contract, or
(b) concerns the adequacy of the price or remuneration, as against the goods or services sold or supplied."

Unfairness in the formation of contracts. Neither of these enactments affects what might be perceived as unfairness in the formation of contracts. In commercial transactions one party may take advantage of his greatly superior bargaining power to drive a very hard bargain: *CTN Cash and Carry v. Gallagher*, below, p. 656. A party may also take advantage of his superior knowledge. In *Turner v. Green* [1895] 2 Ch. 205 the plaintiff, having heard the result of a case, concluded a contract settling a dispute with the defendant, knowing that the defendant had not heard the result of that case and would not have agreed to the settlement if he had known of it. The court thought that this was not the sort of conduct to be expected of solicitors, it was "a shabby trick", but it did not invalidate the contract. Similarly in *Smith v. Hughes* (below, p. 121) Cockburn C.J. put the case of a person who buys an estate knowing that, unknown to the seller, there is a valuable mine under the surface. He thought the case "one in which a man of tender conscience or high honour would be unwilling to take advantage of the ignorance of the seller, but there can be no doubt that the contract for the sale of the estate would be binding . . .". The buyer's conduct might certainly be regarded as "unfair"; but the enactments do not affect it. The general principle of the common law was re-stated by Slade L.J. in the *Banque Financiere* case, below, p. 338. Whether it may be affected by certain developments in case-law is a matter for consideration below, see p. 508, Note 1.

CHAPTER 2

OFFER AND ACCEPTANCE

Section 1. Unilateral Contracts

A unilateral contract is offered when O promises A that he will do something if A will do a certain act, other than make a promise. A accepts O's offer by doing that act. O's promise is binding when the act is completed and not before. O promises A £100 if A will walk to York. If A falls in a faint five yards from the city boundary and completes the journey in an ambulance, he is entitled to nothing. Nor has A committed any breach of contract because he never promised to do anything.

One view is that O's offer is accepted only when A actually gets to York. A difficulty about this view is that, since offers are revocable until accepted, it would appear to follow that O might revoke his offer when A was only five yards from York and going strong, which would seem to be very unjust. An answer might be that O makes a second, implied, offer, namely that he will not revoke the express offer if A embarks on performance. Such an implied offer might, in appropriate circumstances, be thought necessary to give business efficacy to the contract. (Compare *Errington v. Errington*, below, p. 40, with *Luxor v. Cooper*, below, p. 42).

An alternative view is that A accepts O's express offer by embarking on performance, but a condition of his right to recover the £100 is complete performance of the consideration. (Pollock, *Principles of Contract* (13th ed.), p. 19; *Offord v. Davies*, below, p. 78.)

According to both of these theories, O's purported revocation would be a breach of contract entitling A to sue for damages—presumably the value of the lost chance to earn the reward. That would leave open the question whether A would be entitled to claim the promised reward if he insisted on completing performance. *Errington v. Errington*, *White and Carter Councils Ltd. v. McGregor*, below, p. 559 and *Mountford v. Scott*, below, p. 78 suggest that A might succeed.

CARLILL v. CARBOLIC SMOKE BALL CO.

Court of Appeal [1893] 1 Q.B. 256; 62 L.J.Q.B. 257; 67 L.T. 837; 41 W.R. 210;
57 J.P. 325; 4 R. 176

Appeal from a decision of Hawkins J. [1892] 2 Q.B. 484.
The defendants, who were the proprietors and vendors of a medical preparation called "The Carbolic Smoke Ball," inserted in the *Pall Mall Gazette* of November 13, 1891, and in other newspapers, the following advertisement: "£100 reward will be paid by the Carbolic Smoke Ball Company to any person who contracts the increasing epidemic of influenza, colds, or any disease caused by taking cold, after having used the ball three times daily for two weeks according to the printed directions supplied with each ball. £1,000 is deposited with the Alliance Bank, Regent Street, showing our sincerity in the matter.

"During the last epidemic of influenza many thousand carbolic smoke balls were sold as preventatives against this disease, and in no ascertained case was the disease contracted by those using the carbolic smoke ball.

One carbolic smoke ball will last a family several months, making it the cheapest remedy in the world at the price 10s., post free. The ball can be refilled at a cost of

5s. Address, Carbolic Smoke Ball Company, 27 Princes Street, Hanover Square, London."

The plaintiff, a lady, on the faith of this advertisement, bought one of the balls at a chemist's and used it as directed, three times a day from November 20, 1891 to January 17, 1892, when she was attacked by influenza. Hawkins J. held that she was entitled to recover the £100. The defendants appealed.

BOWEN L.J.: We were asked to say that this document was a contract too vague to be enforced.

The first observation which arises is that the document itself is not a contract at all, it is only an offer made to the public. The defendants contend next, that it is an offer the terms of which are too vague to be treated as a definite offer, inasmuch as there is no limit of time fixed for the catching of the influenza, and it cannot be supposed that the advertisers seriously meant to promise to pay money to every person who catches the influenza at any time after the inhaling of the smoke ball. It was urged also, that if you look at this document you will find much vagueness as to the persons with whom the contract was intended to be made—that, in the first place, its terms are wide enough to include persons who may have used the smoke ball before the advertisement was issued; at all events, that it is an offer to the world in general, and, also, that it is unreasonable to suppose it to be a definite offer, because nobody in their senses would contract themselves out of the opportunity of checking the experiment which was going to be made at their own expense. It is also contended that the advertisement is rather in the nature of a puff or a proclamation than a promise or offer intended to mature into a contract when accepted. But the main point seems to be that the vagueness of the document shows that no contract whatever was intended. It seems to me that in order to arrive at a right conclusion we must read this advertisement in its plain meaning, as the public would understand it. It was intended to be issued to the public and to be read by the public. How would an ordinary person reading this document construe it? It was intended unquestionably to have some effect, and I think the effect which it was intended to have, was to make people use the smoke ball, because the suggestions and allegations which it contains are directed immediately to the use of the smoke ball as distinct from the purchase of it. It did not follow that the smoke ball was to be purchased from the defendants directly, or even from agents of theirs directly. The intention was that the circulation of the smoke ball should be promoted, and that the use of it should be increased. The advertisement begins by saying that a reward will be paid by the Carbolic Smoke Ball Company to any person who contracts the increasing epidemic after using the ball. It has been said that the words do not apply only to persons who contract the epidemic after the publication of this advertisement, but include persons who had previously contracted the influenza. I cannot so read the advertisement. It is written in colloquial and popular language, and I think that it is equivalent to this: "£100 will be paid to any person who shall contract the increasing epidemic after having used the carbolic smoke ball three times daily for two weeks." And it seems to me that the way in which the public would read it would be this, that if anybody, after the advertisement was published, used three times daily for two weeks the carbolic smoke ball, and then caught cold, he would be entitled to the reward. Then again it was said: "How long is this protection to endure? Is it to go on forever, or for what limit of time?" I think that there are two constructions of this document, each of which is good sense, and each of which seems to me to satisfy the exigencies of the present action. It may mean that the protection is warranted to last during the epidemic, and it was during the epidemic that the plaintiff contracted the disease. I think, more probably, it means that the smoke ball will be a protection while it is in use. That seems to me the way in which an ordinary person would understand an advertisement about medicine and about a specific against influenza. It could not be supposed that after you have left off using it, you are still to be protected for ever, as if there was to be a stamp set upon your forehead that you were never to catch influenza because you had once used the carbolic smoke ball. I think the immunity is to last during the use of the ball. That is the way in which I should naturally read it, and it seems to me that the subsequent language of the advertisement supports that construction. It says: "During the last epidemic of influenza many thousand carbolic smoke balls were sold, and in no ascertained case was the disease contracted by those using" (not "who had used") "the carbolic smoke ball," and it concludes with saying that one smoke ball will last a family several months (which imports that it is to be efficacious while it is being used), and that the ball can be refilled at a cost of 5s. I, therefore, have myself no hesitation in saying that I think, on the construction of this advertisement, the protection was to enure during the time that the carbolic smoke ball was being used. My brother, the Lord Justice who preceded me, thinks that the contract would be sufficiently definite if you were to read it in the sense that the protection was to be warranted during a reasonable period after use. I have some difficulty myself on that point; but it is not necessary for me to consider it further, because the disease here was contracted during the use of the carbolic smoke ball.

Was it intended that the £100 should, if the conditions were fulfilled, be paid? The advertisement says that £1,000 is lodged at the bank for the purpose. Therefore, it cannot be said that the statement that £100 would be paid was intended to be a mere puff. I think it was intended to be understood by the public as an offer which was to be acted upon.

But it was said there was no check on the part of the persons who issued the advertisement, and that it would be an insensate thing to promise £100 to a person who used the smoke ball unless you could check or superintend his manner of using it. The answer to that argument seems to me to be that if a person chooses to make extravagant promises of this kind he probably does so because it pays him to make them, and, if he has made them, the extravagance of the promises is no reason in law why he should not be bound by them.

It was also said that the contract is made with all the world—that is, with everybody; and that you cannot contract with everybody. It is not a contract made with all the world. There is the fallacy of the argument. It is an offer made to all the world; and why should not an offer be made to all the world which is to ripen into a contract with anybody who comes forward and performs the condition? It is an offer to become liable to anyone who, before it is retracted, performs the condition, and, although the offer is made to the world, the contract is made with that limited portion of the public who come forward and perform the condition on the faith of the advertisement. It is not like cases in which you offer to negotiate, or you issue advertisements that you have got a stock of books to sell, or houses to let, in which case there is no offer to be bound by any contract. Such advertisements are offers to negotiate—offers to receive offers—offers to chaffer, as, I think, some learned judge in one of the cases has said. If this is an offer to be bound, then it is a contract the moment the person fulfils the condition. That seems to me to be sense, and it is also the ground on which all these advertisement cases have been decided during the century; and it cannot be put better than in Willes J.'s judgment in *Spencer v. Harding* (see above, p. 9). "In the advertisement cases," he says, "there never was any doubt that the advertisement amounted to a promise to pay the money to the person who first gave information. The difficulty suggested was that it was a contract with all the world. But that, of course, was soon overruled. It was an offer to become liable to any person who before the offer should be retracted should happen to be the person to fulfil the contract, of which the advertisement was an offer or tender. That is not the sort of difficulty which presents itself here. If the circular had gone on, 'and we undertake to sell to the highest bidder,' the reward cases would have applied, and there would have been a good contract in respect of the persons." As soon as the highest bidder presented himself, says Willes J., the person who was to hold the *vinculum juris* on the other side of the contract was ascertained, and it became settled.

Then it was said that there was no notification of the acceptance of the contract. One cannot doubt that, as an ordinary rule of law, an acceptance of an offer made ought to be notified to the person who makes the offer, in order that the two minds may come together. Unless this is done, the two minds may be apart, and there is not that consensus which is necessary according to the English law—I say nothing about the laws of other countries—to make a contract. But there is this clear gloss to be made upon that doctrine, that as notification of acceptance is required for the benefit of the person who makes the offer, the person who makes the offer may dispense with notice to himself if he thinks it desirable to do so, and I suppose there can be no doubt that where a person in an offer made by him to another person, expressly or impliedly intimates a particular mode of acceptance as sufficient to make the bargain binding, it is only necessary for the other person to whom such offer is made to follow the indicated method of acceptance; and if the person making the offer, expressly or impliedly intimates in his offer that it will be sufficient to act on the proposal without communicating acceptance of it to himself, performance of the condition is a sufficient acceptance without notification.

That seems to me to be the principle which lies at the bottom of the acceptance cases, of which two instances are the well-known judgment of Mellish L.J. in *Harris's* case (L.R. 7 Ch. 587), and the very instructive judgment of Lord Blackburn in *Brogden v. Metropolitan Ry.* ((1876) 2 App. Cas. 666), in which he appears to me to take exactly the line I have indicated.

Now, if that is the law, how are we to find out whether the person who makes the offer does intimate that notification of acceptance will not be necessary in order to constitute a binding bargain? In many cases you look to the offer itself. In many cases you extract from the character of the transaction that notification is not required, and in the advertisement cases it seems to me to follow as an inference to be drawn from the transaction itself that a person is not to notify his acceptance of the offer before he performs the condition, but that if he performs the condition notification is dispensed with. It seems to me that from the point of view of common sense no other idea could be entertained. If I advertise to the world that my dog is lost, and that anybody who brings the dog to a particular place will be paid some money, are all the police or other persons whose business it is to find lost dogs to be expected to sit down and write me a note saying that they have accepted my proposal? Why, of course, they at once look after the dog and as soon as they find the dog they have performed the condition. The essence of the transaction is that the dog should be found, and it is not necessary under such circumstances, as it seems to me, that in order to make the contract binding there should be any notification of acceptance. It follows from the nature of the thing that the performance of the condition is sufficient acceptance without the notification of it, and a person who makes an offer in an advertisement of that kind makes an offer which must be read by the light of that common-sense reflection. He does, therefore, in his offer impliedly indicate that he does not require notification of the acceptance of the offer.

A further argument for the defendants was that this was a *nudum pactum*—that there was no consideration for the promise—that taking the influenza was only a condition, and that the using the smoke ball was only a condition, and that there was no consideration at all; in fact, that there was no request, express or implied, to use the smoke ball. Now, I will not enter into an elaborate discussion upon the law as to requests in this kind of contracts. I will simply refer to *Victors v. Davies* (12 M. & W. 758) and Sergeant Manning's note to *Fisher v. Pyne* (1 M. & G. 265), which everybody ought to read who wishes to embark in this controversy. The short answer, to abstain from academical discussion, is, it seems to me, that there is here a request to use involved in the offer. Then as to the alleged want of consideration. The definition of "consideration" given in Selwyn's *Nisi Prius* (8th ed.), p. 47, which is cited and adopted by Tindal C.J. in the case of *Laythoarp v. Bryant* (3 Scott 238, 250), is this: "Any act of the plaintiff from which the defendant derives a benefit or advantage, or any labour, detriment, or inconvenience sustained by the plaintiff, provided such act is performed or such inconvenience suffered by the plaintiff, with the consent, either express or implied, of the defendant." Can it be said here that if the person who reads this advertisement applies thrice daily, for such time as may seem to him tolerable, the carbolic smoke ball to his nostrils for a whole fortnight, he is doing nothing at all—that it is a mere act which is not to count towards consideration to support a promise (for the law does not require us to measure the adequacy of the consideration). Inconvenience sustained by one party at the request of the other is enough to create a consideration. I think therefore, that it is consideration enough that the plaintiff took the trouble of using the smoke ball. But I think also that the defendants received a benefit from this user, for the use of the smoke ball was contemplated by the defendants as being indirectly a benefit to them, because the use of the smoke balls would promote their sale . . . if you once make up your mind that there was a promise made to this lady who is the plaintiff, as one of the public—a promise made to her that if she used the smoke ball three times daily for a fortnight and got the influenza, she should have £100, it seems to me that her using the smoke ball was sufficient consideration. I cannot picture to myself the view of the law on which the contrary could be held when you have once found who are the contracting parties. If I say to a person, "If you use such and such a medicine for a week I will give you £5," and he uses it, there is ample consideration for the promise.

LINDLEY and A.L. SMITH L.JJ. delivered concurring judgments.

Questions
1. At what moment did the contract come into existence? What was the consideration supplied by Carlill?
2. If the smoke ball had been bought by Carlill's friend and loaned to her, would it have made any difference to the result of this action?
3. If the Smoke Ball Co. published an advertisement on December 8, 1892, in all the newspapers in which the original offer had appeared, saying that the offer was now withdrawn, and Henry, who had been using the smoke ball regularly since November 20, contracted influenza on December 10, would the company be liable?
4. If Carlill had used the smoke ball three times daily for two weeks without knowing anything about the advertisement offering the reward, and had then caught influenza and learned of the advertisement through her doctor, could she have recovered the £100?
5. If Carlill, knowing of the advertisement, used the smoke ball hoping to avoid influenza and, therefore, hoping not to be eligible for the reward, ought she to have recovered the £100? (See the next case.)
6. Did the company promise that Carlill would not catch influenza? Were they in breach of contract when she did? (See below, p. 411.)

WILLIAMS v. CARWARDINE

King's Bench (1833) 5 C. & P. 566; 4 B. & Ad. 621; 1 Nev. & M.(K.B.) 418; 2 L.J.K.B. 101; 172 E.R. 1104

The defendant offered a reward to any person giving information leading to the discovery of a particular murderer. Subsequently, the plaintiff was severely beaten and bruised by one Williams. Believing she had not long to live and to ease her conscience, she gave information which led to Williams's conviction of the murder. The jury found that she was not induced by the offer of the reward but by other motives. Parke J. directed a verdict for the plaintiff.
Curwood moved for a rule to show cause why a nonsuit should not be entered on the ground that the plaintiff was not a meritorious informer; and that she sued on a contract which had in effect been negatived by the finding of the jury.

DENMAN C.J.: Was any doubt suggested as to whether the plaintiff knew of the handbill at the time of her making the disclosure?
Curwood: She must have known of it, as it was placarded all over Hereford, the place at which she lived.

PARKE J.: I take this to have been a contract with anyone who did the thing.

LITTLEDALE J.: If the person knows of the handbill and does the thing, that is quite enough. It does not say, whoever will come forward in consequence of this handbill.

DENMAN C.J.: As the plaintiff is within the terms of the handbill, she is entitled to the reward.

PATTESON J.: The plaintiff being within the terms, her motive is not material.

Rule refused.

R. v. CLARKE

High Court of Australia (1927) 40 C.L.R. 227

A proclamation by the Government of Western Australia offered a reward for information leading to the arrest of certain murderers and a pardon to an accomplice who gave the information. Clarke saw the proclamation in May. On June 6 he gave false information to protect the murderers. On June 10 he gave information which led to their conviction. He admitted that his only object in doing so was to clear himself of a charge of murder and that he had no intention of claiming the reward at that time. He sued the Crown for the reward by petition of right. The High Court (Isaacs A.C.J., Higgins and Starke J.J.), reversing the Full Court of Western Australia, dismissed his claim.

ISAACS A.C.J.: Instances easily suggest themselves where precisely the same act done with reference to an offer would be performance of the condition, but done with reference to a totally distinct object would not be such a performance. An offer of £100 to any person who should swim a hundred yards in the harbour on the first day of the year, would be met by voluntarily performing the feat with reference to the offer, but would not in my opinion be satisfied by a person who was accidentally or maliciously thrown overboard on that date and swam the distance simply to save his life, without any thought of the offer. The offeror might or might not feel morally impelled to give the sum in such a case, but would be under no contractual obligation to do so.

HIGGINS J.: If the case so much relied on for Clarke, the case of *Williams v. Carwardine* (above, p. 36), can be taken as deciding that mutual consent to the terms is not necessary, as well as communication of assent by the offeree, I can only point to higher and more recent authority, such as that of Lord Westbury L.C. in *Chinnock v. Marchioness of Ely* (1865) 4 De G. J. & S. 638 at p. 643: "An agreement is the result of the mutual assent of two parties to certain terms, and if it be clear that there is no *consensus*, what may have been written or said becomes immaterial." This pronouncement is cited by *Leake on Contracts* (7th ed.), p. 2; and the author adds: "A *consensus ad idem* is a prime essential to the validity of a contract." The distinction should be clear between the essential mental assent, and the essential communication of that assent; as in *Re National Savings Bank Association; Hebb's Case* (1867) L.R. 4 Eq. 12; "I am of opinion that an offer does not bind the person who makes it until it has been accepted, *and* its acceptance has been communicated to him or his agent."

But I do not regard *Williams v. Carwardine* as deciding anything to the contrary of this doctrine. That case seems to me not to deal with the essential elements for a contract at all: it shows merely that the *motive* of the informer in accepting the contract offered (and the performing the conditions is usually sufficient evidence of acceptance) has nothing to do with his right to recover under the contract. The reports show (as it was assumed by the judges after the verdict of the jury in favour of the informer), that the informer *knew* of the offer when giving the information, and meant to accept the offer though she had also a *motive* in her guilty conscience. The distinguished jurist, Sir Frederick Pollock, in his Preface to Vol. 38 of the *Revised Reports*, makes comments adverse to the case; but I concur with Burnside J. in his view that we cannot treat such comments as equivalent to an overruling of a clear decision. The case of *Gibbons v. Proctor* (1891) 64 L.T. 594 is much more difficult to explain. There a policeman was held entitled to recover a reward offered by handbills, for information given to the superintendent of police which led to arrest and conviction, although the policeman did not know of the handbills before he sent the information by his agents, or before the handbills reached the superintendent. This would seem to mean that a man can accept an offered contract before he knows that there is an offer—that knowledge of the offer before the informer supplies the information is immaterial to the existence of the contract.[1] *Anson on Contracts* (16th ed.), p. 55, thinks that this decision must be wrong. I venture to think so too, and, though we cannot well overrule it, we ought not to follow it for the purposes of this court. It should be noted in this connection that the great judgment of Lord Blackburn in *Brogden v. Metropolitan Ry.* (1876) 2 App.Cas. 666 is addressed to the other condition of contract, that acceptance must be communicated; but the whole judgment assumes that *consensus* of mind pre-existed— "simple *acceptance in your own mind*, without any intimation to the other party, and expressed by a mere private act, such as putting a letter into a drawer," does not complete a contract (and see *per* Lord Cairns L.C.). The reasoning of Woodruff J. in *Fitch v. Snedaker* (1868) 38 N.Y. 248 seems to me to be faultless; and the decision is spoken of in *Anson* (p. 24) as being undoubtedly correct in principle: "The motive inducing consent may be immaterial, but the consent is vital. Without that there is no contract. How then can there be consent or assent to that of which the party has never heard?" Clarke had seen the offer, indeed; but it was not present to his mind—he had forgotten it, and gave no consideration to it, in his intense excitement as to his own danger. There cannot be assent without knowledge of the offer; and ignorance of the offer is the same thing whether it is due to never hearing of it or forgetting it after hearing. But for this candid confession of Clarke's it might fairly be presumed that Clarke, having once seen the offer, acted on the faith of it, in reliance on it; but he has himself rebutted that presumption.

Questions

1. It is not clear that Clarke had in mind the offer of the pardon. Suppose he had. If two rewards are promised in a single offer and A accepts with only one in view is he entitled (1) only to the reward he has in view; or (2) to both rewards; or (3) to no reward?

---

[1] *Gibbons v. Proctor* has generally been considered to be—and condemned as—a case where the court held that a contract had been formed though the plaintiff did not know of the offer when he gave the information requested. The plaintiff certainly did not know of the offer when he gave the information to a fellow policeman, Coppin. But Coppin gave the information to Inspector Lennan who then wrote to Superintendent Penn. The giving of the information to Penn was the acceptance and, according to the report in (1891) 55 J.P. 616, 617, "The information ultimately reached Penn at a time when the plaintiff knew that the reward had been offered." See Treitel, *Law of Contract* (8th ed.), p. 35, and A. H. Hudson, "*Gibbons* v. *Proctor* Revisited" (1968) 84 L.Q.R. 503. Consider *N.Z. Shipping Co. v. Satterthwaite*, below, p. 290.

2. O offers a reward for information. A, not knowing of the offer, posts the information. Before the information reaches O, A learns of the offer and resolves to claim the reward. Is he entitled to it? If Isaacs A.C.J.'s New Year's Day swimmer happened to know of the reward, should he be entitled to it?

3. *Should* a person be able to recover a reward offered to any member of the public who does a certain act, when he has done that act in ignorance of the offer? See Hudson (1968) 84 L.Q.R. 503. A and B both give information leading to the conviction of bank robbers. A, who is unaware that the Bank has offered a reward, gives the information because he is a public-spirited citizen. B does so only because he knows the Bank has offered a reward. Can A not recover?

Law Revision Committee, 6th Interim Report (Statute of Frauds and the Doctrine of Consideration) (Cmd. 5449) 1937, para. 39 (p. 23)

English law traditionally divides parol contracts into two classes, the bilateral contract of a promise for a promise, and the unilateral contract of a promise for an act. In the case of bilateral contracts one promise is held to be consideration for the other, the agreement therefore becoming effective at the moment when the promises are exchanged. In the case of a unilateral contract, however, the promise does not become binding until the act has been completely performed. A promisor may therefore withdraw his promise at any time before completion of the act, even though he knows that the promisee has already entered upon the performance and nearly completed it. Where performance of the requested act requires considerable time and effort, it is obvious that grave injustice may be done if the offeror is permitted to revoke his offer because he has not as yet received the whole consideration for it. A simple illustration will make this clear: A promises B £50 if he walks from London to York in three days. A can withdraw his promise at any time before B has reached York. It is suggested in some of the books that in these circumstances A is estopped from withdrawing his offer, but this is clearly incorrect, as estoppel is only a rule of evidence and cannot create a cause of action where none exists. It is true that in some cases B can recover on a *quantum meruit* for the services he has rendered, but this may be an unsatisfactory remedy, as the damages in *quantum meruit* are measured by the value of the services to A and not by the loss suffered by B. To avoid this undesirable result the courts have in certain cases implied a second promise on the part of the promisor that he will not do anything to interfere with the promisee's performance of the required act, the consideration for this implied promise being the promisee's beginning of the requested act. This, however, is not satisfactory, for there is considerable doubt at the present time as to when this second promise can be implied and what are its terms. We therefore recommend that a promise made in consideration of the promisee performing an act shall be enforceable as soon as the promisee has entered upon performance of the act, unless the promise includes expressly or by implication a term that it can be revoked before the act has been completed. It is desirable to emphasise that this provision will in no way affect the rule in *Cutter v. Powell* (6 T.R. 320, below, p. 434) that if the promisee fails fully to perform the requested act, he is not entitled to recover anything under the contract. [The Committee's recommendation has never been implemented.]

Question
Estoppel is not a cause of action (see p. 258, below), but is the Committee's argument sound? If B, having reached York, sues for £50, his cause of action is for breach of contract.

He then relies on estoppel. Estoppel would then be invoked (as it usually is) to support an independent cause of action. Is the objection rather that the estoppel would be as to a promise and not a statement of fact? (*Cf. Jorden v. Money* (1854) 5 H.L.Cas. 185, below, p. 252)

Note

The implication of a second promise referred to by the Committee is a solution which has often been proposed (see, *e.g.* McGovney, "Irrevocable Offers" (1914) 27 Harv.L.Rev. 644, 659) and sometimes applied by the English courts (for example, by Denning L.J. in *Errington v. Errington* (below, p. 40). The theory is that when A says to B, "I will pay you £100 if you walk from London to York," he is making two promises, (i) the express promise to pay the £100 when the walk is completed and (ii) a "collateral" promise not to revoke his offer to pay £100 if B sets out on the walk. There are two unilateral contracts. The consideration requested for the first is the complete walk to York. The consideration requested for the second is setting out on the walk. If A "revokes" his offer when B is on his way, B can treat the "revocation" as inoperative (*Mounford v. Scott* below, p. 78) or at least recover damages for the loss of his chance to earn £100.

The Committee questions this solution because of doubts as to when the second promise can be implied. But is it any more uncertain than the implication generally of terms to give "business efficacy" to a contract? Perhaps the solution gives the court a necessary degree of flexibility, because it may not always be right that the offeror should be precluded from revoking his offer. *Cf. Luxor v. Cooper*, below, p. 42.

Wormser, "The True Conception of Unilateral Contracts," 26 Yale Law Journal, 136 Selected Readings 307, 308.

The writer discusses the case where A says to B, "I will give you $100 if you will walk across Brooklyn Bridge." He points out that until the act is done A is not bound since no contract arises until the completion of the act called for. He goes on:

The objection is made, however, that it is very "hard" upon B that he should have walked half-way across the Brooklyn Bridge and should get no compensation. This suggestion, invariably advanced, might be dismissed with the remark that "hard" cases should not make bad law. But going a step further, by way of reply, the pertinent inquiry at once suggests itself, "Was B bound to walk across the Brooklyn Bridge?" The answer to this is obvious. By hypothesis, B was not bound to walk across the Brooklyn Bridge. . . . If B is not bound to continue to cross the bridge, if B is will-free, why should not A also be will-free? Suppose that after B has crossed half the bridge he gets tired and tells A that he refuses to continue crossing. B, concededly, would be perfectly within his rights in so speaking and acting. A would have no cause of action against B for damages. If B has a *locus poenitentiae*, so has A. . . .

Note

In *Offord v. Davies* (below, p. 78 Williams J. asked, during the course of the argument, "suppose I guarantee the price of a carriage to be built for a third party, who, before the carriage is finished, and consequently before I am bound to pay for it, becomes insolvent—may I recall my guarantee?" Counsel (E. James, Q.C.) replied, "Not after the coach-builder has commenced the carriage." Erle C.J. said, "Before it ripens into a contract, either party may withdraw, and so put an end to the matter. But the moment the coach-builder has prepared the materials, he would probably be found by the jury to have contracted."

ERRINGTON v. ERRINGTON AND WOODS

Court of Appeal [1952] 1 K.B. 290; [1952] 1 T.L.R. 231; 96 S.J. 119; [1952] 1 All E.R. 149

Appeal by the plaintiff from the dismissal of her action against her daughter-in-law for the possession of a dwelling house.

DENNING L.J.: The facts are reasonably clear. In 1936 the father bought the house for his son and daughter-in-law to live in. The father put down £250 in cash and borrowed £500 from a building society on the security of the house, repayable with interest by instalments of 15s. a week. He took the house in his own name and made himself responsible for the instalments. The father told the daughter-in-law that the £250 was a present for them, but he left them to pay the building society instalments of 15s. a week themselves. He handed the building society book to the daughter-in-law and said to her: "Don't part with this book. The house will be your property when the mortgage is paid." He said that when he retired he would transfer it into their names. She has in fact paid the building society instalments regularly from that day to this with the result that much of the mortgage has been repaid, but there is a good deal yet to be paid. The rates on the house came to 10s. a week. The couple found that they could not pay those as well as the building society instalments, so the father said he would pay them and did so.

It is to be noted that the couple never bound themselves to pay the instalments to the building society; and I see no reason why any such obligation should be implied. It is clear law that the court is not to imply a term unless it is necessary; and I do not see that it is necessary here. Ample content is given to the whole arrangement by holding that the father promised that the house should belong to the couple as soon as they paid off the mortgage. The parties did not discuss what was to happen if the couple failed to pay the instalments to the building society, but I should have thought it clear that, if they did fail to pay the instalments, the father would not be bound to transfer the house to them. The father's promise was a unilateral contract—a promise of the house in return for their act of paying the instalments. It could not be revoked by him once the couple entered on performance of the act, but it would cease to bind him if they left it incomplete and unperformed, which they have not done. If that was the position during the father's lifetime, so it must be after his death. If the daughter-in-law continues to pay all the building society instalments, the couple will be entitled to have the property transferred to them as soon as the mortgage is paid off; but if she does not do so, then the building society will claim the instalments from the father's estate and the estate will have to pay them. I cannot think that in those circumstances the estate would be bound to transfer the house to them, any more than the father himself would have been ... the couple were licensees, having a permissive occupation short of a tenancy, but with a contractual right, or at any rate, an equitable right to remain so long as they paid the instalments, which would grow into a good equitable title to the house itself as soon as the mortgage was paid. This is, I think, the right view of the relationship of the parties. ... They were not tenants at will but licensees. ... They were licensees with a contractual right to remain. As such they have no right at law to remain, but only in equity, and equitable rights now prevail. ...

In the present case it is clear that the father expressly promised the couple that the property should belong to them as soon as the mortgage was paid, and impliedly promised that so long as they paid the instalments to the building society they should be allowed to remain in possession. They were not purchasers because they never bound themselves to pay the instalments, but nevertheless they were in a position analogous to purchasers. They have acted on the promise, and neither the father nor his widow, his successor in title, can eject them in disregard of it. The result is that in my opinion the appeal should be dismissed and no order for possession should be made.

SOMERVELL and HODSON L.JJ. delivered judgments dismissing the appeal.

Appeal dismissed.

Questions
1. Lord Denning says, "The father's promise was a unilateral contract." Was it a contract? Or was it an offer which, when they "entered on performance", became a contract not to revoke his promise to give them the house when they paid off the mortgage?
2. What was the contract which created a "contractual right . . . to remain so long as they paid the instalments"?
3. What does the case decide, or assume, about the effect of death on (*i*) an offer, (*ii*) a contract? See below, pp. 84, 513.

LUXOR (EASTBOURNE) LTD AND OTHERS v. COOPER

[1941] A.C. 108; [1941] 1 All E.R. 33; 110 L.J.K.B. 131; 164 L.T. 313; 57 T.L.R. 213

On September 23, 1935, the two appellant companies orally agreed that if the respondent introduced a party who should buy the two cinemas owned by the appellants, each of the appellants would pay the respondent £5,000. The respondent introduced a prospective purchaser who agreed, subject to contract, to buy the cinemas for £185,000 and remained throughout ready and willing to buy at that figure. The appellants did not proceed with the sale and the cinemas were ultimately disposed of by way of a sale of shares in the appellant companies to another party. The respondent brought an action claiming £10,000 commission or, alternatively, £10,000 damages for breach of an implied term that the appellants would "do nothing to prevent the satisfactory completion of the transaction so as to deprive the respondent of the agreed commission." The House of Lords, reversing the decision of the Court of Appeal, held (i) that commission was only payable on completion of the sale and (ii) that there was no room for any such implied term as was alleged.

LORD RUSSELL OF KILLOWEN: A few preliminary observations occur to me. (1) Commission contracts are subject to no peculiar rules or principles of their own; the law which governs them is the law which governs all contracts and all questions of agency. (2) No general rule can be laid down by which the rights of the agent or the liability of the principal under commission contracts are to be determined. In each case these must depend upon the exact terms of the contract in question, and upon the true construction of those terms. And (3) contracts by which owners of property, desiring to dispose of it, put it in the hands of agents on commission terms, are not (in default of specific provisions) contracts of employment in the ordinary meaning of those words. No obligation is imposed on the agent to do anything. The contracts are merely promises binding on the principal to pay a sum of money upon the happening of a specified event, which involves the rendering of some service by the agent. There is no real analogy between such contracts, and contracts of employment by which one party binds himself to do certain work, and the other binds himself to pay remuneration for the doing of it.

I do not assent to the view, which I think was the view of the majority in the first *Trollope Case* [1934] 2 K.B. 436, that a mere promise by a property owner to an agent to pay him a commission if he introduces a purchaser for the property at a specified price, or at a minimum price, ties the owner's hands, and compels him (as between himself and the agent) to bind himself contractually to sell to the agent's client who offers that price, with the result that if he refuses the offer he is liable to pay the agent a sum equal to or less than the amount of the commission either (a) on a *quantum meruit* or (b) as damages for breach of a term to be implied in the commission contract. As to the claim on a *quantum meruit*, I do not see how this can be justified in the face of the express provision for remuneration which the contract contains. This must necessarily exclude such a claim, unless it can (upon the facts of a particular case) be based upon a contract subsequent to the original contract, and arising from some conduct on the part of the principal.

As to the claim for damages, this rests upon the implication of some provision in the commission contract, the exact terms of which were variously stated in the course of the argument, the object always being to bind the principal not to refuse to complete the sale to the client whom the agent has introduced.

I can find no safe ground on which to base the introduction of any such implied term. Implied terms, as we all know, can only be justified under the compulsion of some necessity. No such compulsion or necessity exists in the case under consideration. The agent is promised a commission if he introduces a purchaser at a specified or minimum price. The owner is desirous of selling. The chances are largely in favour of the deal going through, if a purchaser is introduced. The agent takes the risk in the hope of a substantial remuneration for comparatively small exertion. In the case of the plaintiff his contract was made on September 23, 1935; his client's offer was made on October 2, 1935. A sum of £10,000 (the equivalent of the remuneration of a year's work by a Lord Chancellor) for work done within a period of eight or nine days is no mean reward, and is one well worth a risk. There is no lack of business efficacy in such a contract, even though the principal is free to refuse to sell to the agent's client.

The position will no doubt be different if the matter has proceeded to the stage of a binding contract having been made between the principal and the agent's client. In that case it can be said with truth that a "purchaser" has been introduced by the agent; in other words the event has happened upon the occurrence of which a right to the promised commission has become vested in the agent. From that moment no act or omission by the principal can deprive the agent of that vested right.

My Lords, for myself, I do not favour the view that an agent who has not earned his commission according to the express terms of the contract is entitled to damages for breach of some term to be implied. I see no necessity which compels the implication.

(Viscount Simon L.C. and Lords Thankerton, Wright and Romer also made speeches allowing the appeal.)

Questions

1. Was Lord Russell accurate (or consistent) in saying that the plaintiff made a contract on September 23, 1935? What consideration did the plaintiff give on that day? Was not an *offer* to make a unilateral contract all that happened that day?

2. It was evidently a breach of contract to revoke the offer in *Errington v. Errington*, not so in *Luxor v. Cooper*. Consider what factors might justify such a difference in result in the two cases.

DAULIA LTD v. FOUR MILLBANK NOMINEES

Court of Appeal [1978] 2 W.L.R. 621; [1978] 2 All E.R. 557

The plaintiffs were keen to buy certain properties from the defendants. Draft contracts were prepared but were never exchanged (see *Eccles v. Bryant*, below, p. 67). The plaintiffs alleged that on December 21, 1976, the defendants promised that, if the plaintiffs procured a bankers' draft for the deposit of £41,250, attended at the defendants' offices before 10 a.m. on December 22, 1976 and tendered the plaintiffs' part of the contract and the bankers' draft, they would enter into a contract to sell the properties. The plaintiffs attended before 10 a.m. with their deposit and part of the contract but the defendants refused to exchange. The plaintiffs' action for damages was dismissed by Brightman J. The plaintiffs appealed.

GOFF L.J. said there were three questions, of which only the first two are now relevant: (i) was there a unilateral contract? (ii) if so, was it unenforceable for want of writing to satisfy section 40 of the Law of Property Act 1925? (Above, pp. 6–7.) He continued: Was there a concluded unilateral contract by the defendants to enter into a contract for sale on the agreed terms?

The concept of a unilateral or "if" contract is somewhat anomalous, because it is clear that, at all events until the offeree starts to perform the condition, there is no contract at all, but merely an offer which the offeror is free to revoke. Doubts have been expressed whether the offeror becomes bound so soon as the offeree starts to perform or satisfy the condition, or only when he has fully done so. In my judgment, however, we are not concerned in this case with any such problem, because in my view the plaintiffs had fully performed or satisfied the condition when they presented themselves at the time and place appointed with a bankers' draft for the deposit and their part of the written contract for sale duly engrossed and signed, and there tendered the same, which I understand to mean proffered it for exchange. Actual exchange, which never took place, would not in my view have been part of the satisfaction of the condition but something additional which was inherently necessary to be done by the plaintiffs to enable, not to bind, the defendants to perform the unilateral contract.

Accordingly in my judgment the answer to the first question must be in the affirmative.

Even if my reasoning so far be wrong the conclusion in my view is still the same for the following reasons. Whilst I think the true view of a unilateral contract must in general be that the offeror is entitled to require full performance of the condition which he has imposed and short of that he is not bound, that must be subject to one important qualification, which stems from the fact that there must be an implied obligation on the part of the offeror not to prevent the condition becoming satisfied, which obligation it seems to me must arise as soon as the offeree starts to perform. Until then the offeror can revoke the whole thing, but once the offeree has

embarked on performance it is too late for the offeror to revoke his offer
. . . [Turning to the second question, his Lordship referred to *Warlow v.
Harrison* (above, p. 21) and continued:] This case affords support for the
plaintiffs' contention as far as it goes, but it is distinguishable, since there
the action was against the auctioneer, not the vendor, and it was not on a
contract by the auctioneer that he himself would sell to the highest bidder
but that his principal would do so.

In these circumstances in my judgment it is necessary to consider how
the matter stands in principle. As I see it the question is whether the
unilateral contract is, and I quote these words from section 40, "a contract
for the sale or other disposition of land or any interest in land." It is clear
to me that ex hypothesi it is not a contract for the sale of land or any
interest in land because it is a separate and independent contract to enter
into such a contract.

In my judgment, however, it is equally clearly a contract for some other
disposition of an interest in land. It is not necessary in my view that the
interest in land to be disposed of should actually exist at the time of the
contract. I cannot doubt that a contract for valuable consideration to grant
an easement over Blackacre would be a contract for the disposition of an
interest in land within the meaning of the section.

Now, in the present case we have a contract to enter into a proper written
contract for the sale of land. Such a contract if entered into would be
specifically enforceable and would therefore give the plaintiffs a right to the
land in equity and so would create and give them an equitable interest in
the land. It follows in my judgment that the unilateral contract was a
contract to dispose of an interest in land, because it was a contract to do
something which would have that effect in law.

The plaintiffs say "But we are not claiming specific performance; only
damages." That, however, in my view is an irrelevant consideration for two
reasons. The first, which is I think conclusive, is that we are not concerned
with whether the "unilateral contract" could be specifically enforced so as
actually to create an interest in land, but whether it is a contract to do that
which, if done, would create such an interest. The words of the section look
only to the contract. The second is that the plaintiffs cannot escape the
impact of the section by limiting the nature of the relief they seek, and,
moreover, the damages for breach of the unilateral contract must, as I see
it, be exactly the same as damages for breach of the contract of sale would
have been if contracts had been exchanged and then broken by the
plaintiffs.

If, however, contrary to my view it be necessary that the unilateral
contract should be one capable of specific performance, in my judgment it
is so. . . . For this purpose one must regard the matter apart from section
40, for if one postulates that the section applies one begs the whole
question. So regarded, I cannot see how a vendor can escape an order for
specific performance by agreeing (with sufficient particularity to be effective in law) to agree to sell rather than by a direct agreement to sell.

The dictum of Lord Wright in *Hillas & Co. Ltd v. Arcos Ltd* (below,
p. 100) "a contract *de praesenti* to enter into what, in law, is an enforceable
contract, is simply that enforceable contract, and no more and no less,"
with which I respectfully agree, does not directly apply, because prior to
exchange of contracts which never took place the plaintiffs were not

themselves bound to purchase or to enter into a contract to purchase. They could have resiled at the very last moment, even after tender, so that this was not a contract between A and B to make a contract between A and B, but a unilateral contract by A to enter into a particular contract with B, but in my view the principle must be the same.

In my judgment, therefore, the unilateral contract in this case is prima facie unenforceable. . . .

Notes and Questions

1. A contract for the disposition of an interest in land which is not in writing signed by both parties is now not merely unenforceable but void: Law of Property (Miscellaneous Provisions) Act 1989, s.2, above, p. 6. "Disposition" has the same meaning in the 1989 as in the 1925 Act: 1989 Act, s.2(6). If the case arose today and Goff L.J.'s reasoning were applied, the result would be the same. The only difference is that it would now be unnecessary to consider Goff L.J.'s third question, that is, whether the doctrine of part performance applied (which it did not). That doctrine has disappeared from the law.

2. What if the defendants had agreed in a writing signed by both parties that if the plaintiffs attended with the draft, etc., they would enter into a contract to sell the properties? Would the writing, under the present law, have become a valid contract by the defendants to sell (though not a contract by the plaintiffs to buy) when the plaintiffs attended as requested? *Cf. Spiro v. Glencrown Properties*, below, p. 104. Is the hypothetical case different from *Spiro* because the written offer was revocable when signed?

3. Why was there not a contract for the sale of land? Was the defendant contractually bound (apart from the lack of written evidence) to sell the land? If it was not a sale of land, what sort of "disposition" was it? Buckley L.J. said, "At the risk of drawing too fine a distinction one might say that, though not a contract of sale, it would be a contract for sale." Is this "too fine a distinction"? What is the difference?

4. Is it accurate to say (as Goff L.J. did when considering the third question) that "the performance of the condition by the offeree [in a unilateral contract] is also the discharge of all his obligations"? Does he have any obligations? Did the plaintiffs incur any obligations? If the parties had been in the act of tendering their parts of the contract could the plaintiffs have withdrawn? Could the defendants?

Section 2. Bilateral Contracts

POWELL v. LEE

King's Bench Division (1908) 99 L.T. 284

The six defendants were the managers of a school. They were minded to appoint a headmaster. The plaintiff applied for the post and with two other candidates was selected for the final choice of the managers. By three votes to two the managers passed a resolution on March 26 that the plaintiff should be appointed. No directions were given by the meeting as to communicating the results of the voting to the plaintiff, but one of the managers, Dismore, was requested by Lee to send a telegram to one of the other candidates, Parker, telling him that he had not been elected. Two of the managers subsequently sought to reopen the question and Lee supported them.

On April 1, without any instruction to do so from the managers as a body, Dismore sent the following telegram to the plaintiff: "The Cranford School managers selected you as headmaster on Tuesday last.—Dismore, Hon. Sec."

On April 2 the managers held a meeting at which all except Dismore were present and passed unanimously a resolution rescinding the resolution of the previous meeting, and appointing Parker headmaster. On April 5 the plaintiff was informed by Lee that Parker had been appointed, and he brought this action, alleging that by breach of a contract to employ him he had suffered damages in loss of salary to the extent of £11 5s.

The county court judge held that there was no contract as there had been no *authorised* communication of intention to contract on the part of the body, that is, the managers, alleged to be a party to the contract.

The plaintiff appealed.

CHANNELL J.: I think the decision of the learned county court judge was right. In my opinion the case depends on this, that where, as in this case, a body of six people, acting not as a corporation or as a board of directors, but as six persons having the power to appoint to a post, vote on the question and resolve to appoint someone, they do not make a concluded contract then and there. There must be something more. There must be a communication made by the body of persons to the selected candidate. In this case the managers authorised a communication to Mr Parker to the effect that he had not been elected; but they did not authorise a communication to Mr Powell to the effect that he had been elected. To my mind, that implies that they reserved the power to consider the matter. Then one of the parties desired to reopen the matter, and he told the plaintiff that there was a difficulty. Later, another party, Mr Dismore, told the plaintiff that he had been elected on March 26. I think Mr Dismore made that communication to the plaintiff acting as an individual, and not for the body of the managers. If the mere knowledge of what happened at the meeting was sufficient to complete the contract, as, for instance, if the result of the voting was overheard at the door, the matter would rest upon a different footing. But I do not think that is sufficient to complete the contract. There must be notice of acceptance from the contracting party in some way, and the mere fact that the managers did not authorise such a communication, which is the usual course adopted, implies that they meant to reserve the power to reconsider the decision at which they had arrived. On these grounds, and on the grounds stated by the learned county court judge, I think his decision was right, and the appeal must be dismissed.

SUTTON J.: I am of the same opinion.

Appeal dismissed.

Questions

1. *Cf. Dickinson v. Dodds*, below, p. 81. Is it true to say that unintended communication of the revocation of an offer is effective when unintended communication of an acceptance is not? If so, why? May the cases be distinguished on the ground that there was no more than a decision to accept in *Powell v. Lee* whereas in *Dickinson v. Dodds* the offeror had done an act inconsistent with the continuance of the offer?

2. Ed applies for a post at the X University. The application states that it is a firm offer to take the post if appointed. The day after the interview Ed receives a letter from R. V. Winkle, the Registrar of the University, informing him that he has been appointed. In fact, the interviewing committee decided to appoint Ted but Winkle had dozed off and misheard the name. Advise Ed.

Note

In *Robophone Facilities Ltd v. Blank* [1966] 1 W.L.R. 1428 Lord Denning held that, where a written offer provided that it should become binding only upon its being signed by the offeree, no contract arose until the offeree signed the document *and notified the offeror* that he had done so. Otherwise, "[The offeree] would be able to keep the form in the office unsigned, and then play fast and loose as they pleased. The [offeror] would not know whether or not there was a contract binding them to supply or him to take. . . ." Diplock L.J. explicitly refrained from, and Harman L.J. did not express, any opinion on this point. Is it arguable that the offeror had waived his right to communication?

FELTHOUSE v. BINDLEY

Common Pleas (1862) 11 C.B. (N.S.) 869; 31 L.J.C.P. 204; 142 E.R. 1037 Exchequer
Chamber (1863) 1 New Rep. 401; 7 L.T. 835; 11 W.R. 429

The plaintiff discussed with his nephew, John, the purchase of a horse belonging to John. A few days later John wrote to the plaintiff, saying that he had learned that there was a misunderstanding as to the price; the plaintiff apparently believed that he had bought the horse for £30, John that he had sold it for 30 guineas. The plaintiff, on January 2, wrote to John proposing to split the difference and adding, "If I hear no more about him, I consider the horse is mine at £30 15s." No reply was sent to this last letter, nor was any money paid, and the horse remained in John's possession. Six weeks later (on February 25) the defendant, an auctioneer, who was employed by John to sell his farming stock, and who had been directed by John to reserve the horse in question, as it had already been sold, by mistake put it up with the rest and sold it.

On February 26 the defendant wrote to the plaintiff admitting that he had been told by John to reserve the horse, but that he had forgotten to do so. On the 27th John wrote to the plaintiff saying that he had told the defendant that "that horse (meaning the one I sold to you) is sold," but that the defendant had, in error, sold it.

In an action for conversion, a verdict was found for the plaintiff, damages £33, leave being reserved to the defendant to enter a nonsuit, if the court should be of the opinion that the objection was well founded.

A rule nisi was obtained on the grounds that "sufficient title or possession of the horse, to maintain the action, was not vested in the plaintiff at the time of the wrong; that the letter of John Felthouse of February 27, 1861, was not admissible in evidence against the defendant; that, if it was admissible, being after the sale of the horse by the defendant, it did not confer title on the plaintiff; and that there was, at the time of the wrong, no sufficient memorandum in writing, or possession of the horse, or payment, to satisfy the Statute of Frauds." (For the Statute of Frauds, see above, p. 5).

WILLES J.: I am of opinion that the rule to enter a nonsuit should be made absolute. [The learned judge stated the facts and continued:] It is clear that there was no complete bargain on January 2: and it is also clear that the uncle had no right to impose upon the nephew a sale of his horse for £30 15s. unless he chose to comply with the condition of writing to repudiate the offer. The nephew might, no doubt, have bound his uncle to the bargain by writing to him; the uncle might also have retracted his offer at any time before acceptance. It stood an open offer; and so things remained until February 25, when the nephew was about to sell his farming stock by auction. The horse in question being catalogued with the rest of the stock, the auctioneer (the defendant) was told that it was already sold. It is clear, therefore, that the nephew in his own mind intended his uncle to have the horse at the price which he (the uncle) had named, £30 15s.: but he had not communicated such his intention to his uncle, or done anything to bind himself. Nothing, therefore, had been done to vest the property in the horse in the plaintiff down to February 25, when the horse was sold by the defendant. It appears to me that, independently of the subsequent letters, there had been no bargain to pass the property in the horse to the plaintiff, and therefore that he had no right to complain of the sale. Then, what is the effect of the subsequent correspondence? The letter of the auctioneer amounts to nothing. The more important letter is that of the nephew, of February 27, which is relied on as showing that he intended to accept and did accept the terms offered by his uncle's letter of January 2. That letter, however, may be treated either as an acceptance then for the first time made by him, or as a memorandum of a bargain complete before February 25, sufficient within the Statute of Frauds. It seems to me that the former is the more likely construction: and, if so, it is clear that the plaintiff cannot recover. But, assuming that there had been a complete parol bargain before February 25, and that the letter of the 27th was a mere expression of the terms of that prior bargain, and not a bargain then for the first time concluded, it would be directly contrary to the decision of the Court of Exchequer in *Stockdale v. Dunlop* (6 M. & W. 224) to hold that that acceptance had relation back to the previous offer so as to bind third persons in respect of a dealing with the property by them in the interim.

BYLES and KEATING JJ. concurred.

In the Court of Exchequer Chamber (Pollock C.B., Mellor and Blackburn JJ., Martin and Wilde BB.), Pollock C.B. said the judgment of the Common Pleas must be affirmed. The Statute of Frauds had not been complied with. There had been no delivery, part payment or memorandum in writing, to vest the property in the plaintiff.

Questions
1. If using the smoke ball three times daily for two weeks was a sufficient acceptance in *Carlill's* case, why was not the nephew's directing the auctioneer to keep the horse out of the sale a sufficient acceptance in *Felthouse v. Bindley?* Cf. C. J. Miller (1972) 35 M.L.R. 489; *Fairline Shipping Corpn. v. Adamson* [1975] Q.B. 180 at 188–189 (Kerr J.).
2. If the horse had died after the nephew had directed the auctioneer to keep it out of the sale, and before the day of the sale, could the nephew have recovered the price from his uncle? (Assuming that the Statute of Frauds was satisfied.)

TAYLOR v. ALLON

Divisional Court [1966] 1 Q.B. 304; [1965] 2 W.L.R. 598; [1965] 1 All E.R. 557

T was convicted of using a motor-car on a road on April 15, 1964, without insurance against third-party risks, contrary to section 201 of the Road Traffic Act, 1960. His insurance had expired on April 5, 1964. The insurance company, in accordance with normal practice, sent him a temporary cover-note for 15 days from April 6. T did not intend, however, to renew that insurance and had obtained a temporary cover-note from a new insurer for 30 days from April 16.

LORD PARKER C.J.: Bearing in mind that a valid insurance for the purposes of the section must arise from an enforceable contract, it seems to me that the contract, if any, contained in the temporary covering note must arise by offer and acceptance. It is conceded that the policy that expired had no provisions for extended cover, and accordingly this document sending this temporary covering note must in my judgment be treated as an offer to insure for the future. It may be, although I find it unnecessary to decide in this case, that there can be an acceptance of such an offer by conduct and without communication with the insurance company. It may well be, as it seems to me, that if a man took his motor-car out on the road in reliance on this temporary cover, albeit that there had been no communication of that fact to the insurance company, there would be an acceptance, and that the contract so created would contain an implied promise by the insured to pay, either in the renewal premium when that was paid, or if it was not paid, for the period for which the temporary cover note had, as it were, been accepted.

I find it unnecessary in the present case to decide that matter, and for this reason, that it seems to me that the defendant must at any rate go to the length of saying that he knew of the temporary cover and that he took out his motor-car in reliance on it. In fact, as I have already said, the defendant never gave any evidence at all. Further, from the justices' clerk's notes, which again we have been allowed to refer to, it appears that when he was stopped by the police and asked to produce his insurance certificate, he produced the old certificate of insurance which expired on April 5, and he also produced the cover note from the new insurance company which commenced on April 16. When the police pointed out that therefore on April 15 he was not covered, he not only did not refer to this temporary cover note, but he said then that he had been negotiating a change of insurance companies, and did not realise that it, presumably the original certificate, had run out. It was only at the hearing, and I think at the second hearing, that this temporary cover note, this extended cover, was produced by the defendant's solicitor.

In those circumstances it seems to me that the defendant has never gone to the length of showing that he knew of the temporary cover, that he acted in reliance on it, and thereby had accepted their offer contained in it. I think the justices came to a correct decision in law and I would dismiss this appeal.

MARSHALL and WIDGERY JJ. agreed.

Problem

Alonzo, who had had discussions with Bertram concerning the sale of Bertram's car, wrote to Bertram on January 1, saying: "I offer you £500 for the car. I am going abroad on January 8 and if I do not hear from you before then I shall consider the car mine at that price and will collect it from you on my return on February 1."

Bertram decided to accept Alonzo's offer, but did not reply. On January 15 Charlie offered Bertram £600 for the car. Bertram replied that he must reluctantly refuse the offer as the car was already sold to Alonzo. Alonzo now refuses to take the car. The market price of cars has fallen considerably. Advise Bertram.

Notes

1. In *Re Selectmove Ltd* [1995] 1 W.L.R. 474, [1995] 2 All E.R. 531, C.A., below, p. 235, Peter Gibson L.J. said that the authorities for the general rule that acceptance cannot be inferred from silence are cases where an offeror sought to impose on the offeree a term that silence would amount to acceptance. He went on: "Where the offeree himelf indicates that an offer is to be taken as accepted if he does not indicate to the contrary by an ascertainable time, he is undertaking to speak if he does not want the agreement to be concluded. I see no reason why that should not be an exceptional circumstance such that the offer can be accepted by silence. But it is unnecessary to express a concluded opinion on the point." Has not the offeree, in the case envisaged, accepted the offer conditionally so as to become bound when the condition is fulfilled?

2. Aggressive sellers have sometimes sent unsolicited goods offering to sell them and advising the offeree that he will be taken to have accepted the goods if he does not reply or return the goods within a certain period. It has always been clear that a contract could not be forced on an unwilling offeree by an ultimatum of this kind. It is now provided by the Unsolicited Goods and Services Act 1971, that the recipient of unsolicited goods may treat the goods as if they were an unconditional gift to him and the sender's rights will be extinguished if the conditions in the Act are satisfied. The conditions are that for a period of six months, or, if the recipient gives notice in the form prescribed by the Act, 30 days from the date of receipt, the sender does not take possession of the goods and the recipient does not unreasonably refuse to permit him to do so.

If the recipient of unsolicited goods were to exercise the rights of an owner over them during the 30 days or six months it is possible that he might be held to have accepted the offer by his conduct and to be bound to pay for the goods. See *Weatherby v. Banham* (1832) 5 C. & P. 228, and *Trinder and Partners v. Haggis* [1951] W.N. 416.

On the inference of contracts from silence and inaction, see Robert Goff L.J. in *Allied Marine Transport v. Vale do Rio Doce* [1985] 2 All E.R. 796 at 805.

HOUSEHOLD FIRE INSURANCE CO. v. GRANT

Court of Appeal (1879) 4 Ex.D. 216; 48 L.J.Ex. 577; 41 L.T. 298; 27 W.R. 858

One Kendrick was the agent of the company in Glamorgan. The defendant handed to Kendrick an application in writing for shares in the company, which stated the defendant had paid to the bankers of the company £5, being a deposit of 1s. per share, and requesting an allotment of 100 shares, and agreeing to pay a further sum of 19s. per share within 12 months of the date of the allotment. Kendrick forwarded the application to the plaintiffs in London and the secretary of the company made out a letter of allotment in favour of the defendant and posted it addressed to the defendant in Swansea. The letter never arrived. The defendant's name was entered on the register of shareholders and he was credited with two dividends amounting to 5s. The company then went into liquidation and the liquidator sued for £94 15s. being the balance due upon the 100 shares.

Lopes J. found for the plaintiff and the defendant appealed.

THESIGER L.J.: In this case the defendant made an application for shares in the plaintiffs' company under circumstances from which we must imply that he authorised the company, in the event of their allotting to him the shares applied for, to send the notice of allotment by post. . . .

Now, whatever in abstract discussion may be said as to the legal notion of its being necessary, in order to the effecting of a valid and binding contract, that the minds of the parties should be brought together at one and the same moment, that notion is practically the foundation of English law upon the subject of the formation of contracts. Unless, therefore, a contract constituted by correspondence is absolutely concluded at the moment that the continuing offer is accepted by the person to whom the offer is addressed, it is difficult to see how the two minds are ever to be brought together at one and the same moment. This was pointed out by Lord Ellenborough in the case of *Adams v. Lindsell* ((1818) 1 B. & A. 681), which is recognised authority upon this branch of the law. But on the other hand it is a principle of law, as well established as the legal notion to which I have referred, that the minds of the two parties must be brought together by mutual communication. An acceptance, which only remains in the breast of the acceptor without being actually and by legal implication communicated to the offeror, is no binding acceptance. How then are these elements of law to be harmonised in the case of contracts formed by correspondence through the post? I see no better mode than that of treating the post office as the agent of both parties, and it was so considered by Lord Romilly in *Hebb's Case* (L.R. 4 Eq. at p. 12) when in the course of his judgment he said: "*Dunlop v. Higgins* (1 H.L.C. 381) decides that the posting of a letter accepting an offer constitutes a binding contract, but the reason of that is, that the post office is the common agent of both parties." Alderson B., also, in *Stocken v. Collin* (7 M. & W. at p. 516), a case of notice of dishonour, and the case referred to by Lord Cottenham, says: "If the doctrine that the post office is only the agent for the delivery of the notice were correct no one could safely avail himself of that mode of transmission." But if the post office be such common agent, then it seems to me to follow that, as soon as the letter of acceptance is delivered to the post office, the contract is made as complete and final and absolutely binding as if the acceptor had put his letter into the hands of a messenger sent by the offerer himself as his agent to deliver the offer and receive the acceptance. What other principle can be adopted short of holding that the contract is not complete by acceptance until and except from the time that the letter containing the acceptance is delivered to the offerer, a principle which has been distinctly negatived? . . . The contract . . . is actually made when the letter is posted. The acceptor, in posting the letter, has, to use the language of Lord Blackburn, in *Brogden v. Directors of Metropolitan Ry.* ((1876) 2 App. Cas. 666) "put it out of his control and done an extraneous act which clenches the matter, and shows beyond all doubt that each side is bound." How then can a casualty in the post, whether resulting in delay, which in commercial transactions is often as bad as no delivery, or in non-delivery, unbind the parties or unmake the contract? To me it appears that in practice a contract complete upon the acceptance of an offer being posted, but liable to be put an end to by an accident in the post, would be more mischievous than a contract only binding upon the parties to it upon the acceptance actually reaching the offerer, and I can see no principle of law from which such an anomalous contract can be deduced.

There is no doubt that the implication of a complete, final, and absolutely binding contract being formed, as soon as the acceptance of an offer is posted, may in some cases lead to inconvenience and hardship. But such there must be at times in every view of the law. It is impossible in transactions which pass between parties at a distance, and have to be carried on through the medium of correspondence, to adjust conflicting rights between innocent parties, so as to make the consequences of mistake on the part of a mutual agent fall equally upon the shoulders of both. At the same time I am not prepared to admit that the implication in question will lead to any great or general inconvenience or hardship. An offerer, if he chooses, may always make the formation of the contract which he proposes dependent upon the actual communication to himself of the acceptance. If he trusts to the post he trusts to a means of communication which, as a rule, does not fail, and if no answer to his offer is received by him, and the matter is of importance to him, he can make inquiries of the person to whom his offer was addressed. On the other hand, if the contract is not finally concluded, except in the event of the acceptance actually reaching the offerer, the door would be opened to the perpetration of much fraud, and, putting aside this consideration, considerable delay in commercial transactions, in which dispatch is, as a rule, of the greatest consequence, would be occasioned; for the acceptor would never be entirely safe in acting upon his acceptance until he had received notice that his letter of acceptance had reached its destination.

Upon balance of conveniences and inconveniences it seems to me, applying with slight alterations the language of the Supreme Court of the United States in *Tayloe v. Merchants Fire Insurance Co.* (9 Howard S. Ct. Rep. 390), more consistent with the acts and declarations of the parties in this case to consider the contract complete and absolutely binding on the transmission of the notice of allotment through the post, as the medium of communication that the parties themselves contemplated, instead of postponing its completion until the notice had been received by the defendant.

BAGGALLAY L.J. delivered a concurring judgment.

BRAMWELL L.J.: If . . . posting a letter which does not reach is a sufficient communication of acceptance of an offer, it is equally a communication of everything else which may be communicated by post, for example, notice to quit. It is impossible to hold, if I offer my landlord to sell him some hay and he writes accepting my offer, and in the same letter gives me notice to quit, and posts his letter which, however, does not reach me, that he has communicated to me his acceptance of my offer, but not his notice to quit. Suppose a man has paid his tailor by cheque or banknote, and posts a letter containing a cheque or banknote to his tailor, which never reaches, is the tailor paid? If he is, would he be if he had never been paid before in that way? Suppose a man is in the habit of sending cheques and banknotes to his banker by post, and posts a letter containing cheques and banknotes, which never reaches. Is the banker liable? Would he be if this was the first instance of a remittance of the sort? In the cases I have supposed, the tailor and banker may have recognised this mode of remittance by sending back receipts and putting the money to the credit of the remitter. Are they liable with that? Are they liable without it? The question then is, is posting a letter which is never received a communication to the person addressed, or an equivalent, or something which dispenses with it? It is for those who say it is to make good their contention. I ask why is it? My answer beforehand to any argument that may be urged is that it is not a communication, and that there is no agreement to take it as an equivalent for or to dispense with a communication. That those who affirm the contrary say the thing which is not. That if Brian C.J. had had to adjudicate on the case, he would deliver the same judgment as that reported. That because a man, who may send a communication by post or otherwise, sends it by post, he should bind the person addressed, although the communication never reaches him, while he would not so bind him if he had sent it by hand, is impossible. There is no reason in it; it is simply arbitrary. I ask whether anyone who thinks so is prepared to follow that opinion to its consequence; suppose the offer is to sell a particular chattel, and the letter accepting it never arrives, is the property in the chattel transferred? Suppose it is to sell an estate or grant a lease, is the bargain completed? The lease might be such as not to require a deed, could be subsequent lessee be ejected by the would-be acceptor of the offer because he had posted a letter? Suppose an article is advertised at so much, and that it would be sent on receipt of a post office order. Is it enough to post the letter? If the word "receipt" is relied on, is it really meant that that makes a difference? If it should be said let the offerer wait, the answer is, maybe he may lose his market meanwhile. Besides, his offer may be by advertisement to all mankind. Suppose a reward for information, information posted does not reach, someone else gives it and is paid, is the offerer liable to the first man?

It is said that a contrary rule would be hard on the would-be acceptor, who may have made his arrangements on the footing that the bargain was concluded. But to hold as contended would be equally hard on the offerer, who may have made his arrangements on the footing that his offer was not accepted; his non-receipt of any communication may be attributable to the person to whom it was made being absent. What is he to do but act on the negative, that no communication has been made to him? Further, the use of the post office is no more authorised by the offerer than the sending an answer by hand, and all these hardships would befall the person posting the letter if he sent it by hand. Doubtless in that case he would be the person to suffer if the letter did not reach its destination. Why should his sending it by post relieve him of the loss and cast it on the other party? It was said, if he sends it by hand it is revocable, but not if he sends it by post, which makes the difference. But it is revocable when sent by post, not that the letter can be got back, but its arrival might be anticipated by a letter by hand or telegram, and there is no case to show that such anticipation would not prevent the letter from binding. It would be a most alarming thing to say that it would. That a letter honestly but mistakenly written and posted must bind the writer if hours before its arrival he informed the person addressed that it was coming, but was wrong and recalled; suppose a false but honest character given, and the mistake found out after the letter posted, and notice that it was wrong given to the person addressed. . . .

I am of opinion that there was no bargain between these parties to allot and take shares, that to make such bargain there should have been an acceptance of the defendant's offer and a communication to him of that acceptance. That there was no such communication. That posting a letter does not differ from other attempts at communication in any of its consequences, save that it is irrevocable as between the poster and post office. The difficulty has arisen from a mistake as to what was decided in *Dunlop v. Higgins* (1 H.L.C. 381), and from supposing that because there is a right to have recourse to the post as a means of communication, that right is attended with some peculiar consequences, and also from supposing that because if the letter reaches it binds from the time of posting, it also binds though it never reaches. Mischief may arise if my opinion prevails. It probably will not, as so much has been said on the matter that principle is lost sight of. I believe equal if not greater, will, if it does not prevail. I believe the latter will be obviated only by the rule being made nugatory by every prudent man saying, "your answer by post is only to bind if it reaches me." But the question is not to be decided on these considerations. What is the law? What is the principle? If Brian C.J. had had to decide this, a public post being instituted in his time, he would have said the law is the same, now there is a post, as it was before, *viz.*, a communication to affect a man must be a communication, that is, must reach him.

Judgment affirmed.

Note

In *Re London and Northern Bank, ex p. Jones* [1990] 1 Ch. 220 at about 7.30 a.m. on October 27 a servant of the Bank took to the G.P.O. in London a letter addressed to Dr Jones in Sheffield accepting his offer to buy shares in the Bank. In the outer precincts of the G.P.O. a postman came by and offered to take the letters. They were handed to him, he took them into the post office and came back and said it was all right. A letter from J withdrawing his offer was delivered at the Bank at 8.30 a.m. on October 27 and opened by the secretary at 9.30 a.m. The letter of acceptance was not delivered to J until 7.30 p.m. that day, having been posted not at the G.P.O. but at a district office. Cozens-Hardy J. held that handing the letter to the postman outside the G.P.O. was not a posting of the letter so as to amount to an acceptance; the Postal Guide expressly stated that town postmen were not allowed to take charge of letters for the post. As the Bank was unable to prove that the letter of acceptance was properly posted before 9.30 a.m. it was held that J's offer was effectively withdrawn.

Questions

1. What would be the position if a letter of acceptance were handed to a postman in a country district where it was customary for the postman to collect the mail?

2. Was the withdrawal complete at 8.30 a.m. or at 9.30 a.m.? *Cf. Byrne v. Van Tienhoven* (below, p. 60).

3. A makes an offer by letter to B. B posts an acceptance which is wrongly addressed and never arrives. Is there a contract?

4. A makes an offer by letter to B. All post office workers then go on strike. B posts an acceptance. Is there a contract? Would the answer be different if the strike began immediately after the posting of the acceptance?

5. What are the answers to the rhetorical questions put by Bramwell L.J. in *Household Fire Insurance Co. v. Grant* above, pp. 53–54.

6. If an offer is sent by telex or fax, is posting a letter an acceptance? *Cf. Quenerduaine v. Cole* (1883) 32 W.R. 185.

HOLWELL SECURITIES LTD v. HUGHES

Court of Appeal [1974] 1 W.L.R. 155; [1974] 1 All E.R. 161; (1973) 26 P. & C.R. 544

On October 19, 1971, the defendant granted the plaintiffs an option to purchase certain freehold property. The agreement provided: "The said option shall be exercisable by notice in writing to [the defendant] at any time within six months from the date hereof." On April 14, 1972, the plaintiffs wrote to the defendant's solicitor purporting to exercise the option. They posted a copy of that letter, with a covering letter properly addressed, to the defendant but these never arrived. The plaintiffs admitted that the letter to the defendant's solicitor was not a sufficient notice. The plaintiffs' action for specific performance of the option agreement, or damages, was dismissed by Templeman J. The plaintiffs appealed.

RUSSELL L.J.: The plaintiffs' main contention below and before this court has been that the option was exercised and the contract for sale and purchase was constituted at the moment that the letter addressed to the defendant with its enclosure was committed by the plaintiffs' solicitors to the proper representative of the postal service, so that its failure to reach its destination is irrelevant.

It is the law in the first place that prima facie acceptance of an offer must be communicated to the offeror. On this principle the law has engrafted a doctrine that, if in any given case the true view is that the parties contemplated that the postal service might be used for the purpose of forwarding an acceptance of the offer, committal of the acceptance in a regular manner to the postal service will be acceptance of the offer so as to constitute a contract, even if the letter goes astray and is lost. Nor, as was once suggested, are such cases limited to cases in which the offer has been made by post. It suffices I think at this stage to refer to *Henthorn v. Fraser*.[1] In the present case, as I read a passage in the judgment below, Templeman J. concluded that the parties here contemplated that the postal service might be used to communicate acceptance of the offer (by exercise of the option); and I agree with that.

But that is not and cannot be the end of the matter. In any case, before one can find that the basic principle of the need for communication of acceptance to the offeror is displaced by this artificial concept of communication by the act of posting, it is necessary that the offer is in its terms consistent with such displacement and not one which by its terms points rather in the direction of actual communication. We were referred to *Henthorn v. Fraser* and to the obiter dicta of Farwell J. in *Bruner v. Moore* [1904] 1 Ch. 305, which latter was a case of an option to purchase patent rights. But in neither of those cases was there apparently any language in the offer directed to the manner of acceptance of the offer or exercise of the option.

The relevant language here is, "the said option shall be exercisable by notice in writing to the Intending Vendor . . .," a very common phrase in an option agreement. There is, of course, nothing in that phrase to suggest that the notification to the defendant could not be made by post. But the requirement of "notice . . . to," in my judgment is language which should be taken expressly to assert the ordinary situation in law that acceptance requires to be communicated or notified to the offeror, and is inconsistent with the theory that acceptance can be constituted by the act of posting, referred to by Anson,[2] as "acceptance *without notification*."

It is of course true that the instrument could have been differently worded. An option to purchase within a period given for value has the characteristic of an offer that cannot be withdrawn. The instrument might have said "The offer constituted by this option may be accepted in writing within six months": in which case no doubt the posting would have sufficed to form the contract. But that language was not used, and, as indicated, in my judgment the language used prevents that legal outcome. Under this head of the case hypothetical problems were canvassed to

---

[1] [1892] 2 Ch. 27. The plaintiff who lived in Birkenhead was handed a note at the defendant's office in Liverpool giving him an option to purchase certain property within 14 days. The next day the defendant posted a letter withdrawing the offer. That letter did not reach Birkenhead until after 5 p.m. In the meantime, the plaintiff had posted a letter at 3.50 p.m. accepting the offer. That letter was delivered after the defendant's office was closed and was opened the following morning. The Court of Appeal held that the plaintiff was entitled to specific performance. Lord Herschell said that it was somewhat artificial to speak of the offeree having the implied authority of the offeror to send his acceptance by post: "Where the circumstances are such that it must have been within the contemplation of the parties that, according to the ordinary usages of mankind, the post might be used as a means of communicating the acceptance of an offer, the acceptance is complete as soon as it is posted."

[2] *Law of Contract* (23rd ed., 1969), p. 47.

suggest difficulties in the way of that conclusion. What if the letter had been delivered through the letterbox of the house in due time, but the defendant had either deliberately or fortuitously not been there to receive it before the option period expired? This does not persuade me that the artificial posting rule is here applicable. The answer might well be that in the circumstances the defendant had impliedly invited communication by use of an orifice in his front door designed to receive communications . . . [His Lordship held that the rule in *Henthorn v. Fraser* was also excluded by section 196 of the Law of Property Act 1925.]

This leaves an alternative contention for the plaintiffs which Templeman J.[1] dismissed with brevity. When the defendant's solicitors received the plaintiffs' solicitors' letter dated April 14[2] they communicated by telephone with the defendant. They did not read the letter to the defendant. . . . [His Lordship quoted the conversation.]

Counsel for the plaintiffs argued that since the defendant knew that the plaintiffs were anxious to exercise the option, and there was in existence a written notice exercising it, therefore there was a "notice in writing to the defendant." I consider this argument to be fallacious. A person does not give notice in writing to another person by sitting down and writing it out and then telephoning to that other saying, "Listen to what I have just written." Moreover, the defendant did not have knowledge of the existence of the combination of two letters which alone could be said to be an exercise of the option. *Dickinson v. Dodds*,[3] which was referred to, does not assist on this point: all it does is to show that an offeree cannot accept a withdrawable offer after he has learnt, by whatever means, that it has been withdrawn.

Accordingly, I would dismiss the appeal . . . (Buckley L.J. agreed).

LAWTON L.J.: Does the rule [in *Henthorn v. Fraser*, above, p. 56, footnote 1] apply in *all* cases where one party makes an offer which both he and the person with whom he was dealing must have expected the post to be used as a means of accepting it? In my judgment, it does not. First, it does not apply when the express terms of the offer specify that the acceptance must reach the offeror. The public nowadays are familiar with this exception to the general rule through their handling of football pool coupons. Secondly, it probably does not operate if its application would produce manifest inconvenience and absurdity. This is the opinion set out in Cheshire and Fifoot's *Law of Contract* (8th ed., 1972), p. 43. It was the opinion of Bramwell B. as is seen by his judgment in *British & American Telegraph Co. v. Colson* ((1871) L.R. 6 Exch. 108), and his opinion is worthy of consideration even though the decision in that case was overruled by this court in *Household Fire and Carriage Accident Insurance Co. Ltd v. Grant* (above, p. 51). The illustrations of inconvenience and absurdity which Bramwell B. gave are as apt today as they were then. Is a stockbroker who is holding shares to the orders of his client liable in damages because he did not sell in a falling market in accordance with the instructions in a letter which was posted but never received? Before the passing of the Law Reform (Miscellaneous Provisions) Act 1970 (which abolished actions for

[1] [1973] 2 All E.R. at 484, [1973] 1 W.L.R. at 765
[2] See [1973] 2 All E.R. at 478, [1973] 1 W.L.R. at 758.
[3] (1876) 2 Ch. 463, below, p. 81.

breach of promise of marriage), would a young soldier ordered overseas have been bound in contract to marry a girl to whom he had proposed by letter, asking her to let him have an answer before he left and she had replied affirmatively in good time but the letter had never reached him? In my judgment, the factors of inconvenience and absurdity are but illustrations of a wider principle, namely, that the rule does not apply if, having regard to all the circumstances, including the nature of the subject-matter under consideration, the negotiating parties cannot have intended that there should be a binding agreement until the party accepting an offer or exercising an option had in fact communicated the acceptance or exercise to the other. In my judgment, when this principle is applied to the facts of this case it becomes clear that the parties cannot have intended that the posting of a letter should constitute the exercise of the option.

The option agreement was one to which section 196 of the Law of Property Act 1925 applied: see subsection (5) which is in these terms:

> "The provisions of this section shall extend to notices required to be served by any instrument affecting property executed or coming into operation after the commencement of this Act unless a contrary intention appears."

The option agreement was an instrument affecting property. A notice in writing had to be given to exercise the option. Giving a notice means the same as serving a notice: see *Re 88 Berkeley Road* [1971] Ch. 648. The object of this subsection was to enable conveyancers to omit from instruments affecting property stipulations as to the giving of notices if they were prepared to accept the statutory ones. As there was nothing in the option agreement to a contrary effect, the statutory stipulations applied in this case. Subsection (4) is in these terms:

> "Any notice required or authorised by this Act to be served shall also be sufficiently served, if it is sent by post in a registered letter addressed to the lessee, lessor, mortgagee, mortgagor, or other person to be served, by name, at the aforesaid place of abode or business, office, or counting-house, and if that letter is not returned through the post-office undelivered; and that service shall be deemed to be made at the time at which the registered letter would in the ordinary course be delivered."

The object of this subsection, as also of subsection (3), is to specify circumstances in which proof of actual knowledge may be dispensed with. This follows from the use of the phrase "any notice . . . shall also be sufficiently served . . ." If the submissions of counsel for the plaintiffs are well-founded, a letter sent by ordinary post the evening before the option expired would have amounted to an exercise of it; but a registered letter posted at the same time and arriving in the ordinary course of post, which would be after the expiration of the option, would not have been an exercise. The parties to the option agreement cannot have intended any such absurd result to follow. When the provisions of section 196(4) are read into the agreement, as they have to be, the only reasonable inference is that the parties intended that the vendor should [*sic* ?not] be fixed with actual knowledge of the exercise of the option save in the circumstances envisaged in the subsection. This, in my judgment, was enough to exclude the rule. I would dismiss the appeal.

Appeal dismissed. Leave to appeal to the House of Lords refused.

Question

The posting of a letter has been held to be equivalent to communication to the addressee in respect of only one legal transaction—the acceptance of an offer. How many of Bramwell B.'s illustrations (above, pp. 53–54) were "apt" when that is borne in mind? Is Lawton L.J.'s illustration of the stockbroker apt?

Note

What is the position where O makes an offer to A by post, A posts an acceptance and then, before the letter arrives, communicates to O (by express letter, telephone or fax) a withdrawal of the acceptance? Logically, if the contract was complete on the posting of the acceptance, A cannot withdraw from it without O's consent. Yet the first that O knows about A's response to his offer is that A does not wish to accept it. Should A be held to have made a contract? *Cf.* Bramwell L.J., above, p. 54.

In a Scottish case, *Countess of Dunmore v. Alexander* (1930) 9 S. 190, the Court of Session, Lord Craigie dissenting, decided that there was no contract where the acceptance and the withdrawal of it reached the offeror together—so, a fortiori, the acceptance would have been invalid if the withrawal had arrived first. But the decision is far from conclusive because of the implications of agency and some rather dubious reasoning.

Alexander, through X, made an offer to Dunmore to enter her service. On November 5 Dunmore posted a letter to X accepting the offer. X forwarded the letter to Alexander. On November 6 Dunmore posted a second letter to X cancelling the first. X forwarded this letter by express and Alexander received both letters together. If X was Alexander's agent to *receive* the acceptance (*cf. Financings Ltd. v. Stimson*, below, p. 80), the contract was complete when X received Dunmore's first letter and her second letter was ineffective. This was the view of Lord Craigie, dissenting. But if X was Alexander's agent only to *transmit* the acceptance, then the acceptance and the withdrawal were received by the offeror simultaneously. The majority seem to have regarded X as an agent only to transmit and reasoned that the case was the same as if—

"a man put an order into the Post Office, desiring his agent to buy stock for him. He afterwards changes his mind but cannot recover his letter from the Post Office. He therefore writes a second letter countermanding the first. They both arrive together, and the result is, that no purchase can be made to bind the principal."

The example is undoubtedly correct—the agent's authority has been revoked before he has done any act to bind his principal—but is it apposite? Did X do anything on behalf of Dunmore that was not authorised by her?

Merton L. Ferson, The Formation of Simple Contracts (1924) 9 Cornell Law Quarterly,
402; Selected Readings, 128, 137

The court squares its decision with the utterance by deeming the post office the common agent of both parties. There is communication, on this assumption, when the letter of acceptance is turned over to the agent post office. It should require no argument, however, to show that the post office is not an agent of both or either party. It may properly be called an "agency" in the sense that it is a means employed, but it is not an "agent" in the technical sense, with everyone who uses it a correlative principal. An acceptance deposited in a hollow tree, if that were by the understanding of the parties a proper receptacle, would, no doubt, give rise instantly to a contract; yet it would be awkward to deem the hollow tree an agent.

BYRNE & CO. v. VAN TIENHOVEN & CO.

Common Pleas (1880) 5 C.P.D. 344; 49 L.J.C.P. 316; 42 L.T. 371

October 1. The defendants, in Cardiff, posted a letter to the plaintiffs, in New York, offering to sell them 1,000 boxes of tinplates.

October 8. The defendants posted a letter revoking their offer.

October 11. The plaintiffs telegraphed acceptance.

October 15. The plaintiffs confirmed their acceptance by letter.

October 20. The defendants' letter of revocation reached the plaintiffs.

LINDLEY J., having stated the facts and held that a revocation, to be effective, must be communicated, continued: I pass, therefore, to the next question, *viz.*, whether posting the letter of revocation was a sufficient communication of it to the plaintiff. The offer was posted on October 1, the withdrawal was posted on the 8th, and did not reach the plaintiff until after he had posted his letter [*sic*] of the 11th accepting the offer. It may be taken as now settled that where an offer is made and accepted by letter sent through the post, the contract is completed the moment the letter accepting the offer is posted: *Harris' Case* (L.R. 7 Ch. 587); *Dunlop v. Higgins* (1 H.L. 381), even although it never reaches its destination. When, however, these authorities are looked at, it will be seen that they are based upon the principle that the writer of the offer has expressly or impliedly assented to treat an answer to him by a letter duly posted as a sufficient acceptance and notification to himself, or, in other words, he has made the Post Office his agent to receive the acceptance and notification of it. But this principle appears to me to be inapplicable to the case of the withdrawal of an offer. In this particular case I can find no evidence of any authority in fact given by the plaintiffs to the defendants to notify a withdrawal of their offer by merely posting a letter; and there is no legal principle or decision which compels me to hold, contrary to the fact, that the letter of October 8 is to be treated as communicated to the plaintiff on that day or on any day before the 20th, when the letter reached them. But before that letter had reached the plaintiffs they had accepted the offer, both by telegram and by post; and they had themselves resold the tinplates at a profit. In my opinion, the withdrawal by the defendants on October 8 of their offer of the 1st was inoperative; and a complete contract binding on both parties was entered into on October 11, when the plaintiffs accepted the offer of the 1st, which they had no reason to suppose had been withdrawn. Before leaving this part of the case it may be as well to point out the extreme injustice and inconvenience which any other conclusion would produce. If the defendants' contention were to prevail no person who had received an offer by post and had accepted it would know his position until he had waited such a time as to be quite sure that a letter withdrawing the offer had not been posted before his acceptance of it. It appears to me that both legal principles, and practical convenience require that a person who has accepted an offer not known to him to have been revoked, shall be in a position safely to act upon the footing that the offer and acceptance constitute a contract binding on both parties . . .

Judgment for the plaintiffs.

Questions

1. Why is an acceptance complete on posting, while a revocation is incomplete until communicated? It has been suggested that "the actual reason for the distinction is that the

former rule was settled in the early part of the nineteenth century, and the latter rule not until the latter half of the century." (Williston, "Mutual Assent in the Formation of Contracts" (1919) 14 *Illinois Law Review*, 85; *Selected Readings*, 119.) The basis for this theory is that the subjective notions of *consensus* which prevailed in the early part of the nineteenth century were replaced in the latter half of the century by the modern, objective, approach. Can the distinction between the rules of acceptance and revocation be justified otherwise than on historical grounds?

2. Is a revocation complete when it arrives or when it is opened? *Cf. Re London and Northern Bank* (above, p. 55).

Problem

On February 1 Rupert wrote to Samuel offering to sell him a house for £30,000, the offer to remain open for a week. On February 2 Samuel posted a letter saying, "£30,000 is too much; but I offer you £25,000." Later the same day, Samuel posted a second letter saying, "I have reconsidered the matter; £30,000 is reasonable and I accept your offer." Rupert received Samuel's first letter on February 3 and at once entered into a contract to sell the house to Thomas. Samuel's second letter arrived on February 4. Advise Rupert.

ENTORES LTD v. MILES FAR EAST CORPORATION

Court of Appeal [1955] 2 Q.B. 327; [1955] 3 W.L.R. 48; 99 S.J. 384; [1955] 2 All E.R. 493; [1955] 1 Lloyd's Rep. 511

The plaintiffs in London made an offer by Telex to the agents in Holland of the defendant corporation in New York. The offer was accepted by a communication received on the plaintiffs' Telex machine in London. The plaintiffs sought leave to serve notice of a writ on the defendants in New York claiming damages for breach of the contract so made. By R.S.C., Ord. 11, r. 1, service out of the jurisdiction is allowed (*inter alia*) to enforce a contract "made within the jurisdiction." The defendants argued that the contract was made in Holland.

The Telex service enable a message to be dispatched by a teleprinter operated like a typewriter in one country and almost instantaneously received and typed in another.

DENNING L.J.: When a contract is made by post it is clear law throughout the common law countries that the acceptance is complete as soon as the letter is put into the post box, and that is the place where the contract is made. But there is no clear rule about contracts made by telephone or by Telex. Communications by these means are virtually instantaneous and stand on a different footing.

The problem can only be solved by going in stages. Let me first consider a case where two people make a contract by word of mouth in the presence of one another. Suppose, for instance, that I shout an offer to a man across a river or a courtyard but I do not hear his reply because it is drowned by an aircraft flying overhead. There is no contract at that moment. If he wishes to make a contract, he must wait till the aircraft is gone and then shout back his acceptance so that I can hear what he says. Not until I have his answer am I bound. I do not agree with the observations of Hill J. in *Newcomb v. De Roos*.[1]

---

[1] (1859) 2 E. & E. 271. Hill J. said that if the parties were on different sides of a district boundary line and an order was verbally given and accepted, the contract would be made in the district in which the order was accepted. The defendant in London wrote to the plaintiff in Stamford instructing him to place advertisements in certain newspapers. The plaintiff did so in Stamford. The court held that the contract was made in Stamford. Was this right? Is it reconcilable with *Entores*?

Now take a case where two people make a contract by telephone. Suppose, for instance, that I make an offer to a man by telephone and, in the middle of his reply, the line goes "dead" so that I do not hear his words of acceptance. There is no contract at that moment. The other man may not know the precise moment when the line failed. But he will know that the telephone conversation was abruptly broken off: because people usually say something to signify the end of the conversation. If he wishes to make a contract, he must therefore get through again so as to make sure that I heard. Suppose next, that the line does not go dead, but it is nevertheless so indistinct that I do not catch what he says and I ask him to repeat it. He then repeats it and I hear his acceptance. The contract is made, not on the first time when I do not hear, but only the second time when I do hear. If he does not repeat it, there is no contract. The contract is only complete when I have his answer accepting the offer.

Lastly, take the Telex. Suppose a clerk in a London office taps out on the teleprinter an offer which is immediately recorded on a teleprinter in a Manchester office, and a clerk at that end taps out an acceptance. If the line goes dead in the middle of the sentence of acceptance, the teleprinter motor will stop. There is then obviously no contract. The clerk at Manchester must get through again and send his complete sentence. But it may happen that the line does not go dead, yet the message does not get through to London. Thus the clerk at Manchester may tap out his message of acceptance and it will not be recorded in London because the ink at the London end fails, or something of that kind. In that case, the Manchester clerk will not know of the failure but the London clerk will know of it and will immediately send back a message "not receiving." Then, when the fault is rectified, the Manchester clerk will repeat his message. Only then is there a contract. If he does not repeat it, there is no contract. It is not until his message is received that the contract is complete.

In all the instances I have taken so far, the man who sends the message of acceptance knows that it has not been received or he has reason to know it. So he must repeat it. But, suppose that he does not know that his message did not get home. He thinks it has. This may happen if the listener on the telephone does not catch the words of acceptance, but nevertheless does not trouble to ask for them to be repeated: or the ink on the teleprinter fails at the receiving end, but the clerk does not ask for the message to be repeated: so that the man who sends an acceptance reasonably believes that his message has been received. *estoppel* The offeror in such circumstances is clearly bound, because he will be estopped from saying that he did not receive the message of acceptance. It is his own fault that he did not get it. But if there should be a case where the offeror without any fault on his part does not receive the message of acceptance—yet the sender of it reasonably believes it has got home when it has not—then I think there is no contract.

My conclusion is, that the rule about instantaneous communications between the parties is different from the rule about the post. The contract is only complete when the acceptance is received by the offeror: and the contract is made at the place where the acceptance is received.

In a matter of this kind, however, it is very important that the countries of the world should have the same rule. I find that most of the European countries have substantially the same rule as that I have stated. Indeed, they apply it to contracts by post as well as instantaneous communications. But in the United States of America it appears as if instantaneous communications are treated in the same way as postal communications. In view of this divergence, I think that we must consider the matter on principle: and so considered, I have come to the view I have stated, and I am glad to see that Professor Winfield in this country (55 *Law Quarterly Review* 514), and Professor Williston in the United States of America (*Contracts* § 82, p. 239), take the same view.

Applying the principles which I have stated, I think that the contract in this case made in London where the acceptance was received. It was, therefore, a proper case for service out of the jurisdiction.

BIRKETT and PARKER L.JJ. delivered concurring judgements.

Appeal dismissed.

Question
Is there any difference in principle between Telex and FAX or Email used in the formation of contracts?

Note
In *The Brimnes* [1975] Q.B. 929; [1974] 3 All E.R. 88, C.A. the defendants hired a ship from the plaintiff shipowners. The contract provided that, if the hire was not paid punctually and regularly, the shipowner was to be at liberty to withdraw the ship. The defendants failed to pay the hire punctually and regularly. The shipowners complained. On April 1 the hire for the following month had not been paid as required by the contract. the shipowners sent a message by Telex, withdrawing the ship from the service, between 17.30 and 18.00 on April 2. It was not until the following morning that the defendants saw the message of withdrawal on the machine. Edmund Davies L.J. said:

> "The learned judge held here that the notice of withdrawal was sent during ordinary business hours, and that he was driven to the conclusion either that the charterers' staff had left the office on April 2 'well before the end of ordinary business hours' or that if they were indeed there, they' neglected to pay attention to the Telex machine in the way they claimed it was their ordinary practice to do.' He therefore concluded that the withdrawal Telex must be regarded as having been 'received' as required by *The Georgios C* ([1971] 1 All E.R. 193; [1971] 1 Q.B. 488), at 17.45 hours on April 2 and that the withdrawal was effected at that time. I propose to say no more than that I respectfully agree with that conclusion. . . ."

The question was whether the withdrawal was complete before the hire was paid because the majority of the Court of Appeal thought that the acceptance of the hire for April in advance would have amounted to waiver of the right to withdraw. It was held that withdrawal was effected some time between 17.30 and 18.00 and that the hire was paid at some time between 17.37 and 18.27. It followed that, on a balance of probabilities, withdrawal had been made before payment.

Notice that this was a case concerning not the formation of a contract but its termination. Would the same principle be applicable to (i) the withdrawal of an *offer*? (ii) the acceptance of an offer? Ought the plaintiffs to have known that the withdrawal had not been received when there was no acknowledgement?

See also *The Laconia* [1977] A.C. 850 and Rose, 30 C.L.P. 213.

Problem
A in London, by Telex, makes an offer to B in Holland at 5 p.m. B replies that he will make a decision in about two hours. At 7 p.m. B sends an acceptance by Telex. There is no acknowledgement but B is not surprised because he knows that A closes his office at 6 p.m. If the message is read by A at 9.30 a.m. the next day, when is the contract made? If the message is not recorded in A's office because the ink fails, is there a contract? Would it make any difference that the failure was due to A's neglect of his Telex machine? *Cf.* note, 72 L.Q.R. 10.

See Brian Coote, "The Instantaneous Transmission of Acceptances" [1971] 4 N.Z.U.L.R. 331.

BRINKIBON LTD v. STAHAG STAHL, etc.

House of Lords [1983] 2 A.C. 34; [1982] 1 All E.R. 293; [1982] 2 W.L.R. 164

The buyers, an English company, by a telex sent from London to Vienna, accepted the terms of sale offered by the sellers, an Austrian company. The buyers issued a writ claiming damages for breach of the contract. The Court of Appeal held that the service of the writ should be set aside because the contract had not been made within the court's jurisdiction. The buyers' appeal to the House of Lords was dismissed, approving and following *Entores v. Miles Far East Corporation* (above, p. 61).

LORD WILBERFORCE: Since 1955 the use of telex communication has been greatly expanded, and there are many variants on it. The senders and recipients may not be the principals to the contemplated contract. They may be servants or agents with limited authority. The message may not reach, or be intended to reach, the designated recipient immediately: messages may be sent out of office hours, or at night, with the intention, or on the assumption, that they will be read at a later time. There may be some error or default at the recipient's end which prevents receipt at the time contemplated and believed in by the sender. The message may have been sent and/or received through machines operated by third persons. And many other variations may occur. No universal rule can cover all such cases; they must be resolved by reference to the intentions of the parties, by sound business practice and in some cases by a judgment where the risks should lie: see *Household Fire and Carriage Accident Insurance Co. Ltd v. Grant* (above, p. 51) *per* Baggallay L.J. and *Henthorn v. Fraser* (above, p. 56) *per* Lord Herschell.

The present case is, as *Entores Ltd v. Miles Far East Corp.* itself, the simple case of instantaneous communication between principals, and, in accordance with the general rule, involves that the contract (if any) was made when and where the acceptance was received. This was on May 3, 1979 in Vienna.

LORD FRASER, having observed that there was little difference in the mechanics of transmission between a telex and a telegram, continued: Nevertheless I have reached the opinion that, on balance, an acceptance sent by telex directly from the acceptor's office to the offeror's office should be treated as if it were an instantaneous communication between principals, like a telephone conversation. One reason is that the decision to that effect in *Entores Ltd v. Miles Far East Corp.* seems to have worked without leading to serious difficulty or complaint from the business community. Secondly, once the message has been received on the offeror's telex machine, it is not unreasonable to treat it as delivered to the principal offeror, because it is his responsibility to arrange for prompt handling of messages within his own office. Thirdly, a party (the acceptor) who tries to send a message by telex can generally tell if his message has not been received on the other party's (the offeror's) machine, whereas the offeror, of course, will not know if an unsuccessful attempt has been made to send an acceptance to him. It is therefore convenient that the acceptor, being in the better position, should have the responsibility of ensuring that his message is received. For these reasons I think it is right that in the ordinary simple case, such as I take this to be, the general rule and not the postal rule should apply. But I agree with both my noble and learned friends that the general rule will not cover all the many variations that may occur with telex messages.

Winfield, Some Aspects of Offer and Acceptance (1939) 55 L.Q.R. 516

Note

Winfield, in the passage below, is discussing a famous case in the United States Supreme Court, *Eliason v. Henshaw* (1819) Wheat. 225; 4 L.Ed. 556. The defendant offered to purchase flour from the plaintiff. The offer was contained in a letter sent by the defendant with a wagoner employed by the plaintiff to haul flour from the plaintiff's mill at Mill Creek to Harper's Ferry where the defendant was. A postscript to the letter read: "Please write by return of wagon whether you accept our offer." Instead of sending a reply by wagon, the plaintiff sent a letter by mail addressed to the defendant at Georgetown, purporting to accept the offer. The mail took considerably longer than the wagon and, when the defendant received the "acceptance," he had already bought all the flour he needed. The plaintiff's action for damages for failure to accept the flour failed. The court said that the purpose of requiring a reply by return of wagon was obviously to enable the defendant to calculate the time at which he would receive an answer—"and therefore it was entirely unimportant, whether it was sent by that, or another wagon, or in any other manner, provided it was sent to Harper's Ferry, and was not delayed beyond the time which was ordinarily employed by wagons engaged in hauling flour from the [plaintiff's] mill to Harper's Ferry. Whatever uncertainty there might have been as to the time when the answer would be received, there was none as to the place to which it was to be sent.... The place ... to which, the answer was to be sent constituted an essential part of the [defendant's] offer."

Now, [writes Winfield] put it that H's postal acceptance had arrived earlier than, or as soon as, a reply by wagon would have done, could E have said, "There is no contract. I told you to accept by wagon, but you have not done so"? H's retort would be, "What of that? You are in exactly the same position as if I had replied by wagon; indeed, if my posted letter reached you earlier than a reply by wagon would have done, you are actually in a better position." ...

But every case must be construed on its own facts. In *Eliason v. Henshaw* it did not appear that E had an exclusive preference for reply by wagon. If, however, he had said, "Reply by wagon only," then a reply in any other way would have been useless. If it be argued that so long as he got his reply in time it was immaterial how he got it, the answer is that if an offeror clearly insists on a particular mode of acceptance, the law ought to respect his wishes. To do anything else would be to dictate to him how he should make his offer, and it is for the parties to make their own contract and not for the judges to make it for them. E might have had good reason for distrusting the post or he might have thought that there was a greater possibility of forgery of an acceptance if it were posted than if it were delivered by wagon. But whether his motives were reasonable or capricious, they are not relevant. The law is concerned with the mode of acceptance laid down by him; it is not concerned with the reason why he selected it.

Question

Do you agree that if the postal reply had arrived at Georgetown earlier than an answer by wagon would have reached Harper's Ferry there would have been a good contract?

Problem

Smith in Nottingham sends an offer by lorry driver to Thomas in London and requests a reply by the same means. Is there a contract (a) when Thomas hands his acceptance to the driver or (b) when it is given to Smith? Would it make any difference that the driver was (i) Smith's employee (ii) Thomas's employee (iii) an independent contractor?

MANCHESTER DIOCESAN COUNCIL FOR EDUCATION v. COMMERCIAL AND GENERAL INVESTMENTS LTD

Chancery Division [1970] 1 W.L.R. 241; [1969] 3 All E.R. 1593; P. & C.R. 38

The plaintiff owned property which could be sold only subject "to the approval of the Secretary of State for Education and Science." The plaintiff decided to sell the property by tender and prepared a form of tender. Clause 4 provided: "The person whose tender is accepted shall be the purchaser and shall be informed of the acceptance of his tender by letter sent to him by post addressed to the address given in the tender." The defendant completed the form of tender and sent it (from 15 Berkeley St.) to the plaintiff's surveyor who, on September 1, informed the defendant's surveyor that he would recommend acceptance and, on September 15, wrote to the defendant's surveyor that the plaintiff had approved the sale and that the approval of the Secretary of State was being sought. That approval was given on November 18. On December 23 the plaintiff's solicitors wrote to the defendant's solicitors that the consent had been given and that the contract was binding. The defendant's solicitors replied that they did not agree. On January 7 the plaintiff's solicitors wrote to the defendant company at the address given by it in the form of tender giving formal notification of acceptance. The plaintiff sued for a declaration that either the letter dated September 15 or that dated January 7 constituted a binding contract.

BUCKLEY J.: The offer contained in the tender was to the effect that in the event of its being accepted in accordance with the conditions of sale on or before the day named therein for that purpose—and none was so named—the defendant would pay the price and complete the purchase. An offeror may by the terms of his offer indicate that it may be accepted in a particular manner. In the present case the conditions included condition 4 which I have read. It is said, on the defendant's behalf, that that condition was not complied with until January 7, 1965; that until that date the offer was never accepted in accordance with its terms; and that consequently nothing earlier than that date can be relied on as an acceptance resulting in a binding contract. If an offeror stipulates by the terms of his offer that it may, or that it shall, be accepted in a particular manner a contract results as soon as the offeree does the stipulated act, whether it has come to the notice of the offeror or not. In such a case the offeror conditionally waives either expressly or by implication the normal requirement that acceptance must be communicated to the offeror to conclude a contract. There can be no doubt that in the present case, if the plaintiff or its authorised agent had posted a letter addressed to the defendant at 15 Berkeley Street on or about September 15 informing the defendant of the acceptance of its tender, the contract would have been complete at the moment when such a letter was posted, but that course was not taken. Condition 4, however, does not say that that shall be the sole permitted method of communicating an acceptance. It may be that an offeror, who by the terms of his offer insists upon acceptance in a particular manner, is entitled to insist that he is not bound unless acceptance is effected or communicated in that precise way, although it seems probable that, even so, if the other party communicates his acceptance in some other way, the offeror may by conduct or otherwise waive his right to insist upon the prescribed method of acceptance. Where, however, the offeror has prescribed a particular method of acceptance, but not in terms insisting that only acceptance in that mode shall be binding, I am of opinion that acceptance communicated to the offeror by any other mode which is no less advantageous to him will conclude the contract. Thus in *Tinn v. Hoffman & Co.* (above, p. 26), where acceptance was requested by return of post, Honeyman J. said at p. 274:

"That does not mean exclusively a reply by letter or return of post, but you may reply by telegram or by verbal message or by any other means not later than a letter written by return of post."

If an offeror intends that he shall be bound only if his offer is accepted in some particular manner, it must be for him to make this clear. Condition 4 in the present case has not, in my judgment, this effect.

Moreover, the inclusion of condition 4 in the defendant's offer was at the instance of the plaintiff, who framed the conditions and the form of tender. It should not, I think, be regarded as a condition or stipulation imposed by the defendant as offeror upon the plaintiff as offeree, but as a term introduced into the bargain by the plaintiff and presumably considered by the plaintiff as being in some way for the protection or benefit of the plaintiff. It would consequently be a term strict compliance with which the plaintiff could waive, provided the defendant was not adversely affected. The plaintiff did not take advantage of the condition which would have resulted in a contract being formed as soon as a letter of acceptance complying with the condition was posted, but adopted another course, which could only result in a contract when the plaintiff's acceptance was actually communicated to the defendant.

For these reasons, I have reached the conclusion that in accordance with the terms of the tender it was open to the plaintiff to conclude a contract by acceptance actually communicated to the defendant in any way; and, in my judgment, the letter of September 15 constituted such an acceptance. It follows that, in my judgment, and subject to a point relating to the need to obtain ministerial consent to which I will refer in a moment, the parties thereupon became contractually bound. . . .

BUCKLEY J. then held that while the power to *complete* a sale was conditional upon ministerial approval, the power to *contract* was not. For the second part of his judgment, in which he considered whether, if no contract was made on September 15, one was concluded on January 7 (see below, p. 83).

ECCLES v. BRYANT

Court of Appeal [1948] Ch. 93; [1948] L.J.R. 418; 177 L.T. 247; [1947] 2 All E.R. 865

LORD GREENE M.R.: The parties were minded to enter into a contract for the sale and purchase of a house. The matter was put into the hands of their respective solicitors in the ordinary way. The basis on which the negotiations were being conducted was that the terms set out in the preliminary correspondence were stated to be subject to contract and survey. We are not troubled with the survey. The important words are "subject to contract"[1] This is one of those cases where quite clearly and admittedly no contract came into existence in the earlier correspondence. It is common ground that the parties contemplated a definitive binding contract which was to come into existence in the future. One thing is quite clear on the facts of this case to my mind, that both firms of solicitors, one of whom—that is the vendor's solicitors—practised in East Grinstead and the other of whom, the purchaser's solicitors, practised in London, when they were instructed to carry this matter through by their respective clients, contemplated and intended from beginning to end to do so in the customary way which is familiar to every firm of solicitors in the country, namely, by preparing the engrossment of the draft contract when agreed in duplicate, the intention being to do what I have no doubt at this very moment is happening in dozens of solicitors' offices all over the country, namely, to exchange the two parts when signed by their respective clients. That indeed, is what anyone would have understood, I think, from the language of the earlier correspondence and the words "subject to contract"—that the contract would be brought about in the way I have mentioned, by an exchange of the two parts signed by the respective parties.

Vaisey J. pointed out that what he called the ceremonial form of exchange, namely, the meeting of solicitors in the office of one of them— the vendors' solicitors office as a rule—and the passing of the two signed engrossments over the table may be taken to have fallen—and indeed, no doubt it has—into disuse to a certain extent, particularly when there are firms of solicitors in different parts of the country. He recognised that an exchange by post would, in many cases, take the place of the old more ceremonial exchange, but that an exchange was contemplated by both firms of solicitors from beginning to end appears to me to be clear from what took place and from the correspondence. I am prepared to assume—and I think I should probably be right in assuming—that their intention was that the exchange should take place by post. When an exchange takes place by post and a contract comes into existance through the act of exchange, the earliest date at which such a contract can come into existence, it appears to me, would be the date when the later of the two documents to be put in the post is actually put in the post. Another view might be that the exchange takes place and the contract thereby comes into existence when, and not before, the respective parties or their solicitors receive from their "opposite numbers" their parts of the contract. It is not necessary here to choose between those two views. I mention them particularly because Mr Hopkins, for the purchaser, here tried to suggest an intermediate stage, that where the parties contemplate an exchange by post the contract is completed not when an exchange takes place, but when one of the parties puts his part into the post. I am afraid I cannot accept that. It seems to me to be a contradiction in terms to speak of that as an exchange. . . .

It was argued that exchange is a mere matter of machinery, having in itself no particular importance and no particular significance. So far as

[1] See below, p. 101.

significance is concerned, it appears to me that not only is it not right to say of exchange that it has no significance, but it is the crucial and vital fact which brings the contract into existence. As for importance, it is of the greatest importance, and that is why in past ages this procedure came to be recognised by everybody to be the proper procedure and was adopted. When you are dealing with contracts for the sale of land, it is of the greatest importance to the vendor that he should have a document signed by the purchaser, and to the purchaser that he should have a document signed by the vendor. It is of the greatest importance that there should be no dispute whether a contract had or had not been made and that there should be no dispute as to the terms of it. This particular procedure of exchange ensures that none of those difficulties will arise. Each party has got what is a document of title, because directly a contract in writing relating to land is entered into, it is a document of title. That can be illustrated, of course, by remembering the simple case where a purchaser makes a sub-sale. The contract is a vital document for the purpose of the sub-sale. If he had not got the vendor's part, signed by the vendor, to show to the sub-purchaser, he would not be able to make a good title.

If the argument for the purchaser is right and the contract comes into existence before exchange takes place, it would mean that neither party could call upon the other to hand over his part. The non-exchanged part would remain the property of the party who signed it, because exchange would be no element in the contract at all and therefore you could get this position, that the purchaser might wish to resell and would have no right to obtain from the vendor the vendor's signed part. . . .

What took place was this: Both parties did in fact sign their respective parts of the contract. The purchaser put his part in the post and it duly arrived. The vendor did not put his part in the post, but instead of doing so he wrote to repudiate the proposed bargain and declined to go on. There was no exchange. The vendor was doing exactly what he would have been entitled to do if the exchange was going to take place over a table. If one assumes that that had taken place and the purchaser had handed over his document to the vendor across the table, no contract would have come into existence if the vendor had said, "I change my mind" and refused to hand his part over. That, in my opinion, is elementary and in this case that is exactly what happened, except that the post was used to hand over the purchaser's part of the contract and not a manual delivery over the table. . . .

It is of the greatest importance, it appears to me, that these principles should be upheld. The inconvenience and chaos into which these matters would be thrown by the adoption of any other rules appear to me to be very great; but ultimately the matter comes down to this: parties become bound by contract when, and in the manner in which, they intend and contemplate becoming bound. That is a question of the facts of each case, but in this case the manner of becoming bound which the parties and their solicitors must have contemplated from the very beginning was the ordinary, customary, convenient method of exchange. From that contemplation neither side and the solicitors to neither side ever resiled, and there is no justification for taking the view that some new method of making the contract was ever contemplated by anybody.

Notes
1. Lord Greene's proposition that "parties become bound by contract when, and in the manner in which they intend and contemplate becoming bound" is now subject to an

exception created by the Law of Property (Miscellaneous Provisions) Act 1989, s.2, above, p. 6. Parties may intend to become bound by a contract for the disposition of an interest in land by offer and acceptance made orally or by correspondence but their intention is ineffective: *Commission for New Towns v. Cooper (GB) Ltd* [1995] 2 All E.R. 929. There is no binding contract until the terms are incorporated into one document and signed or, where contracts are exchanged, in each. The requirement of exchange still depends on the actual or presumed intention of the parties. If they want to dispense with it, they can; but the requirement of a written signed document incorporating all the terms is statutory and overrides the intention of the parties.

2. The formation of a contract to sell a house is frequently complicated by the fact that it is part of a chain of such transactions. X wants to buy Y's house, Y wants to sell the house to X and they have agreed, subject to contract, on the price. X, however, cannot afford to bind himself to buy until he has secured a binding contract to sell his own house to W, who has agreed, subject to contract, to buy it. Y cannot bind himself to sell until he has secured a binding contract to buy Z's house. The formation of the contract between W and X is dependent on the formation of that between X and Y which is dependent on the formation of that between Y and Z. The chain of contracts contemplated may be represented as follows:-

$$W \leftrightarrow X \leftrightarrow Y \leftrightarrow Z$$

If the procedure envisaged in *Eccles v. Bryant* is followed and each contract is concluded only when an exchange through the post is complete, there is a grave risk that X may find that he has committed himself to buy and W has changed his mind; and Y may find that he has committed himself to sell and Z has changed his mind. The risk is inevitable because of the delay involved in the process of exchange. If, however, the solicitors of all four parties could meet together and exchange the signed parts of the contract virtually simultaneously, all risk could be eliminated. It is usually not practicable for them to meet. If they could conclude the contracts on behalf of their clients on the telephone, the risk could be virtually eliminated, because within the space of minutes rather than hours, each party could be assured that every other party was standing by his agreement and the three contracts could be safely concluded. This is the procedure which was in issue in the next case.

DOMB v. ISOZ

Court of Appeal [1980] Ch. 548; [1980] 2 W.L.R. 565; [1980] 1 All E.R. 942

The case involved three transactions.

(i) The sale by the plaintiffs (solicitor, Redstone) of 38 Chelmsford Square to Petsas (solicitors, Lickfolds).
(ii) The purchase by the plaintiffs of 34 Erskine Hill from the defendant (solicitor, Bond).
(iii) The purchase by the defendant of 40 Westbourne Terrace from Holding (solicitor, Brooke).

On December 22 Redstone wrote to Bond, enclosing the plaintiffs' part of the contract to buy 34 Erskine Hill and the balance of the deposit, as follows: "Would you please hold the enclosed contract and deposit cheque to our order until we are able to agree with you on the telephone that contracts may be exchanged and agree a completion date which we are fairly fluid on as we should be receiving in the course of the next day or so our clients' contract for the sale of their present property and we wish to effect simultaneous exchange of contracts on both transactions."

On February 9, Redstone held both parts of the contract relating to transaction (i) and was in a position to exchange if he could tie up transaction (ii). Bond held both parts of the contract relating to transaction (ii) and was in a position to exchange if he could tie up transaction (iii). Bond, after a telephone discussion with Brooke, telephoned Redstone and they agreed on March 2 as completion date for transaction (ii). Redstone proposed that the contracts for transaction (ii) should be treated as immediately exchanged by telephone at the moment they were speaking and that this should be irrevocable. Bond agreed. Redstone then despatched the plaintiffs' contract to sell 38 Chelmsford Square to Lickfolds and Bond despatched the defendant's contract to buy 40 Westbourne Terrace to Brooke, having inserted March 2 as completion date. Holding however insisted on a six-week completion period with the result that transaction (iii) went off. The defendant declined to complete and the plaintiffs' action for specific performance was dismissed. They appealed.

BUCKLEY L.J.: In my judgment, the essential characteristic of exchange of contracts is that each party shall have a document signed by the other party in his possession or control so that, at his own need, he can have the document available for his own use. Exchange of a written contract for sale is in my judgment effected so soon as each part of the contract, signed by the vendor or the purchaser as the case may be, is in the actual or constructive possession of the other party or of his solicitor. Such possession need not be actual or physical possession; possession by an agent of the party or of his solicitor, in such circumstances that the party or solicitor in question has control over the document and can at any time procure its actual physical possession will, in my opinion, suffice. In such a case the possession of the agent is the possession of the principal. A party's solicitor employed to act in respect of such a contract has, subject to express instructions, implied authority to effect exchange of contracts and so to make the bargain binding on his client. This he can, in my judgment, do by any method which is effectual to constitute exchange.

In the present case, in my judgment, Mr Bond on February 9, constituted himself Mr Redstone's agent to hold the defendant's part of the contract to Mr Redstone's order from the moment of the telephonic agreement, and to despatch it to Mr Redstone forthwith, or on Mr Redstone's demand. At the same time Mr Bond became the holder of the plaintiff's part of the contract to the order of his own client, the defendant, and was discharged from any continuing obligation to hold it to Mr Redstone's order as he had therefore been bound to do in pursuance of the letter of December 22. . . .

The judge thought that such a practice was a bad practice. Again with deference, I do not agree. In the present state of the property market, particularly where domestic houses are concerned, chain bargains are of very frequent occurrence. These necessarily require simultaneous contracts for sale and purchase all the way along the chain. Synchronisation of this kind cannot as a practical matter be secured by physical exchange across the table, or by messenger, or by post; the only method which counsel have been able to suggest involves telephonic agreements which are synchronised, or as nearly completely synchronised as is humanly possible. The mechanics for carrying out such an exchange may, I think, vary. There are probably a number of variants that could be adopted; but the essence is that, as the consequence of the telephonic communication, the part of the contract signed by each party must be either physically or constructively in the hands of the other party or his solicitor, free from any claim of the first party which would enable him to control the second party in his right to hold and retain the document and deal with it as he chooses. As the matter must be handled, if not by a party in person, by solicitors, that is to say by professional men of high integrity who are officers of the court, amenable to the control of the court in the conduct of their professional affairs, such a procedure does not, in my view, involve any undesirable degree of risk of its leading to errors or confusion.

On these grounds in my judgment the events which occurred in the present case on February 9 constituted an effective exchange of contracts, and the sale by the defendant to the plaintiffs of 34 Erskine Hill thereby became binding.

BRIDGE L.J. and TEMPLEMAN L.J. allowed the appeal.

Notes

1. The Law Society's *General Conditions of Sale* (1980 ed.), provided:

> "10 Optional Methods of exchange. (1) Exchange of contracts may be effected by post and if so effected the contract shall be made when the last part is posted. (2) The solicitors to the parties may agree by telephone or telex that the contract be immediately effective and thereupon the solicitors holding a part of the contract signed by their client shall hold it irrevocably to the order of the other party."

The provision is discussed in *The Law Society's Gazette*, February 13, 1980 and April 8, 1981.

2. In *Walton's Stores (Interstate) Ltd v. Maher and another* (1987) 164 C.L.R. 387 the High Court of Australia held that W was bound by a contract for the lease of land and liable to pay damages in lieu of specific performance although the parties, acting through solicitors, intended the contract to be made by the exchange of parts and W had deliberately withheld his part.

Agreement had been reached on all the terms of the lease. M, the lessor, was to demolish a building and construct a new one according to W's specification by a specified date. On November 7, 1983 M told W that it was essential that the agreement be concluded within a day or two if he was to complete the work on time and that he did not want to begin to demolish the building until it was clear that there were no problems with the lease. W sent M a redrafted lease incorporating suggested amendments. On November 11, 1983 M sent an executed lease to W "by way of exchange" and began to demolish the building. W then had second thoughts and, being advised by its solicitor that it was not bound to proceed unless parts were exchanged, told him to "go slow." On January 19, 1989 W said that it did not intend to proceed. The building was then 40 per cent. complete.

The High Court of Australia (Mason C.J., Wilson, Brennan, Deane and Gaudron JJ.) held that, although for want of an exchange no binding agreement for a lease had come into existence, W was estopped from denying that it was bound: W must have known that M was proceeding on the assumption that he had an agreement and that the completion of the exchange was a formality. W's inaction encouraged M to proceed on this assumption. It was "estopped from retreating from its implied promise to complete the contract." Deane J. further held that W's conduct had caused M to assume, and to act on the assumption that a binding contract existed. Gaudron J. held that W's conduct had caused M to believe that an exchange had taken place (but the majority said that M did not believe that an exchange had taken place).

Was M, *acting through solicitors*, entitled to assume he had a binding contract? Or that an exchange had taken place? Is the case distinguishable from *A-G for Hong Kong v. Humphreys*, below, p. 90.

The High Court held that New South Wales equivalent of section 40 of the Law of Property Act 1925 (above, pp. 4–5) did not operate to preclude enforcement of the agreement on various grounds—it is not applicable where equitable estoppel treats the defendant as though a contract had been made; estoppel extends to preclude the assertion of unenforceability; estoppel from denying that an exchange had taken place involved an assumption that the exchanged agreement was duly executed by W.

CHAPTER 3

THE DURATION OF AN OFFER

HYDE v. WRENCH

Rolls Court (1840) 3 Beav. 334; 4 Jur. 1106; 49 E.R. 132

June 6. The defendant wrote to the plaintiff offering to sell his farm for £1,000. The plaintiff's agent immediately called on the defendant, and made an offer of £950, which the defendant wished to have a few days to consider.
June 27. The defendant wrote to say that he could not accept this offer.
June 29. The plaintiff wrote "accepting" the offer of June 6. The plaintiff brought an action for specific performance. The defendant filed a general demurrer.

THE MASTER OF THE ROLLS (LORD LANGDALE): Under the circumstances stated in this bill, I think there exists no valid binding contract between the parties for the purchase of the property. The defendant offered to sell it for £1,000, and if that had been at once unconditionally accepted, there would undoubtedly have been a perfect binding contract; instead of that, the plaintiff made an offer of his own, to purchase the property for £950, and he thereby rejected the offer previously made by the defendant. I think that it was not afterwards competent for him to revive the proposal of the defendant, by tendering an acceptance of it; and that, therefore, there exists no obligation of any sort between the parties; the demurrer must be allowed.

BUTLER MACHINE TOOL CO. LTD v. EX-CELL-O CORPORATION (ENGLAND) LTD

Court of Appeal [1979] 1 W.L.R. 401; [1979] 1 All E.R. 965

On May 23, 1969 the plaintiffs offered to sell a machine to the defendants for £75,535. The terms of the offer included a condition that all orders were accepted only on the sellers' terms which were to prevail over any terms and conditions in the buyers' order. There was also a condition that any increase in the cost of manufacture by the date of delivery should be added to the price. On May 27, 1969 the defendants replied ordering the machine but on different terms and conditions, not including a price variation clause. At the foot of the order was a tear-off slip reading, "We accept your order on the Terms and Conditions stated thereon." On June 5, 1969 the plaintiffs signed and returned it, writing, "... your official order ... is being entered in accordance with our revised quotation of 23rd May ..." The plaintiffs recovered an additional £2,892 under the price variation clause. The defendants appealed.

LORD DENNING M.R.: I have much sympathy with the judge's approach to this case. In many of these cases our traditional analysis of offer, counter-offer, rejection, acceptance and so forth is out-of-date. This was observed by Lord Wilberforce in *New Zealand Shipping Co. Ltd v. A. M. Satterthwaite* (below, p. 290). The better way is to look at all the documents passing between the parties and glean from them, or from the conduct of the parties, whether they have reached agreement on all material points, even though there may be differences between the forms and conditions printed on the back of them. As Lord Cairns L.C. said in *Brogden v. Metropolitan Railway Co.* (1877) 2 App. Cas. 666 at 672:

> ". . . there may be a *consensus* between the parties far short of a complete mode of expressing it, and that *consensus* may be discovered from letters or from other documents of an imperfect and incomplete description."

Applying this guide, it will be found that in most cases when there is a "battle of forms" there is a contract as soon as the last of the forms is sent and received without objection being taken to it. That is well observed in *Benjamin on Sale* (9th ed.), pp. 84–85. The difficulty is to decide which form, or which part of which form, is a term or condition of the contract. In some cases the battle is won by the man who fires the last shot. He is the man who puts forward the latest term and conditions: and, if they are not objected to by the other party, he may be taken to have agreed to them. Such was *British Road Services Ltd v. Arthur V. Crutchley & Co. Ltd* [1968] 1 All E.R. at 816–817 per Lord Pearson; and the illustration given by Professor Guest in *Anson's Law of Contract* (24th ed.), pp. 37–38 where he says that "the terms of contract consist of the terms of the offer subject to the modifications contained in the acceptance." That may however go too far. In some cases, however, the battle is won by the man who gets the blow in first. If he offers to sell at a named price on the terms and conditions stated on the back and the buyer orders the goods purporting to accept the offer on an order form with his own different terms and conditions on the back, then, if the difference is so material that it would affect the price, the buyer ought not to be allowed to take advantage of the difference unless he draws it specifically to the attention of the seller. There are yet other cases where the battle depends on the shots fired on both sides. There is a concluded contract but the forms vary. The terms and conditions of both parties are to be construed together. If they can be reconciled so as to give a harmonious result, all well and good. If differences are irreconcilable, so that they are mutually contradictory, then the conflicting terms may have to be scrapped and replaced by a reasonable implication.

In the present case the judge thought that the sellers in their original quotation got their blow in first; especially by the provision that "These terms and conditions shall prevail over any terms and conditions in the Buyer's order." It was so emphatic that the price variation clause continued through all the subsequent dealings and that the buyer must be taken to have agreed to it. I can understand that point of view. But I think that the documents have to be considered as a whole. And, as a matter of construction, I think the acknowledgement of June 5, 1969 is the decisive document. It makes clear that the contract was on the buyers' terms and not on the sellers' terms: and the buyers' terms did not include a price variation clause.

I would therefore allow the appeal and enter judgment for the buyers.

LAWTON L.J.: The modern commercial practice of making quotations and placing orders with conditions attached usually in small print, is indeed likely, as in this case, to produce a battle of forms. The problem is how should that battle be conducted? The view taken by the judge was that the battle should extend over a wide area and the court should do its best to look into the minds of the parties and make certain assumptions. In my judgment, the battle has to be conducted in accordance with set rules. It is a battle more on classical 18th century lines when convention decided who had the right to open fire first rather than in accordance with the modern concept of attrition.

The rules relating to a battle of this kind have been known for the past 130-odd years. They were set out by the then Master of the Rolls, Lord Langdale, in *Hyde v. Wrench* (above, p. 73) and Lord Denning M.R. has already referred to them; and, if anyone should have thought they were obsolescent, Megaw J. in *Trollope & Colls Ltd v. Atomic Power Constructions Ltd* [1962] 3 All E.R. 1035 at 1038, called attention to the fact that those rules are still in force.

When those rules are applied to this case, in my judgment, the answer is obvious. . . .

As I pointed out in the course of argument to counsel for the sellers, if the letter of June 5 which accompanied the form acknowledging the terms which the buyers had specified had amounted to a counter-offer, then in my judgment the parties never were *ad idem*. It cannot be said that the buyers accepted the counter-offer by reason of the fact that ultimately they took physical delivery of the machine. By the time they took physical delivery of the machine, they had made it clear by correspondence that they were not accepting that there was any price escalation clause in any contract which they had made with the plaintiffs.

I agree with Lord Denning M.R. that this appeal should be allowed.

BRIDGE L.J.: delivered judgment allowing the appeal.

Appeal allowed.

Note

The court discussed paras. 1 and 2 of "The Uniform Law on the Formation of Contracts for the International Sale of Goods" in Schedule 2 to the Uniform Laws on International Sales Act 1967. These provide:

1. An acceptance containing additions, limitations, or other modifications shall be a rejection of the offer and shall constitute a counter-offer.
2. However, a reply to an offer which purports to be an acceptance but which contains additional or different terms which do not materially alter the terms of the offer shall constitute an acceptance unless the offeror promptly objects to the discrepancy; if he does not so object, the terms of the contract shall be the terms of the offer with the modifications contained in the acceptance.

The court did not express any opinion on whether para. 2 represented the common law of England. Lord Denning M.R. and Bridge L.J. did, however, say that Anson's *Law of Contract* (24th ed.), pp. 37–38 went too far in saying: "the terms of the contract consist of the terms of the offer subject to the modifications contained in the acceptance."

How can "additional or different terms" fail to "materially alter the terms of the offer?" Is it not for the offeror to say whether he regards the alteration as material? Is it right that the offeree should be able to force these upon him unless he "promptly objects?"

See notes in 95 L.Q.R. 481, 42 M.L.R. 715.

STEVENSON v. McLEAN

Queen's Bench Division (1880) 5 Q.B.D. 346; 49 L.J.Q.B. 701; 42 L.T. 897; 28 W.R. 916

The plaintiffs and the defendant were negotiating about the sale of a quantity of iron for which the defendant held warrants.

Saturday: The defendant wrote: ". . . I would now sell for 40s. net cash, open till Monday."

Monday: The plaintiffs telegraphed: "Please wire whether you would accept forty for delivery over two months, or if not, longest limit you would give."

The defendant received the telegram at 10.01 a.m. and subsequently sold the iron to a third party.

1.25 p.m.: the defendant telegraphed that he had sold the iron.

1.34 p.m.: the plaintiffs having had no reply to their telegram, telegraphed again, accepting the offer to sell at 40s. cash.

1.46 p.m.: the defendant's telegram arrived.

The plaintiff sued for breach of contract, and the defendant objected that the telegram sent by the plaintiffs on the Monday morning was a rejection of the defendant's offer and a new proposal on the plaintiffs' part, and therefore that the defendant had a right to regard it as putting an end to the original negotiation.

LUSH J.: Looking at the form of the telegram, the time when it was sent, and the state of the iron market, I cannot think this is its fair meaning. The plaintiff Stevenson said he meant it only as an inquiry, expecting an answer for his guidance, and this, I think, is the sense in which the defendant ought to have regarded it.

It is apparent throughout the correspondence, that the plaintiffs did not contemplate buying the iron on speculation, but that their acceptance of the defendant's offer depended on their finding someone to take the warrants off their hands. All parties knew that the market was in an unsettled state, and that no one could predict at the early hour when the telegram was sent how the prices would range during the day. It was reasonable that, under these circumstances, they should desire to know before business began whether they were to be at liberty in case of need to make any and what concession as to the time or times of delivery, which would be the time or times of payment, or whether the defendant was determined to adhere to the terms of his letter; and it was highly unreasonable that the plaintiffs should have intended to close the negotiation while it was uncertain whether they could find a buyer or not, having the whole of the business hours of the day to look for one. Then, again, the form of the telegram is one of inquiry. It is not "I offer forty for delivery over two months," which would have likened the case to *Hyde v. Wrench* (above, p. 73). . . . Here there is no counter proposal. The words are, "Please wire whether you would accept forty for delivery over two months, or, if not, the longest limit you would give." There is nothing specific by way of offer or rejection, but a mere inquiry, which should have been answered and not treated as a rejection of the offer. This ground of objection therefore fails.

(The defendant's second objection was that the offer was revoked before it was accepted: see *Byrne v. Van Tienhoven*, above, p. 60. Following that case, Lush J. held that a "revocation is nothing till it has been communicated.")

Questions

1. Was the plaintiffs' telegram an offer capable of acceptance by the defendant?

2. Henry writes to George offering to sell him a farm, and adding, "I expect you to reject this offer upon first consideration, but I want you to consider it further, because I think you will accept when you have thought about it a while." George immediately writes a rejection which Henry ignores. A fortnight later, having thought the matter over, George sends an acceptance. Is Henry bound?

(See Oliphant, "The Duration and Termination of an Offer" 18 Mich.L.R. 201; *Selected Readings on the Law of Contracts*, 251.)

3. V wrote to P offering to sell a house for £30,000. P telegraphed: "Send lowest cash price. Will give £25,000." V telegraphed in reply: "Cannot reduce price." After receiving this telegram, P purported to accept the original offer. Discuss.

Cf. Livingstone v. Evans (Alberta Supreme Court) (1925) 4 D.L.R. 762.

Note

In *Northland Airliners, Ltd v. Dennis Ferranti Meters, Ltd* (1970) 114 S.J. 845; *The Times*, October 23, 1970, the defendants sent a telegram offering to sell aircraft to the plaintiffs for £27,000. The plaintiffs replied by telegram purporting to accept. The Court of Appeal held that there was no contract because the offer required a deposit of £5,000 to be paid in advance but the acceptance stated that £5,000 had been forwarded to the defendants' bank payable to the defendants on delivery; and the offer, being silent as to delivery, required it within a reasonable time, whereas the "acceptance" required delivery within 30 days. (The plaintiffs evidently *intended* only to inquire if delivery would be made within 30 days but the omission of the word, "if," through an error in transmission caused the intended inquiry to appear to be a stipulation; and the judge held that the plaintiffs were bound by the telegram as sent.) It was immaterial that the defendants at first thought that they were bound. The second telegram was a counter-offer.

ROUTLEDGE v. GRANT

Common Pleas (1828) 4 Bing. 653; 1 M. & P. 717; 3 C. & P. 267; 6 L.J.C.P. 166; 29 R.R. 672; 130 E.R. 920

The defendant offered to take a lease of the plaintiff's premises, "a definitive answer to be given within six weeks from March 18, 1825." On April 9 the defendant withdrew his offer, and on April 29 the plaintiff purported to accept it. The Court of Common Pleas held that there was no contract.

BEST C.J.: Here is a proposal by the defendant to take property on certain terms; namely, that he should be let into possession in July. In that proposal he gives the plaintiff six weeks to consider; but if six weeks are given on one side to accept an offer, the other has six weeks to put an end to it. One party cannot be bound without the other. This was expressly decided in *Cooke v. Oxley*, where the defendant proposed to sell, at a certain price, tobacco to the plaintiff, who desired to have till four in the afternoon of that day to agree to or dissent from the proposal; with which terms the defendant complied; and the plaintiff having afterwards sued him for non-delivery of the tobacco, Lord Kenyon put it on the true ground by saying, "At the time of entering into this contract the engagement was all one side; the other party was not bound." Buller J. said, "It has been argued that this must be taken to be a complete sale from the time the condition was complied with: but it was not complied with; for it is not stated that the defendant did agree at four o'clock to the terms of the sale; or even that the goods were kept till that time." I put the present case on the same ground. At the time of entering into this contract the engagement was all on one side. [The Chief Justice then considered *Payne v. Cave* (above, p. 21) and

Adams v. Lindsell (above, p. 51).] . . . As the defendant repudiated the contract on April 9, before the expiration of the six weeks, he had a right to say that the plaintiff should not enforce it afterwards.

Notes
1. In *Mountford v. Scott* [1975] 1 All E.R. 198, C.A., V, in consideration of the payment of £1, granted in writing an option to P to purchase V's house for £10,000, exercisable within six months. Before the option was exercised, V purported to withdraw his offer. P exercised the option and it was held that he was entitled to specific performance of the contract to sell the house. The offer was irrevocable even though the consideration for it might be described as a token payment; and it was the contract for sale which was specifically enforced. The trial judge had wrongly concentrated on the question whether the option agreement was specifically enforceable.

Was not the decision that the option was irrevocable (as distinct from affording a remedy only in damages) specific enforcement of it? The option was a promise to keep the offer open, and the court held that it must remain open.

2. In *Watson v. Canada Permanent Trust Co.* (1972) 27 D.L.R (3d) 735 (British Columbia Supreme Court, Anderson J.) it was held, applying the *Hightrees* principle (below, p. 249) that the grantor of an option to buy certain shares was estopped from withdrawing his offer to sell when he knew that the purchaser intended to act on his promise to keep the offer open. The grant of the option was not under seal and the court held that there was no consideration for it; but the grantor knew that the grantee intended to embark on a "salvage operation" of the company which it would not attempt unless it had the right to buy the shares in the company. He made a promise "which any reasonable optionee would believe was not to be withdrawn." He knew the grantee intended to act on the promise, the grantee did so, he would have suffered great prejudice if the grantor could withdraw his promise, so the grantor would not be allowed to do so.

OFFORD v. DAVIES

Common Bench (1862) 12 C.B.(N.S.) 748; 31 L.J.C.P. 319; 6 L.T. 579; 10 W.R. 578; 9 Jur. 22 133 R.R. 491; 142 E.R. 1336

The plaintiff alleged that the defendants had promised that, in consideration that the plaintiff would, at the request of the defendants, discount bills of exchange to the extent of £600 for Messrs. Davies & Co. of Newtown, the defendants would guarantee "for the space of twelve calendar months" the due payment of all such bills. The plaintiff alleged that he had discounted various bills which were dishonoured and that the defendants had broken their promise and had not paid the sums of money payable by the bills of exchange.

The defendants' plea was that, after the making of the guarantee but before the plaintiff had discounted any bills, the defendants had countermanded the guarantee and had requested the plaintiff not to discount the bills.

To this plea the plaintiff demurred: "for that a party having given a guarantee (for a definite period) has no power to countermand it without the assent of the person to whom it is given."

ERLE C.J.: The declaration alleged a contract by the defendants, in consideration that the plaintiff would at the request of the defendants discount bills for Davies & Co., not exceeding £600, the defendants promised to guarantee the repayment of such discounts *for 12 months*, and the discount, and no repayment. The plea was a revocation of the promise before the discount in question; and the demurrer raises the question whether the defendants had a right to revoke the promise. We are of opinion that they had, and that consequently the plea is good.

This promise by itself creates no obligation. It is in effect conditioned to be binding if the plaintiff acts upon it, either to the benefit of the defendants, or to the detriment of himself. But, until the condition has been at least in part fulfilled, the defendants have the power of revoking it. In the case of a simple guarantee for a proposed loan, the right of revocation before the proposal has been acted on did not appear to be disputed. Then, are the rights of the parties affected either by the promise being expressed to be for 12 months, or by the fact that some discounts had been made before that now in question, and repaid? We think not.

The promise to repay for 12 months creates no additional liability on the guarantor, but, on the contrary, fixes a limit in time beyond which his liability cannot extend. And, with respect to other discounts, which had been repaid, we consider each discount as a separate transaction, creating a liability on the defendant till it is repaid, and, after repayment, leaving the promise to have the same operation that it had before any discount was made, and no more.

Judgment for the defendants.

Note
See Note on Acceptance of Tenders and Standing Offers, above, p. 10.

Law Revision Committee, 6th Interim Report (Statute of Frauds and the Doctrine of Consideration), Cmd. 5449, 1937, para. 38, p. 22

It appears to us to be undesirable and contrary to business practice that a man who has been promised a period, either expressly defined or until the happening of a certain event, in which to decide whether to accept or to decline an offer cannot rely upon being able to accept it at any time within that period. If the offeror wants a consideration for keeping it open, he can stipulate for it and his offer is then usually called an "option." Merely because he does not so stipulate, he ought not to be allowed to revoke his offer with impunity. We consider that the fixing of a definite period should be regarded as evidence of his intention to make a binding promise to keep his offer open, and that his promise should be enforceable. If no period of time is fixed, we think it may be assumed that no contractual obligation was intended.

It may be noted here that according to the law of most foreign countries a promisor is bound by such a promise. It is particularly undesirable that on such a point the English law should accept a lower moral standard.

Notes
1. "A builder may submit a tender in reliance on offers from suppliers of materials expressed to remain 'firm' for a fixed period. If those offers are withdrawn within that period and after his tender has been accepted, he may be gravely prejudiced": Treitel, *Law of Contracts* (8th ed.), p. 141.
2. The proposals of the Law Revision Committee have been reconsidered by the Law Commission in their Working Paper No. 60, "Firm Offers." The principal provisional recommendation made is that "An offeror who has promised that he will not revoke his offer for a definite time should be bound by the terms of that promise for a period not exceeding six years, *provided that* the promise has been made 'in the course of a business' . . ."; and that an offeror who breaks such a promise should be liable to damages.

SHUEY v. UNITED STATES

Supreme Court of the United States (1875) 92 U.S. 73; 23 L.Ed. 697

On April 20, 1865, the Secretary of War caused to be published in the public newspapers and otherwise a proclamation, announcing that "liberal rewards will be paid for any information that shall conduce to the arrest of either of the above-named criminals or their accomplices." The proclamation was not limited in terms to any specific period. On November 24, 1865, the President caused to be issued an order revoking the offer of the reward.

In 1866 the claimant discovered and identified Surratt, one of the named persons, and informed the United States authorities. He was, at all times, unaware that the offer of the reward had been revoked.

The claimant's petition was dismissed by the Court of Claims, and he appealed to the Supreme Court of the United States.

STRONG J.: The offer of a reward for the apprehension of Surratt was revoked on November 24, 1865; and notice of the revocation was published. It is not to be doubted that the offer was revocable at any time before it was accepted, and before anything had been done in reliance upon it. There was no contract until its terms were complied with. Like any other offer of a contract, it might, therefore, be withdrawn before rights had accrued under it; and it was withdrawn through the same channel in which it was made. The same notoriety was given to the revocation that was given to the offer; and the findings of fact do not show that any information was given by the claimant, or that he did anything to entitle him to the reward offered, until five months after the offer had been withdrawn. True, it is found that then, and at all times until the arrest was actually made, he was ignorant of the withdrawal; but that is an immaterial fact. The offer of the reward not having been made to him directly, but by means of a published proclamation, he should have known that it could be revoked in the manner in which it was made.

Judgment affirmed.

Note

In *Financings Ltd v. Stimson* [1962] 1 W.L.R. 1184; [1962] 3 All E.R. 386, the defendant, on March 16, 1961, at the premises of a dealer signed a form by which he offered to take a car on hire-purchase terms from the plaintiffs. On March 18 he paid a deposit of £70 and was allowed to take the car away from the dealer's premises. He was dissatisfied with it and on March 20 returned it to the dealer, saying he did not want it and (believing himself to be bound by a contract) offered to forfeit his deposit. In the night of March 24 the car was stolen from the dealer's premises and badly damaged. On March 25 the plaintiffs, not having been told that the defendant had returned the car, signed the hire-purchase agreement. It was held by the Court of Appeal:

(i) that the defendant had revoked his offer by returning the car to the dealer. Though he thought he was seeking rescission of a contract, not revoking an offer, it was enough that he had made it clear that he did not want to go on with the transaction. Pearson L.J., dissenting, held that the dealer was an agent only to transmit the revocation which, not having been transmitted, was ineffective. *Cf. Dunmore v. Alexander* (above, p. 59).

(ii) In view of an express provision in the form of contract that the defendant had examined the car and satisfied himself that it was in good order and condition, the offer was conditional on the car remaining in substantially the same condition until the moment of acceptance. That condition not being fulfilled, the acceptance was invalid. Lord Denning M.R. said: ". . . suppose an offer is made to buy a Rolls Royce car at a high price on one day and before it is accepted, it suffers the next day severe damage. Can it be accepted and the offeror bound? My answer to that is: no, because the offer is conditional on the goods at the moment of acceptance remaining in substantially the same condition as at the time of the offer." On this case, see Atiyah, "Judicial Techniques and the English Law of Contract," 2 Ottawa Law Rev. 337, 339.

Problems

1. P offered to buy V's garage business for £10,000, the offer to remain open for seven days. Two days later, plans were announced for a by-pass which would divert the bulk of the traffic

from the garage. V posted an acceptance of P's offer before P had an opportunity to revoke it. Is there a contract? (*Cf.* Lord Atkin in *Bell v. Lever Bros.* at p. 492 below.)

2. S offered to ship goods from Port Sudan to Belfast on c.i.f. terms. The Suez Canal was then unexpectedly closed for an indefinite period. B accepted before S could revoke his offer. (*Cf.* Note on p. 531 below.)

DICKINSON v. DODDS

Court of Appeal (1876) 2 Ch.D. 463; 45 L.J.Ch. 777; 34 L.T. 607

On Wednesday, June 10, the defendant delivered to the plaintiff a written offer to sell certain houses, "This offer to be left over until Friday, 9 o'clock a.m., June 12, 1874." In the afternoon of Thursday the plaintiff was informed by a Mr Berry that Dodds had been offering or agreeing to sell the property to one Allan. At about 7.30 that evening the plaintiff left a formal letter of acceptance at the house where Dodds was staying, but it appeared that this letter was overlooked and never delivered to Dodds. On Friday morning at about 7, Berry, who was acting as agent for the plaintiff, handed Dodds a duplicate of the letter of acceptance and explained its purport to him. It appeared that the day before Dodds had signed a formal contract for the sale of property to Allan. Bacon V.-C. made a decree of specific performance against Dodds, who appealed.

JAMES L.J.: It must, to constitute a contract, appear that the two minds were at one, at the same moment of time, that is, that there was an offer continuing up to the time of the acceptance. If there was not such a continuing offer, then the acceptance comes to nothing. Of course it may well be that the one man is bound in some way or other to let the other man know that his mind with regard to the offer has been changed; but in this case, beyond all question, the plaintiff knew that Dodds was no longer minded to sell the property to him as plainly and clearly as if Dodds had told him in so many words, "I withdraw the offer." This is evident from the plaintiff's own statements in the bill. . . . It is to my mind quite clear that before there was any attempt at acceptance by the plaintiff, he was perfectly well aware that Dodds had changed his mind, and that he had in fact agreed to sell the property to Allan. It is impossible, therefore, to say there was ever that existence of the same mind between the two parties which is essential in point of law to the making of an agreement. I am of opinion, therefore, that the plaintiff has failed to prove that there was any binding contract between Dodds and himself.

MELLISH L.J.: If an offer has been made for the sale of property, and before that offer is accepted, the person who has made the offer enters into a binding agreement to sell the property to someone else, and the person to whom the offer was first made receives notice in some way that the property has been sold to another person, can he after that make a binding contract by the acceptance of the offer? I am of the opinion that he cannot. The law may be right or wrong in saying that a person who has given to another a certain time within which to accept an offer is not bound by his promise to give that time; but, if he is not bound by that promise, and may still sell the property to someone else, and if it be the law that, in order to make a contract, the two minds must be in agreement at some one time, that is, at the time of the acceptance, how is it possible that when the person to whom the offer has been made knows that the person who has made the offer has sold the property to someone else, and that, in fact, he has not remained in the same mind to sell it to him, he can be at liberty to accept the offer and thereby make a binding contract? It seems to me that would be simply absurd. If a man makes an offer to sell a particular horse in his stable, and says, "I will give you until the day after tomorrow to accept the offer," and the next day goes and sells the horse to somebody else, and receives the purchase-money from him, can the person to whom the offer was originally made then come and say, "I accept," so as to make a binding contract, and so as to be entitled to recover damages for the non-delivery of the horse? If the rule of law is that a mere offer to sell property, which can be withdrawn at any time, and which is made dependent on the acceptance of the person to whom it is made, is a mere *nudum pactum*, how is it possible that the person to whom the offer has been made can by acceptance make a binding contract after he knows that the person who has made the offer has sold the property to someone else? It is admitted law that, if a man who makes an offer dies the offer cannot be accepted after he is dead, and parting with the property has very much the same effect as the death of the owner, for it makes the performance of the offer impossible. I am clearly of the opinion that, just as when a man who has made an offer dies before it is accepted it is impossible that it can be accepted, so when once the person to whom the offer was made knows that the property has been sold to someone else, it is too late for him to accept the offer, and on that ground I am clearly of opinion that there was no binding contract for the sale of the property by Dodds to Dickinson, and even if there had been, it seems to me that the sale of the property to Allan was first in point of time. However, it is not necessary to consider, if there had been two binding contracts, which of them would be entitled to priority in equity, because there is no binding contract between Dodds and Dickinson.

BAGGALLAY J.A. concurred.

Decision of Bacon V.-C. reversed.

Question

In the headnote to *Dickinson v. Dodds* in the *Law Reports* the following statement appears: "*Semble*, that the sale of the property to a third person would itself amount to a withdrawal of the offer even although the person to whom the offer was first made had no knowledge of the sale."

Do you consider that this is an accurate statement of the law?

Problems

1. On Monday Charles offers to sell Derek his house for £12,000, the offer to remain open for seven days, "unless I sell the property in the meantime." On Tuesday Charles sells the house to Edward for £12,500. On Wednesday Derek, who has heard nothing of the transaction with Edward, communicates his acceptance of the original offer. Advise Charles.

2. On June 1 Angus wrote to Bruce offering to sell his Tudor house for £200,000, the offer to remain open for a week. On June 4 Angus reads in *The Times*: "Mr Bruce has informed the National Trust that he has bought Mr Angus's well-known Tudor Mansion. . . ." Later the same day, Claymore offered Angus £210,000 for the house. Angus accepted, and 'phoned Bruce to say that the offer was no longer available. When the call came through Bruce was just about to leave his office to post a letter of acceptance, written the day before, but overlooked by the office boy. Advise Bruce.

MANCHESTER DIOCESAN COUNCIL FOR EDUCATION v. COMMERCIAL AND GENERAL INVESTMENTS LTD

For the facts, see above, p. 66.

BUCKLEY J. continued: If I am right in thinking that there was a contract on September 15, 1964, that disposes of the case but, in case I should be held to be wrong in that view, I will now consider the other point in the case and will for this purpose assume that no contract was made at that date. On this basis no contract can have been concluded before January 7, 1965. The defendant contends that, as the tender stipulated no time within which it must be accepted, it was an implied term of the offer that it must be accepted, if at all, within a reasonable time. It is said that acceptance on January 7 was not within a reasonable time.

It has long been recognised as being the law that, where an offer is made in terms which fix no time limit for acceptance, the offer must be accepted within a reasonable time to make a contract. (*Chitty* on *Contracts*, (22nd ed., 1961), p. 90, para. 89; *Williams* on *Vendor and Purchaser*, (4th ed., 1936), p. 16; *Halsbury's Laws of England*, (3rd ed., 1954), Vol. 8, p. 71, para. 124). There seems, however, to be no reported case in which the reason for this is explained. There appear to me to be two possible views on methods of approaching the problem. First it may be said that by implication the offer is made upon terms that, if it is not accepted within a reasonable time, it must be treated as withdrawn. Alternatively, it may be said that, if the offeree does not accept the offer within a reasonable time, he must be treated as having refused it. On either view the offer would cease to be a live one upon the expiration of what, in the circumstances of the particular case, should be regarded as a reasonable time for acceptance. The first of these alternatives involves implying a term that if the offer is not accepted within a reasonable time, it shall be treated as withdrawn or lapsing at the end of that period, if it has not then been accepted: the second is based upon an inference to be drawn from the conduct of the offeree, that is, that having failed to accept the offer within a reasonable time he has manifested an intention to refuse it. If in the first alternative the time which the offeror is to be treated as having set for acceptance is to be such a time as is reasonable at the date of the offer, what is reasonable must depend on circumstances then existing and reasonably likely to arise during the continuance of the offer; but it would not be unlikely that the offeror and offeree would make different assessments of what would be reasonable, even if, as might quite possibly not be the case, they based those judgments on identical known and anticipated circumstances. No doubt a court could resolve any dispute about this, but this approach clearly involves a certain degree of uncertainty about the precise terms of the offer. If, on the other hand, the time which the offeror is to be treated as having set for acceptance is to be such a time as turns out to be reasonable in the light of circumstances then existing and of circumstances arising thereafter during the continuance of the offer, whether forseeable or not, an additional element of uncertainty is introduced. The second alternative, on the other hand, involves simply an objective assessment of facts and the determination of the question whether on the facts the offeree should, in fairness to both parties, be regarded as having refused the offer.

It does not seem to me that either party is in greater need of protection by the law in this respect than the other. Until his offer has been accepted it is open to the offeror at any time to withdraw it or put a limit on the time for acceptance. On the other hand, the offeree can at any time refuse the offer or, unless he has been guilty of unreasonable delay, accept it. Neither party is at a disadvantage. Unless authority constrains me to do otherwise, I am strongly disposed to prefer the second alternative to the first. . . .

I have dealt with this part of the case at some length because, if the first alternative were the correct view of the law and if what is reasonable had to be ascertained as at the time of the offer, the subsequent conduct of the parties would be irrelevant to the question how long the offer should be treated as remaining open. In my opinion, however, the subsequent conduct of the parties is relevant to the question, which I think is the right test, whether the offeree should be held to have refused the offer by his conduct.

In my judgment, the letter of September 15, 1964, excludes the possibility of imputing to the plaintiff a refusal of the offer. If that letter does not itself constitute an effective acceptance, it clearly discloses an intention to accept from which there is nothing to suggest a departure before January 7, 1965. Accordingly, if no contract was formed earlier, I am of the opinion that it was open to the plaintiff to accept it on January 7 and that the plaintiff's letter of that date was effectual to bind the defendant contractually.

Order for specific performance and costs.

BRADBURY v. MORGAN

Exchequer (1862) 1 H. & C. 249; 158 E.R. 877; 31 L.J.Ex. 462; 7 L.T. 104; 8 Jur.(N.S.) 918; 10 W.R. 776; 26 Digest 208, 1625

The defendants were the executors of J. M. Leigh who had written the following letter to the plaintiffs:

> 3 George Yard, Lombard St.,
> London, May 3, 1858

Messrs. Bradbury, Greatorex and Co.

Gentlemen,
   I request that you will give credit in the usual way of your business to Henry Jones Leigh, of Leather Lane, Holborn; and in consideration of your doing so, I hereby engage to guarantee the regular payment of the running balance of his account with you, until I give you notice to the contrary, to the extent of one hundred pounds sterling.

> I remain, etc.
> J. M. Leigh.

Limit £100

The plaintiffs thereafter credited H. J. Leigh in the usual way of their business. J. M. Leigh died and the plaintiffs, having no notice or knowledge of his death, continued to supply H. J. Leigh with goods on credit. £100 was owing by H. J. Leigh to the plaintiffs and the defendants declined to pay, arguing that they were not liable as the debts were contracted and incurred after the death of J. M. Leigh and not in his lifetime.

POLLOCK C.B.: We are all of opinion that the plaintiff is entitled to judgment. No doubt, if this were merely an implied contract which arose from a request, it would be revoked by the death of either party. *Blades v. Free* (9 B. & C. 167)[1] is an authority that a request is revoked, but a contract is not put an end to, by death. The language here used, "I request you will give credit," is a mere mode of civil expression, and the party using it never meant to request in that sense which Mr Brown has suggested. Instead of saying, "I will thank you to give credit"; or "you will oblige me by giving credit," he says, "I request you will give credit." Whether his death was contemplated, I do not know. The probability is, that if it had been suggested the plaintiffs would have required some notice before the guarantee was determined; but this is a contract, and the question is whether it is put an end to by the death of the guarantor. There is no direct authority to that effect; and I think that all reason and authority, such as there is, are against that proposition, and that the plaintiffs are therefore entitled to judgment.

BRAMWELL B.: I am of the same opinion. The general rule is thus stated in *Williams on Executors* (5th ed.), p. 1559: "The executors or administrators so completely represent their testator or intestate, with respect to the liabilities above mentioned, that every bond, or covenant, or contract of the deceased includes them, although they are not named in the terms of it; for the executors or administrators of every person are implied in himself."

The only exception is where the contract is in respect of the personal qualification of the testator or intestate, and that does not apply to the present case. If the guarantee had been in these terms: "I request you to deliver to A tomorrow morning goods to the value of £50, and in consideration of your so doing I will pay you," and before the morning the guarantor died, but the goods were duly delivered; I can see no reason why the personal representative of the guarantor should not be liable; and whether a guarantor says, "deliver some goods on a given day," or "deliver a quantity of goods upon any day or days," can make no difference. Very likely a tradesman, who would not trust in the first instance without a guarantee, would not deliver any goods after the death of the guarantor, but, however that may be, the executor must give some timely notice in order to put an end to the contract. Mr Brown relied on the words, "I request you will give credit," but they are of no importance; for this is not a case of authority given by the deceased.

Judgment for the plaintiffs.

Questions
When J.M. Leigh died, had he made a contract or a standing offer? (*Cf. Offord v. Davies*, above, p. 78.) What was the court's view? Is the case an authority on the termination of offers?

[1] T's mistress had authority to bind T by her contracts for necessaries as if she had been his wife. The plaintiff supplied goods to the mistress, not knowing that T had died. It was held that T's executor was not bound to pay for the goods.

Note

In *Coulthart v. Clementson* (1879) 5 Q.B.D. 42 it was held by Bowen J. that a continuing guarantee was revoked where the creditor (a bank) had notice of the guarantor's death and the fact that he had made a will. This amounted to notice of trusts which might be incompatible with the continuance of the guarantee. In *Re Whelan* [1897] 1 I.R. 575 Chatterton V.-C. held that the same principle applied *a fortiori* where the guarantor died intestate; for, while an option to continue the guarantee might exist in the case of a will, it could not do so in the case of intestacy.

In both of these cases the guarantee was an ordinary standing offer and was revocable by the guarantor in his lifetime. The position is different where the guarantee is given for consideration and is therefore irrevocable. So *Coulthart v. Clementson* was distinguished by the Court of Appeal in *Lloyd's v. Harper* (1880) 16 Ch.D. 290 (and see below, p. 306) where the deceased guarantor undertook responsibility for his son's engagements as a Lloyd's underwriter, in consideration of the son's being admitted as such by Lloyd's. It was held that the guarantee, being given for a once for all consideration, was irrevocable in the testator's lifetime and was not revoked by his death.

CHAPTER 4

CONTRACT AS AN AGREEMENT

Section 1. Finality and Completeness

MAY AND BUTCHER v. R.

House of Lords (1929) [1934] 2 K.B. 17n.; 103 L.J.K.B. 556n.; 151 L.T. 246n.

Petition of Right. The suppliants, May and Butcher, alleged that it was mutually agreed between them and the Controller of the Disposals Board for the purchase by the suppliants of the whole of the tentage which might become available for disposal in the United Kingdom up to March 31, 1923.

The relevant terms of the alleged agreement were as follows:
"(3) The price or prices to be paid, and the date or dates on which payment is to be made by the purchasers to the Commission for such old tentage shall be agreed upon from time to time between the Commission and the purchasers as the quantities of the said old tentage become available for disposal, and are offered to the purchasers by the Commission.
(10) It is understood that all disputes with reference to or arising out of this agreement will be submitted to arbitration in accordance with the provisions of the Arbitration Act, 1889."

By demurrer, answer and plea the Attorney-General said that the petition of right disclosed no sufficient and binding contract of sale.
Rowlatt J. held that the arrangement constituted no contract, but merely a series of clauses for adoption if and when contracts were made, because the price, date of payment and period of delivery had still to be agreed; and that the arbitration clause did not apply to differences of opinion on these questions. The Court of Appeal (Scrutton L.J. dissenting) affirmed Rowlatt J.'s decision. The suppliants appealed.

LORD BUCKMASTER: In my opinion there never was a concluded contract between the parties. It has long been a well-recognised principle of contract law that an agreement between two parties to enter into an agreement in which some critical part of the contract matter is left undetermined is no contract at all. It is, of course, perfectly possible for two people to contract that they will sign a document which contains all the relevant terms, but it is not open to them to agree that they will in the future agree upon a matter which is vital to the arrangement between them and has not yet been determined. It has been argued that as the fixing of the price has broken down, a reasonable price must be assumed. That depends in part upon the terms of the Sale of Goods Act, which no doubt reproduces, and is known to have reproduced, the old law upon the matter. That provides in section 8 that "the price in a contract of sale may be fixed by the contract, or may be left to be fixed in manner thereby agreed, or may be determined by the course of dealing between the parties. Where the price is not determined in accordance with the foregoing provisions the buyer must pay a reasonable price"[1]; while, if the agreement is to sell goods on the terms that the price is to be fixed by the valuation of a third party, and such third party cannot or does not make such valuation, section 9 says that the agreement is avoided. I find myself quite unable to understand the distinction between an agreement to permit the price to be fixed by a third party and an agreement to permit the price to be fixed in the future by the two parties to the contract themselves. In principle it appears to me that they are one and the same thing. . . .

The next question is about the arbitration clause, and there I entirely agree with the majority of the Court of Appeal and also with Rowlatt J. The clause refers "disputes with reference to or arising out of this agreement" to arbitration, but until the price has been fixed, the agreement is not there. The arbitration clause relates to the settlement of whatever may happen when the agreement has been completed and the parties are regularly bound. There is nothing in the arbitration clause to enable a contract to be made which in fact the original bargain has left quite open.

VISCOUNT DUNEDIN: I am of the same opinion. This case arises upon a question of sale, but in my view the principles which we are applying are not confined to sale, but are the general principles of the law of contract. To be a good contract there must be a concluded bargain, and a concluded contract is one which settles everything that is necessary to be settled and leaves nothing to be settled by agreement between the parties. Of course it may leave something which still has to be determined, but then that determination must be a determination which does not depend upon the agreement between the parties. In the system of law in which I was brought up, that was expressed by one of those brocards of which perhaps we have been too fond, but which often express very neatly what is wanted: "*Certum est quod certum reddi potest.*" Therefore, you may very well agree that a certain part of the contract of sale, such as price, may be settled by someone else. As a matter of the general law of contract all the essentials have to be settled. What are the essentials may vary according to the particular contract under consideration. We are here dealing with sale, and undoubtedly price is one of the essentials of sale, and if it is left still to be agreed between the parties, then there is no contract. It may be left to the determination of a certain person, and if it was so left and that person either would not or could not act, there would be no contract because the price was to be settled in a certain way and it has become impossible to settle it in that way, and therefore there is no settlement. No doubt as to goods, the Sale of Goods Act, 1893, says that if the price is not mentioned and settled in the contract it is to be a reasonable price. The simple answer in this case is that the Sale of Goods Act provides for silence on the point and here there is no silence, because there is a provision that the two parties are to agree. As long as you have something certain it does not matter. For instance, with regard to price it is a perfectly good contract to say that the price is to be settled by the buyer. I have not had time, or

---

[1] s.15 of the Supply of Goods and Services Act 1982 now makes similar provision for the payment of a reasonable charge for a service.

perhaps I have not been industrious enough, to look through all the books in England to see if there is such a case; but there was such a case in Scotland in 1760, where it was decided that a sale of a landed estate was perfectly good, the price being left to be settled by the buyer himself. I have only expressed in other words what has already been said by my noble friend on the Woolsack. Here there was clearly no contract. There would have been a perfectly good settlement of price if the contract had said that it was to be settled by arbitration by a certain man, or it might have been quite good if it was said that it was to be settled by arbitration under the Arbitration Act so as to bring in a material plan by which a certain person could be put in action. The question then arises, has anything of that sort been done? I think clearly not. The general arbitration clause is one in very common form as to disputes arising out of the arrangements. In no proper meaning of the word can this be described as a dispute arising between the parties; it is a failure to agree, which is a very different thing from a dispute.

As regards the option point, I do not think it can be more neatly put than it was by Rowlatt J. when he said: "It is an option to offer terms on terms that are not agreed. An option to offer a contract which is not a contract seems to me not to carry the case any further than the first way of putting it." For these reasons I agree in the motion.

Appeal dismissed.

Note

In *Foley v. Classique Coaches* [1934] 2 K.B. 1 the plaintiff agreed to sell some land to the defendants for a coach station in consideration of the defendants agreeing to buy all their petrol from him. The agreement concerning the sale of the land and that concerning the sale of the petrol were put into separate documents, the former agreement stating that it was conditional on the defendants' entering into the latter and the latter stating that it was supplemental to the former. The agreement about the petrol provided that it was to be supplied "at a price to be agreed by the parties in writing and from time to time." The land was conveyed and the petrol agreement was acted on for three years. The defendants then repudiated the petrol agreement. The plaintiff succeeded in an action for damages, a declaration that the agreement was binding and an injunction to restrain the defendants from buying petrol from elsewhere. The defendants' appeal was dismissed.

SCRUTTON L.J. said: In the present case the parties obviously believed they had a contract and they acted for three years as if they had; they had an arbitration clause which relates to the subject-matter of the agreement as to the supply of petrol, and it seems to me that this arbitration clause applies to any failure to agree as to the price. By analogy to the case of a tied house there is to be implied in this contract a term that the petrol shall be supplied at a reasonable price and shall be of reasonable quality.

See also *Sykes (F. & G.) Wessex v. Fine Fare* [1967] 1 Lloyd's Rep. 53, C.A.

Questions

1. Is there a valid distinction between an agreement to permit the price to be fixed in the future by the two parties to the agreement and and:

(a) an agreement to permit the price to be fixed by a third party? (See *Campbell v. Edwards*, [1976] 1 W.L.R. 403.)

(b) an agreement to permit the price to be fixed by one of the "agreeing" parties? (Viscount Dunedin's dictum that there may be a good contract where the price is to be settled by the buyer was followed in *Lombard Tricity Finance Ltd. v. Paton* [1989] 1 All E.R. 918, 923, C.A., holding that a provision in a contract of loan allowing the lender to vary the rate of interest at in its absolute discretion was not unlawful: ". . . we do not see that it can be different in a contract of loan, where the borrower has (in theory at any rate) the opportunity to repay the whole outstanding balance.") *Cf.* UTCC Regulations Sched. 3, sub-paras. 1(j) and 2(b) below, pp. 718 and 719. "Solus" agreements (below, p. 690) are not treated as invalid on the ground that the price of petrol is to be fixed by the seller.

2. Can *May and Butcher v. R.* be properly distinguished from *Foley v. Classique Coaches?*
3. What would have been the position if the defendant in *Foley* had repudiated both agreements immediately after they were signed?
4. What if, after the land had been conveyed, he had repudiated the petrol agreement only?
5. In *British Steel Corp. v. Cleveland Bridge and Engineering Co. Ltd* [1984] 1 All E.R. 504 at 511, Robert Goff L.J. said of the facts of that case:

> "In my judgment, the true analysis of the situation is simply this. Both parties confidently expected a formal contract to eventuate. In these circumstances, to expedite performance under that anticipated contract, one requested the other to commence the contract work, and the other complied with that request. If thereafter, as anticipated, a contract was entered into, the work done as requested will be treated as having been performed under that contract; if, contrary to their expectation, no contract was entered into, then the performance of the work is not referable to any contract the terms of which can be ascertained, and the law simply imposes an obligation on the party who made the request to pay a reasonable sum for such work as has been done pursuant to that request, such an obligation sounding in quasi contract or, as we now say, in restitution. Consistently with that solution, the party making the request may find himself liable to pay for work which he would not have had to pay for as such if the anticipated contract had come into existence, for example, preparatory work which will, if the contract is made, be allowed for in the price of the finished work."

What is the difference between the situation found to exist by Robert Goff L.J. and that in *Foley?*

Note

In *A-G of Hong Kong v. Humphreys Estate (Queen's Gardens) Ltd* [1987] 2 All E.R. 387 the Hong Kong government agreed with HKL Ltd, subject to contract, on an exchange of properties. In pursuance of an agreement in principle, the government took possession of HKL's flats, fitted them out, moved in civil servants and disposed of their former residences. HKL entered the Crown property and demolished the buildings with a view to redevelopment. All material term had been agreed and the necessary documents drafted and agreed. Before the agreement was executed HKL withdrew and terminated the government's licence to occupy the flats. It was common ground that the agreement was still subject to contract but the government argued that HKL were estopped from withdrawing from it. The Privy Council held that they were not estopped. Lord Templeman said (p. 395):

> "In the present case the government acted in the hope that a voluntary agreement in principle expressly made 'subject to contract' and therefore not binding would eventually be followed by the achievement of legal relationships in the form of grants and transfers of property. It is possible but unlikely that in circumstances at present unforeseeable a party to negotiations set out in a document expressed to be 'subject to contract' would be able to satisfy the court that the parties had subsequently agreed to convert the document into a contract or that some form of estoppel had arisen to prevent both parties from refusing to proceed with the transactions envisaged by the document. But in the present case the government chose to begin and elected to continue on terms that either party might suffer a change of mind and withdraw."

He distinguished *Salvation Army Ltd v. W. Yorks Metropolitan C.C.* (1980) 41 P. & C.R. 179 where the Bradford City Council told the Army that they intended to acquire the Army's meeting hall for road widening purposes and it was agreed, "subject to contract," that the Army would acquire a new site and build a new hall, receiving £29,097 as compensation. The contract was never executed but the Army acquired the site and built the new hall. The Metropolitan Council, which had taken over the functions of City Council, abandoned the road widening scheme and refused to pay. Woolf J. held that they were bound to do so. The Army "were under a mistaken belief that they were under an obligation to vacate the old site and had a right to purchase the new site . . ."; and the defendant either knew or ought to have known that the plaintiffs were continuing to incur expenditure under that mistaken belief and allowed them to continue to do so. The defendant was estopped from denying that the supposed right and obligation existed. In the Hong Kong case neither party was under any mistake. (On estoppel, see below, p. 258).

SUDBROOK TRADING ESTATE LTD v. EGGLETON

House of Lords [1983] 1 A.C. 444; [1982] 3 W.L.R. 315; [1982] 3 All E.R. 1

A lease gave the lessee an option to purchase the reversion "at such price, not being less than twelve thousand pounds as may be agreed upon by two Valuers one to be nominated by the Lessor and the other by the Lessees or in default of such agreement by an Umpire appointed by the said Valuers. . . ." When the lessee sought to exercise the option the lessor refused to appoint a valuer, claiming that the option clause was void for uncertainty. The House of Lords (Lord Russell dissenting), reversing the Court of Appeal, held that the option was valid and had been effectively exercised and that it should be specifically performed, the price being fixed by a valuation ordered by the court.

LORD DIPLOCK: The option clause cannot be classified as a mere "agreement to make an agreement." There are not any terms left to be agreed between the parties. In modern terminology, it is to be classified as a unilateral or "if" contract. Although it creates from the outset a right on the part of the lessees, which they will be entitled, but not bound, to exercise against the lessors at a future date, it does not give rise to any legal obligations on the part of either party unless and until the lessees give notice in writing to the lessors, within the stipulated period, of their desire to purchase the freehold reversion to the lease. The giving of such notice, however, converts the "if" contract into a synallagmatic or bilateral contract, which creates mutual legal rights and obligations on the part of both lessors and lessees.

The first obligation on each of them, once the contract has become synallagmatic, is to appoint their respective valuers to fix what is the fair and reasonable price for the reversion. That this is a primary obligation under the contract follows from the use of the words "*to be* nominated," but it would, in my view, also be a necessary implication to give business efficacy to the option clause. The requirement that the price to be so fixed is one that will be fair and reasonable as between lessors and lessees appears to me to be a necessary implication from the description "valuers" applied to the persons by whom the price is to be fixed by agreement between them, if possible, and from the description "umpire" applied to the person by whom the price is to be fixed if the valuers cannot agree. The term "valuer" (with a capital "V" at any rate) is used nowadays to denote a member of a recognised profession comprised of persons possessed of skill and experience in assessing the market price of property, particularly real property.

The obligation of both lessors and lessees on appointing their respective valuers is to instruct them to carry out the functions for which the option clause requires that they should be appointed, *viz.* to try to reach agreement with one another on a price for the reversion that is fair and reasonable as between the lessors and the lessees and, failing such agreement, to agree on and appoint a suitably qualified impartial person to fix such price.

The option clause, to which the lessors and lessees alone are parties, cannot of itself impose on the valuers any legal duty to endeavour to reach agreement with one another as to a fair and reasonable price for the reversion or, if they fail to do so, to agree on what person is to be appointed by them jointly as umpire to fix the price. But that this, which is stressed in several of the cases cited by Templeman L.J., presents an obstacle to compelling performance of the contract contained in the option clause is a proposition that on examination proves, in my opinion, to be illusory. If a valuer appointed by the lessors or lessees does not carry out the instructions given him by his appointor, but in default of agreement with his fellow valuer on the price, fails to agree with him on the person to be appointed as umpire, the valuer will be in breach of his own contract with his appointor; his appointment can be revoked and a fresh valuer, who will comply with his instructions, appointed in his stead. In the (improbable) event contemplated, in my view it would by necessary implication be a contractual duty owed by the lessors and lessees to one another under the option clause to adopt this course.

So if both lessors and lessees carry out their primary contractual obligations to one another, under the option clause, the result will be a conveyance by the lessors to the lessees of the reversion in fee simple to the demised premises on the completion date fixed for completion by para. (b) of the clause at a price agreed on between valuers appointed by each party or failing such agreement determined by an umpire appointed jointly by the valuers. Until such conveyance and payment the contract remains executory; but so does any other contract for the sale of land. What Templeman L.J. refers to in his summary of the effect of the authorities as the one central proposition from which the three principles that he states all stem, *viz.* until the price has been fixed by the method provided for in the contract "there is no complete agreement to enforce" (see [1981] 3 All E.R. 105 at 115, [1981] 3 W.L.R. 361 at 373), involves a fundamental fallacy. A contract is complete as a contract as soon as the parties have reached agreement as to what each of its essential terms is or can with certainty be ascertained, for it is an elementary principle of the English law of contract *id certum est quod certum reddi potest.* True it is that the agreement for the sale of land remains executory until transfer of title to the land and payment of the purchase price; but if this is the sense in which the agreement is said not to be complete it is only executory contracts that do require enforcement by the courts; and such enforcement may either take the form of requiring a party to perform his primary obligation to the other party under it (specific performance) or, if he has failed to perform a primary obligation, of requiring him to perform the secondary obligation, that arises only on such failure, to pay monetary compensation (damages) to the other party for the resulting loss that he has sustained.

LORD FRASER made a speech allowing the appeal.

LORD RUSSELL, dissenting, asked: Why should it be thought that potential vendor and purchaser intended the price to be "fair"? The former would intend the price to be high, even though "unfairly" so. And the latter vice versa. Vendors and purchasers are normally greedy.

LORD SCARMAN: The question for decision is as to the true construction to be placed on an option granted to a lessee to buy the freehold reversion. The terms of the option have been set out in full by my noble and learned friend Lord Diplock. Were the parties agreeing to a sale "at a fair valuation," that is, "at a reasonable price"? Or were they treating their chosen mode of ascertaining the price as being of the essence of their contract? What was the object of their contract? A fair and reasonable price? Or a price reached only by the means specified?

Unembarrassed by authority, I would unhesitatingly conclude that the parties intended that the lessee should pay a fair and reasonable price to be determined as at the date when he exercised the option. The valuation formula was introduced into the contract merely as a convenient way of ascertaining the price at that future time. Should we be deterred from so construing the provision by the existence of a line of authority stretching back over 150 years in which provisions remitting to a valuer or arbitrator the ascertainment of a price have been construed as making the machinery of ascertainment an essential term of the contract?

I think not.

LORD BRIDGE made a speech allowing the appeal.

Questions
1. Is an agreement to buy and sell at a price to be fixed by the parties different in kind from an agreement to buy and sell at a price to be fixed by valuers appointed by the parties?
2. Is an agreement to buy and sell at a price to be fixed by the valuers to be appointed by the parties the same as an agreement to buy and sell at a reasonable price?
3. Would a valuer who failed to agree on a person to be appointed umpire be (as Lord Diplock says) in breach of contract? What if he had no confidence in any of the persons his fellow-valuer would agree to?

BRITISH BANK FOR FOREIGN TRADE v. NOVINEX LTD

Court of Appeal [1949] 1 K.B. 623; [1949] L.J.R. 658; 93 S.J. 146; [1949]
1 All E.R. 155

The defendants, by letter to the plaintiffs, agreed to buy from clients of the plaintiffs (Messrs. Pritchard and Gee Trading Co.) 20,000 oilskin suits. In that letter the defendants wrote: "We confirm that we have agreed to cover you on this transaction with a commission of 4d. per oilskin suit. . . . We also undertake to cover you with an agreed commission on any other business transacted with your friends. In return for this you are to put us in direct contact with your friends." The plaintiffs did put the defendants in direct contact with their friends and, in August 1947, the defendants bought from the friends by two transactions 1,000 and 20,000 oilskin suits. The second transaction did not arise directly from the introduction of the plaintiffs, but from the defendants having seen an advertisement in *The Times*.

The defendants denied liability to pay commission on these two transactions on the grounds (1) that no legally enforceable bargain arose under the letter quoted above; and (2) if the arrangement was an enforceable contract, it applied only to business arising directly from the introduction, which the transaction as to the 20,000 skins, at least, did not. Denning J. appears to have accepted both submissions. The plaintiffs appealed.

COHEN L.J. dealt first with the second point, and held that there was nothing in the agreement to limit it to orders directly attributable to the introduction. He then went on: Is this an enforceable agreement? A number of authorities have been cited to us, to which I do not propose to refer in detail, because, in my view, the effect of the authorities is stated correctly in the learned judge's judgment where he said: "The principle to be deduced from the cases is that if there is an essential term which has yet to be agreed and there is no express or implied provision for its solution, the result in point of law is that there is no binding contract. In seeing whether there is an implied provision for its solution, however, there is a difference between an arrangement which is wholly executory on both sides and one which has been executed on one side or the other. In the ordinary way, if there is an arrangement to supply goods at a price "to be agreed" or to perform services on terms "to be agreed," then although, while the matter is still executory, there may be no binding contract, nevertheless, if it is executed on one side, that is, if the one does his part without having come to an agreement as to the price or the terms, then the law will say that there is necessarily implied, from the conduct of the parties, a contract that, in default of agreement, a reasonable sum is to be paid." With that statement of the principle of law, I respectfully agree. My difference with the learned judge is only on the question whether he has correctly applied that statement of principle to the facts of this case.

The learned judge continued: "The difficulty is to apply the distinction in this case. This is not a case of services to be rendered for wages or goods to be supplied for a price. It is an arrangement in regard to repeat transactions or follow-up transactions, in respect of which the person effecting the original introduction has performed no fresh service whatever apart from his original introduction. He has, however, done his part. He has effected the original introduction." Pausing there for a moment, I can see no difference in principle between a case where the service which is rendered is labour and a case where the service is an introduction. Whatever the value of the service may be, the plaintiffs have rendered to the defendants the service which was intended to be the consideration for the agreement to pay commission on future orders. I cannot think that there is a difference in principle between such a service and an agreement to serve an employer as a clerk or in any other capacity. The judge then said that, in his view, it was impossible to apply the principle as regards ordinary service contracts to the present case, because he said that there was so much left in the air. He said: "Is it to be implied that he is to receive a reasonable commission on all follow-up transactions?" I have already dealt with that point. It seems to me on that point the agreement is plain and unambiguous and is so expressed. Then he said: "Is commission to be payable until the crack of doom?" I think the observation applies that if the defendants go on dealing with Pritchard and Gee Trading Co. Ltd, until the crack of doom, they will have to go on paying commission to the plaintiffs, if they are in existence, until that doom occurs. As was pointed out in *Levy v. Goldhill* ([1917] 2 Ch. 297, 300) by Peterson J., parties having entered into a bargain may have it in their power to put an end to it. The defendants in this case need not continue to deal with Messrs. Pritchard and Gee Trading Co., Ltd I feel no difficulty on either of these points. Then the learned judge said: "Is it confined to oilskins or does it apply to business of an entirely different kind, in different commodities, by different departments, and so forth?" Here again I can find no ambiguity in the agreement, and I do not therefore feel any difficulty in answering this question in favour of the second alternative.

Then the judge continued on what, I think, is the principal issue: "And what is the amount of commission to be? If there is no usual or customary commission, how can anyone say what is a reasonable commission for a follow-up transaction or a repeat transaction? That appeared quite clearly from the evidence which showed when parties are negotiating for the price they are going to pay, they take account of any commission they have to pay to agents." Denning J. went on to say that this showed that the agreement was too vague to be enforced. But the agreement had said in terms, instead of by implication: "we also undertake to cover you with a reasonable commission on any other business transacted with your friends." Denning J. seems to have regarded that condition as being too vague to be enforceable. I cannot agree with this view. I think that a court should take the view that a jury properly directed would be able to arrive at a proper conclusion as to what in the circumstances of this case is a reasonable commission.

COHEN L.J. then considered what was a reasonable commission, and held it to be ¼d. per skin.]

The court should, I think, make a declaration that the defendants are liable to pay a reasonable commission on the value of any transaction between the defendants and Messrs. Pritchard and Gee Trading Co. Ltd after December 9, 1946, and order the payment of commission at the figure I have mentioned in respect of the two transactions in August 1947.

BUCKNILL and SINGLETON L.JJ. agreed.

WALFORD AND OTHERS v. MILES AND ANOTHER

House of Lords [1992] 1 All E.R. 453

M owned a company carrying on a photographic processing business. He decided to sell it. P made an offer of £1.9m. W heard the business was for sale. He thought it was "dramatically undervalued" and was enthusiastic to buy it for £2m. W and M reached an agreement by correspondence and telephone, "subject to contract," for the sale. M asked W for a "comfort letter" (see below, p. 187) from W's bankers confirming that they would provide the finance. M agreed that if W provided that letter by a certain day he would terminate negotiations with any third party and consideration of any alternative with a view to concluding an agreement with W. W provided the comfort letter as agreed and M confirmed that he agreed, "subject to contract," to sell the property for £2m. W sent preliminary inquiries and a draft agreement to M's solicitors but M sold the property to P.

W sued for breach of an alleged oral agreement, collateral to the negotiations for the sale that, in consideration of W (i) agreeing to continue the negotiations and not withdraw and (ii) providing the comfort letter, M had agreed to terminate negotiations with, and not deal with, any third party or give further consideration to any alternative. [A "lockout agreement."] By an amendment to his statement of claim, W also alleged that there was a term, necessarily implied to give business efficacy to the contract, that M would continue to negotiate in good faith with W. W claimed that the true value of the property was £3m and that he had lost £1m. (A further point relating to misrepresentation is omitted.)

The Court of Appeal by a majority held that the agreement was nothing more than an agreement to negotiate and was unenforceable. Bingham L.J., dissenting, held that the agreement was enforceable as a contract not to deal with any third party. W appealed.

LORD KEITH OF KINKEL agreed with Lord Ackner.

LORD ACKNER: Mr Naughton (counsel for the appellants) accepted that as the law now stands and has stood for approaching 20 years an agreement to negotiate is not recognised as an enforceable contract. This was first decided in terms in *Courtney & Fairbairn Ltd v. Tolaini Bros. (Hotels) Ltd* [1975] 1 All E.R. 716 at 720, where Lord Denning M.R. said:

> "If the law does not recognise a contract to enter into a contract (when there is a fundamental term yet to be agreed) it seems to me it cannot recognise a contract to negotiate. The reason is because it is too uncertain to have any binding force ... It seems to me that a contract to negotiate, like a contract to enter into a contract, is not a contract known to the law ... I think we must apply the general principle that when there is a fundamental matter left undecided and to be the subject of negotiation, there is no contract."

In that case Lord Denning M.R. rejected as not well founded (and Lord Diplock expressly concurred with this rejection) the dictum of Lord Wright in *Hillas & Co. Ltd v. Arcos Ltd* [1932] All E.R. Rep. 494 at 505:

> "There is then no bargain except to negotiate, and negotiation may be fruitless and end without any contract ensuing; yet even then, in strict theory, there is a contract (if there is good consideration) to negotiate, though in the event of repudiation by one party the damages may be nominal, unless a jury think that the opportunity to negotiate was of some appreciable value to the injured party."

Before your Lordships it was sought to argue that the decision in the *Courtney & Fairbairn Ltd* case was wrong. Although the cases in the United States did not speak with one voice your Lordships' attention was drawn to the decision of the United States Court of Appeals, Third Circuit in *Channel Home Centers Division of Grace Retail Corp. v. Grossman* (1986) 795 F. 2d 291 as being "the clearest example" of the American cases in the appellants' favour. That case raised the issue whether an agreement to negotiate in good faith, if supported by consideration, is an enforceable contract. I do not find the decision of any assistance. While accepting that an agreement to agree is not an enforceable contract, the United States Court of Appeals appears to have proceeded on the basis that an agreement to negotiate in good faith is synonymous with an agreement to use best endeavours and, as the latter is enforceable, so is the former. This appears to me, with respect, to be an unsustainable proposition. The reason why an agreement to negotiate, like an agreement to agree, is unenforceable is simply because it lacks the necessary certainty. The same does not apply to an agreement to use best endeavours. This uncertainty is demonstrated in the instant case by the provision which it is said has to be implied in the agreement for the determination of the negotiations. How can a court be expected to decide whether, *subjectively*, a proper reason existed for the termination of negotiations? The answer suggested depends upon whether the negotiations have been determined "in good faith." However, the concept of a duty to carry on negotiations in good faith is inherently repugnant to the adversarial position of the parties when involved in negotiations. Each party to the negotiations is entitled to pursue his (or her) own interest, so long as he avoids making misrepresentations. To advance that interest he must be entitled, if he thinks it appropriate, to threaten to withdraw from further negotiations or to withdraw in fact in the hope that the opposite party may seek to reopen the negotiations by offering him improved terms. Mr Naughton, of course, accepts that the agreement upon which he relies does not contain a duty to complete the negotiations. But that still leaves the vital question: how is a vendor ever to know that he is entitled to withdraw from further negotiations? How is the court to police such an "agreement?" A duty to negotiate in good faith is as unworkable in practice as it is inherently inconsistent with the position of a negotiating party. It is here that the uncertainty lies. In my judgment, while negotiations are in existence either party is entitled to withdraw from these negotiations, at any time and for any reason. There can be thus no obligation to continue to negotiate until there is a "proper reason" to withdraw. Accordingly, a bare agreement to negotiate has no legal content.

LORD GOFF OF CHIEVELEY, LORD JAUNCEY OF TULICHETTLE and LORD BROWNE-WILKINSON agreed.

Appeal dismissed.

Questions
1. Is a lock-out agreement of any value if it does not imply an agreement to negotiate? What is the use of A's exclusive right to bombard B with offers if B has no obligation to respond in any way?
2. Is there an insuperable difficulty in the notion of an obligation to negotiate in good faith? If, after agreeing to do so, X decides, for whatever reason, that he does not wish to enter into the contemplated contract in any circumstances, he is surely entitled to do so; and thereafter any negotiations would be a sham—*i.e.*, *not* in good faith. On the other hand an obligation *not* to negotiate in bad faith (*i.e.*, to go through the motions of negotiating, having already decided not to conclude any agreement) is readily comprehensible. If so, would it not follow that a promise, "If I negotiate at all, it will be in good faith," would be meaningful? But would it be of any value? See, generally, Carter and Furmston, "Good Faith and Fairness in the Negotiation of Contracts," (1994) 8 J.C.L. 1, 93.
3. Must a valid lock-out agreement always include a term specifying its duration? Why should it not be valid for the time reasonably necessary to make the necessary investigations and to prepare an offer?

PITT v. PHH ASSET MANAGEMENT LTD

Court of Appeal [1994] 1 W.L.R. 327; [1993] 4 All E.R. 961

The defendant placed a property on the market at the asking price of £205,000. Buckle offered £185,000. The plaintiff made an offer of £190,000 which the defendant accepted, subject to contract. Buckle increased her offer to £195,000. The defendant withdrew his acceptance of the plaintiff's offer. The plaintiff and Buckle then each offered £200,000. The defendant accepted the plaintiff's offer, subject to contract. Buckle increased her offer to £210,000. The defendant again withdrew his acceptance of the plaintiff's offer.

Plaintiff, annoyed, told the defendant (i) he would seek an injunction to prevent the sale to Buckle; (ii) he would tell Buckle he was withdrawing, leaving her alone in the field, and advise her to lower her offer; and (iii) he was in a position to exchange as soon as the defendant wanted. On October 3, 1991 the plaintiff and defendant entered into an oral agreement reflected in a letter, as follows, from the plaintiff to the defendant's agent, Mr Roberts.

"Following our telephone conversation of today, I write to confirm the main points discussed. 1. Your client has decided it is in his best interest to stay with my offer of £200,000 (Two hundred thousand pounds), subject to contract for the above property. 2. The Vendor will not consider any further offers for the property on the basis that I will exchange contracts within a period of two weeks of the receipt of that contract. 3. The Vendor will be writing to me to confirm the above."

After some delay a draft contract was sent to the plaintiff's solicitor on November 7. On November 12 the defendant announced their intention to sell to Buckle for £210,000 and subsequently the draft contract with the plaintiff was withdrawn and the property sold to Buckle. The plaintiff's action for breach of the agreement of October 3 succeeded. The defendant appealed.

PETER GIBSON L.J.: In my opinion the crucial paragraph is para (2) of the letter from the plaintiff to Mr Roberts:

"The Vendor will not consider any further offers for the property on the basis that I will exchange contracts within a period of two weeks of the receipt of that contract."

As the learned judge put it in his judgment, there was a clear acceptance that Mr Pitt, the plaintiff, should have a clear run of achieving an exchange of contracts which was to be within two weeks after receipt of the draft. The defendant was agreeing that it would not consider further offers. That was its plain understanding and that is reflected in the letters from the defendant to Mr Roberts and from Mr Roberts to Miss Buckle's agents to the effect that only if the exchange of contracts did not take place within the required time would the defendant reconsider the second offer from Miss Buckle. I can see no reason why that agreement, whereby the defendant was locking itself out from negotiating with other prospective purchasers for a limited period, should be considered to be subject to contract, there being nothing further to agree. Accordingly I would reject Mr Payne's argument on the first point.
[For the second point, see below, p. 294.]

SIR THOMAS BINGHAM M.R.: I agree that this appeal should be dismissed for the reasons given by Peter Gibson L.J.
For very many people their first and closest contact with the law is when they come to buy or sell a house. They frequently find it a profoundly depressing and frustrating experience. The vendor puts his house on the market. He receives an offer which is probably less than his asking price. He agonises over whether to accept or hold out for more. He decides to accept, perhaps after negotiating some increase. A deal is struck. Hands are shaken. The vendor celebrates, relaxes, makes plans for his own move and takes his house off the market. Then he hears that the purchaser who was formerly pleading with him to accept his offer has decided not to proceed. No explanation is given, no apology made. The vendor has to embark on the whole dreary process of putting his house on the market all over again.
For the purchaser the process is, if anything, worse. After a series of futile visits to unsuitable houses he eventually finds the house of his dreams. He makes an offer, perhaps at the asking price, perhaps at what the

agent tells him the vendor is likely to accept. The offer is accepted. A deal is done. The purchaser instructs solitors to act. He perhaps commissions an architect to plan alterations. He makes arrangements to borrow money. He puts his own house on the market. He makes arrangements to move. He then learns that the vendor has decided to sell to someone else, perhaps for the price already offered and accepted, perhaps for an increased price achieved by a covert, unofficial auction. Again, no explanation, no apology. The vendor is able to indulge his self-interest, even his whims, without exposing himself to any legal penalty.

The reasons why purchaser and vendor can act in this apparently unprincipled manner are to be found in two legal rules of long standing: first, the rule that contracts for the sale and purchase of land must be evidenced (or now made) in writing; secondly, the rule that terms agreed subject to contract do not give rise to a binding contract. These rules are deeply imbedded in statute and authority. They make possible the behaviour I have described, but the validity and merits of those rules are not, and could not be, the subject of challenge in this appeal.

For the purchaser there is, however, one means of protection: to make an independent agreement by which the vendor agrees for a clear specified period not to deal with anyone other than that purchaser. The effect is to give that purchaser a clear run for the period in question. The vendor does not agree to sell to that purchaser—such an agreement would be covered by s.2 of the 1989 Act—but he does give a negative undertaking that he will not (for the given period deal with anyone else. That, I am quite satisfied, is what happened here, as the judge rightly held. The vendor and the prospective purchaser made what has come to be called a "lock-out agreement". That was a contract binding on them both. The vendor broke it. He is liable to the prospective purchaser for damages which remain to be assessed. I would dismiss the appeal.

MANN L.J. agreed

Appeal dismissed.

Question
Should the two rules discussed by Bingham M.R. be abolished?

NICOLENE LTD v. SIMMONDS

Court of Appeal [1953] 1 Q.B. 543; [1953] 2 W.L.R. 717; 97 S.J. 247; [1953] 1 All E.R. 882; [1953] 1 Lloyd's Rep. 189

Appeal from Sellers J.

SINGLETON L.J. delivered judgment in favour of the respondent (plaintiff).

DENNING L.J.: This case raises a short, but important, point which can be stated quite simply: the plaintiffs allege that there was a contract for the sale to them of 3,000 tons of steel reinforcing bars, and the seller broke his contract. When the buyers claimed damages the seller set up the defence that, owing to one of the sentences in the letters which constituted the contract, there was no contract at all. The material words are: "We are in agreement that the usual conditions of acceptance apply." There were no usual conditions of acceptance at all, so the words are meaningless. There is nothing to which they can apply. On that account it is said that there was never a contract at all between the parties. In my opinion a distinction must be drawn between a clause which is meaningless and a clause which is yet to be agreed. A clause which is meaningless can often be ignored, whilst still leaving the contract good; whereas a clause which has yet to be agreed may mean that there is no contract at all, because the parties have not agreed on all the essential terms. . . .

I would just say a word about the recent decision of McNair J. in *British Electrical and Associated Industries (Cardiff) Ltd v. Patley Pressings Ltd* [1953] 1 W.L.R. 280, 283, where the contract note contained the clause "subject to *force majeure* conditions. "If the true construction of the documents in that case was that an essential term had yet to be agreed, it would fall within the cases to which I have referred, but if the true view was that the exempting clause was agreed but was "so vague and uncertain as to be incapable of any precise meaning" (which was how McNair J. described it) I should have thought that it could be ignored without impairing the validity of the contract. It was clearly severable from the rest of the contract, whereas the term in *G. Scammell & Nephew, Ltd v. Ouston*[1] was not.

In the present case there was nothing yet to be agreed. There was nothing left to further negotiation. All that happened was that the parties agreed that "the usual conditions of acceptance apply." That clause was so vague and uncertain as to be incapable of any precise meaning. It is clearly severable from the rest of the contract. It can be rejected without impairing the sense or reasonableness of the contract as a whole, and it should be so rejected. The contract should be held good and the clause ignored. The parties themselves treated the contract as subsisting. They regarded it as creating binding obligations between them; and it would be most unfortunate if the law should say otherwise. You would find defaulters all scanning their contracts to find some meaningless clause on which to ride free.

---

[1] In *Scammell v. Ouston* [1941] A.C. 251; [1941] 1 All E.R. 14, the respondents agreed to purchase from the appellants a new motor-van but stipulated that "this order is given on the understanding that the balance of the purchase price can be had on hire-purchase terms over a period of two years." The House of Lords held that this sentence was "so vaguely expressed that it cannot, standing by itself, be given a definite meaning—that is to say, it requires further agreement to be reached between the parties before there would be a complete *consensus ad item*." It might have been different if there had been any well-known "usual terms" in such a contract, but there were not.

In *Hillas and Co Ltd v. Arcos Ltd* (1932) 147 L.T. 503 the appellants agreed to buy 22,000 standards of softwood goods over the season 1930, subject to certain conditions. A clause in the agreement gave them an option to buy a further 100,000 standards during the season 1931. The question was whether this agreement was enforceable. The Court of Appeal held, in the words of Scrutton L.J., that ". . . considering the number of things left undetermined, kinds, sizes and quantities of goods, times and ports and manner of shipment . . . the option clause was not an agreement, but . . . 'an agreement to make an agreement,' which is not an enforceable agreement." The House of Lords allowed the appeal. The view of the Court of Appeal would have excluded the possibility of business men making big forward contracts because of the impossibility of specifying in advance all the details of a complicated performance. That view ignored ". . . the legal implication in contracts of what is reasonable, which runs through the whole of modern English law in relation to business contracts. . . . After all, the parties, being business men, ought to be left to decide what degree of precision it is essential to express in their contracts, if no legal principle is violated."

HODSON L.J. delivered judgment in favour of the respondent.

Appeal dismissed.

WINN v. BULL

Chancery Division (1877) 7 Ch.D. 29; 47 L.J.Ch. 139; 26 W.R. 230

The defendant agreed in writing with the plaintiff to take a lease of a house for a certain term at a certain rent, "subject to the preparation and approval of a formal contract." No other contract was ever entered into between the parties. The plaintiff brought an action for specific performance.

JESSEL M.R.: I am of the opinion there is no contract. I take it the principle is clear. If in the case of a proposed sale or lease of an estate two persons agree to all the terms and say, "We will have the terms put into form," then all the terms being put into writing and agreed to, there is a contract. [See now the Law of Property Act (M.P.) 1989, s.2, above, p. 6.]

If two persons agree in writing that up to a certain point the terms shall be the terms of the contract, but that the minor terms shall be submitted to a solicitor, and shall be such as are approved of by him, then there is no contract, because all the terms have not been settled.

Now with regard to the construction of letters which are relied upon as constituting a contract, I have always thought that the authorities are too favourable to specific performance. When a man agrees to buy an estate, there are a great many more stipulations wanted than a mere agreement to buy the estate and the amount of purchase-money that is to be paid. What is called an open contract is clearly a most perilous thing, and even now, notwithstanding the provisions of a recent Act of Parliament—the Vendor and Purchaser Act 1874—no prudent man who has an estate to sell would sign a contract of that kind, but would stipulate that certain conditions should be inserted for his protection. When, therefore, you see a stipulation as to a formal agreement put into a contract, you may say it was not put in for nothing, but to protect the vendor against that very thing. Indeed, notwithstanding protective conditions, the vendor has not unfrequently to allow a deduction from the purchase-money to induce the purchaser not to press requisitions which the law allows him to make.

All this shows that contracts for purchase of lands should contain something more than can be found in the short and meagre form of an ordinary letter.

When we come to a contract for a lease the case is still stronger. When you bargain for a lease simply, it is for an ordinary lease and nothing more; that is, a lease containing the usual covenants and nothing more; but when the bargain is for a lease which is to be formally prepared, in general no solicitor would, unless actually bound by the contract, prepare a lease not containing other covenants besides, that is, covenants which are not comprised in or understood by the term "usual covenants." It is then only rational to suppose that when a man says there shall be a formal contract approved for a lease he means that more shall be put into the lease than the law generally allows. Now, in the present case, the plaintiff says in effect, "I agree to grant you a lease on certain terms, but subject to something else being approved." He does not say, "Nothing more shall be required beyond what I have already mentioned," but "something else is required" which is not expressed. That being so, the agreement is uncertain in its terms and consequently cannot be sustained.

The distinction between an agreement which is final in its terms, and therefore binding, and an agreement which is dependent upon a stipulation for a formal contract, is pointed out in the authorities. . . .

[The Master of the Rolls then considered certain cases.]

It comes, therefore, to this, that where you have a proposal or agreement made in writing expressed to be subject to a formal contract being prepared, it means what it says; it is subject to and is dependent upon a formal contract being prepared. When it is not expressly stated to be subject to a formal contract it becomes a question of construction, whether the parties intended that the terms agreed on should merely be put into form, or whether they should be subject to a new agreement the terms of which are not expressed in detail. The result is, that I must hold that there is no binding contract in this case, and there must therefore be judgment for the defendant.

Note

An "open contract" for the sale of land is one which specifies merely the names of the parties, the property to be sold and the price. There may be a valid contract even though the parties have agreed on nothing more than these fundamental matters, provided only that the parties have reached the end of their negotiations, and have agreed on everything which they consider requires agreement and, since September 27, 1989, the agreement is in writing and signed in accordance with the Law of Property (M.P.) Act 1989, s.2, above, p. 6 "Open contracts" are unusual because of the difficulties and importance of the issues involved in the sale of land; and, in deciding whether the parties intended to contract, the court may bear in mind the improbability of their intending to bind themselves in such an informal way: *Clifton v. Palumbo* [1944] 2 All E.R. 497.

Questions

1. Why is it essential that the price be fixed in a contract for the sale of land, when it need not be fixed in a sale of goods? (*Cf. May and Butcher v. R.*, above, p. 87).

2. If the parties agree that "the minor terms shall be submitted to a solicitor, and shall be such as are approved of by him . . ." why should there not be a contract? (*Cf.* sections 8 and 9 of the Sale of Goods Act, 1979, discussed above, pp. 87–88 and *Marten v. Whale*, below, p. 415). Is a contract now precluded by section 2 of the Law of Property (M.P.) Act 1989, above, p. 6.

CHILLINGWORTH v. ESCHE

Court of Appeal [1924] 1 Ch. 97, 113; 93 L.J.Ch. 129;129 L.T. 808; 40 T.L.R. 23

SARGANT L.J.: I desire to say one or two words as to the phrase "contract to enter into a contract." This phrase is used by Parker J. in his classic judgment in *Hatzfeldt-Wildenburg v. Alexander* [1912] 1 Ch. 284, but only, I think, as a secondary or less accurate method of stating the alternative. In the strictest sense of the words the court will often enforce a contract to make a contract. The specific performance of a formal agreement of purchase is the enforcement of a contract to make a contract; the ultimate conveyance being often in itself in many respects a contract. The same remarks apply to the specific performance of a clause in a lease giving the lessee an option to purchase the superior interest of the lessor, freehold or leasehold as the case may be. The true meaning of the phrase is that the court will not enforce a contract to make a second contract part of the terms of which are indeterminate and have yet to be agreed, so that there is not any definite contract at all which can be enforced, but only an agreement for a contract some of the terms of which are not yet agreed. . . .

To my mind the words "subject to contract" or "subject to formal contract" have by this time acquired a definite ascertained legal meaning— not quite so definite a meaning perhaps as such expressions as f.o.b. or c.i.f. in mercantile transactions, but approaching that degree of definiteness. The phrase is a perfectly familiar one in the mouths of estate agents and other persons accustomed to deal with land; and I can quite understand a solicitor saying to a client about to negotiate for the sale of his land: "Be sure that to protect yourself you introduce into any preliminary contract you may think of making the words 'subject to contract'." I do not say that the phrase makes the contract containing it necessarily and whatever the context a conditional contract. But they are words appropriate for introducing a condition, and it would require a very strong and exceptional case for this clear prima facie meaning to be displaced.

Question
You can have a contract to make a contract; but can you have an agreement to agree? *Cf. May and Butcher v. R.* above, p. 87.

Note
Agreements "subject to . . ."
An agreement "subject to contract" is not a concluded contract where that phrase signifies (as it usually does) that there is further negotiation to be conducted. The parties have agreed on certain terms but there is further agreement to be reached before they are willing to bind themselves. The principle is that applied in *May & Butcher v. R.* (above, p. 87).

It is common for an agreement to buy land to be made "subject to satisfactory survey, "subject to the purchaser obtaining a satisfactory mortgage" or "subject to planning permission being given." These all present a different problem from the "subject to contract" case because they do not contemplate further agreement between the parties. There will be a binding contract provided that, on its true construction, the clause—

   (i) is sufficiently precise and definite for a court to be able to say when it is satisfied; and
   (ii) it does not leave either of the parties with a discretion whether to go on with the transaction.

If the meaning of the clause is that one party has a complete discretion whether to proceed or not, there cannot be a contract because the essence of a bilateral contract is that both parties bind themselves. But see *Sprio v. Glencrown Properties*, below, p. 104.

In *Marks v. Board* (1930) 46 T.L.R. 424, Rowlatt J. held that a person who agreed to buy land, subject to surveyor's report, "reserved to himself the absolute and undisputed right to say whether he liked the surveyor's report." In *Graham and Scott (Southgate) Ltd v. Oxlade* [1950] 2 K.B. 257 Roxburgh J. and the Court of Appeal said that the buyer was the arbiter of whether the survey was satisfactory or not and Megaw J. made a decision to that effect in relation to the sale of a yacht "subject to satisfactory survey": *Astra Trust Ltd v. Williams* [1969] 1 Lloyds Rep. 81. If this is correct, there is clearly no contract because the buyer has an absolute discretion and, if he is not bound, the seller is not bound either. But it does not follow that the legal position of the parties is the same as where they have agreed, "subject to contract."

In a "subject to contract" case, neither party can make the "agreement" binding without the consent of the other. In a "subject to survey" case, the buyer can bind the seller by having the property surveyed and informing the seller that the survey is satisfactory. "Subject to survey" (as interpreted in the cases cited above) leaves the seller in the position of an offeror. He can revoke his offer to sell at any time before the buyer finds the survey to be satisfactory and, probably until the buyer has so informed him. Once he is so informed, the agreement has become unconditional.

If the clause is, as it appears usually to be, for the exclusive benefit of the buyer, he could also bind the seller by simply informing him that he has waived the condition—he is not going to bother with a survey—whereupon the contract is concluded.

If the arbiter of the satisfactoriness of the survey is a third party, then in principle, there is a contract. A building society may have agreed to give the buyer a mortgage, subject to satisfactory survey. If the buyer were to agree to buy, "subject to the survey being satisfactory to the building society," then the agreement:

    (i) is sufficiently precise and definite because the building society either says that it is satisfied, in which case the contract is on, or it says that it is not satisfied, in which case it is off; and—

   (ii) neither of the *parties* has a discretion, though the building society does. *Cf. Pym v. Campbell* and *Marten v. Whale*, (below, p. 415).

In *Ee v. Kakar* (1979) 40 P. & C.R. 223, Walton J. held that an agreement subject to survey was binding on the seller. The buyer was under an obligation to have the property surveyed and to consider bona fide whether the survey was satisfactory or not. If the survey would satisfy a reasonable person, it might be difficult for the buyer to satisfy the court that his dissatisfaction was bona fide. Though the same words may bear different meanings in different contexts, the decision on this point seems irreconcilable with *Marks v. Board* and the *Astra Trust* case; but Walton J. also held that the condition was for the exclusive benefit of the buyer and so he could waive and had waived it.

The words "subject to the purchaser obtaining a satisfactory mortgage" raise exactly the same issues of principle and have also caused a difference of judicial opinion. In *Lee Parker v. Izzet* [1971] 1 W.L.R. 1688; [1971] 3 All E.R. 1099 Goff J. held that there was a contract, "a satisfactory mortgage" meaning a mortgage to the satisfaction of the purchaser acting reasonably. But in *Lee Parker v. Izzet (No. 2)* [1972] 2 W.L.R. 775; [1972] 2 All E.R. 800, Goulding J. held that a similar phrase was void for uncertainty.

In *Graham v. Pitkin* [1992] 2 All E.R. 235, P.C., Lord Templeman said of that case: "But since the purchaser, if he had the money, could always have declared that a mortgage of £10 from his brother-in-law was 'satisfactory' their Lordships doubt the finding that there was no contract." But if this means, as it seems to, that the purchaser had an absolute discretion as to what was "satisfactory", did not this confirm Goulding J.'s view that there was no contract?

"Subject to planning permission to develop" was held by Russell J. to be sufficiently certain in the context of *Batten v. White* (1960) 12 P. & C.R. 66. The buyer was bound to proceed with due diligence and bona fide to seek the relevant permission.

In *Bishop & Baxter, Ltd v. Anglo-Eastern Trading and Industrial Co. Ltd* [1943] 2 All E.R. 598, B made a counter-offer to buy 20,000 cardigans from S subject to various conditions including "war clause." S accepted. 3,000 cardigans were delivered and accepted by B.S. then repudiated the agreement. It was held by the Court of Appeal that while there had been a sale of the 3,000 cardigans, there was no contract for the sale of 20,000. There were many forms of "war clause" and the joint selection of one form was a necessary preliminary to the contract coming into existence. Scott L.J. said: "The parties may, both of them, . . . have erroneously supposed that a contract in writing was already in existence; but, if they did, it was because they did not realise that the appellants' counter-offer required a further consensual step, before the law could recognise the formation of a completed contract; and their bad law could not make a contract."

SPIRO v. GLENCROWN PROPERTIES LTD AND ANOTHER

Chancery Division [1991] Ch. 537; [1991] 2 W.L.R. 931; [1991] 1 All E.R. 600

By an agreement in two parts, each signed by both parties and exchanged, containing all the agreed terms, the plaintiff granted the first defendant an option to buy a property for £745,000. The option was exercisable by notice in writing to the vendor on the same day and was duly exercised. The purchaser failed to complete. The vendor sued him and his guarantor, the second defendant, for damages for breach of contract.

HOFFMANN J. having quoted section 2(1) of the Law of Property (Miscellaneous Provisions) Act 1989 (above, p. 6): If the "contract for the sale . . . of an interest in land" was for the purposes of section 2(1) the agreement by which the option was *granted*, there is no difficulty. The agreement was executed in two exchanged parts, each of which incorporated all the terms which had been agreed and had been signed by or on behalf of the vendor and purchaser respectively. But the letter which *exercised* the option was of course signed only on behalf of the purchaser. If the contract was made by this document, it did not comply with section 2.

Apart from authority, it seems to me plain enough that section 2 was intended to apply to the agreement which created the option and not to the notice by which it was exercised. Section 2, which replaced section 40 of the Law of Property Act 1925, was intended to prevent disputes over whether the parties had entered into a binding agreement or over what terms they had agreed. It prescribes the formalities for recording their mutual consent. But only the grant of the option depends upon consent. The exercise of the option is a unilateral act. It would destroy the very purpose of the option if the purchaser had to obtain the vendor's counter-signature to the notice by which it was exercised. The only way in which the concept of an option to buy land could survive section 2 would be if the purchaser ensured that the vendor not only signed the agreement by which the option was granted but also at the same time provided him with a counter-signed form to use if he decided to exercise it. There seems to be no conceivable reason why the legislature should have required this additional formality.

The language of section 2 places no obstacle in the way of construing the grant of the option as the relevant contract. An option to buy land can properly be described as a contract for the sale of that land conditional upon the exercise of the option. . . .

Hoffmann J. discussed *Helby v. Matthews* [1895] A.C. 471 a case of a contract for the hire purchase of piano. Hire purchase is a contract of hiring with an option to purchase. Before the hirer had paid all the instalments and exercised the option he pledged the piano with the defendant. The question was whether the pledgee got a good title. If the hirer had "agreed to buy" the piano within the meaning of the Factors Act 1889, by virtue of that Act, he gave a good title to the pledgee. (*Cf.* the provision to the same effect in the Sale of Goods Act 1979, s.25(1) discussed in *Marten v. Whale*, below, p. 415.) It was held that the hirer had not "agreed to buy," and therefore the pledgee had no title, because those words implied an obligation to buy and the hirer was under no such obligation; he was entitled to return the piano and terminate the agreement at any time Hoffmann J. quoted, on the one hand, Lord Macnaghten who described the contract "on the part of the dealer" as "a contract of hiring with *a conditional contract* or undertaking to sell"; and, on the other hand, Lord Herschell L.C. who said that this was not an agreement to sell but "in truth *merely an offer* which cannot be withdrawn"; and Lord Watson who said that the dealer "was in exactly the same position as if he had made *an offer to sell* on certain terms, and had undertaken to keep it open for a definite period."

Referring to the Factors Act 1889, Hoffmann J. continued: The language and purpose of the statute requires one to look at the arrangement from the buyer's point of view. And the essence of an option is that while the seller may be said to be conditionally bound, the buyer is free. In the *Helby v. Matthews* context it was therefore true to say that pending exercise of the option, the position of the buyer was *as if* he had been made an offer which the seller could not withdraw.

But the concept of an offer is of course normally used as part of the technique for ascertaining whether the parties have reached that mutual consent which is a necessary element in the formation of a contract. In this primary sense, it is of the essence of an offer that by itself it gives rise to no legal obligations. It was for this reason that Diplock L.J. said in *Varty (Inspector of Taxes) v. British South Africa Co.* [1965] Ch. 508 at 523:

> "To speak of an enforceable option as an 'irrevocable offer' is juristically a contradiction in terms, for the adjective 'irrevocable' connotes the existence of an obligation on the part of the offeror, while the noun 'offer' connotes the absence of any obligation until the offer has been accepted."

This does not mean that in Diplock L.J.'s opinion, Lord Herschell L.C. and Lord Watson were speaking nonsense. They were not using "offer" in its primary sense but, as often happens in legal reasoning, by way of metaphor or analogy. Such metaphors can be vivid and illuminating but prove a trap for the unwary if pressed beyond their original context. As I said recently in another connection, ". . . there are dangers in reasoning from the metaphor as if it expressed a literal truth rather than from the underlying principle which the metaphor encapsulates" (see *Re K, Re F* [1988] Ch. 310 at 314).

Here the underlying principles are clear enough. The granting of the option imposes no obligation upon the purchaser and an obligation upon the vendor which is contingent upon the exercise of the option. When the option is exercised, vendor and purchaser come under obligations to perform as if they had concluded an ordinary contract of sale. And the analogy of an irrevocable offer is, as I have said, a useful way of describing the position of the purchaser between the grant and exercise of the option. Thus in the recent case of *J. Sainsbury plc v. O'Connor (Inspector of Taxes)* [1990] S.T.C. 516 at 532 Millett J. used it to explain why the grantee of an option to buy shares did not become the beneficial owner until he had exercised the option.

But the irrevocable offer metaphor has much less explanatory power in relation to the position of the vendor. The effect of the "offer" which the vendor has made is, from his point of view, so different from that of an offer in its primary sense that the metaphor is of little assistance. Thus in the famous passage in *London and South Western Rly. Co. v. Gomm* (1882) 20 Ch.D. 562 at 581 Jessel M.R. had no use for it in explaining why the grant of an option to buy land confers an interest in the land upon the grantee:

> "The right to call for a conveyance of the land is an equitable interest or equitable estate. In the ordinary case of a contract for purchase there is no doubt about this, and an option for repurchase is not different in its nature. A person exercising the option has to do two things, he has to give notice of his intention to purchase, and to pay the purchase-money; but as far as the man who is liable to convey is concerned, his estate or interest is taken away from him without his consent, and the right to take it away being vested in another, the

covenant giving the option must give that other an interest in the land."

The fact that the option binds the vendor contingently to convey was the reason why an option agreement was held to fall within section 40 of the Law of Property Act 1925: see *Richards v. Creighton Griffiths (Investments) Ltd* (1972) 225 E.G. 2104, where Plowman J. rejected a submission that it was merely a contract not to withdraw an offer. Similarly in *Weeding v. Weeding* (1861) 1 John & H. 424 at 430–431, 70 E.R. 812 at 815 Page Wood V.-C. held that the grant of an option to buy land was sufficient to deem that land converted into personality for the purposes of the grantor's will, even though the option had not yet been exercised when he died. Page Wood V.-C. said:

> "I cannot agree with the argument that there is no contract. It is as much a conditional contract as if it depended on any other contingency than the exercise of an option by a third person, such as, for example, the failure of issue of a particular person."

Thus in explaining the vendor's position, the analogy to which the courts usually appeal is that of a conditional contract. This analogy might also be said to be imperfect, because one generally thinks of a conditional contract as one in which the contingency does not lie within the sole power of one of the parties to the contract. But this difference from the standard case of a conditional contract does not destroy the value of the analogy in explaining the *vendor's* position. So far as he is concerned, it makes no difference whether or not the contingency is within the sole power of the purchaser. The important point is that his estate or interest is taken away from him without his consent. . . .

. . . The purchaser's argument requires me to say that "irrevocable offer" and "conditional contract" are mutually inconsistent concepts and that I must range myself under one or other banner and declare the other to be heretical. I hope that I have demonstrated this to be a misconception about the nature of legal reasoning. An option is not strictly speaking either an offer or a conditional contract. It does not have *all* the incidents of the standard form of either of these concepts. To that extent it is a relationship *sui generis*. But there are ways in which it resembles each of them. Each analogy is in the proper context a valid way of characterising the situation created by an option. The question in this case is not whether one analogy is true and the other false, but which is appropriate to be used in the construction of section 2 of the Law of Property (Miscellaneous Provisions) Act 1989. . . .

In my judgment there is nothing in the authorities which prevents me from giving section 2 the meaning which I consider to have been the clear intention of the legislature. On the contrary, the purposive approach taken in cases like *Mulholland* encourages me to adopt a similar approach to section 2. And the plain purpose of section 2 was, as I have said, to prescribe the formalities for recording the consent of the parties. It follows that in my view the grant of the option was the only "contract for the sale or other disposition of an interest in land" within the meaning of the section and the contract duly complied with the statutory requirements.

There must be judgment for the plaintiff against both defendants with costs.

Questions

1. What is "an irrevocable offer" if an option is not one, but only analogous to one? Does it exist? If not, how can there be an analogy to it?

2. It may be fair to say that there was a conditional contract to sell; but the question was whether the buyer was bound. Was there a conditional contract to buy?

3. *Does* the word "offer" imply revocability?

4. If the grant of the option was the *only* contract for the sale of land, what was the effect of the exercise of the option by the buyer if it was not to make a contract? By what process did he become bound to buy?

5. Was Hoffmann J. coming to the rescue of Parliament (and the Law Commission whose recommendations Parliament had implemented) who had failed to realise that they were invalidating the exercise of options to buy land?

6. Is a written agreement for the sale of land, "subject to satisfactory survey" and signed by both parties, "a contract for the sale . . . of an interest in land" (i) before, (ii) after, the buyer declares the survey to be satisfactory?

Section 2. Objective and Subjective

The courts used frequently to speak as if an actual agreement, a *consensus ad idem* or "meeting of minds," is an essential of contract. If this was ever the case, it is clear that it is not so today. If you behave in such a manner as to lead me reasonably to believe that you are making an offer to enter into a certain contract and I accept, there is a contract, even though, in fact, you did not intend to make an offer at all. If you make an offer which can reasonably bear only one meaning and I, understanding that offer in its one reasonable sense, accept, you cannot escape liability by saying, however truthfully, that you intended it to mean something else. This is a general, if not universal, principle of our law of contract because otherwise no one could ever safely act on a contract which he reasonably believed he had made. There is always the possibility that the other party might be under some undisclosed, undiscoverable and perhaps fundamental misapprehension as to the existence or nature or effect of the contract. This approach, which attaches importance to what the party said or did instead (where there is a difference) of what he *intended* to say or do, is known as the "objective" approach, distinguishing it from the "subjective," which attempts to ascertain the actual state of the party's mind at the relevant time.

This is not to say that the actual state of mind of the parties is always ignored in the law of contract. Where, for example, the offer, looked at objectively, is so ambiguous that it is impossible to say what is its true meaning but both the parties in fact understood it in the same sense, it would be absurd not to give effect to the contract in the sense which they both actually intended. Even where the contract, looked at objectively, has only one reasonable meaning but both parties intended a different meaning, it would seem to be right to admit evidence as to their actual intention. *Cf. Rose v. Pim*, below, p. 125, the comment of Professor Glanville Williams, and Note 1 below, pp. 127–128. See also, *Ingram v. Little*, below, p. 171 and *Wade v. Simeon*, below, p. 213.

Problems commonly arise because the parties have different notions as to the meaning of the promise given by one or other of them. The promisor intends to give X; the promisee expects to receive Y. If a reasonable man in the position of the promisee would have understood that he was being promised Y, then the contract is to give Y. But if he would have understood that he was being promised X, then the contract is to give X. If the promise is so framed that it may reasonably be understood to mean either X or Y, it seems likely that there is no contract; though it is arguable that the promisee should be able to enforce the promise in the sense that he in good faith gave to it. Consider *Falck v. Williams* (below, p. 119).

It is conceivable that a reasonable person in the position of the promisee would have understood the promise in a third sense, Z, which does not represent the actual intention of either party. In that case, it would seem that the promise should be enforced in sense Z at the suit of either party. "In seeing whether there is a contractor or not, the law can only look to outward appearances. If an intelligent bystander would reasonably infer that a warranty was intended, that will suffice even though neither party in fact had it in mind": *Hornal v. Neuberger Products Ltd* [1957] 1 Q.B. 247 at 257, *per* Denning L.J.; [1956] 3 All E.R. 970. Consider the problem, below, p. 114.

The Role of Estoppel

It has sometimes been said that the basis of the objective test is the doctrine of estoppel. Estoppel takes a variety of different forms but the basic notion is that where one person (the representor) has led another (the representee) to believe that a certain fact or state of affairs exists, intending the representee to act on that belief, and the representee does so act to his detriment, then in any future litigation between them the representor will not be allowed to deny (that is, he will be estopped from denying) that the representation was true. The case will be decided as if the fact or state of affairs existed even if in truth this was not so. The language of estoppel is used in some of the cases on the objective interpretation of contracts. In *Tamplin v. James*, *infra*, Baggallay L.J., though he did not use that term, said: "I think [the defendant] is not entitled to say to any effectual purpose that he was under a mistake . . ."—which is the same idea. And in *Scriven v. Hindley*, (note, below, p. 114) A. T. Lawrence J. looked for but failed to find grounds for an estoppel.

Estoppel not the foundation of the objective test. Estoppel is not, however, a satisfactory explanation. The essence of estoppel lies in the act done in detrimental reliance on the relevant statement; but the objective interpretation of promises does not seem to require detrimental reliance, either in entering into the contract or on it after it has been made. In *Hasham v. Zenab* [1960] A.C. 316 a person who had signed a contract to sell a two acre plot of land under the belief, not induced by fraud or misrepresentation, that the contract related to only half an acre of the plot was held bound although he tore up the agreement within minutes of signing it. Indeed, one of the criticisms (below) of the objective approach is that, under it, a person may acquire rights without any act of reliance other than that of entering into the contract.

Objective meaning displaced by estoppel. Estoppel does however have a part to play in displacing the objective meaning of the contract. As noticed above, if both parties believe that the contract means X and each is aware of the other's belief, then it seems probable that it will be enforced in sense X even though the objective observer would have thought it meant Z. *Cf.* Glanville Williams and Note 1, below, pp. 127–128. (The objective reader of the contract would have thought it was a contract for horsebeans; but if both parties had intended "horse-beans" to mean "feveroles" it would have been a contract for feveroles.) This is certainly so where both parties have acted on the common assumption that the contract means X, for then there will be an "estoppel by convention" precluding either of them from setting up the objective meaning (even though that be the "true" meaning) of the agreement against the other. See *Amalgamated Investment etc. v. Texas Commerce*, below, p. 262; *Salvation Army Ltd v. W. Yorks Metropolitan C.C.*, above, p. 90.

Estoppel may also, in effect, change the meaning of a contract after it has been entered into. If the true meaning of the contract at the time it is made is Z but A leads B to believe that the contract means X and B acts on that belief, A will not be allowed to deny that the contract means X. In effect, the meaning of the contract has changed from Z to X.

TAMPLIN v. JAMES

Chancery Division (1880) 15 Ch.D. 215; 43 L.T. 520; 29 W.R. 311

Property was put up for sale under the description "Lot 1. All that Inn known as 'The Ship,' together with premises adjoining thereto, situate at Newerne, No. 454 and 455 on the tithe map, and containing 20 perches, more or less, now in the occupation of Mrs Knowles and Mr S. Merrick."

At the back of Lot 1 were two plots of ground in the occupation of the tenant of the inn. These plots did not belong to the vendor. At the auction plans of Lot 1 were lying on the table, and the auctioneer called the attention of the persons present to them. These plans showed clearly the extent of Lot 1, and that it excluded the two plots at the back.

Lot 1 was not sold at the auction but the defendant, who had been present, immediately afterwards made an offer for it which was accepted, and signed a contract for the purchase according to the conditions of sale for £750.

The defendant bought in the belief that he was buying all the land in the occupation of the tenant and declined to complete unless the two plots were conveyed to him. He deposed that he had not seen the plans and was not aware that there were any plans in the room; that he had known the property from a boy, and knew that the two plots all along had been occupied with "The Ship Inn."

The vendors brought an action for specific performance.

BAGGALLAY L.J.: The defendant insists in his statement of defence that he signed the memorandum in the reasonable belief that the property comprised therein included the whole of the premises in the occupation of Mrs Knowles and of Mr Samuel Merrick, and not merely the messuages and hereditaments which the plaintiffs allege to be the only property comprised therein, and that such his belief was induced and confirmed by the acts and words of the auctioneer at the sale. The defendant has sworn positively that he had such a belief at the time he signed the memorandum, and I see no reason to doubt the statement so made by him; but was such a belief a reasonable belief?

It is doubtless well established that a court of equity will refuse specific performance of an agreement when the defendant has entered into it under a mistake, and where injustice would be done to him were performance to be enforced. The most common instances of such refusal on the ground of mistake are cases in which there has been some unintentional misrepresentation on the part of the plaintiff (I am not now referring to cases of intentional misrepresentation which would fall rather under the category of fraud), or where from the ambiguity of the agreement different meanings have been given to it by the different parties. The case of *Manser v. Back* (6 Hare 443) is a well-known illustration of this. It is true also that specific performance has been refused in cases not coming under either of these heads, as in *Malins v. Freeman* (2 Keen 25). But where there has been no misrepresentation, and where there is no ambiguity in the terms of the contract, the defendant cannot be allowed to evade the performance of it by the simple statement that he has made a mistake. Were such to be the law the performance of a contract could rarely be enforced upon an unwilling party who was also unscrupulous. I think that the law is correctly stated by Lord Romilly in *Swaisland v. Dearsley* (29 Beav. 430, 433): "The principle on which the court proceeds in cases of mistake is this—if it appears upon the evidence that there was in the description of the property a matter on which a person might bona fide make a mistake, and he swears positively that he did make such mistake, and his evidence is not disproved, this court cannot enforce the specific performance against him. If there appears on the particulars no ground for the mistake, if no man with his senses about him could have misapprehended the character of the parcels, then I do not think it is sufficient for the purchaser to swear that he made a mistake, or that he did not understand what he was about." The observations of Wigram V.-C. in *Manser v. Back* (6 Hare 443, 448) seem to me to tend in the same direction.

Now does it appear, or can it safely be held in this case that the defendant reasonably entertained a belief that the gardens were included in the property purchased by him? I will consider first the terms of the contract itself, and then the allegations as to the acts and words of the auctioneer and other agents of the plaintiffs, for it is possible that although the terms of the agreement taken *per se* may have been free from doubt, enough may have been said or done by the plaintiffs' agents to lead the defendant to attribute a different meaning to its terms.

Mr Pearson admitted, and I think he could not well have avoided admitting, that if the vendors had merely referred to the property as being in the occupation of Mrs Knowles and Mr Merrick without more, there would have been at any rate such an amount of ambiguity that the defendant might reasonably have understood that he was purchasing the whole of the property in their occupation. But the particulars go on to state that the property sold is Nos. 454 and 455 on the tithe map and contains 20 perches. The additional land which the defendant claims to have included is about 20 perches more. Therefore, if he is right in his contention, he would be entitled to double the amount which the printed particulars state the lot to contain. There, no doubt, is force in the argument that a person unaccustomed to measuring would not know whether a property contained 20 perches or 40 perches, but that does not get rid of the effect of the reference to the tithe map. The defendant appears to have purchased in reliance upon his knowledge of the occupation of the premises without looking at the plans, and probably without paying attention to the details of the particulars of Lot 1, but is a person justified in relying upon knowledge of that kind when he has the means of ascertaining what he buys? I think not. I think he is not entitled to say to any effectual purpose that he was under a mistake, when he did not think it worth while to read the particulars and look at the plans. If that were to be allowed, a person might always escape from completing a contract by swearing that he was mistaken as to what he bought, and great temptation to perjury would be offered. Here the description of the property is accurate and free from ambiguity, and the case is wholly unaffected by *Manser v. Back* (6 Hare 443) and the other cases in which the defendant has escaped from performance of a contract on the ground of its ambiguity.

The decision of Baggallay L.J. was affirmed by the Court of Appeal, 15 Ch.D. 219.

Note

The remedy for breach of contract provided by the common law is an award of monetary compensation (damages) for the loss which the plaintiff has suffered as a result of the breach. Where, however, damages are not an adequate remedy equity will compel the defendant actually to perform his contract by a decree of specific performance. Such orders are most commonly made in the case of contracts for the sale of land. No two pieces of land are exactly alike and courts of equity therefore consider that damages are not an adequate remedy for a failure to convey the land agreed upon. In the case of a sale of goods, on the other hand, it will usually be possible for the buyer to obtain exactly similar goods elsewhere; and, if the seller fails to deliver, the buyer will usually be deemed adequately compensated by damages for any extra expense to which he has been put. Specific performance of a sale of goods will be granted only where the goods are of a unique or very unusual character.

DENNY v. HANCOCK

Court of Appeal in Chancery (1870) L.R. 6 Ch.App.1; 23 L.T. 686; 19 W.R. 54

On a sale of a small residential property the plan exhibited showed the western side as bounded by a strip of ground covered with a mass of shrubs or trees. The defendant went with the plan in his hand, inspected the property and found on the western side a belt of shrubs bounded on the west by an iron fence, and including three magnificent trees. He then bid for the property, believing that he was buying everything up to the fence. He afterwards discovered that the three trees and the iron fence stood on the adjoining property, the real boundary being denoted by stumps which were so shrouded by shrubs as not easily to be seen. The plan represented in a conspicuous way all the detached trees standing on the property, none of which was nearly so large as the trees in question, but did not show these trees. It was admitted that the existence of these trees was a material element in the value of the property as a residence.

The defendant declined to complete and Malins V.-C. made a decree of specific performance against him.

Sir W. M. James L.J.: Now when we come to examine the evidence, I am bound to say, with all deference to the Vice-Chancellor's judgment in this matter, that the case is clear in favour of the defendant. The defendant tells just the sort of story that I myself should have told if I had been the intending purchaser, and had gone to inspect the property with the plan in my hand: [His Lordship read passages of the defendant's answer.] He has not been cross-examined, and I must say I have no doubt whatever that if I had done exactly what this gentleman did, and taken that plan in my hand, and gone through the property, and found a shrubbery, or ground covered partly with shrubs and partly with thorns, with an iron fence outside, I should have arrived at exactly the same conclusion as this gentleman did, and I should have gone to the sale and bid in the belief that I was buying the belt up to the iron fence with those trees upon it. Then the defendant's surveyor, who says he has been for 20 years in the profession, says: [His Lordship read an extract from the surveyor's evidence]. This gentleman, again, has not been cross-examined, and there really is not, in my judgment, a shadow of evidence in reply to his evidence that the plan was so made as to lead not only the general public, but persons who, like himself, had practical experience in mapping and planning, to the conclusion that the whole of the belt of shrubs up to the iron fence was included in the sale: [His Lordship then stated the effect of the plaintiff's evidence and continued:] There is no denial in evidence of this fact, that the plan produced was calculated to induce anybody to believe that the whole of the belt, or shrubbery, or whatever you may call it, was included in the property sold. It is urged, however, that the defendant was negligent. The substance of the argument seems to be this: that if he had looked at the plan very minutely he would have seen that the trees in the meadows and in the garden were marked, but these three fine trees, which added so much to the value of the property, were not marked; and it is urged that the absence of these remarkable trees from the plan is a thing calculated to put a man so completely on his guard that he ought not to have been misled, and is not to be believed when he says he was misled. But it seems to me that it never would occur to a person who entertained no doubt whatever about what the thing was that had been sold to him, to make any inquiry about the omission of two or three trees in that which appeared on the plan to be a mass of wood. If this gentleman did as he says, buy it under a mistake as to the property, such mistake was caused by the plan which was presented to him, drawn by the vendors' agent, and also caused by this fact, which alone might have been enough to mislead him, that there was on the ground an apparent visible boundary, quite distinct from the almost invisible real boundary. I think that, independently of the plan, and on this latter ground alone, it would have required great consideration before a court of equity would have fixed the purchaser with this contract, which he swears he entered into in the belief that the property extended to its apparent boundary; but coupling the state of the property with the representation made by the plan, I am of the opinion that it would not be according to the established principles of this court to compel the purchaser to complete his contract. I am also of opinion that the mistake was occasioned by at least *crassa negligentia* on the part of the vendors in respect to what they sent out to the public. I am, therefore, unable to agree with the Vice-Chancellor, and am of opinion that he ought to have dismissed this bill with costs.

The judgment of Sir G. Mellish L.J. is omitted.

Note

The fact that a court of equity dismisses an action for specific performance does not necessarily mean that there was no contract enforceable at law. Equitable remedies are said to be "discretionary." This means that the court may take into account all the circumstances of the case, including, for example, the conduct of the plaintiff and the hardship which the order might cause the defendant, in deciding whether to grant the remedy. Thus where an action for specific performance fails the plaintiff might, nevertheless, recover damages, for breach of contract.

In *Malins v. Freeman* (1837) 2 Keen 25; 48 E.R. 537 the defendant went to an auction intending to bid for property A. He arrived late but in time to hear the auctioneer describe Lot 3 in terms wholly inapplicable to Property A. He began to bid for Lot 3, supposing it to be Property A, and in due course Lot 3 was knocked down to him for an extravagant price. Lot 3 was a quite different property. The defendant's mistake could not be ascribed in any way to the conduct of the plaintiff or his agents, but Lord Langdale M.R. refused to decree specific performance, saying:

"I am of opinion that the defendant never intended to bid for this estate. He was hurried and inconsiderate, and, when his error was pointed out to him, he was not so prompt as he ought to have been in declaring it. It is probable that by his conduct he occasioned some loss to the plaintiff; for that he is answerable, if the contract was valid, and will be left so, notwithstanding the decision to be now made. But I think that he never meant to enter into this contract, and that it would not be equitable to compel him to perform it, whatever may be the responsibility to which he is left liable at law."

Questions

1. The legal position in *Denny v. Hancock* admits of three possibilities:

(1) There was no contract.
(2) There was a contract, not specifically enforceable by the vendor, for the sale of the land bounded by the stumps.

(3) There was a contract for the sale of the land bounded by the iron fence. In such a case equity has jurisdiction to decree specific performance against the vendor and to order compensation to be paid to the purchaser for the discrepancy between what was agreed to be conveyed and what can be conveyed: *Rutherford v. Acton-Adams* [1915] A.C. 866 (P.C.). See Harpum, [1981] C.L.J. 47.

Is it possible to say which was the actual legal position?
2. Can you formulate a general principle of law from the two cases?

Problem

Athelstan is the owner of an inn. To the north of the inn is a yard which does not belong to Athelstan, but which has always been occupied with the inn. To the east of the inn is a field which does belong to Athelstan. Athelstan intends to offer for sale the inn and the field. Unfortunately the auctioneer employed to carry out the sale misunderstands his instructions and prepares plans and a description of the property which include neither the yard nor the field. The property is put up for sale as Lot 2 and attention is drawn to the plan. Beowulf, who has known the property from a boy, is under the impression that Lot 2 includes the yard but excludes the field. Without examining the plan he bids £5,000 for Lot 2, but it is withdrawn. Later Beowulf meets Athelstan in the saleroom and says: "I offer you £6,000 for Lot 2." Athelstan believing that Lot 2 includes the field, says: "I accept." They sign a note: "Lot 2, the Ship Inn, sold for £6,000."

Is there a contract and, if so, what are its terms?

Note

In *Scriven Bros. & Co. v. Hindley and Co.* [1913] 3 K.B. 564, the defendants bid at an auction for two lots, believing both to be hemp. In fact Lot A was hemp but Lot B was tow, a different commodity in commerce (as the jury found) and of very little value. The defendants declined to pay for Lot B and the sellers sued for the price. The defendants' mistake arose from the fact that both lots contained the same shipping mark, "SL," and witnesses stated that in their experience hemp and tow were never landed from the same ship under the same shipping mark. The defendants' manager had been shown bales of hemp as "samples of the 'SL' goods." The auctioneer believed that the bid was made under a mistake but he had reasonable ground for believing that the mistake was merely one as to the value of tow.

A. T. Lawrence J. said that as the parties were not *ad idem* the plaintiffs could recover only if the defendants were estopped from relying upon what was now admittedly the truth. He held that the defendants were not estopped since their mistake had been caused by or contributed to by the negligence of the plaintiffs.

In this case, the sellers' offer was at least ambiguous, as in *Denny v. Hancock*. The decision was that there was no contract for the sale of the bales of tow. Where there is a valid contract for the sale of goods, the judge has no discretion to dismiss the seller's claim for the price (as he has a discretion to dismiss the vendor of land's action for specific performance).

In deciding whether there has been an unequivocal offer and acceptance, the court may consider not merely the words of the alleged offer and acceptance and the relevant surrounding circumstances, but also the history of the negotiations. In *Webster v. Cecil* (1861) 30 Beav. 62; 54 E.R. 812 the defendant, *having refused to sell some property to the plaintiff for £2,000*, wrote a letter in which, as the result of a mistaken calculation, he offered to sell it for £1,250. The plaintiff accepted. Romilly M.R. refused a decree of specific performance, saying that the plaintiff "might bring such action at law as he might be advised." In *Hartog v. Colin and Shields* [1939] 3 All E.R. 566 the defendants offered to sell 30,000 skins to the plaintiff at prices *per pound*. The previous negotiations had been carried on (as was customary in the trade) by reference to the price *per piece*. The value of a piece was about one-third that of a pound. The price stated was absurdly low and the defendants said they had written "pound" in error for "piece." Singleton J. dismissed an action for damages for breach of contract, saying, "The plaintiff could not reasonably have supposed that the offer contained the offerors' real intention."

On the other hand, it has been decided that the history of the negotiations is not admissible in order to *interpret* the contract: *Prenn v. Simmonds* [1971] 1 W.L.R. 1381; [1971] 3 All E.R. 237, H.L., below, p. 137 and *City and Westminster Properties v. Mudd* (below, p. 38). Is this consistent with the cases cited above? The evidence was there admitted, not to interpret the words used, but to show that the words used did not, and could not reasonably be supposed by the other party to, represent the true intention of the parties. Is this a valid distinction? See also, *Roberts v. Leics. C.C.* (below, p. 128).

Questions
   1. Suppose the buyers in *Scriven v. Hindley* had sued the seller for breach of a contract to sell hemp. What would they have had to prove in order to succeed?
   2. The defendants alleged that the auctioneer knew that they were bidding for hemp, not tow. What would have been the effect if they had been able to prove the truth of that allegation? See *Smith v. Hughes*, below, p. 121, *Roberts v. Leicestershire County Council*, below, p. 128.
   3. What would have been the result if the buyers had (as the auctioneer believed) been merely making a mistake as to the value of tow? If the buyers would have been bound, is that reconcilable with *Hartog v. Colin*.

CENTROVINCIAL ESTATES PLC v. MERCHANT INVESTORS ASSURANCE COMPANY LTD

Court of Appeal [1983] Com.L.R. 158; *The Times*, March 8, 1983; 1982 C. 6380
(Lexis transcript)

The defendants were tenants from December 1, 1978 to December 24, 1989 of premises at a yearly rent of £68,320, subject to review from December 25, 1982. Clause 1 of the lease required the lessor and lessee to endeavour, at least six months before December 25, 1982, to reach agreement on the then current market value of the premises and, if able to agree, to certify the amount of the current market rental value. In the event of failure to agree, the matter was to be referred to an independent valuer. The plaintiffs were about to become the landlords. On June 22, 1982, their solicitors wrote to the defendants proposing £65,000 per annum as the appropriate rental value and inviting them to agree this figure. The defendants replied on June 23 agreeing the figure, stating that they had attached the two letters to the lease and asking the plaintiffs to do the same with their copy. The plaintiffs received this letter on June 28 and on that day telephoned the defendants to say that the figure of £65,000 was a mistake and inviting them to treat the letter of June 22 as if it had quoted the figure they had intended to propose, £126,000. The defendants declined to do so. The plaintiffs issued a writ claiming a declaration that there was no binding agreement as to the rental value. They issued a summons for judgment under Order 14 of the Rules of the Supreme Court (see Smith & Bailey, *The Modern English Legal System*, p. 421). They claimed that the defendants were taking advantage of what they knew, or ought reasonably to have known, was an error on the part of the plaintiffs' solicitors; but they conceded that the issue as to the state of the defendant's knowledge could only be resolved at the trial. They nevertheless obtained summary judgment. The defendants appealed.

SLADE L.J., giving the judgment of the Court (SLADE and ROBERT GOFF L.JJ.): This concession having been made, in our opinion correctly, the plaintiffs were confronted with at least formidable difficulties on their application for summary judgment. On the face of it, the letter of June 22, 1982 constituted a formal, unequivocal and unambiguous offer made to the defendants on behalf of the plaintiffs, with an intent to create legal relations, to agree that the "current market rental value" of the demised premises, for the purpose of sub-paragraph A of the rent review provision, was £65,000 per annum. On the face of it, the letter of June 23, 1982 constituted a formal, unequivocal and unambiguous acceptance of that offer by the defendants. The plaintiffs' solicitors indeed assert that they erroneously inserted the figure of £65,000 in the letter of June 22, 1982 in substitution for the figure of £126,000, which they had intended to insert; and like the learned Judge we are prepared to accept the truth of this assertion for the purpose of dealing with the present application. But in the absence of any proof, as yet, that the defendants either knew or ought reasonably to have known of the plaintiffs' error at the time when they purported to accept the plaintiffs' offer, why should the plaintiffs now be allowed to resile from that offer? It is a well-established principle of the English law of contract that an offer falls to be interpreted not subjectively by reference to what has actually passed through the mind of the offeror, but objectively, by reference to the interpretation which a reasonable man in the shoes of the offeree would place on the offer. It is an equally well-established principle that ordinarily an offer, when unequivocally accepted according to its precise terms, will give rise to a legally binding agreement as soon as acceptance is communicated to the offeror in the manner contemplated by the offer, and cannot thereafter be revoked without the consent of the other party. Accepting, as they do, that they have not yet proved that the defendants knew, or ought reasonably to have known, of their error at the relevant time, how can the plaintiffs assert that the defendants have no realistic hope of establishing an agreement of the relevant nature by virtue of the two letters of June 22 and 23, 1982?

Mr Richard Scott in answer has submitted an argument to the following effect. The "agreement" envisaged by sub-paragraphs A and B of the rent review provision is a genuine agreement, a real meeting of the minds. In the present case there was no real meeting of the parties' minds because of the plaintiffs' error. True it is that their intentions would have fallen to be judged objectively, according to their external manifestation, if the defendants had not only purported to accept the offer but had further altered their position as a result. However, so the argument runs, the general rule that the intentions of an offeror must be judged objectively is based on estoppel. Accordingly, if the person who has accepted the offer has not altered his position in reliance on the offer, no such estoppel arises. In the present case, it is submitted, the critical fact is that the figure of £65,000 was lower than the rent currently payable under the Lease immediately before December 25, 1982. In these circumstances, it is said, the defendants in agreeing that figure, did not alter their position in any way. Because of sub-paragraph E of the rent review provision, the current rent of £68,320 would have continued to be payble after December 25, 1982, notwithstanding the agreement. In all the circumstances, it is submitted, the plaintiffs, having proved their error at the relevant time, were at liberty to withdraw the offer contained in the letter of June 22, 1982, even after it had been accepted, and they duly did so at the end of June 1982.

We understand from the learned Judge's judgment that an argument on much the same lines was submitted to him on behalf of the plaintiffs and that, though he regarded it as novel and surprising, he was in the end convinced by it.

As will have appeared, Mr Scott's submissions based on mistake involve the implicit proposition (among other propositions) that the defendants have given no consideration for the agreement on which they now rely; we understood him to accept that if the defendants had altered their position in any material respect in agreeing the figure of £65,000, the argument based on mistake could not avail the plaintiffs. Since, for reasons which we will explain later in this judgment, we have come to the clear conclusion that the defendants did give consideration, the argument based on mistake must in our opinion fail for this reason, if no other, and any further reference to the issue of mistake is not strictly necessary. Furthermore, it is right to record that Mr Scott, in an argument which brevity rendered no less forceful, did not burden (and indeed was not pressed to burden) the Court with citations of authority on this issue. In all the circumstances this judgment on an Order XIV summons is not an appropriate occasion to embark on a lengthy discussion on the law relating to mistake in contract. Nevertheless, we should perhaps attempt to explain briefly (albeit *obiter*) why, quite apart from questions of consideration, we respectfully differ from the learned Judge on the question of mistake, as a matter of broad principle.

The nature of the apparent contract concluded by the two letters of June 22 and 23, 1982 is what is sometimes called a "bilateral contract." It was concluded by

(a) an offer by the plaintiffs to treat £65,000 as the "current market rental value" of the premises for the purpose of the Lease if the defendants would promise to accept that figure as that value, followed by

(b) the giving of a promise by the defendants in those terms. Where the nature of an offer is to enter into a bilateral contract, the contract becomes binding when the offeree gives the requested promise to the promisor in the manner contemplated by the offer; the mutual promises alone will suffice to conclude the contract. In our opinion, subject to what is said below relating to consideration, it is contrary to the well established principles of contract law to suggest that the offeror under a bilateral contract can withdraw an unambiguous offer, after it has been accepted in the manner contemplated by the offer, merely because he has made a mistake which the offeree neither knew nor could reasonably have known at the time when he accepted it. And in this context, provided only that the offeree has given sufficient consideration for the offeror's promise, it is nothing to the point that the offeree may not have changed his position beyond giving the promise requested of him.

For these reasons we think that the plaintiff's submissions based on mistake cannot, as matters stand, suffice to negative the existence of the apparent agreement of the parties to treat £65,000 as the current market rental value for the purpose of the Lease and to deprive the defendants of the right to defend this action on the basis of such agreement, though we are not, of course, saying that the plea of mistake as formulated in the statement of claim will not succeed at the trial.

We did, however, allow Mr Scott to submit another ground in support of the plaintiff's application, even though it appears that it did not emerge clearly in argument in the Court below and is not reflected in any respondents' notice. While the Court will not generally concern itself with the adequacy of consideration, by examining a bargain to see whether it is fair and beneficial to both sides, it will generally require some consideration to support a promise. A party to a contract can only enforce a promise not given under seal if in return for it he has given something of value in the eyes of the law: (see for example *Halsbury's Laws of England* (4th ed.), Vol. 9, paras. 316 and 317 in the cases there cited). Though one promise will by itself generally be sufficient consideration for another promise, in the present case Mr Scott forcefully submitted that, in entering into the agreement alleged by them, the defendants gave nothing whatever of value.

In his submission they conferred no benefit on the plaintiffs, because the effect of the agreement would not have enabled them to claim any more rent than that to which they would have been entitled in its absence. For the same reason, he contended, the agreement subjected the defendants to no detriment; on any footing the agreement had no practical operative effect because of sub-paragraph F of the rent review provision Mr Scott submitted that this argument based on lack of consideration was perfectly capable of being decided on the affidavit and other documentary evidence before the Court and by itself sufficed to negative the existence of an agreement such as alleged by the defendants. . . .

In our opinion, on the assumption that consideration is necessary to support the agreement alleged by them, they have plainly given it, if only because, by their letter of June 23, 1983, they have deprived themselves of the right to put forward any figure other than £65,000 as the relevant "current market rental value" or to have this rental value referred to an independent surveyor or valuer. We appreciate that these rights may be said to be of little value to the defendants, but we are not concerned with the adequacy of the consideration given by them for the plaintiffs' promise; and we are not prepared to say that these rights are of no value. It has to be remembered that, if the defendants had refused to agree any figure at all, considerable inconvenience to the plaintiffs might have resulted; an agreement should at least have had the merit of producing certainty and avoiding future disputes. Furthermore, if in the end the plaintiffs had been driven to have the matter referred to an independent valuer, they would have had to pay one half of the costs of the assessment: (see sub-paragraph F of the rent review provision). In all the circumstances in our judgment the surrender by the defendants of the rights to which we have referred clearly constituted sufficient consideration in law for the alleged agreement so that this last weapon in the plaintiffs' armoury on this present summons does not avail them.

Appeal allowed with unconditional leave to defend.

Questions

1. Professor Atiyah asks:

> "Why should an offeree be entitled to create legal rights for himself by the bare act of acceptance when he has in no way relied upon the offer before being informed that it was made as a result of a mistake and did not in reality reflect the intention of the offeror? Now that liability for misleading statements is an accepted part of tort law, it becomes increasingly anomalous if in a contractual context a party is able to sue upon an unrelied-upon statement, whereas in any other context he is not. A misleading offer is a commercial or perhaps social nuisance which should be discouraged, and for which compensation may be due, if loss is thereby caused, but surely the principles governing such misleading communications ought not to depend upon whether the communication can be classified as an offer or not."

Do you agree? (Atiyah is discussing *The Hannah Blumenthal* [1983] 1 A.C. 834 which, he believes, throws doubt on the *Centrovincial* case and *The Leonidas D* [1985] 2 All E.R. 796, C.A. which he criticises: (1986) 102 L.Q.R. 363 at 368.)

2. How should the trial court have decided the above case if it had been proved (i) that the defendants knew or ought to have known that the plaintiffs were making a gross mistake about the current market value of the premises; or (ii) that the defendants knew or ought to have known that the figure of £65,000 did not represent the real intention of the plaintiffs?

3. The defendants were contracting to pay a less sum than they were already bound to pay under the lease. Why was not the rule in *Pinnel's case* (below, p. 242) applicable?

Note

In *Watkin v. Watson-Smith*, *The Times*, July 3, 1986, the plaintiff, a frail old man of 80, agreed on a purchase price for his bungalow of £2,950 rather than £29,500 by mistake. M. Wheeler Q.C., sitting as a deputy judge of the Chancery Division, held that there was no contract as the defendant knew or ought to have known of the mistake as in *Hartog v. Colin*, above, p. 114 or because the parties were never *ad idem*: *Scriven v. Hindley*, above, p. 114. In any event, he would have set the contract aside as an unconscionable bargain, taking into account the plaintiff's old age with accompanying diminution of capacity and judgment, his desire for a quick sale, the undervalue and the lack of independent advice. *Cf.* below, Chapter 18.

Problem

Al wrote to several contractors, inviting them to tender for the supply and installation of windows in a building which Al was erecting. Ben put in a tender of £200. The prices submitted by the four other contractors who tendered ranged from £1,200 to £1,800. Al posted a letter accepting Ben's tender. Ben has now replied explaining that his clerk had put a decimal point in the wrong place when calculating the square footage of glass required and that the price quoted should be £2,000.

Is there a contract and, if so, what are its terms?

Cf. Imperial Glass Ltd v. Consolidated Supplies Ltd (1960) 22 D.L.R. (2d) 759 and comment in (1961) 39 Can. Bar Rev. 625; *McMaster University v. Wilchar Construction Ltd* (1971) 22 D.L.R. (3d) 9; *Belle River Community Arena v. Kaufmann* (1978) 87 D.L.R. (3d) 761.

FALCK v. WILLIAMS

Privy Council [1900] A.C. 176; 69 L.J.P.C. 17

The plaintiff and the defendant used a code for business purposes. The plaintiff through his agent, Buch, sent an offer in code by telegraph. The offer was ambiguous owing to the absence of punctuation. It was not clear whether an important word of the code ("escorte") went with one sentence or with the sentence following. The defendant accepted the offer. But the plaintiff understood the offer in one sense, the defendant in the other. The effect was that Williams thought the contract was for the carriage of a cargo of shale from Sydney to Barcelona and Falck thought it was a contract for the carriage of a cargo of copra from Fiji to the U.K. The plaintiff's action for breach of contract in the Supreme Court of New South Wales failed. He appealed to the Privy Council. The appeal was dismissed. The judgment of their Lordships was delivered by

LORD MACNAGHTEN: . . . the whole controversy when the matter is threshed out seems to be narrowed down to this question—"Is the word 'escorte' to be read with what has gone before or with what follows?" In their Lordships' opinion there is no conclusive reason pointing one way or the other. The fault lay with the appellant's agent. If he had spent a few more shillings on his message, if he had even arranged the words he used more carefully, if he had only put the word "escorte" before the word "begloom" instead of after it, there would have been no difficulty. It is not for their Lordships to determine what is the true construction of Buch's telegram. It was the duty of the appellant as plaintiff to make out that the construction which he put upon it was the true one. In that he must fail if the message was ambiguous, as their Lordships hold it to be. If the respondent had been maintaining his construction as plaintiff he would have equally failed.

Question

Do you agree with Lord Macnaghten's dictum that if the respondent had been suing as plaintiff he would equally have failed?

RAFFLES v. WICHELHAUS

Exchequer (1864) 2 H. & C. 906; 159 E.R. 375; 33 L.J.Ex. 160

The declaration contained a count upon an agreement for the purchase, by the defendants, of "125 bales of Surat cotton, guaranteed middling fair merchants Dhollerah to arrive ex *Peerless* from Bombay, to be taken from the quay at the price of 17¼ per lb., to be paid within a certain time then agreed upon after the arrival of the goods in England." Averment—That the goods did arrive by the said ship from Bombay in England, and that the plaintiff was ready and offered to deliver, etc. Breach—That the defendants did not nor would, but wholly refused to accept the said goods, or pay the plaintiff for them, and have not paid him for them, by means whereof, etc.

Second plea—That the said ship mentioned in the agreement was meant and intended by the defendants to be the ship called the *Peerless*, which sailed from Bombay, to wit, in October, and that the plaintiff was not ready and willing and did not offer to deliver to the defendants, any bales of cotton which arrived by the last-mentioned ship, but instead thereof was only ready and willing to deliver, and offered to deliver to the defendants, 125 bales of Surat cotton, which arrived by another and different ship, which was also called the *Peerless*, and which sailed from Bombay to wit, in December.

Demurrer, and joinder in demurrer.

Milward, in support of the demurrer: The contract was for the sale of so much cotton of a particular nature, well described, which the plaintiff was ready to deliver. By which ship it should come was immaterial. The words "to arrive," etc., merely mean that, if the ship be lost, the contract is to go off.

[POLLOCK C.B.: You may as well say that a description of goods as those "in a particular warehouse" is no part of the contract. Whether the same *Peerless* was meant by the plaintiff and the defendants is a matter of evidence for the jury.]

It does not appear that the plaintiff had any goods in the other *Peerless*. If the defendants had said their speculation had fallen through in consequence, it might have been different.

[POLLOCK C.B.: If the plea fairly raises the question, it is as good a plea as ever was framed.]

The defendants are not justified in introducing parol evidence into a written contract, which has been performed by the plaintiff. They do not say that he misled them, but only that they fancied the ship was different. Intention is of no use, unless stated at the time of the contract.

The time of the sailing of the ship was no part of the contract; and, for the purposes of the plea, we must take it that both ships sailed on the same day.

Mellish (*Cohen* with him), in support of the plea: The contract was for cotton, "ex *Peerless* from Bombay." There is nothing on the face of the contract to show which *Peerless* was meant; so that this is a plain case of latent ambiguity, as soon as it is shown that there were two *Peerlesses* from Bombay; and parol evidence may be given when it will be found that the plaintiff meant one and the defendants the other. If this was the case, there was no *consensus ad idem*, and therefore no binding contract.

Per curiam (Pollock C.B., Martin B. and Pigott B.).

Judgment for the defendants.

Note

    Where the parties have reduced their contract to writing it is not permissible, as a general rule, to adduce parol (oral) evidence to add to, vary or contradict the written instrument. This rule, known as "the parol evidence rule," is subject to many qualifications or exceptions (see pp. 329, 382, 517, below), one of which, established by *Raffles v. Wichelhaus*, is that parol evidence is admissible to reveal a latent ambiguity. A latent ambiguity is one which does not appear on the face of the instrument, a patent ambiguity one which does so appear: see *Falck v. Williams* (above, p. 119). For further discussion of the parol evidence rule, see Cheshire Fifoot & Furmston, *Law of Contract* (12th ed.), pp. 124–126, and Cross, *Evidence* (7th ed.), pp. 695–710. The Law Commission has recommended that no legislation is required to reform or clarify the rule: (1986) Law Com. No. 154 (Cmnd. 9700).

Questions
1. If the buyer had been thinking of the December *Peerless* would there have been a contract? If so, is this not a type of case in which the court is concerned with the actual state of mind of the parties?
2. Suppose the buyer had discovered his mistake but decided he would like the cargo of the December *Peerless* after all; the seller, having also discovered the mistake, declines to deliver. Has the buyer any rights?
3. The offer in the present case, (by whichever party it was made) was ambiguous. Does it, then, follow that Lord Macnaghten's dictum in *Falck v. Williams* (above, p. 119) is correct? Or is there a difference in the responsibility for the ambiguity which might affect the result?
4. See Gilmore, *The Death of Contract*, pp. 35–44: ". . . the judges, no doubt mistakenly, believed that the identity of the carrying ship was important. . . ." Were the judges mistaken? Does the case show, as Gilmore argues, that the courts "were approaching the problem of formation of contract from a purely subjectivist point of view. . . ."? *Cf.* J. C. Smith, (1979) 13 *The Law Teacher*, p. 73.

SMITH v. HUGHES

Queen's Bench (1871) L.R. 6 Q.B. 597; 40 L.J.Q.B. 221; 25 L.T. 329; 19 W.R. 1059

The plaintiff, a farmer asked the manager of the defendant, who was a trainer of racehorses, if he would like to buy 40 or 50 quarters of oats, and showed him a sample. The manager wrote to say that he would take the whole quantity at 34s. a quarter. The plaintiff delivered a portion of them. The defendant complained that the oats were new oats, whereas he thought he was buying old oats, new oats being useless to him. The plaintiff, who knew that the oats were new—he had no old oats—refused to take them back and sued for the price. There was a conflict of evidence as to what took place between the plaintiff and the manager. According to the plaintiff the manager had said: "I am always a buyer of good oats," to which the plaintiff replied: "I have some good oats for sale." But according to the manager he said to the plaintiff: "I am always a buyer of good *old* oats," to which the plaintiff responded: "I have some good old oats for sale."
The judge left two questions to the jury:
1. Was the word "old" used? If so, verdict for the defendant.
2. If the word "old" was not used, did the plaintiff believe the defendant to believe or to be under the impression that he was contracting for old oats? If so, verdict for the defendant.
The jury found a verdict for the defendant. The plaintiff appealed.

COCKBURN C.J.: It is to be regretted that the jury were not required to give specific answers to the questions so left to them. For, it is quite possible that their verdict may have been given for the defendant on the first ground; in which case there could, I think, be no doubt as to the propriety of the judge's direction; whereas now, as it is possible that the verdict of the jury—or at all events of some of them—may have proceeded on the second ground, we are called upon to consider and decide whether the ruling of the learned judge with reference to the second question was right.

For this purpose we must assume that nothing was said on the subject of the defendant's manager desiring to buy *old* oats, nor of the oats having been said to be old; while on the other hand, we must assume that the defendant's manager believed the oats to be old oats, and that the plaintiff was conscious of the existence of such belief, but did nothing, directly or indirectly, to bring it about, simply offering his oats and exhibiting his sample, remaining perfectly passive as to what was passing in the mind of the other party. The question is whether, under such circumstances, the passive acquiescence of the seller in the self-deception of the buyer will entitle the latter to avoid the contract. I am of opinion that it will not.

The oats offered to the defendant's manager were a specific parcel, of which the sample submitted to him formed a part. He kept the sample for 24 hours, and had, therefore, full opportunity of inspecting it and forming his judgment upon it. Acting on his own judgment, he wrote to the plaintiff, offering him a price. Having this opportunity of inspecting and judging of the sample, he is practically in the same position as if he had inspected the oats in bulk. It cannot be said that, if he had gone and personally inspected the oats in bulk, and then, believing—but without anything being said or done by the seller to bring about such a belief—that the oats were old, had offered a price for them, he would have been justified in repudiating the contract, because the seller, from the known habits of the buyer, or other circumstances, had reason to infer that the buyer was ascribing to the oats a quality they did not possess, and did not undeceive him.

I take the true rule to be, that where a specific article is offered for sale, without express warranty, or without circumstances from which the law will imply a warranty—as where, for instance, an article is ordered for a specific purpose—and the buyer has full opportunity of inspecting and forming his own judgment, if he chooses to act on his own judgment, the rule *caveat emptor* applies. If he gets the article he contracted to buy, and that article corresponds with what it was sold as, he gets all he is entitled to, and is bound by the contract. Here the defendant agreed to buy a specific parcel of oats. The oats were what they were sold as, namely, good oats according to the sample. The buyer persuaded himself they were old oats, when they were not so; but the seller neither said nor did anything to contribute to his deception. He has himself to blame. The question is not what a man of scrupulous morality or nice honour would do under such circumstances. The case put of the purchase of an estate, in which there is a mine under the surface, but the fact is unknown to the seller, is one in which a man of tender conscience or high honour would be unwilling to take advantage of the ignorance of the seller, but there can be no doubt that the contract for the sale of the estate would be binding. . . .

Now, in this case, there was clearly no legal obligation in the plaintiff in the first instance to state whether the oats were new or old. He offered them for sale according to the sample, as he had a perfect right to do, and gave the buyer the fullest opportunity of inspecting the sample, which, practically, was equivalent to an inspection of the oats themselves. What, then, was there to create any trust or confidence between the parties, so as to make it incumbent on the plaintiff to communicate the fact that the oats were not, as the defendant assumed them to be, old oats? If, indeed, the buyer, instead of acting on his own opinion, had asked the question whether the oats were old or new, or had said anything which intimated his understanding that the seller was selling the oats as old oats, the case would have been wholly different; or even if he had said anything which showed that he was not acting on his own inspection and judgment, but assumed as the foundation of the contract that the oats were old, the silence of the seller, as a means of misleading him, might have amounted to a fraudulent concealment, such as would have entitled the buyer to avoid the contract. Here, however, nothing of the sort occurs. The buyer in no way refers to the seller, but acts entirely on his own judgment . . .

It only remains to deal with an argument which was pressed upon us, that the defendant in the present case intended to buy old oats, and the plaintiff to sell new, so the two minds were not *ad idem*; and that consequently there was no contract. This argument proceeds on the fallacy of confounding what was merely a motive operating on the buyer to induce him to buy with one of the essential conditions of the contract. Both parties were agreed as to the sale and purchase of this particular parcel of oats. The defendant believed the oats to be old, and was thus induced to agree to buy them, but he omitted to make their age a condition of the contract. All that can be said is, that the two minds were not *ad idem* as to the age of the oats; they were certainly *ad idem* as to the sale and purchase of them. Suppose a person to buy a horse without a warranty, believing him to be sound, and the horse turns out unsound, could it be contended that it would be open to him to say that, as he had intended to buy a sound horse, and the seller to sell an unsound one, the contract was void, because the seller must have known from the price the buyer was willing to give, or from his general habits as a buyer of horses that he thought the horse was sound? The cases are exactly parallel.

BLACKBURN J.: The rule of law is that stated in *Freeman v. Cooke* (1848) 2 Exch. 654. If, whatever a man's real intention may be, he so conducts himself that a reasonable man would believe that he was assenting to the terms proposed by the other party, and that other party upon that belief enters into the contract with him, the man thus conducting himself would be equally bound as if he had intended to agree to the other party's terms.

The jury were directed that, if they believed the word "old" was used, they should find for the defendant—and this was right; for if that was the case, it is obvious that neither did the defendant intend to enter into a contract on the plaintiff's terms, that is, to buy this parcel of oats without any stipulation as to their quality; nor could the plaintiff have been led to believe he was intending to do so.

But the second direction raises the difficulty. I think that, if from that direction the jury would understand that they were first to consider whether they were satisfied that the defendant intended to buy this parcel of oats on the terms that it was part of his contract with the plaintiff that they were old oats, so as to have the warranty of the plaintiff to that effect, they were properly told that, if that was so, the defendant could not be bound to a contract without any such warranty unless the plaintiff was misled. But I doubt whether the direction would bring to the minds of the jury the distinction between agreeing to take the oats under the belief that they were old, and agreeing to take the oats under the belief that the plaintiff contracted that they were old.

The difference is the same as that between buying a horse believed to be sound, and buying one believed to be warranted sound; but I doubt if it was made obvious to the jury, and I doubt this the more, because I do not see much evidence to justify a finding for the defendant on this latter ground if the word "old" was not used. There may have been more evidence than is stated in the case; and the demeanour of the witnesses may have strengthened the impression produced by the evidence there was; but it does not seem a very satisfactory verdict if it proceeded on this latter ground. I agree, therefore, in the result that there should be a new trial.

HANNEN J.: The rule of law applicable to such a case is a corollary from the rule of morality which Mr Pollock cited from Paley (*Moral and Political Philosophy*, Book III, Chap. 5), that a promise is to be performed "in that sense in which the promiser apprehended at the time the promisee received it," and may be thus expressed: "The promiser is not bound to fulfil a promise in a sense in which the promisee knew at the time the promiser did not intend it." And in considering the question, in what sense a promisee is entitled to enforce a promise, it matters not in what way the knowledge of the meaning in which the promiser made it is brought to the mind of the promisee, whether by express words, or by conduct, or previous dealings, or other circumstances. If by any means he knows that there was no real agreement between him and the promiser, he is not entitled to insist that the promise shall be fulfilled in a sense to which the mind of the promiser did not assent.

If, therefore, in the present case, the plaintiff knew that the defendant, in dealing with him for oats, did so on the assumption that the plaintiff was contracting to sell him old oats, he was aware that the defendant apprehended the contract in a different sense to that in which he meant it, and he is thereby deprived of the right to insist that the defendant shall be bound by that which was only the apparent, and not the real bargain.

This was the question which the learned judge intended to leave to the jury; and, as I have already said, I do not think it was incorrect in its terms, but I think that it was likely to be misunderstood by the jury. The jury were asked, "whether they were of opinion, on the whole of the evidence, that the plaintiff believed the defendant to believe, or to be under the impression that he was contracting for the purchase of old oats? If so, there would be a verdict for the defendant." The jury may have understood this to mean that, if the plaintiff believed the defendant to believe that he was buying old oats, the defendant would be entitled to the verdict; but a belief on the part of the plaintiff that the defendant was making a contract to buy the oats, of which he offered him a sample, under a mistaken belief that they were old, would not relieve the defendant from liability unless his mistaken belief were induced by some misrepresentation of the plaintiff, or concealment by him of a fact which it became his duty to communicate. In order to relieve the defendant it was necessary that the jury should find not merely that the plaintiff believed the defendant to believe that he was buying old oats, but that he believed the defendant to believe that he, the plaintiff, was contracting to sell old oats. . . .

New trial ordered.

Questions
  1. If the word "old" was used, the plaintiff loses. Does he lose because:

(a) there was no contract? or
(b) there was a contract to sell oats which the plaintiff promised were old—that is, a contract which was not performed? *Cf. Roberts v. Leicestershire County Council* (below, p. 128).

2. Suppose the defendant's horses had suffered injury through eating new oats. Could the defendant (if the word "old" was used) have recovered damages from the plaintiff?
(*Cf.* Lord Atkin in *Bell v. Lever Bros.*, below, p. 491.)

3. If the word "old" was not used, but the plaintiff knew that the defendant believed that the plaintiff was contracting to sell old oats, the plaintiff loses. Does he lose because:

(a) there was no contract? or
(b) there was a contract to sell oats which the plaintiff promised were old—that is, a contract which was not performed?

4. The plaintiff wins though he knew the defendant was making a mistake of fact. Should he not, *a fortiori*, have won if he had been making the same mistake? But see *Solle v. Butcher*, below, p. 501 and *William Sindall plc. v. Cambs. C.C.*, below, p. 506.

FREDERICK E. ROSE (LONDON) LTD v. WILLIAM H. PIM JNR. & CO., LTD

Court of Appeal [1953] 2 Q.B. 450; [1953] 3 W.L.R. 497; 97 S.J. 556; [1953] 2 All E.R. 739; 70 R.P.C. 238

The plaintiffs, London merchants, were asked by their Eygptian house for "Moroccan horsebeans described here as feveroles." Their representative did not know what feveroles were, and asked the defendants' representative who, after making inquiries, told him that feveroles were just horsebeans and that his firm could procure them. After negotiations on that basis, written contracts were concluded (1) between North African suppliers and the defendant, (2) between the defendant and the plaintiffs, and (3) between the plaintiffs and Egyptian buyers, for the sale and purchase of "horsebeans," payment to be in London by confirmed irrevocable letters of credit against shipping documents. When the horsebeans, shipped from Tunis, were received by the Egyptian buyers, the latter found that the commodity supplied was not feveroles, but another type of bean; but as they had paid for the goods, they accepted them and claimed damages.

The plaintiffs now sought rectification of their contract with the defendants. The Court of Appeal (Singleton, Denning and Morris L.JJ.) held, reversing Pilcher J., that, as the concluded oral agreement was for horsebeans, and the written contracts were in the same terms, the remedy of rectification was not available.

DENNING L.J. said: I am clearly of opinion that the contract was not a nullity. It is true that both parties were under a mistake, and that the mistake was of a fundamental character with regard to the subject-matter. The goods contracted for—horsebeans—were essentially different from what they were believed to be—"feveroles." Nevertheless, the parties to all outward appearances were agreed. They had agreed with quite sufficient certainty on a contract for the sale of goods by description, namely, horsebeans. Once they had done that, nothing in their minds could make the contract a nullity from the beginning, though it might, to be sure, be a ground in some circumstances for setting the contract aside in equity. In *Ryder v. Woodley* (1862) 10 W.R. 294, where a buyer contracted to buy a commodity described "St. Giles Marais wheat," believing that it was wheat when it was not, the contract was held to be binding on him and not a nullity. In *Harrison & Jones Ltd v. Bunten & Lancaster Ltd* [1953]1 Q.B. 646, where parties contracted for the supply of "Calcutta kapok 'Sree' brand," both believing it to be pure kapok containing no cotton whereas it in fact contained 10 to 12 per cent of cotton, Pilcher J. held that their mistake, although fundamental, did not make the contract a nullity. In *McRae v. Commonwealth Disposals Commission* (below, p. 487), where sellers contracted to sell a stranded oil tanker, described as lying at a specified point off Samarai, believing that there was a tanker at such a place when there was in fact no such tanker there, nor anywhere in the locality, the High Court of Australia held that the mistake, although fundamental, did not make the contract a nullity, and that the buyers were entitled to damages. The court showed convincingly that *Couturier v. Hastie* (below, p. 486) was a case of construction only. It was not a case where the contract was void for mistake. The other old cases at common law can likewise be explained. At the present day, since the fusion of law and equity, the position appears to be that when the parties to a contract are to all outward appearances in full and certain agreement, neither of them can set up his own mistake, or the mistake of both of them, so as to make the contract a nullity from the beginning. Even a common mistake as to the subject-matter does not make it a nullity. Once the contract is outwardly complete, the contract is good unless and until it is set aside for failure of some condition on which the existence of the contract depends, or for fraud, or on some equitable ground: see *Solle v. Butcher* (below, p. 501). Could this contract, then, have been set aside? I think it could, if the parties had acted in time. This contract was made under a common mistake as to the meaning of "feveroles" and "horsebeans." This mistake was induced by the innocent misrepresentation of the defendants made to the buyers and passed on to the sub-buyers. As soon as the buyers and sub-buyers discovered the mistake, they could, I think, have rejected the goods and asked for their money back. The fact that the contract was executed would not be a bar to rescission. But once the buyers and sub-buyers accepted the goods, and treated themselves as the owners of them, they could no longer claim rescission: see *Leaf v. International Galleries*, (below, p. 342).

The buyers now, after accepting the goods, seek to rectify the contract. Instead of it being a contract for "horsebeans" simpliciter, they seek to make it a contract for "horsebeans described in Egypt as feveroles." The judge has granted their request. He has found that there was "a mutual and fundamental mistake" and that the defendants and the plaintiffs, through their respective market clerks, "intended to deal in horsebeans of the feverole type"; and he has held that, because that was their intention—their "continuing common intention"—the court could rectify their contract to give effect to it. In this I think he was wrong. Rectification is concerned with contracts and documents, not with intentions. In order to get rectification it is necessary to show that the parties were in complete agreement on the terms of their contract, but by an error wrote them down wrongly; and in this regard, in order to ascertain the terms of their contract, you do not look into the inner minds of the parties—into their intentions—any more than you do in the formation of any other contract. You look at their outward acts, that is, at what they said or wrote to one another in coming to their agreement, and then compare it with the document which they have signed. If you can predicate with certainty what their contract was, and that it is, by a common mistake, wrongly expressed in the document, then you rectify the document; but nothing less will suffice. It is not necessary that all the formalities of the contract should have been executed so as to make it enforceable at law (see *Shipley Urban District Council v. Bradford Corporation* [1936] Ch. 375); but formalities apart, there must have been a concluded contract. There is a passage in *Crane v. Hegeman-Harris Co. Inc.* [1939] 1 All E.R. 662, 664 which suggests that a continuing common intention alone will suffice; but I am clearly of opinion that a continuing common intention is not sufficient unless it has found expression in outward agreement. There could be no certainty at all in business transactions if a party who had entered into a firm contract could afterwards turn round and claim to have it rectified on the ground that the parties intended something different. He is allowed to prove, if he can, that they *agreed something different*: see *Lovell & Christmas v. Wall*, per Lord Cozens-Hardy M.R. and *per* Buckley L.J. ([1911]) 104 L.T. 85, 88, 93) but not that they *intended* something different.

The present case is a good illustration of the distinction. The parties no doubt intended that the goods should satisfy the inquiry of the Egyptian buyers, namely, "horsebeans described in Egypt as feveroles." They assumed that they would do so, but they made no contract to that effect. Their agreement, as outwardly expressed, both orally and in writing, was for "horsebeans." That is all the defendants ever committed themselves to supply; and all that they should be bound to. There was, no doubt, an erroneous assumption underlying the contract—an assumption for which it might have been set aside on the grounds of misrepresentation or mistake—but that is very different from an erroneous expression of the contract, such as to give rise to rectification.

The matter can best be tested by asking what would have been the position if the contract between the defendants and the plaintiffs had been for "feveroles." Surely, then, the defendants on their side would have stipulated with their Algerian suppliers for the delivery of "feveroles," and the plaintiffs on their side would have agreed with their sub-buyers to deliver "feveroles." It would not be fair to rectify one of the contracts without rectifying all three, which is obviously impossible.

Glanville Williams, Mistake and Rectification in Contract, 17 M.L.R. 154

The writer says with reference to the above case:

Let it be supposed that with the contract as it was in the instant case, both parties had gone into the witness-box and testified that they realised the distinction between the ordinary horsebeans and "feveroles," but that they used the term "horsebeans" to mean "feveroles" and not to mean ordinary horsebeans. In that event, it is clear, the contract would be valid for the sale of feveroles and there would be no contract for the sale of ordinary horsebeans. A contract is not enforced according to its "outward appearance" if both parties concur in intending something else. It is not invariably true, therefore, to say, as Denning L.J. does, that in the formation of a contract "one does not look into the inner minds of the parties." (And see above, p. 121, (question 1) and below, pp. 137, Note 1, 173.

Notes

1. In *London Weekend Television Ltd v. Paris & Griffith* (1969) 113 S.J. 222, Megaw J. is reported as saying, "Where two persons agreed expressly with one another what was the

meaning of a particular phrase but did not record their definition in the contract itself, if one of the parties sought to enforce the agreement on the basis of some other meaning, he could be prevented by an action for rectification."

2. In *Rose v. Pim*, Denning L.J. said that, if rectification is to be ordered, "formalities apart, there must have been a concluded contract" before the document to be rectified was signed. This would appear to be too wide a statement. There need not be an antecedent concluded contract, so long as the parties were in agreement up to the moment when they executed the formal contract and there had been some "outward expression of accord." In *Joscelyne v. Nissen* [1970] 2 Q.B. 86; [1970] 1 All E.R. 1213, a father and daughter were agreed and intended, among other things, that the father should live in the ground floor of the daughter's house, she to pay the gas, electricity and coal bills and the cost of a home help to tend her afflicted mother. The agreement in fact signed by the father and daughter stated that the father should have the ground floor "free of all rent and outgoings of every kind in any event"; and, on ordinary construction, would not require the daughter to pay the gas bills, etc. The Court of Appeal held that the contract should be rectified to provide expressly that the daughter pay the gas bills, etc., Russell L.J. said (p. 99): "We wish to stress that this is a case of rectification based on antecedent expressed accord on a point adhered to in intention by the parties to the subsequent written contract . . ."

ROBERTS AND CO. LTD v. LEICESTERSHIRE COUNTY COUNCIL

[1961] Ch. 555; [1961] 2 W.L.R. 1000; [1961] 2 All E.R. 545

The plaintiffs, building contractors, submitted to the defendants a tender for the erection of a school, in which they offered to undertake to complete the work in 18 months. The defendants replied "accepting" the tender and forwarded contract documents. In these documents they specified, for their own benefit and not that of the company, a period of 30 months, instead of the 18 months referred to in the tender. The officers of the company executed the contract without noticing this change in the contract period. The officers of the county council realised that the plaintiffs were in error as to the contract period but did not draw their attention to the period actually stated and, subsequently, the county council executed the contract. There is a direct relationship between the price and the contract period, and if the company had made its tender on the basis of a 30-month period, the price would have been higher. A dispute having arisen, PENNYCUICK J. held that the contract must be rectified by the substitution of a period of 18 months for that of 30 months. Having held that the plaintiffs were not entitled to rectification on the ground of a common mistake because the parties did not have a common intention as to what period should be inserted in the contract, he went on:

The second ground rests on the principle that a party is entitled to rectification of a contract on proof that he believed a particular term to be included in the contract and that the other party concluded the contract with the omission or a variation of that term in the knowledge that the first party believed the term to be included. Counsel appearing for the council formulated the principle in slightly different terms, as follows, *viz.*, the plaintiff must show that his intention was that the term sought to be introduced by rectification should be included in the contract and, so far as now relevant, that the omission of the term was occasioned by the dishonest conduct of the defendant in acceptance of the formation of the contract without the term, in the knowledge that the plaintiff thought the term was included. Counsel thus introduces into his formulation of the principle the word "dishonest," but he accepts that such conduct by the defendant in his formulation is of its nature dishonest, so that the word "dishonest" appears to carry the matter no further. I do not think that there is any substantial disagreement as to the scope of the principle.

The principle is stated in *Snell's Principles of Equity* (26th ed.), p. 684, as follows: "By what appears to be a species of equitable estoppel, if one party to a transaction knows that the instrument contains a mistake in his favour but does nothing to correct it, he (and those claiming under him) will be precluded from resisting rectification on the ground that the mistake is unilateral and not common."

The exact basis of the principle appears to be in some doubt. If the principle is correctly rested on estoppel it seems to me that it is not an essential ingredient of the right of action to establish any particular degree of obliquity to be attributed to the defendant in such circumstances. If, on the other hand, the principle is rested on fraud, obviously dishonesty must be established. It is well established that a party claiming rectification must prove his facts beyond reasonable doubt, and I think that this high standard of proof must equally apply where the claim is based on the principle indicated above.

Questions

1. The court orders rectification where the contract as recorded differs from the contract which was in fact made. See Cheshire Fifoot & Furmston (12th ed.), pp. 244–246, Treitel (8th ed.), pp. 285–290. Thus Pennycuick J. must have held that the true contract in the above case was for performance in 18 months. What light, then, does the decision cast on the answer to question 3(b) on p. 125, above?

2. In *London Holeproof Hosiery Co. Ltd v. Padmore* (1928) 44 T.L.R. 499 a lessee of a factory which had been destroyed by fire exercised an option to renew the lease, believing that the lessor was promising to rebuild the premises. The lessor knew that the lessee so believed. The Court of Appeal dismissed both the lessee's action for failure to rebuild the premises and the lessor's counterclaim for specific performance of a contract to take the premises in the condition in which they were. Following *Smith v. Hughes*, the court held that the parties were not *ad idem* and that there was no contract. See P.S. Atiyah, 2 Ottawa L.R. (1968), 337.

Is this consistent with the decision in *Roberts v. Leicestershire County Council*? Is it a correct application of *Smith v. Hughes*? And is it right in principle?

3. Would the Misrepresentation Act 1967 (below, p. 352, be of relevance to the situation in *Rose v. Pim* or *Roberts v. Leicestershire County Council*?

Note

In *Thomas Bates & Son Ltd v. Wyndham's (Lingerie) Ltd* [1981] 1 All E.R. 1077 (C.A.), a rent review clause in a lease of a factory by B Ltd to W Ltd stated that the lessee had an option to renew the lease for a specific period at a rent to be agreed between the parties, and, in default of such agreement, at a rent to be fixed by a single arbitrator appointed by the President of the Royal Institution of Chartered Surveyors. When the lease came up for renewal, the provision concerning the reference to arbitration was omitted due to a mistake on the part of B Ltd's managing director. W Ltd knew that he did not realise his mistake, but they signed the lease without the clause concerned. B Ltd applied for rectification of the document.

It was held (Buckley, Eveleigh and Brightman L.JJ.) that rectification would be ordered. For the doctrine of rectification to apply, where there was a mistake on the part of one of the parties only, it had to shown that (1) one party erroneously believed that the document sought to be rectified contained a particular term or provision; (2) the other party was aware of the omission and that it was due to a mistake; (3) the other party had failed to draw the mistake to his attention; and (4) the mistake must be one calculated to benefit the other person. If those requirements were satisfied, the court might regard it as inequitable to allow the other party to resist rectification to give effect to the mistaken party's intention on the ground that the mistake was not, at the time of the execution of the document, a mutual mistake. In the present case the requirements had all been established. (*Roberts v. Leicestershire County Council*, applied.)

RIVERLATE PROPERTIES LTD v. PAUL

Court of Appeal [1975] Ch. 133; [1974] 3 W.L.R. 564; [1974] 2 All E.R. 656; 28 P. & C.R. 220

The plaintiff granted a lease of a maisonette for 99 years to the defendant at a price of £6,500 with a ground rent of £25 per annum. The plaintiff intended that the lessee should pay half of the cost of exterior and structural repairs but the lease put the entire burden on the plaintiff. The defendant's understanding was that she was not responsible for these repairs. The plaintiff's claim for rectification or alternatively rescission of the lease was dismissed by Templeman J. and the Court of Appeal.

RUSSELL L.J., delivering the judgment of the court: What is there in principle, or in authority binding on this court, which requires a person who has acquired a leasehold interest on terms on which he intended to obtain it, and who thought when he obtained it that the lessor intended him to obtain it on those terms, either to lose the leasehold interest, or, if he wish to keep it, to submit to keep it only on the terms which the lessor meant to impose but did not? In point of principle, we cannot find that this should be so. If reference be made to principles of equity, it operates on conscience. If conscience is clear at the time of the transaction, why should equity disrupt the transaction? If a man may be said to have been fortunate in obtaining a property at a bargain price, or on terms that make if a good bargain, because the other party unknown to him has made a miscalculation or other mistake, some high-minded men might consider it appropriate that he should agree to a fresh bargain to cure the miscalculation or mistake, abandoning his good fortune. But if equity were to enforce the views of those high-minded men, we have no doubt that it would run counter to the attitudes of much the greater part of ordinary mankind (not least the world of commerce), and would be venturing on the field of moral philosophy in which it would soon be in difficulties.

Question
What if the defendant had been aware of the plaintiff's misunderstanding when the lease was signed?

COMMISSION FOR NEW TOWNS v. COOPER (GB) LTD

Court of Appeal [1995] Ch. 529; [1995] 2 W.L.R. 677; [1995] 2 All E.R. 929

The question for the court was whether a contract entered into by correspondence between the plaintiff and the defendant (then called CoopInd) granted to the defendant a put option (an option to require the plaintiff to take an assignment of an underlease). Differing from the trial judge, the court held that, on its true construction, the contract did not grant that option. In case they were wrong about that, the court went on to consider whether the contract should be rectified, so as to exclude the option, on the ground that the plaintiff entered into the contract believing that it contained no such option and that CoopInd knew, or at least suspected, that the plaintiff so believed.

STUART-SMITH L.J. referred to the judgment of Slade L.J. in *Agip SpA v. Navigazione Alta SpA, The Nai Genova* [1984] 1 Lloyd's Rep. 353 stating that in all the cases, including *Roberts, Riverplate* and *Bates,* where rectification had been granted on the ground of a unilateral mistake, the defendant had actual knowledge of the plaintiff's mistake at the time the contract was signed and that he inclined to the view that rectification could only be granted where the defendant had actual knowledge. Stuart-Smith L.J. continued: It is only with great diffidence that I venture to think that this may not be an exhaustive statement of the law, although it undoubtedly covers the majority of situations. But were it necessary to do so in this case, I would hold that where A intends B to be mistaken as to the construction of the agreement, so conducts himself that he diverts B's attention from discovering the mistake by making false and misleading statements, and B in fact makes the very mistake that A intends, then notwithstanding that A does not actually know, but merely suspects that B is mistaken, and it cannot be shown that the mistake was induced by any misrepresentation, rectification may be granted. A's conduct is unconscionable and he cannot insist on performance in accordance to the strict letter of the contract; that is sufficient for rescission. But it may also not be unjust or inequitable to insist that the contract be performed according to B's understanding, where that was the meaning that A intended that B should put upon it. That is so here because, although on the assumption that CoopInd's construction is correct and the put option was included, the contract appeared to be a whole package, in truth CoopInd thought they were getting something for nothing.

[His Lordship referred to the analysis of mental states by Peter Gibson J. in *Baden*'s case [1992] 4 All ER 161 at 235 as comprising: "(i) actual knowledge; (ii) wilfully shutting one's eyes to the obvious; (iii) wilfully and recklessly failing to make such inquiries as an honest and reasonable man would make; (iv) knowledge of circumstances which would indicate the facts to an honest and reasonable man; (v) knowledge of circumstances which would put an honest and reasonable man on inquiry." Having cited passages from the trial judge, he continued.]

The judge appears therefore to be holding that only Peter Gibson J.'s category (i) is sufficient. But with all respect to him, this is not so; categories (ii) and (iii) also constitute actual knowledge in law. In my judgment, it must have been plain that neither Mr Hill nor Mr Barton [representatives of the plaintiff] had any idea that they were dealing with the put option, far less agreeing to grant it to CoopInd. It did not suit CoopInd's plan, as the judge found, to draw attention to this or ask any questions about it. Their (CoopInd's representatives') conduct in raising the smokescreen in relation to the side land was dishonest and intended to deceive. If the question is posed as a jury question, I find it impossible to reach any other conclusion but that an honest and reasonable man would have mentioned the point expressly.

EVANS L.J. agreed, saying that "'knowledge' in this context includes 'shut-eye' knowledge."

FARQUHARSON L.J. AGREED.

Question
  Should Peter Gibson J.'s category (iv) or (v) be a ground for rectification of a written contract?

Section 3. Objectivity and Written Contracts

L'ESTRANGE v. GRAUCOB LTD

Divisional Court [1934] 2 K.B. 394; 103 L.J.K.B. 730; 152 L.T. 164

The plaintiff signed a "Sales Agreement" for the purchase of an automatic machine. The agreement was printed on brown paper and included a number of clauses "in regrettably small print but quite legible." The plaintiff did not read the document, it was not read over to her, nor did the defendants call her attention to the words in small type, and she said in evidence that she had no clear idea of what she was signing. The machine failed to work properly. In an action for breach of warranty the defendants were held to be protected by one of the clauses in small print which exempted them from liability.

Scrutton L.J.: When a document containing contractual terms is signed, then, in the absence of fraud, or, I will add, misrepresentation, the party signing it is bound, and it is wholly immaterial whether he has read the document or not.

Signing a Contract without reading it. In cases like *L'Estrange v. Graucob* the defendant is held liable although he does not really, in his mind, assent to the particular terms in the document because he does not know what they are. He has, however, signified his assent to them by his signature. *Cf. Riverlate Properties Ltd v. Paul,* above, p. 130. In *Harris v. Great Western Railway* (1876) 1 Q.B.D. 515, 530 Blackburn J. explained this on the grounds of estoppel. (Above, p. 78) The party who has signed without reading is bound—"on the ground that, by assenting to the contract thus reduced to writing, he represents to the other side that he has made himself acquainted with the contents of that writing and assents to them, and so induces the other side to act upon that representation by entering into the contract with him, and is consequently precluded from denying that he did make himself acquainted with those terms." If this were the basis of the rule, it would seem to follow that the signer should be able to repudiate the contract when the other party knew very well that he had not read the document before signing. There would then be no ground for implying a representation that the signer had read the document and, anyway, the other party would know any such representation to be untrue and so could not be said to act on it. In *McCutcheon v. David MacBrayne Ltd* [1964] 1 W.L.R. 125 (below, p. 155) Lord Devlin thought that Blackburn J.'s dictum might some day have to be examined more closely by their Lordships and went on: "It seems to me that when a party assents to a document forming the whole or part of his contract, he is bound by the terms of the document, read or unread, signed or unsigned, simply because they are in the contract; and it is unnecessary and possibly misleading to say that he is bound by them because he represents to the other party that he has made himself acquainted with them." *Cf. The Polyduke* (1978) 1 Lloyds Rep. 211.

J.R. Spencer in [1973] C.L.J. 104 criticises the rule stated in *L'Estrange v. Graucob* as the product of an excessively objective theory of agreement under which the test is not what the other party would have thought—as in *Smith v. Hughes* and *Hartog v. Colin* (above, pp. 121, 114) but "how things would have appeared to a reasonable fly on the wall," a theory which the author considers to have been applied in *Rose v. Pim* (above, p. 125). Mr Spencer argues that an application of the rule in *Smith v. Hughes* would have enabled L'Estrange to succeed in her action. The case shows that where, at the time of contracting, A knows that B is mistaken as to the terms of the contract, A cannot enforce it in the sense in which he, A, understood it: and

Roberts v. Leicestershire C.C. shows that B may enforce the contract in the sense in which A knew that B understood it. But was L'Estrange under any *mistake* as to the terms of the contract? She knew that the paper contained contractual terms. Did it not appear to Graucob (who was not guilty of fraud or misrepresentation), as well as to the reasonable fly on the wall that she was expressing her assent to those terms, whatever they might be?

TILDEN RENT-A-CAR CO. v. CLENDENNING

Ontario Court of Appeal (1978) 83 D.L.R. (3d) 400

The defendant rented a car from the plaintiff at Vancouver airport. The plaintiff's clerk asked him if he wanted "additional cover" and he said he did. He then signed the front of the contract under the words "I, the undersigned, have read and received a copy of above and reverse side of this contract." He did not read it in fact, as was apparent to the clerk. On the front of the contract it was stated that, in consideration of the payment of $2.00 per day, the customer's liability for damage to the car was limited to nil, but that the customer should be fully liable for collision damage if the vehicle was driven in violation of any provision of the rental agreement. On the reverse, conditions in small, faint type provided that the customer agreed that the vehicle would not be driven in violation of any law and would not be operated by any person who had consumed any intoxicating liquor, whatever the quantity. Subsequently the defendant drove the car into a pole and pleaded guilty to driving while intoxicated. The plaintiff's action in respect of damage to the vehicle was dismissed. He appealed.

DUBIN J.A., having referred to *L'Estrange v. Graucob*: *Consensus ad idem* is as much a part of the law of written contracts as it is of oral contracts. The signature to a contract is only one way of manifesting assent to contractual terms. However, in the case of *L'Estrange v. F. Graucob, Ltd*, there was in fact no *consesus ad idem* . . .

Although the subject of critical analysis by learned authors (see, for example, J.R. Spencer, "Signature, Consent, and the Rule in L'Estrange v. Graucob" [1973] C.L.J. 104), the case has survived, and it is now said that it applies to all contracts irrespective of the circumstances under which they are entered into, if they are signed by the party who seeks to escape their provisions.

Thus, it was submitted that the ticket cases, which in the circumstances of this case would afford a ready defence for the hirer of the automobile, are not applicable.

As is pointed out in Waddams, *The Law of Contracts*, at p. 191: From the 19th century until recent times an extraordinary status has been accorded to the signed document that will be seen in retrospect, it is suggested, to have been excessive.

The justification for the rule in *L'Estrange v. Graucob, Ltd*, appears to have been founded upon the objective theory of contracts, by which means parties are bound to a contract in writing by measuring their conduct by outward appearance rather than what the parties inwardly meant to decide. This, in turn, stems from the classic statement of Blackburn J. in *Smith v. Hughes* (1871) L.R. 6 Q.B. 597 at p. 607: . . .

Even accepting the objective theory to determine whether Mr Clendenning had entered into a contract which included all the terms of the written instrument, it is to be observed that an essential part of that test is whether the other party entered into the contract in the belief that Mr Clendenning was assenting to all such terms. In the instant case, it was apparent to the employee of Tilden Rent-A-Car that Mr Clendenning had not in fact read the document in its entirety before he signed it. It follows under such circumstances that Tilden Rent-A-Car cannot rely on provisions of the contract which it had no reason to believe were being assented to by the other contracting party.

As stated in Waddams, *The Law of Contracts*, p. 191: One who signs a written document cannot complain if the other party reasonably relies on the signature as a manifestation of assent to the contents, or ascribes to words he uses their reasonable meaning. But the other side of the same coin is that only a reasonable expectation will be protected. If the party seeking to enforce the document knew or had reason to know of the other's mistake the document should not be enforced.

In ordinary commercial practice where there is frequently a sense of formality in the transaction, and where there is a full opportunity for the parties to consider the terms of the proposed contract submitted for signature, it might well be safe to assume that the party who attaches his signature to the contract intends by so doing to acknowledge his acquiescence to its terms, and that the other party entered into the contract upon that belief. This can hardly be said, however, where the contract is entered into in circumstances such as were present in this case.

A transaction, such as this one, is invariably carried out in a hurried, informal manner. The speed with which the transaction is completed is said to be one of the attractive features of the services provided.

The clauses relied on in this case, as I have already stated, are inconsistent with the over-all purpose for which the contract is entered into by the hirer. Under such circumstances, something more should be done by the party submitting the contract for signature than merely handing it over to be signed. [The judge quoted from Lord Devlin in *McCutcheon v. MacBrayne*, below, p. 155.]

An analysis of the Canadian cases, however, indicates that the approach in this country has not been so rigid. In the case of *Colonial Investment Co. of Winnipeg, Man. v. Borland* [1911] 1 W.W.R. 171 at p. 189, [affirmed 6 D.L.R. 21], Beck J. set forth the following propositions:

> *Consensus ad idem* is essential to the creation of a contract, whether oral, in writing or under seal, subject to this, that as between the immediate parties (and merely voluntary assigns) apparent—as distinguished from real—consent will on the ground of estoppel effect a binding obligation unless the party denying the obligation proves:
>
> (1) That the other party knew at the time of the making of the alleged contract that the mind of the denying party did not accompany the expression of his consent; or
>
> (2) Such facts and circumstances as show that it was not reasonable and natural for the other party to suppose that the denying party was giving his real consent and he did not in fact give it;

In commenting on the *Colonial Investment Co. of Winnipeg v. Borland* case, Spencer, in the article above cited, observes at p. 121: It is instructive to compare a Canadian approach to the problem of confusing documents which are signed but not fully understood.

And at p. 122 the author concludes his article with the following analysis:

> Policy considerations, but of different kinds, no doubt lay behind both the Canadian and the English approaches to this problem. The Canadian court was impressed by the abuses which would result— and, in England, *have* resulted—from enabling companies to hold ignorant signatories to the letter of sweeping exemption clauses contained in contracts in standard form. The English courts, however, were much more impressed with the danger of furnishing an easy line of defence by which liars could evade contractual liabilities freely assumed. It would be very dangerous to allow a man over the age of legal infancy to escape from the legal effect of a document he has, after reading it, signed, in the absence of any express misrepresentation by the other party of that legal effect. Forty years later, most lawyers would admit that the English courts made a bad choice between two evils.

The significance of the circumstances under which a contract is entered into is noted by Taschereau J. in *Provident Savings Life Ass'ce Society of New York v. Mowat et al.* (1902) 32 S.C.R. 147, as follows at p. 162:
As remarked by Mr Justice Maclennan [27 O.A.R. 675]:

> "The case of a formal instrument like the present, prepared and executed, after a long negotiation, and correspondence delivered and accepted, and acted upon for years, is wholly different from the cases relating to railways and steamship and cloakroom tickets, in which it has been held that conditions qualifying the principal contract of carriage or bailment, not sufficiently brought to the attention of the passenger or bailor are not binding upon him. Such contracts are usually made in moments of more or less haste and confusion and stand by themselves."

I see no real distinction in contracts such as these, where the signature by itself does not truly represent an acquiescence of unusual and onerous terms which are inconsistent with the true object of the contract, and the ticket cases.

. . . In modern commercial practice, many standard form printed documents are signed without being read or understood. In many cases the parties seeking to rely on the terms of the contract know or ought to know that the signature of a party to the contract does not represent the true intention of the signer, and that the party signing is unaware of the stringent and onerous provisions which the standard form contains. Under such circumstances, I am of the opinion that the party seeking to rely on such terms should not be able to do so in the absence of first having taken reasonable measures to draw such terms to the attention of the other party, and, in the absence of such reasonable measures, it is not necessary for the party denying knowledge of such terms to prove either fraud, misrepresentation or *non est factum*.

In the case at bar, Tilden Rent-A-Car took no steps to alert Mr Clendenning to the onerous provisions in the standard form of contract presented by it. The clerk could not help but have known that Mr Clendenning had not in fact read the contract before signing it. Indeed the form of the contract itself with the important provisions on the reverse side and in very small type would discourage even the most cautious customer from endeavouring to read and understand it. Mr Clendenning was in fact unaware of the exempting provisions. Under such circumstances, it was not open to Tilden Rent-A-Car to rely on those clauses, and it was not incumbent on Mr Clendenning to establish fraud, misrepresentation or *non est factum*. Having paid the premium, he was not liable for any damage to the vehicle while being driven by him.

LACOURCIERE J.A. (dissenting), having read the conditions in the contract: These clauses are certainly not irrelevant or foreign to the contract. . . . They do not, for example, purport to exempt Tilden from any implied undertaking as to the road worthy fitness of the vehicle. They are not exemptions from common law liability or statutory liability. . . .

The clause is undoubtedly a strict one. It is not for a Court to nullify its effect by branding it unfair, unreasonable and oppressive. It may be perfectly sound and reasonable from an insurance risk viewpoint, and may indeed be necessary in the competitive business of car rentals, where rates are calculated on the basis of the whole contract. On this point, see the majority judgment delivered by Lord Wilberforce in *New Zealand Shipping Co. Ltd v. A. M. Satterthwaite & Co. Ltd* [1975] A.C. 154 at p. 169, where it was held that the Court must give effect to the clear intent of a commercial document.

I am of the view that, even if the respondent's signature is not conclusive, the terms of the contract are not unusual, oppressive or unreasonable and are binding on the respondent. I would, therefore, allow the appeal with costs, set aside the judgment below and in lieu thereof substitute a judgment for the amount of the agreed damages and costs.

ZUBER J.A. concurs with DUBIN J.A.

Appeal dismissed.

Questions
1. Does the case decide that, in a written but unread contract, clauses which are "stringent" or "onerous" are not binding but the other clauses are?
2. Would the result have been different if the defendant had signed the contract without reading it in the absence of the clerk who did not know whether it had been read or not?
3. Dubin J.A. refers to the "exempting provisions." Were they "exempting provisions?" Did it—or should it—matter? (In England today an exempting provision would have to satisfy the requirement of reasonableness under the Unfair Contract Terms Act 1977, below, p. 467, but the Act makes no such requirement in respect of other provisions.)
4. Was there "in fact no consensus ad idem" in *L'Estrange v. Graucob*? Would Dubin J.A. have held the contract to be void?
5. Did the case decide that the offending clause was not part of the contract? (". . . an essential part of [the objective theory] is whether the other party entered into the contract in the belief that Mr Clendenning was assenting to all such terms"—above p. 134). A ruling that the clause was not part of the contract would settle the matter; but if it were part of the contract, the question in England would now be whether the term, contrary to the requirement of good faith, "causes a significant imbalance in the parties obligations under

the contract to the detriment of the consumer": Unfair Terms Regulations, reg. 4(1), below, p. 716.

Notes

Interpretation of a written contract

(1) In construing a *written* contract, the court is entitled to take account of the circumstances with reference to which the words were used and the object, appearing from those circumstances, which the person using the words had in view; but it may not look at the prior negotiations of the parties as an aid to construction of the written contract resulting from those negotiations: *Prenn v. Simmonds* [1971] 1 W.L.R. 1381; [1971] 3 All E.R. 237, H.L. The reason for excluding evidence of the negotiations is "simply that such evidence is unhelpful. By the nature of things, where negotiations are difficult, the parties' positions, with each passing letter, are changing and until the final agreement, although converging, still divergent. It is only the final document which records a consensus. If the previous documents use different expressions, how does the construction of those expressions, itself a doubtful process, help on the construction of the contractual words? If the same expressions are used, nothing is gained by looking back; indeed something may be lost since the relevant surrounding circumstances may be different."

For an illustration, see *City and Westminster Properties v. Mudd* (below, p. 381) and compare *Roberts v. Leics C.C.* (above, p. 128).

What if the history of the negotiations would show that the parties intended to use a word in a special sense? *Cf.* Glanville Williams and note (1) (above, p. 127). Suppose the first letter says, "Let us agree that 'horsebeans' shall mean 'feveroles'"? Surely this ought to admissible?

(2) It is well settled that "it is not legitimate to use as an aid to the construction of the contract anything which the parties said or did after it was made. Otherwise one might have the result that a contract meant one thing the day it was signed, but by reason of subsequent events meant something different a month or a year later": *James Miller v. Whitworth Estates* [1970] 2 W.L.R. 728; [1970] 1 All E.R. 796 at p. 798, *per* Lord Reid. The House of Lords held that Denning M.R. and Widgery L.J. in the Court of Appeal had been wrong to have regard to the conduct of the parties after the contract was made in order to decide whether they intended the contract to be governed by English or Scottish law. But where both parties have acted on a common assumption as to the meaning of the contract, they will be "estopped by convention" from denying that the meaning on which they have acted is the true meaning.

(3) See *Staffs Area Health Authority v. South Staffs Waterworks* [1978] 3 All E.R. 769 for an interesting discussion and application of rules of construction.

Signature induced by misrepresentation

Where A induces B to enter into a contract with him by fraud or misrepresentation, the contract is voidable at B's option and so he has no difficulty in avoiding liability to A if he wishes to do so when he discovers the truth. If, however, before the contract is avoided, a third person, C, acquires rights under it for value and in good faith, B cannot avoid the contract against C, merely on the grounds of A's fraud or misrepresentation. B will be bound to C unless he can show that the contract with A was not merely voidable but void. If the contract was void, C could acquire no rights under it. Under the doctrine known as *Non est Factum*, "it is not my deed," a signed document may, in the circumstances considered in the following cases, be held to be void.

Section 4. Non est Factum

Non est factum is a doctrine of the common law originating in cases where illiterate or blind persons were induced to make deeds by fraud as to the nature of the document. The signer could, of course, repudiate the contract as against the person who deceived him on the ground of fraud but he could also plead *non est factum*—"it is not my deed"—against an innocent third party who had, or rather believed he had, acquired rights under the document for value. In the leading case of *Foster v. MacKinnon* (1869) L.R. 4 C.P. 704 the plaintiff, as indorsee of a bill of exchange for £3,000, sued the defendant (M) as indorser. There was a question whether the endorsement was the defendant's signature but a witness, Callow, stated that he had produced the bill to M, an elderly man, telling him that the document was a guarantee and that M signed the bill in that belief. Bovill L.C.J. told the jury that if M signed, not knowing that it was a bill and believing it to be a guarantee, and if he was not guilty of any negligence in so signing, he was entitled to the verdict. The jury found for M. The Court of Common Pleas held that this was a correct direction.

This doctrine was subsequently held to apply only where the person signing was misled, not merely as to the contents of the document he signed, but as to its class or character. It was possibly applicable in *Foster v. Mackinnon*, because a guarantee is plainly a document of a different character from a bill of exchange. But a person who signed a promissory note for £1,000, having been told it was a promissory note for £10, would not have been able to rely on the doctrine, because his mistake was merely to the contents—he knew the class of document he was signing.

If a person's mistake as to the character of the document he signed was due to his own negligence, then he might be precluded from relying on the defence of *non est factum*—but only, according to *Carlisle and Cumberland Banking Co. v. Bragg* [1911] 1 K.B. 489, if the document signed was in fact a negotiable instrument. In *Bragg's* case the Court of Appeal put a restrictive interpretation upon *Foster v. Mackinnon* (where the document signed was in fact a negotiable instrument) and held that the principle of that case did not apply where the defendant carelessly signed a guarantee of an overdraft, having been deceived into believing that he was witnessing an insurance document. Notwithstanding his negligence, Bragg successfully pleaded *non est factum* against the bank which had advanced money in reliance on his signature.

The doctrine, as summarised above, was reconsidered by the House of Lords in the following case.

GALLIE v. LEE AND ANOTHER

House of Lords [1971] A.C. 1004; [1970] 3 W.L.R. 1078; [1970] 3 All E.R. 961

Mrs Gallie, a widow aged 78, had made a will leaving her house to her nephew, Parkin. Lee, a friend of Parkin, was heavily in debt and discussed with Parkin how money might be raised on the house. In Parkin's presence, Lee put before Mrs Gallie a document which he told her was a deed of gift of the house to Parkin. Mrs Gallie did not read it because she had broken her spectacles. The deed was in fact a deed of sale of the house to Lee for £3,000, the receipt of which Mrs Gallie acknowledged in the deed but did not in fact receive.

Using this deed, Lee purported to mortgage the house to the second defendant, the Anglia Building Society, and borrowed £2,000. Lee defaulted in instalments on the mortgage and the building society sought to recover possession of the house. Mrs Gallie sued for a declaration that the deed was void—*non est factum*—and for the recovery of the title deeds.

STAMP J. found for the plaintiff: [1968] 2 All E.R. 322. He held that *a deed of gift to X* is a document of a totally different character or class from *a deed of sale to Y*. Mrs Gallie could plead *non est factum* and was not precluded from doing so by any carelessness on her part since the document signed was not a negotiable instrument.

THE COURT OF APPEAL unanimously allowed the appeal: [1969] 2 Ch. 17. DENNING M.R. rejected (i) the distinction between the class of the document and the contents of the document; (ii) the view that mistake as to the person renders the contract void (see below, p. 165 and (iii) the rule in *Bragg's* case that a party may be precluded by his negligence from setting up *non est factum* only where the document signed is a negotiable instrument. He applied the broad principle discussed below. RUSSELL and SALMON L.JJ., while disliking it, felt bound to apply the law as laid down in the earlier authorities (the Master of the Rolls "has sought to wield a broom labelled 'For the use of the House of Lords only'"—*per* RUSSELL L.J.). Applying existing principles, RUSSELL L.J. held (i) that Mrs Gallie had not satisfied the heavy onus of proving that she believed that the conveyance was a deed of gift when she signed it; and (ii) even if she did believe this, it was not a mistake as to the *character* of the document. In determining whether a mistake is as to character, regard must be had to "the object of the exercise." Mrs Gallie knew that the transaction was intended to divest her of her interest in the property, in pursuance of a joint project of Lee and Parkin to raise money on the security of it. The document in fact carried out the object which she intended it to carry out. SALMON L.J. held that the document was binding on Mrs Gallie because she would have executed it even if its true character and class had been explained to her. She was not concerned with the character of the document but was happy to sign anything which P advised her to sign.

Mrs Gallie appealed to the House of Lords.

LORD REID said that he was in general agreement with Lord Pearson. He concluded: I think that in the older authorities difference in practical result was more important than difference in legal character. If a man thinks that he is signing a document which will cost him £10 and the actual document would cost him £1,000 it could not be right to deny him this remedy simply because the legal character of the two was the same. It is true that we must then deal with questions of degree but that is a familiar task for the courts and I would not expect it to give rise to a flood of litigation.

There must I think be a radical difference between what he signed and what he thought he was signing—or one could use the words "fundamental" or "serious" or "very substantial." But what amounts to a radical difference will depend on all the circumstances. If he thinks he is giving property to A whereas the document gives it to B the difference may often be of vital importance, but in the circumstances of the present case I do not think that it is. I think that it must be left to the courts to determine in each case in light of all the facts whether there was or was not a sufficiently great difference. The plea *non est factum* is in sense illogical when applied to a case where the man in fact signed the deed. But it is none the worse for that if applied in a reasonable way.

I would dismiss this appeal.

LORD HODSON and VISCOUNT DILHORNE made speeches dismissing the appeal.

LORD WILBERFORCE: How, then, ought the principle, on which a plea of *non est factum* is admissible, to be stated? In my opinion, a document should be held to be void (as opposed to voidable) only when the element of consent to it is totally lacking; that is, more concretely, when the transaction which the document purports to effect is essentially different in substance or in kind from the transaction intended. Many other expressions, or adjectives, could be used—"basically" or "radically" or "fundamentally." In substance, the test does not differ from that which was applied in the leading cases of *Thoroughgood's Case* and *Foster v. Mackinnon*, except in moving from the character/contents distinction to an area better understood in modern practice.

To this general test it is necessary to add certain amplifications. First, there is the case of fraud. The law as to this is best stated in the words of the judgment in *Foster v. Mackinnon* where it is said that a signature obtained by fraud:

> ". . . is invalid not merely on the ground of fraud, where fraud exists, but on the ground that the mind of the signer did not accompany the signature; in other words, that he never intended to sign, and therefore in contemplation of law never did sign, the contract to which his name is appended."

In other words, it is the lack of consent that matters, not the means by which this result was brought about. Fraud by itself may do no more than make the contract voidable.

Secondly, a man cannot escape from the consequences, as regards innocent third parties, of signing a document if, being a man of ordinary education and competence, he chooses to sign it without informing himself of its purport and effect. This principle is sometimes found expressed in the language that "he is doing something with his estate" (*Hunter v. Walters* (1871) 7 Ch.App. 75, *Howatson v. Webb*) but it really reflects a rule of common sense on the exigency of busy lives.

Thirdly, there is the case where the signer has been careless, in not taking ordinary precautions against being deceived. This is a difficult area. Until 1911 the law was reasonably clear; it had been stated plainly in *Foster v. Mackinnon* that negligence—that is, carelessness—might deny the signer the benefit of the plea. Since *Bragg's* case was decided in 1911 (*Carlisle and Cumberland Banking Co. v. Bragg*) the law has been that, except in relation to negotiable instruments, mere carelessness is not disabling; there must be negligence arising from a duty of care to the third person who ultimately relies on the document. It does not need much force to demolish this battered precedent. It is sufficient to point to two major defects in it. First, it confuses the kind of careless conduct which disentitles a man from denying the effect of his signature with such legal negligence as entitles a person injured to bring an action in tort. The two are quite different things in standard and scope. Secondly, the judgment proceeds on a palpable misunderstanding of the judgment in *Foster v. Mackinnon*; for Byles J., so far from confining the relevance of negligence to negotiable instruments (as *Bragg's* case suggests), clearly thought that the signer of a negotiable instrument would be liable, negligence or no negligence, and that negligence was relevant in relation to documents other than negotiable instruments; for example, (as in the actual case before him) to a guarantee.

In my opinion, the correct rule, and that which in fact prevailed until *Bragg's* case, is that, leaving aside negotiable instruments to which special rules may apply, a person who signs a document, and parts with it so that it may come into other hands, has a responsibility, that of the normal man of prudence, to take care what he signs, which, if neglected, prevents him from denying his liability under the document according to its tenor. I would add that the onus of proof in this matter rests on him, that is, to prove that he acted carefully and not on the third party to prove the contrary. I consider therefore that *Carlisle and Cumberland Banking Co. v. Bragg* was wrong, both in the principle it states and in its decision, and that it should no longer be cited as an authority for any purpose.

The preceding paragraphs contemplate persons who are adult and literate: the conclusion as to such persons is that, while there are cases in which they may successfully plead *non est factum*, these cases will, in modern times, be rare. As to persons who are illiterate, or blind, or lacking in understanding, the law is in a dilemma. On the one hand, the law is traditionally, and rightly, ready to relieve them against hardship and imposition. On the other hand, regard has to be paid to the position of innocent third parties who cannot be expected, and often would have no means, to know the condition or status of the signer. I do not think that a defined solution can be provided for all cases. The law ought, in my opinion, to give relief if satisfied that consent was truly lacking but will require of signers even in this class that they act responsibly and carefully according to their circumstances in putting their signature to legal documents.

This brings me to the present case. The plaintiff was a lady of advanced age, but, as her evidence shows, by no means incapable physically or mentally. It certainly cannot be said that she did not receive sympathetic consideration or the benefit of much doubt from the judge as to the circumstances in which the assignment was executed. But accepting all of this, I am satisfied, with Russell L.J., that she fell short, very far short, of making the clear and satisfactory case which is required of those who seek to have a legal act declared void and of establishing a sufficient discrepancy between her intentions and her act. I am satisfied to adopt, without repetition, the analysis of the facts which appears in the judgment of Russell L.J. as well as that of my noble and learned friend, Lord Pearson.

I would dismiss the appeal.

LORD PEARSON: In my opinion, the plea of *non est factum* ought to be available in a proper case for the relief of a person who for permanent or temporary reasons (not limited to blindness or illiteracy) is not capable of both reading and sufficiently understanding the deed or other document to be signed. By "sufficiently understanding" I mean understanding at least to the point of detecting a fundamental difference between the actual document and the document as the signer had believed it to be. There must be a proper case for such relief. There would not be a proper case if (a) the signature of the document was brought about by negligence of the signer in failing to take precautions which he ought to have taken, or (b) the actual document was not fundamentally different from the document as the signer believed it to be. I will say something later about negligence and fundamental difference.

In the present case the plaintiff was not at the material time a person who could read, because on the facts found she had broken her spectacles and could not effectively read without them. In any case her evidence (unless it was deliberately false, which has not been argued) shows that she had very little capacity for understanding legal documents and property transactions, and I do not think a reasonable jury would have found she was negligent. In my opinion, it would not be right to dismiss the plaintiffs appeal on the ground that the principle stated by the Master of the Rolls is applicable to her case. I do not think it is.

The principle as stated is limited to a case in which it is apparent on the face of the document that it is intended to have legal consequences. That allows for possible success of the plea in a case such as *Lewis v. Clay* (1897) 67 L.J. Q.B. 224, where Clay had been induced to sign promissory notes by the cunning deception of a false friend, who caused him to believe that he was merely witnessing the friend's signature on several private and highly confidential documents, the material parts of which had been covered up. . . .

Suppose that the very busy managing director of a large company has a pile of documents to be signed in a few minutes before his next meeting, and his secretary has arranged them for maximum speed with only the spaces for signature exposed, and he "signs them blind," as the saying is, not reading them or even looking at them. He may be exercising a wise economy of his time and energy. There is the possibility of some extraneous document, involving him in unexpected personal liability, having been fraudulently inserted in the pile, but this possibility is so improbable that a reasonable man would disregard it: *Bolton v. Stone* [1951] A.C. 850, 858. Such conduct is not negligence in any ordinary sense of the word. But the person who signs documents in this way ought to be held bound by them, and ought not to be entitled to avoid liability so as to shift the burden of loss on to an innocent third party. The whole object of having documents signed by him is that he makes them his documents and takes responsibility for them. He takes the chance of a fraudulent substitution. I think the right view of such a case is that the person who signs intends to sign the documents placed before him, whatever they may be, and so there is no basis on which he could successfully plead *non est factum.* . . .

Salmon L.J. has said in his judgment in this case [1969] 2 Ch. 17, 48: "If, . . . a person signs a document because he negligently failed to read it, I think he is precluded from relying on his own negligent act for the purpose of escaping from the ordinary consequences of his signature. In such circumstances he cannot succeed on a plea of *non est factum.* This is not in my view a true estoppel, but an illustration of the principle that no man may take advantage of his own wrong."

I agree.

The degree of difference required: The judgments in the older cases used a variety of expressions to signify the degree or kind of difference that, for the purposes of the plea of *non est factum,* must be shown to exist between the document as it was and the document as it was believed to be. More recently there has been a tendency to draw a firm distinction between (a) a difference in character or class, which is sufficient for the purposes of the plea, and (b) a difference only in contents, which is not sufficient. This distinction has been helpful in some cases, but, as the judgments of the Court of Appeal have shown, it would produce wrong results if it were applied as a rigid rule for all cases. In my opinion, one has to use a more general phrase, such as "fundamentally different" or "radically different" or "totally different."

I would dismiss the appeal.

Appeal dismissed.

Questions
1. What test replaces the distinction between "contents" and "class or character"?
2. Would the following mistakes pass the new test so as to found the plea? (a) D, believing he is witnessing a proposal of insurance, signs a guarantee of X's overdraft with the P. Bank. (b) D signs a contract to hire a car, believing that he is signing a contract for the hire-purchase of the car. (c) D signs a contract to sell a two-acre plot of land, believing that the contract relates to only half an acre of the plot. (*Cf. Hasham v. Zenab* [1960] A.C. 316, P.C., where it was held that the defence was not available because the mistake was not induced by fraud.)
3. Are estoppel and negligence separate grounds on which a person who has made a fundamental mistake may be precluded from relying on the defence? May estoppel be effective against a signer who has not been negligent?
Cf. Professor Stone, "Non Est Factum after *Gallie v. Lee*" (1972) 88 L.Q.R. 190.

NORWICH AND PETERBOROUGH BUILDING SOCIETY v. STEED (NO. 2)

Court of Appeal [1993] Ch. 116; [1992] 3 W.L.R. 669; [1993] 1 All E.R. 330

The appellant, Mr Steed, allowed his mother, his sister and her husband to live in his house while he was living in the United States. The sister and her husband persuaded him to execute a power of attorney in favour of his mother. They then tricked Mrs Steed into executing a transfer of the house to them and, on the same day, borrowed £15,000 from the building society on the security of the property. When they defaulted, the society brought an action for possession of the house. The appellant, who was joined as a party, claimed, inter alia, that he was entitled to rely on *non est factum*. The Court of Appeal did not agree.

SCOTT L.J.: Mr Lloyd Q.C. for the appellant has attacked this part of the judgment by relying heavily on the proposition that Mrs Steed did not know anything about the power of attorney and her status thereunder. In that state of ignorance she could not, when she signed the transfer, have known she was dealing with her son's property. She must have supposed she was dealing, in some way, with her own affairs. So, it was argued, she was mistaken as to the essential character of the document she signed and of the transaction which it effected.

Submissions on these lines, as Butler-Sloss L.J. pointed out during argument, placed Mr Steed on a species of Morton's fork. Let it be supposed that Mrs Steed was a lady of sufficient general understanding and capability to be a suitable donee of the power of appointment. Why then did she not inform herself of the purport and effect of the transfer before signing it? Her failure to do so brings the case within the second of Lord Wilberforce's amplifications. (See p. 140 above.) On the other hand, let it be supposed that she lacked ordinary competence and capacity. Lord Wilberforce referred to persons 'illiterate, or blind, or lacking in understanding'. If Mrs Steed falls into this category, what was Mr Steed about when he appointed her his attorney? The donor of a power of attorney who appoints as his attorney a person incapable of understanding the import of a simple transfer can hardly be allowed, if the donee signs a transfer without any understanding of what he or she is doing, to repudiate the transfer on the ground of a lack of understanding on the part of the donee.

As to Mrs Steed's ignorance of the power of attorney, if she was ignorant of it, the ignorance was attributable to Mr Steed's incomprehensible failure to tell her either that he was about to or that he had made the appointment. It is known that he and she spoke on the telephone at about the time the power of attorney was executed. If it was really the case that he did not mention the power of attorney when speaking to her on that occasion and left her in ignorance of her responsibilities and status, his failure shows, in my opinion, such a want of care as to preclude him from relying, in support of his *non est factum* plea, on her ignorance of the power. As between an innocent third party purchaser such as the building society on the one hand and Mr Steed on the other hand, his failure to take the ordinary precautionary and prudent step of informing his mother of her appointment as his attorney requires, in my judgment, that the building society be preferred. In my judgment, and for substantially the same reasons as those given by the learned judge, the *non est factum* plea fails.

Section 5. Incorporation of Written Terms in Oral Contracts

Cases in this section must be read in the light of the Unfair Contract Terms Act 1977 and the Unfair Terms in Consumer Contract Regulations, below, p. 467 and p. 704.

PARKER v. SOUTH EASTERN RY.

Court of Appeal (1877) 2 C.P.D. 416; 46 L.J.Q.B. 768; 36 L.T. 540; 41 J.P. 644; 25 W.R. 564

The plaintiff deposited a bag in a cloak-room at the defendants' railway station, paid the clerk 2d. and received a paper ticket on which were printed a number and a date and notices as to when the office would be open, and the words "See back." On the other side were printed several clauses including "The company will not be responsible for any package exceeding the value of £10." The plaintiff presented his ticket on the same day, but his bag could not be found. He claimed £24 10s. as the value of his bag, and the company pleaded that they had accepted the goods on the condition that they would not be responsible if the value exceeded £10. The questions left by Pollock B. to the jury were: (1) Did the plaintiff read or was he aware of the special condition upon which the articles were deposited? (2) Was the plaintiff, under the circumstances, under any obligation, in the exercise of reasonable and proper caution, to read or make himself aware of the condition? The jury answered both questions in the negative and the judge directed judgment to be entered for the plaintiff. The defendants moved to enter judgment and obtained an order nisi for a new trial on the ground of misdirection. The order was discharged and the motion refused by the Common Pleas Division. The defendants appealed.

MELLISH L.J.: In this case we have to consider whether a person who deposits in the cloak-room of a railway company, articles which are lost through the carelessness of the company's servants, is prevented from recovering, by a condition on the back of the ticket, that the company would not be liable for the loss of goods exceeding the value of £10. It was argued on behalf of the railway company that the company's servants were only authorised to receive goods on behalf of the company upon the terms contained in the ticket; and a passage from Blackburn J.'s judgment in *Harris v. Great Western Ry.*, 1 Q.B.D. 515 at p. 533, was relied on in support of their contention: "I doubt much—inasmuch as the railway company did not authorise their servants to receive goods for deposit on any other terms, and as they had done nothing to lead the plaintiff to believe that they had given such authority to their servants so as to preclude them from asserting, as against her, that the authority was so limited—whether the true rule of law is not that the plaintiff must assent to the contract intended by the defendants to be authorised, or treat the case as one in which there was no contract at all, and consequently no liability for safe custody." I am of opinion that this objection cannot prevail. It is clear that the company's servants did not exceed the authority given them by the company. They did the exact thing they were authorised to do. They were authorised to receive articles on deposit as bailees on behalf of the company, charging 2d. for each article, and delivering a ticket properly filled up to the person leaving the article. This is exactly what they did in the present case, and whatever may be the legal effect of what was done, the company must, in my opinion, be bound by it. The directors may have thought, and no doubt did think, that delivering the ticket to the person depositing the article would be sufficient to make him bound by the conditions contained in the ticket, and if they were mistaken in that, the company must bear the consequence.

The question then is, whether the plaintiff was bound by the conditions contained in the ticket. In an ordinary case, where an action is brought on a written agreement which is signed by the defendant, the agreement is proved by proving his signature, and, in the absence of fraud, it is wholly immaterial that he has not read the agreement and does not know its contents. The parties may, however, reduce their agreement into writing, so that the writing constitutes the sole evidence of the agreement, without signing it; but in that case there must be evidence independently of the agreement itself to prove that the defendant has assented to it. In that case, also, if it is proved that the defendant has assented to the writing constituting the agreement between the parties, it is, in the absence of fraud, immaterial that the defendant had not read the agreement and did not know its contents. Now if in the course of making a contract one party delivers to another a paper containing writing, and the party receiving the paper knows that the paper contains conditions which the party delivering it intends to constitute the contract, I have no doubt that the party receiving the paper does, by receiving and keeping it, assent to the conditions contained in it, although he does not read them, and does not know what they are. I hold, therefore, that the case of *Harris v. Great Western Rly.* was rightly decided, because in that case the plaintiff admitted, on cross-examination, that she believed there were some conditions on the ticket. On the other hand, the case *of Henderson v. Stevenson*, L.R. 2 Sc. & Div. 470, is a conclusive authority that if the person receiving the ticket does not know that there is any writing upon the back of the ticket, he is not bound by a condition printed on the back. The facts in the cases before us differ from those in both *Henderson v. Stevenson* and *Harris v. Great Western Rly.*, because in both the cases which have been argued before us, though the plaintiffs admitted that they knew there was writing on the back of the ticket, they swore not only that they did not read it, but that they did not know or believe that the writing contained conditions, and we are to consider whether, under those circumstances, we can lay down as a matter of law either that the plaintiff is bound or that he is not bound by the conditions contained in the ticket, or whether his being bound depends on some question of fact to be determined by the jury, and if so, whether, in the present case, the right question was left to the jury.

Now, I am of the opinion that we cannot lay down, as a matter of law, either that the plaintiff was bound or that he was not bound by the conditions printed on the ticket, from the mere fact that he knew there was writing on the ticket, but did not know that the writing contained conditions. I think there may be cases in which a paper containing writing is delivered by one party to another in the course of a business transaction, where it would be quite reasonable that the party receiving it should assume that the writing contained in it no condition, and should put it in his pocket unread. For instance, if a person driving through a turnpike-gate received a ticket upon paying the toll, he might reasonably assume that the object of the ticket was that by producing it he might be free from paying toll at some other turnpike-gate, and might put it in his pocket unread. On the other hand, if a person who ships goods to be carried on a voyage by sea receives a bill of lading signed by the master, he would plainly be bound by it, although afterwards, in an action against the shipowner for the loss of the goods, he might swear that he had never read the bill of lading, and that he did not know that it contained the terms of the contract of carriage, and that the shipowner was protected by the exceptions contained in it. Now the reason why the person receiving the bill of lading would be bound seems to me to be that in the great majority of cases persons shipping goods do know that the bill of lading contains the terms of the contract of carriage; and the shipowner, or the master delivering the bill of lading, is entitled to assume that the person shipping goods has that knowledge. It is, however, quite possible to suppose that a person who is neither a man of business nor a lawyer might on some particular occasion ship goods without the least knowledge of what a bill of lading was, but in my opinion such a person must bear the consequences of his own exceptional ignorance, it being plainly impossible that business could be carried on if every person who delivers a bill of lading had to stop to explain what a bill of lading was.

Now the question we have to consider is whether the railway company were entitled to assume that a person depositing luggage, and receiving a ticket in such a way that he could see that some writing was printed on it, would understand that the writing contained the conditions of contract, and this seems to me to depend upon whether people in general would in fact, and naturally, draw that inference. The railway company, as it seems to me, must be entitled to make some assumptions respecting the person who deposits luggage with them: I think they are entitled to assume that he can read, and that he understands the English language, and that he pays such attention to what he is about as may be reasonably expected from a person in such a transaction as that of depositing luggage in a cloak-room. The railway company must, however, take mankind as they find them, and if what they do is sufficient to inform people in general that the ticket contains conditions, I think that a particular plaintiff ought not to be in a better position than other persons on account of his exceptional ignorance or stupidity or carelessness. But if what the railway company do is not sufficient to convey to the minds of people in general that the ticket contains conditions, then they have received goods on deposit without obtaining the consent of the persons depositing them to the conditions limiting their liability. I am of opinion, therefore, that the proper direction to leave to the jury in these cases is, that if the person receiving the ticket did not see or know that there was any writing on the ticket, he is not bound by the conditions; that if he knew there was writing, and knew or believed that the writing contained conditions, then he is bound by the conditions; that if he knew there was writing on the ticket, but did not know or believe that the writing contained conditions, nevertheless he would be bound, if the delivering of the ticket to him in such a manner that he could see there was writing upon it, was, in the opinion of the jury, reasonable notice that the writing contained conditions.

I have lastly to consider whether the direction of the learned judge was correct, namely, "Was the plaintiff, under the circumstances, under any obligation, in the exercise of reasonable and proper caution, to read or to make himself aware of the condition?" I think that this direction was not strictly accurate, and was calculated to mislead the jury. The plaintiff was certainly under no obligation to read the ticket, but was entitled to leave it unread if he pleased, and the question does not appear to me to direct the attention of the jury to the real question, namely, whether the railway company did what was reasonably sufficient to give the plaintiff notice of the condition.

On the whole, I am of opinion that there ought to be a new trial.

BAGGALLAY L.J. delivered a concurring judgment, while BRAMWELL L.J. held that the question was one of law and judgment ought to be entered for the defendants.

Order absolute for a new trial.

Notes
1. The dictum of Mellish L.J. regarding the turnpike ticket was followed in *Chapelton v. Barry Urban District Council* [1940] 1 K.B. 532, C.A., where the plaintiff received two tickets on taking two deck chairs for which he paid 4d. On the back of the ticket were printed words purporting to exempt the council from liability. They were held ineffective. The ticket was a mere receipt; its object was that the hirer might produce it to prove that he had paid and to show him how long he might use the chair. Slesser L.J. pointed out that a person might sit in one of these chairs for an hour or two before an attendant came round to take his money and give him a receipt.

In *Olley v. Marlborough Court* [1949] 1 K.B. 532 a similar point formed the *ratio decidendi* of the case. It was held that a notice in an hotel bedroom purporting to exempt the proprietors of the defendant hotel from liability for the loss of guests' luggage was not incorporated in the contract between the proprietors and a guest. The contract was made in the hall of the hotel before the plaintiff entered her bedroom and before she had an opportunity to see the notice.

In *Mendelssohn v. Normand Ltd* [1970] 1 Q.B. 177, C.A., the plaintiff had frequently garaged his car at the defendants' garage and always received a ticket which stated that the defendants "will not accept responsibility for any loss or damage sustained by the vehicle, its accessories or contents, however caused." "He may not have read it. But that does not matter. It was plainly a contractual document; and, as he accepted it without objection, he must be taken to have agreed to it"—*per* Lord Denning. (Contrast *Thornton v. Shoe Lane Parking*, below, p. 148.) The plaintiff on previous occasions had locked his car but on this occasion was prevented by the attendant from doing so; he pointed out that the car contained valuable property. The attendant said it was the rule that the car be left unlocked but if the plaintiff would leave the key he would lock the car as soon as he had moved it. The car was unlocked when the plaintiff returned and property had been stolen. Held: notwithstanding the condition in the contract, the defendants were liable because—

(i) The promise to lock up the car was within the ostensible authority of the attendant, was binding on the defendants and took priority over the written condition. (*Cf. Curtis v. Chemical, etc. Co.*, below, p. 446.)

(ii) defendants had agreed to keep the car locked up; instead they left it unlocked.

"This was so entirely different a way of carrying out the contract that the exemption clause cannot be construed as extending to it."—*per* Lord Denning. (*Cf.* below, p. 447.)

2. In *Thompson v. London Midland & Scottish Rly. Co.* [1930] 1 K.B. 41 the plaintiff who could not read gave her niece, A, the money to buy a ticket for an excursion from Manchester to Darwen. A did so. On the face of the ticket was printed "Excursion, For Conditions see back"; and on the back, "Issued subject to the conditions and regulations in the company's time-tables and notices and excursion and other bills." The excursion bills referred to the conditions in the company's timetables, which provided that excursion ticket holders should have no right of action against the company in respect of any injury, however caused. There was only one copy of the time-tables in the booking office and it cost 6d. to buy one. The plaintiff sustained an injury on Darwen station. At the trial the judge left to the jury the question whether the defendants had taken reasonable steps to bring the conditions to the notice of the plaintiff. The jury found that they had not and assessed damages at £176. The judge nevertheless entered judgment for the defendants.

The Court of Appeal held that the judge was right. The Court thought that the verdict of the jury was probably based on the fact that the passenger had to make a considerable search to find the conditions; but that was no answer. There was no evidence on which the jury could find that the company did not take reasonable steps to bring the conditions to the notice of the plaintiff. Lord Hanworth M.R. said that the company had made an offer to intending passengers to carry them on terms which could be ascertained and that offer had been accepted. Anyone who took the ticket was conscious that there were some conditions and it was obvious that the company did not provide for 2s. 7d. (the price of an excursion ticket) what it provided for the usual fare of 5s. 4d. Having regard to the condition of education in this country, it was irrelevant that the plaintiff could not read. Lawrence and Sankey L.JJ. both said that it would have been different if the condition had been unreasonable to the knowledge of the company; but this condition was not unreasonable.

If the condition had applied to regular, as well as excursion services, might the notice have been held to be insufficient?

Consider the effect of the UTCC Regulations 5(1) and Sched. 3 sub-para. 1(i), below, p. 715.

Questions

1. "*Henderson v. Stevenson*, 2 Sc. & Div. 470, is a conclusive authority that if the person receiving the ticket does not know that there is any writing upon the back of the ticket, he is not bound by a condition printed on the back" (*per* Mellish L.J., above, p. 145). The ticket in that case was "complete upon the face of it" and did not refer to the conditions printed on the back. Could a plaintiff rely on his ignorance of the writing on the back of a ticket if any person who "pays such attention to what he is about as may reasonably be expected" would necessarily have known of it?

2. Is a blind man bound by the conditions printed on a ticket in such a way that a person with normal sight could not fail to know of them?

3. "I ask for a ticket to Aberdeen: the clerk in error gives me a ticket for Aberdovey: the inspector points out the error. I cannot get my money back because I have contracted for conveyance to Aberdovey: the ticket constitutes the offer and Aberdovey is printed on it. I must buy another ticket for Aberdeen." (J. D. I. Hughes, "The Constructive Acceptance of Uncommunicated Offers" 47 L.Q.R. 459, 463.) Do you agree?

THORNTON v. SHOE LANE PARKING LTD

Court of Appeal [1971] 2 Q.B. 163; [1971] 2 W.L.R. 585; [1971] 1 All E.R. 686; [1971] R.T.R. 79; [1971] 1 Lloyd's Rep. 289

The plaintiff drove into the entrance to the defendants' car park where a notice stated. "All cars parked at owner's risk." A light changed from red to green as he drove in. He took a ticket from a machine and drove into the garage. He looked at the ticket to see the time printed on it and saw other printed wording which he did not read. When the plaintiff collected the car, there was an accident in which he suffered personal injuries, partly through the negligence of the defendants. The defendants relied on the ticket which stated that it was "issued subject to the conditions of issue as displayed on the premises." Conditions displayed *inside* the garage stated that, "The customer is deemed to be fully insured . . ." and that the defendants should not be liable for any loss, mis-delivery of or damage to the vehicle or injury to the customer. Mocatta J. held that the defendants were liable. They appealed.

LORD DENNING M.R., having referred, *inter alia*, to *Parker v. South Eastern Railway* (above, p. 144), *McCutcheon v. MacBrayne* (below, p. 155) and *Thompson v. L.M.S.* (above, p. 148) continued:

None of those cases has any application to a ticket which is issued by an automatic machine. The customer pays his money and gets a ticket. He cannot refuse it. He cannot get his money back. He may protest to the machine, even swear at it. But it will remain unmoved. He is committed beyond recall. He was committed at the very moment when he put his money into the machine. The contract was concluded at that time. It can be translated into offer and acceptance in this way: the offer is made when the proprietor of the machine holds it out as being ready to receive the money. The acceptance takes place when the customer puts his money into the slot. The terms of the offer are contained in the notice placed on or near the machine stating what is offered for the money. The customer is bound by those terms as long as they are sufficiently brought to his notice before-hand but not otherwise. He is not bound by the terms printed on the ticket if they differ from the notice, because the ticket comes too late. The contract has already been made: see *Olley v. Marlborough Court, Ltd* (above, p. 147). The ticket is no more than a voucher or receipt for the money that has been paid (as in the deckchair case, *Chapelton v. Barry Urban District Council* (above, p. 147), on terms which have been offered and accepted before the ticket is issued.

In the present case the offer was contained in the notice at the entrance giving the charges for garaging and saying "at owner's risk," that is, at the risk of the owner so far as damage to the car was concerned. The offer was accepted when Mr Thornton drove up to the entrance and, by the movement of his car, turned the light from red to green, and the ticket was thrust at him. The contract was then concluded, and it could not be altered by any words printed on the ticket itself. In particular, it could not be altered so as to exempt the company from liability for personal injury due to their negligence.

Assuming, however, that an automatic machine is a booking clerk in disguise—so that the old-fashioned ticket cases still apply to it. We then have to go back to the three questions[1] put by Mellish L.J. in *Parker v. South Eastern Railway Co.*, subject to this qualification: Mellish L.J. used the word "conditions" in the plural, whereas it would be more apt to use the word "condition" in the singular, as indeed the lord justice himself did on the next page. After all, the only condition that matters for this purpose is the exempting condition. It is no use telling the customer that the ticket

---

[1] See Lord Hodson's analysis of *Parker's* case, quoted by Megaw L.J., below, p. 150.

is issued subject to some "conditions" or other, without more: for he may reasonably regard "conditions" in general as merely regulatory, and not as taking away his rights, unless the exempting condition is drawn specifically to his attention. (Alternatively, if the plural "conditions" is used, it would be better prefaced with the word "exempting," because the exempting conditions are the only conditions that matter for this purpose.) Telescoping the three questions, they come to this: the customer is bound by the exempting condition if he knows that the ticket is issued subject to it; or, if the company did what was reasonably sufficient to give him notice of it.

Mr Machin admitted here that the company did not do what was reasonably sufficient to give Mr Thornton notice of the exempting condition. That admission was properly made. I do not pause to inquire whether the exempting condition is void for unreasonableness. All say is that it is so wide and so destructive of rights that the court should not hold any man bound by it unless it is drawn to his attention in the most explicit way. It is an instance of what I had in mind in *J. Spurling, Ltd v. Bradshaw* [1956] 1 W.L.R. 461, 466. In order to give sufficient notice, it would need to be printed in red ink with a red hand pointing to it—or something equally startling. (Lord Denning rejected an argument that the plaintiff knew that the writing contained conditions—the burden of proof was on the defendants and there was no finding to that effect—and said that he would dismiss the appeal.)

MEGAW L.J.: For myself, I would reserve a final view on the question at what precise moment of time the contract was concluded . . .

The essence of the decision in *Parker v. South Eastern Railway Co.* was analysed by Lord Hodson in *McCutcheon v. David MacBrayne, Ltd* as follows: "That case, affirmed in *Hood v. Anchor Line (Henderson Brothers) Ltd* [1918] A.C. 837, established that the appropriate questions for the jury in a ticket case were: (1) Did the passenger know that there was printing on the railway ticket? (2) Did he know that the ticket contained or referred to conditions? and (3) Did the railway company do what was reasonable in the way of notifying prospective passengers of the existence of conditions and where their terms might be considered?"

[The judge held that the first and second questions must be answered in the negative.]

So I come to the third of the three questions. That question, if I may return to the speech of Lord Dunedin in *Hood v. Anchor Line (Henderson Brothers) Ltd* was posed by him in this way: "Accordingly it is in each case a question of circumstance whether the sort of restriction that is expressed in any writing (which, of course, includes printed matter) is a thing that is usual, and whether, being usual, it has been fairly brought before the notice of the accepting party."

That, though it is more fully stated by Lord Dunedin, is essentially the same question, I think, as was formulated by Mellish L.J. in *Parker's* case, at the very end of his judgment, where he said that the question which ought to have been left to the jury was: whether the railway company did what was reasonably sufficient to give the plaintiff notice of *the condition*. (I emphasise the use by Mellish L.J. of the definite article and of the word "condition" in the singular.) I agree with Lord Denning M.R. that the question here is of the particular condition on which the defendants seek to rely, and not of the conditions in general.

When the conditions sought to be attached all constitute, in Lord Dunedin's words, "the sort of restriction . . . that is usual," it may not be necessary for a defendant to prove more than that the intention to attach *some* conditions has been fairly brought to the notice of the other party. But at least where the particular condition relied on involves a sort of restriction that is not shown to be usual in that class of contract, a defendant must show that his intention to attach an unusual condition *of that particular nature* was fairly brought to the notice of the other party. How much is required as being, in the words of Mellish L.J., "reasonably sufficient to give the plaintiff notice of the condition," depends upon the nature of the restrictive condition.

In the present case what has to be sought in answer to the third question is whether the defendant company did what was reasonable fairly to bring to the notice of the plaintiff, at or before the time when the contract was made, the existence of this particular condition. This condition is that part of the clause—a few words embedded in a lengthy clause—which Lord Denning M.R. has read, by which, in the midst of provisions as to damage to property, the defendants sought to exempt themselves from liability for any personal injury suffered by the customer while he was on their premises. Be it noted that such a condition is one which involves the abrogation of the right given to a person such as the plaintiff by statute, the Occupiers' Liability Act, 1957. True, it is open under that statute for the occupier of property by a contractual term to exclude that liability. In my view, however, before it can be said that a condition of that sort, restrictive of statutory rights, has been fairly brought to the notice of a party to a contract there must be some clear indication which would lead an ordinary sensible person to realise, at or before the time of making the contract, that a term of that sort, relating to personal injury, was sought to be included. I certainly would not accept that the position has been reached today in which it is to be assumed as a matter of general knowledge, custom, practice, or whatever is the phrase that is chosen to describe it, that when one is invited to go upon the property of another for such purposes as garaging a car, a contractual term is normally included that if one suffers any injury on those premises as a result of negligence on the part of the occupiers of the premises they shall not be liable.

Even if I were wrong in the view which I take that the third question has to be posed in relation to this particular term, it would still not avail the defendants here. In my view the judge was wholly right on the evidence in the conclusion which he reached that the defendants have not taken proper or adequate steps fairly to bring to the notice of the plaintiff at or before the time when the contract was made that *any* special conditions were sought to be imposed.

I think it is a highly relevant factor in considering whether proper steps were taken fairly to bring that matter to the notice of the plaintiff that the first attempt to bring to his notice the intended inclusion of those conditions was at a time when as a matter of hard reality it would have been practically impossible for him to withdraw from his intended entry upon the premises for the purpose of leaving his car there. It does not take much imagination to picture the indignation of the defendants if their potential customers, having taken their tickets and observed the reference therein to contractual conditions which, they said, could be seen in notices on the premises, were one after the other to get out of their cars, leaving the cars blocking the entrances to the garage, in order to search for, find and peruse the notices! Yet unless the defendants genuinely intended that potential customers should do just that, it would be fiction, if not farce, to treat those customers as persons who have been given a fair opportunity, before the contracts are made, of discovering the conditions by which they are to be bound.

I agree that this appeal should be dismissed.

SIR GORDON WILLMER: It seems to me that the really distinguishing feature of this case is the fact that the ticket on which reliance is placed was issued out of an automatic machine. I think it is right to say—at any rate, it is the fact so far as the cases that have been called to our attention are concerned—that in all the previous so-called "ticket cases" the ticket has been proffered by a human hand, and there has always been at least the notional opportunity for the customer to say—if he did not like the conditions—"I do not like your conditions: I will not have this ticket." But in the case of a ticket which is proffered by an automatic machine there is something quite irrevocable about the process. There can be no *locus poenitentiae*. I do not propose to say any more upon the difficult question which has been raised as to the precise moment when a contract was concluded in this case; but at least it seems to me that any attempt to introduce conditions after the irrevocable step has been taken of causing the machine to operate must be doomed to failure. It may be that those who operate garages of this nature, as well as those who instal other types of automatic machines, should give their attention to this problem. But it seems to me that the judge below was on the right track when he said, towards the end of his judgment, that in this sort of case, if you do desire to impose upon your customers stringent conditions such as these, the least you can do is to post a prominent notice at the entrance to the premises, warning your customers that there are conditions which will apply.

Appeal dismissed with costs.

Questions
1. "Does the law applicable to the purchase of a ticket from a machine in the Underground differ from the law applicable to the purchase of a similar ticket from the clerk in the booth?" (A. L. G. in a note in 87 L.Q.R. 296, 298.)
2. A ticket contains a number of conditions, ranging in nature from the very unusual and far-reaching to the commonplace. Is it possible that the ticket constitutes notice of some but not all of the conditions?

INTERFOTO PICTURE LIBRARY LTD v. STILETTO VISUAL PROGRAMMES LTD

Court of Appeal [1989] Q.B. 433; [1988] 2 W.L.R. 615; [1988] 1 All E.R. 348

The plaintiffs ran a library of photographic transparencies. The defendants required photographs of the 1950's for a client. In response to a telephone inquiry by the defendants (with whom they had not dealt previously) the plaintiffs, on March 5, delivered a bag of 47 transparencies with a delivery note. This clearly stated that the transparencies were to be returned by March 19. Under the prominently printed Heading, "Conditions," Condition 2 stated that all transparencies were to be returned within 14 days from the date of delivery and that "A holding fee of £5.00 plus VAT per day will be charged for each transparency which is retained by you longer than the said period of 14 days." It is unlikely that the defendants read any of the conditions but a director, Mr Beeching, telephoned that one or two of the transparencies could be of interest and that he would get back to them within a few days. He did not do so. The defendants did not use any of the transparencies but put them aside and forgot about them until April 2 when they were returned. The plaintiffs claimed £3,783.50, being the holding charge at £5 per transparency per day from March 19 to April 2. The defendants refused to pay. The judge gave judgment for the plaintiffs. The defendants appealed.

DILLON L.J., having held that a contract was made when Mr Beeching telephoned and having discussed *Parker v. South Eastern Railway Co.*, above, p. 144 and *Thornton v. Shoe Lane Parking Ltd*, above p. 148, continued:

Counsel for the plaintiffs submits that *Thornton v. Shoe Lane Parking Ltd* was a case of an exemption clause and that what their Lordships said must be read as limited to exemption clauses and in particular exemption clauses which would deprive the party on whom they are imposed of statutory rights. But what their Lordships said was said by way of interpretation and application of the general statement of the law by Mellish L.J. in *Parker v. South Eastern Rly. Co.* and the logic of it is applicable to any particularly onerous clause in a printed set of conditions of the one contracting party which would not be generally known to the other party.

Condition 2 of these plaintiffs' conditions is in my judgment a very onerous clause. The defendants could not conceivably have known, if their attention was not drawn to the clause, that the plaintiffs were proposing to charge a "holding fee" for the retention of the transparencies at such a very high and exorbitant rate.

At the time of the ticket cases in the last century it was notorious that people hardly ever troubled to read printed conditions on a ticket or delivery note or similar document. That remains the case now. In the intervening years the printed conditions have tended to become more and more complicated and more and more one-sided in favour of the party who is imposing them, but the other parties, if they notice that there are printed conditions at all, generally still tend to assume that such conditions are only concerned with ancillary matters of form and are not of importance. In the ticket cases the courts held that the common law required that reasonable steps be taken to draw the other parties' attention to the printed conditions or they would not be part of the contract. It is in my judgment a logical development of the common law into modern conditions that it should be held, as it was in *Thornton v. Shoe Lane Parking Ltd*, that, if one condition in a set of printed conditions is particularly onerous or unusual, the party seeking to enforce it must show that that particular condition was fairly brought to the attention of the other party.

In the present case, nothing whatever was done by the plaintiffs to draw the defendants' attention particularly to condition 2; it was merely one of four columns' width of conditions printed across the foot of the delivery note. Consequently condition 2 never, in my judgment, became part of the contract between the parties.

I would therefore allow this appeal and reduce the amount of the judgment which the judge awarded against the defendants to the amount which he would have awarded on a quantum meruit on his alternative findings, that is, the reasonable charge of £3.50 per transparency per week for the retention of the transparencies beyond a reasonable period, which he fixed at 14 days from the date of their receipt by the defendants.

BINGHAM L.J.: In many civil law systems, and perhaps in most legal systems outside the common law world, the law of obligations recognises and enforces an overriding principle that in making and carrying out contracts parties should act in good faith. This does not simply mean that they should not deceive each other, a principle which any legal system must recognise; its effect is perhaps most aptly conveyed by such meta-phorical colloquialisms as "playing fair," "coming clean" or "putting one's cards face upwards on the table." It is in essence a principle of fair and open dealing. In such a forum it might, I think, be held on the facts of this case that the plaintiffs were under a duty in all fairness to draw the defendants' attention specifically to the high price payable if the trans-parencies were not returned in time and, when the 14 days had expired, to point out to the defendants the high cost of continued failure to return them.

English law has, characteristically, committed itself to no such over-riding principle but has developed piecemeal solutions in response to demonstrated problems of unfairness. Many examples could be given. Thus equity has intervened to strike down unconscionable bargains. Parliament has stepped in to regulate the imposition of exemption clauses and the form of certain hire-purchase agreements. The common law also has made its contribution, by holding that certain classes of contract require the utmost good faith, by treating as irrecoverable what purport to be agreed estimates of damage but are in truth a disguised penalty for breach, and in many other ways.

The well-known cases on sufficiency of notice are in my view properly to be read in this context. At one level they are concerned with a question of pure contractual analysis, whether one party has done enough to give the other notice of the incorporation of a term in the contract. At another level they are concerned with a somewhat different question, whether it would in all the circumstances be fair (or reasonable) to hold a party bound by any conditions or by a particular condition of an unusual and stringent nature. . . .

[Having examined the authorities Bingham L.J. continued]: Turning to the present case, I am satisfied for reasons which Dillon L.J. has given that no contract was made on the telephone when the defendants made their initial request. I am equally satisfied that no contract was made on delivery of the transparencies to the defendants before the opening of the Jiffy bag in which they were contained. Once the Jiffy bag was opened and the transparencies taken out with the delivery note, it is in my judgment an inescapable inference that the defendants would have recognised the delivery note as a document of a kind likely to contain contractual terms and would have seen that there were conditions printed in small but visible lettering on the face of the document. To the extent that the conditions so displayed were common form or usual terms regularly encountered in this business, I do not think the defendants could successfully contend that they were not incorporated into the contract.

The crucial question in the case is whether the plaintiffs can be said fairly and reasonably to have brought condition 2 to the notice of the defendants. The judge made no finding on the point, but I think that it is open to this court to draw an inference from the primary findings which he did make. In my opinion the plaintiffs did not do so. They delivered 47 transparencies, which was a number the defendants had not specifically asked for. Condition 2 contained a daily rate per transparency after the initial period of 14 days many times greater than was usual or (so far as the evidence shows) heard of. For these 47 transparencies there was to be a charge for each day of delay of £235 plus value added tax. The result would be that a venial period of delay, as here, would lead to an inordinate liability. The defendants are not to be relieved of that liability because they did not read the condition, although doubtless they did not; but in my judgment they are to be relieved because the plaintiffs did not do what was necessary to draw this unreasonable and extortionate clause fairly to their attention. I would accordingly allow the defendants' appeal and substitute for the judge's award the sum which he assessed on the alternative basis of *quantum meruit*.

In reaching the conclusion I have expressed I would not wish to be taken as deciding that condition 2 was not challengeable as a disguised penalty clause. (See below, pp. 622–631.) This point was not argued before the judge nor raised in the notice of appeal. It was accordingly not argued before us. I have accordingly felt bound to assume, somewhat reluctantly, that condition 2 would be enforceable if fully and fairly brought to the defendants' attention.

Appeal allowed.

Questions

1. What if condition 2 had been printed in red, with a red hand pointing to it and had still not been read?
2. What if the defendants had *signed* the delivery note without reading it?
3. Is it realistic to say, for example, that sufficient notice has been given of conditions 1 and 3 to 9 and that they are part of the contract but that no sufficient notice has been given of condition 2? If the reasonable man would have been aware of any of them, would he not have been aware of all of them?

Note

Notice that neither the Unfair Contract Terms 1977 (below, p. 704) nor the UTCC Regulations 1994 (below, p. 715) would be applicable in this case. The Act did not apply because, though the contract was made on Interfoto's "written standard terms of business" (s. 3(1)), it was not an exclusion clause. The Regulations would not apply as the contract was not a "consumer contract" both because (i) Stiletto was not a "natural person" but a limited company and (ii) it was acting for the purposes of its business. So the matter would still be governed by the common law.

Section 6. Incorporation of Terms by a Course of Dealing

McCUTCHEON v. DAVID MacBRAYNE LTD

House of Lords (Scotland) [1964] 1 W.L.R. 125; [1964] 1 All E.R. 430; [1964] 1 Lloyd's Rep. 16; 1964 S.L.T. 66

McCutcheon's brother-in-law, McSporran, shipped McCutcheon's car on MacBrayne's ship. The ship was negligently sailed into a rock and sank. McCutcheon sued for the value of the car. MacBrayne relied on condition 19 of their elaborate contract of carriage which purported to exempt them from liability for negligence. It was their practice to require consignors to sign "risk notes" containing these conditions; but on the occasion in question the purser forgot to ask McSporran to sign. McSporran had consigned goods on a number of previous occasions. Sometimes he was asked to sign a risk note, sometimes not. He had never read the risk note. He knew it contained conditions but did not know what they were. MacBrayne contended that, because of the knowledge gained by his agent, McSporran, on these previous occasions, McCutcheon was bound by the terms. The House of Lords held that the printed conditions were not part of the contract and MacBrayne was liable.

LORD REID took the view that there had been no consistent course of dealing. Sometimes McSporran was asked to sign and sometimes he was not. He did not know what the conditions were. This time he was offered an oral contract without reference to any conditions, and he accepted the offer in good faith.

LORD HODSON thought it would be scarcely tolerable to treat a contracting party as if he had signed and so bound himself by the terms of a document with conditions embodied in it when, as here, he had done no such thing but may be supposed having regard to his previous experience to have been willing to sign what was put before him if he had been asked.

LORD GUEST: All that the previous dealings in the present case can show is that the appellant and his agent knew that the previous practice of the respondents was to impose special conditions. But knowledge on their part did not and could not by itself import acceptance by them of these conditions, the exact terms of which they were unaware, into a contract which was different in character from those in the previous course of dealing.

LORD DEVLIN: If a man is given a blank ticket without conditions or any reference to them, even if he knows in detail what the conditions usually exacted are, he is not, in the absence of any allegation of fraud or of that sort of mistake for which the law gives relief, bound by such conditions. It may seem a narrow and artificial line that divides a ticket that is blank on the back from one that says "For conditions see time-tables," or something of that sort, that has been held to be enough notice. I agree that it is an artificial line and one that has little relevance to everyday conditions. It may be beyond your Lordships' power to make the artificial line more natural: but at least you can see that it is drawn fairly for both sides and that there is not one law for individuals and another for organisations that can issue printed documents. If the respondents had remembered to issue a risk note in this case, they would have invited your Lordships to give a curt answer to any complaint by the appellant. He might say that the terms were unfair and unreasonable, that he had never voluntarily agreed to them, that it was impossible to read or understand them and that anyway if he had tried to negotiate any change the respondents would not have listened to him. The respondents would expect him to be told that he had made his contract and must abide by it. Now the boot is on the other foot. It is just as legitimate, but also just as vain, for the respondents to say that it was only a slip on their part, that it is unfair and unreasonable of the appellant to take advantage of it and that he knew perfectly well that they never carried goods except on conditions. The law must give the same answer they must abide by the contract they made. What is sauce for the goose is sauce for the gander. It will remain unpalatable sauce for both animals until the legislature, if the courts cannot do it, intervenes to secure that when contracts are made in circumstances in which there is no scope for free negotiation of the terms, they are made upon terms that are clear, fair and reasonable and settled independently as such. That is what Parliament has done in the case of carriage of goods by rail and on the high seas.

LORD PEARCE: It is the consistency of a course of conduct which gives rise to the implication that in similar circumstances a similar contractual result will follow. When the conduct is *not* consistent, there is no reason why it should still produce an invariable contractual result. The respondents having previously offered a written contract, on this occasion offered an oral one.

BRITISH CRANE HIRE CORPORATION LTD v. IPSWICH PLANT HIRE LTD

Court of Appeal [1975] Q.B. 303; [1974] 2 W.L.R. 856; [1974] 1 All E.R. 1059

Plaintiffs and defendants were both in the business of hiring out heavy earth-moving equipment. Defendants, carrying out drainage work themselves, urgently needed a dragline crane. By telephone they agreed to hire one from plaintiffs. Charges were agreed but nothing was said about conditions of hire. Plaintiffs, in accordance with usual practice, sent a printed form to be signed by defendants. Before it was signed, the crane, without anyone's fault, sank in marshy ground. Under the conditions in the printed form, which were similar to those used by all firms in the plant-hiring business, including defendants, defendants were liable to indemnify plaintiffs. Defendants appealed from a finding that the printed conditions were incorporated into the contract.

LORD DENNING M.R. (having referred to *Hollier v. Rambler Motors*, below, p. 158), where Salmon L.J. held that three or four transactions over a period of five years could not be described as "a course of dealing"): That was a case of a private individual who had had his car repaired by the defendants and had signed forms with conditions on three or four occasions. The plaintiff there was not of equal bargaining power with the garage company which repaired the car. The conditions were not incorporated.

But here the parties were both in the trade and were of equal bargaining power. Each was a firm of plant hirers who hired out plant. The defendants themselves knew that firms in the plant-hiring trade always imposed conditions in regard to the hiring of plant; and that their conditions were on much the same lines. The defendants' manager, Mr Turner (who knew the crane), was asked about it. He agreed that he had seen these conditions or similar ones in regard to the hiring of plant. He said that most of them were, to one extent or another, variations of a form which he called "the

Contractors' Plant Association form." The defendants themselves (when they let out cranes) used the conditions of that form. The conditions on the plaintiffs' form were in rather different words, but nevertheless to much the same effect . . . it is clear that both parties knew quite well that conditions were habitually imposed by the supplier of these machines: and both parties knew the substance of those conditions. In particular that, if the crane sank in soft ground, it was the hirer's job to recover it; and that there was an indemnity clause. In these circumstances, I think the conditions on the form should be regarded as incorporated into the contract. I would not put it so much on the course of dealing, but rather on the common understanding which is to be derived from the conduct of the parties, namely, that the hiring was to be on the terms of the plaintiffs' usual conditions.

As Lord Reid said in *McCutcheon v. David MacBrayne Ltd* (above, p. 155), quoting from the Scottish textbook *Gloag on Contract* (2nd ed., 1929), p. 7: "the judicial task is not to discover the actual intentions of each party: it is to decide what each was reasonably entitled to conclude from the attitude of the other." It seems to me that, in view of the relationship of the parties, when the defendants requested this crane urgently and it was supplied at once—before the usual form was received—the plaintiffs were entitled to conclude that the defendants were accepting it on the terms of the plaintiffs' own printed conditions . . .

MEGAW L.J. agreed.

SACHS L.J. said that the case was wholly different from that where the owner and the user are in wholly different walks of life as in *Hollier's* case. He held that the plaintiffs were entitled to conclude that the defendants accepted the plaintiffs' conditions, at any rate if they were reasonable: and he had no doubt but that both parties contracted on the basis of those conditions.

Questions
1. The *All England* headnote states: "Since the bargaining power of the defendants was equal to that of the plaintiffs and the defendants knew that printed conditions in similar terms to those of the plaintiffs were in common use in the business, the plaintiffs were entitled to conclude that the defendants were accepting the crane on the terms of their conditions." Would the plaintiffs not have been entitled so to conclude if the bargaining power had been unequal? Is equality of bargaining power relevant to this issue?
2. Suppose the plaintiffs were a large, powerful and prosperous firm and the defendants were a small, weak firm on the verge of bankruptcy. Should the answer have been different? (*Cf. Lloyds Bank v. Bundy*, below, p. 647).
3. Were the plaintiffs dealing "on [the defendants'] written standard terms of business"? See Unfair Contract Terms Act, s.3(1), below, pp. 470 and 705.

HOLLIER v. RAMBLER MOTORS (A.M.C.), LTD

Court of Appeal [1972] 2 W.L.R. 401; [1972] 1 All E.R. 399; [1972] R.T.R. 190

The plaintiff made an oral contract with the defendants, garage proprietors, for repairs to his car. A fire broke out in the garage through the defendants' negligence and the car was damaged. The plaintiff had had his car repaired or serviced by the defendants three or four times during the previous five years. On two at least of these occasions the plaintiff signed an "invoice" which it was the defendants' practice to require customers to sign, which contained the clause: "The company is not responsible for damage caused by fire to customers' cars on the premises. Customers' cars are driven by staff at owner's risk." The County Court Judge held that the defendants were protected from liability by this clause. The plaintiff appealed, arguing that the clause ought not to be imported into the oral contract; and that if it were, it did not protect the defendants.

SALMON L.J.: I am bound to say that, for my part, I do not know of any other case in which it has been decided or even argued that a term could be implied into an oral contract on the strength of a course of dealing (if it can be so called) which consisted at the most of three or four transactions over a period of five years.

We have been referred to *Hardwick Game Farm v. Suffolk Agricultural Poultry Producers Association* [1969] 2 A.C. 31. That was a case in which some feeding-stuff was sold by some merchants to a farmer. The feeding-stuff was found to be defective. The farmer sued the merchants. The merchants brought in as third party the persons from whom they had purchased the feeding-stuff; they in their turn brought in their suppliers, and there was a long list of many parties brought in right down the chain. As between two of these suppliers a point arose as to whether a term that the buyer under the contract took the responsibility for any latent defects was a term which had been imported into the contract in question by reason of the course of dealing between those parties. It is to be observed that in that case there had been three or four dealings each month between the parties during the previous three years. The course of dealing had been that the feeding-stuff was ordered orally by the buyer and the order was accepted orally by the suppliers. Then on the day of the oral contract, or perhaps the next day, the suppliers sent on to the buyer a sold note. One of the terms appearing on the sold note was that the buyer under the contract took the responsibility for any latent defects. Three or four times each month, year in and year out for three years, sold notes had been sent on to the buyer, and the buyer had never raised any protest or said anything which would have led the sellers to assume that the buyers were doing anything other than accepting the terms of the contract which appeared on the sold note. In that case, although this practice had been going on all that time, and the buyers had received well over 100 sold notes containing the condition to which I have referred, they had not actually read the condition and knew nothing about it. It was argued that, therefore, the condition could not be implied into the contract in question, although it had been made in exactly the same way as all the other contracts, namely, orally, with a sold note in the usual form sent on after the contract had been made. The House of Lords decided that the fact that the buyer had not read the condition on the sold notes, having had every opportunity of doing so, did not avail him, because any reasonable seller in circumstances such as those, having had no intimation from the buyer that he took any objection to the condition, would have had good cause to assume that the buyer was agreeing to the condition.

That case is obviously very different from the present case. The *Hardwick Game Farm* case seems to be a typical case where a consistent course of dealing between the parties makes it imperative for the court to read into the contract the condition for which the sellers were contending.

Everything that the buyer had done, or failed to do, would have convinced any ordinary seller that the buyer was agreeing to the terms in question. The fact that the buyer had not read the term is beside the point. The seller could not be expected to know that the buyer had not troubled to acquaint himself with what was written in the form that had been sent to him so often, year in and year out during the previous three years, in transactions exactly the same as the transaction then in question . . . [The judge then discussed *McCutcheon v. MacBrayne Ltd*, above, p. 155.]

It seems to me that if it was impossible to rely on a course of dealing in *McCutcheon v. David MacBrayne Ltd*, still less would it be possible to do so in this case, when the so-called course of dealing consisted only of three or four transactions in the course of five years.[1] As I read the speeches of Lord Reid, Lord Guest and Lord Pearce, one, but only one amongst many, of the facts to be taken into account in considering whether there had been a course of dealing from which a term was to be implied into the contract was whether the consignor actually knew what were the terms written on the back of the risk note. Lord Devlin said that this was a critical factor. Even on the assumption that Lord Devlin's dictum went further than was necessary for the decision in that case, and was wrong—which I think is the effect of the *Hardwick Game Farm* case [1969] 2 A.C. 31—I do not see how that can help the defendants here. The speeches of the other members of the House and the decision itself in *McCutcheon*'s case [1964] 1 W.L.R. 125 make it plain that the clause upon which the defendants seek to rely cannot in law be imported into the oral contract they made in March 1970. . . . [In case he was wrong on this point, the judge went on to consider what effect the clause would have, had it been incorporated into the contract. See below, p. 451.]

Note

The plaintiff in the *Hardwick Game Farm* case was not a consumer but he might now argue that the contract was made on the seller's "written standard terms of business" and was therefore subject to the test of reasonableness. The UTCC regulations, could not apply because Hardwick was not a "consumer".

[1] *Cf. British Crane Hire v. Ipswich Plant*, above, p. 157.

CHAPTER 5

IDENTITY OF OFFEROR AND OFFEREE

BOULTON v. JONES

(1857) 27 L.J. Ex. 117; 2 H. & N. 564; 157 E.R. 232; 3 Jur. 1156; 6 W.R. 107

Action (in the Passage Court of Liverpool) for goods sold.

Plea, never indebted.

The evidence was, that on January 13 the defendant sent to the shop of one Brocklehurst, who had that day, unknown to the defendant, sold his stock-in-trade and assigned his business to his foreman, the plaintiff, an order in writing, addressed to Brocklehurst, for certain goods. The goods were sent by the plaintiff, and at the trial the written order appeared with Brocklehurst's name struck out, but there was no evidence when that was done. There was contradictory evidence on a collateral point, but none as to whether the defendant had notice of the change of business before the plaintiff sent in an invoice, which was not until after the goods were consumed. The defendant had a running account with, and a set-off against Brocklehurst. The objection was taken that the contract was with him and not the plaintiff, and the learned Assessor reserved the point.

The jury found for the plaintiff, and Mellish had obtained a rule to enter a verdict for the defendant, or to enter a nonsuit. . . .

POLLOCK C.B.: The point raised was this, whether the order in writing did not import, on the part of the buyer, the defendant, an intention to deal exclusively with Brocklehurst; the person who had succeeded him, the plaintiff, having executed the order without any notice to the defendant of the change, until he received the invoice, subsequently to his consumption of the goods. The decision of the jury did not dispose of that point, and it was the point reserved. Now the rule of law is clear, that if you propose to make a contract with A, then B cannot substitute himself for A without your consent and to your disadvantage, securing to himself all the benefit of the contract. The case being, that if B sued, the defendant would have the benefit of a set-off, of which he is deprived by A's suing. If B sued, the defendant could plead his set-off; as B does not sue, but another party, with whom the defendant did not contract, all that he can do is deny that he ever was indebted to the plaintiff.

MARTIN B.: That being the point, there can be no doubt upon the matter. This was not a case of principal and agent at all, because the plaintiff was not Brocklehurst's agent, but his successor in the business, and made the contract on his own account, not for the plaintiff [sic]. Where the facts prove that the defendant never [sic] meant to contract with A alone, B can never force a contract upon him; he has dealt with A, and a contract with no one else can be set up against him.

161

BRAMWELL B.: It is an admitted fact, that the defendant supposed he was dealing with Brocklehurst; and the plaintiff misled him by executing the order unknown to him. It is clear also, that if the plaintiff were at liberty to sue, it would be a prejudice to the defendant, because it would deprive him of a set-off, which he would have had if the action had been brought by the party with whom he supposed he was dealing. And upon that my judgment proceeds. I do not lay it down that because a contract was made in one person's name another person cannot sue upon it, except in cases of agency. But when any one makes a contract in which the personality, so to speak, of the particular party contracted with is important for any reason, whether because it is to write a book or paint a picture, or do any work of personal skill, or whether because there is a set-off due from that party, no one else is at liberty to step in and maintain that he is the party contracted with, that he has written the book or painted the picture, or supplied the goods; and that he is entitled to sue, although, had the party really contracted with sued, the defendant would have had the benefit of his personal skill, or of a set-off due from him. As to the difficulty suggested, that if the plaintiff cannot sue for the price of the goods, no one else can, I do not feel pressed by it any more than I did in such a case as I may suppose, of work being done to my house, for instance, by a party different from the one with whom I had contracted to do it. The defendant has, it is true, had the goods; but it is also true that he has consumed them and cannot return them. And that is no reason why he should pay money to the plaintiff which he never contracted to pay, but upon some contract which he never made, and the substitution of which for that which he did make would be to his prejudice, and involve a pecuniary loss by depriving him of a set-off.

CHANNELL B.: The plaintiff is clearly not in a situation to sustain this action, for there was no contract between himself and the defendant. The case is not one of principal and agent; it was a contract made with B, who had transactions with the defendant and owed him money, and upon which A seeks to sue. Without saying that the plaintiff might not have had a right of action on an implied contract, if the goods had been in existence, here the defendant had no notice of the plaintiff's claim, until the invoice was sent to him, which was not until after he had consumed the goods, and when he could not, of course, have returned them. Without saying what might have been the effect of the receipt of the invoice before the consumption of the goods, it is sufficient to say that in this case the plaintiff clearly is not entitled to sue and deprive the defendant of his set-off.

Rule absolute for a nonsuit.

The above is taken from the *Law Journal* report.

Questions

1. Was not Boulton reasonably entitled to suppose that the offer was made to the owner of the business for the time being? If so, was he not entitled to accept? Was the existence of the set-off material if it was not known to Boulton?

2. If there was no contract, did not the goods remain Boulton's property? Might he not have succeeded in an action for conversion?

Problem

Belfridge, the owner of a chain of department stores (trading under the name "Belfridge's"), at 12 noon on February 1 sold his entire business to Ramage. At 1 p.m. on February 1 Clarence agreed to buy an expensive carpet in one of "Belfridge's" shops. He knew nothing of the sale to Ramage. He now wishes to avoid the contract. Advise him.

See Stoljar, *Mistake and Misrepresentation*, Chap. 4.

LINDSAY v. CUNDY

Queen's Bench Division (1876) 1 Q.B.D. 348; 45 L.J.Q.B. 381; 34 L.T. 314; 24 W.R. 730; 13 Cox C.C. 162

The action was brought by Messrs. Roberts, Lindsay & Co., who are linen manufacturers at Belfast, against Messrs. Cundy for the conversion of 250 dozen handkerchiefs. At the trial before Blackburn J. it appeared that one Alfred Blenkarn, in 1873, hired a third floor at No. 37, Wood Street, and 5, Little Love Lane, Cheapside. There was a well-known firm of William Blenkiron & Sons, which had for many years carried on business at No. 123, Wood Street. Blenkarn wrote letters at the end of 1873 to the plaintiffs; by the first proposing to order, and by the others ordering, a large quantity of handkerchiefs from the plaintiffs. Those letters had a printed heading, "37, Wood Street, Cheapside, London; entrance, second door in Little Love Lane," and were signed "A. Blenkarn & Co." written in such a way that it was evidently intended to be read "A. Blenkiron & Co." One of the plaintiffs had known the firm of Blenkiron & Sons several years before, and knew they were respectable. The plaintiffs wrote several letters addressed to "Messrs. Blenkiron & Co., 37, Wood Street," and they forwarded several lots of hand-kerchiefs to the same address, heading the invoices, "Messrs. Blenkiron and Co., London."

The fraud was afterwards discovered, and Blenkarn was, in April 1874, convicted of obtaining the goods by the false pretence of being Blenkiron & Sons.

In the meantime the defendants had bought of Blenkarn 250 dozen cambric handkerchiefs, and had resold them all to different persons before the fraud of Blenkarn was discovered. The jury found that the defendants were bona fide purchasers of the handkerchiefs, and that they were part of the handkerchiefs sold by the plaintiffs to Blenkarn. The learned judge reserved the question for the court, whether on the facts and findings the action was maintainable.

(The above statement of facts is taken from the judgment of Mellish L.J. in the Court of Appeal (1877) 2 Q.B.D. 98.)

BLACKBURN J. (in the Q.B.D.): I think that judgment should be entered for the defendants. The first question that arises is one of fact, were these goods, which were originally the property of the plaintiffs, Messrs. Lindsay & Co., obtained from them by fraud, so that the property passed from them under a contract, though a contract liable under certain circumstances to be avoided; or did the property never pass from the plaintiffs at all? Upon that question reliance was placed on the case of *Hardman v. Booth* (1 H. & C. 803), and that case unquestionably lays down very good law. The question for us is whether the facts are the same, and whether we ought to draw the same inference from the facts that the Court of Exchequer did in *Hardman v. Booth*. That case lays down this law, that where a person has sold goods to A. B., or has been led to believe he has sold them to A. B., and delivered them as he supposes to A. B., and the person who led him into that belief receives and carries off the goods, and disposes of them to another—there has not been a selling to the person who fraudulently represented himself to be a servant or agent of the supposed purchaser, A. B., and he cannot confer a good title upon anyone else, the property never having vested in him. The facts in *Hardman v. Booth* seem to have been these: The plaintiffs, meaning to deal with Thomas Gandell & Sons, went to their office and took an order from a person who, as they believed, and in point of fact was, the son of Thomas Gandell, and whom they believed to be acting for the firm of Thomas Gandell & Sons; and they took away a card of the firm of Thomas Gandell & Sons, to show to whom they were to send them, and they sent them to Thomas Gandell & Sons' place of business. Edward Gandell, who was the son of Thomas Gandell, had a private business of his own, and he it was who in that office had given the order for Thomas Gandell & Sons without any authority, and he it was, as it was proved upon the trial, who intercepted the goods when they arrived at Messrs. Gandell's, and carried them away, and sold them to the defendant. Upon these facts, the Court of Exchequer drew the inference that there never was any property vested in Edward Gandell as purchaser under a contract voidable through fraud; for there never was intended to be a contract with anybody but Thomas Gandell & Sons, and in point of fact that contract did not exist, because Thomas Gandell and Sons had not meddled in the matter in any way; and what had been done by the plaintiffs did not in the slightest degree constitute a contract with Edward Gandell vesting the property in him. I think that is good law, and the inference would seem upon the evidence to have been correctly drawn.

The same law was applied in the case of *Hollins v. Fowler* (L.R. 7 Q.B. 616; L.R. 7 H.L. 757), which was subsequently affirmed in the House of Lords, the facts there being clear.

When we look at the facts of the present case they are not the same at all. The plaintiffs having received a letter from a person who signed himself with the name of "Blenkarn," looking like "Blenkiron" & Co., of 37, Wood Street, they address all their letters to him, and send the goods to him at 37, Wood Street, and deliver them there, and everything is done with him at 37, Wood Street. The fact was, that there was a highly respectable firm in the name of William Blenkiron & Co., at 123, Wood Street, and this man set up a pretended business at 37, Wood Street, in the hope that people would confuse him with his namesake, and he would get the advantage of his namesake's character. In this particular case he did get the advantage of his namesake's character, and it being found that he did so intentionally, and that it was a fraudulent intention, he was guilty of obtaining the goods under false pretences; but nonetheless was the contract by the plaintiffs made with him . . . upon the facts of this case, the intention of the plaintiffs was to contract with the person who was carrying on the business at 37, Wood Street, and there was therefore a contract with him, although it was obtained by fraud.

The Court of Appeal (Mellish L.J. and Brett and Amphlett JJ.A.) reversed the judgment of the Queen's Bench Division, holding that the plaintiffs intended to deal with Blenkiron & Sons and therefore there was no contract with Blenkarn; that the property in the goods never passed from the plaintiffs; and that they were accordingly entitled to recover in the action: (1877) 2 Q.B.D. 96. The defendant appealed to the House of Lords.

CUNDY v. LINDSAY

House of Lords (1878) 3 App.Cas. 459; 38 L.T. 573; 42 J.P. 483; 26 W.R. 406; 14 Cox C.C. 93

THE LORD CHANCELLOR (LORD CAIRNS): My Lords, you have in this case to discharge a duty which is always a disagreeable one for any court, namely, to determine as between two parties, both of whom are perfectly innocent, upon which of the two the consequences of a fraud practised upon both of them must fall. My Lords, in discharging that duty your Lordships can do no more than apply, rigorously, the settled and well-known rules of law. Now, with regard to the title to personal property, the settled and well-known rules of law may, I take it, be thus expressed: by the law of our country the purchaser of a chattel takes the chattel as a general rule subject to what may turn out to be a certain infirmities in the title. If he purchases the chattel in market overt, he obtains a title which is good against all the world; but if he does not purchase the chattel in market overt, and if it turns out that the chattel has been found by the person who professed to sell it, the purchaser will not obtain a title good as against the real owner. If it turns out that the chattel has been stolen by the person who has professed to sell it, the purchaser will not obtain a title. If it turns out that the chattel has come into the hands of the person who professed to sell it, by a *de facto* contract, that is to say, a contract which has purported to pass the property to him from the owner of the property, there the purchaser will obtain a good title, even although afterwards it should appear that there were circumstances connected with that contract, which would enable the original owner of the goods to reduce it, and to set it aside, because these circumstances so enabling the original owner of the goods, or of the chattel, to reduce the contract and to set it aside, will not be allowed to interfere with a title for valuable consideration obtained by some third party during the interval while the contract remained unreduced.

My Lords, the question, therefore, in the present case, as your Lordships will observe, really becomes the very short and simple one which I am about to state. Was there any contract which, with regard to the goods in question in this case, had passed the property in the goods from the Messrs. Lindsay to Alfred Blenkarn? If there was any contract passing that property, even although, as I have said, that contract might afterwards be open to a process of reduction, upon the ground of fraud, still, in the meantime, Blenkarn might have conveyed a good title for valuable consideration to the present appellants.

Now, my Lords, there are two observations bearing upon the solution of that question which I desire to make. In the first place, if the property in the goods in question passed, it could only pass by way of contract; there is nothing else which could have passed the property. The second observation is this, your Lordships are not here embarrassed by any conflict of evidence, or any evidence whatever as to conversations or as to acts done, the whole history of the whole transaction lies upon paper. The principal parties concerned, the respondents and Blenkarn, never came into contact personally—everything that was done was done by writing. What has to be judged of, and what the jury in the present case had to judge of, was merely the conclusion to be derived from that writing, as applied to the admitted facts of the case.

Now, my Lords, discharging that duty and answering that inquiry, what the jurors have found is in substance this: it is not necessary to spell out the words, because the substance of it is beyond all doubt. They have found that by the form of signatures to the letters which were written by Blenkarn, by the mode in which his letters and his applications to the respondents were made out, and by the way in which he left uncorrected the mode and form in which, in turn, he was addressed by the respondents; that by all those means he led, and intended to lead, the respondents to believe, and they did believe, that the person with whom they were communicating was not Blenkarn, the dishonest and irresponsible man, but was a well-known and solvent house of Blenkiron & Co., doing business in the same street. My Lords, those things are found as matters of fact, and they are placed beyond the range of dispute and controversy in the case.

If that is so, what is the consequence? It is that Blenkarn—the dishonest man, as I call him—was acting here just in the same way as if he had forged the signature of Blenkiron & Co., the respectable firm, to the applications for goods, and as if, when, in return, the goods were forwarded and letters were sent, accompanying them, he had intercepted the goods and intercepted the letters, and had taken possession of the goods, and of the letters which were addressed to, and intended for, not himself but, the firm of Blenkiron & Co. Now, my Lords, stating the matter shortly in that way, I ask the question, how is it possible to imagine that in that state of things any contract could have arisen between the respondents and Blenkarn, the dishonest man? Of him they knew nothing, and of him they never thought. With him they never intended to deal. Their minds never, even for an instant of time rested upon him, and as between him and them there was no consensus of mind which could lead to any agreement or any contract whatever. As between him and them there was merely the one side to a contract, where, in order to produce a contract, two sides would be required. With the firm of Blenkiron & Co. of course there was no contract, for as to them the matter was entirely unknown, and therefore the pretence of a contract was a failure.

The result, therefore, my Lords, is this, that your Lordships have not here to deal with one of those cases in which there is *de facto* a contract made which may afterwards be impeached and set aside, on the ground of fraud; but you have to deal with a case which ranges itself under a completely different chapter of law, the case namely in which the contract never comes into existence. My Lords, that being so, it is idle to talk of the property passing. The property remained, as it originally had been, the property of the respondents, and the title which was attempted to be given to the appellants was a title which could not be given to them.

LORDS HATHERLEY and PENZANCE delivered concurring speeches and LORD GORDON concurred.

Appeal dismissed.

Questions
  1. Which of the following statements is true? Or are they both true?

(i) The plaintiffs intended to contract with Blenkiron & Sons.
(ii) The plaintiffs intended to contract with the person who was carrying on business at 37, Wood Street.

If both statements are true is it possible to decide between the views of the Queen's Bench Division and the House of Lords?
2. Would it have made any difference if Blenkarn had not been fraudulent, but had innocently misled Lindsay into thinking he was Blenkiron & Sons?

KING'S NORTON METAL CO. LTD v. EDRIDGE, MERRETT & CO. LTD

Court of Appeal (1897) 14 T.L.R. 98; 39 Digest 534, *1455*

The plaintiffs were metal manufacturers at King's Norton, Worcestershire, and the defendants were metal merchants at Birmingham. It appeared that in 1896 the plaintiffs received a letter purporting to come from Hallam & Co., Soho Hackle Pin and Wire Works, Sheffield, at the head of which was a representation of a large factory with a number of chimneys, and in one corner was a printed statement that Hallam & Co. had depots and agencies at Belfast, Lille and Ghent. The letter contained a request by Hallam & Co. for a quotation of prices for brass rivet wire. In reply, the plaintiffs quoted prices, and Hallam & Co. then by letter ordered some goods, which were sent off to them. These goods were never paid for. It turned out that a man named Wallis had adopted the name of Hallam & Co., and fraudulently obtained goods by the above means, and that Wallis sold the goods to the defendants, who bought them bona fide, and that with no notice of any defect of title in Wallis. The plaintiffs brought this action to recover damages for the conversion of these goods. It appeared that the plaintiffs had been paid for some goods previously ordered by Hallam & Co., by a cheque drawn by "Hallam & Co." At the trial, the learned judge nonsuited the plaintiffs upon the ground that the property in the goods had passed to Wallis, who sold them to the defendants before the plaintiffs had disaffirmed the contract.

A. L. SMITH L.J. said that the case was a plain one. The question was whether the plaintiffs, who had been cheated out of their goods by a rogue called Wallis, or the defendants were to bear the loss. The law seemed to him to be well settled. If a person, induced by false pretences, contracted with a rogue to sell goods to him and the goods were delivered the rogue could until the contract was disaffirmed give a good title to a bona fide purchaser for value. The facts here were that Wallis, for the purpose of cheating, set up in business as Hallam & Co., and got notepaper prepared for the purpose, and wrote to the plaintiffs representing that he was carrying on business as Hallam & Co. He got the goods in question and sold them to the defendants, who bought them bona fide for value. The question was, With whom, upon this evidence, which was all one way, did the plaintiffs contract to sell the goods? Clearly with the writer of the letters. If it could have been shown that there was a separate entity called Hallam & Co. and another entity called Wallis then the case might have come within the decision in *Cundy v. Lindsay*. In his opinion there was a contract by the plaintiffs with the person who wrote the letters, by which the property passed to him. There was only one entity, trading it might be under an alias, and there was a contract by which the property passed to him. Cave J. said that this was nothing more than a long firm fraud. Did anyone ever hear of an attempt being made by a person who had delivered his goods to a long firm to get his goods back on the ground that he had made no contract with the long firm? The indictment against a long firm was always obtaining the goods by false pretences, which presupposed the passing of the property. For these reasons there was no question to go to the jury, and the nonsuit was right.

RIGBY AND COLLINS L.JJ. delivered judgment to the same effect.

Questions
   1. Would it have made any difference if there had in fact been a firm of the name of Hallam & Co. with all the various attributes stated on Wallis's letterhead (a) if that firm was not known to the plaintiffs? (b) if it was known to them?
   2. Would it have made any difference if Wallis had described his fictitious business as Hallam & Co. Ltd.? See *Newborne v. Sensolid Ltd, infra.*
   3. What would have been the result if Lindsay had sued Blenkarn in contract for the price of the goods? (*Cf.* Atiyah, *Introduction to the Law of Contract* (4th ed.), p. 69.)

Problem
   Twister induces Sparkler, a jeweller, to sell him a ring by representing falsely that his father is Lord X. Is there a contract between Twister and Sparkler (a) if, as Sparkler knows, Lord X has one son? (b) if, as Sparkler knows, Lord X has two sons?
   (*Cf.* Glanville Williams, "Mistake as to Party in the Law of Contract" 23 *Canadian Bar Review*, 271.)

NEWBORNE v. SENSOLID LTD

Court of Appeal [1954] 1 Q.B. 45; [1952] 2 T.L.R. 763; 97 S.J. 209; [1953] 1 All E.R. 708

The plaintiff formed a limited company called Leopold Newborne, Ltd Before the company was registered a contract form, bearing the name and address of Newborne, Ltd, and signed "Yours faithfully, Leopold Newborne (London), Ltd," with the name of Leopold Newborne underneath, was sent to the defendant. The defendant signed it, and thereby agreed to buy certain goods from Leopold Newborne, Ltd. Leopold Newborne, Ltd, issued a writ claiming damages for failure to accept the goods. The plaintiffs' solicitors then discovered that the company had not been registered at the time of the contract, and they took steps to substitute the name of Leopold Newborne for that of the company. The defendants then contended that Newborne was trying to sue on a contract which he had not made, but which purported to have been made by a limited liability company which had not been registered. Parker J. found for the defendant and was affirmed by the Court of Appeal.

LORD GODDARD C.J.: This contract purports to be a contract by the company; it does not purport to be a contract by Mr Newborne. He does not purport to be selling his goods but to be selling the company's goods. The only person who had any contract here was the company, and Mr Newborne's signature merely confirmed the company's signature. . . .
   In my opinion, unfortunate though it may be, as the company was not in existence when the contract was signed there never was a contract, and Mr Newborne cannot come forward and say: "Well, it was my contract." The fact is, he made a contract for a company which did not exist.

Questions
   1. If there was a contract between Wallis and the King's Norton Metal Co. Ltd, why was there no contract between Newborne and Sensolid, Ltd? (*Cf.* (1957) 20 M.L.R. 38.)

2. The Companies Act 1985, s.36(4), provides: "Where a contract purports to be made by a company, or by a person as agent for a company, at a time when the company has not been formed, then subject to any agreement to the contrary the contract shall have effect as a contract entered into by the person purporting to act for the company or as agent for it, and he shall be personally liable on the contract accordingly."

Does this subsection overrule *Newborne v. Sensolid*? It appears to make Newborne liable on the contract. Does it enable him to enforce it? *Cf. Phonogram Ltd v. Lane* [1982] Q.B. 938.

Note

In *Cotronic (U.K.) Ltd v. Dezonie, t/a Wendeland Builders Ltd, The Times*, March 8, 1991, C.A., D, on March 7, 1986 purported to make a contract on behalf of Wendeland Builders Ltd. Unknown to D who had controlled that company, it had been dissolved in 1981. A new company bearing the same name was incorporated in 1988. It was held that there was no contract and that section 36(4) did not apply. It was impossible to say that D purported to act for the new company.

PHILLIPS v. BROOKS LTD

King's Bench Division [1919] 2 K.B. 243; 88 L.J.K.B. 953; 121 L.T. 249

Action tried by Horridge J.

The plaintiff, who was a jeweller, sued the defendants, who were pawn-brokers, for the return of a ring or, alternatively, its value, and damages for its detention.

On April 15, 1918, a man entered the plaintiff's shop and asked to see some pearls and some rings. He selected pearls at the price of £2,550 and a ring at the price of £450. He produced a cheque-book and wrote out a cheque for £3,000. In signing it, he said: "You see who I am, I am Sir George Bullough," and he gave an address in St. James's Square. The plaintiff knew that there was such a person as Sir George Bullough, and finding on reference to a directory that Sir George lived at the address mentioned, he said: "Would you like to take the articles with you?" to which the man replied: "You had better have the cheque cleared first, but I should like to take the ring as it is my wife's birthday tomorrow," whereupon the plaintiff let him have the ring. The cheque was dishonoured, the person who gave it being in fact a fraudulent person named North who was subsequently convicted of obtaining the ring by false pretences. In the meantime, namely on April 16, 1918, North, in the name of Firth, had pledged the ring with the defendants who, bona fide and without notice, advanced £350 upon it.

HORRIDGE J. said: I have carefully considered the evidence of the plaintiff, and have come to the conclusion that, although he believed the person to whom he was handing the ring was Sir George Bullough, he in fact contracted to sell and deliver it to the person who came into his shop, and who was not Sir George Bullough, but a man in the name of North, who obtained the sale and delivery by means of the false pretence that he was Sir George Bullough. It is quite true the plaintiff in re-examination said he had no intention of making any contract with any other person than Sir George Bullough; but I think I have myself to decide what is the proper inference to draw where a verbal contract is made and an article delivered to an individual describing himself as somebody else. . . .

It was argued before me that the principle quoted from Pothier (*Traitè des Obligations*, § 19), in *Smith v. Wheatcroft* (9 Ch.D. 223, 230), namely, "Whenever the consideration of the person with whom I am willing to contract enters as an element into the contract which I am willing to make, error with regard to the person destroys my consent and consequently annuls the contract" applies. I do not think, however, that that passage governs this case, because I think the seller intended to contract with the person present, and there was no error as to the person with whom he contracted, although the plaintiff would not have made the contract if there had not been a fraudulent misrepresentation. Moreover, the case of *Smith v. Wheatcroft* was an action for specific performance, and was between the parties to the contract, and had no relation to rights acquired by third parties innocently under the contract, and misrepresentation would have been an answer to the enforcement of the contract. In this case, I think, there was a passing of the property and the purchaser had a good title, and there must be judgment for the defendants with costs.

Judgment for defendants.

Note

A learned correspondent, discussing *Phillips v. Brooks*, writes in 35 L.Q.R. 289:

What if A, wearing a false nose and beard, had represented to B that he was Lord Rothschild or Mr Bernard Shaw? It could hardly be said that in such a case B would not be in "error with regard to the person" with whom he was contracting. And it is difficult to believe that the element of a false nose and beard makes the difference between a good title and no title.

E.C.S. Wade, Mistaken Identity in the Law of Contract, 38 L.Q.R. 201, 204

Having contrasted *Phillips v. Brooks* and *Cundy v. Lindsay*, the writer continues:

The solution, it seems, of the vexed question as to which of two innocent parties is to suffer for the fraud of a third party is to turn upon the mode by which the parties to the original transaction came into contact. If it be through the medium of written communications, the original owner does not suffer, but can recover his goods, even though in the hands of bona fide purchasers for value. It is otherwise if he had an opportunity of meeting his customer face to face; for he is enabled to rely on his own judgment, as well as the customer's assertion, and not merely upon a written representation. But this distinction is specious; for the seller who relies on a written representation has the opportunity of verifying it at his leisure. And why should he be protected—as he undoubtedly is by *Cundy v. Lindsay*—in the event of his being mistaken? For the shopkeeper, who has in the interests of his business often to decide on the spur of the moment, runs the risk of being unable to have the contract set aside after the pretender has parted with his acquisitions to a purchaser or pawnbroker; this, of course, he invariably hastens to do. It is to be noted, moreover, that the Scottish courts have decided (*Morrison v. Robertson*, 1908 S.C. 332) that such a transaction as took place in *Phillips v. Brooks* is void *ab initio*.

The writer then suggests an alternative view of the facts:

A collation of the various reports of this case shows the following sequence of facts:

(1) A sale of pearls for £2,550 and a ring for £450 by B to A, whereupon
(2) by virtue of section 18 of the Sale of Goods Act, 1893, the property passed from B to A;
(3) a fraudulent misrepresentation by A as to his identity which
(4) successfully induced voluntary delivery of the ring on the part of B to A.

This alternative view of the facts is a possible one, and will support the decision of Horridge J. that the swindler obtained a voidable title to the ring and was able to pass a good title to the pawnbrokers . . . it can be taken that the fraud was practised to induce the plaintiff to deliver the ring, after the contract of sale had been completed.

Note

Whether Professor Wade's explanation of *Phillips v. Brooks* is acceptable may be debated. (*Cf.* Pearce L.J., below, p. 173) However, cases have certainly occurred in which the course of events was similar to that posed in Professor Wade's analysis. In *Dennant v. Skinner* [1948] 2 K.B. 164 a man bid for a car at an auction sale and it was knocked down to him. The auctioneer did not know the bidder. He asked him his name so as to complete the memorandum of sale and the bidder said he was King of King's Motors Oxford. Other cars were knocked down to the bidder and subsequently, by repeating the statement that he represented King's of Oxford (which was false) and other statements, he induced the auctioneer to accept a cheque and allow him to take the cars away. Hallett J. held that the property in the cars passed to the bidder. "At an auction sale, apart from any question of the reserve price, the lot is knocked down to the highest bidder, whoever he might be."

Question

"Did the shopkeeper believe that he was entering into a contract with Sir George Bullough and did North know this? If both answers are in the affirmative then it is submitted that there was no contract. If a blind man makes an offer to A, who is present, in the mistaken belief that he is B, can A, who is aware of the mistake, accept the offer?" (Goodhart, "Mistake as to Identity in Contract" 57 L.Q.R. 228, 240.)

INGRAM AND OTHERS v. LITTLE

Court of Appeal [1961] 1 Q.B. 31; [1960] 3 W.L.R. 504; [1960] 3 All E.R. 332; 104 S.J. 704

Three plaintiffs, Elsie Ingram, Hilda Ingram and Mrs Badger, who were the joint owners of a car, advertised it for sale. A rogue, introducing himself as Hutchinson, offered to buy it. He was taken for a run in the car in the course of which he talked about his family and said that they were in Cornwall but that his home was in Caterham. Later, "Hutchinson" offered Elsie Ingram, who conducted the negotiations for the plaintiffs, £700 and she refused. He then offered £717 which she was prepared to accept. When the rogue pulled out a cheque book, she said that she would not under any circumstances accept a cheque and that the proposed deal was finished. The rogue then said that he was a P. G. M. Hutchinson with business interests in Guildford and living at Stanstead House, Stanstead Road, Caterham. Hilda Ingram checked in the telephone directory that there was such a person as P. G. M. Hutchinson, living at that address. The plaintiffs then let the rogue have the car in exchange for the cheque.

The rogue was not P. G. M. Hutchinson who had nothing to do with the transaction. The cheque was dishonoured. The rogue sold the car to the defendant and then disappeared and remained untraced. The plaintiffs sued the defendant for the return of the car or damages for its conversion. Slade J. gave judgment for the plaintiffs. The defendant appealed.

SELLERS L.J. delivered judgment dismissing the appeal.

PEARCE L.J.: I agree. The question here is whether there was any contract, whether offer and acceptance met. For, as Gresson P. said in *Fawcett v. Star Car Sales Ltd* [1960] N.Z.L.R. 406: "a void contract is a paradox; in truth there is no contract at all." . . .

When an offeror seeks to avoid an apparent contract on the ground of mistaken identity the investigation must start with his actual state of mind. For it would be absurd if he could avoid the contract when he was not really mistaken in his own mind as to the offeree's identity or when the apparent contract was not induced by mistake, when he was equally prepared to make the contract had he not been mistaken. That, as it seems to me, is a preliminary essential. But the courts, in deciding the question whether the apparent contract is non-existent owing to mistake in identity, apply the usual objective test (see *Holmes on the Common Law* (1881), p. 308, Lecture 9), rather than a subjective test which would gravely impair the certainty and stability of contracts. The judge approached the matter on an objective basis. He pointed out, however, that he would have reached the same result by approaching the matter on the subjective test suggested by Pothier. In cases such as this the cheat is fully aware of the offeror's actual state of mind. Moreover, he could not be heard to say that he was not aware of the offeror's state of mind when he has himself deliberately and fraudulently induced it. Thus the objective and subjective tests produce the same result in such a case, and it is the offeror's intention which provides the answer. It is for that reason, I think, that in such cases as this so many observations have been made that are equally referable to the subjective and objective test. . . .

An apparent contract made orally *inter praesentes* raises particular difficulties. The offer is apparently addressed to the physical person present. Prima facie, he, by whatever name he is called, is the person to whom the offer is made. His physical presence identified by sight and hearing preponderates over vagaries of nomenclature. *Praesentia corporis tollit errorem nominis*, said Lord Bacon (*Law Tracts* (1737), p. 102). Yet clearly, though difficult, it is not impossible to rebut the prima facie presumption that the offer can be accepted by the person to whom it is physically addressed. To take two other extreme instances. If a man orally commissions a portrait from some unknown artist who had deliberately passed himself off whether by disguise or merely by verbal cosmetics, as a famous painter, the imposter could not accept the offer. For though the offer is made to him physically, it is obviously, as he knows, addressed to the famous painter. The mistake in identity on such facts is clear and the nature of the contract makes it obvious that identity was of vital importance to the offeror. At the other end of the scale, if a shopkeeper sells goods in a normal cash transaction to a man who misrepresents himself as being some well-known figure, the transaction will normally be valid. For the shopkeeper was ready to sell goods for cash to the world at large and the particular identity of the purchaser in such a contract was not of sufficient importance to override the physical presence identified by sight and hearing. Thus the nature of the proposed contract must have a strong bearing on the question of whether the intention of the offeror (as understood by his offeree) was to make his offer to some other particular identity rather than to the physical person to whom it was orally offered.

In our case, the facts lie in the debatable area between the two extremes. At the beginning of the negotiations, always an important consideration, the name or personality of the false Hutchinson were of no importance and there was no other identity competing with his physical presence. The plaintiffs were content to sell the car for cash to any purchaser. The contractual conversation was orally addressed to the physical identity of the false Hutchinson. The identity was the man present, and his name was merely one of his attributes. Had matters continued thus, there would have clearly been a valid but voidable contract.

I accept the judge's view that there was no contract at the stage when the man pulled out his cheque book. From a practical point of view negotiations reached an impasse at that stage. For the vendor refused to discuss the question of selling on credit. It is argued that there was a contract as soon as the price was agreed at £717 and that from that moment either party could have sued on the contract with implied terms as to payment and delivery. That may be theoretically arguable, but in my view, the judge's more realistic approach was right. Payment and delivery still needed to be discussed and the parties would be expecting to discuss them. Immediately they did discuss them it became plain that they were not *ad idem* and that no contract had yet been created. But, even if there had been a concluded agreement before discussion of a cheque, it was rescinded. The man tried to make Mrs Ingram take a cheque. She declined it and said that the deal was off. He did not demur but set himself to reconstruct the negotiations. For the moment had come, which he must all along have anticipated, as the crux of the negotiations, the vital crisis of the swindle. He wanted to take away the car on credit against his worthless cheque, but she refused. Thereafter, the negotiations were of a different kind from what the vendor had mistakenly believed them to be hitherto. The parties were no longer concerned with a cash sale of goods where the identity of the purchaser was prima facie unimportant. They were concerned with a credit sale in which both parties knew that the identity of the purchaser was one of the utmost importance. She now realised that she was being asked to give him possession of the car on the faith of his cheque.

This was an important stage of the transaction because it demonstrated quite clearly that she was not prepared to sell on credit to the mere physical man in her drawing-room though he represented himself as a man of substance. He proceeded to "give to airy nothing a local habitation and a name." He tried to persuade her to sell to him as P. G. M. Hutchinson of Stanstead House, a personality which no doubt he had selected for the purpose of inspiring confidence into his victim. This was unsuccessful. Only when she had ascertained (through her sister's short excursion to the local post office and investigation of the telephone directory) that there was a P. G. M. Hutchinson of Stanstead House in the directory did she agree to sell on credit. The fact that the man wrote the name and address on the back of the cheque is an additional indication of the importance attached by the parties to the individuality of P. G. M. Hutchinson of Stanstead House.

It is not easy to decide whether the vendor was selling to the man in her drawing-room (fraudulently misrepresented as being a man of substance with the attributes of the real Hutchinson) or to P. G. M. Hutchinson of Stanstead House (fraudulently misrepresented as being the man in her drawing room). Did the individuality of P. G. M. Hutchinson of Stanstead House or the physical presence of the man in her drawing room preponderate? Can it be said that the prima facie predominance of the physical presence of the false Hutchinson identified by sight and hearing was overborne by the identity of the real Hutchinson on the particular facts of the present case?

The judge said: "I have not the slightest hesitation in reaching the conclusion that the offer which the plaintiffs made to accept the cheque for £717 was one made solely to, and one which was capable of being accepted only by, the honest Hutchinson—that is to say Philip Gerald Morpath Hutchinson of Stanstead House, Stanstead Road, Caterham, Surrey, and that it was capable of being accepted only by the honest Hutchinson." In view of the experience of the judge and the care which he devoted to the present case, I should hesitate long before interfering with that finding of fact, and I would only do so if compelled by the evidence or by the view that the judge drew some erroneous inference. Where, as here, a borderline case is concerned with ascertaining the intention of the parties, the views of the trial judge who hears the witnesses should not lightly be discarded. I am not persuaded that on the evidence he should have found otherwise.

[His Lordship then considered *Phillips v. Brooks Ltd* and concluded:] In my view, it was a borderline case decided on its own particular facts, and is in no wise decisive of the case before us. [His Lordship then considered *Hardman v. Booth* (see above, p. 163) and concluded:] That case, however, was a clearer case of there being no contract than is the present one, since there the plaintiffs had gone to the premises of Gandell & Co. to deal with that firm, and on those premises they had dealt with someone who duped them into believing that he was a member of the firm. Had the plaintiffs in the present case gone to Stanstead House especially to deal with the real Hutchinson and been duped on the premises by the false Hutchinson, their case would have been very clear. [His Lordship then considered *Lake v. Simmons* [1927] A.C. 487.]

Each case must be decided on its own facts. The question in such cases is this. Has it been sufficiently shown in the particular circumstances that, contrary to the prima facie presumption, a party was not contracting with the physical person to whom he uttered the offer, but with another individual whom (to the other party's knowledge) he believed to be the physical person present. The answer to that question is a finding of fact.

It is argued that although such a finding might properly have been reached if the cheat had pretended to be some great man or someone known already to the vendor by dealing or by reputation, it could not be so in this case, since the vendor had no knowledge of P. G. M. Hutchinson of Stanstead House. Had it not been for investigation of the telephone directory, that might well be so; but here the entry represented an individual of apparent standing and stability, a person whom the vendor was ready to trust with her car against his cheque. His individuality was less dominating than that of a famous man would be, but that is a question of degree. It does not, I think, preclude the judge from finding that it was with him that the vendor was intending to deal.

DEVLIN L.J. said that the question was: with whom did Miss Ingram intend to contract?—the person to whom she was speaking or the person whom he represented himself to be?—and that this was a mixed question of fact and law which the trial judge, who had seen the witnesses, was no better equipped to answer than the Court of Appeal, who had not. He continued:

In my judgment, the court cannot arrive at a satisfactory solution in the present case except by formulating a presumption and taking it at least as a starting point. The presumption that a person is intending to contract with the person to whom he is actually addressing the words of contract seems to me to be a simple and sensible one and supported by some good authority. It is adopted in *Benjamin on Sale* (8th ed., 1950), p. 102, where two decisions in the United States are referred to, *Edmunds v. Merchants Despatch Co.* and *Phelps v. McQuade.* The reasoning in the former was adopted by Horridge J. in *Phillips v. Brooks Ltd* and the latter case is a decision of the New York Court of Appeals. All these three cases still stand as the law in their respective jurisdictions. *Corbin on Contract* (1951), Vol. 3, s.602, p. 385, cites them and a number of others, and states the general principle in the United States as follows: "The courts hold that if A appeared in person before B, impersonating C, an innocent purchaser from A gets the property in the goods against B."

I do not think that it can be said that the presumption is conclusive, since there is at least one class of case in which it can be rebutted. If the person addressed is posing only as an agent, it is plain that the party deceived has no thought of contracting with him but only with his supposed principal; if then there is no actual or ostensible authority, there can be no contract. *Hardman v. Booth* (above, p. 163) is, I think, an example of this. Are there any other circumstances in which the presumption can be rebutted? It is not necessary to strain to find them, for we are here dealing only with offer and acceptance; contracts in which identity really matters may still be avoided on the ground of mistake. I am content to leave the question open, and do not propose to speculate on what other exceptions there may be to the general rule. What seems plain to me is that the presumption cannot in the present case be rebutted by piling up the evidence to show that Miss Ingram would never have contracted with H. unless she had thought him to be P. G. M. Hutchinson. That fact is conceded and, whether it is proved *simpliciter* or proved to the hilt, it does not go any further than to show that she was the victim of fraud. With great respect to the judge, the question that he propounded as the test is not calculated to show any more than that. He said: "Is it to be seriously suggested that they were willing to accept the cheque of the rogue other than in the belief, created by the rogue himself, that he, the rogue, was in fact the honest P. G. M. Hutchinson of the address in Caterham with the telephone number which they had verified?" In my judgment, there is everything to show that Miss Ingram would never have accepted H's offer if she had known the truth, but nothing to rebute the ordinary presumption that she was addressing her acceptance, in law as well as in fact, to the person to whom she was speaking. I think, therefore, that there was offer and acceptance in form. . . .

There can be no doubt, as all this difference of opinion shows, that the dividing line between voidness and voidability, between fundamental mistake and incidental deceit, is a very fine one. That a fine and difficult distinction has to be drawn is not necessarily any reproach to the law. But need the rights of the parties in a case like this depend on such a distinction? The great virtue of the common law is that it sets out to solve legal problems by the application to them of principles which the ordinary man is expected to recognise as sensible and just; their application in any particular case may produce what seems to him a hard result, but as principles they should be within his understanding and merit his approval.

But here, contrary to its habit, the common law, instead of looking for a principle that is simple and just, rests on theoretical distinctions. Why should the question whether the defendant should or should not pay the plaintiff damages for conversion depend upon voidness or voidability, and upon inferences to be drawn from a conversation in which the defendant took no part? The true spirit of the common law is to override theoretical distinctions when they stand in the way of doing practical justice. For the doing of justice, the relevant question in this sort of case is not whether the contract was void or voidable, but which of two innocent parties shall suffer for the fraud of a third. The plain answer is that the loss should be divided between them in such proportion as is just in all the circumstances. If it be pure misfortune, the loss should be borne equally; if the fault or imprudence of either party has caused or contributed to the loss, it should be borne by that party in the whole or in the greater part. In saying this, I am suggesting nothing novel, for this sort of observation has often been made. But it is only in comparatively recent times that the idea of giving to a court power to apportion loss has found a place in our law. I have in mind particularly the Law Reform Acts of 1935, 1943 and 1945, that dealt respectively with joint tortfeasors, frustrated contracts and contributory negligence. These statutes, which I believe to have worked satisfactory, show a modern inclination towards a decision based on a just apportionment rather than one given in black or in white according to the logic of the law. I believe it would be useful if Parliament were now to consider whether or not it is practicable by means of a similar act of law reform to provide for the victims of a fraud a better way of adjusting their mutual loss than that which has grown out of the common law.

Appeal dismissed with costs.

Law Reform Committee, Twelfth Report (Transfer of Title to Chattels) (Cmnd. 2958 of 1966)

The Report, having referred to the above judgment of Devlin L.J., continues:

9. A power of apportionment is plainly attractive at first sight, and we ourselves would have been in favour of a solution on these lines had we not come to the conclusion that there were overriding objections to it. We think that if the courts were given power to apportion loss in the type of case with which we are concerned it would introduce into a field of law where certainty and clarity are particularly important that uncertainty which inevitably follows the grant of a wide and virtually unrestrained judical discretion. Such a discretion is not appropriate in the case of transactions involving the transfer of property, and we do not regard any change in the law as desirable which is likely to increase litigation and make it more difficult for businessmen and others to obtain reliable legal advice or to assess the likely financial outcome of their dealings and insure against the risks involved.

10. The practical and procedural difficulties to which any system of apportionment would give rise would, in our view, be considerable. Let us suppose that goods belonging to O have been wrongfully obtained by a rogue, R, who sells them to an innocent purchaser, A, from whom they pass in succession to B and C. The title to the goods remains in O. But by virtue

of section 12 of the Sale of Goods Act, 1893, each of the sales from R to A, from A to B, and from B to C contains an implied condition that the seller has a right to sell the goods. Under the present law, if O has not recovered the goods he will have an action in conversion or detinue against C; C will have an action against B for breach of the condition as to title implied by the Sale of Goods Act, and B will have the same against A, who will (in theory) have the same against R. If O, C and B succeed in their actions and if, as usually happens, R cannot be found or is a man of straw, all the damages and costs fall on A. This, of course, is essentially the situation which a power to apportion is designed to remedy, but how would it operate in practice? C, when sued by O, would, presumably, have to establish the fact and extent of O's "negligence"—we put this in inverted commas because it seems clear that O would not be in breach of any common law duty to C—in failing to take adequate care of his goods. (It is true that in *Ingram v. Little* Lord Justice Devlin suggested that where the loss was "pure misfortune" it should be borne equally, but we see no reason why the owner of a chattel, if he is to retain the title to it—a matter with which we deal later in this Report—should be penalised when he has been in no way at fault.) It would, however, be difficult for C to establish negligence against O. He would not be able to give particulars of negligence in his pleading and discovery would be unlikely to assist as there would be no relevant documents in most cases, although interrogatories might sometimes establish a prima facie case. The extent to which C in his turn had acted reasonably would, of course, be relevant in ascertaining the extent of his right to any contribution, and the same difficulties of proof would arise.

11. The situation becomes much more complex when A and B are brought in, as they would have to be if the apportionment were to do justice between all parties. Any contribution which C was able to obtain from O would reduce the amount of damages in his action against B and those in B's action against A. This would be a very fortuitous benefit to A because it would depend on what C could prove about O's lack of care: indeed C would usually have little interest in obtaining contribution from O since the benefit of it would accrue not to him (unless B were insolvent) but to B, and through him to A. Thus the real issue would be between O and A, however many subsequent purchasers there might have been, but this issue could not be settled until all the other purchasers had been brought in. The need to take account of the extent to which any of them had been "negligent" would require the court to disregard any special provisions in the contracts between A and B, B and C, and so on down the chain of purchasers. These difficulties would add greatly to the complications about onus of proof, evidence, and procedure which we have mentioned above and thus to the length and cost of the proceedings. Consideration would have to be given to the case in which any of the parties was insolvent, as well as to the case in which R (the rogue) was found and was worth suing before, or, alternatively, after, an apportionment had taken place. We need not pause to consider the further complications which would arise if any of the contracts had a foreign element.

12. It may be suggested that these difficulties could be avoided if, instead of attempting to apportion the loss among all parties concerned, provision

were to be made merely for contribution as between the two parties directly affected, namely, the owner of the goods and the purchaser in whose hands they are found. This would enable the person having possession of the goods to recover a contribution from the true owner based on the extent to which the latter had failed to take the care which might reasonably have been expected of him. But it would hardly be satisfactory to ignore any negligence on the part of earlier purchasers in the chain as *res inter alios acta* and to do so would certainly be unjust to the owner of the goods. This is underlined by the fact that the good faith of the first purchaser in a chain is often suspect even though it may be difficult to prove anything against him. Moreover, the last purchaser would have little inducement to attempt to establish negligence against the owner when he could recover the whole of his loss from his immediate vendor in an action based on the implied condition as to title. Yet if this right were to be made subject to the right of recovery from the owner the last purchaser might well find himself in a worse position than he is today. We therefore think that any procedure for contribution would inevitably involve bringing in all the earlier purchasers in the chain, a solution which we have already given reasons for rejecting.

(The Committee's second and third recommendations are as follows:

(2) Where goods are stolen the owner should retain his title except where the goods are subsequently bought by a purchaser in good faith by retail at trade premises or at a public auction.

(3) Where goods are sold under a mistake as to the buyer's identity, the contract should, so far as third parties are concerned, be voidable and not void.)

LEWIS v. AVERAY

Court of Appeal [1972] 1 Q.B. 198; [1971] 3 W.L.R. 603; [1971] 3 All E.R. 907

Lewis advertised his car for sale. A man who gave no name rang up and arranged to see the car. He tested it and said he liked it. They went to the flat of Lewis's fiancée. The man told them he was Richard Greene, the well-known actor who played Robin Hood in the "Robin Hood" series. They agreed a price of £450 and he wrote a cheque for £450 signed "R. A. Green." He said he would like the car now and told Lewis not to bother about one or two small jobs he intended to do to the car. Lewis asked if he had anything to prove he was Richard Greene and the man produced an admission pass to Pinewood Studios, bearing an official stamp, the name of "Richard A. Green" and a photograph of the man. They exchanged receipts and Lewis allowed the man to take the car and log book. The cheque was worthless, being taken from a stolen cheque book. The man was not Richard Greene, the well-known actor. He sold the car, in the name of Lewis, for £200 to a bona fide purchaser, Averay, to whom he produced the log book. In the County Court Averay was held liable to Lewis for conversion of the car. Averay appealed.

LORD DENNING M.R., having stated the facts and discussed *Phillips v. Brooks* and *Ingram v. Little,* continued: Who is entitled to the goods? original seller? Or the ultimate buyer? The courts have given different answers. In *Phillips v. Brooks,* the ultimate buyer was held to be entitled to the ring. In *Ingram v. Little* the original seller was held to be entitled to the car. In the present case the deputy county court judge has held the original seller entitled.

It seems to me that the material facts in each case are quite indistinguishable the one from the other. In each case there was, to all outward appearance, a contract: but there was a mistake by the seller as to the identity of the buyer. This mistake was fundamental. In each case it led to the handing over of the goods. Without it the seller would not have parted with them.

This case therefore raises the question: What is the effect of a mistake by one party as to the identity of the other? It has sometimes been said that if a party makes a mistake as to the identity of the person with whom he is contracting there is no contract, or, if there is a contract, it is a nullity and void, so that no property can pass under it. This has been supported by a reference to the French jurist Pothier; but I have said before, and I repeat now, his statement is no part of English law. I know that it was quoted by Lord Haldane in *Lake v. Simmons* [1927] A.C. 487, 501, and, as such, misled Tucker J. in *Sowler v. Potter* [1940] 1 K.B. 271, into holding that a lease was void whereas it was really voidable.[1] But Pothier's statement has given rise to such refinements that it is time it was dead and buried altogether.

For instance, in *Ingram v. Little* the majority of the court suggested that the difference between *Phillips v. Brooks* and *Ingram v. Little* was that in *Phillips v. Brooks* the contract of sale was concluded (so as to pass the property to the rogue) before the rogue made the fraudulent misrepresentation: see [1961] 1 Q.B. 31, 51, 60: whereas in *Ingram v. Little* the rogue made the fraudulent misrepresentation before the contract was concluded. My own view is that in each case the property in the goods did not pass until the seller let the rogue have the goods.

Again it has been suggested that a mistake as to the identity of a person is one thing: and a mistake as to his attributes is another. A mistake as to identity, it is said, avoids a contract: whereas a mistake as to attributes does not. But this is a distinction without a difference. A man's very name is one of his attributes. It is also a key to his identity. If then, he gives a false name, is it a mistake as to his identity? or a mistake as to his attributes? These fine distinctions do no good to the law.

As I listened to the argument in this case, I felt it wrong that an innocent purchaser (who knew nothing of what had passed between the seller and the rogue) should have title depend on such refinements. After all, he has acted with complete circumspection and in entire good faith: whereas it was the seller who let the rogue have the goods and thus enabled him to commit the fraud. I do not, therefore, accept the theory that a mistake as to identity renders a contract void. I think the true principle is that which underlies the decision of this court in *King's Norton Metal Co. Ltd v. Edridge Merret & Co. Ltd* and of Horridge J. in *Phillips v. Brooks*, which has stood

---

[1] In May 1938 the defendant, then known as Ann Robinson, was convicted of permitting disorderly conduct in a café. In June 1938 she applied for a lease of Sowler's premises for use as a café, under the name of Potter. Shortly afterwards she changed her name by deed poll to Potter. The lease was then entered into in August 1938. Sowler's agent, when letting the premises, remembered the conviction of Robinson and would not have let the flat to the defendant had he known she was Robinson. He believed that, whoever he was contracting with, it was not Robinson. Tucker J. held the lease to be void. Since the defendant had submitted a fraudulent reference, he might have avoided the lease on the grounds of fraud. See the criticism of the case by Goodhart, 57 L.Q.R. 228; *Cheshire Fifoot & Furmston* (12th ed.), p. 251; and Denning L.J. in *Solle v. Butcher*, below, p. 501.

for these last 50 years. It is this: When two parties have come to a contract—or rather what appears, on the face of it, to be a contract—the fact that one party is mistaken as to the identity of the other does not mean that there is no contract, or that the contract is a nullity and void from the beginning. It only means that the contract is voidable, that is, liable to be set aside at the instance of the mistaken person, so long as he does so before third parties have in good faith acquired rights under it.

Applied to the cases such as the present, this principle is in full accord with the presumption stated by Pearce L.J. and also Devlin L.J. in *Ingram v. Little.* When a dealing is had between a seller like Mr Lewis and a person who is actually there present before him, then the presumption in law is that there is a contract, even though there is a fraudulent impersonation by the buyer representing himself as a different man than he is. There is a contract made with the very person there, who is present in person. It is liable no doubt to be avoided for fraud, but it is still a good contract under which title will pass unless and until it is avoided. In support of that presumption, Devlin L.J. quoted, at p. 66, not only the English case of *Phillips v. Brooks,* but other cases in the United States where "the courts hold that if A appeared in person before B, impersonating C, an innocent purchaser from A gets the property in the goods against B." That seems to me to be right in principle in this country also.

In this case Mr Lewis made a contract of sale with the very man, the rogue, who came to the flat. I say that he "made a contract" because in this regard we do not look into his intentions, or into his mind to know what he was thinking or into the mind of the rogue. We look to the outward appearances. On the face of the dealing, Mr Lewis made a contract under which he sold the car to the rogue, delivered the car and the logbook to him, and took a cheque in return. The contract is evidenced by the receipts which were signed. It was, of course, induced by fraud. The rogue made false representations as to his identity. But it was still a contract, though voidable for fraud. It was a contract under which this property passed to the rogue, and in due course passed from the rogue to Mr Averay, before the contract was avoided.

Though I very much regret that either of these good and reliable gentlemen should suffer, in my judgment it is Mr Lewis who should do so. I think the appeal should be allowed and judgment entered for the defendant.

PHILLIMORE L.J. allowed the appeal.

MEGAW L.J.: For myself, with very great respect, I find it difficult to understand the basis, either in logic or in practical considerations, of the test laid down by the majority of the court in *Ingram v. Little* [1961] 1 Q.B. 31. That test is, I think, accurately recorded in the headnote, as follows:

"—where a person physically present and negotiating to buy a chattel fraudulently assumed the identity of an existing third person, the test to determine to whom the offer was addressed was how ought the promisee to have interpreted the promise."

The promisee, be it noted, is the rogue. The question of the existence of a contract and therefore the passing of property, and therefore the right of third parties, if this test is correct, is made to depend upon the view which some rogue should have formed, presumably knowing that he is a rogue, as to the state of mind of the opposite party to the negotiation, who does not know that he is dealing with a rogue.

However that may be, and assuming that the test so stated is indeed valid, in my view, this appeal can be decided on a short and simple point. . . . When one looks at the evidence of the plaintiff, Mr Lewis himself, it is, I think, clear . . . that there was not any evidence that would justify the finding that he, Mr Lewis, regarded the identity of the man who called himself Mr Green as a matter of vital importance.

I agree that the appeal should be allowed.

Questions

1. Can *Lewis v. Averay* be reconciled with *Ingram v. Little*? If not, which is right?

2. In *Gallie v. Lee* (above, p. 138) Lord Denning M.R. said in the Court of Appeal [1969] 2 Ch. at p. 116: "I have long had doubts about the theory that, in the law of contract, mistake as to the identity of the person renders the contract a nullity and void. *Cundy v. Lindsay* (above, p. 165) can be explained on the ground that the offer was made to one person (Blenkiron & Co.) and accepted by another person (Alfred Blenkarn) and for that reason there was no contract at all." (See also Lord Denning's dictum in *Solle v. Butcher* (below, p. 501).) Is there any difference between Lord Denning's explanation of *Cundy v. Lindsay* and the theory that mistake as to identity renders the contract void? Are Lord Denning's remarks in *Lewis v. Averay* reconcilable with *Cundy v. Lindsay*?

CHAPTER 6

INTENTION TO CREATE LEGAL RELATIONS

BALFOUR v. BALFOUR

Court of Appeal [1919] 2 K.B. 571; 88 L.J.K.B. 1054; 121 L.T. 346

The defendant, who was a civil servant stationed in Ceylon, in November 1915, came to England with the plaintiff, his wife. They remained in England until August 1916, when the husband's leave was up and he had to return. The plaintiff, on the doctor's advice, remained in England, and the husband, before sailing, promised to give her £30 a month until she returned. He did so after assessing the sum she would require for maintenance in consultation with her. Later the husband wrote saying that it would be better if they remained apart, and in 1918 the wife obtained a decree nisi. The plaintiff sued on the promise to pay her £30 per month. Sargant J. gave judgment for the plaintiff, holding that the husband was under an obligation to support his wife and the parties had contracted that the extent of that obligation should be defined in terms of so much a month. The consent of the wife to that arrangement was a sufficient consideration to constitute a contract which could be sued upon. The husband appealed.

WARRINGTON and DUKE L.JJ. gave judgment allowing the appeal.

ATKIN L.J.: . . . it is necessary to remember that there are agreements between parties which do not result in contracts within the meaning of that term in our law. The ordinary example is where two parties agree to take a walk together, or where there is an offer and an acceptance of hospitality. Nobody would suggest in ordinary circumstances that those agreements result in what we know as a contract, and one of the most usual forms of agreement which does not constitute a contract appears to me to be the arrangements which are made between husband and wife. It is quite common, and it is the natural and inevitable result of the relationship of husband and wife, that the two spouses should make arrangements between themselves—agreements such as are in dispute in this action—agreements for allowances, by which the husband agrees that he will pay to his wife a certain sum of money, per week, or per month, or per year, to cover either her own expenses or the necessary expenses of the household and of the children of the marriage, and in which the wife promises either expressly or impliedly to apply the allowance for the purpose for which it is given. To my mind those agreements, or many of them, do not result in contracts at all, and they do not result in contracts even though there may be what as between other parties would constitute consideration for the agreement. The consideration, as we know, may consist either in some right, interest, profit or benefit accruing to one party or some forbearance, detriment, loss or responsibility given, suffered or undertaken by the other. That is a well-known definition, and it constantly happens, I think, that such arrangements made between husband and wife are arrangements in which there are mutual promises, or in which there is consideration in form within the definition that I have mentioned. Nevertheless, they are not contracts, and they are not contracts because the parties did not intend that they should be attended by legal consequences. To my mind it would be of the worst possible example to hold that agreements such as this resulted in legal obligations which could be enforced in the courts. It would mean this, that when the husband makes his wife a promise to give her an allowance of 30s. or £2 a week, whatever he can afford to give her, for the maintenance of the household and children, and she promises so to apply it, not only could she sue him for his failure in any week to supply the allowance, but he could sue her for non-performance of the obligation, express or implied, which she had undertaken upon her part. All I can say is that the small courts of this country would have to be multiplied one hundredfold if these arrangements were held to result in legal obligations. They are not sued upon, not because the parties are reluctant to enforce their legal rights when the agreement is broken, but because the parties, in the inception of the arrangement, never intended that they should be sued upon. Agreements such as these are outside the realm of contracts altogether. The common law does not regulate the form of agreements between spouses. Their promises are not sealed with seals and sealing wax. The consideration that really obtains for them is that natural love and affection which counts for so little in these cold courts. The terms may be repudiated, varied or renewed as performance proceeds or as disagreements develop, and the principles of the common law as to exoneration and discharge and accord and satisfaction are such as find no place in the domestic code.

COWARD v. MOTOR INSURERS' BUREAU

Court of Appeal [1963] 1 Q.B. 259; [1962] 2 W.L.R. 663; [1962] 1 All E.R. 531; [1962] 1 Lloyd's Rep 583

Coward was a pillion passenger on a motor-cycle owned and driven by Cole when, by an accident due to Cole's negligence, both were killed. In an action by Coward's widow the court thought it necessary to decide whether there was a contract between Coward and Cole. [In *Albert v. Motor Insurers' Bureau, infra,* the majority of the House of Lords held that it was not necessary to decide this question in cases of this kind and *Coward*'s case was disapproved; but it is not necessarily wrong on the question whether there was a contract.]

UPJOHN L.J.: The practice whereby workmen go to their place of business in the motor car or on the motor-cycle of a fellow workman upon the terms of making a contribution to the costs of transport is well known and widespread. In the absence of evidence that the parties intended to be bound contractually, we should be reluctant to conclude that the daily carriage by one of another to work upon payment of some weekly (or it may be daily) sum involved them in a legal contractual relationship. The hazards of everyday life, such as temporary indisposition, the incidence of holidays, the possibility of a change of shift or different hours of overtime, or incompatibility arising, make it most unlikely that either contemplated that the one was legally bound to carry and the other to be carried to work. It is made all the more improbable in this case by reason of the fact that alternative means of transport seem to have been available to Coward.

On the probabilities of the case, therefore, we reach the conclusion that, while admitting the evidence rejected by the judge, which in our judgment clearly proved an arrangement whereby Coward paid a weekly sum to Cole for transporting him to and from his work, neither party intended to enter into a legal contract.

Note

See also *Albert v. Motor Insurers' Bureau* [1971] 3 W.L.R. 291, H.L. In *Simpkins v. Pays* [1955] 1 W.L.R. 975, Sellers J. held binding an arrangement between A, a paying boarder at B's house, B and B's grand-daughter, C. They entered a fashion competition in a Sunday newspaper each week, each filling in one line, but the entry being sent in B's name. Sellers J. found that there was an agreement that, whichever line won, all should share equally, and that A was entitled to recover one-third of the prize from B.

In *Parker v. Clark* [1960] 1 W.L.R. 286, Devlin J. held that an arrangement between relatives to share a house was binding in view particularly of the fact that it was necessary for Parker to take the drastic and irrevocable step of disposing of his own residence in order to adopt the arrangement. The judge could not believe that Clark really believed that the law would allow him, if he chose, "to tell the Parkers when they arrived that he had changed his mind, that they could take their furniture away, and that he was indifferent whether they found anywhere else to live or not."

In *Gage v. King* [1961] 1 Q.B. 188, Diplock J. held that when a husband and wife open a joint banking account, prima facie, there is no intention to enter into legal relations *inter se*. And where a husband promised his wife to buy her a car in an effort to improve their strained matrimonial relationship and entered into a hire-purchase agreement in respect of a car which was delivered at their home, it was held that this was a purely domestic arrangement, not intended to create legal relationships and that, accordingly, the wife acquired no rights in the car or under the hire-purchase agreement: *Spellman v. Spellman* [1961] 1 W.L.R. 921.

In *Merritt v. Merritt* [1970] 1 W.L.R. 1211; [1970] 2 All E.R. 760, the Court of Appeal held that the presumption that agreements between husband and wife are not intended to create legal relations does not apply when they are not living in amity but are separated or about to separate. H had left W and was living with another woman. He agreed to pay W £40 a month, and signed a written agreement that, in consideration of W's paying off the mortgage on their jointly owned house, he would then transfer it to her sole ownership. W paid off the mortgage. Stamp J. made a declaration that W was the sole beneficial owner. H's appeal was dismissed. Lord Denning said: "In all these cases the court does not try to discover the intention by looking into the minds of the parties. It looks at the situation in which they were placed and asks itself: would reasonable people regard this agreement as intended to be binding?"

In *Gould v. Gould* [1970] 1 Q.B. 275, in deciding whether there was an intent to create legal relations, the court had regard to the uncertainty of the words. H on leaving W promised orally to pay her £15 per week "as long as he had it" or "as long as business was O.K." (according to W) or (according to H) "as long as I can manage it." The uncertainty of the words used led Edmund Davies and Megaw L.JJ. to conclude that there was no intent to create legal relations. Lord Denning, dissenting, thought an oral separation agreement, by which H agrees to pay W so much a week, is legally enforceable; terms should not be held void for uncertainty "unless it is utterly impossible to put a meaning on them"; and meaning could be given by implying a term that, if H could not keep up payments, he could determine the agreement by reasonable notice.

In *Jones v. Padavatton* [1969] 1 W.L.R. 328; [1969] 2 All E.R. 616, a mother (M) promised her daughter (D), aged 34, that if D would give up her well-paid job in Washington, D.C., and come to England to study for the bar, M would pay her $200 a month until she had completed her studies. D came to England in 1962 and studied for the bar. Danckwerts and Fenton Atkinson L.JJ. held that M and D did not intend to create legal relations. Salmon L.J. held that there was a binding unilateral contract requiring M to pay D $200 a month for a reasonable time; but a reasonable time could not possibly exceed five years, so she could not rely on the contract in 1968. Fenton Atkinson L.J. relied heavily on the conduct of the parties subsequent to the agreement (but see *Jas. Miller & Partners Ltd. v. Whitworth St. Estates* [1970] 2 W.L.R. 728; [1970] 1 All E.R. 796, above, p. 137).

In *Buckpitt v. Oates* [1968] 1 All E.R. 1145 the plaintiff and defendant, both aged seventeen, were in the habit of riding in each other's cars. The plaintiff sustained injury while riding in the defendant's car through the defendant's negligence. He had paid the defendant 10s. towards the cost of the petrol. John Stephenson J. found that "there was a friendly arrangement, or (I can hardly avoid using the phrase) a 'gentleman's agreement' to go on this trip, which gave rise to no legal obligations or rights, except those which the general law of the land imposes or implies."

In *Edwards v. Skyways Ltd* [1964] 1 W.L.R. 349 the defendant airline company agreed with the British Airline Pilots Association to pay certain "ex gratia" payments "approximating to" a readily ascertainable figure to pilots declared redundant. An action was brought by the plaintiff, a redundant pilot, for his payment under this agreement. It was admitted that consideration had moved from the plaintiff but the defendant company sought to escape liability by showing that the agreement was not intended to create legal relations and was too vague. Megaw J. considered that the subject of the present agreement related to business matters, so that the onus of establishing that there was no intention to create legal relations lay on the defendant company as the party seeking to use it as a defence. The company had not, he thought, discharged that onus. In so far as the term "ex gratia" had been used, he decided that its use had been simply in order to indicate that the company did not admit any pre-existing liability on its part. The words did not mean, to put it another way, that the promise, when accepted, should have no binding effect at law.

The use of the words "approximating to" by the defendant company did not in his lordship's view make the terms of the agreement too vague. On the evidence he took this to mean at most a "rounding off" of a few pounds downwards so as to achieve a round figure. The plaintiff accordingly succeeded.

ROSE AND FRANK CO. v. CROMPTON BROS.

Kings Bench Division [1923] 2 K.B. 261, 276; House of Lords [1925] A.C. 445; 94 L.J.K.B. 120; 132 L.T. 641; 30 Com. Cas. 163

The defendants were an English firm which manufactured paper tissues. In 1913 the defendants entered into an arrangement with the plaintiffs, an American firm, whereby the plaintiffs were constituted sole agents for the sale in the United States of the tissues supplied by the English firm, for three years with an option to extend that time. The document contained the following clause, described as the "Honourable Pledge Clause":

"This arrangement is not entered into, nor is this memorandum written, as a formal or legal agreement, and shall not be subject to legal jurisdiction in the law courts either of the United States or England, but it is only a definite expression and record of the purpose and intention of the three parties concerned to which they each honourably pledge themselves with the fullest confidence, based on past business with each other, that it will be carried through by each of the three parties with mutual loyalty and friendly co-operation."

The agreement was subsequently extended to March 1920, but in 1919 the defendants terminated it without notice. The defendants had received and accepted a number of specific orders for tissues before the termination, and these they refused to execute. The plaintiffs sued for breach of contract and for non-delivery of the goods.

Bailhache J. held that the 1913 arrangement and the orders and acceptances were legally binding contracts. The Court of Appeal (Bankes, Scrutton and Atkin L.JJ.) were unanimous in holding that the 1913 arrangement was not legally binding and they also held by a majority (Atkin L.J. dissenting) that the orders and acceptances did not constitute legally binding contracts.

SCRUTTON L.J.: Now it is quite possible for parties to come to an agreement by accepting a proposal with the result that the agreement concluded does not give rise to legal relations. The reason of this is that the parties do not intend that their agreement shall give rise to legal relations. This intention may be implied from the subject-matter of the agreement, but it may also be expressed by the parties. In social and family relations such an intention is readily implied, while in business matters the opposite result would ordinarily follow. But I can see no reason why, even in business matters, the parties should not intend to rely on each other's good faith and honour, and to exclude all idea of settling disputes by any outside intervention, with the accompanying necessity of expressing themselves so precisely that outsiders may have no difficulty in understanding what they mean. If they clearly express such an intention I can see no reason in public policy why effect should not be given to their intention.

Both legal decisions and the opinions of standard text writers support this view . . . Mr Leake says (7th ed., 1921), p. 3, that "an agreement as the source of a legal contract imports that the one party shall be bound to some performance, which the latter [sic] shall have a legal right to enforce." In Sir Frederick Pollock's language (9th ed., 1921), p. 3, an agreement to become enforceable at law must "be concerned with duties and rights which can be dealt with by a court of justice. And it must be the intention of the parties that the matter in hand shall, if necessary, be so dealt with, or at least they must not have the contrary intention." Sir William Anson requires in contract "a common intention to affect" the legal relations of the parties.

Judged by this test, I come to the same conclusion as the learned judge, that the particular clause in question shows a clear intention by the parties that the rest of their arrangement or agreement shall not affect their legal relations, or be enforceable in a court of law, but in the words of the clause, shall be "only a definite expression and record of the purpose and intention of the three parties concerned to which they each honourably pledge themselves," "and shall not be subject to legal jurisdiction." If the clause stood first in the document, the intention of the parties would be exceedingly plain.

ATKIN L.J.: In this case the defendants by the honourable understanding entered into the vague engagement contained in the document which had as a basis the average turnover for the last three years before the agreement. But whatever the terms of the agreement or understanding, it contemplated, as nearly all such agreements do, that the actual business done under it should be done by particular contracts of purchase and sale upon the terms of the general agreement so far as applicable. The actual business was done in this case, as in countless others, by orders for specific goods given by the "agent" and accepted by the manufacturer or merchant. . . . [His Lordship then examined the correspondence between the parties.] Pausing there, this is the common formula of acceptance in the business world which has been treated as acceptance in countless cases since merchants first wrote to one another. It would be understood as an acceptance passing between two merchants where there was no obligation at all on the part of the vendor to accept. Why it should bear a different meaning in a case where there is an honourable understanding by the merchant to accept up to some vague limit, I am unable to understand.

The House of Lords held (1) that the arrangement of 1913 was not a binding contract, but, (2) the orders given and accepted constituted enforceable contracts of sale.

Letters of Comfort. This device usually takes the form of encouragement by A of B to advance money to C, falling short of a guarantee by A. It appears that it originated in, the United States in the 1960s. Parent companies were reluctant to guarantee the debts of their subsidiaries because guarantees had to be disclosed in their accounts as contingent liabilities. Letters of comfort, not amounting to legal obligations, need not be shown. They appear now to be widely used in international business transactions.

KLEINWORT BENSON LTD v. MALAYSIA MINING CORP Bhd

Court of Appeal [1989] 1 W.L.R. 379, [1989] 1 All E.R. 785

The plaintiff bank agreed to make a loan of up to £10 million to MMC Metals Ltd ("Metals"), a wholly owned subsidiary of the defendants. The plaintiffs had tried to secure the joint and several liability of the defendants and Metals, or a guarantee by the defendants of the liability of Metals to the plaintiffs, but the defendants had refused to assume either form of obligation. Instead the plaintiffs accepted (but with a higher rate of interest) a "letter of comfort" drafted by them and signed by the defendants stating:

> "[2] We confirm that we will not reduce our current financial interest in MMC Metals Ltd until the above facilities have been repaid or until you have confirmed that you are prepared to continue the facilities with new shareholders.
> [3] It is our policy to ensure that the business of MMC Metals Ltd is at all times in a position to meet its liabilities to you under the above arrangements."

It was accepted that [2] created a legal obligation. The issue was whether [3] did so. Hirst J. held that it did. The defendants appealed.

RALPH GIBSON L.J.: The submission in this court for the plaintiffs can be more shortly stated because counsel adopted and relied on the reasoning of the judge. As to the effect and meaning to be given to para. 3, his main submissions were that: (i) the statement in para. 3 was made in a commercial contractual document and it is to be treated as a contractual promise if it appears on the evidence to have been so intended: see *Esso Petroleum Co. Ltd v. Mardon* (below p. 367); (ii) it is shown to have been so intended because the statement was made for the purpose of inducing the plaintiffs to enter into the acceptance credit transaction with Metals under the credit facility and it was plainly of decisive commercial importance to the transaction; (iii) the statement as to present policy must be taken as including a promise that that policy will remain in force. This proposition can be tested, it was said, by taking an example remote from banking: suppose a shop, by notice, announced that "it is our policy to take back all goods purchased and to refund the price, without any questions, on return of the goods in good condition within 14 days of purchase", if a customer should return goods, having bought them in reliance on the notice, the shop could not (said counsel for the plaintiffs) refuse to refund the price on the ground that the notice only stated the shop's policy on the day of purchase so that the shop was free to change its policy within the 14-day period. So in this case it is absurd in commercial terms for the defendants to claim to be free to change their announced policy after money has been advanced in reliance on it. To treat the words of para. 3 as no more than a representation of fact is to give no force to the words "at all times".

For my part, I am persuaded that the main criticisms of the judgment of Hirst J. advanced by counsel for the defendants are well founded and I would, for the reasons which follow, allow this appeal. In my judgment the defendants made a statement as to what their policy was, and did not in para. 3 of the comfort letter expressly promise that such policy would be continued in future. It is impossible to make up for the lack of express promise by implying such a promise, and indeed, no such implied promise was pleaded. My conclusion rests on what, in my judgment, is the proper effect and meaning which, on the evidence, is to be given to para. 3 of the comfort letters. . . .

The central question in this case, in my judgment, is that considered in *Esso Petroleum Co. Ltd v. Mardon*, on which counsel for the plaintiffs relied in this court but which was not cited to Hirst J. That question is whether the words of para. 3, considered in their context, are to be treated as a warranty or contractual promise. Paragraph 3 contains no express words of promise. Paragraph 3 is in its terms a statement of present fact and not a promise as to future conduct. I agree with the submission of counsel for the defendants that, in this regard, the words of para. 3 are in sharp contrast with the words of para. 2 of the letter: "We confirm that we will not" etc. The force of this point is not limited, as Hirst J. stated it, to the absence from para. 3 of the words "We confirm". The real contrast is between the words of promise, namely "We will not" in para. 2, and the words of statement of fact, "It is our policy" in para. 3. Hirst J. held that, by the words of para. 3, the defendants gave an undertaking that now and at all times in the future, so long as Metals should be under any liability to the plaintiffs under the facility arrangements, it is *and will* be the defendants' policy to ensure that Metals is in a position to meet their liabilities. To derive that meaning from the words it is necessary to add the words emphasised, namely "and will be", which do not appear in para. 3. In short, the words of promise as to the future conduct of the defendants were held by Hirst J. to be part of the necessary meaning of the words used in para. 3. The question is whether that view of the words can be upheld. . . .

[RALPH GIBSON L.J. held that that meaning could not be upheld.]

If my view of this case is correct, the plaintiffs have suffered grave financial loss as a result of the collapse of the tin market and the following decision by the defendant company not to honour a moral responsibility which it assumed in order to gain for its subsidiary the finance necessary for the trading operations which the defendants wished that subsidiary to pursue. The defendants have demonstrated, in my judgment, that they made no relevant contractual promise to the plaintiffs which could support the judgment in favour of the plaintiffs. The consequences of the decision of the defendants to repudiate their moral responsibility are not matters for this court.

I would allow this appeal.

NICHOLLS and O'CONNOR L.JJ. agreed.

Appeal allowed.

Note

In *Banque Brussels Lambert v. Australian National Industries Ltd* (1989) 21 NSWLR 502 Rogers C.J. said of the *Kleinwort Benson* case that the judgment of Hirst J. reflected "the bias of experienced commecial judges to pay high regard to the fact that the comfort letters before them came into existence as part and parcel of a commercial banking transaction and that the promises were an important feature of the letters." He said: "The Court of Appeal subjected the letters to minute textual analysis. Courts will become irrelevant in the resolution of commercial disputes if they allow this approach to dominate their consideration of commercial documents. . . . [Ralph Gibson L.J.'s] construction of the letter renders the document a scrap of paper. If the Lord Justice is correct, the writer has not expressed itself on anything relevant as a matter of honour."

Question
If A says to B; "I would like you to advance money to C. It is my intention to indemnify you if C defaults but I am not prepared to enter into any legal obligation to do so. You can rely on my word;" and B, relying on A's "words of comfort", then agrees to make the advance but at a higher rate of interest than if he had received a guarantee, should A be liable to B if C defaults and A declines to pay?

ESSO PETROLEUM LTD v. COMMISSIONERS OF CUSTOMS AND EXCISE

House of Lords [1976] 1 W.L.R. 1; [1976] 1 All E.R. 117

The facts are given above, p. 16.

VISCOUNT DILHORNE (having referred to statements in *Rose and Frank v. Crompton* and *Edwards v. Skyways* that in business matters there is a heavy onus on a party who asserts that legal relations were not intended): I do not wish in any way to criticise or qualify these statements, but I do not feel that they provide a sound foundation for the decision of this appeal.

True it is that Esso are engaged in business. True it is that they hope to promote the sale of their petrol, but it does not seem to me necessarily to follow or to be inferred that there was any intention on their part that their dealers should enter into legally binding contracts with regard to the coins; or any intention on the part of the dealers to enter into any such contract or any intention on the part of the purchaser of four gallons of petrol to do so.

If on the facts of this case the conclusion is reached that there was any such intention on the part of the customer, of the dealer and of Esso, it would seem to exclude the possibility of any dealer ever making a free gift to any of his customers, however negligible its value, to promote his sales.

If what was described as being a gift would be given if something was purchased was something of value to the purchaser, then it could readily be inferred that there was a common intention to enter into legal relations. But here, whatever the cost of production, it is clear that the coins were of little intrinsic value.

I do not consider that the offer of a gift of a free coin is properly to be regarded as a business matter in the sense in which that word was used by Scrutton L.J. in the passage cited above. Nor do I think that such an offer can be comprehended within the "business relations" which were in the *Skyways* case, as Megaw L.J. said, "the subject-matter of the agreement." I see no reason to imply any intention to enter into contractual relations from the statements on the posters that a coin would be given if four gallons of petrol were bought.

Nor do I see any reason to impute to every motorist who went to a garage where the posters were displayed to buy four gallons of petrol any intention to enter into a legally binding contract for the supply to him of a coin. On the acceptance of his offer to purchase four gallons there was no doubt a legally binding contract for the supply to him of that quantity of petrol, but I see again no reason to conclude that because such an offer was made by him, it must be held that, as the posters were displayed, his offer included an offer to take a coin. The gift of a coin might lead to a motorist returning to the garage to obtain another one, but I think the facts in this case negative any contractual intention on his part and on the part of the dealer as to the coin and suffice to rebut any presumption there may be to the contrary. . . .

LORD SIMON OF GLAISDALE: My Lords, I have had the advantage of reading in draft the speech prepared by my noble and learned friend Lord Russell of Killowen. I beg to take advantage of his explanation of the facts that have led to the appeal and the statutory provisions by which they are to be judged.

I am, however, my Lords, not prepared to accept that the promotion material put out by Esso was not envisaged by them as creating legal relations between the garage proprietors who adopted it and the motorists who yielded to its blandishments. In the first place, Esso and the garage proprietors put the material out for their commercial advantage, and designed it to attract the custom of motorists. The whole transaction took place in a setting of business relations. In the second place, it seems to me in general undesirable to allow a commercial promoter to claim that what he has done is a mere puff, not intended to create legal relations (cf. Carlill v. Carbolic Smoke Ball Co. above, p. 31). The coins may have been themselves of little intrinsic value; but all the evidence suggests that Esso contemplated that they would be attractive to motorists and that there would be a large commercial advantage to themselves from the scheme, an advantage in which the garage proprietors also would share. Thirdly, I think that authority supports the view that legal relations were envisaged.

Note

It has often been laid down that "An agreement purporting to oust the jurisdiction of the courts is illegal and void on grounds of public policy" (Halsbury, *Laws of England*, Vol. 9, p. 352). The rule may be illustrated by *Baker v. Jones* (1954) 1 W.L.R. 1005. The rules of the British Amateur Weightlifters' Association provided that the council of the Association should be the sole interpreter of its rules (r. 40(vii)) and that the council's decision in all cases should be final (r. 40(viii)). When a member of the Association claimed a declaration that the use of the Association's funds for a certain purpose was unlawful under the Association's rules, Lynskey J. held that he had jurisdiction to entertain the action. The contract between the plaintiff and the Association could not exclude the jurisdiction of the courts and rule 40(vii) and rule 40(viii), in so far as they purported to do so, were contrary to public policy and void. *Cf.* also *Lee v. Showmen's Guild* (1952) 2 Q.B. 329, 342.

Thus it appears that the parties are at liberty to declare that their arrangement is not a contract at all, but only a gentleman's agreement: *Rose and Frank v. Crompton* (1925) A.C. 445; but they may not make a contract which provides that the courts shall not have jurisdiction over it: *Baker v. Jones*. In effect this seems to mean that the parties are at liberty to provide that their agreement shall not be enforced by any authority whatsoever; but they may not set up some other contract-enforcing authority to the exclusion of the court. If the Weightlifters' Association had included an "Honourable Pledge Clause" in the contract with its members this might have prevented the rules being enforced at all—but that was certainly not what the Association wanted. They wanted the rules to be enforceable by their council; but if the contract is to be enforceable at all, the jurisdiction of the courts cannot be excluded.

Agreements not to enforce particular legal rights stand on a different footing and are generally binding: *Alliance Bank v. Broom*, below, p. 215, *Cook v. Wright*, below, p. 214. In some cases it is contrary to public policy to allow a person to give up his right and, in such a case, a contract to do so is void. Thus a wife's promise not to apply to the Divorce Court for maintenance is not binding on her; "The wife's right to future maintenance is a matter of public concern—which she cannot barter away." (Lord Atkin in *Hyman v. Hyman* [1929] A.C. 601; discussed in *Combe v. Combe* [1951] 2 K.B. 215, below, p. 255.

PART II

CONSIDERATION AND PRIVITY OF CONTRACT

CHAPTER 7

CONSIDERATION

Section 1. Introductory

Corbin, "Does a Pre-existing Duty Defeat Consideration?—Recent Noteworthy Decisions,"
27 Yale L.J. 362, 376

In all contract law our problem is to determine what facts will operate to create legal duties and other legal relations. We find at the outset that bare words of promise do not so operate. Our problem then becomes one of determining what facts must accompany promissory words in order to create a legal duty (and other legal relations). We must know what these facts are in order that we can properly predict the enforcement of reparation, either specific or compensatory, in case of non-performance. We are looking for a sufficient cause or reason for the legal enforcement of a promise. This problem was also before the Roman lawyers and it must exist in all systems of law. With us it is called the problem of consideration.

C. J. Hamson, The Reform of Consideration (1938) 54 L.Q.R. 233, 234, 242

What is today the significance of consideration in the law of simple contract? So far from being an additional and unnecessary mystery, an accidental tom-tit in an otherwise rational theory of contract, consideration in its essential nature is an aspect merely of the fundamental notion of bargain, other aspects of which, no less but no more important, are offer and acceptance. Consideration, offer and acceptance are an indivisible trinity, facets of one identical notion which is that of bargain. Indeed, consideration may conveniently be explained as merely the acceptance viewed from the offeror's side. Acceptance is defined to be the doing of that act (which may be the giving of a promise or the rendering of a performance) which is *requested* by the offeror in exchange for his promise; it is the *response* to the offer. An act done at the request of the offeror in response to his promise is consideration; and consideration in its essence is nothing else but response to such a request. To a gratuitous promise the common law notion of offer and acceptance does not apply. We can no doubt separate offer, acceptance and consideration for our convenience in treating of them: but they are logical and interdependent entities abstracted from the one entire reality which is bargain. We can no more abolish one without destroying the others than we can think of a circle without a circumference. . . .

If it were clear when a party has formed an intention to incur legal obligation, *if* a person did commonly define the obligation he desired to assume in terms which left little doubt as to its nature, it would be unnecessary, and indeed merely foolish, to require an additional test of that

195

intention. It is because persons commonly do not so define their intention, and because the common law recognises that fact, that the common law requires a test. To dismiss the doctrine of consideration as not worth serious attention because "it came into being not as an essential part of a *theory* of the law of contract but more or less fortuitously as an expedient adopted in order to determine when persons injured by the breach of a promise ought to be allowed to bring an action" (paragraph 18 of the 6th interim report of the Law Revision Committee 1937 Cmd. 5449) is, to my mind, to misunderstand what is an essential part of a *practical* law of contract.

P.S. Atiyah, Consideration in Contracts (1971)

. . . to talk of abolition of the doctrine of consideration is nonsensical. Consideration *means* a reason for the enforcement of a promise. Nobody can seriously propose that all promises should become enforceable; to abolish the doctrine of consideration, therefore, is simply to require the Courts to begin all over again the task of deciding what promises are to be enforceable. They will, of course, have to set new technical justifications for this task, and the obvious one that lies to hand is the "intent to create legal relations." No doubt there is something to be said for beginning this task all over again, and for using a new technique for the purpose. Changes in social and commercial conditions, and changes in the moral values of the community, mean that the Courts will not always find the same reasons for the enforcement of promises to be good today as their forbears did; equally it is likely that they will often find good reasons for the enforcement of promises where their predecessors did not. Moreover, I think there is less likelihood of the "intent to create legal relations" formula ossifying into a "doctrine"; though there is the converse danger that its application may create uncertainty as to what promises will be enforceable. But I question whether the "intent to create legal relations" formula will in the long run work any better than the rules of consideration.

Pollock, Principles of Contract (13th ed.) p. 133

The following description of Consideration was given by the Exchequer Chamber in 1875: "A valuable consideration, in the sense of the law, may consist either in some right, interest, profit, or benefit accruing to the one party, or some forbearance, detriment, loss, or responsibility, given, suffered, or undertaken by the other": *Currie v. Misa* (1875) L.R. 10 Ex. at 162.

The second branch of this judicial description is really the more important one. Consideration means not so much that one party is profited as that the other abandons some legal right in the present, or limits his legal freedom of action in the future, as an inducement for the promise of the first. It does not matter whether the party accepting the consideration has any apparent benefit thereby or not: it is enough that he accepts it, and that the party giving it does thereby undertake some burden, or lose something which in contemplation of law may be of value.

An act or forbearance of the one party, or the promise thereof, is the price for which the promise of the other is bought, and the promise thus given for value is enforceable. (Words adopted by Lord Dunedin in *Dunlop v. Selfridge*, below, p. 276.)

J. C. Smith, The Law of Contract—Alive or Dead? 13, The Law Teacher (1979), 73, 77

The language of benefit and detriment is, and I believe long has been, out of date. So is the idea that consideration must be an economic benefit of some kind. All that is necessary is that the defendant should, expressly or impliedly, ask for something in return for his promise, an act or a promise by the offeree. If he gets what he has asked for, then the promise is given for consideration unless there is some vitiating factor. Though lip-service has been paid to the notions of benefit and detriment, they have no substantial meaning, in the light of the principle that the court will not inquire into the adequacy of the consideration. If I make a promise to you in return for your supplying me with three, quite useless, chocolate wrappers, which I will instantly throw away, there is a perfectly good contract provided that the promise was seriously intended (below, p. 206.) I have got what I asked for and that is a sufficient "benefit". You have parted with something that you might have kept and that is a sufficient "detri-ment." But the wrappers are of no value to me, and you are perhaps glad to be rid of them. As for economic value, the judges have recognised, for over a century, the validity of the contract to pay £100 if the promisee will walk to York (a famous example given by Brett J. in *Great Northern Rly. v. Witham* (1873) L.R.9C.P 16); and no one has ever demonstrated what economic value there is in walking to York. Similarly with promises of reward for not smoking; (*Hamer v. Sidway* 27 N.E. 256; 124 N.Y. 538, 1891) or by the father of an illegitimate child to pay the mother an allowance if she proves to him that the child is well looked after and happy (below, p. 223).

Gratuitous Promises and Conditional Gifts

Hamson above, p. 195 stresses the need for a request. See also *Carlill v. Carbolic Smoke Ball Co.*, above p. 31 *Shadwell v. Shadwell*, below, p. 225 and *Combe v. Combe* below, p. 255. These authorities suggest that a promise to pay money, or to do any other act, in a certain event but without any express or implied request to the promisee to bring about, or to promise to bring about, that event, is made without consideration. In *Dickinson v. Abel* [1969] 1 W.L.R. 295; [1969] 1 All E.R. 484, W told A that he was willing to pay £100,000 for a certain farm. A had no proprietary interest in the farm but had transmitted earlier offers for it to the bank who were trustees of it. A asked "What's in it for me?" and was told that he would receive £10,000 if W bought it for £100,000 or less. W did not specify any service to be rendered by A and A did not know what was in W's mind. The sale took place and A received £10,000. Held that it was not taxable because it was not paid under an enforceable contract. Pennycuick J. found that there was no implied request for any service or promise of service [for example, to use his best endeavours to persuade the bank to sell at £100,000 or to act as a go-between—*cf.* the putting in touch with X in *British Bank for Foreign Trade v. Novinex* (above, p. 93). The judge obviously thought that A had told a tall story, but he had to accept the facts in the Case Stated by the Crown.

A similar problem provoked a difference of judicial opinion in *Wyatt v. Kreglinger and Fernau* [1933] 1 K.B. 793. The defendant firm lawfully terminated the employment of the plaintiff who had worked for them for many years. The plaintiff had no right to any pension. The defendants wrote to him and told him that they had *decided* to pay him a pension of £200 a year and that he was at liberty to enter into any other employment or enter any business, "except in the wool trade." The plaintiff did not enter the wool trade but after nine years the defendants stopped the pension. The plaintiff claimed that they were bound by contract to continue the pension. All the judges in the Court of Appeal were agreed that, if there was a contract, it was illegal as being in restraint of trade. Scrutton L.J., agreeing with the trial judge, Macnaghten J., thought there was no contract. The pension was a voluntary gratuitous payment and the words "except in the wool trade" were merely an intimation to Mr Wyatt that if he did enter the wool trade he must not expect them to continue the pension. Slesser and Greer L.JJ. thought that there was a contract but that it was illegal as being in restraint of trade.

If a gratuitous unconditional promise is revocable should it become irrevocable because a condition is added? Suppose that D promises his widowed or divorced daughter-in-law, P, to pay her £5,000 a year. Could he not withdraw the promise on finding himself in straitened circumstances, or on falling out with P, or because she had married a wealthy man? Suppose then that D's promise is to pay the money "so long as you remain unmarried." Is this merely a definition of the limits of a gratuitous promise (as in *Thomas v. Thomas, infra*) or is it an offer to contract, the consideration being P's forbearance from marriage? Might it be different if D, on hearing of P's intention to remarry, were to say, "Please do not remarry. I will pay you £5,000 a year so long as you remain unmarried." In this case D is clearly asking a price for his promise but is he in the former case?

Is there a difference between *requesting* an act and *specifying* an act to be done in return for the promise? Or are these two ways of describing the same thing? See Atiyah, *Consideration in Contracts*, pp.33–34.

Problems

1. William is very worried as to whether he will pass his solicitor's final examination which he has already failed twice. In order to allay his anxiety his father says, "If you fail again I will take you into my book-binding business as a partner." William fails again. His father now refuses to give him the partnership. Advise William.

Would your answer be different if William's father had said, "If you *pass* the examination I will take you, etc.?"

(See Smith, "Unilateral Contracts and Consideration" (1953) 69 L.Q.R. 102; and *cf.* F. H. Lawson, "Analogues of the *Stipulatio* in English Law," *XXth Century Comparative and Conflicts Law*, p. 117 *et seq.*)

(a) A, who has a new Rolls-Royce car, says to B, "I will give you my car if you fetch it from the garage."

(b) A, who has an ancient and dilapidated Rolls-Royce immobilised in his garage says to B, "I will give you my car if you fetch it from the garage."

In what circumstances, if any, would a contract result in either of the above situations?

Section 2. Consideration—Executed, Executory, and Past: and Motive

THOMAS v. THOMAS

Queen's Bench (1842) 2 Q.B. 851; 2 G & D. 226; 11 L.J.Q.B. 104; 6 Jur. 645; 114 E.R. 330

The plaintiff, the widow of John Thomas, sued the defendants, his executors, for breach of a written agreement to convey to her a cottage. The agreement recited that John had left all his estate to his executors by his will but that, shortly before his death, he had declared in the presence of several witnesses that he wished his widow to have the cottage for her life or so long as she continued a widow; and that, though this wish was never put into writing, the executors were convinced that it was his desire and were willing and desirous that it should be put into effect. The agreement stated that "in consideration of such desire" the executors would convey the cottage to the widow for her life or so long as she should continue a widow. It was provided and further agreed that the widow would pay to the executors "the sum of £1 yearly, towards the ground-rent, payable in respect of the said dwelling house," and would keep it in good repair.

The executors refused to convey the cottage. A jury awarded the widow £100 damages and the Queen's Bench discharged a rule to enter a non-suit.

PATTESON J.: The cause for the gift was unquestionably respect for the memory of the testator. But we must not confound motive with consideration. A consideration, such as is recognised and known to our law, means a consideration of some value, moving from the plaintiff. Mere respect for the memory and wishes of a testator cannot be in any way construed as such. It is then argued, that, this being so, there is no consideration for the agreement at all, and that it is an agreement for a voluntary gift on certain conditions; but, looking at the agreement, we find, not a mere proviso, but an express agreement by the plaintiff to pay £1 towards a certain ground-rent, which apparently has been for the first time apportioned, and to pay it to the defendant, who is, I presume, liable to the whole ground-rent. It is not, therefore, a burden incident to the taking of the lease; if it were, it would be to pay to the superior landlord. Then again, as to the repairs: it may be that the original lease from the ground landlord contained covenants compelling repairs to be made by the lessee; but we know nothing of such a lease or such covenants. For anything we know, it is an agreement entered into for the first time, in consequence of this instrument . . .

Questions

1. What was the consideration to support the defendant's promise: (a) expressed in the agreement? (b) found by the court?

2. What promise, express or implied, was made by the plaintiff?

3. Both Lord Denman C.J. and Patteson J. emphasise the need to distinguish between consideration and the motive which induces entry into a contract. Is not the price which one party is to receive for his undertaking a motive for his entry into the contract with the other party?

Note

The court assumes that, if the ground-rent was "a burden incident to the taking of the lease" or (Lord Denman C.J.) "a necessary burden on the premises," the plaintiff's promise to pay it would not have been a sufficient consideration: a promise to make a gift of onerous property is still a mere promise to make a gift, though the promisee agrees to assume the burden. This is questionable. In *Price v. Jenkins* (1877) 5 Ch.D. 619, C.A. (followed in *Johnsey Estates Ltd v. Lewis & Manley (Engineering) Ltd* (1987) 54 P. & C.R. 296, it was held that a settlement of leasehold property was a conveyance for valuable consideration because the donee would have to undertake payment of the rent and performance of the covenants. James L.J. asked, "Can an assignment of leasehold property ever be strictly speaking voluntary?" in *Cheale v. Kenward* (1858) 27 L.J. Ch. 784 it was held that a promise to transfer shares in a company on which no deposit or other sum had been paid was made for consideration when the transferee agreed to do all acts necessary to relieve the transferor of liability in respect of the shares. And *cf. Merritt v. Merritt*, above, p. 185.

Question

Uncle says to nephew: "I intend to give you my shares in the Super Company on your twenty-first birthday. They are worth about a million. You will have to pay calls of about £500. Will you accept them?" Nephew replies with alacrity that he will. Has Uncle contracted to transfer the shares? If he does transfer them, has he made a gift or performed a contract?

LAMPLEIGH v. BRATHWAIT

Common Bench (1615) Hob. 105; Moore K.B. 866; 1 Sm. L.C. (13th ed.) 148; 80
E.R. 255

In assumpsit in the Common Bench, it was alleged that Brathwait, having killed a
man, asked the plaintiff to use his endeavours to obtain him a pardon, wherefore the
plaintiff did go to Royston to the King to get the pardon and, in consideration of
this service, the defendant promised the plaintiff £100. To this declaration, it was
demurred that the consideration was executed before the promise was made. . . .
Nicols, Winch and Hobart held that the action was well laid because it was alleged
that there was a request before the endeavour was made and where there is such a
precedent request, a subsequent assumpsit after the execution of the consideration is
binding.
     First it was agreed, that a mere voluntary curtesy will not have a consideration to
uphold an assumpsit. But if that curtesy were moved by a suit or request of the
party that gives the assumpsit, it will bind, for the promise, though it follows, yet it
is not naked, but couples itself with the suit before, and the merits of the party
procured by that suit, which is the difference.
     (A second point, upon which Warburton J. based a dissenting judgment is
omitted.)

Note
     In *Kennedy v. Broun* (1863) 13 C.B. 677 (Common Pleas) Erle C.J. said that in *Lampleigh v.
Brathwait* "it was assumed that the journeys which the plaintiff performed at the request of the
defendant, and the other services he rendered, would have been sufficient to make any
promise binding if it had been connected therewith in one contract; the peculiarity of the
decision lies in connecting a subsequent promise with a prior consideration after it had been
executed. Probably, at the present day, such service on such request would have raised a
promise by implication to pay what it was worth; and the subsequent promise of a sum certain
would have been evidence for the jury to fix the amount."

Re CASEY'S PATENTS, STEWART v. CASEY

Court of Appeal [1892] 1 Ch. 104; 61 L.J. Ch. 61; 66 L.T. 93; 40 W.R. 180

J. Stewart and T. Charlton wrote to the defendant, Casey, the following
letter:
                     "Stewart and Charlton's Patents
Dear Sir,
     We now have pleasure in stating that in consideration of your services as
the practical manager in working both our patents as above for transit by
steamer or for any land purposes, we hereby agree to give you one third
share of the patents above-mentioned, the same to take effect from this
date. This is in addition to and in combination with our agreement of the
29th November last."
     They later transferred the letters patent to Casey during some negotia-
tions which eventually came to nothing. After the death of Stewart, the
present plaintiffs—his executor and Charlton—asked Casey to return the
letters patent: Casey refused, claiming to be entitled to possession as owner
of a third share, and registered the letter set out above.
     In the present action, the plaintiffs claimed delivery up of the letters
patent and damages for their detention. Romer J. dismissed the action and
his judgment was affirmed by the Court of Appeal (Lindley, Bowen and
Fry L.JJ.).

Inter alia, it was argued before the Court of Appeal that there was no assignment of a share to Casey because there was no consideration for the agreement contained in the letter.

BOWEN L.J.: . . . But then it was said by Mr Daniel, "But there is no consideration, and this document is not under seal." We will see if there is consideration. The consideration is stated, such as it is. It is, "in consideration of your services as the practical manager in working our patents as above for transit by steamer." Then says Mr Daniel, "Yes, but that is a future consideration and a future consideration, if nothing were done under it or nothing was proved to be done, would fail." The answer to that is that the consideration is not the rendering of the services, as is plain from the fact that the document is to take effect in Equity from the date. The consideration must be something other than rendering services in the future. It is the promise to render them which those words imply, that constitutes the consideration; and the promise to render future services, if an effectual promise, is certainly good consideration. Then, driven from that, Mr Daniel said, "Oh! but it is past services that it means, and past services are not a consideration for anything." Well, that raises the old question—or might raise it, if there was not an answer to it—of *Lampleigh v. Brathwait* (above, p. 200), a subject of great interest to every scientific lawyer, as to whether a past service will support a promise. I do not propose to discuss that question, or, perhaps, I should not have finished this week. I should have to examine the whole state of the law as to, and the history of the subject of, consideration, which, I need hardly say, I do not propose to do. But the answer to Mr Daniel's point is clear. Even if it were true, as some scientific students of law believe, that a past service cannot support a future promise, you must look at the document and see if the promise cannot receive a proper effect in some other way. Now, the fact of a past service raises an implication that at the time it was rendered it was to be paid for, and, if it was a service which was to be paid for, when you get in the subsequent document a promise to pay, that promise may be treated either as an admission which evidences or as a positive bargain which fixes the amount of that reasonable remuneration on the faith of which the service was originally rendered. So that here for past services there is ample justification for the promise to give the third share. Therefore, this is an equitable assignment which cannot be impeached.

Questions
1. Would every "past service" raise an implication that it was to be paid for, so as to allow action on a subsequent promise of payment?

2. (a) What is the difference between
     (i) a promise which evidences the amount of payment and
     (ii) a positive bargain which fixes the amount of reasonable remuneration?
   (b) A does services for B for which a reasonable remuneration would be £100.
     (i) Without discussion, B promises to give A £500 for his services;
     (ii) A demands £500, B offers £100. A says he will accept £250. B agrees to pay £250.

Consider the consequences in each case, if B should subsequently refuse to give A the money.

Note
The principles of *Lampleigh v. Brathwait* as interpreted in *Re Casey's Patents* were applied by the Privy Council in *Pao On v. Lau Yiu Long*, [1980] A.C. 614, below, pp. 228 and 654. Lord Scarman said:

"An act done before the giving of a promise to make a payment or to confer some other benefit can sometimes be consideration for the promise. The act must have been done at the promisors' request: the parties must have understood that the act was to be remunerated either by a payment or the conferment of some other benefit: and payment, or the conferment of a benefit, must have been legally enforceable had it been promised in advance. All three features are present in this case. . . .

Their Lordships agree that the mere existence or recital of a prior request is not sufficient in itself to convert what is prima facie past consideration into sufficient consideration in law to support a promise, as they have indicated, it is only the first of three necessary preconditions. As for the second of those preconditions, whether the act done at the request of the promisor raises an implication of promised remuneration or other return is simply one of the construction of the words of the contract in the circumstances of its making."

The Board held that, on the somewhat complex facts of the particular case, it mattered not whether the subsequent promise was regarded as the best evidence of the benefit intended to be conferred or as the positive bargain, the benefit on the faith of which the promise was given.

Question

Is it strictly true to say that "An act done before the giving of a promise to make a payment or to confer some benefit can sometimes be consideration for the promise"? Where the promise is the "best evidence" it only expresses an implied promise (implied in the request). Where it is "a positive bargain," the consideration is to be found in that bargain. *Cf.* question 2(b) above, p. 201.

ROSCORLA v. THOMAS

Queen's Bench (1842) 3 Q.B. 234; 2 G. & D. 508; 11 L.J.Q.B. 214; 6 Jur. 929; 61 R.R. 216; 114 E.R. 496

The relevant facts appear in the judgment of the court delivered by LORD DENMAN C.J.:

This was an action of assumpsit for breach of warranty of the soundness of a horse. The first count of the declaration, upon which alone the question arises, stated that, in consideration that the plaintiff, at the request of the defendant, had bought of the defendant a horse for the sum of £30, the defendant promised that it was sound and free from vice. And it was objected, in arrest of judgment, that the precedent executed consideration was insufficient to support the subsequent promise. And we are of opinion that the objection must prevail.

It may be taken as a general rule, subject to exceptions, not applicable to this case, that the promise must be co-extensive with the consideration. In the present case, the only promise that would result from the consideration, as stated, and be co-extensive with it, would be to deliver the horse upon request. The precedent sale, without a warranty, though at the request of the defendant, imposes no other duty or obligation upon him. It is clear, therefore, that the consideration stated would not raise an implied promise by the defendant that the horse was sound or free from vice.

But the promise in the present case must be taken to be, as in fact it was, express: and the question is, whether that fact will warrant the extension of the promise beyond that which would be implied by law; and whether the consideration, though insufficient to raise an implied promise, will nevertheless support an express one. And we think that it will not.

The cases in which it has been held that, under certain circumstances, a consideration insufficient to raise an implied promise will nevertheless support an express one, will be found collected and reviewed in the note (*a*) to *Wennall v. Adney* (3 Bos. & Pul. 249), and in the case of *Eastwood v. Kenyon* (1840) 11 Ad. & E. 438). There are cases of voidable contracts subsequently ratified, of debts barred by operation of law, subsequently revived, and of equitable and moral obligations, which, but for some rule of law, would of themselves have been sufficient to raise an implied promise. All these cases are distinguishable from, and indeed, inapplicable to, the present, which appears to us to fall within the general rule, that a consideration past and executed will support no other promise than such as would be implied by law.

The rule for arresting the judgment upon the first count must therefore be made absolute.

Rule absolute.

Question
If the precedent sale was at the request of the defendant, who later made the express promise of the guarantee, why should not the guarantee have been enforceable under *Lampleigh v. Brathwait?*

Law Reform Committee, 6th Interim Report, para. 32

The inconvenience of this rule (*sic.* that past consideration is no consideration) is frequently evaded by means of the fiction that the promise made subsequent to the consideration merely fixes the amount due under an earlier promise deemed to exist contemporaneously with the consideration. In a very important class of case, namely, actions upon cheques and other bills of exchange, the rule does not apply and we can see no reason why it should apply at all. The fact that the promisor has already received consideration for his promise before he makes it, so far from enabling him to break his promise seems to us to form an additional reason for making him keep it. We therefore recommend the abolition of this rule.

Question
What is meant here by "past consideration"? (See Hamson, 54 L.Q.R. 233, 251–253.)

Bills of Exchange Act 1882

Section 27(1). Valuable consideration for a bill may be constituted by:
(a) Any consideration sufficient to support a simple contract;
(b) An antecedent debt or liability. Such a debt or liability is deemed valuable consideration whether the bill is payable on demand or at a future time.

(2) Where value has at any time been given for a bill the holder is deemed to be a holder for value as regards the acceptor and all parties to the bill who became parties prior to such time.

(3) Where the holder of a bill has a lien on it arising either from contract or by implication of law, he is deemed to be a holder for value to the extent of the sum for which he has a lien.

Section 30(1). Every party whose signature appears on a bill is prima facie deemed to have become a party thereto for value.

Note

Note the limited nature of the exception created by section 27(1)(*b*), above. In *Thoni Gesellschaft v. RTP Eqpt.* [1979] 2 Lloyd's Rep. 282, C.A., a bill for one million Austrian schillings was given by a debtor to his creditor. Only 400,000 schillings were actually due. It was held that the creditor could recover only 400,000.

Section 3. Sufficiency of Consideration

(a) ADEQUACY OF CONSIDERATION

BAINBRIDGE v. FIRMSTONE

Queen's Bench (1838) 1 P. & D. 2; 8 Ad. & El. 743; 1 W.W. & H. 600; 53 R.R. 234; 112 E.R. 1019

Assumpsit. The declaration stated that, whereas heretofore, to wit, etc., in consideration that the plaintiff, at the request of the defendant, had then consented to allow the defendant to weigh divers, to wit two, boilers of the plaintiff, of great value, etc., defendant promised that he would, within a reasonable time after the said weighing was effected, leave and give up the boilers in as perfect and complete a condition, and as fit for use by plaintiff, as the same were in at the time of the consent so given by plaintiff; and that, although in pursuance of the consent so given, defendant to wit, on, etc., did weigh the same boilers, yet defendant did not nor would, within a reasonable time after the said weighing was effected, leave and give up boilers in as perfect, etc., but wholly neglected and refused so to do, although a reasonable time for that purpose had elapsed before the commencement of this suit; and, on the contrary thereof, defendant afterwards, to wit on, etc., took the said boilers to pieces and did not put the same together again, but left the same in a detached and divided condition, and in many different pieces, whereby plaintiff hath been put to great trouble, etc. Plea, non assumpsit.

On the trial before Lord Denman C.J. at the London sittings after last Trinity term, a verdict was found for the plaintiff.

John Bayley now moved in arrest of judgment. The declaration shows no consideration. There should have been either detriment to the plaintiff, or benefit to the defendant: 1 Selwyn's N.P. 45 (9th ed.). It does not appear that the defendant was to receive any remuneration. Besides, the word "weigh" is ambiguous.

LORD DENMAN C.J.: It seems to me that the declaration is well enough. The defendant had some reason for wishing to weigh the boilers; and he could do so only by obtaining permission from the plaintiff, which he did obtain by promising to return them in good condition. We need not inquire what benefit he expected to derive. The plaintiff might have given or refused leave.

PATTESON J.: The consideration is, that the plaintiff, at the defendant's request, had consented to allow the defendant to weigh the boilers. I suppose the defendant thought he had some benefit; at any rate, there is a detriment to the plaintiff from his parting with the possession for even so short a time.

WILLIAMS AND COLERIDGE JJ. concurred.

Rule refused.

Consideration Need not be Adequate but must be Sufficient

If the promisor gets what he asks for in return for his promise, he has received sufficient consideration and is bound. It is immaterial that his promise is far more valuable than the price he has asked for it. The courts are generally concerned only with the question whether the promisor has made a bargain, not with whether he has made a good bargain. They will not inquire into the adequacy of the consideration he has asked for and received. See *Mountford v. Scott*, above, p. 78, *Centrovincial Estates plc v. Merchant Investors*, above, p. 115, *Thomas v. Thomas* above, p. 198.

There are, however, certain promises and acts which, for various reasons of policy, are deemed to be of no value in law and which are therefore an insufficient consideration. Hence the curious but traditional terminology of the law—the consideration need not be adequate but must be sufficient (or real). If the law deems a promise to be void, it is not sufficient consideration. A wife's promise not to go to court to seek maintenance from her estranged husband was deemed to be void as being contrary to public policy and, consequently, the husband's promise to pay her money in consideration of her agreeing not to go to court was made without consideration and also void: *Gaisberg v. Storr* [1950] 1 K.B. 107, but see, now, Matrimonial Causes Act 1973, s.34, below, p. 220. The doing of an act which there is a public duty to do—for example, attendance as a witness in response to a subpoena (below, p. 216) has similarly been held to have no value in the law and to be insufficient consideration for a promise made in return for the doing of it. A New Zealand court held that an undertaking by the government not to introduce legislation regarding the advertising of cigarettes was incapable of being consideration for a promise by a tobacco company because the government's promise was of no value: it cannot fetter the legislature: *Rothmans of Pall Mall (NZ) Ltd v. Attorney General* [1991] N.Z.L.R. 323.

There are exceptions to the rule that the court will not inquire into the adequacy of the consideration. These apply in some contracts made by minors and generally where because of a special relationship, one party is able to take unfair advantage of another. *Cf. Thorne v. Motor Trade Association*, below, p. 211.

Note

When a gambling club gives chips to a customer to play at the club's tables it does not give consideration for the money paid for the chips by the customer. The chips, according to Lord Templeman, ([1992] 4 All E.R. at p. 518), remain the property of the club and do not give a right to the customer to gamble or take advantage of the other facilities of the club. When the customer gambles with the chips, all the necessary elements of a contract, offer, acceptance and consideration would be present but for the Gaming Act 1845 (below, p. 659) which renders all contracts by way of gaming or wagering null and void; so no consideration is given by the club at this stage either. Consequently, when the gambler has used stolen money to obtain the chips, the true owner is entitled to recover it from the club: *Lipkin Gorman v. Karpnale Ltd* [1992] 4 All E.R. 512. See the interesting (and somewhat puzzling) discussion of the consideration point by Lord Goff at pp. 529–532. Should it be different if the chips did give (or purport to give) the holder a right to gamble or use the other facilities (such as buying drinks) of the club?

In *Crockfords Club v. Mehta* [1992] 2 All E.R. 748, C.A., it was held that, when a member gave the Club a cheque drawn on a company's account in return for chips and the cheque was dishonoured, the Club could sue the member on a loan of money equal to the value of the chips. In the ordinary way, when A gives B cash in return for a cheque, properly drawn on C's account, there is an implied promise by B to pay if the cheque is dishonoured. A has two causes of action—one against B on the debt and one against C on the dishonoured cheque. The question in the case was whether the ordinary rule was displaced by the Gaming Act s.16; and it was held that it was not. But, in the light of *Lipkin Gorman*, above, was there consideration for B's implied promise to pay?

CHAPPELL & CO. LTD v. NESTLÉ CO. LTD

House of Lords [1960] A.C. 87; [1959] 3 W.L.R. 168; [1959] 2 All E.R. 701; 103 S.J. 561

Nestlé Co. entered into a contract with the Hardy Co., manufacturers of gramophone records, to purchase a number of recordings of a piece of music, "Rockin' Shoes," the copyright of which was vested in Chappell & Co. The Hardy Co. supplied the records to Nestlé Co. for 4d. each. Nestlé Co. advertised to the public that the records could be obtained from Nestlé Co. for 1s. 6d. each together with three wrappers from Nestlé's 6d. milk chocolate bars. The wrappers when received were thrown away.

Section 8(1) of the Copyright Act 1956, permits a person to make a record of a musical work for the purpose of its being sold retail, if he gives notice to the owner of the copyright and pays him a royalty of 6¼ per cent of "the ordinary retail selling price." The Hardy Co. gave notice of their intention to manufacture stating 1s. 6d. to be the ordinary retail selling price and offered to pay Chappell & Co. royalties thereon, which Chappell and Co. refused.

Chappell & Co. sought an injunction restraining Nestlé & Co. and the Hardy Co. from manufacturing the records on the ground that the transaction involved breaches of copyright. Upjohn J. granted an order restraining the defendants from infringing Chappell & Co.'s copyright. This decision was reversed by the Court of Appeal (Jenkins and Ormerod L.JJ., Romer L.J. dissenting). Chappell & Co. now appealed to the House of Lords.

VISCOUNT SIMONDS (dissenting): It appears to me that, in order to comply with the provisions of section 8 and thus obtain its protection, there are three relevant conditions to be satisfied by the manufacturer of an article which would otherwise be an infringement of copyright. By "relevant conditions" I mean those conditions about which an issue arises in this case. First, there must be a "sale" of the article in question: secondly, the sale must be a "retail sale": thirdly, it must be possible to predicate of it that there is an "ordinary retailing selling price" of it, for if there is not, an essential part of the prescribed notice cannot be given.

Upon the first point I cannot feel any doubt. It had not been contended in the course of the case that there was not a sale, until during the debate in your Lordships' House that suggestion was made, and I think that, beyond doubt, anyone, who in answer to the advertisement acquired a record, would say that he had bought it and would be surprised that any doubt should be cast upon what he regarded as an obvious fact. Whether the consideration or the price that he paid was 1s. 6d. only or 1s. 6d. and three wrappers is a matter not for him but for your Lordships to determine. . . .

[His Lordship held that the sale was a "retail" sale.]

In my opinion, my Lords, the wrappers are not part of the selling price. They are admittedly themselves valueless and are thrown away and it was for that reason, no doubt, that Upjohn J. was constrained to say that their value lay in the evidence they afforded of success in an advertising campaign. That is what they are. But what, after all, does that mean? Nothing more than that someone, by no means necessarily the purchaser of the record, has in the past bought not from Nestlé's but from a retail shop three bars of chocolate and that the purchaser has thus directly or indirectly acquired the wrappers. How often he acquires them for himself, how often through another, is pure speculation. The only thing that is certain is that, if he buys bars of chocolate from a retail shop or acquires the wrappers from another who has bought them, that purchase is not, or at the lowest is not necessarily, part of the same transaction as his subsequent purchase of a record from the manufacturers. . . . What can be easier than for a manufacturer to limit his sales to those members of the public who fulfil the qualification of being this or doing that? It may be assumed that the manufacturer's motive is his own advantage. It is possible that he achieves his object. But that does not mean that the sale is not a retail sale to which the section applies or that the ordinary retail selling price is not the price at which the record is ordinarily sold, in this case 1s. 6d. I would dismiss the appeal.

LORD KEITH OF AVONHOLME delivered a speech to similar effect.

LORD REID: The manufacturer pays royalty on records which he intends to be sold by retail. Apart from the last purpose set out in condition (c) he is not entitled to make them for any other purpose. And if later someone disposes of a record in some other way no part of the royalty can be recovered.

I can now turn to what appears to me to be the crucial question in this case: was the 1s. 6d. an "ordinary retail selling price" within the meaning of section 8? That involves two questions, what was the nature of the contract between the Nestlé Co. and a person who sent 1s. 6d. plus three wrappers in acceptance of their offer, and what is meant by "ordinary retail selling price" in this context.

To determine the nature of the contract one must find the intention of the parties as shown by what they said and did. The Nestlé Co.'s intention can hardly be in doubt. They were not setting out to trade in gramophone records. They were using these records to increase their sales of chocolate. Their offer was addressed to everyone.

It seems to me clear that the main intention of the offer was to induce people interested in this kind of music to buy (or perhaps get others to buy), chocolate which otherwise would not have been bought. It is, of course, true that some wrappers might come from the chocolate which had already been bought or from chocolate which would have been bought without the offer, but that does not seem to me to alter the case. Where there is a large number of transactions—the notice mentions 30,000 records—I do not think we should simply consider an isolated case where it would be impossible to say whether there had been a direct benefit from the acquisition of the wrappers or not. The requirement that wrappers should be sent was of great importance to the Nestlé Co.; there would have been no point in their simply offering records for 1s. 6d. each. It seems to me quite unrealistic to divorce the buying of the chocolate from the supplying of the records. It is a perfectly good contract if a person accepts an offer to supply goods if he (a) does something of value to the supplier and (b) pays money: the consideration is both (a) and (b). There may have been cases where the acquisition of the wrappers conferred no direct benefit on the Nestlé Co., but there must have been many cases where it did. I do not see why the possibility that in some cases the acquisition of the wrappers did not directly benefit the Nestlé Co. should require us to exclude from consideration the cases where it did. And even where there was no direct benefit from the acquisition of the wrappers there may have been an indirect benefit by way of advertisement.

I do not think that it matters greatly whether this kind of contract is called a sale or not. The appellants did not take the point that this transaction was not a sale. But I am bound to say that I have some doubts. If a contract under which a person is bound to do something as well as pay money is a sale, then either the price includes the obligation as well as the money, or the consideration is the price plus the obligation. And I do not see why it should be different if he has to show that he has done something of value to the seller. It is to my mind illegitimate to argue—this is a sale, the consideration for a sale is the price, price can only include money or something which can be readily converted into an ascertainable sum of money, therefore anything like wrappers which have no money value when delivered cannot be part of the consideration.

The respondents avoid this difficulty by submitting that requiring and delivering the wrappers was merely a condition which gave a qualification to buy and was not part of the consideration for sale. Of course, a person may limit his offer to persons qualified in a particular way, for example, members of a club. But where the qualification is the doing of something of value to the seller, and where the qualification only suffices for one sale and must be reacquired before another sale, I find it hard to regard the repeated acquisitions of the qualification as anything other than parts of the consideration for the sales. The purchaser of records had to send three wrappers for each record, so he had first to acquire them. The acquisition of wrappers by him was, at least in many cases, of direct benefit to the Nestlé Co., and required expenditure by the acquirer which he might not otherwise have incurred. To my mind the acquiring and delivering of the wrappers was certainly part of the consideration in these cases, and I see no good reason for drawing a distinction between these and other cases.

LORD SOMERVELL OF HARROW: My Lords, section 8 of the Copyright Act 1956, provides for a royalty of an amount, subject to a minimum, equal to $6^{1}/_{4}$ per cent of the ordinary retail selling price of the record. This necessarily implies, in my opinion, that a sale to be within the section must not only be retail, but one in which there is no other consideration for the transfer of property in the record but the money price. . . .

The question, then, is whether the three wrappers were part of the consideration or, as Jenkins L.J. held, a condition of making the purchase, like a ticket entitling a member to buy at a co-operative store.

I think they are part of the consideration. They are so described in the offer. "They," the wrappers, "will help you to get smash hit recordings." They are so described in the record itself—all you have to do to get such new record is to send three wrappers from Nestlé's 6d. milk chocolate bars, together with postal order for 1s. 6d." This is not conclusive but, however described, they are, in my view, in law part of the consideration. It is said that when received the wrappers are of no value to Nestlé's. This I would have thought irrelevant. A contracting party can stipulate for what consideration he chooses. A peppercorn does not cease to be good consideration if it is established that the promisee does not like pepper and will throw away the corn. As the whole object of selling the record, if it was a sale, was to increase the sales of chocolate, it seems to me wrong not to treat the stipulated evidence of such sales as part of the consideration. For these reasons I would allow the appeal.

Lord Tucker delivered a speech allowing the appeal.

Appeal allowed.

Questions
1. Suppose that the advertisement had run, "Yours for 1s. 6d.—'Rockin' Shoes.' Offer open only to 'members,' that is, people who have bought three Nestlé bars. To prove you qualify, send three wrappers with your money." Would this be a condition or would the wrappers still constitute part of the consideration? (*Cf.* Wedderburn, 1959 C.L.J. 160.)
2. Would there have been a contract to supply a record if the advertisement had asked only for three wrappers and no money?

In *De La Bere v. Pearson, Ltd* [1908] 1 K.B. 280, the defendants, owners of a newspaper, carried an advertisement in each issue informing readers who wanted financial advice to write to a given address. The plaintiff wrote for such advice and also for the name of a "good stockbroker." The editor passed the letter to a person whom he knew to be an "outside broker" (one who does Stock Exchange business but is not a member of the Exchange) but whose honesty he had no reason to suspect. This person was in fact an undischarged bankrupt who wrote to the plaintiff as being recommended by the editor and who misappropriated the funds sent to him by the plaintiff for investment. The plaintiff sued the defendants for breach of contract to exercise due care in giving him financial advice. The Court of Appeal (Vaughan Williams L.J., Gorell Barnes P., and Bigham J.) affirmed the decision of Lord Alverstone C.J. in favour of the plaintiff. In *Hedley Byrne & Co. v. Heller & Partners* (below, p. 340) Lord Devlin said of this case: ". . . I think that today the result can and should be achieved by the application of the law of negligence. . . . I agree with Sir Frederick Pollock's note on the case of *De La Bere v. Pearson, Ltd* when he wrote in *Pollock on Contracts* (13th ed.), 140 (n. 31) that 'the cause of action is better regarded as arising from default in the performance of a voluntary undertaking independent of contract.' " See further below, pp. 340–342.

Problem
Suppose that a newspaper advertises: "We want letters (which we may publish) from readers seeking advice; and we undertake that, if we give advice, we will exercise all proper care." Is it in any way artificial or unrealistic to regard that as an offer of a contract? But should such an undertaking be implied from a mere invitation to the reader to seek advice?

(b) Forbearance as Consideration

WHITE v. BLUETT

Exchequer (1853) 23 L.J.Ex. 36; 2 C.L.R. 301; 2 W.R. 75

John Bluett had received a promissory note from his son, William, the present defendant, in respect of money lent by him to William. The present action was brought by John's executor, the declaration containing a count on the promissory note and a count for money lent.

Plea that the note was given to secure the loan; that, subsequent to the loan and the giving of the note, the defendant had complained to John Bluett that he had not received equal favourable treatment with John Bluett's other children; that John Bluett had conceded the truth of these complaints and agreed with the defendant that, in consideration that the defendant should cease his complaints and also out of his natural love and affection for the defendant, he would discharge the defendant from all liability in respect of the loan and the note.

The plaintiff demurred that there was no consideration for the agreement between the deceased and the defendant.

T. J. Clark for the defendant argued that the adequacy of consideration is not to be investigated; that the defendant had a right to complain and that promising to forgo that right constituted good consideration.

POLLOCK C.B.: The plea is clearly bad. By the argument a principle is pressed to an absurdity, as a bubble is blown until it bursts. Looking at the words merely, there is some foundation for the argument, and, following the words only, the conclusion may be arrived at. It is said, the son had a right to an equal distribution of his father's property, and did complain to his father because he had not had an equal share, and said to him, I will cease to complain if you will not sue upon this note. Whereupon the father said, if you will promise me not to complain I will give up the note. If such a plea as this could be supported, the following would be a binding promise: A man might complain that another person used the public highway more than he ought to do, and that other might say, do not complain, and I will give you five pounds. It is ridiculous to suppose that such promises could be binding. So, if the holder of a bill of exchange were suing the acceptor, and the acceptor were to complain that the holder had treated him hardly, or that the bill ought never to have been circulated, and the holder were to say, Now, if you will not make any more complaints, I will not sue you. Such a promise would be like that now set up. In reality, there was no consideration whatever. The son had no right to complain for the father might make what distribution of his property he liked; and the son's abstaining from doing what he had no right to do can be no consideration.

ALDERSON B.: If this agreement were good, there could be no such thing as a *nudum pactum*. There is a consideration on one side, and it is said the consideration on the other is the agreement itself: if that were so there could never be a *nudum pactum*.

Judgment for plaintiff.

(The judgment of PARKE B. is omitted; PLATT B. concurred.)

Questions

1. Was it true to say that the son "had no right to complain"? Did he commit any legal wrong by complaining? Why should not his giving up his liberty to complain be consideration? Is it any different from giving up a liberty to smoke? Cf. *Hamer v. Sidway*, above, p. 197. But could refraining, or a promise to refrain, from smoking *cannabis* be sufficient consideration? (It is an offence under section 5 of the Misuse of Drugs Act 1971 to be in possession of cannabis.)

Cf. Hohfeld, *Some Fundamental Legal Conceptions*; Salmond, *Jurisprudence* (12th ed.), p. 217.

2. Is an agreement by a father, made in consideration that his son will not bore him, a binding contract? (Parke B. in the course of argument.)

3. Is an agreement by a husband separately to maintain his wife, if she will not "molest" him, a binding contract?

In *Dunton v. Dunton* (1892) 18 V.L.R. 114 (Supreme Court of Victoria), the Court (Higinbotham and Williams JJ., Hood J. dissenting) held that an agreement between ex-spouses whereby the former husband undertook to pay the former wife £6 per month, "so long as she . . . shall conduct herself with sobriety, and in a respectable, orderly, and virtuous manner" was a valid contract made for a consideration. Williams J. said, "In effect, (the former husband) says to (the former wife): 'If you, who now owe me no duty as a wife, will agree to my stipulation, I will, so long as you observe that stipulation, pay you £6 per month.' Thereupon she signifies her agreement and her assent to the stipulation by signing the agreement . . . there is sufficient consideration to support the agreement sued upon."

Williston, Selections from Williston on Contracts, § 133

. . . courts have not been so strict in denying the validity of consideration where a moral duty was performed, as they have in holding agreements invalid as against public policy where they contemplated a violation of the same duty. In other words, there are differences of degree in immoral conduct; some acts within this category may be classed as immoral liberties, since not specifically punishable by law. Thus, an agreement to get drunk would doubtless be against public policy, but an agreement to refrain from doing so would be sufficient consideration for a return promise. And the same may be said of most other merely moral duties.

THORNE v. MOTOR TRADE ASSOCIATION

[1937] A.C. 797; 106 L.J.K.B. 495; 157 L.T. 399; 53 T.L.R. 810; [1937] 3 All E.R. 157

The M.T.A. by its constitution had a power to put on a stop list the name of a member or person who infringed its rule forbidding the sale of articles at other than the list prices relevant thereto unless such person should pay to the Association a fine within limits to be laid down by the Council of the Association. This was an action by Thorne, a member of the M.T.A., against the Association to determine whether a demand of a sum of money in lieu of placing a person's name on the stop list would constitute a demand of money with menaces and without reasonable or probable cause within section 29 (1)(i) of the Larceny Act 1916. MacKinnon J. found for the defendant and his decision was affirmed by the Court of Appeal (Greer and Greene L.JJ., Talbot J.). On appeal by the plaintiff to the House of Lords.

LORD ATKIN: The ordinary blackmailer normally threatens to do what he has a perfect right to do—namely, communicate some compromising conduct to a person whose knowledge is likely to affect the person threatened. Often, indeed, he has not only the right but also the duty to make the disclosure, as of a felony, to the competent authorities. What he has to justify is not the threat, but the demand of money. The gravamen of the charge is the demand without reasonable or probable cause: and I cannot think that the mere fact that the threat is to do something a person is entitled to do either causes the threat not to be a "menace" within the Act or in itself provides a reasonable or probable cause for the demand. . . .

It appears to me that if a man may lawfully, in the furtherance of business interests, do acts which will seriously injure another in his business he may also lawfully, if he is still acting in the furtherance of his business interests, offer that other to accept a sum of money as an alternative to doing the injurious acts. He must no doubt be acting not for the mere purpose of putting money in his pocket, but for some legitimate purpose other than the mere acquisition of money. . . .

I think that the absence of reasonable or probable cause is in a criminal charge under this subsection a question of fact for the jury. But if the cause is reasonably capable of being associated with the promotion of lawful business interests the judge should not allow the case to go to the jury if there is no evidence of the accused's intention going beyond such lawful business interests. . . . I think this appeal should be dismissed with costs.

LORD WRIGHT: I think the jury should be directed by the judge that the respondent Association had a legal right to put the person's name on the stop list, so long as they did so in order to promote the trade interests of the Association and its members and not with intent to injure, and so long as the money, fine or penalty demanded was reasonable and not extortionate.

. . . (T)here are many cases where a man who has a "right," in the sense of a liberty or capacity of doing an act which is not unlawful, but which is calculated seriously to injure another, will be liable to a charge of blackmail if he demands money from that other as the price of abstaining. . . . Thus a man may be possessed of knowledge of discreditable incidents in the victim's life and may seek to extort money by threatening, if he is not paid, to disclose the knowledge to a wife or husband or employer, though the disclosure may not be libellous. Such is a common type of blackmail. Cases where the non-disclosure to the proper authority is illegal, as amounting to compounding a felony or a misdemeanour of public import, or where the publication would constitute a public libel, are *a fortiori*. Again a legal liberty (that is something that a man may do with legal justification) may form the basis of blackmail. Thus a husband who has proof of his wife's adultery, may threaten the paramour that he will petition in the Divorce Court unless he is bought off. Though it is possible that the facts of such a case might show merely the legitimate compromise of a claim to damages, on the other hand, the facts might be such as to constitute extortion and blackmail of a serious type.

LORDS THANKERTON, RUSSELL OF KILLOWEN and ROCHE also made speeches dismissing the appeal.

Appeal dismissed.

Note
   This decision followed a conflict of authority between the Court of Appeal and the Court of Criminal Appeal. In the civil case of *Hardie & Lane v. Chilton* [1928] 2 K.B. 306, the Court of Appeal had held that a trade association which by its constitution had power to put the name of a person infringing its rules on a stop list, could instead lawfully ask the person concerned to make a money payment by way of compromise. In the Court of Criminal Appeal in *R. v. Denyer* [1926] 2 K.B. 258 it had been held that a request for money in such circumstances did constitute an offence under the Larceny Act 1916, s.29(1)(i). In the present case the House of Lords found that *Hardie & Lane v. Chilton* was correctly decided but not that a demand for money in lieu of placing on the stop list would be lawful in all circumstances.
   The practice, in issue in this case, "collective resale price maintenance," was invalidated by the Resale Prices Act 1964. See now Restrictive Trade Practices Act 1976.

Questions
   1. Where A demands money from B in return for not disclosing B's wrongdoing, A will usually be guilty of blackmail contrary to section 21 of the Theft Act 1968 and, if "the offer"

constitutes a crime, it clearly cannot lead to a contract; but what if B, without any demand, express or implied by A, offers A money not to disclose B's wrongdoing, and A accepts? That is not blackmail, or any offence. Is it a contract?

See, generally, Goodhart, "Blackmail and Consideration in Contracts" 44 L.Q.R. 436.

2. A, a notoriously loose-living man, offers to refrain from publishing his memoirs in a Sunday newspaper, if B will give him £1,000 in recompense for the loss of the fee of £1,000 that he would receive from the newspaper. Consider the validity of the agreement between A and B. Would your answer be different if A asked for £3,000 instead of £1,000?

(*Cf.* Lord Denning's Report, Cmnd. 2152 of 1963, p. 35.)

3. D. Co., who own a chain of multiple stores, agree with E, a private trader, that they will not open a branch in his locality if E will give them £2,500. Consider the validity of the agreement.

4. Does not the court indicate that it is necessary to inquire into the adequacy of the consideration in cases of this type? What principle determines whether a case falls within the category where adequacy of consideration is relevant?

WADE v. SIMEON

Common Pleas (1846) 2 C.B. 548; 135 E.R. 1061

Assumpsit. The first count of the declaration stated that the plaintiff had commenced action against the defendant in the Court of Exchequer to recover two sums of £700 and £1,300, respectively, issue had been joined and the hearing was to take place on December 7, 1844; that the defendant, on December 6, 1844, promised the plaintiff that, if he (plaintiff) would forbear prosecuting the proceedings until December 14, the defendant would on that day pay the money with interest and costs; that the plaintiff, relying on this promise, forbore prosecuting the action until the day named but that the defendant did not pay the money or costs. By his fourth plea, the defendant pleaded that the plaintiff never had any cause of action against the defendant in respect of the £2,000, the subject of the Exchequer proceedings, which the plaintiff, at the commencement of that action and thence until and at the time of the making of the alleged promise, well knew. The plaintiff demurred.

TINDAL C.J.: The only question now remaining is upon the demurrer to the fourth plea. The fourth plea states that the plaintiff never had any cause of action against the defendant in respect of the subject-matter of the action in the Court of Exchequer, which he, the plaintiff, at the time of the commencement of the said action, and thence until the time of the making the promise in the first count mentioned, well knew. By demurring to that plea, the plaintiff admits that he had no cause of action against the defendant in the action therein mentioned, and that he knew it. It appears to me, therefore, that he is estopped from saying that there was any valid consideration for the defendant's promise. It is almost *contra bonos mores*, and certainly contrary to all the principles of natural justice, that a man should institute proceedings against another, when he is conscious that he has no good cause of action. In order to constitute a binding promise, the plaintiff must show a good consideration, something beneficial to the defendant, or detrimental to the plaintiff. Detrimental to the plaintiff it cannot be, if he has no cause of action; and beneficial to the defendant it cannot be; for, in contemplation of law, the defence upon such an admitted state of facts must be successful, and the defendant will recover costs, which must be assumed to be a full compensation for all the legal damage he may sustain. The consideration, therefore, altogether fails. On the part of the plaintiff, it has been urged that the cases cited for the defendant were not cases where actions had already been brought, but only cases of promises to forbear commencing proceedings. I must, however, confess, that, if that were so, I do not see that it would make any substantial difference. The older cases, and some of the modern ones, too, do not afford any countenance to that distinction. . . .

. . . the defendant asserts, and the plaintiff admits, that there never was any cause of action in the original suit, and that the plaintiff knew it. I therefore think the fourth plea affords a very good answer, and that the defendant is entitled to judgment thereon.

CRESSWELL J.: It has been surmised, in the course of the argument, that there is a distinction between abstaining from commencing an action, and forbearing to prosecute one already commenced. In the older cases I find no such distinction. Lord Coke lays it down broadly that the staying of an action that has been unjustly brought is no consideration for a promise to pay money. I cannot help thinking, on broad principles, that the staying proceedings in an action brought without any cause is no good consideration for a promise such as is relied on here. The plea, in plain terms, avers that the plaintiff never had any cause of action, and he well knew it. Are we to assume that the defendant might by some slip in pleading, have failed in his defence to that action, if it had proceeded? I think not.

(The judgments of MAULE and ERLE JJ. are omitted.)

Judgment for the defendant on the fourth plea.

COOK v. WRIGHT

Queen's Bench (1861) 1 B. & S. 559; 30 L.J.Q.B. 321; 4 L.T. 704; 7 Jur. 1121; 124 R.R. 649; 121 E.R. 822

Before the Queen's Bench, after a verdict for the defendant, on a motion that the evidence did not prove want of consideration and that, upon the evidence, the plaintiffs were entitled to a verdict. The relevant facts are stated in the judgment of the court (Cockburn C.J., Wightman and Blackburn JJ.), delivered by BLACKBURN J.: In this case it appeared on the trial that the defendant was agent for a Mrs Bennett, who was non-resident owner of houses in a district subject to a local Act. Works had been done in the adjoining street by the Commissioners for executing the Act, the expenses of which, under the provisions of their Act, they charged on the owners of the adjoining houses. Notice had been given to the defendant, as if he had himself been the owner of the houses, calling on him to pay the proportion chargeable in respect of them. He attended at a board meeting of the Commissioners, and objected both to the amount and nature of the charge, and also stated that he was not the owner of the houses, and that Mrs Bennett was. He was told that, if he did not pay, he would be treated as one Goble had been. It appeared that Goble had refused to pay a sum charged against him as owner of some houses, and the Commissioners had taken legal proceedings against him, and he had then submitted and paid, with costs. In the result, it was agreed between the Commissioners and the defendant that the amount charged upon him should be reduced, and that time should be given to pay it in three instalments; he gave three promissory notes for the three instalments; the first was duly honoured; the others were not, and were the subject of the present action. At the trial it appeared that the defendant was not in fact owner of the houses. As agent for the owner he was not personally liable under the Act. In point of law, therefore, the Commissioners were not entitled to claim the money from him; but no case of deceit was alleged against them. It must be taken that the Commissioners honestly believed that the defendant was personally liable, and really intended to take legal proceedings against him, as they had done against Goble. The defendant, according to his own evidence, never believed that he was liable in law, but signed the notes in order to avoid being sued as Goble was. Under these circumstances the substantial question reserved (irrespective of the form of the plea) was whether there was any consideration for the notes. We are of the opinion that there was.

There is no doubt that a bill or note given in consideration of what is supposed to be a debt is without consideration if it appears that there was a mistake in fact as to the existence of the debt; *Bell v. Gardiner* (4 M. & Gr. 11); and, according to the cases of *Southall v. Rigg* and *Forman v. Wright* (11 C.B. 481), the law is the same if the bill or note is given in consequence of a mistake of law as to the existence of a debt. But here there was no mistake on the part of the defendant either of law or fact. What he did was not merely the making an erroneous account stated, or promising to pay a debt for which he mistakenly believed himself liable. It appeared on the evidence that he believed himself not to be liable; but he knew that the plaintiffs thought him liable, and would sue him if he did not pay, and in order to avoid the expense and trouble of legal proceedings against himself he agreed to a compromise; and the question is, whether a person who has given a note as a compromise of a claim honestly made on him, and which but for that compromise would have been at once brought to a legal decision, can resist the payment of the note on the ground that the original claim thus compromised might have been successfully resisted . . .

In the present case we think that there was sufficient consideration for the notes in the compromise made as it was.

The rule to enter a verdict for the plaintiff must be made absolute.

Notes

1. The court suggests that if the defendant (D) had (wrongly) believed himself to be liable to pay the charges, he would not have been liable on the notes; but, because he (rightly) believed himself not to be liable to pay the charges, he is liable on the notes. *Cf.* Bills of Exchange Act 1882, s.27(1), above, p. 203 (which applies to promissory notes). In neither case is there an "antecedent debt or liability" because D is not in fact liable to pay the charges. In the latter case, however, the commissioners give consideration because they refrain from pursuing the threatened proceedings. In the former case there is no express threat of proceedings to be withdrawn if the defendant pays up promptly because he believes himself to be liable. But suppose that, though believing himself to be liable, he gives a note or cheque only in response to a demand threatening legal proceedings? Is he liable on the note or cheque? If he is, does it really make a difference that he gives the note or cheque promptly on receiving the first demand for payment? Is there not an implicit threat of legal proceedings in even the first demand for payment of a debt? *Cf. Alliance Bank v. Broom*, below.

It seems very unjust that D should have been required to pay Mrs Bennett's debt; but note that he could probably have recovered the money from her as money paid to her use. See generally, *Cheshire, Fifoot and Furmston* (12th ed.), pp. 667–669. The modern doctrine of economic duress would have been of no help to D. See *CTN Cash and Carry Ltd v. Gallagher Ltd*, below, p. 656.

2. In *Alliance Bank v. Broom* (1864) 2 Dr. & Sm. 289; 62 E.R. 631, a firm of Liverpool merchants owed their bank some £22,000 on an overdraft. The bank asked for some security for this amount and the defendant promised by letter to charge certain goods and to pay the proceeds thereof to the bank against the overdraft. On the failure to honour this promise, the bank claimed that they were entitled to a lien on the goods by virtue of the agreement in the letter. The defendant demurred on the ground that there was no consideration for the promise. Overruling the demurrer, Kindersley V.-C. said: "It appears to me that, when the plaintiffs demanded payment of their debt, and in consequence of that application the defendant agreed to give certain security, although there was no promise on the part of the plaintiffs to abstain for any certain time from suing for the debt, the effect was, that the plaintiffs did in effect give, and the defendant received, the benefit of some degree of forbearance; not indeed, for any definite time but, at all events, some extent of forbearance."

3. In *Callisher v. Bischoffsheim* (1870) L.R 5 Q.B. 449 at 451, Cockburn C.J. said: The authorities clearly establish that if an agreement is made to compromise a disputed claim,

forbearance to sue in respect of that claim is good consideration; and whether proceedings to enforce the disputed claim have or have not been instituted makes no difference. If the defendant's contention were adopted, it would result that in no case of a doubtful claim could a compromise be enforced. Every day a compromise is effected on the ground that the party making it has a fair chance of succeeding in it, and if he bona fide believes he has a fair chance of success he has a reasonable ground for suing, and his forbearance to sue will constitute a good consideration.

See also *Miles v. New Zealand Alford Estate Co.* (1886) 32 Ch. D. 266, C.A., and compare the views of Denning L.J. in *Williams v. Williams* (below, p. 217).

(c) COMPLIANCE WITH LEGAL OBLIGATIONS

Law Revision Committee, 6th Interim Report, paragraph 36, p. 21

Three cases must be discussed:

(a) Where A makes a promise to B in consideration of B doing or promising to do something which he is already bound to do by reason of a duty imposed upon him by law, whether by a Statute or otherwise: for instance, the duty of a local polic authority to afford adequate protection to A and his property;

(b) Where A makes a promise to B in consideration of B doing or promising to do something which he is already bound to do under a contract with A;

(c) Where A makes a promise to B in consideration of B doing or promising to do something which he is already bound to do under a contract with C.

In cases (a) and (b) where the thing promised or performed is precisely the thing which the promisor is already bound to do and no more, and there is no dispute that he is bound to do it, there is said to be no consideration or only illusory consideration for the new promise, and it is not enforceable. In case (c) the law is not so clear and frequently other factors are present out of which a consideration for the promise can be manufactured.

In our opinion, in all three cases, a promise made by A to B in consideration of B doing or promising to do something which he is already bound to do should be enforced by the law, provided that in other respects such as legality and compatability with public policy it is free from objection; thus a promise in return for an agreement by a police authority to give precisely the amount of protection it was by law bound to give and no more should be unenforceable as being against public policy.

The dominant factor is that A thought it worth his while to make the promise to B in order that he should feel more certain that B would do the thing bargained for, and we can see no reason in general why A, having got what he wanted, should be allowed to evade his promise. Moreover, why did the promisor make the promise if it was to have no legal effect?

Notes

1. See also Hamson, "The Reform of Consideration" 54 L.Q.R. 233 at 237–240; and Shatwell, "The Doctrine of Consideration in the Modern Law" 1 Sydney L.R. 289.
2. The situations are treated in an order different from that above.

(i) *Imposed by Law*

COLLINS v. GODEFROY

King's Bench (1831) 1 B. & Ad. 950; 109 E.R. 1040; 1 Dowl. 326; 9 L.J.(o.s.) K.B. 158

Assumpsit to recover a remuneration for the plaintiff's loss of time during his attendance upon subpoena as a witness in an action. At the trial before Lord

Tenterden C.J. it appeared that Godefroy brought an action against one Dalton, and caused Collins to be subpoenaed to attend. Collins, who attended for six days but was not called, on November 2, 1829, demanded of Godefroy six guineas as his fee for attendance and commenced his action on the following day. Lord Tenterden was of opinion that the plaintiff was not entitled to recover because, in point of law, he was bound to give evidence pursuant upon a subpoena. The plaintiff was nonsuited but with leave reserved to enter a verdict for six guineas.

A rule nisi having been obtained.

LORD TENTERDEN C.J.: Assuming that the offer to pay the six guineas without costs was evidence of an express promise by the defendant to pay that sum to the plaintiff as a compensation to him for his loss of time, still, if the defendant was not bound by law to pay that sum, the offer to do so not having been accepted will not avail the plaintiff. If it be a duty imposed by law upon a party regularly subpoenaed to attend from time to time to give his evidence then a promise to give him any remuneration for loss of time incurred in such attendance is a promise without consideration. We think that such a duty is imposed by law; and on consideration of the Statute of Elizabeth,[1] and of the cases which have been decided on this subject, we are all of the opinion that a party cannot maintain an action for compensation for loss of time in attending a trial as a witness. We are aware of the practice which has prevailed in certain cases, of allowing, as costs between party and party, so much per day for the attendance of professional men, but that practice cannot alter the law. What the effect of our decision may be, is not for our consideration. We think, on principle, that an action does not lie for a compensation to a witness for loss of time in attendance under a subpoena. The rule, therefore, must be discharged.

Rule discharged.

Note

In *Arrale v. Costain* [1976] 1 Lloyds Rep. 98 the plaintiff who had been injured in the course of his employment in Dubai was paid by his employer, the defendants, the amount of compensation required by the law of Dubai. He signed a document stating that he received the money in full satisfaction of all claims in respect of personal injury. Subsequently he brought an action for negligence in England. The Court of Appeal held that the action was not barred by the agreement. Lord Denning, applying *D. & C. Builders v. Rees*, below, held that there was no true accord and satisfaction—there was inequality of bargaining power and the plaintiff was unaware of his rights at common law. Geoffrey Lane L.J. said that if the defendants were doing no more than perform an obligation already cast upon them by law there was no consideration for the plaintiff's agreement not to sue. He rejected the argument that the defendants had done something more by refraining from setting up certain answers to the claim permitted by the Dubai law; as a matter of policy it was never their intention to do so and "It is no consideration to refrain from a course of action which it was never intended to pursue; see *Cook v. Wright* (1861) 1 B. & S. 559, 589 (above, p. 214)."

Stephenson L.J. agreed that there was no consideration.

WILLIAMS v. WILLIAMS

Court of Appeal [1957] 1 W.L.R. 148; 121 J.P. 93; [1957] 1 All E.R. 305; 101 S.J. 108

The relevant facts appear in the judgment of Denning L.J.

[1] 5 Eliz. 1, c.9 (Perjury Act).

DENNING L.J.: In this case a wife claims sums due to her under a maintenance agreement. No evidence was called in the court below because the facts are agreed. The parties were married on April 25, 1945; they have no children. On January 24, 1952, the wife deserted the husband. On March 26, 1952, they signed the agreement now sued upon which has three clauses: "(1) the husband will pay to the wife for her support and maintenance a weekly sum of One Pound Ten Shillings to be paid every four weeks during the joint lives of the parties so long as the wife shall lead a chaste life the first payment hereunder to be made on the Fifteenth day of April 1952. (2) The wife will out of the said weekly sum or otherwise support and maintain herself and will indemnify the husband against all debts to be incurred by her and will not in any way at any time hereafter pledge the husband's credit. (3) The wife shall not so long as the husband shall punctually make the payments hereby agreed to be made commence or prosecute against the husband any matrimonial proceedings other than proceedings for dissolution of marriage but upon failure of the husband to make the said weekly payments as and when the same become due the wife shall be at full liberty on her election to pursue all and every remedy in this regard either by enforcement of the provisions hereof or as if this agreement had not been made." So far as we know, the parties have remained apart ever since. On June 1, 1955, the husband petitioned for divorce, on the grounds of his wife's desertion, and on October 12, 1955, a decree nisi was made against her. On December 2, 1955, the decree was made absolute. In this action the wife claims maintenance at the rate of £1 10s. a week under the agreement for a period from October 1954 to October 1955. The sum claimed is £30 5s. 9d., which is the appropriate sum after deduction of tax.

The husband disputes the claim, on the ground that there was no consideration for his promise. Let me first deal with clause 3. It is settled law that a wife, despite such a clause as clause 3, can make application to the magistrates or to the High Court for maintenance. If this wife made such an application the husband could set up the fact of desertion as an answer to the claim, but he could not set up clause 3 as a bar to the proceedings. The clause is void and as such no consideration to support the agreement: see *Bennett v. Bennett* (below, p. 702).[1] Now let me deal with clause 2.

Now I agree that in promising to maintain herself whilst she was in desertion, the wife was only promising to do that which she was already bound to do. Nevertheless, a promise to perform an existing duty is, I think, sufficient consideration to support a promise, so long as there is nothing in the transaction which is contrary to the public interest. Suppose that this agreement had never been made, and the wife had made no promise to maintain herself and did not do so. She might then have sought and received public assistance or have pledged her husband's credit with tradesmen: in which case the National Assistance Board might have summoned him before the magistrates, or the tradesmen might have sued him in the county court. It is true that he would have an answer to those claims because she was in desertion, but nevertheless he would be put to all

---

[1] The actual decision of *Bennett v. Bennett* was overruled by the provisions of the Maintenance Agreements Act 1957, s.1(2), now represented by the Matrimonial Causes Act 1973, s.34.

the trouble, worry and expense of defending himself against them. By paying her 30s. a week and taking this promise from her that she will maintain herself and will not pledge his credit, he has an added safeguard to protect himself from all this worry, trouble and expense. That is a benefit to him which is good consideration for his promise to pay maintenance. That was the view which appealed to the county court judge: and I must say it appeals to me also.

There is another ground on which good consideration can be found. Although the wife was in desertion, nevertheless it must be remembered that desertion is never irrevocable. It was open to her to come back at any time. Her right to maintenance was not lost by desertion. It was only suspended. If she made a genuine offer to return which he rejected, she would have been entitled to maintenance from him. She could apply to the magistrates or the High Court for an order in her favour. If she did so, however, whilst this agreement was in force the 30s. would be regarded as prima facie the correct figure. It is a benefit to the husband for it to be so regarded, and that is sufficient consideration to support his promise.

I construe this agreement as a promise by the husband to pay his wife 30s. a week in consideration of her promise to maintain herself during the time she is living separate from him, whether due to her own fault or not.

I would dismiss the appeal accordingly.

HODSON L.J.: Mr Priestley has argued that [as the wife was in desertion when the agreement was made] she had forfeited all right to be maintained by her husband and so she was giving no consideration at all when she said she would maintain herself, because that is what she would have to do anyway. The short answer to that is I think that she had not forfeited her right to be maintained by her husband by being in desertion: she had only suspended her right and not destroyed it. Authority for that proposition is contained in the judgment of Lord Reading C.J. in *Jones v. Newtown and Llanidloes Guardians* [1920] 3 K.B. 381, 384[1]: "There is no doubt that at common law if a wife chooses wilfully and without justification to live away from her husband she cannot, so long as she continues absent, render him liable for the necessaries supplied to her, or for her maintenance by the union, for the reason that she has of her own free will deprived herself of the opportunity which the husband was affording her of being maintained in the home. But the relief of the husband from the obligation of maintenance continues only so long as she voluntarily remains absent. Her absence, although wrongful, does not affect the relationship of husband and wife." That passage applies to this case, looking at it, as we must do, as at the time when the agreement was entered into. The wife had then deserted the husband and was temporarily wrongfully away from home; but she might at any time return. In those circumstances, if she returned or offered to return, her husband's liability to maintain her would revive. So that there was good consideration there to meet that contingency, which was a real contingency and not a fanciful one at that time. . . .

MORRIS L.J.: . . . I consider that we must proceed on the basis that at the date this agreement was entered into, March 26, 1952, the wife was then in

[1] *Cf.* also *Pinnick v. Pinnick* [1957] 1 W.L.R. 644, esp. 653.

desertion. But it seems to me that the wife might thereafter have offered to return and might have ceased to be in desertion, and that clause 2 would at that stage and in that event have been in operation: therefore it does not seem to me that it can be said that clause 2 was not of value to the husband. The probability of the happening of such events need not be measured, for the court does not inquire as to the adequacy of consideration.

I think that for that reason the county court judge came to a correct conclusion. Like my Lord, Hodson L.J., I prefer to base my judgment on that ground rather than on the alternative ground—that apart from any question of an offer by the wife to return, while she was still in desertion, there might have been trouble, expense or embarrassment if the wife had incurred debts.

I, therefore, agree that the appeal fails.

Appeal dismissed.

Questions
1. If the wife were to pledge her husband's credit in these circumstances, she would be guilty of obtaining by false pretences or obtaining credit by fraud under the then law (now obtaining by deception—Theft Act 1968). Should her promise to refrain from so doing constitute good consideration?
2. Is the wife's duty to support herself when in desertion (*cf.* Denning L.J.) a legal duty? Is not the wife while in desertion, bound in law to refrain from pledging her husband's credit? Is her promise not to do so good consideration for the husband's agreement to pay the 30s. per week? Does the case, from this standpoint, require reconciling with *Collins v. Godefroy* (above, p. 216) and *Stilk v. Myrick* (below, p. 230)?
3. If the wife were to return to her husband, would the contract, as found by the court, still be binding upon the parties?

Notes
1. The Matrimonial Causes Act 1973, s.34, provides:
(1) If a maintenance agreement includes a provision purporting to restrict any right to apply to a court for an order containing financial arrangements, then—
   (a) that provision shall be void; but
   (b) any other financial arrangements contained in the agreement shall not thereby be rendered void or unenforceable and shall, unless they are void or unenforceable for any other reason (and subject to sections 35 and 36, below) be binding on the parties to the agreement.

(2) In this and in section 35 below—
"maintenance agreement" means any agreement in writing made, whether before or after the commencement of this Act, between the parties to a marriage, being—
   (a) an agreement containing financial arrangements, whether made during the continuance or after the dissolution or annulment of the marriage; or
   (b) a separation agreement which contains no financial arrangements in a case where no other agreement in writing between the same parties contains such arrangements.
2. In *Pitt v PHH Asset Management Ltd*, above, p. 97, Peter Gibson L.J. said: On the second point, the consideration moving from the plaintiff, Mr Payne submitted that in reality there was no consideration provided by the plaintiff. The plaintiff was expressing himself to be ready, willing and able to proceed to exchange contracts, which was, he submitted, simply what he would have to do in any case. Further, he said that the learned judge rightly described the threat by the plaintiff to issue an injunction as vapid, that is to say of no substance. He accordingly submitted that there was nothing by way of valuable consideration which the defendant received. I cannot accept these submissions either. I accept that the threat of an injunction only had a nuisance value in that I cannot see how the plaintiff could have succeeded in any claim. Nevertheless, that nuisance was something which the defendant was freed from by the plaintiff agreeing to the lock-out agreement. Further, the threat of causing trouble with Miss Buckle was again a matter which could have been a nuisance to the defendant and again removal of that threat provided some consideration. But I also believe

that the promise by the plaintiff to get on by limiting himself to just two weeks if he was to exchange contracts was of some value to the defendant. The defendant had the benefit of knowing that if it chose to give the plaintiff a draft contract to agree, there would be no delay on the plaintiff's part beyond a maximum of two weeks thereafter. The learned judge held that these three items constituted valuable consideration sufficient to support the lock-out agreement and I respectfully agree with him.

Question
Were all or any of the following capable of being consideration?
  (i) The withdrawal of the "vapid" threat to issue an injunction? *Cf. Wade v. Simeon*, above, p. 213, *Williams v. Williams*, above, p. 217.
 (ii) Refraining from advising Buckle that she could lower her offer.
(iii) A promise to return contracts within fourteen days—faster than usual in such circumstances.

GLASBROOK BROS. LTD v. GLAMORGAN COUNTY COUNCIL

House of Lords [1925] A.C. 270; 94 L.J.K.B. 272; 132 L.T. 611; 89 J.P. 29; 41 T.L.R. 213; 69 S.J. 212; 23 L.G.R. 61

Appeal from an order of the Court of Appeal affirming a judgment of Bailhache J.
  The action was brought by the respondents against the appellants to recover the sum of £2,200 11s. 10d. for the services of police specially supplied by the respondents at the request of and by agreement with the appellants.
  The appellants owned a colliery near Swansea, employing about 1,000 men. A general colliery strike in South Wales ended early in July 1921, but work was not resumed at their colliery. After a hostile demonstration by some 500 or 600 of the men, the appellants' colliery manager, James, was informed by the men's committee that the strikers were going to get the "safety men" out. Without the safety men, the mine would have become flooded. James went to the local police superintendent, one Smith, and asked for 100 police to be billeted on the colliery premises, as, otherwise, the safety men, who were frightened, would not come to work. Smith was of opinion that adequate protection could be given by keeping a mobile force ready, who, on warning of danger, could be swiftly moved to the danger area; but, if police were to be billeted in the colliery, 70 would be sufficient. James finally agreed to 70, and signed a requisition form, agreeing on behalf of the appellants to pay for the services of the men provided at certain specified rates *per diem* and also for their travelling expenses and to provide them with food and sleeping accommodation. When the police were billeted in the colliery, the safety men came to work, which they would not have done but for the presence of the police. The police remained on the premises until the end of the strike.
  The defence to the action was that there was no consideration for the promise of payment, it being the duty of the county council to supply police protection; there was also a counterclaim for £1,330 4s., the cost of feeding and housing the police supplied. Bailhache J. gave judgment for the respondents on the claim and dismissed the counterclaim. The Court of Appeal by a majority (Bankes and Scrutton L.JJ., Atkin L.J. dissenting) affirmed the judgment.

VISCOUNT CAVE L.C.: No doubt there is an absolute unconditional obligation binding the police authorities to take all steps which appear to them to be necessary for keeping the peace, for preventing crime, or for protecting property from criminal injury; and the public, who pay for this protection through the rates and taxes, cannot lawfully be called upon to make a further payment for that which is their right. . . . But it has always been recognised that, where individuals desire that services of a special kind which, though not within the obligations of a police authority, can most effectively be rendered by them, should be performed by members of the police force, the police authorities may (to use an expression which is found in the Police Pensions Act 1890) "lend" the services of constables for that purpose in consideration of payment. Instances are the lending of constables on the occasions of large gatherings in and outside private premises, as on the occasions of weddings, athletic or boxing contests or race meetings, and the provision of constables at large railway stations. Of course no such lending could possibly take place if the constables were required elsewhere for the preservation of order; but (as Bankes L.J. pointed out) an effective police force requires a margin of reserve strength in order to deal with emergencies, and to employ that margin of reserve, when not otherwise required, on special police service for payment is to the advantage both of the persons utilising their services and of the public who are thereby relieved from some part of the police charges. Atkin L.J. put the contrary view in the form of a dilemma when he said: "Either they were performing this public duty in giving the protection asked for, in which case I think they cannot charge, or, which no one suggests, they were at the request of an individual doing something which it was not their duty to do, in which case it seems to me both public policy and section 10 of the County Police Act 1839, make the contract illegal and void." With great respect to the learned Lord Justice I am disposed to think that this reasoning rests on an ambiguous use of the word "duty." There may be services rendered by the police which, although not within the scope of their absolute obligations to the public may yet fall within their powers, and in such cases public policy does not forbid their performance. I do not understand the reference in the above passage to section 10 of the Act of 1839.

(His Lordship then proceeded to consider whether in this case the billeting of the police was a special duty for which a charge might be made.)

. . . In this connection I think it important to bear in mind exactly what it was that the learned trial judge had to decide. It was no part of his duty to say—nor did he purport to say—whether in his judgment the billeting of the 70 men at the colliery was necessary for the prevention of violence or the protection of the mines from criminal injury. The duty of determining such questions is cast by law, not upon the courts after the event, but upon the police authorities at the time when the decision has to be taken; and a court which attempted to review such a decision from the point of view of its wisdom or prudence would (I think) be exceeding its proper functions. The question for the court was whether on July 9, 1921, the police authorities acting, reasonably and in good faith, considered a police garrison at the colliery necessary for the protection of life and property from violence, or, in other words, whether the decision of the chief constable in refusing special protection unless paid for was such a decision as a man in his position and with his duties could reasonably take. If in the judgment of the police authorities, formed reasonably and in good faith, the garrison was necessary for the protection of life and property, then they were not entitled to make a charge for it, for that would be to exact a payment for the performance of a duty which they clearly owed to the appellants and their servants; but if they thought the garrison a superfluity and only acceded to Mr James's request with a view to meeting his wishes, then in my opinion they were entitled to treat the garrison duty as special duty and to charge for it. . . .

. . . In my opinion, therefore, this appeal fails and should be dismissed with costs.

VISCOUNT FINLAY AND LORD SHAW OF DUNFERMLINE made speeches to similar effect.

LORD CARSON and LORD BLANESBURGH dissented, holding that, in the circumstances of the case, the billeting of the police was not a special service.

Note

In *Harris v. Sheffield United Football Club* [1987] 2 All E.R. 838 the police authority claimed from the club £51,699 for providing special police services at the club's ground between August 1982 and November 1983. The club contended that in attending the matches the police were merely fulfilling their duty to enforce the law and their attendance did not constitute the provision of "special police services" within section 15(1) of the Police Act 1964. That section provided statutory authority for the long established practice of charging a person who requested "special police services." The judge upheld the authority's claim and the Court of Appeal, considering *Glasbrook v. Glamorgan*, dismissed the appeal. In deciding whether police services are "special" the court will take into account: (1) whether the officers are required to attend on private premises or in a public place; (2) whether violence has already occurred or is imminent—if so, the services cannot be "special"; (3) the nature of the event—public events like elections lie at one end of the spectrum, private events like weddings at the other, and events like football matches somewhere in the middle; (4) whether protection can be provided without using officers who would otherwise be on other duties or off duty.

Questions

1. The Rovers' F.C. secretary telephones the Chief Constable—"The crowd is fighting—police are overwhelmed—send help." The Chief Constable replies, "Only if you agree to pay." The secretary agrees. Does the Club have to pay the bill? If not, why not?—is it a question of consideration? What if, a month before the game, the Chief Constable had advised that 50 officers would be required in the ground but the Club was willing to pay for only 25?

2. In *Sykes v. D.P.P.* [1962] A.C. 528; [1961] 3 All E.R. 33, it was held that the crime of misprision of felony consisted in concealment of or failure to reveal a felony known to have been committed, regardless whether the accused kept silent for profit. Citizens thus had a legal duty to reveal felonies known to them. Does that mean that, in the "reward cases" (above, pp. 31–40), a promise was enforceable, the consideration for which was the performance of an existing legal duty? (Misprision of felony has ceased to be a crime since the Criminal Law Act 1967.)

WARD v. BYHAM

Court of Appeal [1956] 1 W.L.R. 496; 100 S.J. 341; [1956] 2 All E.R. 318

When the parents of an illegitimate child separated, the father paid a neighbour £1 per week to look after the child. Later the mother, having taken a housekeeping job where she could have the child with her, wrote to the father to let her have the child and the £1 per week. The father replied, "I am prepared to let you have (the child) and pay you up to £1 a week allowance for her providing you can prove that she will be well looked after and happy and also that she is allowed to decide for herself whether or not she wishes to come and live with you." It was agreed that the child should go to the mother and the father paid the £1 per week until the mother married her employer, when the father stopped payments. The county court judge gave judgment for the mother in an action brought by her for the £1 per week based upon the father's undertaking. The father appealed.

DENNING L.J.: I look on the father's letter as dealing with two things. One is the handing over of the child to the mother. The father agrees to let the mother have the child, provided the child herself wishes to come and provided also that the mother satisfies the father that she will be well looked after and happy. The other thing is the future maintenance of the child. The father promises to pay the mother up to £1 per week so long as the mother looks after the child. (His Lordship then referred to the fact that the mother of an illegitimate child was bound to maintain it, whereas the father was not under such obligation. (See section 42 of the National Assistance Act 1948.))

I approach the case, therefore, on the footing that, in looking after the child, the mother is only doing what she is legally bound to do. Even so, I think there was sufficient consideration to support the promise. I have always thought that a promise to perform an existing duty, or the performance of it, should be regarded as good consideration, because it is a benefit to the person to whom it is given. Take this very case. It is as much a benefit for the father to have the child looked after by the mother as by a neighbour. If he gets the benefit for which he stipulated, he ought to honour his promise, and he ought not to avoid it by saying that the mother was herself under a duty to maintain the child.

I regard the father's promise in this case as what is sometimes called a unilateral contract, a promise in return for an act, a promise by the father to pay £1 per week in return for the mother's looking after the child. Once the mother embarked on the task of looking after the child, there was a binding contract. So long as she looked after the child, she would be entitled to £1 a week. . . .

MORRIS L.J.: It seems to me, therefore, that the father was saying, in effect: Irrespective of what may be the strict legal position, what I am asking is that you shall prove that the child will be well looked after and happy, and also that you must agree that the child is to be allowed to decide for herself whether or not she wishes to come and live with you. If those conditions were fulfilled, the father was agreeable to pay. On those terms, which in fact became operative, the father agreed to pay £1 a week. In my judgment, there was ample consideration there to be bound for his promise, which I think was binding.

PARKER L.J. concurred.

Appeal dismissed.

Questions
1. What was the consideration for the father's promise as found by:
 (a) Denning L.J.?
 (b) Morris L.J.?

2. Though not under a legal liability to maintain his illegitimate child, the father is under a moral duty to do so. Would the promise of a complete stranger to pay a mother to maintain her illegitimate child be binding on the promisor?
Cf. Williams v. Williams (above, p. 217).

Note
　　Treitel (8th ed.), p. 87 says of *Ward v. Byham*: "One basis of the decision is that the mother had provided consideration by showing that she had made the child happy, etc.: in this way she can be said to have conferred a factual benefit on the father, even though she may not have suffered any detriment." Why is it not a detriment to the mother to have to prove a fact to the father—something she has no prior obligation to do? Treitel adds" But if a son's promise not to bore his father is not good consideration (*White v. Bluett* above, p. 209), it is hard to see why a mother's promise to make her child happy should stand on a different footing. . . ." Can the two cases be reconciled?

(ii) *By Contract with a Third Party*

SHADWELL v. SHADWELL

Common Bench (1860) 9 C.B.(N.S.) 159; 30 L.J.C.P. 145; 7 Jur. 311; 3 L.T. 628; 9 W.R. 163; 127 R.R. 604; 142 E.R. 62

　　The declaration stated that the testator in his lifetime (in consideration that the plaintiff would marry Ellen Nicholl) agreed with and promised the plaintiff, then unmarried, in the terms of and contained in the following letter:

August 11, 1838,
Gray's Inn

My Dear Lancey,
　　I am glad to hear of your intended marriage with Ellen Nicholl, and, as I promised to assist you at starting, I am happy to tell you that I will pay to you one hundred and fifty pounds yearly during my life, and until your annual income derived from your profession of a Chancery barrister shall amount to six hundred guineas, of which your own admission will be the only evidence that I shall receive or require.

Your ever affectionate uncle,
Charles Shadwell.

　　Averment that everything necessary happened to entitle the plaintiff to have the said testator pay to him eighteen of the yearly sums of £150 and that the time therefore elapsed after he had married Ellen Nicholl and during the testator's lifetime and that plaintiff's annual income from his profession as a Chancery barrister never amounted to 600 guineas; that the testator paid 12 of the 18 annual sums and part of the thirteenth but that the residue of that and the 5 subsequent instalments were due and unpaid.
　　Fourth plea, that the plaintiff's marriage with Ellen Nicholl had been arranged before the alleged agreement without any request from the testator and that there was no consideration for the alleged agreement.
　　Second replication to the fourth plea, that the agreement was in the terms of and contained in the letter set out above. Averment that the plaintiff married Ellen Nicholl, relying on the said promise and so married while his income as a Chancery barrister did not amount to 600 guineas per annum. Demurrer to the replication to the fourth plea. Joinder in demurrer.

　　ERLE C.J.: The question raised by the demurrer to the replication to the fourth plea is, whether there was a consideration to support the action on the promise to pay an annuity of £150 per annum. . . . The circumstances are, that the plaintiff had made an engagement to marry Ellen Nicholl, his uncle promising him to assist him at starting, by which, as I understand the words, he meant on commencing his married life. Then the letter containing the promise declared on is said to specify what the assistance would be, namely, £150 per annum during the uncle's life, and until the plaintiff's professional income should be acknowledged by him to exceed 600 guineas; and a further averment, that the plaintiff, relying upon his promise, without any revocation on the part of the uncle, did marry Ellen Nicholl. Then, do these facts show that the promise was in consideration, either of the loss to be sustained by the plaintiff, or the benefit to be derived from the plaintiff to the uncle, at his, the uncle's request? My answer is in the affirmative. First, do these facts show a loss sustained by the plaintiff at the uncle's request? When I answer this in the affirmative, I am aware that a man's marriage with the woman of his choice is in one sense a boon, and in that sense the reverse of a loss; yet, as between the plaintiff and the party promising an income to support the marriage, it may be a loss. The plaintiff may have made the most material changes in his position, and have induced the object of his affections to do the same, and have incurred pecuniary liabilities resulting in embarrassments, which would be in every sense a loss, if the income which had been promised should be withheld; and if the promise was made in order to induce the parties to marry, the promise so made would be, in legal effect, a request to marry. Secondly, do these facts show a benefit derived from the plaintiff to the uncle at his request? In answering again in the affirmative, I am at liberty to consider the relation in which the parties stood, and the interest in the status of the nephew which the uncle declares. The marriage primarily affects the parties thereto; but in the second degree it may be an object of interest with a near relative, and in that sense a benefit to him. This benefit is also derived from the plaintiff at the uncle's request, if the promise of the annuity was intended as an inducement to the marriage; and the averment that the plaintiff, relying on the promise, married, is an averment that the promise was one inducement to the marriage. This is a consideration averred in the declaration, and it appears to me to be expressed in the letter, construed with the surrounding circumstances. No case bearing a strong analogy to the present was cited; but the importance of enforcing promises which have been made to induce parties to marry has been often recognised, and the cases of *Montefiori v. Montefiori* ((1762) 1 W.Bl. 363) and *Bold v. Hutchinson* (1855) 20 Beavan 250) are examples. I do not feel it necessary to add anything about the numerous authorities referred to in the learned arguments addressed to us, because the decision turns on a question of fact, whether the consideration for the promise is proved as pleaded. I think it is, and therefore my judgment on the first demurrer is for the plaintiff.

KEATING J. concurred.

BYLES J. (dissenting): I am of opinion that the defendant is entitled to the judgment of the court on the demurrer to the second replication to the fourth plea. It is alleged by the fourth plea, that the defendant's testator never requested the plaintiff to enter into the engagement to marry, or to marry, and that there never was any consideration for the testator's promise, except what may be collected from the letter itself set out in the declaration. The inquiry, therefore, narrows itself to this question: Does the letter itself disclose any consideration for the promise? The consideration relied on by the plaintiff's counsel being the subsequent marriage of the plaintiff, I think the letter discloses no consideration. It is in these words: [his Lordship read it]. It is by no means clear that the words "at starting" mean "on marriage with Ellen Nicholl," or with anyone else. The more natural meaning seems to me to be, "at starting in the profession," for it will be observed that these words are used by the testator in reciting a prior promise made when the testator had not heard of the proposed marriage with Ellen Nicholl, or, so far as appears, heard of any proposed marriage. This construction is fortified by the consideration that the annuity is not, in terms, made to begin from the marriage, but, as it should seem, from the date of the letter. Neither is it in terms made defeasible if Ellen Nicholl should die before marriage. But even on the assumption that the words "at starting" mean "on marriage," I still think that no consideration appears sufficient to sustain the promise. The promise is one which, by law, must be in writing; and the fourth plea shows that no consideration or request, *dehors* the letter, existed, and, therefore, that no such consideration, or request, can be alluded to by the letter. Marriage of the plaintiff at the testator's express request would be, no doubt, an ample consideration; but marriage of the plaintiff without the testator's request is no consideration to the testator. It is true that marriage is, or may be, a detriment to the plaintiff; but detriment to the plaintiff is not enough, unless it either be a benefit to the testator, or be treated by the testator as such, by having been suffered at his request. Suppose a defendant to promise a plaintiff, "I will give you £500 if you break your leg," would that detriment to the plaintiff, should it happen, be any consideration? If it be said that such an accident is an involuntary mischief, would it have been a binding promise if the testator had said, "I will give you £100 a year while you continue in your present chambers"? I conceive that the promise would not be binding for want of a previous request by the testator. Now, the testator in the case before the court derived, so far as appears, no personal benefit from the marriage. The question, therefore, is still further narrowed to this point: Was the marriage at the testator's request? Express request there was none. Can any request be implied? The only words from which it can be contended that it is to be implied are the words, "I am glad to hear of your intended marriage with Ellen Nicholl." But it appears from the fourth plea that that marriage had already been agreed on, and that the testator knew it. These words, therefore, seem to me to import no more than the satisfaction of the testator at the engagement as an accomplished fact. No request can, as it seems to me, be inferred from them. And, further, how does it appear that the testator's implied request, if it could be implied, or his promise, if that promise alone would suffice, or both together, were intended to cause the marriage, or did cause it, so that the marriage can be said to have taken place at the testator's request, or, in other words, in consequence of that request? It seems to me, not only that this does not appear, but that the contrary appears; for the plaintiff before the letter had already bound himself to marry, by placing himself not only under a moral, but under a legal, obligation to marry, and the testator knew it. The well-known cases which have been cited at the Bar in support of the position, that a promise, based on the consideration of doing that which a man is already bound to do, is invalid, apply to this case; and it is not necessary, in order to invalidate the consideration, that the plaintiff's prior obligation to afford that consideration should have been an obligation to the defendant. It may have been an obligation to a third person: see *Herring v. Dorell* ((1840) 8 Dowl. P.C. 604); *Atkinson v. Settree* ((1744) Willes 482). The reason why the doing what a man is already bound to do is no consideration, is not only because such a consideration is in judgment of law of no value, but because a man can hardly be allowed to say that the prior legal obligation was not his determining motive. But, whether he can be allowed to say so or not, the plaintiff does not say so here. He does, indeed, make an attempt to meet this difficulty, by alleging, in the replication to the fourth plea, that he married relying on the testator's promise; but he shrinks from alleging, that though he had promised to marry before the testator's promise to him, nevertheless, he would have broken his engagement, and would not have married without the testator's promise. A man may rely on encouragements to the performance of his duty, who yet is prepared to do his duty without those encouragements. At the utmost, the allegation that he relied on the testator's promise seems to me to import no more than that he believed the testator would be as good as his word. It appears to me, for these reasons, that this letter is no more than a letter of kindness, creating no legal obligation.

Judgment for the plaintiff

(A second point arising on the fifth plea and replication thereto is omitted.)

Note
    Though this case is always cited on the issue of whether the performance of a contractual obligation owed to a third party can be good consideration, the principal point at issue was whether the testator made an offer of contract at all. Erle C.J. thought he had because he had requested the plaintiff to marry Ellen. Byles J. thought that he had not because he had made no such request. He had no doubt that "Marriage of the plaintiff at the testator's express request would be . . . an ample consideration." In *Jones v. Padavatton* [1969] 1 W.L.R. 328 at 333, above, p. 185, Salmon L.J. said of *Shadwell v. Shadwell*: "I confess that I should have decided it without hesitation in accordance with the views of Byles J., but this is of no consequence." Who was right? Was there a request (express or implied) in the letter or not? (Because writing was required by the Statute of Frauds (above, p. 5), it had to be found there, or not at all.)
    Suppose that nephew had told uncle that he intended to break off the engagement and uncle had written: "I am disappointed to hear you are thinking of breaking off your engagement. Ellen is a splendid girl. If you marry her, I will pay you . . ." How would Byles J. (and, presumably, Salmon L.J.) then have decided the case? *Cf.* Note on *Gratuitous Promises and Conditional Gifts*, above, p. 197.
    Is a promise to give a wedding present binding when the marriage takes place? Does it matter that the present is so substantial that it is a powerful inducement to marry?

PAO ON v. LAU YIU LONG

Privy Council [1980] A.C. 614; [1979] 3 W.L.R. 435; [1979] 3 All E.R. 65

One of the questions raised (see also above, pp. 201, 203 and below p. 292 was whether the plaintiffs had given consideration to the defendants by promising to perform an existing contract between the plaintiffs and a third party, Fu Chip, in the performance of which the defendants had an interest. The plaintiffs had said that they were not going to perform that contract unless the defendants entered into the contract with them which was in issue.

LORD SCARMAN: Their Lordships do not doubt that a promise to perform, or the performance of, a pre-existing contractual obligation to a third party can be valid consideration. In *New Zealand Shipping Co. Ltd v. A. M. Satterthwaite & Co. Ltd (The Eurymedon)*, below, p. 290 the rule and the reason for the rule were stated:

> "An agreement to do an act which the promisor is under an existing obligation to a third party to do, may quite well amount to valid consideration . . . the promisee obtains the benefit of a direct obligation. . . . This proposition is illustrated and supported by *Scotson v. Pegg (supra)* which their Lordships consider to be good law."

Unless, therefore the guarantee was void as having been made for an illegal consideration or voidable on the ground of economic duress, the extrinsic evidence establishes that it was supported by valid consideration.

(Having referred to *Harris v. Watson* and *Stilk v. Myrick*, below, pp. 230–231 his Lordship proceeded:)

When one turns to consider cases where a pre-existing duty imposed by law is alleged to be valid consideration for a promise, one finds cases in which public policy has been held to invalidate the consideration. A promise to pay a sheriff in consideration of his performing his legal duty, a promise to pay for discharge from illegal arrest, are to be found in the books as promises which the law will not enforce: see the cases cited in paragraph 326, footnote 2 of *Halsbury's Laws of England* (4th ed., 1974), Vol. 9. Yet such cases are also explicable upon the ground that a person who promises to perform, or performs, a duty imposed by law provides no consideration. In cases where the discharge of a duty imposed by law has been treated as valid consideration, the courts have usually (but not invariably) found an act over and above, but consistent with, the duty imposed by law: see *Williams v. Williams*, (above, p. 217). It must be conceded that different judges have adopted differing approaches to such cases: contrast, for example, Denning L.J. with the view of the majority in *Williams'* case. But where the pre-existing obligation is a contractual duty owed to a third party, some other ground of public policy must be relied on to invalidate the consideration (if otherwise legal) . . .

[The Board went on to hold that the contract was not voidable for economic duress—see below, pp. 237, 642–658 and Atiyah (1982) 98 L.Q.R. 197 and (1983) 99 L.Q.R. 353 and Tiplady (1983) 99 L.Q.R. 188.]

Notes

1. In *Scotson v. Pegg* (1861) 30 L.J.Ex. 225 the plaintiffs had contracted with a third party, A, to deliver a cargo of coal to A or to the order of A. A sold the cargo to the defendant and directed the plaintiffs to deliver it to the defendant as per contract. The defendant then made an agreement with the plaintiffs in which "in consideration that the plaintiffs, at the request of the defendant, would deliver to the defendant" the cargo of coal, the defendant promised to unload it at a stated rate. The plaintiffs sued for the defendant's failure to honour this promise and the defendant pleaded lack of consideration, the plaintiffs being already under a duty of delivery by the contract with A. The Court of Exchequer (Martin and Wilde BB.) found for the plaintiffs: Wilde B. thought that the plaintiffs might have found it advantageous not to comply with their contract with A so that their agreement with the defendant was a detriment to them; in any event, they agreed to part with the cargo to the defendant which was a benefit to him.

2. It will be noted that in the passage cited from *The Eurymedon*, above, the Privy Council regarded the promise to perform the existing agreement as consideration and that Lord

Scarman made no distinction between the performance of, and the promise to perform, the existing obligation. *Cf. Cheshire, Fifoot & Furmston* (12th ed.) pp. 107–108.

3. In *Jones v. Waite* (1839) 5 Bing. N.C. 341; 132 E.R. 1136 (affirmed on a different ground, 9 Cl. & Fin. 101; 8 E.R. 353) the Court of Exchequer Chamber held that a promise by A to pay existing debts that he owed B was no consideration for a promise by C. Lord Abinger C.B. said: "Now a consideration to support a promise must either operate to the advantage of the party making the promise, or to the detriment of the party who is to perform the consideration. But a man is under a moral and legal obligation to pay his just debts. It cannot therefore be stated, as an abstract proposition, that he suffers any detriment from the discharge of that duty; and the declaration does not show in what way the defendant could have derived any advantage from the plaintiff paying his own debts. The plea therefore shows the insufficiency of that part of the consideration."

Questions

1. Does the duty to pay a debt differ from other legal duties in nature?

2. Might not a debtor legitimately seek release from his creditor? Could not a promise in effect to forgo this liberty constitute consideration?

3. Do you think that the decision in *Jones v. Waite* would be the same today?

(iii) *By Contract with the Promisor*

STILK v. MYRICK

King's Bench (1809) 2 Camp. 317; 11 R.R. 717; 6 Esp. 129, 170 E.R. 1168

This was an action for seaman's wages, on a voyage from London to the Baltic and back.

By the ship's articles, executed before the commencement of the voyage, the plaintiff was to be paid at the rate of £5 a month; and the principal question in the cause was, whether he was entitled to a higher rate of wages. In the course of the voyage two of the seamen deserted; and the captain, having in vain attempted to supply their places at Cronstadt, there entered into an agreement with the rest of the crew, that they should have the wages of the two who had deserted equally divided among them, if he could not procure two other hands at Gottenborg. This was found impossible, and the ship was worked back to London by the plaintiff and eight more of the original crew, with whom the agreement had been made at Cronstadt.

LORD ELLENBOROUGH: I think *Harris v. Watson* was rightly decided; but I doubt whether the ground of public policy, upon which Lord Kenyon is stated to have proceeded, be the true principle on which the decision is to be supported. Here, I say, the agreement is void for want of consideration. There was no consideration for the ulterior pay promised to the mariners who remained with the ship. Before they sailed from London they had undertaken to do all that they could under all the emergencies of the voyage. They had sold all their services till the voyage should be completed. If they had been at liberty to quit the vessel at Cronstadt, the case would have been quite different; or if the captain had capriciously discharged the two men who were wanting, the others might not have been compellable to take the whole duty upon themselves, and their agreeing to do so might have been a sufficient consideration for the promise of an advance of wages. But the desertion of a part of the crew is to be considered an emergency of the voyage as much as their death; and those who remain are bound by the terms of their original contract to exert themselves to the utmost to bring the ship in safety to her destined port. Therefore, without looking to the policy of this agreement, I think it is void for want of consideration, and that the plaintiff can only recover at the rate of £5 a month.

Verdict accordingly.

Note

1. In *Harris v. Watson* (1791) Peake 102; 170 E.R. 94, the plaintiff, a seaman, claimed that the defendant, the captain of his ship, had promised him five guineas over and above his ordinary wages if he would perform some extra work in navigating the ship, the promise having been made, when the ship was in danger, to induce the seamen to exert themselves. Nonsuiting the plaintiff, Lord Kenyon C.J. said, "If this action was to be supported, it would materially affect the navigation of this kingdom. It has been long since determined, that when the freight is lost, the wages are also lost. This rule was founded on a principle of policy, for if sailors were in all events to have their wages, and in times of danger entitled to insist on an extra charge on such a promise as this, they would in many cases suffer a ship to sink, unless the captain would pay an extravagant demand they might think proper to make."

According to the report of *Stilk v. Myrick* in Espinasse, Lord Ellenborough said that "he recognised the principle of the case of *Harris v. Watson* as founded on just and proper policy." See Gilmore, *The Death of Contract*, pp. 22–28. Note that there is no evidence of a demand by the seamen in either *Harris v. Watson* or *Stilk v. Myrick*. Of course, a demand may be implied as well as express; but, if there was no demand, could either case be explained on the ground of duress? Should there be a difference between the case where the demand comes from the seamen and that where the master takes the initiative with a generous offer?

2. In *Hartley v. Ponsonby* (1857) 7 El. & Bl. 872 an able seaman successfully sued the master of the *Mobile* on a promise to pay him £40 if he would assist in taking the ship from Port Philip to Bombay with a crew of 19 hands. The defence was that there was no consideration for the promise because the plaintiff was bound by his existing contract to assist in sailing the ship. The ship had left England with a crew of 36 but, as a result of desertions, only 19 remained and only 4 or 5 of them were able seamen. The Queen's Bench held that the crew was so reduced that it was dangerous to life to sail and unreasonable for the master to require his crew to do so. Their contract had come to an end (see Chapter 14, Frustration, below) and they were in the same position as any other free seamen in Port Philip: "they might stipulate for any amount of remuneration; and, considering the circumstances, £40 might not have been an exorbitant sum"—*per* Erle J.

Suppose £40 had been an "exorbitant" sum. Should it have made any difference? Could not a free seaman in Port Philip properly have taken full advantage of a seller's market? Would it now be regarded as economic duress?

WILLIAMS v. ROFFEY BROS. & NICHOLLS (CONTRACTORS) LTD

Court of Appeal [1990] 2 W.L.R. 1153; [1990] 1 All E.R. 512

The defendants who had contracted to refurbish a block of flats sub-contracted the carpentry work to the plaintiff for a price of £20,000 to be paid in instalments related to the work completed. The plaintiff got into financial difficulties because the price was too low and he did not supervise the work properly. He had received over 80 per cent of the price but still had far more than 20 per cent. of the work to do. The defendants were liable to a penalty clause in the main contract if the work was not completed on time. They were aware of the plaintiff's difficulties and that the price was too low. They met him and agreed to pay him an extra £10,300 at £575 per flat to ensure that he continued with the work and completed on time. The plaintiff completed eight further flats and received a payment of £1,500. He stopped work and sued for the money he alleged to be owing. The defendants denied liability and, in particular, that they were liable to pay any part of the additional £10,300 because their agreement to pay it was not supported by any consideration.

The judge held that the plaintiff was entitled to eight payments of £575, less certain deductions. The defendants appealed.

GLIDEWELL L.J., having reviewed the authorities, concluding with *Pao On v. Lau Yiu*, continued: It is true that *Pao On v. Lau Yiu* is a case of a tripartite relationship, that is, a promise by A to perform a pre-existing contractual obligation owed to B, in return for a promise of payment by C. But Lord Scarman's words seem to me to be of general application, equally applicable to a promise made by one of the original two parties to a contract. Accordingly, following the view of the majority in *Ward v. Byham* and of the whole court in *Williams v. Williams* and that of the Privy Council in *Pao On v. Lau Yiu* the present state of the law on this subject can be expressed in the following proposition: (i) if A has entered into a contract with B to do work for, or to supply goods or services to, B in return for payment by B and (ii) at some stage before A has completely performed his obligations under the contract B has reason to doubt whether A will, or will be able to, complete his side of the bargain and (iii) B thereupon promises A an additional payment in return for A's promise to perform his contractual obligations on time and (iv) as a result of giving his promise B obtains in practice a benefit, or obviates a disbenefit, and (v) B's promise is not given as a result of economic duress or fraud on the part of A, then (vi) the benefit to B is capable of being consideration for B's promise, so that the promise will be legally binding.

As I have said, counsel for the defendants accepts that in the present case by promising to pay the extra £10,300 the defendants secured benefits. There is no finding, and no suggestion, that in this case the promise was given as a result of fraud or duress.

If it be objected that the propositions above contravene the principle in *Stilk v. Myrick*, I answer that in my view they do not: they refine and limit the application of that principle, but they leave the principle unscathed, for example, where B secures no benefit by his promise. It is not in my view surprising that a principle enunciated in relation to the rigours of seafaring life during the Napoleonic wars should be subjected during the succeeding 180 years to a process of refinement and limitation in its application in the present day.

It is therefore my opinion that on his findings of fact in the present case, the judge was entitled to hold, as he did, that the defendants' promise to pay the extra £10,300 was supported by valuable consideration, and thus constituted an enforceable agreement.

As a subsidiary argument, counsel for the defendants submits that on the facts of the present case the consideration, even if otherwise good, did not "move from the promisee." This submission is based on the principle illustrated in the decision in *Tweddle v. Atkinson* (below, p. 275).

My understanding of the meaning of the requirement that "consideration must move from the promisee" is that such consideration must be provided by the promisee, or arise out of his contractual relationship with the promisor. It is consideration provided by somebody else, not a party to the contract, which does not "move from the promisee." This was the situation in *Tweddle v. Atkinson*, but it is, of course, not the situation in the present case. Here the benefits to the defendants arose out of their agreement of April 9, 1986 with the plaintiff, the promisee. In this respect I would adopt the following passage from *Chitty on Contracts* (25th ed., 1983), para. 173, and refer to the authorities there cited:

> "The requirement that consideration must move from the promisee is most generally satisfied where some detriment is suffered by him: for example, where he parts with money or goods, or renders services, in exchange for the promise. But the requirement may equally well be satisfied where the promisee confers a benefit on the promisor without *in fact* suffering any detriment." (*Chitty's* emphasis.)

That is the situation in this case.

I repeat, therefore, my opinion that the judge was, as a matter of law, entitled to hold that there was valid consideration to support the agreement under which the defendants promised to pay an additional £10,300 at the rate of £575 per flat.

For these reasons I would dismiss this appeal.

RUSSELL L.J., having cited the judgments in *Amalgamated Investment and Property Co. Ltd v. Texas Commerce International Bank Ltd* (below, p. 262), continued: These citations demonstrate that while consideration remains a fundamental requirement before a contract not under seal can be enforced, the policy of the law in its search to do justice between the parties has developed considerably since the early nineteenth century when *Stilk v. Myrick* was decided by Lord Ellenborough C.J. In the late twentieth century I do not believe that the rigid approach to the concept of consideration to be found in *Stilk v. Myrick* is either necessary or desirable. Consideration there must still be but in my judgment the courts nowadays should be more ready to find its existence so as to reflect the intention of the parties to the contract where the bargaining powers are not unequal and where the finding of consideration reflects the true intention of the parties.

What was the true intention of the parties when they arrived at the agreement pleaded by the defendants in para. 5 of the amended defence? The plaintiff had got into financial difficulties. The defendants, through their employee Mr Cottrell, recognised that the price that had been agreed originally with the plaintiff was less than what Mr Cottrell himself regarded as a reasonable price. There was a desire on Mr Cottrell's part to retain the services of the plaintiff so that the work could be completed without the need to employ another sub-contractor. There was further a need to replace what had hitherto been a haphazard method of payment by a more formalised scheme involving the payment of a specified sum on the completion of each flat. These were all advantages accruing to the defendants which can fairly be said to have been in consideration of their undertaking to pay the additional £10,300. True it was that the plaintiff did not undertake to do any work additional to that which he had originally undertaken to do but the terms on which he was to carry out the work were varied and, in my judgment, that variation was supported by consideration which a pragmatic approach to the true relationship between the parties readily demonstrates.

For my part I wish to make it plain that I do not base my judgment on any reservation as to the correctness of the law long ago enunciated in *Stilk v. Myrick*. A gratuitous promise, pure and simple, remains unenforceable unless given under seal. But where, as in this case, a party undertakes to make a payment because by so doing it will gain an advantage arising out of the continuing relationship with the promisee the new bargain will not fail for want of consideration. As I read the judgment of the assistant recorder this was his true ratio on that part of the case wherein the absence of consideration was raised in argument. For the reasons that I have endeavoured to outline, I think that the assistant recorder came to a correct conclusion and I too would dismiss this appeal.

PURCHAS L.J.: The question must be posed: what consideration has moved from the plaintiff to support the promise to pay the extra £10,300 added to the lump sum provision? In the particular circumstances which I have outlined above, there was clearly a commercial advantage to both sides from a pragmatic point of view in reaching the agreement of April 9. The defendants were on risk that as a result of the bargain they had struck the plaintiff would not or indeed possibly could not comply with his existing obligations without further finance. As a result of the agreement the defendants secured their position commercially. There was, however, no obligation added to the contractual duties imposed on the plaintiff under the original contract. Prima facie this would appear to be a classic *Stilk v. Myrick* case. It was, however, open to the plaintiff to be in deliberate breach of the contract in order to "cut his losses" commercially. In normal circumstances the suggestion that a contracting party can rely on his own breach to establish consideration is distinctly unattractive. In many cases it obviously would be and if there was any element of duress brought on the other contracting party under the modern development of this branch of the law the proposed breaker of the contract would not benefit. With some hesitation and comforted by the passage from the speech of Lord Hailsham L.C. [in [1972] A.C. 741 at 757–758], to which I have referred, I consider that the modern approach to the question of consideration would be that where there were benefits derived by each party to a contract of variation even though one party did not suffer a detriment this would not be fatal to the establishing of sufficient consideration to support the agreement. If both parties benefit from an agreement it is not necessary that each also suffers a detriment. In my judgment, on the facts as found by the judge, he was entitled to reach the conclusion that consideration existed and in those circumstances I would not disturb that finding. This is sufficient to determine the appeal. The judge found as a fact that the flats were "substantially completed" and that payment was due to the plaintiff in respect of the number of flats substantially completed, which left an outstanding amount due from the defendants to the plaintiff in the absence of the payment of which the plaintiff was entitled to remove from the site. For these reasons and for the reasons which have already been given by Glidewell L.J., I would dismiss this appeal.

Appeal dismissed. (Leave to appeal to the House of Lords was granted but not pursued.)

Questions
1. Do the cases cited by Glidewell L.J. support the conclusion (vi) in his proposition?
2. Was *Stilk v. Myrick* distinguishable as a case where the master secured no benefit by his promise. Was it not a benefit to him to have the crew sail the ship home rather than abandon

him and it in a foreign port? Did not the master "gain an advantage out of the continuing relationship" with the sailors? And *Cf. Atlas Express Ltd. v. Kafko Ltd,* below, p. 653.

3. Is it not always a "benefit" to a contracting party to have the other party perform rather than default? Did the defendants receive any benefit other than (i) the performance of the contract by the plaintiff and (ii) avoidance of the penalty? How if at all did the existence of the penalty clause affect the consideration given by the plaintiff? Did the plaintiff give anything other than the performance of his contract? Is this what counsel had in mind when he argued that consideration (for example, relief from the penalty) did not "move from the promisee?" See *Note, infra.*

4. Does the case suggest that the worse the plight of the promisor (for example, the bigger the penalty clause) the greater the benefit to him and the more likely it is that performance of the contract will be held to be consideration?

5. Would the result have been the same if the original agreed price for the carpentry had been a fair price? Or a generous price?

6. Is the decision reconcilable with *Foakes v. Beer,* below, p. 240? Note that Lord Blackburn was convinced that prompt part payment of a debt is in fact a benefit to the creditor but he abandoned the opinion that it is for that reason consideration for the creditor's promise not to claim the balance.

Note

In *Anangel Atlas Compania Naviera SA v. Ishikawajima Harima Heavy Industries Co. Ltd (No. 2)* [1990] 2 Lloyds Rep. 526 Hirst J. held that it was a clear benefit or an avoidance of a disbenefit to the defendants that the plaintiffs agreed to take delivery of a ship on the contract date since—

> "Their own evidence conclusively demonstrated that their main object was to make sure that the plaintiffs, whom they described as their 'core' customers, did indeed take delivery on July 25, in order to encourage their other reluctant customers to follow suit."

It was the "very substantial practical avoidance of disbenefit" arising from the anticipated behaviour of the other customers which supplied the consideration. This was apparently the distinction discerned by Hirst J. between the case before him and *Stilk v. Myrick* which, he said, still applies where "there is a wholly gratuitous promise." A promise is gratuitous unless the promisee is paying a price for it by giving something in return. Was the existence of the penalty clause in *Williams v. Roffey* or the potential default of the other buyers in *Anangel* an element in the price paid by the respective promisees? Suppose there had been no other likely defaulters in *Anangel.* Would the promise have then been gratuitous? Was the promise in *Atlas Express Ltd v. Kafko Ltd,* below, p. 653, rightly held to be gratuitous?

Re SELECTMOVE LTD

Court of Appeal [1995] 1 W.L.R. 474; [1995] 2 All E.R. 531

S Ltd owed the Revenue large sums of income tax (PAYE) and national insurance (NIC). For the purposes of the decision, it was accepted that, at a meeting on July 15, 1991 with Mr Polland (P), a collector of taxes, S's managing director, Mr ffooks (ff), suggested that it would not be in anyone's interest for the company to be put into compulsory liquidaton and proposed that the company should pay future PAYE and NIC as it fell due and the arrears at £1,000 per month from February 1, 1992. P said that he would have to seek approval and would come back to ff if the proposal was unacceptable. S made two payments under the alleged agreement. S heard no more from the Revenue until October 9, 1991 when they demanded payment of arrears of PAYE and NIC amounting to £24,650 and threatened a winding-up petition. The question was whether the proposal for payment by instalments on July 15, 1991 had become a binding agreement. On the issue of acceptance, see above, p. 55. On the issue of consideration—

PETER GIBSON L.J.: There are two elements to the consideration which the company claims was provided by it to the Crown. One is the promise to pay off its existing liability by instalments from 1 February 1992. The other is the promise to pay future PAYE and NIC as they fell due. Mr Nugee [Counsel for S Ltd] suggested that implicit in the latter was the promise to continue trading. But that cannot be spelt out of Mr ffooks' evidence as to what he agreed with Mr Polland. Accordingly, the second element is no more than a promise to pay that which it was bound to pay under the fiscal legislation at the date at which it was bound to make such payment. If the first element is not good consideration, I do not see why the second element should be either.

PETER GIBSON L.J. considered *Foakes v. Beer, Vanbergen v. St. Edmunds Properties* and *D & C Builders Ltd v. Rees* (below, pp. 240, 245 and 267) and continued] Mr Nugee, however, submitted that an additional benefit to the Crown was conferred by the agreement in that the Crown stood to derive practical benefits therefrom: it was likely to recover more from not enforcing its debt against the company, which was known to be in financial difficulties, than from putting the company into liquidation. He pointed to the fact that the company did in fact pay its further PAYE and NIC liabilities and £7,000 of its arrears. He relied on the decision of this court in *Williams v. Roffey Bros.* (above, p. 231) for the proposition that a promise to perform an existing obligation can amount to good consideration provided that there are practical benefits to the promisee.

[Having discussed *Williams'* case and cited Glidewell L.J.'s six propositions (above, p. 232) PETER GIBSON L.J. continued:] Mr Nugee submitted that although Glidewell L.J. in terms confined his remarks to a case where B is to do the work for or supply goods or services to A, the same principle must apply where B's obligation is to pay A, and he referred to an article by Adams and Brownsword "Contract, Consideration and the Critical Path" (1990) 53 MLR 536 at 539–540 which suggests that *Foakes v. Beer* might need reconsideration. I see the force of the argument, but the difficulty that I feel with it is that if the principle of *Williams'* case is to be extended to an obligation to make payment, it would in effect leave the principle in *Foakes v. Beer* without any application. When a creditor and a debtor who are at arm's length reach agreement on the payment of the debt by instalments to accommodate the debtor, the creditor will no doubt always see a practical benefit to himself in so doing. In the absence of authority there would be much to be said for the enforceability of such a contract. But that was a matter expressly considered in *Foakes v. Beer* yet held not to constitute good consideration in law. *Foakes v. Beer* was not even referred to in *Williams'* case, and it is in my judgment impossible, consistently with the doctrine of precedent, for this court to extend the principle of *Williams'* case to any circumstances governed by the principle of *Foakes v. Beer*. If that extension is to be made, it must be by the House of Lords or, perhaps even more appropriately, by Parliament after consideration by the Law Commission.

In my judgment, the judge was right to hold that if there was an agreement between the company and the Crown it was unenforceable for want of consideration.

[PETER GIBSON L.J. held promissory estoppel was inapplicable because (i) P had no actual or ostensible authority to make the alleged promise and (ii)

S Ltd had failed to honour its promises to pay. STUART-SMITH and BALCOMBE L.JJ. agreed.]

Questions

1. Is there a valid distinction, in the context of consideration, between an obligation to pay money and an obligation to render services? *Cf. Ruxley Electronics*, below, p. 611, and question 3, below, p. 614.

2. Might the court have taken a different view if the offer had come from the Revenue—*e.g.*, "If you will promise to pay by instalments, we will not apply for a winding up order"? Or are *Foakes v. Beer* and *Vanbergen* still an insuperable obstacle?

NORTH OCEAN SHIPPING CO. v. HYUNDAI CONSTRUCTION CO.

Queen's Bench Division [1979] Q.B. 705; [1979] 3 W.L.R. 419; [1978] 3 All E.R. 1170; sub nom. *The Atlantic Baron*, [1979] 1 Lloyd's Rep. 89

Shipbuilders ("the yard") on April 10, 1972, entered into a contract to build a tanker for shipowners ("the owners") for the fixed price of U.S. $30,950,000, payable in five instalments as the work progressed. The contract required the yard to open a letter of credit to provide security for repayment of instalments in the event of their default in performance of the contract. The owners paid the first instalment on April 28, 1972. On February 12, 1973, the U.S. dollar was devalued by 10 per cent. The yard claimed an increase of 10 per cent. on the four remaining instalments. The owners did not agree and offered to submit the dispute to arbitration. The yard declined and by telex on June 26, 1973, said that, if the owners did not agree to pay the extra 10 per cent they would terminate the contract and refund the first instalment. The owners in May, 1973, had entered into a very advantageous agreement to charter the tanker on completion to Shell for three years, and they would have lost this advantage if the yard carried out its threat. Accordingly, the owners replied by telex on June 28,:

> "We are in receipt of your telex dated 26th June, 1973. Although we are convinced we are under no obligation to make additional payments which you ask, we are prepared as you demand in your telex of the 26th June, 1973, and in order to maintain an amicable relationship and without prejudice to our rights, to make an increase of 10 per cent in instalments payable subsequent to the 12th February, 1973. No doubt you will arrange for corresponding increases in the letter of credit provided for in article XI(2)(iii)."

The yard replied acknowledging that the difference of opinion had been settled and promising to increase the letter of credit. The yard did not appreciate the significance of the words, "without prejudice to our rights," the owners realised that this was so and deliberately did not draw the yard's attention to the significance of the reservation. The letter of credit was increased, the instalments were paid with the additional 10 per cent without protest, the final instalment being expressed to be "in full and final settlement"; and the tanker was delivered on November 27, 1974.

On July 30, 1975 the owners claimed the return of the excess 10 per cent. They refrained from claiming until that date because they had a contract with the yard for another tanker and it was suggested that they feared that, if they initiated the claim before the tanker was delivered, the yard might have refused to deliver. The arbitrators found that there was no ground for such an inference.

The arbitrators held that the owners' claim failed and, at the request of the parties, stated their award in the form of a special case.

MOCATTA J., having stated the facts:

Counsel's argument for the owners that the agreement to pay the extra 10 per cent. was void for lack of consideration was based on the well-known principle that a promise by one party to fulfil his existing contractual duty towards his other contracting party is not good consideration: he relied on the well-known case of *Stilk v. Myrick* for this submission. Accordingly there was no consideration for the owner's agreement to pay the further 10 per cent, since the yard were already contractually bound to build the ship and it is common ground that the devaluation of the dollar had in no way lessened the yard's legal obligation to do this. There has of course been some criticism in the books of the decision in *Stilk v. Myrick* which is somewhat differently reported in the two sets of reports, but Campbell's reports have the better reputation and what I have referred to as being the law on this point is referred to as "the present" rule in *Chitty on Contracts*: see, also, *Cheshire and Fifoot*. The law seems still to be the same in Australia: see *T. A. Sundell & Sons Pty Ltd v. Emm Yannoulatos (Overseas) Pty Ltd* [1956] S.R. (N.S.W.) 323.

Counsel for the yard relied on what Denning L.J. said in two cases dealing with very different subject matters. [His Lordship discussed *Ward v. Byham* (above, p. 223) and *Williams v. Williams* (above, p. 217), and pointed out that the other judges in those cases found that there was ample consideration.]

I do not therefore think either of these cases successfully enables counsel for the yard to avoid the rule in *Stilk v. Myrick* . . .

[His Lordship then considered whether the increase of 10 per cent in the letter of credit amounted to consideration.]

I remain unconvinced, however, that by merely securing an increase in the instalments to be paid of 10 per cent the yard automatically became obliged to increase the return letter of credit *pro tanto* and were therefore doing no more than undertaking in this respect to fulfil their existing contractual duty. I think that here they were undertaking an additional obligation or rendering themselves liable to an increased detriment. I therefore conclude, though not without some doubt, that there was consideration for the new agreement. . . .

Having reached the conclusion that there was consideration for the agreement made on June 28 and June 29, 1973, I must next consider whether even if that agreement, varying the terms of the original ship-building contract of April 10, 1972, was made under a threat to break that original contract and that the various increased instalments were made consequentially under the varied agreement, the increased sums can be recovered as money had and received. Counsel for the owners submitted that they could be, provided they were involuntary payments and not made, albeit perhaps with some grumbling, to close the transaction. Certainly this is the well-established position if payments are made, for example, to avoid the wrongful seizure of goods where there is no prior agreement to make such payments.

[His Lordship considered the authorities, including *Smith v. William Charlick Ltd* [1924] 34 C.L.R. 38 at 56 where Isaacs J. said: "It is conceded that the only ground on which the promise to repay could be implied is 'compulsion.' The payment is said by the respondent not to have been 'voluntary' but 'forced' from 'it within the contemplation of the law . . .

'compulsion' in relation to a payment of which refund is sort, and whether it is also variously called 'coercion,' 'extortion,' 'exaction' or 'force,' includes every species of duress or conduct analogous to duress actual or threatened, exacted by or on behalf of the payee and applied to the person or the property or any right of the person who pays. . . . Such compulsion is a legal wrong, and the law provides a remedy by raising a fictional promise to repay."]

Before proceeding further it may be useful to summarise the conclusions I have so far reached. First, I do not take the view that the recovery of money paid under duress other than to the person is necessarily limited to duress to goods falling within one of the categories hitherto established by the English cases. I would respectfully follow and adopt the broad statement of principle laid down by Isaacs J. cited earlier and frequently quoted and applied in the Australian cases. Secondly, from this it follows that the compulsion may take the form of "economic duress" if the necessary facts are proved. A threat to break a contract may amount to such "economic duress." Thirdly, if there has been such a form of duress leading to a contract for consideration, I think that contract is a voidable one which can be avoided and the excess money paid under it recovered.

I think the facts found in this case do establish that the agreement to increase the price by 10 per cent reached at the end of June, 1973, was caused by what may be called "economic duress." The yard were adamant in insisting on the increased price without having any legal justification for so doing and the owners realised that the yard would not accept anything other than an unqualified agreement to the increase. The owners might have claimed damages in arbitration against the yard with all the inherent unavoidable uncertainties of litigation, but in view of the position of the owners *vis-à-vis* their relations with Shell it would be unreasonable to hold that this is the course they should have taken: see *Astley v. Reynolds* (1731) 2 Str. 915. The owners made a very reasonable offer of arbitration coupled with security for any award in the yard's favour that might be made, but this was refused. They then made their agreement, which can truly I think be said to have been made under compulsion, by the telex of June 28, without prejudice to their rights. I do not consider the yard's ignorance of the Shell charter material. It may well be that had they known of it they would have been even more exigent.

If I am right in the conclusion reached with some doubt earlier that there was consideration for the 10 per cent increase agreement reached at the end of June, 1973, and if it be right to regard this as having been reached under a kind of duress in the form of economic pressure, then what is said in *Chitty on Contracts* (24th ed.), para. 442, to which both counsel referred me, is relevant, namely that a contract entered into under duress is voidable and not void—

"that a person who has entered into the contract may either affirm or avoid such contract after the duress has ceased; and if he has so voluntarily acted under it with a full knowledge of all the circumstances he may be held bound on the ground of ratification, or if, after escaping from the duress, he takes no steps to set aside the transaction he may be found to have affirmed it."

[His Lordship reviewed the facts.]

I have come to the conclusion that the important points here are that (i) since there was no danger at this time in registering a protest, (ii) the final payments were made without any qualification, and (iii) were followed by a delay until July 31, 1975, before the owners put forward their claim, the correct inference to draw, taking an objective view of the facts, is that the action and inaction of the owners can only be regarded as an affirmation of the variation in June, 1973, of the terms of the original contract by the agreement to pay the additional 10 per cent In reaching this conclusion I have not, of course, overlooked the findings in the special case [that the owners never intended to affirm the agreement for extra payments] but I do not think that an intention on the part of the owners not to affirm the agreement for the extra payments, not indicated to the yard, can avail them in view of their overt acts. As was said in *Deacon v. Transport Regulation Board* (1958) V.R. 458, 460, in considering whether a payment was made voluntarily or not: "No secret mental reservation of the doer is material. The question is—what would his conduct indicate to a reasonable man as his mental state." I think this test is equally applicable to the decision this court has to make whether a voidable contract has been affirmed or not and I have applied this test in reaching the conclusion I have just expressed.

I think I should add very shortly that having considered the many authorities cited, even if I had come to a different conclusion on the issue about consideration, I would have come to the same decision adverse to the owners on the question whether the payments were made voluntarily in the sense of being made to close the transaction.

Judgment for the yard.

Questions

1. In the light of *Williams v. Roffey*, should Mocatta J. have held that the performance of their contract by the yard was a benefit, and therefore consideration, to the owners because it enabled them to perform their very advantageous charter agreement with Shell (corresponding to the avoidance of the penalty in *Williams* and the encouragement of the potential defaulters in *Anangel*)?

2. Was Mocatta J. right to hold that the automatic obligation to increase the return letter of credit was consideration? If the extra 10 per cent was a gift, was it perhaps an onerous gift like that in *Johnsey Estates Ltd v. Lewis & Manley* and cases cited in the *Note*, above, p. 199.

FOAKES v. BEER

House of Lords (1984) 9 App.Cas. 605; 54 L.J.Q.B. 130; 51 L.T. 833; 33 W.R. 233

Appeal from an order of the Court of Appeal.

On August 11, 1875, the respondent recovered judgment against the appellant for £2,077 17s. 2d. for debt and £13 1s. 10d. for costs. On December 21, 1876, a memorandum of agreement was made and signed by the appellant and respondent in the following terms:

"Whereas the said John Weston Foakes is indebted to the said Julia Beer and she has obtained a judgment in Her Majesty's High Court of Justice, Exchequer Division, for the sum of £2,090 19s. And whereas the said John Weston Foakes has requested the said Julia Beer to give him time in which to pay such judgment, which she has agreed to do on the following conditions. Now this agreement witnesseth that in consideration of the said John Weston

Foakes paying to the said Julia Beer on the signing of this agreement the sum of £500, the receipt whereof she doth hereby acknowledge in part satisfaction of the said judgment debt of £2,090 19s., and on condition of his paying her or her executors, administrators, assigns or nominee the sum of £150 on the 1st day of July and the 1st day of January or within one calendar month after each of the said days respectively in every year until the whole of the said sum of £2,090 19s. shall have been fully paid and satisfied, the first of such payments to be made on the 1st day of July next, then she the said Julia Beer hereby undertakes and agrees that she, her executors, administrators or assigns, will not take any proceedings whatever on the said judgment."

The respondent having in June, 1882, taken out a summons for leave to proceed on the judgment, an issue was directed to be tried between the respondent as plaintiff and the appellant as defendant whether any and what amount was on July 1, 1882, due upon the judgment.

At the trial of the issue before Cave J. it was proved that the whole sum of £2,090 19s. had been paid by instalments, but the respondent claimed interest. The jury under his Lordship's direction found that the appellant had paid all the sums which by the agreement of December 21, 1876, he undertook to pay and within the times therein specified. Cave J. was of the opinion that whether the judgment was satisfied or not, the respondent was, by reason of the agreement, not entitled to issue execution for any sum on the judgment.

The Queen's Bench Division (Watkin Williams and Mathew JJ.) discharged an order for a new trial on the ground of misdirection.

The Court of Appeal (Brett M.R., Lindley and Fry L.JJ.) reversed that decision and entered judgment for the respondent for the interest due with costs: (1883) 11 Q.B.D. 221.

EARL OF SELBORNE L.C.: My Lords, upon the construction of the agreement of December 21, 1876, I cannot differ from the conclusion in which both the courts below were agreed. If the operative part could properly be controlled by the recitals, I think there would be much reason to say that the only thing contemplated by the recitals was giving time for payment, without any relinquishment, on the part of the judgment creditor, of any portion of the amount recoverable (whether for principal or for interest) under the judgment. But the agreement of the judgment creditor, which follows the recitals, is that she "will not take any proceedings whatever on the judgment," if a certain condition is fulfilled. What is that condition? Payment of the sum of £150 in every half year, "until the whole of said sum of £2,090 19s." (the aggregate amount of the principal debt and costs, for which judgment had been entered) "shall have been fully paid and satisfied." A particular "sum" is here mentioned, which does not include the interest then due, or future interest. Whatever was meant to be payable at all, under this agreement, was clearly to be payable by half-yearly instalments of £150 each; any other construction must necessarily make the conditional promise nugatory. But to say that the half-yearly payments were to continue till the whole sum of £2,090 19s., "and interest thereon," should have been fully paid and satisfied, would be to introduce very important words into the agreement which are not there, and of which I cannot say that they are necessarily implied. Although, therefore, I may (as indeed I do) very much doubt whether the effect of the agreement, as a conditional waiver of the interest to which she was by law entitled under the judgment, was really present to the mind of the judgment creditor, still I cannot deny that it might have that effect, if capable of being legally enforced.

The question, therefore, is nakedly raised by this appeal, whether your Lordships are now prepared, not only to overrule, as contrary to law, the doctrine stated by Sir Edward Coke to have been laid down by all the judges of the Common Pleas in *Pinnel's Case* (1602) 5 Co.Rep. 117a, in 1602, and repeated in his note to Littleton, § 344, Co.Litt. 212b, but to treat a prospective agreement, not under seal, for satisfaction of a debt by a series of payments on account to a total amount less than the whole debt, as binding in law, provided these payments are regularly made; the case not being one of a composition with a common debtor, agreed to, *inter se*, by several creditors. . . . The doctrine itself, as laid down by Sir Edward Coke, may have been criticised as questionable in principle by some persons whose opinions are entitled to respect, but it has never been judicially overruled; on the contrary I think it has always, since the sixteenth century, been accepted as law. If so, I cannot think that your Lordships would do right, if you were now to reverse, as erroneous, a judgment of the Court of Appeal, proceeding upon a doctrine which has been accepted as part of the law of England for 280 years. . . .

The distinction between the effect of a deed under seal, and that of an agreement by parol, or by writing not under seal, may seem arbitrary, but it is established in our law; nor is it really unreasonable or practically inconvenient that the law should require particular solemnities to give a gratuitous contract the force of a binding obligation. If the question be (as, in the actual state of the law, I think it is), whether consideration is, or is not, given in a case of this kind, by the debtor who pays down part of the debt presently due from him, for a promise by the creditor to relinquish, after certain further payments on account, the residue of the debt, I cannot say that I think consideration is given, in the sense which I have always understood that word as used in our law. It might be (and indeed I think it would be) an improvement in our law, if a release or acquittance of the whole debt, on payment of any sum which the creditor might be content to receive by way of accord and satisfaction (though less than the whole), were held to be, generally, binding, though not under seal; nor should I be unwilling to see equal force given to a prospective agreement, like the present, in writing though not under seal; but I think it impossible, without refinements which practically alter the sense of the word, to treat such a release or acquittance as supported by any new consideration proceeding from the debtor. All the authorities subsequent to *Cumber v. Wane* (1721) 1 Stra. 426 which were relied upon by the appellant at your Lordships' Bar (such as *Sibree v. Tripp* (1846) 15 M. & W. 23; *Curlewis v. Clark* (1849) 3 Exch. 375 and *Goddard v. O'Brien* (1882) 9 Q.B.D. 37) have proceeded upon the distinction that, by giving negotiable paper or otherwise, there has been some new consideration for a new agreement, distinct from mere money payments in or towards discharge of the original liability.[1] I think it unnecessary to go through those cases, or to examine the particular grounds on which each of them was decided. There are no such facts in the case now before your Lordships. What is called "any benefit, or even any legal possibility of benefit," in Mr Smith's notes to

---

[1] *D. & C. Builders v. Rees* (below, p. 267) decides that there is no material distinction between giving a small sum in cash and giving the same amount by a negotiable instrument.

Cumber v. Wane, is not (as I conceive) that sort of benefit which a creditor may derive from getting payment of part of the money due to him from a debtor who might otherwise keep him at arm's length, or possibly become insolvent, but is some independent benefit, actual or contingent, of a kind which might in law be a good and valuable consideration for any other sort of agreement not under seal.

My conclusion is, that the order appealed from should be affirmed, and the appeal dismissed, with costs, and I so move your Lordships.

LORD BLACKBURN [having held that the agreement was one to take £500 in satisfaction of the whole sum of £2,090 19s., subject to the condition that, unless the balance of the principal debt was paid by instalments, the whole might be enforced with interest, turned to the question whether payment of a lesser sum is good satisfaction:]

This is a question, I think, of difficulty.

In Coke, Littleton 212b., Lord Coke says: "where the condition is for payment of £20, the obligor or feoffor cannot at the time appointed pay a lesser sum in satisfaction of the whole, because it is *apparent* that a lesser sum of money *cannot* be a satisfaction of a greater. . . . If the obligor or feoffor pay a lesser sum either before the day or at another place than is limited by the condition, and the obligee or feoffee receiveth it, this is a good satisfaction." For this he cites *Pinnel's Case*. That was an action on a bond for £16, conditioned for the payment of £8 10s. on November 11, 1600.[1] Plea that defendant, at plaintiff's request, before the said day, to wit, on October 1, paid to the plaintiff £5 2s. 2d., which the plaintiff accepted in full satisfaction of the £8 10s. The plaintiff had judgment for the insufficient pleading.[2] But though this was so, Lord Coke reports that it was resolved by the whole Court of Common Pleas "that payment of a lesser sum on the day in satisfaction of a greater cannot be any satisfaction for the whole, because it appears to the judges that by no possibility a lesser sum can be satisfaction to the plaintiff for a greater sum: but the gift of a horse, hawk, or robe, etc., in satisfaction is good for it shall be intended that a horse, hawk, or robe, etc., might be more beneficial to the plaintiff than the money, in respect of some circumstance, or otherwise the plaintiff would not have accepted it in satisfaction. But when the whole sum is due, by no intendment the acceptance of parcel can be a satisfaction to the plaintiff; but in the case at bar it was resolved that the payment and acceptance of parcel before the day in satisfaction of the whole would be a good satisfaction in regard of circumstance of time; for peradventure parcel of it before the day would be more beneficial to him than the whole at the day, and the value of the satisfaction is not material; so if I am bound in £20 to pay you £10 at Westminster, and you request me to pay you £5 at the

---

[1] The bond was a common form of agreement whereby, *e.g.* C loaned D £8 10s. and D executed a bond (under seal) promising to pay a larger sum, say £16, on a certain day, say, November 11, 1600, subject to a condition that, if he paid £8 10s. before that day, the bond was to be void. See A. W. B. Simpson, "The Penal Bond with Conditional Defeasance" (1966) 82 L.Q.R. 392.

[2] The defendant omitted to plead that he *tendered* the money in full satisfaction: "And always the manner of the tender and of the payment shall be directed by him who made the tender or payment, and not by him who accepts it."

day at York, and you will accept it in full satisfaction for the whole £10, it is a good satisfaction for the whole, for the expenses to pay it at York is sufficient satisfaction."

There are two things here resolved. First, that where a matter paid and accepted in satisfaction of a debt certain might by any possibility be more beneficial to the creditor than his debt, the court will not inquire into the adequacy of the consideration. If the creditor, without any fraud, accepted it in satisfaction when it was not a sufficient satisfaction it was his own fault. And that payment before the day might be more beneficial, and consequently that the plea was in substance good, and this must have been decided in the case.

There is a second point stated to have been resolved, *viz*.: "That payment of a lesser sum on the day cannot be any satisfaction of the whole, because it appears to the judges that by no possibility a lesser sum can be a satisfaction to the plaintiff for a greater sum." This was certainly not necessary for the decision of the case; but though the resolution of the Court of Common Pleas was only a dictum, it seems to me clear that Lord Coke deliberately adopted the dictum, and the great weight of his authority makes it necessary to be cautious before saying that what he deliberately adopted as law was a mistake, and though I cannot find that in any subsequent case this dictum has been made the ground of the decision, except in *Fitch v. Sutton* (1804) 5 East 230, as to which I shall make some remarks later, and in *Down v. Hatcher* (1839) 10 Ad. & El. 121, as to which Parke B., in *Cooper v. Parker* (1855) 15 C.B. 828, said, "Whenever the question may arise as to whether *Down v. Hatcher* is good law, I should have a great deal to say against it," yet there certainly are cases in which great judges have treated the dictum in *Pinnel's Case* as good law.

For instance, in *Sibree v. Tripp*, Parke B. says, "It is clear if the claim be a liquidated and ascertained sum, payment of part cannot be satisfaction of the whole, although it may, under certain circumstances, be evidence of a gift of the remainder." And Alderson B., in the same case, says, "It is undoubtedly true that payment of a portion of a liquidated demand, in the same manner as the whole liquidated demand which ought to be paid, is payment only in part, because it is not one bargain, but two: *viz*., payment of part, and an agreement without consideration to give up the residue. The courts might very well have held the contrary, and have left the matter to the agreement of the parties, but undoubtedly the law is so settled." After such strong expressions of opinion, I doubt much whether any judge sitting in a court of the first instance would be justified in treating the question as open. But as this has very seldom, if at all, been the ground of the decision even in a court of the first instance, and certainly never been the ground of a decision in the Court of Exchequer Chamber, still less in this House, I did think it open in your Lordships' House to reconsider this question. And, notwithstanding the very high authority of Lord Coke, I think it is not the fact that to accept prompt payment of a part only of a liquidated demand can never be more beneficial than to insist on payment of the whole. And if it be not the fact, it cannot be apparent to the judges. . . .

[Having considered the earlier authorities his Lordship continued:]

What principally weighs with me in thinking that Lord Coke made a mistake of fact is my conviction that all men of business, whether merchants or tradesmen, do every day recognise and act on the ground that prompt payment of a part of their demand may be more beneficial to them than it would be to insist on their rights and enforce payment of the whole. Even where the debtor is perfectly solvent, and sure to pay at last, this is often so. Where the credit of the debtor is doubtful it must be more so. I had persuaded myself that there was no such long-continued action on this dictum as to render it improper in this House to reconsider the question. I had written my reasons for so thinking; but as they were not satisfactory to the other noble and learned Lords who heard the case, I do not now repeat them nor persist in them.

I assent to the judgment proposed, though it is not that which I had originally thought proper.

LORDS WATSON and FITZGERALD held that, on the true construction of the agreement, Beer was entitled to recover the interest. The only effect of the agreement was to give Foakes time to pay and not to forgive him anything. If they were wrong about that, they agreed that there was no consideration for a promise to forgo the interest.

Order appealed from affirmed; and appeal dismissed with costs.

Questions
1. What was the meaning of the agreement (a) according to Beer, (b) according to Foakes? Which view was accepted by the majority of the House?
2. What was the expressed "consideration"? Was it (a) the promise of £500, or (b) the payment of £500, or (c) the payment of £500 and the promise of the remainder by instalments?
3. What was the *ratio decidendi* of *Pinnel's Case*? Was the rule in *Pinnel's Case* binding on the House of Lords?
4. Did the judges think the rule they applied was a good one?
5. Cheshire and Fifoot (8th ed.), p. 90, wrote: ". . . Doctor Foakes was not seeking 'legally to enforce the agreement' against Mrs Beer. He was setting it up by way of defence to her application for leave to proceed on the judgment. He was therefore under no necessity to establish a contract and the question of consideration was irrelevant. The learned Lords concentrated on the wrong issue." Do you agree? Was not the question whether Beer's promise not to take proceedings binding?
6. Cheshire, Fifoot and Furmston (12th ed.), p. 93 say "It will be observed that the plaintiff sued in *Pinnel's Case* not in assumpsit but in debt, so that no question of consideration arose." But it was not the promise to pay the debt which was in issue but the promise not to enforce the debt. Did not that raise an issue of consideration?
See also below, pp. 249–272; and see Kelly, 27 M.L.R. (1964) 540.
7. If the parties did not intend the interest to be forgiven, might not the contract have been rectified (if the argument based on consideration had failed)? How would Lord Denning have decided the case? See *D. & C. Builders v. Rees*, below, p. 267.

VANBERGEN v. ST. EDMUNDS PROPERTIES LTD.

Court of Appeal [1933] 2 K.B. 223; 102 L.J.K.B. 369; 149 L.T. 182

Appeal from a decision of Macnaghten J. on the further consideration of an action tried by him with a special jury.

In July 1932 the plaintiff was indebted to the defendants in the sum of £208 odd for costs under a judgment and order.

By his statement of claim, the plaintiff alleged that on July 6, 1932, the defendants by their solicitor, a Mr Kennard, verbally agreed with him that, if he would on July 7, 1932, pay the £208 in cash into a bank at Eastbourne for the credit of the solicitor's firm at the Law Courts branch of the Bank of England, that payment would satisfy all sums that he owed them and a bankruptcy notice which they had issued in respect of part of the debt would not be served on him. On July 7, the plaintiff did pay the £208 to the Eastbourne bank with instructions to remit it as agreed. He alleged that, the same day, he advised the solicitors of the payment and, on July 8, the defendants' clerk; but that, in breach of the agreement, the bankruptcy notice was served on him. He claimed damages for the breach of contract.

The defendants denied the agreement and pleaded that, if it were made, there was no consideration for making it.

The jury found that the agreement was made and returned a verdict for the plaintiff, awarding damages of £500.

On the further consideration of the action, Macnaghten J. held that, as the plaintiff, under the agreement, was to pay not to the creditors but to the credit of their solicitors there was a sufficient consideration.

The defendants appealed.

LORD HANWORTH M.R. [after stating the facts and accepting the principle that a creditor is not bound by an agreement to accept a smaller sum in satisfaction of a larger ascertained amount, unless there be a benefit or even any legal possibility of benefit to the creditor thrown in]: We have, therefore, to consider whether the agreement that was made here on July 6 was an agreement to do anything else than simply to pay on Friday, July 8, into the hand of the creditors the sum which was already ascertained and in respect of which there was not only the legal liability, but a duty enforceable by any mode of execution against the debtor. Was there any sort of advantage, any sort of independent benefit, actual or contingent, of a kind which might be a good and valuable consideration moving towards the creditors?

Macnaghten J. dealt with the question whether the action is maintainable on the ground of the principle of *Foakes v. Beer* (above, p. 240), to which I have referred, and he says: "In the present case the jury, by their verdict, have found that on July 6 Mr Kennard made an offer that if, on the following day, the plaintiff obtained the money and paid it into a bank at Eastbourne with instructions to remit it to the account of Stanley Evans & Co. at the Law Courts branch of the Bank of England, he would not serve the bankruptcy notice. That offer became a contract when the plaintiff accepted it. The plaintiff, by going to Eastbourne, obtaining the money, and remitting it in the manner suggested, made it a binding contract on the part of Mr Kennard that he would not serve the bankruptcy notice." I cannot find out of the evidence any facts which support the view or which justify the inference. The words which I have read are plain: it was Mr Vanbergen who said he was going down to Eastbourne, that he was going down as part of his business, and that he did not think he would be getting back after his business on Thursday in time to pay it on Thursday, and the concession arose out of the question whether or not the debtor could be back in town in time to bring it himself, because he frankly said he was trying to get a little more time. When the creditors found that the debtor had to go down to Eastbourne in any event, then the concession was given by the creditors. But they reaped no advantage; there was nothing moving towards them which could be deemed to be a consideration, with the result that the case is one in which the contract is made, but remains unenforceable in law. . . .

The appeal must be allowed and judgment entered for the defendants with costs.

LAWRENCE and ROMER L.JJ. delivered concurring judgments.

Appeal allowed.

Question
Because the variation in mode of payment is exclusively for the benefit of the debtor it is no consideration to the creditor. But suppose that the creditor accepts the debtor's old car in satisfaction of a debt of £2,000, protesting that he would much rather have the cash and eventually taking the car only because there seems to be no hope of anything better. Can he resile from this agreement when the debtor subsequently comes into money?

Note
In *Couldery v. Bartrum* (1881) 19 Ch.D. 394 at 400, Jessel M.R., discussing the rule in *Pinnel's Case* and compositions with creditors, said ". . . as every debtor had not a stock of canary birds, or tomtits, or rubbish of that kind, to add to his dividend, it was felt desirable to bind the creditors in a sensible way by saying that, if they all agreed, there should be a consideration imported from the agreement constituting an addition to the dividend, so as to make the agreement no longer *nudum pactum*, but an agreement made for valuable consideration, then there would be satisfaction." But in 1937 the Law Revision Committee, 6th Interim Report, para. 22, p. 16, referred to "the problem, still unsolved, of discovering the consideration for a debtor's composition with his creditors."
There is no difficulty in finding consideration between the creditors. Each agrees to accept the dividend in full satisfaction in consideration of every other creditor who is a party to the agreement doing so. If one creditor then sues for the balance of his debt he commits a breach of contract with each of those creditors. But the debtor is not a party to the contract. However in *West Yorkshire Darracq Agency Ltd (in liquidation) v. Coleridge* [1911] 2 K.B. 326, where the debtor (the liquidator) was a party to the agreement between the creditors (the directors of the company), Horridge J. held that "by becoming a party he obtained the benefit of the consideration which each of the directors gave to his co-director by waiving his right to his fees." The basis of the debtor's defence seems to be that the action is a fraud on the other parties to the contract to forbear from suing. See below, pp. 311–316. If that is so, should it make any difference whether the debtor is a party to the *agreement* (he is not a party to the *contract*) or not? Are not the forbearing creditors equally defrauded in either case?
If the creditors decide to rescind their agreement and sue for the full amount of their debts, can the creditor rely on the agreement as a defence, whether or not he was a party to it?
In *Comr. of Stamp Duties v. Bone* [1976] 2 All E.R. 354 at 360 (P.C.) Lord Russell, speaking for five Lords of Appeal, said: "A debt can only be truly released and extinguished by agreement for valuable consideration or under seal. By 'giving' or 'forgiving' or 'releasing' by will a debt to the debtor, a testator, in their Lordships' opinion, is but leaving a legacy of the amount of the debt. . . . The debt remains outstanding as an asset of the estate. . . ."

HIRACHAND PUNAMCHAND v. TEMPLE

Court of Appeal [1911] 2 K.B. 330; 80 L.J.K.B. 1155; 105 L.T. 277; 27 T.L.R. 430

Appeal from the judgment of Scrutton J.
Sir Richard Temple, father of Lt. Temple who was indebted to the plaintiffs as the maker of a promissory note, wrote to the plaintiffs offering an amount less than that of the debt in full settlement of the debt and enclosed a draft for the smaller amount. The plaintiffs, having cashed and retained the proceeds of the draft, brought the present action against Lt. Temple for the balance.
Scrutton J. gave judgment for the plaintiffs for the amount claimed. The defendant appealed.

VAUGHAN WILLIAMS L.J.: . . . In my judgment, this draft having been sent to the plaintiffs by Sir Richard Temple, and retained and cashed by them, we ought to draw the conclusion that the plaintiffs, who kept and cashed the draft, agreed to accept it on the terms upon which it was sent. . . . Under these circumstances, assuming that there was no accord and satisfaction, what form of defence, if any, could be pleaded by the defendant? In my judgment it would be that the plaintiffs had ceased really to be holders of the negotiable instrument on which they sued. They had ceased to be such holders, because, in effect, in their hands the document had ceased to be a negotiable instrument quite as much as if there had been on the acceptance of the draft by the plaintiffs an erasure of the writing of the signature to the note. But, alternatively, assuming that this was not so, and that the instrument did not cease to be a negotiable instrument, then, in my judgment, from the moment when the draft sent by Sir Richard Temple was cashed by the plaintiffs a trust was created as between Sir Richard Temple and the moneylenders in favour of the former, so that any money which the latter might receive upon the promissory note, if they did receive any, would be held by them in trust for him. . . .

. . . then, without any question of resort to a court of equity, there might have been a defence in a court of law on the ground that any money recoverable on the note by the plaintiffs was recoverable by them merely as trustees for Sir Richard Temple, and that, under the circumstances disclosed by the correspondence, the relations between the father and son were such that it was impossible to suppose that the father wished to insist on payment of the note by the son.

Having said thus much, I desire to add a word or two with regard to the case of *Cook v. Lister* (13 C.B.(N.S.) 543) in the Common Pleas. If the judgments in that case are looked at, it will be found that Willes J. said, in explaining the grounds of his judgment that under circumstances like those of the present case, the debt is gone, because it would be a fraud upon the stranger who pays part of a debt in discharge of the whole, that an action should be brought for the debt. I have founded my judgment upon the grounds which I have already expressed, but I do not wish to be understood as thereby negativing the proposition that a defence might be set up on the alternative basis mentioned by Willes J. In my opinion this appeal should be allowed.

FLETCHER MOULTON L.J.: I am of the opinion that by that transaction between the plaintiffs and Sir Richard Temple the debt on the promissory note became extinct. I agree with the view expressed by Willes J. in *Cook v. Lister*. The effect of such an agreement between a creditor and a third party with regard to the debt is to render it impossible for the creditor afterwards to sue the debtor for it. The way in which this is worked out in law may be that it would be an abuse of the process of the court to allow the creditor under such circumstances to sue, or it may be, and I prefer that view, that there is an extinction of the debt; but, whichever way it is put, it comes to the same thing, namely that, after acceptance by the creditor of a sum offered by a third party in settlement of the claim against the debtor, the creditor cannot maintain an action for the balance. . . . [His Lordship then distinguished *Foakes v. Beer* as applying between debtor and creditor.] If a third person steps in and gives a consideration for the discharge of the debtor, it does not matter whether he does it in meal or in malt, or what proportion the amount given bears to the amount of the debt. Here the money was paid by a third person, and I have no doubt that, upon the acceptance of that money by the plaintiffs with full knowledge of the terms on which it was offered, the debt was absolutely extinguished.

FARWELL L.J.: The plaintiffs could only accept the money on the terms upon which it was offered. We were pressed with *Day v. McLea* ((1889) 22 Q.B.D. 610), where the debtor himself sent a cheque for an amount smaller than that of the debt to the creditor on the terms that it should be in satisfaction of the debt. In that case, there being no consideration for the discharge of the balance of the debt, it was held that the creditor could retain the money, and sue for the balance. The same reasoning does not apply where the money is sent by a stranger, in which case it can only be accepted on the terms upon which it is sent. In the former case the creditor can reply to the debtor, "you owe me more than this, and if you sue for a return of this, I shall set off my larger claim against it." In the latter case, the creditor has no excuse or justification for retaining the stranger's money, unless he complies with the conditions on which it was paid. I agree with Fletcher Moulton L.J. that the plaintiffs cannot be heard to say that they have acted dishonestly when an honest construction can be put upon their conduct by treating their acceptance and retention of the money as being upon the terms on which it was offered.

Appeal allowed.

Question
Do you agree with Fletcher Moulton L.J. that refusal of the creditor's claim comes to the same thing as the extinction of the debt? Suppose that the father had later authorised the creditor to sue for the balance of the debt—or required him to do so as trustee (see Vaughan Williams L.J.)? Would the son be liable? Suppose, father being impoverished and son having come into money, the father had required the creditor to sue for the whole sum?

CENTRAL LONDON PROPERTY TRUST LTD v. HIGH TREES HOUSE LTD

King's Bench Division [1947] 1 K.B. 130; [1947] L.J.R. 77; 175 L.T. 333; 62 T.L.R. 557; [1956] 1 All E.R. 256

Action tried by Denning J.

By a lease under seal made on September 24, 1937, the plaintiffs, Central London Property Trust Ltd, granted to the defendants High Trees House Ltd, a subsidiary of the plaintiff company, a tenancy of a block of flats for the term of 99 years from September 29, 1937, at a ground rent of £2,500 a year. The block of flats was a new one and had not been fully occupied at the beginning of the war owing to the absence of people from London. With war conditions prevailing, it was apparent to those responsible that the rent reserved under the lease could not be paid out of the profits of the flats and, accordingly, discussions took place between the directors of the two companies concerned, which were closely associated, and an arrangement was made between them which was put into writing. On January 3, 1940, the plaintiffs wrote to the defendants in these terms, "we confirm the arrangement made between us by which the ground rent should be reduced as from the commencement of the lease to £1,250 per annum," and on April 2, 1940, a confirmatory resolution to the same effect was passed by the plaintiff company. On March 20, 1941, a receiver was appointed by the debenture holders of the plaintiffs and on his death on February 28, 1944, his place was taken by his partner. The defendants paid the reduced rent from 1941 down to the beginning of 1945, by which time all the flats in the block were fully let, and continued to pay it thereafter. In September, 1945, the then receiver of the plaintiff company looked into the matter of the lease and ascertained that the rent actually reserved by it was £2,500. On September 21, 1945, he wrote to the defendants saying that rent must be paid at the full rate and claiming that arrears amounting to £7,916 were due. Subsequently, he instituted the present friendly proceedings to test the legal position in regard to the rate at which the rent was payable. In the action the plaintiffs sought to recover £625, being the amount represented by the difference between rent at the rate of £2,500 and £1,250 per annum for the quarters ending September 29 and December 25, 1945. By their defence the defendants pleaded (1) that the letter of January 3, 1940, constituted an agreement that the rent reserved should be £1,250 only, and that such agreement related to the whole term of the lease, (2) in the alternative, that the plaintiff company were estopped from alleging that the rent exceeded £1,250 per annum, and (3) as a further alternative, that by failing to demand rent in excess of £1,250 before their letter of September 21, 1945 (received by the defendants on September 24), they had waived their rights in respect of any rent, in excess of that at the rate of £1,250, which had accrued up to September 24, 1945.

DENNING J. stated the facts and continued: If I were to consider this matter without regard to recent developments in the law, there is no doubt that, had the plaintiffs claimed it, they would have been entitled to recover ground rent at the rate of £2,500 a year from the beginning of the term, since the lease under which it was payable was a lease under seal which, according to the old common law, could not be varied by an agreement by parol (whether in writing or not), but only by deed. Equity, however, stepped in, and said that if there had been a variation of a deed by a simple contract (which in the case of a lease required to be in writing would have to be evidenced by writing), the courts may give effect to it as is shown in *Berry v. Berry* [1929] 2 K.B. 316. That equitable doctrine, however, could hardly apply in the present case because the variation here might be said to have been made without consideration. With regard to estoppel, the representation made in relation to reducing the rent was not a representation of an existing fact. It was a representation, in effect, as to the future, namely, that payment of the rent would not be enforced at the full rate but only at the reduced rate. Such a representation would not give rise to an estoppel, because, as was said in *Jorden v. Money* (1854) 5 H.L.C. 185 (below, p. 252), a representation as to the future must be embodied as a contract or be nothing.

But what is the position in view of developments in the law in recent years? The law has not been standing still since *Jorden v. Money*. There has been a series of decisions over the past 50 years which, although they are said to be cases of estoppel are not really such. They are cases in which a promise was made which was intended to create legal relations and which, to the knowledge of the person making the promise, was going to be acted on by the person to whom it was made, and which was in fact so acted on. In such cases the courts have said that the promise must be honoured. The cases to which I particularly desire to refer are: *Fenner v. Blake* [1900] 1 Q.B. 426; *Re Wickham* (1917) 34 T.L.R. 158; *Re William Porter & Co. Ltd* [1937] 2 All E.R. 361 and *Buttery v. Pickard* [1946] W.N. 25. As I have said they are not cases of estoppel in the strict sense. They are really promises—

promises intended to be binding, intended to be acted on, and in fact acted on. *Jorden v. Money* can be distinguished, because there the promisor made it clear that she did not intend to be legally bound, whereas in the cases to which I refer the proper inference was that the promisor did intend to be bound. In each case the court held the promise to be binding on the party making it, even though under the old common law it might be difficult to find any consideration for it. The courts have not gone so far as to give a cause of action in damages for the breach of such a promise, but they have refused to allow the party making it to act inconsistently with it. It is in that sense, and that sense only, that such a promise gives rise to an estoppel. The decisions are a natural result of the fusion of law and equity: for the cases of *Hughes v. Metropolitan Railway* (below, p. 254); *Birmingham and District Land Co. v. London & North Western Rly.* (below, p. 255); and *Salisbury (Marquess) v. Gilmore* [1942] 2 K.B. 38, 51, afford a sufficient basis for saying that a party would not be allowed in equity to go back on such a promise. In my opinion, the time has now come for the validity of such a promise to be recognised. The logical consequence, no doubt, is that a promise to accept a smaller sum in discharge of a larger sum, if acted upon, is binding notwithstanding the absence of consideration: and if the fusion of law and equity leads to this result, so much the better. That aspect was not considered in *Foakes v. Beer* (above, p. 240). At this time of day, however, when law and equity have been joined together for over 70 years, principles must be reconsidered in the light of their combined effect. It is to be noticed that in the Sixth Interim Report of the Law Revision Committee, paras. 35, 40, it is recommended that such a promise as that to which I have referred, should be enforceable in law even though no consideration for it has been given by the promisee. It seems to me that, to the extent I have mentioned, that result has now been achieved by the decisions of the courts.

I am satisfied that a promise such as that to which I have referred is binding and the only question remaining for my consideration is the scope of the promise in the present case. I am satisfied on all the evidence that the promise here was that the ground rent should be reduced to £1,250 a year as a temporary expedient while the block of flats was not fully, or substantially fully let, owing to the conditions prevailing. That means that the reduction in the rent applied throughout the years down to the end of 1944, but early in 1945 it is plain that the flats were fully let, and, indeed the rents received from them (many of them not being affected by the Rent Restrictions Acts), were increased beyond the figure at which it was originally contemplated that they would let. At all events the rent from them must have been very considerable. I find that the conditions prevailing at the time when the reduction in rent was made, had completely passed away by the early months of 1945. I am satisfied that the promise was understood by all parties only to apply under the conditions prevailing at the time when it was made, namely, when the flats were only partially let, and that it did not extend any further than that. When the flats became fully let, early in 1945, the reduction ceased to apply.

In those circumstances, under the law as I hold it, it seems to me that rent is payable at the full rate for the quarters ending September 29 and December 25, 1945.

If the case had been one of estoppel, it might be said that in any event the estoppel would cease when the conditions to which the representation applied came to an end, or it also might be said that it would only come to an end on notice. In either case it is only a way of ascertaining what is the scope of the representation. I prefer to apply the principle that a promise intended to be binding, intended to be acted on and in fact acted on, is binding so far as its terms properly apply. Here it was binding as covering the period down to the early part of 1945, and as from that time full rent is payable.

I therefore give judgment for the plaintiff company for the amount claimed.

Judgment for the plaintiff.

Note

Denning J. hints that *Foakes v. Beer* (1884) might have been decided differently if the fusion of law and equity by the Judicature Acts 1873–1875 had been considered. He says that the decisions on which he relies, the most important of which is *Hughes v. Metropolitan Railway* (1877), below, p. 254, were a natural result of that fusion. Why, then was the principle in *Hughes* not applied in *Foakes v. Beer*? Lords Selborne and Blackburn were in both cases. Is the answer that the principle applied in *Hughes* was entirely inapplicable to both *Foakes v. Beer* and *High Trees*? That principle might be formulated as follows: if A tells B (by words or conduct) that B need not perform a contractual (or other) obligation owed by B to A and B takes A at his word and does not perform that obligation, A cannot treat that non-performance as a breach of contract entitling him to damages or to terminate the contract. It would be entirely wrong that A should be allowed to treat as a legal wrong that to which he has consented. It was this principle which applied in *Hughes*. A, the landlord, having (by conduct) told B, his tenant, "You need not fulfil your contractual duty to repair the premises within six months of the notice I have given you," could not forfeit the lease (that is, terminate the contract) on the ground that B had broken his contract.

Foakes v. Beer appears to be an application of a second, quite different, principle: if A tells B that B need not perform a contractual (or other) obligation owed by B to A, A can change his mind and require B to perform that obligation in so far as it is still possible to do so. A is not alleging that B has broken his contract—he is simply saying "Now you must perform—and if you fail to do so, *that* will be a breach of contract."

If *Hughes* was relevant to the decision in *Foakes* it must follow that *Pinnel's Case* was equally relevant to the decision in *Hughes* but it was not cited in the latter case and it would surely have been very surprising if it had been.

Many of the cases which have from time to time been relied on in support of the *High Trees* doctrine are clearly examples of only the first principle. For example, *Panoutsos v. Raymond Hadley* [1917] 2 K.B. 473, C.A., a case frequently cited by Lord Denning: under a contract of sale by A to B, B has a duty to open a *confirmed* credit. A, by words or conduct, tells B that the unconfirmed credit which B has opened will do. A may not terminate the contract on the ground that B has committed a breach by not opening a confirmed credit—but he may insist that B opens a confirmed credit within a reasonable time and, if B does not do so, he will then be in breach of contract.

In *High Trees*, the landlord, having accepted half rent for, say, one year, would clearly have been precluded from asserting, "You have broken your contract and I forfeit the lease." That would have been exactly analogous to *Hughes*. It does not follow that he could not say, "You must now pay me the arrears of rent for the past year." *Foakes v. Beer* says he could do that. Denning J. denies it. It is the doctrine that the promise has this wider effect which is known as "equitable estoppel" or, more commonly, "promissory estoppel." See *Maharaj v. Chand* [1986] 3 All E.R. 107, P.C.

JORDEN v. MONEY

(1854) 5 H.L.C. 185; 10 E.R. 868

M had borrowed £1,200 from J's brother, C, for an unsuccessful financial speculation with other persons. Judgment for the sum had been entered against M but not executed. M gave C a bond and warrant of attorney to secure repayment of the money. On C's death, J as his executrix became entitled to the bond and warrant. J often stated that she never intended to enforce the claim secured, saying that she believed M to have been unfairly treated in being obliged to enter into the securities. Such statements were made by J, among other occasions, in circumstances which were calculated to lead and did lead to their being communicated to relatives of the intended wife of M at the time when his marriage was in course of preparation. His prospective parents in law wanted assurance that he was free from all liability in respect of the debt of £1,200 and the bond and warrant. In consequence of J's assurances, the marriage of M and his wife took place. M now brought an action, by Bill in Chancery praying that the debt secured by the bond and warrant be declared to have been abandoned, that J be decreed to have released M from the bond, that the warrant of attorney be delivered up to be cancelled and that satisfaction be entered upon the judgment which had been obtained against M by C. Romilly M.R. granted an injunction restraining J from enforcing the judgment on the warrant of attorney. On appeal, the Court of the Lords Justices was divided, Knight-Bruce L.J. supporting the order of the Master of the Rolls and Lord Cranworth L.J. thinking that it should be reversed, and accordingly the order of the Master of the Rolls stood. J then appealed to the House of Lords. Their Lordships (Lord Cranworth L.C. and Lord Brougham, Lord St. Leonards dissenting) allowed the appeal and ordered that the case go back to the Court of Chancery with a declaration that the Bill should be dismissed without costs.

LORD CRANWORTH L.C.: There are two grounds upon which it is said that the parties have lost their right to enforce the bond. The one is, that previously to William Money's marriage, Mrs Jorden, then Miss Marnell, represented that the bond had been abandoned, that she had given up her legal right upon it, and upon the faith of that representation the marriage was contracted. And then it is said that upon a principle well known in the law, founded upon good faith and equity, a principle equally of law and of equity, if a person makes any false representation to another, and that other acts upon that false representation, the person who has made it shall not afterwards be allowed to set up that what he said was false, and to assert the real truth in place of the falsehood which has so misled the other. That is a principle of universal application, and has been particularly applied to cases where representations have been made as to the state of the property of persons about to contract marriage, and where, upon the faith of such representations, marriage has been contracted. There the person who has made the false representations has in a great many cases been held bound to make his representations good.

[Having considered various authorities, his Lordship proceeded:] I am bound to state my view of the case: I think that the doctrine does not apply to a case where the representation is not a representation of fact but a statement of something which the party intends or does not intend to do. In the former case it is a contract, in the latter it is not; what is here contended for is this, that Mrs Jorden, then Miss Marnell, over and over again represented that she abandoned the debt. Clothe that in any words you please, it means no more than this, that she would never enforce the debt: she does not mean, in saying that she had abandoned it, to say that she had executed a release of the debt so as to preclude her legal right to sue. All that she could mean, was that she positively promised that she would never enforce it. My opinion is, that if all the evidence had come up to the mark, which, for reasons I shall presently state, I do not think it did, that if upon the very eve of the marriage she had said, "William Money, I never will enforce the bond against you," that would not bring it within these cases.[1]

LORD BROUGHAM: In my opinion, there was a misrepresentation by Louisa Marnell of an intention as to her will, and a promise was made by her; but of misrepresentation of fact there was none. She simply stated what was her intention; she did not misrepresent her intention; and I have no manner of doubt that at the time she made that statement, she had the intention which it is stated she professed, of never putting William Bailey Money in trouble, by proceeding upon the bond. . . . I certainly have, after very considerable doubt upon some parts of the case, but after fully viewing the whole particulars, and examining those depositions, come to the conclusion by which my noble and learned friend abides, the conclusion to which he arrived in the court below, that there was not an abandonment of the debt, by Mrs Jorden; not only that there was not an abandonment of it, but that there was rather a refusal of abandonment, when you come to examine in what sense, and with what intent the word "abandonment" has been used.

LORD ST. LEONARDS made a dissenting speech.

Appeal allowed.

Note

Atiyah, *Consideration in Contracts*, pp. 53–58, argues that the facts in *Jorden v. Money* really reveal a contract with good consideration which would have been enforceable at law, had it not lacked the evidence in writing then necessary, for a promise given in consideration of marriage, under the Statute of Frauds, above. The plaintiff was thus attempting to evade the Statute by calling his cause of action estoppel instead of contract. Atiyah is able to reach this conclusion because he believes the promisee's action in reliance on the promise constitutes consideration even though it is not requested. Jorden did not request Money to marry, but he acted on her promise. But *cf.* the insistence upon the need for a request by all judges in *Shadwell v. Shadwell* (above, p. 225) only six years later—though, admittedly, the majority were able to discern a request in rather unpromising material. And see above, pp. 195–198.

See also *Argy Trading Development Co. Ltd v. Lapid Developments Ltd* [1977] 3 All E.R. 785 at 796 *per* Croom-Johnson J.

Question

Suppose that Mrs Jorden had said to Money, "I have executed a release of the debt under seal," whereafter Money got married. If she had subsequently sued him for the sum, what would be the effect of her previous statement?

HUGHES v. METROPOLITAN RLY. CO.

House of Lords (1877) 2 App. Cas. 439; 46 L.J.C.P. 583; 36 L.T. 932; 25 W.R. 680

A landlord had, in October 1874, given his tenant six months' notice to repair the premises, the lease being forfeitable if the tenant failed to comply with the notice. The tenant replied, agreeing to do the necessary repairs but also suggesting that the landlord who owned the freehold might like to purchase the lease and indicating that repairs would not be effected while negotiations on this suggestion were in

---

[1] The second ground, concerning the Statute of Frauds, is omitted.

progress. In November the landlord began negotiations with the tenant for the surrender of the lease but these were broken off on December 31. Meanwhile the tenant had done no repairs on the premises. When six months from the original notice had expired, the landlord claimed to treat the lease as forfeit.

The House of Lords (Lord Cairns L.C., Lords O'Hagan, Selborne, Blackburn and Gordon) held that the tenant was entitled to relief in equity against the forfeiture, the landlord's opening of negotiations having been the reason for the tenant's failure to do any repairs, the six months allowed therefor should run from the failure of the negotiations.

LORD CAIRNS L.C.: It is the first principle upon which all courts of equity proceed, that if parties who have entered into definite and distinct terms involving certain legal results—certain penalties or legal forfeiture— afterwards by their own act or with their own consent enter upon a course of negotiation which as the effect of leading one of the parties to suppose that the strict rights arising under the contract will not be enforced, or will be kept in suspense, or held in abeyance, the person who otherwise might have enforced those rights will not be allowed to enforce them where it would be inequitable having regard to the dealings which have thus taken place between the parties.

Note

In *Birmingham and District Land Co. v. L. & North Western Rly.* (1888) 40 Ch.D. 268; 60 L.T. 527, C.A., BOWEN L.J. (referring to the principle expressed by Lord Cairns in *Hughes'* case above) said: "Now, it was suggested by (counsel) that that proposition only applied to cases where penal rights in the nature of forfeiture, or analogous to those of forfeiture, were sought to be enforced. I entirely fail to see any such possible distinction. The principle has nothing to do with forefeiture. . . . It was applied in *Hughes v. Metropolitan Rly.* in a case in which equity could not relieve against forfeiture upon the mere ground that it was a forfeiture, but could interfere only because there had been something in the nature of acquiescence, or negotiations between the parties, which made it inequitable to allow the forfeiture to be enforced. The truth is that the proposition is wider than cases of forfeiture. It seems to me to amount to this, that if persons who have contractual rights against others induce by their conduct those against whom they have such rights to believe that such rights will either not be enforced or will be kept in suspense or abeyance for some particular time, those persons will not be allowed by a court of equity to enforce the rights until such time has elapsed, without at all events placing the parties in the same position as they were before. That is the principle to be applied. I will not say it is not a principle that was recognised by courts of law as well as of equity. It is not necessary to consider how far it was always a principle of common law."

COMBE v. COMBE

Court of Appeal [1951] 2 K.B. 215; [1951] 1 T.L.R. 811; 95 S.J. 317; [1951] 1 All E.R. 767

Appeal from Byrne J.

The parties, a husband and wife, were married in 1915, but separated in 1939. On February 1, 1943, on the wife's petition, a decree nisi of divorce was pronounced. On February 9, 1943, the wife's solicitor wrote to the husband's solicitor. "With regard to permanent maintenance, we understand that your client is prepared to make her an allowance of £100 per year, free of income tax." On February 19, 1943, the husband's solicitor replied that the husband had "agreed to allow your client £100 per annum, free of tax." On August 11, 1943, the decree was made absolute. The wife's solicitor wrote for the first instalment of £25 on August 26, and asking that future instalments should be paid on November 11, February 11, May 11, and August 11. The husband, himself, replied that he could not be expected to pay in advance. In fact, he never made any payment. The wife pressed for payment but made no application to the Divorce Court for maintenance. She had an income of between £700 and £800 a year. Her husband had only £650 a year.

On July 28, 1950, the wife brought an action in the King's Bench Division claiming from her husband £675, being arrears of payments at the rate of £100 per year for six and three-quarter years. Byrne J. held that the first three quarterly instalments of £25 were barred by the Limitation Act 1939, but gave judgment for the wife for £600. He held on the authority of *Gaisberg v. Storr* [1950] 1 K.B. 107 that there was no consideration for the husband's promise to pay his wife £100, but nevertheless he held that the promise was enforceable on the principle stated in *Central London Property Trust, Ltd v. High Trees House, Ltd* (above, p. 249) and *Robertson v. Minister of Pensions* [1949] 1 K.B. 227, because it was an unequivocal acceptance of liability, intended to be binding, intended to be acted on and, in fact, acted on.

The husband appealed.

DENNING L.J. [after stating the facts]: Much as I am inclined to favour the principle stated in the *High Trees* case, it is important that it should not be stretched too far, lest it be endangered. That principle does not create new causes of action where none existed before. It only prevents a party from insisting upon his strict legal rights, when it would be unjust to allow him to enforce them, having regard to the dealings which have taken place between the parties. That is the way it was put in *Hughes v. Metropolitan Rly.* (above, p. 254), the case in the House of Lords in which the principle was first stated, and in *Birmingham etc., Land Company v. London and North Western Rly.* (above, p. 255), the case in the Court of Appeal where the principle was enlarged. . . . It is also implicit in all the modern cases in which the principle has been developed. That is, I think, its true function. It may be part of a cause of action, but not a cause of action in itself.

(Having reviewed the authorities his Lordship proceeded):

The principle, as I understand it, is that, where one party has, by his words or conduct, made to the other a promise or assurance which was intended to affect the legal relations between them and to be acted on accordingly, then, once the other party has taken him at his word and acted on it, the one who gave the promise or assurance cannot afterwards be allowed to revert to the previous legal relations as if no such promise or assurance had been made by him, but he must accept their legal relations subject to the qualification which he himself has so introduced, even though it is not supported in point of law by any consideration but only by his word.

Seeing that the principle never stands alone as giving a cause of action in itself, it can never do away with the necessity of consideration when that is an essential part of the cause of action. The doctrine of consideration is too firmly fixed to be overthrown by a side-wind. Its ill-effects have been largely mitigated of late, but it still remains a cardinal necessity of the formation of a contract, though not of its modification or discharge. I fear that it was my failure to make this clear which misled Byrne J. in the present case. He held that the wife could sue on the husband's promise as a separate and independent cause of action by itself, although as he held there was no consideration for it. That is not correct. The wife can only enforce it if there was consideration for it. That is, therefore, the real question in the case: was there sufficient consideration to support the promise?

If it were suggested that, in return for the husband's promise, the wife expressly or impliedly promised to forbear from applying to the court for maintenance—that is, a promise in return for a promise—there would clearly be no consideration, because the wife's promise was not binding on her and was therefore worth nothing. Notwithstanding her promise, she could always apply to the Divorce Court for maintenance—maybe only with leave—and no agreement by her could take away that right: *Hyman v. Hyman* [1929] A.C. 601, as interpreted by this court in *Gaisberg v. Storr*.

There was, however, clearly no promise by the wife, express or implied, to forbear from applying to the court. All that happened was that she did in fact forbear—that is, she did an act in return for a promise. Is that sufficient consideration? Unilateral promises of this kind have long been enforced, so long as the act or forbearance is done on the faith of the promise and at the request of the promisor, express or implied. The act done is then in itself sufficient consideration for the promise even though it arises *ex post facto*, as Parker J. pointed out in *Wigan v. English and Scottish Law Life Assurance Association* [1909] 1 Ch. 291, 298. If the findings of Byrne J. were accepted, they would be sufficient to bring this principle into play. His finding that the husband's promise was intended to be binding, intended to be acted upon, and was, in fact, acted on—although expressed to be a finding on the *High Trees* principle—is equivalent to a finding that there was consideration within this long settled rule, because it comes to the same thing expressed in different words: see *Oliver v. Davis* [1949] 2 K.B. 727. But my difficulty is to accept the finding of Byrne J. that the promise was "intended to be acted upon." I cannot find any evidence of any intention by the husband that the wife should forbear from applying to the court for maintenance, or, in other words, any request by the husband, express or implied, that the wife should so forbear. He left her to apply if she wished to do so. She did not do so and I am not surprised, because it is very unlikely that the Divorce Court would have then made any order in her favour, seeing that she had a bigger income than her husband. Her forbearance was not intended by him, nor was it done at his request. It was, therefore, no consideration. . . .

ASQUITH L.J.: The judge has decided that, while the husband's promise was unsupported by any valid consideration, yet the principle in *Central London Property Trust, Ltd v. High Trees House, Ltd* entitles the wife to succeed. It is unnecessary to express any view as to the correctness of that decision, though I certainly must not be taken to be questioning it; and I would remark, in passing, that it seems to me a complete misconception to suppose that it struck at the roots of the doctrine of consideration. But assuming, without deciding, that it is good law, I do not think, however, that it helps the plaintiff at all. What that case decides is that when a promise is given which (1) is intended to create legal relations, (2) is intended to be acted upon by the promisee, and (3) is in fact so acted upon, the promisor cannot bring an action against the promisee which involves the repudiation of his promise or is inconsistent with it. It does not, as I read it, decide that a promisee can sue on the promise. On the contrary, Denning J. expressly stated the contrary. Neither in the *High Trees*, case nor in *Minister of Pensions v. Robertson* (another decision of my Lord which is relied upon by the plaintiff) was an action brought by the promisee on the promise. In the first of those two cases the plaintiff was in effect the promisor or a person standing in the shoes of the promisor, while in the second the claim, though brought by the promisee, was brought upon a cause of action which was not the promise but was an alleged statutory right. . . .

(The concurring judgment of BIRKETT L.J. is omitted.)

Appeal allowed.

(iv) *Estoppel and Causes of Action*

In *Robertson v. Minister of Pensions* the War Office wrote to the plaintiff stating, "Your disability has been accepted as attributable to military service." On the faith of that assurance the plaintiff took no steps to obtain an independent medical opinion as otherwise he would have done. Subsequently a pensions appeal tribunal decided that his injury was not due to war service. Denning J., following *inter alia* the High Trees case, held that the assurance by the War Office was binding on the Minister of Pensions, both being agents of the Crown. An award must issue that the injury *was* attributable to war service. Arguably, this was an ordinary estoppel, being a representation of fact. Whatever its nature, it enabled plaintiff to make out his cause of action on his legal right to a pension. The oft-cited dictum of Birkett L.J. (quoting counsel for the husband) in *Combe v. Combe*, that the *High Trees* doctrine can be used as a shield but not a sword, is misleading. Like estoppel generally, it may be part of the armoury of the attacker just as readily as that of the defender. Estoppel (with the possible exception of "proprietary estoppel") is never a cause of action in the sense of breach of contract, tort, or breach of trust, because it is not a recognised legal injury: but it may assist to establish the conditions necessary for the success of any cause of action, no less than it may establish the conditions necessary for a defence. See Brandon L.J. in *Amalgamated Investment v. Texas Commerce*, below, p. 262.

The so-called "proprietary estoppel" has been held to arise where A purports to give, but does not effectively convey, or promises to give, land or an interest in land to B, knowing that B will expend money or otherwise act to his detriment in reliance on the supposed or promised gift. When B does so act, this gives him an "equity" to require A to complete the gift. In *Dillwyn v. Llewellyn* (1862) 4 De G.F. & J. 517, C.A. in Chancery, a father, wishing his son to reside near him, signed a memorandum "presenting [a freehold estate] to my son for the purpose of furnishing him with a dwelling-house." The son took possession and expended a large sum in building a house and generally improving the property. The father never conveyed the estate and, after his death, the son, claiming to be the equitable owner in fee simple, sued for and obtained an order that the trustees convey the estate to him. Lord Westbury L.C. said that "the subsequent expenditure by the son with the approbation of the father supplied a valuable consideration, originally wanting." The case might therefore be explained simply as one of unilateral contract (above, p. 31), the element of request being implicit in the father's wish that his son live near him; but later cases are not readily explicable on this ground. See, for example, *Inwards v. Baker* [1965] 2 Q.B. 29, C.A. Perhaps the explanation is that the action in reliance on the promise creates the "equity" in the nature of a constructive trust and the plaintiff sues on that. *Cf. Re Basham* [1987] 1 All E.R. 405 (Nugee Q.C.).

CRABB v. ARUN DISTRICT COUNCIL

Court of Appeal [1976] Ch. 179; [1975] 3 W.L.R. 847; [1975] 3 All E.R. 865

The plaintiff owned a plot of land, the adjacent portion to which had been sold by his predecessor in title to the defendant for the erection of houses. It was the intention of the parties that the council should build a new road between the two pieces of land and, in the conveyance, the plaintiff was granted access (at point A) and a right of way over the road. Before the development was started, the plaintiff decided that it would be to his advantage to divide his land into two portions in such a way that he would need access to the road at a second point. He informed the council of his plan and at a meeting with council representatives, received a clear impression that he would be given the second access point (point B), but no formal grant of a right of way was ever made. The council built the road and fenced it off from the plaintiff's land, leaving a gap at point B. Subsequently, the plaintiff sold the part of his land with access at point A so that he was dependent for access to the land that he retained at point B. However, the council fenced off this access point and refused either to reopen it or to grant the plaintiff an easement save on payment. The plaintiff claimed a declaration that he was entitled to a right of way and an injunction. Brightman J. dismissed the claim. The plaintiff appealed.

LORD DENNING M.R.: When counsel for Mr Crabb said that he put his case on an estoppel, it shook me a little, because it is commonly supposed that estoppel is not itself a cause of action. But that is because there are estoppels and estoppels. Some do give rise to a cause of action. Some do not. In the species of estoppel called proprietary estoppel, it does give rise to a cause of action. We had occasion to consider it a month ago in *Moorgate Mercantile Co. Ltd v. Twitchings* [1975] 3 All E.R. 314 where I said that the effect of estoppel on the true owner may be that—

"his own title to the property, be it land or goods, has been held to be limited or extinguished, and new rights and interests have been created therein. And this operates by reason of his conduct—what he has led the other to believe—even though he never intended it."

... The question then is: were the circumstances here such as to raise an equity in favour of Mr Crabb? True the council on the deeds had the title to their land, free of any access at point B. But they led Mr Crabb to believe that he had or would be granted a right of access at point B. At the meeting of July 26, 1967, Mr Alford and Mr Crabb told the council's representative that Mr Crabb intended to split the two acres into two portions and wanted to have an access at point B for the back portion, and the council's representative agreed that he should have this access. ...

The judge found that there was "no definite assurance" by the council's representative, and "no firm commitment," but only an "agreement in principle," meaning I suppose that, as Mr Alford said, there were "some further processes" to be gone through before it would become binding. But if there were any such processes in the minds of the parties, the subsequent conduct of the council was such as to dispense with them. The council actually put up the gates at point B at considerable expense. That certainly led Mr Crabb to believe that they had agreed that he should have the right of access through point B without more ado.

The judge also said that, to establish this equity or estoppel, the council must have known that Mr Crabb was selling the front portion without reserving a right of access for the back portion. I do not think this was necessary. The council knew that Mr Crabb *intended* to sell the two portions separately and that he would need an access at point B as well as point A. Seeing that they knew of his intention—and they did nothing to disabuse him, but rather confirmed it by erecting gates at point B—it was their conduct which led him to act as he did; and this raises an equity in favour against them. . . .

I would, therefore, hold that Mr Crabb, as the owner of the back portion, has a right of access at point B over the verge on to Mill Park Road and a right of way along that road to Hook Lane without paying compensation. I would allow the appeal and declare that he has an easement, accordingly.

LAWTON L.J.: I ask myself whether any principle of equity applies. I am grateful to counsel for the defendants for having drawn our attention this morning to *Ramsden v. Dyson* (1866) L.R. 1 H.L. 129. If there had been any doubt in my mind about the application of principles of equity to the facts as I have recounted them, that case would have dissipated it. As was pointed out to counsel for the defendants in the course of the argument, if one changes the parties in a passage in the speech of Lord Cranworth L.C. L.R. 1 H.L. at 142 into the names of the parties in this case, one has a case for the intervention of equity which Lord Cranworth regarded with favour. The passage to which I refer is in these terms:

> ". . . if I had come to the conclusion that Thornton, when he erected his building in 1837, did so in the belief that he had against Sir John an absolute right to the lease he claims, and that Sir John knew that he was proceeding on that mistaken notion, and did not interfere to set him right, I should have been much disposed to say that he was entitled to the relief he sought."

The answer of counsel for the defendants was that the plaintiff had not got an absolute right to have the gates put up. For the reasons I have stated, I am of the opinion that he had in the sense that he had been given a firm undertaking. The defendants, knowing that the plaintiff intended to sell part of his land, stood by when he did so and, without a word of warning, allowed him to surround himself with a useless piece of land from which there was no exit. I would allow this appeal and grant relief in the terms indicated by Lord Denning M.R.

SCARMAN L.J., having stated that the enquiry must be whether an equity was established and, if so, what was its extent and appropriate remedy: In pursuit of that enquiry I do not find helpful the distinction between promissory and proprietary estoppel. This distinction may indeed be valuable to those who have to teach or expound the law, but I do not think that, in solving the particular problem raised by a particular case, putting the law into categories is of the slightest assistance. . . .

What is needed to establish an equity? In the course of an interesting addition to his submissions this morning, counsel for the defendants cited *Ramsden v. Dyson*[1] to support his proposition that in order to establish an equity by estoppel, there must be a belief by the plaintiff in the existence of a right created or encouraged by the words or actions of the defendant. With respect, I do not think that that is today a correct statement of the law. I think the law has developed so that today it is to be considered as

---

[1] (1866) L.R. 1 H.L. 129, 142.

correctly stated by Lord Kingsdown in his dissenting speech in *Ramsden v. Dyson*. Like Lord Denning M.R., I think that the point of dissent in *Ramsden v. Dyson* was not on the law but on the facts. Lord Kingsdown's speech, insofar as it dealt with propositions of law, has been often considered, and recently followed, by this court in *Inwards v. Baker* [1965] 2 Q.B. 29. Lord Kingsdown said:[1]

> "The rule of law applicable to the case appears to me to be this: If a man, under a verbal agreement with a landlord for a certain interest in land, or what amounts to the same thing, *under an expectation, created or encouraged by the landlord* [my italics], that he shall have a certain interest, takes possession of such land, with the consent of the landlord, and upon the faith of such promise or expectation, with the knowledge of the landlord, and without objection by him, lays out money upon the land, a Court of equity will compel the landlord to give effect to such promise or expectation."

Counsel for the defendants, in the course of an interesting and vigorous submission, drew the attention of the court to the necessity of finding something akin to fraud before the equity sought by the plaintiff could be established. "Fraud" was a word often in the mouths of those robust judges who adorned the bench in the 19th century. It is less often in the mouths of the more wary judicial spirits who sit today on the Bench. But it is clear that whether one uses the word "fraud" or not, the plaintiff has to establish as a fact that the defendant, by setting up his right, is taking advantage of him in a way which is unconscionable, inequitable or unjust. It is to be observed . . . that the fraud or injustice alleged does not take place during the course of negotiation, but only when the defendant decides to refuse to allow the plaintiff to set up his claim against the defendant's undoubted right. The fraud, if it be such, arises after the event, when the defendant seeks by relying on his right to defeat the expectation which he by his conduct encouraged the plaintiff to have. There need not be anything fraudulent or unjust in the conduct of the actual negotiations—the conduct of the transaction by the defendant.

Appeal allowed.

Questions
1. It has been suggested (Atiyah, 91 L.Q.R. 174) that the decision could have been based on contract in that the plaintiff's acting to his detriment would constitute consideration. The council did not ask him to sell the plot dependent on point B. Can unrequested detriment to a promisee constitute consideration? See above, pp. 195–199. See also Millett, 92 L.Q.R. 342.
2. If there had been a contract to grant an easement it would have been a contract for the sale or disposition of an interest in land and so unenforceable in the absence of a memorandum in writing: Law of Property Act 1925, s.40, above, and now void under the L.P. (M.P.) Act 1989. So the "equity" is better than a contract?
3. The Council led Mr Crabb to believe that "he had or would be granted a right of access." Is there a significant difference between "had" and "would be granted?" Does not the one indicate a statement of fact and the other a promise? Is there a similar distinction between the passages from Lord Cranworth and Lord Kingsdown quoted from *Ramsden v. Dyson* by Lawton and Scarman L.JJ. respectively?

[1] (1866) L.R. 1 H.L. 129, 170.

4. Lord Denning and Scarman L.J. appear to differ as to the practical significance of categorising an estoppel as "proprietary." Who is right? *Cf. Jorden v. Money*, above.

See also *Pascoe v. Turner* [1979] 2 All E.R. 945; *Greasley v. Cooke* [1980] 3 All E.R. 710; *Taylor Fashions Ltd v. Liverpool Victoria Trustees Co. Ltd* [1981] 1 All E.R. 897; and the next case.

AMALGAMATED INVESTMENT & PROPERTY CO. LTD (IN LIQUIDATION) v. TEXAS COMMERCE INTERNATIONAL BANK LTD

Court of Appeal [1982] Q.B. 84; [1981] 3 W.L.R. 565; [1981] 3 All E.R. 577

The plaintiff (AIP) requested the defendant (the bank) to make advances to AIP's subsidiary (ANPP) in the Bahamas and covenanted to pay on demand money owed by ANPP to the bank (the guarantee). To circumvent Bahamian restrictions, money was advanced by the bank to a Bahamian company (Portsoken) which advanced the same sum to ANPP (the NASSAU loan). The guarantee was a standing offer to repay any money advanced by the bank to ANPP. No such money was ever advanced. Both parties, however, believed the guarantee to be binding and effective. The mistake originated with the bank but AIP represented to the bank and encouraged it to believe that the guarantee was binding and effective. Robert Goff J. dismissed a claim by AIP that it was under no liability to the bank under the guarantee. AIP appealed.

LORD DENNING M.R. AND EVELEIGH L.J. delivered judgments dismissing the appeal.

BRANDON L.J.: The judge . . . based his decision on the question of estoppel on three matters. The first matter was that, from 1974 to 1976, both the bank and AIP conducted the transactions which took place between them in what must for present purposes be regarded as the mistaken belief that the guarantee relating to the Nassau loan effectively bound AIP to discharge any indebtedness of ANPP to Portsoken in respect of that loan. The second matter was that, although it had originally been due to the bank's own error that it came to hold its mistaken belief, AIP, being under the same mistaken belief itself, by its conduct encouraged and reinforced the mistaken belief held by the bank. The third matter was that the bank, in reliance on the mistaken belief concerned, accorded various indulgences to, and refrained from exercising various rights against, AIP in a way which, but for the bank's mistaken belief, it would never have done. . . .

Two main arguments against the existence of an estoppel were advanced on behalf of AIP both before Robert Goff J. and before us. The first argument was that, since the bank came to hold its mistaken belief in the first as a result of its own error alone, and AIP had at most innocently acquiesced in that belief which it also held, there was no representation by AIP to the bank on which an estoppel could be founded. The second argument was that, in the present case, the bank was seeking to use estoppel not as a shield, but as a sword, and that that was something which the law of estoppel did not permit.

I consider first the argument based on the origin of the bank's mistaken belief. In my opinion this argument is founded on an erroneous view of the kind of estoppel which is relevant in this case. The kind of estoppel which is relevant in this case is not the usual kind of estoppel in pais based on a representation made by A to B and acted on by B to his detriment. It is rather the kind of estoppel which is described in Spencer Bower and Turner on Estoppel by Representation (3rd ed., 1977), pp. 157–160 as estoppel by convention:

> "This form of estoppel is founded, not on a representation of fact made by a representor and believed by a representee, but on an agreed statement of facts the truth of which has been assumed, by the convention of the parties, as the basis of a transaction into which they are about to enter. When the parties have acted in their transaction upon the agreed assumption that a given state of facts is to be accepted between them as true, then as regards that transaction each will be estopped as against the other from questioning the truth of the statement of facts so assumed."

Applying that description of estoppel by convention to the present case, the situation as I see it is this. First, the relevant transactions entered into by AIP and the bank were the making of new arrangements with regard to the overall security held by the bank in relation to both the U.K. and Nassau loans. Second, for the purposes of those transactions, both the bank and AIP assumed the truth of a certain state of affairs, namely that the guarantee given in relation to the Nassau loan effectively bound AIP to discharge any indebtedness of ANPP to Portsoken. The transactions took place on the basis of that assumption, and their course was influenced by it in the sense that, if the assumption had not been made, the course of the transactions would without doubt have been different.

Those facts produce, in my opinion, a classic example of the kind of estoppel called estoppel by convention as described in the passage from Spencer Bower and Turner on Estoppel by Representation and so deprive the first argument advanced on behalf of AIP of any validity which, if the case were an ordinary one of estoppel by representation, it might otherwise have.

I turn to the second argument advanced on behalf of AIP, that the bank is here seeking to use estoppel as a sword rather than a shield, and that that is something which the law of estoppel does not permit. Another way in which the argument is put is that a party cannot found a cause of action on an estoppel.

In my view much of the language used in connection with these concepts is no more than a matter of semantics. Let me consider the present case and suppose that the bank had brought an action against AIP before it went into liquidation to recover moneys owed by ANPP to Portsoken. In the statement of claim in such an action the bank would have pleaded the contract of loan incorporating the guarantee, and averred that, on the true construction of the guarantee, AIP was bound to discharge the debts owed by ANPP to Portsoken. By their defence AIP would have pleaded that, on the true construction of the guarantee, AIP was only bound to discharge debts owed by ANPP to the bank, and not debts owed by ANPP to Portsoken. Then in their reply the bank would have pleaded that, by reason of an estoppel arising from the matters discussed above, AIP were precluded from questioning the interpretation of the guarantee which both parties had, for the purpose of the transactions between them, assumed to be true.

In this way the bank, while still in form using the estoppel as a shield, would in substance be founding a cause of action on it. This illustrates what I would regard as the true proposition of law, that, while a party cannot in terms found a cause of action on an estoppel, he may, as a result of being able to rely on an estoppel, succeed on a cause of action on which, without being able to rely on that estoppel, he would necessarily have failed. That, in my view, is, in substance, the situation of the bank in the present case.

It follows from what I have said above that I would reject the second argument against the existence of an estoppel put forward on behalf of AIP as well as the first. It further follows, from my rejection of both arguments against the existence of an estoppel, that I would answer the second of the two questions which I formulated earlier by holding that, if AIP did not, by the contract relating to the Nassau loan, undertake to the bank to discharge any indebtedness of ANPP to Portsoken, it is nevertheless estopped from denying that it did so by reason of the basis, accepted by both the bank and AIP, on which the transactions between them were later conducted during the period from 1974 to 1976.

Appeal dismissed.

Note

It appears that, if the parties to a contract misconstrue their agreement and act upon that misconstruction, there will be an estoppel by convention; and, if a dispute arises, the contract will be enforced, not according to its real meaning but according to the "false" meaning put upon it by the parties. What if the parties enter into the contract under a common misapprehension as to the effect of their agreement? Is the contract to be enforced in its true or false meaning? What if, in performing the contract, the parties act on the assumption that the false meaning is the true one? Has not the formerly false meaning now become the "true" meaning?

TOOL METAL MANUFACTURING CO. LTD v. TUNGSTEN ELECTRIC CO. LTD

House of Lords [1955] 1 W.L.R. 761; 99 S.J. 470; [1955] 2 All E.R. 657; 72 R.P.C. 209

In 1938 the Tool Metal Manufacturing Co. Ltd. (T.M.M.C.) who owned certain patents entered into a formal agreement with the Tungsten Electric Co. Ltd (T.E.C.O.), whereby T.M.M.C. gave T.E.C.O. a licence to deal in the products protected by the patents (styled "contract materials") until 1947, terminable by six months' notice in writing on either side, in consideration of T.E.C.O.'s paying a royalty of 10 per cent on the net value of all contract material used by T.E.C.O. other than material supplied by T.M.M.C. Clause 5 of the agreement provided that, if in any month the contract material used by T.E.CO. exceeded a quota of 50 kilograms, T.E.C.O. should pay to T.M.M.C. "compensation" equal to 30 per cent of the net value of the excess contract material. After the outbreak of war in 1939 the payment of compensation was suspended but royalties were paid down to March 1942. In 1942 T.M.M.C. orally intimated to T.E.C.O. that they would prepare a new agreement and would not, meantime, claim compensation and would be satisfied with a flat royalty of 10 per cent, as the national interest required the maximum output of contract material: no compensation was claimed during the war and T.E.C.O. regulated their production accordingly. In September 1944 T.M.M.C. submitted to T.E.C.O. the draft of a proposed new agreement which contained a provision for the revival of compensation and which was rejected by T.E.C.O. In 1945, T.E.C.O. brought an action against T.M.M.C. for fraudulent misrepresentation or breach of contract in the 1938 agreement and alleged in their claim for damages that it had been agreed that no compensation should be payable after December 31, 1939. T.M.M.C. denied the alleged agreement and maintained that if there were such agreement there was no consideration for it: and they counterclaimed, alleging that since 1942, T.E.C.O., in breach of their contract, had not paid royalties or compensation on the contract material they had used. They did not seek compensation for the period December 31, 1939–May 31, 1945, but sought compensation in respect of material used since June 1, 1945.

The Court of Appeal (Somervell, Singleton and Cohen L.JJ.), affirming in part the decision of Devlin J., held ((1952) 69 R.P.C. 108, 112) that there had been no contract for the final termination of the payment of compensation, only a temporary arrangement pending a new agreement; but, on the principle of *Hughes v. Metropolitan Ry.* and *Birmingham and District Land Co. v. L. & North Western Rly.* this arrangement to suspend the payment of compensation was binding in equity upon T.M.M.C. until terminated by proper notice and the presentation of the draft new agreement in 1944 did not constitute such notice.

In 1950, T.M.M.C. commenced an action claiming compensation as from January 1, 1947, treating their delivery of the counterclaim in the first action as a sufficient notice to determine the agreement to suspend payment of compensation. T.E.C.O. pleaded *inter alia*, that the counterclaim was not sufficient notice because no time was specified in it for the termination of the arrangement. The House of Lords (Viscount Simonds, Lords Oaksey, Tucker, and Cohen), reversing the decision of the Court of Appeal ([1954] 1 W.L.R. 862), restored the decision of Pearson J. ((1954) 71 R.P.C. 1) in favour of T.M.M.C.

LORD TUCKER: My Lords, the parties to the present action are estopped from disputing the correctness of the decision of the Court of Appeal in the first action to the effect that circumstances existed which gave rise to the application of the equitable principle in *Hughes v. Metropolitan Rly.*, and that no sufficient intimation to terminate the period of suspension of payment had been given prior to the counterclaim in that action, but it would be wrong, in my opinion, if the view were to prevail that your Lordships in the present case are tacitly accepting the correctness of that decision. . . .

The sole question . . . before the courts on this issue in the present action has been throughout: Was the counterclaim in the first action a sufficient intimation to determine the period of suspension which has been found to exist?

LORD COHEN: [The findings of the Court of Appeal in the first case] necessarily involve that, in the present case, equity required T.M.M.C. to give some form of notice to T.E.C.O. before compensation would become payable. But it has never been decided that in every case notice should be given before a temporary concession ceases to operate. It might, for instance, cease automatically on the occurrence of a particular event. Still less has any case decided that, where notice is necessary, it must take a particular form.

Romer L.J. seems to have taken the view that the counterclaim could not be a notice, because you cannot terminate an agreement by repudiating it.

With all respect, the fallacy of this argument consists in treating the arrangement found to exist by the Court of Appeal in the first action as an agreement binding in law. It was not an agreement, it was a voluntary concession by T.M.M.C. which, for reasons of equity, the court held T.M.M.C. could not cease to allow without plain intimation to T.E.C.O. of their intention to do so. The counterclaim seems to me a plain intimation of such change of intention operating as from June 1, 1945, and for the future. Nonetheless, the intimation would fall short of what was required if it was the duty of T.M.M.C. to specify in the intimation the reasonable time which they would allow after receipt of the intimation to enable T.E.C.O. to readjust their business to the altered conditions. I see no reason why equity should impose this burden on T.M.M.C..

(v) *Promissory Estoppel—Suspensory or Extinctive?*

There has been much discussion as to whether promissory estoppel extinguishes or merely suspends the estopped party's rights. The answer seems reasonably clear: as regards existing obligations it is extinctive, as regards future obligations it is suspensory. Both these points emerge in the *Tool Metal* case. T.M.M.C.'s right to the 20 per cent balance of "compensation" during the period of operation of the estoppel was gone for ever. They sued for it and Devlin J. and the Court of Appeal in the first action held that they failed. This is obviously what Denning J. intended in the *High Trees* case. If, during the war years, the landlord could have required payment of the whole of the back rent, the doctrine would have achieved precisely nothing; that would have been no more than an application of *Foakes v. Beer*. If, on the other hand, during the war years, the landlord had told the tenant that, from a reasonable period, say three months, hence, he must again begin to pay the full rent, that according to *Tool Metal* (but perhaps not Denning J.) would have been effective. This would have been the same as T.M.M.C. resuming its right to the full amount of compensation for the future. The suspensory aspect can apply only when there is a continuing series of obligations some of which are in the future—to pay rent, royalties, interest, or whatever.

The problem of reconciling the dictum in *High Trees* and the decision of the Court of Appeal in *Tool Metal* with *Foakes v. Beer* remains. Denning J. apparently took the view that they were irreconcilable, *Foakes v. Beer* having been decided *per incuriam* through overlooking a principle of equity. The irreconcilability may be accepted—what is the difference between agreeing to forgo interest which would otherwise accrue from day to day and agreeing to forgo rent or royalties which would otherwise accrue from time to time? The opinion that the Law Lords forgot about equity is harder to swallow. It will be noted that in *Tool Metal* their Lordships were concerned to make it clear that they were not deciding that promissory estoppel applied to the facts of the case. As between the parties, it had been finally decided by the Court of Appeal in the first action that it did apply—the parties were estopped by the record (a different kind of estoppel) from denying it—but the House was not saying that that decision was right or wrong. Given that a promissory estoppel was in operation, the only question for them was whether a sufficient notice had been given to bring it to an end. The House may be taken to have decided only that, if there is a doctrine of promissory estoppel which operates in these circumstances, its operation may be terminated by reasonable notice; and, in the circumstances, reasonable notice had been given.

Notwithstanding the enormous amount of discussion of the *High Trees* case, the occasions for its application seem to have been very few. Most of the cases in which it has been cited were decided, or could have been decided, on the basis of previously recognised principles of estoppel or the principle of *Hughes v. Metropolitan Railway* as stated in the *Note*, above, p. 252. Indeed, the only two cases which directly raise the apparent conflict with *Foakes v. Beer* seem to be *D. & C. Builders v. Rees* and the *Tool Metal* case. In the former case, below, *Foakes v. Beer* was applied. In the *Tool Metal* case, the Court of Appeal, though purporting to apply *Hughes*, went beyond that case, at least as interpreted above, p. 252 and applied the extension of it favoured by Denning J. in *High Trees*—though without mentioning that case.

In *F. A. Ajayi v. R. T. Briscoe (Nigeria) Ltd* [1964] 1 W.L.R. 1326; [1964] 3 All E.R. 556, Lord Hodson, delivering the judgment of the J.C.P.C. said:

"Their Lordships are of opinion that the principle of law as defined by Bowen L.J. has been confirmed by the House of Lords in the case of *Tool Metal Manufacturing Co. Ltd v. Tungsten Electric Co. Ltd* where the authorities were reviewed and no encouragement was given to the view that the principle was capable of extension so as to create rights in the promisee for which he had given no consideration. The principle, which has been described as quasi-estoppel and perhaps more aptly as promissory estoppel, is that when one party to a contract in the absence of fresh consideration agrees not to enforce his rights an equity will be raised in favour of the other party. This equity is, however, subject to the qualifications (1) that the other party has altered his position, (2) that the promissor can resile from his promise on giving reasonable notice, which need not be a formal notice, giving the promisee reasonable opportunity of resuming his position, (3) the promise only becomes final and irrevocable if the promisee cannot resume his positon."

Note

See also Denning, "Recent Developments in the Doctrine of Consideration" 15 M.L.R. 1; Wilson, "Recent Developments in Estoppel," 67 L.Q.R. 330; Fridman, "Promissory Estoppel," 35 Can. Bar Rev. 279; Stoljar, "Modification of Contracts," 35 Can. Bar Rev. 485; Gordon, 1963 C.L.J. 222; Wilson 1965 C.L.J. 93.

D. & C. BUILDERS LTD v. REES

Court of Appeal [1966] 2 Q.B. 617; [1966] 2 W.L.R. 288; [1965] 3 All E.R. 837

LORD DENNING M.R.: D. & C. Builders Ltd ("the plaintiffs") are a little company. "D." stands for Mr Donaldson, a decorator, "C." for Mr Casey, a plumber. They are jobbing builders. The defendant, Mr Rees, has a shop where he sells builders' materials.

In the spring of 1964 the defendant employed the plaintiffs to do work at his premises, 218 Brick Lane. The plaintiffs did the work and rendered accounts in May and June, which came to £746 13s. 1d. altogether. The defendant paid £250 on account. In addition the plaintiffs made an allowance of £14 off the bill. So in July 1964 there was owing to the plaintiffs the sum of £482 13s. 1d. At this stage there was no dispute as to the work done. But the defendant did not pay.

On August 31, 1964, the plaintiffs wrote asking the defendant to pay the remainder of the bill. He did not reply. On October 19, 1964, they wrote again, pointing out that the "outstanding account of £480 is well overdue." Still the defendant did not reply. He did not write or telephone for more than three weeks. Then on Friday, November 13, 1964, the defendant was ill with influenza. His wife telephoned the plaintiffs. She spoke to Mr Casey. She began to make complaints about the work: and then said: "My husband will offer you £300 in settlement. That is all you'll get. It is to be in satisfaction." Mr Casey said he would have to discuss it with Mr

Donaldson. The two of them talked it over. Their company was in desperate financial straits. If they did not have the £300, they would be in a state of bankruptcy. So they decided to accept the £300 and see what they could do about the rest afterwards. Thereupon Mr Donaldson telephoned the defendant's wife. He said to her: "£300 will not even clear our commitments on the job. We will accept £300 and give you a year to find the balance." She said: "No, we will never have enough money to pay the balance. £300 is better than nothing." He said: "We have no choice but to accept." She said: "Would you like the money by cash or by cheque. If it is cash you can have it on Monday. If by cheque, you can have it tomorrow (Saturday)." On Saturday, November 14, 1964, Mr Casey went to collect the money. He took with him a receipt prepared on the company's paper with the simple words: "Received the sum of £300 from Mr Rees." She gave him a cheque for £300 and asked for a receipt. She insisted that the words "in completion of the account" be added. Mr Casey did as she asked. He added the words to the receipt. So she had the clean receipt: "Received the sum of £300 from Mr Rees in completion of the account. Paid, M. Casey." Mr Casey gave in evidence his reason for giving it: "If I did not have the £300 the company would have gone bankrupt. The only reason we took it was to save the company. She knew the position we were in."

The plaintiffs were so worried about their position that they went to their solicitors. Within a few days, on November 23, 1964, the solicitors wrote complaining that the defendant had "extricated a receipt of some sort or other" from them. They said that they were treating the £300 as a payment on account. On November 28, 1964, the defendant replied alleging bad workmanship. He also set up the receipt which Mr Casey gave to his wife, adding: "I assure you she had no gun on her." The plaintiffs brought this action for the balance. The defendant set up a defence of bad workmanship and also that there was a binding settlement. The question of settlement was tried as a preliminary issue. The judge made these findings:

> "I concluded that by the middle of August the sum due to the plaintiffs was ascertained and not then in dispute. I also concluded that there was no consideration to support the agreement of November 13 and 14. It was a case of agreeing to take a lesser sum, when a larger sum was already due to the plaintiffs. It was not a case of agreeing to take a cheque for a smaller amount instead of receiving cash for a larger amount. The payment by cheque was an incidental arrangement."

The judge decided, therefore, the preliminary issue in favour of the plaintiffs. The defendant appeals to this court. He says there was here an accord and satisfaction—an *accord* when the plaintiffs agreed, however reluctantly, to accept £300 in settlement of the account—and *satisfaction* when they accepted the cheque for £300 and it was duly honoured. The defendant relies on the cases of *Sibree v. Tripp* (1846) 15 M. & W. 23) and *Goddard v. O'Brien* ((1882) 9 Q.B.D. 37) as authorities in his favour.

This case is of some consequence: for it is a daily occurrence that a merchant or tradesman, who is owed a sum of money, is asked to take less. The debtor says he is in difficulties. He offers a lesser sum in settlement, cash down. He says he cannot pay more. The creditor is considerate. He accepts the proffered sum and forgives him the rest of the debt. The question arises: is the settlement binding on the creditor? The answer is that, in point of law, the creditor is not bound by the settlement. He can sue the next day sue the debtor for the balance, and get judgment. The law was so stated in 1602 by Lord Coke in *Pinnel's Case* ((1602) 5 Co.Rep. 117a)— and accepted in 1884 by the House of Lords in *Foakes v. Beer* (above, p. 240).

Now, suppose that the debtor, instead of paying the lesser sum in cash, pays it by cheque. He makes out a cheque for the amount. The creditor accepts the cheque and cashes it. Is the position any different? I think not. No sensible distinction can be taken between payment of a lesser sum by cash and payment of it by cheque. The cheque, when given, is conditional payment. When honoured, it is actual payment. It is then just the same as cash. If a creditor is not bound when he receives payment by cash, he should not be bound when he receives payment by cheque. This view is supported by the leading case of *Cumber v. Wane* ((1721) 1 Stra. 426), which has suffered many vicissitudes but was, I think, rightly decided in point of law.

The case of *Sibree v. Tripp* ((1846) 15 M. & W. 23) is easily distinguishable. There the plaintiffs brought an action for £500. It was settled by the defendant giving three promissory notes amounting in all to £250. Those promissory notes were given on a new contract, in substitution for the debt sued for, and not as conditional payment. The plaintiff's only remedy thenceforward was on the notes and not on the debt. The case of *Goddard v. O'Brien* ((1882) 9 Q.B.D. 37) is not so easily distinguishable. There a creditor was owed £125 for some slates. He met the debtor and agreed to accept £100 in discharge of it. The debtor gave a cheque for £100. The creditor gave a written receipt "in settlement on the said cheque being honoured." The cheque was clearly given by way of conditional payment. It was honoured. The creditor sued the debtor for the balance of £25. He lost, because the £100 was paid by cheque and not by cash. The decision was criticised by Fletcher Moulton L.J. in *Hirachand Punamchand v. Temple* (above, p. 247), and by the editors of *Smith's Leading Cases* (13th ed.), Vol. 1, p. 380. It was, I think, wrongly decided. In point of law payment of a lesser sum, whether by cash or by cheque, is no discharge of a greater sum.

This doctrine of the common law has come under heavy fire. It was ridiculed by Sir George Jessel M.R. in *Couldery v. Bartrum* ((1881) 19 Ch.D. 394 at p. 399). It was held to be mistaken by Lord Blackburn in *Foakes v. Beer*. It was condemned by the Law Revision Committee in their Sixth Interim Report (Cmnd. 5449), para. 20 and para. 22. But a remedy has been found. The harshness of the common law has been relieved. Equity has stretched out a merciful hand to help the debtor. The courts have invoked the broad principle stated by Lord Cairns L.C. in *Hughes v. Metropolitan Rly.* (above, p. 254):

> ". . . it is the first principle upon which all courts of equity proceed, that if parties, who have entered into definite and distinct terms involving certain legal results . . . afterwards by their own act, or with their own consent, enter upon a course of negotiation which has the effect of leading one of the parties to suppose that *the strict rights arising under the contract will not be enforced*, or will be kept in suspense, or

held in abeyance, the person who otherwise might have enforced those rights *will not be allowed to enforce them where it would be inequitable, having regard to the dealings which have taken place between the parties.*"

It is worth noting that the principle may be applied, not only so as to suspend strict legal rights, but also so as to preclude the enforcement of them.

This principle has been applied to cases where a creditor agrees to accept a lesser sum in discharge of a greater. So much so that we can now say that, when a creditor and a debtor enter on a course of negotiation, which leads the debtor to suppose that, on payment of the lesser sum, the creditor will not enforce payment of the balance, and on the faith thereof the debtor pays the lesser sum and the creditor accepts it as satisfaction: then the creditor will not be allowed to enforce payment of the balance when it would be inequitable to do so. This was well illustrated during the last war. Tenants went away to escape the bombs and left their houses unoccupied. The landlords accepted a reduced rent for the time they were empty. It was held that the landlords could not afterwards turn round and sue for the balance: see *Central London Property Trust Ltd v. High Trees House Ltd* (above, p. 249). This caused at the time some eyebrows to be raised in high places. But they have been lowered since. The solution was so obviously just that no one could well gainsay it.

In applying this principle, however, we must note the qualification. The creditor is barred from his legal rights only when it would be *inequitable* for him to insist on them. Where there has been a *true accord*, under which the creditor voluntarily agrees to accept a lesser sum in satisfaction, and the debtor *acts on* that accord by paying the lesser sum and the creditor accepts it, then it is inequitable for the creditor afterwards to insist on the balance. But he is not bound unless there has been truly an accord between them.

In the present case, on the facts as found by the judge, it seems to me that there was no true accord. The debtor's wife held the creditor to ransom. The creditor was in need of money to meet his own commitments, and she knew it. When the creditor asked for payment of the £480 due to him, she said to him in effect: "We cannot pay you the £480. But we will pay you £300 if you will accept it in settlement. If you do not accept it on those terms, you will get nothing. £300 is better than nothing." She had no right to say any such thing. She could properly have said: "We cannot pay you more than £300. Please accept it on account." But she had no right to insist on his taking it in settlement. When she said: "We will pay you nothing unless you accept £300 in settlement," she was putting undue pressure on the creditor. She was making a threat to break the contract (by paying nothing) and she was doing it so as to compel the creditor to do what he was unwilling to do (to accept £300 in settlement): and she succeeded. He complied with her demand. That was on recent authority a case of intimidation (see *Rookes v. Barnard* [1964] A.C. 1129, and *J. T. Stratford & Son Ltd v. Lindley* [1965] A.C. 269 at pp. 283, 284). In these circumstances there was no true accord so as to found a defence of accord and satisfaction (see *Day v. McLea* (1889) 22 Q.B.D. 610). There is also no equity in the defendant to warrant any departure from the due course of law. No person can insist on a settlement procured by intimidation.

In my opinion there is no reason in law or equity why the creditor should not enforce the full amount of the debt due to him. I would, therefore, dismiss this appeal.

DANCKWERTS L.J. gave a judgment concurring with Lord Denning M.R.

WINN L.J.: . . . The question to be decided may be stated thus. Did the defendant's agreement to give his own cheque for £300 in full settlement of his existing debt to the plaintiffs of £482 13s. 1d. and the plaintiffs' agreement to accept it in full payment of that debt, followed by delivery and due payment of such a cheque, constitute a valid accord and satisfaction discharging the debt in law?

Apart altogether from any decided cases bearing on the matter, there might be a good deal to be said, as a matter of policy, in favour of holding any creditor bound by his promise to discharge a debtor on his paying some amount less than the debt due: some judges no doubt so thought when they held readily that acceptance by the creditor of something of a different nature from that to which he was entitled was a satisfaction of the liability (*cf. Pinnel's Case* (1602) 5 Co. Rep. 117a, *Smith v. Trowsdale* (1854) 3 E. & B. 83, *Cooper v. Parker* (1855) 15 C.B. 882). A like approach might at some time in the past have been adopted by the courts to all serious assurances of agreement, but as English law developed, it does not now permit in general of such treatment of mere promises. In the more specific field of discharge of monetary debt there has been some conflict of judicial opinion.

Where a cheque for a smaller sum than the amount due is drawn by a person other than the debtor and delivered in satisfaction of his debt, it is clear that the debt is discharged if the cheque be accepted on that basis and duly paid (*cf. Hirachand Punamchand v. Temple*, above, p. 247).

In the instant case the debtor's own cheque was accepted, though not stipulated for by the creditor, as the equivalent of cash, conditionally of course on its being duly paid on presentation: such is the modern usage in respect of payments of money due, common, though not yet universal, in domestic no less than commercial transactions. This court must now decide the effect of that transaction.

[Having discussed *Goddard v. O'Brien*, his lordship continued:] I interpose the comment that I find it impossible in the instant case to visualise any benefit or legal possibility of benefit to the builders which might derive from the receipt of the defendant's cheque for £300 instead of the same amount of cash.

Only two years after the decision in *Goddard's* case the House of Lords, in the case of *Foakes v. Beer* (above, p. 240), had to consider the effect of an agreement between a judgment debtor and a judgment creditor that in consideration of the debtor paying down part of the judgment debt and costs and paying the residue by instalments, the creditor would not take any proceedings on the judgment. The House held this to be a *nudum pactum*, being without consideration, and that it did not prevent the creditor after payment of the whole debt and costs from proceeding to enforce payment of interest on the judgment. *Pinnel's Case* and *Cumber v. Wane* were expressly followed.

[Having discussed *Foakes v. Beer* and *Hirachand Punamchand v. Temple*, his lordship proceeded:] In my judgment it is an essential element of a valid accord and satisfaction that the agreement which constitutes the accord should itself be binding in law, and I do not think that any such agreement can be so binding unless it is either made under seal or supported by consideration. Satisfaction, *viz.*, performance, of an agreement of accord does not provide retroactive validity to the accord, but depends for its effect on the legal validity of the accord as a binding contract at the time when it is made: this I think is apparent when it is remembered that, albeit rarely, existing obligations of debt may be replaced effectively by a contractually binding substitution of a new obligation.

In my judgment this court should now decline to follow the decision in *Goddard v. O'Brien* and should hold that where a debtor's own cheque for a lesser amount than he indisputably owes to his creditor is accepted by the creditor in full satisfaction of the debt, the creditor is to be regarded, in any case where he has not required the payment to be made by cheque rather than in cash, as having received the cheque merely as conditional payment of part of what he was entitled to receive: he is free in law, if not in good commercial conscience, to insist on payment of the balance of the amount due to him from the debtor.

I would dismiss this appeal.

Appeal dismissed.

Questions

1. Lord Denning recognises that *Foakes v. Beer* continues to represent the common law and, apparently, is glad to follow it. But he considers that the *High Trees* principle will prevail where this is equitable. Is this a satisfactory principle or does it leave too much discretion to the judge in deciding whether it is "equitable" to apply the principle?

2. In the absence of the element of intimidation, would the decision have been unanimous?

3. "Accord and satisfaction is the purchase of a release from an obligation, whether arising under contract or tort, by means of any valuable consideration, not being the actual performance of the obligation itself": Salmond and Williams on *Contracts* 328, adopted in *British Russian Gazette v. Associated Newspapers Ltd* [1933] 2 K.B. 616 at 643–644. The accord is the agreement, the satisfaction is the consideration; so this is merely the name for a particular type of contract. Is agreement generally precluded by the fact that one party takes advantage of another's weak position? Suppose that X, knowing that D. & C. Builders are desperate for work, beats them down until they agree to do work at very low cost. Are they bound by the agreement? Was there any less of an "accord" in the actual case than in that example? Is the difference that Rees was threatening to break his contract by not paying at all?

4. If a threat to break a contract is intimidation, why was there no intimidation in *High Trees* when the tenant said, "We cannot pay the full rent?" Is there a difference between "we can't" and "we won't?" *Cf. Williams v. Roffey Bros.*, above, p. 231 and *Atlas Express Ltd v. Kafko Ltd*, below, p. 653.

5. Lord Denning says that *Sibree v. Tripp* was easily distinguishable because there was a "new contract." There was no dispute as to the amount due in that case. How can promissory notes for £250 be consideration for £500—except by regarding the notes as something different from cash?

Note

In *Woodhouse A.C. Israel Cocoa Ltd S.A. v. Nigerian Produce Marketing Co. Ltd* [1972] A.C. 741, Lord Hailsham of St. Marylebone L.C. said (p. 758): "I desire to add that the time may soon come when the whole sequence of cases based on promissory estoppel since the war beginning with *Central London Property Trust Ltd v. High Trees House Ltd* (above, p. 249), may need to be reviewed and reduced to a coherent body of doctrine by the courts. I do not mean to say that any are to be regarded with suspicion. But as is common with an expanding doctrine they do raise problems of coherent exposition which have never been systematically explored." See also Lord Pearson at p. 762. The time has still not come.

See Dugdale and Yates, "Variation, Waiver and Estoppel—A Re-Appraisal" (1976) 39 M.L.R. 680.

CHAPTER 8

PRIVITY OF CONTRACT

Section 1. Consideration and Privity

In the first part of this chapter we are concerned with the question whether a person who is not a party to a contract can acquire rights under it. The short answer is that, subject to certain exceptions, he cannot. There are said to be two principles involved. The first is that only a promisee can enforce the promise. A promises B, for consideration supplied by B, that he will do something for the benefit of C. C acquires no rights.

$$A \longleftrightarrow B$$
$$C$$

The second principle is that "consideration must move from the promisee." A promises B *and* C, for consideration supplied by B, that he will do something for the benefit of C.

$$A \longleftrightarrow B$$
$$\searrow C$$

C is no better off in the second case than in the first. In the first case he acquires no rights because he is not a party to the agreement. In the second case, he acquires no rights because, though he is a "promisee," the consideration does not move from him. Since it is immaterial whether C is a promisee or not, it is clear that the crucial principle is the second one. The question is not whether C is a promisee or not but whether he is a contracting party or not; and, while he may be a party to the *agreement*, he is not a *contracting* party unless he gives consideration. The doctrine of privity of contract is nothing more than an application of the doctrine of consideration which is why it is considered in this book at this point instead of, as is common, at a much later stage. The supposed first principle cannot truly be said to be a principle at all since the operation of the second leaves no room for the application of the first.

This analysis is based on the traditional view of the second principle. It should be noted, however, that it has been strenuously argued in recent years that one joint promisee may sue even though the consideration was supplied exclusively by the other. This theory has the support of the *dicta* of four out of five judges of the High Court of Australia in *Coulls v. Bagot's Executor and Trustee Co. Ltd* (1967) 119 C.L.R. 460 and of Professors Atiyah (*Consideration in Contracts: A Fundamental Restatement*, pp. 41–42), Treitel (*Law of Contract* (8th ed.), p. 523) and Waddams (*The Law of Contracts* (2nd ed.), p. 200). The contrary has been cogently argued by Professor Coote, "Consideration and the Joint Promisee" [1978] C.L.J. 300. Most important is the fact that the traditional view has the support of the leading case, the decision of the House of Lords in *Dunlop v. Selfridge*, below, p. 276. Consider the note, below, p. 280.

Even according to the traditional view, C acquires rights in the following cases.

(i) B gives consideration on behalf of himself and C. B deposits money in a bank in the names of B and C. Whether the money belongs to B alone (or indeed to C alone) is simply not the bank's business. The consideration has been supplied on behalf of both and that is the end of the matter. The question was discussed, *obiter*, by Lord Atkin in *McEvoy v. Belfast Banking Corporation* [1935] A.C. 24. C's claim

273

against the bank failed on other grounds but, rejecting the argument that C could in no circumstances succeed, he said:

> "My Lords, to say this is to ignore the vital difference between a contract purporting to be made by B with the bank to pay B or C and a contract purporting to be made by B and C with the bank to pay B or C. In both cases of course payment to C would discharge the bank whether the bank contracted with B alone or with B and C. But the question is whether in the case put C has any rights against the bank if payment to him is refused. I have myself no doubt that in such a case C can sue the bank. The contract on the face of it purports to be made with B and C, and I think with them jointly and severally. B purports to make the contract on behalf of C as well as himself and the consideration supports such a contract. If B has actual authority from C to make such a contract, C is a party to the contract *ab initio*. If he has not actual authority then subject to the ordinary principles of ratification C can ratify the contract purporting to have been made on his behalf and his ratification relates back to the original formation of the contract. If no events had happened to preclude C from ratifying, then on compliance with the contract conditions, including notice and production of the deposit receipt, C would have the right to demand from the bank so much of the money as was due on the deposit account.
>
> In my view, therefore, if nothing had happened to prevent the son from ratifying the contract, he could sue the bank on the original deposit account. . . . I think the case is rightly put on ratification, for I can find no sufficient evidence that the father had the actual authority of the son to enter into this contract on the son's behalf."[1]

(ii) Where, though it is expected that B will supply the consideration, C will be bound to supply it if he does not. C is a contracting party because he is (usually impliedly) promising that he will supply the consideration, at least if B does not. So in *Lockett v. Charles* [1938] 4 All E.R. 170 a wife successfully sued a restaurateur in contract for supplying unfit food although her husband had paid the bill. In *Olley v. Marlborough Court*, (above, p. 147), the wife's action against the hotel succeeded although the husband booked the accommodation and paid the bill.

Coulls v. Bagot's Executor presents a more difficult problem. In consideration of a payment of £5, B gave A the right to quarry on B's land and A promised to pay a royalty. B authorised A to pay the royalty to B and C (A's wife) as joint tenants. The agreement was signed by A, B and C. On B's death, the question was whether the royalties were payable to B's estate or to C. The majority held that the contract was between A and B with a revocable mandate from B to pay moneys to C. The mandate was revoked by B's death so the money was payable to B's executor. Four of the judges thought that, if it had been a contract by A to pay B and C jointly, C would have been entitled to sue, although she personally gave no consideration. Barwick C.J. and Windeyer J., dissenting, thought C was a party to the contract. Barwick C.J. treated the case as if it fell within case (i), above:—

> ". . . as I construe this writing, we have here not a promise by A with B for consideration supplied by B to pay C. It was, in my opinion, a promise by A made to B and C for consideration to pay B and C. In such a case it cannot lie in the mouth of A, in my opinion, to question whether the consideration which he received for his promise moved from both B and C or, as between themselves, only from one of them. His promise is not a gratuitous promise as

---

[1] The identification of the parties in Lord Atkin's dictum has been altered to conform with that used above and throughout this Chapter.

between himself and the promisees as on the view I take of the agreement it was a promise in respect of which there was privity between A on the one hand and B and C on the other. . . . I find nothing in *Dunlop Pneumatic Tyre Co. Ltd v. Selfridge & Co. Ltd* to suggest that [A could successfully deny either privity or consideration]"

The difficulty about this approach is that the reality, known to all the parties, was that only B, the owner of the land, was doing anything for A. Windeyer J. said:

"Still, it was said, no consideration moved from [C]. But that, I consider, mistakes the nature of a contract made with two or more persons jointly. The promise is made to them collectively. It must, of course, be supported by consideration, but that does not mean by considerations furnished by them separately. It means a consideration given on behalf of them all, and therefore moving from all of them. In such a case the promise of the promisor is not gratuitous; and, as between him and the joint promisees, it matters not how they were able to provide the price of his promise to them."

If C was joining in the promise by B to provide A with the price of his promise, there was consideration. As Coote points out [1978] C.L.J. at 311) "the benefit to the quarrying company . . . would have been, not her provision of the quarry but her accountability in law should her husband have defaulted." The difficulty is to see that she did join in the promise. Accepted principles support Coote's conclusion:

"To sum up, then it is submitted that the joint promisee doctrine enunciated in *Coulls v. Bagot's Executor and Trustee Co. Ltd* was based on a misapprehension of what constitutes the provision of consideration and of what constitutes a 'party' to a contract. The requirement of the common law remains that consideration move from the promisee. To that requirement joint promisees are no exception."

TWEDDLE v. ATKINSON

Queen's Bench (1861) 1 B. & S. 393; 30 L.J.Q.B. 265; 4 L.T. 468; 9 W.R. 781; 8 Jur. 332; 124 R.R. 610

The declaration stated that the plaintiff was the son of John Tweddle, deceased, and, before the making of the agreement hereafter mentioned, married the daughter of William Guy, deceased; that, before the said marriage, John Tweddle and William Guy each orally promised to give a marriage portion to his child in consideration of the marriage, which promises were unperformed; that, after the marriage, John Tweddle and William Guy, as a mode of giving effect to their said oral promises, entered into the following agreement in writing:

"High Coniscliffe,
July 11, 1855

Memorandum of an agreement made this day between William Guy, of etc., of the one part, and John Tweddle, of etc., of the other part. Whereas it is mutually agreed that the said William Guy shall and will pay the sum of £200 to William Tweddle, his son-in-law, and the said John Tweddle, father to the aforesaid William Tweddle, shall and will pay the sum of £100 to the said William Tweddle, each and severally the said sums on or before the 21st day of August, 1855. And it is hereby further agreed by the aforesaid William Guy and the said John Tweddle that the said William Tweddle has full power to sue the said parties in any court of law or equity for the aforesaid sums hereby promised and specified."

The plaintiff claimed that afterwards and before this suit, he and his wife ratified the agreement, he being the William Tweddle mentioned; that August 21, 1855, passed and all things necessary to entitle the plaintiff to have the £200 paid by William Guy or his executor had happened; but that the money remained unpaid.
Demurrer and joinder thereon.
Mellish, for the plaintiff, argued that, though in general an action must be brought by the person from whom the consideration moved, there was an exception in the case of contracts made by parents for the purpose of providing for their children, citing *Dutton v. Poole*, 2 Lev. 210; *Bourne v. Mason*, 1 Ventr. 6.

CROMPTON J.: It is admitted that the plaintiff cannot succeed unless this case is an exception to the modern and well-established doctrine of the action of assumpsit. At the time when the cases which have been cited were decided the action of assumpsit was treated as an action of trespass upon the case, and therefore in the nature of a tort; and the law was not settled, as it now is, that natural love and affection is not a sufficient consideration for a promise upon which an action may be maintained; nor was it settled that the promisee cannot bring an action unless the consideration for the promise moved from him. The modern cases have, in effect, overruled the old decisions; they show that the consideration must move from the party entitled to sue upon the contract. It would be a monstrous proposition to say that a person was a party to the contract for the purpose of suing upon it for his own advantage, and not a party to it for the purpose of being sued. It is said that the father in the present case was agent for the son in making the contract, but that argument ought also to make the son liable upon it. I am prepared to overrule the old decisions and to hold that, by reason of the principles which now govern the action of assumpsit, the present action is not maintainable.
(The judgments of WIGHTMAN and BLACKBURN JJ. are omitted.)

Judgment for the defendant.

Note
Consider the criticisms of the doctrine of privity by Steyn L.J. in the *Darlington* case, below, pp. 308–310.

DUNLOP PNEUMATIC TYRE CO. LTD v. SELFRIDGE & CO. LTD

House of Lords [1915] A.C. 847; 84 L.J.K.B. 1680; 113 L.T. 386; 31 T.L.R. 399

Appeal from an order of the Court of Appeal reversing a judgment of Phillimore J.
The appellants were manufacturers of motor tyres.
The respondents were retailers, part of whose business consisted of retailing to the public motor tyres, etc., among them those of the appellants' manufacture.
On October 12, 1911, by a written agreement between the appellants and Dew and Co., who were dealers in motor accessories, Dew and Co. bought certain of the appellants' products as trade customers, and agreed, *inter alia*, that, in allowing a discount of up to 10 per cent. off list prices, to "persons legitimately engaged in the

motor trade," they would, as agents for the appellants in that behalf, obtain from such trader a written undertaking that he would observe appellants' list prices. etc., current at the time of sale in any resale by him, and that they would forward all such undertakings to the appellants upon demand and refuse trade discounts to any persons if such written undertaking was not previously obtained.

On December 22, 1911, the respondents accepted an order from one Jameson, and on January 1, 1912, an order from one Strauss, for certain Dunlop goods at prices below the appellants' current price lists. On January 2, respondents ordered these goods from Dew & Co. who obtained them from appellants and delivered them the same day, together with a price maintenance agreement for the respondents to sign, the material parts of which were as follows:

"PRICE MAINTENANCE AGREEMENT

To be entered into by Trade Purchasers of Dunlop Motor Tyres.
Messrs Selfridge & Co. to Messrs. A. J. Dew & Co.

January 2, 1912

Dear Sir,

In consideration of your allowing us a trade discount of 10 per cent. for prompt monthly payments off the list prices for motor tyres, covers, tubes and repairs contained in the Dunlop Pneumatic Tyre Co.'s list current from time to time. . . .

(2) We will not sell or offer any Dunlop motor tyres, covers or tubes to any private customers or to any co-operative society at prices below those mentioned in the said price list current at the time of sale, nor give to any such customer or society any cash or other discounts or advantages reducing the same. We will not sell or offer any Dunlop motor tyres, covers or tubes to any other person, firm or company at prices less than those mentioned in the said price list. . . .

(5) We agree to pay to the Dunlop Pneumatic Tyre Co. Ltd. the sum of £5 for each and every tyre, cover or tube sold or offered in breach of this agreement, as and by way of liquidated damages and not as a penalty, but without prejudice to any other rights or remedies you or the Dunlop Pneumatic Tyre Co. Ltd may have hereunder."

This agreement was in due course signed by respondents' manager and returned to Dew & Co. In the meantime, respondents had delivered to Jameson the cover he had ordered at the price agreed on; they later informed Strauss that they could supply him with the goods he ordered only at the list price.

The appellants commenced an action against the respondents for an injunction and damages in respect of the breach of the agreement of January 2, which they claimed to be an agreement made by respondents and appellants through Dew and Co. as their agents.

Phillimore J. gave judgment for the appellants for £10, the liquidated damages in respect of two breaches, and gave an injunction restraining the respondents from selling Dunlop goods below the appellants' current list prices. The Court of Appeal (Vaughan Williams, Kennedy, and Swinfen Eady L.JJ.) reversed this decision. They held that the contract of January 2 was not a contract between the appellants and the respondents at all, but between Dew and Co. and the respondents only.

VISCOUNT HALDANE L.C.: My Lords, in my opinion this appeal ought to fail.

Prior to January 2, 1912, Messrs. Dew had entered into a contract with the appellants to purchase a quantity of tyres and other goods from them at the prices in their list, in consideration of receiving certain discounts. As part of their contract Messrs. Dew undertook, among other things, not to sell to certain classes of customer at prices below the current list prices of the appellants. They were, however, to be at liberty to sell to a class of customer that included the respondents at a discount which was substantially less than the discount they were themselves to receive from the appellants, but in the case of any such sale they undertook, as the appellants' agents in this behalf, to obtain from the customer a written undertaking that he similarly would observe the terms so undertaken to be observed by themselves. This contract was embodied in a letter dated October 12, 1911.

On January 2 the respondents contracted with Messrs. Dew, in terms of a letter of that date addressed to them, that, in consideration of the latter allowing them discounts on goods of the appellants' manufacture which the respondents might purchase from Messrs. Dew, less, in point of fact, than the discount received by the latter from the appellants, the respondents, among other things, would not sell the appellants' goods to private customers at prices below those in the appellants' current list, and that they would pay to the appellants a penalty for every article sold in breach of this stipulation.

The learned judge who tried the case has held that the respondents sold goods of the appellants' manufacture supplied through Messrs. Dew at less than the stipulated prices, and the question is whether, assuming his finding to be correct, the appellants, who were not in terms parties to the contract contained in the letter of January 2, can sue them.

My Lords, in the law of England certain principles are fundamental. One is that only a person who is a party to a contract can sue on it. Our law knows nothing of a *jus quaesitum tertio* arising by way of contract. Such a right may be conferred by way of property, as, for example, under a trust, but it cannot be conferred on a stranger to a contract as a right to enforce the contract *in personam*. A second principle is that if a person with whom a contract not under seal has been made is to be able to enforce it consideration must have been given by him to the promisor or to some other person at the promisor's request. These two principles are not recognised in the same fashion by the jurisprudence of certain Continental countries or of Scotland, but here they are well established. A third proposition is that a principal not named in the contract may sue upon it if the promisee really contracted as his agent. But again, in order to entitle him so to sue, he must have given consideration either personally or through the promisee, acting as his agent in giving it.

My Lords, in the case before us, I am of opinion that the consideration, the allowance of what was in reality part of the discount to which Messrs. Dew, the promisees, were entitled as between themselves and the appellants, was to be given by Messrs. Dew on their own account, and was not in substance, any more than in form, an allowance made by the appellants. The case for the appellants is that they permitted and enabled Messrs. Dew, with the knowledge and by the desire of the respondents, to sell to the latter on the terms of the contract of January 2, 1912. But it appears to me that even if this is so the answer is conclusive. Messrs. Dew sold to the respondents goods which they had a title to obtain from the appellants independently of this contract. The consideration by way of discount under the contract of January 2, was to come wholly out of

Messrs. Dew's pocket, and neither directly nor indirectly out of that of the appellants. If the appellants enabled them to sell to the respondents on the terms they did, this was not done as any part of the terms of the contract sued on.

No doubt it was provided as part of these terms that the appellants should acquire certain rights, but these rights appear on the face of the contract as *jura quaesita tertio*, which the appellants could not enforce. Moreover, even if this difficulty can be got over by regarding the appellants as the principals of Messrs. Dew in stipulating for the rights in question, the only consideration disclosed by the contract is one given by Messrs. Dew, not as their agents, but as principals acting on their own account.

The conclusion to which I have come on the point as to consideration renders it unnecessary to decide the further question as to whether the appellants can claim that a bargain was made in this contract by Messrs. Dew as their agents; a bargain which, apart from the point as to consideration, they could therefore enforce. If it were necessary to express an opinion on this further question, a difficulty as to the position of Messrs. Dew would have to be considered. Two contracts—one by a man on his own account as a principal, and another by the same man as agent, may be validly comprised in the same piece of paper. But they must be two contracts and not one as here. I do not think that a man can treat one and the same contract as made by him in two capacities. He cannot be regarded as contracting for himself and for another *uno flatu*.

My Lords, the form of the contract which we have to interpret leaves the appellants in this dilemma, that, if they say that Messrs. Dew contracted on their behalf, they gave no consideration, and if they say they gave consideration in the shape of a permission to the respondents to buy, they must set up further stipulations, which are neither to be found in the contract sued upon nor are germane to it, but are really inconsistent with its structure. That contract has been reduced to writing, and it is in the writing that we must look for the whole of the terms made between the parties. These terms cannot, in my opinion consistently with the settled principles of English law, be construed as giving to the appellants any enforceable rights as against the respondents.

I think that the judgment of the Court of Appeal was right, and I move that the appeal be dismissed with costs.

LORD DUNEDIN: My Lords, I am content to adopt from a work of Sir Frederick Pollock, to which I have often been under obligation, the following words as to consideration: "An act on forbearance of one party, or the promise thereof, is the price for which the promise of the other is bought, and the promise thus given for value is enforceable." (*Pollock on Contracts* (8th ed.), p. 175.)

Now the agreement sued on is an agreement which on the face of it is an agreement between Dew and Selfridge. But speaking for myself, I should have no difficulty in the circumstances of this case in holding it proved that the agreement was truly made by Dew as agent for Dunlop, or in other words that Dunlop was the undisclosed principal, and as such can sue on the agreement. Nonetheless, in order to enforce it he must show consideration, as above defined, moving from Dunlop to Selfridge.

In the circumstances, how can he do so? The agreement in question is not an agreement for sale. It is only collateral to an agreement for sale; but that agreement for sale is an agreement entirely between Dew and Selfridge. The tyres, the property in which upon the bargain is transferred to Selfridge, were the property of Dew, not of Dunlop, for Dew under his agreement with Dunlop held these tyres as proprietor, and not as agent. What then did Dunlop do, or forbear to do, in a question with Selfridge? The answer must be, nothing. He did not do anything, for Dew, having the right of property in the tyres, could give a good title to anyone he liked, subject, it might be, to an action of damages at the instance of Dunlop for breach of contract, which action, however, could never create a *vitium reale* in the property of the tyres. He did not forbear in anything, for he had no action against Dew which he gave up, because Dew had fulfilled his contract with Dunlop in obtaining, on the occasion of the sale, a contract from Selfridge in the terms prescribed.

To my mind, this ends the case.

LORD ATKINSON, having held that Dunlop gave no consideration to Selfridge. It was also urged on behalf of the appellants that it was competent for the latter to show that Dew & Co. entered into this contract of January 2, 1912, as agents for undisclosed principals, namely, the appellants in the present action.

Even if that were so, and the appellants were to be treated as parties to the contract contained in this letter, it does not get over the difficulty. The contract is as to them a nudum pactum, since no consideration moves from them to the respondents, or to any other person or body at the respondents' request.

LORD PARKER OF WADDINGTON: My Lords, even assuming that the undertaking upon which this action is founded was given by the respondents to Messrs. A. J. Dew & Co. as agents for the appellants, and was intended to enure for their benefit, the appeal cannot succeed unless the undertaking was founded on a consideration moving from the appellants, and in my opinion there was no such consideration.

LORD SUMMER: The true question . . . is that of consideration. . . . The appellants, as alleged promisees, neither did nor suffered nor forbore anything, nor promised to do any of these things, or anything at all, in exchange for the undertaking purporting to be given by the respondents. . . . The appellants have sued on a *nudum pactum*.

LORD PARMOOR.: Kennedy L.J. in his judgment in the Court of Appeal states his conclusion that it would be inconsistent with the terms of the contract itself to admit the claim of the appellants to be regarded as undisclosed principals with a consequent right to bring an action to enforce certain of its conditions. I agree with this conclusion, and it is sufficient to dispose of the case.

Note

Since the Restrictive Trade Pratices Act 1956, now replaced by the Restrictive Trade Practices Act 1976, contracts for the maintenance of minimum prices such as that in issue in *Dunlop v. Selfridge* have been void. This in no way affects the authority of *Dunlop v. Selfridge* on the principles of the common law concerning privity and consideration.

It will have been observed that Lord Haldane stated that the rule that only a person who is a party to a contract can sue on it is different from the rule that consideration must move from the promisee (see above, p. 273); but that all the judges, except Lord Parmoor, based their decision on the fact that Dunlop gave no consideration to Selfridge. *Tweddle v. Atkinson* is expressly based on the principle that consideration must move from the promisee. The leading cases on privity are in fact cases on consideration.

Dew were certainly not acting as agent for Dunlop in the contract of sale because Dew, and not Dunlop, were the sellers; but were not Dew clearly Dunlop's agent in extracting from Selfridge the promise not to sell below list price and to pay Dunlop £5 if they did? No reasonable person (and particularly a person in commerce like Selfridge) could fail to realise that the promise was obtained with Dunlop's authority and for Dunlop's benefit. But was Dunlop a promisee? Is *Coulls v. Bagot's Executor* (above, p. 274) distinguishable on the ground that Dunlop was not a promisee? Was Dew Dunlop's agent to receive Selfridge's promise?

Section 2. Contract and Tort

Where A negligently performs his contract with B and causes damage to a third party, C, C may sometimes have a remedy in the tort of negligence. It depends on whether the law imposes a duty on A to take reasonable care not to cause the injury in question to C. Such duties have long been recognised in the case of physical injury to person or property. The leading case is *Donoghue v. Stevenson* [1932] A.C. 562 where the injured consumer of defective ginger beer successfully sued the manufacturer although there was no contract between them. Modern cases have extended the principle to purely economic loss. For example, in *Ross v. Caunters* [1980] Ch. 297 solicitors (A) negligently allowed the husband of the plaintiff (C) to attest a will drawn up on the instructions of the testator (B) with the result that a gift made by B to C in the will was invalidated. Megarry V.C. held that C was entitled to damages from A. A owed a duty of care to C when carrying out his contract with B.

The same result was reached, Lords Keith and Mustill dissenting, in *White v. Jones* [1995] 1 All E.R. 691, H.L. Solicitors (A) negligently delayed in carrying out B's instructions to prepare a new will. Consequently, it remained unexecuted when B died. C recovered damages for the loss of the legacy which she would have received if the will had been prepared within a reasonable time and executed by B. Lord Goff said that "an ordinary action in tortious negligence on the lines proposed by Megarry V.C. in *Ross v. Caunters* must . . . be regarded as inappropriate, because it does not meet any of the conceptual problems which have been raised"; but it was open to the House "to fashion a remedy to fill a lacuna in the law and so prevent the injustice which would otherwise occur . . ." So they should extend to C a remedy under the *Hedley Byrne* principle (below, p. 340) "by holding that the assumption of responsibility by the solicitor towards his client should be held in law to extend to the intended beneficiary who (as the solicitor can reasonably foresee) may, as a result of the solicitor's negligence, be deprived of his intended legacy in circumstances in which neither the testator nor his estate will have a remedy against the solicitor."

Lord Mustill, dissenting, said that "it does not conduce to the orderly development of the law, or to the certainty which practical convenience demands, if duties are simply conjured up as a matter of positive law, to answer the injustice of an individual case." He could see nothing special about the calling of a solicitor to distinguish him from others in a much broader category. "If the claim in the present case is sound . . . it must be sound in every instance of the general situation which I have already indentified, namely: where A promises B for reward to perform a service for B, in circumstances where it is foreseeable that performance of the service with care will cause C a benefit and that failure to perform it may cause C not to benefit. To hold that a duty exists, even prima facie, in such a situation would be to go far beyond anything so far contemplated by the law of negligence."

What was Lord Goff doing by extending the doctrine of *Hedley Byrne* if he was not allowing the "ordinary action in tortious negligence" which he had just characterised as inappropriate? Were not the "conceptual problems" left unmet? If the decision establishes the broad principle stated (and deplored) by Lord Mustill, does it not make a substantial inroad into the privity rule? An earlier decision of the House which seemed to do so was *Junior Books v. Veitch* [1983] A.C. 520. Though probably wrongly decided, it still provides interesting material for discussion.

Junior Books (C) engaged a building contractor (B) to build a factory for them. C's architects nominated Veitchi (A) as specialist sub-contractors to lay a concrete floor with a special surface. A then entered into a contract with B, the main contractor, to carry out that work. There was no contractual relationship between A and C. Two years after it had been laid the floor developed cracks, requiring constant maintenance to keep it usable. C brought an action in negligence against A, claiming the cost of replacing the floor and consequential economic loss. No explanation was offered why C did not sue B on what would seem to have been a straightforward action for breach of contract. It has subsequently emerged that C had already settled a contractual claim against B. Presumably the damage had turned out to be worse than they had realised so they were coming back for more. This may reduce their claim to sympathy but it has no effect on the law—it is the same as if they had never sued B because, for example, B was insolvent. A claimed that C's pleading did not disclose a good cause of action because there was no contractual relationship between A and C and because C did not claim that the floor was a danger to health or safety of any person or to any other property belonging to A. The House of Lords, Lord Brandon dissenting, held that A was liable to C for the economic loss caused.

A's duty to lay the floor arose out of their contract with B. If they had never lifted a finger, only B could have sued. The same applies to their duty to lay a good floor—one which was reasonably fit for the purpose envisaged in the contract. Contractual duties are usually strict and, even if there had been no evidence of negligence, C would probably have been liable to B (who might in turn have been liable to A) for failure to provide a floor which was fit for its purpose. But if all that could be proved was a breach of that strict duty there would have been no question of C's liability in tort to A. It was only because there was a *negligent* failure to make the floor fit that the case got off the ground. But to say that (i) A owed no duty to C to provide a fit floor but (ii) A owed a duty to C to take reasonable care to provide a fit floor looks very odd. The decision seems to be, in substance, that an action would lie for damages for a negligent breach of a contract to lay a proper floor; and the plaintiff, C, was not a party to that contract. Lord Roskill in his speech set out no fewer than eight facts which he regarded as crucial to the decision; but there is nothing to avoid the conclusion that the defendant was liable because he had negligently performed a contract to which the plaintiff was not a party. The decision was heavily criticised. The courts noted its possible wide-ranging effects and sprang to the defence of privity as a doctrine which it was necessary to preserve. In *Balsamo v. Medici* [1984] 2 All E.R. 304 Walton J. said:

> "If the principle [in *Junior Books*] does not have some certain limits, it will come perilously close to abrogating completely the concept of privity of contract. A sub-bailee will be liable directly to the bailor, and the sub-agent will be directly liable to the principal for all negligent breaches of whatever agreement he makes with the bailor or agent as the case may be, at any rate over a wide field. I do not think the law has yet got to this point, if it ever will."

In *Simaan v. Pilkington Glass* (No. 2) [1988] 1 All E.R. 791, 805, Dillon L.J. went so far as to say that he found it difficult to see that the future citation of *Junior Books* could serve any useful purpose. In *D & F Estates Ltd v. Church Commissioners* [1988] 2 All E.R. 992 the House of Lords applied the dissenting dicta of Lord Brandon, not the decision of the majority. They held that, in the absence of a contractual relationship between the parties, the cost of repairing a defect in a chattel or structure which was discovered before the defect had caused personal injury or physical damage was not recoverable in negligence. The lessees of a block of flats could not recover from the builders the cost of work necessary to remedy negligent plastering work. This was pure economic loss. It would probably have been different if the negligently applied plaster had fallen off and injured a plaintiff's person or property.

Section 3. Privity and defences

The cases examined so far concern the question whether C can sue on, or because of, a contract made by A and B. The following cases are concerned with the question whether C can rely on the contract made by A and B when he is sued. They happen to be mainly concerned with contracts for the carriage of goods, particularly carriage by sea. They involve a bill of lading which, according to Lord Blackburn on Sale, 275—

> "is a writing signed on behalf of the owner of the ship in which goods are embarked, acknowledging the receipt of the goods, and undertaking to deliver them at the end of the voyage, subject to such conditions as may be mentioned in the bill of lading."

There is some debate as to whether the bill contains the contract of carriage or is merely evidence of its terms (see Debattista, "The Bill of Lading as the Contract of Carriage" (1982) 45 M.L.R. 652) but that is not material for present purposes. The reader will find that the shipper (the person who sends the goods) and the consignee (the person to whom they are sent) tend to be treated as if they were one and the same, *vis-à-vis* the carrier. This is because the delivery of the bill of lading transfers not only the ownership in the goods but also the contractual relationship with the carrier from shipper to consignee. The Bills of Lading Act 1855, s.1 provides:

> "Every consignee of goods named in a bill of lading, and every endorsee of a bill of lading, to whom the property in the goods therein mentioned shall pass upon or by reason of such consignment or endorsement, shall have transferred to and vested in him all rights of suit, and be subject to the same liabilities in respect of such goods as if the contract contained in the bill of lading had been made with himself."

The significance of bailment. A feature of this group of cases is that they involve the law of bailment as well as that of contract. A bailment arises when the owner of goods (the bailor) gives possession of the goods to another (the bailee) for some specified purpose, while retaining ownership for himself. A delivers goods to B to be carried to a named place, or to be stored in a warehouse, or to be repaired, or to be cleaned. There will, of course, usually be a contract between A and B as well as a bailment. It is when B makes a sub-bailment to C, and C damages or loses the goods, that a problem arises. Unless B was acting as A's agent in making a contract with C, there is no privity of contract between A and C. C may however owe a duty of care to A under the law of the tort of negligence. The question arises whether C can rely on the terms on which B accepted the goods from A to exclude or limit his liability. In the leading case of *Scruttons Ltd* which follows, the majority considered only the law of contract. Only Lord Denning, in his dissenting speech, invoked the law of bailment which led him to differ from the majority. But in *The Pioneer*

Container, below, p. 296, the Privy Council (four Law Lords and Sir Thomas Eichelbaum) applied Lord Denning's opinion, expressed obiter in *Morris v. Martin*, below, p. 294. The importance of his lordship's full and brilliant analysis in *Scruttons Ltd* is therefore enhanced.

The law of bailment is, of course, irrelevant where the question is one of liability for injury to the person.

SCRUTTONS LTD v. MIDLAND SILICONES LTD

House of Lords [1962] A.C. 446; [1962] 2 W.L.R. 186; 106 S.J. 34; [1962] 1 All E.R. 1

A drum of chemicals was shipped to the plaintiffs (the consignees) on a ship owned by United States Lines Inc. (the carrier) under a bill of lading which incorporated the United States Carriage of Goods by Sea Act 1936, and limited the liability of the carrier for damage to $500. The defendants, a stevedoring company, were engaged by the carrier to discharge their vessels in London and to act as agents in the delivery of goods to consignees, by a contract which limited the liability of the stevedores to $500. They negligently dropped the drum, causing damage to the value of £593. The plaintiffs sued the defendants in tort, claiming £593. Diplock J. held ([1959] 2 Q.B. 171) that the plaintiffs could recover that sum, rejecting the defendants' arguments that they were protected by the bill of lading. He held that the bill of lading did not purport to govern the relations between the consignees and the stevedores; that it was impossible to say that the stevedores were undisclosed principals of the carrier; that the *Elder, Dempster* case[1] was not an authority for the doctrine of "vicarious immunity from liability for torts" laid down by Scrutton L.J. in *Mersey Shipping & Transport Co. Ltd v. Rea Ltd* ((1925) 21 Lloyd's Rep. at p. 378); that if, as in the *Elder, Dempster* case A invites B to do something to A's goods which B is under no antecedent contractual duty to do, it may be reasonable to imply an agreement between A and B as to the terms on which that thing shall be done; but, as the plaintiffs in the present case never invited the defendants to do anything, no contract between them could be implied; that Denning L.J.'s observations in the *Snipes Hall* case ([1949] 2 K.B. 500; [1949] 2 All E.R. 179), in *White v. John Warwick & Co. Ltd* ([1953] 1 W.L.R. 1285; [1953] 2 All E.R. 1021) and *Adler v. Dickson* ([1955] 1 Q.B. 158; [1954] 3 All E.R. 397) were *obiter* and seemed in direct conflict with *Dunlop v. Selfridge* (above, p. 276) and *Cosgrove v. Horsfall* (below, p. 300) which were binding on him; and that the defendants could not limit their liability to the plaintiffs in tort by relying on a contract between the plaintiffs and a third party to which they were not parties and for which they gave no consideration to the plaintiffs. The Court of Appeal (Hodson, Pearce and Upjohn L.JJ.) affirmed the decision. The defendants now appealed to the House of Lords.

---

[1] [1924] A.C. 522. The plaintiffs sued the charterers and owners of the ship, *Grelwen*, for damage caused by bad stowage to oil shipped by the plaintiffs on the *Grelwen*. The bills of lading issued by the charterers provided that "the shipowners" should not be liable for any damage caused by bad stowage. It was not disputed that the term "shipowners" included the charterers but it was argued that the clause could not protect the owners from liability for the negligence of their servants since "they neither knew nor cared anything about the bills of lading." Allowing an appeal from the Court of Appeal where Scrutton L.J. dissented, the House of Lords held that the owners were protected. The precise juristic basis for this rule remains obscure; but it will be noted that the situation in which it operates is a highly specialised one: the master of the ship who takes possession of the goods shipped is the servant of the shipowners, who thus acquire possession directly from the shipper. While the shipowners are exempt, it does not by any means necessarily follow that the master or any member of the crew would be exempt if he were sued personally for his negligence: *Cf.* Jenkins L.J. at [1955] 1 Q.B. 194.

VISCOUNT SIMONDS made a speech dismissing the appeal.

LORD REID: Although I may regret it, I find it impossible to deny the existence of the general rule that a stranger to a contract cannot in a question with either of the contracting parties take advantage of provisions of the contract, even where it is clear from the contract that some provision in it was intended to benefit him. That rule appears to have been crystallised a century ago in *Tweddle v. Atkinson* (above, p. 275) and finally established in this House in *Dunlop Pneumatic Tyre Co. Ltd v. Selfridge & Co. Ltd* (above, p. 276). There are, it is true, certain well-established exceptions to that rule—though I am not sure that they are really exceptions and do not arise from other principles. But none of these in any way touches the present case.

The actual words used by Lord Haldane in the *Dunlop* case were made the basis of an argument that, although a stranger to a contract may not be able to sue for any benefit under it, he can rely on the contract as a defence if one of the parties to it sues him in breach of his contractual obligation—that he can use the contract as a shield though not as a sword. I can find no justification for that. If the other contracting party can prevent the breach of contract well and good, but if he cannot I do not see how the stranger can. As was said in *Tweddle v. Atkinson*, the stranger cannot "take advantage" from the contract.

It may be that in a roundabout way the stranger could be protected. If A, wishing to protect X, gives to X an enforceable indemnity, and contracts with B that B will not sue X, informing B of the indemnity, and then B does sue X in breach of his contract with A, it may be that A can recover from B as damages the sum which he has to pay X under the indemnity, X having had to pay it to B. But there is nothing remotely resembling that in the present case.

The appellants in this case seek to get round this rule in three different ways. In the first place, they say that the decision in *Elder, Dempster & Co. Ltd v. Paterson, Zochonis & Co. Ltd* ([1924] A.C. 522) establishes an exception to the rule sufficiently wide to cover the present case. I shall later return to consider this case. Secondly, they say that through the agency of the carrier they were brought into contractual relation with the shipper and that they can now found on that against the consignees, the respondents. And thirdly, they say that there should be inferred from the facts an implied contract, independent of the bill of lading, between them and the respondents. It was not argued that they had not committed a tort in damaging the respondents' goods.

I can see a possibility of success of the agency argument if (first) the bill of lading makes it clear that the stevedore is intended to be protected by the provisions in it which limit liability, (secondly) the bill of lading makes it clear that the carrier, in addition to contracting for these provisions on his own behalf, is also contracting as agent for the stevedore that these provisions should apply to the stevedore, (thirdly) the carrier has authority from the stevedore to do that, or perhaps later ratification by the stevedore would suffice, and (fourthly) that any difficulties about consideration moving from the stevedore were overcome. And then to affect the consignee it would be necessary to show that the provisions of the Bills of Lading Act 1855, apply.

But again there is nothing of that kind in the present case. I agree with your Lordships that "carrier" in the bill of lading does not include stevedore, and if that is so I can find nothing in the bill of lading which states or even implies that the parties to it intended the limitation of liability to extend to stevedores. Even if it could be said that reasonable men in the shoes of these parties would have agreed that the stevedores should have this benefit, that would not be enough to make this an implied term of the contract. And even if one could spell out of the bill of lading an intention to benefit the stevedore, there is certainly nothing to indicate that the carrier was contracting as agent for the stevedore in addition to contracting on his own behalf. So it appears to me that the agency argument must fail.

And the implied contract argument seems to me to be equally unsound. From the stevedores' angle, they are employed by the carrier to deal with the goods in the ship. They can assume that the carrier is acting properly in employing them, and they need not know whom the goods belong to. There was in their contract with the carrier a provision that they should be protected, but that could not by itself bind the consignee. They might assume that the carrier would obtain protection for them against the consignee and feel aggrieved when they found that the carrier did not or could not do that. But a provision in the contract between them and the carrier is irrelevant in a question between them and the consignee. Then from the consignees' angle they would know that stevedores would be employed to handle their goods, but if they read the bill of lading they would find nothing to show that the shippers had agreed to limit the liability of the stevedores. There is nothing to show that they ever thought about this or that if they had they would have agreed or ought as reasonable men to have agreed to this benefit to the stevedores. I can find no basis in this for implying a contract between them and the stevedores. It cannot be said that such a contract was in any way necessary for business efficiency.

So this case depends on the proper interpretations of the *Elder, Dempster* case. What was there decided is clear enough. The ship was under time charter, the bill of lading made by the shippers and the charterers provided for exemption from liability in the event which happened and this exemption was held to enure to the benefit of the shipowners who were not parties to the bill of lading but whose servant the master caused damage to the shippers' goods by his negligence. The decision is binding on us but I agree that the decision by itself will not avail the present appellants because the facts of this case are very different from those in the *Elder, Dempster* case. For the appellants to succeed it would be necessary to find from the speeches in this House a *ratio decidendi* which would cover this case and then to follow that *ratio decidendi*. . . .

It can hardly be denied that the *ratio decidendi* of the *Elder, Dempster* decision is very obscure. A number of eminent judges have tried to discover it, hardly any two have reached the same result, and none of the explanations hitherto given seems to me very convincing. If I had to try, the result might depend on whether or not I was striving to obtain a narrow *ratio*. So I turned to the decision itself. Two quite separate points were involved in the case. The first was whether the damage to the cargo was caused by bad stowage or by the ship being unseaworthy. This was very fully considered and the decision was bad stowage. On the conditions in the bill of lading this clearly freed the charterer of liability. The other question was whether those conditions were also available as a defence to the shipowner. From the report of the case it would seem that this was not very fully argued, and none of the three noble Lords who spoke devoted more than a page of print to it. They cannot have thought that any important question of law or any novel principle was involved. Lord Finlay said that a decision against the shipowner would be absurd and the other noble Lords probably thought the same. They must all have thought that they were merely applying an established principle to the facts of the particular case.

But when I look for such a principle I cannot find it, and the extensive and able arguments of counsel in this case have failed to discover it. . . .

(Having discussed the case and the dissenting judgment of Scrutton L.J. in the Court of Appeal [1923] 1 K.B. 420, his Lordship proceeded): I must treat the decision as an anomalous and unexplained exception to the general principle that a stranger cannot rely for his protection on provisions in a contract to which he is not a party. The decision of this House is authoritative in cases of which the circumstances are not reasonably distinguishable from those which gave rise to the decision. The circumstances in the present case are clearly distinguishable in several respects. Therefore I must decide this case on the established principles of the law of England apart from that decision and on that basis I have no doubt that this appeal must be dismissed.

LORD KEITH OF AVONHOLME: made a speech dismissing the appeal.

LORD DENNING: (having referred to the statement of Scrutton L.J. in *Mersey Shipping and Transport Co., Ltd v. Rea, Ltd* (1925) 21 Lloyd's Rep. at p. 378 that "where there is a contract which contains an exemption clause, the servants or agents who act under that contract have the benefit of the exemption clause," his Lordship proceeded): My Lords, it is said that, in stating this proposition, for once Homer nodded and that this great master of our commercial law—and the members of this House too—overlooked the "fundamental principle" that no one who is not a party to a contract can sue or be sued upon it or take advantage of the stipulations or conditions that it contains. I protest they did nothing of the kind. You cannot understand the *Elder, Dempster* case without some knowledge of the previous law and I would draw the attention of your Lordships to it.

First of all let me remind your Lordships that this "fundamental principle" was a discovery of the nineteenth century. Lord Mansfield and Buller J. knew nothing of it. But in the nineteenth century it was carried to the most extravagant lengths. It was held that, where a duty to use reasonable care arose out of a contract, no one could sue or be sued for a breach of that contract except a party to it, see *Winterbottom v. Wright* ((1842) 10 M. & W. 109), *Alton v. Midland Ry.* ((1865) 19 C.B.(N.S.) 213). In the nineteenth century if a goods owner had sought to sue stevedores for negligence, as he has in this case, he would have failed utterly. The reason being that the duty of the stevedores to use reasonable care arose out of their contract with the carrier; and no one could sue them for a breach of that duty except the other party to the contract, namely, the carrier. If the goods were damaged, the only remedy of the owner of the goods was against the carrier with whom he contracted, and not against the stevedores with whom he had no contract. If proof were needed that the doctrine was carried so far, it is provided by the many cases in the middle of the nineteenth century where the owner of goods sent them by railway for "through transit" to a destination on another line. The first carrier carried them safely over his line but they were damaged by the negligence of the second carrier. It was repeatedly held that the goods owner had no remedy against the second carrier: for the simple reason that he had no contract with him. The owner's only remedy was against the first carrier with whom he contracted, see *Scothorn v. South Staffordshire Ry.* ((1853) 8 Exch. 341): and not against the second carrier with whom he had no contract, see *Mytton v. Midland Ry.* ((1859) 4 H. & N. 615), *Coxon v. Great Western Ry.* ((1860) 5 H. & N. 274). If the first carrier was exempted from liability by the conditions of the contract, the goods owner had no remedy at all: none against the first carrier because he was protected by the conditions: and none against the second carrier because he was "not liable at all." It was so held by this House in *Bristol and Exeter Ry. v. Collins* ((1859) 7 H.L.Cas. 194). See especially what Lord Chelmsford said with the entire agreement of Lord Brougham and what Lord Cranworth said.

What an irony is here! This "fundamental principle" which was invoked 100 years ago for the purpose of holding that the agents of the carrier were "not liable at all" is now invoked for the purpose of holding that they are inescapably liable, without the benefit of any of the conditions of carriage. How has this come about?

The reason is because in the nineteenth century negligence was not an independent tort. If you wished to sue a man for negligence, you had to show some special circumstances which put him under a duty of care towards you. You might do it by reason of a contract, by a bailment, by his inviting you on to his premises on business, by his leaving about a thing which was dangerous in itself, and in other ways. But apart from some such special circumstances, there was no general duty to use care. . . . Suppose in those days that you tried to show that the defendant was under a duty of care, then if you could only show it by reason of contract, your remedy lay only in contract and not in tort. But if you could show it, not only by reason of contract, but also for some other reason, as for instance by reason of his inviting you to his premises, you could sue either in contract or in tort. It was by a development of this principle that, in the "through transit" cases, the courts eventually found a way of making the second carrier liable. It was held that if, on through transit, the second carrier accepted a person as a passenger, the second carrier was under a duty, irrespective of contract, to carry him with reasonable care. . . . Likewise, if a second carrier accepted goods for carriage, so that they were lawfully on his premises, he was under a duty to the owner to use reasonable care, although there was no contract between them. . . . But when the courts found this way of making the second carrier liable, they did not thereby open a way by which the injured person could escape the conditions of carriage. If he had agreed that the carriage was to be "at owner's risk" for the whole journey, he was held to his agreement, even when he sued the second carrier in tort . . . the only acceptable explanation of the "through transit" cases, to my mind, is that the second carrier falls within Scrutton L.J.'s proposition, being an "agent," that is, a sub-contractor employed to carry out the contract to the first carrier, and so entitled to the benefit of the conditions.

This brings me to the *Elder, Dempster* case itself. . . . It is said that the decision is anomalous and contrary to principle, but that is only because you are looking at it through the spectacles of 1961 and not those of 1924. Since the decision of *Donoghue v. Stevenson* ([1932] A.C. 562) in 1932 we have had negligence established as an independent tort in itself. Small wonder, then, that nowadays it is said that the tortfeasor cannot rely for his protection on provisions in a contract to which he was not a party. But the very point in the *Elder, Dempster* case was that the negligence there was not an independent tort in itself. It was negligence in the very course of performing the contract—done, it is true, by the sub-contractor and not by the principal—but if you permit the owner of the goods to sue the sub-contractor in tort for what is in truth a breach of the contract of carriage, then at least you should give him the protection of the contract. Were it otherwise there would be an easy way round the conditions of the contract of carriage. That is how the judges in the *Elder, Dempster* case looked at it and I am not prepared to say they were wrong. I am sure that the profession looked at it, too, at that time in the same way. If the draftsmen of the Hague Rules had thought in those days that the goods owner could get round the exceptions by suing the stevedores or the master in tort, they would surely have inserted provisions in those Rules to protect them. They did not do so because they did not envisage their being made liable at all.

But if you look at the *Elder, Dempster* case with the spectacles of 1961, then there is a way in which it can be supported. It is this: Even though negligence is an independent tort, nevertheless it is an accepted principle of the law of tort that no man can complain of an injury if he has voluntarily consented to take the risk of it on himself. This consent need not be embodied in a contract. Nor does it need consideration to support it. Suffice it that he consented to take the risk of injury on himself. So in the case of through transit, when the shipper of goods consigns them "at owner's risk" for the whole journey, his consent to take the risk avails the second carrier as well as the first, even though there is no contract between the goods owner and the second carrier. Likewise in the *Elder, Dempster* case the shipper, by exempting the charterers from bad stowage, may be taken to have consented to exempt the shipowners also. But I am afraid that this reasoning would not avail the stevedores in the present case: for the simple reason that the bill of lading is not expressed so as to protect the stevedores but only the "carrier." The shipper has therefore not consented to take on himself the risk of the negligence of the stevedores and is not to be defeated on that ground. But if the bill of lading were expressed in terms by which the owner of the goods consented to take on himself the risk of loss in excess of $500, whether due to the negligence of the carrier or the stevedores, I know of no good reason why his consent, if freely given, should not be binding on him. . . .

I suppose, however, that I must be wrong about all this: because your Lordships, I believe, take a different view. But it means that I must go on to consider the second question, namely, whether the stevedores can avail themselves of the protection clause in their own "stevedoring contract." Here your Lordships are untrammelled by authority. The cases in the High Court of Australia and in the United States Supreme Court do not touch the point. The stevedores in those two cases, for aught that appears, had agreed to do their work on a "bald" stevedoring contract "with unrestricted liability": where as here they stipulated that they should "have such protection as is afforded by the terms, conditions and exceptions of the bill of lading."

It is said here again that the owners of the goods cannot be affected by the "stevedoring contract" to which they were not parties: but it seems to me that we are now in a different branch of the law. When considering the contract between the carrier and the stevedores, it is important to remember that the carrier of goods, like a hirer, is a bailee: and the law of bailment is governed by somewhat different principles from those of contract or of tort: for "bailment," as Sir Percy Winfield said, "is more fittingly regarded as a distinct branch of the Law of Property, under the title Possession than as appropriate to either the law of contract or the law of tort," see *The Province of the Law of Tort*, p. 100. One special feature of the law of bailment is that the bailee can make a contract in regard to the goods which will bind the owner, although the owner is no party to the contract and cannot sue or be sued upon it. . . .

Applying this principle, the question is: Did the owners of the goods impliedly authorise the carrier to employ the stevedores on the terms that their liability should be limited to $500? I think they did. Put in simple language, the shipper said to the carrier: "Please carry these goods to London and deliver them to the consignee. You may take it that they are not worth more than $500 so your liability is limited to $500. If they were worth more, we would declare it to you." The carrier carries them to London and says to the stevedores: "Please deliver these goods to the consignee. They have not been declared as being in excess of $500, so you need not insure them for more. You are to have the same protection as I have, namely, your liability is limited to $500." It is quite plain that the consignee cannot sue the carrier for more than $500, and the carrier cannot sue the stevedores for more than $500. But can the consignee turn round and say to the stevedores: "Although the goods were not declared as being worth more than $500, yet they were worth in fact $1,500 and I can make you liable for it"? I do not think our law permits him to do this. The carrier simply passed on the self-same limitation as he himself had, and this must have been within his implied authority. It seems to me that when the owner of goods allows the person in possession of them to make a contract in regard to them, then he cannot go back on the terms of the contract, if they are such as he expressly or impliedly authorised, that is to say, consented to be made, even though he was no party to the contract and could not sue or be sued upon it. It is just the same as if he stood by and watched it being made. And his successor in title is in no better position.

I would allow the appeal.

LORD MORRIS made a speech dismissing the appeal.

NEW ZEALAND SHIPPING COMPANY LTD v. A. M. SATTERTHWAITE & CO. LTD

THE EURYMEDON

Privy Council [1975] A.C. 154; [1974] 2 W.L.R. 865; [1974] 1 All E.R. 1015

The question was whether the stevedore could obtain the benefit of a provision discharging the carrier from all liability unless action was brought within one year after delivery of the goods. The bill of lading between the consignors and the carrier contained the following provision: "It is hereby expressly agreed that no servant or agent of the Carrier (including every independent contractor from time to time employed by the Carrier) shall in any circumstances whatsoever be under any liability whatsoever to the Shipper, Consignee or Owner . . . and . . . every exemption, limitation, condition and liberty herein contained . . . shall also be available and shall extend to protect every such servant or agent of the Carrier . . . and for the purpose of all the foregoing provisions of this clause the Carrier is or shall be deemed to be acting as agent or trustee on behalf of and for the benefit of all persons who are or might be his agents from time to time (including independent contractors as aforesaid) . . ."

Reversing the New Zealand Court of Appeal and restoring the judgment of Beattie J., the Privy Council (Viscount Dilhorne and Lord Simon of Glaisdale dissenting) held that it could. LORD WILBERFORCE, delivering the majority opinion, said that the question was whether the contract satisfied the four propositions which Lord Reid declared to be necessary to argue that the carriers acted as agents for the stevedore (above, p. 285).

His Lordship continued: It was on this point that the Court of Appeal differed from Beattie J., holding that it had not been shown that any consideration for the shippers' promise as to exemption moved from the promisee, that is, the stevedore.

If the choice, and the antithesis, is between a gratuitous promise and a promise for consideration, as it must be, in the absence of a *tertium quid*, there can be little doubt which, in commercial reality, this is. The whole contract is of a commercial character, involving service on one side, rates of payment on the other, and qualifying stipulations as to both. The relations of all parties to each other are commercial relations entered into for business reasons of ultimate profit. To describe one set of promises, in this context, as gratuitous, or *nudum pactum*, seems paradoxical and is prima facie implausible. It is only the precise analysis of this complex of relations into the classical offer and acceptance, with identifiable consideration, that seems to present difficulty, but this same difficulty exists in many situations of daily life, for example, sales at auction; supermarket purchases; boarding an omnibus; purchasing a train ticket; tenders for the supply of goods; offers of reward; acceptance by post; warranties of authority by agents; manufacturers' guarantees; gratuitous bailments; bankers' commercial credits. These are all examples which show that English law, having committed itself to a rather technical and schematic doctrine of contract, in application takes a practical approach, often at the cost of forcing the facts to fit uneasily into the marked slots of offer, acceptance and consideration.

In their Lordships' opinion the present contract presents much less difficulty than many of those above referred to. It is one of carriage from Liverpool to Wellington. The carrier assumes an obligation to transport the goods and to discharge at the port of arrival. The goods are to be carried and discharged, so the transaction is inherently contractual. It is contemplated that a part of this contract, *viz.*, discharge, may be performed by independent contractors—*viz.*, the stevedore. By clause 1 of the bill of lading the shipper agrees to exempt from liability the carrier, his servants and independent contractors in respect of the performance of this contract of carriage. Thus, if the carriage, including the discharge, is wholly carried out by the carrier, he is exempt. If part is carried out by him, and part by his servants, he and they are exempt. If part is carried out by him and part by an independent contractor, he and the independent contractor are exempt. The exemption is designed to cover the whole carriage from loading to discharge, by whomsoever it is performed: the performance attracts the exemption or immunity in favour of whoever the performer turns out to be. There is possible more than one way of analysing this business transaction into the necessary components; that which their Lordships would accept is to say that the bill of lading brought into existence a bargain initially unilateral but capable of becoming mutual, between the shippers and the stevedore, made through the carrier as agent. This became a full contract when the stevedore performed services by discharging the goods. The performance of these services for the benefit of the shipper was the consideration for the agreement by the shipper that the stevedore should have the benefit of the exemptions and limitations contained in the bill of lading. The conception of a "unilateral" contract of this kind was recognised in *Great Northern Railway Co. v. Witham* (above, p. 11) and is well established. This way of regarding the matter is very close to, if not identical to, that accepted by Beattie J. in the Supreme Court; he analysed the transaction as one of an offer open to acceptance by action such as was found in *Carlill v. Carbolic Smoke Ball Co.* (above, p. 31). But whether one describes the shipper's promise to exempt as an offer to be accepted by performance or as a promise in exchange for an act seems in the present context to be a matter of semantics. The words of Bowen L.J. in *Carlill v. Carbolic Smoke Ball Co.*," . . . why should not an offer be made to all the world which is to ripen into a contract with anybody who comes forward and performs the condition?" seem to bridge both conceptions: he certainly seems to draw no distinction between an offer which matures into a contract when accepted and a promise which matures into a contract after performance, and, though in some special contexts (such as in connection with the right to withdraw) some further refinement may be needed, either analysis may be equally valid. On the main point in the appeal, their Lordships are in substantial agreement with Beattie J.

The following other points require mention:

1. In their Lordships' opinion, consideration may quite well be provided by the stevedore, as suggested, even though (or if) it was already under an obligation to discharge to the carrier. (There is no direct evidence of the existence or nature of this obligation, but their Lordships are prepared to assume it.) An agreement to do an act which the promisor is under an existing obligation to a third party to do, may quite well amount to valid consideration and does so in the present case: the promisee obtains the benefit of a direct obligation which he can enforce. This proposition is illustrated and supported by *Scotson v. Pegg* (above, p. 229) which their Lordships consider to be good law.

2. The consignee is entitled to the benefit of, and is bound by, the stipulations in the bill of lading by his acceptance of it and request for delivery of the goods thereunder. This is shown by *Brandt v. Liverpool, Brazil and River Plate Steam Navigation Co. Ltd* ([1924] 1 K.B. 575, C.A.) and a line of earlier cases. The Bills of Lading Act, 1855, s.1 (in New Zealand the Mercantile Law Act, 1908, s.13) gives a partial statutory recognition to this rule, but, where the statute does not apply, as it may well not do in this case, the previously established law remains effective.

3. The stevedore submitted, in the alternative, an argument that, quite apart from contract, exemptions from, or limitation of, liability in tort may be conferred by mere consent on the part of the party who may be injured. As their Lordships consider that the stevedore ought to succeed in contract, they prefer to express no opinion on this argument: to evaluate it requires elaborate discussion.

4. A clause very similar to the present was given effect by a United States District Court in *Carle and Montanari Inc. v. American Export Isbrandtsen Lines Inc.* ([1968] 1 Lloyd's Rep. 260). The carrier in that case contracted, in an exemption clause, as agent for, *inter alias*, all stevedores and other independent contractors and although it is no doubt true that the law in the United States is more liberal than ours as regards third party contracts, their Lordships see no reason why the law of the Commonwealth should be more restrictive and technical as regards agency contracts. Commercial consideration should have the same force on both sides of the Pacific.

In the opinion of their Lordships, to give the stevedore the benefit of the exemptions and limitations contained in the bill of lading is to give effect to the clear intentions of a commercial document and can be given within existing principles. They see no reason to strain the law or the facts in order to defeat these intentions. It should not be overlooked that the effect of denying validity to the clause would be to encourage actions against servants, agents and independent contractors in order to get round exemptions (which are almost invariable and often compulsory) accepted by shippers against carriers, the existence, and presumed efficacy, of which is reflected in the rates of freight. They see no attraction in this consequence.

VISCOUNT DILHORNE (dissenting): The clause does not in my opinion either expressly or impliedly contain an offer by the shippers to the carriers to enter into an agreement whereby if the appellants performed services in relation to the goods the shippers would give them the benefit of every exemption from, and limitation of, liability contained in the bill of lading. I see no difficulty in expressing such an offer in clear and unequivocal language, and if the clause contained such an offer, I would have been in favour of allowing the appeal.

What the clause records is not an offer but an agreement, and one agreement only, made between the shippers and the carriers acting in a dual capacity, on their own behalf and on behalf of all persons who were or might be their servants or employed by them as independent contractors, and an agreement to which all such persons are or are to be deemed to be parties.

I agree with Turner P. in thinking that the terms of clause 1 cannot be read as constituting such an offer. If the terms of the expressed agreement fail to constitute a legally binding contract between the shippers and the appellants, to read them as merely constituting an offer by the shippers capable of acceptance by conduct by the appellants is to rewrite the clause.

LORD SIMON OF GLAISDALE (dissenting): The difference between the two ways of putting the case can be illustrated by two simple types of unilateral contract. In the first, A says to B, "If you will dig over my kitchen garden next Tuesday I will give you £2." B replies, "Agreed! If I dig over your kitchen garden next Tuesday I will get £2 from you." Though there has been what the stevedore's second proposition calls "a bargain," neither party is contractually bound at this stage, and A can, at any reasonable period before the time for performance, communicate the withdrawal of his offer without incurring liability. But, if the offer is not so withdrawn, and if B on Tuesday does dig over A's kitchen garden (the mode of performance being clearly indicated), the contract is complete and A is bound to pay B £2. The acceptance is verbal, and performance furnishes the consideration moving from B. In the second type, A may say to B, "If you dig over my kitchen garden next Tuesday, I will pay you £2." B does not verbally communicate his acceptance of the offer, A having impliedly waived such requirement. But if A does not communicate any withdrawal of his offer, and if B on Tuesday does dig over A's kitchen garden, the offer is accepted by the stipulated mode of performance, which also provides the considera- tion: A is bound to pay B £2. This latter type of unilateral contract—the *Carlill* type contract—is that propounded in the stevedore's third proposi- tion; the former type of unilateral contract in the stevedore's second proposition. As counsel for the stevedore rightly submitted, they are mutually exclusive. Nevertheless, both require an offer, and one stipulating a mode of performance. Here, for the reasons given in the Court of Appeal and heretofore, there was no offer, and no sufficient stipulation of a mode of performance which would constitute acceptance. Counsel for the ste- vedore relied for his second proposition on *Great Northern Railway Co. v. Witham*, above p. 11, a well-known case the soundness of which has never been doubted. But it is far removed from the instant.

Note

In *Port Jackson Stevedoring Pty Ltd v. Salmond & Spraggon Pty (Australia) Ltd* [1980] 1 W.L.R. 138, [1980] 3 All E.R. 257, P.C. the Board said, obiter, that *Satterthwaite* was not only a decision in principle that the *Himalaya* clause (below, p. 300, *Note*) is capable of conferring on a third person falling within the description, "servant or agent of the Carrier (including every independent contractor from time to time employed by the Carrier)", defences and immu- nities conferred by the bill of lading, but also that stevedores employed by the carrier may and normally will come within that protection. It involved no new principle. Its importance, quoting an Australian court, lay in "the manner in which on the bare facts of the case their Lordships were able to discern a contract between the shipper and the stevedore". Agreed, but did their Lordships discern a contract which was not really there? See Viscount Dilhorne's and Lord Simon's dissent, *supra*.

MORRIS v. C.W. MARTIN & SONS LTD

Court of Appeal [1966] 1 Q.B. 716; [1965] 3 W.L.R. 276; [1965] 2 All E.R. 725

The plaintiff sent a mink stole to Beder, a furrier, to be cleaned. With the plaintiff's consent Beder sent the fur to the defendants, well-known and reputable cleaners. Beder made the contract with the defendants as principal and not as agent for the plaintiff. It contained exempting clauses. The defendants' servant, whose duty it was to clean the fur, stole it from their premises. It was never recovered. The plaintiff failed in the county court on the ground that the servant's act was not done in the course of his employment. The Court of Appeal held, following *Lloyd v. Grace, Smith & Co.* [1912] A.C. 716 and overruling *Cheshire v. Bailey* [1905] 1 K.B. 237, that the servant's act was done in the course of his employment. LORD DENNING M.R., having so held, went on:

Now comes the question: Can the defendants rely, as against the plaintiff, on the exempting conditions although there was no contract directly between them and her? There is much to be said on each side. On the one hand, it is hard on the plaintiff if her just claim is defeated by exempting conditions of which she knew nothing and to which she was not a party. On the other hand, it is hard on the defendants if they are held liable to a greater responsibility than they agreed to undertake. As long ago as 1601 Lord Coke advised a bailee to stipulate specially that he would not be responsible for theft, see *Southcote's Case* (1601) 4 Co. Rep. 83b, a case of theft by a servant. It would be strange if his stipulation was of no avail to him. The answer to the problem lies, I think, in this: the owner is bound by the conditions if he has expressly or impliedly consented to the bailee making a sub-bailment containing those conditions, but not otherwise. Suppose the owner of a car lets it out on hire, and the hirer sends it for repair, and the repairer holds it for a lien. The owner is bound by the lien because he impliedly consented to the repairs being done, since they were reasonably incidental to use of the car: see *Tappenden v. Argus* [1964] 2 Q.B. 185. So also if the owner of a ship accepts goods for carriage on a bill of lading containing exempting conditions (that is, a "bailment upon terms") the owner of the goods (although not a party to the contract) is bound by those conditions if he impliedly consented to them as being in "the known and contemplated form": see the words of Lord Sumner in *Elder, Dempster & Co. v. Paterson, Zochonis & Co. Ltd* [1924] A.C. 522 which were regarded by Dixon C.J. and Fullagar J. as stating the *ratio decidendi*: see *Wilson v. Darling Island Stevedoring & Lighterage Co. Ltd* (1956) 95 C.L.R. 43; [1956] 1 Lloyds' Rep. 346 with whose judgment Viscount Simonds entirely agreed in *Scruttons Ltd v. Midland Silicones Ltd* [1962] A.C. 446, 472, and also the cases to which I referred in that case [1962] A.C. 446, 489, 491.

In this case the plaintiff agreed that Beder should send the fur to the defendants, and by so doing I think she impliedly consented to his making a contract for cleaning on the terms usually current in the trade. But when I come to study the conditions I do not think they are sufficient to protect the cleaners. We also construe such conditions strictly. Clause 9 applies only to "goods belonging to customers," that is, goods belonging to Beder, and not to goods belonging to his customers such as the plaintiff. The conditions themselves draw a distinction between "customer" and "his own customer": see clause 16. Clause 14 only applied to "the loss of or damage to the goods during processing." The loss here was not during processing. It was before or after processing.

DIPLOCK AND SALMON L.JJ. agreed that the exemption clauses were inapplicable to the facts of the present case and reserved the question whether they would have protected the defendants had they been applicable; but Salmon L.J. said that he was "strongly attracted" by the view of the Master of the Rolls.

Appeal allowed.

Note

In *Harris Ltd v. Continental Express Ltd and Another* [1961] 1 Lloyds' Rep. 251 (Paull J.) the plaintiffs entered into a contract with forwarding agents, X, for the dispatch of the plaintiffs' goods by X's postal service. X had a contract with the second defendants, Y, under which Y lent vans to X for use in X's business and supplied drivers. It was provided that Y should not be responsible for goods carried and that X should indemnify them in all claims relating thereto. The plaintiffs' goods were collected in a van bearing X's name and coloured in the manner of X's own vans, but in fact owned by Y and driven by Y's servant. Owing to the negligence of Y's servant, the goods were stolen.

The plaintiffs' action against X failed because of a clause in the contract between the plaintiffs and X providing that X should not be liable in any circumstances whatsoever for any theft of the goods. The plaintiffs' action in negligence against Y succeeded. The contract between X and Y could not in any way affect the plaintiffs. But, in third-party proceedings brought by Y against X, Y was entitled to an indemnity from X under the terms of the contract between them. Thus X had to pay in the end.

It will be noted that the plaintiffs thought that they were dealing with X throughout. If this had been the case, of course they would have failed. It was purely fortuitous, so far as they were concerned, that X had employed a sub-contractor; and thus purely fortuitous that they were able to recover damages which, in the end, were paid by X. But why should not the *Elder Dempster* case (above, p. 284, footnote) have applied? See also *Johnson Matthey & Co. Ltd v. Constantine Terminals Ltd* [1976] 2 Lloyd's Rep. 215 and Beatson, 1977, Can. Bar Rev. 746.

THE PIONEER CONTAINER KH ENTERPRISE v. PIONEER CONTAINER

Privy Council [1994] 2 All E. R. 250

The plaintiffs (A) contracted with carriers (B) for the carriage of B's goods from Taiwan to Hong Kong by bills of lading which provided that B was entitled to sub-contract "on any terms" the whole or any part of the carriage. B sub-contracted the carriage to the defendants (C) on bills of lading which provided that the contract was governed by Chinese law and any dispute was to be determined in Taiwan ("the exclusive jurisdiction clause"). The ship sank and the question was whether A could sue C in Hong Kong. It was accepted that there was no contract between A and C. The Hong Kong Court of Appeal held that A was bound by the exclusive jurisdiction clause. The Privy Council, applying the principle stated by Lord Denning in *Morris v. Martin*, dismissed A's appeal. C became a bailee of the goods for reward and both A and B had concurrently the rights of a bailor against C. The obligation owed by C to A (as well as to B) was that of a bailee for reward, (A bailee for reward owes a higher obligation than a gratuitous bailee) although the reward was payable not by A but by B. It would be inconsistent to impose on the bailee two different standards of care in respect of the goods entrusted to him.

LORD GOFF (259): In *Morris v C W Martin & Son*, [1966] 1 Q.B. 716 at 729 Lord Denning M.R. expressed his opinion on this point in clear terms, though on the facts of the case his opinion was obiter. He said:

"The answer to the problem lies, I think, in this: the owner is bound by the conditions if he has expressly or impliedly consented to the bailee making a sub-bailment containing those conditions, but not otherwise."

... In order to decide whether ... to accept the principle so stated by Lord Denning M.R., it is necessary to consider the relevance of the concept of "consent" in this context. It must be assumed that, on the facts of the case, no direct contractual relationship has been created between the owner and the sub-bailee, the only contract created by the sub-bailment being that between the bailee and the sub-bailee. Even so, if the effect of the sub-bailment is that the sub-bailee voluntarily receives into his custody the goods of the owner and so assumes towards the owner the responsibility of a bailee, then to the extent that the terms of the sub-bailment are consented to by the owner, it can properly be said that the owner has authorised the bailee so to regulate the duties of the sub-bailee in respect of the goods entrusted to him, not only towards the bailee but also towards the owner. . . .

Such a conclusion, finding its origin in the law of bailment rather than the law of contract, does not depend for its efficacy either on the doctrine of privity of contract or on the doctrine of consideration. That this may be so appears from the decision of the House of Lords in *Elder Dempster & Co Ltd v. Paterson Zochonis & Co Ltd* [above, p. 284, footnote]. In that case, shippers of cargo on a chartered ship brought an action against the shipowners for damage caused to the cargo by bad stowage, for which the shipowners were responsible. It is crucial to observe that the cargo was shipped under charterers' bills of lading, so that the contract of carriage contained in or evidenced by the bills of lading was between the shippers and the charterers. The shipowners nevertheless sought to rely, as against the shippers, upon an exception in the bill of lading which protected the charterers from liability for damage due to bad stowage. It was held that the shipowners were entitled to do so, the preferred reason upon which the House so held . . . being found in the speech of Lord Sumner where he said ([1924] AC 522 at 564 . . .):

> ". . . in the circumstances of this case the obligations to be inferred from the reception of the cargo for carriage to the United Kingdom amount to a bailment upon terms, which include the exceptions and limitations of liability stipulated in the known and contemplated form of bill of lading."

Of course, there was in that case a bailment by the shippers direct to the shipowners, so that it was not necessary to have recourse to the concept of sub-bailment. Even so, notwithstanding the absence of any contract between the shippers and the shipowners, the shipowners' obligations as bailees were effectively subject to the terms upon which the shipowners implicitly received the goods into their possession. Their Lordships do not imagine that a different conclusion would have been reached in the *Elder Dempster* case if the shippers had delivered the goods, not directly to the ship, but into the possession of agents of the charterers who had, in their turn, loaded the goods on board; because in such circumstances, by parity of reasoning, the shippers may be held to have impliedly consented that the sub-bailment to the shipowners should be on terms which included the exemption from liability for bad stowage.

. . . once it is recognised that the sub-bailee, by voluntarily taking the owner's goods into his custody, ipso facto becomes the bailee of those goods vis-à-vis the owner, it must follow that the owner's rights against the sub-bailee will only be subject to terms of the sub-bailment if he has consented to them, *i.e.* if he has authorised the bailee to entrust the goods to the sub-bailee on those terms. Such consent may, as Lord Denning M.R. pointed out, be express or implied; and in this context the sub-bailee may also be able to invoke, where appropriate, the principle of ostensible authority. . . .

Their Lordships wish to add that this conclusion . . . produces a result which in their opinion is both principled and just. They incline to the opinion that a sub-bailee can only be said for these purposes to have voluntarily taken into his possession the goods of another if he has sufficient notice that a person other than the bailee is interested in the goods so that it can properly be said that (in addition to his duties to the bailee) he has, by taking the goods into his custody, assumed towards that other person the responsibility for the goods which is characteristic of a bailee. This they believe to be the underlying principle. Moreover, their Lordships do not consider this principle to impose obligations on the sub-bailee which are onerous or unfair, once it is recognised that he can invoke against the owner terms of the sub-bailment which the owner has actually (expressly or impliedly) or even ostensibly authorised. In the last resort the sub-bailee may, if necessary and appropriate, be able to invoke against the bailee the principle of warranty of authority.

Questions
   1. Does the failure of the majority in *Scruttons Ltd* to consider the law of bailment mean that that case was decided *per incuriam*?
   2. Has the *Elder Dempster* case, written off by Lord Reid as "an anomalous and unexplained exception," now been rehabilitated as an authority on general principle?

NORWICH CITY COUNCIL v. HARVEY AND OTHERS

Court of Appeal [1989] 1 W.L.R. 828; [1989] 1 All E.R. 1180

The plaintiffs employed contractors to extend a swimming pool. The contract provided (clause 20) that the risk of loss or damage by fire should be on the employer who was required to maintain adequate insurance. The contractor sub-contracted roofing work to the second defendant. The invitation to the sub-contractor to tender identified the main contract and expressly stated that clause 20 would apply. It stated: ". . . acceptance of this order binds the Sub-contractors . . . to the same terms and conditions as those of the Main contract."

The sub-contractor's employee, the first defendant, while using a blow torch set fire to the building. It was not disputed that, if the sub-contractors owed any duty to take care to avoid damage by fire to plaintiffs' property, they were in breach. Garland J. held that there was no privity of contract between the plaintiffs and the sub-contractors and that the main contractor was not acting as agent or trustee for the sub-contractors; but that the duty of care which the defendants would otherwise have owed had been so qualified by the terms of the contracts that it would not be just and reasonable to hold that the defendants owed any duty to the plaintiffs to avoid damage by fire. The plaintiffs appealed.

MAY L.J.: I trust I do no injustice to the plaintiffs' argument in this appeal if I put it shortly in this way. There is no dispute between the employer and the main contractor that the former accepted the risk of fire damage: see *James Archdale & Co. Ltd v. Comservices Ltd* [1954] 1 All E.R. 210, [1954] 1 W.L.R. 459 and *Scottish Special Housing Association v. Wimpey Construction UK Ltd* [1986] 2 All E.R. 957, [1986] 1 W.L.R. 995. However clause 20[C] does not give rise to any obligation on the employer to indemnify the sub-contractor. That clause is primarily concerned to see that the works were completed. It was intended to operate only for the mutual benefit of the employer and the main contractor. If the judge and the sub-contractors are right, the latter obtain protection which the rules of privity do not provide. Undoubtedly the sub-contractors owed duties of care in respect of damage by fire to other persons and in respect of other property (for instance the lawful visitor, employees of the employer or other buildings outside the site); in those circumstances it is impracticable juridically to draw a sensible line between the plaintiffs on the one hand and others on the other to whom a duty of care was owed. The employer had no effective control over the terms on which the relevant sub-contract was let and no direct contractual control over either the sub-contractors or any employee of theirs.

In addition, the plaintiffs pointed to the position of the first defendant, the sub-contractors' employee. *Ex hypothesi* he was careless and, even if his employers are held to have owed no duty to the building employers, on what grounds can it be said that the employee himself owed no such duty? In my opinion, however, this particular point does not take the matter very much further. If in principle the sub-contractors owed no specific duty to the building owners in respect of damage by fire, then neither in my opinion can any of their employees have done so.

In reply the defendants contend that the judge was right to hold that in all the circumstances there was no duty of care on the sub-contractors in this case. Alternatively they submit that the employers' insurers have no right of subrogation to entitle them to maintain this litigation against the sub-contractors. . . .

[His Lordship discussed the cases on duty of care in the law of tort.]

In the instant case it is clear that as between the employer and the main contractor the former accepted the risk of damage by fire to its premises arising out of and in the course of the building works. Further, although there was no privity between the employer and the sub-contractor, it is equally clear from the documents passing between the main contractors and the sub-contractors to which I have already referred that the sub-contractors contracted on a like basis. In *Scottish Special Housing Association v. Wimpey Construction UK Ltd* [1986] 2 All E.R. 957, [1986] 1 W.L.R. 995 the House of Lords had to consider whether, as between the employer and main contractors under a contract in precisely the same terms as those of the instant case, it was in truth intended that the employer should bear the whole risk of damage by fire, even fire caused by the contractor's negligence. The position of sub-contractors was not strictly in issue in the *Scottish Housing* case, which I cannot think the House did not appreciate, but having considered the terms of clauses 18, 19 and 20[C] of the same standard form as was used in the instant case Lord Keith, in a speech with which the remainder of their Lordships agreed, said ([1986] 2 All E.R. 957 at 959, [1986] 1 W.L.R. 995 at 999): "I have found it impossible to resist the conclusion that it is intended that the employer shall bear the whole risk of damage by fire, including fire caused by the negligence of the contractor or that of sub-contractors."

As Lord Keith went on to point out, a similar conclusion was arrived at by the Court of Appeal in England in *James Archdale & Co. Ltd v. Comservices Ltd* [1954] 1 All E.R. 210, [1954] 1 W.L.R. 459 on the construction of similarly but not identically worded corresponding clauses in a predecessor of the standard form used in the *Scottish Housing* and instant cases. Again the issue only arose in the earlier case as between employer and main contractor, but approaching the question on the basis of what is just and reasonable I do not think that the mere fact that there is no strict privity between the employer and the sub-contractor should prevent the latter from relying on the clear basis on which all the parties contracted in relation to damage to the employer's building caused by fire, even when due to the negligence of the contractors or sub-contractors.

Appeal dismissed

Questions

1. It does not appear whether the sub-contractors were insured against the loss. May they not reasonably have omitted to insure in reliance on clause 20? Should that be relevant? Would it have assisted the defence of the first defendant, their employee?

2. Assuming that the plaintiffs fulfilled their obligation to insure, the action was brought for the benefit, not of the Norwich City Council, but for that of the insurers. If the action had succeeded, future sub-contractors in the same situation would have been well advised to insure against the same risk. Is that a result which the law should strive to avoid?

3. Can the decision be reconciled with *Scruttons Ltd v. Midland Silicones* (above, p. 284), which was cited in argument but not mentioned by the court. Is it easier for the court to hold that a duty of care in tort is negatived than to hold that a limitation clause is effective?

4. What do you think of the proposition that the sub-contractors had no duty to take care not to burn down the building? Suppose that the plaintiffs had discovered that the sub-contractors were following a dangerous practice. Would they have had no remedy?

Note

In *Cosgrove v. Horsfall* (1945) 62 T.L.R. 140, C.A., a bus driver was held liable to a passenger travelling on a free pass containing a term that neither the company *nor its servants* would be liable to him for injury, however caused; the driver "was not a party to and has no right by virtue of the licence or contract." In *Adler v. Dickson* [1955] 1 Q.B. 158, C.A., the captain and boatswain of a P. & O. steamship, *Himalaya*, were held liable for their negligence in causing injury to a passenger, notwithstanding a clause in the ticket that the *company* should not be liable for any injury. Denning L.J. agreed in the result but, differing from his brethren, thought that the servants would have had a good defence if the clause had, in express terms, purported to cover them. (Such a clause is now commonly known as a "Himalaya clause"—see above, p. 294.) This view is inconsistent with the speeches of the majority in *Scruttons Ltd v. Midland Silicones Ltd* but in that case, too, it will be noted, the clause did not in express terms purport to cover the stevedores. (*Cf.* Furmston, "Return to *Dunlop v. Selfridge?*" (1960) 23 M.L.R. 373). And see *N.Z. Shipping Co. v. Satterthwaite* (above, p. 290) and *Port Jackson v. Salmond & Spraggon* (above p. 294).

In *Adler v. Dickson* both Denning and Morris L.JJ. said that an injured party could be deprived of his rights at common law only by a contract. This is a difficult proposition to sustain (and Lord Denning seems to have had second thoughts in *Scruttons Ltd v. Midland Silicones Ltd* above p. 284). Consider *Wilkie v. L.P.T.B.* [1947] 1 All E.R. 258. In *Ashdown v. Samuel Williams & Sons Ltd* [1957] 1 Q.B. 409, C.A., it was held that an occupier had excluded his liability for the negligence of his servants towards a licensee by giving proper notice to her of the terms on which she might cross his land. The rules about notice laid down in *Parker v. South Eastern Ry.* (above, p. 144) were held to be equally applicable to the case of a non-contractual licence. No question was raised in that case as to the possible liability of the occupier's servants for their negligence; and *Cosgrove v. Horsfall* clearly suggests that they would not be protected. See also *White v. Blackmore* [1972] 2 Q.B. 651; [1972] 3 W.L.R. 296, C.A.

Section 4. Enforcement of the Contract by a Contractor for the Benefit of a Non-Contractor

Even if, in the situations envisaged on p. 273, above, C is not able to enforce the contract himself, there remains the possibility that B may be able to sue A for the benefit of C. If the contract is a specifically enforceable one, B may be able to obtain a decree that A carry out the contract for the benefit of C. If the contract is not specifically enforceable, B will be able to recover damages from A if A fails, in breach of contract, to confer the promised benefit on C. Selfridge's refusal to pay £5 to Dunlop was clearly a breach of contract with Dew for which Dew could have recovered damages. The difficulty is that B (in that case, Dew) will usually have suffered no damage and so, prima facie, will be entitled only to nominal damages. See, however Lord Pearce in *Beswick v. Beswick*, below, p. 302. Where B has contracted as trustee for C the contractual right against A belongs in law to B but in equity to C and B can then recover the substantial damages which belong in equity to C and C himself may sue: below, p. 316.

BESWICK v. BESWICK

House of Lords [1968] A.C. 58; [1967] 2 All E.R. 1197; [1967] 3 W.L.R. 932

Peter Beswick was assisted in his business of coal merchant by his nephew, the defendant. In March 1962, when Peter was over seventy and in ill-health, he entered into an agreement with the defendant under which he assigned the business to the defendant in consideration of the defendant employing him as consultant for the remainder of his life at £6 10s. 0d a week and paying an annuity of £5 a week to his widow after his death, to be charged on the business. Peter died in November 1963. The defendant paid the widow the first £5 but thereafter refused to pay any more. The widow sued as administratix of her husband's estate and in her personal capacity for arrears of the annuity, for a declaration and for specific performance of the agreement. Burgess V.-C in the Chancery Court of the County Palatine of Lancaster dismissed the action: [1965] 3 All E.R. 858. The plaintiff appealed. The Court of Appeal (Denning M.R., Danckwerts and Salmon L.JJ.) allowed the appeal, declaring that the agreement to pay the annuity should be specifically enforced. The defendant appealed to the House of Lords. It was not argued in the House that the widow was entitled to enforce her claim at common law in her own name.

LORD REID [having stated the facts and the arguments of the appellant]: the respondent's first answer is that the common law has been radically altered by section 56(1) of the Law of Property Act 1925, and that that section entitles her to sue in her personal capacity and recover the benefit provided for her in the agreement although she was not a party to it.

[Having considered the background to section 56, particularly section 5 of the Real Property Act 1845 which it replaced, his Lordship proceeded:]

"A person may take an immediate or other interest in land or other property, or the benefit of any condition, right of entry, covenant or agreement over or respecting land or other property, although he may not be named as a party to the conveyance or other instrument. . . ."

If the matter stopped there it would not be difficult to hold that section 56 does not substantially extend or alter the provisions of section 5 of the Act of 1845. But more difficulty is introduced by the definition section of the Act of 1925 (section 205) which provides:

"(1) In this Act unless the context otherwise requires, the following expressions have the meanings hereby assigned to them respectively, that is to say: . . . (xx) "Property includes any thing in action, and any interest in real or personal property."

[His lordship discussed earlier authorities on s.56.]

I can now return to consider the meaning and scope of section 56. It refers to any "agreement over or respecting land or other property." If "land or other property" means the same thing as "tenements or hereditaments" in the Act of 1845 then this section simply continues the law as it was before the Act of 1925 was passed, for I do not think that the other differences in phraseology can be regarded as making any substantial change. So any obscurities in section 56 are obscurities which originated in 1845. . . .

Perhaps more important is the fact that the section does not say that a person may take the benefit of an agreement although he was not a party to it: it says that he may do so although he was not named as a party in the instrument which embodied the agreement . . . if the definition [of "property" in s.205(xx), above] is applied the result is to make section 56 go far beyond the pre-existing law. Holding that the section has such an effect would involve holding that the invariable practice of Parliament has been departed from *per incuriam*, so that something has got into this consolidation Act which neither the draftsman nor parliament can have intended to be there. I am reinforced in this view by two facts. The language of section 56 is not at all what one would have expected if the intention had been to bring in all that the application of the definition would bring in and, secondly, section 56 is one of twenty-five sections which appear in the Act under the cross-heading "Conveyances and other Instruments." The other twenty-four sections come appropriately under that heading and so does section 56 if it has a limited meaning: but, if its scope is extended by the definition of property, it would be quite inappropriately placed in this part of the Act. For these reasons I am of opinion that section 56 has no application to the present case.

The respondent's second argument is that she is entitled in her capacity of administratrix of her deceased husband's estate to enforce the provision of the agreement for the benefit of herself in her personal capacity, and that a proper way of enforcing that provision is to order specific performance. That would produce a just result, and, unless there is some technical objection, I am of opinion that specific performance ought to be ordered. . . . This appeal should be dismissed.

LORDS HODSON and GUEST delivered speeches holding that section 56 excludes the definition of "property" in section 205(1)(xx) and is confined to real property; but that the respondent was entitled to a decree of specific performance.

LORD PEARCE: My Lords, if the annuity had been payable to a third party in the lifetime of Beswick senior and there had been default, he could have sued in respect of the breach. His administratrix is now entitled to stand in his shoes and to sue in respect of the breach which has occurred since his death. It is argued that the estate can recover only nominal damages and that no other remedy is open, either to the estate or to the personal plaintiff. Such a result would be wholly repugnant to justice and common sense. And if the argument were right it would show a very serious defect in the law.

In the first place, I do not accept the view that damages must be nominal. Lush L.J. in *Lloyd's v. Harper* (below, p. 306) said:

"Then the next question which, no doubt, is a very important and substantial one, is, that Lloyd's, having sustained no damage themselves, could not recover for the losses sustained by third parties by reason of the default of Robert Henry Harper as an underwriter. That, to my mind, is a startling and alarming doctrine, and a novelty, because I consider it to be an established rule of law that where a contract is made with A for the benefit of B, A can sue on the contract for the benefit of B, and recover all that B could have recovered if the contract had been made with B himself."

(See also *Drimmie v Davies* [1899] 1 I.R. 176.) I agree with the comment of Windeyer J. in the case of *Coulls v. Bagot's Executor and Trustee Co., Ltd* (1967) 40 A.L.J.R. 471, 486, in the High Court of Australia that the words of Lush L.J. cannot be accepted without qualification and regardless of context and also with his statement:

"I can see no reason why in such cases the damages which A would suffer upon B's breach of his contract to pay C $500 would be merely nominal: I think that in accordance with the ordinary rules for the assessment of damages for breach of contract they could be substantial. They would not necessarily be $500; they could I think be less or more."

In the present case I think that the damages, if assessed, must be substantial. It is not necessary, however, to consider the amount of damages more closely since this is a case in which, as the Court of Appeal rightly decided, the more appropriate remedy is that of specific performance.

The administratrix is entitled, if she so prefers, to enforce the agreement rather than accept its repudiation, and specific performance is more convenient than an action for arrears of payment followed by separate actions as each sum falls due. Moreover, damages for breach would be a less appropriate remedy since the parties to the agreement were intending an annuity for a widow; and a lump sum of damages does not accord with this. And if (contrary to my view) the argument that a derisory sum of damages is all that can be obtained be right, the remedy of damages in this case is manifestly useless.

The present case presents all the features which led the equity courts to apply their remedy of specific performance. The contract was for the sale of a business. The defendant could on his part clearly have obtained specific performance of it if Beswick senior or his administratrix had defaulted. Mutuality is a ground in favour of specific performance.

Moreover, the defendant on his side has received the whole benefit of the contract and it is a matter of conscience for the court to see that he now performs his part of it. Kay J. said in *Hart v. Hart* (1881) 18 Ch.D. 670 at p. 685:

". . . when an agreement for valuable consideration . . . has been partially performed, the court ought to do its utmost to carry out that agreement by a decree for specific performance."

What, then, is the obstacle to granting specific performance? It is argued that since the widow personally had no rights which she personally could enforce the court will not make an order which will have the effect of enforcing those rights. I can find no principle to this effect. The condition as to payment of an annuity to the widow personally was valid. The estate (though not the widow personally) can enforce it. Why should the estate be barred from exercising its full contractual rights merely because in doing so it secures justice for the widow who, by a mechanical defect of our law, is unable to assert her own rights? Such a principle would be repugnant to justice and fulfil no other object than that of aiding the wrongdoer. I can find no ground on which such a principle should exist.

(Having discussed previous authorities, his Lordship continued):

Recently in *Coulls v. Bagot's Executor and Trustee Co., Ltd* the learned Chief Justice of Australia, Sir Garfield Barwick, in commenting on the report of the Court of Appeal's decision in the present case, said:

"I would myself, with great respect, agree with the conclusion that where A promises B for a consideration supplied by B to pay C that B may obtain specific performance of A's promise, at least where the nature of the consideration given would have allowed the debtor to have obtained specific performance. I can see no reason whatever why A in those circumstances should not be bound to perform his promise. That C provided no part of the consideration seems to me irrelevant."

It is argued that the court should be deterred from making the order because there will be technical difficulties in enforcing it. In my opinion, the court should not lightly be deterred by such a consideration from making an order which justice requires. But I do not find this difficulty.

R.S.C., Ord. 45, r. 9(1), provides under the heading "Execution by or against a person not being a party":

"Any person not being a party to a cause or matter, who obtains any order or in whose favour any order is made, shall be entitled to enforce obedience to the order by the same process as if he were a party."

This would appear by its wide terms to enable the widow for whose benefit the annuity is ordered to enforce its payment by the appointment of a receiver, by writ of fi. fa., or even by judgment summons. I see no reason to limit the apparent meaning of the words of the rule, which would appear to achieve a sensible purpose.

In my opinion, the plaintiff as administratrix is entitled to a decree of specific performance. [His Lordship went on to hold that section 56 had no relevance to the case. He was inclined to the view of the section expressed by Lord Upjohn.]

LORD UPJOHN [having held that the plaintiff was entitled to a decree of specific performance and having considered the history behind section 56]: Bearing in mind the wide import of the word "property" apart from any definition, I find it difficult in the context to limit that word to an interest in real property. Without expressing any concluded view, I think it may be that the true answer is that Parliament (as sometimes happens in consolidation statutes) inadvertently did alter the law in section 56 by abrogating the old common law rule in respect of contracts affecting personal property as well as real property. But it cannot have done more. Parliament *per incuriam* it may be, went back to the position under the Act of 1845 but I am convinced that it never intended to alter the fundamental rule laid down in *Tweddle v. Atkinson* (above, p. 275).

The real difficulty is as to the true scope and ambit of the section. My present views, though *obiter* and tentative, are these. Section 56, like its predecessors, was only intended to sweep away the old common law rule that in an indenture *inter partes* the covenantee must be named as a party to the indenture to take the benefit of an immediate grant or the benefit of a covenant; it intended no more. So that for the section to have any application it must be to relieve from the consequences of the common law, and in my opinion three conditions must be satisfied. If all of them are not satisfied then the section has no application and the parties are left to their remedies at common law.

First let me assume for a moment that the agreement in this case is an indenture *inter partes* under seal—does section 56 help B? Plainly not. C did not purport to covenant with or make any grant to B; he only covenanted with A. Had C purported to covenant with B to pay the annuity to B though B was not a party, then any difficulty B might have had in suing might be saved by section 56.

The narrow view which I take of section 56 is, I think, supported by the observations of Simonds J. (as he then was) in *White v. Bijou Mansions* [1937] Ch. 610 when he said:

"Just as under section 5 of the Act of 1845 only that person could call it in aid who, although not a party, was a grantee or covenantee, so under section 56 of this Act only that person can call it in aid, who, although not named as a party to the conveyance or other instrument, is yet a person to whom that conveyance or other instrument purports to grant some thing or with which some agreement or covenant is purported to be made."

See to the same effect Wynn–Parry J. in *in Re Miller's Agreement* [1947] Ch. 615. That was another example of the familiar case where, upon the dissolution of a partnership, the continuing partners covenanted with the retiring partner to pay as from his death annuities to his three daughters. the learned judge said:

"In my view the plaintiffs [the daughters] are not persons to whom the deed purports to grant something, or with whom some agreement or covenant is purported to be made. . . ."

So B does not satisfy this condition.

The second condition is that the reference to the "conveyance or other instrument" in the section is, in my opinion, limited to documents under seal. This does no violence to the definitions of "conveyance" or "instrument" in section 205 of the Law of Property Act.

The third condition is that, in my opinion, the section refers only to documents strictly *inter partes* (*Cooker v. Child* (1673) 2 Lev. 74).

The agreement satisfies none of these conditions.

Section 56 does not help the appellant, but, for reasons given earlier, I would dismiss this appeal.

Appeal dismissed.

Questions
1. Lord Pearce, above, p. 302 seems to have been alone in thinking that substantial damages might have been recoverable. In a simple contract by A with B to pay C £500, how would the damages be estimated? On the basis of B's loss of gratification at the benefit to C? How could that be evaluated? Or on the basis of the consideration supplied to A by B and now "wasted"? *Cf.* the cases on damages for wasted expenditure, below, p. 599.
2. If the deceased had appointed an executor who had declined to sue the nephew, would the widow have had any remedy?
3. Suppose the hypothetical executor had agreed to release the nephew from his obligation to pay the annuity, in consideration of the payment of £100, which he had then applied for the benefit of those entitled (not the widow) under the supposed will. Would the widow have had any redress? *Cf. Re Schebsman* (below, p. 318).
4. Suppose the hypothetical executor had wished to compel the nephew to carry out the contract, but the persons entitled to the estate had instructed him to seek to compromise as in question 4. What is the executor's duty?
5. Lord Upjohn said: "Let me assume (contrary to the fact) that B died with substantial assets but also many creditors. The legal position is that prima facie the duty of B [the administratrix] is to carry out her intestate's contracts and compel A [the nephew] to pay C [the widow]; but the creditors may be pressing and the agreement may be considered onerous;

so it may be her duty to try and compromise the agreement with A and save something for the estate even at the expense of C." [1967] 2 All E.R. 1220. In what sense is A under a legal duty to enforce the contract with C for the benefit of B? Was A, in his lifetime under such a duty?

6. Would section 56, in the opinion of any of the judges, have enabled the plaintiff in *Tweddle v. Atkinson* (above, p. 275) to succeed?

JACKSON v. HORIZON HOLIDAYS LTD

Court of Appeal [1975] 1 W.L.R. 1468; [1975] 3 All E.R. 92

The plaintiff entered into a contract for a holiday for himself, his wife and two children, in Ceylon. The price including air fares was £1,200. The holiday provided failed to comply with the description given by the defendants in important respects. The judge, following *Jarvis v. Swan's Tours Ltd* below, awarded £1,100 damages. He said that he could only consider the distress to the plaintiff, not that to the wife and children. The defendants appealed against the amount of the damages.

LORD DENNING M.R. dealing with a submission that the plaintiff was entitled to damages for his wife and children:

We have had an interesting discussion as to the legal position when one person makes a contract for the benefit of a party. In this case it was a husband making a contract for the benefit of himself, his wife and children. Other cases readily come to mind. A host makes a contract with a restaurant for a dinner for himself and his friends. The vicar makes a contract for a coach trip for the choir. In all these cases there is only one person who makes the contract. It is the husband, the host, or the vicar, as the case may be. Sometimes he pays the whole price himself. Occasionally he may get a contribution from the others. But in any case it is he who makes the contract. It would be a fiction to say that the contract was made by all the family, or all the guests, or all the choir, and that he was only an agent for them. Take this very case. It would be absurd to say that the twins of three years old were parties to the contract or that the father was making the contract on their behalf as if they were principals. It would equally be a mistake to say that in any of these instances there was a trust. The transaction bears no resemblance to a trust. There was no trust fund and no trust property. No, the real truth is that in each instance, the father, the host or the vicar, was making a contract himself for the benefit of the whole party. In short, a contract by one for the benefit of third persons.

What is the position when such a contract is broken? At present the law says that the only one who can sue is the one who made the contract. None of the rest of the party can sue, even though the contract was made for their benefit. But when that one does sue, what damages can he recover? Is he limited to his own loss? Or can he recover for the others? Suppose the holiday firm puts the family into a hotel which is only half built and the visitors have to sleep on the floor? Or suppose the restaurant is fully booked and the guests have to go away, hungry and angry, having spent so much on fares to get there? Or suppose the coach leaves the choir stranded half-way and they have to hire cars to get home? None of them individually can sue. Only the father, the host or the vicar can sue. He can, of course, recover his own damages. But can he not recover for the others? I think he can. The case comes within the principle stated by Lush L.J. in *Lloyd's v. Harper* (below, p. 316) ". . . I consider it to be an established rule of law that where a contract is made with A. for the benefit of B., A. can sue on the contract for the benefit of B. and recover all that B. could have recovered if the contract had been made with B. himself." It has been suggested that Lush L.J. was thinking of a contract in which A. was trustee for B. But I do not think so. He was a common lawyer speaking of the common law. His words were quoted with considerable approval by Lord Pearce in *Beswick* v. *Beswick*. I have myself often quoted them. I think they should be accepted as correct, at any rate so long as the law forbids the third persons themselves to sue for damages. It is the only way in which a just result can be achieved. Take the instance I have put. The guests ought to recover from the restaurant their wasted fares. The choir ought to recover the cost of hiring the taxis home. There is no one to recover for them except the one who made the contract for their benefit. He should be able to recover the expense to which they have been put, and pay it over to them. Once recovered, it will be money had and received to their use. (They might even, if desired, be joined as plaintiffs.) If he can recover for the expense, he should also be able to recover for the discomfort, vexation and upset which the whole party have suffered by reason of the breach of contract, recompensing them accordingly out of what he recovers.

Applying the principles to this case, I think that the figure of £1,100 was about right. It would, I think, have been excessive if it had been awarded only for the damage suffered by Mr Jackson himself. But when extended to his wife and children I do not think it is excessive. . . .

I would therefore dismiss this appeal.

ORR L.J. I agree.

JAMES L.J. delivered judgment dismissing the appeal.

Appeal dismissed.

Questions
George, the secretary of the University Law Society arranged the Society's annual dinner at the Majestic Hotel. All the diners suffered food poisoning but there was no negligence on the part of the Hotel. All the members of the Society paid for their meals but their guests, Box and Cox L.JJ., did not. What damages can be recovered and by whom?

Note
In *Woodar Investment Development Ltd v. Wimpey Construction U.K. Ltd* [1980] 1 W.L.R. 277; 1 All E.R. 571; *Jackson's* case was "explained" Lord Wilberforce said: The majority of the Court of Appeal followed, in the case of Goff L.J. with expressed reluctance, its previous decision in *Jackson v. Horizon Holidays Ltd*. I am not prepared to dissent from the actual decision in that case. It may be supported either as a broad decision on the measure of damages [*per* James L.J.) or possibly as an example of a type of contract—examples of which are persons contracting for family holidays, ordering meals in restaurants for a party, hiring a taxi for a group—calling for special treatment. As I suggested in *New Zealand Shipping Co. Ltd v. A.M. Satterthwaite & Co., Ltd* above, p. 290, there are many situations of daily life which do not fit neatly into conceptual analysis, but which require some flexibility in the law of contract. *Jackson's* case may well be one.

I cannot however agree with the basis on which Lord Denning M.R. put his decision in that case. The extract on which he relied from the judgment of Lush L.J. in *Lloyd's v. Harper* (1880) 16 Ch.D. 290, 321 was part of a passage in which the Lord Justice was stating as an "established rule of law" that an agent (sc. an insurance broker) may sue on a contract made by him on behalf of the principal (sc. the assured) if the contract gives him such a right, and is no authority for the proposition required in *Jackson's* case, still less for the proposition required here, that, if Woodar made a contract for a sum of money to be paid to Transworld,

Woodar can, without showing that it has itself suffered loss or that Woodar was agent or trustee for Transworld, sue for damages for non-payment of that sum. That would certainly not be an established rule of law, nor was it quoted as such authority by Lord Pearce in *Beswick v. Beswick*, above, p. 301.

Lord Russell of Killowen, while dissenting from the decision, said: I do not criticise the outcome of *Jackson*'s case: the plaintiff had bought and paid for a high class family holiday, he did not get it, and therefore was entitled to substantial damages for the failure to supply *him* with one. It is to be observed that the order of the Court of Appeal as drawn up did not suggest that any part of the damages awarded to him were "for the use and benefit of" any member of his family. It was a special case quite different from the instant case on the Transworld point.

I would not, my Lords, wish to leave the *Jackson* case without adverting with respectful disapproval to the reliance there placed by Lord Denning M.R.—not for the first time—on an extract taken from the judgment of Lush L.J. in *Lloyd's v. Harper*. That case was plainly a case in which a trustee or agent was enforcing the rights of a beneficiary or principal, there being therefore a fiduciary relationship. [His Lordship cited Lord Denning's discussion of *Lloyd's v. Harper*.]

I have already indicated that in all the other judgments the matter proceeded upon a fiduciary relationship between A and B: and Lush L.J. in the same passage makes it plain that he does also; for he says: "It is true that the person [B] who employed him [the broker A] has a right, if he pleases, to take action himself and sue upon the contract made by the broker for him, for he [B] *is a principal party to the contract*."

To ignore that passage is to divorce the passage quoted by Lord Denning from the fiduciary context in which it was uttered, the context of principal and agent, a field with which it may be assumed Lush L.J. was familiar. I venture to suggest that the brief quotation should not be used again as support for a proposition which Lush L.J. cannot have intended to advance.

[For other aspects of *Woodar* see below, p. 555. See also Rose, 1977, Can. Bar. Rev. 333.]

DARLINGTON BOROUGH COUNCIL v. WILTSHIER NORTHERN LTD and ANOTHER

Court of Appeal [1995] 1 W.L.R. 68; [1995] 3 All E. R. 895

W entered into contracts with MG, a finance company, to build, and built, a recreational centre for the Council on the Council's land. In accordance with an agreement with the Council, MG assigned to the Council all rights and causes of action against W arising out of the contracts with MG. The Council claimed that the building work was defective. As assignee of MG's rights, they would be able to recover only such damages as MG might have recovered. On a preliminary issue as to the Council's right of action, Judge Newey Q.C. held that MG, having no proprietary right in the Centre and not being liable for the cost of repairs, could have recovered only nominal damages. The Council appealed.

DILLON L.J. said that he would allow the appeal by the direct application of the rule in *Dunlop v. Lambert* (1839) 6 Cl. & F. 600, H.L. (discussed by Steyn L.J., below) as applied in a building contract context in Lord Browne-Wilkinson's speech in *Linden Gardens Trust Ltd v. Lenesta Sludge Disposals Ltd* [1994] A.C. 85 at 114–115; and added that if, before any assignment, MG had sued in its own name it would have recovered damages as constructive trustee for the Council, by analogy to *Lloyds v. Harper* (below, p. 306).

STEYN L.J.: The case for recognising a contract for the benefit of a third party is simple and straightforward. The autonomy of the will of the parties should be respected. The law of contract should give effect to the reasonable expectations of contracting parties. Principle certainly requires that a burden should not be imposed on a third party without his consent. But there is no doctrinal, logical or policy reason why the law should deny effectiveness to a contract for the benefit of a third party where that is the expressed intention of the parties. Moreover, often the parties, and particularly third parties, organise their affairs on the faith of the contract. They rely on the contract. It is therefore unjust to deny effectiveness to such a contract. I will not struggle further with the point since nobody seriously asserts the contrary; but see a valuable article by Jack Beatson, a law commissioner, now Rouse Ball Professor of English Law at Cambridge, "Reforming the Law of Contracts for the Benefit of Third Parties: a Second Bite at the Cherry" (1992) 45 C.L.P. 1.

The genesis of the privity rule is suspect. It is attributed to *Tweddle v. Atkinson* (above, p. 275). It is more realistic to say that the rule originated in the misunderstanding of *Tweddle v. Atkinson*: see Atiyah, *The Rise and Fall of Freedom of Contract* (1979), p. 414 and Simpson, *A History of the Law of Contract: the Rise of the Action of Assumpsit* (1975), p. 475. While the privity rule was barely tolerable in Victorian England, it has been recognised for half a century that it has no place in our more complex commercial world. Indeed, as early as 1915, in *Dunlop Pneumatic Tyre Co. Ltd v. Selfridge & Co. Ltd* [1915] A.C. 847, 855, when the House of Lords restated the privity rule, Lord Dunedin observed in a dissenting speech that the rule made

> "it possible for a person to snap his fingers at a bargain deliberately made, a bargain not in itself unfair, and which the person seeking to enforce it has a legitimate interest to enforce."

Among the majority, Viscount Haldane L.C. asserted as a self-evident truth, at p. 853, that "only a person who is a party to a contract can sue on it." Today the doctrinal objection to the recognition of a stipulatio alteri continues to hold sway. While the rigidity of the doctrine of consideration has been greatly reduced in modern times, the doctrine of privity of contract persists in all its artificial technicality.

In 1937 the Law Revision Committee in its Sixth Report (Cmd. 5449, para. 41–48) proposed the recognition of a right of a third party to enforce the contract which by its express terms purports to confer a benefit directly on him. In 1967, in *Beswick v. Beswick* (above, p. 301), Lord Reid observed that if there was a long period of delay in passing legislation on the point the House of Lords might have to deal with the matter. Twelve years later Lord Scarman, who as a former chairman of the Law Commission usually favoured legislative rather than judicial reform where radical change was involved, reminded the House that it might be necessary to review all the cases which "stand guard over this unjust rule:" *Woodar Investment Development Ltd v. Wimpey Construction U.K. Ltd* [1980] 1 W.L.R. 277, 300G. See also Lord Keith of Kinkel, at pp. 297H–298A. In 1981 Dillon J. described the rule as "a blot on our law and most unjust:" *Forster v. Silvermere Golf and Equestrian Centre* (1981) 125 S.J. 397. In 1983 Lord Diplock described the rule as "an anachronistic shortcoming that has for many years been regarded as a reproach to English private law:" *Swain v. The Law Society* [1983] 1 A.C. 598, 611D.

But as important as judicial condemnations of the privity rule is the fact that distinguished academic lawyers have found no redeeming virtues in it:

see, for example, Markesinis (1987) 103 L.Q.R. 354; Reynolds (1989) 105 L.Q.R. 1; Beatson (1992) 44 C.L.P. 1 and Adams and Brownsword (1993) 56 M.L.R. 722. And we do well to remember that the civil law legal systems of other members of the European Union recognise such contracts. That our legal system lacks such flexibility is a disadvantage in the single market. Indeed it is a historical curiosity that the legal system of a mercantile country such as England, which in other areas of the law of contract (such as, for example, the objective theory of the interpretation of contracts) takes great account of the interests of third parties, has not been able to rid itself of this unjust rule deriving from a technical conception of a contract as a purely bilateral vinculum juris.

In 1991 the Law Commission revisited this corner of the law. In cautious language appropriate to a consultation paper the Law Commission has expressed the provisional recommendation that "there should be a (statutory) reform of the law to allow third parties to enforce contractual provisions made in their favour:" Privity of Contract: Conflicts for the Benefit of Third Parties. Consultation Paper No. 121, p. 132. The principal value of the consultation paper lies in its clear analysis of the practical need for the recognition of a contract for the benefit of third parties, and the explanation of the unedifying spectacle of judges trying to invent exceptions to the rule to prevent demonstrable unfairness. No doubt there will be a report by the Law Commission in the not too distant future recommending the abolition of the privity of contract rule by statute. What will then happen in regard to the proposal for legislation? The answer is really quite simple: probably nothing will happen.

But on this occasion I can understand the inaction of Parliament. There is a respectable argument that it is the type of reform which is best achieved by the courts working out sensible solutions on a case by case basis, e.g., in regard to the exact point of time when the third party is vested with enforceable contractual rights: see Consultation Paper, No. 121, para. 5.8. But that requires the door to be opened by the House of Lords reviewing the major cases which are thought to have entrenched the rule of privity of contract. Unfortunately, there will be few opportunities for the House of Lords to do so. After all, by and large, courts of law in our system are the hostages of the arguments deployed by counsel. And Mr Furst for the council, the third party, made it clear to us that he will not directly challenge the privity rule if this matter should go to the House of Lords. He said that he is content to try to bring his case within exceptions to the privity rule or what Lord Diplock in *Swain v. The Law Society* [1983] 1 A.C. 598, 611D, described as "juristic subterfuges . . . to mitigate the effect of the lacuna resulting from the non-recognition of a jus quaesitum tertio . . ."

[His Lordship discussed the issues in the present case] That brings me to the speech of Lord Browne-Wilkinson in the *Linden Gardens* case [1994] A.C. 85. In his speech Lord Browne-Wilkinson rested his decision on the exception to the rule that a plaintiff can only recover damages for his own loss which was enunciated in *The Albazero* [1977] A.C. 774 in the context of carriage of goods by sea, bills of lading and bailment. The relevant passage from Lord Diplock's speech in *The Albazero* reads, at p. 847:

> "The only way in which I find it possible to rationalise the rule in *Dunlop v. Lambert* so that it may fit into the pattern of the English law

is to treat it as an application of the principle, accepted also in relation to policies of insurance upon goods, that in a commercial contract concerning goods where it is in the contemplation of the parties that the proprietary interests in the goods may be transferred from one owner to another after the contract has been entered into and before the breach which causes loss or damage to the goods, an original party to the contract, if such be the intention of them both, is to be treated in law as having entered into the contract for the benefit of all persons who have or may acquire an interest in the goods before they are lost or damaged, and is entitled to recover by way of damages for breach of contract the actual loss sustained by those for whose benefit the contract is entered into."

Clearly, this passage did not exactly fit the material facts in the *Linden Gardens* case. But Lord Browne-Wilkinson extracted the rationale of the decision and by analogy applied it to the purely contractual situation in *Linden Gardens*. He particularly justified this extension of the exception in *The Albazero* by invoking Lord Diplock's words in *The Albazero*:

"there may still be occasional cases in which the rule would provide a remedy where no other would be available to a person sustaining loss which under a rational legal system ought to be compensated by the person who has caused it."

Lord Browne-Wilkinson's conclusion was supported by all members of the House of Lords, although, it is right to say, Lord Griffiths wished to go further. Relying on the exception recognised in the *Linden Gardens* case, as well as on the need to avoid a demonstrable unfairness which no rational legal system should tolerate, I would rule that the present case is within the rationale of Lord Browne-Wilkinson's speech. I do not say that the relevant passages in his speech precisely fit the material facts of the present case. But it involves only a very conservative and limited extension to apply it by analogy to the present case. For these reasons I would hold that the present case is covered by an exception to the general rule that a plaintiff can only recover damages for his own loss.

WAITE L.J.: agreed with Dillon and Steyn L.JJ. that the appeal be allowed by the direct application of the rule in *Dunlop v. Lambert* and also on the constructive trust ground mentioned by Dillon L.J.

Appeal allowed.

The House of Lords gave leave to appeal.

Question

If the case for recognising a contract for the benefit of a third party is, as Steyn L.J. says, simple and straightforward, how can it be argued (as Steyn L.J. says it can) that reform is best achieved by the courts on a case by case basis?

GORE v. VAN DER LANN (LIVERPOOL CORPORATION INTERVENING)

Court of Appeal [1967] 2 Q.B. 31; [1967] 2 W.L.R. 358; [1967] 1 All E.R. 360

The plaintiff was injured while boarding a Liverpool corporation bus. It was presumably in the light of *Adler v. Dickson*, above, p. 300 and *Wilkie v. LPTB, infra,* that she sued only the conductor and not the corporation for negligence, counting on the fact that, if the conductor were held liable, the corporation would feel obliged, perhaps by trade union pressure, to pay the damages. Gore, a pensioner, held "a free pass" which she had obtained by signing an application form stating: "In consideration of my being granted a free pass . . . I agree that the use of such pass by me shall be subject to the conditions overleaf, which have been read to or by me prior to signing." Condition 4 provided that neither the corporation nor any of its servants or agents should be liable to her for loss of life or injury however caused.

The defendant, who entered the employment of the corporation after the pass had been issued, relied on Condition 4 and alleged that he had ratified the action of the corporation in obtaining the undertaking from the plaintiff. The corporation applied for an order under section 41 of the Judicature Act 1925 to stay the action on the ground that they were obliged to satisfy any judgment obtained against the defendant. The application was dismissed and the plaintiff appealed.

It was held by Willmer and Salmon L.JJ. that the pass constituted a contract and consequently the condition was void under section 151 of the Road Traffic Act 1960 (now replaced by section 29 of the Public Passenger Vehicles Act 1981) which invalidates a contract for the conveyance of a passenger in a public service vehicle in so far as it purports to negative or restrict the liability of a person in respect of death or bodily injury to the passenger. So the plaintiff could, after all, have sued the corporation directly, as being vicariously liable for the conductor's negligence. The court distinguished its earlier decision in *Wilkie v. London Passenger Transport Board* (1946) 62 T.L.R. 327 where a free pass issued by the Board was held to be only a licence, not a contract, so that the Road Traffic Act provision which was re-enacted in section 151 did not apply and the exclusionary condition was effective to protect the Board. The distinction taken was that Wilkie was an employee and the pass was issued as a matter of course as one of the privileges of his employment—there was, Willmer L.J. said, no contractual *animus* in that case, but there was in this.

WILLMER L.J.: That is sufficient to dispose of the appeal; but I think it right to add that, even if I had thought that the issue of the free pass amounted to no more than the grant of a licence subject to conditions, I should still have arrived at the same conclusion so far as this application is concerned. It is true that the conditions accepted by the plaintiff when she accepted the offer of a free pass included a provision that the employees of the corporation were not to be liable to her for any injury or loss; but I cannot construe this provision as a promise by the plaintiff not to institute proceedings against an employee. If the corporation desired such a promise from the holder of a free pass, it could have said so in clear and unambiguous terms. In my judgment the conditions are to be construed strictly against the corporation who put them forward. It is not enough to say that a promise not to sue the employee is to be implied. At the best for the corporation, the condition relied on is ambiguous, and any ambiguity must be resolved in favour of the plaintiff.

In these circumstances the corporation has not satisfied me that it has any justification for interfering with the plaintiff's prima facie right at common law to bring proceedings against the defendant whom she accuses of negligence. On this ground also I am of opinion that the judge came to the right conclusion, and that the appeal should be dismissed.

Since preparing this judgment I have had the advantage of reading the judgment of HARMAN L.J. I should desire to express my concurrence with his view that, since it has not been shown that there was any contract between the corporation and the defendant rendering the corporation liable in law to indemnify the defendant, there is no ground on which the corporation could be held to have an interest entitling it to relief under section 41 of the Act of 1925. On this ground, also, in addition to those which I have already set out, I am satisfied that the corporation's application was rightly dismissed.

HARMAN L.J., who said that he did not propose to offer an opinion on "the difficult question" whether the free pass constituted a contract or a licence: The question, therefore, is whether before the Supreme Court of Judicature Act 1873,[1] the corporation would have been entitled to apply to restrain the action. This would have been done by a bill in Chancery. The ground stated is that the prosecution of the action would be a fraud on the corporation, and the fraud alleged apparently is that, if the action succeeded and damages were obtained against the conductor, the corporation would in some way be liable to indemnify him. It is here in my judgment that the case breaks down, for I do not see how the corporation could be liable in law for what would said to be supported by a decision of DU PARCQ L.J. in *Cosgrove v. Horsfall* (above, p. 300), where the lord justice suggested that the corporation might in somewhat similar circumstances obtain redress under section 41; but as I read the judgment that is only suggested on the footing that the corporation could be shown to have been in danger of suffering damage by the supposed breach by the plaintiff of the condition attached to her free pass. DU PARCQ L.J., said this:

> "The London Passenger Transport Board may well be entitled to some redress against the plaintiff, though, before expressing a positive opinion on this matter, I should wish to know what claim they make and what answer to it the plaintiff may have. The board are not a party to these proceedings. They may be entitled to recover damages, and if they were shown to have suffered loss through the plaintiff's breach of the condition the circumstances might be such that the damages would be more than nominal. I will express no opinion on the question, which counsel for the defendant told us he had considered, whether the board could have applied successfully to stay the present action under section 41 of the Supreme Court of Judicature (Consolidation) Act, 1925 (see especially proviso (b)). We are not now concerned with the rights of the board, but it must not be assumed that if the plaintiff caused them to suffer loss by a breach of the condition, they were without remedy and are now necessarily without redress. I doubt, however, whether the board are in any way affected by what the plaintiff has chosen to do."

There is no suggestion in the instant case that there is any contract between the corporation and the defendant making the corporation liable for the torts of the latter, and in its absence I cannot see that the corporation is liable at law and, if not, I think that the corporation has no interest which would entitle it to relief under the section.

[1] Now replaced by the Supreme Court Act 1981, s.49(3) which provides:
    3. Nothing in this act shall affect the power of the Court of Appeal or the High Court to stay any proceedings before it, where it thinks fit to do so, either of its own motion or on the application of any person, whether or not a party to the proceedings.

SALMON L.J.: Even had there been no contract in the present case, I would have come to the clear conclusion that the corporation must fail. For the corporation to obtain the relief which it claims, it would be necessary for it to show (as HARMAN L.J. points out) that, before the Supreme Court of Judicature Act 1873, it would have been entitled to apply to the court in Chancery to restrain the plaintiff from bringing her action against the defendant. In order to succeed, the corporation would have had to establish that the action was a fraud on the corporation either (i) because the plaintiff had agreed with the corporation for good consideration not to bring such an action, or (ii) because of some other good reason. As to (i) this presupposes a contractual promise by the plaintiff not to sue the corporation's servant. I do not think that any such promise can be implied. Even if it could, it would mean that there was a contract between the plaintiff and the defendant which, in so far as it purported to negative or restrict the plaintiff's right to sue, would be void under section 151 of the Road Traffic Act 1960. As to (ii), the only other reason for holding that the plaintiff's action could be a fraud on the corporation would be that the corporation would in law be obliged to indemnify its servant, the defendant, against his liability to the plaintiff in negligence. Clearly there is no such legal obligation on the corporation. I appreciate that the corporation would not wish to leave the defendant personally to bear the burden of this action, and moreover that it might face trouble with his trade union if it did so; but this is not, in my view, sufficient to stigmatise the plaintiff's action against the defendant as a fraud on the corporation.

Appeal dismissed.

SNELLING v. JOHN G. SNELLING LTD AND OTHERS

Queen's Bench Division [1972] 2 W.L.R. 588; [1972] 1 All E.R. 79

The plaintiff and the second and third defendants were brothers and directors of the defendant company. The company was financed by loans from each brother. In 1968 the company raised money on mortgage from a finance company. The brothers were parties to the mortgage and each covenanted with the finance company, but not with each other, that he would not reduce his loan to the company below the amount outstanding on March 31. On March 22 the brothers entered in an agreement with each other, to which the company was not a party, which was to remain in force until the loan from the finance company had been repaid, that if any of them resigned from his directorship he would forfeit the money due to him from the defendant company and the remaining directors would use the money to repay the finance company.

The plaintiff resigned and sued the company for the repayment of his loan. His brothers applied to be joined as defendants, adopting the company's defence and counterclaiming a declaration that the sum due to the plaintiff on the loan account had been forfeited.

ORMROD J. held that the defendant brothers were entitled to a declaration that the plaintiff was bound by the agreement of March 22, but that the company, not being a party to the agreement, was not entitled to rely on it. Having referred to the holding of the Court of Appeal in *Gore v. Van der Lann* that the exemption clause "was not sufficiently precise in its terms to justify the granting of a stay," he continued:

So in the present case counsel for the plaintiff says that there was no specific promise by the plaintiff not to sue the defendant company and consequently the court should refuse to stay the plaintiff's action. I do not think that the Court of Appeal can have intended to lay down a general proposition of law that the court will not stay proceedings in such circumstances unless the plaintiff has expressly undertaken not to sue. Such a ruling would appear to put an unjustified fetter on the discretionary powers of the court under section 41. I do not think that the Court of Appeal intended to go further than to say that the promise which is to be enforced by the granting of a stay must be clear and unambiguous. In this connection an observation by Kelly C.B. in *Slater v. Jones* (1873) L.R. 8 Exch. 186 at 189, is of assistance. In that case, which concerned the effect of a resolution of creditors to accept a composition, he said: ". . . I think that a person who is bound by such a resolution is also bound, by necessary implication, not to sue the debtor before the time for payment comes, and until defaut is made."

So here, it is a necessary implication of clause 4 of the agreement of March 22, 1968 that the plaintiff will not sue the company.

In my judgment, therefore, the second and third defendants have made out an unambiguous case and have shown that the interests of justice require that the plaintiff be not permitted to recover against the defendant company. It follows that this is a proper case in which to grant a stay of all further proceedings in the plaintiff's action against the company.

Counsel for the defendants, however, has submitted that he is entitled to go further and ask for the plaintiff's claim against the company to be dismissed. He relies on three cases: *West Yorkshire Darracq Agency Ltd v. Coleridge* [1911] 2 K.B. 326, *Hirachand Punamchand v. Temple* (above) and *Re William Porter & Co. Ltd* [1937] 2 All E.R. 361. In the *West Yorkshire* case all the directors of a company in liquidation agreed to forgo their respective claims to outstanding directors' fees. The liquidator was a party to an oral agreement to this effect. Horridge J. held that the company was entitled to rely on the agreement as a good defence to a subsequent claim by one of the directors for his fees. The basis of the judgment was that the company, through the liquidator, was a party to the agreement, although no consideration moved from it to the plaintiff. In *Re William Porter & Co. Ltd* the opposite situation arose. Following a resolution passed by the directors of a company that no directors' fees be paid until a further resolution was passed, the trustee in bankruptcy of the governing director submitted a proof in the liquidation of the company for subsequent fees due to the director. The liquidator rejected the proof. Simonds J. held that the company was not a party to any agreement with the directors and that the *West Yorkshire* case did not apply. He went on to hold, however, that the directors, by assenting to the postponement or abrogation of their rights, had induced the company to a course of conduct from which it could have abstained. He, therefore, upheld the rejection of the proof by the liquidator.

In the present case the defendant company was not specifically mentioned as a party to the agreement of March 22, 1968 which, in form at any rate, was an agreement between the three directors concerned. On the other hand, the minutes of the defendant company contain references to it and it was an important item on the agenda at two meetings of the board of directors. There being no liquidator there was no physical person other than the directors who could have been a party to it on behalf of the defendant company, and they themselves never applied their minds to the question whether the company was to be a party to it or not. They regarded the business, the company and its associated companies, and themselves as an amalgam for most purposes, and their intention was to act for the benefit of the amalgam. However, it is not possible to distinguish this case on its facts from *Re William Porter & Co. Ltd* in this respect. I must, therefore, hold that the defendant company was not a party to the agreement. I have no evidence that the defendant company took any action in reliance on the agreement which it would not otherwise have done so that Simonds J.'s decision cannot be relied on to support the view that the company is entitled to have this action dismissed.

Hirachand Punamchand v. Temple (above, p. 247), . . . was a wholly different case on the facts, . . .

I am inclined to the view that in a case such as this where the promisees under the agreement and the party to be benefited by the agreement are all before the court and the promisees have succeeded against the plaintiff on their counterclaim, the right view is that the plaintiff's claim should be dismissed. I think that this accords with section 41 of the 1925 Act. If the action was left with no more than an order staying further proceedings on the claim, the plaintiff could start another action only to have it also stayed and so on ad infinitum. The reality of the matter is that the plaintiff's claim fails and the order of the court ought, if possible, clearly to reflect that fact.

The plaintiff's action against the defendant company dismissed.

Questions

1. Would the company have had a defence if (i) the two brothers had declined to join in the action as defendants? Or if all three brothers had sued the company for the return of their money.

2. Does it matter whether the company, not being a party to the *contract*, is a party to the *agreement* or not?

PRIVITY OF CONTRACT AND THE TRUST CONCEPT

If it be shown that, in a contract made by A and B whereby A undertakes to do something for C, B was acting as trustee for C (that is, holding his contractual rights in trust for C) then C can directly enforce A's obligation in equity. Originating in the Old Court of Chancery (*Cf. Tomlinson v. Gill* (1756) Amb. 330 and *Gregory and Parker v. Williams* (1817) 3 Mer. 582), the principle was accepted after the Judicature Act 1873, in *Lloyd's v. Harper* (above, p. 306). In this case, Lloyd's and a creditor of an insolvent underwriter were allowed to sue on a guarantee which had been given to Lloyd's by a person then deceased, in respect of the liabilities which might be incurred by the underwriter. Whether or not Lush L.J. in that case was a "common lawyer speaking of the common law"—Lord Denning says (*supra*) it is clear that Fry J. at first instance and James and Cotton L.JJ. in the Court of Appeal proceeded on the basis that there was a trust. The possibility of implying a trust in a contract made by A for the benefit of C was confirmed by the acceptance of the concept by the House of Lords in *Les Affréteurs Réunis Société Anonyme v. Leopold Walford (London) Ltd*, below, p. 389 though there are abundant instances of the use of the concept before that decision. In *Walford*'s case, indeed, it was held by the House of Lords that C could sue in his own name without joining the other contracting party. While it is a convenient way of in fact allowing a third party to secure an enforceable benefit under a contract, the use of the concept depends upon the readiness of the court to construe a trust in such cases. Hence there has been a number of seemingly inconsistent decisions (see, for example, *Re Flavell* (1883) 25 Ch.D.89 and *Re Englebach's Estate* [1924] 2 Ch. 348) showing the doctrine of the implied trust to be one of uncertain application—on this, see Corbin, "Contracts for the Benefit of Third Persons." 46 L.Q.R. 12 and Williams, "Contracts for Third Parties" 7 M.L.R. 123.

The turning point in the use of the trust concept was historically *Vandepitte v. Preferred Accident Insurance Corporation of New York* [1933] A.C. 70, a decision of the Judicial Committee of the Privy Council. In that case, V had incurred injuries in a motor accident and recovered judgment against B, a minor who had been driving her father's vehicle with his permission. B's father had insured his car with the respondent company which undertook to indemnify him and those driving his car with his permission. A British Columbia statute provided that where someone recovered judgment for injury or damage against an insured person and the judgment was unsatisfied, the judgment creditor could proceed against the insurers for the amount of the judgment. V's judgment against B remaining unsatisfied, V brought the present action against the respondents, arguing that B was insured by them, either as a party directly to the insurance contract which had been effected by her father or as *cestui que trust* of the promise of indemnity made by the respondents in the contract with B's father. The Judicial Committee of the Privy Council rejected both contentions.

B could be a direct party to the insurance contract only if she had had *animus contrahendi* but she had had no part in the contract which had been concluded entirely by her father and the respondents; on the second contention in the words of Lord Wright, "the intention to constitute a trust must be affirmatively proved; the intention cannot necessarily be inferred from the mere general words of the policy. . . ."

There followed a long period in which the trust concept was scarcely mentioned in the context of third party beneficiaries of a contract. Thus Lord Greene M.R. in *Re Schebsman* (below, p. 318—the first case fairly to raise the issue after *Vandepitte*— said, "it is not legitimate to import into the contract the idea of a trust when the parties have given no indication that such was their intention. To interpret this contract as creating a trust would, in my judgment, be to disregard the dividing line between the case of a trust and the simple case of a contract made between two persons for the benefit of a third." Subsequent cases have shown a similar disregard for the trust concept: for example, *Green v. Russell* [1959] 2 Q.B. 229, where an employer, B, insured the life of his employee, C, with A who agreed to pay the insurance money to C's representatives; the Court of Appeal held that neither C nor his representatives had any right in law or equity to recover the insurance money. The concept does not even appear in *Beswick v. Beswick* in the House of Lords (above, p. 301). Not the least reason why the trust concept has found relatively little favour is the irrevocability of a trust. If the court finds that a trust in favour of C has been created by a contract between A and B, it is in effect saying that A and B have put it out of their power to alter or modify their own positions in the future.

Nevertheless, the trust concept cannot be regarded as defunct. See the opinions of Dillon and Waite L.JJ. in the *Darlington* case, above, p. 308. In *A. Tomlinson (Hauliers) Ltd v. Hepburn* [1966] A.C. 451, the plaintiffs entered into a contract with Imperial Tobacco subsidiary, Players, whereby they agreed to carry goods and to insure them comprehensively while in transit. The plaintiffs insured the goods with the defendant. Two lorry loads of cigarettes were stolen without any fault on the part of the plaintiffs. The plaintiffs claimed the full value of the goods lost. The defendant contended that the policy covered only the liability which the plaintiffs might incur to Players; and they incurred none.

The Court of Appeal [1966] 1 Q.B. 21, affirming Roskill J., decided for the plaintiffs. They held that, where B and C each has an insurable interest in goods and B effects a policy covering the totality of the insurable interest, intending to insure C's as well as his own interest, B may sue on the policy *as trustee* for C. Distinguishing *Green v. Russell (supra)*, Pearson L.J. said (at p. 51): "The distinguishing feature of the present case . . . is that where two persons, bailor and bailee, having [*sic*] concurrent interests in the same goods, so that it would be reasonable and natural and economical for one of them to insure for the benefit of both. In the sphere of insurance on goods, it would be unrealistic and productive of injustice to require from the party taking out the insurance an express declaration or conscious assumption of trusteeship. The existence of the intention is sufficient."

Affirming the decision, the House of Lords ([1966] A.C. 451) regarded the case as one depending on a special rule governing the insurance of goods by a bailee for the benefit of a bailor rather than as an application of the trust concept. Lord Reid said (pp. 470–471): "No doubt the principle preventing *just quaesitum tertio* has been firmly established for at least half a century. But it does not appear to me to be a primeval or necessary principle of the law of England. We must uphold it until it is altered. But I do not think that we are bound to be astute to extend it on a logical basis so as to cut down an exception, if it be an exceptions . . ." Lord Pearce drew attention to the special position of the bailee of goods who has a right to sue for conversion and said (p. 480): "It would seem irrational, therefore, if he could not also insure for their full value." However the dictum of Pearson L.J. be regarded in the future, the circumstances of "insurance of goods" cases are manifestly distinguishable from the *Vandepitte, Re Schebsman, Beswick* situations.

But while rejecting the possible enforcement of the contract by the intended third party beneficiary himself these later cases have established that the performance of the agreement by the contracting party for the benefit of the third party—although it would have been unenforceable by that party—is in itself a valid performance of the contract with the other contracting party. This has had peripheral consequences illustrated by *Re Schebsman (infra)* and *Re Miller's Agreement* [1947] Ch. 615. In that case, a deed of dissolution of partnership between A, B, and C, on the retiral of A, provided that A transferred his share of the goodwill to B and C in consideration of a lump sum and an annuity for life and a covenant that B and C would pay certain annuities to A's daughters. B and C entered into a covenant to pay annuities as from A's death. On A's death, B, and C did pay the annuities to A's daughters. The question was whether the daughters were liable to pay estate and succession duty in respect of the annuities. Wynn-Parry J., holding that the covenants, being *res inter alios acta*, gave the daughters no interest in property that would be protected in a court of law or equity, held that the payments to them by B and C were gratuitous and so attracted neither duty.

Re SCHEBSMAN

Court of Appeal [1944] Ch.83; 113 L.J. Ch.33; 170 L.T. 9; 60 T.L.R. 128; 88 S.J. 17; [1943] 2 All E.R. 768

Appeal from Uthwatt J.

An agreement was made dated September 20, 1940, between a Swiss company of the first part, an English company associated in business with the Swiss company of the second part, and J.W. Schebsman, deceased (hereafter called "the debtor"), of the third part, upon the termination of the debtor's employment with the two companies. It was agreed, *inter alia*, that the English company should pay to the debtor a sum of £5,500 to be paid in the manner specified in the schedule to the agreement and would make "all payments due to" the debtor's widow or daughter under the terms of the agreement. By the schedule, it was provided that the £5,500 should be payable to the debtor in six annual instalments, payable on March 31, 1941 to 1946 inclusive; that, if the debtor died during this period, the English company was thereafter to make payments to his widow in the manner specified in the schedule by equal weekly instalments; and that, if the widow died at any time before March 31, 1950, the schedule should, after her death, be read as though the name of the debtor's daughter appeared instead of the widow's. The debtor was adjudicated bankrupt on March 5, 1942, and died on May 12, 1942. On April 9, 1943, the trustee in bankruptcy launched a motion to which the English company and the debtor's widow and daughter were respondents claiming a declaration that all sums payable by the English company under the agreement of September 20, 1940, formed part of the estate of the debtor.

Uthwatt J. held (1) that under the agreement the debtor was neither a trustee nor an agent for his wife and daughter; (2) that, as a matter of law, payment to the widow was due performance of the agreement, unless a term was to be implied—which was not the case—entitling the debtor or his sequels in title to intercept the sums agreed to be paid to her; (3) that the agreement did not constitute a settlement within section 42(1) of the Bankruptcy Act 1914. The trustee in bankruptcy appealed.

Roxburgh K.C. and *Pennycuick* for the trustee; *Denning K.C.* and *G.F.R. Morris* for the widow and daughter.

LORD GREENE M.R. gave judgment dismissing the appeal.

DU PARCQ L.J.: It is, in my opinion, convenient to approach the problems raised in this appeal by first considering the position of the parties at common law. It is clear that Mrs Schebsman, who was not a party to the agreement of September 20, 1940, acquired no rights under it and has never been in a position to maintain an action on it. It is common ground, also, that the personal representatives of the debtor could not have recovered any sums which had been paid to Mrs Schebsman under the agreement as money had and received or by any process known to the common law. It is not disputed that the English company, which under the agreement was liable to make the payments, properly performed that agreement by paying into the hands of Mrs Schebsman those sums which it had bound itself to pay to Mrs Schebsman, and, at common law, could not be called on to pay them to the personal representatives of the debtor. Nor, I think, is it disputed, and it may be said to be self-evident, that the English company's agreement to pay these moneys into the hands of Mrs Schebsman was a valid agreement, a breach of which would be regarded by the courts as an "unlawful act" and a "legal wrong."

So far there is general agreement. I may now express my own agreement with a proposition submitted by Mr Roxburgh. He said that the duty to pay into the hands of a nominated person is discharged when the money has been paid to that person, and the party bound to make a payment has no control over its destination. As a general proposition, that is true and can hardly be questioned. In the case before us Mrs Schebsman, being no party to the contract, is clearly under no obligation to the English company to apply the money in any particular way, nor is the English company concerned with any agreement which she may choose to make with third parties binding herself to apply it in a particular manner, but the proposition, accurate as it is, may be misleading unless it is considered together with another proposition which I take to be equally unexceptionable and which I will now state.

It is open to parties to agree that, for a consideration supplied by one of them, the other will make payments to a third person for the use and benefit of that third person and not for the use and benefit of the contracting party who provides the consideration. Whether or not such an agreement has been made in a given case is clearly a question of construction, but, assuming that the parties have manifested their intention so to agree, it cannot, I think, be doubted that the common law would regard such an agreement as valid and as enforceable (in the sense of giving a cause of action for damages for its breach to the other party to the contract), and would regard the breach of it as an unlawful act. If the party from whom the consideration moved somehow succeeded in intercepting a payment intended for the named payee he would be guilty of a tort, and, in certain circumstances, of a crime, and he would also be breaking his contract, since it would be implicit in his agreement with the other party that he would do nothing to prevent the money paid from reaching the payee. If he sought to argue that because he had himself provided the consideration he alone was interested in the destination of the money, the answer would be that the other contracting party had not agreed (and, perhaps, might never have thought of agreeing) to make a payment either to him or for his benefit. If he can persuade the payee to hand the money over to him by lawful means, he is, of course, at liberty to do so, and there may be circumstances dehors the contract which give him rights against the payee. Subject to that qualification he can never, in the case of such a contract as I have supposed, lawfully claim payment of the money for himself while the contract remains unaltered. That the common law allows it to be varied nobody doubts. At any time the parties may agree that payment shall in future be made, not to the payee named in the contract, but to the party from whom the consideration moved, or, for that matter, to any other person, but in the case of such a contract there cannot be a variation at the will of one of the parties any more than a condition introduced into a contract for the benefit of both parties can be waived by only one of them. . . .

I may now summarise the position at common law as follows: 1. It is the right as well as the duty of the company to make the prescribed payments to Mrs Schebsman and to no other person. 2. Mrs Schebsman may dispose of the sums so received as she pleases and is not accountable for them to the personal representatives of the debtor or to anyone claiming to stand in the shoes of the debtor. 3. If anyone standing in the shoes of the debtor were to intercept the sums payable to Mrs Schebsman and refuse to account to her for them, he would be guilty of a breach of the debtor's contract with the company. 4. The obligation undertaken by the company cannot be varied at the will of the other party to the contract, but may be varied consensually at any time although the debtor is no longer living, as it could have been in his lifetime.

It now remains to consider the question whether, and if so to what extent, the principles of equity affect the position of the parties. It was argued by Mr Denning that one effect of the agreement of September 20, 1940, was that a trust was thereby created, and that the debtor constituted himself trustee for Mrs Schebsman of the benefit of the covenant under which payments were to be made to her. Uthwatt J. rejected this contention, and the argument has not satisfied me that he was wrong. It is true that, by the use possibly of unguarded language, a person may create a trust, as Monsieur Jourdain talked prose, without knowing it, but unless an intention to create a trust is clearly to be collected from the language used and the circumstances of the case, I think that the court ought not to be astute to discover indications of such an intention. I have little doubt that in the present case both parties (and certainly the debtor) intended to keep alive their common law right to vary consensually the terms of the obligation undertaken by the company, and if circumstances had changed in the debtor's lifetime injustice might have been done by holding that a trust had been created and that those terms were accordingly unalterable. On this point therefore, I agree with Uthwatt J.

(The judgment of LUXMOORE L.J. is omitted.)

Appeal dismissed.

Section 5. The Imposition of Burdens on Third Parties

It would be surprising if a contract between A and B could impose burdens or obligations on C and the general principle is that it cannot do so. (But *Cf. Morris v. Martin,* above, p. 298.) The only established exceptions to this rule are part of the law of property rather than that of contract. Covenants in a lease are binding not only on the original parties but also on their successors in title. In addition, covenants restricting the use of land are binding in equity not only on the original covenantor but also on subsequent purchasers of the land with notice of the covenant, provided that the covenantee has retained other land for the benefit of which the covenant was taken. This is the doctrine of *Tulk v. Moxhay* (1848) 2 Ph. 74. In *Taddy v. Sterious* [1904] 1 Ch. 354 Swinfen Eady J. declined to extend a similar principle to goods. The plaintiffs, manufacturers of tobacco, attached a notice to each packet stating that it was sold on the express condition that retailers would not sell it below stipulated prices, adding that

> "acceptance of the goods will be deemed a contract between the purchaser and Taddy & Co. that he will observe these stipulations. In the case of a purchase by a retail dealer through a wholesale dealer, the latter shall be deemed to be the agent of Taddy & Co."

The defendants who had purchased through a wholesaler with notice of the conditions were held not bound by them.

A publisher of paperback books inserts the following in the front of the book.

> "This book is sold subject to the condition that it shall not, by way of trade or otherwise, be lent, re-sold, hired out, or otherwise circulated without the publisher's prior consent in any form of binding or cover other than that in which it is published and without a similar condition including this condition being imposed on the subsequent purchaser."

Consider whether this is binding on C who purchases the book from a retailer and wishes to re-bind it and use it in a private lending library. In *De Mattos v. Gibson* (1858) 4 De G. & J. 276 at 282 enunciated a broad principle:

> "Reason and justice seem to prescribe that, at least as a general rule, where a man, by gift or purchase, acquires property from another, with knowledge of a previous contract, lawfully and for valuable consideration made by him with a third person, to use and employ the property for a particular purpose in a specified manner, the acquirer shall not, to the material damage of the

third person, in opposition to the contract and inconsistently with it, use and employ the property in a manner not allowable to the giver or seller. This rule, applicable alike in general as I conceive to moveable and immoveable property, and recognised and adopted, as I apprehend, by the English law, may, like other general rules, be liable to exceptions arising from special circumstances; but I see at present no room for any exception in the instance before us."

The validity of this principle is, to say the least, controversial. It has received its fullest judicial consideration in the following judgment of Browne-Wilkinson J. (The case subsequently went to the Court of Appeal and the House of Lords [1981] 2 W.L.R. 893; [1981] 2 All E.R. 449, which decided the case on other grounds, not affecting this aspect of Browne-Wilkinson J.'s opinion. The facts of the case are omitted.)

SWISS BANK CORPORATION v. LLOYDS BANK LTD

Chancery Division [1979] 3 W.L.R. 201; [1979] 2 All E.R. 853

BROWNE-WILKINSON J.: How then do the authorities stand? In *De Mattos v. Gibson* itself the plaintiff had chartered a ship from its owner Curry. Curry had subsequently charged the ship to Gibson, who had actual notice of the charterparty. Curry got into financial difficulties and was unable to continue the voyage. Gibson was proposing to sell the ship of which he had taken possession. In the action the plaintiff claimed an injunction against Gibson restraining him from interfering with the charterparty. The plaintiff applied for an interim injunction, which was granted on appeal. The grounds for the decision of Knight Bruce L.J. were those set out in the passage [quoted, above]. The decision of Turner L.J. was founded entirely on balance of convenience, but one of the three questions he said would have to be decided at the trial was whether the plaintiff, even if not entitled to specific performance of the charterparty, was entitled to an injunction to restrain a breach of the charterparty. In due course the action came on for trial before Page Wood V.-C. (from whose decision there was an appeal to the Lord Chancellor). Lord Chelmsford L.C. held that no injunction should be granted against Gibson. He referred expressly to the three questions posed by Turner L.J., and after holding that the charterparty could not be specifically performed, said that Gibson having taken with full knowledge of the charter could be restrained from doing any act which would have the immediate effect of preventing its performance. But Lord Chelmsford L.C. went on to show that on the facts there was no real possibility of Curry performing the charterparty whatever Gibson did, and therefore there was no question of any act by Gibson constituting an interference by Gibson with the plaintiff's contractual rights. In my judgment that case is an authority binding on me that a person taking a charge on property which he knows to be subject to a contractual obligation can be restrained from exercising his rights under the charge in such a way as to interfere with the performance of that contractual obligation. In my judgment the *De Mattos v. Gibson* principle is merely the equitable counterpart of the tort. But two points have to be emphasised about the decision in *De Mattos v. Gibson*: first, the ship was acquired with actual knowledge of the plaintiff's contractual rights; secondly, that no such injunction will be granted against the third party if it is clear that the original contracting party cannot in any event perform his contract. It is this second point which in my judgment accounts for the fact that the *De Mattos v. Gibson* principle is not applicable to restrictive covenants: the original contracting party (even if traceable) could not carry out his contract relating to the land, or the chattel once he had parted with it.

In *Lord Strathcona Steamship Co. Ltd v. Dominion Coal Co.* [1926] A.C. 108 the facts were that a ship which was the subject-matter of a charterparty to Dominion was sold to Strathcona expressly subject to the rights of Dominion under the charterparty. The Privy Council held that an injunction could be granted restraining Strathcona from interfering with Dominion's rights under the charterparty. It will be noted that the *Strathcona* case is of the type I considered under category (b) above, that is, Strathcona bought expressly subject to Dominion's rights. And certainly one ground of decision is that, in the circumstances, Strathcona was a constructive trustee. It is not clear to me whether this was the only ground of decision since the passages in the judgment dealing with *De Mattos v. Gibson* (which was held to be good law) certainly seem to proceed on the basis of knowing interference with another's contract. The Privy Council accepted that, in order to get an injunction, the plaintiff had to have a continuing interest in the property but undoubtedly held that a bare contractual right, as opposed to a property interest, was a sufficient interest for this purpose.

There are parts of the judgment in the *Strathcona* case which I find difficult to follow but in my judgment it certainly decides (i) that *De Mattos v. Gibson* is good law and (ii) that an injunction can be granted to restrain a subsequent purchaser of a chattel from using it so as to cause a breach of a contract of which he has express notice.

In *Port Line Ltd v. Ben Line Steamers Ltd* [1958] 2 Q.B. 146, 168 Diplock J. stated that he thought the *Strathcona* case was wrongly decided and refused to follow it. In that case Port had chartered a vessel from Silver. Silver then sold to Ben but subject to an immediate recharter by Ben to Silver. Under the charterparty between Port and Silver the requisitioning of the vessel did not determine the charter; under the charterparty between Ben and Silver it did. The vessel was requisitioned and Port was claiming from Ben compensation received by Ben for the requisition. It is important to notice that Port could only succeed if it showed either that it had a positive right to possession of the vessel or that Ben was accountable for the compensation as constructive trustee. Diplock J. was not concerned with the question whether Port was entitled to a negative injunction to restrain the tort.

It is not necessary for me to express any view as to whether the *Strathcona* case was rightly decided so far as it was a decision based on constructive trusteeship, which was all that Diplock J. was concerned with: the *Strathcona* case itself decided that there was no right to specific performance of the charterparty. However, although I of course differ from Diplock J. with diffidence, in my judgment the *Strathcona* case was rightly decided on the basis that Dominion was entitled to an injunction against Strathcona to prevent Strathcona from interfering with the contract between Dominion and the original charterer. Diplock J. explained *De Mattos v. Gibson* on that ground and gave as an alternative ground for his decision that actual, as opposed to constructive, notice was necessary in such a case. To that extent his decision supports my own view.

In my judgment there is in any event a decision of the Court of Appeal which is binding on me, namely *Manchester Ship Canal Co. v. Manchester Racecourse Co.* [1901] 2 Ch. 37. In that case the racecourse company had granted the canal company a right of first refusal over certain land. The racecourse company, without giving proper effect to such a right of first refusal, had entered into a contract to sell the land to a third party, Trafford. The Court of Appeal held (whether rightly or wrongly does not for this purpose matter) that the right of first refusal did not create any property interest in the land, but even so granted an injunction against Trafford restraining them from completing their contract to purchase. The Court of Appeal founded its decision expressly on the basis that Trafford, having full knowledge, was proposing to do something which would cause a breach of the contract between the canal company and the racecourse company, that is, to commit the tort. In my judgment this is a decision of the Court of Appeal that the court will restrain a person from enforcing his contractual rights so as to cause a breach of another contract of which he had full knowledge when he entered into his own contract. As such, it covers the present case. But it is to be noted that Trafford in that case had actual knowledge, as opposed to constructive notice, of the contract between the canal company and the racecourse company.

In *Binions v. Evans* [1972] Ch. 359, 371 Megaw L.J. indicated that he thought the case could properly have been decided on the basis that an injunction to restrain the tort should be granted. This again supports the existence of the jurisdiction.

What then are the authorities which suggest that the *De Mattos v. Gibson* principle is not good law? In my judgment apart from the *Port Line* case they are all cases falling within category (a) above; that is to say not cases in which the plaintiff sought an injunction to restrain the defendant from committing the tort but cases where the plaintiff was seeking to make the defendant positively perform a contract to which he was not a party. In particular, it is in my judgment, clear that the remarks of Scrutton J. (as he then was) in *London County Council v. Allen* [1914] 3 K.B. 642 and Scrutton L.K. in *Barker v. Stickney* [1919] 1 K.B. 121 are to be read in their context as cases where the plaintiff was seeking to enforce performance of the contract against the defendant who was not a party to the contract. So far as I can see, in neither of those cases was there any consideration of the rights of the plaintiff to a negative injunction restraining the defendant from causing someone else to breach the contract with the plaintiff.

Therefore, in my judgment the authorities establish the following propositions. (i) The principle stated by Knight Bruce L.J. in *De Mattos v. Gibson* is good law and represents the counterpart in equity of the tort of knowing interference with contractual rights. (ii) A person proposing to deal with property in such a way as to cause a breach of a contract affecting that property will be restrained by injunction from so doing if when he acquired that property he had actual knowledge of that contract. (iii) A plaintiff is entitled to such an injunction even if he has no proprietary interest in the property: his right to have his contract performed is a sufficient interest. (iv) There is no case in which such an injunction has been granted against a defendant who acquired the property with only constructive, as opposed to actual, notice of the contract. In my judgment constructive notice is not sufficient, since actual knowledge of the contract is a requisite element in the tort.

Section 6. Exceptions to the Doctrine of Privity

Some of the cases which are often treated as exceptions to the doctrine of privity are not really exceptions. *The Eurymedon* and *The New York Star* (above, pp. 290, 294) do not create exceptions because the courts found, however deviously and improbably, that there was a separate contract between the shipper or consignee and the stevedore. Nor do the cases on collateral contracts such as *Shanklin v. Detel Products*, below, p. 383. In all these cases, C is found to be a contracting party, not the beneficiary of a contract between A and B. Whether the trust cases, above, p. 316 and the doctrine of the undisclosed principal, above, pp. 278–280 should be regarded as "exceptions" is a matter of taste. Genuine exceptions to the rule so far encountered are:—

1. The *Elder Dempster* case, above, p. 284 footnote.
2. The principle that a contract by the bailee in relation to the bailed goods may be binding on the bailor: *The Pioneer Container*, above, p. 296
3. The principle that a bailor can sue on a contract of insurance of the bailed goods made by the bailee for the benefit of the bailor: above, p. 318.

In addition, the following exceptions or quasi-exceptions should be noted.
4. The principle that, where A and B, when making a contract concerning B's goods or land, contemplate that B's proprietary interest may be transferred to another, (C), before the breach causes loss or damage, B may recover the loss sustained by C: *Dunlop v. Lambert* as applied in the *Linden Gardens* and *Darlington* cases, above, p. 308.
5. Assignment of contractual obligations. Both at law under the Law of Property Act 1925, s.136, and in equity it is possible for B to assign to C certain rights arising under a contract between A and B which C may then enforce against A. See Cheshire, Fifoot and Furmston, *Law of Contract*, (12th ed.), Chap. 16.
6. Certain covenants in land law. Covenants in a lease of land granted by A to B bind successors in title of either party on the basis of "privity of estate." And see *Tulk v. Moxhay*, above, p. 321.
7. Statutory exceptions. In some cases Parliament has intervened to overcome what were seen to be injustices and inconveniences arising from the privity rule. The following are examples.

Married Women's Property Act 1882, s.11

A policy of assurance effected by any man on his own life and expressed to be for the benefit of his wife, or of his children, or of his wife and children, or any of them, or by any woman on her own life, and expressed to be for the benefit of her husband, or of her children, or of her husband and children, or any of them, shall create a trust in favour of the objects therein named, and the moneys payable under any such policy shall not, so long as any object of the trust remains unperformed, form part of the estate of the insured, or be subject to his or her debts.

Marine Insurance Act 1906, s.14(2)

A mortgagee, consignee, or other person having an interest in the subject-matter insured may insure on behalf and for the benefit of other persons interested as well as for his own benefit.

Law of Property Act 1925

Section 47(1)—Where after the date of any contract for sale or exchange of property, money becomes payable under any policy of insurance maintained by the vendor in respect of any damage to or destruction of property included in the contract, the money shall, on completion of the contract, be held or receivable by the vendor on behalf of the purchaser and paid by the vendor to the purchaser on completion of the sale or exchange, or as soon thereafter as the same shall be received by the vendor.

Section 56(1).—A person may take an immediate or other interest in land or other property, or the benefit of any condition, right of entry, covenant or agreement over or respecting land or other property, although he may not be named as a party to the conveyance or other instrument.

Road Traffic Act 1988, s.148(7)

Notwithstanding anything in any enactment, a person issuing a policy of insurance under section 145 of this Act shall be liable to indemnify the persons or classes of persons specified in the policy in respect of any liability which the policy purports to cover in the case of those persons or classes of persons.

Defective Premises Act 1972

Note

An agreement of June 17, 1946, between the Minister of Transport and the Motor Insurers' Bureau contains the following provision: "If judgment in respect of any liability which is required to be covered by a policy of insurance or a security (hereinafter called 'a contract of insurance') under Part II of the Road Traffic Act 1930, is obtained against any person or persons in any court in Great Britain, whether or not such person or persons be in fact covered by a contract of insurance or if judgment in respect of any liability which is not so required to be covered by reason only of the provisions of subsection (4) of section 35 of the said Act is in fact covered by a contract of insurance and any such judgment is not satisfied in full within seven days from the date upon which the person or persons in whose favour the judgment was given became or would apart from the provisions of the Courts (Emergency Powers) Act 1939, or similar legislation have become entitled to enforce it, then M.I.B. will, subject to the provisions of clauses 5 and 6 of these presents, pay or satisfy or cause to be paid or satisfied to or to the satisfaction of the person or persons in whose favour the judgment was given any sum payable or remaining payable thereunder in respect of the aforesaid liability including taxed costs (or such proportion thereof as is attributable to the aforesaid liability) whatever may be the cause of the failure of the judgment debtor to satisfy the judgment."

In *Hardy v. Motor Insurers' Bureau* [1964] 2 Q.B. 745, 757, Lord Denning M.R. said of the above agreement: "This was, on the face of it, a contract between two parties for the benefit of a third person. No point is taken by the Motor Insurers' Bureau that it is not enforceable by the third person. I trust no such point will ever be taken."

PART III

OBLIGATIONS ARISING FROM THE CONTRACT AND ITS FORMATION

CHAPTER 9

STATEMENTS MADE DURING NEGOTIATIONS FOR A CONTRACT AND THEIR EFFECT

It is common for one party to make statements during the course of negotiations for a contract with the object and perhaps the effect of inducing the other party to contract. Sometimes such statements may be held to amount to promises and to become part of the contract so that, if they are unfulfilled, an action for breach of contract will lie. The circumstances in which such a statement becomes part of the contract are considered in detail below, pp. 361 *et seq.*

On other occasions, the statement will be held not to form part of the contract. For example, where a contract of sale has been reduced to writing, assurances which were given by the seller as to his land or his goods, as the case may be, will probably be held not to form part of the contract if they are not referred to in the document. The parol evidence rule, though subject to many exceptions (above, pp. 120–121, below, pp. 382, 517) will generally apply to exclude evidence which would add to, vary or contradict the written document. A statement which induces a contract without forming part of it is not necessarily devoid of effect, if it is false. If the misrepresentation was made fraudulently (that is, the maker knew it was false or was reckless whether it was true or false: *Derry v. Peek* (1889) 14 App.Cas. 337, 374, *per* Lord Herschell) then the party who was misled into contracting in reliance on it could, at common law, rescind the contract—that is, treat it as avoided *ab initio*— and sue to recover damages for the tort of deceit. If the misrepresentation was made innocently (that is, the maker believed it to be true, whether reasonably or not) the common law, until the decision in 1963 in *Hedley Byrne v. Heller & Partners* (below, p. 340), afforded no remedy. In equity, however, the party who was misled into contracting in reliance on it, might be allowed to rescind the contract and to recover an indemnity. The question of the nature of the indemnity is considered below, p. 349. The cases which follow this note are concerned with the circumstances in which the equitable remedy of rescission for innocent misrepresentation is available. There follows the case of *Hedley Byrne & Co. v. Heller & Partners*, which established that, in certain circumstances, damages might be recovered at common law for an innocent misrepresentation proved to have been made negligently. These cases are followed by the Misrepresentation Act 1967, which has made important additions to the law as set out in the decisions.

Section 1. Misrepresentation in Equity

REDGRAVE v. HURD

Court of Appeal (1881) 20 Ch.D. 1; 51 L.J.Ch. 113; 45 L.T. 485; 30 W.R. 251

The plaintiff, a solicitor, inserted in the *Law Times* an advertisement offering to "take as partner an efficient lawyer and advocate, about forty, who would not object to purchase advertiser's suburban residence. . . ." The defendant replied to the advertisement, and had two interviews with the plaintiff, at which, as Fry J. found, the plaintiff had represented that his business was bringing in either about £300 a year, or from £300 to £400 a year. At a third interview the plaintiff produced summaries of business done in 1877, 1878 and 1879. These summaries showed gross receipts not quite amounting to £200 a year. The defendant asked how the difference was made up and the plaintiff produced a quantity of letters and papers which, he stated, related to other business which he had done. The defendant did not examine the books and papers thus produced, but only looked cursorily at them, and ultimately agreed to purchase the house and take a share in the business for £1,600. Fry J. came to the conclusion that the letters and papers, if examined, would have shown business of only £5 or £6 a year.

The defendant signed a written agreement to purchase the house for £1,600 and paid £100 deposit. Finding, as he alleged, that the practice was utterly worthless, he refused to complete, and the plaintiff brought an action for specific performance. The defendant alleged that he was induced to enter into the contract by misrepresentations, and counterclaimed for rescission of the contract.

Fry J. gave judgment for the plaintiff, holding that the defendant must be taken not to have relied on the oral representations as to the value of the business: "If he had intended to rely upon that parol representation, . . . having the materials before him, he would have made some inquiry into it": and that he "must be taken to have accepted the statements which were in those papers." The defendant appealed.

JESSEL M.R.: As regards the rescission of a contract, there was no doubt a difference between the rules of courts of equity and the rules of courts of common law—a difference which, of course, has now disappeared by the operation of the Judicature Act, which makes the rules of equity prevail. According to the decisions of courts of equity it was not necessary, in order to set aside a contract obtained by material false representation, to prove that the party who obtained it knew at the time when the representation was made that it was false. It was put in two ways, either of which was sufficient. One way of putting the case was, "A man is not to be allowed to get a benefit from a statement which he now admits to be false. He is not to be allowed to say, for the purpose of civil jurisdiction, that when he made it he did not know it to be false; he ought to have found that out before he made it." The other way of putting it was this: "Even assuming that moral fraud must be shown in order to set aside a contract, you have it where a man, having obtained a beneficial contract by a statement which he now knows to be false, insists upon keeping that contract. To do so is a moral delinquency: no man ought to seek to take advantage of his own false statements." The rule in equity was settled, and it does not matter on which of the two grounds it was rested. As regards the rule of common law there is no doubt it was not quite so wide. There were, indeed, cases in which, even at common law, a contract could be rescinded for misrepresentation, although it could not be shown that the person making it knew the representation to be false. They are variously stated, but I think, according to the later decisions, the statement must have been made recklessly and without care whether it was true or false, and not with the belief that it was true. But, as I have said, the doctrine in equity was settled beyond controversy, and it is enough to refer to the judgment of Lord Cairns in the *Reese River Silver Mining Co. v. Smith*, L.R. 4 H.L. 64, in which he lays it down in the way which I have stated.

There is another proposition of law of very great importance which I think it is necessary for me to state, because, with great deference to the very learned judge from whom this appeal comes, I think it is not quite accurately stated in his judgment. If a man is induced to enter into a contract by a false representation it is not a sufficient answer to him to say, "If you had used due diligence you would have found out that the statement was untrue. You had the means afforded to you of discovering its falsity, and did not choose to avail yourself of them." I take it to be a settled doctrine of equity, not only as regards specific performance but also as regards rescission, that this is not an answer unless there is such delay as constitutes a defence under the Statute of Limitations. That, of course, is quite a different thing. Under the statute delay deprives a man of his right to rescind on the ground of fraud, and the only question to be considered is from what time the delay is to be reckoned. It had been decided, and the rule was adopted by the statute, that the delay counts from the time when by due diligence the fraud might have been discovered. Nothing can be plainer, I take it, on the authorities in equity than that the effect of false representation is not got rid of on the ground that the person to whom it was made has been guilty of negligence. One of the most familiar instances in modern times is where men issue a prospectus in which they make false statements of the contracts made before the formation of a company, and then say that the contracts themselves may be inspected at the offices of the solicitors. It has always been held that those who accepted those false statements as true were not deprived of their remedy merely because they neglected to go and look at the contracts. Another instance with which we are familiar is where a vendor makes a false statement as to the contents of a lease, as, for instance, that it contains no covenant preventing the carrying on of the trade which the purchaser is known by the vendor to be desirous of carrying on upon the property. Although the lease itself might be produced at the sale, or might have been open to the inspection of the purchaser long previously to the sale, it has been repeatedly held that the vendor cannot be allowed to say, "You were not entitled to give credit to my statement." It is not sufficient, therefore, to say that the purchaser had the opportunity of investigating the real state of the case, but did not avail himself of that opportunity. It has been apparently supposed by the learned judge in the court below that the case of *Attwood v. Small*, 6 Cl. & F. 232, conflicts with that proposition. He says this: "He inquired into it to a certain extent, and if he did that carelessly and inefficiently it is his own fault. As in *Attwood v. Small*, those directors and agents of the company who made ineffectual inquiry into the business which was to be sold to the company were nevertheless held by their investigation to have bound the company, so here, I think, the defendant who made a cursory investigation into the position of things on February 17 must be taken to have accepted the statements which were in those papers." I think that those remarks are inaccurate in law, and are not borne out by the case to which the learned judge referred.

[His Lordship then considered the speeches in *Attwood v. Small*.]

... the two grounds taken by Lord Brougham are that there was no misrepresentation, and that the purchaser did not rely on the representations. He agreed in one with Lord Cottenham and in the other with Lord Devon. The three grounds taken by the three noble Lords, one of which grounds was taken by one only of the Lords, and each of the others by two, were that there was no fraud—that there was actual knowledge of the facts before the contract, and that no reliance was placed upon the representation. In no way, as it appears to me, does the decision, or any of the grounds of decisions, in *Attwood v. Small*, support the proposition that it is a good defence to an action for rescission of a contract on the ground of fraud that the man who comes to set aside the contract inquired to a certain extent, but did it carelessly and inefficiently, and would, if he had used reasonable diligence, have discovered the fraud. . . .

. . . the learned judge came to the conclusion either that the defendant did not rely on the statement, or that if he did rely upon it he had shown such negligence as to deprive him of his title to relief from this court. As I have already said, the latter proposition is in my opinion not founded in law, and the former part is not founded in fact; I think also it is not founded in law, for when a person makes a material representation to another to induce him to enter into a contract, and the other enters into the contract, it is not sufficient to say that the party to whom the representation is made does not prove that he entered into the contract relying upon the representation. If it is a material representation calculated to induce him to enter into the contract, it is an inference of law that he was induced by the representation to enter into it, and in order to take away his title to be relieved from the contract on the ground that the representation was untrue, it must be shown either that he had knowledge of the facts contrary to the representation, or that he stated in terms, or showed clearly by his conduct, that he did not rely on the representation. If you tell a man, "You may enter into partnership with me, my business is bringing in between £300 and £400 a year," the man who makes that representation must know that it is a material inducement to the other to enter into the partnership, and you cannot investigate as to whether it was more or less probable that the inducement would operate on the mind of the party to whom the representation was made. Where you have neither evidence that he knew facts to show that the statement was untrue, or that he said or did anything to show that he did not actually rely upon the statement, the inference remains that he did so rely, and the statement being a material statement, its being untrue is a sufficient ground for rescinding the contract.

BAGGALLAY and LUSH L.JJ.: delivered concurring judgments.

Appeal allowed.

BISSET v. WILKINSON

Privy Council [1927] A.C. 177; 96 L.J.P.C. 12; 136 L.T. 97; 42 T.L.R. 727

The respondent purchased from the appellant two blocks of land in New Zealand for the purpose of sheep-farming. During the negotiations the appellant told the respondent that, if the place was worked properly, it would carry two thousand sheep. The respondent, it was admitted, bought the place believing that it would carry two thousand sheep. As both parties were aware, the appellant had not and, so far as appeared, no other person had at any time carried on sheep-farming on the land. In an action for rescission for misrepresentation, Sim J. said:

"In ordinary circumstances, any statement made by an owner who has been occupying his own farm as to its carrying capacity would be regarded as a statement of fact. . . . This, however, is not such a case. . . . In these circumstances . . . the defendants were not justified in regarding anything said by the plaintiff as to the carrying capacity as being anything more than an expression of his opinion on the subject."

Their Lordships concurred in this view of the matter, and therefore held that the purchaser had no right to rescind the contract,

"... since an erroneous opinion stated by the party affirming the contract, though it may have been relied upon and have induced the contract on the part of the party who seeks rescission, gives no title to relief unless fraud is established. ... If a reasonable man with the vendor's knowledge could not have come to the conclusion he stated, the description of that conclusion as an opinion would not necessarily protect him against rescission for misrepresentation, but what was actually the capacity in competent hands of the land the purchasers purchased had never been, and never was practically ascertained."

Note
   Cf. Esso Petroleum Co. Ltd v. Mardon, below, p. 367.

Section 2. Silence and Misrepresentation

In *Banque Financiere v. Westgate Insurance Co.* [1989] 2 All E.R. 952, 1010, (affirmed on other grounds by the House of Lords, [1990] 2 All E.R. 947) Slade L.J., quoting from Blackburn J. in *Smith v. Hughes* (above, p. 121) and citing Lord Atkin's example in *Bell v. Lever Bros* (below, p. 491) of the horse, the picture, the lease and the garage, said:

"The general principle that there is no obligation to speak within the context of negotiations for an ordinary commercial contract (though qualified by the well-known special principles relating to contracts *uberrimae fidei*, fraud, undue influence, fiduciary duty etc.) is one of the foundations of our law of contract, and must have been the basis of many decisions over the years. There are countless cases in which one party to a contract has in the course of negotiations failed to disclose a fact known to him which the other party would have regarded as highly material, if it had been revealed. However, ordinarily in the absence of misrepresentation, our law leaves that other party entirely without remedy."

WALES v. WADHAM

Family Division. [1977] 1 W.L.R. 199; [1977] 2 All E.R. 125

On February 15, 1973, Wales and his wife (now Mrs Wadham) reached a compromise agreement whereby he would pay her £13,000 out of his half-share of the proceeds of the sale of their matrimonial home if she would not make any further claim for maintenance. (*Cf.* Matrimonial Causes Act 1973, above, p. 220). The agreement was embodied in a consent order made on July 6 on the grant to the wife of a decree nisi. Wales sought rescission of the agreement on the ground, *inter alia*, that he would not have entered into the agreement on February 15 had he known that his wife then intended to remarry. The agreement was intended to commute his liability for periodical payments, a liability which, in the event, he would never have had. She had stated on several occasions in 1971 that she would never remarry. She did not reveal her intention to marry Mr Wadham because she did not wish him to be involved in the divorce proceedings.

TUDOR EVANS J.: It is submitted that even if the wife's statement that she would never remarry was honestly held, she was under a duty to tell the husband of her changed circumstances, but that she failed to do so. Counsel has referred me to *With v. O'Flanagan* [1936] Ch. 575 in the Court of Appeal. In that case, during the course of negotiations for the sale of a medical practice, the vendor made representations to the purchaser, about the existing nature of the practice which, by the time when the contract was signed, were untrue. The value of the practice had declined in the meantime because of the vendor's inability to attend to it through illness. Lord Wright M.R. quoted, with approval, observations of Fry J. in *Davies v. London and Provincial Marine Insurance Co.* (1878) 8 Ch.D. 469, 475 where he said:

> "So again, if a statement has been made which is true at the time, but which during the course of negotiations becomes untrue, then the person who knows that it has become untrue is under an obligation to disclose to the other the change of circumstances."

The representations in both of these cases related to existing fact and not to a statement of intention in relation to future conduct. A statement of intention is not a representation of existing fact, unless the person making it does not honestly hold the intention he is expressing, in which case there is a misrepresentation of fact in relation to the state of that person's mind. That does not arise on the facts as I have found them. On the facts of this case, the wife made an honest statement of her intention which was not a representation of fact, and I can find no basis for holding that she was under a duty in the law of contract to tell the husband of her change of mind. Counsel for the wife submits that, apart from any other consideration, the wife's objection to remarriage after divorce and her specific statements to the husband that she would not remarry, do not have the quality of representations in the sense that at her age she could not seriously be taken as representing that she would never change her mind. I accept that submission. It seems to me that when after a marriage which had lasted for some 26 years the wife told the husband she would never marry again she was not representing to the husband that, she then being barely 50, she would never change her mind. The wife's objections to remarriage on religious grounds could not, in themselves, amount to a representation. They were simply general opinions expressed during the existence of the marriage, and not in any way made in contemplation by either party of a contract. With respect to the specific statements, as I have said, I am satisfied that the wife made them in an attempt to save her marriage and I am satisfied she was not representing that she would never change her mind.

I must now consider the submission of the husband that the contract in this case was one requiring *uberrima fides*. Such contracts are an exception to the common law rule that a party may remain silent about material facts when negotiating a contract, and that such silence does not amount to a misrepresentation. I have been referred to *Bell v. Lever Bros Ltd* [1962] A.C. 161, 232, where Lord Thankerton said:

> "The most familiar of these exceptions is found in the case of policies of insurance, as to which Blackburn J. says, in *Fletcher v. Krell* (1873) 42 L.J.Q.B. 55, 'mercantile custom has established the rule with regard to concealment of material facts in policies of assurance, but in other cases there must be an allegation of moral guilt or fraud.' Other exceptions are found in case of trustee and cestui que trust and of a company issuing a prospectus and an applicant for shares, but the number of exceptions is limited, and no authority has been cited which extends the exceptions to cover a case such as the present."

Further examples are contracts of partnership and suretyship but there is no case in which the principle has been extended to contracts between a husband and wife, although counsel for the husband has referred to a number of authorities in the 19th century concerned with deeds of separation, in which he submits the duty to disclose has been recognised. I shall refer to these cases at a later stage. The first submission is that the contract in the present case is similar to a contract of insurance. It is pointed out that contracts of insurance are speculative in nature in the sense that an insurer can only compute his risk on the basis of what he is told by the proposed assured. I have been referred to an early case, *Carter v. Boehm* (1766) 3 Burr. 1905 at 1909, where Lord Mansfield C.J. said:

> "Insurance is a contract upon speculation. The special facts, upon which the contingent chance is to be computed, lie most commonly in the knowledge of the *insured* only: the under-writer trusts to his representation, and proceeds upon confidence that he does not keep back any circumstance in his knowledge, to mislead the under-writer into a belief that the circumstance does not exist . . ."

It is said that the husband in the present case was computing or compromising in a single sum a future and uncertain liability to maintain the wife and that the likelihood of the wife's remarriage was a material fact in the computation which should have been disclosed. I cannot accept that there is any analogy between a contract of insurance and the contract in the present case. In contracts of insurance, the material facts on which the insurer decides whether to assume the risk and, if so, on what terms, lie exclusively within the knowledge of the insured. Contracts requiring *uberrima fides* are based on the fact that, from the very necessity of the case, only one party possesses knowledge of all the material facts. In the case of life assurance, for example, only the proposed assured can know the state of his health, past or present. The contract in the present case was one in which material facts on both sides were withheld. Neither side made full disclosure. The husband admitted in cross-examination that he did not disclose his income. Nor was anything said about Mrs Turner's financial position.[1] The wife stated in evidence that although she knew the sources

---

[1] The husband left the wife to live with Mrs Turner.

of the husband's capital assets, that is his interest in Dean Cottage and his share capital, she had no real idea of his income although she pressed him for details. . . . On the wife's side, she did not disclose that between the end of October 1972, when the husband made the offer, and February 1973, when counsel agreed the terms in settlement of all the wife's claims for ancillary relief for maintenance, that she had an arrangement to marry Mr Wadham. No questions were asked of the wife's financial position nor whether she intended to marry at any time in the future. It seems to me that the negotiations and the agreement reached was a compromise without full disclosure on either side. I can find no similarity at all to a contract of insurance.

Judgment for the wife.

Questions

Is it true to say that a statement of intention is not a representation of existing fact where the person making it honestly holds the intention expressed? It is not a *mis*representation because it is true; but that does not prevent it being a representation of fact. Is *With v. O'Flanagan* properly distinguishable?

LAMBERT v. CO-OPERATIVE INSURANCE SOCIETY LTD

Court of Appeal [1975] 2 Lloyd's Rep. 485

In April 1963 Mrs Lambert signed a proposal form for an insurance policy to cover her own and her husband's jewellery. Her answers to questions on the form were filled in by an agent of the insurance company. No questions were asked about previous convictions and Mrs Lambert gave no information about them. She knew that her husband had been convicted some years earlier of stealing cigarettes and fined £25. The company issued a policy providing that it should be void if there was an omission to state any fact material to the risk. The policy was renewed from year to year, the last application to renew being made in March 1972. In December 1971 the husband had been convicted of conspiracy to steal and theft and sentenced to 15 months imprisonment. Mrs Lambert knew of the conviction but did not disclose it and the policy was renewed. On April 30, 1972, seven items of the insured jewellery, valued at £311, were lost or stolen. Mrs Lambert's claim was repudiated on the grounds (i) that she had failed to disclose her husband's first conviction; (ii) that she had failed to disclose his second conviction. Judge Ranking dismissed the wife's claim on the ground that the 1971 conviction was a material fact and that a prudent insurer, knowing of it, would not have continued the risk.

The plaintiff appealed.

MACKENNA J.: Everyone agrees that the assured is under a duty of disclosure and that the duty is the same when he is applying for a renewal as it is when he is applying for the original policy. The extent of that duty is the matter in controversy. There are, at least in theory, four possible rules or tests which I shall state. (1) The duty is to disclose such facts only as the particular assured believes to be material. (2) It is to disclose such facts as a reasonable man would believe to be material. (3) It is to disclose such facts as the particular insurer would regard as material. (4) It is to disclose such facts as a reasonable or prudent insurer might have treated as material.

Section 18 of the Marine Insurance Act, 1906, chooses the fourth. Sub-section (1) of that section provides that:

The assured must disclose to the insurer, before the contract is concluded, every material circumstance which is known to the assured, and the assured is deemed to know every circumstance which, in the ordinary course of business ought to be known by him. If the assured fails to make such disclosure, the insurer may avoid the contract.

Sub-section (2) is in these words:

Every circumstance is material which would influence the judgment of a prudent insurer in fixing the premium, or determining whether he will take the risk.

There is no obvious reason why there should be a rule in marine insurance different from the rules in other forms of insurance and, in my opinion, there is no difference. [His Lordship examined various authorities, concluding with the Report of the Law Reform Committee (Cmnd. 62 of 1957)].

After stating their decision to exclude marine insurance from the scope of their inquiries, because of the lack of interest by the general public in the subject, the committee went on to state their view about non-disclosure. I quote from paragraph 4 of the report.

The effect of non-disclosure may be considered first, since it is a consequence of the general law relating to insurance contracts and does not involve any express term or condition. We take it to be well settled law (a) that the duty of disclosure of material facts—or the rule of *uberrima fides* as it is often called—applies to all classes of insurance, and (b) that the question in every case is whether the fact not disclosed was material to the risk, and not whether the insured, whether reasonably or otherwise, believed or understood it to be so.

Further, we see no reason to doubt that the definition of "material," adopted by the Privy Council in *Mutual Life Insurance Co. of New York v. Ontario Metal Products Co. Ltd* for the purposes of life assurance—namely that the fact, if disclosed, might have led a reasonable insurer to decline the risk or to stipulate for a higher premium—would be applied in all classes of insurance. This definition is substantially the same as that laid down in the Marine Insurance Act, 1906, and has been adopted by an English Court as a definition of materiality for the purpose of subsections (3) and (5) of section 10 of the Road Traffic Act 1934.

That last reference is of course to the *Zurich General Accident and Liability Insurance Co. v. Morrison.*

The report continues:

The practical effect of the law on this point is that insurers are entitled to repudiate liability wherever they can show that a fact within the knowledge of the insured was not disclosed which, according to current insurance practice, would have affected their judgment of the risk. Whether the insuring public at large is aware of this it is difficult to say; but it seems to us to follow from the accepted definition of materiality that a fact may be material to insurers, in the light of the great volume of experience of claims available to them, which would not necessarily appear to a proposer for insurance, however honest and careful, to be one which he ought to disclose. [—They went on to recommend a change in the law. I will quote the first of three recommendations in paragraph 14 of the report:—] (1) That for the purpose of any contract of insurance no fact should be deemed material unless it would have been considered material by a reasonable insured.

We are, in effect, invited to say that the committee misunderstood the matter and that what they proposed as a change in the law is the existing rule. I am not prepared to accept this invitation. Recognising that there are expressions in some of the cases which favour the appellant's argument, I think the committee got it right and that their statement of the existing law was correct. . . . I cannot say that the Judge's view was wrong. I am content to act upon his finding of fact which is, I think, sufficiently supported by evidence, and to take the law as stated by the Law Reform Committee.

I would only add to this long judgment the expression of my personal regret that the Committee's recommendation has not been implemented. The present case shows the unsatisfactory state of the law. Mrs Lambert is unlikely to have thought that it was necessary to disclose the distressing fact of her husband's recent conviction when she was renewing the policy on her little store of jewellery. She is not an under-writer and has presumably no experience in these matters. The defendant company would act decently if, having established the point of principle, they were to pay her. It might be thought a heartless thing if they did not, but that is their business, not mine. I would dismiss the appeal.

LAWTON and CAIRNS L.JJ. delivered judgments dismissing the appeal.

The duty to disclose: mutuality; and remedies

The duty of disclosure of facts which are material to the risk in insurance contracts is mutual, that is, it is imposed on the insurer as well as the insured. In *Banque Financière v. Westgate Insurance* [1990] 2 All E.R. 947, 960, H.L., Lord Jauncey said that the duty is limited to facts which are material to the risk insured, that is, facts which would influence a prudent insurer in deciding whether to accept the risk and, if so, on what terms, and a prudent insured in entering into the contract on the terms proposed by the insurer; but that there is no duty to disclose supervening facts which come to the knowledge of either party after the conclusion of the contract. There have been no reported cases involving the failure of an insurer to disclose material facts to an insured. The example given by Lord Mansfield in *Carter v. Boehm* (1766) 3 Burr. 1905, 1909, is of an insurer who insured a ship knowing that she had already arrived. Another example would be the insurance against fire of a house which the insurer knew had been demolished.

In *Banque Financière*, Steyn J. had held that an action for damages lies for breach of the obligation of utmost good faith in an insurance contract—a proposition for which there was no previous authority—but the Court of Appeal decided that no such action lies. There was some suggestion in earlier cases that the duty of disclosure rests upon an implied promise in the contract that full disclosure had been made. If that were so, the non-disclosure would be a breach of contract as soon as the contract came into existence and an action for damages would lie. But the court (pp. 993–996) held that the duty is imposed by law and arises entirely outside the contract. (A holding followed in *Bank of Novia Scotia v. Hellenic Mutual* [1989] 3 All E.R. 628, 659, C.A.) Nor was there any authority to the effect that non-disclosure constitutes a tort and the court was not prepared to create a new one. The court assumed (p. 1001), without deciding, that any conduct which is capable of giving rise to an estoppel by conduct is capable of giving rise to a claim for misrepresentation; but mere silence, even where there is a duty to speak does not constitute a misrepresentation, (p. 1003). For the purposes of the 1967 Act (below, p. 703) a misrepresentation must be "made." This is not apt to include a failure to make a statement which ought to have been made, (see p. 1004).

Materiality and inducement

A circumstance is material (p. 337, above) if a prudent insurer would consider it in deciding whether to accept the risk and, if so, on what terms, even though, after that consideration, the circumstance would not affect his decision on either of these matters: The House of Lords so held in *Pan Atlantic Insurance Co. Ltd v. Pine Top Insurance Co. Ltd* [1994] 3 All E. R. 581, H.L. (Lords Templeman and Lloyd dissenting), rejecting the "decisive influence test"; but they went on to hold unanimously, applying the "actual inducement test", that an insurer can avoid a policy for a misrepresentation or non-disclosure only if (a) it was material *and* (b) it induced the making of the policy on the relevant terms. So the duty of the insured to disclose extends to facts which the prudent insurer would take into account even though they would, in the end, have no influence on his decision. But a failure to disclose such a fact would have no effect unless the the particular insurer, being of more than ordinary prudence, would either have refused to take the risk or charged a higher premium if he had known of the fact.

Law Commission Working Paper No. 73: Insurance Law—Non-disclosure and breach of warranty

After referring to judicial criticism of the law in *Lambert v. Co-op. Ins.*, the Law Commission go on[1]:

38. It has been pointed out that many laymen are not aware that a duty of disclosure exists and that it may be very difficult if not impossible for those who are aware of the duty to know what information would be regarded as material by a prudent insurer. One writer has observed that the duty imposes an especially heavy burden on insureds who hold a policy which is renewable year by year as they are most unlikely to realise that the duty arises on each successive renewal. Another has raised the problem of the extent of the duty to an insured when he applies over the telephone for the issue of a cover-note by an insurer.

39. The general rule of the present law whereby an insured is not relieved of his duty of disclosure even where the insurer has asked questions of him in a proposal form, has been criticised on the ground that the insured may well have been led to suppose that no further information was required to be disclosed by him.

40. In endeavouring to ascertain the materiality of particular facts, the courts will hear the expert evidence of other insurers; such evidence will be produced by the insurer who will select its expert witnesses. Some judicial doubt has been cast on the cogency of such evidence. For instance, it has

---

[1] Footnotes are omitted.

been thought odd that an insurer who would not himself have regarded a non-disclosed fact as material should be able to call evidence that a prudent insurer would have done so.

41. Criticism has also been directed to judicial decisions as to the materiality of particular types of fact. It will suffice to mention two such decisions. One is *Regina Fur v. Bossom* [1957] 2 Lloyd's Rep. 466 in which an insurer was held entitled to repudiate on the grounds of the insured's failure to disclose a conviction that had taken place 23 years earlier. Another is *Locker & Woolf Ltd. v. Western Australian Insurance Co.* [1936] 1 K.B. 408 in which the non-disclosed fact held to be material was a previous rejection with regard to an entirely different type of insurance from that which was being applied for.

42. We are impressed by these criticisms and have reached the conclusion that the law as to non-disclosure should be reformed.

See the Law Commission's Report, Law Com. No. 104, (Cmnd. 8064).

Section 3. Damages for Innocent Misrepresentation at Common Law

HEDLEY BYRNE & CO. v. HELLER & PARTNERS

House of Lords [1964] A.C. 465; [1963] 3 W.L.R. 101; [1963] 2 All E.R. 575; [1963] 1 Lloyd's Rep. 485

Hedley Byrne were a firm of advertising agents who had placed advertising orders for £8,000–£9,000 on behalf of a client, Easipower Ltd. They wanted to know whether Easipower Ltd was creditworthy, and asked their bank, the National Provincial, to find out. The National Provincial got in touch with Heller & Partners, Easipower's bankers. Heller told the National Provincial, "in confidence and without responsibility on our part," that Easipower were good for £100,000 per annum on advertising contracts. Hedley Byrne relied on this statement in placing further orders on behalf of Easipower Ltd and, as a result, lost more than £17,000 when Easipower went into liquidation. They sought to recover this loss as damages. McNair J. held that Heller were negligent but that they owed no duty of care to Hedley Byrne. The Court of Appeal affirmed that there was no duty of care and did not find it necessary to decide whether Heller was negligent. Hedley Byrne appealed.

LORDS REID, MORRIS, HODSON and DEVLIN made speeches dismissing the appeal.

LORD PEARCE: My Lords, Viscount Haldane L.C. in *Nocton v. Lord Ashburton* [1914] A.C. 932 at 948 said:

"Although liability for negligence in word has in material respects been developed in our law differently from liability for negligence in act, it is none the less true that a man may come under a special duty to exercise care in giving information or advice. I should accordingly be sorry to be thought to lend countenance to the idea that recent decisions have been intended to stereotype the cases in which people can be held to have assumed such a special duty. Whether such a duty has been assumed must depend on the relationship of the parties, and it is at least certain that there are a good many cases in which that relationship may be properly treated as giving rise to a special duty of care in statement."

The law of negligence has been deliberately limited in its range by the courts' insistence that there can be no actionable negligence *in vacuo* without the existence of some duty to the plaintiff. For it would be impracticable to grant relief to everybody who suffers damage through the carelessness of another.

The reason for some divergence between the law of negligence in word and that of negligence in act is clear. Negligence in word creates problems different from those of negligence in act. Words are more volatile than deeds. They travel fast and far afield. They are used without being expended and take effect in combination with innumerable facts and other words. Yet they are dangerous and can cause vast financial damage. . . .

Denning L.J. in his dissenting judgment in *Candler v. Crane, Christmas & Co.* [1951] 2 K.B. at 179 . . . reached the conclusion that in respect of reports and work that resulted in such reports there was a duty of care laid on

"those persons such as accountants, surveyors, valuers and analysts, whose profession and occupation it is to examine books, accounts, and other things and to make reports on which other people—other than their clients—rely in the ordinary course of business."

The duty is in his opinion owed (apart from contractual duty to their employer)

"to any third person to whom they themselves show the accounts, or to whom they know their employer is going to show the accounts so as to induce him to invest money or take some other action on them."

He excludes strangers of whom they have heard nothing and to whom their employer without their knowledge may choose to hand their accounts, and continues:

"The test of proximity in these cases is: did the accountants know that the accounts were required for submission to the plaintiff and use by him?"

. . . I agree with those words. In my opinion they are consonant with earlier cases and with the observations of Lord Haldane.

It is argued that so to hold would create confusion in many aspects of the law and infringe the established rule that innocent misrepresentation gives no right to damages. I cannot accept that argument. The true rule is that innocent misrepresentation *per se* gives no right to damages. If the misrepresentation was intended by the parties to form a warranty between two contracting parties, it gives on that ground a right to damages (*Heilbut, Symons & Co. v. Buckleton* (below, p. 363). If an innocent misrepresentation is made between parties in a fiduciary relationship it may, on that ground, give a right to claim damages for negligence. There is also in my opinion a duty of care created by special relationships which, though not fiduciary, give rise to an assumption that care as well as honesty is demanded.

Was there such a special relationship in the present case as to impose on the respondents a duty of care to the appellants as the undisclosed principals for whom National Provincial Bank Ltd was making the inquiry? The answer to that question depends on the circumstances of the transaction. If, for instance, they disclosed a casual social approach to the inquiry no such special relationship or duty of care would be assumed (see *Fish v. Kelly* (1864) 17 C.B. (N.S.) 194). To import such a duty the representation must normally, I think, concern a business or professional transaction whose nature makes clear the gravity of the inquiry and the importance and influence attached to the answer. It is conceded that Salmon J. rightly found a duty of care in *Woods v. Martins Bank Ltd* [1959] 1 Q.B. 55, but the facts in that case were wholly different from those in the present case. A most important circumstance is the form of the inquiry and of the answer. Both were here plainly stated to be without liability. Counsel for the appellants argues that those words are not sufficiently precise to exclude liability for negligence. Nothing, however, except negligence could, in the facts of this case, create a liability (apart from fraud, to which they cannot have been intended to refer and against which the words would be no protection since they would be part of the fraud). I do not, therefore, accept that, even if the parties were already in contractual or other special relationship, the words would give no immunity to a negligent answer. But in any event they clearly prevent a special relationship from arising. They are part of the material from which one deduces whether a duty of care and a liability for negligence was assumed. If both parties say expressly (in a case where neither is deliberately taking advantage of the other) that there shall be no liability, I do not find it possible to say that a liability was assumed. . . .

I would, therefore, dismiss the appeal.

Appeal dismissed.

Section 4. Losing the Right to Rescind

LEAF v. INTERNATIONAL GALLERIES

Court of Appeal [1950] 2 K.B. 86; 66 T.L.R. (Pt. 1) 1031; [1950] 1 All E.R. 693

In March 1944 the plaintiff purchased from the defendants a picture called "Salisbury Cathedral" for £85. At the time of purchase the defendants represented that the picture was painted by John Constable, but when, five years later, the plaintiff tried to sell it, he was informed that it was not by Constable. Thereupon he returned it to the defendants and asked them to refund the £85. The plaintiff brought an action for rescission. The county court judge found that the defendants had made an innocent misrepresentation and that the picture had not been painted by Constable. He gave judgment for the defendant, holding, on the authority of *Angel v. Jay*,[1] that the equitable remedy of rescission was not available in the case of an executed contract.

---

[1] See below, p. 353 and Misrepresentation Act 1967, s.1(*b*), below, p. 703.

DENNING L.J.: The question is whether the plaintiff is entitled to rescind the contract on the ground that the picture in question was not painted by Constable. I emphasise that it is a claim to rescind only: there is no claim in this action for damages for breach of condition or breach of warranty. The claim is simply one for rescission. At a very late stage before the county court judge counsel did ask for leave to amend by claiming damages for breach of warranty, but it was not allowed. No claim for damages is before us at all. The only question is whether the plaintiff is entitled to rescind.

The way in which the case is put by Mr Weitzman, on behalf of the plaintiff, is this: he says that this was an innocent misrepresentation and that in equity he is, or should be, entitled to claim rescission even of an executed contract of sale on that account. He points out that the judge has found that it is quite possible to restore the parties to their original position. It can be done by simply handing back the picture to the defendants.

In my opinion, this case is to be decided according to the well-known principles applicable to the sale of goods. This was a contract for the sale of goods. There was a mistake about the quality of the subject-matter, because both parties believed the picture to be a Constable; and that mistake was in one sense essential or fundamental. But such a mistake does not avoid the contract: there was no mistake at all about the subject-matter of the sale. It was a specific picture, "Salisbury Cathedral." The parties were agreed in the same terms on the same subject-matter, and that is sufficient to make a contract: see *Solle v. Butcher* (below, p. 501).

There was a term in the contract as to the quality of the subject-matter: namely, as to the person by whom the picture was painted—that it was by Constable. That term of the contract was, according to our terminology, either a condition or a warranty. If it was a condition, the buyer could reject the picture for breach of the condition at any time before he accepted it, or is deemed to have accepted it; whereas, if it was only a warranty, he could not reject it at all but was confined to a claim for damages.

I think it right to assume in the buyer's favour that this term was a condition, and that if he had come in proper time he could have rejected the picture; but the right to reject for breach of condition has always been limited by the rule that, once the buyer has accepted, or is deemed to have accepted, the goods in performance of the contract, then he cannot thereafter reject, but is relegated to his claim for damages: see section 11(1)(c) of the Sale of Goods Act 1893 (See now s.11(4) of the 1979 Act below, p. 400), and *Wallis, Son & Wells v. Pratt & Haynes* [1910] 2 K.B. 1003; [1911] A.C. 394 (below, p. 417).

The circumstances in which a buyer is deemed to have accepted goods in performance of the contract are set out in section 35 of the Act, which says that the buyer is deemed to have accepted the goods, amongst other things, "when, after the lapse of a reasonable time, he retains the goods without intimating to the seller that he has rejected them." In this case the buyer took the picture into his house and, apparently, hung it there, and five years passed before he intimated any rejection at all. That, I need hardly say, is much more than a reasonable time. It is far too late for him at the end of five years to reject this picture for breach of any condition. His remedy after that length of time is for damages only, a claim which he has not brought before the court.

Is it to be said that the buyer is in any better position by relying on the representation, not as a condition, but as an innocent misrepresentation?. . .

Although rescission may in some cases be a proper remedy, it is to be remembered that an innocent misrepresentation is much less potent than a breach of condition; and a claim to rescission for innocent misrepresentation must at any rate be barred when a right to reject for breach of condition is barred. A condition is a term of the contract of a most material character, and if a claim to reject on that account is barred, it seems to me *a fortiori* that a claim to rescission on the ground of innocent misrepresentation is also barred.

So, assuming that a contract for the sale of goods may be rescinded in a proper case for innocent misrepresentation, the claim is barred in this case for the self-same reason as a right to reject is barred. The buyer has accepted the picture. He had ample opportunity for examination in the first few days after he had bought it. Then was the time to see if the condition or representation was fulfilled. Yet he has kept it all this time. Five years have elapsed without any notice of rejection. In my judgment he cannot now claim to rescind. His only claim, if any, as the county court judge said, was one for damages, which he has not made in this action. In my judgment, therefore, the appeal should be dismissed.

JENKINS L.J. and EVERSHED M.R. delivered concurring judgments.

PEYMAN v. LANJANI

Court of Appeal [1985] Ch. 457; [1985] 2 W.L.R. 154; [1984] 3 All E.R. 703

The plaintiff entered into an agreement to purchase from the defendant the lease of a restaurant for £55,000 to be paid by the plaintiff selling his house to the defendant for £32,000, the balance to be paid in cash. The defendant had obtained the landlord's consent to the assignment to him of the lease by fraud ("the first impersonation"). On February 9, when the plaintiff was reluctant to proceed with the transaction, he learned of the impersonation. The solicitor who was acting for both parties urged him to proceed. A month later the plaintiff consulted new solicitors who advised him that the defendant's title was defective because of the fraud and that he had a right to rescind; and the plaintiff gave notice to the defendant of his intention to do so. The judge held that the plaintiff had affirmed the contract because on February 22, after he knew of the impersonation, he had proceeded with the contract, taken possession of the restaurant and paid £10,000 to the defendant.

The plaintiff appealed. The Court of Appeal held that the plaintiff was not deprived of his right to rescind because, knowing *of the facts* which give rise to the right to rescind, he proceeded with the contract, unless he also knew that he had *the right* to rescind. The plaintiff (an Iranian who spoke no English) did not know he had such a right. As he did not know he had such a right, he could not be said to have elected to affirm the contract by his actions.

SLADE L.J.: Where the other stated conditions for the operation of the common law doctrine of "election" are present, a person may be held to his election even though the other party has not in any way acted to his detriment in reliance on the relevant communication; the mere facts of the unequivocal act or statement, coupled with the communication thereof to the other party, suffice to bring the doctrine into play. For this reason, if no other, as appears from the judgments of Stephenson and May L.JJ. a clear distinction has to be drawn between election on the one hand and estoppel or waiver by conduct on the other hand.

The relevant argument in the present case has primarily been directed to election. Before us it has been common ground that the injured party to a contract who has a right of rescission cannot be said to have elected to affirm it at a time before he became aware of the facts which give rise to this right. However, as Stephenson L.J. has demonstrated, statements of the highest authority seem at first sight to give conflicting answers to the question whether knowledge of the existence of the legal right to rescind is also a condition precedent to an effective election.

Lord Blackburn in *Kendall v. Hamilton* (1879) 4 App.Cas. 504 at 542, said: ". . . there cannot be election until there is knowledge of the right to elect." For the reasons given by Stephenson and May L.JJ., I am of the opinion that this statement, which was cited by Lord Porter in *Young v. Bristol Aeroplane Co. Ltd* [1946] A.C. 163 at 186 as being the foundation of the principle of election, still correctly represents the law. With Stephenson and May L.JJ., I do not think that a person (such as Mr Peyman in the present case) can be held to have made the irrevocable choice between rescission and affirmation which election involves unless he had knowledge of his legal right to choose and actually chose with that knowledge.

I would like to make a few observations as to the practical consequences of this court's decision on this point, as I see them. If A wishes to allege that B, having had a right of rescission, has elected to affirm a contract, he should in his pleadings, so it seems to me, expressly allege B's knowledge of the relevant right to rescind, since such knowledge will be an essential fact on which he relies. The court may, and no doubt often will, be asked to order A to give further and better particulars of the allegation (see RSC Ord. 18, r. 12(4)). In many cases the best particulars that A will be able to give will be to invite the court to infer knowledge from all the circumstances. However strong that prima facie inference may be, it will still be open to the court at the trial, after hearing evidence as to B's true state of mind, to hold on the balance of probabilities that he did not in fact have the requisite knowledge. In the latter event A's plea that B has elected will fail. Yet it should not be thought that injustice to A will necessarily follow. For, if A has acted to his detriment in reliance of [*sic*] an *apparent* election by B, he will in most cases be able to plead and rely on an estoppel by conduct, in the alternative. If, on the other hand, A has *not* acted to his detriment in reliance on any such apparent election, justice would not seem to preclude B from sheltering behind his ignorance of his legal rights. These brief observations may perhaps serve to highlight the distinction between election and estoppel.

Since Mr Peyman had no knowledge of his legal right to rescind the restaurant agreement, until he consulted new solicitors, his conduct in entering into possession of the restaurant and paying £10,000 to Mr Lanjani, for this reason if no other, cannot in my opinion have amounted to an *election* to affirm the contract; the only remaining question can be whether Mr Peyman by that conduct has estopped himself from relying on his right to rescind.

However, even if I am wrong in thinking that knowledge of the relevant legal right is a precondition to an effective election, the result on the facts of the present case is, in my opinion, still the same for these reasons. Whatever knowledge may be requisite, the passages which I have cited above . . . in my opinion make it quite clear that a person who has the right to rescind a contract cannot be treated as having elected to affirm it unless and until he has done an unequivocal act, or made an unequivocal statement, which demonstrates to the other party to the contract that he still intends to proceed with it, notwithstanding the relevant breach. An unequivocal act or unequivocal statement on the part of Mr Peyman is no less necessary if Mr Lanjani is to rely on an estoppel by conduct.

The judge considered that the arrangements by which Mr Peyman took possession of the restaurant and paid Mr Lanjani £10,000 of the purchase price did amount to "an unequivocal affirmation of the contract." He thought that Mr Lanjani acted on this affirmation by giving up possession of the restaurant and going away to Iran. Mr Peyman, he considered, by these arrangements, "accepted the title through his solicitor . . . and that as between him and Mr Lanjani is that."

This conduct of Mr Peyman on February 22, 1979 undeniably indicated that, at least for the time being, he intended to proceed with the restaurant agreement. In my opinion, however, this does not by itself suffice to indicate any·relevant final choice on his part. The question is whether his conduct on February 22, 1979 would have led Mr Lanjani and his legal advisers reasonably to infer he did not intend to object to *the particular defect in title which had arisen through the first impersonation.*

For my part, I do not think that Mr Lanjani or his legal advisers could reasonable have drawn any such inference . . .

Note

Compare the principles stated by Lord Denning in *Leaf v. International Galleries*, above, p. 342 governing rescission of a contract for the sale of goods, and see Lord Goff in *The Kanchenjunga* [1990] 1 Lloyd's Rep. 391 at 398: "Generally . . . it is a prerequisite of election that the party making the election must be aware of the facts which have given rise to the existence of his new right. This may not always be so. For example, in the law of sale of goods, where goods have been tendered to the buyer which are not in conformity with the contract, he may, if he has had a reasonable opportunity to examine them, be deemed in certain circumstances to have accepted them, thereby electing not to exercise his right to reject them, even though he has not actually examined the goods and discovered the defect (see sections 34 and 35 of the Sale of Goods Act 1979). This may flow from the fact that he has waived his right to examine them—yet another example of waiver. I add in parenthesis that, for present purposes, it is not necessary for me to consider certain cases in which it has been held that, as a prerequisite of election, the party must be aware not only of the facts giving rise to his rights but also of the rights themselves, because it is not in dispute here that the owners were aware both of the relevant facts and of their relevant rights."

Section 5. How to Rescind

CAR AND UNIVERSAL FINANCE CO. LTD v. CALDWELL

[1965] 1 Q.B. 525; [1964] 2 W.L.R. 600; [1964] 1 All E.R. 290

The defendant sold his car on January 12, 1960, to Norris who took it away leaving a deposit of £10 and a cheque for £965. The cheque was dishonoured when the defendant presented it the next day. He immediately informed the police and the Automobile Association of the fraudulent transaction. Subsequently Norris sold the car to X who sold it to Y who sold it to Z who sold it to the plaintiffs. In interpleader proceedings one of the issues to be tried was whether the defendant's conduct and representations on or about January 13 amounted to a rescission of the contract of sale. Lord Denning M.R. held that, where a seller of goods had a right to avoid a contract for fraud, he sufficiently exercised his election if, on discovering the fraud, he immediately took all possible steps to regain the goods, even though he could not find the purchaser or communicate with him; and that the contract of sale was therefore rescinded on January 13. The plaintiffs appealed.

SELLERS L.J. delivered judgment dismissing the appeal.

UPJOHN L.J.: Where one party to a contract has an option unilaterally to rescind or disaffirm it by reason of the fraud or misrepresentation of the other party, he must elect to do so within a reasonable time, and cannot do so after he has done anything to affirm the contract with knowledge of the facts giving rise to the option to rescind. In principle and on authority, however, he must, in my judgment, in the ordinary course communicate his intention to rescind to the other party. This must be so because the other party is entitled to treat the contractual nexus as continuing until he is made aware of the intention of the other to exercise his option to rescind. So the intention must be communicated and an uncommunicated intention, for example, by speaking to a third party or making a private note, will be ineffective. The textbooks to which we were referred are unanimous on the subject. "If a party elects to rescind he must within a reasonable time manifest that election by communicating to the other party his intention to rescind the transaction and claim no interest under it. The communication need not be formal provided it is a distinct and positive repudiation of the transaction": *Kerr on Fraud and Mistake* (7th ed., 1952), p. 530. See also *Benjamin on Sale* (8th ed., 1950), p. 441; *Pollock on Contracts* (13th ed., 1950), p. 467.

Mr Caplan, for the plaintiffs, of course also relies strongly on the well-known words of Lord Blackburn in *Scarf v. Jardine*, 7 App.Cas. 345, 349, 360, to the effect that in general an election must be communicated to the other side, though that was not a case of contract. Further, with all respect to the judgment of Lord Denning M.R., Lord Hatherley's observations in *Reese River Silver Mining Co. v. Smith* (1869) L.R. 4 H.L. 64, 74, in my view support the same conclusion.

Such in my view must be the general principle. Does it admit of any exception? Mr Caplan concedes that there is one: Where the subject-matter of the contract is a transfer of property, then the party entitled to do so may disaffirm the contract by retaking possession of the property. Mr Caplan, however, submits this is really a method of communication, though for my part I do not see how that can be true of every case that can be suggested. Is there any other exception? Mr Caplan submits not and that, apart from recaption, there should be a universal rule of law that communication is essential to break the nexus. On the facts of this case it is clear that Norris intended quite deliberately to disappear and render it impossible for the defendant to communicate with him or to recover the car. While I appreciate Mr Caplan's argument that this point can only arise in cases between the vendor and a third party, I agree with Sellers L.J. that this problem must be solved by consideration of the rights between the two contracting parties. Admittedly one of two innocent parties must suffer for the fraud of a third, but that cannot be helped and does not assist to solve the problem. One thing is quite clear—that neither Lord Blackburn nor Lord Hatherley in the cases above mentioned nor the textbook writers had in mind circumstances remotely resembling these. It is indeed strange that there is no authority in point.

If one party, by absconding, deliberately puts it out of the power of the other to communicate his intention to rescind which he knows the other will almost certainly want to do, I do not think he can any longer insist on his right to be made aware of the election to determine the contract. In these circumstances communication is a useless formality. I think that the law must allow the innocent party to exercise his right of rescission otherwise than by communication or repossession. To hold otherwise would be to allow a fraudulent contracting party by his very fraud to prevent the innocent party from exercising his undoubted right. I would hold that in circumstances such as these the innocent party may evince his intention to disaffirm the contract by overt means falling short of communication or repossession.

We heard much interesting argument on the position where one party makes an innocent misrepresentation which entitles the other to elect to rescind and then innocently so acts that the other cannot find him to communicate his election to him. I say nothing about that case and would leave it to be decided if and when it arises. I am solely concerned with the fraudulent rogue who deliberately makes it impossible for the other to communicate with him or to retake the property.

Mr Caplan further argued that even if, in the circumstances of the case, communication to Norris was not necessary, yet what the plaintiff did on January 13, when the cheque was dishonoured, did not amount to an unequivocal election to disaffirm; and it was further said that he could have done more to contact Norris. On the facts of this case I do not see what the plaintiff could reasonably have done, nor how he could have made his position plainer.

Davies L.J. delivered judgment dismissing the appeal.

Appeal dismissed.

Notes

1. The Law Reform Committee (Twelfth Report (Transfer of Title to Chattels), Cmnd. 2958, para. 16) thought that the decision in the above case "goes far to destroy the value of section 23 of the Sale of Goods Act, 1893 (see now 1979 Act), which provides that where the seller of goods has a voidable title which has not been avoided at the time of sale, the buyer acquires a good title to the goods provided he buys them in good faith and without notice of the seller's defect of title. We think that unless and until notice of the rescission of the contract is communicated to the other contracting party an innocent purchaser from the latter should be able to acquire a good title. No doubt this will mean that the innocent purchaser will do so in the great majority of cases since it will usually be impracticable for the original owner of the goods to communicate with the rogue who has deprived him of them."

Why should the innocent purchaser's rights depend on whether or not notice has been given to his seller since, by definition, the innocent purchaser knows nothing of it?

2. The party who seeks rescission must be in a position to restore whatever benefits he has received under the contract. If he is not, he can no longer rescind. "If you are fraudulently induced to buy a cake you may return it and get back the price; but you cannot both eat your cake and return your cake," *per* Crompton J. in the course of the argument in the next case.

CLARKE v. DICKSON

Queen's Bench (1858) 120 E.R. 463; El.Bl. & El. 148

In 1853 the plaintiff was induced to take shares in a company by the misrepresentation of the defendants. In 1857 the company was in bad circumstances and was, with the plaintiff's assent, registered as a company with limited liability. It was afterwards wound up, and during the winding up the plaintiff discovered the falsity of the representations for the first time. He brought an action to recover the money which he had paid for the shares. The Court of Queen's Bench held that the action failed.

CROMPTON J.: When once it is settled that a contract induced by fraud is not void, but voidable at the option of the party defrauded, it seems to me to follow that, when that party exercises his option to rescind the contract, he must be in a state to rescind; that is, he must be in such a situation as to be able to put the parties into their original state before the contract. Now here I will assume, what is not clear to me, that the plaintiff bought his shares from the defendants and not from the company, and that he might at one time have had a right to restore the shares to the defendants if he could, and demand the price from them. But then what did he buy? Shares in a partnership with others. He cannot return those; he has become bound to those others. Still stronger, he has changed their nature: what he now has and offers to restore are shares in a quasi corporation now in process of being wound up. That is quite enough to decide this case. The plaintiff must rescind *in toto* or not at all; he cannot both keep the shares and recover the whole price. That is founded on the plainest principles of justice. If he cannot return the article he must keep it, and sue for his real damage in an action on the deceit. Take the case I put in the argument, of a butcher buying live cattle, killing them, and even selling the meat to his customers. If the rule of law were as the plaintiff contends, that butcher, might, upon discovering a fraud on the part of the grazier who sold him the cattle, rescind the contract and get back the whole price: but how could that be consistent with justice? The true doctrine is, that a party can never repudiate a contract after, by his own act, it has become out of his power to restore the parties to their original condition.

Note
    In *O'Sullivan v. Management Agency* [1985] 3 All E.R. 351, 365, Dunn L.J., after a detailed examination of the case law, concluded: This analysis of the cases shows that the principle of *restitutio in integrum* is not applied with its full rigour in equity in relation to transactions entered into by persons in breach of a fiduciary relationship, and that such transactions may be set aside even though it is impossible to place the parties precisely in the position in which they were before, provided that the court can achieve practical justice between the parties by obliging the wrongdoer to give up his profits and advantages, while at the same time compensating him for any work that he has actually performed pursuant to the transaction. *Erlanger v. New Sombrero Phosphate Co.* (1878) 3 App.Cas. 1218 is a striking example of the application of this principle.

Section 6. The Right to Indemnity

For an innocent but "negligent" misrepresentation the injured party may now recover damages as well as rescind the contract: Misrepresentation Act 1967, below,

p. 352. In the rare case where a contract is rescinded for an innocent non-negligent misrepresentation, the injured party may not recover damages (unless the misrepresentation has become a term of the contract), but he has a right to indemnity.

NEWBIGGING v. ADAM

Court of Appeal (1886) 34 Ch.D. 582; 56 L.J.Ch. 275; 55 L.T. 794; 35 W.R. 597; 3 T.L.R. 259

The plaintiff was induced by the defendants by innocent misrepresentations to enter into a contract of partnership. The plaintiff bound himself to bring in £10,000 to the capital of the firm. Of this, he brought in £9,700 and also paid, in discharge of the liabilities of the partnership, £324. The business proved unsuccessful. In an action for the dissolution of the partnership Bacon V.-C. ordered the defendants to repay the sums brought into the partnership by the plaintiff, and to indemnify him against all liabilities to which he had become or might become liable on account of the partnership. The defendants appealed and argued that this order amounted to giving the plaintiff damages for innocent misrepresentation.

BOWEN L.J. said: If we turn to the question of misrepresentation, damages cannot be obtained at law for misrepresentation which is not fraudulent, and you cannot, as it seems to me, give in equity any indemnity which corresponds with damages. If the mass of authority there is upon the subject were gone though I think it would be found that there is not so much difference as is generally supposed between the view taken at common law and the view taken in equity as to misrepresentation. At common law it has always been considered that misrepresentations which strike at the root of the contract are sufficient to avoid the contract on the ground explained in *Kennedy v. Panama, New Zealand, and Australian Royal Mail Company*, L.R. 2 Q.B. 580; but when you come to consider what is the exact relief to which a person is entitled in a case of misrepresentation it seems to me to be this, and nothing more, that he is entitled to have the contract rescinded, and is entitled accordingly to all the incidents and consequences of such rescission. It is said that the injured party is entitled to be replaced *in status quo*. It seems to me that when you are dealing with innocent misrepresentation you must understand that proposition that he is to be replaced *in status quo* with this limitation—that he is not to be replaced in exactly the same position in all respects, otherwise he would be entitled to recover damages, but is to be replaced in his position so far as regards the rights and obligations which have been created by the contract into which he has been induced to enter. That seems to me to be the true doctrine. . . .

[His Lordship then considered the case of *Redgrave v. Hurd* (above, p. 329) and continued:] . . . the Master of the Rolls . . . treats the relief as being the giving back by the party who made the misrepresentation of the advantages he obtained by the contract. Now those advantages may be of two kinds. He may get an advantage in the shape of an actual benefit, as when he receives money; he may also get an advantage if the party with whom he contracts assumes some burthen in consideration of the contract. In such a case it seems to me that complete rescission would not be effected unless the misrepresenting party not only hands back the benefits which he has himself received—but also reassumes the burthen which under the contract the injured person has taken upon himself. Speaking only for myself I should not like to lay down the proposition that a person is to be restored to the position which he held before the misrepresentation was made, nor that the person injured must be indemnified against loss which arises out of the contract, unless you place upon the words "out of the contract" the limited and special meaning which I have endeavoured to shadow forth. Loss arising out of the contract is a term which would be too wide. It would embrace damages at common law, because damages at common law are only given upon the supposition that they are damages which would naturally and reasonably follow from the injury done. I think *Redgrave v. Hurd* shows that it would be too wide, because in that case the court excluded from the relief which was given the damages which had been sustained by the plaintiff in removing his business, and other similar items. There ought, as it appears to me, to be a giving back and a taking back on both sides, including the giving back and taking back of the obligations which the contract has created, as well as the giving back and the taking back of the advantages. There is nothing in the case of *Rawlins v. Wickham*, 3 De G. & J. 304, which carries the doctrine beyond that. In that case, one of three partners having retired, the remaining partners introduced the plaintiff into the firm, and he, under his contract with them, took upon himself to share with them the liabilities which otherwise they would have borne in their entirety. That was a burthen which he took under the contract and in virtue of the contract. It seems to me, therefore, that upon this principle indemnity was rightly decreed as regards the liabilities of the new firm. I have not found any case which carries the doctrine further, and it is not necessary to carry it further in order to support the order now appealed from. A part of the contract between the plaintiff and Adam & Co. was that the plaintiff should become and continue for five years partner in a new firm and bring in £10,000. By this very contract he was to pledge his credit with his partners in the new firm for the business transactions of the new firm. It was a burthen or liability imposed on him by the very contract. It seems to me that the £9,000 odd, and, indeed, all the moneys brought in by him or expended by him for the new firm up to the £10,000 were part of the actual moneys which he undertook by the true contract with Adam & Co. to pay. Of course he ought to be indemnified as regards that. I think, also, applying the same doctrine, he ought to be indemnified against all the liabilities of the firm, because they were liabilities which under the contract he was bound to take upon himself.

COTTON and FRY L.JJ. delivered concurring judgments.

Appeal dismissed.

On appeal, the House of Lords varied the decision of the Vice-Chancellor, there having been financial adjustments between the parties: 13 App.Cas. 308.

WHITTINGTON v. SEALE-HAYNE

Chancery Division (1900) 82 L.T. 49; 16 T.L.R. 181

The plaintiffs, breeders of prize poultry, were induced to take a lease of the defendant's premises by the defendant's oral innocent representation that the premises were in a thoroughly sanitary condition. Under the lease the plaintiff covenanted to execute all such works as might be required by any local or public authority. Owing to the insanitary condition of the premises the water supply was poisoned, the plaintiff's manager and his family became very ill, and the poultry either died or became valueless for breeding purposes. The plaintiffs sought indemnity against the following losses: value of stock lost, £750; loss of profit on sales, £100; loss of breeding season, £500; removal of storage and rent, £75; services on behalf of the manager, £100.

Farwell J. rescinded the lease, and, following the judgment of Bowen L.J. in *Newbigging v. Adam*, held that the plaintiff could recover the rents, rates, and repairs under the covenants in the lease but nothing more.

Section 7. Misrepresentation Act 1967

The Misrepresentation Act, 1967, (below, p. 703) made important changes in the law relating to misrepresentation in three areas: (a) rescission of contracts; (b) damages; and (c) the effect of exception clauses.

(a) RESCISSION

As will be apparent from the preceeding cases, an innocent misrepresentation has long been a ground for rescission of a contract provided that two conditions were satisfied:

(a) It was a misrepresentation of *fact* and not of law or opinion. Failure to fulfil a promise or a statement of intention was not a misrepresentation, but a misstatement of present intention was.

(b) It misled the representee and he contracted relying on its truth. He could not rescind if he never knew of it, or knew it to be untrue, or did not believe it, or if he was entirely uninfluenced by it.

The Act extends the right to rescind in two respects:

(i) *Where a misrepresentation is incorporated as a term*

The law before the Act was clear enough where a misrepresentation made in the course of negotiations was not subsequently incorporated into the contract. It might happen, however that it was so incorporated. Suppose that Seller tells Buyer, "the horse is sound," and thereby induces him to contract. The horse is not sound. All the conditions are fulfilled to entitle Buyer to rescind. But suppose that they then enter into a written contract which states as one of its terms, "Seller warrants the horse to be sound." This term, according to the traditional theory (which is now known to be inadequate (see below, pp. 421, 423, 426) but which will suffice for present purposes) is either a condition or a warranty. The distinction is that if the term is a condition, breach of it entitles the injured party to terminate the contract; if the term is a warranty, breach of it does not (below, pp. 411, 417). If the term were held to have the status of a condition, there was no problem—the buyer could return the horse if it was unsound. If, however, the term were held to have the status merely of a warranty, there was an apparent conflict, the misrepresentation rules stating that Buyer could return the horse, the rules relating to terms saying that he could not. Such authority as there was (and there was not much) suggested that the rules relating to terms prevailed; with the anomalous result that Buyer might be worse off if the misrepresentation was incorporated into the contract than if it were left outside as a "mere representation."

This absurdity, if it ever was the law, is repealed by section 1(a). If a misrepresentation during negotiations would otherwise give rise to a right to rescind, it does not fail to do so because the misrepresentation has become incorporated as a term of the contract. In that case, if the term is a warranty, the contract may not be terminated for breach but it may be rescinded for misrepresentation.

(ii) *Where the contract has been performed*

Section 1(b) is also concerned with preserving to the representee a right of rescission which would, before the Act, have been lost. Once again there was no conclusive authority for saying what the law was, but there was at least respectable authority for the proposition that when a contract was performed (or "executed") any right of rescission for innocent misrepresentation, which had existed up to that moment, ceased to exist. In *Angel v. Jay* [1911] 1 K.B. 666 a lessor innocently misrepresented during negotiations for a lease that the drains were in good order. The lease for a term of three years was executed and the tenant occupied the premises. He then discovered the falsity of the representation and sought to rescind the lease. It was held by a divisional court that he could not do so; the right to rescind the contract for the lease terminated on the execution of the lease. Earlier, the same doctrine had been held applicable to a contract for the sale of shares in a company, so that a right to rescind the contract for innocent misrepresentation was lost when the shares were transferred. Under the Misrepresentation Act, in neither of these cases would the right to rescind be lost merely on the ground that the contract had been performed. But it should be noted that failure to rescind within a reasonable time after discovering the truth would be held to be evidence of an affirmation of the contract.

Section 1(*b*) is more far-reaching than the clause proposed by the Law Reform Committee. They recommended that contracts for the sale of land should be excepted from this provision—that is, they thought that such contracts should not be capable of rescission after execution. Their view was:

> ". . . in the case of sales of land finality should be the predominant consideration. The vendor will often have spent the proceeds of sale on the purchase of another house and so be unable to repay them. The purchase of a house is commonly linked with the raising of a mortgage and perhaps a sequence of other transactions. Rescission of one sale may thus start a chain reaction. The purchaser who buys a house in reliance on the vendor's representations and without an adequate survey, like one who buys without fully investigating the title, must know that he is taking a risk."

In spite of this, and against the advice of all of the professional bodies consulted, the government decided against excluding contracts for the sale of land. The difficulties feared to do not seem in fact to have arisen. It must be remembered that the court will order rescission only where the parties can be restored to substantially the position they were in before the contract. If the vendor has spent the proceeds on another house and is unable to repay them, it seems most improbable that rescission will be ordered. The purchaser certainly does not wish to give up the house without getting his money back; and to require the vendor to re-sell his new house in order to pay back the price of his old one would probably be thought too harsh. The case for refusing rescission in these circumstances is greatly strengthened by the new discretionary power given by the Act (below, p. 355) to award damages in lieu of rescission for innocent misrepresentation. Where the vendor has agreed to buy another house "subject to contract" (above, pp. 101–104) the rescission of his contract to sell may certainly set up a chain reaction—but this frequently happens anyway, since the vendor may withdraw at will from the arrangement. If the vendor has entered into a binding contract to purchase another property, he of course remains bound, whether his contract to sell be rescinded or not.

The other objection to the extension of the new section to land was that contracts for the sale of land are contracts in which the principle *caveat emptor* ought to apply in its full rigour, since the prudent buyer has the title investigated by his solicitor and the property inspected by his surveyor. But the solicitor and the surveyor may in fact be misled by the vendor or his agents, just as the purchaser himself may be; and it has never been regarded as an answer to a claim for rescission that the party who has been misled could have found out the truth if only he had been more diligent.

(b) DAMAGES

Damages have always been recoverable at common law for a fraudulent misrepresentation through the action of deceit—an action in tort. If a vendor represents that the drains of a house are in good order, when either he knows that they are not in good order, or he is aware that he does not know whether they are in good order or not, he commits a fraudulent misrepresentation. If, however, he genuinely believes that the drains are in good order, whether his belief is based on reasonable grounds or not, his misrepresentation is categorised as innocent. Until 1964 it was thought that no damages could be recovered at common law for a non-fraudulent misrepresentation—the only possible remedy was rescission of the contract. The decision of the House of Lords in *Hedley Byrne & Co. v. Heller & Partners* [1964] A.C. 465 (above, p. 340), established that, in some circumstances, damages might be recoverable if it were proved that the innocent misrepresentation was made negligently; but the extent of this rule remains very uncertain.

The Misrepresentation Act now provides that damages may be recovered for innocent misrepresentation in two situations:

(a) Under section 2(1) where the representor is unable to prove that he had reasonable grounds to believe that the misrepresentation was true—that is, he is unable to disprove negligence: though he can prove that he honestly believed the drains to be in good order, he cannot prove that he had reasonable grounds for that belief.

(b) Under section 2(2) where the representee has rescinded or is asking for rescission; and the court holds that he is entitled to rescission but that it would be more equitable to award damages. Here damages may be awarded even though the representor's belief was honest and based on reasonable grounds. The point is that the more drastic remedy of rescission is being refused in the representor's own interest.

(i) *Damages for misrepresentation not reasonably believed to be true*

An action for damages for innocent misrepresentation will lie under section 2(1) where the following four conditions are satisfied:

1. The action is brought by a party to a contract against a party to that contract.

2. A misrepresentation was made by the defendant to the plaintiff before the contract was entered into and the defendant cannot prove that he had reasonable grounds to believe and did believe that it was true. (The misrepresentation may have been made by an agent; but the agent is not personally liable under the subsection, according to Mustill J. in *The Skopas* [1983] 2 All E.R. 1).

3. As a result, the plaintiff suffered loss.

4. The defendant would have been liable in damages had the misrepresentation been made fraudulently.

This last seems a strange and circuitous way of making innocent misrepresentations actionable. Suppose that the defendant has said that the drains are in good order, honestly believing this to be true. The Act now requires us to ask, what would have been the position had he made this statement not believing it to be true? This sends us to the law of the tort of deceit which is thus incorporated by reference into the Act.

This fiction, if applied literally, could lead to some very curious results. Suppose Vendor says in all good faith: "*In my opinion*, the drains are in good order." They are not. Since this is a mere expression of opinion it is not such a misrepresentation as would have given rise to a right to rescind or to liability in any shape or form before the Act. If, however, we are now required to pretend that Vendor was fraudulent, he will be liable in damages; if, knowing the drains are in bad condition, he says, "In my opinion, the drains are in good order," he is lying and, if the Purchaser buys the property relying on such a fraudulent statement of opinion, Vendor is liable in deceit. If this be correct, the perfectly innocent Vendor, who has cautiously made it clear that he is doing no more than expressing an opinion, might find himself liable to pay damages.

The only way to avoid this result is to give a narrow meaning to "misrepresentation." That is, to construe it as meaning such misrepresentations as would formerly have given rise to a right to rescind—and thus to exclude misrepresentations of law or opinion. This would seem to be the preferable course.

Section 2(1) appears to create a new statutory tort, with the consequence that the tort and not the contract rules concerning damages apply. In two cases Lord Denning M.R. expressed the opinion that the contractual measure of damages applies but the Court of Appeal has now decided that the tort rules apply: *Chesnau v. Interhome Ltd* (1983) 134 N.L.J. 341; *Royscot Trust Ltd v. Maidenhead Honda Centre* [1991] 3 All E.R. 294. In the latter case the court had to decide the further point, whether the tortious measure is that of fraudulent misrepresentation (deceit) or that of negligent (*Hedley Byrne*, above, p. 340) misrepresentation. Not following a number of academic opinions, the court held that the plain words of the section require the court to apply the rules of fraudulent misrepresentation.

Whereas in contract the object of the damage is usually to put the plaintiff in the position he would have been in had the contract been performed, in tort it is to put him in the position he would have been in had the tort not been committed. In *Royscot* the court applied *Doyle v. Olby Ltd* [1969] 2 Q.B. 158, C.A., where Lord Denning said:

> "In contract, the damages are limited to what may reasonably be supposed to have been in the contemplation of the parties. In fraud, they are not so limited. The defendant is bound to make reparation for all the actual damage directly flowing from the fraudulent inducement. The person who has been defrauded is entitled to say: 'I would not have entered into this bargain at all but for your representation. Owing to your fraud, I have not only lost all the money I paid you, but, what is more, I have been put to a large amount of extra expense as well and suffered this or that extra damages.' All such damages can be recovered: and it does not lie in the mouth of the fraudulent person to say that they could not reasonably have been foreseen."

This is all very well where the defendant has really been guilty of fraud; but is it fair where, as under section 2(1), the fraud is entirely fictional? Assuming that *Hedley Byrne* damages are less severe, is it defensible that a tortfeasor who is proved to have been negligent should be better off than one who is deemed a tortfeasor because he cannot satisfy the court that he had reasonable grounds to believe that his representation was true?

(ii) *Damages in lieu of rescission*

Damages under section 2(1) may, presumably, be recovered where the contract is rescinded as well as where it is not—as is the case with fraudulent misrepresentation. Damages under section 2(2) may be recovered only where the court refuses rescission or (a new concept) reconstitutes a rescinded contract. Where the contract is rescinded for an innocent non-negligent misrepresentation, only an indemnity and not damages are recoverable.

In *William Sindall plc v. Cambridgeshire County Council* [1994] 3 All E.R. 932 WS in 1988 bought land for development from CCC for over £5 million. In 1990 WS discovered that a sewer was buried under the land which, unless it could be re-routed, would prevent the proposed development. They purported to rescind the contract for misrepresentation and mistake. (As to mistake, see below, p. 506) The judge held that WS were entitled to rescind for innocent misrepresentation, and, declining to exercise his discretion under section 2(2) to award damages in lieu of rescission, ordered CCC to repay the full purchase price with interest. In 1990 the property was worth less than half the price paid. The cost of diverting the sewer was £18,000. The Court of Appeal held that there had been no misrepresentation but considered, *obiter*, how the discretion under section 2(2) should have been applied if there had been.

Hoffmann L.J. said that there were three particular matters to which the court must have regard:

(i) The importance of the representation in relation to the subject-matter of the contract. In this case, a defect which would cost £18,000 to rectify was of relatively minor importance in the context of a £5 million sale.

(ii) The loss which would be caused by the misrepresentation if the contract were upheld. Section 2(2) gave power to award damages which would not previously have been recoverable. Whereas section 2(1) was concerned with damage flowing from having entered into the contract, section 2(2) was concerned with the damage caused by the property being not what it was represented to be; and should never exceed the sum which would have been awarded if the representation had been a warranty.

(iii) The loss which would be caused to CCC by rescission. They would have to return about £8 million (purchase price + interest) in exchange for land worth less than £2 million.

Accordingly, he would have exercised his discretion to award damages in lieu of rescission.

(c) Avoidance of Provisions Excluding Liability for Misrepresentation

The effect of section 3 is that a term purporting to exclude liability for misrepresentation is ineffective, unless the party relying on it satisfies the court that it was a fair and reasonable term to be included, in the following actions:

(a) Under section 2(1) for an innocent negligent misrepresentation.

(b) Under section 2(2) for an innocent misrepresentation whether negligent or not.

If the misrepresentation is a fraudulent one, liability may not be avoided. A clause purporting to exclude liability for fraudulent misrepresentation is probably void at common law and section 3 is unlikely to be construed as giving the court a discretion to uphold such a clause.

Whether section 3 is applicable at all to an action for breach of contract, as distinct from an action for fraudulent, negligent or innocent misrepresentation, is a more difficult question. Suppose that a misrepresentation is later incorporated into a contract in which there is a clause excluding liability for both misrepresentation and breach of contract. If the plaintiff claims damages under section 2(1) or rescission for misrepresentation, then, clearly, the clause may be struck down under section 3. But what if he claims damages for breach of contract or to avoid for breach of condition? One view is that the defendant still cannot rely on the exclusion clause. "The point is that the section does not invalidate a provision only *to the extent* that it excludes or restricts a liability or remedy arising from a misrepresentation; it invalidates the whole provision, though subject to the discretion of the court." (Atiyah and Treitel, 30 M.L.R. at p. 383.)

If there are two exclusion clauses, one excluding liability for misrepresentation and the other excluding liability for breach of contract, it is clear that these will be separate "provisions" and that section 3 applies only to the first and not to the second. Against the view stated above, it might be argued that it would be absurd that it should make any difference whether substantially the same provisions are put into one clause of a contract rather than into two: and that a single clause which purports to exclude liability (a) for misrepresentation and (b) for breach of contract really constitutes two "provisions," the former being valid and the second invalid. (*Cf.* the cases on severance of void provisions (below, p. 695)).

If this view be correct, section 3 does not limit the right of a party to a contract to exclude liability for contractual promises as to matters of fact, whether or not they amounted to misrepresentation before the conclusion of the contract. Whether this view is correct or not, section 3 does not limit his right to exclude liability for contractual promises as to future conduct. In a great many contracts, this will not matter, because the purported exclusion of contractual liability will be subject to the same "fair and reasonable" test of the Unfair Contract Terms Act 1977, below, p. 700. But, whereas section 3 applies to all contracts, the 1977 Act does not. Where the contract is one of those excluded by the 1977 Act, the scope of section 3 is material. The Law Reform Committee proposed that provisions excluding liability for negligent misrepresentations should be entirely void. It was apparently thought that such a rule might work hardly against a party relying on an exclusion clause in a big commercial contract negotiated at arm's length (foreign buyers were referred to in Parliament); and the draft clause was amended in the interests of the party seeking to exclude liability. He may be able to do so, notwithstanding his negligence, to the extent that the court thinks it fair and reasonable.

For criminal sanctions for false statements, see Theft Act 1968, ss.15 and 16, Theft Act 1978, ss.1 and 2, and Trade Descriptions Act 1968, generally.

HOWARD MARINE & DREDGING CO. LTD v. A. OGDEN & SONS (EXCAVATIONS) LTD

Court of Appeal. [1978] Q.B. 574; [1978] 2 W.L.R. 515; [1978] 2 All E.R. 1134; [1978] 1 Lloyd's Rep. 334

The defendants wished to hire two sea-going barges to carry earth and dump it at sea. On April 10, 1974, the plaintiffs quoted a price for the hire of two barges in a letter which stated that the cubic capacity of each was 850 cubic metres but made no mention of weight. At a meeting on July 11 the plaintiffs' representative, O'Loughlin, was asked about the carrying capacity in tonnes and replied that it was about 1,600 tonnes. The answer was given honestly but was wrong. It was based on O'Loughlin's recollection of the deadweight figure given in Lloyd's Register of 1,800 tonnes. This was wrong, the true figure being 1,195 tonnes. The correct figure was given in shipping documents which O'Loughlin had seen but forgotten. The defendants hired the barges but the work was held up because of their limited carrying capacity. They refused to pay the hire. The plaintiffs withdrew the barges and sued for the outstanding payments. The defendants counterclaimed damages, *inter alia*, for misrepresentation under the Misrepresentation Act 1967, s.2(1).

LORD DENNING M.R. (dissenting) held (1) that there was no collateral warranty; (2) that there was nothing to give rise to a duty of care so as to make the plaintiffs liable for negligence at common law; and, having cited section 2(1) of the Misrepresentation Act 1967, (below, p. 703), be examined the judge's finding that O'Loughlin was not negligent.

It seems to me that, when one examines the details, the judge's view was entirely justified. He found that Mr O'Loughlin's state of mind was this. Mr O'Loughlin had examined Lloyd's register and had seen there that the deadweight capacity of each barge was 1,800 tonnes. That figure stuck in his mind. The judge found that "the 1,600 tonnes was arrived at by knocking off what he considered a reasonable margin for fuel, and so on, from the 1,800 tonnes summer deadweight figure in Lloyd's Register, which was in the back of his mind." The judge said that Mr O'Loughlin had seen at some time the German shipping documents and had seen the deadweight figure of 1,055.135 tonnes, but it did not register. All that was in his mind was the 1,800 tonnes in Lloyd's Register which was regarded in shipping circles as the bible. That afforded reasonable ground for him to believe that the barges could each carry 1,600 tonnes payload; and that is what Mr O'Loughlin believed.

So on this point, too, I do not think we should fault the judge. It is not right to pick his judgment to pieces, by subjecting it (or the shorthand note) to literal analysis. Viewing it fairly, the judge (who had section 2(1) in front of him) must have been of opinion that the burden of proof was discharged.

The exception clause

If I be wrong so far, however, there remains the exception clause in the charterparty. It was, as I have said, included throughout all the negotiations; and no objection was ever taken to it. The important words are:

> ". . . Charterers acceptance of handing over the vessel shall be conclusive that [she is] . . . in all respects fit for the intended and contemplated use by the Charterers and in every other way satisfactory to them."

In the old days we used to construe such an exception clause strictly against the party relying on it; but there is no need, and I suggest no warrant, any longer for construing it so strictly. The reason is that now by section 3 of the Misrepresentation Act 1967 the provision is of no effect except to the extent that the court may allow reliance on it as being fair and reasonable in the circumstances of the case. Under this section the question is not whether the provision itself is reasonable, but only whether "reliance on it [is] fair and reasonable in the circumstances of the case."[1]

If the clause itself is reasonable, that goes a long way towards showing that reliance on it is fair and reasonable. It seems to me that the clause was itself fair and reasonable. The parties here were commercial concerns and were of equal bargaining power. The clause was not foisted by one on the other in a standard printed form. It was contained in all the drafts which passed between them, and it was no doubt given close consideration by both sides, like all the other clauses, some of which were amended and others not. It was a clause common in charterparties of this kind; and is familiar in other commercial contracts, such as construction and engineering contracts. . . . It is specially applicable in cases where the contractor has the opportunity of checking the position for himself. It tells him that he should do so; and that he should not rely on any information given

---

[1] Note that, under the amended s.3, the test is the requirement of reasonableness in s.11(1) of the Unfair Contract Terms Act—whether the term was a fair and reasonable one *to be included*: below, pp. 704 and 708.

beforehand, for it may be inaccurate. Thus it provides a valuable safeguard against the consequences of innocent misrepresentation.

Even if the clause were somewhat too wide (I do not think it is), nevertheless this is, I think, a case where it would be fair and reasonable to allow reliance on it. Here is a clause by which Ogdens accepted that the barges were "in all respects fit for the intended and contemplated use by the charterers." Ogdens had had full inspection and examination of the barges. They had had an "on-hire condition" survey by their surveyors. Any expert could have given them a reliable estimate as to the dead-weight capacity. Yet they seek to say that the barges were not fit for the use for which they intended them, in that they were of too low carrying capacity. And in support of their case they have no written representation to go on. They only have two telephone conversations and one interview, as to which there is an acute conflict of evidence. It is just such conflicts which commercial men seek to avoid by such a clause as this. I would do nothing to impair its efficacy. I would allow Howards to rely on it. . . .

BRIDGE L.J., having held that there was no evidence of a collateral warranty, cited section 2(1) of the Misrepresentation Act 1967 and continued: The first question then is whether Howards would be liable in damages in respect of Mr O'Loughlin's misrepresentation if it had been made fraudulently, that is to say, if he had known that it was untrue. An affirmative answer to that question is inescapable. The judge found in terms that what Mr O'Loughlin said about capacity of the barges was said with the object of getting the hire contract for Howards, in other words with the intention that it should be acted on. This was clearly right. Equally clearly the misrepresentation was in fact acted on by Ogdens. It follows, therefore, on the plain language of the 1967 Act that, although there was no allegation of fraud, Howards must be liable unless they proved that Mr O'Loughlin had reasonable ground to believe what he said about the barges' capacity.

It is unfortunate that the learned judge never directed his mind to the question whether Mr O'Loughlin had any reasonable ground for his belief. The question he asked himself, in considering liability under the 1967 Act, was whether the innocent misrepresentation was negligent. He concluded that if Mr O'Loughlin had given the inaccurate information in the course of the April telephone conversations he would have been negligent to do so but that in the circumstances obtaining at the Otley interview in July there was no negligence. I take it that he meant by this that on the earlier occasions the circumstances were such that he would have been under a duty to check the accuracy of his information, but on the later occasions he was exempt from such duty. I appreciate the basis of this distinction, but it seems to me, with respect, quite irrelevant to any question of liability under the 1967 Act. If the representee proves a misrepresentation which, if fraudulent, would have sounded in damages, the onus passes immediately to the representor to prove that he had reasonable ground to believe the facts represented. In other words the liability of the representor does not depend on his being under a duty of care the extent of which may vary according to the circumstances in which the representation is made. In the course of negotiations leading to a contract the 1967 Act imposes an absolute obligation not to state facts which the representor cannot prove he had reasonable ground to believe. . . .

I am fully alive to the dangers of trial by transcript and it is to be assumed that Mr O'Loughlin was perfectly honest throughout. But the question remains whether his evidence, however benevolently viewed, is sufficient to show that he had an objectively reasonable ground to disregard the figure in the ship's documents and to prefer the Lloyd's Register figure. I think it is not. The fact that he was more interested in cubic capacity could not justify reliance on one figure of deadweight capacity in preference to another. The fact that the deadweight figure in the ship's documents was a freshwater figure was of no significance since, as he knew, the difference between freshwater and sea water deadweight capacity was minimal. Accordingly I conclude that Howards failed to prove that Mr O'Loughlin had reasonable ground to believe the truth of his misrepresentation to Mr Redpath.

Having reached a conclusion favourable to Ogdens on the issue of liability under the Misrepresentation Act 1967, I do not find it necessary to express a concluded view on the issue of negligence at common law. As at present advised I doubt if the circumstances surrounding the misrepresentation at the Otley interview were such as to impose on Howards a common law duty of care for the accuracy of the statement. If there was such a duty, I doubt if the evidence established a breach of it.

There remains the question whether Howards can escape from their liability under the 1967 Act in reliance on clause I of the charterparty, which provides: . . .

[See above, p. 358].

A clause of this kind is to be narrowly construed. It can only be relied on as conclusive evidence of the charterers' satisfaction in relation to such attributes of the vessel as would be apparent on an ordinary examination of the vessel. I do not think deadweight capacity is such an attribute. It can only be ascertained by an elaborate calculation or by an inspection of the ship's documents. But even if, contrary to this view, the clause can be read as apt to exclude liability for the earlier misrepresentation, Howards still have to surmount the restrictions imposed by section 3 of the 1967 Act, which provides: . . .

[His Lordship quoted the section.]

What the learned judge said in this matter was: "If the wording of the clause is apt to exempt from responsibility for negligent misrepresentation as to carrying capacity, I hold that such exemption is not fair and reasonable . . ." The judge having asked himself the right question and answered it as he did in the exercise of the discretion vested in him by the 1967 Act, I can see no ground on which we could say that he was wrong.

I would accordingly allow the appeal to the extent of holding that Ogdens have established liability against Howards under section 2(1) of the 1967 Act for any damages they have suffered as a result of Mr O'Loughlin's misrepresentation at the Otley interview in the terms as found by the learned judge.

SHAW L.J., having held that there was no evidence of a warranty, but (differing from the other members of the Court and Bristow J.) that Ogden had a cause of action in negligence at common law continued:

There remains the issue raised by the claim under section 2(1) of the Misrepresentation Act 1967. I do not regard the telephone conversation of

April and the interview of July 11, 1974 as being so casual as to give rise to no legal consequences. Certainly I find myself unable to dismiss what was said at the interview in July as inconsequential. I share the opinion expressed in this regard in the judgment of Bridge L.J. which is based on the finding of the learned judge. I entirely agree, furthermore, with Bridge L.J.'s analysis of the evidence, together with the learned judge's findings in this regard, and I agree also with the views expressed by Bridge L.J. as to the operation and effect of the relevant provisions of the 1967 Act. I cannot do better than respectfully to adopt his reasoning without seeking to repeat it and I agree with his conclusions.

On this ground as well as in relation to the claim based on negligence at common law I would allow the appeal.

Appeal allowed.

Question
If O'Loughlin made the statement about the barges with the intention that Ogden should act on it by entering into the contract of hire, why was there no evidence of a collateral warranty? See cases discussed in *Note*, below p. 367 and *Schawel v. Reade*, below p. 378.

Section 8. When a Representation Becomes a Term

The problem to be considered in this section is the extent of the contractual obligation. Assuming that a contract has been concluded according to the rules of offer, acceptance and consideration already considered, there may still be a problem of ascertaining what promises have been made by each party. If the contract is an oral one, this may involve an examination of a long history of negotiations. For instance, the offer and acceptance in a contract for the sale of a car may consist simply of, "I offer you £500 for the car"; "I accept." It is unlikely that this is the whole contract between the parties. During previous negotiations the buyer may have received assurances that the car is a 1980 model, that the seller has owned it since it was new, that it has a reconditioned engine, that it has done a certain mileage, and so on. Such assurances will, as the seller knows, have contributed to the buyer's decision to make his offer and been present to his mind when he did so. If they are false, they amount to misrepresentations with the consequences which are considered above; but it may very well be that they amount to contractual undertakings by the seller. When the contract has been reduced to writing, the parol evidence rule applies to exclude evidence which would add to, vary or contradict the terms of the document. Generally, therefore, we will be confined to interpreting the document. But this rule is subject to important exceptions and cases will be considered in which, by one means or another, the court succeeds certainly in adding to, and perhaps varying or even contradicting, the document, by reference to the negotiations which precede it.

The cases in this section are concerned with the question whether a particular statement or "representation" is, or is not, part of the contract. If it is not part of the contract, it is commonly described as a "mere representation." In spite of the new remedies for innocent misrepresentation provided by the Misrepresentation Act, it will frequently be important to determine whether a statement has, or has not, become part of the contract. For example, the defendant may be able to prove that he believed on reasonable grounds that his misrepresentation was true, in which case he will not be liable under the Act (above, p. 354). His honest and reasonable belief will not, however, afford him a defence if he is held to have given a contractual undertaking as to its truth.

The problem of determining the extent of the contractual obligation is not at an end when we have classified all the statements which have been made as either mere representations or contractual terms. A contract may be held to include terms which have never been put into words, whether written or oral. In the example of the sale of the car, for instance, it will almost certainly be held that the seller promises that he has a right to sell it, even though he has never said so. This is "something so obvious that it goes without saying." Such "implied terms" are just as much a part of the contractual obligation as the express terms. The circumstances in which the courts will imply terms are considered in detail in Chapter 10 below.

Even when both the express and implied terms have been ascertained, the interpreter's task is not necessarily at an end, for terms differ in their nature. Traditionally, they were divided into two categories: conditions and warranties. Conditions are the essential promises in a contract, while warranties are of a subsidiary nature. Breach of either kind of term entitles the injured party to sue for damages. The importance of the distinction is that, in the case of the breach of condition only, the injured party has the *additional* remedy of terminating the contract, if he so wishes. If the plaintiff is suing for damages it will not be necessary for the court to determine whether the term alleged to be broken is a condition or a warranty; the damages will be the same in either case. The two words are commonly loosely used by the courts, especially in the older cases: and the fact that either word is used must not be taken to mean that the court has evaluated the terms as an essential or subsidiary one unless the question of its value was actually in issue. The value of the term will be in issue in two main types of case: (i) where the plaintiff seeks to terminate the contract for breach, there having been no actionable misrepresentation, and (ii) where there is a clause in the contract excluding liability for warranties but not conditions.

It is now apparent that a division of contractual terms into conditions and warranties is an over-simplification. The most widely held view is that there is a third category of terms a breach of which may or may not entitle the injured party to rescind, depending on the nature of the breach and its effect: *Hong Kong Fir Shipping Co. Ltd v. Kawasaki Kisen Kaisha Ltd* (below). Since there is no accepted name for such terms they may conveniently be styled "innominate terms." Another view is that there are only two categories: conditions, any breach of which justifies termination of the contract; and warranties, breach of which justifies termination only if the effect of the breach is to deprive the other party of the consideration for which he bargained. See Ormrod L.J. in the *Hansa Nord* [1976] Q.B. 44 and Lord Devlin, "The Treatment of Breach of Contract" [1966] C.L.J. 192 at 202. The "Guide," below, adopts the former view.

A GUIDE TO MISREPRESENTATION AND TERMS

The law concerning misrepresentation and terms of the contract may have been improved by the Misrepresentation Act, but it has certainly become more complicated. The following summary may assist the reader in considering the subsequent cases. It should be noted that the terms "rescind" and "avoid" are often used in books, cases and statutes to mean *either* (i) to nullify the contract *ab initio* or (ii) to nullify the contract from the moment of "rescission" or "avoidance"; but in this note, "rescind" means to nullify the contract *ab initio* and "terminate" means to bring the contract to an end from the moment of the act of termination—usually on notice by P (the representee) to D (the representor).

(i) *Where the Misrepresentation leads to the Conclusion of a Contract*

(1) Where the misrepresentation is a term of the contract. The term may be:

(a) a condition. If so, P may recover *damages*, and *terminate* the contract for breach.

(b) a warranty. If so, P may recover *damages* but he may not *terminate* the contract for breach.

(c) an innominate term. If so, P may recover *damages* and, if the breach and its consequences are sufficiently grave, *terminate* the contract for breach.

P may alternatively *rescind* the contract for misrepresentation, although the misrepresentation has become a term of the contract and the contract has been performed: Misrepresentation Act, 1967, s.1; *and* recover *damages* under section 2 of that Act as in (2) below.

(2) Where the misrepresentation is *not a term* of the contract:

P may recover damages under section 2(1) of the Misrepresentation Act, 1967 (above, p. 354) *and* rescind the contract, *unless* D can prove that he had reasonable grounds to believe and did believe the facts represented to be true. If D can so prove, P's only remedy is rescission in equity and an indemnity (but damages might be awarded in lieu of rescission, if it were equitable to do so, under section 2(2) of the Misrepresentation Act, 1967 (above, p. 355; below, p. 703).

(ii) *Where the Misrepresentation does not lead to the Conclusion of a Contract*

P may recover damages:
 (a) for deceit, if he can prove that the misrepresentation was made fraudulently: *Derry v. Peek* (1889) 14 App.Cas. 337; or
 (b) Under *Hedley Byrne & Co. v. Heller and Partners* [1964] A.C. 465 (above, p. 340, if he can prove that D had assumed, and was in breach of, a duty to exercise care in making the representation.
(There is no point in P's pursuing these common law remedies where the misrepresentation leads to a contract since, by doing so, he would incur the onus of proof which lies on D where action is brought under section 2(1) of the Misrepresentation Act; but a plaintiff may sue in deceit instead of under the Act if he wishes: *Archer v. Brown* [1984] 2 All E.R. 267 (Peter Pain J.)).

HEILBUT, SYMONS & CO. v. BUCKLETON

House of Lords [1913] A.C. 30; 82 L.J.K.B. 245; 107 L.T. 769

VISCOUNT HALDANE L.C.: My Lords, the appellants, who were rubber merchants in London in the spring of 1910 underwrote a large number of shares in a company called the Filisola Rubber and Produce Estates Ltd, a company which was promoted and registered by other persons about that time. They instructed a Mr Johnston, who was the manager of their Liverpool business, to obtain applications for shares in Liverpool. Johnston, who had seen a draft prospectus in London but had at the time no copy of the prospectus, mentioned the company to several people in Liverpool, including a Mr Wright, who sometimes acted as broker for the respondent. On April 14 the respondent telephoned to Johnston from Wright's office. As to what passed there is no dispute. The respondent said: "I understand you are bringing out a rubber company." The reply was: "we are." The respondent then asked whether Johnston had any prospectuses, and his reply was in the negative. The respondent then asked "if it was all right," and Johnston replied: "We are bringing it out," to which the respondent rejoined: "That is good enough for me." He went on to ask how many shares he could have, and to say that he would take almost any number. He explained in his evidence in chief that his reason for being willing to do this was that the position the appellants occupied in the rubber trade was of such high standing that "any company they should see fit to bring out was a sufficient warranty" to him "that it was all right in every respect." Afterwards, as the result of the conversation, a large number of shares were allotted to the respondent. [The contract was embodied on two letters dated April 15, the day after the conversation].

About this time the rubber boom of 1910 was at its height and the shares of the Filisola Company were, and for a short time remained, at a premium. Later on it was discovered that there was a large deficiency in the rubber trees which were said in the prospectus to exist on the Filisola Estate, and the shares fell in value. The respondent brought an action against the appellants for fraudulent misrepresentation, and alternatively for damages for breach of warranty that the company was a rubber company whose main object was to produce rubber.

The action was tried at Liverpool Assizes before Lush J. and a special jury. The jury found that there was no fraudulent representation by the appellants or Johnston, but they found that the company could not be properly described as a rubber company, and that the appellants or Johnston, or both, had warranted that the company was a rubber company. . . .

It is contrary to the general policy of the law of England to presume the making of such a collateral contract in the absence of language expressing or implying it, and I think the learned judge who tried the case ought to have informed the jury that on the issue of warranty there was no case to go to it, and that on this issue he and the Court of Appeal ought to have given judgment for the appellants. The strongest presentation of the case for the respondents seems to me that of Farwell L.J. to the effect that there was a contract that the shares should be shares in a rubber company, and that the jury has found that the company was not a rubber company. But even on the basis of this finding I do not think that the account given by the learned Lord Justice of the transaction properly describes it. The respondent did not ask the technical question whether the company of which he had heard vaguely was correctly described as a rubber company. That he was not thinking of this point seems to me clear from the fact that when he received the letters informing him that he was to have shares in the Filisola Rubber and Produce Estates (a description which was in accordance with that in the prospectus) he made no further inquiry. What he from the first wanted to know was whether Johnston thought the company was "all right," a question to which Johnston simply replied that the appellants were bringing it out, an answer which, to my mind, simply conveyed that a firm of their standing would not be bringing it out if they did not believe it to be all right. From the evidence of the respondents, which immediately follows in the passage I have quoted, it seems to me plain that this was accepted by the respondent as the answer he wanted. . . .

Neither the respondent nor Johnston appears to have had any question in his mind other than whether some company dealing with rubber, as to the identity of which there was no question raised, was being brought out by the appellants. For the respondent says that the position of the appellants in the rubber trade was such that "any company that they should see fit to bring out was a sufficient warranty" to him "that it was all right in every respect." His interest was in the shares for which he was minded to apply, and all he was really asking for was the assurance I have mentioned. Had Johnston thought that he was being asked to do anything else than answer the question whether the appellants were bringing out the company, he might well have refused to pledge himself, and I do not believe that either he or the respondent, regard being had to the character of the conversation, was thinking of any other question. But if not, there was in point of law no evidence to go to the jury on the issue as to warranty, and this issue ought not to have been submitted to it. In reality the only contract entered into seems to have been the contract reduced into writing by the two letters of April 15 for procuring an allotment of shares in what was described as the Filisola "Rubber and Produce Estates" Company. . . .

LORD MOULTON, having stated the facts, went on:
It is evident, both on principle and on authority, that there may be a contract the consideration for which is the making of some other contract. "If you will make such and such a contract I will give you one hundred pounds," is in every sense of the word a complete legal contract. It is collateral to the main contract, but each has an independent existence, and they do not differ in respect of their possessing to the full the character and status of a contract. But such collateral contracts must from their very nature be rare. The effect of a collateral contract such as that which I have instanced would be to increase the consideration of the main contract by £100, and the more natural and usual way of carrying this out would be by so modifying the main contract and not by executing a concurrent and collateral contract. Such collateral contracts, the sole effect of which is to vary or add to the terms of the principal contract, are therefore viewed with suspicion by the law. They must be proved strictly. Not only the terms of such contracts but the existence of an *animus contrahendi* on the part of all the parties to them must be clearly shown. Any laxity on these points would enable parties to escape from the full performance of the obligations of contracts unquestionably entered into by them and more especially would have the effect of lessening the authority of written contracts by making it possible to vary them by suggesting the existence of verbal collateral agreements relating to the same subject-matter. There is in the present case an entire absence of any evidence to support the existence of such a collateral contract. . . .
In the history of English law we find many attempts to make persons responsible in damages by reason of innocent misrepresentations, and at times it has seemed as though the attempts would succeed. . . .
On the common law side of the court the attempts to make a person liable for an innocent misrepresentation have usually taken the form of attempts to extend the doctrine of warranty beyond its limits and to find that a warranty existed in cases where there was nothing more than an innocent misrepresentation. The present case is, in my opinion, an instance of this. But in respect of the question of the existence of a warranty the courts have had the advantage of an admirable enunciation of the true principle of law which was made in very early days by Holt C.J. with respect to the contract of sale. He says: "An affirmation at the time of the

sale is a warranty, provided it appears on evidence to be so intended." So far as decisions are concerned, this has, on the whole, been consistently followed in the courts of common law. But from time to time there have been dicta inconsistent with it which have, unfortunately, found their way into textbooks and have given rise to confusion and uncertainty in this branch of the law. For example, one often sees quoted the dictum of Bayley J. in *Cave v. Coleman*, 3 Man. & Ry. 2, where, in respect of a representation made verbally during the sale of a horse, he says that, "being made in the course of dealing, and before the bargain was complete, it amounted to a warranty"—a proposition that is far too sweeping and cannot be supported. A still more serious deviation from the correct principle is to be found in a passage in the judgment of the Court of Appeal in *De Lassalle v. Guildford* [1901] 2 K.B. 215, 221, which was cited to us in the argument in the present case. In discussing the question whether a representation amounts to a warranty or not the judgment says: "In determining whether it was so intended, a decisive test is whether the vendor assumes to assert a fact of which the buyer is ignorant, or merely states an opinion or judgment upon a matter of which the vendor has no special knowledge, and on which the buyer may be expected also to have an opinion and to exercise his judgment."

With all deference to the authority of the court that decided that case, the proposition which it thus formulates cannot be supported. It is clear that the court did not intend to depart from the law laid down by Holt C.J. and cited above, for in the same judgment that dictum is referred to and accepted as a correct statement of the law. It is, therefore, evident that the use of the phrase, "decisive test" cannot be defended. Otherwise it would be the duty of a judge to direct a jury that if a vendor states a fact of which the buyer is ignorant, they must, as a matter of law, find the existence of a warranty, whether or not the totality of the evidence shows that the parties intended the affirmation to form part of the contract; and this would be inconsistent with the law as laid down by Holt C.J. It may well be that the features thus referred to in the judgment of the Court of Appeal in that case may be criteria of value in guiding a jury in coming to a decision whether or not a warranty was intended; but they cannot be said to furnish decisive tests, because it cannot be said as a matter of law that the presence or absence of those features is conclusive of the intention of the parties. The intention of the parties can only be deduced from the totality of the evidence, and no secondary principles of such a kind can be universally true.

> Order of the Court of Appeal reversed and
> judgment entered for the appellants.

Questions

1. What did the respondent want to know when he telephoned? On what matter or matters was he seeking assurance? Did he make it clear to Johnston that it was of importance to him to know whether it was a "rubber" company?

2. Was Johnston negligent in describing the company as a "rubber company" (assuming this was a misdescription)? Would negligence in such circumstances afford a remedy today? *Cf. Hedley Byrne & Co. v. Heller & Partners* [1964] A.C. 465 (above, p. 340 and Misrepresentation Act, below, p. 703.

Note

A warranty is often described as a "collateral" term of a contract. By this is meant that it relates to the subject-matter of another promise made by the warrantor and exists, side by side with that promise, in a single contract. In the Sale of Goods Act 1979 (s.61(1))

" 'Warranty' . . . means an agreement with reference to goods which are the subject of a contract of sale, but collateral to the main purpose of such contract, the breach of which gives rise to a claim for damages, but not to a right to reject the goods and treat the contract as repudiated."

A promises to sell a horse to B and warrants that it is sound. The warranty is subordinate to A's promise to sell the horse in the sense that it is only made because of that promise. In normal circumstances it would be pointless for A to give B a warranty of the soundness of A's horse unless A also transferred the property in the horse (or hired it, etc.) to B. (*Cf.*, however, *Shanklin Pier Ltd v. Detel Products Ltd*, below.) Though "collateral," a warranty is generally part of a single contract containing the main promise. Suppose that Buckleton had obtained from Johnston a firm assurance that the company was a rubber company in the technical sense and that, subsequently, an oral contract had been concluded for the sale of the shares. It would surely not have been unreasonable to say that it was a term in that contract that the shares were shares in a rubber company. In fact, the contract was concluded in writing and the judges were no doubt inhibited by the parol evidence rule (above) from holding that the representation amounted to a warranty in that written contract (though see Chapter 10 on Implied Terms, below). Buckleton's counsel therefore argued that the warranty was contained in a separate contract; that is, "If you will buy shares in the company, I will promise you that it is a rubber company." Buckleton's entering into the main contract for the purchase of the shares would then have been the consideration for the promise. Had this contention been made out, a quite distinct and separate contract would have come into existence at the same moment as the main contract.

Such a contract, existing side by side with the main contract, is described as "a collateral contract."[1] It is clearly quite a different concept from an ordinary warranty which is not a separate contract. The epithet "collateral" is applied to both concepts and it is not always clear to which the courts are referring. The collateral contract is an extremely useful device, particularly in that the parol evidence rule is no bar to its use. It was well known before *Heilbut v. Buckleton*. In *Morgan v. Griffith* (1871) L.R. 6 Ex. 70 and *Erskine v. Adeane* (1873) L.R. 8 Ch.App. 756 lessors were held liable to their tenants for failing to keep down the game on the demised land although they had refused to allow any promise that they would do so to be inserted in the leases, when it was proved that the tenant in each case declined to sign the lease until he had such an undertaking and signed on the faith of it. In *De Lassalle v. Guildford* a tenant had declined to hand over his counterpart of a lease until he had the landlord's oral assurance that the drains were in good order and was held entitled to damages for breach of that undertaking. The decision appears to be sound in spite of Lord Moulton's observations on the dicta of A.L. Smith M.R. For another type of collateral contract, see *Warlow v. Harrison*, above, p. 21 and *Cf. Howard Marine v. Ogden*, above, p. 357.

Heilbut v. Buckleton (and especially Lord Moulton's judgment) is almost always cited when the question of warranty or no warranty is in issue. Yet in spite of Lord Moulton's suspicion of collateral contracts, the courts seem to have made more and more use of them in recent years. It has been held that there may even be a contract collateral to a contract for the sale of land required by section 2 of the Law of Property (Miscellaneous Provisions Act 1989, above, p. 6, to be in writing and to incorporate all the terms expressly agreed in one document: *Record v. Bell* [1991] 4 All E.R. 471, Ch. D. See also *Webster v. Higgin* [1948] 2 All E.R. 127, *Couchman v. Hill* (below, p. 378), *Harling v. Eddy*, (below, p. 379), *City and Westminster Properties Ltd v. Mudd*, (below, p. 381), *Esso v. Mardon infra* and *Strongman Ltd v. Sincock* (below, p. 671). *Cf. Evans v. Merzario* [1976] 1 W.L.R. 1078.

ESSO PETROLEUM CO. LTD v. MARDON

Court of Appeal [1976] 2 W.L.R. 583; [1976] 2 All E.R. 5

Esso's experienced representative told Mardon that Esso estimated that the throughput of petrol on a certain site would reach 200,000 gallons in the third year of operation and so persuaded Mardon to enter into a tenancy agreement in April

---

[1] This proposition should be considered in the light of *Bell v. Lever Bros.* (below, p. 491) and *Smith v. Hughes* (above, p. 121).

1963 for three years. Mardon did all that could be expected of him as tenant but the site was not good enough to achieve a throughput of more than 60,000–70,000 gallons. In July 1964 Mardon gave notice to quit but Esso granted him a new tenancy at a reduced rent. Mardon continued to lose money and by August 1966 was unable to pay for petrol supplied. Esso claimed possession of the site and money due. Mardon claimed damages in respect of the representation alleging that it amounted (i) to a warranty; (ii) to a negligent misrepresentation. Lawson J. rejected the claim for breach of warranty but held Esso liable in negligence. The Court of Appeal affirmed the finding of negligence under the principle of *Hedley Byrne v. Heller* [1964] A.C. 465: above, p. 340 (The Misrepresentation Act 1967 was inapplicable because the misrepresentation was made before the Act came into force: see section 5 below, p. 704). On the issue of warranty:

LORD DENNING M.R.: Ever since *Heilbut Symons & Co. v. Buckleton* (above, p. 363) we have had to contend with the law as laid down by the House of Lords that an innocent misrepresentation gives no right to damages. In order to escape from that rule, the pleader used to allege—I often did it myself—that the misrepresentation was fraudulent, or alternatively a collateral warranty. At the trial we nearly always succeeded on collateral warranty. We had to reckon, of course, with the dictum of Lord Moulton that "such collateral contracts must from their very nature be rare." But more often than not the court elevated the innocent misrepresentation into a collateral warranty; and thereby did justice—in advance of the Misrepresentation Act, 1967. I remember scores of cases of that kind, especially on the sale of a business. A representation as to the profits that had been made in the past was invariably held to be a warranty. Besides that experience, there have been many cases since I have sat in this court where we have readily held a representation—which induces a person to enter into a contract—to be a warranty sounding in damages. I summarised them in *Dick Bentley Products Ltd v. Harold Smith (Motors) Ltd* [1965] 2 All E.R. 65 at 67; [1965] 1 W.L.R. 623 at 627, below, p. 377). . . .

Counsel for Esso retaliated, however, by citing *Bisset v. Wilkinson* (above, p. 332) where the Privy Council said that a statement by a New Zealand farmer that an area of land "would carry 2,000 sheep" was only an expression of opinion. He submitted that the forecast here of 200,000 gallons was an expression of opinion and not a statement of fact; and that it could not be interpreted as a warranty or promise.

Now, I would quite agree with counsel for Esso that it was not a warranty—in this sense—that it did not guarantee that the throughput *would be* 200,000 gallons. But, nevertheless, it was a forecast made by a party, Esso, who had special knowledge and skill. It was the yardstick (the "e a c") by which they measured the worth of a filling station. They knew the facts. They knew the traffic in the town. They knew the throughput of comparable stations. They had much experience and expertise at their disposal. They were in a much better position than Mr Mardon to make a forecast. It seems to me that if such a person makes a forecast—intending that the other should act on it and he does act on it—it can well be interpreted as a warranty that the forecast is sound and reliable in this sense that they made it with reasonable care and skill. It is just as if Esso said to Mr Mardon: "Our forecast of throughput is 200,000 gallons. You can rely on it as being a sound forecast of what the service station should do. The rent is calculated on that footing." If the forecast turned out to be an unsound forecast, such as no person of skill or experience should have made, there is a breach of warranty. Just as there is a breach of warranty when a forecast is made "expected to load" by a certain date if the maker has no reasonable grounds for it: see *Samuel Sanday v. Keighley Maxted & Co.* ((1922) 27 Com.Cas. 296); or bunkers "expected 600/700 tons": see *The Pantanassa* ([1958] 2 Lloyd's Rep. 449 at 455–457) by Diplock J. It is very different from the New Zealand case where the land had never been used as a sheep farm and both parties were equally able to form an opinion as to its carrying capacity.

In the present case it seems to me that there was a warranty that the forecast was sound, that is that Esso had made it with reasonable care and skill. That warranty was broken. Most negligently Esso made a "fatal error" in the forecast they stated to Mr Mardon, and on which he took the tenancy. For this they are liable in damages.

ORMROD and SHAW L.JJ. delivered judgments allowing the appeal.

Appeal allowed.

Note
   Cf. Kleinwort Benson Ltd v. Malaysia Mining Corp. Bhd., above, p. 188.

OSCAR CHESS LTD v. WILLIAMS

Court of Appeal [1957] 1 W.L.R. 370; 101 S.J. 186; [1957] 1 All E.R. 325

In March 1954 the defendant's mother acquired a second-hand Morris car on the footing that it was a 1948 model. The registration book showed that it was first registered on April 13, 1948, with five changes of ownership between 1948 and 1954. In May 1955 the defendant acquired a new car on hire-purchase terms through the plaintiffs who took the Morris in part exchange. The defendant described the car as a 1948 Morris and produced the registration book. The plaintiffs' salesman, who was familiar with the car, having often had lifts in it, checked the current price for a 1948 Morris in *Glass's Guide* which was £290 and made the defendant an allowance for that sum against the price of the new car.

Eight months later the plaintiffs discovered that the car was not made in 1948 but in 1939, the appearance of the model not having changed in the meantime. If they had known that it was a 1939 model they would have allowed only £175. They brought an action to recover £115 as damages for breach of an express term that the car was a 1948 model. The county court judge found that it was a condition of the contract that the car was a 1948 model. The defendant appealed.

DENNING L.J. stated the facts set out above, and said that in describing the car as a 1948 Morris the defendant was perfectly innocent; he honestly believed it was a 1948 model; and so no doubt did the previous sellers. Someone in 1948 must have fraudulently altered the log-book, but he could not now be traced. His Lordship continued: I entirely agree with the judge that both parties assumed that the Morris was a 1948 model and that this assumption was fundamental to the contract. But this does not prove that the representation was a term of the contract. The assumption was based by both of them on the date given in the registration book as the date of first registration. They both believed it was a 1948 model whereas it was only a

1939 one. They were both mistaken and their mistake was of fundamental importance.

The effect of such a mistake is this: It does not make the contract a nullity from the beginning, but it does in some circumstances enable the contract to be set aside in equity. If the buyer had come promptly, he might have succeeded in getting the whole transaction set aside in equity on the ground of this mistake[1]: see *Solle v. Butcher* (below, p. 501); but he did not do so and it is too late for him to do it: see *Leaf v. International Galleries* (above, p. 342). His only remedy is in damages, and to recover these he must prove a warranty.

In saying that he must prove a warranty, I use the word "warranty" in its ordinary English meaning to denote a binding promise. Everyone knows what a man means when he says "I guarantee it" or "I warrant it" or "I give you my word on it." He means that he binds himself to it. That is the meaning it has borne in English law for 300 years from the leading case of *Chandelor v. Lopus* (1603) Cro.Jac. 4 onwards. During the last fifty years, however, some lawyers have come to use the word "warranty" in another sense. They use it to denote a subsidiary term in a contract as distinct from a vital term which they call a "condition." In so doing they depart from the ordinary meaning, not only of the word "warranty" but also of the word "condition." There is no harm in their doing this, so long as they confine this technical use to its proper sphere, namely, to distinguish between a vital term, the breach of which gives the right to treat the contract as at an end, and a subsidiary term which does not. But the trouble comes when one person uses the word "warranty" in its ordinary meaning and another uses it in its technical meaning. When Holt C.J., in *Crosse v. Gardner* (1689) Carth. 90 (as glossed by Buller J. in *Pasley v. Freeman* (1789) 3 Term Rep. 51, 57) and *Medina v. Stoughton* (1700) 1 Salk. 210, made his famous ruling that an affirmation at the time of a sale is a warranty, provided it appears on evidence to be so intended, he used the word "warranty" in its ordinary English meaning of a binding promise: and when Lord Haldane L.C. and Lord Moulton in 1913 in *Heilbut, Symons & Co. v. Buckleton* (above, p. 363), adopted his ruling, they used it likewise in its ordinary meaning. These different uses of the word seem to have been the source of confusion in the present case. The judge did not ask himself, "Was the representation (that it was a 1948 Morris) intended to be a warranty?" He asked himself, "Was it fundamental to the contract?" He answered it by saying that it was fundamental; and therefore it was a condition and not a warranty. By concentrating on whether it was fundamental, he seems to me to have missed the crucial point in the case which is whether it was a term of the contract at all. The crucial question is: was it a binding promise or only an innocent misrepresentation? The technical distinction between a "condition" and a "warranty" is quite immaterial in this case, because it is far too late for the buyer to reject the car. He can at best only claim damages. The material distinction here is between a statement which is a term of the contract and a statement which is only an innocent misrepresentation. This distinction is best expressed by the ruling of Lord Holt: Was it intended as a warranty or not? using the word warranty there in its ordinary English meaning: because it gives the exact shade of meaning that is required. It is something to which a man must be taken to bind himself.

[1] *Cf. Prenn v. Simmonds* [1971] 1 W.L.R. 1381, above, p. 137.

In applying Lord Holt's test, however, some misunderstanding has arisen by the use of the word "intended." It is sometimes supposed that the tribunal must look into the minds of the parties to see what they themselves intended. That is a mistake. Lord Moulton made it quite clear that "The intention of the parties can only be deduced from the totality of the evidence." The question whether a warranty was intended depends on the conduct of the parties, on their words and behaviour, rather than on their thoughts. If an intelligent bystander would reasonably infer that a warranty was intended, that will suffice. And this, when the facts are not in dispute, is a question of law. That is shown by *Heilbut, Symons & Co. v. Buckleton* itself, where the House of Lords upset the finding by a jury of a warranty.

It is instructive to take some recent instances to show how the courts have approached this question. When the seller states a fact which is or should be within his own knowledge and of which the buyer is ignorant, intending that the buyer should act on it, and he does so, it is easy to infer a warranty: see *Couchman v. Hill* (below, p. 378), where the farmer stated that the heifer was unserved, and *Harling v. Eddy* (below, p. 379), where he stated that there was nothing wrong with her. So also if he makes a promise about something which is or should be within his own control: see *Birch v. Paramount Estates Ltd* (unreported), decided on October 2, 1956, in this court, where the seller stated that the house would be as good as the show house. But if the seller, when he states a fact, makes it clear that he has no knowledge of his own but has got his information elsewhere and is merely passing it on, it is not so easy to imply a warranty. Such a case was *Routledge v. McKay* [1954] 1 W.L.R. 615, 636, where the seller "stated that it was a 1942 model and pointed to the corroboration found in the book," and it was held that there was no warranty.

Turning now to the present case, much depends on the precise words that were used. If the seller says "I believe it is a 1948 Morris. Here is the registration book to prove it," there is clearly no warranty. It is a statement of belief, not a contractual promise. But if the seller says "I guarantee that it is a 1948 Morris. This is borne out by the registration book, but you need not rely solely on that. I give you my own guarantee that it is," there is clearly a warranty. The seller is making himself contractually responsible, even though the registration book is wrong.

In this case much reliance was placed by the judge on the fact that the buyer looked up *Glass's Guide* and paid £290 on the footing that it was a 1948 model: but that fact seems to me to be neutral. Both sides believed the car to have been made in 1948 and in that belief the buyer paid £290. That belief can be just as firmly based on the buyer's own inspection of the logbook as on a contractual warranty by the seller.

Once that fact is put on one side I ask myself: What is the proper inference from the known facts? It must have been obvious to both that the seller had himself no personal knowledge of the year when the car was made. He only became owner after a great number of changes. He must have been relying on the registration book. It is unlikely that such a person would warrant the year of manufacture. The most he would do would be to state his belief, and then produce the registration book in verification of it. In these circumstances the intelligent bystander would, I suggest, say that the seller did not intend to bind himself so as to warrant that it was a 1948 model. If the seller was asked to pledge himself to it, he would at once have said "I cannot do that. I have only the log-book to go by, the same as you."

The judge seems to have thought that there was a difference between written contracts and oral contracts. He thought that the reason why the buyer failed in *Heilbut, Symons & Co. v. Buckleton* and *Routledge v. McKay* was because the sales were afterwards recorded in writing, and the written contracts contained no reference to the representation. I agree that that was an important factor in those cases. If an oral representation is afterwards recorded in writing, it is good evidence that it was intended as a warranty. If it is not put into writing, it is evidence against a warranty being intended. But it is by no means decisive. There have been many cases where the courts have found an oral warranty collateral to a written contract such as *Birch v. Paramount Estates*. But when the purchase is not recorded in writing at all it must not be supposed that every representation made in the course of the dealing is to be treated as a warranty. The question then is still: Was it intended as a warranty? In the leading case of *Chandelor v. Lopus* in 1603 a man by word of mouth sold a precious stone for £100 affirming it to be a bezar stone whereas it was not. The declaration averred that the seller affirmed it to be a bezar stone, but did not aver that he warranted it to be so. The declaration was held to be ill because "the bare affirmation that it was a bezar stone, without warranting it to be so, is no cause of action." That has been the law from that day to this and it was emphatically reaffirmed by the House of Lords in *Heilbut, Symons & Co. v. Buckleton*.

One final word: It seems to me clear that the motor-dealers who bought the car relied on the year stated in the log-book. If they had wished to make sure of it, they could have checked it then and there, by taking the engine number and chassis number and writing to the makers. They did not do so at the time, but only eight months later. They are experts, and, not having made that check at the time, I do not think they should now be allowed to recover against the innocent seller who produced to them all the evidence he had, namely, the registration book. I agree that it is hard on the dealers to have paid more than the car is worth: but it would be equally hard on the seller to make him pay the difference. He would never have bought the Hillman at all unless he had got the allowance of £290 for the Morris. The best course in all these cases would be to "shunt" the difference down the train of innocent sellers until one reaches the rogue who perpetrated the fraud: but he can rarely be traced, or if he can, he rarely has the money to pay the damages. So one is left to decide between a number of innocent people who is to bear the loss. That can only be done by applying the law about representations and warranties as we know it: and that is what I have tried to do. If the rogue can be traced, he can be sued by whomsoever has suffered the loss: but if he cannot be traced, the loss must lie where it falls. It should not be inflicted on innocent sellers, who sold the car many months perhaps many years before and have forgotten all about it and have conducted their affairs on the basis that the transaction was concluded. Such a seller would not be able to recollect after all this length of time the exact words he used, such as whether he said "I believe it is a 1948 model," or "I warrant it is a 1948 model." The right course is to let the buyer set aside the transaction if he finds out the mistake quickly and comes promptly before other interests have irretrievably intervened; otherwise the loss must lie where it falls: and that is, I think, the course prescribed by law. I would allow this appeal accordingly.

HODSON L.J. delivered a concurring judgment.

MORRIS L.J. dissented, holding that the defendant's statement amounted to a condition in the contract. He said: The statement related to a vitally important matter: it described the subject-matter of the contract then being made and the statement directed the parties to, and was the basis of, their agreement as to the price to be paid or credited to the defendant. In the language of Scott L.J. (in *Coachman v. Hill*, below, p. 378 it seems to me that the statement made by the defendant was "an item in the description" of what was being sold and that it constituted a substantial ingredient in the identity of the thing sold.

Question
Might the result in the above case have been different if the seller had been the car dealer and the buyer the layman? Consider what effect, if any, the Misrepresentation Act (below, p. 703) or the Unfair Contract Terms Act (below, p. 704) might have on this case.

HARLINGDON & LEINSTER ENTERPRISES LTD v. CHRISTOPHER HULL FINE ART LTD

Court of Appeal [1990] 3 W.L.R. 13; [1990] 1 All E.R. 737

In 1984 Hull, the owner of the defendant company, was asked to dispose of two oil paintings which were described in an auction catalogue of 1980 as the work of Gabriele Münter (1877–1962), an artist of the German expressionist school. Hull, who specialised in British contemporary artists had no training, experience or knowledge which would enable him to identify a painting as the work of Münter. He took the paintings to Christies who expressed interest. Earlier he had been told that the plaintiff company had a good reputation as dealers in German art and in fact they had a special interest in buying and selling German expressionist paintings. Hull telephoned the plaintiffs that he had two paintings by Münter to sell. They expressed interest and sent their Mr Runkel to view them. Hull told Runkel he did not know much about the paintings, he had never heard of Münter and thought little of the paintings. He made it absolutely plain that he was not an expert in them and "to a certain extent" made it clear that he was relying on Runkel. Runkel saw a copy of the 1980 catalogue and asked no questions about the provenance of the paintings. There was some bargaining as to price but Runkel agreed to the asking price of £6,000 for one of the paintings, provided he could find a customer. When he did so, Hull made out an invoice:

"GABRIELE MÜNTER (1877–1962)   December 3rd, 1984
  Dorfstrasse in Oberbayern
  oil on board
   39 × 48 cm

                                £6,000"

In February 1985 the customer discovered that the painting was not by Münter but was a forgery. The plaintiffs took it back and refunded the price. The defendants refused to take it back. The plaintiffs sued, alleging a breach of a contract; (i) for the sale of goods by description (Sale of Goods Act, s.13(1), below, p. 401; (ii) that the painting was of merchantable quality (s.14(2)); (iii) that the painting would be reasonably fit for a particular purpose (s.14(3)); and (iv) a misrepresentation under the Misrepresentation Act 1967 (above, p. 352). The judge held in favour of the defendants on all four points. Only the first and second were pursued in the Court of Appeal. The concept of "merchantable quality" in the Sale of Goods Act has now been replaced by that of "satisfactory quality" and judgments on that issue are therefore omitted.

NOURSE L.J., having cited certain authorities:
It is suggested that the significance which some of these authorities attribute to the buyer's reliance on the description is misconceived. I think that that criticism is theoretically correct. In theory it is no doubt possible for a description of goods which is not relied on by the buyer to become an essential term of a contract for their sale. But in practice it is very difficult, and perhaps impossible, to think of facts where that would be so. The description must have a sufficient influence in the sale to become an essential term of the contract and the correlative of influence is reliance. Indeed, reliance by the buyer is the natural index of a sale by description. It is true that the question must, as always, be judged objectively and it may be said that previous judicial references have been to subjective or actual reliance. But each of those decisions, including that of Judge Oddie in the present case, can be justified on an objective basis. For all practical purposes, I would say that there cannot be a contract for the sale of goods by description where it is not within the reasonable contemplation of the parties that the buyer is relying on the description. For those purposes, I think that the law is correctly summarised in these words of *Benjamin*, p. 641, which should be understood to lay down an objective test:

"Specific goods may be sold as such . . . where, though the goods are described, the description is not relied upon, as where the buyer buys the goods such as they are."

In giving his decision on this question Judge Oddie said:

"There can clearly be a sale by description where the buyer has inspected the goods if the description relates to something not apparent on inspection. Every item in a description which constitutes a substantial ingredient in the identity of the thing sold is a condition."

Later, having said that he had not been referred to any similar case where a sale in reliance on a statement that a painting was by a particular artist had been held to be a sale by description, the judge continued:

"In my judgment such a statement could amount to a description and a sale in reliance on it to a sale by description within the meaning of the 1979 Act. However, on the facts of this case I am satisfied that the description by Mr Hull before the agreement was not relied on by Mr Runkel in making his offer to purchase which was accepted by Mr Hull. I conclude that he bought the painting as it was. In these circumstances there was not in my judgment a sale by description."

I agree. On a view of their words and deeds as a whole the parties could not reasonably have contemplated that the defendants were relying on the plaintiff's statement that the painting was by Gabriele Münter. On the facts which he found the judge could not, by a correct application of the law, have come to any other decision.

STUART-SMITH L.J. (dissenting): In my judgment the matter can be tested in this way. If following the telephone conversation Mr Runkel had arrived at the defendants' gallery, seen the painting, bargained about the price and agreed to buy it, it seems to me beyond argument that it would have been a sale by description. And indeed counsel for the defendants was at one time disposed to concede as much. Had the invoice been a contractual document, as it frequently is, again it seems to me clear that the sale would have been a sale by description. In fact the invoice was written out subsequently to the oral contract; but the judge held, rightly as it seems to me, that it gave effect to what had been agreed. It was cogent evidence of the oral contract.

How does it come about that what would otherwise be a sale by description in some way ceased to be one? It can only be as a result of the conversation between Mr Hull and Mr Runkel before the bargain was actually struck. If Mr Hull had told Mr Runkel that he did not know one way or the other whether the painting was by Münter in spite of the fact that he had so described it or that he could only say that the painting was attributed to Münter, and that Mr Runkel must make up his mind for himself on this point, I can well see that the effect of what had previously been said about the identity of the painter might have been cancelled or withdrawn and was no longer effective at the time of the contract. But Mr Hull did not say that, as the judge found. And I cannot see that this is the effect of what was said. Merely to say that he knew nothing of the painter and did not like her paintings does not in any way to my mind necessarily mean that he was cancelling or withdrawing what he had previously said, based as it was on the auction catalogue. Nor does the fact that it was recognised that the plaintiffs were more expert in German expressionist art than Mr Hull advance the matter. It would, in my judgment, be a serious defect in the law if the effect of a condition implied by statute could be excluded by the vendor's saying that he was not an expert in what was being sold or that the purchaser was more expert than the vendor. That is not the law; it has long been held that conditions implied by statute can only be excluded by clear words. There is nothing of that kind in this case.

SLADE L.J.: While some judicial dicta seem to support the view that there can be no sale by description unless there is actual reliance on the description by the purchaser, I am not sure that this is strictly correct in principle. If a party to a contract wishes to claim relief in respect of a misrepresentation as to a matter which did not constitute a term of the contract, his claim will fail unless he is able to show that he relied on this representation in entering into the contract; in general, however, if a party wishes to claim relief in respect of a breach of a *term* of the contract (whether it be a condition or warranty) he need prove no actual reliance.

Nevertheless, where a question arises whether a sale of goods was one by description, the presence or absence of reliance on the description may be very relevant in so far as it throws light on the intentions of the parties at the time of the contract. If there was no such reliance by the purchaser, this may be powerful evidence that the parties did not contemplate that the authenticity of the description should constitute a term of the contract, in other words, that they contemplated that the purchaser would be buying the goods *as they were*. If, on the other hand, there was such reliance (as in *Varley v. Whipp* [1900] 1 Q.B. 513, where the purchaser had never seen the goods) this may be equally powerful evidence that it was contemplated by both parties that the correctness of the description would be a term of the contract (so as to bring it within section 13(1)).

So far as it concerns section 13(1), the issue for the court in the present case was and is, in my judgment, this: on an objective assessment of what the parties said and did at and before the meeting at Motcomb Street, and of all the circumstances of the case, is it right to impute to them the common intention that the authenticity of the attribution to Gabriele Münter should be a term of the contract of sale? The proper inferences to be drawn from the evidence and the findings of primary fact by the judge are matters on which different minds can take different views, as the cogent judgments of Nourse and Stuart-Smith L.JJ. have shown. However, I for my part feel no doubt that the answer to the crucial issue is, No. . . .

I do not say that in the present case section 13 has been excluded by any contract term: my analysis of the position is that the contract was not one for the sale of goods by description. Nevertheless, in my judgment, the provisions of the 1977 Act support the view that the very fact that two parties to the negotiations for the sale of a specific chattel are dealers in that class of chattel is a relevant factor in considering whether or not an attribution of origin made by one dealer to the other during the course of negotiation should be treated as rendering the transaction a "sale by description."

The form of the invoice subsequently made out in favour of the plaintiffs does not, in my judgment, assist the plaintiffs' case. By that time the contract had already been concluded. While the reference to Gabriele Münter in the invoice is quite consistent with the parties having made the origin of the picture a term of the contract, it can equally well be read as merely a convenient mode of reference to a particular picture which both parties knew to have been attributed to Gabriele Münter (and indeed both still thought to be her work).

Appeal dismissed.

Questions

1. *Oscar Chess. v. Williams* (above, p. 369) is not mentioned in the report. Was it not a powerful authority in favour of the seller?

2. Would it have been different if the buyer had been not an art dealer but, say, a stockbroker, buying a picture for his house? (In a consumer sale liability for breach of the undertaking as to description implied by section 13 cannot be excluded: Unfair Contract Terms Act 1977, s.6(2), (below, p. 706); but this only applies where the contract *is* "a contract for the sale of goods by description.")

3. The judges suggest that a description may be an essential term though it is not in fact relied on; but can it be a term if the seller makes it clear that his description is not to be relied on?

4. Might it have been argued that, in the absence of any undertaking that the picture was by Münter, the contract was void for failure of a common assumption which was the foundation of the contract (below, p. 483), that is, that the picture was by Münter? Or that, if not void, it was voidable for common mistake as to an essential quality (*Solle v. Butcher*, below, p. 501)? The fact that the buyer was not relying on the seller would be irrelevant. (The judge found

that Hull and Runkel both believed the painting was by Münter and, if either had not believed that, the deal would not have been made.)

DICK BENTLEY PRODUCTIONS LTD AND ANOTHER v. HAROLD SMITH (MOTORS) LTD

Court of Appeal [1965] 1 W.L.R. 623; [1965] 2 All E.R. 65

Bentley asked Smith, a car dealer, to find him a "well-vetted" Bentley car. Smith found a car which he told Bentley had done only 20,000 miles since it had been fitted with a replacement engine and gear box. This statement was untrue and, on the car proving unsatisfactory, Bentley sued and recovered damages for breach of warranty. Smith appealed.

LORD DENNING M.R.: I endeavoured to explain in *Oscar Chess Ltd v. Williams* (above, p. 369) that the question whether a warranty was intended depends on the conduct of the parties, on their words and behaviour, rather than on their thoughts. If an intelligent bystander would reasonably infer that a warranty was intended, that will suffice. What conduct, then? What words and behaviour, lead to the inference of a warranty?

Looking at the cases once more, as we have done so often, it seems to me that if a representation is made in the course of dealings for a contract for the very purpose of inducing the other party to act on it, and it actually induces him to act on it by entering into the contract, that is prima facie ground for inferring that the representation was intended as a warranty. It is not necessary to speak of it as being collateral. Suffice it that the representation was intended to be acted on and was in fact acted on. But the maker of the representation can rebut this inference if he can show that it really was an innocent misrepresentation, in that he was in fact innocent of fault in making it, and that it would not be reasonable in the circumstances for him to be bound by it. [His Lordship referred to the *Oscar Chess* case and continued:] . . . in the present case it is very different. The inference is not rebutted. Here we have a dealer, Mr Smith, who was in a position to know, or at least to find out, the history of the car. He could get it by writing to the makers. He did not do so. Indeed it was done later. When the history of this car was examined, his statement turned out to be quite wrong. He ought to have known better. There was no reasonable foundation for it. . . .

DANCKWERTS L.J.: I agree with the judgment of Lord Denning M.R.

SALMON L.J.: I agree. I have no doubt at all that the learned county court judge reached a correct conclusion when he decided that Mr Smith gave a warranty to the second plaintiff, Mr Bentley, and that that warranty was broken. Was what Mr Smith said intended and understood as a legally binding promise? If so, it was a warranty and as such may be part of the contract of sale or collateral to it. In effect, Mr Smith said: "If you will enter into a contract to buy this motor car from me for £1,850, I undertake that you will be getting a motor car which has done no more than twenty thousand miles since it was fitted with a new engine and a new gear box." I have no doubt at all that what was said by Mr Smith was so understood and was intended to be so understood by Mr Bentley. . . .

Appeal dismissed.

Question

When a seller warrants the quality of his goods, is it relevant, in an action on the warranty, whether he had reasonable grounds to believe his statement to be true or whether he was "completely innocent of any fault"? *Cf.* the case where the buyer is suing on section 2(1) of the Misrepresentation Act 1967. Are the *Oscar Chess* and *Dick Bentley* cases properly distinguishable? *Cf. Beale v. Taylor* [1967] 1 W.L.R. 1193 and note by K.L. Koh [1968] C.L.J. 11.

Contractual Term or Mere Representation? A series of cases concerning the sale of animals is instructive. In *Schawel v. Reade* [1913] 2 Ir. Rep. 81, H.L., the owner of a horse said to a potential buyer who was examining it, "You need not look for anything. The horse is perfectly sound. If there was anything the matter with the horse I would tell you." The buyer thereupon terminated the examination and three weeks later bought the horse. It was unfit for stud purposes. The jury answered in the affirmative the judge's question: "Did the defendant at the time of the sale represent to the plaintiff in order that the plaintiff might purchase the horse, that the horse was fit for stud purposes and did the plaintiff act upon that representation in the purchase of the horse?" The House of Lords held that the jury's answer amounted to a finding of a warranty. Lords MacNaghten and Atkinson said that the question contained all the ingredients of a warranty. Lord Moulton said that the essence of a warranty is that it is made plain by the words and actions that it is intended that the responsibility for soundness shall rest upon the vendor; and the vendor, at the conversation three weeks before the sale, could not have indicated more clearly that he intended to take upon himself the responsibility of the fitness of the horse.

In an earlier case, *Hopkins v. Tanqueray* (1854) 15 C.B. 130 an almost identical conversation took place the day before the sale by auction at Tattersalls of a horse, California. The seller was emphatic: "I assure you he is perfectly sound in every respect"; and the buyer responded, "If you say so, I am perfectly satisfied." He bought the horse at the auction. It was unsound. The Court of Common Pleas found that there was no evidence to support the jury's finding that there was a warranty embodied in the contract of sale. The explanation seems to be that both parties knew at the time of the conversation that the sale was to be by auction at Tattersalls, that the well-known course of business there is that sales are without a warranty and that the parties could not have intended a warranty since they could not have supposed that the buyer would be in a better position than other bidders at the sale. The court expressed doubts about the legality of a private warranty at a public auction without a warranty; but the decision is that no warranty was intended.

In *Couchman v. Hill* [1947] K.B. 554 the plaintiff purchased a heifer at an auction. The heifer was described in the catalogue as "unserved" but the catalogue and the exhibited conditions of sale made it clear that the accuracy of any description was not guaranteed and the lots were to be sold with all errors of description. The plaintiff required an unserved heifer for service by his own bull. Before the sale when the heifers were in the ring he asked both the defendant, the owner, and the auctioneer if they could confirm that the heifer was unserved. They both answered, "Yes." After he had bought the heifer it was found to be in calf and died from carrying a calf at too young an age. The Court of Appeal ruled that the answers of the defendant and auctioneer amounted to an offer of a warranty overriding the conditions of sale, that the offer was accepted by the plaintiff's bid and that the misdescription amounted to a breach of condition, which the plaintiff was entitled to treat as a breach of warranty and recover damages. *Hopkins v. Tanqueray* was not cited and an editorial note in the Law Reports stated that: "Since bidders at an auction have the right to suppose that they are all bidding on equal terms, it is a very grave question whether a private bargain for a warranty, when it is publicly announced that the sale is without warranty" could be upheld.

HARLING v. EDDY

Court of Appeal [1951] 2 K.B. 739; [1951] 2 T.L.R. 245; 95 S.J. 501; [1951]
2 All E.R. 212

The defendant put up a heifer for sale at Ashford Cattle Market on June 30, 1950. Condition 12 of the printed conditions of sale provided: "No animal . . . is sold with a 'warranty' unless specially mentioned at the time of offering, and no warranty so given shall have any legal force or effect unless the terms thereof appear on the purchaser's account." When the heifer appeared in the auction ring no one made a bid, owing to her unpromising appearance. Thereupon the defendant said that there was nothing wrong with the heifer, that he would absolutely guarantee her in every respect, and that he would be willing to take her back if she turned out not to be what he stated she was. Bidding then began and the heifer was knocked down to the plaintiff. Within three months the heifer had died from advanced tuberculosis.

EVERSHED M.R. [after stating the facts]: The real question is whether the statement which the defendant made at the sale immediately before the bidding entitles the plaintiff now to say that the animal was not, as the defendant stated her to be, sound in every respect, and that he now takes advantage of the offer which the defendant made and claims from the defendant the price paid for the animal, or equivalent damages. The real difficulty arises from the circumstance that condition 12, prima facie, seems intended to render nugatory any mere warranty given at the sale. The first answer, in my judgment, to the defence based on condition 12 is that, in the circumstances, this statement by the defendant was a condition.

It has been said many times, and particularly in *Wallis, Son & Wells v. Pratt & Haynes* (below, p. 417), that whether any statement is to be regarded as a condition or a warranty must depend upon the intention to be inferred from the particular statement. A statement that an animal is sound in every respect would, prima facie, be but a warranty; but in this case the judge quite clearly found as a fact that the defendant went further: he promised that he would take the animal back if she were no good. . . .

The defendant's statement having, therefore, included words to the effect, "If there is anything wrong I will take it back," it seems to me quite plain that the words which he used could not have been intended merely as a warranty; for a warranty would give no right of rejection to the purchaser. The final words involve necessarily a right in the purchaser to reject, that is, to return the animal; and they convert the statement, to my mind, from a warranty into a condition.

If, then, it is a condition, what would be the right of the plaintiff? Mr Laskey has argued forcibly that the plaintiff must at least exercise his right of rejection in due time. He plainly purported to do so on September 21, when he called upon the defendant to take the animal back. In my judgment, in the circumstances of the case, the period between July 1 and the middle of September would not be unreasonable; but, however that may be, it is plain also from *Wallis, Son & Wells v. Pratt & Haynes* that a person entitled to the benefit of a condition, as was the plaintiff here, can turn the condition, in effect, into a warranty by claiming damages as for breach of warranty instead of his exercising his right or rejection. By the time this claim had been formulated, the animal was dead, and the plaintiff could, in truth, not do otherwise than he has done here—namely, to claim damages; and in my judgment he was entitled to treat the condition to that extent as though it were a warranty.

If that is right, the question still remains whether condition 12 of the conditions apply. In my opinion, the answer is No. Condition 12 is limited in its terms to a statement which is a mere warranty and is not a condition, and the second part of it," . . . and no warranty so given shall have any legal force or effect . . ." can only refer to the warranty previously mentioned, namely, a statement which is a warranty and no more. In other words, condition 12 cannot be relied on by the defendant to defeat the right of the plaintiff to sue for damages for the breach of the condition.

[His Lordship then considered *Couchman v. Hill*]

The terms of the printed conditions in this case differ from the terms of the printed conditions in *Couchman v. Hill* (above, p. 378), and the language used by the two defendants differs also. Bearing the facts in mind, and in particular the initial silence which greeted the entry of this animal into the ring, and the fact that bidding only began when the defendant's statement had been made, the question may properly be formulated thus: did the defendant imply by this statement that the animal should be sold on the faith of what he stated, to the exclusion of the printed condition 12, or of any other condition which might be found in the auction particulars which would of itself appear to exclude any oral statement? Mr Laskey argued that neither party may have had in mind, when this particular incident occurred, what were the exact terms of the conditions of sale. I should, however, suppose that, both being experienced in the buying and selling of cattle, they would be aware, according to common practice, that there would be stultifying conditions of some kind in the auction particulars.

If that were the question to be posed, in my judgment it should be answered affirmatively on the facts as found by the judge. I therefore, for my part, would hold that, even if the language used here were a warranty only and not a condition, the plaintiff nevertheless would be entitled to succeed.

[His Lordship then discussed a question of pleading which arose at the trial, and continued:] Before leaving *Couchman v. Hill* I would like to say one further word about it. To the report in the *All England Law Reports* there is an editorial note referring to a case of 100 years ago, *Hopkins v. Tanqueray* (above, p. 378), relating to the sale of a horse at Tattersalls. In that case the seller and the buyer happened to have met not at the sale, but the day before it, and the conversation which is related in this note formed no part of the transaction which occurred at the sale itself. At this meeting between the seller and the buyer a statement was made about the soundness of the horse, and later the auction took place. The question in that case was whether what had passed in that previous conversation could affect a stultifying condition in the auction particulars. But the court in *Hopkins v. Tanqueray* found that what was said—the promise made by the seller in his private conversation—formed no part of the contract: the contract was formed as a result of the sale at the auction and comprehended the conditions set out in the auction particulars. It is plain, therefore, that that case is wholly distinguishable from *Couchman v. Hill*, and equally from this case. I say that because the note to which I have alluded suggests that, had

Hopkins v. Tanqueray been referred to at the time of the hearing in this court of *Couchman v. Hill*, the later decision might have been different. I do not think so. Having considered this editorial note, it seems to me that the earlier case was entirely distinguishable from *Couchman v. Hill*, and to my mind there is no reason for suggesting that *Couchman v. Hill* was otherwise than rightly decided on the issues raised before the court. It binds this court in any case; but I desire to express my entire concurrence with that decision, without, however, committing myself either way on the question whether a private bargain for a warranty, as distinguished from a public bargain, as the bargain was in this case, is assailable on the ground of illegality.

DENNING L.J., CONCURRING: The decision of this court in *Couchman v. Hill* is to the same effect. *Hopkins v. Tanqueray* is distinguishable because there was no warranty. I have before me Scott L.J.'s copy of the *All England Law Reports* containing the report of *Couchman v. Hill*, and I can see that he has noted in his own handwriting: "*Hopkins v. Tanqueray*, a case of a conversation a day before the sale is distinguishable. My attention was drawn to it by the editor of the Law Reports, February 22, 1947."

ROXBURGH J. concurred.

Questions
  1. Does this case settle the question whether a private bargain for a warranty is enforceable when it has been publicly announced that the sale is to be without warranty? How could Evershed M.R. express his "entire concurrence" with *Couchman v. Hill* without committing himself on the question? What should be the answer to the question?
  2. A racehorse, Scattercash, is to be sold by auction without a warranty. Al alone has received a private assurance as to Scattercash's fitness from the owner. When the bidding reaches £10,000, all the bidders except Al and Ben fall out. Al would fall out too, if he had not received the warranty. He continues to bid up to £14,000. Ben bids £14,500 and the horse is knocked down to him. He then learns the truth. Is the contract binding?
  3. Is *Hopkins v. Tanqueray* distinguishable because the conversation took place the day before the sale? *Cf. Schawel v. Reade*, above, p. 378 and note that the jury found that the representation made three weeks earlier was made "at the time of the sale." Does it matter when the words were uttered if the buyer was reasonably relying on them at the time of the sale?
  4. Consider the effect of the Misrepresentation Act 1967, below, p. 703 the Unfair Contract Terms Act 1977, ss.6 and 12(2), below, p. 704.

CITY AND WESTMINSTER PROPERTIES (1934) LTD v. MUDD

[1959] Ch. 129; [1958] 3 W.L.R. 312; 102 S.J. 582; [1958] 2 All E.R. 733

In 1941 the defendant became the tenant of a lock-up shop for three years. He was allowed by the landlords (the plaintiffs) to sleep in the shop. In 1944 the plaintiffs granted the defendant a second lease for three years, in which the defendant covenanted not to use the premises except as a shop for his business as an antique dealer. He continued to sleep there and fitted up the basement as a residence. The plaintiffs knew that he slept there but not that the premises were his residence. In 1947 a draft of a new lease was prepared which contained covenants by the lessee not to use the premises as a place for lodging, dwelling or sleeping. The defendant objected to this clause and his solicitors deleted it from the draft but the plaintiffs insisted on retaining it, fearing that to permit the defendant to reside on the premises might bring them within the Rent Restriction Acts. The defendant told the plaintiffs' agent that he would not sign a lease with a clause about not sleeping there. The agent then told the defendant orally that, if he would sign the lease, the plaintiffs would not object to his sleeping there. In consequence the defendant was willing to complete and the lease and counterpart were exchanged. The words about lodging dwelling or sleeping were omitted—according to the plaintiffs' solicitor, through inadvertence in his office. The covenant to use the premises for trade purposes only, however, remained.

In 1956 the defendant applied for a new lease for twenty-one years. The plaintiffs noticed that he was living there and brought an action for forfeiture of the lease, alleging a breach of the covenant not to use the premises except for trade purposes.

Harman J. held that he was not entitled to use the negotiations and the drafts as an aid to construction (the defendant having relied on the omission of the words "lodging, dwelling or sleeping" as evidence that he was to be allowed to sleep there. Nor was the defendant entitled to rectification for there was no common intention that a clause permitting him to reside should be inserted in the lease. Nor did the fact that the plaintiffs knew that the defendant was sleeping there amount to a release of the covenant or a new letting. The learned judge continued:

There remains the so-called question of estoppel. This, in my judgment, is a misnomer and the present case does not raise the controversial issue of the *Central London Property Trust v. High Trees, Ltd* decision (above p. 249). This is not a case of a representation made after contractual relations existed between the parties to the effect that one party to the contract would not rely on his rights. If the defendant's evidence is to be accepted, as I hold it is, it is a case of a promise made to him before the execution of a lease that if he would execute it in the form put before him, the landlord would not seek to enforce against him personally the covenant about using the property as a shop only. The defendant says that it was in reliance on this promise that he executed the lease and entered on the onerous obligations contained in it. He says, moreover, that but for the promise made he would not have executed the lease, but would have moved to other premises available to him at the time. If these be the facts, there was a clear contract acted upon by the defendant to his detriment and from which the Plaintiffs cannot be allowed to resile. The case is truly analogous to *Re William Porter & Co. Ltd* [1937] 2 All E.R. 361. . . .

The plea that this was a mere licence retractable at the plaintiff's will does not bear examination. The promise was that as long as the defendant personally was tenant, so long would the landlords forbear to exercise the rights which they would have if he signed the lease. He did sign the lease on this promise and is therefore entitled to rely on it so long as he is personally in occupation of the shop.

Judgment for the defendant.

Questions

1. Would the application of the *High Trees* doctrine have protected the defendant as effectively as the collateral contract?

2. In *Henderson v. Arthur* [1907] 1 K.B. 10, an action on a covenant in a lease for payment of the rent quarterly in advance, the lessee's defence was that, antecedently to the execution of the lease, the lessor had agreed to take a bill payable at three months for each quarter's rent in advance as it became due. The Court of Appeal, reversing Lord Alverstone C.J., held that the evidence of the agreement was inadmissible. Collins M.R. said: ". . . to admit evidence of such an agreement as being so available would be to violate one of the first principles of the law of evidence; because, in my opinion, it would be to substitute the terms of an antecedent parol agreement for the terms of a subsequent formal contract under seal dealing with the same subject-matter. I do not see how, in this case, the covenant in the lease and the antecedent parol agreement can co-exist and the subsequent deed has the effect of wiping out any previous agreement dealing with the same subject-matter . . . it is not a merely collateral agreement, but provides in another and contradictory manner for doing what was subsequently provided for by the lease."

Is *Mudd's* case reconcilable with *Henderson v. Arthur*? Is there a difference between an antecedent agreement (which is wiped out) and a coincident agreement (which is not)?

SHANKLIN PIER LTD v. DETEL PRODUCTS LTD

King's Bench Division [1951] 2 K.B. 854; 95 S.J. 563; [1951] 2 All E.R. 471, [1951] 2 Lloyd's Rep. 187

The plaintiffs, the owners of a pier, entered into a contract with contractors to have the pier repainted with two coats of bituminous paint. The plaintiffs had the right, under this contract, to vary the specification. A director of the defendant company went to Shanklin with the object of securing for his company the contract for supplying the paint. He assured the plaintiffs' representatives that a certain paint manufactured by the defendants and known as D.M.U. would have a life of at least seven to ten years. On the faith of this representation the plaintiffs amended their specification by the substitution of D.M.U. That paint was bought by the contractors from the defendants and applied to the pier but it proved to be unsatisfactory and lasted only about three months. The plaintiffs, by their statement of claim, alleged that, in consideration of the plaintiffs' specifying that the contractors should use for repainting the pier two coats of a paint known as D.M.U., the defendants warranted that the paint would be suitable for repainting the pier and would have a life of from seven to ten years.

McNAIR J.: This case raises an interesting and comparatively novel question whether or not an enforceable warranty can arise as between parties other than parties to the main contract for the sale of the article in respect of which the warranty is alleged to have been given. . . . [His Lordship then stated the facts, and reviewed the evidence about the negotiations which led to the contract for D.M.U. paint.]

In the result, I am satisfied that, if a direct contract of purchase and sale of the D.M.U. had then been made between the plaintiffs and the defendants, the correct conclusion on the facts would have been that the defendants gave to the plaintiffs the warranties substantially in the form alleged in the statement of claim. In reaching this conclusion, I adopt the principles stated by Holt C.J. in *Crosse v. Gardner* (1689) Comb. 142, and *Medina v. Stoughton* (1700) 1 Salk. 210, that an affirmation at the time of sale is a warranty, provided it appear on evidence to have been so intended.

Counsel for the defendants submitted that in law a warranty could give rise to no enforceable cause of action except between the same parties as the parties to the main contract in relation to which the warranty was given. In principle, this submission seems to me to be unsound. If, as is elementary, the consideration for the warranty in the usual case is the entering into of the main contract in relation to which the warranty is given, I see no reason why there may not be an enforceable warranty between A and B supported by the consideration that B should cause C to enter into a contract with A or that B should do some other act for the benefit of A.

Judgment for the plaintiffs.

Note

The principle of the *Shanklin Pier* case was applied to the common transaction in which a dealer induced his customer to take goods by representations about the goods whereupon the customer entered into a contract of credit sale or hire-purchase, not with the dealer, but with a finance company to which the dealer sold the goods. In *Andrews v. Hopkinson* [1957] 1 Q.B. 289, the dealer said, "It's a good little bus. I would stake my life on it. You will have no trouble with it." The plaintiff entered into a written contract with a finance company to take the car on hire-purchase. The car was unroadworthy. McNair J. held that there was a warranty by the dealer, enforceable by the customer. The consideration given by the customer was the entry into the hire-purchase agreement. Notice that the warranty was probably enforceable only against the dealer and not against the finance company. Consider the effect upon such transactions of section 14(3) of the Sale of Goods Act 1979, below.

WELLS (MERSTHAM) LTD v. BUCKLAND SAND AND SILICA LTD

Queen's Bench Division [1964] 2 W.L.R. 453; [1964] 1 All E.R. 41; 108 S.J. 177

The plaintiffs were chrysanthemum growers and the defendants, sand merchants. The plaintiffs' manager visited the defendants and was assured by their manager that deliveries of sand could be relied on as conforming to an analysis which showed that the sand had a low iron oxide content. Subsequently the plaintiffs placed an order for the defendants' sand with a third party (in order to save transport costs) who bought the sand from the defendants and resold it to the plaintiffs. The third party did not tell the defendants that the sand was for the plaintiffs and the defendants did not know that it was for horticultural purposes. The sand did not correspond with the analysis, having a high iron oxide content which caused damage agreed at £2,500 to the plaintiffs. Having held that a warranty was intended that the sand conformed to the analysis, EDMUND DAVIES J. went on:

Then does it make any difference that, the warranty having been given to the plaintiffs, all the purchases other than the first were made by the plaintiffs from a third party? If that question demands in law an affirmative answer, the result would not be justice, for, as I have said, it was purely fortuitous that all the loads were not sold by the defendants direct to the plaintiffs. But in my judgment such an affirmative answer is not required, as several reported decisions indicate. Thus, in *Brown v. Sheen and Richmond Car Sales Ltd* [1950] 1 All E.R. 1102, *Shanklin Pier Ltd v. Detel Products Ltd* (above, p. 383) and *Andrews v. Hopkinson* [1957] 1 Q.B. 289, all tried at first instance, and *Yeoman Credit Ltd v. Odgers* [1962] 1 W.L.R. 215, the warranty given by the defendant was held enforceable notwithstanding that the main contract was subsequently entered into between the plaintiff and a third party. As McNair J. said in the second case, "If, as is elementary, the consideration for the warranty in the usual case is the entering into of the main contract in relation to which the warranty is given, I see no reason why there may not be an enforceable warranty between A and B supported by the consideration that B should cause C to enter into a contract with A or that B should do some other act for the benefit of A." And if Clark gave the warranty I have found he did, it would be absurd in the circumstances of the case to regard that warranty as being impliedly restricted to orders placed directly by the plaintiffs with the defendants.

As between A (a potential seller of goods) and B (a potential buyer), two ingredients, and two only, are in my judgment required in order to bring about a collateral contract containing a warranty: (1) a promise or assertion by A as to the nature, quality or quantity of the goods which B may reasonably regard as being made *animo contrahendi*, and (2) acquisition by B of the goods in reliance on that promise or assertion. As K. W. Wedderburn expresses it in "Collateral Contracts" in *Cambridge Law Journal*, 1959, at p. 79: ". . . the consideration given for the promise is no more than the act of entering into the main contract. Going ahead with that bargain is a sufficient price for the promise, without which it would not have gone ahead at all." And a warranty may be enforceable notwithstanding that no specific main contract is discussed at the time it is given, though obviously an *animus contrahendi* (and, therefore, a warranty) would be unlikely to be inferred unless the circumstances show that it was within the present contemplation of the parties that a contract based upon the promise would shortly be entered into. Furthermore, the operation of the warranty must have a limitation in point of time which is reasonable in all the circumstances. But none of these considerations gives rise to difficulty in the present case.

Judgment for the plaintiffs for £2,500.

Questions

1. What consideration did the plaintiffs supply to the defendants? When did the warranty become binding?

2. Suppose the third party had held a stock of the defendants' sand and had supplied the plaintiffs from that: would there still have been a warranty?

3. Suppose the plaintiffs had already held stocks of the defendants' sand and had sent their manager to find out if it was suitable for growing chrysanthemums: could the plaintiffs have recovered damages? (*Cf. Hedley Byrne & Co. v. Heller & Partners* [1964] A.C. 465, above, p. 340.

4. Is the case the same as those cited by Edmund Davies J.? In each of those cases a transaction with a third party was clearly contemplated by the party giving the warranty. Should this make a difference?

5. Henry advertises on television that his sand (which can be obtained from any gardening shop) is ideal for growing chrysanthemums. In reliance on the advertisement, several hundred people buy Henry's sand. Because of its high iron oxide content, their chrysanthemums die. Advise Henry.

CHAPTER 10

IMPLIED TERMS

Glanville Williams, Language and the Law, 61 L.Q.R., p. 401

The courts will generally enforce consequences logically implied in the language of contracts, wills, statutes, and other legal documents and transactions. The point now to be noticed is that the legal doctrine of implied terms goes much farther than this. Judges are accustomed to read into documents and transactions many terms that are not logically implied in them. As an academic matter non-logical implication may be classified into three kinds: (i) of terms that the parties (the plural shall throughout include the singular) probably had in mind but did not trouble to express; (ii) of terms that the parties, whether or not they actually had them in mind, would probably have expressed if the question had been brought to their attention; and (iii) of terms that the parties, whether or not they had them in mind or would have expressed them if they had foreseen the difficulty, are implied by the court because of the court's view of fairness or policy or in consequence of rules of law. Of these three kinds of non-logical implication (i) is an effort to arrive at actual intention; (ii) is an effort to arrive at hypothetical or conditional intention—the intention that the parties would have had if they had foreseen the difficulty; (iii) is not concerned with the intention of the parties except to the extent that the term implied by the court may be excluded by an expression of positive intention to the contrary. . . .

The view may perhaps be held that this particular process is not very happily called "implication." It is not so much the interpretation of a pre-existing and expressed intent as legislation amending or supplementing the expressed intent. Terms so read into the contract might better be called "constructive" than "implied." However, this is simply a question of nomenclature; and in any case no fixed nomenclature can be maintained in practice, because terms of classes (i), (ii) and (iii) merge into each other. There is no legal difference between the three classes, and the only practical difference is that the courts are more ready to imply terms of class (i) than of classes (ii) and (iii). Terms of classes (ii) and (iii) are mainly of specified types and are comparatively rarely added to, though it is always open to the court to add to them. . . .

It is a matter of taste whether implied terms of classes (ii) and (iii) be styled implied terms or rules of law. They are in fact merely rules of law that apply in the absence of an expression of contrary intent: whether we choose to call them implied terms or not is simply a matter of terminology. Our terminology as we now have it is not consistent, for there are some rules of law that are indistinguishable from implied terms in their practical effect, yet which are never called implied terms. Such, for instance, are the rules of interpretation. So, also we do not say that the rule that a contract is voidable for innocent misrepresentation is an implied term, although it can be derogated from by agreement; yet some judges and writers have been known to declare that the law of frustration, the duty to disclose in contracts *uberrimae fidei*, and even part of the law of mistake in contract, rest upon implied terms or conditions. With all respect to those who hold a contrary opinion, it is submitted that the question is purely terminological and has (or should have) no practical importance.

HUTTON v. WARREN

Exchequer of Pleas (1836) 1 M. & W. 466; 2 Gale 71; 1 Tyr. & G. 646;
5 L.J.Ex. 234; 150 E.R. 517

The defendant was the landlord, and the plaintiff the tenant of a certain farm. At Michaelmas 1833 the defendant gave the plaintiff notice to quit at the Lady Day following. In October 1833 the defendant insisted that the plaintiff was bound to continue to cultivate the farm in due course of husbandry according to the custom of the country, and gave him formal notice to that effect. The plaintiff quitted in accordance with the notice and now alleged that he was entitled to a fair allowance for seeds and labour on the arable land. It was proved that by the custom of the country a tenant was bound to farm according to a certain course of husbandry for the whole of his tenancy, and, on quitting, was entitled to a fair allowance for seeds and labour on the arable land. The judgment of the court was delivered by PARKE B.:

We are of opinion that this custom was, by implication, imported into the lease. It has long been settled, that, in commercial transactions, extrinsic evidence of custom and usage is admissible to annex incidents to written contracts, in matters with respect to which they are silent. The same rule has also been applied to contracts in other transactions of life, in which known usages have been established and prevailed; and this has been done upon the principle of presumption that, in such transactions, the parties did not mean to express in writing the whole of the contract by which they intended to be bound, but a contract with reference to those known usages. Whether such a relaxation of the strictness of the common law was wisely applied, where formal instruments have been entered into, and particularly leases under seal, may well be doubted; but the contrary has been established by such authority, and the relations between landlord and tenant have been so long regulated upon the supposition that all customary obligations, not altered by the contract, are to remain in force, that it is too late to pursue a contrary course; and it would be productive of much inconvenience if this practice were now to be disturbed.

The common law, indeed, does so little to prescribe the relative duties of landlord and tenant, since it leaves the latter at liberty to pursue any course of management he pleases, provided he is not guilty of waste, that it is by no means surprising that the courts should have been favourably inclined to the introduction of those regulations in the mode of cultivation which custom and usage have established in each district to be the most beneficial to all parties. . . .

[Parke B. referred to a number of cases including *Senior v. Armitage*, reported in Holt's Nisi Prius Cases 197, where the question was whether a tenant was entitled to compensation for seeds and labour. He continued]:
Mr Holt appears to have stated the case too strongly when he said that the court held the custom to be operative, "unless the agreement in express

terms excluded it"; and probably he has not been quite accurate in attributing a similar opinion to the Lord Chief Baron Thompson, who presided on the second trial. It would appear that the court held that the custom operated, unless it could be collected from the instrument, either expressly or impliedly, that the parties did not mean to be governed by it.

On the second trial, the Lord Chief Baron Thompson held that the custom prevailed, although the written instrument contained an express stipulation that all the manure made on the farm should be left at the end of the tenancy, without any compensation being paid. Such a stipulation certainly does not exclude by implication the tenant's right to receive a compensation for seed and labour. . . .

The question then is, whether, from the terms of the lease now under consideration it can be collected that the parties intended to exclude the customary obligations to make allowances for seed and labour.

The only clause relating to the management of the farm (except the covenant to repair) is one which stipulated that the plaintiff shall spend and consume on the farm three-fourths of the hay and straw arising not only from the farm itself, but from the demised tithes of the whole parish, and spread the manure, leaving such as should not be spread at the end of the term for the use of the landlord, on paying a reasonable price for the same. This provision introduces and has a principal reference to a subject to which the custom of the country does not apply at all, namely, the tithes, and imposes a new obligation on the tenant dehors that custom, and then qualifies that obligation by an engagement on the landlord's part to give a remuneration, by re-purchasing a part of the produce in a particular event. It is by no means to be inferred from this provision that this is the only compensation which the tenant is to receive on quitting. If, indeed, there had been a covenant by the tenant to plough and sow a certain portion of the demised land in the last year, being such as the custom of the country required, he being paid on quitting for the ploughing, or to plough, sow, and manure, he being paid for the manuring, the principle of *expressum facit cessare tacitum*, which governed the decision in *Webb v. Plummer* (1819) 2 B. & Ald. 746, would have applied; but that is not the case here. The custom of the country as to the obligation of the tenant to plough and sow, and the corresponding obligation of the landlord to pay for such ploughing and sowing in the last year of the term, is in no way varied. The only alteration made in the custom is, that the tenant is obliged to spend more than the produce of the farm on the premises being paid for it in the same way as he would have been for that which the custom required him to spend.

Note

In *Les Affréteurs Réunis Société Annonyme v. Leopold Walford (London) Ltd* [1919] A.C. 801; 121 L.T. 393, H.L., above, p. 316, Bailhache J. held that there was a custom in the shipping trade that a chartering broker's commission was payable only in respect of hire duly earned under the charterparty. He therefore rejected W.'s claim for commission as broker in effecting a charter of ss. *Flore* since the ship was requisitioned by the French Government and never entered upon service under the charterparty. The charterparty, however, provided that the commission should be payable "on signing this charter (ship lost or not lost)"; and the Court of Appeal and the House of Lords held that the custom could have no application since it was inconsistent with the express terms of the charterparty.

THE MOORCOCK

Court of Appeal (1889) 14 P.D. 64; 58 L.J.P. 73; 60 L.T. 654; 37 W.R. 439

The appellants were wharfingers possessed of a wharf abuffing on, and a jetty extending into, the River Thames. The respondent was the owner of the steamship Moorcock.

In November 1887 it was agreed between the appellants and the respondent that the vessel should be discharged and loaded at the wharf, and for that purpose should be moored alongside the jetty where she would take the ground at low water.

No charge was made in respect of the vessel being moored alongside, or lying at, the jetty but the shipowner paid for the use of the cranes in discharging the cargo, and rates were payable to the appellants on all goods landed, shipped, or stored.

Whilst the Moorcock was lying moored at the extremity of the jetty discharging her cargo, the tide ebbed and, when she ceased to be waterborne, she sustained damage, owing to the centre of the vessel settling on a ridge of hard ground beneath the mud.

Butt J. came to the conclusion that there was no warranty by the wharfingers that the place was safe for the vessel to lie in, and that the evidence negatived any express representation by them that the place was suitable for the vessel, but the learned judge held that as the use of the wharfingers' premises by the owner of the Moorcock required that the vessel should take the ground when moored alongside the jetty, there was an implied representation by the wharfingers that they had taken reasonable care to ascertain that the bottom of the river at the jetty was in such a condition as not to endanger the vessel.

The defendants appealed.

BOWEN L.J.: The question which arises here is whether when a contract is made to let the use of this jetty to a ship which can only use it, as is known by both parties, by taking the ground, there is any implied warranty on the part of the owners of the jetty, and if so, what is the extent of the warranty. Now, an implied warranty, or, as it is called, a covenant in law, as distinguished from an express contract or express warranty, really is in all cases founded on the presumed intention of the parties, and upon reason. The implication which the law draws from what must obviously have been the intention of the parties, the law draws with the object of giving efficacy to the transaction and preventing such a failure of consideration as cannot have been within the contemplation of either side; and I believe if one were to take all the cases, and they are many, of implied warranties or covenants in law, it will be found that in all of them the law is raising an implication from the presumed intention of the parties with the object of giving to the transaction such efficacy as both parties must have intended that at all events it should have. In business transactions such as this, what the law desires to effect by the implication is to give such business efficacy to the transaction as must have been intended at all events by both parties who are business men; not to impose on one side all the perils of the transaction, or to emancipate one side from all the chances of failure, but to make each party promise in law as much, at all events, as it must have been in the contemplation of both parties that he should be responsible for in respect of those perils or chances.

Now what did each party in a case like this know? For if we are examining into their presumed intention we must examine into their minds as to what the transaction was. Both parties knew that this jetty was let out for hire, and knew that it could only be used under the contract by the ship taking the ground. They must have known that it was by grounding that she used the jetty; in fact, except so far as the transport to the jetty of the cargo in the ship was concerned, they must have known, both of them, that unless the ground was safe the ship would be simply buying an opportunity of danger, and that all consideration would fail unless some care had been taken to see that the ground was safe. In fact the business of the jetty could not be carried on except upon such a basis. The parties also knew that with regard to the safety of the ground outside the jetty the shipowner could know nothing at all, and the jetty owner might with reasonable care know everything. The owners of the jetty, or their servants, were there at high and low tide, and with little trouble they could satisfy themselves, in case of doubt, as to whether the berth was reasonably safe. The ship's owner, on the other hand, had not the means of verifying the state of the jetty, because the berth itself opposite the jetty might be occupied by another ship at any moment.

Now the question is how much of the peril of the safety of this berth is it necessary to assume that the shipowner and the jetty owner intended respectively to bear—in order that such a minimum of efficacy should be secured for the transaction, as both parties must have intended it to bear? Assume that the berth outside had been absolutely under the control of the owners of the jetty, that they could have repaired it and made it fit for the purpose of the unloading and the loading. If this had been the case, then the case of *The Mersey Docks Trustees v. Gibbs*, L.R. 1 H.L. 93, shows that those who owned the jetty, who took money for the use of the jetty, and who had under their control the *locus in quo*, would have been bound to take all reasonable care to prevent danger to those who were using the jetty—either to make the berth outside good, or else not to invite ships to go there—either to make the berth safe, or to advise persons not to go there. But there is a distinction in the present instance. The berth outside the jetty was not under the actual control of the jetty owners. It is in the bed of the river, and it may be said that those who owned the jetty had no duty cast upon them by statute or common law to repair the bed of the river, and that they had no power to interfere with the bed of the river, unless under the licence of the Conservators. Now it does make a difference, it seems to me, where the entire control of the *locus in quo*—be it canal, or be it dock, or be it river berth—is *not* under the control of the persons who are taking toll for accommodation which involves its user, and, to a certain extent, the view must be modified of the necessary implication which the law would make about the duties of the parties receiving the remuneration. This must be done exactly for the reason laid down by Lord Holt in his judgment in *Coggs v. Bernard*, Ld.Raym. 909, 918, where he says: "it would be unreasonable to charge persons with a trust further than the nature of the thing puts it in their power to perform." Applying that modification, which is one of reason, to this case, it may well be said that the law will not imply that the persons who have not the control of the place have taken reasonable care to make it good, but it does not follow that they are relieved from all responsibility. They are on the spot. They must know that the jetty cannot be used unless reasonable care is taken, if not to make it safe, at all events to see whether it is safe. No one can tell whether reasonable safety has been secured except themselves, and I think if they let out their jetty for use they at all events imply that they have taken reasonable care to see whether the berth, which is the essential part of the use of the jetty, is safe, and if it is not safe, and if they have not taken such reasonable care, it is their duty to warn persons with whom they have dealings that they have not done so. This is a business transaction as to which at any moment the parties may make any bargain they please, and either side may by the contract throw upon the other the burden of the unseen and existing danger. The question is what inference is to be drawn where the parties are dealing with each other on the assumption that the negotiations are to have some fruit, and where they say nothing about the burden of this kind of unseen peril, leaving the law to raise such inferences as are reasonable from the very nature of the transaction. So far as I am concerned I do not wish it to be understood that I at all consider this is a case of any duty on the part of the owners of the jetty to see to the access to the jetty being kept clear. The difference between access to the jetty and the actual use of the jetty seems to me, as Mr Finlay says it is, only a question of degree, but when you are dealing with implications which the law directs, you cannot afford to neglect questions of degree, and it is just that difference of degree which brings one case on the line and prevents the other from approaching it. I confess that on the broad view of the case I think that business could not be carried on unless there was an implication to the extent I have laid down, at all events in the case where a jetty like the present is so to be used, and, although the case is a novel one, and the cases which have been cited do not assist us, I feel no difficulty in drawing the inference that this case comes within the line.

LORD ESHER M.R. and FRY L.J. delivered judgment to the same effect.

Question
   Bowen L.J. speaks in this case of an implied warranty. Might he have held the term to be a condition if that had been necessary to the decision? Did the wharfingers impliedly promise (a) that the berth was safe?; (b) that they had taken reasonable steps to make it safe?; (c) that they had taken reasonable steps to find out whether it was safe?

REIGATE v. UNION MANUFACTURING CO.

Court of Appeal [1918] 1 K.B. 592, 605, 87 L.J.K.B. 724; 118 L.T. 479

SCRUTTON L.J.: The first thing is to see what the parties have expressed in the contract; and then an implied term is not to be added because the court thinks it would have been reasonable to have inserted it in the contract. A term can only be implied if it is necessary in the business sense to give efficacy to the contract; that is, if it is such a term that it can confidently be said that if at the time the contract was being negotiated someone had said to the parties, "What will happen in such a case?" they would both have replied: "Of course, so and so will happen; we did not trouble to say that; it is too clear." Unless the court comes to some such conclusion as that, it ought not to imply a term which the parties themselves have not expressed.

Note

In the above case the Court of Appeal held that where, in consideration of the plaintiff investing £1,000 in the capital of the defendant company, the company had appointed him their sole agent for the sale of certain goods for seven years, no term could be implied that the company could terminate the agency at any time by ceasing to carry on business. "If this matter had been mooted at the time when the contract had been negotiated, I expect that the parties would at once have disagreed as to what the position was. Unless we are satisfied that it is an implication which must necessarily have been in the minds of both parties, we cannot imply a term which they have not expressed, especially when I see that they have thought sufficiently about the matter to express two conditions on which the agreement is to be determined, first the obvious one on the death of the agent; and secondly, by six months' notice after the expiration of seven years"—*per* Scrutton L.J. at p. 605.

SHIRLAW v. SOUTHERN FOUNDRIES LTD

Court of Appeal [1939] 2 K.B. 206, 227; 108 L.J.K.B. 747; 160 L.T. 353; 55 T.L.R. 611; 83 S.J. 357; [1939] 2 All E.R. 113

MACKINNON L.J.: I recognise that the right or duty of a court to find the existence of an implied term or implied terms in a written contract is a matter to be exercised with care; and a court is too often invited to do so upon vague and uncertain grounds. Too often also such an invitation is backed by the citation of a sentence or two from the judgment of Bowen L.J. in *The Moorcock* (above, p. 390). They are sentences from an extempore judgment as sound and sensible as all the utterances of that great judge; but I fancy that he would have been rather surprised if he could have foreseen that these general remarks of his would come to be a favourite citation of a supposed principle of law, and I even think that he might sympathise with the occasional impatience of his successors when *The Moorcock* is so often flushed for them in that guise.

For my part, I think that there is a test that may be at least as useful as such generalities. If I may quote from an essay which I wrote some years ago, I then said: "Prima facie that which in any contract is left to be implied and need not be expressed is something so obvious that it goes without saying; so that, if, while the parties were making their bargain, an officious bystander were to suggest some express provision for it in their agreement, they would testily suppress him with a common 'Oh, of course!'"

At least it is true, I think, that, if a term were never implied by a judge unless it could pass that test, he could not be held to be wrong.

Note

Applying the above test, MacKinnon L.J. held that there were implied terms in a company's contract, appointing the plaintiff, a director, to be its managing director for 10 years, (i) that the company would not remove him during that time from his *directorship*, since such removal would automatically terminate his appointment as managing director; and (ii) that the company would not alter its articles of association so as to create a right in itself or another to remove him. Goddard L.J. agreed, but Greene M.R. dissented on the first point. The House of Lords ([1940] A.C. 701) dismissed an appeal by a majority of three to two; but none of their Lordships held that term (ii) (above) should be implied; and, of the majority, Lord Wright stated that the removal of the plaintiff from his directorship was a breach of an express, not an implied term. *Cf. General Publicity Services Ltd v. Best's Brewery Ltd* [1951] 2 T.L.R. 875 (C.A.); [1951] W.N. 507.

For interesting applications of MacKinnon L.J.'s test, see *Forbes v. Kemsley Newspapers, Ltd* [1951] 2 T.L.R. 656 and *Spring v. National Amalgamated Stevedores and Dockers Society* [1956] 1

W.L.R. 585 at 598–599. See also *Trollope & Colls Ltd v. N.W. Hospital Board* [1973] 2 All E.R. 260.

LIVERPOOL CITY COUNCIL v. IRWIN AND ANOTHER

House of Lords [1977] A.C. 239; [1976] 2 W.L.R. 562; [1976] 2 All E.R. 39

The plaintiff owned a tower block containing about 70 flats. Access was by a common staircase and two lifts. Tenants were provided with an internal chute for the discharge of rubbish. In July 1966 the defendants became tenants of a flat. The tenancy agreement imposed obligations on the tenant but said nothing of the obligations of the landlord. The conditions of the block deteriorated seriously, partly because of the activities of vandals and lack of co-operation by the tenants. The defendants and other tenants refused to pay rent by way of protest at the conditions. The plaintiff sought an order for possession and the defendants counterclaimed alleging, *inter alia*, a breach of an implied covenant for quiet enjoyment. The judge granted the order for possession but awarded the defendants £10 damages on their counterclaim. The plaintiff appealed. The Court of Appeal allowed the appeal. Roskill and Ormrod L.JJ. held that no covenant could be implied, since it was not *necessary* to do so. Lord Denning M.R. held that the court could imply a term if it was *reasonable* to do so; that a term should be implied that the Council would take reasonable care to keep the lifts and staircase reasonably fit for use; but that there was no evidence that they had not done so. The defendants' appeal to the House of Lords was dismissed.

LORD WILBERFORCE: I consider first the appellants' claim insofar as it is based on contract. The first step must be to ascertain what the contract is. This may look elementary, even naive, but it seems to me to be the essential step and to involve, from the start, an approach different, if simpler, from that taken by the members of the Court of Appeal. We look first at documentary material. As is common with council lettings there is no formal demise or lease or tenancy agreement. There is a document headed "Liverpool Corporation, Liverpool City Housing Department" and described as "Conditions of Tenancy." This contains a list of obligations on the tenant—he shall do this, he shall not do that, or he shall not do that without the corporation's consent. This is an amalgam of obligations added to from time to time, no doubt, to meet complaints, emerging situations, or problems as they appear to the council's officers. In particular there have been added special provisions relating to multi-storey flats which are supposed to make the conditions suitable to such dwellings. We may note under "Further special notes" some obligations not to obstruct staircases and passages, and not to permit children under 10 to operate any lifts. I mention these as a recognition of the existence and relevance of these facilities. At the end there is a form for signature by the tenant stating that he accepts the tenacy. On the landlords' side there is nothing, no signature, no demise, no covenant; the contract takes effect as soon as the tenants sign the form and are let into possession.

We have then a contract which is partly, but not wholly, stated in writing. In order to complete it, in particular to give it a bilateral character, it is necessary to take account of the actions of the parties and the circumstances. As actions of the parties, we must note the granting of possession by the corporation and reservation by it of the "common parts"—stairs, lifts, chutes, etc. As circumstances we must include the nature of the premises, *viz.* a maisonette for family use on the ninth floor of a high block, one which is occupied by a large number of other tenants, all using the common parts and dependent on them, none of them having any expressed obligation to maintain on repair them.

To say that the construction of a complete contract out of these elements involves a process of "implication" may be correct: it would be so if implication means the supplying of what is not expressed. But there are varieties of implications which the courts think fit to make and they do not necessarily involve the same process. Where there is, on the face of it, a complete, bilateral contract, the courts are sometimes willing to add terms to it, as implied terms; this is very common in mercantile contracts where there is an established usage; in that case the courts are spelling out what both parties know and would, if asked, unhesitatingly agree to be part of the bargain. In other cases, where there is an apparently complete bargain, the courts are willing to add a term on the ground that without it the contract will not work—this is the case, if not of *The Moorcock* (above, p. 390) itself on its facts, at least of the doctrine of *The Moorcock* as usually applied. This is, as was pointed out by the majority in the Court of Appeal, a strict test—though the degree of strictness seems to vary with the current legal trend, and I think that they were right not to accept it as applicable here. There is a third variety of implication, that which I think Lord Denning M.R. favours, or at least did favour in this case, and that is the implication of reasonable terms. But though I agree with many of his instances, which in fact fall under one or other of the preceding heads, I cannot go so far as to endorse his principle; indeed, it seems to me, with respect, to extend a long, and undesirable, way beyond sound authority.

The present case, in my opinion, represents a fourth category or, I would rather say, a fourth shade on a continuous spectrum. The court here is simply concerned to establish what the contract is, the parties not having themselves fully stated the terms. In this sense the court is searching for what must be implied.

What then should this contract be held to be? There must first be implied a letting, that is, a grant of the right of exclusive possession to the tenants. With this there must, I would suppose, be implied a covenant for quiet enjoyment, as a necessary incident of the letting. The difficulty begins when we consider the common parts. We start with the fact that the demise is useless unless access is obtained by the staircase; we can add that, having regard to the height of the block, and the family nature of the dwellings, the demise would be useless without a lift service; we can continue that there being rubbish chutes built in to the structures and no other means of disposing of light rubbish there must be a right to use the chutes. The question to be answered—and it is the only question in this case—is what is to be the legal relationship between landlord and tenant as regards these matters.

There can be no doubt that there must be implied (i) an easement for the tenants and their licensees to use the stairs, (ii) a right in the nature of an easement to use the lifts and (iii) an easement to use the rubbish chutes.

But are these easements to be accompanied by any obligation on the landlord, and what obligation? There seem to be two alternatives. The first, for which the corporation contends, is for an easement coupled with no legal obligation, except such as may arise under the Occupiers' Liability Act, 1957, as regards the safety of those using the facilities, and possibly such other liability as might exist under the ordinary law of tort. The alterative is for easements coupled with some obligation on the part of the landlords as regards the maintenance of the subject of them, so that they are available for use.

My Lords, in order to be able to choose between these, it is necessary to define what test is to be applied, and I do not find this difficult. In my opinion such obligation should be read into the contract as the nature of the contract itself implicitly requires, no more, no less; a test in other words of necessity. The relationship accepted by the corporation is that of landlord and tenant; the tenant accepts obligations accordingly, in relation, *inter alia*, to the stairs, the lifts and the chutes. All these are not just facilities, or conveniences provided at discretion; they are essentials of the tenancy without which life in the dwellings, as a tenant, is not possible. To leave the landlord free of contractual obligation as regards these matters, and subject only to administrative or political pressure, is, in my opinion, totally inconsistent with the nature of this relationship. The subject-matter of the lease (high-rise blocks) and the relationship created by the tenancy demands, of its nature, some contractual obligation on the landlord.

I do not think that this approach involves any innovation as regards the law of contract. The necessity to have regard to the inherent nature of a contract and of the relationship thereby established was stated in this House in *Lister v. Romford Ice & Cold Storage Co. Ltd* ([1957] A.C. 555). That was a case between master and servant and of a search for an "implied term." Viscount Simonds made a clear distinction between a search for an implied term such as might be necessary to give "business efficacy" to the particular contract and a search, based on wider considerations, for such a term as the nature of the contract might call for, or as a legal incident of this kind of contract. If the search were for the former, he said ([1957] A.C. at 576): "I should lose myself in the attempt to formulate it with the necessary precision." We see an echo of this in the present case, when the majority in the Court of Appeal, considering a "business efficacy term," that is, a "*Moorcock*" ((1889) 14 P.D. 64) term, found themselves faced with five alternative terms and therefore rejected all of them. But that is not, in my opinion, the end, or indeed the object, of the search.

We have some guidance in authority for the kind of term which this typical relationship (of landlord and tenant in multi-occupational dwellings) requires in *Miller v. Hancock*. There Bowen L.J. said ([1893] 2 Q.B. 177 at 180, 181):

> "The tenants could only use their flats by using the staircase. The defendant, therefore, when he let the flats, impliedly granted to the tenants an easement over the staircase, which he retained in his own occupation, for the purpose of the enjoyment of the flats so let. Under those circumstances, what is the law as to the repairs of the staircase? It was contended by the defendant's counsel that, according to the common law, the person in enjoyment of an easement is bound to do the necessary repairs himself. That may be true with regard to easements in general, but it is subject to the qualification that the grantor of the easement may undertake to do the repairs either in

express terms or by necessary implication. This is not the mere case of a grant of an easement without special circumstances. It appears to me obvious, when one considers what a flat of this kind is, and the only way in which it can be enjoyed, that the parties to the demise of it must have intended by necessary implication, as a basis without which the whole transaction would be futile, that the landlord should maintain the staircase, which is essential to the enjoyment of the premises demised, and should keep it reasonably safe for the use of the tenants, and also of those persons who would necessarily go up and down the stairs in the ordinary course of business with the tenants; because, of course, a landlord must know when he lets a flat that tradesmen and other persons having business with the tenant must have access to it. It seems to me that it would render the whole transaction inefficacious and absurd if an implied undertaking were not assumed on the part of the landlord to maintain the staircase so far as might be necessary for the reasonable enjoyment of the demised premises."

Certainly that case, as a decision concerning a claim by a visitor, has been overruled (*Fairman v. Perpetual Investment Building Society* ([1923] A.C. 74)). But I cite the passage for its common sense as between landlord and tenant, and you cannot overrule common sense. . . .

I accept, of course, the argument that a mere grant of an easement does not carry with it any obligation on the part of the servient owner to maintain the subject-matter. The dominant owner must spend the necessary money, for example, in repairing a drive leading to his house. And the same principle may apply when a landlord lets an upper floor with access by a staircase; responsibility for maintenance may well rest on the tenant. But there is a difference between that case and the case where there is an essential means of access, retained in the landlord's occupation, to units in a building of multi-occupation; for unless the obligation to maintain is, in a defined manner, placed on the tenants, individually or collectively, the nature of the contract, and the circumstances, require that it be placed on the landlord.

It remains to define the standard. My Lords, if, as I think, the test of the existence of the term is necessity the standard must surely not exceed what is necessary having regard to the circumstances. To imply an absolute obligation to repair would go beyond what is a necessary legal incident and would indeed be unreasonable. An obligation to take reasonable care to keep in reasonable repair and usability is what fits the requirements of the case. Such a definition involves—and I think rightly—recognition that the tenants themselves have their responsibilities. What it is reasonable to expect of a landlord has a clear relation to what a reasonable set of tenants should do for themselves. . . .

I would hold therefore that the corporation's obligation is as I have described. And in agreement, I believe, with your Lordships, I would hold that it has not been shown in this case that there was any breach of that obligation. On the main point therefore I would hold that the appeal fails.

My Lords, it will be seen that I have reached exactly the same conclusion as that of Lord Denning M.R., with most of whose thinking I respectfully agree. I must only differ from the passage in which, more adventurously, he suggested that the courts had power to introduce into contracts any terms they thought reasonable or to anticipate legislative recommendations of the Law Commission. A just result can be reached, if I am right, by a less dangerous route.

LORD SALMON, having cited the passage of the judgment of Bowen L.J. in *Miller v. Hancock* quoted by Lord Wilberforce, continued: Could it in reality have been contemplated by the corporation or its tenants that the corporation undertook no responsibility to take, at any rate, reasonable care to keep the lifts in order and the staircases lit? No doubt the tenants also owed a duty to use the lifts and staircases reasonably; indeed, so much was clearly implied in the printed terms of the tenancy. Can a pregnant woman accompanied by a young child be expected to walk up 15, or for that matter nine, storeys in the pitch dark to reach her home? Unless the law, in circumstances such as these, imposes an obligation on the corporation at least to use reasonable care to keep the lifts working properly and the staircase lit, the whole transaction becomes inefficacious, futile and absurd. I cannot go so far as Lord Denning M.R. and hold that the courts have any power to imply a term into a contract merely because it seems reasonable to do so. Indeed, I think that such a proposition is contrary to all authority. To say, as Lord Reid ([1969] 1 A.C. 454 at 465) said in *Young and Marten, Ltd v. McManus Childs, Ltd* that "no warranty ought to be implied in a contract unless it is in all the circumstances reasonable" is, in my view, quite different from saying that any warranty or term which is, in all the circumstances, reasonable ought to be implied in a contract. I am confident that Lord Reid meant no more than that unless a warranty or term is in all the circumstances reasonable there can be no question of implying it into a contract, but before it is implied much else besides is necessary, for example, that without it the contract would be inefficacious, futile and absurd. . . .

I find it difficult to think of any term which it could be more necessary to imply than one without which the whole transaction would become futile, inefficacious and absurd as it would do if in a 15-storey block of flats or maisonettes, such as the present, the landlords were under no legal duty to take reasonable care to keep the lifts in working order and the staircases lit.

It may be that further codification of the law of landlord and tenant is desirable. The recommendations of the Law Commission referred to in the Court of Appeal may be translated into Acts sooner or later—perhaps much later. I respectfully agree with Lord Denning M.R. that, in the meantime, the law should not be condemned to sterility and that the judges should take care not to abdicate their traditional role of developing the law to meet even the advent of tower blocks. . . . Since, however, only an absolute obligation was pleaded against the corporation to which it had a complete answer, I do not think it would be right for the reasons I have already given to find against it on the ground that it failed to take reasonable care. I would accordingly dismiss the appeal insofar as it relates to the lifts and staircase.

Questions
1. Why was the *Moorcock* doctrine considered inapplicable?
2. If the contract without the implied term would have been "futile, inefficacious and absurd," how could it be that the Liverpool Council (as a reasonable council) would not have

agreed to it if it had been proposed by the officious bystander? Is it to be assumed that they intended a futile, inefficacious and absurd contract?

3. Did not Bowen L.J. in the passage from *Miller v. Hancock* (approved by a majority of the House) apply the "business efficacy" principle?

4. If the test was necessity, but not necessity to give business efficacy, for what purpose was the term required to be "necessary"?

5. Why should the House be persuaded of the necessity for a general rule implying a term into a class of contracts when it was not persuaded of the necessity for implying the term into that particular contract? What are the "wider considerations" applicable in stating a general rule? Did the House lay down a rule which they thought reasonable rather than necessary?

6. Does not the *Moorcock* itself establish a rule for a class of contracts—wharfingers' contracts?

Exclusion of terms prima facie to be implied In *Liverpool City Council v. Irwin* [1977] A.C. at 254 Lord Cross said:

> "When it implies a term in a contract the court is sometimes laying down a general rule that in all contracts of a certain type—sale of goods, master and servant, landlord and tenant, and so on—some provision is to be implied unless the parties have expressly excluded it."

This passage has been quoted in recent cases to show that only express exclusion will keep the term out: *The Maira* [1989] 1 All E.R. 213, 219, C.A.; *Elawadi v. Bank of Credit and Commerce SA* [1989] 1 All E.R. 242, 251 (Hutchison J.). *Cf.* the discussion by Parke B. of *Senior v. Armitage*, above, p. 388. Did Lord Cross, like Mr Holt, put the case too strongly by allowing only for *express* exclusion? What if the clear *implication* of the contract is that the alleged term is not to apply?

SALE OF GOODS ACT 1979

(As Amended by the Sale and Supply of Goods Act 1994)

Conditions and Warranties

Stipulations about time

10.—(1) Unless a different intention appears from the terms of the contract, stipulations as to time of payment are not of the essence of a contract of sale.

(2) Whether any other stipulation as to time is or is not of the essence of the contract depends on the terms of the contract.

(3) In a contract of sale "month" prima facie means calendar month.

PART II

When condition to be treated as warranty

11.—(1) This section does not apply to Scotland.

(2) Where a contract of sale is subject to a condition to be fulfilled by the seller, the buyer may waive the condition, or may elect to treat the breach of the condition as a breach of warranty and not as a ground for treating the contract as repudiated.

(3) Whether a stipulation in a contract of sale is a condition, the breach of which may give rise to a right to treat the contract as repudiated, or a warranty, the breach of which may give rise to a claim for damages but not to a right to reject the goods and treat the contract as repudiated, depends

in each case on the construction of the contract; and a stipulation may be a condition, though called a warranty in the contract.

(4) Where a contract of sale is not severable and the buyer has accepted the goods or part of them, the breach of a condition to be fulfilled by the seller can only be treated as a breach of warranty, and not as a ground for rejecting the goods and treating the contract as repudiated, unless there is an express or implied term of the contract to that effect.

[(5) Repealed]

(6) Nothing in this section affects a condition or warranty whose fulfilment is excused by law by reason of impossibility or otherwise.

(7) Paragraph 2 of Schedule 1 below applies in relation to a contract made before April 22, 1967 or (in the application of this Act to Northern Ireland) July 28, 1967.

Implied terms about title, etc.

12.—(1) In a contract of sale, other than one to which subsection (3) below applies, there is an implied term on the part of the seller that in the case of a sale he has a right to sell the goods, and in the case of an agreement to sell he will have such a right at the time when the property is to pass.

(2) In a contract of sale, other than one to which subsection (3) below applies, there is also an implied term that—

(a) the goods are free, and will remain free until the time when the property is to pass, from any charge or encumbrance not disclosed or known to the buyer before the contract is made, and

(b) the buyer will enjoy quiet possession of the goods except so far as it may be disturbed by the owner or other person entitled to the benefit of any charge or encumbrance so disclosed or known.

(3) This subsection applies to a contract of sale in the case of which there appears from the contract or is to be inferred from its circumstances an intention that the seller should transfer only such title as he or a third person may have.

(4) In a contract to which subsection (3) above applies there is an implied term that all charges or encumbrances known to the seller and not known to the buyer have been disclosed to the buyer before the contract is made.

(5) In a contract to which subsection (3) above applies there is also an implied term that none of the following will disturb the buyer's quiet possession of the goods, namely—

(a) the seller;

(b) in a case where the parties to the contract intend that the seller should transfer only such title as a third person may have, that person;

(c) anyone claiming through or under the seller or that third person otherwise than under a charge or encumbrance disclosed or known to the buyer before the contract is made.

(5A) As regards England and Wales and Northern Ireland, the term implied by subsection (1) above is a condition and the terms implied by subsections (2), (4) and (5) above are warranties.

(6) Paragraph 3 of Schedule 1 below applies in relation to a contract made before May 18, 1973.

Sale by description

13.—(1) Where there is a contract for the sale of goods by description, there is an implied term that the goods will correspond with the description.

(1A) As regards England and Wales and Northern Ireland, the term implied by subsection (1) above is a condition.

(2) If the sale is by sample as well as by description it is not sufficient that the bulk of the goods corresponds with the sample if the goods do not also correspond with the description.

(3) A sale of goods is not prevented from being a sale by description by reason only that, being exposed for sale or hire, they are selected by the buyer.

(4) Paragraph 4 of Schedule 1 below applies in relation to a contract made before May 18, 1973.

Implied terms about quality or fitness

14.—(1) Except as provided by this section and section 15 below and subject to any other enactment, there is no implied term about the quality or fitness for any particular purpose of goods supplied under a contract of sale.

(2) Where the seller sells goods in the course of a business, there is an implied term that the goods supplied under the contract are of satisfactory quality.

(2A) For the purposes of this Act, goods are of satisfactory quality if they meet the standard that a reasonable person would regard as satisfactory, taking account of any description of the goods, the price (if relevant) and all the other relevant circumstances.

(2B) For the purposes of this Act, the quality of goods includes their state and condition and the following (among others) are in appropriate cases aspects of the quality of goods—

(a) fitness for all the purposes for which goods of the kind in question are commonly supplied,
(b) appearance and finish,
(c) freedom from minor defects,
(d) safety, and
(e) durability.

(2C) The term implied by subsection (2) above does not extend to any matter making the quality of goods unsatisfactory—

(a) which is specifically drawn to the buyer's attention before the contract is made,
(b) where the buyer examines the goods before the contract is made, which that examination ought to reveal, or
(c) in the case of a contract for sale by sample, which would have been apparent on a reasonable examination of the sample.

(3) Where the seller sells goods in the course of a business and the buyer, expressly or by implication, makes known—

(a) to the seller, or
(b) where the purchase price or part of it is payable by instalments and the goods were previously sold by a credit-broker to the seller, to that credit-broker,

any particular purpose for which the goods are being bought, there is an implied term that the goods supplied under the contract are reasonably fit for that purpose, whether or not that is a purpose for which such goods are commonly supplied, except where the circumstances show that the buyer does not rely, or that it is unreasonable for him to rely, on the skill or judgment of the seller or credit-broker.

(4) An implied term about quality or fitness for a particular purpose may be annexed to a contract of sale by usage.

(5) The preceding provisions of this section apply to a sale by a person who in the course of a business is acting as agent for another as they apply to a sale by a principal in the course of a business, except where that other is not selling in the course of a business and either the buyer knows that fact or reasonable steps are taken to bring it to the notice of the buyer before the contract is made.

(6) As regards England and Wales and Northern Ireland, the terms implied by subsections (2) and (3) above are conditions.

(7) Paragraph 5 of Schedule 1 below applies in relation to a contract made on or after May 18, 1973 and before the appointed day, and paragraph 6 in relation to one made before May 18, 1973.

(8) In subsection (7) above and paragraph 5 of Schedule 1 below references to the appointed day are to the day appointed for the purposes of those provisions by an order of the Secretary of State made by statutory instrument.

[Section 15 (Sale by sample) is omitted)

Modification of remedies for breach of condition in non-consumer cases.
   15A.—(1) Where in the case of a contract of sale—

(a) the buyer would, apart from this subsection, have the right to reject goods by reason of a breach on the part of the seller of a term implied by section 13, 14 or 15 above, but
(b) the breach is so slight that it would be unreasonable for him to reject them,

then, if the buyer does not deal as consumer, the breach is not to be treated as a breach of condition but may be treated as a breach of warranty.

(2) This section applies unless a contrary intention appears in, or is to be implied from, the contract.

(3) It is for the seller to show that a breach fell within subsection (1)(b) above.

(4) This section does not apply to Scotland.

   55.—(1) Where a right, duty or liability would arise under a contract of sale of goods by implication of law, it may (subject to the Unfair Contract Terms Act 1977) be negatived or varied by express agreement, or by the course of dealing between the parties, or by such usage as binds both parties to the contract.

(2) An express term does not negative a term implied by this Act unless inconsistent with it.

(3) Paragraph 11 of Schedule 1 below applies in relation to a contract made on or after May 18, 1973 and before February 1, 1978, and paragraph 12 in relation to one made before May 18, 1973.

Note
Provisions corresponding to sections 12, 13, 14, 15 (Sale by sample) and 55 of the Sale of Goods Act are to be found, for hire-purchase contracts, in the Supply of Goods (Implied Terms) Act 1973, ss.8–12; for other contracts for the transfer of property in goods (such as contracts for work and materials or barter), in the Supply of Goods and Services Act 1982, ss.2–5 and 16; and, for contracts for the hire of goods, in ss.7–10 and 16 of the same Act. Similar provisions for goods exchanged for trading stamps are in the Trading Stamps Act 1964, as amended by the Supply of Goods (Implied Terms) Act 1973.

Implied Terms on the Sale or Lease of Land and Houses

At common law, there is no implied term in a contract for the sale or lease of land that the land is fit for any particular purpose: for example, for building upon or for cultivation. Where there is a contract for the sale (or letting) of a piece of land with a house on it there is no implied term that the house is fit for human habitation. By the Housing Act 1957, s.6, in the case of leases of small houses of a specified value, a condition that the house is and will be kept fit for human habitation is implied, notwithstanding any stipulation to the contrary; and certain repairing covenants are implied by the Landlord and Tenant Act 1985, ss.8–10, in leases of houses for less than three years. Certain "covenants for title" are implied in an instrument effecting a disposition (including a term of years) of property (including a thing in action and any interest in real or personal property), whether or not the disposition is for valuable consideration: Law of Property (Miscellaneous Provision) Act 1994.

Subject to such statutory exceptions, however, the maxim *caveat emptor* is applied rigorously and it is for the buyer or his surveyor to inspect the house and make up his own mind as to its fitness. In the case of a lease of *furnished* premises, however, there is an implied condition that the premises are fit for human habitation at the beginning of the tenancy; so if the house is infested with bugs (*Smith v. Marrable* (1843) 11 M. & W. 5) or if the drainage is out of order (*Wilson v. Finch-Hatton* (1877) 2 Ex.D. 336) or if it was recently occupied by a person suffering from pulmonary tuberculosis (*Collins v. Hopkins* [1923] 2 K.B. 617), the tenant may rescind the contract. But there is no implied undertaking that the premises will continue fit during the term; so that where a person living in the same house as the demised premises caught scarlet fever after the commencement of the term, this did not constitute a breach of contract by the landlord (*Sarson v. Roberts* [1895] 2 Q.B. 395). The reason for the distinction between furnished and unfurnished premises is obscure. Even where, as in *Wilson v. Finch-Hatton*, the defect is *only* in the building and not in the furniture, the tenant's right depends on the fact that the building was furnished.

Where the defect in unfurnished premises is one easily discoverable on inspection it is, perhaps, reasonable that there should be no warranty; but where it is not discoverable the reasonableness of the rule is more doubtful. Professor Glanville Williams suggests (5 M.L.R. 194, 199) that the law *ought to be* that the condition as to reasonable fitness is implied in leases of both furnished and unfurnished premises, "unless in either case the lessor has reason to believe that the lessee is taking it with his eyes open." At present, there is no implied contractual duty; but, if the vendor is the builder, he may be liable in tort to the purchaser or a visitor to the premises who is injured as a result of negligent construction.

Where the contract is to sell, not a completed house, but a piece of land on which the seller agrees to erect a house, or complete a partially built house, then a term is implied at common law that the house, when completed, will be reasonably fit for human habitation: *Miller v. Cannon Hill Estates Ltd* [1931] 2 K.B. 113; *Jennings v. Taverner* [1955] 1 W.L.R. 932. See also the Defective Premises Act 1972, *infra*.

DEFECTIVE PREMISES ACT 1972

Duty to build dwellings properly

1.—(1) A person taking on work for or in connection with the provision of a dwelling (whether the dwelling is provided by the erection or by the conversion or enlargement of a building) owes a duty—

(a) if the dwelling is provided to the order of any person, to that person; and

(b) without prejudice to paragraph (a) above, to every person who acquires an interest (whether legal or equitable) in the dwelling;

to see that the work which he takes on is done in a workman-like or, as the case may be, professional manner, with proper materials and so that as regards that work the dwelling will be fit for habitation when completed.

(2) A person who takes on any such work for another on terms that he is to do it in accordance with instructions given by or on behalf of that other shall, to the extent to which he does it properly in accordance with those instructions, be treated for the purposes of this section as discharging the duty imposed on him by subsection (1) above except where he owes a duty to that other to warn him of any defects in the instructions and fails to discharge that duty.

(3) A person shall not be treated for the purposes of subsection (2) above as having given instructions for the doing of work merely because he has agreed to the work being done in a specified manner, with specified materials or to a specified design. . . .

6.—(3) Any term of an agreement which purports to exclude or restrict, or has the effect of excluding or restricting, the operation of any of the provisions of this Act, or any liability arising by virtue of any such provision, shall be void.

LYNCH v. THORNE

Court of Appeal [1956] 1 W.L.R. 303; 100 S.J. 225; [1956] 1 All E.R. 744

The plaintiff agreed to purchase from the defendant, a builder, a plot of land with a partially erected house on it. The defendant agreed to complete the house in accordance with the plan and specification produced by the defendant and attached to the agreement. The specification provided that the walls were to be nine-inch brick walls. The house was built precisely in accordance with specification, with sound material and good workmanship, but turned out to be unfit for human habitation because rain penetrated the walls. Of three architects who gave evidence one would have expected a nine-inch wall to allow driving rain to penetrate and the other two were not at all surprised that it did. The defendant appealed from the judgment of a county court judge, awarding damages for breach of an implied warranty that the house when completed would be reasonably fit for human habitation.

EVERSHED M.R.: Where there is a written contract expressly setting forth the bargain between the parties it is, as a general rule, also well established that you only imply terms under the necessity of some compulsion. It was thus that Lord Russel of Killowen expressed himself in *Luxor (Eastbourne) Ltd v. Cooper* (above, p. 42), and similarly Scrutton L.J. in the case to which Mr Garland referred us of *Reigate v. Union Manufacturing Co. (Ramsbottom) Ltd* (above, p. 392). I am, however, prepared to assume for the purposes of this judgment that, whether or not it can be said that any necessity so compels in the case where a vendor contracts to sell the land and also to complete the building, in such a case prima facie there is an implied covenant on the vendor builder's part that he will complete the house so as to make it habitable. Still, such a term prima facie to be implied must, according to well-established principle, always yield to the express letter of the bargain. . . .

Here there was an express contract as to the way in which the house was to be completed. The express provisions were exactly complied with, and any variation from them which would have rendered this wall water proof would (as Parker L.J. observed during the course of the argument) have been a deviation from the express language of the contract.

Mr Garland has sought to avoid that result in one of two ways. He has said, first, as I have followed him: even though there is here an express contract precisely prescribing the way in which this work is to be done, still there is an overriding promise or warranty that the edifice, when built in strict accordance with those terms, will be a habitable house. That seems to me to involve an extension of the principle of implied terms for which I can find no authority, and which indeed seems to me to be in direct conflict with the authorities to which I have already referred. Then, secondly, he says—and Mr Garland uses this rather to emphasise and support the main contention already stated: after all, the plaintiff, the unfortunate Mr Lynch, no expert himself in the mysteries of architecture and house building, relied, and the judge found that he relied, upon the skill and judgment of the defendant, the builder. I am unable to derive from that fact the conclusion which commended itself to the judge. Of course, if a skilled person promises to do a job, that is, to produce a particular thing, whether a house or a motor-car or a piece of machinery, and he makes no provision as a matter of bargain as to the precise structure or articles he will create, then it may well be that the buyer of the structure or article relies upon the judgment and skill of the other party to produce that which he says he will produce. But that, after all, is only another way of formulating the existence in such circumstances of an implied warranty. On the other hand, if two parties elect to make a bargain which specifies in precise detail what one of them will do, then, in the absence of some other express provision, it would appear to me to follow that the bargain is that which they have made; and so long as the party doing the work does that which he has contracted to do, that is the extent of his obligation. For the plaintiff obviously one cannot help feeling a great deal of sympathy; but a grown adult man is presumably capable of taking competent skilled advice if he wants to; and if he elects not to do so but to make a bargain in precise terms with someone else, then, though no doubt he does rely upon the skill of the other party in a sense, he only does so in the sense that he assumes that the other party, as was the fact in this case, will do the job he has promised to do competently and, at best, that he believes that the house he is going to build will be a habitable house. But that is far short of importing into the transaction any such overriding condition or warranty as that for which Mr Garland has contended. It would appear almost to involve the result that because the plaintiff elected not to take advice himself, therefore there was some duty of care thrust upon the defendant which should more properly have been borne by somebody engaged by the plaintiff. These considerations seem to me to find no place in the authorities, as I have understood them, and since, as I think, there was here what Romer L.J. has called an express contract as to the way in which the house was to be completed, I can find no room for an implied warranty, the only effect of the operation of which would, so far as I can see, be to create an inconsistency with the express language of the bargain made.

BIRKETT AND PARKER L.JJ. delivered concurring judgments.

Appeal allowed.

Questions
1. In *Harbutt's Plasticine v. Wayne Tank* (below, p. 621) the defendants supplied machinery using "Drapipe" in accordance with the specification in the contract. Durapipe was unsuitable for the purpose and the court said that stainless steel pipes should have been specified. It would have been a breach of the express contract to supply stainless steel pipes (*per* Widgery L.J. [1970] 1 Q.B. at p. 471, and see Cross L.J. at p. 474). The court held that the defendants were liable for the faulty specification, thus holding that the defendants promised both (i) to do the work according to a particular specification, and (ii) (impliedly) that the work so done would be reasonably fit for the purpose for which it was done. It was impossible to fulfil both promises; work done in accordance with the specification was inevitably unfit for the purpose. Did not the court in *Harbutt* do what it held to be impossible in *Lynch v. Thorne*? In *Basildon D.C. v. J.E. Lesser Ltd* [1985] 1 All E.R. 20, 27, Judge John Newey distinguished *Lynch v. Thorne* "in which the court concentrated its attention on the agreed defective plan and did not consider whether if the builder was its author he was in breach of an implied term either on account of its faults or in failing to warn against the use of it." See also, *Cullinane v. British Rema* [1954] Q.B. 292 and *Baldry v. Marshall* [1925] 1 K.B. 90, C.A.
2. In the latter case the plaintiff asked the defendants, specialists in the sale of Bugatti cars, about the Bugatti eight-cylinder, saying that he wanted a car suitable for touring purposes. The defendants said the Bugatti would be suitable. The plaintiff entered into a contract to buy a Bugatti "fully equipped and finished to standard specification as per the car inspected." A car similar to that inspected and apparently complying with specification was delivered, but it was not suitable for touring purposes. The plaintiff succeeded in an action for breach of section 14(1) of the Sale of Goods Act 1893 (s.14(3) of the 1979 Act, above, pp. 401–402). Is this case reconcilable with the reasoning in *Lynch v. Thorne*?
3. How is the position in *Lynch v. Thorne* affected by the Defective Premises Act 1972, above, p. 404.

WETTERN ELECTRIC LTD v. WELSH DEVELOPMENT AGENCY

Queen's Bench Division [1983] Q.B. 796; [1983] 2 W.L.R. 897;
[1983] 2 All E.R. 629

The defendants gave the plaintiffs a licence to occupy a factory unit for 12 months. Serious structural defects made the premises unsafe and the plaintiffs had to leave. They claimed damages for loss of production, etc., relying on an implied term that the premises would be reasonably suitable for their purposes.

JUDGE NEWEY Q.C.: My view is that it is possible for terms as to fitness for purpose to be implied in licences, but that, except perhaps in relation to safety, there are none which the courts imply prima facie in the way that such terms are implied in sale of goods, hire and the like. If any term as to suitability was to be implied in the contractual licence in this case it must, I think, be on the application of the test propounded in *The Moorcock*, as clarified by *Reigate v. Union Manufacturing Co. (Ramsbotton) Ltd* and by *Liverpool City Council v. Irwin*, (above, pp. 390, 392 and 394) or because it is necessary to complete an incomplete contract as in *Irwin*, or both. . . .

Asking, as *The Moorcock* test requires, whether it was necessary in order to give efficacy to the licence agreement that the defendant should have warranted as set out in (a) of the issue that unit 7 was of sound construction or reasonably fit for the purposes required by the plaintiffs, namely the manufacture of plastics and composite materials, I think that the answer must be Yes. The sole purpose of the licence was to enable the plaintiffs to have accommodation in which to carry on and expand their business while their existing factory was being enlarged. If anyone had said to the plaintiff and the defendants' directors and executives at the time when the licence was being granted, "Will the premises be sound and suitable for the plaintiffs' purposes?" they would assuredly have replied, "Of course; there would be no point in the licence if that were not so." The term was required to make the contract workable.

The defendants' letter of June 21, 1979 which the plaintiffs were required to approve was not unlike the conditions of tenancy which the tenants in *Liverpool City Council v. Irwin* were required to sign. In each case the terms provided were one-sided. If I had not thought that a warranty of soundness and suitability for the plaintiffs' purposes was to be implied on the application of *The Moorcock* test, I would have thought that an identical term would have had to be implied in order to complete the contract as the parties must clearly have intended.

Questions

1. Why should a term be implied in a licence when it would not be implied in a lease? Is it not odd that "a mere licensee" should be better off than a lessee?

2. What is the difference between implying a term (i) to give business efficacy to the contract and (ii) "to complete the contract?" Are not both operations "to complete the contract?"

WILLIAM CORY & SON LTD v. LONDON CORPORATION

Court of Appeal [1951] 2 K.B. 476; [1951] 2 T.L.R. 174; 115 J.P. 371; 95 S.J. 465; [1951] 2 All E.R. 85; [1951] 1 Lloyd's Rep. 475

London Corporation, acting as sanitary authority under the Public Health (London) Act 1936, made a contract in 1936 with the claimants, barge and lighter owners, for the removal of refuse from the city to Essex. In April 1948 the corporation, acting as port public health authority, sealed by-laws to come into effect on November 1, 1950, which made regulations as to coamings and coverings far more onerous than those contained in the contract of 1936. The claimants alleged that the sealing of this by-law amounted to a repudiation of the contract by anticipatory breach and they claimed rescission. The corporation did not dispute that the passing of the by-law made the contract commercially impossible of performance as from November 1, 1950, and the contract was frustrated as from that date. The Court of Appeal, affirming Goddard L.C.J., held that there had been no repudiation of the contract by anticipatory breach.

LORD ASQUITH: The claimants argue that it is an implied term of every, or almost every, contract between A and B (and certainly of this contract) that A shall not prevent or disable B from performing the contract and vice versa, and that this was just what the corporation did by the act in question. In general, no doubt, it is true that a term is necessarily implied in any contract whose other terms do not repel the implication, that neither party shall prevent the other from performing it, and that a party so preventing the other is guilty of a breach.

But an act cannot be a breach of a term of the contract—express or implied—(let alone a repudiation) unless the term in question is valid. There can be no breach, if the term in question is illegal, contrary to public policy, or (in the case of a corporation) *ultra vires* the contracting party, or for some other reason waste paper, because in such a case there is no binding obligation, and only a binding obligation can be violated. . . .

If the suggested term were express, it would have to take some such form as this: "True we are charged by Parliament with the duty of making such by-laws with reference to refuse as may be called for from time to time by considerations of public health. But even if these considerations call, and call peremptorily, for a provision not less stringent than that made by the 1948 by-laws, even if a second plague of London is likely to occur, unless such provision is made, we undertake in such an event to neglect or violate our statutory duty so far as the requirement of such a by-law may exceed the requirements imposed by clause 1 of our contract with the claimants." Such a contractual provision would seem to be plainly invalid.

Notes

1. For anticipatory breach, see below, p. 551.

2. *Performance rendered impossible by a party's own act.* In *Thompson v. Asda-MFI Group plc* [1988] 2 All E.R. 722 the plaintiff, as an employee of Wades Ltd, a wholly owned subsidiary of Asda, was eligible to acquire, and did acquire for £1, share options under a scheme established for the benefit of the employees of Asda and its subsidiaries. The rules provided that the option should lapse if the holder should cease to hold office or employment by virtue of which he was eligible to participate in the scheme. In January 1985 Asda sold Wades and informed the plaintiff that, in accordance with the rules of the scheme, his options had lapsed. The plaintiff sued for damages for wrongful repudiation of the share option agreement, relying on the principle that a party to a contract cannot take advantage of his own acts to avoid his obligations, or to defeat the rights of the other party, under the contract. SCOTT J., having extensively reviewed the authorities held that the action failed: ". . . the law is now, in my judgment, as stated by Lord Diplock in *Cheall v. Association of Professional Executive Clerical and Computer Staff* [1983] 2 A.C. 180 at 189. In order to attract the principle that a party is not entitled to rely on his own acts as fulfilling a condition subsequent and bringing a contract to an end, the act must be a breach of duty and (*per* Lord Diplock)—

". . . the duty must be one that is owed to the other party under that contract; breach of a duty whether contractual or non-contractual owed to a stranger to the contract does not suffice."

. . . In this area of the law of contract English law proceeds, in my view, by means of implied terms. If a term can be implied that a party will not do an act that, if done, would prevent the fulfilment of a condition precedent, then the doing of that act will be a breach of contract; if a term can be implied that a party will not do an act that, if done, would cause a condition subsequent to be fulfilled, then the doing of that act will be a breach of contract. But if a suitable term cannot be implied into the contract then in my judgment, the contract will take effect according to its tenor. The condition precedent will fail and the condition subsequent will be fulfilled.

In the present case, Asda was entitled to sell its shareholding in Wades. The sale did not represent any breach of duty owed to the plaintiff. Nor, for that matter, was the sale wrongful in any other sense. A term to the effect that Asda would not sell its Wades shares cannot be implied into the rules. So the rules take effect as they stand. . . .'

Would it be reasonable to hold that a term was necessarily implied in the share option contract that Asda would not sell Wades because that sale would defeat the option agreement? *Cf. General Publicity Services Ltd v. Best's Brewery Ltd* [1951] 2 T.L.R. 875.

If the principle is (as commonly stated) that a person cannot take advantage of his own wrong (as distinct from "his own act") was there any "wrong" by Asda? *Cf. Micklefield v. SAC Technology Ltd* [1991] 1 All E.R. 275, Ch.D., where an employee was wrongfully dismissed shortly before becoming entitled to exercise a share option but the principle was nevertheless held to be excluded by the terms of the scheme.

In *Alghussein Establishment v. Eton College* [1991] 1 All E.R. 267 the House of Lords found it unnecessary to decide whether there is "an absolute rule of law and morality which prevents a party taking advantage of his own wrong whatever the terms of the contract"; and Lord Jauncey said that for his part he had no doubt that the weight of authority favoured the view that the principle is a rule of construction rather than a rule of law. An agreement with a developer ("the Tenant") provided (clause 4, proviso) that "if for any reason due to the wilful default of the Tenant the development shall remain uncompleted on the 29th day of September 1983 the lease shall forthwith be granted . . ." The Tenant claimed that, if they were in "wilful default," the landlord was bound to grant them a lease. The court suspected that the word "not" had been missed out of the relevant clause but there was no claim for rectification and the word could not be inserted. Reading the contract as a whole and applying the rule of construction, the House held that the Tenant was not entitled to invoke the proviso to clause 4.

Cf. the case where a contract has become impossible of performance by reason of a frustrating event which is alleged to have been self-induced: *"The Super Servant Two,"* below, p. 535 Why should the nature of the fault differ according to whether the "condition subsequent" is express (as in *Thompson v. Asda*) or implied (as in frustration)?

CHAPTER 11

THE NATURE AND EFFECT OF CONTRACTUAL TERMS

Section 1. The Nature of a Condition

The word "condition" is used in many senses. One writer[1] discerns no fewer than 12. So far, the word has been used in this book mainly as meaning a promise in a contract of so important a nature that a failure to perform it entitles the other party to terminate the contract as well as to sue for damages. In this sense, the word is contrasted with "warranty" which, it will be recalled, also means a promise, but one of a subsidiary nature, the breach of which entitles the injured party to damages only and not to terminate the contract.

It is now time to notice that the word "condition" is used in the law of contract in a second, different and (it may be thought) more proper sense. It may be used to describe some fact or event, on the existence or occurrence of which some or all of the rights and duties under the contract are made to depend. It is not necessary that anyone should promise that that fact or event exists or will occur, but, if it does not exist or occur, the rights and duties dependent on it will be inoperative. When Carlill had used the smoke ball for two weeks (above, p. 31) she had a contract with the Smoke Ball Company. But the company was under no duty to do anything until a certain event occurred—that is, Carlill caught influenza. Catching influenza was, then, a condition of the company's obligation to pay £100. Notice that it was not held that the company promised that she would not catch influenza.[2] Notice also that Carlill did not promise that she would, or would not do so. This was not an "act" by her, but simply the happening of an event. As this was a unilateral contract, only one party undertook any obligation. In a bilateral contract the obligations of either or both parties may be made subject to a condition. It has been seen (above, p. 88) that the Sale of Goods Act 1979, s.9, provides that where the parties to a contract for the sale of goods agree that the price is to be fixed by a third party and the third party cannot or does not fix the price, the agreement is thereby avoided. Here the fixing of the price is a condition of the obligations of both parties. Again, there is no promise by either buyer or seller that the third party will fix the price. The proper interpretation of this situation would seem to be that there is a contract as soon as the parties have completed their agreement but no duties to perform arise unless and until the specified event, in this case the fixing of the price, occurs. The specified event may be an act by one of the parties: see *Trans Trust S.P.R.L. v. Danubian Trading Co. Ltd* (below, p. 416); and see *Bentworth Finance Ltd v. Lubert and Another* [1968] 1 Q.B. 680. That party is not necessarily obliged to do the act; but, if he does not, the contract will never become operative.

These are examples of conditions *precedent*, because the condition must be fulfilled before the obligation exists or becomes operative.

With conditions precedent are contrasted conditions *subsequent*, which are said to occur where the happening of the event operates to destroy an existing obligation. True examples of such conditions are hard to find. The example usually given is *Head v. Tattersall* (1871) L.R. 7 Ex. 7, where A sold a horse to B and warranted that it had been hunted with the Bicester hounds. There was an express condition that if

---

[1] Stoljar, "The Contractual Concept of Condition" 69 L.Q.R. 485.

[2] It was argued, [1892] 2 Q.B. 484, 486, before Hawkins J., that the defendants warranted that the plaintiff would not catch influenza, with liquidated damages in the event of breach; but that was not the decision. (*Cf. Lambert v. Lewis* [1980] 1 All E.R. 978, 1002.)

411

the horse did not answer the description it could be returned before five o'clock on the following Wednesday. It was held that B, on finding that the horse did not answer the description, could return it within the time limited, although in the meantime it had suffered an injury (in no way B's fault) which reduced its value. It is difficult to see, however, that this condition was *subsequent* to anything. At the time of the making of the contract, the condition either was or was not fulfilled. The true interpretation of the contract would seem to be that *not having been hunted with the Bicester hounds* was a condition *precedent* to B's right to reject the horse. In fact, he had such a right from the moment the contract was made though he did not know it until he discovered the horse's lack of connection with the Bicester hounds.[1] Perhaps a better example is the "promissory warranty" in a contract of marine insurance because the effect of a breach of that warranty by the insured is that, while the contract may survive, the insurer is automatically discharged from liability as from the date of the breach: *The Good Luck* [1991] 3 All E.R. 1, H.L., applying the Marine Insurance Act 1906, s.33(3). When the ship, in breach of such a warranty, entered a prohibited zone in the Persian Gulf, the insurer's obligations automatically ceased. Unlike the ordinary case of breach of condition, the termination of the obligations is not dependent on any decision by the insurer. But even in this case, the House used the language of condition precedent, citing Lord Blackburn in *Thomson v. Weems* (1884) 9 App.Cas. 671 at 684: "compliance with that warranty is a condition precedent to the attaching of the risk."

Conditions subsequent are sometimes confused with *limitations*—that is, clauses defining the extent of the promise. In the *High Trees* case (above, p. 249) the plaintiff's promise not to demand the full rent was held to be subject to an implied limitation in that it was only to be operative while the war-time conditions prevailed. In *Wyatt v. Kreglinger* (above, p. 197) the entry of the plaintiff into the wool trade was a limitation on the defendants' promise (void, as it turned out, for another reason) to pay the pension. The distinction is that a condition subsequent avoids the liability *ab initio*, so that the promise is treated as never having been made.[2] But in *High Trees* it was certainly not *intended* that the plaintiffs should be able to demand arrears of rent on the cessation of war-time conditions (notice that whether that intention should be effective is a different question and one to which Denning J. devoted most of his judgment). Nor, in *Wyatt v. Kreglinger*, was it the intention that the plaintiff's right to the pension he had already received should be avoided on his subsequent entry into the wool trade. Both these clauses, then, were limitations and not conditions subsequent. When this distinction is borne in mind conditions subsequent become even harder to find and the conclusion of one writer that "the famous condition subsequent is nothing but a ghost"[3] is hard to resist.

Conditions are sometimes also described as "concurrent." For example, section 28 of the Sale of Goods Act provides that "Payment and delivery are concurrent conditions." This would appear to mean that the seller's obligation to deliver is conditional on the price having been paid and that the buyer's obligation to pay the price is conditional on the goods having been delivered. If this were the case, clearly the statute would have created a legal stalemate in which neither party is bound to act.[4] In fact, however, the Act goes on to explain what it means: ". . . that is to say, the seller must be ready and willing to give possession of the goods to the buyer in exchange for the price, and the buyer must be ready and willing to pay the price in exchange for possession of the goods." This makes it clear that the seller's readiness and willingness to give possession is a condition *precedent* to the buyer's duty to pay the price and vice versa. The truth is that "'concurrent condition'" is an elliptical expression for a condition precedent where performances are due at the same time." (*Restatement of Contracts*, p. 363.)

---

[1] *Cf.* Stoljar's discussion of the case, 69 L.Q.R. 510.
[2] Montrose, 15 Can.Bar Rev. 319.
[3] Stoljar, *op. cit.* 508.
[4] See Salmond and Williams, *Contracts*, 54.

It is clear that in describing as "conditions" both (a) the essential as opposed to the subsidiary promises in a contract and (b) those facts or events on the occurrence of which the duty to perform contractual promises depends, we are using the same word to describe two very different things. The distinction between a condition, strictly so-called, and a promise is clearly explained by Professor Montrose:[1]

"I promise you £5 if you go to Rome: you promise to go to Rome. There are two terms of the contract, the subject-matter of which is going to Rome: there is a condition annexed by my promise and there is your promise. Each has a distinct function and so your going to Rome has a dual operation. It is a fulfilment of the condition annexed to my promise and also the performance of your promise. I must pay you the £5 not because you have performed your promise as such, but because such performance operates as a fulfilment of the condition annexed to my promise. Likewise, of course, your not going to Rome has a dual operation. There is a failure of the condition annexed to my promise and you have committed a breach of your promise. Because of the failure of the condition I do not have to pay you £5: because of the non-performance of your promise you are liable to me in damages. The event which brings about the failure of the condition operates also as a breach of your promise. Failure of the condition is followed by your liability to pay damages but is not the cause of it. The breach of your promise is followed by release from my promise but is not the cause of it."

The English usage which describes an essential promise in a contract as a condition is misleading, not because there is not a condition in the contract, but because the term is applied to the wrong thing. A offers B an old picture, of unknown authorship, for £100. After examining it and forming the opinion that it is a Constable, B says: "I will give you £100 for it provided it is a genuine Constable." A accepts. Clearly B's promise is subject to a condition and equally clearly A gives no undertaking as to the authorship of the picture. There is a condition, but no promise. Now if the facts were that A had given an *assurance* that the picture was by Constable, without which he knew B would not have contracted, the same condition would have been present, for B clearly did not intend to pay unless the painting was a Constable; but, in addition, there is now a promise by A for which he could be held liable in damages.

Professor Williston[2] described the use of the word "condition" to mean a certain kind of promise as "astonishing," expressing the opinion that "the difference between conditions and promises is so radical in its consequences that there is no excuse for a nomenclature which fails to recognise the distinction." The usage is nevertheless well established and was defended by Stephenson L.J. in *Wickman Sales v. Schuler* [1972] 1 W.L.R. 840 at pp. 859–861 and the student of English law must be on his guard to ascertain in which sense the term is being used in any case.

PYM v. CAMPBELL

Queen's Bench (1856) 6 El. & Bl. 379; 119 E.R. 903

The plaintiff alleged that the defendants agreed in writing to purchase a share in an invention of the plaintiff's. The defendants gave evidence that they had agreed on the price at which the invention should be purchased, if bought at all, and had arranged for a meeting at which the plaintiff was to explain his invention to two engineers appointed by the defendants. If they approved, the machine should be bought. At the appointed time the defendants and the two engineers, Fergusson and Abernethie, attended, but the plaintiff did not come and the engineers went away.

---

[1] Conditions, Warranties and Other Contractual Terms," 15 Can.Bar Rev. 308, 323.
[2] Selections from Williston, *Contracts*, subsection 665.

Shortly after they were gone the plaintiff arrived. Fergusson was found, and expressed a favourable opinion; but Abernethie could not then be found. It was then proposed that, as the parties were all present, and might find it troublesome to meet again, an agreement should be then drawn up and signed which, if Abernethie approved of the invention, should be the agreement, but, if Abernethie did not approve, should not be one. Abernethie did not approve of the invention when he saw it; and the defendants contended that there was no bargain.

The Lord Chief Justice told the jury that, if they were satisfied that, before the paper was signed, it was agreed amongst them all that it should not operate as an agreement until Abernethie approved of the invention, they should find for the defendants. Verdict for the defendants. The plaintiff obtained a rule nisi for a new trial on the ground of misdirection.

ERLE J.: I think that this rule ought to be discharged. The point made is that this is a written agreement, absolute on the face of it, and that evidence was admitted to show it was conditional: and if that had been so it would have been wrong. But I am of opinion that the evidence showed that in fact there was never any agreement at all. The production of a paper purporting to be an agreement by a party, with his signature attached, affords a strong presumption that it is his written agreement; and, if in fact he did sign the paper *animo contrahendi*, the terms contained in it are conclusive, and cannot be varied by parol evidence: but in the present case the defence begins one step earlier: the parties met and expressly stated to each other that, though for convenience they would then sign the memorandum of the terms, yet they were not to sign it as an agreement until Abernethie was consulted. I grant the risk that such a defence may be set up without ground; and I agree that a jury should therefore always look on such a defence with suspicion: but, if it be proved that in fact the paper was signed with the express intention that it should not be an agreement, the other party cannot fix it as an agreement upon those so signing. The distinction in point of law is that evidence to vary the terms of an agreement in writing is not admissible, but evidence to show that there is not an agreement at all is admissible.

CROMPTON J. and LORD CAMPBELL C.J. delivered concurring judgments.

Rule discharged.

Questions

1. Was it accurate to say that there was never any agreement at all? Was there (a) any disagreement? (b) any outstanding matter on which agreement was required? *Cf.* Corbin, *Contracts*, Vol. I, 66. For the parol evidence rule, see above, pp. 120–121, 329.

2. Suppose that the defendant has announced that he would not buy the invention, whatever the result of Abernethie's inspection and before he had had a reasonable opportunity to carry it out. Would the plaintiff have had any remedy? Compare the case where the parties to a sale of goods agree that the price is to be fixed by a third party. The Sale of Goods Act 1979, s.9(2), provides that if either the seller or the buyer prevents the fixing of the price, the party not in fault may maintain an action for damages against the party in fault. What is the cause of action in such a case?

3. Suppose that the defendant had said that, notwithstanding Abernethie's disapproval, he wanted the invention. Would the plaintiff have been bound to sell it? *Cf. Aquis Estates Ltd v. Minton* [1975] 3 All E.R. 1043 (C.A.); *Heron Ltd v. Moss* [1974] 1 All E.R. 421 (Brightman J.).

4. In *Wood Preservation Ltd v. Prior* [1969] 1 W.L.R. 1077; [1969] 1 All E.R. 364, C.A. B agreed to buy from S, Ltd. the whole of the shares in the WP Co. Ltd. subject to the production within one month of a letter from a German Co., giving an assurance that it would

continue certain rights in favour of WP Ltd. The question (for tax purposes) was: Did the beneficial ownership in the shares pass before the condition was satisfied or (as in fact happened) was waived? S, Ltd. said it did not pass because there was no binding contract until the condition was waived. Held: there was a binding contract; S, Ltd. could have been restrained by injunction from selling the shares to anyone else; it could not declare any bonus or dividend; and it would have been bound to transfer the shares if B had waived the condition. S, Ltd. was no longer "beneficial owner"; its ownership was a mere legal shell.

Cf. Pym v. Campbell: could not the seller in that case have been similarly restrained from selling to another, pending Abernethie's inspection? And could not the buyer have waived the condition of Abernethie's approval, since it was exclusively for the buyer's benefit?

MARTEN v. WHALE

Court of Appeal [1917] 2 K.B. 480; 86 L.J.K.B. 1305; 117 L.T. 137; 33 T.L.R. 330

The plaintiff and one Thacker entered into an agreement by which Thacker agreed to sell and the plaintiff to buy a plot of land for the sum of £385, "subject to purchaser's solicitors' approval of title and restrictions." In consideration of that transaction the plaintiff agreed to sell and Thacker to buy a motor-car for £300, "completion of such sale and purchase to be carried out simultaneously with above transaction." The plaintiff let Thacker have the car "on loan," and Thacker sold it to the defendant who bought in good faith and without notice of the plaintiff's rights. Subsequently, the plaintiff's solicitors refused to approve the restrictions in connection with the land. If Thacker was a person who had "agreed to buy" the car then he had given a good title under section 25(2) of the Sale of Goods Act 1893 [s.25(1) of the 1979 Act]. In an action to recover the car and damages for its detention Rowlatt J. gave judgment for the defendant. The plaintiff appealed.

SCRUTTON L.J.: The plaintiff contends that Thacker only agreed to buy the car if the plaintiff carried through the transaction for the purchase of the land from Thacker, which transaction the plaintiff might at his option repudiate, and that, as the carrying through of the transaction as to the land was at the plaintiff's option, it cannot be said that the plaintiff had entered into a binding agreement to sell, and that Thacker had "agreed to buy," the car. On the other hand, the defendant says that the sale of the car was to be carried out whether or not the sale of the land went through. If that is so, it is clear that Thacker had agreed to buy. The defendant further says that, if the two parts of the agreement are interdependent, the matter did not rest only on the plaintiff's option; that the plaintiff had to appoint a solicitor, and the solicitor had to give an honest opinion as to approving of the restrictions, and that therefore there was an agreement to buy the car. I am inclined to think that the two parts of the document are dependent on each other, and I will deal with the case upon this assumption. What is the nature of the transaction? I cannot read the first part of the document as giving the plaintiff a mere option. There is an implied provision that the plaintiff shall appoint a solicitor and shall consult him in good faith, and that the solicitor shall give his honest opinion. That is not an option; it is a conditional contract, and I agree with Swinfen Eady L.J. that a conditional agreement to buy is an agreement to buy within the Act.

SWINFEN EADY L.J and BRAY J. delivered judgment to the same effect.

Appeal dismissed.

Questions

1. If the plaintiff had refused to appoint a solicitor would Thacker have had any remedy? If the solicitor, appointed in good faith, had given his honest opinion disapproving of title and

restrictions would Thacker have had any remedy? (Assume that Thacker had not behaved dishonestly.) *Cf. Ee v. Kakar*, above, p. 104.

2. If there was a conditional contract in this case, was there not one also in *Pym v. Campbell*?

3. Was it a contract for sale of goods or an exchange of land for a car and £85?

Conditional Contracts

The agreements in *Pym v. Campbell* and *Marten v. Whale* may properly be described as "conditional contracts" because both parties were bound, subject to a condition, the approval of Abernethie in the one case and the solicitor in the other. It will be noted that Scrutton L.J. distinguished a conditional contract from an option. The grantor of an option for consideration or under seal has undertaken an obligation but the grantee, of course, has not. The essence of the option is that the grantee has a choice whether to become bound or not. But in *Spiro v. Glencrown Properties* (above, p. 104) Hoffmann J. held that the grant of an option to purchase land was "a contract for the sale of an interest in land"—"An option to buy land can properly be described as a contract for the sale of that land conditional upon the exercise of the option." The grantor may fairly be said to have made a conditional contract to sell—his obligation to sell is dependent on an event outside his control and it may be thought immaterial that the event is the act, not of a third party as in *Marten v. Whale*, but of the other party to the proposed contract. But can the grantee be said to have made any sort of contract to buy? Like any offeree, he is entirely free to accept or not as he thinks fit.

TRANS TRUST S.P.R.L. v. DANUBIAN TRADING CO. LTD

[1952] 2 Q.B. 297; [1952] 1 T.L.R. 1066; 96 S.J. 312; [1952] 1 All E.R. 970; [1952] 1 Lloyd's Rep. 348

The defendants contracted to buy a quantity of steel from the plaintiffs. It was provided that payment by the defendants should be by cash against shipping documents from a confirmed credit to be opened at a named bank. The defendants never opened the credit and eventually repudiated the contract. McNair J. awarded the plaintiffs their loss of profit on the transaction as damages for breach of contract. The defendants' appeal against the award of damages was dismissed.

DENNING L.J., referring to the provision for the opening of the confirmed credit, said: What is the legal position of such a stipulation? Sometimes it is a condition precedent to the formation of a contract, that is, it is a condition which must be fulfilled before any contract is concluded at all. In those cases the stipulation "subject to the opening of a credit" is rather like a stipulation "subject to contract." (See above, p. 101) If no credit is provided, there is no contract between the parties. In other cases a contract is concluded and the stipulation for a credit is a condition which is an essential term of the contract. In those cases the provision of the credit is a condition precedent, not to the formation of a contract, but to the obligation of the seller to deliver the goods. If the buyer fails to provide the credit, the seller can treat himself as discharged from any further performance of the contract and can sue the buyer for damages for not providing the credit.

The first question is: what was the nature of the stipulation in this case? When the buyers sent their order, they stated in writing on September 25, 1950, that a "credit will be opened forthwith." . . . The statement was a firm promise by the buyers by which they gave their personal assurance that a credit would be opened forthwith . . . the stipulation for a credit was not a condition precedent to the formation of any contract at all. It was a condition which was an essential term of a contract actually made. [The judgments in this case were concerned mainly with the measure of damages recoverable.]

Questions

There seem to be three possible situations:

    (a) the buyer undertakes that a credit will be opened;

    (b) the buyer undertakes that he will use reasonable diligence to procure the opening of a credit: *Cf. Re Anglo-Russian Merchant Traders Ltd.* [1917] 2 K.B. 679

    (c) the buyer says that he will open a credit if he thinks fit.

Is any of these cases the same in legal effect as a stipulation "subject to contract"? In the third case is there any contract at all (i) before the buyer opens a credit? (ii) after he does so?

Problem

A agrees to sell goods to B, "subject to the opening of a credit by B." Before B has had a reasonable opportunity to open the credit, A repudiates the contract. B has to buy the goods at a higher price elsewhere. Has he any remedy?

Section 2. Conditions, Warranties and Innominate Terms

WALLIS, SON & WELLS v. PRATT AND HAYNES

Court of Appeal [1910] 2 K.B. 1003; House of Lords [1911] A.C. 394; 80 L.J.K.B. 1058; 105 L.T. 146; 27 T.L.R. 431; 55 S.J. 496

The defendants sold to the plaintiffs by sample a quantity of seed described as "common English sainfoin." Seed equal to sample was delivered, and a portion of it was resold by the plaintiffs as common English sainfoin. When it came up, it was found to be, not common English, but giant sainfoin, a seed which is indistinguishable but of inferior quality. The plaintiffs reasonably and properly settled a claim brought against them by the sub-purchaser and sued to recover the amount so paid. The defendants relied on a term in the written contract: "Sellers give no warranty, express or implied, as to growth, description, or any other matters. . . ." Bray J. gave judgment for the plaintiffs, but was reversed by the Court of Appeal. Vaughan Williams and Farwell L.JJ. held that the plaintiffs, having accepted and resold the seed, had put it out of their power to treat the description of the article sold as common English sainfoin as a condition, and could treat it only as a warranty, but that the condition relied on by the defendants excluded all liability for breach of warranty. The decision of the Court of Appeal was reversed by the House of Lords, on the grounds given by Fletcher Moulton L.J., dissenting in the Court of Appeal.

FLETCHER MOULTON L.J.: . . . A party to a contract who has performed, or is ready and willing to perform, his obligations under that contract is entitled to the performance by the other contracting party of all the obligations which rest upon him. But from a very early period of our law it has been recognised that such obligations are not all of equal importance. There are some which go so directly to the substance of the contract or, in other words, are so essential to its very nature that their non-performance may fairly be considered by the other party as a substantial failure to perform the contract at all. On the other hand, there are other obligations which, though they must be performed, are not so vital that a failure to perform them goes to the substance of the contract. Both classes are equally obligations under the contract, and the breach of any one of them entitles the other party to damages. But in the case of the former class he has the alternative of treating the contract as being completely broken by the non-performance and (if he takes the proper steps) he can refuse to perform any of the obligations resting upon himself and sue the other party for a total failure to perform the contract. Although the decisions are fairly consistent in recognising the distinction between the two classes of obligations under a contract there has not been a similar consistency in the nomenclature applied to them. I do not, however, propose to discuss this matter, because later usage has consecrated the term "condition" to describe an obligation of the former class and "warranty" to describe an obligation of the latter class. I do not think that the choice of terms is happy, especially so far as regards the word "condition," for it is a word which is used in many other connections and has considerable variety of meaning. But its use with regard to the obligations under a contract is well known and recognised, and no confusion need arise if proper regard be had to the context.

This usage has been followed in the codification of the law of the contract of sale in the Sale of Goods Act. The word "condition" is used in the text of the Act, though no formal definition is given to it. But in the interpretation clause "warranty" is expressly defined in the followed terms: "'Warranty' as regards England and Ireland means an agreement with reference to goods which are the subject of a contract of sale, but collateral to the main purposes of such contract, the breach of which gives rise to a claim for damages, but not to a right to reject the goods and treat the contract as repudiated." It is clear from this definition that a breach of warranty entitles the other contracting party to damages only. In contrast to this the additional right in the case of a breach of a condition is fully recognised in section 11. In all this the Act adopts the well-settled law that existed at the date when it was passed. . . .

Now it is admitted that the vendors committed a breach of this contract in that they delivered seed of giant sainfoin, which is a different article of inferior value. Inasmuch as by the law the obligation to deliver the kind of goods stipulated for in a contract of sale is an obligation which has the status of a condition, this breach gave to the purchasers the choice of the two remedies, either of rejecting the goods and treating the contract as repudiated or suing for damages for delivery of the inferior article. But the purchasers resold the goods in ignorance of the breach (the two kinds of seed bearing a close resemblance to one another in appearance), and by the fact that they have resold the goods they have prevented themselves from exercising the higher right. They must, therefore, content themselves with suing for damages for breach on the vendors' part of the obligation which lay upon them under the contract. This they are doing, and we are asked to say whether their claim is a good one.

I confess that for my own part I can see no possible answer to it. . . .

Note

Fletcher Moulton L.J. went on to reject the argument that, as the vendors could not now reject the goods, the condition had *become* a warranty and was caught by the exclusion clause. He pointed out that section 11(1) of the Sale of Goods Act 1893 (s.11(4) of the 1979 Act, above, p. 400) does not say that a condition *becomes* a warranty but only that the "higher remedy" is no longer available. Once a condition, always a condition, apparently.

If a term is so important that non-performance of it may fairly be considered as a substantial failure to perform the contract at all, it is a condition; but note that this is not an exclusive definition of "condition." See the dictum of Blackburn J. quoted by Lord Reid, *infra* and *Bunge v. Tradax*, below, p. 426.

L. SCHULER A.G. v. WICKMAN MACHINE TOOL SALES LTD

House of Lords [1974] A.C. 235; [1973] 2 W.L.R. 683; [1973] 2 All E.R. 39; [1973] 2 Lloyd's Rep. 53

Schuler agreed to give the claimants Wickman sole selling rights of presses manufactured by Schuler for 4½ years. Clause 7(b) of the agreement provided that "It shall be a condition of this agreement that (i) [Wickman] shall send its representative to visit" the six largest U.K. motor manufacturers "at least once in every week" to solicit orders. No other term in the 20 clauses was described as a condition. Clause 11 provided that either party might determine the agreement if the other committed a "material breach" of its obligations and failed to remedy it within 60 days of being required to do so in writing. Wickman committed material breaches of clause 7(b) in the first eight months but these were waived by the respondents. In the next six months they committed some immaterial breaches but Schuler terminated the contract, relying on clause 11. Wickman claimed damages. Schuler's amended defence relied on Wickman's breach of the "express condition" in clause 7(b). The arbitrator construed "condition" in clause 7(b) as referable to clause 11 and awarded in favour of Wickman. Mocatta J. held the word, "condition," gave Schuler the right to repudiate the agreement if Wickman committed a single breach of the visiting obligation. Wickman's appeal to the Court of Appeal was allowed, Stephenson L.J. dissenting. Schuler appealed to the House of Lords.

LORD REID: In the ordinary use of the English language "condition" has many meanings, some of which have nothing to do with agreements. In connection with an agreement it may mean a pre-condition: something which must happen or be done before the agreement can take effect. Or it may mean some state of affairs which must continue to exist if the agreement is to remain in force. The legal meaning on which Schuler rely is, I think, one which would not occur to a layman; a condition in that sense is not something which has an automatic effect. It is a term the breach of which by one party gives to the other an option either to terminate the contract or to let the contract proceed and, if he so desires, sue for damages for the breach.

Sometimes a breach of a term gives that option to the aggrieved party because it is of a fundamental character going to the root of the contract, sometimes it gives that option because the parties have chosen to stipulate that it shall have that effect. Blackburn J. said in *Bettini v. Gye* (below, p. 422): "Parties may think some matter, apparently of very little importance, essential; and if they sufficiently express an intention to make the literal fulfilment of such a thing a condition precedent, it will be one."

In the present case it is not contended that Wickman's failures to make visits amounted in themselves to fundamental breaches. What is contended is that the terms of clause 7 "sufficiently express an intention" to make any breach, however small, of the obligation to make visits a condition so that any such breach shall entitle Schuler to rescind the whole contract if they so desire.

Schuler maintains that the use of the word "condition" is in itself enough to establish this intention. No doubt some words used by lawyers do have a rigid inflexible meaning. But we must remember that we are seeking to discover intention as disclosed by the contract as a whole. Use of the word "condition" is an indication—even a strong indication—of such an intention but it is by no means conclusive. The fact that a particular construction leads to a very unreasonable result must be a relevant consideration. The more unreasonable the result the more unlikely it is that the parties can have intended it, and if they do intend it the more necessary it is that they shall make that intention abundantly clear.

Clause 7(b) requires that over a long period each of the six firms shall be visited every week by one or other of two named representatives. It makes no provision for Wickman being entitled to substitute others even on the death or retirement of one of the named representatives. Even if one could imply some right to do this, it makes no provision for both representatives being ill during a particular week. And it makes no provision for the possibility that one or other of the firms may tell Wickman that they cannot receive Wickman's representative during a particular week. So if the parties gave any thought to the matter at all they must have realised the probability that in a few cases out of the 1,400 required visits a visit as stipulated would be impossible. But if Schuler's contention is right failure to make even one visit entitles them to terminate the contract however blameless Wickman might be. This is so unreasonable that it must make me search for some other possible meaning of the contract. If none can be found then Wickman must suffer the consequences. But only if that is the only possible interpretation.

If I have to construe clause 7 standing by itself then I do find difficulty in reaching any other interpretation. But if clause 7 must be read with clause 11 the difficulty disappears. The word "condition" would make any breach of clause 7(b), however excusable, a material breach. That would then entitle Schuler to give notice under clause 11(a)(i) requiring the breach to be remedied. There would be no point in giving such a notice if Wickman were clearly not in fault but if it were given Wickman would have no difficulty in showing that the breach had been remedied. If Wickman were at fault then on receiving such a notice they would have to amend their system so that they could show that the breach had been remedied. If they did not do that within the period of the notice then Schuler would be entitled to rescind.

In my view, that is a possible and reasonable construction of the contract and I would therefore adopt it. The contract is so obscure that I can have no confidence that this is its true meaning but for the reasons which I have given I think that it is the preferable construction. It follows that Schuler were not entitled to rescind the contract as they purported to do. So I would dismiss this appeal.

I must add some observations about a matter which was fully argued before your Lordships. The majority of the Court of Appeal ([1972] 1 W.L.R. 840) were influenced by a consideration of actings subsequent to the making of the contract. In my view, this was inconsistent with the decision of this House in *James Miller and Partners Ltd v. Whitworth Street Estates (Manchester) Ltd* (above, p. 137). . . . We were asked by Wickman to reconsider that decision on this point and I have done so. As a result I see no reason to change the view which I expressed in that case.

LORDS MORRIS, SIMON AND KILBRANDON made speeches dismissing the appeal.

LORD WILBERFORCE: Does clause 7(b) amount to a "condition" or a "term?" (to call it an important or material term adds, with all respect, nothing but some intellectual assuagement). My Lords, I am clear in my own mind that it is a condition, but your Lordships take the contrary view. On a matter of construction of a particular document, to develop the reasons for a minority opinion serves no purpose. I am all the more happy to refrain from so doing because the judgments of Mocatta J., Stephenson L.J. and indeed of Edmund Davies L.J. on construction, give me complete satisfaction and I could in any case add little of value to their reasons. I would only add that, for my part, to call the clause arbitrary, capricious or fantastic, or to introduce as a test of its validity the ubiquitous reasonable man (I do not know whether he is English or German) is to assume, contrary to the evidence, that both parties to this contract adopted a standard of easy-going tolerance rather than one of aggressive, insistent punctuality and efficiency. This is not an assumption I am prepared to make, nor do I think myself entitled to impose the former standard on the parties if their words indicate, as they plainly do, the latter. I note finally, that the result of treating the clause, so careful and specific in its requirements, as a term is, in effect, to deprive the appellants of any remedy in respect of admitted and by no means minimal breaches. The arbitrator's finding that these breaches were not "material" was not, in my opinion, justified in law in the face of the parties' own characterisation of them in their document: indeed the fact that he was able to do so, and so leave the appellants without remedy, argues strongly that the legal basis of his finding—that clause 7(b) was merely a term—is unsound.

I would allow this appeal.

Appeal dismissed.

Note

Cf. The Chikuma [1981] 1 All E.R. 652. A time charter provided, ". . . failing the punctual and regular payment of the hire . . . the Owners shall be at liberty to withdraw the vessel. . . ." An instalment of hire fell due on January 22, 1976. On that day the charterers caused the owners' bank to be credited with the amount of the hire but on terms that interest would not begin to run until January 26. If the owners had withdrawn the money, as the could have done, on January 22, they would probably have had to pay interest on it to their bank until January 26. The House of Lords, restoring a judgment of Robert Goff J. and allowing an appeal from the Court of Appeal, held that there was no payment in cash, as the contract required, on January 22 and the owners had acted within their rights in withdrawing the ship on January 24. Lord Bridge, with whom all their Lordships agreed, said: "It has often been pointed out that shipowners and charterers bargain at arm's length. Neither class has such a preponderance of bargaining power as to be in a position to oppress the other. They should be in a position to look after themselves by contracting only on terms which are acceptable to them. Where, as here, they embody in their contracts common form clauses, it is, to my mind, of overriding importance that their meaning and legal effect should be certain and well understood. The ideal at which the courts should aim, in construing such clauses, is to produce a result such that in any given situation both parties seeking legal advice as to their rights and obligations can expect the same clear and confident answer from their advisers and neither will be tempted to embark on long and expensive litigation in the belief that victory depends on winning the sympathy of the court. This ideal may never be fully attainable, but we shall certainly never even approximate to it unless we strive to follow clear and consistent principles and steadfastly refuse to be blown off course by the supposed merits of individual cases."

Innominate Terms

For many years writers on the law of contract assumed that there were only two classes of contractual term and that every term was a condition or a warranty. The

Sale of Goods Act 1893 (see ss.10–14 of the 1979 Act, above, p. 399) seems to have been drafted on this assumption. The Sale and Supply of Goods Act 1994 replaced the words "condition" and "warranty" by "term"; but then made clear that, for English, but not Scots, law, every implied term was either a condition or a warranty. Whether an injured party had a right to determine the contract depended, according to this theory, on the nature of the term which had been broken. If it was a condition he could do so. If it was a warranty, he could not. The nature of the term was settled when the contract was made. The nature of the breach was immaterial. That principle is qualified by the 1994 Act, section 15A, in non-consumer cases: in such cases, a breach of a condition by the seller which is so slight that it would be unreasonable to reject the goods is to be "treated as a breach of warranty".

This was the theory at common law; but in practice the court does seem often to have had regard to the effect of the breach in deciding whether the injured party could treat the contract as at an end. Standard examples of a warranty and a condition, used in the pre-1962 editions of Anson and Cheshire and Fifoot, were the cases of *Bettini v. Gye* (1876) 1 Q.B.D. 183 and *Poussard v. Spiers* (1876) 1 Q.B.D. 351. The plaintiff in each case was a singer who, because of illness, was unable to be present on the day on which his presence was first required. The defendant in each case terminated the contract and the plaintiff sued for damages. Bettini was required by his contract to be present six days before the first performance for rehearsals and arrived three days late. His engagement was to sing in theatres, halls and drawing-rooms from March 30 to July 13, 1875. His failure to arrive on time clearly did not prevent the contract from being substantially carried out. If the engagement had been a very short one it might have been different. The Queen's Bench Division thought the failure did not go to the root of the matter. The defendant was not entitled to dismiss the plaintiff. Poussard was taken ill five days before the first performance. Her illness appeared to be a serious one of uncertain duration and it was held that the defendant was justified in terminating her contract and engaging another artiste.

Bettini was considered by the writers to have committed a breach of warranty and Poussard a breach of condition. In neither case, however, did the court scrutinise the contract at the time it was made and identify a term as a condition or warranty. It looked at the effect of the failure to perform in the circumstances existing at the time of the failure. Thus, if a *temporary* substitute for Poussard, capable of performing the part adequately, could have been obtained on reasonable terms, the defendant would not have been justified in dismissing her. The plaintiff's failure went to the root of the matter because no such substitute was available. The term broken seems to have been the same in both cases—the promise to be available on a certain day. The difference was in the nature and effect of the breach of the term.

Another example is *Aerial Advertising Co. v. Batchelor's Peas Ltd* [1938] 2 All. E.R. 788. The plaintiffs contracted to advertise the defendants' product by flying an aircraft trailing a banner reading "Eat Batchelor's Peas." The pilot flew over Salford main square on Armistice Day during the two minute silence, causing outrage. The defendants terminated the contract. Atkinson J. held that they were entitled to do so. Further flights might have re-kindled public anger so it was unreasonable to expect them to continue. The term of the contract that was broken seems to have been that which required the pilot to consult the defendants as to where he was going each day. Clearly, on any other day, a breach of the same term would have been relatively innocuous. It was not the nature of the term that was important so much as the nature of the breach and its effect.

The "innominate term," a term which is neither a condition nor a warranty, is thus not a recent invention. The courts utilised the concept for many years before they or the writers identified it. The *Hong Kong Fir* case seems to have been the first in which it was expressly recognised.

HONG KONG FIR SHIPPING CO. LTD v. KAWASAKI KISEN KAISHA LTD

[1962] 2 Q.B. 26; [1962] 2 W.L.R. 474; [1962] 1 All E.R. 474;
[1961] 2 Lloyd's Rep. 478

By a time charter the plaintiffs agreed to let and the defendants to hire the vessel *Hong Kong Fir* for 24 months from the date of delivery "she being fitted in every way for ordinary cargo service." The vessel was delivered and sailed from Liverpool to Newport News, U.S.A., and loaded a cargo for Osaka. The engine room staff were inefficient and the engines were very old with the result that she was held up for repairs for five weeks on her way to Osaka where it was found that further repairs, requiring 15 weeks to complete, were necessary to make her seaworthy. The charterparty still had 20 months to run. The charterers repudiated the contract and the owners sued for wrongful repudiation.

Salmon J. found that the vessel was unseaworthy, having regard to her engine room staff, but that the owners' breach of contract did not entitle the charterers to rescind the contract and that the contract was not frustrated. The charterers appealed to the Court of Appeal.

Sellers and Upjohn L.JJ. delivered judgment dismissing the appeal.

DIPLOCK L.J.: Every synallagmatic[1] contract contains in it the seeds of the problem: in what event will a party be relieved of his undertaking to do that which he has agreed to do but has not yet done? The contract may itself expressly define some of these events, as in the cancellation clause in a charterparty; but, human prescience being limited, it seldom does so exhaustively and often fails to do so at all. In some classes of contracts such as sale of goods, marine insurance, contracts of affreightment evidenced by bills of lading and those between parties to bills of exchange, Parliament has defined by statute some of the events not provided for expressly in individual contracts of that class; but where an event occurs the occurrence of which neither the parties nor Parliament have expressly stated will discharge one of the parties from further performance of his undertakings, it is for the court to determine whether the event has this effect or not.

The test whether an event has this effect or not has been stated in a number of metaphors all of which I think amount to the same thing: does the occurrence of the event deprive the party who has further undertakings still to perform of substantially the whole benefit which it was the intention of the parties as expressed in the contract that he should obtain as the consideration for performing those undertakings?

This test is applicable whether or not the event occurs as a result of the default of one of the parties to the contract, but the consequences of the event are different in the two cases. Where the event occurs as a result of the default of one party, the party in default cannot rely upon it as relieving himself of the performance of any further undertakings on his part, and the innocent party, although entitled to, need not treat the event as relieving him of the further performance of his own undertakings. This is only a specific application of the fundamental legal and moral rule that a man should not be allowed to take advantage of his own wrong. Where the event occurs as a result of the default of neither party, each is relieved of the

---

[1] "Synallagmatic" means "bilateral." See above, p. 4.

further performance of his own undertakings, and their rights in respect of undertakings previously performed are now regulated by the Law Reform (Frustrated Contracts) Act, 1943 (below, p. 544).

This branch of the common law has reached its present stage by the normal process of historical growth, and the fallacy in Mr Ashton Roskill's contention that a different test is applicable when the event occurs as a result of the default of one party from that applicable in cases of frustration where the event occurs as a result of the default of neither party lies, in my view, from a failure to view the cases in their historical context. The problem: in what event will a party to a contract be relieved of his undertaking to do that which he has agreed to do but has not yet done? has exercised the English courts for centuries, probably ever since assumpsit emerged as a form of action distinct from covenant and debt and long before even the earliest cases which we have been invited to examine; but until the rigour of the rule in *Paradine v. Jane* (below, p. 511) was mitigated in the middle of the last century by the classic judgments of Blackburn J. in *Taylor v. Caldwell* (below, p. 511) and Bramwell B. in *Jackson v. Union Marine Insurance Co. Ltd* (below, p. 516), it was in general only events resulting from one party's failure to perform his contractual obligations which were regarded as capable of relieving the other party from continuing to perform that which he had undertaken to do. . . .

Once it is appreciated that it is the event and not the fact that the event is a result of a breach of contract which relieves the party not in default of further performance of his obligations, two consequences follow. (1) The test whether the event relied upon has this consequence is the same whether the event is the result of the other party's breach of contract or not, as Devlin J. pointed out in *Universal Cargo Carriers Corporation v. Citati* [1957] 2 Q.B. 401, 434.[1] (2) The question whether an event which is the result of the other party's breach of contract has this consequence cannot be answered by treating all contractual undertakings as falling into one of two separate categories: "conditions" the breach of which gives rise to an event which relieves the party not in default of further performance of his obligations, and "warranties" the breach of which does not give rise to such an event.

Lawyers tend to speak of this classification as if it were comprehensive, partly for the historical reasons which I have already mentioned and partly because Parliament itself adopted it in the Sale of Goods Act 1893, as respects a number of implied terms in contracts for the sale of goods and has in that act used the expressions "condition" and "warranty" in that meaning. But it is by no means true of contractual undertakings in general at common law.

No doubt there are many simple contractual undertakings, sometimes express but more often because of their very simplicity ("It goes without saying") to be implied, of which it can be predicated that every breach of such an undertaking must give rise to an event which will deprive the party not in default of substantially the whole benefit which it was intended that he should obtain from the contract. And such a stipulation, unless the parties have agreed that breach of it shall not entitle the non-defaulting party to treat the contract as repudiated, is a "condition."[2] So too there may

[1] But see *Bunge v. Tradax*, below, p. 426.
[2] The passage from the beginning of this paragraph is criticised in *Bunge v. Tradax*, below, p. 427.

be other simple contractual undertakings of which it can be predicated that *no* breach can give rise to an event which will deprive the party not in default of substantially the whole benefit which it was intended that he should obtain from the contract; and such a stipulation, unless the parties have agreed that breach of it shall entitle the non-defaulting party to treat the contract as repudiated, is a "warranty."

There are, however, many contractual undertakings of a more complex character which cannot be categorised as being "conditions" or "warranties," if the late nineteenth-century meaning adopted in the Sale of Goods Act, 1893, and used by Bowen L.J. in *Bentsen v. Taylor, Sons & Co.* [1893] 2 Q.B. 274, 280, be given to those terms. Of such undertakings all that can be predicated is that some breaches will and others will not give rise to an event which will deprive the party not in default of substantially the whole benefit which it was intended that he should obtain from the contract; and the legal consequences of a breach of such an undertaking, unless provided for expressly in the contract, depend upon the nature of the event to which the breach gives rise and do not follow automatically from a prior classification of the undertaking as a "condition" or a "warranty." For instance, to take Bramwell B.'s example in *Jackson v. Union Marine Insurance Co. Ltd* itself, breach of an undertaking by a shipowner to sail with all possible dispatch to a named port does not necessarily relieve the charterer of further performance of his obligation under the charterparty, but if the breach is so prolonged that the contemplated voyage is frustrated it does have this effect. . . .

As my brethren have already pointed out, the shipowner's undertaking to tender a seaworthy ship has, as a result of numerous decisions as to what can amount to "unseaworthiness," become one of the most complex of contractual undertakings. It embraces obligations with respect to every part of the hull and machinery, stores and equipment and the crew itself. It can be broken by the presence of trivial defects easily and rapidly remediable as well as by defects which must inevitably result in a total loss of the vessel.

Consequently the problem in this case is, in my view, neither solved nor soluble by debating whether the shipowner's express or implied undertaking to tender a seaworthy ship is a "condition" or a "warranty." It is like so many other contractual terms an undertaking one breach of which may give rise to an event which relieves the charterer of further performance of his undertakings if he so elects and another breach of which may not give rise to such an event but entitle him only to monetary compensation in the form of damages. It is, with all deference to Mr Ashton Roskill's skilful argument, by no means surprising that among the many hundreds of previous cases about the shipowner's undertaking to deliver a seaworthy ship there is none where it was found profitable to discuss in the judgments the question whether that undertaking is a "condition" or a "warranty"; for the true answer, as I have already indicated, is that it is neither, but one of that large class of contractual undertakings one breach of which may have the same effect as that ascribed to a breach of "condition" under the Sale of Goods Act, 1893, and a different breach of which may have only the same effect as that ascribed to a breach of "warranty" under that act . . .

What the judge had to do in the present case, as in any other case where one party to a contract relies upon a breach by the other party as giving him a right to elect to rescind the contract, and the contract itself makes no express provision as to this, was to look at the events which had occurred as a result of the breach at the time at which the charterers purported to rescind the charterparty and to decide whether the occurrence of those events deprived the charterers of substantially the whole benefit which it was the intention of the parties as expressed in the charterparty that the charterers should obtain from the further performance of their own contractual undertakings.

One turns therefore to the contract, the Baltime 1939 charter, of which Sellers L.J. has already cited the relevant terms. Clause 13, the "due diligence" clause, which exempts the shipowners from responsibility for delay or loss or damage to goods on board due to unseaworthiness, unless such delay or loss or damage has been caused by want of due diligence of the owners in making the vessel seaworthy and fitted for the voyage, is in itself sufficient to show that the mere occurrence of the events that the vessel was in some respect unseaworthy when tendered or that such unseaworthiness had caused some delay in performance of the charterparty would not deprive the charterer of the whole benefit which it was the intention of the parties he should obtain from the performance of his obligations under the contract—for he undertakes to continue to perform his obligations notwithstanding the occurrence of such events if they fall short of frustration of the contract and even deprives himself of any remedy in damages unless such events are the consequence of want of due diligence on the part on the shipowner.

The question which the judge had to ask himself was, as he rightly decided, whether or not at the date when the charterers purported to rescind the contract, namely, June 6, 1957, or when the shipowners purported to accept such rescission, namely, August 8, 1957, the delay which had already occurred as a result of the incompetence of the engine-room staff, and the delay which was likely to occur in repairing the engines of the vessel and the conduct of the shipowners by that date in taking steps to remedy these two matters, were, when taken together, such as to deprive the charterers of substantially the whole benefit which it was the intention of the parties they should obtain from further use of the vessel under the charterparty.

In my view, in his judgment—on which I would not seek to improve—the judge took into account and gave due weight to all the relevant considerations and arrived at the right answer for the right reasons.

Appeal dismissed.

Question
Is the shipowner's obligation to tender a seaworthy ship a single obligation or a "bundle of obligations of varying importance"? (See Cheshire Fifoot & Furmston, *Law of Contract* (12th ed.), p. 151.) If the latter, is it necessary to modify the traditional categorisation of all terms as either conditions or warranties? See above.

BUNGE CORPORATION, NEW YORK v. TRADAX EXPORT SA, PANAMA

Court of Appeal [1980] 1 Lloyd's Rep. 294; [1981] 2 All E.R. 513

A contract for the sale of 5,000 long tons, 5 per cent. more or less, of soya bean flour, required the buyers to give at least 15 consecutive days notice of probable readiness of vessel(s) and of approximate quantity to be loaded. A Gulf port of loading was then to be nominated by the seller. The buyer gave notice on June 17, 1975, less than 15 days before the end of the shipment period, June 30. On June 20 the seller repudiated the contract. The market price having fallen by $60 per metric ton, the seller claimed and was awarded damages of $317,500 by the umpire whose decision was upheld by the Trade Association appeal board but reversed by Parker J. Parker J. held that the term requiring 15 days notice was an innominate term and that the breach did not go to the root of the contract. The Court of Appeal (Megaw, Browne and Brightman L.JJ.) allowed the seller's appeal, holding that the term was a condition.

MEGAW L.J.: I come back to the purpose of the notice of probable readiness term in the present contract. The commercial reasons why advance notice is required are, I think obvious. The sellers have to nominate the loading port. Is loading going to be possible, and if possible convenient, at Port A, or Port B, or Port C? Until the probable date of readiness is known, it may be impossible to answer those questions. Until they are answered, the sellers cannot perform their contractual duty of nominating the port. When the port is decided, arrangements have to be made to have the contract quantity (to be defined by the buyers by reference to "5 per cent. more or less") of the contract goods available when the vessel is ready. What is involved in making such arrangements? It may involve, or include, buying goods, arranging for them to be moved by road, rail or water from wherever they may be; for warehousing them or moving them from one warehouse to another. Of course, in any given case, some or all of these tasks may be simply achieved, or their achievement may be possible in less than 15 days, in order to have the goods ready for loading where and when the vessel is ready for loading. It obviously cannot be predicated that 14 days' notice, instead of 15 days, would necessarily and in all circumstances cause sellers serious difficulties in respect of a contract containing these terms. What can and should be accepted is that the parties have agreed that, for the purposes of this contract, the reasonable time required to enable the sellers to perform their contractual obligations as to delivery of the goods is 15 days' notice of the probable readiness of the vessel to load. . . .

[Having quoted Diplock L.J. in *Hong Kong Fir*, above, p. 424, footnote 1 "No doubt there are many simple contractual undertakings, sometimes express but more often because of their very simplicity ('It goes without saying') to be implied, of which it can be predicated that every breach of such an undertaking must give rise to an event which will deprive the party not in default of substantially the whole benefit which it was intended that he should obtain from the contract. And such a stipulation, unless the parties have agreed that breach of it shall not entitle the non-defaulting party to treat the contract as repudiated, is a 'condition.'"]

If that statement is intended to be a definition of the requirements which must always be satisfied, in all types of contract and all types of clauses, in order that a term may qualify as a condition, I would very respectfully express the view that it is not a correct statement of the law. . . .

[Having quoted from *United Scientific v. Burnley Council* [1978] A.C. 904:]

In the light of what was said by their Lordships in that case, I think it can fairly be said that in mercantile contracts stipulations as to time not only may be, but usually are, to be treated as being "of the essence of the contract," even though this is not expressly stated in the words of the contract. It would follow that in a mercantile contract it cannot be predicated that, for time to be of the essence, any and every breach of the term as to time must necessarily cause the innocent party to be deprived of substantially the whole of the benefit which it was intended that he should have. . . .

[Having referred again to Diplock L.J. in *Hong Kong Fir*:]

In its literal sense, the words there used would mean that the test whether a term is a condition is whether *every* breach of such an undertaking *must* give rise to an event which will deprive the party not in default of *substantially the whole benefit which it was intended that he should obtain from the contract* (I underline various words to which I have given emphasis in reading it.) If this is a definition of the requirements which, in English law, must always be fulfilled before any contractual term (in the absence, of course, of express words) can achieve the legal status of a condition, then the term with which we are here concerned would not pass the test. The view which I have expressed that it is a condition would necessarily be wrong.

There are various reasons why I do not think that this was intended to be a literal, definitive and comprehensive statement of the requirements of a condition; and also, if it were, why, with great respect, I do not think that it represents the law as it stands today.

First, if it were intended to cover terms as to time in mercantile contracts, how could the requirements be said to be met in respect of stipulations in contracts of types in which, as Lord Diplock has recently said, time may be of the essence: for example, in respect of a stipulated time for delivery? It could never be said, as I see it, in any real sense, that *any* breach of such a stipulation *must necessarily* cause the innocent party to be deprived of *substantially all the benefit*.

Secondly, and following on what I have just said, I do not see how any contractual term, whether as to time or otherwise, could ever pass the test. Conditions would no longer exist in the English law of contract. For it is always possible to suggest hypothetically some minor breach or breaches of any contractual term which might, without undue use of the imagination, be wholly insufficient to produce serious effects for the innocent party, let alone the loss of sustantially all the benefit.

Thirdly, English law does recognise as conditions contractual terms which do not pass that test. For example, *Bowes v. Shand* (1877) 2 App.Cas. 455 and, I think, a substantial number of other cases which are binding, at least, on this Court.

Fourthly, it is clear law, reaffirmed by the House of Lords since *Hong Kong Fir* was decided, that where there has been a breach of a condition the innocent party is entitled to elect whether or not to treat the contract as repudiated. . . . How could this right of election be anything other than a legal fiction, a chimera, if the election can arise only in circumstances in which, as a result of the breach, an event has happened which will deprive the innocent party of substantially the whole benefit which it was intended that he should receive? This test, it is to be observed, is regarded (*Hong Kong Fir*, above p. 423) as applying also where the term is an intermediate term, except that you then look to what has actually happened in order to see if the innocent party has lost substantially all the benefit. So, again, if the test be right, the former principle of English law that the innocent party has the right to elect is no longer anything but an empty shadow, for a right to elect to continue a contract, with the result that the innocent party will be bound to continue to perform his own contractual obligations, when he will, by definition, have lost substantially all his benefit under the contract, does not appear to me to make sense.

Fifthly, the same considerations as I have set out in the previous paragraph apply if the test be that a breach of contract gives a right to the innocent party to treat it as a repudiation only if the events which in fact have flowed from the breach would, if they had come about otherwise than by a breach of contract, amount to frustration of the contract. Lord Radcliffe's classical definition of frustration in *Davis Contractors Ltd v. Fareham Urban District Council* (below, p. 526), is:

> ... without default of either party a contractual obligation has become incapable of being performed because the circumstances in which performance is called for would render it a thing radically different from that which was undertaken by the contract. *Non haec in foedera veni.*[1] It was not this that I promised to do. . . . There must be ... such a change in the significance of the obligation that the thing undertaken would, if performed, be a different thing from that contracted for.

If that, with the substitution of "default" for "no default" as being the cause of "the different thing," were the universal test which must be applied before there can be a condition or a breach of condition, then there can never be an election by the innocent party to proceed with the contract, despite the other party's default. For, as appears dramatically in the Virgilian quotation, it would not be the same contract. Yet the law has never ceased to recognise that there may be a right of election, when the innocent party is faced with a repudiatory breach, to keep the contract alive: the same contract, not a different one, as it would, necessarily and invariably, be on the frustration test.

Counsel for the sellers submitted that the test of a condition suggested in the paragraph which I have quoted, at least if it fell to be treated in its literal sense and as a comprehensive definition of the requirements of a condition, in all types of contracts and all types of contractual stipulations, is not a part of the ratio decidendi of the *Hong Kong Fir* case. I would, with very great respect, feel obliged to agree. Lord Justice Upjohn, in the opening words of his judgment, said that he—

> ... [entirely agreed] with the judgment which has just been delivered.

That judgment was the judgment of Lord Justice Sellers. As I understand it, the ratio of the judgment of Lord Justice Sellers, as to the test of a condition, is to be found in the paragraph in which he said:

---

[1] Sir John Megaw in a letter to *The Times*, December 20, 1980, refers to this quotation and asks "Have those eminent jurists, beginning with Lord Cairns in 1876, who have used that quotation to throw light on the circumstances in which a contract is frustrated, considered the context? Do the words not come, only slightly distorted, from the *Aeneid*, Book 4, lines 338 and 339: *'nec . . . haec in foedera veni?'* If so, they are a part of Aeneas's shabby excuses for his planned desertion of Queen Dido. Hardly, perhaps, the most attractive basis for a doctrine which involves releasing people from their contracts!"

"The formula for deciding whether a stipulation is a condition or a warranty is well recognised; the difficulty is in its application. It is put in a practical way by Lord Justice Bowen in *Bentsen v. Taylor Sons & Co.* [1893] 2 Q.B. 274, at p. 281: 'There is no way of deciding that question except by looking at the contract in the light of the surrounding circumstances, and then making up one's mind whether the intention of the parties, as gathered from the instrument itself, will best be carried out by treating the promise as a warranty sounding only in damages, or as a condition precedent by the failure to perform which the other party is relieved of his liability.'"

Applying that test for the reasons which I have sought to give I would hold that the term here in question is a condition.

The decision of the Court of Appeal was affirmed by the House of Lords, [1981] 1 W.L.R. 711; [1981] 2 All E.R. 513; [1981] 2 Ll.R. 1.

LORD WILBERFORCE, having referred to the "inescapable conclusion" of the Court of Appeal in *Hong Kong Fir* that the obligation of seaworthiness was not a condition: Diplock L.J. then generalised this particular consequence into the analysis which has since become classical. The fundamental fallacy of the appellants' argument lies in attempting to apply this analysis to a time clause such as the present in a mercantile contract, which is totally different in character. As to such a clause there is only one kind of breach possible, namely to be late, and the questions which have to be asked are: first, what importance have the parties expressly ascribed to this consequence? and, second, in the absence of expressed agreement, what consequence ought to be attached to it having regard to the contract as a whole?

The test suggested by the appellants was a different one. One must consider, they said, the breach actually committed and then decide whether that default would deprive the party not in default of substantially the whole benefit of the contract. They even invoked certain passages in the judgment of Diplock L.J. in *Hong Kong Fir* to support it. One may observe in the first place that the introduction of a test of this kind would be commercially most undesirable. It would expose the parties, after a breach of one, two, three, seven and other numbers of days, to an argument whether this delay would have left time for the seller to provide the goods. It would make it, at the time, at least difficult, and sometimes impossible, for the supplier to know whether he could do so. It would fatally remove from a vital provision in the contract that certainty which is the most indispensable quality of mercantile contracts, and lead to a large increase in arbitrations. It would confine the seller, perhaps after arbitration and reference through the courts, to a remedy in damages which might be extremely difficult to quantify. These are all serious objections in practice. But I am clear that the submission is unacceptable in law. The judgment of Diplock L.J. does not give any support and ought not to give any encouragement to any such proposition; for beyond doubt it recognises that it is open to the parties to agree that, as regards a particular obligation, any breach shall entitle the party not in default to treat the contract as repudiated. Indeed, if he were not doing so he would, in a passage which does not profess to be more than clarificatory, be discrediting a long and uniform series of cases, at least from *Bowes v. Shand* (1877) 2 App.Cas. 455 onwards, which have been referred to by my noble and learned friend Lord Roskill. It remains true, as Roskill L.J. has pointed out in *Cehave NV v. Bremer Handelsgesellschaft mbH* [1976] Q.B. 44 at 70–71, that the courts should not be too ready to interpret contractual clauses as conditions. And I have myself commended, and continue to commend, the greater flexibility in the law of contracts to which *Hong Kong Fir* points the way (see *Reardon Smith Line Ltd v. Hansen-Tangen* [1976] 3 All E.R. 570 at 576, [1976] 1 W.L.R. 989 at 998). But I do not doubt that, in suitable cases, the courts should not be reluctant, if the intentions of the parties as shown by the contract so indicate, to hold that an obligation has the force of a condition, and that indeed they should usually do so in the case of time clauses in mercantile contracts. To such cases the "gravity of the breach" approach of *Hong Kong Fir* would be unsuitable. I need only add on this point that the word "expressly" used by Diplock L.J. in *Hong Kong Fir* [1962] 1 All E.R. 474 at 487, [1962] 2 Q.B. 26 at 70 should not be read as requiring the actual use of the word "condition"; any term or terms of the contract, which, fairly read, have the effect indicated, are sufficient. Lord Diplock himself has given recognition to this in this House (see *Photo Production Ltd v. Securicor Transport Ltd* [1980] A.C. 827 at 849). I therefore reject that part of the appellants' argument which was based on it, and I must disagree with the judgment of the trial judge in so far as he accepted it. I respectfully indorse, on the other hand, the full and learned treatment of this issue in the judgment of Megaw L.J. in the Court of Appeal.

LORD SCARMAN: I read the *Hong Kong Fir* case as being concerned as much with the construction of the contract as with the consequences and effect of breach. The first question is always, therefore, whether, on the true construction of a stipulation and the contract of which it is part, it is a condition, an innominate term, or only a warranty. If the stipulation is one which on the true construction of the contract the parties have not made a condition, and breach of which may be attended by trivial, minor or very grave consequences, it is innominate, and the court (or an arbitrator) will, in the event of dispute, have the task of deciding whether the breach that has arisen is such as the parties would have said, had they been asked at the time they made their contract, "It goes without saying that, if that happens, the contract is at an end."

Where, therefore, as commonly happens, the parties do not identify a stipulation as a condition, innominate term or warranty, the court will approach the problem of construction in the way outlined by Upjohn L.J. [1962] 2 Q.B. 26 at 63–64:

> "Where, however, on the true construction of the contract, the parties have not made a particular stipulation a condition, it would be unsound and misleading to conclude that, being a warranty, damages is a sufficient remedy."

Unless the contract makes it clear, either by express provision or by necessary implication arising from its nature, purpose and circumstances ("the factual matrix" as spelt out for example, by Lord Wilberforce in his speech in *Reardon Smith Line Ltd v. Hansen-Tangen* [1976] 1 W.L.R. 989 at

995–997), that a particular stipulation is a condition or only a warranty, it is an innominate term the remedy for a breach of which depends on the nature, consequences and effect of the breach.

[After some hesitation, Lord Scarman concluded that the term in the present case was not an innominate term but a condition.]

Question
   Diplock L.J. says that a breach gives rise to a right to terminate a contract only if the event caused by the breach is so fundamental that, if it had happened without breach, it would have frustrated the contract. (For frustration, see Chapter 14, below.) *Bunge* makes it clear that this is not so regarding breach of a condition. Is it true for breach of an innominate term? Was the event in the *Aerial Advertising* case, above, p. 422, such that, if it had occurred without breach (that is, the pilot had flown over Salford with the approval of Batchelors and produced the same wrath on the part of the populace), would the contract have been frustrated? Would a party having the right to terminate for breach of an innominate term ever exercise his option to affirm if, *ex hypothesi*, the contract were frustrated?

THE MIHALIS ANGELOS

[1971] 1 Q.B. 164; [1970] 3 W.L.R. 601; [1970] 3 All E.R. 125;
[1970] 2 Lloyd's Rep. 43

In a charterparty a shipowner (S) undertook that the ship, "expected ready to load . . . about July 1, 1965," would proceed to Haiphong and there load a cargo, the charterer (C) to have the option of cancelling the charter if the ship was not ready to load by July 20.
   On July 17, C, being unable to get a cargo, cancelled the charter, alleging that it was frustrated. It was accepted at the trial that the charter was not frustrated merely by C's inability to procure a cargo, but it was argued that C was entitled to avoid the contract on July 17 by reason of a breach of contract by S—that is, that he had impliedly promised that he had reasonable grounds for his expectation that the ship would be ready to load on July 1, and that there were no such grounds. Mocatta J. held that there was a breach of this term, but the term was not a condition and the breach was not so fundamental as to afford a right to terminate the contract.
   The Court of Appeal held that the term was a condition and that C had properly avoided the contract even though he had done so on the ground that the contract was frustrated when this was not the case. "The fact that a contracting party gives a bad reason for determining it does not prevent him from afterwards relying on a good reason when he discovers it"—*per* Lord Denning, following *British & Beningtons Ltd v. Cachar Tea Co. Ltd* [1923] A.C. 48.

MEGAW L.J., discussing the term "expected ready to load . . .": In my judgment, such a term in a charterparty ought to be regarded as being a condition of the contract, in the old sense of the word "condition"; that is that when it has been broken, the other party can, if he wishes, by intimation to the party in breach, elect to be released from performance of his further obligations under the contract; and he can validly do so without having to establish that, on the facts of the particular case, the breach has produced serious consequences which can be treated as "going to the root of the contract" or as being "fundamental," or whatever other metaphor may be thought appropriate for a frustration case.
   I reach that conclusion for four interrelated reasons. First, it tends towards certainty in the law. One of the essential elements of law is some measure of uniformity. One of the important elements of the law is

predictability. At any rate in commercial law, there are obvious and substantial advantages in having, where possible, a firm and definite rule for a particular class of legal relationship; for example as here, the legal categorisation of a particular, definable type of contractual clause in common use. It is surely much better, both for shipowners and charterers (and, incidentally, for their advisers), when a contractual obligation of this nature is under consideration, and still more when they are faced with the necessity for an urgent decision as to the effects of a suspected breach of it, to be able to say categorically: "If a breach is proved, then the charterer can put an end to the contract," rather than that they should be left to ponder whether or not the courts would be likely, in the particular case, when the evidence had been heard, to decide that in the particular circumstances the breach was or was not such as "to go to the root of the contract." Where justice does not require greater flexibility, there is everything to be said for, and nothing against, a degree of rigidity in legal principle.

Second, it would, in my opinion, only be in the rarest case, if ever, that a ship-owner could legitimately feel that he had suffered an injustice by reason of the law having given to a charterer the right to put an end to the contract because of the breach by the ship-owner of a clause such as this. If a ship-owner has chosen to assert contractually, but dishonestly or without reasonable grounds, that he expects his vessel to be ready to load on such and such a date, wherein does the grievance lie? Third, it is, as Mocatta J. held, clearly established by authority binding on this court that where a clause "expected ready to load" is included in a contract for the sale of goods to be carried by sea, that clause is a condition, in the sense that any breach of it enables the buyer to reject the goods without having to show that the dishonest or unreasonable expectation of the seller has in fact been prejudicial to the buyer. . . .

It would, in my judgment, produce an undesirable anomaly in our commercial law if such a clause—"expected ready to load"—were to be held to have a materially different legal effect where it is contained in a charterparty from that which it has when it is contained in a sale of goods contract. . . .

The fourth reason why I think that the clause should be regarded as being a condition when it is found in a charterparty is that that view was the view of Scrutton L.J. so expressed in his capacity as the author of *Scrutton on Charterparties*.

Notes

1. In *The Naxos* [1990] 3 All E.R. 641, the principle that a stipulation as to time in a mercantile contract will usually be interpreted as a condition, was applied by the House of Lords to a clause requiring the seller of sugar to have it available at the port of loading immediately on the arrival of the ship. Lord Brandon, dissenting, pointed out that two other stipulations as to time, breach of which, would result in delay in loading the ship (the buyer's obligation to present the ship, and the seller's obligation to complete loading, within a specified time), were clearly intended to be only warranties. He continued:

> "In each case what matters to the party to whom the obligation is owed is the result of the breach, namely delay in the loading of the ship, and not the form or nature of the obligation itself. It seems to me that the logical way to interpret the contract . . . is to classify all the obligations of either party, the breach of which would cause delay in the loading of the ship, in the same way, that is to say as warranties and not as conditions."

2. In *Torvald Klaveness A/S v. Arni Maritime Corp* [1994] 4 All E.R. 998, H.L. the term in question was that specifying the date for the redelivery of a ship under a time charter. In the

Court of Appeal Simon Brown L.J. said that this was clearly established *not* to be a condition properly so called. In the House of Lords, Lord Mustill, with whom the majority agreed, said ". . . although it is well established that certain obligations under charterparties do have the character of conditions I would not for my part wish to enlarge the category unduly, given the opportunity which this provides for a party to rely on an innocuous breach as a means of escaping from an unwelcome bargain." He inclined to the view that this particular obligation is "innominate" and that a short delay in redelivery would not justify the termination of the contract. (The vessel was in fact redelivered eight days late.)

The charterer had given an order for a voyage which, in the circumstances then existing, could have been performed within the charter period. After circumstances had so changed that this was impossible, they persisted in it. Lord Mustill said that "the charterer's persistence in [the original order] after it had become invalid showed that they did not intend to perform their obligations under the charter. That is to say, they 'evinced an intention no longer to be bound' by the charter. This was an anticipatory breach entitling the owners to treat the contract as ended." What if the anticipated breach had been a delay of only one day? For anticipatory breach, see below, p. 551.

Section 3. Partial or Substituted Performance of Conditions

The problems considered in this section may be summarised as follows.

Where A and B have contracted that the performance of a defined act by A shall be a condition of the liability of B, and A either partly performs that act but fails to complete it or completely performs a similar but not identical act, what are the rights of the parties? Can B repudiate his own obligations under the contract and yet retain any benefit which A's performance may have conferred on him without payment? Does it make any difference that the part of the act which A failed to do was large or very small, or that the act completely performed differed widely or only slightly from the defined act?

CUTTER v. POWELL

King's Bench (1795) 6 T.R. 320; 2 Sm.L.C., 13th ed., 1; 3 R.R. 185; 101 E.R. 573

To assumpsit for work and labour done by the intestate, the defendant pleaded the general issue. And at the trial at Lancaster the jury found a verdict for the plaintiff for £31 10s. subject to the opinion of this court on the following case.

The defendant being at Jamaica subscribed and delivered to T. Cutter, the intestate, a note, whereof the following is a copy: "Ten days after the ship Governor Parry, myself master, arrives at Liverpool, I promise to pay to Mr T. Cutter the sum of thirty guineas, provided he proceeds, continues and does his duty as second mate in the said ship from hence to the port of Liverpool. Kingston, July 31, 1793." The ship Governor Parry sailed from Kingston on August 2, 1793, and arrived in the port of Liverpool on October 9 following. T. Cutter went on board the ship on July 31, 1793, and sailed in her on August 2, and proceeded, continued and did his duty as second mate in her from Kingston until his death, which happened on September 20 following, and before the ship's arrival in the port of Liverpool. The usual wages of a second mate of a ship on such a voyage, when shipped by the month out and home is four pounds per month: but when seamen are shipped by the run from Jamaica to England, a gross sum is usually given. The usual length of a voyage from Jamaica to Liverpool is about eight weeks.

It was argued for the plaintiff, the intestate's widow, that she was entitled to recover a proportionable part of the wages on a *quantum meruit* for work and labour done duing that part of the voyage that he lived and served the defendant. The defendant replied that where there is an express contract between the parties they cannot resort to an implied one; that this was an entire and indivisible contract, and the intestate's continuing to perform his duty during the whole voyage was a condition precedent to his recovering anything.

LORD KENYON C.J.: I should be extremely sorry that in the decision of this case we should determine against what had been the received opinion in the mercantile world on contracts of this kind, because it is of great importance that the laws by which the contracts of so numerous and so useful a body of men as the sailors are supposed to be guided should not be overturned. Whether these kind of notes are much in use among the seamen, we are not sufficiently informed; and the instances now stated to us from Liverpool are too recent to form anything like usage. But it seems to me at present that the decision of this case may proceed on the particular words of this contract and the precise facts here stated, without touching marine contracts in general. That where the parties have come to an express contract none can be implied has prevailed so long as to be reduced to an axiom in the law. Here the defendant expressly promised to pay the intestate 30 guineas, provided he proceeded, continued and did his duty as second mate in the ship from Jamaica to Liverpool; and the accompanying circumstances disclosed in the case are that the common rate of wages is four pounds per month, when the party is paid in proportion to the time he serves: and that this voyage is generally performed in two months. Therefore if there had been no contract between these parties, all that the intestate could have recovered on a *quantum meruit* for the voyage would have been eight pounds; whereas here the defendant contracted to pay 30 guineas provided the mate continued to do his duty as mate during the whole voyage, in which case the latter would have received nearly four times as much as if he were paid for the number of months he served. He stipulated to receive the larger sum if the whole duty were performed, and nothing unless the whole of that duty were performed: it was a kind of insurance. On this particular contract my opinion is formed at present; at the same time I must say that if we were assured that these notes are in universal use, and that the commercial world have received and acted upon them in a different sense, I should give up my own opinion.

The concurring judgments of ASHURST, GROSE and LAWRENCE JJ. are omitted.

Notes
1. The rights of seamen in respect of wages are now regulated by the Merchant Shipping Act 1970.
2. A *quantum meruit* action may be contractual or quasi-contractual. It is contractual where there is a real contract, but no price has been fixed for the plaintiff's services or other consideration supplied by him. It is quasi-contractual where the plaintiff, not relying on a contract, claims the value of a benefit conferred by him on a defendant who had an option to accept or reject it (see *Sumpter v. Hedges*, below, p. 437) and accepted it. So where the plaintiff rendered services in pursuance of a supposed contract which turned out to be *void* he could recover the value of his services in *quantum meruit*: *Craven-Ellis v. Canons Ltd* [1936] 2 K.B. 403. Since, however, the action is based on an implied promise, it cannot lie where there is in existence an inconsistent express contract: *Britain v. Rossiter* (1879) 11 Q.B.D. 123.
3. Was the defendant's note to Cutter merely an offer of a unilateral contract which Cutter never succeeded in accepting?—like the offeree who, through no fault of his, fails to walk to York, or use the smoke ball three times daily for two weeks—above, p. 31. Or do the words, "duty as second mate," and the circumstances imply that Cutter undertook obligations—a bilateral contract?
Cf. Glanville Williams, "Partial Performance of Entire Contracts" 57 L.Q.R. 373; Stoljar, "The Great Case of *Cutter v. Powell*" 34 Can. Bar Rev. 288; Beck, "The Doctrine of Substantial

Performance: Conditions and Conditions Precedent" (1975) 38 M.L.R. 413. In connection
with *Cutter v. Powell*, see also the Frustrated Contracts Act, ss.1(3), 2(3), below p. 545) *et seq.*

VIGERS v. COOK

Court of Appeal [1919] 2 K.B. 475; 88 L.J.K.B. 1132; 121 L.T. 357; 35 T.L.R. 605

The plaintiff, a funeral undertaker, contracted with the defendant for the conduct
of the funeral of the defendant's son. By the terms of the contract the coffin was to
be taken into a certain church where a part of the funeral service was to be read over
the body. The body was in an advanced state of decomposition. The plaintiff
supplied a lead coffin, in which he left a vent for the escape of gas resulting from
decomposition, and the coffin with the body in it was taken to a mortuary. Owing to
a complaint by the mortuary authorities of an offensive smell from the coffin, the
plaintiff had the vent closed, in consequence of which by the time the funeral had
reached the church the coffin had burst and was leaking, and the smell was so
offensive that it was impossible to take the coffin into the church, and the service
had to be read without it. In consequence the defendant refused to pay the
plaintiff's bill. The county court judge found that the plaintiff had broken his
contract and disallowed the cost of the lead coffin and the plaintiff's profits, and
gave judgment for the plaintiff for the reduced sum of £42 as upon a *quantum meruit*.
The defendant appealed to a divisional court (A. T. Lawrence and Lush JJ.) which
held that this was one entire contract, to conduct the service in a proper manner,
and as this had not been done, the plaintiff could recover nothing. The plaintiff
appealed to the Court of Appeal.

BANKES L.J.: In my opinion the contract which was made between the
parties included, as I have said, as an essential term the conveying of the
body into the church for a part of the service, subject to this condition, that
the body was in such a state as to permit of that being done. The body in
this coffin was not in that state, but the onus was on the plaintiff to
establish that it was not in that state owing to no default on his part. In my
opinion he did not discharge that onus. In considering whether he
discharged the onus it is necessary to see what it was prima facie possible
for him to have done. When on August 3 the body left the mortuary for
Richmond the plaintiff knew that there was within the coffin a very
considerable accumulation of gas, such an accumulation as raised a
question of doubt whether it could safely be removed on that journey. He
considered it, and came to the conclusion that the risk could be safely
taken. Assuming he had come to the conclusion that the risk could not
safely be taken, as it turned out it could not, what was it possible to have
done? It was possible to reopen the aperture and allow the gas to escape.
Whether it was practicable was a different question, and the onus rested
upon the plaintiff to prove that, though possible, it was not practicable. No
evidence was given on that point. Another question arose which it was
necessary to consider. Assuming it to be both possible and practicable to
reopen the aperture, would the condition of things with the aperture
reopened have been equally offensive as it was with the coffin burst, or at
any rate so offensive that the body could not have been carried into the
church? There again the onus rested upon the plaintiff. It may well be that
the condition of things was such that, even if the hole had been reopened,
it would not have been possible, reverently and decently, to take the body

into the church. At present that is left unsettled. In these two matters I think that, although the plaintiff down to the time of the closing of the aperture did nothing other than what a competent and careful undertaker would do, in the difficult circumstances which arose when he felt it necessary to close the aperture, he has not shown that it was owing to no fault on his part that one essential term of his contract was not fulfilled; and it being one entire contract, in my opinion he fails in proving that he is entitled to any portion of the one entire price which was payable for the entire contract.

SCRUTTON AND ATKIN L.JJ. agreed.

Questions
Why did the court consider that this case turned on whether the plaintiff was negligent or not, when nothing was said about negligence in *Cutter v. Powell*?

It is possible for a contract to allow alternative modes of performance, depending upon some condition: for example, "The concert will be held on the lawn if it is fine; but in the hall if it is wet." Might it not be that it was implicit in the contract in *Vigers v. Cook* that if, *after all proper steps had been taken*, the condition of the body made it impossible to take the coffin into church, then the coffin should be left outside? If so, would not Vigers, then, have fully performed his contract if he had been able to show that he was not negligent?

On the question of burden of proof on the negligence issue, compare the *Constantine Steamship* case, below, p. 539.

SUMPTER v. HEDGES

Court of Appeal [1898] 1 Q.B. 673; 67 L.J.Q.B. 545; 78 L.T. 378; 46 W.R. 454

The plaintiff, a builder, contracted with the defendant to erect certain buildings upon the defendant's land for £565. The plaintiff did part of the work to the value of about £333 and received payment of part of the price. He then informed the defendant that he had no money and could not go on with the work. The defendant finished the buildings on his own account, using for that purpose certain materials which the plaintiff had left on the site. In an action for work done and materials provided Bruce J. found that the plaintiff had abandoned the contract and gave judgment for him for the value of the materials used by the defendant, but allowed him nothing for the work done. The plaintiff appealed.

A.L. Smith and Chitty L.JJ. gave judgment dismissing the appeal.

COLLINS L.J.: I agree. I think the case is really concluded by the finding of the learned judge to the effect that the plaintiff had abandoned the contract. If the plaintiff had merely broken his contract in some way so as not to give the defendant the right to treat him as having abandoned the contract, and the defendant had then proceeded to finish the work himself, the plaintiff might perhaps have been entitled to sue on a *quantum meruit* on the ground that the defendant had taken the benefit of the work done. But that is not the present case. There are cases in which, though the plaintiff has abandoned the performance of a contract, it is possible for him to raise the inference of a new contract to pay for the work done on a *quantum meruit* from the defendant's having taken the benefit of that work, but, in order that that may be done, the circumstances must be such as to give an option to the defendant to take or not to take the benefit of the work done. It is only where the circumstances are such as to give that option that there is any evidence on which to ground the inference of a new contract. Where, as in the case of work done on land, the circumstances are such as to give the defendant no option whether he will take the benefit of the work or not, then one must look to other facts than the mere taking the benefit of the work in order to ground the inference of a new contract. In this case I see no other facts on which such an inference can be founded. The mere fact that a defendant is in possession of what he cannot help keeping, or even has done work upon it, affords no ground for such an inference. He is not bound to keep unfinished a building which in an incomplete state would be a nuisance on his land. I am therefore of opinion that the plaintiff was not entitled to recover for the work which he had done.

Appeal dismissed.

SALE OF GOODS ACT 1979

Delivery of wrong quantity.

30.—(1) Where the seller delivers to the buyer a quantity of goods less than he contracted to sell, the buyer may reject them, but if the buyer accepts the goods so delivered he must pay for them at the contract rate.

(2) Where the seller delivers to the buyer a quantity of goods larger than he contracted to sell, the buyer may accept the goods included in the contract and reject the rest, or he may reject the whole.

(2A) A buyer who does not deal as consumer may not—

(a) where the seller delivers a quantity of goods less than he contracted to sell, reject the goods under subsection (1) above, or
(b) where the seller delivers a quantity of goods larger than he contracted to sell, reject the whole under subsection (2) above,

if the shortfall or, as the case may be, excess is so slight that it would be unreasonable for him to do so.

(2B) It is for the seller to show that a shortfall or excess fell within subsection (2A) above.

Section 30(1) and (2) enacted the rule of the common law, requiring strict performance as a condition. Delivery of 143 bottles, instead of the gross contracted for, entitled the buyer to reject. In a consumer contract, it still does. The consumer may reject, however unreasonable it is for him to do so. But, for other contracts, section 30(2)A, inserted by the Sale and Supply of Goods Act 1994, reduces the term regarding quantity, in effect to an innominate term. See also pp. 421, 433–434, above.

APPLEBY v. MYERS

Exchequer Chamber (1867) L.R. 2 C.P. 651; 36 L.J.C.P. 331; 16 L.T. 669

The plaintiffs contracted with the defendant to erect a steam engine and machinery on premises in the possession of the defendant. The specification divided the work into 10 different parts and stated the price to be charged for each part. The contract concluded with these words: "We offer to make and erect the whole of the machinery . . . and to put it to work, for the sums above named respectively, and to keep the whole in order, under fair wear and tear, for two years from the date of completion. . . ." The total cost of the works to be done amounted to £459. When all parts of the work were far advanced towards completion, though none of them had been absolutely completed, an accidental fire entirely destroyed the premises and the works which had been erected thereon. The plaintiff sued to recover £419 for work done and materials provided. The judgment of the Court of Common Pleas in favour of the plaintiff was reversed by the Court of Exchequer Chamber. Blackburn J., delivering the judgment of the court (Martin B., Blackburn J., Bramwell B., Shee and Lush JJ.), held, differing from the court below, that there was no absolute promise or warranty by the defendant that the premises should continue in a fit state to enable the plaintiffs to perform the work upon them. The destruction of the premises excused both parties, but gave a cause of action to neither. He went on:

Then it was argued before us, that, inasmuch as this was a contract of that nature which would in pleading be described as a contract for work, labour, and materials, and not as one of bargain and sale, the labour and materials necessarily became the property of the defendant as soon as they were worked into his premises and became part of them, and therefore were at his risk. We think that, as to a great part at least of the work done in this case, the materials had not become the property of the defendant; for, we think that the plaintiffs, who were to complete the whole for a fixed sum, and keep it in repair for two years, would have had a perfect right, if they thought that a portion of the engine which they had put up was too slight, to change it and substitute another in their opinion better calculated to keep in good repair during the two years, and that without consulting or asking the leave of the defendant. But, even on the supposition that the materials had become unalterably fixed to the defendant's premises, we do not think that, under such a contract as this, the plaintiffs could recover anything unless the whole work was completed. It is quite true that materials worked by one into the property of another become part of that property. This is equally true, whether it be fixed or movable property. Bricks built into a wall become part of the house; thread stitched into a coat which is under repair, or planks and nails and pitch worked into a ship under repair, become part of the coat or the ship; and therefore, generally, and in the absence of something to show a contrary intention, the bricklayer, or tailor, or shipwright, is to be paid for the work and materials he has done and provided, although the whole work is not complete. It is not material whether in such a case the non-completion is because the shipwright did not choose to go on with the work, as was the case in *Roberts v. Havelock*, 3 B. & Ad. 404, or because in consequence of a fire he could not go on with it, as in *Menetone v. Athawes*, 3 Burr. 1592. But, though this is the prima facie contract between those who enter into contracts for doing work and supplying materials, there is nothing to render it either illegal or absurd in the workman to agree to complete the whole, and be paid when the whole is complete, and not till then: and we think that the plaintiffs in the present case had entered into such a contract. Had the accidental fire left the defendant's premises untouched, and only injured a part of the work which the plaintiffs had already done, we apprehend that it is clear the plaintiffs under such a contract as the present must have done that part over again, in order to fulfil their contract to complete the whole and "put it to work for the sums above named respectively." As it is, they are, according to the principle laid down in *Taylor v. Caldwell* (below, p. 511), excused from completing the work; but they are not therefore entitled to any compensation for what they have done, but which has, without any fault of the defendant, perished. The case is in principle like that of a shipowner who has been excused from the performance of his contract to carry goods to their destination, because his ship has been disabled by one of the excepted perils, but who is not therefore entitled to any payment on account of the part-performance of the voyage, unless there is something to justify the conclusion that there has been a fresh contract to pay freight *pro rata*.

Note
    This case must now be considered in the light of the Frustrated Contracts Act, 1943. See especially sections 1(3) and 2(3), below, pp. 544–546.

FORMAN & CO. PROPRIETARY LTD. v. THE SHIP "LIDDESDALE"

Privy Council [1900] A.C. 190; 69 L.J.P.C. 44; 82 L.T. 33]; 9 Asp.M.C. 45

The *Liddesdale* ran aground and sustained damage off the coast of Western Australia. The plaintiffs contracted with the shipowner to effect certain specified repairs for a fixed sum. The plaintiffs did do repairs which were good work, and which added value to the ship; but the work was not—and the plaintiffs did not assert that it was—the *stipulated* work. The plaintiffs did allege that it was equivalent to the stipulated work, or something better. For example, the plaintiffs had used iron girders where their contract required steel. The iron girders were more expensive and, the plaintiffs alleged, to the advantage of the ship—though the defendants denied this. The Privy Council held that the plaintiffs could recover nothing; they could not recover under the express contract, because they had not done what they had undertaken to do; nor under an implied contract for the work actully done, because there had been no acquiescence in, or ratification of that work by the defendants. "The mere fact that the defendant took the ship which was his own property and made the best he could of it cannot give the plaintiffs any additional right. It is not like the case of an acceptance of goods which were not previously the property of the acceptor. . . ."

Note
    Cf. Ruxley Electronics, below, p. 611, and question 2, below, p. 614.

HOENIG v. ISAACS

Court of Appeal [1952] 1 T.L.R. 1360; [1952] 2 All E.R. 176

The plaintiff was an interior decorator and furniture designer. The defendant, the owner of a one-room flat, employed the plaintiff to decorate it and provide it with furniture, including bedstead and wardrobe and bookcase fitments, for a sum of £750, the terms of payment being "net cash, as the work proceeds; and balance on completion." On April 12, 1950, the defendant paid £150, and on April 19 he paid a further £150. On August 28, the plaintiff said that he had carried out the work in compliance with the contract and requested payment of the balance of £450. The defendant replied complaining of faulty design and bad workmanship, but he sent the plaintiff a further £100, entered into occupation of the flat, and used the furniture. On a claim by the plaintiff for the balance of £350, the defendant alleged that the plaintiff had failed to perform his contract, and, alternatively, that the work was done negligently, unskilfully, and in an unworkmanlike manner. The official referee held that the door of a wardrobe required replacing, and that a bookshelf, which was too short, would have to be remade, which would require alterations being made to a bookcase. The defendant contended that this was an entire contract which had not been performed, and, therefore, the plaintiff could not recover. The official referee held that there had been a substantial compliance with the contract and that the defendant was liable for £350 less the cost of remedying the defects which he assessed at £55 18s. 2d., and he gave judgment for £294 1s. 10d.

SOMERVELL L.J., having stated the facts, continued: Counsel for the defendant submits that the decision of the official referee is wrong in law. He submits that this is an entire contract which, on the findings of fact, has not been performed. On the well-known principle applied to the facts of that case in *Cutter v. Powell* (above, p. 434) he submitted that the plaintiff cannot, therefore, recover on his contract. He was not concerned to dispute that on this basis the plaintiff might on the facts of this case be entitled to recover on a *quantum meruit*. Such a claim has never been put forward. If it were, he submits that the amount recoverable would be the fair value of what was done and delivered. The learned official referee found that there had been a substantial compliance with the contract. Counsel submits that, if his first point is right, this does not enable the plantiff to succeed. If necessary, he submits that on his findings of fact the learned official referee was wrong as a matter of law in holding that there had been substantial compliance. [His Lordship referred to the official referee's findings as to the wardrobe door, the bookshelf, and the bookcase, and continued:] If any issue arises whether the breaches were substantial, I think it must be based on the items to which I have referred, bearing in mind, of course, that there were some additional minor defects.

The official referee regarded the principle laid down in *H. Dakin & Co. Ltd v. Lee* [1916] 1 K.B. 566 as applicable. The contract in that case was for repairs to a house. The official referee before whom the case came in the first instance found that the work as completed did not accord with the contract in certain respects. He proceeded to hold that the plaintiff could not recover any part of the contract price or any sum in respect of the contract work. This decision was reversed in the Divisional Court and their decision was affirmed by this court. In support of the official referee's decision it was argued that the plaintiff could not recover either on the contract or on a *quantum meruit*. No new contract on the latter basis could be implied from the fact that the defendant by continuing to live in her house had enjoyed the benefit of what had been done.

In *Eshelby v. Federated European Bank Ltd* [1932] 1 K.B. 423, Greer L.J. ([1932] 1 K.B. 431) clearly felt some difficulty about H. *Dakin & Co. Ltd v. Lee* as possibly inconsistent with *Cutter v. Powell*, and the cases following that decision and deciding that where work is to be done for a sum named neither that sum nor any part of it can be recovered while the work remains undone. We were referred to a number of these cases and I have considered those authorities and others. Each case turns on the construction of the contract. In *Cutter v. Powell* the condition for the promissory note sued on was that the sailor should proceed to continue and do his duty as second mate in the ship from Jamaica to the port of

Liverpool. The sailor died before the ship reached Liverpool and it was held his estate could not recover either on the contract or on a *quantum meruit*. It clearly decided that his continuing as mate during the whole voyage was a condition precedent to payment. It did not decide that if he had completed the main purpose of the contract, namely, serving as mate for the whole voyage, the defendant could have repudiated his liability by establishing that in the course of the voyage the sailor had, possibly through inadvertence, failed on some occasion in his duty as mate whereby some damage had been caused. In these circumstances, the court might have applied the principle applied to ordinary contracts for freight. The shipowner can normally recover nothing unless the goods are carried to their agreed destination. On the other hand, if this is done, his claim is not defeated by the fact that some damage has been done to the goods in transit which has resulted from a breach of the contract. The owner of the goods has his remedy by cross-action: *Dakin v. Oxley* (1864) 15 C.B.(N.S.) 646; 143 E.R. 938. The damage might, of course, be so great as to raise the question whether what was agreed to be carried had substantially arrived. *Sinclair v. Bowles* (1829) 9 B. and Co. 92; 109 E.R. 35, is often cited as an illustration of the *Cutter v. Powell* principle. The plaintiff had undertaken to repair chandeliers and make them "complete" or "perfect." This he, quite plainly on the evidence and findings of the jury, failed to do. It may, perhaps, be regarded as a case where, on the construction of the contract, having regard to the subject-matter, there was no scope for terms collateral to the main purpose.

The principle that fulfilment of every term is not necessarily a condition precedent in a contract for a lump sum is usually traced back to a short judgment of Lord Mansfield C.J. in *Boone v. Eyre* (1779) 1 Hy. Bl. 273n. the sale of the plantation with its slaves. Lord Mansfield said: ". . . where mutual covenants go to the whole of the consideration on both sides, they are mutual conditions, the one precedent to the other. But where they go only to a part, where a breach may be paid for in damages, there the defendant has a remedy on his covenant, and shall not plead it as a condition precedent." One is very familiar with the application of this principle in the law relating to the sale of goods. *Quoad* stipulations which are conditions, the *Cutter v. Powell* principle is applicable. If they are not all performed the other party can repudiate, but there will not have been, as there was in *Cutter v. Powell*, a partial performance. But there may be other terms, collateral to the main purpose, the breach of which in English law gives rise to a claim for damages, but not to a right to reject the goods and treat the contract as repudiated: see definition of warranty, Sale of Goods Act, 1893, s.62(1).[1]

In a contract to erect buildings on the defendant's land for a lump sum, the builder can recover nothing on the contract if he stops before the work is completed in the ordinary sense—in other words, abandons the contract. He is also usually in a difficulty in recovering on a *quantum meruit* because no new contract can be inferred from the mere fact that the defendant

---

[1] "Warranty . . . means an agreement with reference to goods which are the subject of a contract of sale, but collateral to the main purpose of such contract, the breach of which gives rise to a claim for damages, but not to a right to reject the goods and treat the contract as repudiated." See now the Sale of Goods Act 1979, s.61(1).

remains in possession of his land: *Sumpter v. Hedges.* In *Appleby v. Myers* while the work was in progress the premises and the work so far done on them were destroyed by fire and the court held both parties excused. At the end of his judgment Blackburn J., after referring to *Cutter v. Powell, Sinclair v. Bowles,* and that line of cases, said: ". . . the plaintiffs, having contracted to do an entire work for a specific sum, can recover nothing unless the work be done. . . ." In *H. Dakin & Co. Ltd v. Lee* Lord Cozens-Hardy M.R., I think, had this principle in mind when he said: "The work was finished—and when I say this I do not wish to prejudice matters, but I cannot think of a better word to use at the moment."

The question here is whether in a contract for work and labour for a lump sum payable on completion the defendant can repudiate liability under the contract on the ground that the work though "finished" or "done" is in some respects not in accordance with the contract. *H. Dakin & Co. Ltd v. Lee* is, of course, binding on us, but counsel for the defendant submitted that it was an exception to a general rule applying to contracts such as that in issue here and should be confined within as narrow limits as possible. I agree with the learned editor of the notes to *Cutter v. Powell* in Smith's *Leading Cases,* (13th ed.), Vol. 2, p. 21, that *H. Dakin & Co. Ltd v. Lee,* so far from being an exception, reaffirmed the true position on the construction of this class of contract on which doubts had been thrown by taking certain observations out of their context. . . .

The learned official referee regarded *H. Dakin & Co. Ltd v. Lee* as laying down that the price must be paid subject to set-off or counterclaim if there was a substantial compliance with the contract. I think on the facts of this case where the work was finished in the ordinary sense, though in part defective, this is right. It expresses in a convenient epithet what is put from another angle in the Sale of Goods Act, 1893. The buyer cannot reject if he proves only the breach of a term collateral to the main purpose. I have, therefore, come to the conclusion that the first point of counsel for the defendant fails.

The learned official referee found that there was substantial compliance. Bearing in mind that there is no appeal on fact, was there evidence on which he could so find? The learned official referee having, as I hold, properly directed himself, this becomes, I think, a question of fact. The case on this point was, I think, near the border line, and if the finding had been the other way I do not think we could have interfered. Even if I had felt we could interfere, the defendant would be in a further difficulty. The contract included a number of chattels. If the defendant wished to repudiate his liability under the contract he should not, I think, have used those articles, which he could have avoided using. On this view, though it is not necessary to decide it, I think he put himself in the same position as a buyer of goods who by accepting them elects to treat a breach of condition as a breach of warranty.

I now come to the final question, the measure of damages. It seems from the argument that the defendant regards the price of £750 as excessive irrespective of any relief by way of reduction of price or on his counterclaim. He was anxious to put the plaintiff in the position of having to sue on a *quantum meruit* for the value of the work done and he was anxious to tender evidence designed, no doubt, to show that the work done was worth much less than £750. The learned official referee excluded this evidence. The measure he applied was the cost of putting the work in accordance with the contract and on this basis such evidence was rightly excluded. The defendant is bound, he held, to pay for the furniture supplied less the cost of putting right the defects. This I think is, as the learned official referee thought, in accordance with *H. Dakin & Co. Ltd v. Lee*. Lord Cozens-Hardy M.R. there said: ". . . the builders are entiled to recover the contract price, less so much as it is found ought to be allowed in respect of the items which the official referee has found to be defective." This seems to follow what was said by Parke B. in *Mondel v. Steel*. In dealing with the procedural point he said that the defendant need not bring a cross-action but can diminish the price ". . . by showing how much less the subject-matter of the contract was worth, by reason of the breach of contract."

DENNING AND ROMER L.JJ. delivered concurring judgments.

Appeal dismissed.

Notes
1. In *Bolton v. Mahadeva* [1972] 1 W.L.R. 1009 the Court of Appeal applied the rule to defeat an action by a contractor for the agreed price of £560 for the installation of a combined heating and domestic hot water system. The county court judge, though he assessed the deficiencies at £174, held that there had been substantial performance. Cairns L.J. said: "if a central heating system when installed is such that it does not heat the house adequately and is such, further, that fumes are given out, so as to make living rooms uncomfortable, and if the putting right of these defects is not something which can be done by some slight amendment of the system, then I think that the contract is not substantially performed." Sachs L.J. said: "This rule does not work hardly upon a contractor if only he is prepared to remedy the defects before seeking to resort to litigation to recover the lump sum. It is entirely the fault of the contractor in this instant case that he has placed himself in a difficulty by his refusal, on December 4, 1969, to remedy the defects of which complaint was being made."
2. Of the plaintiffs, Cutter, Vigers, Sumpter, Appleby, and Forman & Co., who were in breach of contract? Who were excused because the contract became impossible of performance without fault? Where the contract has become impossible of performance without the plaintiff's fault he may now have a remedy under section 1(3) and 2(3) of the Frustrated Contracts Act 1943, below, p. 544. Where the plaintiff was in breach of contract, however, the Act does not help him. The plight of the party in breach of contract is one of the matters considered by the Law Commission in Working Paper No. 65 (1975) and in its Report, "Pecuniary Restitution on Breach of Contract" Law Com. No. 121, (1983). It is recommended that the party who has failed to complete and who would have no right to recover under the present law should be entitled to recover from the other party to the contract a sum representing the value of what he has done under the contract to that person who has had the benefit of it, whether he is a party to the contract or not. The court would have no discretion to reduce or disallow the claim, because of the conduct of the party in breach but the sum awarded would not exceed the proportion of the sum payable on completion as is equal to the proportion of the work done to that promised. The party not in breach would be able to counterclaim for damages and the normal rules relating to remoteness and mitigation would apply.

CHAPTER 12

EXCLUSION CLAUSES

"Exclusion" or "exemption" or "exceptions" clauses are terms which exclude or limit, or purport to exclude or limit, a liability which would otherwise arise at common law, or by statute, or under the terms of a contract. Such a clause may exclude or limit a liability which would otherwise arise under the express or implied terms of a contract, but the effect of these clauses is not confined to contractual liability. Duties imposed by the common law or by statute may sometimes be excluded by the terms of a contract or, indeed, by a notice not having contractual effect. The common law of bailment imposes duties on the bailee to take proper care of the goods but this duty might be restricted or excluded by a contract or notice accompanying the bailment. The Occupiers' Liability Act 1957, s.2(1), imposes on the occupier of premises a "common duty of care" to all his visitors but does not prevent him from restricting, modifying or excluding this duty "by agreement or otherwise." An exclusion clause in a contract or, indeed, in a notice not forming part of a contract, may thus amount to a defence to an action for a breach of a common law or statutory duty.

Suppliers of goods and services have often sought to exclude or limit their possible legal liability by the inclusion of far-reaching exclusion clauses in their standard forms of contract. The courts have long been hostile to such clauses. They are not freely negotiated but are in effect imposed by the one party on the other. The supplier declares that he will contract on his standard terms and no other and his customer frequently has to accept those terms or go without the service he wants. There is no "equality of bargaining power." because of their sympathy with the weaker party, the courts have applied the rules concerning the formation and interpretation of contracts strictly in his favour, resolving any doubts against the stronger party. Thus, they have frequently held exclusion clauses to be inoperative—

(1) by holding the clause not to be part of the contract because notice of it was insufficient or too late. The relevant cases are to be found above, pp. 144–160.

(2) By construing the clause strictly against the person relying on it (*contra proferentem*) and holding it inapplicable to the events which have occured; and

(3) more controversially, by invoking the "doctrine of fundamental breach"—that a person who has committed a breach of a fundamental term or a fundamental breach of an innominate term is precluded from relying on any exemption clause, at least if the contract has been terminated as a result of the breach. The House of Lords has now twice stated that there is no rule of law to this effect—it is only an aspect of the rule of strict construction. The first case, *Suisse Atlantique*, below, p. 459, was restrictively interpreted or ignored altogether by lower courts; but, the second, *Photo Production v. Securicor*, below, p. 463 has been more effective.

Injustice arising from the use of exclusion clauses has attracted the attention of Parliament from time to time and the reader has encountered examples of statutes which invalidate such clauses in particular circumstances. Attention is drawn to the following:

(1) Road transport: Public Passenger Vehicles Act 1981, s.29 (p. 312).
(2) Liability for misrepresentation: Misrepresentation Act 1967, s.3 (p. 356).
(3) Defective Premises Act 1972, s.6 (p. 404).

As noted above, p. 28, there are now two more general and far reaching enactments—the Unfair Contract Terms Act 1977 and the Unfair Terms in

445

Consumer Contracts Regulations 1995—though neither is quite so far-reaching as it sounds. The Act came into force on February 1, 1978, and applies to contracts made on or after (but not before) that date and to liability for loss or damage suffered on or after (but not before) that date. Its title is misleading in two respects. (i) It is not concerned with all contract terms which might be thought "unfair" but with only two types of term: exclusion clauses and indemnity clauses. (ii) It is not confined to contractual terms. It applies to cases where there is no contractual relationship between the parties and an attempt is made to exclude tortious or other liability by means of a notice or other disclaimer. (*Cf. Ashdown v. Samuel Williams* (above, p. 300).)

The Regulations apply only to terms in "consumer contracts" which have not been individually negotiated and, for these purposes, only natural persons, not limited companies or other corporations, are consumers.

Far-reaching though these enactments are, the common law continues to be of importance because (i) some very important classes of contracts are outside the scope of both; and (ii) where an enactment provides that an exclusion clause is valid if reasonable the plaintiff may argue (a) that it is not part of the contract at all or (b) that, on its true construction, it does not apply to the situation which has arisen—in which case it is ineffective even if it is a reasonable clause. It is probable that the common law principles will not be applied with the same degree of strictness as before. On this consider the observations of Lord Wilberforce in the *Securicor case*, below, p. 463 and of Lord Denning in *Mitchell v. Finney Lock Seeds*, below, p. 473.

For detailed studies of the law, see Brian Coote, *Exception Clauses* (1964); David Yates, *Exclusion Clauses in Contracts* (1978); Richard Lawson, *Exclusion Clauses after the Unfair Contract Terms Act* (1978); Palmer and Yates "The Future of the Unfair Contract Terms Act" [1981] C.L.J. 108 and G. Howells, *Consumer Contract Legislation*. See annotations of the Unfair Contract Terms Act by Rogers and Clarke in *Current Law Statutes*.

Section 1. The Effect of Misrepresentation

CURTIS v. CHEMICAL CLEANING AND DYEING CO.

Court of Appeal [1951] 1 K.B. 805; [1951] 1 T.L.R. 452; 95 S.J. 253; [1951] 1 All E.R. 631

The plaintiff took a white satin wedding dress to the shop of the defendants for cleaning. On being requested by a shop assistant to sign a paper headed "Receipt," the plaintiff asked why her signature was required and was told that it was because the defendants would not accept liability for certain specified risks, including the risk of damage by or to the beads and sequins with which the dress was trimmed. The plaintiff then signed the "Receipt" which, in fact, contained the following condition: "This article is accepted on condition that the company is not liable for any damage howsoever arising." When the dress was returned there was a stain on it which could not be explained.

The county court judge found for the plaintiff. The defendants appealed.

DENNING L.J., having referred to *L'Estrange v. Graucob*, (above, p. 132) and asked, "what is a sufficient misrepresentation?" went on: In my opinion any behaviour, by words or conduct, is sufficient to be a misrepresentation if it is such as to mislead the other party about the existence or extent of the exemption. If it conveys a false impression, that is enough. If the false impression is created knowingly, it is a fraudulent misrepresentation; if it is created unwittingly, it is an innocent misrepresentation; but either is sufficient to disentitle the creator of it to the benefit of the exemption. In *R. v. Kylsant (Lord)* [1932] 1 K.B. 442 it was held that a representation might be literally true but practically false, not because of what it said, but because of what it left unsaid; in short, because of what it implied. This is as true of an innocent misrepresentation as it is of a fraudulent misrepresentation. When one party puts forward a printed form for signature, failure by him to draw attention to the existence or extent of the exemption clause may in some circumstances convey the impression that there is no exemption at all, or at any rate not so wide an exemption as that which is in fact contained in the document. The present case is a good illustration. The customer said in evidence: "When I was asked to sign the document I asked why? The assistant said I was to accept any responsibility for damage to beads and sequins. I did not read it all before I signed it." In those circumstances, by failing to draw attention to the width of the exemption clause, the assistant created the false impression that the exemption only related to the beads and sequins, and that it did not extend to the material of which the dress was made. It was done perfectly innocently, but nevertheless a false impression was created. It was probably not sufficiently precise and unambiguous to create an estoppel: *Low v. Bouverie* [1891] 3 Ch. 82, but nevertheless it was a sufficient misrepresentation to disentitle the cleaners from relying on the exemption, except in regard to beads and sequins. . . .

In my opinion when the signature to a condition, purporting to exempt a person from his common law abilities, is obtained by an innocent misrepresentation, the party who has made that misrepresentation is disentitled to rely on the exemption. . . . I therefore agree that the appeal should be dismissed.

(The judgment of SOMERVELL L.J. is omitted. SINGLETON L.J. agreed.)

Appeal dismissed.

Questions
1. What would have been the position if only the beads and sequins had been damaged?
2. What would have been the position if the plaintiff had signed the document without asking for an explanation of it?
3. The Conditions of Acceptance approved by the National Federation of Dyers and Cleaners included the following term: "None of our agents or employees has any authority to alter, vary or qualify in any way these terms and conditions." Would this term have protected the defendants in the *Curtis* case? Consider note, above p. 446, *Overcombe Estates v. Glencombe Properties Ltd* [1974] 2 All E.R. 511 and UTCC Regulations 5(1) and Sched. 3, sub-para. 1(n).

Section 2. The Interpretation of the Clause

Regulation 6 of the Unfair Terms Regulations 1994 provides:

"**Construction of written contracts.** A seller or supplier shall ensure that any written term of a contract is expressed in plain, intelligible language, and if there is any doubt about the meaning of a written term, the interpretation most favourable to the consumer shall prevail."

The first half of this provision seems little more than a pious exhortation to sellers and suppliers; but the second half is, in substance, the *contra proferentem* rule of construction which, in English law, applies not only to sale and supply contracts with consumers but to contracts generally. See particularly the examples discussed below, pp. 451–459.

"ISTROS" (OWNERS) v. F. W. DAHLSTROEM & CO.

King's Bench Division [1931] 1 K.B. 247; 18 Asp.M.L.C. 177

A charterparty provided by clause 8: "Captain to prosecute all voyages with utmost dispatch ..."; and by clause 12: "Owners only to be responsible ... for delay ... if ... caused by want of due diligence on the part of owners or their manager in making steamer seaworthy and fitted for the voyage, or any other personal act or omission, or default of owners or their manager." The captain failed to prosecute the voyage with the utmost dispatch and the charterer withheld part of the hire in respect of the delay. An umpire ordered that the sum withheld should be paid; and the question for the court was whether this award was right in law.

WRIGHT J.: In my opinion the award is right in law and I, therefore, order that it shall stand. Clause 12 appears to me, so far as the facts of this particular case are concerned, to be quite clear. There has been no want of due diligence on the part of the owner or his manager in making the ship seaworthy and fitted for the voyage, and there has been no other personal act, or omission, or default on the part of either of them. Any neglect or default that there has been, has been that of the owner's servants. The umpire has found that there was neglect or default by the master and that that caused the delay. That seems to me to come within the precise words of clause 12.

It is not necessary here to consider whether every possible case that may arise under clause 8 of a failure on the part of the captain to prosecute all voyages with utmost dispatch is covered by clause 12. I have not in my mind at this moment any specific type of a breach of clause 8 by act of the captain for which, notwithstanding clause 12, the owner would be responsible. There may be such cases, but it seems to me that clause 12 must receive effect where the case comes within its clear terms.

If the effect is to render the owner free from any liability for loss or delay where there is a failure on the part of the captain to prosecute the voyage with the utmost dispatch, then I think that the owner is entitled to the full benefit of that clause. Clause 8, it may be said, has then no practical effect. It has a practical effect to the extent that it contains clear recognition of the duty of the captain so to act, and the effect of clause 12 is not to modify or qualify the existence of that duty, although it may operate if an action is brought against the owner for damages as a defence. In one sense, every exception clause is *pro tanto* inconsistent with the primary or express obligation which at law or by contract rest upon an owner or a master in respect of the goods entrusted to his charge and the duties arising under a charterpary, but, notwithstanding those obligations, exception clauses must receive in due course, if their language and the circumstances require it, their appropriate effect as a shield to a claim for damages.

I see nothing in the circumstances of this case to prevent the owner from relying here on the protection afforded to him by clause 12 of the charterparty.

Award upheld.

Questions
1. In what sense was the captain under a duty to prosecute the voyage with the utmost dispatch?
2. Was the failure of the captain a breach of contract by the owners?

Note
For a criticism of the approach to exception clauses adopted by Wright J. in the above case, see Brian Coote, *Exception Clauses*, especially Chapters 1 and 8. Professor Coote's view is that "Instead of being mere sheilds to claims based on breach of accrued rights, exception clauses substantively delimit the rights themselves" (p. 17); that is, that in the above case, it ought to have been held that there was no right to performance with the utmost dispatch—and, therefore, of course, no duty so to perform. Coote divides exception clauses into two classes: "Type A: exception clauses whose effect, if any, is upon the accrual of particular primary rights. . . . Type B: exception clauses which qualify primary or secondary rights without preventing the accrual of any particular primary right" (p. 9). Examples of Type A are that in the above case and those in *Harling v. Eddy* (above, p. 379), *Wallis v. Pratt* (above, p. 417), *Andrews v. Singer (infra)* and *Thompson v. L.M.S.* (above, p. 148). It will be found that in each of these cases the object of the clause was to exclude entirely an obligation which would otherwise arise. Type B clauses, however, merely limit the time within which a claim might be brought, as in *Smeaton Hanscomb v. Setty* [1953] 1 W.L.R. 1468 or limit the amount which might be recovered on a claim, as in *Parker v. S.E. Ry.* (above, p. 144). *Scruttons v. Midland Silicones* (above, p. 284) and *Alderslade v. Hendon Laundry* (below, p. 452).
Coote argues: "What makes the distinction between the two types significant and important is that if the effect of clauses of Type A is upon whether particular primary rights shall arise from a promise, they are directly relevant to the existence or otherwise in that promise, or substantive contractual content."
Coote conceded, however, that the current approach of the courts even to clauses of Type A was to regard them as no more than shields to breaches of accrued rights and duties.
See now, *Photo Production v. Securicor*, below, p. 463.

ANDREWS BROS. LTD v. SINGER & CO. LTD

Court of Appeal [1934] 1 K.B. 17; 103 L.J.K.B. 90; 150 L.T. 172; 39 Com.Cas. 96;
50 T.L.R. 33

The plaintiffs entered into a contract to buy "new Singer cars" from the defendants. Clause 5 of the contract provided: "All cars sold by the company are subject to the terms of the warranty set out in Schedule No. 3 of this agreement and all conditions, warranties and liabilities implied by common law, statute or otherwise are excluded." (*Cf. L'Estrange v. Graucob*, above, p. 132) The plaintiffs succeeded in an action for damages before Goddard J. on the ground that one of the cars delivered, having run a considerable mileage, was not a new car. The defendants appealed.

SCRUTTON L.J.: . . . The judge has found, and his view is not now contested, that the car tendered in this case was not a new Singer car. Does then clause 5 prevent the vendors being liable in damages for having tendered and supplied a car which is not within the express terms of the contract? Clause 5 says this: "All conditions, warranties and liabilities implied by statute, common law or otherwise are excluded." There are well-known obligations in various classes of contracts which are not expressly mentioned but are implied. During the argument Greer L.J. mentioned an apt illustration, namely, where an agent contracts on behalf of A he warrants that he has authority to make the contract on behalf of A although no such warranty is expressed in the contract. Mr Pritt relied on section 13 of the Sale of Goods Act, 1893, (see section 13 of the 1979 Act, above,

p. 401) which provides that "where there is a contract for the sale of goods by description, there is an implied condition that the goods shall correspond with the description . . .," and from that he says it follows that this particular condition comes within the words employed by the section. That, I think, is putting a very strained meaning on the word "implied" in the section. Where goods are expressly described in the contract and do not comply with that description, it is quite inaccurate to say there is an implied term; the term is expressed in the contract. Suppose the contract is for the supply of a car of 1932 manufacture, and a car is supplied which is of 1930 manufacture, there has not been a breach of an implied term; there has been a breach of an express term of the contract. It leads to a very startling result if it can be said that clause 5 allows a vendor to supply to a purchaser an article which does not comply with the express description of the article in the contract, and then, though the purchaser did not know of the matter which prevented the article supplied from complying with the express terms of the contract, to say, "We are under no liability to you because this is a condition implied by statute and we have excluded such liability."

In my view there has been in this case a breach of an express term of the contract. If a vendor desires to protect himself from liability in such a case he must do so by much clearer language than this, which, in my opinion, does not exempt the defendants from liability where they have failed to comply with the express term of the contract. For these reasons I think Goddard J. came to a correct conclusion, and this appeal therefore fails.

GREER L.J. delivered a concurring judgment and EVE J. agreed.

Note

In *L'Estrange v. Graucob* (above, p. 132) the clause provided: "This agreement contains all the terms and conditions under which I agree to purchase the machine specified above and any express or implied condition, statement, or warranty, statutory or otherwise not stated herein is hereby excluded." Scrutton L.J. referred to *Wallis v. Pratt* (above, p. 417) and *Andrews v. Singer* and said: "The clause here in question would seem to have been intended to go further than any of the previous clauses, and in order to avoid the result of these decisions, to include all terms denoting collateral stipulations." The document stated that the contract was for "One Six Column Junior Ilam Automatic Machine." The machine supplied did not work satisfactorily but it does not appear that it did not comply with the description. Would the clause have protected the seller if it had not so complied?—if, for example, a *Five* Column Junior Ilam Automatic Machine had been supplied? (Benjamin's *Sale of Goods* (1974), para. 960, suggests that the case is wrongly decided if the fundamental breach cases, decided before *Suisse Atlantique* (below, p. 459), are rightly decided.) Consider the effect of section 55 of the Sale of Goods Act 1979, above, p. 402.

Benjamin on Sale (8th ed., by Finnemore and James, 1950) 622

Referring to *Andrews v. Singer* the editors wrote: It is a little curious that the judgment in this case give a hint that the defendants might have protected themselves by a more carefully chosen wording. It is submitted that by no words can a seller avoid the strict legal consequences of a sale by description. He cannot do it by excluding all implied conditions; and it is difficult to see how he can exclude an express condition. A man cannot in one and the same contract expressly include a term (whether condition or warranty) and also exclude it; there would be no contract at all. Of course he may say that he gives no guarantee, whether condition or warranty, but that would not touch the description. Once it is established that a certain phrase is a description, and the contract is a sale by description, that is the contract, and the sale is of described goods and of nothing else. The defendant in the present case might have said: "We will appoint you agent to sell new Singer cars, but we do not bind ourselves that the cars will always be new; they may occasionally be as good as new," but then it follows that "new" would have been no part of the description. Once the court has decided that the sale was a sale by description of "new Singer cars" then nothing else could satisfy the contract and by no artifice could the seller avoid the obligation to provide new Singer cars. Startling results would follow otherwise, for, if the seller can ignore one of the three descriptive words, he can ignore the others; the article need not be a Singer car, or even a car. The seller might supply a second-hand pedal bicycle or a child's perambulator! In a sale by description one is selling a described thing or things and that is fundamental and one need not really consider conditions or warranties express or implied as ordinarily understood. A contract for the sale of one thing can never be performed by the supply of another. The questions in cases of this kind will be: (1) Was this a sale by description? (2) What was the description? The answer to the second question gives the subject-matter of the contract. Scrutton L.J. said, "In my opinion this was a contract for the sale of a new Singer car" and, it is submitted, that concluded the matter.

(See also Benjamin's *Sale of Goods* (1974, by Guest and others), paras. 936–938.)

Note

In *White v. John Warwick & Co. Ltd* [1953] 1 W.L.R. 1285 the plaintiff hired a tradesman's cycle from the defendants under a written agreement which provided that "nothing in this agreement shall render the owners liable for any personal injuries." While the plaintiff was riding the cycle the saddle titled forward and he was injured. The Court of Appeal held that the defendants were liable in negligence. In the absence of the exemption clause, the defendants might have been liable in contract for supplying a defective machine even if they were not negligent. The operation of the clause had to be confined to that stricter liability. (For a valuable note on this case, see L.C.B. Gower, 17 M.L.R. 155.)

HOLLIER v. RAMBLER MOTORS (A.M.C.), LTD

Court of Appeal [1972] 2 W.L.R. 401; [1972] 1 All E.R. 399; [1972] R.T.R. 190

For the facts and the judgment on the first point in the case, see above, p. 158.

SALMON L.J.: The principles are stated by Scrutton L.J. with his usual clarity in *Rutter v. Palmer* [1922] 2 K.B. 87, 92[1]: "For the present purposes a rougher test will serve. In construing an exemption clause certain general rules may be applied: First the defendant is not exempted from liability for the negligence of his servants unless adequate words are used; secondly, the liability of the defendant apart from the exempting words must be ascertained; then the particular clause in question must be considered; and

[1] The plaintiff left his car with the defendant, a dealer, for sale on commission. The defendant's driver, when showing the car to a prospective purchaser, negligently collided with a lamp-post.

if the only liability of the party pleading the exemption is a liability for negligence, the clause will more readily operate to exempt him."

Scrutton L.J. was far too great a lawyer, and had far too much robust common sense, if I may be permitted to say so, to put it higher than that "if the only liability of the party pleading the exemption is a liability for negligence, the clause will more readily operate to exempt him." He does not say that "if the only liability of the party pleading the exemption is a liability for negligence, the clause will necessarily exempt him." After all, there are many cases in the books dealing with exemption clauses, and in every case it comes down to a question of construing the alleged exemption clause which is then before the court. It seems to me that in *Rutter v. Palmer*, although the word "negligence" was never used in the exemption clause, the exemption clause would have conveyed to any ordinary, literate and sensible person that the garage in that case was inserting a clause in the contract which excluded their liability for the negligence of their drivers. The clause being considered in that case—and it was without any doubt incorporated in the contract—was: "Customers' cars are driven by your staff at customers' sole risk." Any ordinary man knows that when a car is damaged it is not infrequently damaged because the driver had driven it negligently. He also knows, I suppose, that if he sends it to a garage and a driver in the employ of the garage takes the car on the road for some purpose in connection with the work which the customer has entrusted the garage to do, the garage could not conceivably be liable for the car being damaged in an accident unless the driver was at fault. It follows that no sensible man could have thought that the words in that case had any meaning except that the garage would not be liable for the negligence of their own drivers. That is a typical case where, on the construction of the clause in question, the meaning for which the defendant was there contending was the obvious meaning of the clause.

The next case to which I wish to refer is the well-known case of *Alderslade v. Hendon Laundry, Ltd* [1945] 1 K.B. 189. In that case articles were sent by the plaintiff to the defendants' laundry to be washed, and they were lost. In an action by the plaintiff against the defendants for damages, the defendants relied on the following condition to limit their liability: "The maximum amount allowed for lost or damaged articles is 20 times the charge made for laundering." Again, this was a case where negligence was not expressly excluded. The question was: what do the words mean? I have no doubt that they would mean to the ordinary housewife who was sending her washing to the laundry that, if the goods were lost or damaged in the course of being washed through the negligence of the laundry, the laundry would not be liable for more than 20 times the charge made for the laundering. I say that for this reason. It is, I think, obvious that when a laundry loses or damages goods it is almost invariably because there has been some neglect or default on the part of the laundry. It is said that thieves break in and steal, and the goods (in that case handkerchiefs) might have been stolen by thieves. That of course is possible, but I should hardly think that a laundry would be a great allurement to burglars. It is a little far-fetched to think of burglars breaking into a laundry to steal the washing when there are banks, jewellers, post offices, factories, offices and homes likely to contain money and articles far more attractive to burglars. I think that the ordinary sensible housewife, or indeed anyone else who sends washing to the laundry, who saw that clause must have appreciated that almost always goods are lost or damaged because of the laundry's negligence, and, therefore, this clause could apply only to limit the liability of the laundry, when they were in fault or negligent.

Mr Tuckey has drawn our attention to the way in which the matter was put by Lord Greene M.R. in delivering the leading judgment in this court, and he contends that Lord Greene M.R. was in fact making a considerable extension to the law as laid down by Scrutton L.J. in the case to which I have referred. For this proposition he relies on the following passage in Lord Greene M.R.'s judgment at p. 192: "The effect of those authorities can I think be stated as follows: where the head of damage in respect of which limitation of liability is sought to be imposed by such a clause is one which rests on negligence and nothing else, the clause must be construed as extending to that head of damage, because it would otherwise lack subject-matter."

If one takes that word "must" au pied de la lettre that passage does support Mr Tuckey's contention. However, we are not here construing a statute, but a passage in an unreserved judgment of Lord Greene M.R., who was clearly intending no more than to restate the effect of the authorities as they then stood. It is to be observed that MacKinnon L.J., who gave the other judgment in this court, set out the rule or principle which he said was very admirably stated by Scrutton L.J. in *Rutter v. Palmer* [1922] 2 K.B. 87. He said at p. 195: "Applying that principle to the facts of the case, I think that the clause in question does avail to protect the proprietors of the laundry in respect of liability for negligence, which must be assumed to be the cause of these handkerchiefs having disappeared."

And clearly it did, for the reasons I have already given. I do not think that Lord Greene M.R. was intending to extend the law in the sense for which Mr Tuckey contends. If it were so extended, it would make the law entirely artificial by ignoring that rules of construction are merely our guides and not our masters; in the end you are driven back to construing the clause in question to see what it means. Applying the principles laid down by Scrutton L.J., they lead to the result at which the court arrived in *Alderslade v. Hendon Laundry Ltd* [1945] 1 K.B. 189. In my judgment these principles lead to a very different result in the present case. The words are: "The company is not responsible for damage caused by fire to customer's cars on the premises." What would that mean to any ordinarily literate and sensible car owner? I do not suppose that any such, unless he is a trained lawyer, has an intimate or, indeed, any knowledge of the liability of bailees in law. If you asked the ordinary man or woman: "Supposing you send your car to the garage to be repaired, and there is a fire, would you suppose that the garage would be liable?" I should be surprised if many of them did not answer, quite wrongly; "Of course they are liable if there is a fire." Others might be more cautious and say; "Well, I had better ask my solicitor," or, "I do not know. I suppose they may well be liable." That is the crucial difference, to my mind, between the present case and *Alderslade v. Hendon Laundry, Ltd* and *Rutter v. Palmer*. In those two cases, any ordinary man or woman reading the conditions would have known that all that was being excluded was the negligence of the laundry, in the one case, and the garage, in the other. But here I think the ordinary man or woman would be equally surprised and horrified to learn that if the garage was so negligent that a fire was caused which damaged their car, they would be without remedy because of the words in the condition. I can quite understand that the ordinary man or woman would consider that, because of these words, the mere fact that there was a fire would not make the garage liable. Fire can occur from a large variety of causes, only one of which is negligence on the part of the occupier of the premises, and that is by no means the most frequent cause. The ordinary man would I think say to himself: "Well, what they are telling me is that if there is a fire due to any cause other than their own negligence they are not responsible for it." To my mind, if the defendants were seeking to exclude their responsibility for a fire caused by their own negligence, they ought to have done so in far plainer language than the language here used.

[Salmon L.J. then discussed *Olley v. Marlborough Court, Ltd* (above, p. 147) which the court had also considered on the basis that the notice did become part of the contract and that the defendants were not common innkeepers (who, in the absence of agreement to the contrary, are subject to strict liability in respect of the goods of guests).]

Denning L.J. said at p. 550: "Ample content can be given to the notice by construing it as a warning that the hotel company is not liable, in the absence of negligence. As such it serves a useful purpose. It is a warning to the guest that he must do his part to take care of his things himself, and, if need be, insure them. It is unnecessary to go further and to construe the notice as a contractual exemption of the hotel company from their common law liability for negligence."

Similarly, I think, in this case the words at the bottom of this form can be given ample content by construing them as a warning in the sense that I have already indicated. It seems plain that if the notice in the bedroom of the hotel had read as follows: "Proprietors will not hold themselves responsible for articles lost or stolen, nor for the damage or destruction of articles caused by fire," and then there had been a full stop, and the notice went on to say that to avoid articles being lost or stolen they should be handed to the manageress for safe custody, by a parity of reasoning the court must have come to the conclusion that the notice would not have excluded the hotel proprietors from liability for the loss of articles by a fire caused by their own negligence.

Stamp L.J. and Latey J. delivered judgment allowing the appeal.

Appeal allowed.

Questions

1. Would the clause in *Hollier* have protected the defendant if the plaintiff's car had been damaged by negligent *driving?* Cf. the discussion of *Rutter v. Palmer.* Could the clause (p. 159) be so construed that one half of it excluded liability for negligence while the other did not?

2. Lord Greene's statement in *Alderslade* (above, pp. 452–453) related to *limitation of liability.* Was it not correct for limitation, as distinct from exclusion of liability? A limitation clause cannot have the declaratory function attributed by the court to an exclusion clause. There could be no point in limiting a liability which could never arise. If the only liability which could arise would be in negligence, does it not follow that the clause, if it has any meaning at all, *must,* as Lord Greene said, apply to liability in negligence?

Note

The courts distinguish between cases where, in the absence of any exclusion clause, (i) the defendant may be held liable only if he is negligent (N) and (ii) the defendant may be held liable if he is negligent or even if he is not (strict liability (SL)). This may be illustrated diagramatically:

(i)   (ii)

If the clause is held to be not merely declaratory of the position at common law but to be intended to affect the relationship between the parties and is not expressed to cover negligence then it will be construed to limit or exclude the liability for negligence in (i) because there is nothing else for it to apply to; but to exclude only the strict liability in (ii); thus;

(i)   (ii)

There is the possibility, however, that the defendant may have been guilty of something worse than negligence; for example, being the bailee of a fur coat for cleaning, he has given it away to his girlfriend. No reasonable man would suppose that even the most far-reaching clause in a dry-cleaning contract entitled the cleaner to do that. Imagine reaction to a suggestion by the officious bystander that this was what they were agreeing to. There is thus the possibility of a third type of liability which, for want of a better term, may be called fundamental breach (FB). A complete diagram of potential liability is then as follows:

(i)   (ii)

If we apply the exclusion clause envisaged above to this situation we reach the following result:

(i)   (ii)

Where goods have been lost, there may be no direct evidence of either negligence or of fundamental breach and the question of onus of proof is then of crucial importance.

In *Woolmer v. Delmer Price* [1955] 1 Q.B. 291 the plaintiff left a mink coat with the defendants for storage or resale. The defendants failed to comply with a demand for the return of the coat and were unable to adduce satisfactory evidence as to what had happened to it. In an action in detinue the defendants relied on a clause in their receipt, "All goods left at customer's risk." McNair J. said that it must be assumed that there was negligence on the part of the launderer in the *Alderslade* case (above, p. 452) whereas in the present case it was not proved whether the loss did or did not occur through negligence. The coat might have been sold in mistake and its sale mistakenly recorded as that of another coat [would not this have been negligence]? or it may have been put into store at a place not permitted by the contract which would have been a fundamental breach. The implication is that if the defendants had been able to prove that they lost the coat through negligence, they would have been protected by the clause.

In *Hunt & Winterbotham v. B.R.S. (Parcels) Ltd* [1962] 1 Q.B. 617, which concerned a contract of carriage, the Court of Appeal agreed that the onus was on the carrier to show that the loss of the goods was not due to his negligence but said that was a very different thing from saying that he must also prove the absence of any fundamental breach. There was, however, no allegation of fundamental breach in that case.

LEVISON AND ANOTHER v. PATENT STEAM CARPET CLEANING CO. LTD

Court of Appeal [1978] Q.B. 69; [1977] 3 W.L.R. 90; [1977] 3 All E.R. 498

The plaintiffs telephoned the defendants and asked them to collect a carpet for cleaning. It was a Chinese carpet worth £900. At the defendant's van driver's request, Mr L signed the defendant's order form. He did not read it. By clause 2(a), the maximum value of the carpet, based on its area, was deemed to be £40. Clause 5 provided "All merchandise is expressly accepted at the owner's risk" and recommended owners to insure their goods. The carpet was lost. The plaintiffs recovered £900 damages. The defendants appealed, contending that they were exempt from liability for negligence by virtue of clause 5, that on a balance of probabilities the loss was due to their negligence, not a fundamental breach, and the burden of proving that the loss was due to fundamental breach lay on the plaintiffs.

LORD DENNING M.R. said that, on the construction of the contract, the liability of the defendants was limited to £40; but that, notwithstanding *Suisse Atlantique*, the doctrine of fundamental breach still applied to standard form contracts where there was inequality of bargaining power. [But see *Photo Productions v. Securicor*, below, p. 463.] His Lordship continued:

This brings me to the crux of the case: on whom is the burden of proof? Take the present case. Assuming that clause 2(a) or clause 5, or either of them, limits or exempts the cleaners from liability for negligence, but not for a fundamental breach. On whom is the burden to prove that there was fundamental breach?

On principle, I should have thought that the burden was on the cleaners to prove that they were not guilty of a fundamental breach. After all, Mr Levison does not know what happened to it. The cleaners are the ones who know, or should know, what happened to the carpet, and the burden should be on them to say what it was. It was so held by McNair J. in *Woolmer v. Delmer Price Ltd* (above, p. 455); and by me in *J. Spurling Ltd v. Bradshaw* [1956] 1 W.L.R. at 466, and by the East African Court of Appeal in *United Manufacturers Ltd v. WAF Co. Ltd.* A contrary view was expressed by this court in *Hunt & Winterbotham (West of England) Ltd v. B.R.S. (Parcels) Ltd* (above, p. 455); and there is a long line of shipping cases in which it has been held that, if a shipowner makes a prima facie case that the cause of the loss was one of the excepted perils, the burden is on the shipper to prove that it was not covered by the exception: see the cases from *The Glendarroch* [1894] P. 266, and *Munro, Brice & Co. v. War Risks Association Ltd* [1918] 2 K.B. 78, to which there may be added *Joseph Constantine Steamship Line Ltd v. Imperial Smelting Corpn. Ltd, The Kingswood* (below, p. 539).

It is, therefore, a moot point for decision. On it I am clearly of opinion that, in a contract of bailment, when a bailee seeks to escape liability on the ground that he was not negligent or that he was excused by an exception or limitation clause, then he must know what happened to the goods. He must prove all the circumstances known to him in which the loss or damage occurred. If it appears that the goods were lost or damaged without any negligence on his part, then, of course, he is not liable. If it appears that they were lost or damaged by a slight breach, not going to the root of the contract, he may be protected by the exemption or limitation clause. But, if he leaves the cause of loss or damage undiscovered and unexplained, then I think he is liable: because it is then quite likely that the goods were stolen by one of his servants; or delivered by a servant to the wrong address; or damaged by reckless or wilful misconduct; all of which the offending servant will conceal and not make known to his employer. Such conduct would be a fundamental breach against which the exemption or limitation clause will not protect him.

The cleaning company in this case did not show what had happened to the carpet. They did not prove how it was lost. They gave all sorts of excuses for non-delivery and eventually said it had been stolen. Then I would ask: by whom it was stolen? Was it by one of their servants? or with his connivance? Alternatively, was it delivered by one of their servants to the wrong address? In the absence of any explanation, I would infer that it was one of these causes. In none of them would the cleaning company be protected by the exemption or limitation clause.

ORR L.J. and SIR DAVID CAIRNS held that the words of clause 5 exempted the defendants from liability for negligence but were not sufficiently clear or strong to exempt them from liability for so fundamental or radical a breach as, say, misdelivery of the carpet; and they agreed with Lord Denning that the onus of proving that the loss was not due to fundamental breach was on the defendants and that they had not discharged it.

Appeal dismissed.

Questions
1. Suppose that the carpet had been misdelivered because of a mistake by the van driver, Why would not that be negligence and so covered by cl. 5?
2. Suppose that the carpet was stolen by one of the defendants' employees. The defendants may have been negligent in employing him, or they may not. Should the company be held to have committed "a fundamental breach" when the *company*—the directors and managerial staff—were not even negligent?
3. Consider the effect of the Unfair Contract Terms Act, s.2(2) and s.3 and of reg. 4 of the Regulations. Is it unreasonable or unfair for a cleaning company to say that they will accept a carpet only if the owner agrees to take the risk, against which they advise him to insure? *Cf.* S. M. Males [1978] C.L.J. 24, 26: ". . . even if the defendants had pointed out the exemption clause, why should Mr Levison have worried? He was insured. Indeed, knowing himself to be insured, he had no need even to bother to read the form." Does the decision benefit anyone but the insurance company?

SZE HAI TONG BANK LTD v. RAMBLER CYCLE CO. LTD

Privy Council [1959] A.C. 576; [1959] 3 W.L.R. 214; 103 S.J. 567; [1959] 3 All E.R. 182; [1959] 2 Lloyd's Rep. 114

The respondent shipped goods under a bill of lading which required delivery "unto order or his or their assigns" and provided that the responsibility of the carrier should cease absolutely after the goods had been discharged from the ship. After the goods had been discharged into a warehouse in Singapore the carrier-agents released them to the consignee without requiring production of the bill of lading. The consignee never paid for the goods. The carrier was held liable for breach of contract and conversion of the goods.

LORD DENNING: . . . it is contended that [the exemption clause] is wide enough to absolve the shipping company from responsibility for the act of which the Rambler Cycle Co. complains, that is to say, the delivery of the goods to a person who, to their knowledge, was not entitled to receive them. If the exemption clause upon its true construction absolved the shipping company from an act such as that, it seems that by parity of reasoning they would have been absolved if they had given the goods away to some passer-by or had burnt them or had thrown them into the sea. If it had been suggested to the parties that the condition exempted the shipping company in such a case, they would both have said: "Of course not." There is, therefore, an implied limitation on the clause, which cuts down the extreme width of it: and, as matter of construction, their Lordships decline to attribute to it the unreasonable effect contended for.

But their Lordships go further. If such an extreme width were given to the exemption clause, it would run counter to the main object and intent of the contract. For the contract, as it seems to their Lordships, has, as one of its main objects, the proper delivery of the goods by the shipping company "unto order or his or their assigns," against production of the bill of lading. It would defeat this object entirely if the shipping company were at liberty, at its own will and pleasure, to deliver the goods to somebody else, not entitled at all, without being liable for the consequences. The clause must therefore be modified to the extent necessary to enable effect to be given to the main object and intent of the contrat: see *Glynn v. Margetson & Co.* [1893] A.C. 351, 357; *G. H. Renton & Co. Ltd v. Palmyra Trading Corpn. of Panama* [1956] 1 Q.B. 462, 501.

To what extent is it necessary to limit or modify the clause? It must at least be modified so as not to permit the shipping company deliberately to disregard its obligations as to delivery. For that is what has happened here. The shipping company's agents in Singapore acknowledged: "We are doing something we know we should not do." Yet they did it. And they did it as agents in such circumstances that their acts were the acts of the shipping company itself. And they deliberately disregarded one of the prime obligations of the contract. No court can allow so fundamental a breach to pass unnoticed under the cloak of a general exemption clause: see *The Cap Palos* [1909] A.C. 369.

The self-same distinction runs through all the cases where a fundamental breach has disentitled a party from relying on an exemption clause. In each of them there will be found a breach which evinces a deliberate disregard of his bounden obligations. Thus, in *Bontex Knitting Works Ltd v. St. John's Garage* (1943) 60 T.L.R. 44, the lorry driver left the lorry unattended for an hour, in breach of an express agreement for immediate delivery. In *Alexander v. Railway Executive* [1951] 2 K.B. 882 the cloak-room official allowed an unauthorised person to have access to the goods, in breach of the regulations in that behalf. In *Karsales (Harrow) Ltd v. Wallis* [1956] 1 W.L.R. 936 the agent of the finance company delivered a car which would not go in breach of its obligation to deliver one that would go. . . . It might have been different if the servant had merely been negligent or inadvertent.

Note

Exclusion or limitation? There are three important distinctions between a clause which purports to exclude liability altogether and one which purports to limit liability. Thus—

1. An exclusion clause may be inconsistent with an express term (and therefore have to give way to it) whereas a limitation clause may be quite compatible with the same express term. Thus—

      (i) "We undertake to exercise due care . . ." and—
      (ii) "We are not to be liable for our negligence . . ."—

are inconsistent in that (ii), if valid, destroys (i) as a contractual undertaking. But

      (i) "We undertake to exercise due care . . ." and

(ii) "If we fail to exercise due care our liability shall be limited to £1,000"
—are perfectly compatible.

2. An exclusion clause may have the merely declaratory function attributed by the Court to the clause in *Hollier v. Rambler Motors* above, p. 158, so that the clause has no effect on the rights and duties of the parties; but a limitation clause cannot be declaratory and therefore must limit at least some kind of liability which might arise. (*Alderslade v. Hendon Laundry* and Question 2 and Note, above p. 454.)
3. A limitation clause is not to be construed as rigidly and strictly as an exclusion clause.

AILSA CRAIG FISHING CO. LTD v. MALVERN FISHING CO. LTD AND ANOTHER

House of Lords [1983] 1 W.L.R. 964; [1983] 1 All E.R. 101

Securicor agreed to provide a security service to Ailsa Craig Ltd's fishing boats in Aberdeen harbour. Because of negligence consisting in a total or partial failure to provide the service contracted for, a fishing boat belonging to Ailsa Craig sank and took with it another boat belonging to Malvern. The contract contained both an exclusion and a limitation clause. The Court of Session held that liability had been limited but not excluded. Ailsa Craig appealed against that decision insofar as it held that liability had been limited. The House of Lords unanimously dismissed the appeal.

LORD FRASER, having referred to the strict principles to be applied when construing exclusion clauses went on—

"In my opinion these principles are not applicable in their full rigour when considering the effect of clauses merely limiting liability. Such clauses will of course be read *contra proferentem* and must be clearly expressed, but there is no reason why they should be judged by the specially exacting standards which are applied to exclusion and indemnity clauses. The reason for imposing such standards on these clauses is the inherent improbability that the other party to a contract including such a clause intended to release the proferens from a liability that would otherwise fall upon him. But there is no such high degree of improbability that he would agree to a limitation of the liability of the proferens, especially when, as explained in condition (4) (i) of the present contract, the potential losses that might be caused by the negligence of the proferens or its servants are so great in proportion to the sums that can reasonably be charged for the services contracted for. It is enough in the present case that the clause must be clear and unambiguous."

SUISSE ATLANTIQUE SOCIÉTÉ D'ARMEMENT MARITIME S.A. v. N.V. ROTTERDAMSCHE KOLEN CENTRALE

House of Lords [1967] 1 A.C. 361; [1966] 2 W.L.R. 944; [1966] 2 All E.R. 61

By a charterparty dated December, 1956, the respondents agreed to charter a vessel from the appellants for the carriage of coal from the United States to Europe. The charter was to remain in force for a total of two years' consecutive voyages. The vessel had with all possible dispatch to sail and proceed to a port in the United States and, having loaded a cargo of coal, proceed with all possible dispatch to a port in Europe. She had to be loaded at a specified rate per running day and, if she was detained beyond the loading time, the respondents were to pay $1,000 a day demurrage. Similarly, if she were detained longer than was required to unload her at the stipulated rate per day and that was not due to strikes, etc., or other causes beyond the control of the respondents, the respondents, who were to discharge the cargo, were to pay demurrage at the rate of $1,000 a day. In September, 1957, the appellants regarded themselves as entitled to treat the charterparty as repudiated by reason of the respondents' delays in loading and discharging the vessel. That was not accepted by the respondents, and, in October, 1957, the appellants and respondents agreed, without prejudice to their dispute, that from thenceforward the charterparty would be carried out. Between then and the end of the charter the vessel made eight round voyages. The appellants alleged that, due to delays in loading and unloading for which the respondents were responsible, the vessel did not make as many voyages as she should have done, with the result that they were deprived of the freights they would have earned on the additional voyages and, after giving credit for the demurrage payments received by them, claimed damages from the respondents in respect of voyages which, they said, ought to have been completed between October 19, 1957, and the end of the charterparty. The appellants contended that, if the delays for which the respondents were responsible were such as to entitle the appellants to treat the charterparty as repudiated, the demurrage provisions did not apply and they were entitled to recover the full loss that they had suffered.

Mocatta J. gave judgment in favour of the respondents and the appellants' appeal to the Court of Appeal was dismissed. The appellants appealed to the House of Lords.

VISCOUNT DILHORNE and LORDS REID, HODSON and UPJOHN delivered opinions in favour of the respondents.

LORD WILBERFORCE: . . . The appellants' main argument in law is formulated as follows: First, they say that a breach of contract which goes to the root of the contract or which conflicts with its main purpose is a deviation from or a repudiation or fundamental breach of such contract. Secondly, they contend that exceptions clauses do not apply to breaches which are deviations from or repudiations or fundamental breaches of the contract. These propositions contain in themselves implicitly or explicitly several distinct lines of argument. It is necessary to separate the strands before attempting to examine them. It is convenient first to segregate the reference to what is sometimes (and conveniently) described as the main purpose rule. This is a rule of construction, a classic statement of which is found in Lord Halsbury's speech in *Glynn v. Margetson* [1893] A.C. 351 at p. 357: it can be summed up in his words:

"Looking at the whole of the instrument, and seeing what one must regard, as its main purpose, one must reject words, indeed whole provisions, if they are inconsistent with what one assumes to be the main purpose of the contract."

The decision in that case was that printed words in a document intended to be used in a variety of contracts of affreightment between a variety of ports ought to be restricted so as to be consistent with the purpose of the particular charterparty which was for a voyage from Malaga to Liverpool. There is no difficulty as to this, and I shall consider in due course whether it has any application to the relevant clause (that is, the demurrage clause) in the contract.

Next for consideration is the argument based on "fundamental breach" or, which is presumably the same thing, a breach going "to the root of the contract." . . .

The conception . . . of "fundamental breach" as one which, through ascertainment of the parties' contractual intention, falls outside an exceptions clause is well recognised and comprehensible. Is there any need, or authority, in relation to exceptions clauses, for extension of it beyond this? In my opinion there is not. The principle that the contractual intention is to be ascertained—not just grammatically from words used, but by consideration of those words in relation to commercial purpose (or other purpose according to the type of contract)—is surely flexible enough, and though it may be the case that adhesion contracts give rise to particular difficulties in ascertaining or attributing a contractual intent, which may require a special solution, those difficulties need not be imported into the general law of contract nor be permitted to deform it.

The only new category of "fundamental breach" which in this context I understand to have been suggested is one of "deliberate" breaches. This most clearly appears in the Privy Council case of *Sze Hai Tong Bank Ltd v. Rambler Cycle Co. Ltd* (above, p. 457). The decision itself presents no difficulty and seems to have been based on construction: it was that an exceptions clause referring to "discharge" of the goods did not apply to a discharge wholly outside the contract, a case I would have thought well within the principle of the "deviation" cases. But the appellants rely on one passage in the judgment of the Board which seems to suggest that "deliberate" breaches may, of themselves, form a separate category, citing three previous English decisions. Two of them *Alexander v. Railway Executive* [1951] 2 K.B. 882 and *Karsales (Harrow) Ltd v. Wallis* [1956] 1 W.L.R. 936 (on which I have already commented) are straightforward cases of "total departure" from what is contractually contemplated and present no difficulty. The third *Bontex Knitting Works Ltd v. St. John's Garage* (1943) 60 T.L.R. 44, does not appear to be based on the deliberate character of the breach. The decision may be justified on the basis that there was a breach of contract equivalent to a deviation, but if it goes beyond this I would regard it as of doubtful validity. The "deliberate" character of a breach cannot, in my opinion, of itself give to a breach of contract a "fundamental" character, in either sense of that word. Some deliberate breaches there may be of a minor character which can appropriately be sanctioned by damages: some may be, on construction, within an exceptions clause (for example, a deliberate delay for one day in loading). This is not to say that "deliberateness" may not be a relevant factor: depending on what the party in breach "deliberately" intended to do, it may be possible to say that the parties never contemplated that such a breach would be excused or limited; and a deliberate breach may give rise to a right for the innocent party to refuse further performance because it indicates the other party's attitude towards future performance. All these arguments fit without difficulty into the general principle: to create a special rule for deliberate acts is unnecessary and may lead astray.

I now come to the facts of the present case. First, it is necessary to decide what is the legal nature of the demurrage clause: is it a clause by which damages for breach of the contract are agreed in advance, a liquidated damages clause as such provisions are commonly called, or is it, as the appellants submit, a clause limiting damages? If it is the latter, the appellants are evidently a step nearer the point when they can invoke cases in which clauses of exception, or exemption, do not apply to particular breaches of contract. The appellants' strongest argument here rests on the discrepancy which they assert to exist between the demurrage rate of $1,000 per diem and the freight rate for which the charterparty provides. The extent of the discrepancy is said to be shown by the difference between the appellants' claim for lost freight (which is of the order of $900,000 on one calculation and $600,000 on another) and the amount which they would receive under the demurrage provision, which is approximately $150,000. So, the argument runs, the $1,000 per diem cannot be a pre-estimate of damage: it must be a limit in the charterer's favour.

I am unable to accept this. Leaving aside that the figures quoted for lost freight represent merely the owners' claim, it must be borne in mind that the $1,000-a-day figure has to cover a number of possible events. There might have been delay for one day or a few days beyond the laytime, in which case the owners might, and probably would, lose nothing in the way of freight and only suffer through increased overheads in port. Even if a case were to arise where freight was lost, over a period of two years circumstances might well change which would affect adversely the owners' anticipated rate of profit. So I am far from satisfied that any such discrepancy has been shown between the agreed figure and reality as requires the conclusion that the clause is not what on its face it purports to be—particularly when one bears in mind that each side derives an advantage from having the figure fixed and so being assured of payment without the expense and difficulty of proof.

The form of clause is, of course, not decisive, nor is there any rule of law which requires that demurrage clauses should be construed as clauses of liquidated damages; but it is the fact that the clause is expressed as one agreeing a figure and not as imposing a limit: and as a matter of commercial opinion and practice demurrage clauses are normally regarded as liquidated damage clauses. (This has the authority of *Scrutton on Charter-parties* (10th and following editions), and see *Chandris v. Isbrandtsen Moller Co. Inc.* [1951] 1 K.B. 240 at p. 249, *per* Devlin J.)

The clause being, then, one which fixes, by mutual agreement, the amount of damages to be paid to the owners of the vessel if "longer detained" than is permitted by the contract, is there any reason why it should not apply in the present case in either of the assumed alternatives, that is, either that the aggregated delays add up to "frustrating" breach of contract, or that the delays were "deliberate" in the special sense? In answering these questions it is necessary to have in mind what happened. It appears that there was an initial dispute between the owners and the charterers in which the owners claimed that they were entitled to treat the charterers as having repudiated the charterparty. This dispute was resolved by an agreement on October 8, 1957, under which the charterers agreed to pay an agreed sum as demurrage, leaving it to arbitration to decide whether the owners' claim was correct and, if so, what damages they should recover. It was further agreed that the charterparty should be performed for the remainder of the agreed two-year period. The manner in which it was performed is set out in a schedule to the consultative case. There were eight voyages in all, the last terminating on March 7, 1959, three days before the termination date. It is as regards these eight voyages that it is claimed that the delays in question occurred. During the whole of the period, although the periods spent in port on either side of the Atlantic (in fact at Rotterdam and, in every case but the first, Newport News) must have been known to the owners, who must also have been in a position to ascertain the availability of cargo and of loading and discharging facilities, the owners took no steps which would indicate that they regarded the charterparty as repudiated: they did not sail their vessel away but allowed it to continue with further voyages and took demurrage at the agreed rate for the delays. So there is no question here of any termination of the contract having taken place. Is there, then, any basis upon which the owners can escape from their bargain as regards detention of the vessel? In my opinion there is not. The arbitrators can (on the assumptions required) only find that the breach of contract falls within one, or other, or both of the two stated categories, namely, that they "frustrate the commercial purpose of the charterparty," or that the delays were "deliberate" (in the special sense). In either case, why should not the agreed clause operate? Or what reason is there for limiting its application to such delays as fall short of such as "frustrate the commercial purpose" or such as are not "deliberate"? I can see no such reason for limiting a plain contractual provision, nor is there here any such conflict between the demurrage clause and the main purpose of the contract as to bring into play the doctrine of *Glynn v. Margetson & Co.* On a consideration of the nature of this clause, together with the events which took place, and in particular the fact that the owners did not during its currency put an end to the contract, I reach the conclusion that the owners are clearly bound by it and can recover no more than the appropriate amount of demurrage.

Note

If the first dispute had not been resolved by the agreement of October 8, 1957, and the owners had sailed their ship away, it is plain that the clause in the charterparty would have had no further application; the charterers would not have been able to detain the ship when loading or unloading. The owners (assuming that they were justified in repudiating) would presumably have recovered as damages the difference between the profit they would have made under the charterparty and that which they made by employing the ship on other work. The application of the particular clause depended on the fact that the contract was affirmed. In *Harbutt's Plasticine Ltd v. Wayne Tank and Pump Co. Ltd* [1970] 1 Q.B. 447 the Court of Appeal wrongly deduced from this, and from certain dicta in the case, that the doctrine of fundamental breach was excluded only where the contract continued in existence after the breach. If the contract came to an end as a result of the breach, the effect was to avoid the exclusion clause *ab initio*, though it was (and is) well established that both frustration and avoidance for breach are not retrospective but terminate the contract only from the occurrence of the frustrating event or the act of avoidance. The contract "remains alive for the awarding of damages either for previous breaches, or for the breach which constitutes the repudiation": *Heyman v. Darwins* [1942] A.C. 356, 379, *per* Lord Wright. In that case the House held that an arbitration clause in a contract applied when one party had repudiated the contract and the other had accepted the breach. *Harbutt's* case (on this point) was overruled by the next case.

PHOTO PRODUCTION LTD v. SECURICOR TRANSPORT LTD

House of Lords [1980] A.C. 827; [1980] 2 W.L.R. 283; [1980] 1 All E.R. 556

In 1968, for a fee of £8 15s. 0d. a week the defendants agreed to provide security services, including night patrols, at the plaintiff's factory. The defendants' employee, Musgrove, while carrying out a night patrol, deliberately started a small fire which got out of control and destroyed the factory and stock, together valued at £615,000. There was no evidence that the defendants were negligent in employing Musgrove. In an action for damages, the defendants relied on the following clause in the contract.

> "Under no circumstances shall the company [Securicor] be responsible for any injurious act or default by any employee of the company unless such act or default could have been foreseen and avoided by the exercise of due diligence on the part of the company as his employer; nor, in any event, shall the company be held responsible for (a) any loss suffered by the customer through burglary, theft, fire or any other cause, except in so far as such loss is solely attributable to the negligence of the company's employees acting within the course of their employment. . . ."

MacKenna J. dismissed the action. The Court of Appeal allowed an appeal, following the *Harbutt's Plasticine* case and holding that a fundamental breach of the contract had brought it to an end and that it followed that the exemption clause could no longer be relied on. Alternatively, the clause was to be construed so as not to apply to the event which had occurred. The defendants appealed.

LORD WILBERFORCE said that the *ratio decidendi* of the *Suisse Atlantique* case was correctly summarised in the headnote: "That the question whether an exceptions clause was applicable where there was a fundamental breach of contract was one of the true construction of the contract."

His Lordship, having discussed the speeches in *Suisse Atlantique*, continued:

1. The doctrine of "fundamental breach" in spite of its imperfections and doubtful parentage has served a useful purpose. There was a large number of problems, productive of injustice, in which it was worse than unsatisfactory to leave exception clauses to operate. Lord Reid referred to these in the *Suisse Atlantique* case, pointing out at the same time that the doctrine of fundamental breach was a dubious specific. But since then Parliament has taken a hand: it has passed the Unfair Contract Terms Act 1977. This Act applies to consumer contracts and those based on standard terms and enables exception clauses to be applied with regard to what is just and reasonable. It is significant that Parliament refrained from legislating over the whole field of contract. After this Act, in commercial matters generally, when the parties are not of unequal bargaining power, and when risks are normally borne by insurance, not only is the case for judicial intervention undemonstrated, but there is everything to be said, and this seems to have been Parliament's intention, for leaving the parties free to apportion the risks as they think fit and for respecting their decisions.

At the stage of negotiation as to the consequences of a breach, there is everything to be said for allowing the parties to estimate their respective claims according to the contractual provisions they have themselves made, rather than for facing them with a legal complex so uncertain as the doctrine of fundamental breach must be. What, for example, would have been the position of the respondents' factory if instead of being destroyed it had been damaged, slightly or moderately or severely? At what point does the doctrine (with what logical justification I have not understood) decide, *ex post facto*, that the breach was (factually) fundamental before going on to ask whether legally it is to be regarded as fundamental? How is the date of "termination" to be fixed? Is it the date of the incident causing the damage, or the date of the innocent party's election, or some other date? All these difficulties arise from the doctrine and are left unsolved by it.

At the judicial stage there is still more to be said for leaving cases to be decided straightforwardly on what the parties have bargained for rather than upon analysis, which becomes progressively more refined, of decisions in other cases leading to inevitable appeals. The learned judge was able to decide this case on normal principles of contractual law with minimal citation of authority. I am sure that most commercial judges have wished to be able to do the same: see *Trade and Transport Inc v. Iino Kaiun Kaisha Ltd* [1973] 1 W.L.R. 210, 232, *per* Kerr J. In my opinion they can and should.

2. The case of *Harbutt* must clearly be overruled. It would be enough to put that upon its radical inconsistency with the *Suisse Atlantique* case (above, p. 459). But even if the matter were *res integra* I would find the decision to be based upon unsatisfactory reasoning as to the "termination" of the contract and the effect of "termination" on the plaintiff's claim for damage. I have, indeed, been unable to understand how the doctrine can be reconciled with the well accepted principle of law, stated by the highest modern authority, that when in the context of a breach of contract one speaks of "termination," what is meant is no more than that the innocent party or, in some cases, both parties, are excused from further performance. Damages, in such cases, are then·claimed under the contract, so what reason in principle can there be for disregarding what the contract itself says about damages—whether it "liquidates" them, or limits them, or excludes them? These difficulties arise in part from uncertain or inconsistent terminology. A vast number of expressions are used to describe situations where a breach has been committed by one party of such a character as to entitle the other party to refuse further performance: discharge, rescission, termination, the contract is at an end, or dead, or displaced; clauses cannot survive, or simply go. I have come to think that some of these difficulties can be avoided; in particular the use of "rescission," even if distinguished from rescission *ab initio*, as an equivalent for discharge, though justifiable in some contexts (see *Johnson v. Agnew* [1980] A.C. 367) may lead to confusion in others. To plead for complete uniformity may be to cry for the moon. But what can and ought to be avoided is to make use of these confusions in order to produce a concealed and unreasoned legal innovation: to pass, for example, from saying that a party, victim of a breach of contract, is entitled to refuse further performance, to saying that he may treat the contract as at an end, or as rescinded, and to draw from this the proposition, which is not analytical but one of policy, that all or (arbitrarily) some of the clauses of the contract lose, automatically, their force, regardless of intention.

If this process is discontinued the way is free to use such words as "discharge" or "termination" consistently with principles as stated by modern authority which *Harbutt's* case disregards. I venture with apology to relate the classic passages. In *Heyman v. Darwins Ltd* [1942] A.C. 356, 399 Lord Porter said:

> "To say that the contract is rescinded or has come to an end or has ceased to exist may in individual cases convey the truth with sufficient accuracy, but the fuller expression that the injured party is

thereby absolved from future performance of his obligations under the contract is a more exact description of the position. Strictly speaking, to say that on acceptance of the renunciation of a contract the contract is rescinded is incorrect. In such a case the injured party may accept the renunciation as a breach going to the root of the whole of the consideration. By that acceptance he is discharged from further performance and may bring an action for damages, but the contract itself is not rescinded."

And similarly Lord Macmillan at p. 373: see also *Boston Deep Sea Fishing and Ice Co. v. Ansell* (1888) 39 Ch.D. 339, 361, *per* Bowen L.J. In *Lep Air Services Ltd v. Rolloswin Investments Ltd* [1973] A.C. 331, 350, my noble and learned friend, Lord Diplock, drew a distinction (relevant for that case) between primary obligations under a contract, which on "rescission" generally come to an end, and secondary obligations which may then arise. Among the latter he includes an obligation to pay compensation, that is, damages. And he states in terms that this latter obligation "is just as much an obligation arising from the contract as are the primary obligations that it replaces." My noble and learned friend has developed this line of thought in an enlightening manner in his opinion which I have now had the benefit of reading.

These passages I believe to state correctly the modern law of contract in the relevant respects: they demonstrate that the whole foundation of *Harbutt's* case is unsound . . .

3. I must add to this, by way of exception to the decision not to "gloss" the *Suisse Atlantique* [1967] 1 A.C. 361 a brief observation on the deviation cases, since some reliance has been placed upon them, particularly upon the decision of this House in *Hain Steamship Co. Ltd v. Tate and Lyle Ltd* (1936) 155 L.T. 177 (so earlier than the *Suisse Atlantique*) in the support of the *Harbutt* doctrine. I suggested in the *Suisse Atlantique* that these cases can be regarded as proceeding upon normal principles applicable to the law of contract generally *viz.*, that it is a matter of the parties' intentions whether and to what extent clauses in shipping contracts can be applied after a deviation, that is, a departure from the contractually agreed voyage or adventure. It may be preferable that they should be considered as a body of authority *sui generis* with special rules derived from historical and commercial reasons. What on either view they cannot do is to lay down different rules as to contracts generally from those later stated by this House in *Heyman v. Darwins Ltd* [1942] A.C. 356 . . .

4. It is not necessary to review fully the numerous cases in which the doctrine of fundamental breach has been applied or discussed. Many of these have now been superseded by the Unfair Contract Terms Act 1977. Others, as decisions, may be justified as depending upon the construction of the contract (see *Levison v. Patent Steam Carpet Cleaning Co. Ltd*, above, p. 455), in the light of well known principles such as that stated in *Alderslade v. Hendon Laundry Ltd*, above, p. 452.

In this situation the present case has to be decided. As a preliminary, the nature of the contract has to be understood. Securicor undertook to provide a service of periodical visits for a very modest charge which works out at 26p. per visit. It did not agree to provide equipment. It would have no knowledge of the value of the plaintiffs' factory: that, and the efficacy of their fire precautions, would be known to the respondents. In these circumstances nobody could consider it unreasonable, that as between these two equal parties the risk assumed by Securicor should be a modest one, and that the respondents should carry the substantial risk of damage or destruction.

The duty of Securicor was, as stated, to provide a service. There must be implied an obligation to use due care in selecting their patrol-men, to take care of the keys and, I would think, to operate the service with due and proper regard to the safety and security of the premises. The breach of duty committed by Securicor lay in a failure to discharge this latter obligation. Alternatively it could be put upon a vicarious responsibility for the wrongful act of Musgrove—*viz.*, starting a fire on the premises: Securicor would be responsible for this upon the principle stated in *Morris v. C. W. Martin & Sons Ltd*, (above, p. 294). This being the breach, does condition 1 apply? It is drafted in strong terms, "Under no circumstances" . . . "any injurious act or default by any employee." These words have to be approached with the aid of the cardinal rules of construction that they must be read *contra proferentem* and that in order to escape from the consequences of one's own wrongdoing, or that of one's servant, clear words are necessary. I think that these words are clear. The respondents in fact relied upon them for an argument that since they exempted from negligence they must be taken as not exempting from the consequence of deliberate acts. But this is a perversion of the rule that if a clause can cover something other than negligence, it will not be applied to negligence. Whether, in addition to negligence, it covers other, for example, deliberate, acts, remains a matter of construction requiring, of course, clear words. I am of opinion that it does, and being free to construe and apply the clause, I must hold that liability is excluded. On this part of the case I agree with the judge and adopt his reasons for judgment. I would allow the appeal.

LORD DIPLOCK made a speech allowing the appeal.

LORD SALMON made a speech allowing the appeal. He agreed with Lord Wilberforce's analysis of *Suisse Atlantique*.

LORDS KEITH OF KINKEL and SCARMAN agreed with Lord Wilberforce.

Appeal allowed.

Questions
1. Does the decision support Professor Coote's theory of the construction of exemption clauses? (See above, p. 449, Note, and L. S. Sealy [1980] C.L.J. 252.) Did the judges decide that the clause excluded liability for a breach that had been committed or that it excluded a duty and so prevented a breach being committed? See Palmer and Yates [1981] C.L.J. 108.
2. Was the House right to assume that there was equality of bargaining power? Should the result have been different if the plaintiffs had been a new, struggling, small business? See A. Nicol and R. Rawlings (1980) 43 M.L.R. 567.
3. The first half of the exemption clause (above, p. 464) clearly exempted the defendants from either a duty or a liability for breach of a duty; but what about the second half? Did it not implicitly restrict the first half? Or does it apply to *foreseeable* acts or defaults?

Section 3. The Unfair Contract Terms Act 1977 and the Unfair Terms in Consumer Contracts Regulations 1995.

The Regulations (set out below, p. 715), which came into force on July 1, 1995, implement EEC Council Directive 93/13 on unfair terms in consumer contracts.

They were enacted without any revision of, and on top of, the statutory protection against unfair terms already existing in English law, such as the Misrepresentation Act 1967, section 3 and the 1977 Act. The result is that the 1977 Act and the Regulations (hereafter, "the Act" and "the Regulations") overlap in a rather disorderly way. Some types of contract are covered by both enactments, some only by one and some only by the other. Section 26 and schedule 1 of the Act and schedule 1 of the Regulations (below, pp. 713, 717) specify types of contract to which the Act and Regulations do not apply. The lists do not coincide, so it may be necessary to consult both. If the type of contract is not excluded by an enactment, then it is necessary to consider whether the type of term is covered.

Terms affected by the Act and terms affected by the Regulations.

(i) *The Act.*

Part I of the Act applies to terms which exclude or restrict liability and section 13(1) states "to the extent that [Part I] prevents the exclusion or restriction of liability it also prevents—

    (a) making the liability or its enforcement subject to restrictive or onerous conditions;

    (b) excluding or restricting any right or remedy in respect of the liability, or subjecting any person to any prejudice in consequence of his pursuing any such right or remedy;

    (c) excluding or restricting rules of evidence or procedure; and (to that extent) sections 2 and 5 to 7 also prevent excluding or restricting liability by reference to terms and notices which exclude or restrict the relevant obligation or duty."

Clauses requiring claims or complaints to be made within a specified time or in a specified form would be covered by paragraph (a). Paragraph (b) would apply to clauses excluding the right to rescind or avoid a contract or to withhold part of the price because of defects in the goods or services supplied. A clause stating that a customer's signature should be conclusive proof that goods comply with a contract or have a particular value would fall foul of paragraph (c).

Agreements to submit differences to arbitration, on the other hand, are not to be treated as excluding or restricting liability (section 13(2)) and so are unaffected by the Act. While a clause which *limits* the amount of damages payable on a breach of contract is covered, a clause which *fixes* the amount is probably not, and is valid if it is a liquidated damages clause (see *Suisse Atlantique*, above, p. 459) but void if it is a penalty clause (below, p. 622).

An agreement to settle an action for damages is an agreement to exclude or restrict liability but it relates to an existing liability, whereas the Act is concerned with prospective liability—liability which the parties contemplate might arise under a contract which they are about to enter into. Though section 15 provides that the Act does not affect the validity of such a settlement in Scotland and there is no corresponding provision for England, it has been held that the Act is not intended to, and does not, apply to such a settlement: *Tudor Grange Holdings Ltd v. Citibank NA* [1991] 4 All E.R. 1, Ch. D., Browne-Wilkinson V.C.

(ii) *The Regulations.*

The Regulations, on the other hand, apply to all terms in consumer contracts except—

    (i) terms which have been individually negotiated;

    (ii) terms defining the subject-matter of the contract; and

(iii) terms fixing the price or remuneration where its adequacy is in issue.

It appears that the Regulations may apply to an arbitration clause or a liquidated damages clause; but not a contract for the settlement of a dispute because that could hardly be called a consumer contract.

A long "indicative and illustrative list of terms which may be regarded as unfair" is provided in schedule 3, below, p. 718.

Consumer contracts

Both enactments use the same partial definition of "business":

> "'business' includes a profession and the activities of any government department or local or public authority:" (section 14 and reg. 2)

Sections 2 to 7 of the Act apply only to "business liability" as defined in section 1(3); so only a person who is carrying on a business will be disadvantaged by these provisions.

On the other hand, a person can benefit from the provisions of both enactments relating to consumers (some provisions of the Act, but not the Regulations, apply to parties who are not consumers) only if he is *not* acting in the course of a business. The Act provides that

> "a party to a contract 'deals as consumer' in relation to another party if—
>
> (a) he neither makes the contract in the course of a business nor holds himself out as doing so; and
> (b) The other party does make the contract in the course of a business; . . ."

The Regulations (reg. 2) provide that

> "'consumer' means a natural person who in making a contract to which these Regulations apply, is acting for purposes which are outside his business."

So a corporation, not being a "natural person," cannot benefit from the consumer provisions of the Regulations but it may be protected by the Act. It is difficult to imagine a limited company making contracts otherwise than in the course of its business; but a corporation which is a charity probably does not carry on a business and so could be a "consumer" for the purposes of the Act but not the Regulations.

Avoidance of liability for negligence

Both enactments apply to an attempt to avoid liability to a consumer for negligence but the Act also protects persons who are not consumers. Where death or personal injury is caused by negligence, the Act rules out absolutely any exclusion or restriction of liability whereas under the Regulations it is only a term "which may be regarded as unfair": schedule 3. So the injured consumer, or his personal representatives if he is dead, will be protected by the Act and there is no room for the application of the Regulations. Where the term purports to exclude or limit liability for damage to property caused by negligence, it will be invalid under the Act unless it is shown to satisfy the "requirement of reasonableness" and, under the Regulations, unless it is shown not to be an "unfair term" within the meaning of reg. 4. It is not clear that there is any material difference between the two tests. Compare schedule 2 of the Act ("Guidelines" for the Application of Reasonableness Test) with schedule 2 of the Regulations (Assessment of Good Faith). As the Act will generally be the applicable enactment, we will concentrate particularly on it.

The effect of the Act on liability for negligence

Negligence is defined by section 1(1) to include the breach of any duty to take reasonable care or exercise reasonable skill arising out of a contract or imposed by the common law or the Occupier's Liability Act 1957. The common law duty will include duties imposed by the tort of negligence and the law of bailment (see Palmer, 128 N.L.J. 887). In order to satisfy the requirement of reasonableness, a contract term must be a fair and reasonable one to be included having regard to the circumstances which were, or ought reasonably to have been, known to or in the contemplation of the parties *when the contract was made*: section 11(1). In the case of a notice not having contractual effect the requirement is that it should be fair and reasonable to allow reliance on it, having regard to all the circumstances obtaining *when the liability arose* or (but for the notice) would have arisen: section 11(3). Where the term or notice purports to restrict liability to a specified sum of money, the court must have regard to the resources which the defendant could expect to have to meet the liability and how far it was open to him to cover himself by insurance: section 11(4). The onus is on the party relying on the term to establish that it satisfies the requirement of reasonableness: section 11(5). Where a term, considered as a whole, is unreasonable, a party cannot rely on a part of the term which, considered in isolation, might be reasonable: *Stewart Gill Ltd v. Horatio Myer & Co. Ltd* [1992] 2 All E.R. 257.

A notice may be relevant evidence that the defendant has satisfied a duty of care by giving warning of a danger; but a term or notice may not negative a duty which would otherwise arise: section 13(1), which provides that sections 2 and 5 to 7 prevent the exclusion or restriction of an obligation or duty to the same extent as they prevent the exclusion or restriction of liability for breach of the duty or obligation: *Smith v. Eric S. Bush*, below, p. 477. So the words, "without responsibility on our part," which saved the defendants in *Hedley Byrne v. Heller* (above) from liability would not be effective unless the defendants persuaded the court (as they well might and as an estate agent succeeded in doing in *McCullagh v. Lane Fox and Partners Ltd*, *The Times*, December 22, 1995) that the disclaimer satisfied the requirement of reasonableness. (For discussion of section 13(1), see Palmer and Yates, [1981] C.L.J. 108, 126–134.)

Section 2(3) of the Act imposes some restriction on the defence to an action in negligence that the plaintiff had voluntarily assumed the risk—*volenti non fit injuria*. At one time it was held that a warning on the dashboard in front of the passenger seat of a private car that the passenger travelled at his own risk was effective: *Buckpitt v. Oates* [1968] 1 All E.R. 1145; *Bennett v. Tugwell* [1971] 2 All E.R. 248. These decisions were reversed by section 148(3) of the Road Traffic Act 1972 which invalidated agreements between drivers and passengers that negatived or restricted liability for personal injury or death caused while driving on a road. That section, now replaced by section 149 of the Road Traffic Act 1988, provides a more effective protection to the passenger than the Unfair Contract Terms Act because it is not confined to business liability—it would apply to the commercial traveller picking up a hitch-hiker whether he was on his way to secure an order or to the races. If a similar notice were displayed otherwise than in a motor vehicle while driving on a road, reliance on those decisions by a "business" defendant would now be subject to the provision in section 2(3) that a person's agreement to or awareness of such a notice is not of itself to be taken as indicating his voluntary assumption of any risk. It is difficult to see what would be enough, if this is not.

Avoidance of liability in contract (other than breaches consisting in negligence)

(i) *Consumer contracts.*

Here both the Act (section 3) and the Regulations operate in favour of a consumer. A term which has been individually negotiated with a consumer is, however, liable to be held invalid only under the Act, not (see reg. 3) under the

Regulations. On the other hand, there are two limitations in the Act which are not in the Regulations:

(i) Where the contract is one of sale or hire-purchase, or one under which the title to goods passes, it is a consumer transaction for the purposes of the Act only if the goods are of a type ordinarily supplied for private use or consumption. A natural person who bought a steam-roller for his private collection would probably not be able to rely on the Act, but could rely on the Regulations.

(ii) Sales by auction or competitive tender are not, in any circumstances, to be regarded as consumer transactions for the purposes of the Act, but they may be under the Regulations. A buyer of a car at an auction sale might now successfully argue that a term relating to the condition of the car was unfair.

(ii) *Non-consumer contracts on written standard terms.*

The Act, but not the Regulations, operates in favour of one who is not a consumer but who is dealing on the other party's written standard terms of business. So a limited company or a businessman may invoke the protection of the Act where he has accepted the other party's written standard terms. The party proffering the standard terms is, *ex hypothesi*, making the contract in the course of a business but the other party may or may not be. Clearly, terms will not fail to qualify as "standard" because particular matters are negotiated—price, time of performance, etc. If the whole of the written terms have been specially drafted for the particular contract, clearly they are not "standard." Standard terms may be prepared by a trade or professional organisation, for example, the R.I.B.A., or by the individual contractor. Standard terms are not necessarily signed. Parties may agree to contract on the terms stated in a catalogue, price list, sold note, ticket, etc.

The effect of section 3. The effect of section 3 is that the business party in a consumer contract or the party proffering the standard terms cannot—

(a) when in breach of contract, exclude or restrict liability, except insofar as the contract term satisfies the requirement or reasonableness; or

(b) claim to be entitled to render a contractual performance substantially different from that which was reasonably expected of him, or to tender no performance at all except insofar as the contract term authorising him to do so satisfies the requirement of reasonableness.

Para. (a) is applicable only when the defendant is in breach. If the term in question excludes the alleged promise there is no breach. See note, above, p. 449, and *Photo Production v. Securicor,* above, p. 463 (Section 13, which prevents the exclusion or restriction of obligations does not apply to section 3.) If, on the other hand, the term purports to exclude liability for breach of the promise, it is caught by the paragraph and is ineffective unless it satisfies the requirement of reasonableness.

However, the importance of the freedom of the defendant to exclude a promise under (a) is much diminished, if not entirely eliminated by para. (b). The different performance or non-performance contemplated by (b) is not a breach of contract—if it were it would be covered by (a). Para. (b) assumes that there are two ways of performing the contract. Each is a "contractual performance" but only one is "reasonably expected." Performing the contract in the other way will be a statutory breach of contract unless the term authorising it satisfies the requirement of reasonableness.

Suppose that standard terms provide—

"(i) Accommodation will be provided in the Majestic Hotel . . .

(xi) If accommodation in the Majestic Hotel is not available it will be provided in another hotel of comparable quality."

If clause (xi) is held to be an attempt to exclude liability for breach of a promise to provide accommodation in the Majestic, it is caught by para. (a) and is inoperative unless it satisfies the requirement of reasonableness; but if it is held to provide for an alternative mode of performance of the contract and the plaintiff reasonably expected to be accommodated in the Majestic, it is caught by para. (b) and is a statutory breach of contract unless the defendant shows that the term satisfies the requirement of reasonableness.

The provision in section 9(1), that an exclusion clause which is required to be reasonable survives the termination of the contract either by breach or the exercise of a right to avoid it, was designed to overrule one aspect of *Harbutt's Plasticine v. Wayne Tank* (above, p. 406). Since that case was overruled in *Photo Production Ltd v. Securicor* the subsection may, with one possible qualification, be regarded as a declaration of the common law. The qualification is that the subsection appears to acknowledge that a contract may be terminated by breach, a proposition not previously recognised; though it may be noted that in *Photo Production* Lord Wilberforce said, ". . . when in the context of a breach of contract one speaks of 'termination' what is meant is no more than that the innocent party or, *in some cases, both parties*, are excused from further performance."

Section 9(2) makes it clear that a party who, after breach, affirms the contract, may recover damages despite an exclusion clause which does not satisfy the requirement of reasonableness.

(iii) *Contracts under which Possession or Ownership of Goods Passes*
Section 6 relates to terms implied under the Sale of Goods Act 1979 and the Supply of Goods (Implied Terms) Act 1973, which governs contracts of hire-purchase; and section 7 relates to other contracts under which ownership or possession of goods passes—for example, barter, hiring or contracts for work and materials. Section 6 provides that liability for breach of the terms of section 12 of the Sale of Goods Act can never be excluded or restricted; and that liability for breach of the terms of sections 13, 14 and 15 can never be excluded or restricted against a consumer and, as against others, only insofar as the clause satisfies the test of reasonableness. The same rules apply to the corresponding provisions of the Supply of Goods Act. Where these provisions apply, there is no room for the application of the Regulations.

Section 7 makes the same provision for the other contracts, with one exception. The supplier may exclude liability for failure to give a good title if the term satisfies the requirement of reasonableness. But the new section 3(A) introduced by the Supply of Goods and Services Act 1982 substantially removes this exception because it prohibits the exclusion of liability for failure to give a good title under contracts within that Act, which include most of the contracts to which section 7 applies.

"Guidelines" for the application by the court of the reasonableness test under sections 6 and 7 are set out in Schedule 2.

(iv) *Guarantees of Consumer Goods*
Section 5 is concerned with the relationship between a manufacturer or distributor of goods and the consumer. It does not apply as between the parties to a contract under or in pursuance of which ownership or possession of goods passes. So if goods are manufactured by A, distributed by B and retailed by C to the consumer, D, the section may apply as between A and D or between B and D but not as between C and D. D will have ample remedies against C under the Sale of Goods Act. The section is concerned with saving D's rights in tort against A and B, or under any collateral contract with A or B (see p. 366 above).

A or B may offer D a guarantee of the goods in consideration of D's surrendering his potential rights of action under *Donoghue v. Stevenson* [1932] A.C. 562 or under any collateral contract there may be. Any such purported surrender of rights is invalidated by the section. If death or personal injury is caused, the term or notice is invalid under section 2 of the Act. Reliance need be placed on section 5 only in respect of damage to property or such other economic loss as may be recoverable at common law.

The section does not create any new liability. If goods merely prove useless in consumer use, section 5 does not give any remedy to the consumer against the manufacturer or distributor with whom he has no contract. Indeed, it has been suggested (see Rogers and Clark, *Current Law Statutes*) that such rights as the consumer may formerly have acquired under the guarantee have been lost since the consideration for the guarantee (the surrender of the consumer's common law rights) may have been removed because that surrender is now void.

Consider the definition of "consumer use." Is a car supplied to an employee in "consumer use" if he is allowed to use it for private as well as business purposes?

(v) *Indemnity clauses*

Section 4 applies only in favour of consumers (see section 12). A consumer may not be required by contract to indemnify any other person against a liability incurred by that other for negligence or breach of contract—unless it is shown that the requirement of reasonableness is satisfied. Suppose that D, the owner of a car ferry, obtains from P, the owner of a car, a promise to indemnify D, or D's servants, against claims arising from the negligent manoeuvring of the car. If injury is caused to a third party (whether to person or property) P can be required to indemnify D only if D shows the clause to be reasonable. If personal injury or death is caused to P himself, the clause appears to be void since section 2(1) prevents exclusion of liability and section 13(1)(b) prevents "subjecting a person to any prejudice in consequence of his pursuing any such right or remedy." A person is clearly subjected to prejudice in pursuing a remedy if he is required immediately to repay what is recovered by exercising the remedy. If the clause is void by section 2 it can hardly be saved by section 4, even if reasonable.

GEORGE MITCHELL (CHESTERHALL) LTD v. FINNEY LOCK SEEDS LTD

House of Lords [1983] 2 A.C. 803; [1983] 3 W.L.R. 163; [1983] 2 All E.R. 737; [1983] 2 Lloyd's Rep. 272

In December 1973, the appellants, seed merchants, agreed to supply the respondents, farmers, with 30 lbs of Dutch winter cabbage seed for £201.60. The seed was delivered with an invoice containing a clause purporting to limit the liability of the seller, in the event of the seed not complying with the express terms of the contract to replacing defective seed or repaying the price. The seed supplied was of a different and inferior variety with result that the crop failed and had to be ploughed in. Parker J. awarded the respondents £61,513.78 damages and £30,756 interest. The Court of Appeal dismissed the appeal, Oliver and Kerr L.JJ, Lord Denning dissenting, on the ground (i) that the clause, on its true construction, did not apply to the breach which had occurred; and, (ii), Lord Denning concurring, that it would not be fair and reasonable to permit reliance on the clause and section 55(4) of the Sale of Goods Act 1979 (above p. 402) as substituted in Schedule 1 of that Act. The House of Lords dismissed the appeal on ground (ii), agreeing with Lord Denning that the clause on its true construction did apply to the breach.

LORD DENNING M.R. (in his last judgment), having reviewed the case law and the Unfair Contract Terms Act 1977 ([1983] 1 All E.R. 108, 115):

The effect of the changes

What is the result of all this? To my mind it heralds a revolution in our approach to exemption clauses; not only where they exclude liability altogether and also where they limit liability; not only in the specific categories in the Unfair Contract Terms Act 1977, but in other contracts too. Just as in other fields of law we have done away with the multitude of cases on "common employment," "last opportunity," "invitees" and "licensees" and so forth, so also in this field we should do away with the multitude of cases on exemption clauses. We should no longer have to go through all kinds of gymnastic contortions to get round them. We should no longer have to harass our students with the study of them. We should set about meeting a new challenge. It is presented by the test of reasonableness. . . .

Fair and reasonable

There is only one case in the books so far on this point. It is *R. W. Green Ltd v. Cade Bros. Farm* [1978] 1 Lloyd's Rep. 602. There Griffiths J. held that it was fair and reasonable for seed potato merchants to rely on a limitation clause which limited their liability to the contract price of the potatoes. That case was very different from the present. The terms had been evolved over 20 years. The judge said (at 607): "They are therefore not conditions imposed by the strong upon the weak; but are rather a set of trading terms upon which both sides are apparently content to do business." The judge added (at 608): "No moral blame attaches to either party; neither of them knew, nor could be expected to know, that the potatoes were infected." In that case the judge held that the clause was fair and reasonable and that the seed merchants were entitled to rely on it.

Our present case is very much on the borderline. There is this to be said in favour of the seed merchants. The price of this cabbage seed was small: £192. The damages claimed are high: £61,000. But there is this to be said on the other side. The clause was not negotiated between persons of equal bargaining power. It was inserted by the seed merchants in their invoices without any negotiation with the farmers.

To this I would add that the seed merchants rarely, if ever, invoked the clause. Their very frank director said: "The trade does not stand on the strict letter of the clause . . . Almost invariably when a customer justifiably complains, the trade pays something more than a refund." The papers contain many illustrations where the clause was not invoked and a settlement was reached.

Next, I would point out that the buyers had no opportunity at all of knowing or discovering that the seed was not cabbage seed, whereas the sellers could and should have known that it was the wrong seed altogether. The buyers were not covered by insurance against the risk. Nor could they insure. But, as to the seed merchants, the judge said ([1981] 1 Lloyd's Rep. 476 at 480):

> "I am entirely satisfied that it is possible for seedsmen to insure against this risk. I am entirely satisfied that the cost of so doing would not materially raise the price of seeds on the market. I am entirely satisfied that the protection of this clause for the purposes of protecting against the very rare case indeed, such as the present, is not reasonably required. If and in so far as it may be necessary to consider the matter, I am also satisfied that it is possible for seedsmen to test seeds before putting them on to the market."

To that I would add this further point. Such a mistake as this could not have happened without serious negligence on the part of the seed merchants themselves or their Dutch suppliers. So serious that it would not be fair to enable them to escape responsibility for it.

In all the circumstances I am of opinion that it would not be fair or reasonable to allow the seed merchants to rely on the clause to limit their liability.

I would dismiss the appeal accordingly.

In the House of Lords, LORD DIPLOCK said that he agreed with Lord Denning and Lord Bridge; and LORDS SCARMAN, ROSKILL and BRIGHTMAN agreed with Lord Bridge.

LORD BRIDGE: My Lords, it seems to me, with all due deference, that the judgments of the learned trial judge and of Oliver L.J. on the common law issue come dangerously near to re-introducing by the back door the doctrine of "fundamental breach" which this House in *Securicor 1* [1980] A.C. 827, had so forcibly evicted by the front. The learned judge discusses what I may call the "peas and beans" or "chalk and cheese" cases, sc. those in which it has been held that exemption clauses do not apply where there has been a contract to sell one thing, for example, a motor car, and the seller has supplied quite another thing, for example, a bicycle. I hasten to add that the judge can in no way be criticised for adopting this approach since counsel appearing for the appellants at the trial had conceded "that if what had been delivered had been beetroot seed or carrot seed, he would not be able to rely upon the clause": [1981] 1 Lloyd's Rep. 476, 479. Different counsel appeared for the appellants in the Court of Appeal, where that concession was withdrawn.

The question of relative bargaining strength under paragraph (*a*) and of the opportunity to buy seeds without a limitation of the seedsman's liability under paragraph (*b*) were inter-related. The evidence was that a similar limitation of liability was universally embodied in the terms of trade between seedsmen and farmers and had been so for very many years. The limitation had never been negotiated between representative bodies but, on the other hand, had not been the subject of any protest by the National Farmers' Union. These factors, if considered in isolation, might have been equivocal. The decisive factor, however, appears from the evidence of four witnesses called for the appellants, two independent seedsmen, the chairman of the appellant company, and a director of a sister company (both being wholly-owned subsidiaries of the same parent). They said that it had always been their practice, unsuccessfully attempted in the instant case, to negotiate settlements of farmers' claims for damages in excess of the price of the seeds, if they thought that the claims were "genuine" and "justified." This evidence indicated a clear recognition by seedsmen in general, and the appellants in particular, that reliance on the limitation of liability imposed by the relevant condition would not be fair or reasonable.

Two further factors, if more were needed, weight the scales in favour of the respondents. The supply of autumn, instead of winter, cabbage seeds was due to the negligence of the appellants' sister company. Irrespective of its quality, the autumn variety supplied could not, according to the appellants' own evidence, be grown commercially in East Lothian. Finally, as the trial judge found, seedsmen could insure against the risk of crop failure caused by supplying the wrong variety of seeds without materially increasing the price of seeds.

My Lords, even if I felt doubts about the statutory issue, I should not, for the reasons explained earlier, think it right to interfere with the unanimous original decision of that issue by the Court of Appeal. As it is, I feel no such doubts. If I were making the original decision, I should conclude without hesitation that it would not be fair or reasonable to allow the appellants to rely on the contractual limitation of their liability.

I would dismiss the appeal.

Note

The modified s.55 of the Sale of Goods Act applied in *Mitchell v. Finney Lock* applies to contracts made between May 18, 1973 and February 1, 1978. Contracts made on or after February 1, 1978 are governed by the Unfair Contract Terms Act. Note that under section 55 the question is whether it is fair and reasonable "to allow reliance on the term" whereas under s.11 of the Unfair Contract Terms Act the question is whether the term was a fair and reasonable one "to be included" in the contract. In a case like *Mitchell v. Finney Lock* where the contract was made after February 1, 1978 would it be possible to take into account the fact that the sellers were guilty of serious negligence? Or of anything else occurring after the contract was made?

WALKER v. BOYLE

Chancery Division [1982] 1 W.L.R. 495; [1982] 1 All E.R. 634

The vendor of a house relied on her husband to conduct her affairs. He replied to a preliminary enquiry, believing his answer to be true, that there were no boundary disputes. The vendor knew there was a boundary dispute. Contracts were exchanged, using the National Conditions of Sale, condition 17(1) of which provided, "no error, mis-statement or omission in any preliminary answer . . . shall annul the sale." DILLON J. held that condition 17 did not apply to misrepresentations where the true facts were within the vendor's knowledge. Alternatively, the condition was invalid under section 3 of the Misrepresentation Act 1967 and section 11(1) of the Unfair Contract Terms Act 1977. He said:

It has been submitted by counsel for Mrs Boyle that as there were solicitors acting for both parties, it would be a very strong thing to say that any term of the contract which resulted is not a fair and reasonable one in the circumstances. That argument would have great force, no doubt, if the solicitors had specifically directed their minds to the problem and had evolved the clause which was under attack. In fact, however, neither solicitor directed his mind to condition 17, and they have both told me, and they are men of not inconsiderable experience as conveyancing solicitors, that they have never come across a case where any question under condition 17 has arisen. It was submitted that it was the duty of the purchaser's solicitor to advise his client, Mr Walker of the implications of condition 17 and of the other terms of the contract which Mr Walker was going to enter into, and he must be taken to have discharged that duty and satisfied himself and Mr Walker that the terms were reasonable. It is, of course, the duty of a solicitor to advise his client about any abnormal or unusual term in a contract, but I think it is perfectly normal and proper for a solicitor to use standard forms of conditions of sale such as the National Conditions of Sale. I do not think he is called on to go through the small print of those somewhat lengthy conditions with a tooth-comb every time he is advising a purchaser or to draw the purchaser's attention to every problem which on a careful reading of the conditions might in some circumstance or other conceivably arise. I cannot believe that purchasers of house property throughout the land would be overjoyed at having such lengthy explanations of the National Conditions of Sale ritually foisted on them.

It has also been submitted by counsel for Mrs Boyle that the court should be very slow to hold that a common-form clause like condition 17 is not fair and reasonable. Of course it is true that there are common-form clauses which have been evolved by negotiation between trade associations, associations of merchants or associations of growers or trade unions or other such bodies concerned to protect the rights of their members, which can be regarded as representing what consensus in the trade regards as fair and reasonable. Again, the National Conditions of Sale are not the product of negotiation between such bodies and it is plain . . . that what now appears in condition 17 has come down through the ages despite very drastic limitations imposed on it by the courts. I do not think it can be said that its precarious survival until 1977 entitles it to the automatic accolade of fairness and reasonableness.

Note
  In *Phillips Products Ltd v. Hyland* [1987] 1 W.L.R. 659 the plaintiff hired an excavator and driver from the defendant. The contract provided that the hirer was to be responsible for all damage arising in connection with the operation of the plant by the driver. The driver drove the plant into the plaintiff's buildings and caused damage. Kenneth Jones J. was not satisfied that the term was a fair and reasonable one to be included and held the defendant liable. Since the judge had not proceeded upon some erroneous principle and was not plainly and obviously wrong in his conclusion, the defendant's appeal was dismissed. In *Thompson v. T. Lohan (Plant Hire) and Another* [1987] 1 W.L.R. 649, the facts were similar except that the injury was to a third party, the plaintiff's husband, who was killed as a result of the driver's negligence. The plaintiff recovered damages. It was held that section 2 of the 1977 Act does not affect arrangements between the wrongdoer and others as to the sharing of the burden of compensation and that the term was effective to require the hirer to indemnify the owner.

SMITH v. ERIC S. BUSH (a firm)

HARRIS AND ANOTHER v. WYRE FOREST DISTRICT COUNCIL AND ANOTHER

House of Lords [1989] 2 All E.R. 514

In both these cases the question was whether a surveyor who was instructed by a mortgagee to value a house owed to the purchaser a duty of care in tort and whether a disclaimer of liability for negligence by or on behalf of the surveyor was effective. The House of Lords held that a surveyor who knew that the purchaser intended to buy the house and would rely on the valuation for which he had paid the mortgagee did owe such a duty. On the question of the effect of the disclaimer on the Unfair Contract Terms Act 1977:

LORD TEMPLEMAN: In *Harris v. Wyre Forest DC* the Court of Appeal (Kerr, Nourse L.JJ. and Caulfield J.) accepted an argument that the 1977 Act did not apply because the council by their express disclaimer refused to obtain a valuation save on terms that the valuer would not be under any obligation to Mr and Mrs Harris to take reasonable care or exercise reasonable skill. The council did not exclude liability for negligence but excluded negligence so that the valuer and the council never came under a duty of care to Mr and Mrs Harris and could not be guilty of negligence. This construction would not give effect to the manifest intention of the 1977 Act but would emasculate the Act. The construction would provide no control over standard form exclusion clauses which individual members of the public are obliged to accept. A party to a contract or a tortfeasor could opt out of the 1977 Act by declining, in the words of Nourse L.J. to recognise "their own answerability to the plaintiff's". Caulfield J. said that the Act "can only be relevant where there is on the facts a potential liability." But no one intends to commit a tort and therefore any notice which excludes liability is a notice which excludes a potential liability. Kerr L.J. sought to confine the Act to "situations where the existence of a duty of care is not open to doubt" or where there is "an inescapable duty of care." I can find nothing in the 1977 Act or in the general law to identify or support this distinction. In the result the Court of Appeal held that the Act does not apply to "negligent misstatements where a disclaimer has prevented a duty of care from coming into existence" *per* Nourse L.J. My Lords, this confuses the valuer's report with the work which the valuer carries out in order to make his report. The valuer owed a duty to exercise reasonable skill and care in his inspection and valuation. If he had been careful in his work, he would not have made a "negligent misstatement" in his report.

Section 11(3) of the 1977 Act provides that, in considering whether it is fair and reasonable to allow reliance on a notice which excludes liability in tort, account must be taken of "all the circumstances obtaining when the liability arose or (but for the notice) would have arisen." Section 13(1) of the Act prevents the exclusion of any right or remedy and (to that extent) section 2 also prevents the exclusion of liability "by reference to . . . notices which exclude . . . the relevant obligation or duty." Nourse L.J. dismissed section 11(3) as "peripheral" and made no comment on section 13(1). In my opinion both these provisions support the view that the 1977 Act requires that all exclusion notices which would in common law provide a defence to an action for negligence must satisfy the requirement of reasonableness. . . .

LORD GRIFFITHS: Section 11(3) provides:

> "In relation to a notice (not being a notice having contractual effect), the requirement of reasonableness under this Act is that it should be fair and reasonable to allow reliance on it, having regard to all the circumstances obtaining when the liability arose or (but for the notice) would have arisen."

And section 13(1) provides:

> "To the extent that this Part of this Act prevents the exclusion or restriction of any liability it also prevents—(*a*) making the liability or its enforcement subject to restrictive or onerous conditions; (*b*)

excluding or restricting any right or remedy in respect of the liability, or subjecting a person to any prejudice in consequence of his pursuing any such right or remedy; (c) excluding or restricting rules of evidence or procedure; and (to that extent) sections 2 and 5 to 7 also prevent excluding or restricting liability by reference to terms and notices which exclude or restrict the relevant obligation or duty."

I read these provisions as introducing a "but for" test in relation to the notice excluding liability. They indicate that the existence of the common law duty to take reasonable care, referred to in section 1(1)(b), is to be judged by considering whether it would exist "but for" the notice excluding liability. The result of taking the notice into account when assessing the existence of a duty of care would result in removing all liability for negligent misstatements from the protection of the Act. It is permissible to have regard to the second report of the Law Commission on *Exemption Clauses* (Law Com. No. 69), which is the genesis of the Unfair Contract Terms Act 1977, as an aid to the construction of the Act. Paragraph 127 of that report reads:

"Our recommendations in this Part of the report are intended to apply to exclusions of liability for negligence where the liability is incurred in the course of a person's business. We consider that they should apply even in cases where the person seeking to rely on the exemption clause was under no legal obligation (such as a contractual obligation) to carry out the activity. This means that, for example, conditions attached to a licence to enter on to land, and disclaimers of liability made where information or advice is given, should be subject to control . . ."

I have no reason to think that Parliament did not intend to follow this advice and the wording of the Act is, in my opinion, apt to give effect to that intention. This view of the construction of the Act is also supported by the judgment of Slade L.J. in *Phillips Products Ltd v. Hyland* [1987] 1 W.L.R. 659, when he rejected a similar argument in relation to the construction of a contractual term excluding negligence.

Finally, the question is whether the exclusion of liability contained in the disclaimer satisfies the requirement of reasonableness provided by section 2(2) of the 1977 Act. The meaning of reasonableness and the burden of proof are both dealt with in section 11(3), which provides:

"In relation to a notice (not being a notice having contractual effect), the requirement of reasonableness under this Act is that it should be fair and reasonable to allow reliance on it, having regard to all the circumstances obtaining when the liability arose or (but for the notice) would have arisen."

It is clear, then, that the burden is on the surveyor to establish that in all the circumstances it is fair and reasonable that he should be allowed to rely on his disclaimer of liability.

I believe that it is impossible to draw up an exhaustive list of the factors that must be taken into account when a judge is faced with this very difficult decision. Nevertheless, the following matters should, in my view, always be considered.

(1) Were the parties of equal bargaining power? If the court is dealing with a one-off situation between parties of equal bargaining power the requirement of reasonableness would be more easily discharged than in a case such as the present where the disclaimer is imposed on the purchaser who has no effective power to object.

(2) In the case of advice, would it have been reasonably practicable to obtain the advice from an alternative source taking into account considerations of costs and time? In the present case it is urged on behalf of the surveyor that it would have been easy for the purchaser to have obtained his own report on the condition of the house, to which the purchaser replies that he would then be required to pay twice for the same advice and that people buying at the bottom end of the market, many of whom will be young first-time buyers, are likely to be under considerable financial pressure without the money to go paying twice for the same service.

(3) How difficult is the task being undertaken for which liability is being excluded? When a very difficult or dangerous undertaking is involved there may be a high risk of failure which would certainly be a pointer towards the reasonableness of excluding liability as a condition of doing the work. A valuation, on the other hand, should present no difficulty if the work is undertaken with reasonable skill and care. It is only defects which are observable by a careful visual examination that have to be taken into account and I cannot see that it places any unreasonable burden on the valuer to require him to accept responsibility for the fairly elementary degree of skill and care involved in observing, following up and reporting on such defects. Surely it is work at the lower end of the surveyor's field of professional expertise.

(4) What are the practical consequences of the decision on the question of reasonableness? This must involve the sums of money potentially at stake and the ability of the parties to bear the loss involved, which, in its turn, raises the question of insurance. There was once a time when it was considered improper even to mention the possible existence of insurance cover in a lawsuit. But those days are long past. Everyone knows that all prudent, professional men carry insurance, and the availability and cost of insurance must be a relevant factor when considering which of two parties should be required to bear the risk of a loss. We are dealing in this case with a loss which will be limited to the value of a modest house and against which it can be expected that the surveyor will be insured. Bearing the loss will be unlikely to cause significant hardship if it has to be borne by the surveyor but it is, on the other hand, quite possible that it will be a financial catastrophe for the purchaser who may be left with a valueless house and no money to buy another. If the law in these circumstances denies the surveyor the right to exclude his liability, it may result in a few more claims but I do not think so poorly of the surveyors' profession as to believe that the floodgates will be opened. There may be some increase in surveyors' insurance premiums which will be passed on to the public, but I cannot think that it will be anything approaching the figures involved in the difference between the Abbey National's offer of a valuation without liability and a valuation with liability discussed in the speech of my noble and learned friend Lord Templeman. The result of denying a surveyor, in

the circumstances of this case, the right to exclude liability will result in distributing the risk of his negligence among all house purchasers through an increase in his fees to cover insurance, rather than allowing the whole of the risk to fall on the one unfortunate purchaser.

I would not, however, wish it to be thought that I would consider it unreasonable for professional men in all circumstances to seek to exclude or limit their liability for negligence. Sometimes breathtaking sums of money may turn on professional advice against which it would be impossible for the adviser to obtain adequate insurance cover and which would ruin him if he were to be held personally liable. In these circumstances it may indeed be reasonable to give the advice on a basis of no liability or possibly of liability limited to the extent of the adviser's insurance cover.

[The House held that the disclaimers failed to satisfy the requirement of reasonableness and were ineffective.]

Note
See a discussion of *Smith v. Bush* by Professor M. P. Furmston in [1989] All E.R. Annual Review 79. The case was considered by the House of Lords in *Caparo Industries plc. v. Dickman* [1990] 1 All E.R. 568 and by Hoffmann J. in *Morgan Crucible Co. plc. v. Hill Samuel Bank Ltd* [1990] 3 All E.R. 330.

CHAPTER 13

INITIAL IMPOSSIBILITY AND MISTAKE

This and the following chapter deal with (i) a group of cases which normally appear in textbooks in a chapter on "Mistake," and (ii) cases which are normally dealt with in a chapter on "Frustration" in a part of the textbook concerned with "Discharge of the Contract." In both types of case there is a complete agreement between the parties. (The cases of "mistake" where the parties never reach a true agreement are thought to raise a quite different problem—one of offer and acceptance—and are therefore considered in Part I of this book.) The problem in each chapter is basically the same: Does the occurrence (or non-occurrence) of some event or the existence (or non-existence) of some fact destroy the obligations which would otherwise arise under the contract? The only difference is that in (i) the fact or event exists or occurs *before* the formation of the contract, in (ii) *after* its formation. A contracts that he will sell his car to B next week. Unknown to either of them, it was destroyed five minutes ago. That is typical of the first group of problems. It is destroyed five minutes later. That is typical of the second group. If the parties had agreed, "This contract shall be avoided if the car shall be destroyed now or at any time before the completion of the sale and delivery," it would be obvious that the existence of the car was a condition precedent to the existence or the performance of the contract. If, as is usually the case, the parties have not adverted to the possibility of the occurrence of such an event and the court nevertheless holds that its effect is to avoid the contract, the most obvious explanation (in the light of the traditional common law view that the court will neither make nor amend a bargain) would seem to be that this has been done by virtue of an implied condition precedent. This theory has played an important part in the development of the law but has been regarded with considerable scepticism by modern writers and judges.

Where the subject-matter of a contract has ceased to exist before the contract was made, or has never existed, an implied term theory would seem to allow three possible solutions:

(i) A impliedly promised B that the thing existed.
(ii) A impliedly promised B that he had taken reasonable care to ascertain that the thing existed.
(iii) A and B proceeded on a common assumption, for which neither was more responsible than the other, that the thing existed and its existence was a condition precedent to the contract.

When the thing did not exist, A would be liable for damages in (i), and, if he had not taken reasonable care, in (ii); whereas in (iii), and in (ii) if A had taken reasonable care, both parties would be discharged from liability—that is, the contract would be effectively void.

Which is the right term to imply depends on the circumstances, particularly the relative means of knowledge of the parties and whether one was relying on the other. Is there some merit in an implied term theory which admits of flexibility and permits the court to adopt the solution which most nearly fits the assumptions and intentions on which the contracting parties, as reasonable men, appear to have proceeded?

HASTIE v. COUTURIER

Exchequer Chamber (1853) 9 Ex. 102; 156 E.R. 43

The plaintiffs, merchants at Smyrna, shipped a cargo of Indian corn at Salonica and sent the charterparty and bill of lading to their London agent, who employed the defendant to sell the cargo. On May 15, 1848, the defendant sold the cargo to Callender and sent him a bought note which stated that he had bought of them "1,180 quarters of Salonica Indian corn of fair average quality when shipped at 27s. per quarter, free on board, and including freight and insurance to a safe port in the United Kingdom, payment at two months from this date upon handing over shipping documents." The vessel sailed from Salonica on February 23 and met with tempestuous weather. The cargo became so heated and fermented that the vessel was obliged to put into Tunis Bay, where the cargo was found to be unfit to be carried further and sold. On May 23 Challender gave the plaintiffs notice that he repudiated the contract on the ground that at the time of the sale to him the cargo did not exist. The defendant was a *del credere* agent (one who guarantees the performance of their contracts by persons whom he introduces to his principal) and the plaintiffs brought an action against him to recover the price of the cargo. The question, therefore, was whether the purchaser was bound to pay for the cargo, because, if he was, the defendant was liable to make good his default. Martin B ruled that the contract imported that, at the time of sale, the corn was in existence as such and capable of delivery, and that, as it had been sold, the plaintiffs could not recover.

The Court of Exchequer held, Pollock C.B. dissenting, that the true meaning of the contract was that the purchaser bought the cargo if it existed at the date of the contract; but that if it had been damaged or lost, he bought the benefit of the insurance. Parke B., delivering the judgment of the court, said: "It is very true that, when there is a sale of a specific chattel (not a contract to sell and deliver a chattel *in futuro*), there is an implied undertaking that it exists; and if there were nothing in this case but a bargain and sale of a certain cargo on May 15, there would be an engagement by the vendor, or a condition, that the cargo was in existence at that time; but in this case there is a great deal more." Having considered the terms of the contract, he concluded: "We think, therefore, that the true meaning of the contract was, that the purchaser bought the cargo, if it existed at the date of the contract; but if it had been damaged or lost, he bought the benefit of the insurance, but no more" (155 E.R. 1250; 8 Ex. 40).

On a bill of exceptions the judgment of the Court of Exchequer Chamber was delivered by—

COLERIDGE J.: for the plaintiffs in error[1] [the defendant] it was contended, that the parties plainly contracted for the sale and purchase of goods, that the price to be paid was for goods, and that for the price the purchaser was to have the benefit of a contract to carry them and a policy of insurance; that a vendor of goods undertakes that they exist, and that they are capable of being transferred, although he may not stipulate for their condition; and that as the goods in question had been sold and delivered to other parties before the contract in question was made, there was nothing on which it could operate; and *Barr v. Gibson*[2] (3 M. & W. 390) and *Strickland v. Turner*[3] (7 Exch. 208) were cited.

On the other hand, it was argued that this was not a mere contract for the sale of an ascertained cargo, but that the purchaser bought the

---

[1] *i.e.* the party who sued out a writ of error. *Cf.* Sutton and Shannon, *Personal Actions at Common Law*, Chap. 8.

[2] B paid S £4,200 for a ship then on a voyage. At the time of the sale it had been stranded and the hull was eventually sold for £10. B's action for breach of a covenant that S had power to sell failed. The ship still existed at the time of the sale; it would have been otherwise had it ceased to exist.

[3] B bought from S an annuity on the life of X who, unknown to B and S, was already dead. It was held that B was able to recover the whole price, the consideration having totally failed.

adventure, and took upon himself all risks from the shipment of the cargo. It was said that the mention of the condition of the cargo at the time of shipment was a proof of the intention of the parties that the buyer should take all risks from that time; that its condition at the time of sale, or the fact of its existence, could not then be ascertained, and therefore the purchaser must be supposed to have taken the risks; that if it had existed, however much deteriorated, the purchaser must have taken it, although the loss had been all but total, and therefore there was no reason for excluding total loss from the risk that he was to bear; that if it had ceased to exist the consideration would not fail, for the purchaser would have the shipping documents. It was further argued that the stipulation for payment, which would probably have to be made before the arrival of the cargo, indicated an intention that the purchaser was in all events to pay for it, on account of the inconvenience that would ensue, if he might have to reclaim the money back. It was not disputed that the cases of *Barr v. Gibson* (3 M. & W. 390) and *Strickland v. Turner* (7 Exch. 208) were well decided.

It appears to us that the contract in question was for the sale of a cargo supposed to exist, and to be capable of transfer, and that, inasmuch as it had been sold and delivered to others by the captain before the contract in question was made, the plaintiffs cannot recover in this action. With regard to the description of the cargo as "of fair average quality when shipped," we think that, if those words had not been introduced, it must have been held that the purchaser of a cargo on a voyage would take upon himself the chance of what its condition at the time of purchase might be, and that this clause was introduced for his benefit, by enabling him to object, if the fact were so, that the cargo was bad when shipped. If, in *Barr v. Gibson*, there had been a stipulation that the ship, when she sailed on the voyage during which she was sold, was seaworthy, that would not have made the purchaser liable, if a total loss had occurred before the contract was entered into. It has been said, that if the loss had been all but total, if the cargo had become all but worthless, yet, if it existed *in specie*, the purchaser must unquestionably have been bound, and therefore there is no reason for holding that he was not also to take the risk of a total loss. The same argument would have applied in *Strickland v. Turner*. If the annuitant, at the time of the sale of the annuity, had been *in extremis*, and had died the next hour, the purchaser would have been bound, and could not have recovered the purchase-money, but was held to be so entitled, the annuitant having died before the sale. Again, it has been supposed that there is an inconsistency in saying that, if the cargo had sustained sea damage, constituting an average loss covered by the policy, it would pass to the purchaser so as to secure to him an indemnity, but would not pass in the event of a total loss. This seems to depend upon the same point, and not to be attended with any real difficulty.

If the contract for sale of the cargo was valid, the shipping documents would pass as accessories to it; but if, in consequence of the previous sale of the cargo, the contract failed as to the principal subject-matter of it, the shipping documents would not pass. Although we cannot find any decision in point, there is a case of *Sutherland* v. *Pratt* (11 M. & W. 296), where this subject was mentioned. In that case, the plaintiff had bought goods on a voyage, and effected an insurance, lost or not lost. They had sustained sea damage before the sale, and the purchaser sued on the policy. The underwriters pleaded that the goods were damaged before the plaintiff had acquired any interest in them. On demurrer, it was held that the plea was bad; but the very learned counsel who argued for the plaintiff admitted, in answer to a question put by Parke B., that, if the goods had been totally lost before his contract of purchase was made, there would not have been an insurable interest, as a person cannot buy a thing that has been totally lost.

For these reasons, it appears to us that the basis of the contract in this case was the sale and purchase of goods, and that all the other terms in the bought note were dependent upon that, and that we cannot give to it the effect of a contract for goods lost or not lost. The consequence is, that the judgment of the court below must be reversed, and entered for the plaintiffs in error [the defendant] according to arrangement between the parties.

Judgment reversed.

Questions

1. Would the buyer have been bound to pay the price if the cargo, in good order when shipped, had been damaged at the time of the sale?

2. Did the success of the action in *Strickland v. Turner* imply that there was no contract or merely that any contract there may have been was not performed? Was S guilty of a breach of contract because X was dead? Would it be reasonable to impute to him a promise that X was alive? If, because of X's death, neither S nor B was under any obligation, does it not follow that the contract was void?

3. If the seller in *Barr v. Gibson* had warranted that the ship was seaworthy when she sailed, would he have been able to keep the price if the ship had already (i) been stranded, (ii) become a total loss, through unseaworthiness?

COUTURIER v. HASTIE

House of Lords (1856) 5 H.L.C. 673; 25 L.J.Ex. 253; 28 L.T. 240; 2 Jur.(N.S.) 1241; 10 E.R. 1065

On a writ of error to the House of Lords the judges were summoned and unanimously expressed the opinion that the judgment of the Exchequer Chamber was right and that of the Court of Exchequer wrong.

THE LORD CHANCELLOR (LORD CRANWORTH): My Lords, that being so, I have no hesitation in advising your Lordships, and at once moving that the judgment of the court below should be affirmed. It is hardly necessary, and it has not ordinarily been usual for your Lordships to go much into the merits of a judgment which is thus unanimously affirmed by the judges who are called in to consider it, and to assist the House in forming its judgment. But I may state shortly that the whole question turns upon the construction of the contract which was entered into between the parties. . . . [His Lordship then considered the construction of the contract.] The contract plainly imports that there was something which was to be sold at the time of the contract, and something to be purchased. No such thing existing, I think the Court of Exchequer Chamber has come to the only reasonable conclusion upon it, and consequently that there must be judgment given by your Lordships for the defendants in error [the defendant].

Questions

1. Did the courts in this case decide:

(a) that there was no contract? or
(b) that there was a contract, but that it was not performed?

2. What consideration was to be supplied by the seller according to (a) the seller, (b) the buyer? Which view was accepted by the court?
3. Suppose the buyer had suffered damage (for example, through loss of a sub-contract). Does the case decide that he could not have recovered damages for the seller's failure to deliver?

LEVER BROTHERS LTD v. BELL

(1931) 1 K.B. 557

WRIGHT J. said: "The simplest and oldest illustration of such a mistake [that is, 'mistake of subject-matter, or substance, or essence, or fundamental basis'] is where the parties contracted to buy and sell a specific chattel which at the date of the contract, though both parties thought it existing, had ceased to exist: in that event, however absolute the terms of the contract, there is in law no binding contract, and this principle is now embodied in the Sale of Goods Act, 1893, s.6. The principle was applied in a sense to the sale of a cargo sold c.i.f. which had, before the date of the contract, owing to sea damage, been properly sold by the shipmaster at a port of refuge, and hence became, without the knowledge of either party, incapable of delivery, though it may be that it still existed: *Couturier v. Hastie*."

Sale of Goods Act 1979, s.6

Where there is a contract for the sale of specific goods, and the goods without the knowledge of the seller have perished at the time when the contract is made, the contract is void.

Question
Is *Couturier* v. *Hastie* an authority for the proposition stated by Wright J., above, or for that contained in the Sale of Goods Act, s.6?

McRAE v. THE COMMONWEALTH DISPOSALS COMMISSION

High Court of Australia, 84 C.L.R. 377; [1951] Argus L.R. 771

The defendants invited tenders for the purchase of an oil tanker described as lying on Jourmand Reef off Papua, together with its contents, which were stated to be oil. The plaintiffs made a tender of £285 which was accepted. They then incurred considerable expenditure in modifying a vessel they owned for salvage work, in purchasing equipment and engaging a crew, and on travelling expenses, etc. There was in fact no oil tanker anywhere near the latitude and longitude specified by the Commission, nor was there any place known as Jourmand Reef. The plaintiffs brought an action for (1) breach of contract, (2) deceit, and (3) negligence. Webb J. gave judgment for the plaintiffs in the action for deceit. He held that *Couturier v. Hastie* obliged him to hold that the contract of sale was void and the claim for breach of contract failed. The plaintiffs appealed and the defendants cross-appealed.

DIXON AND FULLAGAR JJ.: The first question to be determined is whether a contract was made between the plaintiffs and the Commission. The argument that the contract was void, or, in other words, that there was no contract, was based, as has been observed, on *Couturier v. Hastie*. It is true that *Couturier v. Hastie* has been commonly treated in the textbooks as a case of a contract avoided by mutual mistake, and it is found cited in the company of such cases as *Gompertz v. Bartlett* (1853) 2 E. & B. 849, and *Strickland v. Turner* (1852) 7 Ex. 208. Section 7 of the English Sale of Goods Act, 1893, is generally regarded as expressing the effect of the case. The case has not, however, been universally regarded as resting on mistake, and Sir Frederick Pollock in his Preface to Vol. 101 of the *Revised Reports*, at p. vi, says "*Couturier v. Hastie* shows how a large proportion of the cases which swell the rubric of relief against mistake in the textbooks (with or without protest from the textwriter) are really cases of construction." And in *Solle v. Butcher* (below, p. 501) Denning L.J. observed that the cases which it had been usual to classify under the head of "mistake" needed reconsideration since the decision of the House of Lords in *Bell v. Lever Bros. Ltd* (below, p. 491). No occasion seems to have arisen for a close examination of *Couturier v. Hastie*, but such an occasion does now arise.

The facts of the case were simple enough. . . . [The learned judges then stated the facts of *Couturier v. Hastie*.]

In considering *Couturier v. Hastie* it is necessary to remember that it was, in substance, a case in which a vendor was suing for the price of goods which he was unable to deliver. If there had been nothing more in the case, it would probably never have been reported: indeed the action would probably never have been brought. But the vendor founded his claim on the provision for "payment upon handing over shipping documents." He was not called upon to prove a tender of the documents, because the defendant had "repudiated" the contract, but he was able and willing to hand them over, and his argument was, in effect, that by handing them over he would be doing all that the contract required of him. The question thus raised would seem to depend entirely on the construction of the contract, and it appears really to have been so treated throughout. [The learned judges then quoted from the judgments in *Couturier v. Hastie* and Lord Atkin's reference to that case in *Bell v. Lever Bros. Ltd*.

The observation of Lord Atkin in *Bell v. Lever Bros. Ltd* (see below, p. 494, n. 1) seems entirely appropriate to *Couturier v. Hastie*. In that case there was a failure of consideration, and the purchaser was not bound to pay the price; if he had paid it before the truth was discovered, he could have recovered it back as money had and received. The construction of the contract was the vital thing in the case because, and only because, on the construction of the contract depended the question whether the consideration had really failed, the vendor maintaining that, since he was able to hand over the shipping documents, it had not failed. The truth is that the question whether the contract was void, or the vendor excused from performance by reason of the non-existence of the supposed subject-matter, did not arise in *Couturier v. Hastie*. It would have arisen if the purchaser had suffered loss through non-delivery of the corn and had sued the vendor for damages. If it had so arisen, we think that the real question would have been whether the contract was subject to an implied condition precedent that the goods were in existence. Prima facie, one would think, there would be no such implied condition precedent, the position being simply that the vendor *promised* that the goods *were* in existence. That is the real meaning of the direction of Martin B. to the jury, and so the argument for the defendant, as has already been pointed out, included the proposition that a "vendor of goods undertakes that they exist and that they are capable of being transferred, although he may not stipulate for their condition." So in *Barr v. Gibson* (1838) 3 M. & W. 390, where the contract was for the sale of a ship, Parke B. said: "And therefore the sale in this case of a ship implies a contract that the subject of transfer did exist in the character of a ship." It should be noted in this connection that in *Solle v. Butcher* Denning L.J. said that the doctrine of French law, as enunciated by Pothier, is not part of English law. His Lordship was without doubt thinking of the passage quoted from Pothier in a note to the report of the argument in the House of Lords in *Couturier v. Hastie*. Although we would not be prepared to assent to everything that is said by Denning L.J. in the course of this judgment, we respectfully agree with this observation. When once the common law had made up its mind that a promise supported by consideration ought to be performed, it was inevitable that the theorisings of the civilians about "mistake" should mean little or nothing to it. On the other hand, the question whether a promisor was excused from performance by existing or supervening impossibility without fault on his part was a practical everyday question of which the common law has been vividly conscious, as witness *Taylor v. Caldwell* (below, p. 511), with its innumerable (if sometimes dubious) successors. But here too the common law has generally been true to its theory of simple contract, and it has always regarded the fundamental question as being: "What did the promisor really promise?" Did he promise to perform his part at all events, or only subject to the mutually contemplated original or continued existence of a particular subject-matter? So questions of intention or "presumed intention" arise, and these must be determined in the light of the words used by the parties and reasonable inferences from all the surrounding circumstances. That the problem is fundamentally one of construction is shown clearly by *Clifford v. Watts* (1870) L.R. 5 C.P. 577.

If the view so far indicated be correct, as we believe it to be, it seems clear that the case of *Couturier v. Hastie* does not compel one to say that the contract in the present case was void. But, even if the view that *Couturier v. Hastie* was a case of a void contract be correct, we would still think that it could not govern the present case. Denning L.J. indeed says in *Solle v. Butcher*: "Neither party can rely on his own mistake to say it was a nullity from the beginning, no matter that it was a mistake which to his mind was fundamental, and no matter that the other party knew he was under a mistake. A *fortiori* if the other party did not know of the mistake, but shared it." But, even if this be not wholly and strictly correct, yet at least it must be true to say that a party cannot rely on mutual mistake where the mistake consists of a belief which is, on the one hand, entertained by him without any reasonable ground, and, on the other hand, deliberately induced by him in the mind of the other party. . . . [The learned judge held that there was no evidence that the officials of the Commission were guilty of fraud; but that they were guilty of the grossest negligence.] Having no reasonable grounds for such a belief, they asserted by their advertisement to the world at large, and by their later specification of locality to the plaintiffs, that they had a tanker to sell. They must have known that any tenderer would rely implicitly on their assertion of the existence of a tanker, and they must have known that the plaintiffs would rely implicitly on their later assertion of the existence of a tanker in the latitude and longitude given. They took no steps to verify what they were asserting, and any "mistake" that existed was induced by their own culpable, conduct. In these circumstances it seems out of the question that they should be able to assert that no contract was concluded. It is not unfair or inaccurate to say that the only "mistake" the plaintiffs made was that they believed what the Commission told them.

The position so far, then, may be summed up as follows: It was not decided in *Couturier v. Hastie* that the contract in that case was void. The question whether it was void or not did not arise. If it had arisen, as in an action by the purchaser for damages, it would have turned on the ulterior question whether the contract was subject to an implied condition precedent. Whatever might then have been held on the facts of *Couturier v. Hastie*, it is impossible in this case to imply any such term. The terms of the contract and the surrounding circumstances clearly exclude any such implication. The buyers relied upon, and acted upon, the assertion of the seller that there was a tanker in existence. It is not a case in which the parties can be seen to have proceeded on the basis of a common assumption of fact so as to justify the conclusion that the correctness of the assumption was intended by both parties to be a condition precedent to the creation of contractual obligation. The officers of the Commission made an assumption, but the plaintiffs did not make an assumption in the same sense. They knew nothing except what the Commission had told them. If they had been asked, they would certainly not have said: "Of course, if there is no tanker, there is no contract." They would have said: "We shall have to go and take possession of the tanker. We simply accept the Commission's assurance that there is a tanker and the Commission's promise to give us that tanker." The only proper construction of the contract is that it included a promise by the Commission that there was a tanker in the position specified. The Commission contracted that there was a tanker there. "The sale in this case of a ship implies a contract that the subject of the transfer did exist in the character of a ship" (*Barr v. Gibson*). If, on the other hand, the case of *Couturier v. Hastie* and this case ought to be treated as cases raising a question of "mistake," then the Commission cannot in this case rely on any mistake as avoiding the contract, because any mistake was induced by the serious fault of their own servants, who asserted the existence of a tanker recklessly and without any reasonable ground. There *was* a contract, and the Commission contracted that a tanker existed in the position specified. Since there was no such tanker, there has been a breach of contract, and the plaintiffs are entitled to damages for that breach.

Before proceeding to consider the measure of damages one other matter should be briefly mentioned. The contract was made in Melbourne, and it would seem that its proper law is Victorian law. Section 11 of the Victoria Goods Act, 1928, corresponds to section 6 of the English Sale of Goods Act, 1893, and provides that "where there is a contract for the sale of specified goods, and the goods without the knowledge of the seller have perished at the time when the contract is made the contract is void." This has been generally supposed to represent the legislature's view of the effect of *Couturier v. Hastie*. Whether it correctly represents the effect of the decision in that case or not, it seems clear that the section has no application to the facts of the present case. Here the goods never existed, and the seller ought to have known that they did not exist.

The conclusion that there was an enforceable contract makes it unnecessary to consider the other two causes of action. . . .

McTIERNAN J.: concurred in the conclusions of the above judgment.

Glanville Williams, Mistake and Rectification in Contract 17 M.L.R. 154

In *McRae v. Commonwealth Disposals Commission*, Dixon and Fullagar JJ. analysed *Couturier v. Hastie* and thought that it did not decide that the contract was void for initial impossibility, but only that the seller could not get the price. These judges left open the question whether a contract is void for initial impossibility of performance. The language of Denning L.J. in [*Rose v. Pim*, above, p. 125] seems to suggest that had it not been for the particular wording of the contract in *Couturier v. Hastie* the result would have been different. But this is hard to believe, for if the subsequent destruction of specific goods frustrates an agreement for the sale of those goods, as it does under *Taylor v. Caldwell* (below, p. 511, *N.B.* footnote on p. 512) and section 7 of the Sale of Goods Act, it is common sense that prior destruction must have a similar vitiating effect. Moreover, the common understanding of the rule in *Couturier v. Hastie* is affirmed by section 6 of the Sale of Goods Act.

Questions
1. Could not section 6 be excluded by the expressed intention of the parties? *Cf.* section 55 of the Sale of Goods Act 1979 (above, p. 402) and the *Hansa Nord* [1976] Q.B. 44. Suppose, for example, that a seller assures a doubting buyer that the cargo is in existence in order to induce him to buy, and perhaps even puts an undertaking to that effect into the written contract. *If* the section can be excluded by an express term, why not by an implied one, if that appears to have been the intention of the parties?
2. Even if section 6 does lay down a rigid rule which does not yield to a contrary intention, would it not be in accordance with the principle that the consequences of both initial and subsequent impossibility—arising otherwise than through the perishing of goods—should depend upon the intention of the parties, that is, upon an implied term?
3. With reference to the views of Professor Williams (above), may it not be reasonable to impute to the owner of a ship or a theatre a promise that it exists and yet unreasonable to impute to him a promise that it will *continue to exist* at some future time? *Cf.* Atiyah, *Introduction to the Law of Contract* (4th ed.), pp. 198–200. Alternatively, might not a case like the *McRae* case be decided on the ground that the seller undertakes merely that he has taken reasonable steps to find out whether the ship exists? *Cf. The Moorcock* (above, p. 390), *Esso Petroleum v. Mardon* (above, p. 367), *Liverpool City Council v. Irwin* (above, p. 394) and *The Mihalis Angelos* (above, p. 432).

Note
See K.O. Shatwell, "The Supposed Doctrine of Mistake in Contract: A Comedy of Errors" (1955) 33 Can. Bar Rev. 164; P.S. Atiyah, "*Couturier v. Hastie* and the Sale of Non-existent Goods" (1957) 73 L.Q.R. 340. For the damages aspect of the *McRae* case, see below.

BELL v. LEVER BROTHERS LTD

House of Lords [1932] A.C. 161; 101 L.J.K.B. 129; 146 L.T. 258; 48 T.L.R. 133; 76 S.J. 50, 37 Com.Cas. 98

The Lever Company, which had a controlling interest in the Niger Company, in 1923 appointed Bell chairman, and Snelling vice-chairman, of the board of the Niger Company, at salaries of £8,000 and £6,000 a year respectively. In 1926 the arrangement was renewed to run for five years. While acting as chairman and vice-chairman Bell and Snelling, by speculating in the company's business, committed breaches of duty which would have justified the Lever Company in terminating their appointments. In 1929 the Niger Company amalgamated with another company, and the appointments of Bell and Snelling became redundant. D'Arcy Cooper, the chairman of Levers, being unaware of the breaches of duty, arranged on behalf of the Lever Company, to pay Bell £30,000 and Snelling £20,000 as compensation for terminating their services. Bell and Snelling agreed to accept these sums and they were paid. On discovering the breaches, the Lever Company and the Niger Company brought an action alleging fraudulent misrepresentation and claiming rescission of the compensation agreements and repayment of the sums paid thereunder. The jury found that if the Lever Company had been aware of the breaches of duty by the defendants, they would have terminated their agreements and dismissed them from office without compensation; and that, when entering into the compensation agreements, the defendants did not fraudulently conceal, but had not present to their minds, or did not appreciate the effect of, the breaches of duty they had committed.

Wright J. and the Court of Appeal held that the compensation agreements were void as having been made under a common mistake. The defendants appealed.

Lord Blanesburgh held that, after an action based exclusively on fraud had failed, it was not open to the plaintiffs on the pleadings to raise a case of mutual mistake, implying good faith on the part of the defendants; but if it were open to the plaintiffs to raise the issue, then he agreed with Lord Atkin and Lord Thankerton.

Lord Warrington, with whom Lord Hailsham agreed, held, dissenting, that the erroneous assumption made by both parties was as fundamental to the bargain as any that could be imagined and that the contract was void.

LORD ATKIN [having stated the facts]: Two points present themselves for decision: Was the agreement of March 19, 1929, void by reason of a mutual mistake of Mr D'Arcy Cooper and Mr Bell?

Could the agreement of March 19, 1929, be avoided by reason of the failure of Mr Bell to disclose his misconduct in regard to the cocoa dealings?

My Lords, the rules of law dealing with the effect of mistake on contract appear to be established with reasonable clearness. If mistake operates at all it operates so as to negative or in some cases to nullify consent. The parties may be mistaken in the identity of the contracting parties, or in the existence of the subject-matter of the contract at the date of the contract, or in the quality of the subject-matter of the contract. These mistakes may be by one party, or by both, and the legal effect may depend upon the class of mistake above mentioned. Thus a mistaken belief by A that he is contracting with B, whereas in fact he is contracting with C, will negative consent where it is clear that the intention of A was to contract only with B. So the agreement of A and B to purchase a specific article is void if in fact the article had perished before the date of sale. In this case, though the parties in fact were agreed about the subject-matter, yet a consent to transfer or take delivery of something not existent is deemed useless, the consent is nullified. As codified in the Sale of Goods Act the contract is expressed to be void if the seller was in ignorance of the destruction of the specific chattel. I apprehend that if the seller with knowledge that a chattel was destroyed purported to sell it to a purchaser, the latter might sue for damages for non-delivery though the former could not sue for non-acceptance, but I know of no case where a seller has so committed himself. This is a case where mutual mistake certainly and unilateral mistake by the seller of goods will prevent a contract from arising. Corresponding to mistake as to the existence of the subject-matter is mistake as to title in cases where, unknown to the parties, the buyer is already the owner of that which the seller purports to sell to him. The parties intended to effectuate a transfer of ownership: such a transfer is impossible: the stipulation is *naturali ratione inutilis*. This is the case of *Cooper v. Phibbs*, where A agreed to take a lease of a fishery from B, though contrary to the belief of both parties at the time A was tenant for life of the fishery and B appears to have had no title at all. To such a case Lord Westbury applied the principle that if parties contract under a mutual mistake and misapprehension as to their relative and respective rights the result is that the agreement is liable to be set aside as having proceeded upon a common mistake. Applied to the context the statement is only subject to the criticism that the agreement would appear to be void rather than voidable. Applied to mistake as to rights generally it would appear to be too wide. Even where the vendor has no title, though both parties think he has, the correct view would appear to be that there is a contract: but that the vendor has either committed a breach of a stipulation as to title, or is not able to perform his contract. The contract is unenforceable by him but is not void.

Mistake as to quality of the thing contracted for raises more difficult questions. In such a case a mistake will not affect assent unless it is the mistake of both parties, and is as to the existence of some quality which makes the thing without the quality essentially different from the thing as it was believed to be. Of course, it may appear that the parties contracted that the article should possess the quality which one or other or both mistakenly believed it to possess. But in such a case there is a contract and the inquiry is a different one, being whether the contract as to quality amounts to a condition or a warranty, a different branch of law. The principles to be applied are to be found in two cases which, as far as my knowledge goes, have always been treated as authoritative expositions of the law. The first is *Kennedy v. Panama Royal Mail Co.* (1867) L.R. 2 Q.B. 580, 586.

In that case the plaintiff had applied for shares in the defendant company on the faith of a prospectus which stated falsely but innocently that the company had a binding contract with the Government of New Zealand for the carriage of mails. On discovering the true facts the plaintiff brought an action for the recovery of the sums he had paid on calls. The defendants brought a cross-action for further calls. Blackburn J., in delivering the judgment of the court (Cockburn C.J., Blackburn, Mellor and Shee JJ.), said: "The only remaining question is one of much greater difficulty. It was contended by Mr Mellish, on behalf of Lord Gilbert Kennedy, that the effect of the prospectus was to warrant to the intended shareholders that there really was such a contract as is there represented, and not merely to represent that the company bona fide believed it; and that the difference in substance between shares in a company with such a contract and shares in a company whose supposed contract was not binding, was a difference in substance in the nature of the thing; and that the shareholder was entitled to return the shares as soon as he discovered this, quite independently of fraud, on the ground that he had applied for one thing and got another. And, if the invalidity of the contract really made the shares he obtained different things in substance from those which he applied for, this would, we think, be good law. The case would then resemble *Gompertz v. Bartlett*, 2 E. & B. 849, and *Gurney v. Womersley* (1854) 4 E. & B. 133, where the person who had honestly sold what he thought a bill without recourse to him, was nevertheless held bound to return the price on its turning out that the supposed bill was a forgery in the one case, and void under the stamp laws in the other; in both cases the ground of this decision being that the thing handed over was not the thing paid for. A similar principle was acted on in *Ship's Case* (1865) 2 De G.J. & S. 544. There is, however, a very important difference between cases where a contract may be rescinded on account of fraud, and those in which it may be rescinded on the ground that there is a difference in substance between the thing bargained for and that obtained. It is enough to show that there was a fraudulent representation as to any part of that which induced the party to enter into the contract which he seeks to rescind; but where there has been an innocent misrepresentation or misapprehension, it does not authorise a rescission unless it is such as to show that there is a complete difference in substance between what was supposed to be and what was taken, so as to constitute a failure of consideration. For example, where a horse is bought under a belief that it is sound, if the purchaser was induced to buy by a fraudulent representation as to the horse's soundness, the contract may be rescinded. If it was induced by an honest misrepresentation as to its soundness, though it may be clear that both vendor and purchaser thought that they were dealing about a sound horse and were in error, yet the purchaser must pay the whole price unless there was a warranty; and even if there was a warranty, he cannot return the horse and claim back the whole price, unless there was a condition to that effect in the contract: *Street v. Blay* (1831) 2 B. & Ad. 456."

The court came to the conclusion in that case that, though there was a misapprehension as to that which was a material part of the motive inducing the applicant to ask for the shares, it did not prevent the shares from being in substance those he applied for.

The next case is *Smith v. Hughes* (above, p. 121). [His Lordship then stated the facts and quoted from the judgments in that case.]

The court ordered a new trial. It is not quite clear whether they considered that if the defendant's contention was correct, the parties were not *ad idem* or there was a contractual condition that the oats sold were old oats. In either case the defendant would succeed in defeating the claim.

In these cases I am inclined to think that the true analysis is that there is a contract, but that the one party is not able to supply the very thing whether goods or services that the other party contracted to take; and therefore the contract is unenforceable by the one if executory, while if executed the other can recover back money paid on the ground of failure of the consideration.[1]

We are now in a position to apply to the facts of this case the law as to mistake so far as it has been stated. It is essential on this part of the discussion to keep in mind the finding of the jury acquitting the defendants of fraudulent misrepresentation or concealment in procuring the agreements in question. Grave injustice may be done to the defendants

---

[1] This paragraph is the "observation" referred to in *McRae v. The Commonwealth Disposals Commission* (above).

and confusion introduced into the legal conclusion, unless it is quite clear that in considering mistake in this case no suggestion of fraud is admissible and cannot strictly be regarded by the judge who has to determine the legal issues raised. The agreement which is said to be void is the agreement contained in the letter of March 19, 1929, that Bell would retire from the Board of the Niger Company and its subsidiaries, and that in consideration of his doing so Levers would pay him as compensation for the termination of his agreements and consequent loss of office the sum of £30,000 in full satisfaction and discharge of all claims and demands of any kind against Lever Brothers, the Niger Company or its subsidiaries. The agreement, which as part of the contract was terminated, had been broken so that it could be repudiated. Is an agreement to terminate a broken contract different in kind from an agreement to terminate an unbroken contract, assuming that the breach has given the one party the right to declare the contract at an end? I feel the weight of the plaintiffs' contention that a contract immediately determinable is a different thing from a contract for an unexpired term, and that the difference in kind can be illustrated by the immense price of release from the longer contract as compared with the shorter. And I agree that an agreement to take an assignment of a lease for five years is not the same thing as to take an assignment of a lease for three years, still less a term for a few months. But, on the whole, I have come to the conclusion that it would be wrong to decide that an agreement to terminate a definite specified contract is void if it turns out that the agreement had already been broken and could have been terminated otherwise. The contract released is the identical contract in both cases, and the party paying for release gets exactly what he bargains for. It seems immaterial that he could have got the same result in another way, or that if he had known the true facts he would not have entered into the bargain. A buys B's horse; he thinks the horse is sound and he pays the price of a sound horse; he would certainly not have bought the horse if he had known, as the fact is, that the horse is unsound. If B has made no representation as to soundness and has not contracted that the horse is sound, A is bound and cannot recover back the price. A buys a picture from B; both A and B believe it to be the work of an old master, and a high price is paid. It turns out to be a modern copy. A has no remedy in the absence of representation or warranty. A agrees to take on lease or to buy from B an unfurnished dwelling-house. The house is in fact uninhabitable. A would never have entered into the bargain if he had known the fact. A has no remedy, and the position is the same whether B knew the facts or not, so long as he made no representation or gave no warranty. A buys a roadside garage business from B abutting on a public thoroughfare: unknown to A, but known to B, it has already been decided to construct a by-pass road which will divert substantially the whole of the traffic from passing A's garage. Again A has no remedy. All these cases involve hardship on A and benefit B, as most people would say, unjustly. They can be supported on the ground that it is of paramount importance that contracts should be observed, and that if parties honestly comply with the essentials of the formation of contract—for example, agree in the same terms on the same subject-matter—they are bound, and must rely on the stipulations of the contract for protection from the effect of facts unknown to them.

This brings the discussion to the alternative mode of expressing the result of a mutual mistake. It is said that in such a case as the present there is to be implied a stipulation in the contract that a condition of its efficacy is that the facts should be as understood by both parties—namely, that the contract could not be terminated till the end of the current term. The question of the existence of conditions, express or implied, is obviously one that affects not the formation of contract, but the investigation of the terms of the contract when made. A condition derives its efficacy from the consent of the parties, express or implied. They have agreed, but on what terms? One term may be that unless the facts are or are not of a particular nature, or unless an event has or has not happened, the contract is not to take effect. With regard to future facts such a condition is obviously contractual. Till the event occurs the parties are bound. Thus the condition (the exact terms of which need not here be investigated) that is generally accepted as underlying the principle of the frustration cases is contractual, an implied condition. Sir John Simon formulated for the assistance of your Lordships a proposition which should be recorded: "Whenever it is to be inferred from the terms of a contract or its surrounding circumstances that the consensus has been reached upon the basis of a particular contractual assumption, and that assumption is not true, the contract is avoided: that is, it is void *ab initio* if the assumption is of present fact and it ceases to bind if the assumption is of future fact."

I think few would demur to this statement, but its value depends upon the meaning of "a contractual assumption," and also upon the true meaning to be attached to "basis," a metaphor which may mislead. When used expressly in contracts, for instance, in policies of insurance, which state that the truth of the statements in the proposal is to be the basis of the contract of insurance, the meaning is clear. The truth of the statements is made a condition of the contract, which failing, the contract is void unless the condition is waived. The proposition does not amount to more than this: that, if the contract expressly or impliedly contains a term that a particular assumption is a condition of the contract, the contract is avoided if the assumption is not true. But we have not advanced far on the inquiry how to ascertain whether the contract does contain such a condition. Various words are to be found to define the state of things which make a condition. "In the contemplation of both parties fundamental to the continued validity of the contract," "a foundation essential to its existence," "a fundamental reason for making it," are phrases found in the important judgment of Scrutton L.J. in the present case. The first two phrases appear to me to be unexceptionable. They cover the case of a contract to serve in a particular place, the existence of which is fundamental to the service, or to procure the services of a professional vocalist, whose continued health is essential to performance. But "a fundamental reason for making a contract" may, with respect, be misleading. The reason of one party only is presumedly not intended, but in the cases I have suggested above, of the sale of a horse or of a picture, it might be said that the fundamental reason for making the contract was the belief of both parties that the horse was sound or the picture an old master, yet in neither case would the condition as I think exist. Nothing is more dangerous than to allow oneself liberty to construct for the parties contracts which they have not in terms made, by importing implications which would appear to make the contract more businesslike or more just. The implications to be made are to be no more than are "necessary" for giving business efficacy to the transaction, and it appears to me that, both as to existing facts and future facts, a condition would not be implied unless the new state of facts makes the contract something different in kind from the contract in the original state of facts. Thus, in *Krell v. Henry* (below, p. 517), Vaughan Williams L.J. finds that the subject of the contract was "rooms to view the procession": the postponement, therefore, made the rooms not rooms to view the procession. This also is the test finally chosen by Lord Sumner in *Bank Line v. Arthur Capel & Co.* [1919] A.C. 435, agreeing with Lord Dunedin in *Metropolitan Water Board v. Dick Kerr* [1918] A.C. 119, 128, where, dealing with the criterion for determining the effect of interruption in "frustrating" a contract, he says: "An interruption may be so long as to destroy the identity of the work or service, when resumed, with the work or service when interrupted." We therefore get a common standard for mutual mistake, and implied conditions whether as to existing or as to future facts. Does the state of the new facts destroy the identity of the subject-matter as it was in the original state of facts? To apply the principle to the infinite combinations of facts that arise in actual experience will continue to be difficult, but if this case results in establishing order into what has been a somewhat confused and difficult branch of the law it will have served a useful purpose.

I have already stated my reasons for deciding that in the present case the identity of the subject-matter was not destroyed by the mutual mistake, if any, and need not repeat them. [His Lordship then went on to hold that the defendants owed no duty to the Lever Company to disclose the impugned transactions.]

LORD THANKERTON delivered judgment to the same effect as Lord Atkin.

Notes

1. As to the duty of disclosure, see above, p. 333.

2. Was the substance of the matter that Bell was selling his right to continue in Levers' employment (a right which did not exist)? And that Levers were buying the right to terminate Bell's employment (a right which they already owned)? If so, should not the contract have been held to be void under the principles stated by Lord Atkin? If the subject-matter of the contract was Bell's contract of service, the mistake of the parties related only to a quality of it; but, if it was Bell's right to be employed, it did not exist; and, it was Levers' right to terminate, the case was like *Cooper v. Phibbs*. How is the subject-matter best regarded?

3. In the *Harvela* case, above, p. 13 the vendors' acceptance of Sir Leonard's "referential bid" was held by Peter Gibson J. to conclude a valid (though not specifically enforceable) contract. The belief of both parties that the vendors were bound to accept Sir Leonard's offer was a mistake of law which did not affect the formation of the contract. The House of Lords held that there was no such contract, following Buckley J. in *Beesly v. Hallwood Estates* [1960] 2 All E.R. 314 at 322. Buckley J. said:

"Any transaction between two or more parties can, in my judgment, only result in a contract between them if they enter into that transaction with an intention to create binding contractual obligations or in circumstances in which such an intention must be attributed to them. The facts of the present case negative such an intention, for, as I find, these letters were written with the intention of carrying out what were thought to be existing obligations, not of creating any new obligation."

Is this explanation satisfactory? Where A and B have made a *valid* contract to make a contract (above, pp. 102–103) the second contract is certainly a good one although the intention of the parties is to carry out existing obligations, not to create new ones. The parties in *Harvela* in fact intended to create legal relations but the common assumption on which that intention was based was false. Is the principle similar to that which (in the opinion of some judges) rendered void the contract in *Cooper v. Phibbs* where the parties were also making a mistake of law?

4. In *Griffith v. Brymer* (1903) 19 T.L.R. 434 Wright J. held the contract void where, at 11 a.m. on June 24, 1902, the plaintiff had entered into an oral agreement for the hire of a room to view the coronation procession on June 26, but the decision to operate on the King, which rendered the procession impossible, had been taken at about 10 a.m. on June 24. The agreement was made on a missupposition of facts which went to the whole root of the matter: and the plaintiff was entitled to recover his £100. (What if the contract had been made at 9.00 a.m.? *Cf. Krell v. Henry* (below, p. 517), and the *Fibrosa* case (below, p. 540).)

5. In an American case, *Sherwood v. Walker* (Supreme Court of Michigan, 1887, 66 Mich. 568; 33 N.W. 919; 11 Am.St.Rep. 531), the defendants agreed to sell and the plaintiff to buy a cow, "Rose 2nd of Aberlone," for $80. The defendants believed the cow to be barren, but, before she was delivered, they discovered she was in calf. As a breeding cow she was worth $750–$1,000 and the defendants refused to deliver.

The majority of the court held that the parties contracted on the understanding and belief that she was incapable of breeding and of no use as a cow; that the mistake of both parties was "not of the mere quality of the animal, but went to the very nature of the thing," there being as much difference between them as between an ox and a cow; that "the thing sold and bought had in fact no existence" and there was "no contract to sell or sale of the cow as she actually was." The plaintiff's action of replevin failed.

Sherwood J., dissenting, held that the defendants believed the cow to be barren but that the plaintiff thought she could be made to breed; that "there was no difference between the parties, nor misapprehension, as to the substance of the thing bargained for which was a cow supposed to be barren by one party and believed not to be by the other."

Questions

1. Can *Griffith v. Brymer* stand with *Bell v. Lever Bros.*?

2. How would an English court have decided *Sherwood v. Walker* (a) if they had accepted the majority's interpretation of the facts? (b) if they had accepted Sherwood J.'s version?

ASSOCIATED JAPANESE BANK LTD v. CREDIT DU NORD SA AND ANOTHER

Queen's Bench Division (Commercial Court) [1988] 3 All E.R. 902

Bennett contracted (i) to sell to, and (ii) to lease back from, the plaintiff (A.J.B.) four machines. The defendant (C.D.N.) guaranteed the performance by Bennett of his obligations under the lease. Bennett was fraudulent. The machines did not exist. The plaintiff sued the defendant on the guarantee.

STEYN J.: held that, on a sensible construction of the guarantee against its objective setting, it was subject to an express or, if not express an implied, condition precedent that the machines existed. As the machines did not exist the guarantee was void and the action failed.

Although this was determinative of the case Steyn J. went on to consider (treating this as a different ground) whether contract was void for mistake. Discussing *Bell v. Lever Bros.*, he said: Lord Atkin held:

> ". . . a mistake will not affect assent unless it is the mistake of both parties, and is as to the existence of some quality which makes the thing without the quality essentially different from the thing as it was believed to be."

In my view none of the other passages in Lord Atkin's speech detract from that statement of the law. Lord Thankerton came to a similar conclusion. He held that common mistake "can only properly relate to something which both must necessarily have accepted in their minds as an essential and integral part of the subject-matter" (see [1932] AC 161 at 235).

That seems to me exactly the same test as Lord Atkin enunciated. Clearly, Lord Atkin did not conceive of any difference between his formulation and that of Lord Thankerton. . . .

When Lord Denning M.R. referred to *Magee v. Pennine Insurance Co. Ltd* (below, p. 509) to the views of commentators he may have had in mind comments in Cheshire and Fifoot, *Law of Contract* (6th ed., 1964), p. 196. In substance the argument was that the actual decision in *Bell v. Lever Bros. Ltd*, contradicts the language of the speeches. If the test was not satisfied there, so the argument runs, it is difficult to see how it could ever be satisfied: see the latest edition of this valuable textbook for the same argument (Cheshire, Fifoot and Furmston, *Law of Contract* (11th ed., 1986), pp. 225–226). This is a point worth examining because at first glance it may seem persuasive. *Bell v. Lever Bros. Ltd* was a quite exceptional case; all their Lordships were agreed that common mistake had not been pleaded and would have required an amendment in the House of Lords if it were to succeed. The speeches do not suggest that the employees were entitled to keep both the gains secretly made and the golden handshakes. The former were clearly recoverable from them. Nevertheless, the golden handshakes were very substantial. But there are indications in the speeches that the so-called "merits" were not all in favour of Lever Bros. The company was most anxious, because of a corporate merger, to terminate the two service agreements. There was apparently a doubt whether the voidability of the service agreements if revealed to the company *at the time of the severance contract* would have affected the company's decision. Lord Thankerton said ([1932] A.C. 161 at 236, [1931] All E.R. Rep. 1 at 37):

> ". . . I do not find sufficient material to compel the inference that the appellants, at the time of the contract, regarded the indefeasibility of the service agreements as an essential and integral element in the subject-matter of the bargain."

Lord Atkin clearly regarded it as a hard case on the facts, but concluded "on the whole" that the plea of common mistake must fail (see [1932] A.C. 161 at 223). It is noteworthy that Lord Atkin commented on the scarcity of evidence as to the subsidiaries from the boards of which the two employees resigned (see [1932] A.C. 161 at 212). Lord Blanesburgh's speech was directed to his conclusion that the amendment ought not to be allowed. He did, however, make clear that "the mistake must go to the whole consideration," and pointed to the advantages (other than the release from the service agreements) which Lever Bros. received (see [1932] A.C. 161 at 181). Lord Blanesburgh emphasised that Lever Bros. secured the *future* co-operation of the two employees for the carrying through of the amalgamation (see [1932] A.C. 161 at 181). And the burden, of course, rested squarely on Lever Bros. With due deference to the distinguished authors who have argued that the actual decision in *Bell v. Lever Bros. Ltd* contradicts the principle enunciated in the speeches it seems to me that their analysis is altogether too simplistic, and that the actual decision was rooted in the particular facts of the case. In my judgment there is no reason to doubt the substantive reasons emerging from the speeches of the majority. . . .

It is clear, of course, that in this case both parties, the creditor and the guarantor, acted on the assumption that the lease related to existing machines. If they had been informed that the machines might not exist, neither A. J. B. nor C. D. N. would for one moment have contemplated entering into the transaction. That, by itself, I accept, is not enough to sustain the plea of common law mistake. I am also satisfied that C. D. N. had reasonable grounds for believing that the machines existed. That belief was based on C. D. N.'s discussions with Mr Bennett, information supplied by National Leasing, a respectable firm of lease brokers, and the confidence created by the fact that A. J. B. were the lessors.

The real question is whether the subject matter *of the guarantee* (as opposed to the sale and lease) was essentially different from what it was reasonably believed to be. The real security of the guarantor was the machines. The existence of the machines, being profit-earning chattels, made it more likely that the debtor would be able to service the debt. More importantly, if the debtor defaulted and the creditor repossessed the machines, the creditor had to give credit for $97^1/_2$ per cent. of the value of the machines. If the creditor sued the guarantor first, and the guarantor paid, the guarantor was entitled to be subrogated to the creditor's rights in respect of recovery against the debtor: see Goff and Jones, *Law of Restitution* (3rd ed., 1986), pp. 533–536). No doubt the guarantor relied to some extent on the creditworthiness of Mr Bennett. But I find that the prime security to which the guarantor looked was the existence of the four machines as described to both parties. For both parties the guarantee of obligations under a lease with non-existent machines was essentially different from a guarantee of a lease with four machines which both parties at the time of the contract believed to exist. The guarantee is an accessory contract. the non-existence of the subject matter of the principal contract is therefore of fundamental importance. Indeed the analogy of the classic res extincta cases, so much discussed in the authorities, is fairly close. In my judgment, the stringent test of common law mistake is satisfied; the guarantee is void *ab initio*.

Questions

1. Suppose that Steyn J. had decided that there was no express or implied term. Would that decision have left room for any inquiry whether the contract was void for mistake? Would it not have established that the parties intended the contract to be binding in the circumstances which existed? See Smith (1994) 110 L.Q.R. pp. 400, 406–409.

2. Steyn J. suggests that, if Levers had known of the voidability of Bell's service agreement, it would not have affected their decision to pay him £30,000. Is this suggestion reconcilable with the finding of the jury that Levers would have exercised their right to dismiss Bell if they had known they could do so? See Smith, *op. cit.*, pp. 411–418.

3. Steyn J. refers to Lord Blanesborough's point that an operative mistake must go to the whole consideration. Lord Blanesborough pointed out that £30,000 was far more than was necessary to compensate Bell for his loss of employment. It was intended partly (i) as a recognition of outstanding services Bell had rendered to Levers and (ii) to secure his *future* (Steyn J.'s emphasis) co-operation in the amalgamation. The former was a past consideration. The latter may have been Levers' motive for their apparent generosity but can it be regarded as part of the consideration in the light of Levers' letter of March 19, 1929 which embodied the agreement with Bell: ". . . from May 1 next you will on that date retire from the boards . . . and in consideration of your doing so Lever Bros. Ltd. will pay you as compensation for the termination of your agreement . . .?" Co-operation is not mentioned in the letter. Suppose Bell had failed to co-operate. Could Levers have sued him?

SOLLE v. BUTCHER

Court of Appeal [1950] 1 K.B. 671; 66 T.L.R. (Pt. 1) 448; [1949] 2 All E.R. 1107

In 1947 the plaintiff, a surveyor, and the defendant were partners in the business of estate agents. In 1931 a dwelling-house had been converted into five flats. In 1938 Flat No. 1 was let for three years at an annual rent of £140. In 1947 the defendant took a long lease of the building, intending to repair bomb damage and do substantial alterations. The plaintiff and the defendant discussed the rents to be charged after the work had been completed. The plaintiff told the defendant that he could charge £250 for Flat 1, both parties being satisfied that the rent of £140 in 1938 did not apply as the "standard rent." The defendant said that he relied on the plaintiff in the matter of rents. He took no steps to calculate the additions to £140 which, if that were the standard rent, would have been permitted by the Rent Act 1938 because of the improvements made to the flat. Those additions would have brought the rent up to about £250.

In September 1947 Flat No. 1 was let by the defendant to the plaintiff for a term of seven years at a yearly rent of £250. Once this lease was executed no notice of intention to increase the rent could be given under the Rent Restriction Acts during the contractual tenancy.

The plaintiff paid rent at £250 per year for some time and then took proceedings in the county court for a declaration that the standard rent of the flat was £140 and that he was entitled to recover from the landlord the amount overpaid since the commencement of the tenancy. The defendant contended that the flat had become a new and separate dwelling by reason of change of identity, but the county court judge found as a fact that the flat was not a new and separate dwelling. The defendant counterclaimed for rescission of the lease on the ground of mutual mistake of fact, but the county court judge rejected this claim, saying, "I find that there was no mistake of fact—possibly a mistake of law—in that both parties for some obscure reason imagined that the Rent Acts did not apply. I do not think they ever addressed their minds to the material issue of identity." He held also that the plea of estoppel was no defence against the provisions of the Rent Restriction Acts. He made an order for the recovery of the amount of the rent overpaid. The defendant appealed.

BUCKNILL L.J. held that the lease must be set aside on the ground that both parties having, in his opinion (contrary to that of the county court judge), addressed their minds to the question whether the flat had changed its identity, the mistake which each had made was that the work done had made such a substantial alteration to the building as to make it a different flat—a common mistake of fact.

DENNING L.J., having held that the flat had not changed its identity and therefore the raising of the rent from £140 to £250 was invalid; and that, just as parties cannot contract out of the Rent Acts, so they cannot defeat them by any estoppel, went on: In this plight the landlord seeks to set aside the lease. He says, with truth, that it is unfair that the tenant should have the benefit of the lease for the outstanding five years of the term at £140 a year, when the proper rent is £250 a year. If he cannot give a notice of increase now, can he not avoid the lease? The only ground on which he can avoid it is on the ground of mistake. It is quite plain that the parties were under a mistake. They thought that the flat was not tied down to a controlled rent, whereas in fact it was. In order to see whether the lease can be avoided for this mistake it is necessary to remember that mistake is of two kinds: first, mistake which renders the contract void, that is, a nullity from the beginning, which is the kind of mistake which was dealt with by the courts of common law; and, secondly, mistake which renders the contract not void, but voidable, that is, liable to be set aside on such terms as the court thinks fit, which is the kind of mistake which was dealt with by the courts of equity. Much of the difficulty which has attended this subject has arisen because, before the fusion of law and equity, the courts of common law, in order to do justice in the case in hand, extended this doctrine of mistake beyond its proper limits and held contracts to be void which were really only voidable, a process which was capable of being attended with much injustice to third persons who had bought goods or otherwise committed themselves on the faith that there was a contract. In the well-known case of *Cundy v. Lindsay* (above, p. 165), Cundy suffered such an injustice. He bought the handkerchiefs from the rogue, Blenkarn, before the Judicature Acts came into operation. Since the fusion of law and equity, there is no reason to continue this process, and it will be found that only those contracts are now held void in which the mistake was such as to prevent the formation of any contract at all.

Let me first consider mistakes which render a contract a nullity. All previous decisions on this subject must now be read in the light of *Bell v. Lever Bros. Ltd* (above, p. 491). The correct interpretation of that case, to my mind, is that, once a contract has been made, that is to say, once the parties, whatever their inmost states of mind, have to all outward appearances agreed with sufficient certainty in the same terms on the same subject-matter, then the contract is good unless and until it is set aside for failure of some condition on which the existence of the contract depends, or for fraud, or on some equitable ground. Neither party can rely on his own mistake to say it was a nullity from the beginning, no matter that it was a mistake which to his mind was fundamental, and no matter that the other party knew that he was under a mistake. A *fortiori*, if the other party did not know of the mistake, but shared it. The cases where goods have perished at the time of sale, or belong to the buyer, are really contracts which are not void for mistake but are void by reason of an implied condition precedent, because the contract proceeded on the basic assumption that it was possible of performance.[1] So far as cases later than *Bell v. Lever Bros. Ltd* are concerned, I do not think that *Sowler v. Potter* (above, p. 179, footnote) can stand with *King's Norton Metal Co. Ltd v. Edridge* (above, p. 167), which shows that the doctrine of French law as enunciated by Pothier is no part of English law. Nor do I think that the contract in *Nicholson and Venn v. Smith-Marriott* (1947) 177 L.T. 189[2] was void from the beginning.

Applying these principles, it is clear that here there was a contract. The parties agreed in the same terms on the subject-matter. It is true that the landlord was under a mistake which was to him fundamental: he would not for one moment have considered letting the flat for seven years if it meant

---

[1] Compare this sentence with that footnoted on p. 533.

[2] S put up for auction table-napkins "with the crest of Charles I and the authentic property of that monarch." B, relying on the description, bought the napkins for £787. In fact they were Georgian and worth only £105. Hallett J. awarded B damages but said B might have treated the contract as void.

that he could only charge £140 a year for it. He made the fundamental mistake of believing that the rent he could charge was not tied down to a controlled rent; but, whether it was his own mistake or a mistake common to both him and the tenant, it is not a ground for saying that the lease was from the beginning a nullity. Any other view would lead to remarkable results, for it would mean that, in the many cases where the parties mistakenly think a house is outside the Rent Restriction Acts when it is really within them, the tenancy would be a nullity, and the tenant would have to go; with the result that the tenants would not dare to seek to have their rents reduced to the permitted amounts lest they should be turned out.

Let me next consider mistakes which render a contract voidable, that is, liable to be set aside on some equitable ground. Whilst presupposing that a contract was good at law, or at any rate not void, the court of equity would often relieve a party from the consequences of his own mistake, so long as it could do so without injustice to third parties. The court, it was said, had power to set aside the contract whenever it was of opinion that it was unconscientious for the other party to avail himself of the legal advantage which he had obtained: *Torrance v. Bolton* (1872) L.R. 8 Ch. 118, 124, *per* James L.J.

The court had, of course, to define what it considered to be unconscientious, but in this respect equity has shown a progressive development. It is now clear that a contract will be set aside if the mistake of the one party has been induced by a material misrepresentation of the other, even though it was not fraudulent or fundamental; or if one party, knowing that the other is mistaken about the terms of an offer, or the identity of the person by whom it is made, lets him remain under his delusion and concludes a contract on the mistaken terms instead of pointing out the mistake. That is, I venture to think, the ground on which the defendant in *Smith v. Hughes* (above, p. 121) would be exempted nowadays,[1] and on which, according to the view by Blackburn J. of the facts, the contract in *Lindsay v. Cundy* was voidable and not void; and on which the lease in *Sowler v. Potter* was, in my opinion, voidable and not void.

A contract is also liable in equity to be set aside if the parties were under a common misapprehension either as to facts or as to their relative and respective rights, provided that the misapprehension was fundamental and that the party seeking to set it aside was not himself at fault. That principle was first applied to private rights as long ago as 1730 in *Lansdown v. Lansdown* (1730) Mos. 364. There were four brothers, and the second and third of them died. The eldest brother entered on the lands of the deceased brothers, but the youngest brother claimed them. So the two rival brothers consulted a friend who was a local schoolmaster. The friend looked up a book which he then had with him called *The Clerk's Remembrancer* and gave it as his opinion that the lands belonged to the youngest brother. He recommended the two of them to take further advice, which at first they intended to do, but they did not do so; and, acting on the friend's opinion, the elder brother agreed to divide the estate with the younger brother, and executed deeds and bonds giving effect to the agreement. Lord Chancellor

---

[1] The defendant *was* exempted if the plaintiff knew he was mistaken as to the terms of the offer, but not if he was (or appeared to be) merely mistaken as to the age of the oats.

King declared that the documents were obtained by a mistake and by a misrepresentation of the law by the friend and ordered them to be given up to be cancelled. He pointed out that the maxim *ignorantia juris non excusat* only means that ignorance cannot be pleaded in excuse of crimes. Eighteen years later, in the time of Lord Hardwicke, the same principle was applied in *Bingham v. Bingham* (1748) 1 Ves.Sen. 126.

If and in so far as those cases were compromises of disputed rights,[2] they have been subjected to justifiable criticism, but, in cases where there is no element of compromise, but only of mistaken rights, the House of Lords in 1867 in the great case of *Cooper v. Phibbs* (1867) L.R. 2 H.L. 149, 170, affirmed the doctrine there acted on as correct. In that case an uncle had told his nephew, not intending to misrepresent anything, but being in fact in error, that he (the uncle) was entitled to a fishery; and the nephew, after the uncle's death, acting in the belief of the truth of what the uncle had told him, entered into an agreement to rent the fishery from the uncle's daughters, whereas it actually belonged to the nephew himself. The mistake there as to the title to the fishery did not render the tenancy agreement a nullity. If it had done, the contract would have been void at law from the beginning and equity would have had to follow the law. There would have been no contract to set aside and no terms to impose. The House of Lords, however, held that the mistake was only such as to make it voidable, or, in Lord Westbury's words, "liable to be set aside" on such terms as the court thought fit to impose; and it was so set aside.

The principle so established by *Cooper v. Phibbs* has been repeatedly acted on: see, for instance, *Earl Beauchamp v. Winn* (1873) L.R. 6 H.L. 223, 234, and *Huddersfield Banking Co. Ltd v. Lister* [1895] Ch. 273. It is in no way impaired by *Bell v. Lever Bros. Ltd*, which was treated in the House of Lords as a case at law depending on whether the contract was a nullity or not. If it had been considered on equitable grounds, the result might have been different. In any case, the principle of *Cooper v. Phibbs* has been fully restored by *Norwich Union Fire Insurance Society, Ltd v. William H. Price, Ltd* (below p. 506).

Applying that principle to this case, the facts are that the plaintiff, the tenant, was a surveyor who was employed by the defendant, the landlord, not only to arrange finance for the purchase of the building and to negotiate with the rating authorities as to the new rateable values, but also to let the flats. He was the agent for letting, and he clearly formed the view that the building was not controlled. He told the valuation officer so. He advised the defendant what were the rents which could be charged. He read to the defendant an opinion of counsel relating to the matter, and told him that in his opinion he could charge £250 and that there was no previous control. He said that the flats came outside the Act and that the defendant was "clear." The defendant relied on what the plaintiff told him, and authorised the plaintiff to let at the rentals which he had suggested. The plaintiff not only let the four other flats to other people for a long period of years at the new rentals, but also took one himself for seven years at £250 a year. Now he turns round and says, quite unashamedly, that he wants to take advantage of the mistake to get the flat at £140 a year for seven years instead of the £250 a year, which is not only the rent he agreed to pay but

---

[2] *Cf. Cook v. Wright* above, p. 214, distinguishing *Bell v. Gardiner*.

also the fair and economic rent; and it is also the rent permitted by the Acts on compliance with the necessary formalities. If the rules of equity have become so rigid that they cannot remedy such an injustice, it is time we had a new equity, to make good the omissions of the old. But, in my view, the established rules are amply sufficient for this case.

On the defendant's evidence, which the judge preferred, I should have thought there was a good deal to be said for the view that the lease was induced by an innocent material misrepresentation by the plaintiff. It seems to me that the plaintiff was not merely expressing an opinion on the law: he was making an unambiguous statement as to private rights; and a misrepresentation as to private rights is equivalent to a misrepresentation of fact for this purpose: *MacKenzie v. Royal Bank of Canada* [1934] A.C. 468. But it is unnecessary to come to a firm conclusion on this point, because, as Bucknill L.J. has said, there was clearly a common mistake, or, as I would prefer to describe it, a common misapprehension, which was fundamental and in no way due to any fault of the defendant; and *Cooper v. Phibbs* affords ample authority for saying that, by reason of the common misapprehension, this lease can be set aside on such terms as the court thinks fit.

[His Lordship then held that the fact that the lease had been executed was no bar to this relief. See above, p. 353.]

The terms will be complicated by reason of the Rent Restriction Acts, but it is not beyond the wit of man to devise them. Subject to any observations which the parties may desire to make, the terms which I suggest are these: the lease should only be set aside if the defendant is prepared to give an undertaking that he will permit the plaintiff to be a licensee of the premises pending the grant of a new lease. Then, whilst the plaintiff is a licensee, the defendant will in law be in possession of the premises, and will be able to serve on the plaintiff, as prospective tenant, a notice under section 7(4) of the Act of 1938 increasing the rent to the full permitted amount. The defendant must further be prepared to give an undertaking that he will serve such a notice within three weeks from the drawing up of the order, and that he will, if written request is made by the plaintiff, within one month of the service of the notice, grant him a new lease at the full permitted amount of rent, not, however, exceeding £250 a year, for a term expiring on September 29, 1954, subject in all other respects to the same covenants and conditions as in the rescinded lease. If there is any difference of opinion about the figures stated in the notice, that can, of course, be adjusted during the currency of the lease. If the plaintiff does not choose to accept the licence or the new lease, he must go out. He will not be entitled to the protection of the Rent Restriction Acts because, the lease being set aside, there will be no initial contractual tenancy from which a statutory tenancy can spring.

JENKINS L.J. [dissenting]: . . . But whether the parties failed to ask themselves the right question or, having asked it, answered it wrongly, I find it impossible to hold that a mutual mistake of the character here involved affords a good ground for rescission. The defendant meant to grant and the plaintiff meant to take a lease in the terms in which the lease was actually granted of the premises which the lease as granted actually comprised. They knew all the material facts bearing upon the effect of the

Rent Restriction Acts on a lease of those premises. But they mutually misapprehended the effect which, in that state of facts, those Acts would have on such a lease. That is a mistake of law of a kind which, so far as I am aware, has never yet been held to afford good ground for rescission. It is a mistake not as to the subject-matter nature, or purport of the contract entered into, nor as to any question of private right affecting the basis of the contract entered into (see *Cooper v. Phibbs*), but simply a mistake as to the effect of certain public statutes on the contract made, being in all respects precisely the contract the parties intended to make.

The mistaken conclusion, to the effect that on the facts of the case (all relevant facts being known to both parties) the Rent Restriction Acts did not have the effect of making £140 the standard rent of the flat in question was, as it seems to me, equally a mistake of law whether it was due to a failure to appreciate and apply the test of identity or proceeded from an application of that test followed by an erroneous inference or opinion drawn from the facts, to the effect that the flat in question was not in substance the same dwelling-house as the flat formerly let to Howard Taylor. The application of the test, if it was indeed applied, was merely a step in the reasoning leading from the facts to the conclusion of law.

> *Appeal allowed. Rescission of the lease on the terms*
> *stated in the judgment of Denning L.J.*

Note

In *Norwich Union Fire Insurance Society v. Price* [1934] A.C. 455, P.C., the plaintiff insurance company paid to the insured the value of a cargo of lemons which the plaintiffs believed to have been damaged by a peril insured against and sold in consequence. It was ascertained later that the lemons had not been so damaged, but had been sold because they were found to be ripening. The Privy Council held that the plaintiffs could recover the sum paid by them as money paid under a mistake of fact.

Lord Wright, delivering the judgment of their Lordships, said: "The mistake was as vital as that in *Cooper v. Phibbs* (1867) L.R. 2 H.L. 149, 170, in respect of which Lord Westbury used these words: 'If parties contract under a mutual mistake and misapprehension as to their relative and respective rights, the result is that that agreement is liable to be set aside as having proceeded upon a common mistake.' At common law such a contract (or *simulacrum* of a contract) is more correctly described as void, there being in truth no intention to a contract. Their Lordships find nothing tending to contradict or overrule these established principles in *Bell v. Lever Bros. Ltd*" (above, p. 491). Was the court concerned with the question whether a contract existed or not? Or whether a contract was voidable or not? Or neither?

Question

Rescission is normally (for example, for misrepresentation) a remedy of which the injured party may avail himself without recourse to any court. But *Solle v. Butcher* allows rescission only "on terms." Is this, then, a different concept of rescission from that met elsewhere?

WILLIAM SINDALL plc v. CAMBRIDGESHIRE COUNTY COUNCIL

Court of Appeal [1994] 3 All E.R. 932

The trial judge held that the plaintiff buyer of land was entitled to rescind the contract for misrepresentation and common mistake as to the existence of a sewer. As to misrepresentation, see above, p. 356. As to mistake:—

HOFFMANN L.J.: The judge found that in the absence of any actionable misrepresentations Sindall was entitled to rescind the contract for a common mistake as to the existence of a sewer. This is at first sight a startling result. As Steyn J. said in *Associated Japanese Bank (International) Ltd v. Crédit du Nord SA* (above, p. 498).

> "Logically, before one can turn to the rules as to mistake, whether at common law or in equity, one must first determine whether the contract itself, by express or implied condition precedent or otherwise, provides who bears the risk of the relevant mistake. It is at this hurdle that many pleas of mistake will either fail or prove to have been unnecessary. Only if the contract is silent on the point is there scope for invoking mistake."

When the judge speaks of the contract allocating risk "by express or implied condition precedent or otherwise" I think he includes rules of general law applicable to the contract and which, for example, provide that, in the absence of express warranty, the law is caveat emptor. This would, in my view, allocate the risk of an unknown defect in goods to the buyer, even though it is not mentioned in the contract. Similarly, the rule in *Hill v. Harris* [1965] 2 All E.R. 358, [1965] 2 Q.B. 601 that a lessor or vendor does not impliedly warrant that the premises are fit for any particular purpose means that the contract allocates the risk of the premises being unfit for such a purpose. I should say that neither in *Grist v. Bailey*, (below, p. 508) nor in *Laurence v. Lexcourt Holdings Ltd* (below, p. 508) did the judges who decided those cases at first instance advert to the question of contractual allocation of risk. I am not sure that the decisions would have been the same if they had.

In this case the contract says in express terms that it is subject to all easements other than those of which the vendor knows or has the means of knowledge. This allocates the risk of such incumbrances to the buyer and leaves no room for rescission on the grounds of mistake.

EVANS L.J.: Logically, there remains the question whether the contract, notwithstanding that on its true construction it covers the situation which has arisen, and that it cannot be set aside for misrepresentation, nevertheless may be rescinded on the ground of equitable mistake, as defined by Denning L.J. in *Solle v. Butcher*. It must be assumed, I think, that there is a category of mistake which is "fundamental" so as to permit the equitable remedy of rescission, which is wider than the kind of "serious and radical" mistake which means that the agreement is void and of no effect in law: see *Chitty on Contracts* (26th edn, 1989) vol 1, para 401, Treitel *The Law of Contract* (8th edn, 1991) p. 276; and *Cheshire Fifoot and Furmston's Law of Contract* (11th edn, 1986) p. 245. The difference may be that the common law rule is limited to mistakes with regard to the subject matter of the contract, whilst equity can have regard to a wider and perhaps unlimited category of "fundamental" mistake. However that may be, I am satisfied that the judge's finding in the present case was vitiated by his assumption that the presence of the sewer and of the city's easement had serious consequences for the proposed development, even if the sewer was incorporated into the public sewer that was envisaged for the development itself (Option 2A). This would not involve the loss of seven houses and three flats, as the judge appears to have thought, but, at most, of one three-bedroomed house. The additional cost of the alterations to the sewer would not have exceeded about £20,000. Given the breadth of the contract terms, in particular condition No. 14, which on its face was intended to cover precisely such a situation as this, and the relatively minor consequences of the discovery of the sewer, even if some period of delay as well as additional cost was involved, it is impossible to hold, in my judgment, that there is scope for rescission here.

RUSSELL L.J. agreed with both judgments.

Appeal allowed

Notes

1. *Solle v. Butcher* has always been difficult to reconcile with established principles of the common law. *Smith v. Hughes*, above, p. 121, decides that there may be a contract enforceable by the seller even where the seller is aware that the buyer is making a mistake as to a (to him) fundamental quality of the goods; and, if that is right, this must, a fortiori, be so where the seller shares the mistake. If A sells to B a painting which both believe to be of small value, is the contract to be voidable if the painting turns out to be an old master? *If* there are degrees of "fundamentalness" (see below), this mistake is more fundamental than that in *Solle v. Butcher*. But it would undermine the certainty of commercial transactions if such contracts were liable to be set aside at the discretion of the court. Hoffmann L.J.'s dictum, above, would exclude *Solle v. Butcher* in cases of this kind. It seems obvious that an express term on the point, like that in *Sindall*, should be conclusive; but if we must also look at the "rules of general law applicable to the contract", what room, if any, does that leave for the application of the doctrine? Was not the dissent by Jenkins L.J. (above, p. 505) in *Solle v. Butcher* an application of the "rules of general law applicable to the contract"? Is it likely that Lord Denning would have agreed with Hoffmann L.J.? He thought (above, p. 503) that "the defendant in *Smith v. Hughes* would be exempted nowadays."

A second difficulty with *Solle v. Butcher* is that the misapprehension must be "fundamental", yet, ex hypothesi, not so fundamental as to make the contract void, for then there would be nothing to rescind. Evans L.J., in the passage cited, appears to accept that "fundamental" may have a variable meaning; but earlier in his judgment, he questions whether "simultaneously the mistake can be fundamental yet the land not 'essentially and radically different' from what it was supposed to be . . ."

2. In *Grist v. Bailey* [1967] Ch. 532 the defendant entered into a contract to sell a freehold house to the plaintiff for £850, "subject to the existing tenancy thereof." The defendant believed, and the plaintiff's agent assumed, that there was a protected tenant in occupation. The agent would not have expected to get the property with vacant possession for anything like £850. But, unknown to the defendant, the tenant and the tenant's spouse had died. It was uncertain whether their son was entitled to protection under the Act but he never claimed it and vacated the house. The value of the property with vacant possession was about £2,250. The plaintiff sued for specific performance and the defendant counterclaimed for rescission on the ground that the contract was void or voidable for mistake.

GOFF J. said that the mistake in *Bell v. Lever Bros.* was more fundamental than any made in the present case and Lord Atkin's examples of the horse, picture and garage (above, p. 495) would apply to prevent the mistake being sufficient to avoid the agreement; but *Solle v. Butcher* was binding on him. In this case there was a common mistake, namely that there was a subsisting protected tenancy, it was fundamental (£850 as against £2,250) and the defendant was not so at fault as to disentitle him to relief. The plaintiff's action was dismissed and rescission ordered.

In *Laurence v. Lexcourt Holdings Ltd.* [1978] 2 All E.R. 810 plaintiffs offered to let a building for use as offices, overlooking the fact that planning permission for office use extended to part only of the building. Defendants, assuming that planning permission existed, accepted. Dillon Q.C. dismissed a claim for specific performance because (i) the description of the premises as offices was a misrepresentation that planning permission for use as offices was available and (ii) the belief of both parties that planning permission was available was a common mistake of the same character as these in *Solle v. Butcher* and *Grist v. Bailey*.

Questions

1. If a case with exactly the same facts as *Bell v. Lever Bros. Ltd* had come before Goff J., how do you think he would have decided it? If he would have granted rescission, does it follow that *Bell v. Lever Bros. Ltd* was decided *per incuriam*?

2. Would rescission have granted if the conveyance had been executed?

3. Would the case put by Cockburn C.J. of the sale of an estate in which, unknown to the vendor, there is a mine under the surface (above, p. 122) still be decided as he thought? Cf. Professor Atiyah (1968) 2 Ottawa Law Rev. 337, 350.

MAGEE v. PENNINE INSURANCE CO. LTD

Court of Appeal [1969] 2 Q.B. 507; [1969] 2 W.L.R. 1278; [1969] 2 All E.R. 891;
[1969] 2 Lloyd's Rep. 378

In 1961 the plaintiff (M) bought a car for his son to drive. He signed an insurance proposal form filled in by the seller of the car, which stated that M held a provisional licence. M had no licence. He was not dishonest but had not read what he signed. It was the basis of the contract of insurance that M's answers were true. In 1965 the car, driven by the son, was involved in an accident and completely wrecked. M claimed £600 from the insurers, the defendants, (P). P offered M £385 in settlement of his claim. M accepted. P then discovered that M had never had a licence and refused to pay. The county court judge held that M could not sue on the policy because of the misrepresentation, but that the offer and acceptance of a promise to pay £385 was a binding contract of compromise. (See above, pp. 214–216) P appealed.

LORD DENNING M.R., having accepted, after some doubt, that there had been a contract of compromise: But then comes the next point. Accepting that the agreement to pay £385 was an agreement of compromise. Is it vitiated by mistake? The insurance company were clearly under a mistake. They thought that the policy was good and binding. They did not know, at the time of that letter, that there had been misrepresentation in the proposal form. If Mr Magee knew of their mistake—if he knew that the policy was bad—he certainly could not take advantage of the agreement to pay £385. He would be "snapping at an offer which he knew was made under a mistake": and no man is allowed to get away with that. But I prefer to assume that Mr Magee was innocent. I think we should take it that both parties were under a common mistake. Both parties thought that the policy was good and binding. The letter of May 12, 1968, was written on the assumption that the policy was good whereas it was in truth voidable.

What is the effect in law of this common mistake? Mr Taylor said that the agreement to pay £385 was good, despite this common mistake. He relied much on *Bell v. Lever Brothers Ltd* (above, p. 491), and its similarity to the present case. He submitted that, in as much as the mistake there did not vitiate that contract, the mistake here should not vitiate this one. I do not propose today to go through the speeches in that case. They have given enough trouble to commentators already. I would simply say this: A common mistake, even on a most fundamental matter, does not make a contract void at law: but it makes it voidable in equity. I analysed the cases in *Solle v. Butcher* (above, p. 501), and I would repeat what I said there, at [1950] 1 K.B. 671, 693: "A contract is also liable in equity to be set aside if the parties were under a common misapprehension either as to facts or as to their relative and respective rights, provided that the misapprehension was fundamental and that the party seeking to set it aside was not himself at fault."

Applying that principle here, it is clear that, when the insurance company and Mr Magee made this agreement to pay £385, they were both under a common mistake which was fundamental to the whole agreement. Both thought that Mr Magee was entitled to claim under the policy of insurance, whereas he was not so entitled. That common mistake does not make the agreement to pay £385 a nullity, but it makes it liable to be set aside in equity.

This brings me to a question which has caused me much difficulty. Is this a case in which we ought to set the agreement aside in equity? I have hesitated on this point, but I cannot shut my eyes to the fact that Mr Magee had no valid claim on the insurance policy: and, if he had no claim on the policy, it is not equitable that he should have a good claim on the agreement to pay £385, seeing that it was made under a fundamental mistake. It is not fair to hold the insurance company to an agreement which they would not have dreamt of making if they had not been under a mistake. I would, therefore, uphold the appeal and give judgment for the insurance company.

WINN L.J. (dissenting): referred to the speeches of Lords Atkin and Thankerton in *Bell v. Lever Bros*, (above, p. 491) and continued: For my part, I think that here there was a misapprehension as to rights, but no misapprehension whatsoever as to the subject-matter of the contract, namely, the settlement of the rights of the assured with regard to the accident that happened. The insurance company was settling his rights, if he had any. He understood them to be settling his rights; but each of them, on the assumption that the county court judge's view of the facts was right, thought his rights against the insurers were very much more valuable than in fact they were, since in reality they were worthless: the insurers could have repudiated—or avoided, that being the more accurate phrase—on the basis of the mis-statements which my Lord has narrated.

FENTON ATKINSON L.J. agreed with Lord Denning.

Appeal allowed.

Questions
1. Is *Cook v. Wright*, above, p. 214 distinguishable?
2. Should the plaintiff have been entitled to recover his premiums?

CHAPTER 14

SUBSEQUENT IMPOSSIBILITY AND FRUSTRATION

PARADINE v. JANE

King's Bench (1647) Aleyn 26; 82 E.R. 897

In debt the plaintiff declares upon a lease for years rendering rent at the four usual feasts; and for rent behind for three years, ending at the Feast of the Annunciation, 21 Car., brings his action; the defendant pleads, that a certain German prince, by name Prince Rupert, an alien born, enemy to the King and kingdom, had invaded the realm with an hostile army of men; and with the same force did enter upon the defendant's possession, and him expelled, and held out of possession from July 19, 18 Car., till the Feast of the Annunciation, 21 Car., whereby he could not take the profits; whereupon the plaintiff demurred, and the plea was resolved insufficient.

1. Because the defendant hath not answered to one quarter's rent.

2. He hath not averred that the army were all aliens, which shall not be intended, and he hath his remedy against them; and Bacon cited 33 H.6.1.e. where the gaoler in bar of an escape pleaded, that alien enemies broke the prison, etc., and exception taken to it, for that he ought to shew of what countrey they were, *viz.*, Scots, etc.

3. It was resolved, that the matter of the plea was insufficient; for though the whole army had been alien enemies, yet he ought to pay his rent. And this difference was taken, that where the law creates a duty or charge, and the party is disabled to perform it without any default in him, and hath no remedy over, there the law will excuse him. As in the case of waste, if a house be destroyed by tempest, or by enemies, the lessee is excused. Dyer 33.a. Inst.53.d.283.a.12 H.4.6. so of an escape. Co.4.84.b. 33H.6.1. So in 9E.3.16. a supersedeas was awarded to the justices, that they should not proceed in a cessavit upon a cesser during the war, but when the party by his own contract creates a duty or charge upon himself, he is bound to make it good, if he may, notwithstanding any accident by inevitable necessity, because he might have provided against it by his contract. And therefore if the lessee covenant to repair a house, though it be burnt by lightning, or thrown down by enemies, yet he ought to repair it. Dyer 33.a.E.3.6.h. Now the rent is a duty created by the parties upon the reservation, and had there been a covenant to pay it, there had been no question but the lessee must have made it good, notwithstanding the interruption by enemies, for the law would not protect him beyond his own agreement, no more then [sic] in the case of reparations; this reservation then being a covenant in law, and whereupon an action of covenant hath been maintained (as Roll said) it is all one as if there had been an actual covenant. Another reason was added, that as the lessee is to have the advantage of casual profits, so he must run the hazard of casual losses, and not lay the whole burthen of them upon his lessor; and Dyer 56.6 was cited for this purpose, that though the land be surrounded, or gained by the sea, or made barren by wildfire, yet the lessor shall have his whole rent: and judgment was given for the plaintiff.

TAYLOR v. CALDWELL

Queen's Bench (1863) 3 B. & S. 826; 32 L.J.Q.B. 164; 8 L.T. 356; 11 W.R. 726; 2 Sm.L.C., 13th ed., 601; 122 E.R. 309

The plaintiffs claimed expenses, agreed at £58, necessarily incurred in preparation for a series of concerts at the defendants' Music Hall.

BLACKBURN J.: In this case the plaintiffs and defendants had, on May 27, 1861, entered into a contract by which the defendants agreed to let the plaintiffs have the use of the Surrey Gardens and Music Hall on four days then to come, *viz.*, June 17, July 15, August 5 and August 19, for the purpose of giving a series of four grand concerts, and day and night fêtes at the Gardens and Hall on those days respectively; and the plaintiffs agreed to take the Gardens and Hall on those days, and pay £100 for each day.

The parties inaccurately call this a "letting" and the money to be paid a "rent"; but the whole agreement is such as to show that the defendants were to retain the possession of the Hall and Gardens so that there was to be no demise of them, and that the contract was merely to give the plaintiffs the use of them on those days. Nothing, however, in our opinion, depends on this. The agreement then proceeds to set out various stipulations between the parties as to what each was to supply for these concerts and entertainments, and as to the manner in which they should be carried on. The effect of the whole is to show that the existence of the Music Hall in the Surrey Gardens in a state fit for a concert was essential for the fulfilment of the contract—such entertainments as the parties contemplated in their agreement could not be given without it.

After the making of the agreement, and before the first day on which a concert was to be given, the Hall was destroyed by fire. This destruction, we must take it on the evidence, was without the fault of either party, and was so complete that in consequence the concerts could not be given as intended. And the question we have to decide is whether, under these circumstances, the loss which the plaintiffs have sustained is to fall upon the defendants. The parties when framing their agreement evidently had not present to their minds the possibility of such a disaster, and have made no express stipulation with reference to it, so that the answer to the question must depend upon the general rules of law applicable to such a contract.

There seems no doubt that where there is a positive contract to do a thing, not in itself unlawful, the contractor must perform it or pay damages for not doing it, although in consequence of unforeseen accidents, the performance of his contract has become unexpectedly burthensome or even impossible. The law is so laid down in 1 Roll.Abr. 450, Condition (G), and in the note (2) to *Walton v. Waterhouse* (2 Wms.Saund. 421 a, 6th ed.), and is recognised as the general rule by all the judges in the much discussed case of *Hall v. Wright* (E.B. & E. 746). But this rule is only applicable when the contract is positive and absolute, and not subject to any condition either express or implied: and there are authorities which, as we think, establish the principle that where, from the nature of the contract, it appears that the parties must from the beginning have known that it could not be fulfilled unless when the time for the fulfilment of the contract arrived some particular specified thing continued to exist, so that, when entering into the contract, they must have contemplated such continuing existence as the foundation of what was to be done; there, in the absence of any express or implied warranty that the thing shall exist,[1] the contract is not to be construed as a positive contract, but as subject to an implied

---

[1] Notice that Blackburn J. saw no reason why a party should not promise that a thing would exist. *Cf.* the *McRae* case (above, p. 487) and Professor Williams's argument (above, p. 491).

condition that the parties shall be excused in case, before breach, performance becomes impossible from the perishing of the thing without default
of the contractor.

There seems little doubt that this implication tends to further the great
object of making the legal construction such as to fulfil the intention of
those who entered into the contract. For in the course of affairs men in
making such contracts in general would, if it were brought to their minds,
say that there should be such a condition.

Accordingly, in the civil law, such an exception is implied in every
obligation of the class which they call *obligatio de certo corpore*. The rule is
laid down in the Digest, lib. XLV., tit. 1, de verborum obligationibus, 1.33.
"Si Stichus certo die dari promissus, ante diem moriatur: non tenetur
promissor." The principle is more fully developed in 1.23. "Si ex legati
causa, aut ex stipulatu hominem certum mihi debeas: non aliter post
mortem ejus tenearis mihi, quam si per te steterit, quominus vivo eo eum
mihi dares: quod ita fit, si aut interpellatus non dedisti, aut occidisti eum."
The examples are of contracts respecting a slave, which was the common
illustration of a certain subject used by the Roman lawyers, just as we are
apt to take a horse; and no doubt the propriety, one might almost say
necessity, of the implied condition is more obvious when the contract
relates to a living animal, whether man or brute, than when it relates to
some inanimate thing (such as in the present case a theatre) the existence
of which is not so obviously precarious as that of the live animal, but the
principle is adopted in the civil law as applicable to every obligation of
which the subject is a certain thing. The general subject is treated of by
Pothier, who in his *Traité des Obligations*, Partie 3, Chap. 6, Art. 3. § 668,
states the result to be that the debtor *corporis certi* is freed from his
obligation when the thing has perished, neither by his act, nor his neglect,
and before he is in default, unless by some stipulation he has taken on
himself the risk of the particular misfortune which has occurred.

Although the civil law is not, of itself, authority in an English court, it
affords great assistance in investigating the principles on which the law is
grounded. And it seems to us that the common law authorities establish
that in such a contract the same condition of the continued existence of the
thing is implied by English law.

There is a class of contracts in which a person binds himself to do
something which requires to be performed by him in person; and such
promises, for example, promises to marry, or promises to serve for a certain
time, are never in practice qualified by an express exception of the death of
the party; and therefore in such cases the contract is in terms broken if the
promisor dies before fulfilment. Yet it was very early determined that, if
the performance is personal, the executors are not liable: *Hyde v. The Dean
of Windsor* (Cro.Eliz. 552, 553). See 2 Wms.Exors. 1560, 5th ed., where a
very apt illustration is given. "Thus," says the learned author, "if an author
undertakes to compose a work, and dies before completing it, his executors
are discharged from this contract: for the undertaking is merely personal in
its nature, and, by the intervention of the contractor's death, has become
impossible to be performed." For this he cites a dictum of Lord Lyndhurst
in *Marshall v. Broadhurst* (1 Tyr. 348, 349), and a case mentioned by
Patteson J. in *Wentworth v. Cock* (10 A. & E. 42, 45–46). In *Hall v. Wright*
(E.B. & E. 746, 749) Crompton J., in his judgment, puts another case.

"Where a contract depends upon personal skill, and the act of God renders it impossible, as, for instance, in the case of a painter employed to paint a picture who is struck blind, it may be that the performance might be excused."

It seems that in those cases the only ground on which the parties or their executors can be excused from the consequences of the breach of the contract is, that from the nature of the contract there is an implied condition of the continued existence of the life of the contractor, and perhaps, in the case of the painter, of his eyesight. In the instances just given, the person, the continued existence of whose life is necessary to the fulfilment of the contract, is himself the contractor, but that does not seem in itself to be necessary to the application of the principle; as is illustrated by the following example. In the ordinary form of an apprentice deed the apprentice binds himself in unqualified terms to "serve until the full end and term of seven years to be fully complete and ended," during which term it is convenated that the apprentice his master "faithfully shall serve," and the father of the apprentice in equally unqualified terms binds himself for the performance by the apprentice of all and every covenant on his part. (See the form, 2 *Chitty on Pleading*, 370, 7th ed., by Greening.) It is undeniable that if the apprentice dies within the seven years, the covenant of the father that he shall perform his covenant to serve for seven years is not fulfilled, yet surely it cannot be that an action would lie against the father? Yet the only reason why it would not is that he is excused because of the apprentice's death.

These are instances where the implied condition is of the life of a human being, but there are others in which the same implication is made as to the continued existence of a thing. For example, where a contract of sale is made amounting to a bargain and sale, transferring presently the property in specific chattels, which are to be delivered by the vendor at a future day; there, if the chattels, without the fault of the vendor, perish in the interval, the purchaser must pay the price and the vendor is excused from performing his contract to deliver, which has thus become impossible.

That this is the rule of the English law is established by the case of *Rugg v. Minett* (11 East 210), where the article that perished before delivery was turpentine, and it was decided that the vendor was bound to refund the price of all those lots in which the property had not passed; but was entitled to retain without deduction the price of those lots in which the property had passed, though they were not delivered, and though in the conditions of sale, which are set out in the report, there was no express qualification of the promise to deliver on payment. It seems in that case rather to have been taken for granted than decided that the destruction of the thing sold before delivery excused the vendor from fulfilling his contract to deliver on payment.

This is also the rule in the civil law, and it is worth noticing that Pothier, in his celebrated *Traité de Contrat de Vente* (see Part 4, § 307, etc.; and Part 2, Chap. 1, Sect. 1, Art. 4, § 1), treats this as merely an example of the more general rule that every obligation *de certo corpore* is extinguished when the thing ceases to exist. See *Blackburn on the Contract of Sale*, p. 173.

The same principle seems to be involved in the decision of *Sparrow v. Sowgate* (W. Jones 29), where, to an action of debt on an obligation by bail, conditioned for the payment of the debt or the render of the debtor, it was held a good plea that before any default in rendering him the principal debtor died. It is true that was the case of a bond with a condition, and a distinction is sometimes made in this respect between a condition and a contract. But this observation does not apply to *Williams v. Lloyd* (W. Jones 179). In that case the count, which was in assumpsit, alleged that the plaintiff had delivered a horse to the defendant, who promised to redeliver it on request. Breach, that though requested to redeliver the horse he refused. Plea, that the horse was sick and died, and the plaintiff made the request after its death; and on demurrer it was held a good plea, as the bailee was discharged from his promise by the death of the horse without default or negligence on the part of the defendant. "Let it be admitted," say the court, "that he promised to deliver it on request, if the horse die before, that is become impossible by the act of God, so the party shall be discharged, as much as if an obligation were made conditioned to deliver the horse on request, and he died before it." And Jones, adds the report, cited 22 Ass. 41, in which it was held that a ferryman who had promised to carry a horse safe across the ferry was held chargeable for the drowning of the animal only because he had overloaded the boat, and it was agreed that notwithstanding the promise no action would have lain had there been no neglect or default on his part.

It may, we think, be safely asserted to be now English law, that in all contracts of loan of chattels or bailments if the performance of the promise of the borrower or bailee to return the things lent or bailed, becomes impossible because it has perished, this impossibility (if not arising from the fault of the borrower or bailee from some risk which he has taken upon himself) excuses the borrower or bailee from the performance of his promise to redeliver the chattel.

The great case of *Coggs v. Bernard* (1 Smith's L.C. 171, 5th ed.; 2 Ld.Raym. 909) is now the leading case on the law of bailments, and Lord Holt, in that case, referred so much to the civil law that it might perhaps be thought that this principle was there derived direct from the civilians, and was not generally applicable in English law except in the case of bailments; but the case of *Williams v. Lloyd* (W. Jones 179), above cited, shows that the same law had been already adopted by the English law as early as The Book of Assizes. The principle seems to us to be that, in contracts in which the performance depends on the continued existence of a given person or thing, a condition is implied that the impossibility of performance arising from the perishing of the person or thing shall excuse the performance.

In none of these cases is the promise in words other than positive, nor is there any express stipulation that the destruction of the person or thing shall excuse the performance; but that excuse is by law implied, because from the nature of the contract it is apparent that the parties contracted on the basis of the continued existence of the particular person or chattel. In the present case, looking at the whole contract, we find that the parties contracted on the basis of the continued existence of the Music Hall at the time when the concerts were to be given; that being essential to their performance.

We think, therefore, that the Music Hall having ceased to exist, without fault of either party, both parties are excused, the plaintiffs from taking the gardens and paying the money, the defendants from performing their promise to give the use of the Hall and Gardens and other things.

Problem

A grants a lease (not a licence) to B of A's music hall as from a future date. Without the fault of either party, the music hall is destroyed by fire before the date arrives. Is A discharged from his obligation to provide a music hall? Is B discharged from his obligation to pay the rent?

Cf. Paradine v. Jane (above, p. 511), *Matthey v. Curling* [1922] 2 A.C. 180; *National Carriers Ltd v. Panalpina Ltd* (below, p. 524); [1940] 4 M.L.R. 256–260 and [1941] 5 M.L.R. 140.

JACKSON v. UNION MARINE INSURANCE CO. LTD

Exchequer Chamber (1874) L.R. 10 C.P. 125; 44 L.J.C.P. 27; 31 L.T. 789; 23 W.R. 169; 2 Asp.M.C. 435

The plaintiff, a shipowner, in November 1871 entered into a charterparty by which the ship to proceed with all possible dispatch (dangers and accidents of navigation excepted) from Liverpool to Newport, and there load a cargo of iron rails for San Francisco. The plaintiff effected an insurance on the chartered freight for the voyage. The ship sailed from Liverpool on January 2, 1872, and on the 3rd ran aground in Carnarvon Bay. She was got off on February 18 and repaired, the time necessary for the completion of the repairs extending to the end of August. On February 15 the charterers threw up the charter and chartered another ship. At the trial before Brett J. the jury found that (1) the time necessary for getting the ship off and repairing her so as to be a cargo-carrying ship, was so long as to make it unreasonable for the charterers to supply the agreed cargo at the end of the time, and (2) the delay was so long as to put an end in a commercial sense to the commercial speculation entered upon by the shipowner and charterers. The question was whether the plaintiff could have maintained an action against the charterers for not loading (for if he could, there had not been a loss of the chartered freight by any of the perils insured against). Brett J. being of opinion that there was no evidence of a loss of freight by the perils insured against, directed a verdict for the defendants. The Court of Common Pleas made an absolute rule to enter a verdict for the plaintiff, and this judgment was affirmed by the Court of Exchequer Chamber (Bramwell B., Blackburn, Mellor and Lush JJ. and Amphlett B., Cleasby B. dissenting).

BRAMWELL B., delivering the judgment of the majority, said he understood the jury to have found that "the voyage the parties contemplated had become impossible; that a voyage undertaken after the ship was sufficiently repaired would have been a different voyage, not, indeed, different as to the ports of loading and discharge, but different as a different adventure—a voyage for which at the time of the charter the plaintiff had not in intention engaged the ship, nor the charterers the cargo; a voyage as different as though it had been described as intended to be a spring voyage, while the one after the repair would be an autumn voyage." If the charterparty were read as a charter for a definite adventure there was *necessarily* an implied condition that the vessel should arrive at Newport in time for it. This implied stipulation was not repugnant to the express stipulation requiring all possible dispatch. The latter stipulation was not a condition precedent, the former was. Not arriving in time put an end to the contract though, as it arose from an excepted peril, it gave no cause of action. The effect of the exception clause for delay caused by perils of the sea was to excuse the shipowner, but not to give him any right. "The exception is an excuse for him who is to do the act, and operates to save him from an action and makes his non-performance not a breach of contract, but does not operate to take away the right the other party would have had, if the non-performance had been a breach of contract, to retire from the engagement: and, if one party may, so may the other."

KRELL v. HENRY

Court of Appeal [1903] 2 K.B. 740; 72 L.J.K.B. 794; 89 L.T. 328

On June 17, 1902, the defendant noticed an announcement in the windows of the plaintiff's flat at 56A Pall Mall to the effect that windows to view the coronation procession were to be let. The defendant interviewed the housekeeper on the subject, when it was pointed out to him what a good view of the procession could be obtained from the premises and he agreed to take the suite for June 26 and 27, the days on which the coronation processions were to take place. On June 20 the defendant agreed in writing to pay £75 for the entire use of the rooms on the two days. The writing did not mention the procession. He paid £25 then and agreed to pay £50 on June 24. The procession did not take place owing to the serious illness of the King and the defendant declined to pay the £50. The plaintiff sued for that sum, and the defendant counterclaimed for the return of the £25 which he had paid. Darling J. gave judgment for the defendant on the claim and counterclaim. The plaintiff appealed.

VAUGHAN WILLIAMS L.J. read the following judgment: The real question in this case is the extent of the application in English law of the principle of the Roman law which has been adopted and acted on in many English decisions, and notably in the case of *Taylor v. Caldwell* (above, p. 511). That case at least makes it clear that "where, from the nature of the contract, it appears that the parties must from the beginning have known that it could not be fulfilled unless, when the time for the fulfilment of the contract arrived, some particular specified thing continued to exist, so that when entering into the contract they must have contemplated such continued existence as the foundation of what was to be done; there, in the absence of any express or implied warranty that the thing shall exist, the contract is not to be considered a positive contract, but as subject to an implied condition that the parties shall be excused in case, before breach, performance becomes impossible from the perishing of the thing without default of the contractor." Thus far it is clear that the principle of the Roman law has been introduced into the English law. The doubt in the present case arises as to how far this principle extends. The Roman law dealt with *obligationes de certo corpore*. Whatever may have been the limits of the Roman law, the case of *Nickoll v. Ashton* [1901] 2 K.B. 126 makes it plain that the English law applies the principle not only to cases where the performance of the contract becomes impossible by the cessation of existence of the thing which is the subject-matter of the contract, but also to cases where the event which renders the contract incapable of performance is the cessation or non-existence of an express condition or state of things, going to the root of the contract, and essential to its performance. It is said, on the one side, that the specified thing, state of things, or condition the continued existence of which is necessary for the fulfilment of the contract, so that the parties entering into the contract must have contemplated the continued existence of that thing, condition, or state of things as the foundation of what was to be done under the contract, is limited to things which are either the subject-matter of the contract or a condition or state of things, present or anticipated, which is expressly mentioned in the contract. But, on the other side, it is said that the condition or state of things need not be expressly specified, but that it is sufficient if that condition or state of things clearly appears by extrinsic evidence to have been assumed by the parties to be the foundation or basis of the contract, and the event which causes the impossibility is of such a character that it cannot reasonably be supposed to have been in the contemplation of the contracting parties when the contract was made. In such a case the contracting parties will not be held bound by the general words which, though large enough to include, were not used with reference to a possibility of a particular event rendering performance of the contract impossible. I do not think that the principle of the civil law as introduced into the English law is limited to cases in which the event causing the impossibility of performance is the destruction or non-existence of some thing which is the subject-matter of the contract or of some condition or state of things expressly specified as a condition of it. I think that you first have to ascertain, not necessarily from the terms of the contract, but, if required, from necessary inferences, drawn from surrounding circum- stances recognised by both contracting parties, what is the substance of the contract, and then to ask the question whether that substantial contract needs for its foundation the assumption of the existence of a particular state of things. If it does, this will limit the operation of the general words, and in such case, if the contract becomes impossible of performance by reason of the non-existence of the state of things assumed by both contracting parties as the foundation of the contract, there will be no breach of the contract thus limited. Now what are the facts of the present case? . . .

[His Lordship stated the facts.] In my judgment the use of the rooms was let and taken for the purpose of seeing the Royal procession. It was not a demise of the rooms, or even an agreement to let and take the rooms. It is a licence to use rooms for a particular purpose and none other. And in my judgment the taking place of those processions on the days proclaimed along the proclaimed route, which passed 56A Pall Mall, was regarded by both contracting parties as the foundation of the contract; and I think that it cannot reasonably be supposed to have been in the contemplation of the contracting parties, when the contract was made, that the coronation would not be held on the proclaimed days, or the processions not take place on those days along the proclaimed route; and I think that the words imposing on the defendant the obligation to accept and pay for the use of the rooms for the named days, although general and unconditional, were not used with reference to the possibility of the particular contingency which afterwards occurred. It was suggested in the course of the argument that if the occurrence, on the proclaimed days, of the coronation and the pro- cession in this case were the foundation of the contract, and if the general words are thereby limited or qualified, so that in the event of the non- occurrence of the coronation and procession along the proclaimed route they would discharge both parties from further performance of the contract, it would follow that if a cabman was engaged to take someone to Epsom on Derby Day at a suitable enhanced price for such a journey, say £10, both parties to the contract would be discharged in the contingency of the race at Epsom for some reason becoming impossible; but I do not think this follows, for I do not think that in the cab case the happening of the race would be the foundation of the contract. No doubt the purpose of the engager would be to go to see the Derby, and the price would be proportionately high; but the cab had no special qualifications for the purpose which led to the selection of the cab for this particular occasion. Any other cab would have done as well. Moreover, I think that, under the cab contract, the hirer, even if the race went off, could have said, "Drive me to Epsom; I will pay you the agreed sum; you have nothing to do with the purpose for which I hired the cab," and that if the cabman refused he would have been guilty of a breach of contract, there being nothing to qualify his promise to drive the hirer to Epsom on a particular day. Whereas in the case of the coronation, there is not merely the purpose of the hirer to see the coronation procession, but it is the coronation procession and the relative position of the rooms which is the basis of the contract as much for the lessor as the hirer; and I think that if the King, before the coronation day and after the contract, had died, the hirer could not have insisted on having the rooms on the days named. It could not in the cab case be reasonably said that seeing the Derby race was the foundation of the contract, as it was of the licence in this case. Whereas in the present case, where the rooms were offered and taken, by reason of their peculiar suitability from the position of the rooms for a view of the coronation procession, surely the view of the coronation procession was the foundation of the contract, which is a very different thing from the purpose of the man who engaged the cab—namely, to see the race—being held to be the foundation of the contract. Each case must be judged by its own circumstances. In each case one must ask oneself, first, what, having regard to all the circumstances, was the foundation of the contract? Secondly, was the performance of the contract prevented? Thirdly, was the event which prevented the performance of the contract of such a character that it cannot reasonably be said to have been in the contemplation of the parties at the date of the contract? If all these questions are answered in the affirmative (as I think they should be in this case), I think both parties are discharged from further performance of the contract. I think that the coronation procession was the foundation of this contract, and that the non-happening of it prevented the performance of the contract; and, secondly, I think that the non-happening of the procession, to use the words of Sir James Hannen in *Baily v. De Crespigny* (1869) L.R. 4 Q.B. 185, was an event "of such a character that it cannot reasonably be supposed to have been in the contemplation of the contracting parties when the contract was made, and that they are not to be held bound by general words, which, though large enough to include, were not used with reference to the possibility of the particular contingency which afterwards happened." The test seems to be whether the event which causes the impossibility was or might have been anticipated and guarded against. It seems difficult to say, in a case where both parties anticipate the happening of an event, which anticipation is the foundation of the contract, that either party must be taken to have anticipated, and ought to have guarded against, the event which prevented the performance of the contract. In both *Jackson v. Union Marine Insurance Co.* (above, p. 516) and *Nickoll v. Ashton* [1901] 2 K.B. 126 the parties might have anticipated as a possibility that perils of the sea might delay the ship and frustrate the commercial venture: in the former case the carriage of the

goods to effect which the charterparty was entered into; in the latter case
the sale of the goods which were to be shipped on the steamship which was
delayed. But the court held in the former case that the basis of the contract
was that the ship would arrive in time to carry out the contemplated
commercial venture, and in the latter that the steamship would arrive in
time for the loading of the goods the subject of the sale. I wish to observe
that cases of this sort are very different from cases where a contract or
warranty or representation is implied such as was implied in *The Moorcock*
(above, p. 390) and refused to be implied in *Hamlyn v. Wood* [1891] 2 Q.B.
488. But *The Moorcock* is of importance in the present case as showing that
whatever is the suggested implication—be it condition, as in this case, or
warranty or representation—one must, in judging whether the implication
ought to be made, look not only at the words of the contract but also at the
surrounding facts and the knowledge of the parties of those facts. There
seems to me to be ample authority for this proposition. Thus in *Jackson v.
Union Marine Insurance Co.*, in the Common Pleas, the question whether
the object of the voyage had been frustrated by the delay of the ship was
left as a question of fact to the jury, although there was nothing in the
charterparty defining the time within which the charterers were to supply
the cargo of iron rails for San Francisco, and nothing on the face of the
charterparty to indicate the importance of time in the venture; and that was
a case in which, as Bramwell B. points out in his judgment at p. 148, *Taylor
v. Caldwell* (above, p. 511), was a strong authority to support the conclusion
arrived at in the judgment—that the ship not arriving in time for the
voyage contemplated, but at such time as to frustrate the commercial
venture, was not only a breach of the contract but discharged the charterer,
though he had such an excuse that no action would lie. And, again, in
Harris v. Dreesman (1854) 23 L.J.Ex. 210, the vessel had to be loaded, as no
particular time was mentioned, within a reasonable time; and, in judging of
a reasonable time, the court approved of evidence being given that the
defendants, the charterers, to the knowledge of the plaintiffs, had no
control over the colliery from which both parties knew that the coal was to
come; and that, although all that was said in the charterparty was that the
vessel should proceed to Spital Tongue's Spout (the spout of the Spital
Tongue's Colliery), and there take on board from the freighters a full and
complete cargo of coals, and five tons of coke, and although there was no
evidence to prove any custom in the port as to loading vessels in turn.
Again it was held in *Mumford v. Gething* (1859) 7 C.B.(N.S.) 305, that, in
construing a written contract of service under which A was to enter the
employ of B, oral evidence is admissible to show in what capacity A was to
serve B. See also *Price v. Mouat* (1862) 11 C.B. (N.S.) 508. The rule seems to
be that which is laid down in *Taylor on Evidence*, Vol. ii, § 1082: "It may be
laid down as a broad and distinct rule of law that extrinsic evidence of
every material fact which will enable the court to ascertain the nature and
qualities of the subject-matter of the instrument, or, in other words, to
identify the persons and things to which the instrument refers, must of
necessity be received." And Lord Campbell in his judgment says: "I am of
opinion that, when there is a contract for the sale of a specific subject-
matter, oral evidence may be received, for the purpose of showing what that
subject-matter was, of every fact within the knowledge of the parties before
and at the time of the contract." See *per* Campbell C.J., *Macdonald v.*

Longbottom (1859) 1 E. & E. 977, at p. 983. It seems to me that the language of Willes J. in *Lloyd v. Guibert* (1865) 35 L.J.Q.B. 74, 75, points in the same direction. I myself am clearly of opinion that in this case, where we have to ask ourselves whether the object of the contract was frustrated by the non-happening of the coronation and its procession on the days proclaimed, parol evidence is admissible to show that the subject of the contract was rooms to view the coronation procession, and was so to the knowledge of both parties. When once this is established, I see no difficulty whatever in the case. It is not essential to the application of the principle of *Taylor v. Caldwell* that the direct subject of the contract should perish or fail to be in existence at the date of performance of the contract. It is sufficient if a state of things or condition expressed in the contract and essential to its performance perishes or fails to be in existence at that time. In the present case the condition which fails and prevents the achievement of that which was, in the contemplation of both parties, the foundation of the contract, is not expressly mentioned either as a condition of the contract or the purpose of it; but I think for the reasons which I have given that the principle of *Taylor v. Caldwell* ought to be applied. This disposes of the plaintiff's claim for £50 unpaid balance of the price agreed to be paid for the use of the rooms. The defendant at one time set up a cross-claim for the return of the £25 he paid at the date of the contract. As that claim is now withdrawn it is unnecessary to say anything about it. I have only to add that the facts of this case do not bring it within the principle laid down in *Stubbs v. Holywell Ry.* (1867) L.R. 2 Ex. 311, that in the case of contracts falling directly within the rule of *Taylor v. Caldwell* the subsequent impossibility does not affect rights already acquired, because the defendant had the whole of June 24 to pay the balance, and the public announcement that the coronation and processions would not take place on the proclaimed days was made early on the morning of the 24th, and no cause of action could accrue till the end of that day. I think this appeal ought to be dismissed.

Romer and Stirling L.JJ. concurred.

Questions
1. Was the plaintiff able to provide what he had promised (a) in express terms? (b) in the light of the parol evidence?
2. The Bus Co. advertises an "Excursion to Epsom on Derby Day." X buys a ticket. The Derby is cancelled. Is the contract frustrated?
3. The X University Law Society contracts to hire a coach to go to the wedding of one of their number. The wedding is cancelled. Is the contract frustrated?

Cheshire & Fifoot, Law of Contract (5th ed.), p. 467

In *Krell v. Henry*, where it is unlikely that the cancellation of the procession occurred to the parties as a possibility, it was no doubt just and reasonable to treat the contract as discharged, but it is incompatible with the character of the hard bargainer to say that the owner of the room would have agreed to this had the proposal been put to him during the negotiations. It was a property owner's market in which the demand for suitable premises in all probability exceeded supply, and there can be little doubt that had the possibility of a cancellation have been put to the owner his reply would have been: "You must take your chance of that."

McElroy and Williams, The Coronation Cases, 4 M.L.R. 241, 247

Krell v. Henry was an action against the hirer of the rooms for the payment of money, and there was no impossibility, in the legal sense, in the payment of money. The defendant was held to be excused because there was a total failure of the consideration for his promise to pay. . . .

It is thought that if the test . . ., "What did he buy?" be applied to the case of *Krell v. Henry* it throws much light on the true ground of the decision in the latter case. The answer in that case is that he bought "rooms to view the procession. . . ."

The plaintiff's failure to provide that view, though it arose from no default of his, and therefore did not amount to a breach, was a failure going to the whole of the consideration, and *this* excused the defendant from his promise to pay.

HERNE BAY STEAM BOAT COMPANY v. HUTTON

Court of Appeal [1903] 2 K.B. 683; 72 L.J.K.B. 879; 89 L.T. 422

It had been publicly announced that the royal naval Review at Spithead would be held on June 28, 1902. The defendant wished to charter a steam boat to take paying passengers to see the review, and he entered into a contract with the plaintiffs, the owners of steamboat *Cynthia*, in these terms: "The *Cynthia* to be at Mr Hutton's disposal . . . on the morning of June 28 . . . to take out a party . . . for the purpose of viewing the naval review and for a day's cruise round the fleet; also on Sunday, June 29 for similar purposes . . . Price £250 payable, £50 down, balance before ship leaves Herne Bay."

Upon signing the agreement the defendant paid the £50 deposit. On June 25, 1902, an official announcement cancelling the review was published. The plaintiffs thereupon wired to the defendant, "What about *Cynthia*? She ready to start six tomorrow," but received no answer. The plaintiff then employed the ship on her ordinary sailings. On the two days in question, although the review was cancelled, the fleet remained anchored at Spithead. The plaintiffs sued for the balance of £200. The defendant alleged that it was a condition of the agreement that the naval review should take place on June 28, and that the consideration for the agreement wholly failed. The Court of Appeal (Vaughan Williams, Romer and Stirling L.JJ.), held, reversing Grantham J., that the plaintiffs could recover the £200 less the profits they had made by the use of the ship on the two days in question.

VAUGHAN WILLIAMS L.J.: I see nothing that makes this contract differ from a case where, for instance, a person has engaged a brake to take himself and a party to Epsom to see the races there, but for some reason or other, such as the spread of an infectious disease, the races are postponed. In such a case it could not be said that he could be relieved of his bargain. So in the present case it is sufficient to say that the happening of the naval review was not the foundation of the contract.

ROMER L.J.: The ship (as a ship) had nothing particular to do with the review or the fleet except as a convenient carrier of passengers to see it; and other ships suitable for carrying passengers would have done equally as well.

McElroy and Williams, The Coronation Cases, 4 M.L.R. 241, 254

Comparing the two above cases:

It is difficult to appreciate the soundness of this distinction. It may be replied that the number of ships suitable for seeing the review which could have been in that neighbourhood at the time was not unlimited. Moreover, the same argument could be applied equally well to *Krell v. Henry*. It could be said with equal truth that there was no particular fitness in the room which was let in that case. Any other room on the route of the procession would have done as well, and there must have been quite as many rooms overlooking the route of the procession as there were ships in the vicinity of Spithead capable of being hired for this particular purpose of viewing the fleet.

Sir Frederick Pollock, 20 L.Q.R. 4

In point of fact the fleet was still there, as Stirling L.J. observed, and, as the writer of these lines can bear witness, it was very well worth seeing without the review.

Question
What if the fleet had sailed away? Or if the procession had been held without the King?

BLACKBURN BOBBIN CO. LTD v. T. W. ALLEN & SONS LTD

Court of Appeal [1918] 2 K.B. 467; 87 L.J.K.B. 1085; 119 L.T. 215; 34 T.L.R. 508; 23 Com.Cas. 471

Early in 1914 the defendants, timber merchants at Hull, agreed to sell to the plaintiffs a quantity of Finland birch timber. Delivery was to commence about June or July and to continue until about November 1914. No deliveries had been made when war broke out in August 1914. Prior to the war the invariable practice was to load the timber into vessels at ports in Finland for direct sea carriage to English ports, and English timber merchants did not hold stocks of Finnish timber: but these facts were unknown to the plaintiffs. As soon as war broke out imports of timber from Finland stopped at once owing to the presence of German warships in the Baltic. The defendants alleged that the contract was dissolved by the outbreak of war. The plaintiffs claimed damages. The Court of Appeal (Pickford, Bankes and Warrington L.JJ.), affirming McCardie J., held that they were entitled to succeed.

PICKFORD L.J.: Why should a purchaser of goods, not specific goods, be deemed to concern himself with the way in which the seller is going to fulfil his contract by providing the goods he has agreed to sell? The sellers in this case agreed to deliver the timber free on rail at Hull, and it was no concern of the buyers as to how the sellers intended to get the timber there. I can see no reason for saying—and to free the defendants from liability this would have to be said—that the continuance of the normal mode of shipping the timber from Finland was a matter which both parties contemplated as necessary for the fulfilment of the contract. To dissolve the contract the matter relied on must be something which both parties had in their minds when they entered into the contract, such for instance as the existence of the music-hall in *Taylor v. Caldwell* (above, p. 511) or the continuance of the vessel in readiness to perform the contract, as in *Jackson v. Union Marine Insurance Co.* (above, p. 516). Here there is nothing to show that the plaintiffs contemplated, and there is no reason why they should be deemed to have contemplated, that the sellers should continue to have the ordinary facilities for dispatching the timber from Finland. As I have said, that was a matter which to the plaintiffs was wholly immaterial. It was not a matter forming the basis of the contract they entered into.

Questions
1. Would it have made any difference if the goods had been specific?
2. Can a contract for the sale of non-specific goods ever be frustrated? If so in what way?
(See *Howell v. Coupland* (1876) 1 Q.B.D. 258.)

NATIONAL CARRIERS LTD v. PANALPINA (NORTHERN) LTD

House of Lords [1981] A.C. 675; [1981] 2 W.L.R. 45; [1981] 1 All E.R. 161

Appellants leased a warehouse from respondents for a term of 10 years from January 1, 1974 at a rent of £6,500 per annum for the first five years and £13,300 for the second five years. In May 1979 the local authority closed the street giving the only access to the warehouse because of the dangerous condition of a listed building opposite which could not be demolished without the consent of the Minister. It was contemplated that the closure would last for a year or a little longer. At the time of the case, it seemed likely to last just over 18 months, leaving the lease with three more years to run. The closure prevented the appellants from using the premises for the only purpose contemplated, that is, as a warehouse. They stopped paying rent, claiming that the lease was frustrated. Sheen J. affirmed the judgment by the master for the respondents under Order 14, on the ground that the doctrine of frustation could not apply to a lease. The appellants appealed directly to the House of Lords.

LORD HAILSHAM OF ST. MARYLEBONE, L.C., having reviewed the theories of frustration, and expressed his preference for the formulation by Lord Radcliffe in *Davis v. Fareham* below, pp. 529–530 continued:

This discussion brings me to the central point at issue in this case, which, in my view, is whether or not there is anything in the nature of an executed lease which prevents the doctrine of frustration, however formulated, applying to the subsisting relationship between the parties. That the point is open in this House is clear from the difference of opinion expressed in the *Cricklewood* case [1945] A.C. 221 between Lord Russell and Lord Goddard on the one hand, who answered the question affirmatively, and Viscount Simon L.C. and Lord Wright on the other, who answered it negatively, with Lord Porter reserving his opinion until the point arose definitively for consideration. The point, though one of principle, is a narrow one. It is the difference immortalised in HMS Pinafore between "never" and "hardly ever," since both Viscount Simon L.C. and Lord Wright clearly conceded that, though they thought the doctrine applicable in principle to leases, the cases in which it could properly be applied must be extremely rare.

With the view of Viscount Simon L.C. and Lord Wright I respectfully agree. It is clear from what I have said already that, with Lord Radcliffe in the passage I have cited, I regard these cases as a sub-species of the class of case which comes so regularly before the courts, as to which of two innocent parties must bear the loss as the result of circumstances for which neither is at all to blame. Apart from Law Reform (Frustrated Contracts) Act 1943, the doctrine of frustration brings the whole contract to an end, and in the present case, apart from any adjustment under that Act and any statutory right to compensation under the closure order, the effect of frustration, had it been applicable, would have been to throw the whole burden of interruption for 20 months on the landlord, deprived as he would be of all his rent, and imposed, as he would have, on his shoulders the whole danger of destruction by fire and the burden of reletting after the interruption. As it is, with the same qualification as to possible compensation, the tenant has to pay the entire rent during the period of interruption without any part of the premises being usable at all, together with the burden (such as it may be) of the performance of the other tenant's covenants which include covenants to insure and repair. These are no light matters.

[His Lordship reviewed the authorities and continued:]

I conclude that the matter is not decided by authority and that the question is open to your Lordships to decide on principle. In my view your Lordships ought now so to decide it. Is there anything in principle which ought to prevent a lease from ever being frustrated? I think there is not. In favour of the opposite opinion, the difference in principle between real and chattel property was strongly urged. But I find it difficult to accept this, once it has been decided, as has long been the case, that time and demise charters even of the largest ships and of considerable duration can in principle be frustrated. This was sufficiently well established by 1943 to make these charters worthy of an express exception on an exception in the Law Reform (Frustrated Contracts) Act 1943, s.2(5), and since then the Suez cases have supervened. There would be something anomalous in the light of what has been going on recently in the Shatt al Arab to draw a distinction between a leased oil tank and a demise-chartered oil tanker. Other anomalies would follow if the absolute principle were to be applied to leases. Goff J. appears to have found no difficulty in applying frustration to an agreement for a lease (which creates an equitable estate in the land capable of being specifically enforced and thereby converted into a legal estate operating as from the beginning of the equitable interest): see *Rom Securities Ltd v. Rogers (Holdings) Ltd* (1968) 205 Estates Gazette 427. Personally I find the absurdities postulated by Megarry and Wade (Law of Real Property (4th ed., 1975), p. 675) in the case of the destruction by fire of the upper flat of a tenement building (already referred to) unacceptable if the "never" doctrine were rigidly applied, and I am attracted by Professor Treitel's argument (Law of Contract (5th ed., 1979), p. 669) of the inequitable contrast between a contract for the provision of holiday accommodation which amounted to a licence, and thus subject to the rule in *Taylor v. Caldwell*, and a similar contract amounting to a short lease. Clearly the contrast would be accentuated if Goff J.'s view be accepted as to the applicability of the doctrine to agreements for a lease (see above).

I accept of course that systems of developed land law draw a vital distinction between land, which is relatively permanent, and other types of property, which are relatively perishable. But one can overdo the contrast. Coastal erosion as well as the "vast convulsion of nature" postulated by Viscount Simon L.C. in the *Cricklewood* case [1945] 1 All E.R. 252 at 255–256, [1945] A.C. 221 at 229 can, even in this island, cause houses, gardens, even villages and their churches to fall into the North Sea, and, although the law of property in Scotland is different, as may be seen from

Tay Salmon Fisheries Co. Ltd v. Speedie 1929 S.C. 593, whole estates can there, as Lord President Clyde points out (at 600), be overblown with sand for centuries and so fall subject to the rei interitus doctrine of the civil law. In *Taylor v. Caldwell* (1863) 3 B. & S. 826 at 834, itself Blackburn J., after referring to the Digest (lib XLV, title 1) on the subject of "obligatio de certo corpore" on which in part he founds his new doctrine, expressly says:

> ". . . no doubt the propriety, one might almost say the necessity, of the implied condition is more obvious when the contract relates to a living animal, whether man or brute, than when it relates to some inanimate thing (*such as in the present case a theatre*) [emphasis mine] the existence of which is not so obviously precarious as that of the live animal, but the principle is adopted in the Civil law as applicable to every obligation of which the subject is a certain thing."

He then refers to Pothier, Traité des Obligations (partie 3, ch. 6, Art. 3, § 668) in support of his contention.

No doubt a long lease, say for example, one for 999 years, is almost exactly identical with the freehold for this purpose, and therefore subject to the ordinary law regarding the incidence of risk (recognised as regards chattels in section 7 of the former Sale of Goods Act 1893). But there is no difference between chattels in this respect and real property except in degree. Long term speculations and investments are in general less easily frustrated than short term adventures and a lease for 999 years must be in the longer class. I find myself persuaded by the argument presented by Atkin L.J. in his dissenting judgment in *Matthey v. Curling* [1922] 2 A.C. 180 at 199–200 and quoted with approval by Viscount Simon L.C. in the *Cricklewood* case [1945] A.C. 221 at 230. In that passage Atkin L.J. said:

> ". . . it does not appear to me conclusive against the application to a lease of the doctrine of frustration that the lease, in addition to containing contractual terms, grants a term of years. Seeing that the instrument as a rule expressly provides for the lease being determined at the option of the lessor upon the happening of certain specified events, I see no logical absurdity in implying a term that it shall be determined absolutely on the happening of other events—namely, those which in an ordinary contract work a frustration."

I pause here only to observe that, in the instant case, the lease gave the lessor a contingent right of determination in case of destruction by fire or in a case of a need for the use of the premises in connection with the railways, and to point out that in the War Damage Acts the lessee was given a statutory right, albeit different in kind from the doctrine of frustration, to disclaim a current lease on the happening of other events as the result of enemy action.

In the result, I come down on the side of the "hardly ever" school of thought. No doubt the circumstances in which the doctrine can apply to leases are, to quote Viscount Simon L.C. in the *Cricklewood* case [1945] A.C. 221 at 231, "exceedingly rare." Lord Wright appears to have thought the same, whilst adhering to the view that there are cases in which frustration can apply (see [1945] 1 All E.R. 252 at 263, [1945] A.C. 221 at 241). But, as he said in the same passage: "The doctrine of frustration is modern and flexible and is not subject to being constricted by an arbitrary formula." To this school of thought I respectfully adhere. Like Lord Wright, I am struck by the fact that there appears to be no reported English case where a lease has ever been held to have been frustrated. I hope this fact will act as a suitable deterrent to the litigious, eager to make legal history by being first in this field. But I am comforted by the reflexion of the authority referred to in the Compleat Angler (Pt. i, ch. 5) on the subject of strawberries: "Doubtless God could have made a better berry, but doubtless God never did." I only append to his observation of nature the comment that it does not follow from these premises that He never will, and, if it does not follow, an assumption that He never will becomes exceedingly rash.

In the event my opinion is that the appeal should be dismissed with costs.

Lords Wilberforce, Simon of Glaisdale and Roskill delivered speeches to similar effect.

Lord Russell of Killowen said: It is my understanding of the law that the purchaser of land, whether for a freehold or a leasehold interest, takes the risk that it may be or may turn out to be less suitable or quite unsuitable for the purpose he has in mind, unless the vendor or lessor has taken on himself by warranty or otherwise some liability in that event. A freehold purchaser cannot in that event, after completion, return the land and ask for his money back, though in an appropriate case he might be able to resist specific performance while the contract remained outstanding. So also in the case of a lease for which a premium has been paid in addition to rent, the lessee cannot require repayment of the premium and refuse to pay the rent; nor where there is no premium can he refuse to pay the covenanted rent.

Under the bargain between lessor and lessee the land for the term has passed from the lessor to the lessee, with all its advantages and disadvantages. In the instant case a disadvantage existed, or rather supervened, in that access to the building preventing its use for any purpose was blocked by administrative action which we must assume was legally permitted, and for which we were not told that any compensation could be claimed. If a principle of achieving justice be anywhere at the root of the principle of frustration, I ask myself why should justice require that a useless site be returned to the lessor rather than remain the property of the lessee? (It is not suggested that a just solution can be achieved by somehow sharing the bad luck between lessor and lessee by, for example, a reduction of rent.)

I would reserve consideration of cases of physical destruction of flying leaseholds and of the total disappearance of the site comprised in the lease into the sea so that it no longer existed in the form of a piece of terra firma and could not be the subject of re-entry or forfeiture. In that last case I would not need the intervention, of any court to say that the term of years could not outlast the disappearance of its subject matter: the site would no longer have a freeholder lessor, and the obligation to pay rent, which issues out of the land, could not survive its substitution by the waves of the North Sea.

Appeal dismissed

DAVIS CONTRACTORS LTD v. FAREHAM URBAN DISTRICT COUNCIL

House of Lords [1956] A.C. 696; [1956] 3 W.L.R. 37; [1956] 2 All E.R. 145;
54 L.G.R. 289

In July 1946 the contractors entered into a contract with the council to build 78 houses for the sum of £92,425 within a period of eight months. They had attached to their tender, in March 1946, a letter stating that the tender was subject to adequate supplies of labour and building materials being available. No such provision was included in the written contract entered into in July. Owing to unexpected circumstances and without the fault of either party, there was a serious shortage of skilled labour and of building materials and the work took 22 months to complete, with the result that the contractors properly and unavoidably incurred additional expense, amounting to £17,651. They contended that the contract (i) was subject to adequate supplies of labour being available, by reason of the letter of March 1946; (ii) was frustrated by reason of the long delay; and that they were entitled to a sum in excess of the contract price on *a quantum meruit* basis. On a case stated by an arbitrator, Goddard L.C.J. held that the contractors could recover because the letter was incorporated into the contract; but thought that the contract was not frustrated. The Court of Appeal held that the letter was not incorporated into the contract and that the contract was not frustrated. The House of Lords (Viscount Simonds, Lords Morton, Reid, Radcliffe and Somervell) affirmed the Court of Appeal on both points.

VISCOUNT SIMONDS AND LORDS MORTON AND REID made speeches dismissing the appeal.

LORD RADCLIFFE, having held that the letter was not incorporated into the contract, went on:

The theory of frustration belongs to the law of contract and it is represented by a rule which the courts will apply in certain limited circumstances for the purpose of deciding that contractual obligations, *ex facie* binding, are no longer enforceable against the parties. The description of the circumstances that justify the application of the rule and, consequently, the decision whether in a particular case those circumstances exist, are, I think, necessarily questions of law.

It has often been pointed out that the descriptions vary from one case of high authority to another. Even as long ago as 1918 Lord Sumner was able to offer an anthology of different tests directed to the factor of delay alone, and delay, though itself a frequent cause of the principle of frustration being invoked, is only one instance of the kind of circumstance to which the law attends (see *Bank Line Ltd v. Arthur Capel & Co.* [1919] A.C. 435). A full current anthology would need to be longer yet. But the variety of description is not of any importance so long as it is recognised that each is only a description and that all are intended to express the same general idea. I do not think that there has been a better expression of that general idea than the one offered by Lord Loreburn in *F.A. Tamplin Steamship Co. Ltd v. Anglo-Mexican Petroleum Products Co. Ltd* [1916] 2 A.C. 397, 403. It is shorter to quote than to try to paraphrase it: ". . . a court can and ought to examine the contract and the circumstances in which it was made, not of course to vary, but only to explain it, in order to see whether or not from the nature of it the parties must have made their bargain on the footing that a particular thing or state of things would continue to exist. And if they must have done so, then a term to that effect will be implied, though it be not expressed in the contract . . . no court has an absolving power, but it can infer from the nature of the contract and the surrounding circumstances that a condition which is not expressed was a foundation on which the parties contracted." So expressed, the principle of frustration, the origin of which seems to lie in the development of commercial law, is seen to be a branch of a wider principle which forms part of the English law of contract as a whole. But, in my opinion, full weight ought to be given to the requirement that the parties "must have made" their bargain on the particular footing. Frustration is not to be lightly invoked as the dissolvent of a contract.

Lord Loreburn ascribes the dissolution to an implied term of the contract that was actually made. This approach is in line with the tendency of English courts to refer all the consequences of a contract to the will of those who made it. But there is something of a logical difficulty in seeing how the parties could even impliedly have provided for something which *ex hypothesi* they neither expected nor foresaw; and the ascription of frustration to an implied term of the contract has been criticised as obscuring the true action of the court which consists in applying an objective rule of the law of contract to the contractual obligations that the parties have imposed upon themselves. So long as each theory produces the same result as the other, as normally it does, it matters little which theory is avowed (see *British Movietonews Ltd v. London and District Cinemas Ltd* [1952] A.C. 166, 184, *per* Viscount Simon). But it may still be of some importance to recall that, if the matter is to be approached by way of implied term, the solution of any particular case is not to be found by inquiring what the parties themselves would have agreed on had they been, as they were not, forewarned. It is not merely that no one can answer that hypothetical question: it is also that the decision must be given "irrespective of the individuals concerned, their temperaments and failings, their interest and circumstances" (*Hirji Mulji v. Cheong Yue Steamship Co. Ltd* [1926] A.C. 497, 510; 42 T.L.R. 359). The legal effect of frustration "does not depend on their intention or their opinions, or even knowledge, as to the event." On the contrary, it seems that when the event occurs "the meaning of the contract must be taken to be, not what the parties did intend (for they had neither thought nor intention regarding it), but that which the parties, as fair and reasonable men, would presumably have agreed upon if, having such possibility in view, they had made express provision as to their several rights and liabilities in the event of its occurrence" (*Dahl v. Nelson* (1881) 6 App.Cas. 38, *per* Lord Watson).

By this time it might seem that the parties themselves have become so far disembodied spirits that their actual persons should be allowed to rest in peace. In their place there rises the figure of the fair and reasonable man. And the spokesman of the fair and reasonable man, who represents after all no more than the anthropomorphic conception of justice, is and must be the court itself. So perhaps it would be simpler to say at the outset that frustration occurs whenever the law recognises that without default of either party a contractual obligation has become incapable of being performed because the circumstances in which performance is called for would render it a thing radically different from that which was undertaken by the contract. *Non haec in foedera veni.* It was not this that I promised to do. [The formulation preferred by Lord Hailsham, above, p. 524].

There is, however, no uncertainty as to the materials upon which the court must proceed. "The data for decision are, on the one hand, the terms and construction of the contract, read in the light of the then existing circumstances, and on the other hand the events which have occurred" (*Denny, Mott & Dickson Ltd v. James B. Fraser & Co. Ltd* [1944] A.C. 265, 274–275, *per* Lord Wright). In the nature of things there is often no room for any elaborate inquiry. The court must act upon a general impression of what its rule requires. It is for that reason that special importance is necessarily attached to the occurrence of any unexpected event that, as it were, changes the face of things. But, even so, it is not hardship or inconvenience or material loss itself which calls the principle of frustration into play. There must be as well such a change in the significance of the obligation that the thing undertaken would, if performed, be a different thing from that contracted for.

I am bound to say that, if this is the law, the appellants' case seems to me a long way from a case of frustration. Here is a building contract entered into by a housing authority and a big firm of contractors in all the uncertainties of the post-war world. Work was begun shortly before the formal contract was executed and continued, with impediments and minor stoppages but without actual interruption, until the 78 houses contracted for had all been built. After the work had been in progress for a time the appellants raised the claim, which they repeated more than once, that they ought to be paid a larger sum for their work than the contract allowed; but the respondents refused to admit the claim and, so far as appears, no conclusive action was taken by either side which would make the conduct of one or the other a determining element in the case.

That is not in any obvious sense a frustrated contract. But the appellants' argument, which certainly found favour with the arbitrator, is that at some stage before completion the original contract was dissolved because it became incapable of being performed according to its true significance and its place was taken by a new arrangement under which they were entitled to be paid, not the contract sum, but a fair price on *quantum meruit* for the work that they carried out during the 22 months that elapsed between commencement and completion. The contract, it is said, was an eight months' contract, as indeed it was. Through no fault of the parties it turned out that it took 22 months to do the work contracted for. The main reason for this was that, whereas both parties had expected that adequate supplies of labour and material would be available to allow for completion in eight months, the supplies that were in fact available were much less than adequate for the purpose. Hence, it is said, the basis or the footing of the contract was removed before the work was completed; or, slightly altering the metaphor, the footing of the contract was so changed by the circumstance that the expected supplies were not available that the contract built upon that footing became void. These are the findings which the arbitrator has recorded in his supplemental award.

In my view, these are in substance conclusions of law, and I do not think that they are good law. All that anyone, arbitrator or court, can do is to study the contract in the light of the circumstances that prevailed at the time when it was made and, having done so, to relate it to the circumstances that are said to have brought about its frustration. It may be a finding of fact that at the time of making the contract both parties anticipated that adequate supplies of labour and material would be available to enable the contract to be completed in the stipulated time. I doubt whether it is, but, even if it is, it is no more than to say that when one party stipulated for completion in eight months, and the other party undertook it, each assumed that what was promised could be satisfactorily performed. That is a statement of the obvious that could be made with regard to most contracts. I think that a good deal more than that is needed to form a "basis" for the principle of frustration.

The justice of the arbitrator's conclusion depends upon the weight to be given to the fact that this was a contract for specified work to be completed in a fixed time at a price determined by those conditions. I think that his view was that, if without default on either side the contract period was substantially extended, that circumstance itself rendered the fixed price so unfair to the contractor that he ought not to be held to his original price. I have much sympathy with the contractor, but, in my opinion, if that sort of consideration were to be sufficient to establish a case of frustration, there would be an untold range of contractual obligations rendered uncertain and, possibly, unenforceable.

Two things seem to me to prevent the application of the principle of frustration to this case. One is that the cause of the delay was not any new state of things which the parties could not reasonably be thought to have foreseen. On the contrary, the possibility of enough labour and materials not being available was before their eyes and could have been the subject of special contractual stipulation. It was not made so. The other thing is that, though timely completion was no doubt important to both sides, it is not right to treat the possibility of delay as having the same significance for each. The owner draws up his conditions in detail, specifies the time within which he requires completion, protects himself both by a penalty clause for time exceeded and by calling for the deposit of a guarantee bond and offers a certain measure of security to a contractor by his escalator clause with regard to wages and prices. In the light of these conditions the contractor makes his tender, and the tender must necessarily take into account the margin of profit that he hopes to obtain upon his adventure and in that any appropriate allowance for the obvious risks of delay. To my mind, it is useless to pretend that the contractor is not at risk if delay does occur, even serious delay. And I think it a misuse of legal terms to call in frustration to get him out of his unfortunate predicament.

LORD SOMERVELL made a speech dismissing the appeal.

Appeal dismissed.

Note

The closure of the Suez Canal on November 2, 1956, gave rise to a similar problem in three different cases: *Carapanayoti & Co. Ltd v. E.T. Green Ltd* [1959] 1 Q.B. 131; *Tsakiroglou & Co. Ltd v. Noblee Thorl* [1960] 2 Q.B. 318 and *Albert D. Gaon & Co. v. Société Inter-Professionelle des Oléagineaux Fluides Alimentaires* [1960] 2 Q.B. 334. By a c.i.f. contract sellers agreed to ship goods from Port Sudan to Belfast (in the first case) to Hamburg (in the second) and to a Mediterranean port (in the third). In each case the parties contemplated that the shipment would be via the Suez Canal (but did not so stipulate in the contract) and the goods had to go round the Cape, more than two and a half times as far in the first case and more than four times as far in the third. There was no evidence that the longer voyage would have caused the goods (cottonseed cake in the first case and groundnuts in the second and third) to depreciate appreciably in quality or in weight. In each case the sellers failed to deliver the goods.

In the first case, McNair J. asked himself three questions and answered them all in the affirmative: (i) the availability of the canal *was* the basis of the contract; (ii) the closure of the canal *did* transmute the obligation into one of a different kind; (iii) if the officious bystander (see above, p. 393) had asked: "What is to happen if the canal should be closed?" the parties, as reasonable men, *would* have replied: "The contract is off." He therefore held that the contract was frustrated.

In the second case Diplock J. had before him a finding of fact by arbitrators that shipment via the Cape was not commercially or fundamentally different from shipment via Suez. Diplock J. held that this finding was unassailable; there was evidence to support it and there was no indication that the arbitrators had misdirected themselves as to the meaning of "commercially or fundamentally different." He therefore held that the contract was not frustrated. But he emphasised that he was not saying that McNair J. was wrong. This was a case in which a jury, properly directed, could have held either way.

In the third case Ashworth J. disagreed directly with McNair J. He denied that the closure of the canal transmuted the obligation into one of a different character: both before and after the closure, the thing undertaken was arranging the shipment of goods from Port Sudan to the Mediterranean. This was not rendered impossible—as, for example, a contract would be if it provided for shipment of goods from a Black Sea port to the Mediterranean and the Dardanelles were closed for an indefinite period. The mere fact that the performance of the same obligation became much more onerous was not sufficient to frustrate the contract.

The second and third cases went to the Court of Appeal and the decisions of Diplock and Ashworth JJ. were affirmed. The first case was overruled: [1960] 2 Q.B. 348; [1960] 2 W.L.R. 869. The court thought that Diplock J. should have felt free to review the finding of the arbitrator which involved a question of law or at least was a question of mixed fact and law (*per* Ormerod L.J.) or was a finding of a secondary fact, namely, an inference from primary facts, and, as such, open to review (*per* Harman L.J.). Ashworth J.'s view was approved. The House of Lords affirmed the decision of the Court of Appeal in the *Tsakiroglou* case: [1962] A.C. 93; [1961] 2 W.L.R. 633; [1961] 2 All E.R. 179.

Questions
  1. Did McNair J. ask the wrong questions or give the wrong answers?
  2. Do you think that the result in the Suez sale cases ought to have been different if either (a) there had been a stipulation in the contract that the goods were to go via the Suez Canal, or (b) the goods had been of a perishable nature and would not have survived the journey round the Cape?

OCEAN TRAMP TANKERS CORPORATION v. V.O. SOVFRACHT, THE EUGENIA

Court of Appeal [1964] 2 Q.B.226; [1964] 2 W.L.R. 114; [1964] 1 All E.R. 161; [1963] 2 Lloyd's Rep. 231

The *Eugenia* was chartered for a "trip out to India via the Black Sea" from the time the vessel was delivered at Genoa. When the negotiations took place both parties realised the possibility that the Suez Canal might be closed; but the parties were unable to agree on any provision to meet this contingency. A "war clause" forbade the charterers from bringing the vessel into a dangerous zone, without the consent of the owners. The vessel, having sailed from Genoa, via Odessa, arrived at Port Said at a time when it was a "dangerous zone" and became trapped in the canal. The charterers alleged that the charter was frustrated. The owners denied this but treated the charterers' conduct as a repudiation and sued for hire during the period for which the ship was trapped.

LORD DENNING M.R., having held that the charterer had broken the war clause by entering the Canal zone, went on: The second question is whether the charterparty was frustrated by what took place. The arbitrator has held it was not. The judge has held that it was. Which is right? One thing that is obvious is that the charterers cannot rely on the fact that the *Eugenia* was trapped in the canal; for that was their own fault. They were in breach of the war clause in entering it. They cannot rely on a self-induced frustration, see *Maritime National Fish Ltd v. Ocean Trawlers Ltd.* (below, p. 538). But they seek to rely on the fact that the canal itself was blocked. They assert that even if the *Eugenia* had never gone into the canal, but had stayed outside (in which case she would not have been in breach of the war clause), nevertheless she would still have had to go round by the Cape. And that, they say, brings about a frustration, for it makes the venture fundamentally different from what they contracted for. The judge has accepted this view. He has held that on November 16, 1956, the charter-party was frustrated. The reason for taking November 16, 1956, was this: before November 16, 1956, mercantile men (even if she had stayed outside) would not have formed any conclusion as to whether the obstructions in the canal were other than temporary. There was insufficient information available to form a judgment. On November 16, 1956, mercantile men would conclude that the blockage of the southern end would last till March or April 1957; so that by that time it would be clear that the only thing to do (if the ship had never entered the canal) would be to go round the Cape. The judge said: "I hold that the adventure, involving a voyage round the Cape, is basically or fundamentally different from the adventure involving a voyage via the Suez Canal." So he held the contract frustrated. He was comforted to find in *The Massalia* [1961] 2 Q.B. 278 Pearson J. came to a similar conclusion.

I must confess that I find it difficult to apply the doctrine of frustration to a hypothetical situation, that is, to treat this vessel as if she had never entered the canal and then ask whether the charter was frustrated. The doctrine should be applied to the facts as they really are. But I will swallow this difficulty and ask myself what would be the position if the vessel had never entered the canal but stayed at Port Said. Would the contract be frustrated?

This means that once again we have had to consider the authorities on this vexed topic of frustration. But I think the position is now reasonably clear. It is simply this: if it should happen, in the course of carrying out a contract, that a fundamentally different situation arises for which the parties made no provision—so much so that it would not be just in the new situation to hold them bound to its terms—then the contract is at an end.

It was originally said that the doctrine of frustration was based on an implied term. In short, that the parties, if they had foreseen the new situation, would have said to one another: "If that happens, of course, it is all over between us." But the theory of an implied term has now been discarded by everyone, or nearly everyone, for the simple reason that it does not represent the truth.[1] The parties would not have said: "It is all over between us." They would have differed about what was to happen. Each would have sought to insert reservations or qualifications of one kind or another. Take this very case. The parties realised that the canal might

---

[1] Compare the sentence footnoted on p. 502 above. If an implied condition is the proper explanation of the common mistake cases, why not of the frustration cases? Or has Lord Denning changed his mind?

become impassable. They tried to agree on a clause to provide for the contingency. But they failed to agree. So there is no room for an implied term.

It has frequently been said that the doctrine of frustration only applies when the new situation is "unforeseen" or "unexpected" or "uncontemplated," as if that were an essential feature. But it is not so. The only thing that is essential is that the parties should have made no provision for it in their contract. The only relevance of it being "unforeseen" is this: If the parties did not foresee anything of the kind happening, you can readily infer they have made no provision for it: whereas if they did foresee it, you would expect them to make provision for it. But cases have occurred where the parties have foreseen the danger ahead, and yet made no provision for it in the contract. Such was the case in the Spanish Civil War when a ship was let on charter to the republican government. The purpose was to evacuate refugees. The parties foresaw that she might be seized by the nationalists. But they made no provision for it in their contract. Yet, when she was seized, the contract was frustrated, see *W.J. Tatem Ltd v. Gamboa* [1939] 1 K.B. 132. So here the parties foresaw that the canal might become impassable: it was the very thing they feared. But they made no provision for it. So there is room for the doctrine to apply if it be a proper case for it.[1]

We are thus left with the simple test that a situation must arise which renders performance of the contract "a thing radically different from that which was undertaken by the contract," see *Davis Contractors Ltd v. Fareham Urban District Council* (above, p. 526) by Lord Radcliffe. To see if the doctrine applies, you have first to construe the contract and see whether the parties have themselves provided for the situation that has arisen. If they have provided for it, the contract must govern. There is no frustration. If they have not provided for it, then you have to compare the new situation with the situation for which they did provide. Then you must see how different it is. The fact that it has become more onerous or more expensive for one party than he thought is not sufficient to bring about a frustration. It must be more than merely more onerous or more expensive. It must be positively unjust to hold the parties bound. It is often difficult to draw the line. But it must be done. And it is for the courts to do it as a matter of law: see *Tsakiroglou & Co. Ltd v. Noblee Thorl G.m.b.H.* [1962] A.C. 93, 116, 119, by Lord Simonds and by Lord Reid.

Applying these principles to this case, I have come to the conclusion that the blockage of the canal did not bring about a "fundamentally different situation" such as to frustrate the venture. My reasons are these: (1) The venture was the whole trip from delivery at Genoa, out to the Black Sea, there load cargo, thence to India, unload cargo, and redelivery. The time for this vessel from Odessa to Vizagapatam via the Suez Canal would be 26 days, and via the Cape, 56 days. But that is not the right comparison. You have to take the whole venture from delivery at Genoa to redelivery at Madras. We were told that the time for the whole venture via the Suez Canal would be 108 days and via the Cape 138 days. The difference over the whole voyage is not so radical as to produce a frustration. (2) The cargo was iron and steel goods which would not be adversely affected by the longer voyage, and there was no special reason for early arrival. The vessel

[1] See the criticism in Treitel, *Law of Contract* (8th ed.).

and crew were at all times fit and sufficient to proceed via the Cape. (3) The cargo was loaded on board at the time of the blockage of the canal. If the contract was frustrated, it would mean, I suppose, that the ship could throw up the charter and unload the cargo wherever she was, without any breach of contract. (4) The voyage round the Cape made no great difference except that it took a good deal longer and was more expensive for the charterers than a voyage through the canal.

The only hesitation I have had about this case is because of the views expressed by Pearson J. in *The Massalia*. That case can be distinguished because there was a sentence in the charter which read: "Captain also to telegraph to 'Maritsider Genoa' on passing Suez Canal." Pearson J. held that that meant there was actually an obligation to pass the Suez Canal, and hence the contract was frustrated by impossibility. I think he attached too much significance to the clause. I think that there, as here, there was no obligation to go through Suez Canal, but only to go by the route which was customary at the time of performance; and that there is no legitimate distinction to be drawn between that case and this. That was a voyage charter and this a time charter. That makes no difference except that the burden fell on the owners and not the charterers. Pearson J. held that the route via the Cape was fundamentally different from the route via the Suez Canal and that the charter was frustrated on that ground also. I am afraid I cannot take that view. It is important to notice also that since that case the House of Lords have held that, with goods sold c.i.f. Sudan to Hamburg, the contract of sale was not frustrated by the closure of the Suez Canal, see *Tsakiroglou & Co. Ltd v. Noblee Thorl G.m.b.H.* I know that a contract of affreightment is different from a contract for the sale of goods, but I should find it strange if, in the case of a ship loaded with cargo, the contract of affreightment was frustrated by the closure of the canal and the contract of sale was not frustrated. It would lead to endless complications.

I come, therefore, to the conclusion that the decision of Pearson J. in *The Massalia* was wrong and should be overruled. It is to be noticed that both in that case and in this the arbitrators held there was no frustration. I think they were right. I would allow this appeal and hold that the contract was not frustrated.

On this footing I gather there is no other point which needs to be decided.

Donovan L.J. delivered judgment allowing the appeal and Danckwerts L.J. concurred.

Appeal allowed.

J. LAURITZEN A.S. v. WIJSMULLER B.V.

THE "SUPER SERVANT TWO"

Court of Appeal [1990] 1 Lloyd's L. Rep. 1

On July 7, 1980 the defendants contracted to carry the plaintiffs' drilling rig (*Dan King*) from Japan to Rotterdam, using as the "transportation unit," *Super Servant*

One or *Super Servant Two*. The defendants intended to use *Super Servant Two* but on January 29, 1981 it sank. The defendants had entered into contracts with other persons which they could perform only by using *Super Servant One*. They decided to use *Super Servant One* for those other contracts. Among preliminary questions for the court was (2), whether the *Dan King* contract was frustrated if the loss of *Super Servant Two* was caused (a) without the defendants' negligence or (b) by the defendants' negligence.

BINGHAM L.J. Mr Clarke for Wijsmuller submitted that the extraneous supervening event necessary to found a plea of frustration occurred when *Super Servant Two* sank on January 29, 1981. The *Dan King* contract was not, however, thereupon frustrated but remained alive until Wijsmuller decided a fortnight later that that contract could not be, or would not be, performed. There was, he submitted, factually, no break in the chain of causation between the supervening event and the non-performance of the contract. He acknowledged that *Maritime National Fish Ltd*, below, p. 538, contained observations on their face inimical to his argument, but distinguished that as a decision on causation confined to its own peculiar facts and laying down no general rule. For authoritative support Mr Clarke relied on cases dealing with the application of *force majeure* clauses in commodity contracts, and in particular on an unreported judgment of Robert Goff J., as he then was, adopted with approval by the Court of Appeal in *Bremer Handelsgesellschaft m.b.H. v. Continental Grain Co.* [1983] 1 Lloyd's Rep. 269 at p. 292:

> . . . the question resolves itself into a question of causation; in my judgment, at least in a case in which a seller can (as in the present case) claim the protection of a clause which protects him where fulfilment is hindered by the excepted peril, subsequent delivery of his available stock to other customers will not be regarded as an independent cause of shortage, provided that in making such delivery the seller acted reasonably in all the circumstances of the case. . . .

A similar approach was reflected in other cases, see, for example, *Intertradex S.A. v. Lesieur—Tourteaux S.A.R.L.* [1977] 2 Lloyd's Rep. 146 at p. 115, *per* Donaldson J. as he then was; [1978] 2 Lloyd's Rep. 509 at p. 513, *per* Lord Denning, M.R. Reliance was also placed on passages in The Law of Contract (7th ed.) by Professor Treitel, which the Judge quoted in his judgment at p. 152. Thus, Mr Clarke urged, this was a case in which Wijsmuller could not perform all their contracts once *Super Servant Two* was lost; they acted reasonably (as we must assume) in treating the *Dan King* contract as one they could not perform; so the sinking had the direct result of making that contract impossible to perform.

Mr Legh-Jones answered that since the contract provided for the carriage to be performed by one or other vessel the loss of one did not render performance radically different, still less impossible. That apart, Wijsmuller's argument fell foul of the principles summarised above since (among other things) the frustration they sought to establish did not bring the contract to an end forthwith, without more and automatically and was not independent of the act or election of Wijsmuller. The *force majeure* cases were good law so far as they went, but it was one thing to construe and apply a consensual *force majeure* clause, another to determine whether the facts were such that the law should hold the contract to be discharged. . . .

Had the *Dan King* contract provided for carriage by *Super Servant Two* with no alternative, and that vessel had been lost before the time for performance, then assuming no negligence by Wijsmuller (as for purposes of this question we must), I feel sure the contract would have been frustrated. The doctrine must avail a party who contracts to perform a contract of carriage with a vessel which, through no fault of his, no longer exists. But that is not this case. The *Dan King* contract did provide an alternative. When that contract was made one of the contracts eventually performed by *Super Servant One* during the period of contractual carriage of *Dan King* had been made, the other had not, at any rate finally. Wijsmuller have not alleged that when the *Dan King* contract was made either vessel was earmarked for its performance. That, no doubt, is why an option was contracted for. Had it been foreseen when the *Dan King* contract was made that *Super Servant Two* would be unavailable for performance, whether because she had been deliberately sold or accidentally sunk, Lauritzen at least would have thought it no matter since the carriage could be performed with the other. I accordingly accept Mr Legh-Jones's submission that the present case does not fall within the very limited class of cases in which the law will relieve one party from an absolute promise he has chosen to make.

But I also accept Mr Legh-Jones's submission that Wijsmuller's argument is subject to other fatal flaws. If, as was argued, the contract was frustrated when Wijsmuller made or communicated their decision on February 16, it deprives language of all meaning to describe the contract as coming to an end automatically. It was, indeed, because the contract did not come to an end automatically on January 29, that Wijsmuller needed a fortnight to review their schedules and their commercial options. I cannot, furthermore, reconcile Wijsmuller's argument with the reasoning or the decision in *Maritime National Fish Ltd* (below, p. 538). In that case the Privy Council declined to speculate why the charterers selected three of the five vessels to be licensed but, as I understand the case, regarded the interposition of human choice after the allegedly frustrating event as fatal to the plea of frustration. If Wijsmuller are entitled to succeed here, I cannot see why the charterers lost there. The cases on frustrating delay do not, I think, help Wijsmuller since it is actual and prospective delay (whether or not recognised as frustrating by a party at the time) which frustrates the contract, not a party's election or decision to treat the delay as frustrating. I have no doubt that *force majeure* clauses are, where their terms permit, to be construed and applied as in the commodity cases on which Wijsmuller relied, but it is in my view inconsistent with the doctrine of frustration as previously understood on high authority that its application should depend on any decision, however reasonable and commercial, of the party seeking to rely on it. . . .

Question 2(b)

The issue between the parties was short and fundamental: what is meant by saying that a frustrating event, to be relied on, must occur without the fault or default, or without blame attaching to, the party relying on it?

Mr Clarke's answer was that a party was precluded from relying on an event only when he had acted deliberately or in breach of an actionable duty in causing it. Those conditions were not met here since it was not alleged Wijsmuller sank *Super Servant Two* deliberately. . . .

Mr Legh-Jones argued for a less restrictive approach. He relied on what Lord Justice Griffiths, as he then was, said in *The Hannah Blumenthal*, [1982] 1 Lloyd's Rep. 582, p. 592; [1983] 1 A.C. 854 at p. 882:

> [*Denmark Productions Ltd v. Boscobel Productions Ltd* [1969] 1 Q.B. 699] best illustrates what is meant by default in the context of frustration. The essence of frustration is that it is caused by some unforeseen supervening event over which the parties to the contract have no control and for which they are therefore not responsible. To say that the supervening event occurs without the default or blame or responsibility of the parties is, in the context of the doctrine of frustration, but another way of saying it is a supervening event over which they had no control. The doctrine has no application and cannot be invoked by a contracting party when the frustrating event was at all times within his control; still less can it apply in a situation in which the parties owed a contractual duty to one another to prevent the frustrating event occurring.

I do not pause to ask whether Lord Justice Griffith's opinion is formally binding upon us since in my judgment it clearly indicates the path which the law should follow. When, in *Bank Line Ltd* [1919] A.C. 435, 452, Lord Sumner made his famous observation that "Reliance cannot be placed on a self-induced frustration" he was contrasting a self-induced frustration with one arising "without blame or fault on either side." As the Judge observed—

> "... in some respects the doctrine of frustration and the concept of 'self-inducement' are simply opposite sides of the same coin."

Wijsmuller's test would, in my judgment, confine the law in a legalistic strait-jacket and distract attention from the real question, which is whether the frustrating event relied upon is truly an outside event or extraneous change of situation or whether it is an event which the party seeking to rely on it had the means and opportunity to prevent but nevertheless caused or permitted to come about. A fine test of legal duty is inappropriate; what is needed is a pragmatic judgment whether a party seeking to rely on an event as discharging him from a contractual promise was himself responsible for the occurrence of that event.

Lauritzen have pleaded in some detail the grounds on which they say that *Super Servant Two* was lost as a result of the carelessness of Wijsmuller, their servants or agents. If those allegations are made good to any significant extent Wijsmuller would (even if my answer to Question 2(a) is wrong) be precluded from relying on their plea of frustration.

Dillon L.J. delivered judgment to the same effect.

Notes

1. *Maritime National Fish Ltd v. Ocean Trawlers Ltd* [1935] A.C. 524, P.C., concerned the charter of a trawler, *St. Cuthbert*. Both parties knew that it could only be used with an otter trawl and that under Canadian law it was an offence to use an otter trawl without a licence. The charterers were operating five trawlers and applied for five licences but were granted only three and were asked to nominate the trawlers. They nominated three trawlers other than *St.*

Cuthbert and, when sued for the hire, claimed that the contract was frustrated. The Privy Council held that they were liable, any frustration having resulted from their deliberate act. They could not rely on a "self-induced frustration."

2. The party who has induced the frustration cannot rely on it. As against him, the "frustrated" contract continues in force. But if he attempts to sue on that contract, he will fail. He cannot rely on his own wrong to say "Because the frustrating event was my fault, the contract is not frustrated": *F.C. Shepherd & Co. Ltd v. Jerrom* [1986] 3 All E.R. 589, below, p. 570.

3. On the nature of the fault required to render the frustration "self-induced," *Thompson v. Asda-MFI*, above p. 408.

A, a pianist, has undertaken to perform at a concert on June 1. What is the position if (i) on May 29 she takes an overdose of aspirin with intent to commit suicide, survives, but is disabled from performing on June 1? or (ii) on May 29 she absent-mindedly steps in front of a bus and is severely injured? or (iii) on May 29 she assaults a constable and is remanded in custody for a week?

JOSEPH CONSTANTINE STEAMSHIP LINE LTD v. IMPERIAL SMELTING CORPORATION LTD

House of Lords [1942] A.C. 154; 110 L.J.K.B. 433; 165 L.T. 27; 46 Com.Cas. 258; 57 T.L.R. 485; 70 Ll.L.Rep. 1; [1941] 2 All E.R. 165

The respondents chartered the appellants' steamship, *Kingswood*, to proceed to Port Pirie, Australia, to load a cargo. On January 3, 1937, while the ship was anchored in the roads off Port Pirie—she was due to berth on January 4—an explosion of great violence occurred which resulted in such delay that, as was admitted, the commercial object of the adventure was frustrated. The respondents claimed damages. The arbitrator found that, though various hypotheses were put forward, no one had given a satisfactory explanation of the cause of the disaster; he was not satisfied that the true cause of the explosion had as yet been suggested. The Court of Appeal held, reversing Atkinson J., that a party, prima facie guilty of a failure to perform his contract, cannot escape under the plea of frustration, unless he proves that the frustration occurred without his default; that the appellants had failed to discharge that onus, and the respondents were entitled to damages. The House of Lords (Viscount Simon L.C., Viscount Maugham, Lords Russell, Wright and Porter) allowed the appeal.

LORD SIMON L.C., having referred to the judgment of the Court of Appeal, said: . . . if this were correct there must be many cases in which, although in truth frustration is complete and unavoidable, the defendant will be held liable because of his inability to prove a negative—in some cases, indeed, a whole series of negatives. Suppose that a vessel while on the high seas disappears completely during a storm. Can it be that the defence of frustration of the adventure depends on the owner's ability to prove that all his servants on board were navigating the ship with adequate skill and that there was no "default" which brought about the catastrophe? Suppose that a vessel in convoy is torpedoed by the enemy and sinks immediately with all hands. Does the application of the doctrine require that the owners should affirmatively prove that those on board were keeping a good look-out, were obscuring lights, were steering as directed, and so forth? There is no reported case which requires us so to hold. The doctrine on which the defence of frustration depends is nowhere so stated as to place this onus of proof on the party relying on it. . . .

Every case in this branch of the law can be stated as turning on the question whether from the express terms of the particular contract a further term should be implied which, when its conditions are fulfilled, puts an end to the contract.

If the matter is regarded in this way, the question is as to the construction of a contract taking into consideration its express and implied terms. The implied term in the present case may well be—"This contract is to cease to be binding if the vessel is disabled by an overpowering disaster, provided that disaster is not brought about by the default of either party." This is very similar to an express exception of "perils of the seas," as to which it is ancient law that by an implied term of the contract the shipowner cannot rely on the exception if its operation was brought about either (a) by negligence of his servants, or (b) by his breach of the implied warranty of seaworthiness. If a ship sails and is never heard of again the shipowner can claim protection for loss of the cargo under the express exception of perils of the seas. To establish that, must he go on to prove (a) that the perils were *not* caused by negligence of his servants, and (b) were not caused by any unseaworthiness? I think clearly not. He proves a prima facie case of loss by sea perils, and that he is within the exception. If the cargo owner wants to defeat that plea it is for him by rejoinder to allege and prove either negligence or unseaworthiness. The judgment of the Court of Appeal in *The Glendarroch* [1894] P. 266 is plain authority for this. . . .

FIBROSA SPOLKA AKCYJNA v. FAIRBAIRN LAWSON COMBE BARBOUR LTD

House of Lords [1943] A.C. 32; 111 L.J.K.B. 433; 167 L.T. 101; 58 T.L.R. 308; [1942] 2 All E.R. 122

On July 12, 1939, the respondents, an English company, agreed to sell, and the appellants, a Polish company, agreed to purchase machinery for £4,800 of which one-third was to be paid with the order. Delivery was to be made, within three or four months of the settlement of final details, at Gdynia, Poland. Only £1,000 was in fact paid with the order. On September 3 Britain declared war on Germany, and on September 23 Gdynia was occupied by the Germans. The appellants sued for the return of the £1,000. Tucker J. and the Court of Appeal held that the contract was frustrated and that, under the principle of *Chandler v. Webster*,[1] the claim must fail.

Viscount Simon L.C.: If we are to approach this problem anew, it must be premised that the first matter to be considered is always the terms of the particular contract. If, for example, the contract is "divisible" in the sense that a sum is to be paid over in respect of completion of a defined portion of the work, it may well be that the sum is not returnable if completion of

---

[1] In *Chandler v. Webster* [1904] 1 K.B. 493, C.A., the defendant agreed to let to the plaintiff a room for the purpose of viewing the coronation procession of June 26, 1902, for the sum of £141 15s. payable immediately. The procession subsequently became impossible owing to the illness of the King. The plaintiff had paid £100 on account and the balance remained unpaid. The plaintiff sued to recover the £100 paid by him as on a total failure of consideration, and the defendant counterclaimed for the sum of £41 15s.

The Court of Appeal (Collins M.R., Romer and Matthew L.JJ.) held that the plaintiff's action failed and the defendant's counterclaim succeeded. The defendant's right to payment of the whole sum had accrued before the procession became impossible, and the effect of frustration was not to wipe out the contract altogether but only to release the parties from further performance.

the whole work is frustrated. If the contract itself on its true construction stipulates for a particular result which is to follow in regard to money already paid, should frustration afterwards occur, this governs the matter. The ancient and firmly established rule that freight paid in advance is not returned if the completion of the voyage is frustrated: *Byrne v. Schiller*, L.R. 6 Ex. 319, should, I think, be regarded as a stipulation introduced into such contracts by custom, and not as the result of applying some abstract principle. And so, *a fortiori*, if there is a stipulation that the prepayment is "out and out." To take an example, not from commerce, but from sport, the cricket spectator who pays for admission to see a match cannot recover the entrance money on the ground that rain has prevented play if, expressly or by proper implication, the bargain with him is that no money will be returned. Inasmuch as the effect of frustration may be explained as arising from an implied term: see *Joseph Constantine Steamship Line Ltd v. Imperial Smelting Corporation Ltd*; it is tempting to speculate whether a further term could be implied as to what was to happen, in the event of frustration, to money already paid, but, if the parties were assumed to have discussed the point when entering into the contract, they could not be supposed to have agreed on a simple formula which would be fair in all circumstances, and all that could be said is that, in the absence of such agreement, the law must decide. The question now to be determined is whether, in the absence of a term in the contract dealing with the matter, the rule which is commonly called the rule in *Chandler v. Webster* should be affirmed. . . .

The *locus classicus* for the view which has hitherto prevailed is to be found in the judgment of Collins M.R. in *Chandler v. Webster*. It was not a considered judgment, but it is hardly necessary to say that I approach this pronouncement of the then Master of the Rolls with all the respect due to so distinguished a common lawyer. When his judgment is studied, however, one cannot but be impressed by the circumstance that he regarded the proposition that money in such cases could not be recovered back as flowing from the decision in *Taylor v. Caldwell* (above, p. 511). *Taylor v. Caldwell*, however, was not a case in which any question arose whether money could be recovered back, for there had been no payment in advance, and there is nothing in the judgment of Blackburn J., which, at any rate in terms, affirms the general proposition that "the loss lies where it falls." The application by Collins M.R. of *Taylor v. Caldwell* to the actual problem with which he had to deal in *Chandler v. Webster* deserves close examination. He said: "The plaintiff contends that he is entitled to recover the money which he has paid on the ground that there has been a total failure of consideration. He says that the condition on which he paid the money was that the procession should take place, and that, as it did not take place, there had been a total failure of consideration. That contention does no doubt raise a question of some difficulty, and one which has perplexed the courts to a considerable extent in several cases. The principle on which it has been dealt with is that which was applied in *Taylor v. Caldwell*—namely, that where, from causes outside the volition of the parties, something which was the basis of, or essential to the fulfilment of, the contract has become impossible, so that, from the time when the fact of that impossibility has been ascertained, the contract can no further be performed by either party, it remains a perfectly good contract up to that point, and everything previously done in pursuance of it must be treated as rightly done, but the parties are both discharged from further performance of it. If the effect were that the contract were wiped out altogether, no doubt the result would be that money paid under it would have to be repaid as on a failure of consideration. But that is not the effect of the doctrine; it only releases the parties from further performance of the contract. Therefore the doctrine of failure of consideration does not apply."

It appears to me that the reasoning in this crucial passage is open to two criticisms: (a) The claim of a party, who has paid money under a contract, to get the money back, on the ground that the consideration for which he paid it has totally failed, is not based on any provision contained in the contract, but arises because, in the circumstances that have happened, the law gives a remedy in quasi-contract to the party who has not got that for which he bargained. It is a claim to recover money to which the defendant has no further right because in the circumstances that have happened the money must be regarded as received to the plaintiff's use. It is true that the effect of frustration is that, while the contract can no further be performed, "it remains a perfectly good contract up to that point, and everything previously done in pursuance of it must be treated as rightly done," but it by no means follows that the situation existing at the moment of frustration is one which leaves the party that has paid money and has not received the stipulated consideration without any remedy. To claim the return of money paid on the ground of total failure of consideration is not to vary the terms of the contract in any way. The claim arises not because the right to be repaid is one of the stipulated conditions of the contract, but because, in the circumstances that have happened, the law gives the remedy. It is the failure to distinguish between (1) the action of assumpsit for money had and received in a case where the consideration has wholly failed, and (2) an action on the contract itself, which explains the mistake which I think has been made in applying English law to this subject-matter. Thus, in *Blakeley v. Muller & Co.* [1903] 2 K.B. 760n., 761n., Lord Alverstone C.J. said: "I agree that *Taylor v. Caldwell* applies, but the consequence of that decision is that neither party here could have sued on the contract in respect of anything which was to be done under it after the procession had been abandoned." That is true enough, but it does not follow that because the plaintiff cannot sue "on the contract" he cannot sue *dehors* the contract for the recovery of a payment in respect of which consideration has failed. In the same case, Wills J. relied on *Appleby v. Myers* (above, p. 438), where a contract was made for the erection by A of machinery on the premises of B, to be paid for on completion. There was no prepayment and in the course of the work the premises were destroyed by fire. It was held that both parties were excused from further performance, and that no liability accrued on either side, but the liability referred to was liability under the contract, and the learned judge seems to have thought that no action to recover money in such circumstances as the present could be conceived of unless there was a term of the contract, express or implied, which so provided. Once it is realised that the action to recover money for a consideration that has wholly failed rests, not on a contractual bargain between the parties, but, as Lord Sumner said in *Sinclair v. Brougham* [1914] A.C. 398, 452, "upon a notional or imputed promise to repay," or (if it is preferred to omit reference to a fictitious promise) upon an obligation to repay arising from the circumstances, the difficulty in the way of holding that a prepayment made under a contract which has been frustrated can be recovered back appears to me to disappear. (b) There is, no doubt, a distinction between cases in which a contract is "wiped out altogether," for example, because it is void as being illegal from the start or as being due to fraud which the innocent party has elected to treat as avoiding the contract, and cases in which intervening impossibility "only releases the parties from further performance of the contract." But does the distinction between these two classes of case justify the deduction of Collins M.R. that "the doctrine of failure of consideration does not apply" where the contract remains a perfectly good contract up to the date of frustration? This conclusion seems to be derived from the view that, if the contract remains good and valid up to the moment of frustration, money which has already been paid under it cannot be regarded as having been paid for a consideration which has wholly failed. The party that has paid the money has had the advantage, whatever it may be worth, of the promise of the other party. That is true, but it is necessary to draw a distinction. In English law, an enforceable contract may be formed by an exchange of a promise for a promise, or by the exchange of a promise for an act—I am excluding contracts under seal—and thus, in the law relating to the formation of contract, the promise to do a thing may often be the consideration, but when one is considering the law of failure of consideration and of the quasi-contractual right to recover money on that ground, it is, generally speaking, not the promise which is referred to as the consideration, but the performance of the promise. The money was paid to secure performance and, if performance fails, the inducement which brought about the payment is not fulfilled.

If this were not so, there could never be any recovery of money, for failure of consideration, by the payer of the money in return for a promise of future performance, yet there are endless examples which show that money can be recovered, as for a complete failure of consideration, in cases where the promise was given but could not be fulfilled: see the notes in Bullen and Leake's *Precedents of Pleading*, (9th ed.), p. 263. In this connection the decision in *Rugg v. Minett*, 11 East 210, is instructive. There the plaintiff had bought at auction a number of casks of oil. The contents of each cask were to be made up after the auction by the seller to the prescribed quantity so that the property in a cask did not pass to the plaintiff until this had been done. The plaintiff paid in advance a sum of money on account of his purchases generally, but a fire occurred after some of the casks had been filled up, while the others had not. The plaintiff's action was to recover the money he had paid as money received by the defendants to the use of the plaintiffs. The Court of King's Bench ruled that this cause of action succeeded in respect of the casks which at the time of the fire had not been filled up to the prescribed quantity. A simple illustration of the same result is an agreement to buy a horse, the price to be paid down, but the horse not to be delivered and the property not to pass until the horse had been shod. If the horse dies before the shoeing, the price can unquestionably be recovered as for a total failure of consideration, notwithstanding that the promise to deliver was given. This is the case of a contract *de certo corpore* where the *certum corpus* perishes after the contract is made, but, as Vaughan Williams L.J.'s judgment in *Krell v. Henry* (above, p. 517) explained, the same doctrine applies "to cases where the event which renders the contract incapable of performance is the cessation or non-existence of an express condition or state of things, going to the root of the contract, and essential to its performance." I can see no valid reason why the right to recover prepaid money should not equally arise on frustration arising from supervening circumstances as it arises on frustration from destruction of a particular subject-matter. The conclusion is that the rule in *Chandler v. Webster* is wrong, and that the appellants can recover their £1,000.

While this result obviates the harshness with which the previous view in some instances treated the party who had made a prepayment, it cannot be regarded as dealing fairly between the parties in all cases, and must sometimes have the result of leaving the recipient who has to return the money at a grave disadvantage. He may have incurred expenses in connection with the partial carrying out of the contract which are equivalent, or more than equivalent, to the money which he prudently stipulated should be prepaid, but which he now has to return for reasons which are no fault of his. He may have to repay the money, though he has executed almost the whole of the contractual work, which will be left on his hands. These results follow from the fact that the English common law does not undertake to apportion a prepaid sum in such circumstances— contrast the provision, now contained in section 40 of the Partnership Act, 1890, for apportioning a premium if a partnership is prematurely dissolved. It must be for the legislature to decide whether provision should be made for an equitable apportionment of prepaid moneys which have to be returned by the recipient in view of the frustration of the contract in respect of which they were paid. I move that the appeal be allowed, and that judgment be entered for the appellants.

LORDS ATKIN, RUSSELL, MACMILLAN, WRIGHT, ROCHE AND PORTER made concurring speeches.

Appeal allowed.

Law Reform (Frustrated Contracts) Act 1943 (As amended by Sale of Goods Act 1979)

1. Adjustment of rights and liabilities of parties to frustrated contracts.—
(1) Where a contract governed by English law has become impossible of performance or been otherwise frustrated, and the parties thereto have for that reason been discharged from the further performance of the contract, the following provisions of this section shall, subject to the provisions of section 2 of this Act, have effect in relation thereto.
(2) All sums paid or payable to any party in pursuance of the contract before the time when the parties were so discharged (in this Act referred to as "the time of discharge") shall, in the case of sums so paid, be recoverable from him as money received by him for the use of the party by whom the sums were paid, and in the case of sums so payable, cease to be so payable:
Provided that, if the party to whom the sums were so paid or payable incurred expenses before the time of discharge in, or for the purpose of, the performance of the contract, the court may, if it considers it just to do so having regard to all the circumstances of the case, allow him to retain or, as the case may be, recover the whole or any part of the sums so paid or payable, not being an amount in excess of the expenses so incurred.

(3) Where any party to the contract has, by reason of anything done by any other party thereto in, or for the purpose of, the performance of the contract, obtained a valuable benefit (other than a payment of money to which the last foregoing subsection applies) before the time of discharge, there shall be recoverable from him by the said other party such sum (if any), not exceeding the value of the said benefit to the party obtaining it, as the court considers just, having regard to all the circumstances of the case and, in particular—

(a) the amount of any expenses incurred before the time of discharge by the benefited party in, or for the purpose of, the performance of the contract, including any sums paid or payable by him to any other party in pursuance of the contract and retained or recoverable by that party under the last foregoing subsection, and

(b) the effect, in relation to the said benefit, of the circumstances giving rise to the frustration of the contract.

(4) In estimating, for the purposes of the foregoing provisions of this section, the amount of any expenses incurred by any party to the contract, the court may, without prejudice to the generality of the said provisions, include such sum as appears to be reasonable in respect of overhead expenses and in respect of any work or services performed personally by the said party.

(5) In considering whether any sum ought to be recovered or retained under the foregoing provisions of this section by any party to the contract, the court shall not take into account any sums which have, by reason of the circumstances giving rise to the frustration of the contract, become payable to that party under any contract of insurance unless there was an obligation to insure imposed by an express term of the frustrated contract or by or under any enactment.

(6) Where any person has assumed obligations under the contract in consideration of the conferring of a benefit by any other party to the contract upon any other person, whether a party to the contract or not, the court may, if in all the circumstances of the case it considers it just to do so, treat for the purposes of subsection (3) of this section any benefit so conferred as a benefit obtained by the person who has assumed the obligations as aforesaid.

2. Provision as to application of this Act.—(1) This Act shall apply to contracts, whether made before or after the commencement of this Act, as respects which the time of discharge is on or after the first day of July, nineteen hundred and forty-three, but not to contracts as respects which the time of discharge is before the said date.

(2) This Act shall apply to contracts to which the Crown is a party in like manner as to contracts between subjects.

(3) Where any contract to which this Act applies contains any provision which, upon the true construction of the contract, is intended to have effect in the event of circumstances arising which operate, or would but for the said provision operate, to frustrate the contract, or is intended to have effect whether such circumstances arise or not, the court shall give effect to the said provision and shall only give effect to the foregoing section of this Act to such extent, if any, as appears to the court to be consistent with the said provision.

(4) Where it appears to the court that a part of any contract to which this Act applies can properly be severed from the remainder of the contract, being a part wholly performed before the time of discharge, or so performed except for the payment in respect of that part of the contract of sums which are or can be ascertained under the contract, the court shall treat that part of the contract as if it were a separate contract and had not been frustrated and shall treat the foregoing section of this Act as only applicable to the remainder of that contract.

(5) This Act shall not apply—

(a) to any charterparty, except a time charterparty or a charterparty by way of demise, or to any contract (other than a charterparty) for the carriage of goods by sea; or

(b) to any contract of insurance, save as is provided by subsection (5) of the foregoing section; or

(c) to any contract to which section 7 of the Sale of Goods Act, 1979 (which avoids contracts for the sale of specific goods which perish before the risk has passed to the buyer) applies, or to any other contract for the sale, or for the sale and delivery, of specific goods, where the contract is frustrated by reason of the fact that the goods have perished.

3. Short title and interpretation.—(1) This Act may be cited as the Law Reform (Frustrated Contracts) Act, 1943.

(2) In this Act the expression "court" means, in relation to any matter, the court or arbitrator by or before whom the matter falls to be determined.

Note

For a detailed examination of the Act, see Glanville Williams, *The Law Reform (Frustrated Contracts) Act 1943*. Remarkably, the first reported case on the Act is the following.

B.P. EXPLORATION CO. (LIBYA) LTD v. HUNT (No. 2)

Queen's Bench Division [1979] 1 W.L.R. 783; [1982] 1 All E.R. 925

Hunt was the owner of an oil concession in Libya. He contracted to transfer a half-share in the concession to B.P., who agreed to transfer to him certain "farm-in" contributions in cash and oil and to undertake the exploration of the concession and, if oil was found, the development and production, providing all necessary finance until the field came on stream. Then, B.P. were to receive one half of all oil produced plus "reimbursement oil," being three eighths of Hunt's share, until they had received 125 per cent of their farm-in contributions and 50 per cent of the money spent on exploration and development before the field came on stream. Thereafter, the cost of production and development was to be borne by the two parties equally.

B.P. discovered a giant oilfield and expended many millions of pounds on exploration and development. The field came on stream in January 1967. In December 1971 the Libyan government passed a law expropriating B.P.'s interest which frustrated the contract. Hunt continued to export some oil under increasing difficulties until June 1973 when the Libyan government expropriated his interest. The government paid both parties compensation for the book value of facilities in Libya but nothing for the loss of the concession itself. The plaintiffs claimed the award of a just sum under section 1(3) of the Frustrated Contracts Act.

ROBERT GOFF J. said that the principle common to both section 1(2) and (3) and the fundamental principle underlying the Act, is the prevention of unjust enrichment of either party at the other's expense. Section 1(2) provided for the restitution of a net benefit but, under section 1(3), the net benefit simply provided an upper limit to the award. An award under section 1(2) is generally simply an award for the repayment of money. Under section 1(3) it has to be shown that the defendant has obtained a valuable benefit (other than a payment of money) which has to be identified and valued and forms the upper limit of the award. The court may then award a just sum, not exceeding the value of the benefit. Where the services rendered by the plaintiff have an end-product, section 1(3) shows that the value of the end-product is the benefit. Where a contract is frustrated by a fire which destroys a building on which work has been done, the award will be nil. Sometimes the services will have no end-product, as where the work is surveying or transporting goods. Then the benefit must be the value of the services. The benefit must be valued at the date of the frustration, making no allowance for "the time value of money," that is, the notional benefit derived from the fact that the defendant has had the use of the benefit for a period before the frustration. The expenses incurred by the defendant must be deducted from the value of the benefit.

A just sum must then be assessed. The court may have regard to the consideration in the contract as evidence of the appropriate level of remuneration. If a prospector employed for a fee discovered a gold mine before the frustration a rateable part of the contract fee might provide useful evidence of the just sum. If he was to receive a stake in the concession, the just sum might be enhanced. It may be unjust to compel the defendant to pay more than the consideration, or a rateable part of it, that he has agreed to pay—though it was unnecessary to decide whether this will always be so.

Section 2(3) should be given its natural meaning and not limited to provisions *clearly* intended to have effect in the event of frustration; but the fact that the contract is "entire" should not automatically preclude an award under section 1(3). Only if, upon a true construction of the contract, the plaintiff has contracted on terms that he is to receive no payment in the event which has occurred, will the fact that the contract is "entire" preclude an award.

Applying these principles, Hunt's benefits were identified as (in addition to the farm-in payments) the development of a bare concession of unknown potential into a giant oilfield in production, in which Hunt held a half-share. The benefit was to be identified as the product of the work; but it was very greatly reduced by the frustration to, broadly, the benefit of the oil Hunt obtained and benefit of the settlement with the Libyan government. Only half of that benefit should be attributed to B.P.'s work, the other half being attributed to Hunt's own contribution, namely the concession. The court was looking at events which occurred after frustration as the best evidence of the value of Hunt's share at that time. Hunt's benefit was valued at $84,951,000.

In assessing the just sum, regard was had to the consideration which B.P. were to receive—the half share in the concession which they had received, and the reimbursement oil. If they had received the whole, no sum would have been awarded. In fact there remained a balance of 16,899,189 barrels and the equivalent in oil of $550,032. The just sum was valued at $35,403,146—considerably less than the benefit obtained by Hunt ($84,951,000).

Hunt argued that section 2(3) applied because clause 6 of the agreement said that he was to be under no personal liability to repay and section 9(e) of the operating agreement provided that B.P.'s right of recovery was to be out of production. But if A advanced £100,000 to be invested in a business, the contract providing that he was to be repaid only out of the profits of the business, the contract might be frustrated the day after the advance was made. Similarly where A agreed to buy all the apples to be grown in a certain orchard and paid the price in advance, the orchard being seized by the government next day. It might have happened that the day after the field came on stream, B.P. but not Mr Hunt was expropriated and he might have drawn an immense fortune for years. Clause 6 and section 9 were not intended to be effective in the radically changed circumstances. The award of a just sum was not precluded by section 2(3).

Robert Goff J.'s decision was affirmed by the Court of Appeal, [1981] 1 W.L.R. 232; [1982] 1 All E.R. 978 and the House of Lords, [1983] 2 A.C. 352; [1982] 2 W.L.R. 253; [1982] 1 All E.R. 986.

Questions
What would be the effect—if any—of the Frustrated Contracts Act upon the decisions in:
1. *Cutter v. Powell?* (above, p. 434).
2. *Sumpter v. Hedges?* (above, p. 437).
3. *Appleby v. Myers?* (above, p. 438).
4. *The Fibrosa case?* (above, p. 540).

PART IV

RIGHTS AND REMEDIES OF THE INJURED PARTY

CHAPTER 15

PERFORMANCE AND RESCISSION

Section 1. Anticipatory Breach

FROST v. KNIGHT

Exchequer Chamber (1872) L.R. 7 Exch. 111; 41 L.J. Ex. 78; 26 L.T. 77; 20 W.R. 471

The defendant promised to marry the plaintiff on the death of the defendant's father. During his father's lifetime the defendant announced his intention of not fulfilling his promise and broke off the engagement. The plaintiff, without waiting for the father's death, sued for breach of contract.[1] The Court of Exchequer, Martin B. dissenting, made absolute a rule to arrest a judgment in favour of the plaintiff. The case was brought on error before the Court of Exchequer Chamber.

COCKBURN C.J.: . . . The law with reference to a contract to be performed at a future time, where the party bound to performance announces prior to the time his intention not to perform it, as established by the cases of *Hochster v. De la Tour*, 2 E. & B. 678,[2] and *The Danube and Black Sea Co. v. Xenos* on the one hand, and *Avery v. Bowden*, 5 E. & B. 714,[3] *Reid v. Hoskins*, 6 E. & B. 953, and *Barwick v. Buba*, 2 C.B. (N.S.) 563, on the other, may be thus stated. The promisee, if he pleases, may treat the notice of intention as inoperative, and await the time when the contract is to be executed, and then hold the other party responsible for all the consequences of non-performance: but in that case he keeps the contract alive for the benefit of the

---

[1] The action for breach of promise of marriage was abolished by the Law Reform (Miscellaneous Provisions) Act 1970, s.1(1); but the principles enunciated in this case are of general application in the law of contract.

[2] In *Hochster v. de la Tour* the defendant, on April 12, 1852, agreed to engage the plaintiff as a courier, on June 1, 1852, to travel on the Continent of Europe. On May 11, 1852, the defendant wrote to the plaintiff that he had changed his mind, and did not require the plaintiff's services. The plaintiff commenced an action on May 22. The defendant's counsel objected that there could be no breach of contract before June 1. Lord Campbell C.J. said that ". . . where there is a contract to do an act on a future day, there is a relation constituted between the parties in the meantime by the contract, and that they impliedly promise that in the meantime neither will do anything to the prejudice of the other inconsistent with that relation . . . from the day of the hiring till the day when the employment was to begin, they were engaged to each other; and it seems to be a breach of an implied contract if either of them renounces the engagement . . ."

[3] In *Avery v. Bowden* the defendant chartered the plaintiff's ship, *Lebanon* and agreed to load her with a cargo at Odessa within 45 days. The ship proceeded to Odessa and remained there a great part of the 45 days. The defendant told the captain of the ship that he had no cargo for him, and repeatedly advised him to go away. The captain remained at the port in the hope that the defendant would fulfil his contract. Before the 45 days had elapsed, the Crimean War broke out, rendering the performance of the contract thereafter illegal. The plaintiff's action failed. It would have been otherwise if, assuming the defendant's action amounted to a repudiation (which the court doubted), the plaintiff had sailed away before the declaration of war.

other party as well as his own; he remains subject to all his own obligations and liabilities under it, and enables the other party not only to complete the contract, if so advised, notwithstanding his previous repudiation of it, but also to take advantage of any supervening circumstances which would justify him in declining to complete it.

On the other hand, the promisee may, if he thinks proper, treat the repudiation of the other party as a wrongful putting an end to the contract, and may at once bring his action as on a breach of it; and in such action he will be entitled to such damages as would have arisen from the non-performance of the contract at the appointed time, subject, however, to abatement in respect of any circumstances which may have afforded him the means of mitigating his loss.

Considering this to be now settled law, notwithstanding anything that may have been held or said in the cases of *Philpotts v. Evans*, 5 M. & W. 475, and *Ripley v. McClure*, 4 Ex. at p. 359, we should have had no difficulty in applying the principle of the decision in *Hochster v. De la Tour* to the present case, were it not for the difference which undoubtedly exists between that case and the present, *viz.*, that, whereas there the performance of the contract was to take place at a fixed time, here no time is fixed, but the performance is made to depend on a contingency, namely, the death of the defendant's father during the lifetime of the contracting parties. It is true that in every case of a personal obligation to be fulfilled at a future time, there is involved the possible contingency of the death of the party binding himself, before the time of performance arrives; but here we have a further contingency depending on the life of a third person, during which neither party can claim performance of the promise. This being so, we thought it right to take time to consider whether an action would lie before the death of the defendant's father had placed the plaintiff in a position to claim the fulfilment of the defendant's promise.

After full consideration we are of opinion that, notwithstanding the distinguishing circumstances to which I have referred, this case falls within the principle of *Hochster v. De la Tour*, and that, consequently, the present action is well brought.

The considerations on which the decision in *Hochster v. De la Tour* is founded are that the announcement of the contracting party of his intention not to fulfil the contract amounts to a breach, and that it is for the common benefit of both parties that the contract shall be taken to be broken as to all its incidents, including non-performance at the appointed time; as by an action being brought at once, and the damages consequent on non-performance being assessed at the earliest moment, many of the injurious effects of such non-performance may possibly be averted or mitigated.

It is true, as is pointed out by the Lord Chief Baron, in his judgment in this case, that there can be no actual breach of a contract by reason of non-performance so long as the time for performance has not yet arrived. But, on the other hand, there is—and the decision in *Hochster v. De la Tour* proceeds on that assumption—a breach of the contract when the promisor repudiates it and declares he will no longer be bound by it. The promisee has an inchoate right to the performance of the bargain, which becomes complete when the time for performance has arrived. In the meantime he has a right to have the contract kept open as a subsisting and effective contract. Its unimpaired and unimpeached efficacy may be essential to his interests. His rights acquired under it may be dealt with by him in various ways for his benefit and advantage. Of all such advantage the repudiation of the contract by the other party, and the announcement that it never will be fulfilled, must of course deprive him. It is therefore quite right to hold that such an announcement amounts to a violation of the contract in omnibus, and that upon it the promisee, if so minded, may at once treat it as a breach of the entire contract, and bring his action accordingly.

The contract having been thus broken by the promisor, and treated as broken by the promisee, performance at the appointed time becomes excluded, and the breach by reason of the future non-performance becomes virtually involved in the action as one of the consequences of the repudiation of the contract; and the eventual non-performance may therefore, by anticipation, be treated as a cause of action, and damages be assessed and recovered in respect of it, though the time for performance may yet be remote.

It is obvious that such a course must lead to the convenience of both parties; and though we should be unwilling to found our opinion on grounds of convenience alone, yet the latter tend strongly to support the view that such an action ought to be admitted and upheld. By acting on such a notice of the intention of the promisor, and taking timely measures, the promisee may in many cases avert, or at all events materially lessen, the injurious effects which would otherwise flow from the non-fulfilment of the contract; and in assessing the damages for breach of performance, a jury will of course take into account whatever the plaintiff has done, or has had the means of doing, and as a prudent man, ought in reason to have done, whereby his loss has been, or would have been, diminished.

It appears to us that the foregoing considerations apply to the case of a contract the performance of which is made to depend on a contingency, as much as to one in which the performance is to take place at a future time; and we are, therefore, of opinion that the principle of the decision of *Hochster v. De la Tour* is equally applicable to such a case as the present. . . .

KEATING AND LUSH JJ. concurred in the judgment of the Chief Justice, and BYLES J. delivered a judgment to the same effect.

Judgment reversed.

1. **"Accepting" an anticipatory breach.** An anticipatory breach differs from other breaches of contract in that the injured party, A, must "accept" it before he can sue for damages. If A elects to keep the contract alive, the repudiating party, B, may yet perform, in which case A will suffer no loss. Because the word "accept" has been traditionally used, it has sometimes been assumed that something like offer and acceptance in the formation of contract is required. In *Denmark Productions Ltd v. Boscobel Productions Ltd* [1968] 3 All E.R. 513 at 527 Winn L.J. said

> "It seems to me that the process of ending or indeed of varying a contract by repudiation is the converse of that of making the same contract; each process operates by offer and acceptance or their equivalents; each is essentially bilateral. Where A and B are parties to an executory contract, if A intimates by word or conduct that he no longer intends, or is unable, to perform it, or to perform it in a particular manner, he is, in effect, making an offer to B to treat the contract as resolved or varied so far as it relates to the future."

Insofar as this relates to repudiation as distinct from variation, this seems an inappropriate analogy. Suppose that in *Hochster v. De la Tour* (above, p. 551) the plaintiff (P), on receiving the defendant (D)'s letter of May 11, had immediately offered his services to X and, without a word to D, gone off to South America. D, meanwhile, having changed his mind, on May 30, delivers to P's address items to be taken to Europe. P has accepted the fact that the contract is at an end but done nothing to accept any "offer" by D. Is it really to be said that P is now liable to D for damages for breach of contract? P is surely entitled to take D at his word. As Lord Campbell C.J. said at p. 690, "It seems strange that the defendant, after renouncing the contract, and absolutely declaring that he will never act under it, should be permitted to object that faith is given to his assertion and that an opportunity is not left to him of changing his mind."

Or suppose that in, *Frost v. Knight*, D, having contracted to marry P on the death of D's father, writes to P during father's lifetime, "I wouldn't marry you if you were the last woman on earth," whereupon P promptly marries another. Not unnaturally, she does not reply to D. Next day, father dies and D calls upon P to marry him. Could D really have succeeded (before 1970) in an action for breach of promise?

There is however an ambiguity in the word "repudiation." A fundamental breach of contract is sometimes described as a repudiatory breach. See para. 2, below. The party, A, who has committed such a breach, far from declaring the contract to be at an end, may be very anxious that it should continue. Then, B, if he wishes to terminate the contract must notify A to that effect See *Car and Universal Finance Co Ltd v. Caldwell*, above, p. 346.

Vitol SA v. Norelf Ltd [1995] 3 All E.R. 971 raises, as Nourse L.J. said, a question of general importance in the law of contract: "Can an innocent party accept a repudiation of the contract merely by failing to perform his own obligations under it?" The case concerned a contract for the sale by N to V of a cargo to be loaded on the Santa Clara. V, believing that loading was unlikely to be completed until well outside the contractual period sent N a telex stating "In view of the breach of this condition we must reject the cargo and repudiate the contract." V was apparently in error in supposing that there had been a breach of condition by N because it was not disputed that this telex was an anticipatory breach of contract by V. On March 11 N informed V that loading had been completed; and on March 15 N resold the cargo. There was no further communication between them until N claimed damages of $U.S.1 million, the difference between the contract price and resale price. The arbitrator took the view that, until V's breach was accepted by N, it was of no effect but that N's failure to take any further steps to perform the contract, as by tendering a bill of lading, a failure which was apparent to V, constituted a sufficient communication of acceptance. On appeal to the Queen's Bench Division, Phillips J. held that all he had to decide was whether mere failure to perform contractual obligations can *ever* constitute acceptance of an anticipatory breach by the other party. He held that it could, and dismissed V's appeal. The Court of Appeal disagreed. A failure to perform contractual obligations was not sufficiently clear and unequivocal to amount to acceptance of a repudiation because it was equally consistent with misunderstanding, indecision or inadvertence by the innocent party. Because of their limited jurisdiction on appeal from an arbitrator, the question whether the resale was an acceptance of the breach was not considered by the courts. In principle, however, it seems that the resale of the cargo must have put an end to the contract, no less than the supposed marriage in the above example based on *Frost v. Knight*.

2. The nature and extent of the threatened breach. The threatened breach may be of (i) the whole contract, or (ii) a condition, or (iii) an innominate term, or (iv) a warranty. Clearly threat (i) entitles the other party to terminate the contract. It might be expected that threat (ii) would have the same effect, whatever the extent of the threatened breach, since any actual breach justifies termination. Where, however, there is an express term for terminating the contract on the occurrence of a particular breach it appears that only the actual breach, not the threat of it, justifies termination: *The Afovos* [1983] 1 All E.R. 449, H.L. Lord Diplock, with whom the whole House agreed, said that the doctrine of anticipatory breach applies only to a fundamental breach, meaning, apparently, a breach which would deprive the other party of substantially the whole benefit of the contract—which is not true of every breach of condition. See Treitel, *Law of Contract* (9th ed.) 773. In the case of (iii) the answer presumably depends on the extent of the threatened breach. See *Federal Commerce, etc. v. Molena Apha Inc.* [1979] A.C. 757 where the majority of their lordships held that the relevant clause was an innominate term and proceeded to consider whether the threatened breach of it was so fundamental as to amount to a repudiation of the contract. *Cf. Torvald Klaveness v. Arni*, above, p. 433. As the actual breach of a mere warranty (by definition) does not justify termination, the threatened breach can hardly do so.

Notes

1. *Specific Performance.* A party who declines to accept an anticipatory breach as putting an end to the contract can bring no action for damages until the time for performance arrives and the other party fails to perform. But, if the contract is one capable of specific performance, an action for that remedy will lie at once: *Hasham v. Zenab* [1960] A.C. 316, P.C. By a written contract, the defendant agreed to sell the plaintiff a plot of land in Nairobi. A few minutes after signing the contract, the defendant repudiated it by tearing it up. The last day for completion was August 19 and the plaintiff instituted proceedings on July 2. It was held that the institution of the proceedings was not premature. There was a fallacy in equating a right to sue for specific performance with a cause of action at law. The purchaser had an equitable interest in the land which would have enabled him to get an injunction to prevent the vendor disposing of it. All he needed to show were circumstances justifying the intervention of a court of equity.

2. *"Anticipatory breach" is a present breach.* In *The Mihalis Angelos* (above, p. 432) the Court of Appeal considered what would be the position if they were wrong in holding that C had properly terminated the contract on July 17. In that event, C, by declaring on July 17 that he would not provide a cargo when the ship arrived, was guilty of an anticipatory breach of contract. But since the ship could not possibly have been ready to load by July 20 he could and would have rightly cancelled the charterparty on that day. Mocatta J. at first instance had nevertheless held that S was entitled to £4,000 damages for the anticipatory breach. His view was that "the assumed and, in law, inevitable failure to perform is one at the date in the future when performance would have been required had there been no anticipatory breach"; and that damages had to be assessed in relation to that assumed future breach. This was wrong.

Lord Denning said, "The words 'anticipatory breach' are misleading. The cause of action is not the future breach. It is the renunciation itself . . . the damages must be assessed by compensating the injured party for the loss he has suffered by the renunciation. One must take into account all contingencies which might have reduced or extinguished that loss . . . if the defendant has, under the contract, an option which would reduce or extinguish the loss, it will be assumed that he would exercise it. . . . In short, the plaintiff must be compensated for such loss as he would have suffered if there had been no renunciation. . . . Seeing that the charterers would, beyond doubt, have cancelled, I am clearly of opinion that the shipowners suffered no loss and would be entitled at most to nominal damages."

Question

It is clear that the term of the contract which is broken by anticipatory breach is a condition, for the breach entitles the injured party to terminate the contract as well as to sue for damages. What is the promise which is broken in these cases? *Cf.* Montrose in (1937) 15 Can.Bar Rev. 309, 315: "The time for performance does not affect the inception of the promise: an obligation comes into existence as soon as the contract is concluded. This is shown in English law by the action for an anticipatory breach of contract." What is this obligation?

WOODAR INVESTMENT DEVELOPMENT LTD v. WIMPEY CONSTRUCTION U.K. LTD

House of Lords [1980] 1 W.L.R. 277; [1980] 1 All E.R. 571

Woodar contracted to sell to Wimpey 14 acres of land for development. It was provided by clause E(a)(iii) that Wimpey should be entitled to rescind the contract if prior to completion a statutory authority "shall have commenced" compulsorily to acquire the property. As both parties knew, the Minister had commenced compulsory purchase proceedings for 2.3 acres of the property before the time of the contract. Land prices fell dramatically. Wimpey purported to rescind, relying on clause E(a)(iii), Woodar claimed a declaration that Wimpey were not entitled to rescind and Wimpey counterclaimed for a declaration that they had validly rescinded the contract. Woodar then brought a second action claiming that the notice of rescission and the counterclaim amounted to a repudiation which they accepted and claimed damages. The two actions were consolidated. The trial judge held that Wimpey were not entitled to rescind: clause E(a)(iii) applied only to compulsory purchase proceedings commenced after the date of the contract. This finding was not challenged in the higher courts. The judge awarded £462,000 damages. The Court of Appeal affirmed his decision but reduced the damages to £272,943. Wimpey appealed.

LORD WILBERFORCE: My Lords, . . . in considering whether there has been a repudiation by one party, it is necessary to look at his conduct as a whole. Does this indicate an intention to abandon and to refuse performance of the contract? In the present case, without taking Wimpey's conduct generally into account, Woodar's contention, that Wimpey had repudiated, would be a difficult one. So far from repudiating the contract, Wimpey were relying on it and invoking one of its provisions, to which both parties had given their consent. And unless the invocation of that provision were totally abusive, or lacking in good faith, (neither of which is contended for), the fact that it has proved to be wrong in law cannot turn it into a repudiation. At the lowest, the notice of rescission was a neutral document consistent either with an intention to preserve, or with an intention to abandon, the contract, and I will deal with it on this basis, more favourable to Woodar. In order to decide which is correct Wimpey's conduct has to be examined.

One point can, in my opinion, be disposed of at once. Woodar, in March 1974, started proceedings against Wimpey: this is one of the actions consolidated in the litigation before us. They claimed a declaration that Wimpey's notice of rescission was not valid, and Wimpey, by their defence asserted the contrary and they counterclaimed for a declaration to that effect. Woodar now contend that if the original notice did not amount to a repudiation, the defence and counterclaim did. I regard this contention as hopeless. Wimpey's pleading carried the matter no further: it simply rested the matter on the contract. It showed no intention to abandon the contract whatever the result of the action might be. If the action were to succeed (that is if Wimpey lost) there was no indication that Wimpey would not abide by the result and implement the contract.

The facts indicative of Wimpey's intention must now be summarised. It is clear in the first place that, subjectively, Wimpey in 1974 wanted to get out of the contract. Land prices had fallen, and they thought that if the contract was dissolved, they could probably acquire it at a much lower price. But subjective intention is not decisive: it supplied the motive for serving the notice of rescission; there remains the question whether, objectively regarded, their conduct showed an intention to abandon the contract.

In early 1974 there was a possibility that some planning permission might be granted. If it were, and unless Wimpey could take valid objection to it, completion would (under the conditions) have to follow in two months. Therefore, if a notice of rescission were to be given, it had to be served without delay, that is before the planning permission arrived. In this situation, Wimpey's advisers arranged a meeting with a Mr Cornwell, who was acting for Woodar, or as an intermediary with power to commit Woodar, to discuss the matter. This took place on March 7, 1974 and is recorded as a disclosed aide memoire dated the next day. This document was prepared by Wimpey, and we have not had the benefit of Mr Cornwell's evidence on it: he died before the trial. But the rest of the correspondence is fully in line with it and I see no reason to doubt its general accuracy. After recording each side's statement of position, the document contained, *inter alia*, these passages: "He [Mr Cornwell] stated that if we attempted to rescind the contract, then he would take us to court and let the judge decide whether the contract could be rescinded on the point we were making." This "point" was undoubtedly that relating to the compulsory purchase of the 2.5 (*sic*) acres. The aide memoire continues:

> "I told him that our Legal Department would be serving the Notice to Rescind the Contract within a short while—this would ensure that the company was fully protected and was prudent. He assured me that he would accept it on that basis and not regard it as a hostile act."

The notice was then served on March 20, 1974. On March 22, Woodar's solicitors wrote that they did not accept its validity. On May 30, 1974 Mr Cornwell wrote a long letter to Sir Godfrey Mitchell, president of Wimpey. I refer to one passage:

> "... within a few days of the original meeting, a notice of rescission was served upon the vendor company by your organisation that the contract was to be rescinded. Simultaneously with that notice of rescission, proceedings were instituted and there the matter remains so far as the legal situation is concerned and both parties, from the legal point of view, must now await the decision of the court as to the validity of the claim made by Messrs. George Wimpey & Co. Limited that they are entitled to rescind this contract upon the grounds which they have so stated."

On June 4, 1974 Mr Cornwell wrote again: "All I need say now is that we will retire to our battle stations and it goes without saying I am sure that you will abide by the result as I will."

My Lords, I cannot find anything which carries the matter one inch beyond, on Wimpey's part an expressed reliance on the contract (in condition E(a)(iii)), on Woodar's side an intention to take the issue of the validity of the notice (nothing else) to the courts, and an assumption, not disputed by Wimpey, that both sides would abide by the decision of the court. This is quite insufficient to support the case for repudiation. . . .

My Lords, in my opinion, it follows, as a clear conclusion of fact, that Wimpey manifested no intention to abandon, or to refuse future performance of, or to repudiate the contract. And the issue being one of fact, citation of other decided cases on other facts is hardly necessary. I shall simply state that the proposition that a party who takes action relying simply on the terms of the contract and not manifesting by his conduct an ulterior intention to abandon it is not to be treated as repudiating it, is supported by *James Shaffer Ltd v. Findlay Durham & Brodie* [1953] 1 W.L.R. 106 and *Sweet & Maxwell Ltd v. Universal News Services Ltd* [1964] 2 Q.B. 699.

In contrast to these is the case in this House of *Federal Commerce and Navigation Co. Ltd v. Molena Alpha Inc.* [1979] A.C. 757 at 780 which fell on the other side of the line. Of that I said:

"The two cases relied on by the owners (*James Shaffer Ltd v. Findlay Durham & Brodie* and *Sweet & Maxwell Ltd v. Universal News Services Ltd*) . . . would only be relevant here if the owners' action had been confined to asserting their own view, possibly erroneous, as to the effect of the contract. They went, in fact, far beyond this when they threatened a breach of contract with serious consequences."

Spettabile Consorzio Veneziano di Armamento e Navigazione v. Northumberland Shipbuilding Co. Ltd (1919) 121 L.T. 628, though in some factual respects distinguishable from the present, is nevertheless, in my opinion, clear support for Wimpey.

In my opinion, therefore, Wimpey are entitled to succeed on the repudiation issue, and I would only add that it would be a regrettable development of the law of contract to hold that a party who bona fide relies on an express stipulation in a contract in order to rescind or terminate a contract should, by that fact alone, be treated as having repudiated his contractual obligations if he turns out to be mistaken as to his rights. Repudiation is a drastic conclusion which should only be held to arise in clear cases of a refusal, in a matter going to the root of the contract, to perform contractual obligations. To uphold Woodar's contentions in this case would represent an undesirable extension of the doctrine.

LORD SALMON, dissenting: I do not understand how Wimpey's honest belief in a bad point of law can in any way avail them. In *Federal Commerce Navigation Co. Ltd v. Molena Alpha Inc.* [1978] Q.B. 927, 979 Lord Denning M.R. said:

"I have yet to learn that a party who breaks a contract can excuse himself by saying that he did it on the advice of his lawyers; or that he was under an honest misapprehension. Nor can he excuse himself on those grounds from the consequences of a repudiation."

I gratefully adopt that passage which seems to me to be particularly apt in the present case. It certainly was never questioned in your Lordships' House when the appeal from the decision of the Court of Appeal in the *Federal Commerce* case was dismissed. . . .

(His Lordship quoted from other cases.)

I do not recall that any of these definitions of a repudiation of a contract have ever, until now, been questioned. The fact that a party to a contract mistakenly believes that he has the right to refuse to perform it cannot avail him. Nor is there any authority for the proposition that if a party to a contract totally refuses to perform it, this refusal is any the less a repudiation of the contract because he honestly but mistakenly believes that he is entitled by a condition of the contract to refuse to perform it.

It would indeed be unfortunate if the law were otherwise. A mistake in the construction of a contractual condition, even such a glaringly obvious mistake as the present, can apparently easily be made especially perhaps when the market price has fallen far below the contract price. It is acknowledged in this case that the mistake was an honest one. If, however, a case arose in which a mistake of this kind was alleged to be an honest mistake, but not acknowledged to be so, it would be extremely difficult, if not impossible to prove the contrary. . . .

LORD RUSSELL made a dissenting speech

LORD KEITH AND SCARMAN made speeches allowing the appeal

Appeal allowed.

(For another aspect of this case, see above, p. 307)

Questions
1. Would the answer have been different if it had been proved that Wimpey knew very well that, in the circumstances, clause E(a)(iii) did not entitle them to rescind? Should it make any difference? The loss suffered by Woodar would be the same.
2. Wimpey purported to rely on an express provision in the contract. Would it have been different if they had purported to determine the contract in the mistaken belief that Woodar had committed a breach of condition or fundamental breach?
3. Does the decision depend on the fact that it concerned a conveyancing transaction? See J. W. Carter [1980] C.L.J. 256: ". . . in a commercial charterparty or sale of goods . . . there will usually be no room for nice considerations as to whether or not a promisor has acted in good faith."
4. "In this case, Woodar did mitigate and resold the land in 1975 for £330,000. However, it must follow from the House of Lords decision that this resale was wrongful. If Wimpey's notice of rescission was not repudiatory, the contract was still alive and Woodar committed an anticipatory breach by selling the land." (A). Nicol and R. Rawlings (1980) 43 M.L.R. 696 at 698. Suppose that the price of land had then shot up. Could Wimpey have recovered damages from Woodar?

WHITE & CARTER (COUNCILS) LTD v. McGREGOR

House of Lords (Scotland) [1962] A.C. 413; [1962] 2 W.L.R. 17; [1961] 3 All E.R. 1178; 1962 S.C.(H.L.) 1

The facts appear sufficiently in the speech of Lord Reid.

LORD REID: My Lords, the pursuers supply to local authorities litter bins which are placed in the streets. They are allowed to attach to these receptacles plates carrying advertisements, and they make their profit from payments made to them by the advertisers. The defender carried on a garage in Clydebank and in 1954 he made an agreement with the pursuers under which they displayed advertisements of his business on a number of these bins. In June 1957 his sales manager made a further contract with the pursuers for the display of these advertisements for a further period of three years. The sales manager had been given no specific authority to make this contract and when the defender heard of it later on the same day he at once wrote to the pursuers to cancel the contract. The pursuers refused to accept this cancellation. They prepared the necessary plates for attachment to the bins and exhibited them on the bins from November 2, 1957, onwards.

The defender refused to pay any sums due under the contract and the pursuers raised the present action in the Sheriff Court craving payment of £196 4s., the full sum due under the contract for the period of three years.

After sundry procedure the Sheriff-Substitute on March 15,1960, dismissed the action. He held that the sales manager's action in renewing the contract was within his apparent or ostensible authority and that is not now disputed. The ground on which he dismissed the action was that in the circumstances an action for implement of the contract was inappropriate. He relied on the decision in *Langford & Co., Ltd v. Dutch*, (1952), S.C. 15, and cannot be criticised for having done so.

The pursuers appealed to the Court of Session and on November 2, 1960, the Second Division refused the appeal. The present appeal is taken against their interlocutor of that date. That interlocutor sets out detailed findings of fact and, as this case began in the Sheriff Court, we cannot look beyond those findings. The pursuers must show that on those findings they are entitled to the remedy which they seek.

The case for the defender (now the respondent) is that, as he repudiated the contract before anything had been done under it, the appellants were not entitled to go on and carry out the contract and sue for the contract price: he maintains that in the circumstances the appellants' only remedy was damages, and that, as they do not sue for damages, this action was rightly dismissed.

The contract was for the display of advertisements for a period of 156 weeks from the date when the display began. This date was not specified but admittedly the display began on November 2, 1957, which seems to have been the date when the former contract came to an end. The payment stipulated was 2s. per week per plate together with 5s. per annum per plate, both payable annually in advance, the first payment being due seven days after the first display. The reason why the appellants sued for the whole sum due for the three years is to be found in clause 8 of the conditions: "In the event of an instalment or part thereof being due for payment, and remaining unpaid for a period of four weeks or in the event of the advertiser being in any way in breach of this contract then the whole amount due for the 156 weeks or such part of the said 156 weeks as the advertiser shall not yet have paid shall immediately become due and payable."

A question was debated whether this clause provides a penalty or liquidated damages, but on the view which I take of the case it need not be pursued. The clause merely provides for acceleration of payment of the stipulated price if the advertiser fails to pay an instalment timeously. As the respondent maintained that he was not bound by the contract he did not pay the first instalment within the time allowed. Accordingly, if the appellants were entitled to carry out their part of the contract notwithstanding the respondent's repudiation, it was hardly disputed that this clause entitled them to sue immediately for the whole price and not merely the first instalment.

The general rule cannot be in doubt. It was settled in Scotland at least as early as 1848 and it has been authoritatively stated time and again in both Scotland and England. If one party to a contract repudiates it in the sense of making it clear to the other party that he refuses or will refuse to carry out his part of the contract, the other party, the innocent party, has an option. He may accept that repudiation and sue for damages for breach of contract, whether or not the time for performance has come; or he may if he chooses disregard or refuse to accept it and then the contract remains in full effect. . . .

I need not refer to the numerous authorities. They are not disputed by the respondent but he points out that in all of them the party who refused to accept the repudiation had no active duties under the contract. The innocent party's option is generally said to be to *wait* until the date of performance and then to claim damages estimated as at that date. There is no case in which it is said that he may, in face of the repudiation, go on and incur useless expense in performing the contract and then claim the contract price. The option, it is argued, is merely as to the date as at which damages are to be assessed.

Developing this argument, the respondent points out that in most cases the innocent party cannot complete the contract himself without the other party doing, allowing or accepting something, and that it is purely fortuitous that the appellants can do so in this case. In most cases by refusing co-operation the party in breach can compel the innocent party to restrict his claim to damages. Then it was said that, even where the innocent party can complete the contract without such co-operation, it is against the public interest that he should be allowed to do so. An example was developed in argument. A company might engage an expert to go abroad and prepare. an elaborate report and then repudiate the contract before anything was done. To allow such an expert then to waste thousands of pounds in preparing the report cannot be right if a much smaller sum of damages would give him full compensation for his loss. It would merely enable the expert to extort a settlement giving him far more than reasonable compensation.

[His Lordship then considered *Langford & Co., Ltd v. Dutch*, (1952), S.C. 15, and continued:] *Langford & Co., Ltd v. Dutch* is indistinguishable from the present case. Quite properly the Second Division followed it in this case as a binding authority and did not develop Lord Cooper's reasoning: they were not asked to send this case to a larger court. We must now decide whether that case was rightly decided. In my judgment it was not. It could only be supported on one or other of two grounds. It might be said that, because in most cases the circumstances are such that an innocent party is unable to complete the contract and earn the contract price without the assent or co-operation of the other party, therefore in cases where he can do so he should not be allowed to do so. I can see no justification for that.

The other ground would be that there is some general equitable principle or element of public policy which requires this limitation of the contractual rights of the innocent party. It may well be that, if it can be shown that a person has no legitimate interest, financial or otherwise, in performing the contract rather than claiming damages, he ought not to be allowed to saddle the other party with an additional burden with no benefit to himself. If a party has no interest to enforce a stipulation, he cannot in general enforce it: so it might be said that, if a party has no interest to insist on a particular remedy, he ought not to be allowed to insist on it. And, just as a party is not allowed to enforce a penalty, so he ought not to be allowed to penalise the other party by taking one course when another is equally advantageous to him. If I may revert to the example which I gave of a company engaging an expert to prepare an elaborate report and then repudiating before anything was done, it might be that the company could show that the expert had no substantial or legitimate interest in carrying out the work rather than accepting damages: I would think that the *de minimis* principle would apply in determining whether his interest was substantial, and that he might have a legitimate interest other than an immediate financial interest. But if the expert had no such interest then that might be regarded as a proper case for the exercise of the general equitable jurisdiction of the court. But that is not this case. Here the respondent did not set out to prove that the appellants had no legitimate interest in completing the contract and claiming the contract price rather than claiming damages; there is nothing in the findings of fact to support such a case, and it seems improbable that any such case could have been proved. It is, in my judgment, impossible to say that the appellants should be deprived of their right to claim the contract price merely because the benefit to them, as against claiming damages and reletting their advertising space, might be small in comparison with the loss to the respondent: that is the most that could be said in favour of the respondent. Parliament has on many occasions relieved parties from certain kinds of improvident or oppressive contracts, but the common law can only do that in very limited circumstances. Accordingly, I am unable to avoid the conclusion that this appeal must be allowed and the case remitted so that decree can be pronounced as craved in the initial writ.

LORD MORTON OF HENRYTON made a dissenting speech.

LORD KEITH OF AVONHOLM: . . . Much argument and citation of authority was advanced on the topic of anticipatory repudiation. That, in my view, was largely beside the point. There is no doubt that there was here an anticipatory repudiation, for the contract was repudiated by the defender the very day it was made and some months before it could come into operation. But the pursuers did not choose to act on that repudiation and sue the defender for what has sometimes been called an anticipatory breach. The real question at issue is what were the rights of parties when the contract fell to be put into operation, the defender having maintained his repudiation throughout. . . .

Repudiation of a contract is nothing but a breach of contract. Except where it is accepted as an anticipatory breach and as a ground for a claim of damages, a repudiation can never be said to be accepted by the other party except in the sense that he acquiesces in it and does not propose to take any action. Otherwise he founds on it as a cause of action.

The late Professor Gloag in his work on *Contract* (2nd ed.), p. 592, considering the rights arising on breach of contract, said: "The primary rights of the creditor in a contractual obligation may be said to be to secure performance by invoking the assistance of the court to compel it, or, where that remedy is inappropriate, to obtain compensation damages." . . . in the case of a repudiation of a contract when performance is tendered, or due to be given by the other party, the repudiation cannot be said to be writ in water. It gives rise immediately to a cause of action. This does not involve acceptance of the repudiation. There has been a breach of contract which the complaining party denies the other had any right to commit. I know of no authority for saying that the offended party can go quietly on as if the contract still continued to be fully operative between both parties. He is put to his remedy at the date of the breach. It has been said that when an anticipatory repudiation is not treated as a cause of action the contract remains alive. It does until the contract would become operative, when the repudiation, if still maintained, then becomes a cause of action and all pleas and defences then existing are available to the respective parties.

The party complaining of the breach also has a duty to minimise the damage he has suffered, which is a further reason for saying that after the date of breach he cannot continue to carry on his part of an executory contract. A breach of a contract of employment will serve to illustrate the nature of this duty. A person is engaged to serve for a certain period, say three months, to commence at a future date. When that date arrives the prospective employer wrongfully refuses to honour the engagement. The servant is not entitled to see out the three months and then sue the recalcitrant employer for three months' wages. He must take steps by seeking other employment to minimise his loss. It is true, of course, that a servant cannot invoke a contract to force himself on an unwilling master, any more than a master can enforce the service of an unwilling servant. But if the appellants' contention is sound, it is difficult to see why, by parity of reasoning, it should not apply to a person who keeps himself free to perform the duties of his contract of service during the whole period of the contract and is prevented from doing so by the refusal of the other contracting party. Yet in *Hochster v. De la Tour* (above, p. 551, n. 2), from which the whole law about anticipatory repudiation stems, Lord Campbell plainly indicated that if the courier in that case, instead of accepting as he did the repudiation of his engagement as a cause of action, before it was due to commence, had waited till the lapse of the three months of the engagement he could not have sued as for a debt. The jury, he said, would be entitled to look at all that might "increase or mitigate the loss of the plaintiff down to the day of trial." There is no difference in this matter between the law of England and the law of Scotland (*Ross v. M'Farlane* (1894) 21 R. 396). . . .

I find the argument advanced for the appellants a somewhat startling one. If it is right it would seem that a man who has contracted to go to Hong Kong at his own expense and make a report, in return for remuneration of £10,000, and who, before the date fixed for the start of the journey and perhaps before he has incurred any expense, is informed by the other contracting party that he has cancelled or repudiates the contract, is entitled to set off for Hong Kong and produce his report in order to claim in debt the stipulated sum. Such a result is not, in my opinion, in accordance with principle or authority, and cuts across the rule that where one party is in breach of contract the other must take steps to minimise the loss sustained by the breach. (*Cf.* below, p. 621, note.)

It may also be put in another way, that the pursuers are precluded from carrying on with their performance by the notice from the defender, albeit in breach of contract, that he does not intend to pay them if they do. Lord President Dunedin said very much this in *Johannesburg Municipal Council v. D. Stewart & Co. (1909) Ltd*, (1909), S.C. 860, 877, in the following passage: "When two parties are bound together under contract, of course each must perform to the other his mutual stipulations. If one of the parties is in breach of a stipulation of the contract, what is the position of the other? . . . If the stipulation which is broken goes to the root and essence of the contract, the other party is entitled to say—now you have so broken the contract that I am entitled to say that it is at an end through your fault, I shall not perform any more of my stipulations, because you have precluded me, and I shall claim damages."

There remains for consideration the alternative case made for the appellants upon condition 8 of the contract. Their claim is, that in respect of the defender's repudiation and breach of contract he is liable in damages, and that under the clause the damages are fixed at three years' rent which, they say, is liquidated damages, and not a penalty. But the clause, in my opinion, is only intended to take effect after the contract comes in operation. This is clear in the first event mentioned in the clause, because there can be no failure of payment until the advertising plates have been displayed in terms of the agreement. This could not happen on the hypothesis, which must be accepted on this part of the case, that the pursuers were not entitled to go on with the contract. The clause is, in my opinion, just a debt clause ancillary to the conditions for the payment of rent and providing for instant payment of the whole rent in the event of failure in punctual payment of the instalments. No very convincing suggestions were given as to what was meant to be covered by the second event. But, in my opinion, this also must refer to some breaches in the course of performance of the contract, which will again involve instant payment of the full rent. I fail to see how the clause can be at one and the same time a contractual clause sounding in payment of debt and a damages clause for repudiation of the contract. The clause accordingly has, in my opinion, no operation here, and I find it unnecessary to consider whether, if it had, it is a clause for liquidated damages, or for a penalty.

I would dismiss the appeal.

LORD HODSON, with whom LORD TUCKER concurred, made a speech allowing the appeal.

Appeal allowed.

Questions
1. Would it have made any difference if the contract had been that the defenders should supply the pursuers with details of the advertisements and the defenders had repudiated and declined to do so? See *Finelli et al. v. Dee et al.* (1968) 67 D.L.R. (2d) 393.
2. Would it have made any difference if clause 8 had been omitted from the contract?

Problems
1. A delivers his car to B's garage and B accepts A's instructions to install a new engine. Before B has started the work, A countermands his instructions. B refuses to return the car and installs the new engine. Advise A.
2. A contracts with B that he will deliver his car to B's garage on June 1 and pay £100 for the installation of new engine. A refuses to deliver the car. Advise B.

HOUNSLOW LONDON BOROUGH COUNCIL v. TWICKENHAM GARDEN DEVELOPMENTS LTD

Chancery Division [1971] Ch. 233; [1970] 3 W.L.R. 538; [1970] 3 All E.R. 326; 69 L.G.R. 109

The defendant contractor was employed by the borough to do building work on the borough's land. The contract provided that if the contractor failed to proceed diligently with the work, the architect might give him notice specifying the default and, if the default continued for 14 days, the borough might by notice determine the contract. The contractor was given possession of the site in 1966 and in January 1970 the borough gave notice under the above procedure to determine the contract. The contractor refused to accept the repudiation of the contract and continued with the work. The borough issued a writ claiming damages for trespass and an injunction, and, by notice of motion, sought an order restraining the contractor until judgment in the action from entering, remaining or otherwise trespassing on the site.

MEGARRY J. held that the licence given to the contractor to carry out works on the site was created by the contract and was in terms irrevocable, unless the notices were valid, and equity would not assist the borough to revoke the licence in breach of contract. The borough was not entitled to an injunction unless there was a high degree of assurance that the validity of the notices would be established at the trial; and the judge felt no such assurance.

The contractor relied, *inter alia*, on *White and Carter (Councils) Ltd v. McGregor*. MEGARRY J. referred to the "Hong Kong" example and continued: The examples discussed in argument before me applied the doctrine to cases concerning land. A contract to erect buildings on land is let; a few days later the landowner unexpectedly learns that he can obtain a far more advantageous planning permission for developing the land, and he thereupon repudiates the contract; but the contractor insists on performing it, even though the landowner must then either abandon the more valuable development and accept the far less profitable buildings or else pull those buildings down when they have been completed and then carry out the more fruitful scheme. Another landowner lets a contract to erect an extravagant building which his wealth can afford; before much work has been done his fortune collapses, and he can pay for the building only by using all that is left to him; yet the contractor insists on performing the contract. A third landowner contracts with an artist to paint extensive frescoes in a new building over a period of two years; the landowner then receives a handsome offer for the unadorned building, provided vacant possession is delivered forthwith; yet the artist insists on painting on for the rest of the two years.

Examples such as these suggest that there may well be limits to the doctrine. Lord Morton and Lord Keith both stressed the duty to mitigate damages: and he who is bound to mitigate can hardly be entitled to insist on aggravating. However, theirs were dissenting speeches which rejected the doctrine *in toto*. Accordingly I must turn to the speech of Lord Reid. Although it was his voice, with the voices of Lord Tucker and Lord Hodson, that carried the day, two important limitations appear in Lord Reid's speech. First, he pointed out that the peculiarity of the case was that the agents could perform the contract without any co-operation by the proprietor. He said at [1962] A.C. 413, 429: "Of course, if it had been necessary for the defender to do or accept anything before the contract could be completed by the pursuers, the pursuers could not and the court would not have compelled the defender to act, the contract would not have been completed and the pursuers' only remedy would have been damages."

This, I think, was in effect an acceptance of the argument to which Lord Reid had referred on p. 428: "the respondent points out that in most cases the innocent party cannot complete the contract himself without the other party doing, allowing or accepting something, and that it is purely fortuitous that the appellants can do so in this case. In most cases by refusing co-operation the party in breach can compel the innocent party to restrict his claim to damages."

The other limitation, cautiously expressed, at p. 431, was that "it may well be" that if a person has no legitimate financial or other interest in performing the contract rather than claiming damages, "he ought not to be allowed to saddle the other party with an additional burden with no benefit to himself": and this principle might apply to the example of the expert report. However, no such absence of a legitimate interest in the agents had been established, and so the possible principle did not apply.

It seems to me that the decision is one which I should be slow to apply to any category of case not fairly within the contemplation of their Lordships. The case before me is patently one in which the contractor cannot perform the contract without any co-operation by the borough. The whole machinery of the contract is geared to acts by the architect and quantity surveyor, and it is a contract that is to be performed on the borough's land. True, the contractor already has *de facto* possession or control of the land, there is no question of the borough being required to do the act of admitting the contractor into possession, and so in that respect the contractor can perform the contract without any "co-operation" by the borough. But I do not think that the point can be brushed aside so simply. Quite apart from questions of active co-operation, cases where one party is lawfully in possession of property of the other seem to me to raise issues not before the House of Lords in *White and Carter (Councils), Ltd v. McGregor* (above, p. 559). Suppose that A, who owns a large and valuable painting, contracts with B, a picture restorer, to restore it over a period of three months. Before the work is begun, A receives a handsome offer from C to purchase the picture, subject to immediate delivery of the picture in its unrestored state, C having grave suspicions of B's competence. If the work of restoration is to be done in A's house, he can effectually exclude B by refusing to admit him to the house: without A's "co-operation" to this extent B cannot perform his contract. But what if the picture stands in A's locked barn, the key of which he has lent to B so that he may come and go freely, or if the picture has been removed to B's premises? In these cases can B insist on performing his contract, even though this makes it impossible for A to accept C's offer? In the case of the barn, A's co-operation may perhaps be said to be requisite to the extent of not barring B's path to the barn or putting another lock on the door: but if the picture is on B's premises, no active co-operation by A is needed. Nevertheless, the picture is A's property, and I find it difficult to believe that Lord Reid intended to restrict the concept of "co-operation" to active co-operation. In *White and Carter (Councils), Ltd v. McGregor* no co-operation by the proprietor, either active or passive, was required: the contract could be performed by the agents wholly without reference to the proprietor or his property. The case was far removed from that of a property owner being forced to stand impotently aside while a perhaps ill-advised contract is executed on property of his which he has delivered into the possession of the other party, and is powerless to retrieve.

Accordingly, I do not think that *White and Carter (Councils) Ltd v. McGregor* has any application to the case before me. I say this, first, because a considerable degree of active co-operation under the contract by the borough is requisite, and second, because the work is being done to property of the borough. I doubt very much whether the *White* case can have been intended to apply where the contract is to be performed by doing acts to property owned by the party seeking to determine it. I should add that it seems to me that the ratio of the *White* case involves acceptance of Lord Reid's limitations, even though Lord Tucker and Lord Hodson said nothing of them: for without Lord Reid there was no majority for the decision of the House. Under the doctrine of precedent, I do not think that it can be said that a majority of a bare majority is itself the majority.

ATTICA SEA CARRIERS CORPORATION v. FERROSTAAL POSEIDON BULK REEDEREI G.M.B.H.

THE PUERTO BUITRAGO

Court of Appeal [1976] 1 Lloyd's L.Rep. 250

The charterers chartered the Puerto Buitrago from the shipowners for a period of 17 months. Clause 15, "Conditions on Redelivery," provided that the charterer should return the vessel in the same good order and condition as on delivery, ordinary wear and tear excepted, and should do all necessary repairs. The vessel developed engine trouble and was eventually towed to Kiel. Repairs were estimated to cost $2 million and the value of the vessel when repaired would be $1 million. Charterers admitted liability for $400,000 of repairs and redelivered vessel unrepaired. The shipowners refused to accept redelivery contending that the charterers were bound to repair the vessel and to pay the charter hire until it was repaired. They relied on *White & Carter v. McGregor*.

LORD DENNING M.R. referred to that case and continued: The decision has been criticised in a leading textbook (Cheshire & Fifoot (8th ed.), pp. 600 and 601). It is said to give a "grotesque" result. Even though it was a Scots case, it would appear that the House of Lords, as at present constituted, would expect us to follow it in any case that is precisely on all fours with it. But I would not follow it otherwise. It has no application whatever in a case where the plaintiff ought, in all reason, to accept the repudiation and sue for damages—provided that damages would provide an adequate remedy for any loss suffered by him. The reason is because, by suing for the money, the plaintiff is seeking to enforce specific performance of the contract—and he should not be allowed to do so when damages would be an adequate remedy. Take a servant, who has a contract for six months certain, but is dismissed after one month. He cannot sue for his wages for each of the six months by alleging that he was ready and willing to serve. His only remedy is damages. Take a finance company which lets a machine or motor-car on hire purchase, but the hirer refuses to accept it. The finance company cannot sue each month for the instalments. Its only remedy is in damages: see *National Cash Register Co. v. Stanley*, [1921] 3 K.B. 292; *Karsales (Harrow) v. Wallis*, [1956] 1 W.L.R. 936 (2nd point). So here, when the charterers tendered redelivery at the end of the period of the charter—in breach of the contract to repair—the shipowners ought in all reason to have accepted it. They cannot sue for specific performance—either of the promise to pay the charter hire, or of the promise to do the repairs—because damages are an adequate remedy for the breach. What is the alternative which the shipowners present to the charterers? Either the charterers must pay the charter hire for years to come, whilst the vessel lies idle and useless for want of repair. Or the charterers must do repairs which would cost twice as much as the ship would be worth when repaired—after which the shipowners might sell it as scrap, making the repairs a useless waste of money. In short, on either alternative, the shipowners seek to compel specific performance of one or other of the provisions of the charter—with most unjust and unreasonable consequences—when damages would be an adequate remedy. I do not think the law allows them to do this. I think they should accept redelivery and sue for damages. The charterers are, we are told, good for the money. That should suffice.

ORR AND BROWNE L.JJ. agreed.

CLEA SHIPPING CORP. v. BULK OIL INTERNATIONAL LTD

THE ALASKAN TRADER

Queen's Bench Division (Commercial Court) [1984] 1 All E.R. 129

By a charter dated October 19, 1979 the owners chartered the Alaskan Trader to charterers for a period of approximately 24 months. After nearly a year the ship suffered an engine breakdown whereupon the charterers said they had no further use for it. The owners repaired it and on April 7, 1981 informed the charterers that the ship was again at their disposal. The charterers considered the charter-party to have ended and declined to give the master any instructions; but the owners maintained the ship at anchor with a full crew ready to sail until the time charter expired in December 1981. The question was whether the charterers could recover the hire paid for the period April to December 1981. An arbitrator held that the owners had no legitimate interest in pursuing a claim for hire rather than damages.

LLOYD J., having examined the authorities: In addition to arguing that what Lord Reid had said about legitimate interest was only a quotation from counsel, and in any event *obiter*, arguments with which I have already dealt, counsel for the owners submitted that Lord Reid was, quite simply, wrong. It seems to me that it would be difficult for me to take that view in the light of what was said by all three members of the Court of Appeal in *The Puerto Buitrago* (above, p. 567). Whether one takes Lord Reid's language, which was adopted by Orr and Browne L.JJ. in *The Puerto Buitrago*, or Lord Denning M.R.'s language in that case ("in all reason"), or Kerr J.'s language in *The Odenfeld* [1978] 2 Lloyd's Rep. 357 ("wholly unreasonable . . . quite unrealistic, unreasonable and untenable"), there comes a point at which the court will cease, on general equitable principles, to allow the innocent party to enforce his contract according to its strict legal terms. How one defines that point is obviously a matter of some difficulty, for it involves drawing a line between conduct which is merely unreasonable (see *per* Lord Reid in *White & Carter v. McGregor* criticising the Lord President in *Langford & Co. Ltd v. Dutch*) and conduct which is *wholly* unreasonable (see *per* Kerr J. in *The Odenfeld* at 374). But however difficult it may be to define the point, that there *is* such a point seems to me to have been accepted both by the Court of Appeal in *The Puerto Buitrago* and by Kerr J. in *The Odenfeld*.

I turn last to the alternative ground on which the arbitrator based his decision, that this was a contract which called for co-operation between the parties, and therefore fell within Lord Reid's first limitation. Counsel for the charterers argued that a time charter is a contract for services, to be performed by the owners through the master and crew, and through the use of their vessel. As a contract for services, it is, as Lord Diplock pointed out in *The Scaptrade* [1983] 2 All E.R. 763 at 766, [1983] 3 W.L.R. 203 at 207—

"the very prototype of a contract of which before the fusion of law and equity a court would never grant specific performance . . ."

As in any other contract for services the owners earn their remuneration by performing the services required. If they are wrongfully prevented from performing any services, then, as in any other contract for services, the only remedy lies in damages. The fact that the owners' remuneration in this case, called hire, is payable in advance makes no difference. Counsel for the owners, on the other hand, argued that the owners earned their hire simply by holding the vessel and the services of their master and crew at the charterers' disposal. He concedes that in the case of master and servant, where the master has wrongfully dismissed the servant, the servant cannot earn remuneration by holding himself at the disposal of his master. He is confined to his remedy in damages. But counsel for the owners submits that a time charter is different. In view of my decision on the legitimate interest point, it is unnecessary for me to decide between these rival arguments, or to explore the nature of a time charter contract any further. All I will say is that, at first blush, there seemed much to be said for the argument of counsel for the charterers. I say no more, because in *The Odenfeld* Kerr J. found a similar argument unimpressive.

For the reasons I have given I would dismiss the owners' appeal and uphold the award.

Appeal dismissed.

Note

It has sometimes been said that the general principle, that a wrongful repudiation does not bring a contract to an end unless the other party accepts it as doing so, is subject to one exception. In *Vine v. National Dock Labour Board* [1956] 1 Q.B. 658 at 674, Jenkins L.J. said, *obiter*, "In the ordinary case of master and servant . . . the repudiation or the wrongful dismissal puts an end to the contract, and a claim for damages arises. It is necessarily a claim for damages and nothing more. The nature of the bargain is such that it can be nothing more." In the House of Lords Viscount Kilmuir agreed saying, ". . . if the master wrongfully dismisses the servant, either summarily or by giving insufficient notice, the employment is effectively terminated, albeit in breach of contract." In *Sanders v. Ernest A. Neale Ltd* [1974] 3 All E.R. 327 Sir John Donaldson P. said that "the repudiation of a contract of employment is an exception to the general rule. It terminates the contract without the necessity for acceptance by the injured party." The basis for the alleged exception appears to lie in the fact that the contract for personal services cannot be specifically enforced.

This opinion has not been accepted in some other cases. In *Decro-Wall International SA v. Practitioners in Marketing Ltd* [1971] 2 All E.R. 216 Salmon and Sachs L.JJ. expressed their doubts (though Salmon LJ. had appeared to accept that the contract was terminated by breach in *Denmark Productions Ltd v. Boscobel Productions Ltd* [1969] 1 Q.B. 699). In *Thomas Marshall (Exports) Ltd v. Guinle* [1978] 3 All E.R. 193 Megarry V.-C. held that a contract of service was not terminated when repudiated by the employee and granted an injunction restraining the employee from soliciting orders from the employer's customers and from disclosing his trade secrets. The Vice-Chancellor thought it impossible to reconcile the opinions in the preceding paragraph with the cases deciding that an employee who had repudiated his contract could be restrained by injunction from acting in breach of it: *Lumley v. Wagner* (1852) 1 De G.M. & G. 604, *Warner Bros. Pictures Inc. v. Nelson* [1937] 1 K.B. 209. The "automatic determination" cases had not dealt with the question whether, by repudiation, the servant could release himself not only from any further obligations to serve but also from other restrictions, imposed by the contract or implied by law only while the contract exists.

In *Gunton v. London Borough of Richmond* [1980] 3 All E.R. 577 the Court of Appeal held that the wrongful dismissal employee did not put an end to the contract of service. The ordinary principles of contract apply. The fact that a contract of personal service cannot be specifically enforced makes no difference for there are innumerable contracts to which specific performance is inapplicable. (*Cf. Frost v. Knight*, above, p. 551) ". . . the servant cannot sue in debt under the contract for remuneration in respect of any period after the wrongful dismissal, because the right to receive remuneration and the obligation to render services are mutually inter-dependent"—*per* Buckley L.J. [But do not both the right and the obligation continue, if the servant can elect to keep the contract alive?] ". . . the servant must come under an immediate obligation to mitigate his damages and so must almost invariably be bound to seek other employment. . . ."—*per* Buckley L.J. [But is not seeking other employment accepting the repudiation and, if he is obliged to seek other employment, is he not thereby obliged to accept the repudiation?] Brightman L.J., agreeing that the servant could not sue for wages, said that the status or relationship of master and servant was determined, but not the contract.

Shaw L.J., dissenting on this point, said that the practical basis for according an election to the injured party has no reality in relation to a contract of service where there is a total repudiation which is at once destructive of the contractual relationship. To preserve the bare contractual relationship is an empty formality. It might be different where the repudiation is "oblique," for example where the employer seeks to change the nature of the work required to be done.

Even if the law is as stated in *Vine*'s case, it appears that there is an exception to it in the rare case where an injunction may be granted so as, in effect, to compel specific performance of the contract: *Hill v. C. A. Parsons & Co. Ltd.*

In *Hare v. Murphy Bros. Ltd* [1973] I.C.R. 331 (N.I.R.C.) the plaintiff, a foreman employed by the defendants, was sentenced in June 1971 to 12 months' imprisonment for unlawful wounding. On his release in February 1972 the defendants told him that there was no job for him. He claimed compensation for unfair dismissal. It was held that the sentence of imprisonment was "a breach by him of his contract of so serious a nature, bearing in mind the length of time during which he would be away from work and importance of his position as foreman, that it went to the root and constituted a repudiation of his contract of employment." The contract had come to an end as a result of the repudiation and the consequent sentence of imprisonment, so there could be no unfair dismissal in February 1972.

However, in *F. C. Shepherd & Co. Ltd v. Jerrom* [1986] 3 All E.R. 589, the Court of Appeal held that *Hare*'s case was not a binding authority on this point. The contract of an apprentice who had been sentenced to borstal training had come to an end, not because the apprentice had repudiated it, but because it had been frustrated by the sentence of the court. It was not open to the apprentice, who alleged that he had been unfairly dismissed, to claim that this was a self-induced frustration and so not effective to terminate the contract (see above) because he could not be allowed to take advantage of his own wrong.

Section 2. Specific Performance and Injunction

CASES concerning the principles according to which specific performance is granted or refused are *Gibson v. Manchester City Council* (above, p. 7), *Tamplin v. James* (above, p. 110), *Denny v. Hancock* (above, p. 112), *Beswick v. Beswick* (above, p. 301), and *Redgrave v. Hurd* (above, p. 329). *Cf. White & Carter (Councils) Ltd v. McGregor* (above). For further details, see Cheshire, Fifoot and Furmston, *Law of Contract* (12th ed.), pp. 628–636; Treitel, *Law of Contract* (8th ed.), pp. 902–919.

CO-OPERATIVE INSURANCE SOCIETY LTD v. ARGYLL STORES (HOLDINGS) LTD

Court of Appeal, CHANI 95/1247/B, December 21, 1995

The defendants were tenants for 35 years from August 1979 of a property comprising 30 per cent of the total letting area of the Hillsborough Shopping Centre, Sheffield. It was the anchor unit in the centre and played a key role. The lease required the defendants to keep the demised premises open for retail trade during the usual hours of business. The current rent was £140,000 a year. After the property had made a loss of £70,000 in its last trading year the defendants decided in May 1995 to sell it (together with 26 other supermarkets), well knowing of the "keep open" covenant. The plaintiff landlord wrote asking the defendant to keep open for trading until an assignee could be found. The defendants did not respond and, on May 19, 1995, stripped out the shop. It would cost £1 million to reinstate. Judge Maddocks Q.C. gave summary judgment for damages to be assessed but refused an order for specific performance. The plaintiff appealed.

LEGGATT L.J., having stated the facts: Felicitously expressed by Slade J. in *Braddon Towers Ltd v. International Stores Ltd* [1987] 1 E.G.L.R. 209, Ch.D. is the state of authority in 1979, which has not changed materially since. Defendant tenants had covenanted to keep premises intended to be used as a supermarket open at all normal times as a first-class shop, with a display window suitably and attractively placed and to use their utmost endeavours to develop, improve and extend the business and not to do or suffer anything to injure the goodwill. The venture proved to be unprofitable and the defendants decided, in deliberate breach of their covenant, and without prior consultation with the plaintiffs, to close the supermarket. The landlords applied for an interlocutory mandatory injunction. A clear statement of the law was to be found in *Dowty v. Wolverhampton Corporation* [1971] 1 W.L.R. 204 in which Pennycuick J. rejected an application for an injunction to compel the maintenance of an airfield as a going concern. He remarked that that would involve continuing acts of management including the upkeep of runways and buildings, the employment of staff, and in effect the carrying on of a business. He added at page 211—

> "It is very well established that the court will not order specific performance of an obligation to carry on a business or, indeed, any comparable series of activities."

That case reproduced the effect of *Hooper v. Brodrick* (1840) 11 Sim. 47 and *Attorney General v. Colchester Corporation* [1955] 2 Q.B. 207. . .

In *Braddon Towers* counsel submitted that it was due (1) to the court's unwillingness to supervise the doing of continuous, successive acts, and (2) to the fact that the terms of a mandatory injunction must be clear and definite. In the present case the requirement to keep open for retail trade during usual business hours and in keeping with a good class parade of shops was quite intelligible to the respondents, while they were carrying on business there. By reference to that standard and without descending to excessive detail the court would be well able to tell the respondents what is expected of them. If the premises are to be run as a business, it cannot be in the respondents' interest to run it half-heartedly or inefficiently, still less in a way that involves the appellants in continual recourse to the court. Conversely, as Slade J. said at page 213.

> "I am not persuaded that . . . if they themselves thereafter acted in good faith, they would have any real difficulty in knowing how to comply with it, without risk of successful contempt proceedings."

In *Powell v. Duffryn Steam Coal Co. v. Taff Vale Railway Co.* (1874) 9 Ch.App. 331 James L.J., with whom Mellish L.J. agreed, said at page 335—

> "The plaintiffs fail only because of the difficulty in the way of this court's enforcing such a right—a difficulty which to my mind is insuperable."

The modern position has however been stated by Lord Wilberforce in *Shiloh Spinners Ltd v. Harding* [1973] A.C. 691, 724 as follows:

> "Where it is necessary, and, in my opinion right, to move away from some 19th century authorities, is to reject as a reason against granting relief, the impossibility for the courts to supervise the doing of work."

The House of Lords was in effect adopting the view of Megarry J. in *C. H. Giles & Co. v. Morris* (below, p. 576) that the so called rule that contracts involving the continuous performance of services would not be specifically enforced was plainly not absolute and without exception. . . .

Slade J. referred also to a judgment of his own in which he had remarked that—

> ". . . it cannot now be regarded as an absolute and inflexible rule that the court will never grant an injunction requiring a person to do a series of acts requiring the continuous employment of persons over a number of years, though the jurisdiction was one that would be exercised only in exceptional circumstances."

Finally, he quoted from the forceful judgment of Bacon V.-C. in *Greene v. West Cheshire Railway Co.* (1870) 13 Eq. 44 in which he ordered specific performance of an agreement to construct and maintain a siding alongside a railway line upon land belonging to the plaintiffs. He rejected the argument that a court of equity should refrain from granting relief and leave it to the plaintiffs to recover damages at law. At page 51 he characterised with contumely the defendant's attitude:

> "I can, but I will not perform the obligation I have entered into; and instead of keeping faith and honestly fulfilling my promise, I will leave you to take the chances of an action for damages, and reserve to myself the power of endeavouring to defeat your claim; and, instead of acknowledging your just rights, will compel you to receive, instead of them, such a sum as I may be able to persuade a jury will compensate you for the loss and injury and disappointment which my wilful wrongdoing may have occasioned to you."

Referring to the fact that the Vice-Chancellor was, however, not confronted by three adverse cases, as he was himself, Slade J. said—

> "Whether or not this may be properly described as a rule of law, I do not doubt that for many years practitioners have advised their clients that it is the settled and invariable practice of this court never to grant mandatory injunctions requiring persons to carry on business."

After reflecting that the application that he was concerned with was interlocutory, he expressed the conclusion that—

> "The rationale which lies behind the rule or practice may perhaps need rethinking, at least in relation to those cases where it would be possible to define with sufficient certainty the obligations of the person enjoined to carry on a business."

The approach of this court

What is said against that course in this case is that the respondents may have been advised when they entered into their lease that if they found it unprofitable they could disregard their promise to keep the shop open upon payment of damages representing such loss as their dereliction could be proved to have caused. There is no evidence that any such advice was given. Even if it was, they should have been advised also that the making of an order is discretionary, with the result that an order to keep open might be made if the court considered that to be the appropriate remedy.

The judge said that it seemed to him to be a case in which the principles applied in *Braddon Towers* should be applied. He did not, however, say why. Whilst disclaiming any intention to criticise the plaintiffs for not applying for an order before the store was closed, the judge thought that a vastly disproportionate amount of costs would be incurred if an order was made to reopen the store. He seemed to think that that was a good reason for awarding damages instead of specific performance. Whilst acknowledging that there might be some difficulty in the assessment of damages he declared without considering its implications that it is a task which can readily be carried out by the court. Finally, he asserted that "specific relief in this case would be too far reaching and beyond the scope of control which the court should seek to impose." He did not explain these conclusions, but merely asserted that damages provide a more suitable remedy.

The judge's approach was conditioned by his belief in a "settled practice". That prompted or encouraged him to find that damages are the appropriate remedy. If such an exercise of discretion were always to be treated as unexceptionable, this court could never interfere to correct the practice. In my judgment because the judge showed an unwarrantable reluctance to order specific performance, this court should intervene and exercise the discretion afresh unfettered by shibboleths which will otherwise continue to be unthinkingly applied.

In my judgment this is a proper case in which to grant specific performance. It would do the court no credit, if in these circumstances the court refrained from granting an injunction on the ground that it had become the practice not to do so. If this court were to follow that course, the result in practice would be that the common form words of this covenant would hardly ever, if ever, be construed as meaning what they say. If the parties want to contract that a failure to keep open will sound only in damages, they are quite at liberty to do so. But where a responsible and substantial company such as the respondents have undertaken to keep one of their stores open for a stipulated period, I see no reason why they should not be held to their bargain. That in recessionary times may entail trading at a loss; but it by no means entails that they will have to do so for the duration of the lease. In any event there is provision made for assignment with the landlords' consent, and that may provide the respondents with an escape in this case. That they stripped out their store rather than respond to the landlords' cautionary letter was their own idea. They did it at their peril, and have only themselves or their legal advisers to blame for having done so precipitately.

The appellants would have very considerable difficulty in trying to prove their loss. An award of damages would be unlikely to compensate them fully; and the losses of the other tenants of the Shopping Centre would be irrecoverable, except in so far as they might be mitigated by reduced rents. The respondents have acted with gross commercial cynicism, preferring to resist a claim for damages rather than keep an unambiguous promise. This is not a court of morals, but there is no reason why its willingness to grant specific performance should not be affected by a sense of fair dealing.

I would allow the appeal and grant the order of specific performance.

LORD JUSTICE ROCH delivered judgment allowing the appeal.

MILLETT L.J., having reviewed the authorities and noted that it was the settled practice of the court not to grant a final injunction or decree of specific performance which would have the effect of compelling the defendant to carry on a business indefinitely, continued: In my opinion there is a fundamental objection to such an order. If granted for any length of time or for an indefinite period it is oppressive. To compel a defendant for an indefinite period to carry on a business which he considers is not viable, or which for his own commercial reasons he has decided to close down, is to expose him to potentially large unquantifiable and unlimited losses which may be out of all proportion to the loss which his breach of contract has caused to the plaintiff.

The competing arguments in the present case, and the difference in the views of the members of this court, reflect a controversy which has persisted since the dispute between Sir Edward Coke and Lord Ellesmere L.C. Sir Edward Coke resented the existence of an equitable jurisdiction which deprived the defendant of what he regarded as a fundamental freedom to elect whether to carry out his promise or to pay damages for the breach. Modern economic theory supports Sir Edward Coke; an award of damages reflects normal commercial expectations and ensures a more efficient allocation of scarce economic resources. The defendant will break his contract only if it pays him to do so after taking the payment of damages into account; the plaintiff will be fully compensated in damages; and both parties will be free to allocate their resources elsewhere. Against this there is the repugnance felt by those who share the view of Fuller C.J. in *Union Pacific Railway Co. v. Chicago Rock Island and Pacific Railway Co.* (1896) US 564, 600 that it is an intolerable travesty of justice that a party should be allowed to break his contract at pleasure by electing to pay damages for the breach.

English law has adopted a pragmatic approach in resolving this dispute. Equitable relief is discretionary and exceptional. Courts of Equity have never enforced the performance of all contracts, whatever their nature. Over the centuries rules of practice have evolved so that the parties can know in advance which contractual obligations will be specifically enforced and which sound in damages only. The leading principle is usually said to be that equitable relief is not available where damages are an adequate remedy. In my view it would be more accurate to say that equitable relief will be granted where it is appropriate and not otherwise; and that where damages are an adequate remedy it is inappropriate to grant equitable relief.

But this is not the only test of the appropriateness of equitable relief. It is always necessary to consider the consequence to the defendant of granting such relief as well as the consequence to the plaintiff of leaving him to his remedy in damages. Equitable remedies are instruments of justice; they should be refused where they would be potential instruments of oppression. In *Isenberg v. East India Estate Co.* (1863) 3 De G. J. & S. 263 at page 273 Lord Westbury L.C. pointed out that it was not the proper function of a court of equity "by granting a mandatory injunction, to deliver over the defendants to the plaintiff bound hand and foot, in order to be made subject to any extortionate demand that he may by possibility make. . ."

In the present case the Defendants' Lease had 19 years to run at the date of the hearing before the Judge. If the Defendants were unable to find a purchaser willing to take on the Lease and the obligation of operating the premises as a supermarket, a decree of specific performance would have the effect of compelling the Defendants to continue to operate a supermarket on the site regardless of the financial consequences. Even if the Defendants found such a purchaser, he would in turn be amenable to a similar decree if he should find that the business could not be carried on at a profit. Any order would, therefore, have an effective duration of 19 years.

The moral strength of the Plaintiffs' claim to a decree of specific performance is that the court would be doing no more than requiring the Defendants to do that which they have undertaken to do. But the rule in *Doherty v. Allman* (1878) 3 App.Cas. 709, 720 has never been rigorously applied to the grant of a mandatory injunction or a decree of specific performance. Such orders do not issue simply because the defendant has deliberately committed a breach of a negative undertaking and in the face of the plaintiff's protests. They will be refused where the injury to the plaintiff is small and the grant of an injunction or decree will cause disproportionate loss to the defendant. That is not this case. The injury to the Plaintiffs is substantial and difficult, though not impossible, to assess. But the potential loss to the Defendants is enormous, unquantifiable and unlimited, as well as being out of all proportion to any uncompensatable loss which the Plaintiffs may sustain.

This is true of any order which would have the effect of compelling a party to carry on a business as a going concern for an indefinite period. Is he to be driven into bankruptcy? The court cannot know what will be the consequences of its own order. The courts have never before made such an order, and in my opinion their reluctance to do so is well-founded. Over the years countless tenants with the benefit of legal advice have entered into commercial leases containing terms similar to those found in Clause 4(19) of the present Lease. If they had asked their legal advisers whether this meant that they could be compelled to keep the premises open for business regardless of the financial consequences, I have no doubt that they would have been told that it did not; they would have been advised that such a covenant sounds in damages only. If the courts were willing to compel performance, I do not see how any tenant properly advised could safely enter such an obligation.

This affords a secondary reason for refusing to depart from the practice which the courts have consistently followed for so long. Consistent practice, no less than common error, makes the law. The equitable jurisdiction should not be exercised in a manner which would defeat the commercial expectations of the parties at the time when they entered into their contractual obligations.

Since writing the above I have had the advantage of reading in draft the judgment of Leggatt L.J. It is true that there is no evidence of the advice which the parties received when they entered into the Lease, but that does not detract from the dangers inherent in disturbing past transactions based on the known practice of the court. Nor is it sufficient to say that the parties should have been advised that the grant of specific performance is discretionary and that an order might be made if the court thought that it was just. Such advice would be incomplete unless accompanied by a statement that, save in exceptional circumstances, it was not the practice to make an order.

I agree that it would do the court no credit if it declined to make an order merely on the ground that it had become the practice not to do so. The court is entitled and bound to re-examine its practice to see whether it accords with modern requirements. I would willingly see a departure from some of the grounds which have been advanced in the past for declining to make an order. But I remain firmly of the view that the court ought not compel party to carry on a business for an indefinite period regardless of the financial consequences of doing so. The effect of such an order could be far more oppressive than that of an order to pull down a building. Withholding equitable relief does not, of course, mean that a covenant to keep a shop open could safely be ignored. The covenant would sound in damages; such damages could be substantial; and it is an open question whether in an appropriate case they might not include an element of what are sometimes— I believe erroneously—called restitutionary damages.

I would dismiss this appeal.

Appeal allowed.

Note

In *C. H. Giles & Co. v. Morris* [1972] 1 W.L.R. 307, a contract relating to the reorganisation of certain companies provided that A Ltd should adopt new articles of association, reorganise its share capital and sell certain of its shares to B Ltd on certain terms, *inter alia*, a term that, before completion, C should be appointed managing director of A Ltd. Completion date passed without the condition being satisfied and eventually B Ltd claimed specific performance. In proceedings for committal for contempt of directors of A Ltd and sequestration of A Ltd for failure to comply with a consent order for specific performance of the Master, the question arose whether the presence of the term for the appointment of C to the board of A Ltd prevented the court from decreeing specific performance, since that provision was one for personal services. Megarry J. held that there was a distinction between an order *to perform* a contract for services and an order *to procure the execution of* such a contract; the mere fact that the contract to be made was one of which the court would not decree specific performance was not a ground for refusing to decree that the contract be entered into. He further held that, in any case, the mere presence in a contract of one provision which, by itself, would not be specifically enforceable, did not prevent the contract as a whole from being specifically enforced. *Cf. Beswick v. Beswick*, (above, p. 301.) The contract was, accordingly, specifically enforceable.

CHAPTER 16

DAMAGES

Section 1. The Objects of an Award of Damages

SURREY COUNTY COUNCIL and ANOTHER v. BREDERO HOMES LTD

Court of Appeal [1993] 3 All E.R. 705

In 1980 two councils sold freehold land to the defendant (B) for £1.25 million, subject to B's obtaining planning permission to develop the land in accordance with the councils' scheme. B obtained planning permission and the land was transferred, B covenanting with the councils to develop the land in accordance with that permission. B, in breach of the covenant, subsequently obtained planning permission to build, and did build, a larger number of houses on the site, thus making a greater profit. The councils, though aware of the breach, did not seek an injunction or specific performance of the covenants. After B had sold all the houses, the councils sued for damages equal to the amount that they might have extracted from B in return for agreeing to the more profitable development. Ferris J. held that they were entitled only to nominal damages. The councils appealed.

DILLON L.J.: delivered judgment dismissing the appeal.

STEYN L.J.: An award of compensation for breach of contract serves to protect three separate interests. The starting principle is that the aggrieved party ought to be compensated for loss of his positive or expectation interests. In other words, the object is to put the aggrieved party in the same financial position as if the contract had been fully performed. But the law also protects the negative interest of the aggrieved party. If the aggrieved party is unable to establish the value of a loss of bargain he may seek compensation in respect of his reliance losses. The object of such an award is to compensate the aggrieved party for expenses incurred and losses suffered in reliance of the contract. These two complementary principles share one feature. Both are pure compensatory principles. If the aggrieved party has suffered no loss he is not entitled to be compensated by invoking these principles. The application of these principles to the present case would result in an award of nominal damages only.

There is, however, a third principle which protects the aggrieved party's restitutionary interest. The object of such an award is not to compensate the plaintiff for a loss, but to deprive the defendant of the benefit he gained by the breach of contract. The classic illustration is a claim for the return of goods sold and delivered where the buyer has repudiated his obligation to pay the price. It is not traditional to describe a claim for restitution following a breach of contract as damages. What matters is that a coherent law of obligations must inevitably extend its protection to cover certain restitutionary interests. How far that protection should extend is the essence of the problem before us. . . .

The introduction of restitutionary remedies to deprive cynical contract breakers of the fruits of their breaches of contract will lead to greater uncertainty in the assessment of damages in commercial and consumer disputes. It is of paramount importance that the way in which disputes are likely to be resolved by the courts must be readily predictable. Given the premise that the aggrieved party has suffered no loss, is such a dramatic extension of restitutionary remedies justified in order to confer a windfall in each case on the aggrieved party? I think not. In any event such a widespread availability of restitutionary remedies will have a tendency to discourage economic activity in relevant situations. In a range of cases such liability would fall on underwriters who have insured relevant liability risks. Inevitably underwriters would have to be compensated for the new species of potential claims. Insurance premiums would have to go up. That, too, is a consequence which militates against the proposed extension. The recognition of the proposed extension will in my view not serve the public interest. It is sound policy to guard against extending the protection of the law of obligations too widely. For these substantive and policy reasons I regard it as undesirable that the range of restitutionary remedies should be extended in the way in which we have been invited to do so. . . .

I would dismiss the appeal.

ROSE L.J. delivered judgment dismissing the appeal

Appeal dismissed.

Section 2. Remoteness of Damage and Measure of Damages

VICTORIA LAUNDRY (WINDSOR) LTD v. NEWMAN INDUSTRIES LTD

Court of Appeal [1949] 2 K.B. 528; 65 T.L.R. 274; 93 S.J. 371; [1949] 1 All E.R. 997

The plaintiffs, launderers and dyers, wanted a boiler of much greater capacity than the one they possessed in order to expand their business. The defendants, engineers, agreed to sell to the plaintiffs for £2,150 a large boiler then installed on the defendants' premises. Delivery was arranged for June 5, 1946. The boiler was damaged while being dismantled by third parties employed by the defendants and delivery was delayed until November 8, 1946. The plaintiffs claimed as damages for loss of profit due to the defendants' breach of contract:

1. £16 a week for the very large number of new customers whom they could and would have taken on—the demand for laundry services at that time being insatiable.

2. £262 a week which they could and would have earned under dyeing contracts with the Ministry of Supply.

Streatfeild J. awarded £110 under certain minor heads, but held that, under the second rule in *Hadley v. Baxendale* (1854) 9 Ex. 341 (below, pp. 579, 585–586), the defendants were not liable for loss of profits because the special object for which the plaintiffs were acquiring the boiler had not been drawn to the defendants' attention.

The plaintiffs appealed.

The judgment of the court (Tucker, Asquith and Singleton L.JJ.) was delivered by ASQUITH L.J. After stating the facts and emphasising that the defendants knew that the plaintiffs were launderers and dyers and that they required the boiler for immediate use in their business, the learned judge continued:

The authorities on recovery of loss of profits as a head of damage are not easy to reconcile. At one end of the scale stand cases where there has been non-delivery or delayed delivery of what is on the face of it obviously a profit-earning chattel; for instance, a merchant or passenger ship: see *Fletcher v. Tayleur* (1855) 17 C.B. 21; *Re Trent and Humber Company, ex p. Cambrian Steam Packet Company* (1868) L.R. 6 Eq. 396; or some essential part of such a ship; for instance, a propeller, in *Wilson v. General Ironscrew Company* (1878) 47 L.J.Q.B. 23, or engines, *Saint Line v. Richardson* [1940] 2 K.B. 99. In such cases loss of profit has rarely been refused. A second and intermediate class of case in which loss of profit has often been awarded is where ordinary mercantile goods have been sold to a merchant with knowledge by the vendor that the purchaser wanted them for resale; at all events, where there was no market in which the purchaser could buy similar goods against the contract on the seller's default, see, for instance, *Borries v. Hutchinson* (1865) 18 C.B.(N.S.) 445. At the other end of the scale are cases where the defendant is not a vendor of the goods, but a carrier, see, for instance, *Hadley v. Baxendale* (below, pp. 585–586), and *Gee v. Lancashire and Yorkshire Ry.*, 6 H. & N. 211. In such cases the courts have been slow to allow loss of profit as an item of damage. This was not, it would seem, because a different principle applies in such cases, but because the application of the same principle leads to different results. A carrier commonly knows less than a seller about the purposes for which the buyer or consignee needs the goods, or about other "special circumstances" which may cause exceptional loss if due delivery is withheld.

Three of the authorities call for more detailed examination. First comes *Hadley v. Baxendale* itself. Familiar though it is, we should first recall the memorable sentence in which the main principles laid down in this case are enshrined: "Where two parties have made a contract which one of them has broken, the damages which the other party ought to receive in respect of such breach of contract should be such as may fairly and reasonably be considered as either arising naturally, that is according to the usual course of things, from such breach of contract itself, or such as may reasonably be supposed to have been in the contemplation of both parties, at the time they made the contract, as the probable result of the breach of it." The limb of this sentence prefaced by "either" embodies the so-called "first" rule; that prefaced by "or" the "second." In considering the meaning and application of these rules, it is essential to bear clearly in mind the facts on which *Hadley v. Baxendale* proceeded. The head-note is definitely misleading in so far as it says that the defendant's clerk, who attended at the office, was told that the mill was stopped and that the shaft must be delivered immediately. The same allegation figures in the statement of facts which are said on p. 344 to have "appeared" at the trial before Crompton J. If the Court of Exchequer had accepted these facts as established, the court must, one would suppose, have decided the case the other way round; must, that is, have held the damage claimed was recoverable under the second rule. But it is reasonably plain from Alderson B.'s judgment that the court rejected this evidence, for on p. 355 he says: "We find that the only circumstances here communicated by the plaintiffs to the defendants at the time when the contract was made were that the article to be carried was the broken shaft of a mill and that the plaintiffs were the millers of that mill," and it is on this basis of fact that he proceeds to ask, "How do these circumstances show reasonably that the profits of the mill must be stopped by an unreasonable delay in the delivery of the broken shaft by the carrier to the third person?" *British Columbia Sawmills v. Nettleship* (1868) L.R. 3 C.P. 499 annexes to the principle laid down in *Hadley v. Baxendale* a rider to the effect that where knowledge of special circumstances is relied on as enhancing the damage recoverable, that knowledge must have been brought home to the defendant at the time of the contract and in such circumstances that the defendant impliedly undertook to bear any special loss referable to a breach in those special circumstances. The knowledge which was lacking in that case on the part of the defendant was knowledge that the particular box of machinery negligently lost by the defendants was one without which the rest of the machinery could not be put together and would therefore be useless.

Cory v. Thames Ironworks Company, L.R. 3 Q.B. 181, 187—a case strongly relied on by the plaintiffs—presented the peculiarity that the parties contemplated respectively different profit-making uses of the chattel sold by the defendant to the plaintiff. It was the hull of a boom derrick, and was delivered late. The plaintiffs were coal merchants, and the obvious use, and that to which the defendants believed it was to be put, was that of a coal store. The plaintiffs, on the other hand, the buyers, in fact intended to use it for transhipping coals from colliers to barges, a quite unprecedented use for a chattel of this kind, one quite unsuspected by the sellers and one calculated to yield much higher profits. The case accordingly decides, *inter alia*, what is the measure of damage recoverable when the parties are not *ad idem* in their contemplation of the use for which the article is needed. It was decided that in such a case no loss was recoverable beyond what would have resulted if the intended use had been that reasonably within the contemplation of the defendants, which in that case was the "obvious" use. This special complicating factor, the divergence between the knowledge and contemplation of the parties respectively, has somewhat obscured the general importance of the decision, which is in effect that the facts of the case brought it within the first rule of *Hadley v. Baxendale* and enabled the plaintiff to recover loss of such profits as would have arisen from the normal and obvious use of the article. The "natural consequence," said Blackburn J., of not delivering the derrick was that £420 representing those normal profits was lost. Cockburn C.J., interposing during the argument, made the significant observation: "No doubt in order to recover damage arising from a special purpose the buyer must have communicated the special purpose to the seller; but there is one thing which must always be in the knowledge of both parties, which is that the thing is bought for the purpose of being in some way or other profitably applied." This observation is apposite to the present case. These three cases have on many occasions been approved by the House of Lords without any material qualification.

What propositions applicable to the present case emerge from the authorities as a whole, including those analysed above? We think they include the following:

(1) It is well settled that the governing purpose of damages is to put the party whose rights have been violated in the same position, so far as money

can do so, as if his rights had been observed: *Sally Wertheim v. Chicoutimi Pulp Company* [1911] A.C. 301. This purpose, if relentlessly pursued, would provide him with a complete indemnity for all loss *de facto* resulting from a particular breach, however improbable, however unpredictable. This, in contract at least, is recognised as too harsh a rule. Hence.

(2) In cases of breach of contract the aggrieved party is only entitled to recover such part of the loss actually resulting as was at the time of the contract reasonably foreseeable as liable to result from the breach.

(3) What was at the time reasonably so foreseeable depends on the knowledge then possessed by the parties or, at all events, by the party who later commits the breach.

(4) For this purpose, knowledge "possessed" is of two kinds; one imputed, the other actual. Everyone, as a reasonable person, is taken to know the "ordinary course of things" and consequently what loss is liable to result from a breach of contract in that ordinary course. This is the subject-matter of the "first rule" in *Hadley v. Baxendale*. But to this knowledge, which a contract-breaker is assumed to possess whether he actually possesses it or not, there may have to be added in a particular case knowledge which he actually possesses, of special circumstances outside the "ordinary course of things," of such a kind that a breach in those special circumstances would be liable to cause more loss. Such a case attracts the operation of the "second rule" so as to make additional loss also recoverable.

(5) In order to make the contract-breaker liable under either rule it is not necessary that he should actually have asked himself what loss is liable to result from a breach. As has often been pointed out, parties at the time of contracting contemplate not the breach of the contract, but its performance. It suffices that, if he had considered the question, he would as a reasonable man have concluded that the loss in question was liable to result (see certain observations of Lord du Parcq in the recent case of *Monarch Steamship Co. Ltd v. A/B Karlshamns Oljefabriker* [1949] A.C. 196).

(6) Nor, finally, to make a particular loss recoverable, need it be proved that upon a given state of knowledge the defendant could, as a reasonable man, foresee that a breach must necessarily result in that loss. It is enough if he could foresee it was likely so to result. It is indeed enough, to borrow from the language of Lord du Parcq in the same case, at p. 158, if the loss (or some factor without which it would not have occurred) is a "serious possibility" or a "real danger." For short, we have used the word "liable" to result. Possibly the colloquialism "on the cards" indicates the shade of meaning with some approach to accuracy.

If these, indeed, are the principles applicable, what is the effect of their application to the facts of this case? We have, at the beginning of this judgment, summarised the main relevant facts. The defendants were an engineering company supplying a boiler to a laundry. We reject the submission for the defendants that an engineering company knows no more than the plain man about boilers or the purposes to which they are commonly put by different classes of purchasers, including laundries. The defendant company were not, it is true, manufacturers of this boiler or dealers in boilers, but they gave a highly technical and comprehensive description of this boiler to the plaintiffs by letter of January 19, 1946, and offered both to dismantle the boiler at Harpenden and re-erect it on the plaintiffs' premises. Of the uses or purposes to which boilers are put, they would clearly know more than the uninstructed layman. Again, they knew they were supplying the boiler to a company carrying on the business of laundrymen and dyers, for use in that business. The obvious use of a boiler, in such a business, is surely to boil water for the purpose of washing or dyeing. A laundry might conceivably buy a boiler for some other purpose; for instance, to work radiators or warm bath water for the comfort of its employees or directors, or to use for research, or to exhibit in a museum. All these purposes are possible, but the first is the obvious purpose which, in the case of a laundry, leaps to the average eye. If the purpose then be to wash or dye, why does the company want to wash or dye, unless for purposes of business advantage, in which term we, for the purposes of the rest of this judgment, include maintenance or increase of profit, or reduction of loss? (We shall speak henceforward not of loss of profit, but of "loss of business.") No commercial concern commonly purchases for the purposes of its business a very large and expensive structure like this—a boiler 19 feet high and costing over £2,00—with any other motive, and no supplier, let alone an engineering company, which has promised delivery of such an article by a particular date, with knowledge that it was to be put into use immediately on delivery, can reasonably contend that it could not foresee that loss of business (in the sense indicated above) would be liable to result to the purchaser from a long delay in the delivery thereof. The suggestion that, for all the supplier knew, the boiler might have been needed simply as a "standby", to be used in a possibly distant future, is gratuitous. . . .

[His Lordship then quoted from the judgment of Streatfeild J. and continued:] The answer to this reasoning has largely been anticipated in what has been said above, but we would wish to add: First, that the learned judge appears to infer that because certain "special circumstances" were, in his view, not "drawn to the notice of" the defendants and therefore, in his view, the operation of the "second rule" was excluded, *ergo* nothing in respect of loss of business can be recovered under the "first rule." This inference is, in our view, no more justified in the present case than it was in the case of *Cory v. Thames Ironworks Company*. Secondly, that while it is not wholly clear what were the "special circumstances" on the non-communication of which the learned judge relied, it would seem that they were, or included, the following: (a) the "circumstance" that delay in delivering the boiler was going to lead "necessarily" to loss of profits. But the true criterion is surely not what was bound "necessarily" to result, but what was likely or liable to do so, and we think that it was amply conveyed to the defendants by what was communicated to them (plus what was patent without express communication) that delay in delivery was likely to lead to "loss of business"; (b) the "circumstance" that the plaintiffs needed the boiler "to extend their business." It was surely not necessary for the defendants to be specifically informed of this, as a precondition of being liable for loss of business. Reasonable persons in the shoes of the defendants must be taken to foresee without any express intimation that a laundry which, at a time when there was a famine of laundry facilities, was paying £2,000 odd for plant and intended at such a time to put such plant "into use" immediately, would be likely to suffer in pocket from five months' delay in delivery of the plant in question, whether they intended by means of it to extend their business, or merely to maintain it, or to reduce a loss; (c) the "circumstance" that the plaintiffs had the assured expectation of special contracts, whch they could only fulfil by securing punctual delivery of the boiler. Here, no doubt, the learned judge had in mind the particularly lucrative dyeing contracts to which the plaintiffs looked forward and which they mention in para. 10 of the statement of claim. We agree that in order that the plaintiffs should recover specifically and as such the profits expected on these contracts, the defendants would have had to know, at the time of their agreement with the plaintiffs, of the prospect and terms of such contracts. We also agree, that they did not in fact know these things. It does not, however, follow that the plaintiffs are precluded from recovering some general (and perhaps conjectural) sum for loss of business in respect of dyeing contracts to be reasonably expected, any more than in respect of laundering contracts to be reasonably expected.

Thirdly, the other point on which Streatfeild J. largely based his judgment was that there is a critical difference between the measure of damages applicable when the defendant defaults in supplying a self-contained profit-earning whole and when he defaults in supplying a part of that whole. In our view, there is no intrinsic magic, in this connection, in the whole as against a part. The fact that a part only is involved is only significant in so far as it bears on the capacity of the supplier to foresee the consequences of non-delivery. . . .

Appeal allowed.

Question

In *Parsons v. Uttley Ingham* and *Wroth v. Tyler*, (below, p. 590) it was held that what must be contemplated is damage of a particular type, not its degree or quantum. Was the damage caused by loss of the particularly lucrative dyeing contracts different in "type" from that caused by the loss of other, less lucrative, dyeing contracts?

THE HERON II

House of Lords [1969] 1 A.C. 350; [1967] 3 W.L.R. 1491; [1967] 3 All E.R. 686; [1967] 2 Lloyd's Rep. 259

LORD REID: My Lords, by charterparty of October 15, 1960, the respondents chartered the appellant's vessel, *Heron II*, to proceed to Constanza, there to load a cargo of 3,000 tons of sugar; and to carry it to Basrah, or, in the charterers' option, to Jeddah. The vessel left Constanza on November 1. The option was not exercised and the vessel arrived at Basrah on December 2. The umpire has found that "a reasonably accurate prediction of the length of the voyage was 20 days." But the vessel had in breach of contract made deviations which caused a delay of nine days.

It was the intention of the respondent charterers to sell the sugar "promptly after the arrival at Basrah and after the inspection by merchants." The appellant shipowner did not know this, but he was aware of the fact that there was a market for sugar at Basrah. The sugar was in fact sold at Basrah in lots between December 12 and 22 but shortly before that time the market price had fallen partly by reason of the arrival of another cargo of sugar. It was found by the umpire that if there had not been this delay of nine days the sugar would have fetched £32 10s. per ton. The actual price realised was only £31 2s. 9d. per ton. The charterers claim that they are entitled to recover the difference as damage for breach of contract. This shipowner admits that he is liable to pay interest for nine days on the value of the sugar and certain minor expenses but denies that fall in market value can be taken into account in assessing damages in this case.

McNair J., following the decision in *The Parana*[1] (1877) 2 P.D. 118, decided this question in favour of the appellant. He said:

"In those circumstances it seems to me almost impossible to say that the shipowner must have known that the delay in prosecuting the voyage would probably result, or be likely to result, in this kind of loss."

The Court of Appeal by a majority (Diplock and Salmon L.JJ., Sellers L.J. dissenting) reversed the decision of the trial judge. The majority held that *The Parana* laid down no general rule, and, applying the rule (or rules) in *Hadley v. Baxendale* as explained in *Victoria Laundry (Windsor) Ltd v. Newman Industries Ltd* (above, p. 578), they held that the loss due to fall in market price was not too remote to be recoverable as damages.

It may be well first to set out the knowledge and intention of the parties at the time of making the contract so far as relevant or argued to be relevant. The charterers intended to sell the sugar in the market at Basrah on arrival of the vessel. They could have changed their mind and exercised their option to have the sugar delivered at Jeddah, but they did not do so. There is no finding that they had in mind any particular date as the likely date of arrival at Basrah or that they had any knowledge or expectation that in late November or December there would be a rising or a falling market. The shipowner was given no information about these matters by the charterers. He did not know what the charterers intended to do with the sugar. But he knew there was a market in sugar at Basrah, and it appears to me that, if he had thought about the matter, he must have realised that at least it was not unlikely that the sugar would be sold in the market at market price on arrival. He must also be held to have known that in any ordinary market prices are apt to fluctuate from day to day: but he had no reason to suppose it more probable that during the relevant period such fluctuation would be downwards rather than upwards—it was an even chance that the fluctuation would be downwards.

So the question for decision is whether a plaintiff can recover as damages for breach of contract a loss of a kind which the defendant, when he made the contract, ought to have realised was not unlikely to result from a breach of contract causing delay in delivery. I use the words "not unlikely" as denoting a degree of probability considerably less than an even chance but nevertheless not very unusual and easily foreseeable.

For over a century everyone has agreed that remoteness of damage in contract must be determined by applying the rule (or rules) laid down by a court including Parke, Martin and Alderson BB. in *Hadley v. Baxendale*; but many different interpretations of that rule have been adopted by judges at different times. So I think that one ought first to see just what was decided in that case, because it would seem wrong to attribute to that rule a meaning which, if it had been adopted in that case, would have resulted in a contrary decision of that case.

---

[1] The facts of *The Parana* appear below, pp. 588–589.

In *Hadley v. Baxendale* the owners of a flour mill at Gloucester, which was driven by a steam engine, delivered to common carriers, Pickford & Co., a broken crank shaft to be sent to engineers in Greenwich. A delay of five days in delivery there was held to be in breach of contract, and the question at issue was the proper measure of damages. In fact the shaft was sent as a pattern for a new shaft and until it arrived the mill could not operate. So the owners claimed £300 as loss of profit for the five days by which resumption of work was delayed by this breach of contract; but the carriers did not know that delay would cause loss of this kind. Alderson B. delivering the judgment of the court said:

". . . we find that the only circumstances here communicated by the plaintiffs to the defendants at the time the contract was made were that the article to be carried was the broken shaft of a mill and that the plaintiffs were the millers of that mill. But how do these circumstances show reasonably that the profits of the mill must be stopped by an unreasonable delay in the delivery of the broken shaft by the carrier to the third person? Suppose the plaintiffs had another shaft in their possession put up or putting up at the time, and that they only wished to send back the broken shaft to the engineer who made it; it is clear that this would be quite consistent with the above circumstances, and yet the unreasonable delay in the delivery would have no effect upon the intermediate profits of the mill. Or, again, suppose that at the time of the delivery to the carrier the machinery of the mill had been in other respects defective, then, also, the same result would follow."

Then, having said that in fact the loss of profit was caused by the delay, he continued:

"But it is obvious that, in the great multitude of cases of millers sending off broken shafts to third persons by a carrier under ordinary circumstances, such consequences would not, in all probability, have occurred. . . ."

Alderson B. clearly did not and could not mean that it was not reasonably foreseeable that delay might stop the resumption of work in the mill. He merely said that in the great multitude—which I take to mean the great majority—of cases this would not happen. He was not distinguishing between results which were foreseeable and unforeseeable, but between results which were likely because they would happen in the great majority of cases, and results which were unlikely because they would only happen in a small minority of cases. He continued:

"It follows, therefore, that the loss of profits here cannot reasonably be considered such a consequence of the breach of contract as could have been fairly and reasonably contemplated by both the parties when they made this contract."

He clearly meant that a result which will happen in the great majority of cases should fairly and reasonably be regarded as having been in the contemplation of the parties, but that a result which, though foreseeable as a substantial possibility, would happen only in a small minority of cases should not be regarded as having been in their contemplation. He was referring to such a result when he continued:

"For such loss would neither have flowed naturally from the breach of this contract in the great multitude of such cases occurring under ordinary circumstances, nor were the special circumstances, which, perhaps, would have made it a reasonable and natural consequence of such breach of contract, communicated to or known by the defendants."

I have dealt with the latter part of the judgment before coming to the well-known rule, because the court were there applying the rule and the language which was used in the latter part appears to me to throw considerable light on the meaning which they must have attached to the rather vague expressions used in the rule itself. The rule is that the damages

". . . should be such as may fairly and reasonably be considered either arising naturally, that is, according to the usual course of things, from such breach of contract itself, or such as may reasonably be supposed to have been in the contemplation of both parties at the time they made the contract as the probable result of the breach of it."

I do not think that it was intended that there were to be two rules or that two different standards or tests were to be applied. The last two passages which I quoted from the end of the judgment applied to the facts before the court, which did not include any special circumstances communicated to the defendants; and the line of reasoning there is that, because in the great majority of cases loss of profit would not in all probability have occurred, it followed that this could not reasonably be considered as having been fairly and reasonably contemplated by both the parties, for it would not have flowed naturally from the breach in the great majority of cases.

I am satisfied that the court did not intend that every type of damage which was reasonably foreseeable by the parties when the contract was made should either be considered as arising naturally, that is, in the usual course of things, or be supposed to have been in the contemplation of the parties. Indeed the decision makes it clear that a type of damage which was plainly foreseeable as a real possibility but which would only occur in a small minority of cases cannot be regarded as arising in the usual course of things or be supposed to have been in the contemplation of the parties: the parties are not supposed to contemplate as grounds for the recovery of damage any type of loss or damage which, on the knowledge available to the defendant, would appear to him as only likely to occur in a small minority of cases.

In cases like *Hadley v. Baxendale* or the present case it is not enough that in fact the plaintiff's loss was directly caused by the defendant's breach of contract. It clearly was so caused in both. The crucial question is whether, on the information available to the defendant when the contract was made, he should, or the reasonable man in his position would, have realised that such loss was sufficiently likely to result from the breach of contract to make it proper to hold that the loss flowed naturally from the breach or that loss of that kind should have been within his contemplation.

The modern rule in tort is quite different and it imposes a much wider liability. The defendant will be liable for any type of damage which is reasonably foreseeable as liable to happen even in the most unusual case, unless the risk is so small that a reasonable man would in the whole circumstances feel justified in neglecting it; and there is good reason for the difference. In contract, if one party wishes to protect himself against a risk which to the other party would appear unusual, he can direct the other party's attention to it before the contract is made, and I need not stop to consider in what circumstances the other party will then be held to have

accepted responsibility in that event. In tort, however there is no opportunity for the injured party to protect himself in that way, and the
tortfeasor cannot reasonably complain if he has to pay for some very
unusual but nevertheless foreseeable damage which results from his
wrongdoing. I have no doubt that today a tortfeasor would be held liable
for a type of damage as unlikely as was the stoppage of Hadley's Mill for
lack of a crank shaft: to any one with the knowledge the carrier had that
may have seemed unlikely, but the chance of it happening would have been
seen to be far from negligible. But it does not at all follow that *Hadley v.
Baxendale* would today be differently decided.

[His Lordship then considered some of the authorities, in particular *Re
R. & H. Hall Ltd and W. H. Pim (Jnr.) and Co.'s Arbitration* (1928) 139 L.T.
50, and continued:]

It may be that there was nothing very new in this, but I think that *Hall's*
case must be taken to have established that damages are not to be regarded
as too remote merely because, on the knowledge available to the defendant
when the contract was made, the chance of the occurrence of the event
which caused the damage would have appeared to him to be rather less
than an even chance. I would agree with Lord Shaw that it is generally
sufficient that that event would have appeared to the defendant as not
unlikely to occur. It is hardly ever possible in this matter to assess
probabilities with any degree of mathematical accuracy. But I do not find
in that case, or in cases which preceded it, any warrant for regarding as
within the contemplation of the parties any event which would not have
appeared to the defendant, had he thought about it, to have a very
substantial degree of probability.

Then it has been said that the liability of defendants has been further
extended by *Victoria Laundry (Windsor) Ltd v. Newman Industries Ltd.* I do
not think so . . . A large part of the profits claimed would have resulted
from some specially lucrative contracts which the plaintiffs could have
completed if they had had the boiler: that was rightly disallowed because
the defendants had no knowledge of these contracts. Asquith L.J. said:

"It does not, however, follow that the plaintiffs are precluded from
recovering some general (and perhaps conjectural) sum for loss of business
in respect of dyeing contracts to be reasonably expected, any more than in
respect of laundering contracts to be reasonably expected."

It appears to me that this was well justified on the earlier authorities. It
was certainly not unlikely on the information which the defendants had
when making the contract that delay in delivering the boiler would result
in loss of business: indeed it would seem that that was more than an even
chance. And there was nothing new in holding that damages should be
estimated on a conjectural basis. This House had approved of that as early
as 1813 in *Hall v. Ross* (1813) 1 Dow. 201.

What is said to create a "landmark," however, is the statement of
principles by Asquith L.J. This does to some extent go beyond the older
authorities and in so far as it does so, I do not agree with it. In para. (2) it is
said that the plaintiff is entitled to recover "such part of the loss actually
resulting as was at the time of the contract reasonably foreseeable as liable
to result from the breach." To bring in reasonable forseeability appears to
me to be confusing measure of damages in contract with measure of
damages in tort. A great many extremely unlikely results are reasonably

foreseeable: it is true that Asquith L.J. may have meant foreseeable as a likely result, and if that is all he meant I would not object farther than to say that I think that the phrase is liable to be misunderstood. For the same reason I would take exception to the phrase "liable to result" in para.(5). Liable is a very vague word, but I think that one would usually say that when a person foresees a very improbable result he foresees that it is liable to happen.

I agree with the first half of para.(6). For the best part of a century it has not been required that the defendant could have foreseen that a breach of contract must necessarily result in the loss which has occurred; but I cannot agree with the second half of para.(6). It has never been held to be sufficient in contract that the loss was foreseeable as "a serious possibility" or "a real danger" or as being "on the cards." It is on the cards that one can win £100,000 or more for a stake of a few pence—several people have done that; and anyone who backs a hundred to one chance regards a win as a serious possibility—many people have won on such a chance. Moreover, *The Wagon Mound (No. 2); Overseas Tankship (U.K.) Ltd v. Miller Steamship Co. Pty. Ltd* [1967] 1 A.C. 617 could not have been decided as it was unless the extremely unlikely fire should have been foreseen by the ship's officer as a real danger. It appears to me that in the ordinary use of language there is a wide gulf between saying that some event is not unlikely or quite likely to happen and saying merely that it is a serious possibility, a real danger, or on the cards. Suppose one takes a well-shuffled pack of cards, it is quite likely or not unlikely that the top card will prove to be a diamond: the odds are only three to one against; but most people would not say that it is quite likely to be the nine of diamonds for the odds are then fifty-one to one against. On the other hand I think that most people would say that there is a serious possibility or a real danger of its being turned up first and, of course, it is on the cards. If the tests of "real danger" or "serious possibility" are in future to be authoritative, then the *Victoria Laundry* case would indeed be a landmark because it would mean that *Hadley v. Baxendale* would be differently decided today. I certainly could not understand any court deciding that, on the information available to the carrier in that case, the stoppage of the mill was neither a serious possibility nor a real danger. If those tests are to prevail in future, then let us cease to pay lip service to the rule in *Hadley v. Baxendale*. But in my judgment to adopt these tests would extend liability for breach of contract beyond what is reasonable or desirable. From the limited knowledge which I have of commercial affairs I would not expect such an extension to be welcomed by the business community, and from the legal point of view I can find little or nothing to recommend it.

[His Lordship then examined the case of *Monarch Steamship Co., Ltd v. A/B Karlshamns Oliefabriker* [1949] A.C. 196.]

It appears to me that, without relying in any way on the *Victoria Laundry* case, and taking the principle that had already been established, the loss of profit claimed in this case was not too remote to be recoverable as damages. So it remains to consider whether the decision in *The Parana* established a rule which, though now anomalous, should nevertheless still be followed. In that case owing to the defective state of the ship's engines a voyage which ought to have taken sixty-five to seventy days took 127 days, and as a result a cargo of hemp fetched a much smaller price than it would have done if there had been no breach of contract. The Court of Appeal held, however, that the plaintiffs could not recover this loss as damages. The vital part of their judgment was as follows:

"In order that damages may be recovered, we must come to two conclusions—first that it was reasonably certain that the goods would not be sold until they did arrive; and secondly, that it was reasonably certain that they would be sold immediately after they arrived, and that that was known to the carrier at the time when the bills of lading were signed."

If that was the right test then the decision was right, and I think that that test was in line with a number of cases decided before or about that time (1877); but, as I have already said, so strict a test has long been obsolete; and, if one substitutes for "reasonably certain" the words "not unlikely" or some similar words denoting a much smaller degree of probability, then the whole argument in the judgment collapses.

For the reasons which I have given I would dismiss this appeal.

LORDS MORRIS, HODSON, PEARCE and UPJOHN also made speeches dismissing the appeal.

LORD MORRIS thought the "illuminating judgment" of the Court of Appeal in the *Victoria Laundry* case a most valuable analysis of the rule in *Hadley v. Baxendale* which it neither added to nor modified. LORD HODSON thought the phrase, "liable to result," used by the Court of Appeal in *Victoria Laundry*, perhaps a colourless expression but one on which he could not improve. LORD PEARCE thought there was nothing startling or novel about the *Victoria Laundry* case; ". . . it represented (in felicitous language) the approximate view of *Hadley v. Baxendale* taken by many judges in trying ordinary cases of breach of contract." LORD UPJOHN thought that the *Victoria Laundry* case did not alter the law.

All of their Lordships, however, deprecated the use of the phrase, "on the cards," as not having a sufficiently clear meaning (Lord Morris) and as capable of denoting a most improbable and unlikely event (Lord Upjohn).

Problems

1. Baxendale negligently drops Hadley's mill shaft while performing a contract to carry it to Greenwich. In conseqence, the operation of Hadley's mill has to be suspended for a month. Baxendale was unaware that Hadley did not have a spare shaft. Advise Hadley whether he should sue in contract or in tort.

2. If the defendants in the *Victoria Laundry* case were guilty of a tort (for example the ownership in the boiler had passed to the plaintiffs before it was negligently dropped) might the plaintiffs have recovered the loss on the "particularly lucrative dyeing contracts"? (See *Street on Damages*, Chapter 11.)

3. Should *Hadley v. Baxendale* be decided the same way today in the light of the interpretation now put upon that case?

Sale of Goods Act 1979

Damages for non-acceptance: section 50

(2) The measure of damages is the estimated loss directly and naturally resulting, in the ordinary course of events, from the buyer's breach of contract.

(3) Where there is an available market for the goods in question the measure of damages is prima facie to be ascertained by the difference between the contract price and the market or current price at the time or

times when the goods ought to have been accepted or (if no time was fixed for acceptance) at the time of the refusal to accept.

Damages for non-delivery: section 51

(2) The measure of damages is the estimated loss directly and naturally resulting, in the ordinary course of events, from the seller's breach of contract.

(3) Where there is an available market for the goods in question the measure of damages is prima facie to be ascertained by the difference between the contract price and the market or current price of the goods at the time or times when they ought to have been delivered or (if no time was fixed) then at the time of the refusal to deliver.

Note

In *W.L. Thompson v. Robinson (Gunmakers) Ltd* [1955] Ch. 177 the defendants refused to accept delivery of a "Vanguard" car which they had contracted to buy from the plaintiffs. The plaintiffs returned the car to the suppliers who took it back free from any claim for damages. The plaintiffs claimed as damages their loss of profit. The defendants said that the plaintiffs had suffered no loss of profit and that the damages should be nominal. It was admitted that there was no shortage of Vanguard cars to meet all immediate demands in the locality. It was held by Upjohn J. that the plaintiffs' loss was the loss of their bargain and they were entitled to recover the loss of profit. Section 50(3) did not apply because there was no available market.

In *Charter v. Sullivan* [1957] 2 Q.B. 117 the facts were similar except that the car was a Hillman and the plaintiff could sell all the Hillman cars that he could get. The Court of Appeal held that the plaintiff was entitled only to nominal damages, for he had shown no "loss directly and naturally resulting from the defendant's breach of contract." *Cf. Re Vic Mill* [1913] 1 Ch. 465; *Interoffice Telephones Ltd v. Robert Freeman Co. Ltd* [1958] 1 Q.B. 190.

In *Lazenby Garages Ltd v. Wright* [1976] 1 W.L.R. 459 the defendant repudiated a contract to buy a secondhand BMW car for £1,670. The sellers who had paid £1,325 for the car claimed £345 as loss of profit. They resold it for £1,770. The trial judge held that there was a 50:50 chance that the sellers would have sold another car and awarded £172.50. The Court of Appeal held that *Thompson v. Robinson* was inapplicable to the sale of a secondhand car. There was no "available market" for secondhand cars. Each car is unique. It was not proved that the buyer must have contemplated that the seller would sell one car less. The sellers had suffered no loss.

Would it have been different if the second buyer had been about to buy another car from the sellers when the BMW became available because of the defendant's breach of contract?

Problem

Alfred, a painter of portraits, takes a month to paint a portrait and charges 1,000 guineas. He is fully booked up for the next two years. Bertrand, who has contracted to sit for his portrait in two months' time, repudiates the contract. Advise Alfred.

H. PARSONS (LIVESTOCK) LTD v. UTTLEY INGHAM & CO. LTD

[1978] Q.B. 791; [1977] 3 W.L.R. 990; [1978] 1 All E.R. 525;
[1977] 2 Lloyd's Rep. 522

The plaintiffs, pig farmers, bought from the defendants, manufacturers of bulk food storage hoppers, a hopper which the defendants agreed to erect at the plaintiffs' farm. The hopper was described as "fitted with ventilated top." The defendants sealed the ventilator for the purpose of carriage and, after erecting it, forgot to unseal it. As the ventilator was 28 feet above ground, the plaintiffs could not detect that it was closed. Because of the lack of ventilation the pignuts stored in the hopper became mouldy. As a result of eating mouldy nuts many of the plaintiffs' pigs suffered a rare type of intestinal infection, E coli, of which 254 of them died.

The plaintiffs brought an action for breach of contract of the sale of the hopper, claiming the value of the pigs, £10,000, and lost sales and turnover amounting to a further £10,000–£20,000. The defendants argued that the plaintiffs were entitled only to the extra cost of bagged food (used while the mouldy nuts were taken away for examination), £18.02. Swanwick J. found that the parties could not reasonably be supposed to have contemplated that there was a serious possibility that the illness which in fact occurred would result from the breach of contract but he held that the death and sickness of the pigs were the direct result of a breach of section 14(1) of the Sale of Goods Act 1893 (see now section 14(3) of the Sale of Goods Act 1979, above, p. 401) and that the damages claimed were recoverable under s.53(2) of that Act.

LORD DENNING M.R., having discussed *The Heron II* and observed that in the law of tort there was emerging a distinction between economic loss and physical damage:

It seems to me that in the law of *contract*, too, a similar distinction is emerging. It is between loss of profit consequent on a breach of contract and physical damage consequent on it.

Loss of profit cases

I would suggest as a solution that in the former class of case, loss of profit cases, the defaulting party is only liable for the consequences if they are such as, at the time of the contract, he ought reasonably to have contemplated as a *serious* possibility or real danger. You must assume that, at the time of the contract, he had the very kind of breach in mind, such a breach as afterwards happened, as for instance, delay in transit, and then you must ask: ought he reasonably to have contemplated that there was a serious possibility that such a breach would involve the plaintiff in loss of profit? If Yes, the contractor is liable for the loss unless he has taken care to exempt himself from it by a condition in the contract as, of course, he is able to do if it was the sort of thing which he could reasonably contemplate. The law on this class of case is now covered by the three leading cases of *Hadley v. Baxendale* (above, pp. 579, 585), *Victoria Laundry (Windsor) Ltd v. Newman Industries Ltd* (above, p. 578) and *The Heron II*, (above, p. 583). These were all "loss of profit" cases, and the test of "reasonable contemplation" and "serious possibility" should, I suggest, be kept to that type of loss or, at any rate, to economic loss.

Physical damage cases

In the second class of case, the physical injury or expense case, the defaulting party is liable for any loss or expense which he ought reasonably to have foreseen at the time of the breach as a possible consequence, even if it was only a *slight* possibility. You must assume that he was aware of his breach, and then you must ask: ought he reasonably to have foreseen, at the time of the breach, that something of this kind might happen in consequence of it? This is the test which has been applied in cases of tort, ever since *The Wagon Mound* cases [1961] A.C. 388 and [1967] 1 A.C. 617. But there is a long line of cases which support a like test in cases of contract. One class of case which is particularly apposite here concerns latent defects in goods. In modern words: "product liability." In many of these cases the manufacturer is liable in contract to the immediate party for a breach of his duty to use reasonable care, and is liable in tort to the ultimate consumer for the same want of reasonable care. The ultimate consumer can either sue the retailer in contract and pass the liability up the chain to the manufacturer, or he can sue the manufacturer in tort and thus by-pass the chain. The liability of the manufacturer ought to be the same in either case. In nearly all these cases the defects were outside the range of anything that was in fact contemplated, or could reasonably have been contemplated by the manufacturer or by anyone down the chain to the retailers. Yet the manufacturer and others in the chain have been held liable for the damage done to the ultimate user, as for instance the death of the young pheasants in *Henry Kendall & Sons (a firm) v. William Lillico & Sons Ltd* [1969] 2 A.C. 31 and of the mink in *Ashington Piggeries Ltd v. Christopher Hill Ltd* [1972] A.C. 441. Likewise the manufacturers and retailers were held liable for the dermatitis caused to the wearer in the woollen underwear case of *Grant v. Australian Knitting Mills Ltd* [1936] A.C. 85, even though they had not the faintest suspicion of any trouble. So were the manufacturers down the chain to the subcontractors for the disintegrating roofing-tiles in *Young and Marten Ltd v. McManus Childs Ltd* [1969] 1 A.C. 454.

Another familiar class of case is where the occupier of premises is under the common duty of care, both in pursuance of a contract with a visitor or under the Occupiers Liability Act 1957. If he fails in that duty and a visitor is injured, the test of remoteness must be the same no matter whether the injured person enters by virtue of a contract or as a visitor by permission without a contract. No matter whether in contract or tort, the damages must be the same. Likewise when a contractor is doing work on premises for a tenant, and either the tenant or a visitor is injured, the test of remoteness is the same no matter whether the person injured is a tenant under the contract or a visitor without a contract; see *A.C. Billings & Sons Ltd v. Riden* [1958] A.C. 620.

Yet another class of case is where a hospital authority renders medical services in contract to a paying patient and gratuitously to another patient without any contract. The paying patient can sue in contract for negligence. The poor patient can sue in tort; see *Cassidy v. Ministry of Health* [1951] 3 K.B. at 359, 360. The test of remoteness should be the same whether the hospital authorities are sued in contract or in tort; see *Esso Petroleum Co. Ltd v. Mardon* (above, p. 367).

Instances could be multiplied of injuries to persons or damage to property where the defendant is liable for his negligence to one man in contract and to another in tort. Each suffers like damage. The test of remoteness is, and should be, the same in both.

Coming to the present case, we were told that in some cases the makers of these hoppers supply them direct to the pig farmer under contract with him, but in other cases they supply them through an intermediate dealer who buys from the manufacturer and resells to the pig farmer on the self-same terms, in which the manufacturer delivers, direct to the pig farmer. In the one case the pig farmer can sue the manufacturer in contract. In the other in tort. The test of remoteness should be the same. It should be the test in tort.

Conclusion

The present case falls within the class of case where the breach of contract causes physical damage. The test of remoteness in such cases is similar to that in tort. The contractor is liable for all such loss or expense as could reasonably have been foreseen, at the time of the breach, as a possible consequence of it. Applied to this case, it means that the makers of the hopper are liable for the death of the pigs. They ought reasonably to have foreseen that, if the mouldy pig nuts were fed to the pigs, there was a possibility that they might become ill. Not a serious possibility. Nor a real danger. But still a slight possibility. On that basis the makers were liable for the illness suffered by the pigs. They suffered from diarrhoea at the beginning. This "triggered off" the deadly E coli. That was a far worse illness than could then be foreseen. But that does not lessen this liability. The type or kind of damage was foreseeable even though the extent of it was not; see *Hughes v. Lord Advocate* [1963] A.C. 837. The makers are liable for the loss of the pigs that died and of the expenses of the vet, and such like. But not for the loss of profits on future sales or future opportunities of gain; see *Simon v. Pawson & Leafs Ltd* (1932) 38 Com.Cas. 151.

So I reach the same result as Swanwick J., but by a different route. I would dismiss the appeal.

ORR L.J. said that he would dismiss the appeal for the reasons to be given by Scarman L.J.

SCARMAN L.J.: My conclusion in the present case is the same as that of Lord Denning M.R. but I reach it by a different route. I would dismiss the appeal. I agree with him in thinking it absurd that the test for remoteness of damage should, in principle, differ according to the legal classification of the cause of action, though one must recognise that parties to a contract have the right to agree on a measure of damages which may be greater or less than the law would offer in the absence of agreement. I also agree with him in thinking that, notwithstanding the interpretation put on some dicta in *The Heron II*, the law is not so absurd as to differentiate between contract and tort save in situations where the agreement, or the factual relationship, of the parties with each other requires it in the interests of justice. I differ from him only to this extent: the cases do not, in my judgment, support a distinction in law between loss of profit and physical damage. Neither do I think it necessary to develop the law judicially by drawing such a distinction. Of course (and this is a reason for refusing to draw the distinction in law) the type of consequence, loss of profit or market or physical injury, will always be an important matter of fact in determining whether in all the circumstances the loss or injury was of a type which the parties could reasonably be supposed to have in contemplation. [His Lordship quoted Swanwick J.'s conclusion:]

> "On this interpretation the inevitable conclusion from the findings I have already made would be that this hopper was not reasonably fit for that purpose and that this caused the nuts to become toxic and that the illness of the pigs was a direct and natural consequence of such breach and toxicity, and that the plaintiffs do not have to prove that the toxicity or its results were foreseeable to either party. To put it another way, once the question of foreseeability of the breach is eliminated, as it is by the absolute warranty, the consequences of the breach flow naturally from it."

Counsel for the defendant criticises strongly this part of the judgment. He says it is based on a misunderstanding of *Hadley v. Baxendale*; and he referred us to the well-known passage in Lord Reid's speech in *The Heron II*, where he said that it is not enough that in fact the plaintiff's loss was directly caused by the defendant's breach of contract. Lord Reid said:

> "The crucial question is whether, on the information available to the defendant when the contract was made, he should, or the reasonable man in his position would, have realised that such loss was sufficiently likely to result from the breach of contract to make it proper to hold that the loss flowed naturally from the breach or that loss of that kind should have been within his contemplation."

Notwithstanding his choice of language, I think the judge was making the approach which, according to Lord Reid, is the correct one. He was saying, in effect, that the parties to this contract must have appreciated that, if, as happened in the event, the hopper, unventilated, proved not to be suitable for the storage of pig nuts to be fed to the plaintiffs' pigs, it was not unlikely, there was a serious possibility, that the pigs would become ill. The judge put it in this way:

> "The *natural* result of feeding toxic food to animals is damage to their health and maybe death, which is what occurred, albeit from a hitherto unknown disease and to particularly susceptible animals. There was therefore no need to invoke the question of *reasonable* contemplation in order to make the defendants liable." (My emphasis.)

The judge in this critical passage of his judgment is contrasting a natural result, that is one which people placed as these parties were would consider as a serious possibility, with a special, specific result, that is E coli disease, which, as he later found, the parties could not at the time of contract reasonably have contemplated as a consequence. He distinguishes between "presumed contemplation" based on a special knowledge from ordinary understanding based on general knowledge and concludes that the case falls within the latter category. He does so because he has held that the assumption, or hypothesis, to be made is that the parties had in mind at the time of contract not a breach of warranty limited to the delivery of mouldy nuts but a warranty as to the fitness of the hopper for its purpose. The assumption is of the parties asking themselves not what is likely to happen if she nuts are mouldy but what is likely to happen to the pigs if the hopper is unfit for storing nuts suitable to be fed to them. While, on his finding, nobody at the time of contract could have expected E coli to ensue from eating mouldy nuts, he is clearly, and, as a matter of common sense, rightly, saying that people would contemplate, on the second assumption, the serious possibility of injury and even death among the pigs.

And so the question becomes; was he right to make the assumption he did? In my judgment, he was (see *Grant v. Australian Knitting Mills Ltd* [1936] A.C. 85, esp. at 98, 99, and particularly the well-known passage in the speech of Lord Wright).

I would agree with Mr McGregor in his work on Damages that—

> "in contract as in tort, it should suffice that, if physical injury or damage is within the contemplation of the parties, recovery is not to

be limited because the degree of physical injury or damage could not have been anticipated."

This is so, in my judgment, not because there is, or ought to be, a specific rule of law governing cases of physical injury but because it would be absurd to regulate damages in such cases on the necessity of supposing the parties had a prophetic foresight as to the exact nature of the injury that does in fact arise. It is enough if on the hypothesis predicated physical injury must have been a serious possibility. Though in loss of market or loss of profit cases the factual analysis will be very different from cases of physical injury, the same principles, in my judgment, apply. Given the situation of the parties at the time of contract, was the loss of profit, or market, a serious possibility, something that would have been in their minds had they contemplated breach?

It does not matter, in my judgment, if they thought that the chance of physical injury, loss of profit, loss of market, or other loss as the case may be, was slight or that the odds were against it provided they contemplated as a serious possibility the type of consequence, not necessarily the specific consequence, that ensued on breach. Making the assumption as to breach that the judge did, no more than common sense was needed for them to appreciate that food affected by bad storage conditions might well cause illness in the pigs fed on it.

Appeal dismissed. Leave to appeal to the House of Lords granted.

Questions
1. If there had been only a slight possibility of injury to the pigs, would the plaintiff have succeeded?
2. Did Scarman L.J. correctly interpret the findings of Swanwick J.? See 94 L.Q.R. 171.
3. Was the illness which occurred of the same type as an illness which might have been contemplated? See Hadjihambis, 41 M.L.R. 483.
4. Why does it help the plaintiffs to consider the consequences of the hopper being unfit instead of the consequences of the nuts being mouldy? The first consequence of the hopper being unfit was that the nuts were mouldy; so is there any difference? Or are we supposed to consider some other type of unfitness which the parties would have known was likely to cause serious injury—but was not present?
5. Should the rules relating to damages be the same in contract and tort? The same negligent act is commonly both a breach of contract and a tort. See *Midland Bank Trust Co. Ltd v. Hett, Stubbs and Kemp* [1978] 3 W.L.R. 167.

Note
In *Wroth v. Tyler*, below, p. 607, Megarry applied a principle similar to that stated by McGregor on Damages to a case of economic loss. In *Brown v. KMR Services Ltd* [1994] 4 All E.R. 385, 399, where a Lloyd's "name" sued his agent for breach of contract in negligently placing him with a high-risk syndicate, Gatehouse J., following *Parsons v. Uttley Ingham*, said: "It is most unlikely that any professional member of Lloyd's foresaw the magnitude of the financial disasters that struck in the middle-to-late 1980's. . . . But losses of the type that occurred were undoubtedly foreseeable and in fact foreseen even though their scale was not. That is enough for the plaintiff. . . . The plaintiff's losses were the natural and obvious result of his being a member of the 'disaster' syndicates."

CHAPLIN v. HICKS

Court of Appeal [1911] 2 K.B. 786; 80 L.J.K.B. 1292; 105 L.T. 285; 27 T.L.R. 458

The defendant by an advertisement in the Daily Express newspaper offered theatrical engagements for three years to twelve ladies, four at £5, four at £4 and four at £3 per week. Applicants were to submit photographs and a fee of one shilling. The readers of the newspaper in each of ten districts were to select the five whom they considered the most beautiful. The defendant would then select from the fifty chosen by the districts the twelve to fill the places offered. Six thousand photographs were submitted. The plaintiff topped the pole in her district but was not given a reasonable opportunity of presenting herself for final selection. At the trial before Pickford J. the jury awarded £100 damages. On appeal it was argued that the damages were too remote and unassessable.

FLETCHER MOULTON L.J., having held that the damages were not too remote: Then the learned counsel takes up a more hopeful position. He says that the damages are difficult to assess, because it is impossible to say that the plaintiff would have obtained any prize. This is the only point of importance left for our consideration. Is expulsion from a limited class of competitors an injury? To my mind there can be only one answer to that question; it is an injury and may be a very substantial one. Therefore the plaintiff starts with an unchallengeable case of injury, and the damages given in respect of it should be equivalent to the loss. But it is said that the damages cannot be arrived at because it is impossible to estimate the quantum of the reasonable probability of the plaintiff's being a prize-winner. I think that, where it is clear that there has been actual loss resulting from the breach of contract, which it is difficult to estimate in money, it is for the jury to do their best to estimate; it is not necessary that there should be an absolute measure of damages in each case. There are no doubt well-settled rules as to the measure of damages in certain cases, but such accepted rules are only applicable where the breach is one that frequently occurs. In such cases the Court weighs the pros and cons and gives advice, and I may almost say directions, to the jury as regards the measure of damages. This is especially the case in actions relating to the sale of goods of a class for which there is an active and ready market. But in most cases it may be said that there is no recognized measure of damages, and that the jury must give what they think to be an adequate solatium under all the circumstances of the case. Is there any such rule as that, where the result of a contract depends on the volition of an independent party, the law shuts its eyes to the wrong and says that there are no damages? Such a rule, if it existed, would work great wrong. Let us take the case of a man under a contract of service to serve as a second-class clerk for five years at a salary of £200 a year, which expressly provides that, at the end of that period, out of every five second-class clerks two first-class clerks will be chosen at a salary of £500 a year. If such a clause is embodied in the contract, it is clear that a person thinking of applying for the position would reckon that he would have the advantage of being one of five persons from whom the two first-class clerks must be chosen, and that that might be a very substantial portion of the consideration for his appointment. If, after he has taken the post and worked under the contract of service, the employers repudiate the obligation, is he to have no remedy? He has sustained a very real loss, and there can be no possible reason why the law should not leave it to the jury to estimate the value of that of which he has been deprived. Where by contract a man has a right to belong to a limited class of competitors, he is possessed of something of value, and it is the duty of the jury to estimate the pecuniary value of that advantage if it is taken from him. The present case is a typical one. From a body of six thousand, who sent in their photographs, a smaller body of fifty was formed, of which the plaintiff was one, and among that smaller body twelve prizes were allotted for distribution; by reason of the defendant's breach of contract she has lost all the advantage of being in the limited competition, and she is entitled to have her loss estimated. I cannot lay down any rule as to the measure of damages in such a case; this must be left to the good sense of the jury. They must of course give effect to the consideration that the plaintiff's chance is only one out of four and that they cannot tell whether she would have ultimately proved to be the winner. But having considered all this they may well think that it is of considerable pecuniary value to have got into so small a class, and they must assess the damages accordingly.

This consideration decides the case, but I wish to refer to the decision of Jelf J. in *Sapwell v. Bass* [1910] 2 K.B. 486. That decision was, in my opinion, right on the facts of the particular case. The plaintiff had acquired by contract a right to send a mare during the following year to a renowned stallion belonging to the defendant, and the defendant broke his contract. The right to send the mare was coupled with the payment of a fee of 300 guineas. Jelf J. held that for the breach of contract the plaintiff was only entitled to nominal damages. The ground of the decision was that there was no evidence to shew that the right was worth more to the plaintiff than the 300 guineas which he would have had to pay for the services of the stallion, and that there was therefore no evidence that the damages were more than nominal. If, however, the learned judge meant to hold that there were no damages for breach of an undertaking to serve the mare, there is, in my opinion, no justification for such a view. The contract gave the plaintiff a right of considerable value, one for which many people would give money; therefore to hold that the plaintiff was entitled to no damages for being deprived of such a right because the final result depended on a contingency or chance would have been a misdirection. This appeal must be dismissed.

VAUGHAN WILLIAMS and FARWELL L.JJ. delivered judgment dismissing the appeal.

Section 3. Supervening Events

BEOCO LTD v. ALFA LAVAL CO. LTD v. AND ANOTHER

Court of Appeal [1994] 4 All E.R. 464

Alfa (A) installed a heat exchanger in Beoco (B)'s factory. 20 months later on August 24, 1988 the exchanger was found to be cracked. B employed the second defendant (X) to repair the defect. The repair was only partially successful and the exchanger failed a pressure test. B nevertheless put it back into use without an inspection, which would have revealed that it was defective. Two months later it exploded causing damage to B's plant and loss of production.

Chadwick J. held that (i) A was liable for breach of warranty because the exchanger had defects which were latent until the cracks appeared; (ii) X was liable for breach of contract in failing to repair it properly; but (iii) the cause of the explosion was B's recklessness in failing to carry out the proper tests to ascertain that the repair had been successful. He gave judgment against A for damages, to be assessed, for the loss which B would have incurred in replacing or repairing the exchanger if the explosion had not occurred. The first ground of appeal concerned the pleadings in the case.

STUART-SMITH L.J.: The second ground of appeal raises an interesting point of law upon which there does not appear to be any authority directly in point. Can the plaintiff recover damages which he would have incurred by way of loss of profit on lost production during the period necessary to repair the defect in goods or materials supplied by the defendant and caused by his breach of contract, where because of some supervening event those repairs are not carried out or are subsumed in other more extensive repairs?

The supervening event in this case was the negligence of the plaintiff's engineers, who when they discovered the hitherto latent defect in the heat exchanger, put it back into service without making proper tests to see that the repair had been correctly carried out, in circumstances where they knew of the risk of explosion if it was not. But the supervening event might equally have been caused by the breach of contract or negligence of the second defendant, if it had been responsible for making all proper tests before the heat exchanger was put back into service; or it may have been some extraneous event, like a fire in the factory for which no one could be held to blame.

It is common ground in this case that the first defendant is liable for the cost of making good the defective casing of the heat exchanger. This is because what was damaged in the explosion was not a sound heat exchanger with 18 years' life in it, but a defective one with much less. The plaintiff's loss *caused by the explosion* was therefore much less than it would otherwise have been. And it could have recovered from its insurers, or the second defendant as the case may be, only the value of the defective heat exchanger.

Mr Knight submits that the same principle should apply to the loss of profit which could have resulted during the time taken to make good the defect. The cause of action for damages for breach of contract arises at the time of the breach, even though this may not be quantifiable until later. On 24 August 1988, therefore, the plaintiff had a claim against the defendant for breach of contract, the measure of which was the cost of repair and the as yet unquantified claim for lost profit. It is immaterial, he submits, that that loss was never in fact incurred or quantified because of the explosion.

Although there do not appear to be any cases in contract, there are a number of authorities in tort which bear upon the point.

[Having examined the authorities in the law of tort, STUART-SMITH L.J. held that the same principles applied in contract and that the question he posed in the first paragraph, above, should be answered in the negative.]

PETER GIBSON and BALCOMBE L.JJ. agreed.

Appeal allowed.

Section 4. Recovery of Wasted Expenditure

McRAE v. THE COMMONWEALTH DISPOSALS COMMISSION

High Court of Australia 84 C.L.R. 377; [1951] Argus L.R. 771

The facts are given above, p. 487. The plaintiffs recovered the expenditure which they had incurred in sending a salvage expedition to look for the tanker.

DIXON AND FULLAGAR JJ. Mr Tait (for the Commission) contended that . . . it could not be held that the alleged damage flowed from the alleged breach. Let it be supposed, he said in effect, that the plaintiffs acted reasonably in what they did, and let it be supposed that the Commission ought reasonably to have contemplated that they would so act. Still, he said, the plaintiffs are faced with precisely the same difficulty with which they are faced if the case is regarded as a simple and normal case of breach by non-delivery. Suppose there had been a tanker at the place indicated. *Non constat* that the expenditure incurred by the plaintiffs would not have been equally wasted. If the promise that there was a tanker *in situ* had been performed, she might still have been found worthless or not susceptible of profitable salvage operations or of any salvage operations at all. How, then, he asked, can the plaintiffs say that their expenditure was *wasted because* there was no tanker in existence?

The argument is far from being negligible. But it is really, we think, fallacious. If we regard the case as a simple and normal case of breach by non-delivery, the plaintiffs have no starting-point. The burden of proof is on them, and they cannot establish that they have suffered any damage unless they can show that a tanker delivered in performance of the contract would have had some value, and this they cannot show. But when the contract alleged is a contract that there was a tanker in a particular place, and the breach assigned is that there was no tanker there, and the damages claimed are measured by expenditure incurred on the faith of the promise that there was a tanker in that place, the plaintiffs are in a very different position. They have now a starting-point. They can say: (1) this expense was incurred; (2) it was incurred because you promised us that there was a tanker; (3) the fact that there was no tanker made it certain that this expense would be wasted. The plaintiffs have in this way a starting-point. They make a prima facie case. The fact that the expense was wasted flowed prima facie from the fact that there was no tanker; and the first fact is damage, and the second fact is breach of contract. The burden is now thrown on the Commission of establishing that, if there had been a tanker, the expense incurred would equally have been wasted. This, of course, the Commission cannot establish. The fact is that the impossibility of assessing damages on the basis of a comparison between what was promised and what was delivered arises not because what was promised was valueless but because it is impossible to value a non-existent thing. It is the breach of contract itself which makes it impossible even to undertake an assessment on that basis. It is not impossible, however, to undertake an assessment on another basis, and, in so far as the Commission's breach of contract itself reduces the possibility of an accurate assessment, it is not for the Commission to complain.

HAYES AND ANOTHER v. JAMES & CHARLES DODD (A FIRM)

Court of Appeal [1990] 2 All E.R. 815

In 1982 the plaintiffs were considering the purchase of new and larger premises for their motor business. Access for vehicles at the rear of the property which they had in view was critical to the success of the business. The owners of the land over which the access ran asserted that there was no right of way. The defendants who were the plaintiffs' solicitors informed them that the right of way was secure and in reliance on that assurance the plaintiffs purchased the property. There was no right of way and within days of completion the access was blocked with disastrous consequences to the plaintiffs' business. After 12 months they closed it down and attempted unsuccessfully to sell the property as a single unit. Eventually they sold a maisonette on the property in 1986 and the workshop a year later. The defendants appealed on the quantum of damages.

STAUGHTON L.J.: The first question in this appeal relates to the basis on which damages should be assessed. Like Hirst J. I start with the principle stated by Lord Blackburn in *Livingstone v. Rawyards Coal Co.* (1880) 5 App.Cas. 25 at 39:

"... you should as nearly as possible get at that sum of money which will put the party who has been injured, or who has suffered, in the same position as he would have been in if he had not sustained the wrong for which he is now getting his compensation or reparation."

One must therefore ascertain the actual situation of the plaintiffs and compare it with their situation if the breach of contract had not occurred.

What then was the breach of contract? It was not the breach of any warranty that there was a right of way: the defendant solicitors gave no such warranty. This is an important point: see *Perry v. Sidney Phillips & Son (a firm)* [1982] 3 All E.R. 705. The breach was of the solicitors' promise to use reasonable skill and care in advising their clients. If they had done that, they would have told the plaintiffs that there was no right of way; and it is clear that, on the receipt of such advice, the plaintiffs would have decided not to enter into the transaction at all. They would have bought no property, spent no money and borrowed none from the bank.

That at first sight is the situation which one should compare with the actual financial state of the plaintiffs. I will call this the "no-transaction method." There are, however, authorities which show that instead one takes for the first element in the comparison the situation which the plaintiff would have been in if the transaction had gone through in accordance with his legitimate expectations. This I call the "successful-transaction method." Thus, in *Perry*'s case, the plaintiff recovered from negligent surveyors the difference between the value of the house at the date when he bought it if it had not been defective and its actual value at that date. However, it appears to have been found, or assumed, in that case that the plaintiff would still have bought the house if he had been given correct advice as to its condition, albeit at a lower price. It was not a case where he would never have entered into the transaction at all. . . .

The difference between the two methods is unlikely to be of importance in a case which concerns some commodity that is readily saleable, such as peas or beans, and if there is no difficulty or delay in ascertaining that a breach has occurred. A plaintiff who has agreed to buy beans at the current market price and has received a quantity which is defective can sell them forthwith and realise their actual value. If he intended to perform a profitable sub-contract, he can buy other beans in the market for that purpose. In such a case it makes no difference whether damages are assessed on the no-transaction method, so that he recovers the price paid less the sum realised on disposition of the defective beans, or on the successful-transaction method, which gives him the difference between the value of sound beans and the value of defective beans.

However, this case is not concerned with a readily saleable commodity: it took the plaintiffs nearly five years from the date of their purchase to dispose of the maisonette, and another year expired before they were free from the obligations imposed by the lease of the workshop and yard. During all that period they were incurring expenses, such as rent and other items, together with interest on the money which they had borrowed from the bank. Furthermore, they did not receive, until the first year had almost expired, any acknowledgment by the defendants that there was in fact no right of way; that only happened on July 6, 1983, whereas they had completed their purchase on July 28, 1982, and the right of way had first been challenged two days later.

I am quite satisfied that Hirst J. was entitled to award damages in this case on the no-transaction basis, and that he was right to do so. Indeed it may well be that the plaintiffs were, as he held, entitled to elect between that method and the successful-transaction method; but I need not express any concluded view on that. So they should recover all the money which they spent, less anything which they subsequently recovered, provided always that they acted reasonably in mitigating their loss. But they were quite properly denied any sum for the profit which they would have made if they had operated their business successfully.

[Staughton L.J. considered the damages under various heads and came to "G. Mental distress."]

Hirst J. awarded £1,500 to each of the plaintiffs under this head. There can be no doubt, and it was accepted in this court, that each of them suffered vexation and anguish over the years to a serious extent, for which the sum awarded was but modest compensation. There is, however, an important question of principle involved.

For my part I would have wished for a rather more elaborate argument than we received on this point, before deciding it, since the law seems to be in some doubt. But I would be most reluctant to impose on the plaintiffs, on top of their other misfortunes, two or three days of scholarly argument whether and in what circumstances damages can be awarded for mental distress consequent on breach of contract in a business transaction, possibly at their expense, when the sum involved is only £3,000 or roughly 3 per cent. of their total claim. The difficulty is that almost any other case where a plaintiff claims to have suffered mental distress would present a similar problem, that the individual plaintiff ought not to be expected to bear the burden and perhaps also the cost of an elaborate argument. If, as I think, the law needs clarification, it is to be hoped that a case can be found where that will be provided by the House of Lords. Or it may be that the Law Commission can supply it.

Like the judge, I consider that the English courts should be wary of adopting what he called "the United States practice of huge awards." Damages awarded for negligence or want of skill, whether against professional men or anyone else, must provide fair compensation, but no more than that. And I would not view with enthusiasm the prospect that every shipowner in the Commercial Court, having successfully claimed for unpaid freight or demurrage, would be able to add a claim for mental distress suffered while he was waiting for his money.

In a sense, the wrong done to the plaintiffs in this action, for which they seek compensation under this head, lay in the defendants' failure to admit liability at an early stage. On July 6, 1983 the defendants acknowledged that there was no right of way, but denied negligence. Had they on that very day admitted liability and tendered a sum on account of damages, or offered interim reparation in some other form, the anxiety of the plaintiffs, and their financial problems, could have been very largely relieved. But liability was not admitted until January 1987. I believe that in one or more American states damages are awarded for wrongfully defending an action. But there is no such remedy in this country so far as I am aware. . . .

I am not convinced that it is enough to ask whether mental distress was reasonably foreseeable as a consequence, or even whether it should reasonably have been contemplated as not unlikely to result from a breach of contract. It seems to me that damages for mental distress in contract are, as a matter of policy, limited to certain classes of case. I would broadly follow the classification provided by Dillon L.J. in *Bliss v. South East Thames Regional Health Authority* [1987] I.C.R. 700 at 718:

"... where the contract which has been broken was itself a contract to provide peace of mind or freedom from distress ..."

It may be that the class is somewhat wider than that. But it should not, in my judgment, include any case where the object of the contract was not comfort or pleasure, or the relief of discomfort, but simply carrying on a commercial activity with a view to profit. So I would disallow the item of damages for anguish and vexation.

SIR GEORGE WALLER and PURCHAS L.J. delivered judgments to similar effect.

Note
See also *Watts v. Morrow* [1991] 4 All E.R. 937, C.A.

C. & P. HAULAGE (A FIRM) v. MIDDLETON

Court of Appeal [1983] 1 W.L.R. 1461; [1983] 3 All E.R. 94

The appellant was granted by the respondents a contractual licence to occupy premises for the purposes of his business on a renewable six-monthly basis. It was expressly provided that any fixtures he put in were not to be removed at the end of the licence. Ten weeks before the end of a six-month period, he was unlawfully ejected by the respondents. He was given temporary permission by the local authority to use his own home for the work which he continued to do until well after the six-month term would have expired. He claimed the cost of the improvements he had made to the premises. The judge awarded only nominal damages. He appealed.

ACKNER L.J.: The case which I have found of assistance—and I am grateful to counsel for their research—is a case in the British Columbia Supreme Court: *Bowlay Logging Ltd v. Domtar Ltd* [1978] 4 W.W.R. 105. Berger J, in a very careful and detailed judgment, goes through various English and American authorities and refers to the leading textbook writers, and I will only quote a small part of his judgment. At the bottom of p. 115 he refers to the work of Professor L. L. Fuller and William R. Perdue, Jr., in "The Reliance Interest in Contract Damages: 1" (1936), 46 Yale Law Jour. 52 and their statement, at p. 79: "We will not in a suit for reimbursement for losses incurred in reliance on a contract knowingly put the plaintiff in a better position than he would have occupied had the contract been fully performed." Berger J., at p. 116, then refers to *L. Albert & Son v. Armstrong Rubber Co.* (1949) 178 F.2d 182 in which Learned Hand C.J., speaking for the Circuit Court of Appeals, Second Circuit: "held that on a claim for compensation for expenses in part performance the defendant was entitled to deduct whatever he could prove the plaintiff would have lost if the contract had been fully performed." What Berger J. had to consider was this, p. 105: "The parties entered into a contract whereby the plaintiff would cut timber under the defendant's timber sale, and the defendant would be responsible for hauling the timber away from the site of the timber sale. The plaintiff claimed the defendant was in breach of the contract as the defendant had not supplied sufficient trucks to make the plaintiff's operation, which was losing money, viable, and claimed not for loss of profits but for compensation for expenditures. The defendant argued that the plaintiff's operation lost money not because of a lack of trucks but because of the plaintiff's inefficiency, and, further, that even if the defendant had breached the contract the plaintiff should not be awarded damages because its operation would have lost money in any case."

This submission was clearly accepted because the plaintiff was awarded only nominal damages, and Berger J. said, at p. 117: "The law of contract compensates a plaintiff for damages resulting from the defendant's breach; it does not compensate a plaintiff for damages resulting from his making a bad bargain. Where it can be seen that the plaintiff would have incurred a loss on the contract as a whole, the expenses he has incurred are losses flowing from entering into the contract, not losses flowing from the defendant's breach. In these circumstances, the true consequence of the defendant's breach is that the plaintiff is released from his obligation to complete the contract—or in other words, he is saved from incurring further losses. If the law of contract were to move from compensating for the consequences of breach to compensating for the consequences of entering into contracts, the law would run contrary to the normal expectations of the world of commerce. The burden or risk would be shifted from the plaintiff to the defendant. The defendant would become the insurer of the plaintiff's enterprise. Moreover, the amount of the damages would increase not in relation to the gravity or consequences of the breach but in relation to the inefficiency with which the plaintiff carried out the contract. The greater his expenses owing to inefficiency, the greater the damages. The fundamental principle upon which damages are measured under the law of contract is *restitutio in integrium*. The principle contended for here by the plaintiff would entail the award of damages not to compensate the plaintiff but to punish the defendant."

It is urged here that the garage itself was merely an element in the defendant's business; it was not a profit-making entity on its own. Nevertheless, if as a result of being kept out of these premises the defendant had found no other premises to go to for a period of time, his claim would clearly have been a claim for such loss of profit as he could establish his business suffered.

In my judgment, the approach of Berger J. is the correct one. It is not the function of the courts where there is a breach of contract knowingly, as this would be the case, to put a plaintiff in a better financial position than if the contract had been properly performed. In this case the defendant who is the plaintiff in the counterclaim, if he was right in his claim, would indeed be in a better position because, as I have already indicated, had the contract been lawfully determined as it could have been in the middle of December, there would have been no question of his recovering these expenses.

Fox L.J. agreed, pointing out that the case was different from *Anglia Television v. Reed* and *Lloyd v. Stanbury, infra*, in that, in the present case, it was equally likely that the expenditure would be wasted if there had been no breach. The reality was that the appellant had made a very unsatisfactory and dangerous bargain.

Appeal dismissed—judgment for the appellant for nominal damages of £10.

Notes

1. In *C.C.C. Films Ltd v. Impact Quadrant Films Ltd* [1984] 3 All E.R. 298 the plaintiffs paid the defendants $12,000 for a licence to exploit, distribute and exhibit three films. In breach of contract, the defendants failed to deliver the films. The plaintiffs were unable to produce any evidence of loss of profits and instead claimed to recover the $12,000 as wasted expenditure. Hutchinson J. held that the onus lay on the defendants to prove that, if they had not broken their contract, the plaintiffs would not have succeeded in recouping their expenditure. He followed Berger J. in the *Bowlay Logging* case, above, p. 603 and *Albert v. Armstrong Rubber*, above, p. 603, quoting from the judgment of Learned Hand C.J.:

> "In cases where the venture would have proved profitable to the promisee there is no reason why he should not recover his expenses. On the other hand, on those occasions in which the performance would not have covered the promisee's outlay, such a result imposes the risk of the promisee's contract upon the promisor. We cannot agree that the promisor's default in performance should under this guise make him an insurer of the promisee's venture; yet it does not follow that the breach should not throw upon him the duty of showing that the value of the performance would in fact have been less than the promisee's outlay. It is often very hard to learn what the value of the performance would have been; and it is a common expedient, and a just one, in such situations to put the peril of the answer upon that party who by his wrong has made the issue relevant to the rights of the other. On principle therefore the proper solution would seem to be that the promisee may recover his outlay in preparation for the performance, subject to the privilege of the promisor to reduce it by as much as he can show that the promisee would have lost, if the contract had been performed."

Cf. the position where the question is whether the promisee acted reasonably to mitigate the damage, below, p. 617.

2. Damages may be recovered for costs incurred *before* the contract was entered into if they are—

(i)   legal costs of approving and executing the contract; or

(ii) costs of performing an act required to be done by the contract, notwithstanding that the act is performed in anticipation of the contract: *Lloyd v. Stanbury* [1971] 1 W.L.R. 535; [1971] 2 All E.R. 267 (Brightman J.); or

(iii) "such as would reasonably be in the contemplation of the parties as likely to be wasted if the contract was broken": *Anglia Television v. Reed* [1972] 1 Q.B. 60; [1971] 3 All E.R. 690, C.A.

In *Lloyd v. Stanbury* [1971] W.L.R. 535 the defendant agreed to sell part of his land including a farmhouse to the plaintiff. The defendant intended to build a bungalow on the remaining land and the contract provided that the plaintiff should provide a caravan for use of the defendant until the bungalow was built. While the contract was in draft, the plaintiff moved a caravan to the land. Contracts were exchanged and the plaintiff went into occupation, but the defendant wrongly refused to complete. Held, that the plaintiff was entitled to damages under head (i), above, and under head (ii) for costs of removing the caravan.

The plaintiff did *not* recover damages for cost of installation of a power circuit and erection of a television aerial at the farmhouse while he was in occupation because it will not usually be regarded as being in the contemplation of the parties that a buyer will spend money on improving the property before it has been conveyed to him. (Contrast *Mason v. Burningham* [1949] 2 K.B. 545, C.A., where the buyer of a second-hand typewriter, who had to return it to the true owner because the seller had no title to it, was held entitled to recover not only the price of the typewriter but also the cost of having it overhauled. Having the typewriter overhauled was the "ordinary and natural thing" to do in the circumstances.)

In *Anglia Television v. Reed* [1972] 1 Q.B. 60 the plaintiffs incurred expense in preparation for filming a television play. Subsequently they entered into a contract with the defendant to play the leading role. The defendant repudiated the contract. The plaintiffs tried hard to find a substitute but failed. They abandoned the play. Held: they were entitled to recover the whole of the wasted expenditure—"[R] must have known perfectly well that much expenditure had already been incurred on director's fees and the like. He must have contemplated—or, at any rate, it is reasonably to be imputed to him—that if he broke his contract, all that expenditure would be wasted, whether or not it was incurred before or after the contract"—*per* Lord Denning.

Question

Is the loss of pre-contract expenditure *caused* by the breach of contract? Does not a party who incurs expenditure before a contract has been concluded do so at his own risk? See A.I. Ogus (1972) 35 M.L.R. 423.

JOHNSON AND ANOTHER v. AGNEW

House of Lords [1980] A.C. 367; [1979] 2 W.L.R. 487; [1979] 1 All E.R. 883; (1979) 38 P. & C.R. 424

The vendors agreed to sell a house and land which were subject to separate mortgages. The purchaser failed to complete on January 21, 1974, which had been fixed as the final date by a notice making time of the essence. The vendor obtained an order for specific performance on June 27 but it was not drawn up and entered until November 26. By then the mortgagees of the house had obtained an order for possession. On March 7, 1975 the mortgagees of the land also obtained an order for possession and they contracted to sell the land on April 3. The vendors who had taken no action to enforce the order for specific performance were not in a position to convey the land after April 3. The vendors sought a declaration that they entitled to treat the contract as repudiated, and damages.

The House of Lords held that, where it becomes impossible to enforce an order for specific performance, the plaintiff has a right to ask the court to discharge the order and terminate the contract. The contract is then not rescinded *ab initio* but remains in existence until terminated: *Heyman v. Darwins Ltd* [1942] A.C. 356, 359, above, pp. 463, 465–466. The court will grant such an order only when it is just to do so, as it was in the present case where the non-completion and ultimate impossibility of completion was the fault of the purchaser.

LORD WILBERFORCE: It is now necessary to deal with questions relating to the measure of damages. The Court of Appeal, while denying the vendors' right to damages at common law, granted damages under Lord Cairns's Act. Since on the view which I take, damages can be recovered at common law, two relevant questions now arise: (1) whether Lord Cairns's Act provides a different measure of damages from the common law? If so, the respondents would be in a position to claim the more favourable basis to them; and (2) if the measure of damages is the same, on what basis they should be calculated?

Since the decision of this House, by a majority, in *Leeds Industrial Co-operative Society Ltd v. Slack* [1924] A.C. 851, it is clear that the jurisdiction to award damages in accordance with section 2 of Lord Cairns's Act (accepted by the House as surviving the repeal of the Act) may arise in some cases in which damages could not be recovered at common law; examples of this would be damages in lieu of *a quia timet* injunction and damages for breach of a restrictive covenant to which the defendant was not a party. To this extent the Act created a power to award damages which did not exist before at common law. But apart from these, and similar cases where damages could not be claimed at all at common law, there is sound authority for the proposition that the Act does not provide for the assessment of damages on any new basis. The wording of section 2 that damages "may be assessed in such manner as the court shall direct" does not so suggest, but clearly refers only to procedure.

In *Ferguson v. Wilson* (1866) L.R. 2 Ch.App. 77, 88 Turner L.J., sitting in a court which included Cairns L.J. himself, expressed the clear opinion that the purpose of the Act was to enable a court of equity to grant those damages which another court might give; a similar opinion was strongly expressed by Kay J. in *Rock Portland Cement Co. v. Wilson* (1882) 48 L.T. 386, and Fry on Specific Performance (6th ed.) 602 is of the same opinion. In *Wroth v. Tyler* [1974] Ch. 36 however, Megarry J., relying on the words "in lieu of specific performance," reached the view that damages under the Act should be assessed as on the date when specific performance could have been ordered, in that case as at the date of the judgment of the court. This case was followed in *Grant v. Dawkins* [1973] 1 W.L.R. 1406. If this establishes a different basis from that applicable at common law, I could not agree with it, but in *Horsler v. Zorro* [1975] Ch. 302, 316, Megarry J. went so far as to indicate his view that there is no inflexible rule that common law damages must be assessed as at the date of the breach. Furthermore, in *Malhotra v. Choudhury* [1978] 3 W.L.R. 825 the Court of Appeal expressly decided that, in a case where damages are given in substitution for an order for specific performance, both equity and the common law would award damages on the same basis, in that case as on the date of judgment. On the balance of these authorities and also on principle, I find in the Act no warrant for the court awarding damages differently from common law damages, but the question is left open on what date such damages, however awarded, ought to be assessed.

The general principle for the assessment of damages is compensatory, that is that the innocent party is to be placed, so far as money can do so, in the same position as if the contract had been performed. Where the contract is one of sale, this principle normally leads to assessment of damages as at the date of the breach, a principle recognised and embodied section 51 of the Sale of Goods Act 1893. But this is not an absolute rule; if to follow it would give rise to injustice, the court has power to fix such other date as may be appropriate in the circumstances.

In cases where a breach of a contract for sale has occurred, and the innocent party reasonably continues to try to have the contract completed, it would to me appear more logical and just rather than tie him to the date of the original breach, to assess damages as at the date when (otherwise than by his default) the contract is lost. Support for this approach is to be found in the cases. In *Ogle v. Earl Vane* (1867) L.R. 2 Q.B. 275 the date was fixed by reference to the time when the innocent party, acting reasonably, went into the market; in *Hickman v. Haynes* (1875) L.R. 10 C.P. 598 at a reasonable time after the last request of the defendants (the buyers) to withhold delivery. In *Radford v. de Froberville* [1977] 1 W.L.R. 1262, where the defendant had covenanted to build a wall, damages were held measurable as at the date of the hearing rather than at the date of the defendant's breach, unless the plaintiff ought reasonably to have mitigated the breach at an earlier date.

In the present case if it is accepted, as I would accept, that the vendors acted reasonably in pursuing the remedy of specific performance, the date on which that remedy became aborted (not by the vendors' fault) should logically be fixed as the date on which damages should be assessed. Choice of this date would be in accordance both with common law principle, as indicated in the authorities I have mentioned, and with the wording of the Act "in substitution for . . . specific performance." The date which emerges from this is April 3, 1975, the first date on which mortgagees contracted to sell a portion of the property. I would vary the order of the Court of Appeal by substituting this date for that fixed by them, *viz.* November 26, 1974. The same date (April 3, 1975) should be used for the purpose of limiting the respondents' right to interest on damages. Subject to these modifications I would dismiss the appeal.

Note

In *Wroth v. Tyler* the defendant contracted to sell a bungalow for £6,050. He failed to complete on the date fixed. The value of the house on that day was £7,500. Megarry J. refused the plaintiff an order for specific performance on the ground that the defendant could give vacant possession only if he took legal proceedings against his wife which would not necessarily succeed. The plaintiff was however entitled to damages "in substition for such . . . specific performance" under the Chancery Amendment Act 1858 (Lord Cairns's Act). The value of the house at the date of judgment was £11,500. Megarry J. held that damages assessed at the date of breach in accordance with the "normal rule" would be £1,500 which would not be a true substitute for a decree to convey land which, at the time of decree, was worth £5,500 more than the contract price. Whatever the position at common law, the appropriate damages under Lord Cairns's Act were £5,500.

It was sufficient to satisfy the rules in *Hadley v. Baxendale* that a rise in the price of houses was in the contemplation of the parties when the contract was made. It was immaterial that they may not have contemplated a rise which nearly doubled the price. The "second rule" in *Hadley v. Baxendale* required contemplation of a head or type of damage, not its quantum. *Cf. Parsons v. Uttley Ingham*, above, p. 590.

Section 5. Irrecoverable Damage

ADDIS v. GRAMOPHONE COMPANY, LTD

[1909] A.C. 488; 78 L.J.K.B. 1122; 101 L.T. 466

The plaintiff was employed by the defendants at a salary of £15 per week and commission on the trade done. He could be dismissed by six months' notice. The defendants gave him six months' notice but, at the same time, appointed a successor and prevented the plaintiff from acting as manager. The jury awarded £340 in respect of lost commission and £600 in respect of wrongful dismissal. The House of Lords (Lord Loreburn L.C. and Lords James, Atkinson, Gorrell and Shaw) held that he was entitled only to the commission and salary which he had lost.

LORD ATKINSON: . . . The damages plaintiff sustained by this illegal dismissal were (1) the wages for the period of six months during which his formal notice would have been current; (2) the profits or commission which would, in all reasonable probability, have been earned by him during the six months had he continued in the employment; and possibly (3) damages in respect of the time which might reasonably elapse before he could obtain other employment. He has been awarded a sum possibly of some hundreds of pounds, not in respect of any of these heads of damage, but in respect of the harsh and humiliating way in which he was dismissed, including, presumably, the pain he experienced by reason, it is alleged, of the imputation upon him conveyed by the manner of his dismissal. This is the only circumstance which makes the case of general importance, and this is the only point I think it necessary to deal with. . . .

I have always understood that damages for breach of contract were in the nature of compensation, not punishment, and that the general rule of law applicable to such cases was that in effect stated by Cockburn C.J. in *Engel v. Fitch* (1868) L.R. 3 Q.B. 314, 330, in these words: "By the law of England as a general rule a vendor who from whatever cause fails to perform his contract is bound, as was said by Lord Wensleydale in the case referred to, to place the purchaser, so far as money will do it, in the position he would have been in if the contract had been performed. If a man sells a cargo of goods not yet come to hand, but which he believes to have been consigned to him from abroad, and the goods fail to arrive, it will be no answer to the intended purchaser to say that a third party who had engaged to consign the goods to the seller has deceived or disappointed him. The purchaser will be entitled to the difference between the contract price and the market price."

In *Sikes v. Wild* (1861) 1 B. & S. 587, at p. 594, Lord Blackburn says: "I do not see how the existence of misconduct can alter the rule of law by which damages for breach of contract are to be assessed. It may render the contract voidable on the ground of fraud or give a cause of action for deceit, but surely it cannot alter the effect of the contract itself."

. . . in actions of tort motive, if it may be taken into account to aggregate [*sic*] damages, as it undoubtedly may be, it may also be taken into account to mitigate them, as may also the conduct of the plaintiff himself who seeks redress. Is this rule to be applied to actions of breach of contract? There are few breaches of contract more common than those which arise where men omit or refuse to repay what they have borrowed, or to pay for what they have bought. Is the creditor or vendor who sues for one of such breaches to have the sum he recovers lessened if he should be shown to be harsh, grasping, or pitiless, or even insulting, in enforcing his demand, or lessened because the debtor has struggled to pay, has failed because of misfortune, and has been suave, gracious, and apologetic in his refusal? On the other hand, is that sum to be increased if it should be shown that the debtor could have paid readily without any embarrassment, but refused with expression of contempt and contumely, from a malicious desire to injure his creditor?

Few parties to contracts have more often to complain of ingratitude and baseness than sureties. Are they, because of this, to be entitled to recover from the principal, often a trusted friend, who has deceived and betrayed them, more than they paid on that principal's behalf? If circumstances of aggravation are rightly to be taken into account in actions of contract at all, why should they not be taken into account in the case of the surety, and the rules and principles applicable to cases of tort applied to the full extent?

In many other cases of breach of contract there may be circumstances of malice, fraud, defamation, or violence, which would sustain an action of tort as an alternative remedy to an action for breach of contract. If one should select the former mode of redress, he may, no doubt, recover exemplary damages, or what is sometimes styled vindictive damages; but if he should choose to seek redress in the form of an action for breach of contract, he lets in all the consequences of that form of action: *Thorpe v. Thorpe* (1832) 3 B. & Ad. 580. One of these consequences is, I think, this: that he is to be paid adequate compensation in money for the loss of that which he would have received had his contract been kept, and no more.

I can conceive nothing more objectionable and embarrassing in litigation than trying in effect an action of libel or slander as a matter of aggravation in an action for illegal dismissal, the defendant being permitted, as he must in justice be permitted, to traverse the defamatory sense, rely on privilege, or raise every point which he could raise in an independent action brought for the alleged libel or slander itself.

Questions

1. Does the case decided that only damages for pecuniary loss are recoverable in contract? Could the plaintiff in *Hobbs v. L. & S.W. Ry.* (1875) L.R. 10 Q.B. 411 recover damages for inconvenience today? (*Cf.* Street, *Damages*, pp. 237–240.)

2. Does the case decide that damages for loss of reputation can never be recovered in contract? (*Cf.* Street, *loc. cit.*).

JARVIS v. SWAN'S TOURS

Court of Appeal [1973] 1 Q.B. 233; [1972] 3 W.L.R. 954; [1973] 1 All E.R. 71

Defendants, travel agents, advertised in glowing terms a houseparty in Switzerland, promising "a great time." The plaintiff booked the holiday with the defendants and paid £63.45. He went during his annual fortnight's holiday. There were only 13 guests there during the first week and none during the second. The hotel proprietor could not speak English. The holiday failed to comply with the description in the brochure in numerous respects. The county court judge awarded £31.72 damages. The plaintiff appealed.

LORD DENNING M.R.: What is the legal position? I think that the statements in the brochure were representations or warranties. The breaches of them give Mr Jarvis a right to damages. It is not necessary to decide whether they were representations or warranties; because, since the Misrepresentation Act, 1967, there is a remedy in damages for misrepresentation as well as for breach of warranty.

The one question in the case is: what is the amount of damages? The judge seems to have taken the difference in value between what he paid for and what he got. He said that he intended to give "the difference between the two values and no other damages" under any other head. He thought that Mr Jarvis had got half of what he paid for. So the judge gave him half the amount which he had paid, namely, £31.72. Mr Jarvis appeals to this court. He says that the damages ought to have been much more. . . .

What is the right way of assessing damages? It has often been said that on a breach of contract damages cannot be given for mental distress. Thus in *Hamlin v. Great Northern Railway Co.* ((1856) 1 H. & N. 408 at 411) Pollock C.B. said that damages cannot be given "for the disappointment of mind occasioned by the breach of contract." And in *Hobbs v. London & South Western Railway Co.* ((1875) L.R. 10 Q.B. 111 at 122) Mellor J. said that— ". . . for the mere inconvenience, such as annoyance and loss of temper, or vexation, or for being disappointed in a particular thing which you have set your mind upon, without real physical inconvenience resulting, you cannot recover damages." The courts in those days only allowed the plaintiff to recover damages if he suffered physical inconvenience, such as, having to walk five miles home, as in *Hobbs'* case; or to live in an overcrowded house: see *Bailey v. Bullock* ([1950] 2 All E.R. 1167).

I think that those limitations are out of date. In a proper case damages for mental distress can be recovered in contract, just as damages for shock can be recovered in tort. One such case is a contract for a holiday, or any other contract to provide entertainment and enjoyment. If the contracting party breaks his contract, damages can be given for the disappointment, the distress, the upset and frustration caused by the breach. I know that it is difficult to assess in terms of money, but it is no more difficult than the assessment which the courts have to make every day in personal injury cases for loss of amenities. Take the present case. Mr Jarvis has only a fortnight's holiday in the year. He books it far ahead, and looks forward to it all that time. He ought to be compensated for the loss of it.

A good illustration was given by Edmund Davies L.J. in the course of the argument. He put the case of a man who has taken a ticket for Glyndbourne. It is the only night on which he can get there. He hires a car to take him. The car does not turn up. His damages are not limited to the mere cost of the ticket. He is entitled to general damages for the disappointment he has suffered and the loss of the entertainment which he should have had. Here, Mr Jarvis's fortnight's winter holiday has been a grave disappointment. It is true that he was conveyed to Switzerland and back and had meals and bed in the hotel. But that is not what he went for. He went to enjoy himself with all the facilities which the defendants said he would have. He is entitled to damages for the lack of those facilities, and for his loss of enjoyment. . . . I think the damages in this case should be the sum of £125.

EDMUND-DAVIES L.J., having stated that he did not accept the observations of Mellor J. in *Hobbs'* case: Be that as it may, Mellor J. was dealing with a contract of carriage and the undertaking of the railway company was entirely different from that of the defendants in the present case. These travel agents made clear by their lavishly illustrated brochure with its ecstatic text that what they were contracting to provide was not merely air travel, hotel accommodation and meals of a certain standard. To quote the assurance which they gave regarding the Morlialp House Party Centre, "No doubt you will be in for a great time, when you book this houseparty holiday." The result was that they did *not* limit themselves to the obligation to ensure that an air passage was booked, that hotel accommodation was reserved, that food was provided and that these items would measure up the standards they themselves set up. They went further than that. They assured and undertook to provide a holiday of a certain quality, with "Gemutlichkeit" (that is to say, geniality, comfort and cosiness) as its overall characteristics, and "a great time," the enjoyable outcome which would surely result to all but the most determined misanthrope. . . .

STEPHENSON L.J. delivered judgment allowing the appeal.

Appeal allowed; damages of £125 awarded.

Questions
  1. I was Lord Denning right in saying that the damages would be the same under section 2(1) of the Misrepresentation Act? See above, p. 354.
  2. Should damages for vexation and disappointment be recoverable for breach of contract generally? Or is a contract to provide pleasure different. *cf. Addis v. Gramophone Co., Ltd* above, p. 608); *Jackson v. Horizon Holidays* (above, p. 306) and *Hayes v. Dodd*, above, p. 600 at 601.

RUXLEY ELECTRONICS AND CONSTRUCTION LTD v. FORSYTH

House of Lords [1995] 3 W.L.R 118; [1995] 3 All E.R. 268

F contracted with R to build a swimming pool, with a maximum depth of 7ft. 6in. in F's garden. After the pool was complete, F discovered that the maximum depth was only 6ft. 9in. F refused to pay the outstanding balance of the contract price. R sued for it and F counterclaimed for breach of contract. The judge found that the pool as constructed was perfectly safe for diving and that the shortfall in depth had not decreased its value; the only practicable way to achieve a pool of the specified depth would be to demolish the existing pool and build a new one at a cost of £21,560; he was not satisfied that F intended to build a pool at that cost; to do so would be wholly disproportionate to the disadvantage of having the shallower pool; and he awarded damages for loss of amenity of £2,500. The Court of Appeal, (Staughton and Mann L.JJ., Dillon L.J. dissenting), allowed F's appeal: the only way F could achieve his contractual object was to rebuild the pool which was accordingly a reasonable venture. R appealed to the House of Lords.

F's counsel, Jacob, Q.C., argued that the award to his client of £2,500 was contrary to principle and unsupported by authority; that the judge had only two alternatives: to award the cost of rebuilding or the loss of value—*i.e.*, nothing; and since F had undoubtedly suffered a loss the judge was bound to award the cost of rebuilding.

LORD KEITH, LORD BRIDGE and LORD JAUNCEY delivered opinions allowing the appeal.

LORD MUSTILL: There are not two alternative measures of damage, at opposite poles, but only one: namely the loss truly suffered by the promisee. In some cases the loss cannot be fairly measured except by reference to the full cost of repairing the deficiency in performance. In others, and in particular those where the contract is designed to fulfil a purely commercial purpose, the loss will very often consist only of the monetary detriment brought about by the breach of contract. But these remedies are not exhaustive, for the law must cater for those occasions where the value of the promise to the promisee exceeds the financial enhancement of his position which full performance will secure. This excess, often referred to in the literature as the "consumer surplus" (see *e.g.* the valuable discussion by Harris, Ogus and Phillips, "Contract Remedies and the Consumer Surplus" (1979) 95 LQR 581) is usually incapable of precise valuation in terms of money, exactly because it represents a personal, subjective and non-monetary gain. Nevertheless, where it exists the law should recognise it and compensate the promisee if the misperformance takes it away. The lurid bathroom tiles, or the grotesque folly instanced in argument by my noble and learned friend Lord Keith of Kinkel, may be so discordant with general taste that in purely economic terms the builder may be said to do the employer a favour by failing to instal them. But this is too narrow and materialistic a view of the transaction. Neither the contractor nor the court has the right to substitute for the employer's individual expectation of performance a criterion derived from what ordinary people would regard as sensible. As my Lords have shown, the test of reasonableness plays a central part in determining the basis of recovery, and will indeed be decisive in a case such as the present when the cost of reinstatement would be wholly disproportionate to the non-monetary loss suffered by the employer. But it would be equally unreasonable to deny all recovery for such a loss. The amount may be small, and since it cannot be quantified directly there may be room for difference of opinion about what it should be. But in several fields the judges are well accustomed to putting figures to intangibles, and I see no reason why the imprecision of the exercise should be a barrier, if that is what fairness demands.

. . . The judgment of the trial judge acknowledges that the employer has suffered a true loss and expresses it in terms of money. Since there is no longer any issue about the amount of the award, as distinct from principle, I would simply restore his judgment by allowing the appeal.

LORD LLOYD, having cited the judgment of Cardozo J. in *Jacob & Youngs Inc. v. Kent* (1921) 230 N.Y. 239: Cardozo J.'s judgment is important because it establishes two principles which I believe to be correct and which are directly relevant to the present case: first, the cost of reinstatement is not the appropriate measure of damages if the expenditure would be out of all proportion to the good to be obtained, and secondly, the appropriate measure of damages in such a case is the difference in value, even though it would result in a nominal award.

The first of these principles is contrary to Staughton L.J.'s view that the plaintiff is entitled to reinstatement, however expensive, if there is no cheaper way of providing what the contract requires. The second principle is contrary to the whole thrust of Mr Jacob's argument that the judge had no alternative but to award the cost of reinstatement, once it became apparent that the difference in value produced a nil result. . . .

[Having cited various authorities, LORD LLOYD continued]. It seems to me that in the light of these authorities . . . Mr McGuire Q.C. [counsel for R] was right when he submitted, and Dillon L.J. was right when he held, that mitigation is not the only area in which the concept of reasonableness has an impact on the law of damages.

If the court takes the view that it would be unreasonable for the plaintiff to insist on reinstatement, as where, for example, the expense of the work involved would be out of all proportion to the benefit to be obtained, then the plaintiff will be confined to the difference in value. If the judge had assessed the difference in value in the present case at, say, £5,000, I have little doubt that the Court of Appeal would have taken that figure rather than £21,560. The difficulty arises because the judge has, in the light of the expert evidence, assessed the difference in value as nil. But that cannot make reasonable what he has found to be unreasonable. . . .

How then does Mr Jacob seek to support the majority judgment? It can only be, I think, by attacking the judge's finding of fact that the cost of rebuilding the pool would have been out of all proportion to the benefit to be obtained. Mr Jacob argues that this was not an ordinary commercial contract but a contract for a personal preference. This was the line taken by Mann L.J. in the Court of Appeal. . . .

I am far from saying that personal preferences are irrelevant when choosing the appropriate measure of damages ("predilections" was the word used by Ackner L.J. in *GW Atkins Ltd v. Scott* (1980) 7 Const LJ 215 at 221, adopting the language of Oliver J. in *Radford v. De Froberville* [1977] 1 WLR 1262). But such cases should not be elevated into a separate category with special rules. If, to take an example mentioned in the course of argument, a landowner wishes to build a folly in his grounds, it is no answer to a claim for defective workmanship that many people might regard the presence of a well-built folly as reducing the value of the estate. The eccentric landowner is entitled to his whim, provided the cost of reinstatement is not unreasonable. But the difficulty of that line of argument in the present case is that the judge, as is clear from his judgment, took Mr Forsyth's personal preferences and predilections into account. Nevertheless, he found as a fact that the cost of reinstatement was unreasonable in the circumstances. The Court of Appeal ought not to have disturbed that finding. . . .

In the present case the judge found as a fact that Mr Forsyth's stated intention of rebuilding the pool would not persist for long after the litigation had been concluded. In these circumstances it would be "mere pretence" to say that the cost of rebuilding the pool is the loss which he has in fact suffered. This is the critical distinction between the present case and the example given by Staughton L.J. of a man who has had his watch stolen. In the latter case, the plaintiff is entitled to recover the value of the watch because that is the true measure of his loss. He can do what he wants with the damages. But if, as the judge found, Mr Forsyth had no intention of rebuilding the pool, he has lost nothing except the difference in value, if any.

Addis v Gramophone Co Ltd (above, p. 608) established the general rule that in claims for breach of contract, the plaintiff cannot recover damages for his injured feelings. But the rule, like most rules, is subject to exceptions. One of the well-established exceptions is when the object of the contract is to afford pleasure, as, for example, where the plaintiff has booked a holiday with a tour operator. If the tour operator is in breach of contract by failing to provide what the contract called for, the plaintiff may recover damages for his disappointment (see *Jarvis v. Swans Tours Ltd* (above, p. 609) and *Jackson v. Horizon Holidays Ltd* (above, p. 306).

This was, as I understand it, the principle which Judge Diamond applied in the present case. He took the view that the contract was one "for the provision of a pleasurable amenity". In the event, Mr Forsyth's pleasure was not so great as it would have been if the swimming pool had been 7ft 6in deep. This was a view which the judge was entitled to take. If it involves a further inroad on the rule in *Addis v. Gramophone Co Ltd* then so be it. But I prefer to regard it as a logical application or adaptation of the existing exception to a new situation. I should, however, add this note of warning. Mr Forsyth was, I think, lucky to have obtained so large an award for his disappointed expectations. But as there was no criticism from any quarter as to the quantum of the award as distinct from the underlying principle, it would not be right for your Lordships to interfere with the judge's figure.

Appeal allowed.

Questions
1. What if, on discovering the shortfall, F had immediately contracted with another builder to rebuild the pool with a depth of 7ft. 6in?
2. F argued at the trial that this was an "entire contract". The judge held that it was not because the price was payable by a deposit and thereafter by instalments. The point was not argued on appeal. Suppose the price had been payable in a lump sum on completion. Could F have refused to pay anything? If he had paid before discovering the shortfall, could he have recovered his money? *Cf.* pp. 434–444, especially the *Liddesdale* case, p. 440, above. *If it would have been different, should* the fact that the price is payable in a lump sum be so significant?
3. The contract as originally entered into was for a pool 6ft. 6in. deep. Subsequently at F's request R agreed to make it 7ft. 6in. *without extra charge.* The point was apparently never taken; but could R have contended that the original contract stood, there being no consideration for the promise to provide the extra depth?
4. In *White Arrow Express Ltd v. Lamey's Distribution Ltd*, The Times, July 21, 1995, C.A., Bingham M.R., having stated that, unless a plaintiff could show that his financial position had been injured, he could recover only nominal damages, gave the following examples.

> "If A hired and paid in advance for a four-door saloon at £200 a day and received delivery of a two-door saloon available for £100 a day, he suffered loss.
>
> If B ordered and paid in advance for a five-course meal costing £50 and was served with a three-course meal costing £30, he suffered loss.
>
> If C agreed and paid in advance to be taught the violin by a world famous celebrity at £500 an hour and was in the event taught by a musical nonentity whose charging rate was £25 an hour, he suffered loss."

Bingham M.R. said that it would defy common sense to suggest that A, B and C had suffered no loss and were not financially disadvantaged by the breach. They would be entitled to damages amounting to the difference between the price paid, or, if it was lower, the market value of what was contracted for, and the market value of what was obtained. What is the difference between these cases and *Ruxley*?

Section 6. Contributory Negligence

BARCLAYS BANK plc. v. FAIRCLOUGH BUILDING LTD

Court of Appeal [1995] 1 All E.R. 289

The defendant (F) contracted with the plaintiff (B) to carry out work on B's premises, including the cleaning of roofs. In breach of an express term that F would execute the work in an expeditious, efficient and workmanlike manner, F's sub-contractor caused the premises to become contaminated with asbestos, requiring remedial work costing £4 million. B owed a duty to its employees to prevent the premises becoming contaminated. B's safety officer and architect failed to take steps to prevent the contamination. F relied on the Contributory Negligence Act 1945. The judge found that F was the party primarily at fault; the fault of B was a failure to prevent F from committing that fault; and he reduced B's damages by 40 per cent. B appealed.

BELDAM L.J: Section 4 of the 1945 Act defines "fault" as follows:

> "'fault' means negligence, breach of statutory duty or other act or omission which gives rise to a liability in tort or would, apart from this Act, give rise to the defence of contributory negligence."

It is generally agreed that the first part of the definition relates to the defendant's fault and the second part to the plaintiff's but debate has focused on the words "or other act or omission which gives rise to a liability in tort" in the first part and "other act or omission which . . . would, apart from this Act, give rise to the defence of contributory negligence" in the second part. It has been argued that, merely because the plaintiff frames his cause of action as a breach of contract, if the acts or omissions on which he relies could equally well give rise to a liability in tort, the defendant is entitled to rely on the defence of contributory negligence. Examples frequently cited are claims for damages against an employer or by a passenger against a railway or bus company where the plaintiff may frame his action either in tort or in contract and the duty relied on in either case is a duty to take reasonable care for the plaintiff's safety. Contributory negligence has been a defence in such actions for many years. So it is argued that in all cases in which the contractual duty broken by a defendant is the same as and is co-extensive with a similar duty in tort, the defendant may now rely upon the defence. An opposing view based upon the second part of the definition is that if the plaintiff framed his action for breach of contract, contributory negligence at common law was never regarded as a defence to his claim and so cannot be relied on under the 1945 Act.

Under the first part of the definition, if the plaintiff claims damages for breach of a contractual term which does not correspond with a duty in tort to take reasonable care, the defendant's acts or omissions would not give rise to a liability in tort and accordingly no question of contributory negligence could arise.

These arguments have led courts to classify contractual duties under three headings.

(1) Where a party's liability arises from breach of a contractual provision which does not depend on a failure to take reasonable care.

(2) Where the liability arises from an express contractual obligation to take care which does not correspond to any duty which would exist independently of the contract.

(3) Where the liability for breach of contract is the same as, and co-extensive with, a liability in tort independently of the existence of a contract.

This analysis was adopted by Hobhouse J. in *Forsikringsaktieselskapet Vesta v. Butcher* [1986] 2 All E.R. 488 at 508 and by the Court of Appeal ([1988] 2 All E.R. 43, [1989] A.C. 852). The judgments in the Court of Appeal in that case assert that in category (3) cases the Court of Appeal is bound by the decision in *Sayers v. Harlow UDC* [1958] 2 All E.R. 342, [1958] 1 W.L.R. 623 to admit the availability of the defence.

Since I do not regard the case before the court as being in that category, I am content to accept that decision . . .

In my judgment therefore in the present state of the law contributory negligence is not a defence to a claim for damages founded on breach of a strict contractual obligation. I do not believe the wording of the 1945 Act can reasonably sustain an argument to the contrary. Even if it did, in the present case the nature of the contract and the obligation undertaken by the skilled contractor did not impose on the bank any duty in its own interest to prevent the contractor from committing the breaches of contract. To hold otherwise would, I consider, be equivalent to implying into the contract an obligation on the part of the bank inconsistent with the express terms agreed by the parties. The contract clearly laid down the extent of the obligations of the bank as architect and of the contractor. It was the contractor who was to provide appropriate supervision on site, not the architect.

SIMON BROWN L.J.: The very imposition of a strict liability upon the defendant is to my mind inconsistent with an apportionment of the loss. And not least because of the absurdities that the contrary approach carries in its wake. Assume a defendant, clearly liable under a strict contractual duty. Is his position to be improved by demonstrating that besides breaching that duty he was in addition negligent? Take this very case. Is this contract really to be construed so that the respondents are advantaged by an assertion of their own liability in nuisance or trespass as well as in contract? Are we to have trials at which the defendant calls an expert to implicate him in tortious liability, whilst the plaintiffs' expert seeks paradoxically to exonerate him? The answer to all these questions is surely No. Whatever arguments exist for apportionment in other categories of case—and these are persuasively deployed in the 1993 Law Commission Report, *Contributory Negligence as a Defence in Contract* (Law Com. No. 219)—to my mind there are none in the present type of case and I for my part would construe the contract accordingly.

NOURSE L.S. agreed with Beldam L.J.

Appeal allowed.

Section 7. Mitigation of Damage

PAYZU LTD v. SAUNDERS

King's Bench Division: Court of Appeal [1919] 2 K.B. 581; 89 L.J.K.B. 17; 121 L.T. 563; 35 T.L.R. 657

A contract for the sale of goods by the defendant to the plaintiffs provided that delivery should be as required over a period of nine months and that payment be made within one month of delivery. The plaintiffs failed to make prompt payment for the first instalment. The defendant, in breach of contract (*cf.* section 10 of the Sale of Goods Act 1979, above, p. 399), refused to deliver any more instalments under the contract, but offered to deliver the goods at the contract price if the plaintiffs would agree to pay cash with each other. The plaintiffs refused to do so and brought an action for breach of contract. They claimed the difference between the contract price and the market price which had risen.

McCARDIE J.: . . . Now a serious question of law arises on the question of damages. I find as a fact that the defendant was ready and willing to supply the goods to the plaintiffs at the times and prices specified in the contract, provided the plaintiffs paid cash on delivery. Mr Matthews argued with characteristic vigour and ability that the plaintiffs were entitled to ignore that offer on the ground that a person who has repudiated a contract cannot place the other party to the contract under an obligation to diminish his loss by accepting a new offer made by the party in default.

The question is one of juristic importance. What is the rule of law as to the duty to mitigate damages? I will first refer to the judgment of Cockburn C.J. in *Frost v. Knight* (above, p. 551), where he said: "In assessing the damages for breach of performance, a jury will of course take into account whatever the plaintiff has done, or has had the means of doing, and, as a prudent man, ought in reason to have done, whereby his loss has been, or would have been, diminished." This rule is strikingly exemplified in *Brace v. Calder* [1895] 2 Q.B. 253. There the plaintiff claimed damages for wrongful dismissal. He had been employed as manager of a business carried on by four persons in partnership. In the course of his employment two of the partners retired, and the business continued to be carried on by the two remaining partners. The plaintiff resented his technical dismissal which resulted from the dissolution of the partnership, and declined to serve the two remaining partners; and he brought an action against the original firm claiming damages for wrongful dismissal. There was a difference of opinion in the Court of Appeal as to whether the plaintiff had been wrongly dismissed, but the members of the court were unanimously of opinion that the plaintiff as a prudent, reasonable man should have accepted the offer of the two remaining partners to retain him in their service, and that he was therefore entitled to nominal damages only. I think that the substance of the rule which I have indicated was also laid down by the House of Lords in *British Westinghouse Electric and Manufacturing Co. v. Underground Electric Railways Co. of London* [1912] A.C. 673, 689, when Lord Haldane said: "The fundamental basis is thus compensation for pecuniary loss naturally flowing from the breach; but this first principle is qualified by a second, which imposes on a plaintiff the duty of taking all reasonable steps to mitigate the loss consequent on the breach, and debars him from claiming any part of the damage which is due to his neglect to take such steps."

The question, therefore, is what a prudent person ought reasonably to do in order to mitigate his loss arising from a breach of contract. I feel no inclination to allow in a mercantile dispute an unhappy indulgence in far-fetched resentment or an undue sensitiveness to slights or unfortunately worded letters. Business often gives rise to certain asperities. But I agree that the plaintiffs in deciding whether to accept the defendant's offer were fully entitled to consider the terms in which the offer was made, its bona fides or otherwise, its relation to their own business methods and financial position, and all the circumstances of the case; and it must be remembered that an acceptance of the offer would not preclude an action for damages for the actual loss sustained. Many illustrations might be given of the extraordinary results which would follow if the plaintiffs were entitled to reject the defendant's offer and incur a substantial measure of loss which would have been avoided by their acceptance of the offer. The plaintiffs were in fact in a position to pay cash for the goods, but instead of accepting the defendant's offer, which was made perfectly bona fide, the plaintiffs permitted themselves to sustain a large measure of loss which as prudent and reasonable people they ought to have avoided. . . .

Judgment for plaintiffs.

The plaintiffs appealed on the question of damages.

BANKS L.J. delivered judgment dismissing the appeal.

SCRUTTON L.J. I am of the same opinion. Whether it be more correct to say that a plaintiff must minimise his damages, or to say that he can recover no more than he would have suffered if he had acted reasonably, because any further damages do not reasonably follow from the defendant's breach, the result is the same. . . . Mr Matthews has contended that in considering what steps should be taken to mitigate the damage all contractual relations with the party in default must be excluded. That is contrary to my experience. In certain cases of personal service it may be unreasonable to expect a plaintiff to consider an offer from the other party who has grossly injured him; but in commercial contracts it is generally reasonable to accept an offer from the party in default. However, it is always a question of fact. About the law there is no difficulty.

EVE J. delivered judgment dismissing the appeal.

Appeal dismissed.

Note

   Where the question is whether the claimant acted reasonably to mitigate the damage, it appears that the onus of proof is on the defendant to satisfy the court that he did not do so, notwithstanding a ruling to the contrary in *Selvanayagam v. University of West Indies* [1983] 1 W.L.R. 585, P.C. See Kemp (1983) 99 L.Q.R. 497. *Cf. C.C.C. Films Ltd v. Impact Quadrant Films Ltd,* above, p. 604.

THE SOLHOLT

Court of Appeal [1983] Lloyds' Rep. 605; [1983] Com. L.R. 114

Respondents agreed to sell the Solholt to appellants for $5 million, delivery not later than August 31, 1979, failing which buyers were to have right of cancellation.

Sellers were unable to deliver until after August 31 and buyers exercised right of cancellation on September 3, 1979 although market value of vessel was now $5.5 million. Buyers then offered to buy for $4.75 million but the offer was not accepted and buyers claimed damages. Staughton J. held that the prima facie measure of damages was the difference between the market value and the contract price, that is, $.5 million, but dismissed buyers' claim on the ground that they had failed to mitigate their loss by negotiating a further contract for purchase at the original contract price. The buyers appealed.

SIR JOHN DONALDSON M.R.: A plaintiff is under no duty to mitigate his loss, despite the habitual use by the lawyers of the phrase "duty to mitigate." He is completely free to act as he judges to be in his best interests. On the other hand, a defendant is not liable for all loss suffered by the plaintiff in consequence of his so acting. A defendant is only liable for such part of the plaintiff's loss as is properly to be regarded as caused by the defendants' breach of duty. As Viscount Haldane, L.C., put it in *British Westinghouse Electric and Manufacturing Co. Ltd v. Underground Electric Railways Co. of London Ltd*, [1912] A.C. 673 at p. 689:

"The fundamental basis is thus compensation for pecuniary loss naturally flowing from the breach; but this first principle is qualified by a second, which imposes on a plaintiff the duty of taking all reasonable steps to mitigate the loss consequent on the breach, and debars him from claiming any part of the damage which is due to his neglect to take such steps."

As we have already accepted as being trite law, the buyers had an unfettered right in the circumstances of this case to affirm the original contract of sale or to cancel it. No question of mitigation arose at that stage. They decided to cancel and in consequence they suffered a loss of U.S. $500,000. As a matter of causation, this loss, unless avoidable by some reasonable *further* action, was directly attributable to the sellers' breach of contract. The learned Judge held that it was in fact avoidable by *further* action and that such action would have been reasonable. It is nothing to the point that this *further* action *might*, in effect, have reversed the cancellation of the old contract. We say *might* because the new contract which the learned Judge held that the buyers could and should have made might not have been on the same terms as to price although, on the evidence, he held that it would have been.

Whether a loss is avoidable by reasonable action on the part of the plaintiff is a question of fact not law. This was decided in *Payzu Ltd v. Saunders* (above, p. 617). . . .

[His Lordship discussed *Payzu v. Saunders* and *Strutt v. Whitnell* [1975] 2 All E.R. 510 and continued]: We therefore turn to the evidence. The buyers are in the business of shipowning and there is no suggestion that there was any material change in their circumstances or intentions between the time when they agreed to buy the vessel and the time when they cancelled. They wanted a vessel then, and there is no suggestion that they did not want one at the beginning of September, 1979. If they could have found a different but identical ship, clearly it would have been reasonable that they should have bought it and the price of that purchase would have established the measure of their loss. However there is no suggestion that any such vessel was available. This left them with the alternative of buying *Solholt*. The buyers might have been able to allege and prove that she had some fatal defect which made her unsuitable for their purposes, but no such suggestion was made. On the contrary, the buyers recognised that she remained suitable for their purposes and offered to buy her for U.S. $4.75 million. Had that offer been accepted, their loss of U.S. $500,000 would have been extinguished and they would have made an incidental profit of U.S. $250,000. But it was rejected and they did nothing further. . . . Dicta in the judgments in [*Strutt* v. *Whitnell*] are undoubtedly helpful to the buyers. If the House of Lords ever had to consider the decision, it might well hold that the judgments totally confuse the proposition that in deciding whether to rescind or affirm a contract the innocent party need have no regard to considerations of mitigation of loss with the proposition that, having made such an election, he will be able to recover such loss as was unavoidable following that election and that in some, perhaps exceptional, circumstances it may be reasonable at a stage after the decision to rescind or affirm the contract to adopt a course of action which will nullify the effect of that decision. However, no such comment is open to us in this Court. In this Court all that can be said is that the decision has to be reconciled with that in *Payzu Ltd v. Saunders* and that this can only be done by treating it as a decision turning on reasonableness and its own special facts. We so regard it. [His Lordship found nothing in the evidence to contradict Staughton J.'s conclusion that the buyers had failed to take reasonable steps to mitigate their loss by offering $5 million dollars, an offer which would have been accepted.]

Appeal dismissed.

Note

The victim of a breach of contract is under no "duty" to mitigate in the sense that he commits no legal wrong by not doing so. No one has any right that he should do so. On the victim's right to affirm or avoid the contract, compare *White and Carter (Councils) Ltd v. McGregor*, above, p. 559, and Note 1, p. 621.

What would have been the position in *The Solholt* if the buyers, at the time of the breach, had decided they no longer wanted a ship?

PILKINGTON v. WOOD

[1953] Ch. 770; [1953] 2 All E.R. 810; 97 S.J. 572

The plaintiff, because of the negligence of the defendant, his solicitor, bought a house with a defective title. Harman J. held that the plaintiff was entitled to recover the difference between the market value of the property at the time of breach with a good title and its value at that time with a defective title. He rejected the defendant's contention that the plaintiff should have mitigated his damage by suing the vendor on the covenant for title implied under section 76 of and Schedule 2 to the Law of Property Act 1925, provided that (1) an adequate indemnity against costs were offered; (2) the vendor appeared to be solvent; and (3) there was a good prima facie right of action. Harman J. said it might be conceded that the indemnity would be adequate and that the vendor was a man of substance, but it was clear that he would resist the claim. He went on:

I do not propose to attempt to decide whether an action against Colonel Wilks [the vendor] would lie or be fruitful. I can see it would be one attended with no little difficulty. I am of opinion that the so-called duty to mitigate does not go so far as to oblige the injured party, even under an indemnity, to embark on a complicated and difficult piece of litigation against a third party. The damage to the plaintiff was done once and for all directly the voidable conveyance to him was executed. This was the direct result of the negligent advice tendered by his solicitor, the defendant, that a good title had been shown; and, in my judgment, it is no part of the plaintiff's duty to embark on the proposed litigation in order to protect his solicitor from the consequences of his own carelessness.

Note 1

It will be recalled that where there has been an anticipatory breach of contract, the injured party has an option either to acceopt the breach as putting an end to the contract and to sue at once for damages or to treat the breach as entirely inoperative and to await the time for performance: *Frost v Knight* (above, p. 551). If the injured party adopts the former course, then he is under "a duty" to mitigate the damage. So where a person who has agreed to buy goods at a future date declares that he will not accept them when that date arrives, the seller who accepts the breach may be under a duty to sell the goods at the first opportunity, if that is the course which a reasonable business man who desired to mitigate the loss would take: *Roth & Co. v. Tayson, Townsend & Co.* (1895) 1 Com.Cas. 240. The loss must not be increased by any act which the plaintiff ought not to have done or by the omission to do any act which the plaintiff ought to have done. The standard required of the injured party is not a strict one; his duty is only not to act unreasonably: the wrongdoer has no right to expect from the man whom he has wronged the utmost amount diligence, the utmost amount of skill and the most accurate conclusion in a matter of judgment: *Dunkirk Colliery Co. v. Lever* (1880) 41 L.T. 633, *per* James L.J.

The position may be different, however, where the injured party declines to accept the breach as putting an end to the contract. Here there may be no duty to mitigate: *White & Carter (Councils) Ltd v. McGregor* (above, p. 559). In *Tredegar Iron and Coal Co. Ltd v. Hawthorn Bros. & Co.* (1902) 18 T.L.R. 716 the defendants had contracted to buy coal at 16s. a ton from the plaintiffs, to be delivered in February. On February 16, the defendants repudiated the contract; but they procured and communicated to the plaintiffs an offer from a third party to buy the coal at 16s. 3d. a ton. The plaintiffs refused this offer and insisted on the performance of the contract. The defendants having failed to take delivery, the plaintiffs ultimately sold the coal for only 15s. a ton. The Court of Appeal, reversing Phillimore J., held that the plaintiffs were entitled to damages amounting to 1s. a ton. The repudiation, not having been accepted as such, was a nullity and there was no breach of contract until the expiration of the time for the delivery of the goods.

Problem

Needle, a tailor, enters into a contract with Nash to make him a suit for £200. Before Needle has started to make the suit, Nash informs him that he no longer wants it and will not take delivery of it. Needle nevertheless makes the suit which, since Nash is of an unusual build, cannot be disposed of elsewhere. The cost to Needle of the labour and materials for making the suit was £100. Advise him.

Note 2

Where property is damaged by breach of contract, is the plaintiff entitled to (i) the cost of reinstating the property, or (ii) the difference in value of the property before and after breach?

The answer seems to depend on whether, in all the circumstances, the reasonable course for the plaintiff is to reinstate the property or to buy new property. In *Harbutt's* case (above, pp. 406, 463) the plaintiff recovered the cost of reinstatement—£30,000 more than the difference in value of the old mill before and after the fire. "[The plaintiffs] had no choice. They were bound to replace it as soon as they could, not only to keep their business going, but also to mitigate the loss of profit (for which they would be able to charge the defendants)"— *per* Lord Denning. "It was reasonable for the plaintiffs to rebuild their factory, because there was no other way in which they could carry on their business and retain their labour force," *per* Widgery L.J. The plaintiffs did not have to give credit under the heading of "betterment" because the new factory was modern in design and materials. "To do so would be the equivalent of forcing the plaintiffs to invest their money in the modernising of their plant which might be highly inconvenient for them"—*per* Widgery L.J. (If they had added extra accommodation, it would have been different.)

On the other hand, "If the article damaged is a motor-car of popular make the plaintiff cannot charge the defendant with the cost of repair when it is cheaper to buy a similar car on the market"—*per* Widgery L.J. See the discussion in Street, *Principles of the Law of Damages*, pp. 210–212, and of this aspect of *Harbutt* in (1970) 86 L.Q.R. 524. *Harbutt* was followed in *Dominion Mosaics Co. Ltd v. Trafalgar Trucking Co. Ltd* [1990] 2 All E.R. 246, C.A.

Section 8. Penalties and Liquidated Damages

The parties to a contract may anticipate the possibility of a breach and include a term in their agreement that a certain sum shall be paid to the injured party by the party in default in the event of a specified breach or breaches. See the *Suisse Atlantique* case, above, p. 459. If the sum fixed is a genuine estimate of the actual damage likely to be suffered by the injured party in the event of the specified breach, then it is recoverable and is known as "liquidated damages." If it is not a genuine estimate of the amount of damage likely to be caused but is much less, it may still be liquidated damages, for a party may properly limit his liability: *Cellulose Acetate Silk Co. v. Widness Foundry (1925) Ltd* [1933] A.C. 20. But if the sum fixed is greater than any loss which the injured party could suffer as a result of the breach and, therefore, is intended to operate as a threat to keep a potential defaulter to his bargain, it is described as a "penalty." Courts of Equity gave relief against penalties and allowed the injured party to recover no more than his actual loss. Where, for example, a hire-purchase agreement provided that if, as the result of a breach by the hirer, the letter terminated the agreement, the hirer should pay, as compensation for depreciation, 75 per cent of the total sum due under the agreement, the Court of Appeal held that this was a penalty and irrecoverable. If the hirer had failed to pay the first instalment, the letter, according to the agreement, would have recovered a car that had hardly depreciated at all *and* 75 per cent of its value; and, on the actual facts of the case, he would have been £136 better of as a result of the breach than if the agreement had been carried out: *Lamdon Trust Co. v. Hurrel* [1955] 1 W.L.R. 391.

If a plaintiff sues for a penalty he can recover no more than the sum stipulated, even though he has suffered damage in excess of that sum. But it is open to him to ignore the penalty clause and sue for damages in which case he can recover the whole of his loss: *Wall v. Rederiaktiebolaget Luggude* [1915] 3 K.B. 66 and *Jobson v. Johnson*, below, p. 628.

DUNLOP PNEUMATIC TYRE CO. LTD v. NEW GARAGE AND MOTOR CO. LTD

[1915] A.C. 79; 83 L.J.K.B. 1574; 111 L.T. 862; 30 T.L.R. 625

The appellants, manufacturers, supplied their goods to the respondents (dealers) under an agreement whereby the respondents, in consideration of a trade discount, undertook not to tamper with marks on the goods, not to sell below list prices, not to supply certain persons named by the appellants, not to exhibit or export any of the goods, and to pay £5 "by way of liquidated damages and not as a penalty" for every item of the goods sold or offered in breach of the agreement.

The respondents sold a tyre manufactured by the appellants below list price. There was evidence that the whole of the appellants' business was carried on through the trade, that all their customers were required to sign agreements of this nature, and that the probable effect of underselling by any one customer was to compel other customers to deal elsewhere. The Court of Appeal (Vaughan Williams and Swinfen Eady L.JJ., Kennedy L.J. dissenting), reversing the finding of a master, held that the £5 was a penalty and that the plaintiffs were entitled to nominal damages only. The House of Lords (Lords Dunedin, Atkinson, Parker and parmoor) held, assuming without deciding that the sum of £5 applied to all the undertakings in the agreement, that it was liquidated damages.

LORD DUNEDIN: . . . I shall content myself with stating succinctly the various propositions which I think are deducible from the decisions which rank as authoritative:

1. Though the parties to a contract who use the words "penalty" or "liquidated damages" may prima facie be supposed to mean what they say, yet the expression used is not conclusive. The court must find out whether the payment stipulated is in truth a penalty or liquidated damages. This doctrine may be said to be found *passim* in nearly every case.

2. The essence of a penalty is a payment of money stipulated as *in terrorem* of the offending part; the essence of liquidated damages is a genuine covenanted pre-estimate of damage (*Clydebank Engineering and Shipbuilding Co. v. Don Jose Ramos Yzquierdo y Castaneda* [1905] A.C. 6).

3. The question whether a sum stipulated is penalty or liquidated damages is a question of construction to be decided upon the terms and inherent circumstances of each particular contract, judged of as at the time of the making of the contract, not as at the time of the breach (*Public Works Commissioner v. Hills* [1906] A.C. 368 and *Webster v. Bosanquet* [1912] A.C. 394).

4. To assist this task of construction various tests have been suggested, which if applicable to the case under consideration may prove helpful, or even conclusive. Such are:

(a) It will be held to be a penalty if the sum stipulated for is extravagant and unconscionable in amount in comparison with the greater loss that could conceivably be proved to have followed from the breach. (Illustration given by Lord Halsbury in *Clydebank* case.)

(b) It will be held to be a penalty if the breach consists only in not paying a sum of money, and the sum stipulated is a sum greater than the sum which ought to have been paid (*Kemble v. Farren* 6 Bing. 141). This, though one of the most ancient instances, is truly a corollary to the last test. Whether it had its historical origin in the doctrine of the common law that when A promised to pay B a sum of money on a certain day and did not do so, B could only recover the sum with, in certain cases, interest, but could never recover further damages for non-timeous payment, or whether it was a survival of the time when equity reformed unconscionable bargains merely because they were unconscionable—a subject which much exercised Jessel M.R. in *Wallis v. Smith*, 21 Ch.D. 243—is probably more interesting than material.

(c) There is a presumption (but no more) that it is penalty when "a single lump sum is made payable by way of compensation, on the occurrence of one or more or all of several events, some of which may occasion serious and others but trifling damage" (Lord Watson in *Lord Elphinstone v. Monkland Iron and Coal Co.*, 11 App.Cas. 332).

On the other hand:

(d) It is no obstacle to the sum stipulated being a genuine pre-estimate of damage, that the consequences of the breach are such as to make precise pre-estimation almost an impossibility. On the contrary, that is just the situation when it is probable that pre-estimated damage was the true bargain between the parties (*Clydebank* case, Lord Halsbury; *Webster v. Bosanquet*, Lord Mersey).

Turning now to the facts of the case, it is evident that the damage apprehended by the appellants owing to the breaking of the agreement was an indirect and not a direct damage. So long as they got their price from the respondents for each article sold, it could not matter to them directly what the respondents did with it. Indirectly it did. Accordingly, the agreement is headed "Price Maintenance Agreement," and the way in which the appellants would be damaged if prices were cut is clearly explained in evidence by Mr Baisley, and no successful attempt is made to controvert that evidence. But though damage as a whole from such a practice would be certain, yet damage from any one sale would be impossible to forecast. It is just, therefore, one of those cases where it seems quite reasonable for parties to contract that they should estimate that damage at a certain figure, and provided that figure is not extravagant there would seem no reason to suspect that it is not truly a bargain to assess damages, but rather a penalty to be held *in terrorem*.

Note

Penalties and liquidated damages have one thing in common: they are both sums of money which, by the terms of the contract, are payable on the occurrence of a breach of contract. If a contract provides that a sum of money shall become payable on the occurrence of some event other than a breach of contract, then this sum cannot be either a penalty or liquidated damages as these concepts have been traditionally understood and, prima facie, the sum will be recoverable in full whether it bears any relation to any loss which may have been suffered by the party suing or not. If A promises B that, if B, having used one of A's carbolic smoke balls three times daily for two weeks, catches influenza, he (A) will pay £100—or £10,000—B can, on the happening of the event, recover the specified sum even though it vastly exceeds the injury which B has suffered through catching influenza. The position might well be different if A had *promised* B that, if B used the smoke ball as specified, he would not catch influenza and that if B did, A would pay him a certain sum. The money would then be payable on a breach of contract and the question would arise whether it was a penalty or liquidated damages. (*Cf.* p. 622, above.)

In *Alder v. Moore* [1961] 2 Q.B. 57, C.A., the defendant, a professional footballer, was insured by his Union against permanent total disablement from playing professional football. He suffered an injury which the underwriters were satisfied amounted to permanent total disablement. As required by the policy, he signed a declaration that he would take no part, as a playing member, in any form of professional football and that "in the event of infringement of this condition, he will be subject to a penalty of the amount paid him in settlement of his claim."

Four months later the defendant started playing professional football again and the underwriters sued to recover £500. The defence was what the clause was a penalty and that the underwriters had suffered no damage through his playing football again. The Court of Appeal, allowing an appeal from Paull J., held that, notwithstanding the use of the term "penalty," this was a contract for the payment of a certain sum in a certain event which was not a breach of contract (there was no "*contractual* ban upon the defendant from playing professional football again"—*per* Slade J.) and, that event having happened, the sum was payable. Devlin L.J. dissenting, took the view that the underwriters had called the clause "a penalty" so there was an onus on them to satisfy the court that they did not mean what they said; that the underwriters had in fact exacted a promise from the defendant that he would not play football again and he was not prepared to rewrite this as a contingent promise to pay in the event of his playing football again.

The problem has arisen in an acute form in hire-purchase agreements which commonly provide that, if the hirer determines the agreement, he will bring his payments up to a specified sum as compensation for depreciation of the goods. If the hirer exercises his option to return the goods this is not a breach of contract—it is the exercise of a contractual right—and no question of penalty or liquidated damages prima facie arises. If, however, the hirer repudiates the contract, and the latter resumes possession, there is clearly a breach of contract and the sum specified is recoverable only if it amounts to liquidated damages and not a penalty.

BRIDGE v. CAMPBELL DISCOUNT CO. LTD

House of Lords [1962] A.C. 600; [1962] 2 W.L.R. 439; [1962] 1 All E.R. 385

The hirer of a car under a hire-purchase agreement paid an initial sum of £105 and one monthly instalment. He then informed the finance company that he could not keep up the payments and returned the car to them. By clause 6 the hirer had a right to terminate the hiring at any time and return the car but, if he did so, by clause 9, he was required to pay, "by way of agreed compensation for depreciation" such sum as would make his total payments up to two-thirds of the purchase price. Under this clause, the company claimed £206 3s. 4d.

The Court of Appeal, allowing an appeal from the county court judge, held that the amount claimed was not a penalty but was the sum payable as compensation to the company for the hirer's exercise of his right under clause 6. The House of Lords interpreted the hirer's conduct as a repudiation of the contract and not the exercise of his right under clause 6 and, accordingly, held that this was a claim for a penalty.

VISCOUNT SIMONDS, having stated that he dissented from the interpretation put upon the hirer's conduct by their Lordships and preferred the view of the Court of Appeal, went on: Clause 6 is not a penal clause. It confers on the hirer a right for which he agrees to pay a price. He need not exercise it if he does not want to. . . . I must dissent, as Harman L.J. did, from the suggestion that there is a general principle of equity which justifies the court in relieving a party to any bargain if in the event it operates hardly against him. In particular cases, for example, of expectant heirs or of fiduciary relationship, a court of equity (and now any court) will if the circumstances justify it grant relief. So also if there is duress or fraud "which unravels all." In the present case there is nothing which would justify the court in granting relief to a hirer who exercised his rights under clause 6. [His Lordship went on to say that if, as the majority held, the hirer had committed a breach of contract, he agreed that the claim was for a penalty.]

LORD MORTON said that if the appellant had exercised his option under clause 6, he would have agreed with the Court of Appeal; but that he thought the appellant had broken his contract and that clause 9 was a penal provision.

LORD RADCLIFFE: . . . Having regard to the view that your Lordships have taken as to the true facts of the case, our decision does not, I take it, conclude the question of an owner's rights under such agreements, when the hiring is determined under a hirer's option or by an event specified in the contract but not involving a breach. Such questions are closely related to what we have to consider here, but it does not follow that the legal arguments that sustain the hirer, when he is sued on breach, would be capable of sustaining him in these other situations. Indeed, although I wish to decide nothing, I appreciate that the doctrine of penalties can only be applied to those situations by the construction of almost a new set of arguments that would not arise naturally out of the arguments and considerations that have prevailed with courts, either of equity or of common law, when relieving against penalties in the past. "Unconscionable" must not be taken to be a panacea for adjusting any contract between competent persons when it shows a rough edge of one side or the other, and equity lawyers are, I notice, sometimes both surprised and discomfited by the plenitude of jurisdiction, and the imprecision of rules that are attributed to "equity" by their more enthusiastic colleagues. . . .

LORD DENNING: Having pointed out that, according to the view of the Court of Appeal, if Bridge, finding himself unable to keep up the payments and being a conscientious man, gave notice of termination and returned the car, he was liable to pay the "penal sum of £206 3s. 4d. without relief of any kind," went on: Let no one mistake the injustice of this. It means that equity commits itself to this absurd paradox: it will grant relief to a man who breaks his contract but will penalise the man who keeps it. If this be the state of equity today, then it is in sore need of an overhaul, so as to restore its first principles. But I am quite satisfied that such is not the state of equity today. This can be brought within long-established principles without recourse to any new equity. From the very earliest times equity has relieved not only against penalties for breach of contract, but also against penalties for non-performance of a condition. . . .

If I am wrong about all this, however, and there is no jurisdiction to grant the relief unless the hirer is in breach, then I would be prepared to hold in this case Bridge was in breach. . . .

LORD DEVLIN, having held that the case was one of breach of contract and that the sum claimed was penal, went on: When your Lordships have determined that clause 9(b), when it comes into operation as the result of a breach, is a penalty clause, your Lordships must also have determined that the clause contained no genuine estimate of the loss caused to the owner by depreciation and no genuine agreement that a sum should be paid in respect of it. There is no half-way house between a penalty and liquidated damages. However large the sum stipulated may be, if it is a genuine, covenanted pre-estimate of damage it is not stipulated as *in terrorem* and so cannot be a penalty. If, therefore, your Lordships had taken clause 9(b) at its face value and had supposed that, as it states, there was really an agreement about the sum to be paid as compensation for depreciation (I do not mean necessarily a separate collateral agreement; an estimate in which the defendant acquiesced would serve the purpose) the plaintiffs would inevitably have succeeded in their claim. . . .

My Lords, I do not see how an agreement can be genuine for one purpose and a sham for another. If it is a sham, it means that it was never made and does not exist; if it does not exist, it must be ignored altogether. . . .

On this comparatively narrow ground I should (if I had construed the letter of September 3 as the exercise of an option) have held that the defendant was nevertheless entitled to succeed. . . .

Appeal allowed.

Question
Z, a footballer, being apparently disabled, received £500 from an insurance company. Having started to play football again, he is sued for the return of the money. Advise him, assuming that, when he received the £500, he signed a form which stated: "I undertake that I will not in the future play football and, should I do so, will repay the insurance moneys."

Would it be different if the form read: "I undertake that, if I should play football in the future, I will refund the insurance moneys"?

The Law Commission Working Paper No. 61: Penalty Clauses and Forfeiture of Monies Paid

The Law Commission having referred to the paradox stated by Lord Denning in *Bridge v. Campbell Discount (supra)*, continue:

22. Our provisional view is that the court should have the power to deal with such clauses in the same way whether or not they come into operation by breach. There is however a problem of some difficulty, and that centres on the statutory description of contractual provisions to which this power will apply, since we do not envisage the power being confined to minimum payment clauses in hire-purchase agreements. It would not, we think, be possible to confer such a power in relation to all contractual provisions calling for payment of a sum of money for it is not our intention that every price payable under a contract should be subject to judicial control. . . .

25. The South African Conventional Penalties Act 1962 equates stipulations which provide that a party is to remain liable for the performance of some obligation upon withdrawal from an agreement with stipulations for penalties or liquidated damages.[1] A provision on these lines might deal with clauses which come into operation on a voluntary termination of an agreement, but we think that the phrase "upon withdrawal from an agreement" is too narrow to cover all the circumstances in which penalty clauses might come into operation.

Proposal for reform

26. A more acceptable approach would, we think, be this. There are in essence two separate matters which are being considered. There is first the contractual obligation which is being challenged as penal—typically (though not necessarily) an obligation to pay money in specified circumstances. Such an obligation might arise, for example, on the non-performance of some other act, or on the termination of an agreement voluntarily or on death or bankruptcy. The second matter is the act or result which is the true purpose of the contract, although its non-performance or non-fulfilment may not constitute a breach of the contract. Our proposal is that the rules as to penalties should be applied wherever the object of the disputed contractual obligation is to secure the act or result which is the true purpose of the contract. If, for example, a building contract were to provide for completion of the building by a certain date unless delayed by bad weather there would be no breach of contract if completion were delayed by bad weather. If the contract were also to provide that the builder should pay £50 for every day's delay caused by bad weather, the recoverability of the specified sum would depend on its being a genuine pre-estimate of the loss caused by delay. We should welcome views on this provisional proposal.

Note

See the Consumer Credit Act 1974, s.100(1) and (3).

---

[1] Act No. 15 of 1962, as amended by Act No. 102 of 1967. On the Act, see P.M.A. Hunt in [1962] *Annual Survey of South African Law*, p. 94 and C.I. Belcher (1964) 81 S.A.L.J. 80. See also B.A. Hepple (1961) 78 S.A.L.J. 445 on the Bill which led to the Act.

JOBSON v. JOHNSON

Court of Appeal [1989] 1 All E.R. 621

The defendant agreed to buy shares in Southend United Football Club for £351,688 by an initial payment of £40,000 and six half-yearly instalments of £51,948. Clause 6(b) of the agreement provided that if the defendant defaulted on the second or any subsequent instalment, he must return the shares to the seller for £40,000. The defendant paid £140,000 and the shares were transferred to him. He then defaulted and the plaintiff, the assignee of the seller, obtained an order for specific performance of the agreement to re-transfer the shares. The defendant appealed arguing that clause 6(b) was a penalty clause and unenforceable.

DILLON L.J. delivered judgment allowing the appeal to the extent indicated below.

NICHOLLS L.J.:

Equitable relief

In considering this appeal it is right to have in mind that the legal principles applicable today regarding penalty clauses in contracts and those applicable regarding relief from forfeiture stem from a common origin. A penalty clause in a contract, as that expression is normally used today, is a provision which, on breach of the contract, requires the party in default to make a payment to the innocent party of a sum of money which, however it may be labelled, is not a genuine pre-estimate of the damage likely to be sustained by the innocent party, but is a payment stipulated *in terrorem* of the party in default. For centuries equity has given relief against such provisions by not permitting the innocent party to recover under the penal provision more than his actual loss. In *Wyllie v. Wilkes* (1780) 2 Doug K.B. 519 at 522–523, Lord Mansfield observed that in the reign of Henry VIII Sir Thomas More had attempted unsuccessfully to persuade the judges to give relief in respect of money bonds:

> "For he summoned them to a conference concerning the granting relief at law, after the forfeiture of bonds, upon payment of principal, interest, and costs; and when they said they could not relieve against the penalty, he swore by the body of God, he would grant an injunction."

Likewise with forfeiture. Take the simple case of a provision for forfeiture of a lease on non-payment of rent. That provision was regarded by equity as a security for the rent. So that, where conscience so required, equity relieved against the forfeiture on payment of the rent with interest. Again with mortgages: . . .

Penalty clauses

The particular procedure by which the Court of Chancery prevented a party seeking payment under a penalty clause in a contract, including a bond, from recovering more than his actual loss seems to have differed a little according to whether the penalty was intended to secure only a payment of money on a specified date or was intended to secure the performance of an obligation other than a payment of money. The details are not material for the purpose of this appeal. . . .

Thus today, when law and equity are administered concurrently in the same courts, and the rules of equity prevail whenever there is any conflict or variance between the rules of equity and the rules of the common law with reference to the same matter (section 49 of the Supreme Court Act 1981), a penalty clause in a contract is, in practice, a dead letter. An obligation to make a money payment stipulated in terrorem will not be enforced beyond the sum which represents the actual loss of the party seeking payment, namely, principal, interest and, if appropriate, costs, in those cases where (to use modern terminology) the primary obligation is to pay money, or where the primary obligation is to perform some other obligation, beyond the sum recoverable as damages for breach of that obligation. (For convenience I shall hereafter refer to that sum as "the actual loss of the innocent party.") Hence normally there is no advantage in suing on the penalty clause. In *Wall* v. *Rederiaktiebolaget Luggude* [1915] 3 K.B. 66 at 73 Bailhache J. concluded his examination of the history of this matter in the context of a penalty clause in a charterparty with these words:

> "This being the state of the law as I understand it, one easily sees why in charterparty cases no one sues on the penalty clause now. You cannot under it recover more than the proved damages, and if the proved damages exceed the penal sum you are restricted to the lower amount. As the penalty clause may be disregarded it always is disregarded and has become a dead letter, or from another point of view a 'brutum fulmen'. . . ."

Although in practice a penalty clause in a contract as described above is effectively a dead letter, it is important in the present case to note that, contrary to the submissions of counsel for the defendant, the strict legal position is not that such a clause is simply struck out of the contract, as though with a blue pencil, so that the contract takes effect as if it had never been included therein. Strictly, the legal position is that the clause remains in the contract and can be sued on, but it will not be enforced by the court beyond the sum which represents, in the events which have happened, the actual loss of the party seeking payment. There are many cases which make this clear. . . .

Accordingly, once a court becomes aware that the amount claimed by the plaintiff is a penalty arising on default of payment of a specific sum of money the legal consequence which follows, as day follows night, is that the amount claimed will be scaled down by the court to a sum equal to the unpaid principal, with interest and costs. That consequence, albeit having its historical origin in equity, is not dependent on the court exercising a discretion to grant or withhold relief having regard to all the circumstances. It is a consequence which for many years has followed automatically, regardless of the circumstances of the default.

In this respect, as the law has developed, a distinction has arisen between the enforcement of penalty clauses in contracts and the enforcement of forfeiture clauses. A penalty clause will not be enforced beyond the sum which equals the actual loss of the innocent party. A forfeiture clause, of which a right of re-entry under a lease on non-payment of rent is the classic example, may also be penal in its effect. Such a clause frequently subjects the defaulting party, in the event of non-payment of rent or breach of some other obligation, to a sanction which damnifies the defaulting party, and benefits the other party, to an extent far greater than the actual loss of the innocent party. For instance, the lease may be exceedingly valuable and the amount of unpaid rent may be small. But in such a case the court will lend its aid in the enforcement of the forfeiture, by making an order for possession, subject to any relief which in its discretion the court may grant to the party in default. Normally the granting of such relief is made conditional on the payment of the rent with interest and costs. If that condition is not complied with, and subject to any further application by the tenant or other person in default for yet more time, the forfeiture provision will be enforced. Thus the innocent party is in a better position when seeking to enforce a forfeiture clause than when seeking to enforce a penalty clause in a contract . . .

Property and not money

I return to penalty clauses. The scaling-down exercise which is carried out automatically by equity is straightforward when the penalty clause provides for payment of a sum of money. More difficult, and more unusual, is the case where the penal obligation triggered by the breach is an obligation to transfer property to the party not in default, as under clause 6(b). Even in such a case there is no difficulty where the value of the property at the time when the court is making its order does not exceed the actual loss of the innocent party. In that event there can be no more objection to the court specifically enforcing the obligation to transfer the property than there would be to the court making an order for the payment of a sum of money stipulated in a (pecuniary) penalty clause where, in the event, that sum does not exceed the actual loss of the innocent party. The difficulty arises where the value of the property agreed to be transferred exceeds the actual loss of the innocent party. A precisely comparable scaling-down exercise would not provide an acceptable solution, at any rate where the property consists of a single piece of land, or a block of shares in a company such as Southend United Football Club Ltd, whose shares are not traded in one of the securities markets. It could not be right to order specific performance of clause 6(b) in part only, namely in respect of the reduced number of shares whose value does not exceed the actual loss of the plaintiff. That, indeed, would be to make a new bargain for the parties.

In the present case we do not know what is the current value of the shares comprised in clause 6(b), even in approximate terms. I shall return later to the question of what, in that circumstance, can and should be done. For the moment it is sufficient to note that, apart from the difference between shares and money, clause 6(b) possesses all the essential characteristics of a penalty clause. In principle, and subject to the complication arising from the difficulty of "scaling-down" an obligation to transfer shares, there can be no difference between an obligation to pay a stipulated sum of money arising on a default and an obligation to transfer specified property arising on a default. The essential vice is the same in each case. In principle, so far as this can be achieved, the parties' respective positions should be no better, or worse, than they would be if clause 6(b) had stipulated for payment of money rather than a transfer of shares.

[The court offered the plaintiff two alternative forms of relief: (a) an order for the sale of the shares by the court and payment of the unpaid instalments and interest to the plaintiff out of the proceeds or (b) an inquiry as to the value of the shares and, if it did not exceed the amount of the unpaid instalments and interest by £40,000, an order for specific performance of the agreement. KERR L.J., thinking neither alternative offered sufficient justice to the plaintiff, would have offered a third alternative.]

PART V

VITIATING FACTORS

CHAPTER 17

INCAPACITY

The general rule of English law is that any person is competent to bind himself to any contract he chooses to make, provided that it is not illegal or void for reasons of public policy. (See below, Chapter 19.) At common law there are exceptions to this rule in the case of corporations, minors, married women, mentally incompetent and intoxicated persons. The exceptions are now greatly reduced in scope. A series of statutes from 1870 to 1949 abolished the married woman's disabilities and she now enjoys full contractual capacity. The present state of the other exceptions requires a little further explanation.

(a) *Corporations*

A corporation created by Royal Charter has always had the same contractual capacity as an ordinary person but a company incorporated under the Companies Act could, until recently, only make such contracts as were within the scope of the objects set out in its memorandum of association. Anything beyond that was *ultra vires* and void.

In the leading case of *Ashbury Railway Carriage and Iron Co. Ltd v. Riche* (1875) L.R. 7 H.L. 653 the objects set out in the company's memorandum were "to make and sell, or lend on hire, railway carriages and waggons, and all kinds of railway plant, fittings, machinery and rolling stock; to carry on the business of mechanical engineers and general contractors; to purchase, lease, work and sell mines, minerals, land and buildings; to purchase and sell as merchants, timber, coal, metals, or other materials, and to buy any such materials on commission or as agents." The directors purchased a concession for making a railway in Belgium and purported to contract with Riche that he should have the construction of the line. Riche's action for breach of the alleged contract failed since the House of Lords held that the construction of a railway, as distinct from rolling stock, was *ultra vires* the company and that therefore the contract was void. Even if every shareholder of the company had expressed his approval of the act, it would have made no difference, for it was an act which the company had no power, in law, to do. Important changes were made by section 108 of the Companies Act 1989, substituting a new section 35 of the Companies Act 1985. Under that new section it remains the duty of the directors to observe any limitations on their powers flowing from the company's memorandum (section 35(3)) and a member of a company may bring proceedings to restrain the doing of an act in excess of those powers (section 35(2)); but, by section 35(1):

> "The validity of an act done by a company shall not be called into question on the ground of lack of capacity by reason of anything in the company's memorandum."

So, by applying the modern law to the *Ashbury* case, the directors committed a breach of duty by making the contract and might have been restrained by action by a member; but once the contract was made its validity could not be questioned provided that the making of the contract was "an act done by the company." It might be objected that it was not such an act because the directors had no power to make the contract. This objection is met by section 35A(1):

> "In favour of a person dealing with a company in good faith, the power of the board of directors to bind the company, or authorise others to do so, shall be deemed to be free of any limitation under the company's constitution."

635

A person is presumed to have acted in good faith unless the contrary is proved and is not to be regarded as acting in bad faith merely because he knows the act is beyond the directors' powers. An *ultra vires* act by the directors may now be ratified, but only by special resolution which does not affect any liability incurred by the directors or any other person—any such relief must be agreed to separately by special resolution.

Formerly a corporation's contracts were invalid unless made under the corporate seal but, since the Corporate Bodies' Contracts Act 1960, a corporation may make contracts in the same manner as a natural person—that is the contract may be made orally unless a special rule requires a written contract—as in contracts for the sale or disposition of an interest in land—or evidence in writing—as in the case of a guarantee within section 4 of the Statute of Frauds 1677.

(b) *Minors*

At common law persons under the age of 21 were designated "infants" and had only a limited capacity to contract. From January 1, 1970, the Family Law Reform Act 1969 reduced the age of majority to 18 and authorised the term "minor" as an alternative to "infant." "Minor" is now the preferred term. The capacity of a minor to contract is still regulated by the common law, modified by the Minors' Contracts Act 1987 which repealed a troublesome statute, the Infants Relief Act 1874.

The general principle is that a contract made by a minor with an adult is binding on the adult but not on the minor. If, after attaining his majority, he ratifies it by an act confirming the promise he made when a minor, he is bound. There need be no consideration for the act of ratification. A contract by a minor is not void and any money or property transferred by him under the contract can be recovered only if there has been a total failure of consideration. There are three exceptional cases where a minor is to some extent bound.

Necessaries. A minor is bound to pay for necessaries supplied to him under a contract. The Sale of Goods Act 1979 s.3, re-enacting the Act of 1893, provides:

> ". . . where necessaries are sold and delivered to an infant (or minor) . . . he must pay a reasonable price therefor.
>
> 'Necessaries' in this section means goods suitable to the condition of life of such infant (or minor) . . . and to his actual requirements at the time of sale and delivery."

"Necessaries" are those things without which a person cannot reasonably exist and include food, clothing, lodging, education or training in a trade and essential services. The "condition of life" of the minor means his social status and his wealth. What is regarded as necessary for the minor residing in a stately home may be unnecessary for the resident of a council flat. Whatever the minor's status, the goods must be suitable to his actual requirements—if he already has enough fancy waistcoats, more cannot be necessary: *Nash v. Inman* [1908] 2 K.B. 1, C.A.

The nature of the minor's liability for necessary goods is uncertain. The fact that the Sale of Goods Act makes him liable only for goods "sold and delivered" and to pay, not any agreed price, but a reasonable price, suggests quasi-contractual liability—he must pay, not because he has contracted to do so, but because the law requires him to recompense the seller for a benefit conferred and accepted. Some dicta support this view but others treat the minor's liability as contractual. In *Roberts v. Gray* [1913] K.B. 520, C.A., a minor was held liable for his failure to perform a contract for a tour with the plaintiff, a noted billiards player. It was a contract for the instruction of the minor. The contract was wholly executory and the minor had received no benefit but it was held that the contract was binding on him from its formation. It may be thought that there is a distinction between necessary goods and necessary services but this is difficult to justify logically or historically. Perhaps the contract in *Roberts v. Gray* belongs more properly to the category of beneficial contracts of service, below.

A contract is not binding on a minor merely because it is proved to be for the minor's benefit; but a contract which would otherwise be binding as a contract for necessaries is not so if it contains harsh and onerous terms: *Fawcett v. Smethurst* (1914) 84 L.J.K.B. 473, (Atkin J.).

Beneficial contracts of service. It is for the minor's benefit that he should be able to obtain employment which would be difficult if he could not make a binding contract. The law allows him to do so, provided that the contract, taken as a whole, is manifestly for his benefit. So where a young railway porter agreed to join an insurance scheme and to forgo any claims he might have under the Employers' Liability Act, he had forfeited his rights under the Act, the contract as a whole being for his benefit: *Clements v. London & North Western Railway* [1894] 2 Q.B. 482, C.A. Contracts enabling a minor to pursue a career as a professional boxer and as an author have been held binding as being for their benefit.

Acquisition of property with obligations. When a minor acquires "a subject of a permanent nature . . . with certain obligations attached to it"—such as a leasehold, or shares in a company—he is bound by the obligations as long as he retains the subject. He must pay the rent or calls on the shares: *London & North Western Railway v. M'Michael* (1850) 5 Ex. 114. The contract is voidable by the minor—he may repudiate it at any time during his minority or within a reasonable time thereafter. It is uncertain whether avoidance here means rescission *ab initio* or avoidance of only future obligations; but, whether it is retrospective or not, it seems that the minor cannot recover money which he has already paid unless there has been a total failure of consideration: *Steinberg v. Scala Ltd* [1923] 2 Ch. 452, C.A.

Restitution by a minor. Where a minor has obtained property under a contract which is not enforceable against him, the adult party who can neither sue for the price nor get the property back may suffer an injustice. Even where the minor has lied about his age, no action in deceit will lie because this would, in effect, enable the contract to be enforced against him; and for the same reason it is improbable that the minor would be estopped from asserting his true age. The Minors' Contracts Act 1987, s.3, now affords a limited measure of redress. Where a contract made after the commencement of the Act is unenforceable against a defendant because he was a minor when it was made:

"... the court may, if it is just and equitable to do so, require the defendant to transfer to the plaintiff any property acquired by the defendant under the contract or any property representing it."

This may assist the plaintiff where the property is identifiable but where the plaintiff has loaned money it will usually not be. The plaintiff will then be able to recover in equity only if he is able to prove that he loaned the money for the express purpose of enabling the minor to buy necessaries and that he in fact did so: *Lewis v. Alleyne* (1888) 4 T.L.R. 560.

The 1987 Act, s.2, provides "Nothing in this section shall be taken to prejudice any other remedy available to the plaintiff." The plaintiff might rely on the equitable doctrine which required a fraudulent minor to return property which he had obtained by deception and which was still identifiable in his possession: *R. Leslie Ltd v. Shiell* [1914] 3 K.B. 607, C.A.; but it is not clear that there would be any advantage in doing so, since the remedy under section 1 appears to overlap the equitable remedy and does not require proof of fraud.

Guarantee of a minor's contract. Section 3 of the 1987 Act provides that a guarantee of a minor's contract is not unenforceable against the guarantor merely because the contract made by the minor is unenforceable against him on the ground that he is a minor. The section does not apply if the contract made by the minor is unenforceable against him for some other reason, for example misrepresentation or duress by the adult party. In such a case the guarantor would not be bound.

(c) *Mental Incompetents.*

The ancient rule of the common law was that a lunatic could not set up his own insanity (though his heir might) so as to avoid an obligation which he had undertaken. But by 1847 Pollock C.B. was able to say, in delivering the judgment of the Court of Exchequer Chamber in *Moulton v. Camroux*, 2 Ex. 487, that "the rule had in modern times been relaxed, and unsoundness of mind would now be a good defence to an action upon a contract, if it could be shown that the defendant was not of the capacity to contract 'and the plaintiff knew it.'" *Cf. Imperial Loan Co. v. Stone* [1892] 1 Q.B. 599, C.A. Section 3 of the Sale of Goods Act 1979 makes the same provision for persons who are incompetent to contract by reason of mental incapacity as for minors (see above).

A lunatic so found by inquisition was held to be incapable of making a valid *inter vivos* disposition of property (although he could make a valid will) since this would be inconsistent with the position of the Crown under the Lunacy Acts: *Re Walker* [1905] 1 Ch. 160. Presumably the position of a lunatic so found with respect to contracts not effecting *inter vivos* dispositions of his property was the same as that of a lunatic not so found; that is, he would be bound unless he could show that he was not in fact of capacity to contract and that the plaintiff knew it. The Lunacy Acts have been repealed, but an order under the Mental Health Act 1983, may have the same effect as a finding of lunacy.

(d) *Intoxicated persons*

The authorities are scanty; but in *Gore v. Gibson* (1845) 13 M. & W. 621; 153 E.R. 260, it was held that a contract made by a person so intoxicated as not to know the consequences of his act is not binding on him if his condition is known to the other party. It appears, however, that such a contract is not void but merely voidable, for it was held in *Matthews v. Baxter* (1873) L.R. 8 Ex. 132 that if the drunken party, upon coming to his senses, ratifies the contract, he is bound by it.

Section 3 of the Sale of Goods Act 1979 makes the same provision for persons who are incompetent to contract by reason of "drunkenness" as for minors and the mentally incompetent. No doubt, the same rule would be applied to persons intoxicated by drugs other than alcoholic drink, either by a broad interpretation of "drunkenness," or at common law.

CHAPTER 18

DURESS, UNDUE INFLUENCE AND INEQUALITY OF BARGAINING POWER

WILLIAMS v. BAYLEY

House of Lords (1866) L.R. 1 H.L. 200; 35 L.J.Ch. 717; 12 Jur. 875; 14 L.T. 802; 148 R.R. 396

The respondent's son gave to the appellants, bankers, promissory notes upon which he had forged the indorsements of the respondent. Both the respondent and his son had accounts with the appellants. At a meeting of all the parties at the appellants' bank, one of them said to the respondent: "If the bills are yours we are all right; if they are not, we have only one course to pursue; we cannot be parties to compounding a felony." The solicitor for the appellants said it was a serious matter and the respondent's own solicitor added, "a case of transportation for life." After further discussion as to how the son's liabilities might be met, the appellants' solicitor said that they could only look to the respondent. The respondent's solicitor refused to be a party to the respondent making himself liable for the whole amount and prepared to leave the room, when the respondent said: "What be I to do? How can I help myself? You see these men will have their money?"

The respondent then agreed to make an equitable mortgage to the appellants in consideration of the return of the promissory notes. The respondent succeeded in an action for cancellation of the agreement.

LORD CRANWORTH L.C. and LORD CHELMSFORD made speeches in favour of the respondent.

LORD WESTBURY, having held that the basis of the transaction was not, as alleged by the appellants, the possible civil liability of the father for the debt but the criminal liability of the son, continued: The question, therefore, my Lords, is whether a father appealed to under such circumstances, to take upon himself an amount of civil liability with the knowledge that, unless he does so, his son will be exposed to a criminal prosecution, with the certainty of conviction, can be regarded as a free and voluntary agent? I have no hesitation in saying that no man is safe, or ought to be safe, who takes a security for the debt or a felon, from the father of a felon, under such circumstances. A contract to give security for the debt of another, which is a contract without consideration, is, above all things, a contract that should be based upon the free and voluntary agency of the individual who enters into it. But it is clear that the power of considering whether he ought to do it or not, whether it is prudent to do it or not, is altogether taken away from a father who is brought into the situation of either refusing, and leaving his son in that perilous condition, or of taking on himself the amount of that civil obligation.

I have, therefore, my Lords, in that view of the case no difficulty in saying that, as far as my opinion is concerned, the security given for the debt of the son by the father under such circumstances, was not the security of a man who acted with that freedom and power of deliberation that must, undoubtedly, be considered as necessary to validate a transaction of such a description.

My Lords, I would add to that, the great folly, nay, impropriety, of the bankers proceeding to take this security from the defenceless old man after his solicitor had left him, protesting in such an emphatic manner against the proceedings which he knew they were about to enter upon. The respondent's solicitor remained so long as a valid contract, namely, that touching the property of William Bayley, was regarded as possible. When that was impossible, and the bankers began to exert pressure on the father, the solicitor left, remonstrating with all parties against the impropriety of what they were about to do. . . .

Appeal dismissed.

BARTON v. ARMSTRONG

Privy Council [1975] 2 W.L.R. 1050; [1975] 2 All E.R. 465

Armstrong, the former chairman of a company, "Landmark," threatened Barton, the managing director, with death if Landmark did not agree to pay a large sum in cash and to purchase Armstrong's shares in Landmark. There was some evidence that Barton thought the proposed agreement was a satisfactory business arrangement both from his own point of view and that of Landmark. Barton executed a deed on behalf of Landmark carrying out the agreement. He sought a declaration that the deed was executed under duress and was void. Street J. in the Supreme Court of New South Wales held that Barton, though apprehensive as to the safety of himself and his family, was not overborne by Armstrong but exercised free and independent judgment and entered into the contract for reasons of commercial necessity and that his claim failed. The Court of Appeal of New South Wales affirmed the judge's decision.

LORD CROSS: (with whom LORD KILBRANDON and SIR GARFIELD BARWICK agreed), having discussed the facts:

Their Lordships turn now to consider the question of law which provoked a difference of opinion in the Court of Appeal Division. It is hardly surprising that there is no direct authority on the point, for if A threatens B with death if he does not execute some document and B, who takes A's threats seriously, executes the document it can be only in the most unusual circumstances that there can be any doubt whether the threats operated to induce him to execute the document. But this is a most unusual case and the findings of fact made below do undoubtedly raise the question whether it was necessary for Barton in order to obtain relief to establish that he would not have executed the deed in question but for the threats. In answering this question in favour of Barton Jacobs J.A. relied both on a number of old common law authorities on the subject of "duress" and also—by way of analogy—on later decisions in equity with regard to the avoidance of deeds on the ground of fraud. Their Lordships do not think that the common law authorities are of any real assistance for it seems most unlikely that the authors of the statements relied on had the sort of problem which has arisen here in mind at all. On the other hand they think that the conclusion to which Jacobs J.A. came was right and that it is supported by the equity decisions. The scope of common law duress was very limited and at a comparatively early date equity began to grant relief in cases where the disposition in question had been procured by the exercise of pressure which the Chancellor considered to be illegitimate— although it did not amount to common law duress. There was a parallel development in the field of dispositions induced by fraud. At common law the only remedy available to the man defrauded was an action for deceit but equity in the same period in which it was building up the doctrine of "undue influence" came to entertain proceedings to set aside dispositions which had been obtained by fraud: see Holdsworth's *History of English Law* (Vol. 38), p. 51. There is an obvious analogy between setting aside a disposition for duress or undue influence and setting it aside for fraud. In each case—to quote the words of Holmes J. in *Fairbanks v. Snow* (1887) 13 N.E. at 598)—"the party has been subjected to an improper motive for action." Again the similarity of the effect in law of *metus* and *dolus* in connection with dispositions of property is noted by Stair in his *Institutions of the Law of Scotland* (Book IV, tit. 40, 25). Had Armstrong made a fraudulent misrepresentation to Barton for the purpose of inducing him to execute the deed of January 17, 1967, the answer to the problem which has arisen would have been clear. If it were established that Barton did not allow the representation to affect his judgment then he could not make it a ground for relief even though the representation was designed and known by Barton to be designed to affect his judgment. If on the other hand Barton relied on the misrepresentation Armstrong could not have defeated his claim to relief by showing that there were other more weighty causes which contributed to his decision to execute the deed, for in this field the court does not allow an examination into the relative importance of contributory causes. "Once make out that there has been anything like deception, and no contract resting in any degree on that foundation can stand" *per* Lord Cranworth L.J. in *Reynell v. Spyre* (1852) 1 De G.M. & G. 660 at 708); see also the other cases referred to in Cheshire and Fifoot's *Law of Contract* (8th ed. 1972), p. 250, 251. Their Lordships think that the same rule should apply in cases of duress and that if Armstrong's threats were "a" reason for Barton's executing the deed he is entitled to relief even though he might well have entered into the contract if Armstrong had uttered no threats to induce him to do so.

[Their Lordships went on to hold that the onus was on Armstrong to prove that the threats he made contributed nothing to Barton's decision to sign; and that the proper inference was "that though it may be that Barton would have executed the documents even if Armstrong had made no threats and exerted no unlawful pressure to induce him to do so, the threats and unlawful pressure in fact contributed to his decision to sign . . ."]

LORDS WILBERFORCE AND SIMON, dissenting, held that there was no justification for interfering with the findings of fact made by the courts below.

Appeal allowed.

Questions
1. Their Lordships follow the traditional view that operative duress makes a contract merely voidable and not void. If A points a gun at B and says, "Sell me your watch for a penny—or

else . . ." is there really a contract if A hands over his watch? See Lanham (1966) 29 M.L.R. 615.

2. What if, in the above problem, A's offer had been £5 for a watch which he believed to be very valuable and B, knowing the watch was worth £2, had happily accepted?

BARCLAYS BANK plc v. O'BRIEN AND ANOTHER

House of Lords [1994] 1 A.C. 340; [1993] 3 W.L.R. 286; [1993] 4 All E.R. 417

O'Brien (O), a shareholder in a manufacturing company, arranged with the company's bank an overdraft facility for the company of £135,000. O was to guarantee repayment and his liability to the Bank was to be secured by a second charge over the matrimonial home, jointly owned by O and his wife (W). The bank manager's instructions that O and W should be made fully aware of the effect of the security documents were not carried out. Both O and W signed the documents without reading them. When the company's indebtedness increased, the Bank brought proceedings against O and W to enforce the guarantee. W's defence was that O had (i) put undue pressure on her to sign and (ii) misrepresented that the effect of the charge was limited to £60,000 and that it would last only three weeks. The judge gave judgment for the Bank, finding that (i) O had not unduly influenced W and (ii) that O had misrepresented the effect of the charge but that the Bank was not responsible for that misrpresentation. The Court of Appeal held that the Bank was under a duty, which it had not satisfied, to take reasonable steps to ensure that W had an adequate understanding of the transaction so that it was not enforceable against her except to the extent of £60,000. The Bank appealed.

Lord Browne-Wilkinson:

Policy considerations

The large number of cases of this type coming before the courts in recent years reflects the rapid changes in social attitudes and the distribution of wealth which have recently occurred. Wealth is now more widely spread. Moreover a high proportion of privately owned wealth is invested in the matrimonial home. Because of the recognition by society of the equality of the sexes, the majority of matrimonial homes are now in the joint names of both spouses. Therefore in order to raise finance for the business enterprises of one or other of the spouses, the jointly owned home has become a main source of security. The provision of such security requires the consent of both spouses.

In parallel with these financial developments, society's recognition of the sexes has led to a rejection of the concept that the wife is subservient to the husband in the management of the family's finances. A number of the authorities reflect an unwillingness in the court to perpetuate law based on this outmoded concept. Yet, as Scott L.J. in the Court of Appeal rightly points out, although the concept of the ignorant wife leaving all financial decisions to the husband is outmoded, the practice does not yet coincide with the ideal (see [1993], Q.B. 109 at 139). In a substantial proportion of marriages it is still the husband who has the business experience and the wife is willing to follow his advice without bringing a truly independent mind and will to bear on financial decisions. The number of recent cases in this field shows that in practice many wives are still subjected to, and yield to, undue influence by their husbands. Such wives can reasonably look to the law for some protection when their husbands have abused the trust and confidence reposed in them.

On the other hand. it is important to keep a sense of balance in approaching these cases. It is easy to allow sympathy for the wife who is threatened with the loss of her home at the suit of a rich bank to obscure an important public interest, *viz* the need to ensure that the wealth currently tied up in the matrimonial home does not become economically sterile. If the rights secured to wives by the law renders vulnerable loans granted on the security of matrimonial homes, institutions will be unwilling to accept such security, thereby reducing the flow of loan capital to business enterprises. It is therefore essential that a law designed to protect the vulnerable does not render the matrimonial home unacceptable as security to financial institution. . . .

Undue influence

A person who has been induced to enter into a transaction by the undue influence of another (the wrongdoer) is entitled to set that transaction aside as against the wrongdoer. Such undue influence is either actual or presumed. In *Bank of Credit and Commerce International SA v. Aboody* (1988) [1990] 1 Q.B. 923 at 953 the Court of Appeal helpfully adopted the following classification.

Class 1: actual undue influence. In these cases it is necessary for the claimant to prove affirmatively that the wrongdoer exerted undue influence on the complainant to enter into the particular transaction which is impugned.

Class 2: presumed undue influence. In these cases the complainant only has to show, in the first instance, that there was a relationship of trust and confidence between the complainant and the wrongdoer of such a nature that it is fair to presume that the wrongdoer abused that relationship in procuring the complainant to enter into the impugned transaction. In class 2 cases therefore there is no need to produce evidence that actual undue influence was exerted in relation to the particular transaction impugned: once a confidential relationship has been proved, the burden then shifts to the wrongdoer to prove that the complainant entered into the impugned transaction freely, for example by showing that the complainant had independent advice. Such a confidential relationship can be established in two ways, *viz*:

Class 2A. Certain relationships (for example solicitor and client, medical advisor and patient) as a matter of law raise the presumption that undue influence has been exercised.

Class 2B. Even if there is no relationship falling within class 2A, if the complainant proves the *de facto* existence of a relationship under which the complainant generally reposed trust and confidence in the wrongdoer, the existence of such relationship raises the presumption of undue influence. In a class 2B case therefore, in the absence of evidence disproving undue influence, the complainant will succeed in setting aside the impugned transaction merely by proof that the complainant reposed trust and confidence in the wrongdoer without having to prove that the wrongdoer exerted actual undue influence or otherwise abused such trust and confidence in relation to the particular transaction impugned.

As to dispositions by a wife in favour of her husband, the law for long remained in an unsettled state. In the nineteenth century some judges took the view that the relationship was such that it fell into class 2A, *i.e.* as a matter of law undue influence by the husband over the wife was presumed. It was not until the decisions in *Howes v Bishop* [1909] 2 K.B. 390 and *Bank of Montreal v Stuart* [1911] A.C. 120 that it was finally determined that the relationship of husband and wife did not as a matter of law raise a presumption of undue influence within class 2A.

[Lord Browne-Wilkinson examined the authorities in detail.]

Summary

I can therefore summarise my views as follows. Where one cohabitee has entered into an obligation to stand as surety for the debts of the other cohabitee and the creditor is aware that they are cohabitees: (1) the surety obligation will be valid and enforceable by the creditor unless the suretyship was procured by the undue influence, misrepresentation or other legal wrong of the principal debtor; (2) if there has been undue influence, misrepresentation or other legal wrong by the principal debtor, unless the creditor has taken reasonable steps to satisfy himself that the surety entered into the obligation freely and in knowledge of the true facts, the creditor will be unable to enforce the surety obligation because he will be fixed with constructive notice of the surety's right to set aside the transaction; (3) unless there are special exceptional circumstances, a creditor will have taken such reasonable steps to avoid being fixed with constructive notice if the creditor warns the surety (at a meeting not attended by the principal debtor) of the amount of her potential liability and of the risks involved and advises the surety to take independent legal advice.

I should make it clear that in referring to the husband's debts I include the debts of a company in which the husband (but not the wife) has a direct financial interest.

The decision of this case

Applying those principles to this case, to the knowledge of the bank Mr and Mrs O'Brien were man and wife. The bank took a surety obligation from Mrs O'Brien, secured on the matrimonial home, to secure the debts of a company in which Mr O'Brien was interested but in which Mrs O'Brien had no direct pecuniary interest. The bank should therefore have been put on inquiry as to the circumstances in which Mrs O'Brien had agreed to stand as surety for the debt of her husband. If the Burnham branch had properly carried out the instructions from Mr Tucker of the Woolwich branch, Mrs O'Brien would have been informed that she and the matrimonial home were potentially liable for the debts of a company which had an existing liability of £107,000 and which was to be afforded an overdraft facility of £135,000. If she had been told this, it would have counteracted Mr O'Brien's misrepresentation that the liability was limited to £60,000 and would last for only three weeks. In addition according to the side letter she would have been recommended to take independent legal advice.

Unfortunately Mr Tucker's instructions were not followed and to the knowledge of the bank (through the clerk at the Burnham branch) Mrs O'Brien signed the documents without any warning of the risks or any recommendation to take legal advice. In the circumstances the bank (having failed to take reasonable steps) is fixed with constructive notice of the wrongful misrepresentation made by Mr O'Brien to Mrs O'Brien. Mrs O'Brien is therefore entitled as against the bank to set aside the legal charge on the matrimonial home securing her husband's liability to the bank.

For these reasons I would dismiss the appeal with costs.

Lords Templeman, Lowry, Slynn and Woolf agreed.

Appeal dismissed.

Note

See also *British Crane Hire Corporation Ltd v. Ipswich Plant Hire Ltd* (above, p. 157) *A. Schroeder Publishing Co. Ltd v. Macaulay* (below, p. 694), *North Ocean Shipping v. Hyundai* (above, p. 237) and Unfair Contract Terms Act 1977, Sched. 2 (below, p. 714).

NATIONAL WESTMINSTER BANK plc v. MORGAN

House of Lords [1985] A.C. 686; [1985] 2 W.L.R. 588; [1985] 1 All E.R. 821

Mr Morgan's business was in financial difficulties. He was unable to meet the mortgage repayments on his home which he owned jointly with his wife. The building society obtained a possession order. Mr Morgan asked the Bank to "refinance" the building society loan. The Bank was prepared to make a loan of £14,500 to pay off the building society loan subject to the completion of a new unlimited mortgage on the house, that is, one which would cover all the husband's liabilities to the bank. The bank manager, Mr Barrow, called at the house to obtain Mrs Morgan's signature. She had no confidence in her husband's business abilities and was concerned that the document she was being asked to sign might enable him to borrow for business purposes. Mr Barrow assured her in good faith but incorrectly that the charge only secured the amount required to refinance the mortgage. It was, however, the intention of the bank to treat the charge as so limited and it at no time sought to use it for any other purpose. Mrs Morgan had no independent legal advice. The bank now claimed possession of the house from Mrs Morgan. Her defence that the charge had been obtained by undue influence was rejected by the trial judge but upheld by the Court of Appeal. The bank appealed.

Lord Scarman: As to the facts, I am far from being persuaded that the trial judge fell into error when he concluded that the relationship between the bank and Mrs Morgan never went beyond the normal business relationship of banker and customer. Both Lords Justices saw the relationship between the bank and Mrs Morgan as one of confidence in which she was relying on the bank manager's advice. Each recognised the personal honesty, integrity, and good faith of Mr Barrow. Each took the view that the confidentiality of the relationship was such as to impose upon him a "fiduciary duty of care." It was his duty, in their view, to ensure that Mrs Morgan had the opportunity to make an independent and informed decision; but he failed to give her any such opportunity. They, therefore, concluded that it was a case for the presumption of undue influence.

My Lords, I believe that the Lords Justices were led into a misrepresentation of the facts by their use, as is all too frequent in this branch of the law, of words and phrases such as "confidence," "confidentiality," "fiduciary duty." There are plenty of confidential relationships which do not give rise to the presumption of undue influence (a notable example is that of husband and wife, *Bank of Montreal* v. *Stuart* [1911] A.C. 120); and there are plenty of nonconfidential relationships in which one person relies upon the advice of another for example, many contracts for the sale of goods. Nor am I persuaded that the charge, limited as it was by Mr Barrow's declaration to securing the loan to pay off the Abbey National debt and interest during the bridging period, was disadvantageous to Mrs Morgan. It meant for her the rescue of her home upon the terms sought by her—a short-term loan at a commercial rate of interest. The Court of Appeal has not, therefore, persuaded me that the judge's understanding of the facts was incorrect.

But, further, the view of the law expressed by the Court of Appeal was, as I shall endeavour to show, mistaken. Dunn L.J., at p. 90, while accepting that in all the reported cases to which the court was referred the transactions were disadvantageous to the person influenced, took the view that in cases where public policy requires the court to apply the presumption of undue influence there is no need to prove a disadvantageous transaction. Slade L.J. also clearly held that it was not necessary to prove a disadvantageous transaction where the relationship of influence was proved to exist. Basing himself on the judgment of Cotton L.J. in *Allcard v. Skinner* (1887) 36 Ch.D. 145, 171, he said, at p. 92:

"Where a transaction has been entered into between two parties who stand in the relevant relationship to one another, it is still possible that the relationship and influence arising therefrom has been abused, even though the transaction is, on the face of it, one which, in commercial terms, provides reasonably equal benefits for both parties."

I can find no support for this view of the law other than the passage in Cotton L.J.'s judgment in *Allcard v. Skinner*, to which Slade L.J. referred.

[Having considered the judgment of Cotton L.J. in *Allcard v. Skinner*, Lord Scarman went on:]

Like Dunn L.J., I know of no reported authority where the transaction set aside was not to the manifest disadvantage of the person influenced. It would not always be a gift: it can be a "hard and inequitable" agreement (*Ormes v. Beadel* (1860) 2 Gif. 166, 174); or a transaction "immoderate and irrational" (*Bank of Montreal v. Stuart* [1911] A.C. 120, 137) or "unconscionable" in that it was a sale at an undervalue (*Poosathurai v. Kannappa Chettiar* (1919) L.R. 47 I.A. 1, 3–4). Whatever the legal character of the transaction, the authorities show that it must constitute a disadvantage sufficiently serious to require evidence to rebut the presumption that in the circumstances of the relationship between the parties it was procured by the exercise of undue influence. In my judgment, therefore, the Court of Appeal erred in law in holding that the presumption of undue influence can arise from the evidence of the relationship of the parties without also evidence that the transaction itself was wrongful in that it constituted an advantage taken of the person subjected to the influence which, failing proof to the contrary, was explicable only on the basis that undue influence had been exercised to procure it.

[Having quoted extensively from the judgment of Lindley L.J. in *Allcard v. Skinner* and that of Lord Shaw in *Poosathurai v. Kannappa Chesttiar* (1919) L.R. 47 Ind.App. 1 at 3, his Lordship continued:]

The wrongfulness of the transaction must, therefore, be shown: it must be one in which an unfair advantage has been taken of another. The doctrine is not limited to transactions of gift. A commercial relationship can become a relationship in which one party assumes a role of dominating influence over the other. In *Poosathurai*'s case, L.R. 47 I.A. 1 the Board recognised that a sale at an undervalue could be a transaction which a court could set aside as unconscionable if it was shown or could be presumed to have been procured by the exercise of undue influence. Similarly a relationship of banker and customer may become one in which the banker acquires a dominating influence. If he does and a manifestly disadvantageous transaction is proved, there would then be room for the court to presume that it resulted from the exercise of undue influence.

This brings me to *Lloyds Bank Ltd v. Bundy* [1975] Q.B. 326, C.A. It was, as one would expect, conceded by counsel for the respondent that the relationship between banker and customer is not one which ordinarily gives rise to a presumption of undue influence: and that in the ordinary course of banking business a banker can explain the nature of the proposed transaction without laying himself open to a charge of undue influence. This proposition has never been in doubt, though some, it would appear, have thought that the Court of Appeal held otherwise in *Lloyds Bank Ltd v. Bundy*. If any such view has gained currency, let it be destroyed now once and for all time: see Lord Denning M.R. [1975] Q.B. at p. 336F, Cairns L.J. at p. 340D, and Sir Eric Sachs, at pp. 341H–342A. Your Lordships are, of course, not concerned with the interpretation put upon the facts in that case by the Court of Appeal: the present case is not a rehearing of that case. The question which the House does have to answer is: did the court in *Lloyds Bank Ltd v. Bundy* accurately state the law?

Lord Denning M.R. believed that the doctrine of undue influence could be subsumed under a general principle that English courts will grant relief where there has been "inequality of bargaining power" (p. 339). He deliberately avoided reference to the will of one party being dominated or overcome by another. The majority of the court did not follow him: they based their decision on the orthodox view of the doctrine as expounded in *Allcard v. Skinner*. The opinion of the Master of the Rolls, therefore, was not the ground of the court's decision, which was to be found in the view of the majority, for whom Sir Eric Sachs delivered the leading judgment.

Nor has counsel for the respondent sought to rely on Lord Denning M.R.'s general principle; and, in my view, he was right not to do so. The doctrine of undue influence has been sufficiently developed not to need the support of a principle which by its formulation in the language of the law of contract is not appropriate to cover transactions of gift where there is no bargain. The fact of an unequal bargain will, of course, be a relevant feature in some cases of undue influence. But it can never become an appropriate basis of principle of an equitable doctrine which is concerned with transactions "not to be reasonably accounted for on the ground of friendship, relationship, charity, or other ordinary motives on which ordinary men act" (Lindley L.J. in *Allcard v. Skinner* at p. 185). And even in the field of contract I question whether there is any need in the modern law to erect a general principle of relief against inequality of bargaining power. Parliament has undertaken the task—and it is essentially a legislative task—of enacting such restrictions upon freedom of contract as are in its judgment necessary to relieve against the mischief: for example, the hire-purchase and consumer protection legislation of which the Supply of

Goods (Implied Terms) Act 1973, Consumer Credit Act 1974, Consumer Safety Act 1978, Supply of Goods and Services Act 1982 and Insurance Companies Act 1982 are examples. I doubt whether the courts should assume the burden of formulating further restrictions.

For these reasons, I would allow the appeal. In doing so, I would wish to give a warning. There is no precisely defined law setting limits to the equitable jurisdiction of a court to relieve against undue influence. This is the world of doctrine, not of neat and tidy rules. The courts of equity have developed a body of learning enabling relief to be granted where the law has to treat the transaction as unimpeachable unless it can be held to have been procured by undue influence. It is the unimpeachability at law of a disadvantageous transaction which is the starting-point from which the court advances to consider whether the transaction is the product merely of one's own folly or of the undue influence exercised by another. A court in the exercise of this equitable jurisdiction is a court of conscience. Definition is a poor instrument when used to determine whether a transaction is or is not unconscionable: this is a question which depends upon the particular facts of the case."

LORDS KEITH, ROSKILL, BRIDGE and BRANDON agreed.

Appeal allowed.

CIBC MORTGAGES plc v. PITT AND ANOTHER

House of Lords [1993] 4 All E.R. 433

In 1986 Mr and Mrs Pitt's home was valued at £270,000, subject to a mortgage for £16,700. Mr Pitt (H) wanted to borrow money on the house to buy shares. Mrs Pitt (W) was unhappy about this but eventually, under pressure, agreed. H and W signed an application form for a loan by the plaintiffs of £150,000 for the stated purpose of paying off the existing mortgage and buying a holiday home. H and W signed a mortgage offer and legal charge. W received no independent advice and no one suggested to her that she should. She did not read the documents before signing them and did not know the amount being borrowed. H used the loan to speculate on the stock market. When the market crashed in October 1987 he was unable to keep up the mortgage repayments and the plaintiff applied for an order for possession of the house. W contested the application on the ground that she had been induced to sign by H's misrepresentation, fraud and duress. The judge held that H had exercised actual undue influence and that the transaction was manifestly disadvantageous to her but, since H had not acted as the plaintiff's agent and this was not a case of W standing surety for H's debt but a loan jointly to H and W, W's claim failed. The Court of Appeal dismissed W's appeal on the ground that the transaction was *not* manifestly disadvantageous. W appealed.

LORD BROWNE-WILKINSON: I have no doubt that the decision in *Morgan* (above, p. 645) does not extend to cases of actual undue influence. Despite two references in Lord Scarman's speech to cases of actual undue influence, as I read his speech he was primarily concerned to establish that disadvantage had to be shown, not as a constituent element of the cause of action for undue influence, but in order to raise a presumption of undue influence within class 2. (See above, p. 643) That was the only subject matter before the House of Lords in *Morgan* and the passage I have already cited was directed solely to that point. With the exception of a passing reference to *Ormes v. Beadel* (1860) 2 Giff 166, 66 ER 70 all the cases referred to by Lord Scarman were cases of presumed undue influence. In the circumstances, I do not think that this House can have been intending to lay down any general principle applicable to all claims of undue influence, whether actual or presumed.

Whatever the merits of requiring a complainant to show manifest disadvantage in order to raise a class 2 presumption of undue influence, in my judgment there is no logic in imposing such a requirement where actual undue influence has been exercised and proved. Actual undue influence is a species of fraud. Like any other victim of fraud, a person who has been induced by undue influence to carry out a transaction which he did not freely and knowingly enter into is entitled to have that transaction set aside as of right. No case decided before *Morgan* was cited (nor am I aware of any) in which a transaction proved to have been obtained by actual undue influence has been upheld nor is there any case in which a court has even considered whether the transaction was, or was not, advantageous. A man guilty of fraud is no more entitled to argue that the transaction was beneficial to the person defrauded than is a man who has procured a transaction by misrepresentation. The effect of the wrongdoer's conduct is to prevent the wronged party from bringing a free will and properly informed mind to bear on the proposed transaction which accordingly must be set aside in equity as a matter of justice.

I therefore hold that a claimant who proves actual undue influence is not under the further burden of proving that the transaction induced by undue influence was manifestly disadvantageous: he is entitled as of right to have it set aside.

I should add that the exact limits of the decision in *Morgan* may have to be considered in the future. The difficulty is to establish the relationship between the law as laid down in *Morgan* and the long standing principle laid down in the abuse of confidence cases, *viz* the law requires those in a fiduciary position who enter into transactions with those to whom they owe fiduciary duties to establish affirmatively that the transaction was a fair one. . . . The abuse of confidence principle is founded on considerations of general public policy, *viz* that in order to protect those to whom fiduciaries owe duties *as a class* from exploitation by fiduciaries *as a class*, the law imposes a heavy duty on fiduciaries to show the righteousness of the transactions they enter into with those to whom they owe such duties. This principle is in sharp contrast with the view of this House in *Morgan* that in cases of presumed undue influence (a) the law is not based on considerations of public policy and (b) that it is for the claimant to prove that the transaction was disadvantageous rather than for the fiduciary to prove that it was not disadvantageous. Unfortunately, the attention of this House in *Morgan* was not drawn to the abuse of confidence cases and therefore the interaction between the two principles (if indeed they are two separate principles) remains obscure: see also 48 M.L.R. 579 and *Wright v. Carter* [1903] 1 Ch 27, [1900–3] All E.R. Rep. 706.

Notice

Even though, in my view, Mrs Pitt is entitled to set aside the transaction as against Mr Pitt, she has to establish that in some way the plaintiff is affected by the wrongdoing of Mr Pitt so as to be entitled to set aside the legal charge as against the plaintiff.

Applying the decision of this House in *O'Brien*, Mrs Pitt has established actual undue influence by Mr Pitt. The plaintiff will not however be affected by such undue influence unless Mr Pitt was, in a real sense, acting as agent of the plaintiff in procuring Mrs Pitt's agreement or the plaintiff had actual or constructive notice of the undue influence. The judge has correctly held that Mr Pitt was not acting as agent for the plaintiff. The plaintiff had no actual notice of the undue influence. What, then, was known to the plaintiff that could put it on inquiry so as to fix it with constructive notice?

So far as the plaintiff was aware, the transaction consisted of a joint loan to the husband and wife to finance the discharge of an existing mortgage on 26 Alexander Avenue and, as to the balance, to be applied in buying a holiday home. The loan was advanced to both husband and wife jointly. There was nothing to indicate to the plaintiff that this was anything other than a normal advance to a husband and wife for their joint benefit.

Mr Price Q.C. for Mrs Pitt argued that the invalidating tendency which reflects the risk of there being class 2B undue influence (above, p. 643) was, in itself, sufficient to put the plaintiff on inquiry. I reject this submission without hesitation. It accords neither with justice nor with practical common sense. If third parties were to be fixed with constructive notice of undue influence in relation to every transaction between husband and wife, such transactions would become almost impossible. On every purchase of a home in joint names, the building society or bank financing the purchase would have to insist on meeting the wife separately from her husband, advise her as to the nature of the transaction and recommend her to take legal advice separate from that of her husband. If that were not done, the financial institution would have to run the risk of a subsequent attempt by the wife to avoid her liabilities under the mortgage on the grounds of undue influence or misrepresentation. To establish the law in that sense would not benefit the average married couple and would discourage financial institutions from making the advance.

What distinguishes the case of the joint advance from the surety case is that, in the latter, there is not only the possibility of undue influence having been exercised but also the increased risk of it having in fact been exercised because, at least on its face, the guarantee by a wife of her husband's debts is not for her financial benefit. It is the combination of these two factors that puts the creditor on inquiry.

For these reasons I agree with the Court of Appeal and would dismiss the appeal.

Lords Templeman, Lowry, Slynn and Woolf agreed.

Appeal dismissed.

ALEC LOBB (GARAGES) LTD AND OTHERS v. TOTAL OIL G.B. LTD

Court of Appeal [1985] 1 All E.R. 303 [1985] 1 W.L.R. 173

Alec Lobb (Garages) Ltd (the company) carried on a garage business on a site of which it owned the freehold. It was a private company and Alec Lobb and his mother were the only directors and shareholders. The company was indebted to Total and in serious financial difficulties. Mr Lobb made a proposal to Total to solve these difficulties and, after negotiation, in 1969 the company leased the site of the garage to Total for 51 years at a peppercorn rent in consideration of a premium of £35,000 paid by Total; and a sublease (the lease-back) was granted by Total to Mr and Mrs Lobb (not the company) for a term of 21 years, with a right for either party to terminate at the end of the seventh or fourteenth years, at an initial rent of £2,250. The lease-back contained an absolute prohibition on assignment and tie provisions throughout the term requiring the lessees to take all their petrol from Total and to provide a proper and efficient service at all reasonable times.

In an action commenced in 1979 the company and Mr and Mrs Lobb claimed to set aside the lease and lease-back on the grounds (*inter alia*) that the tie constituted an unreasonable restraint of trade. (See below, p. 662.) The trial judge held that the tie provisions were unreasonable and void but severable from the remaining provisions. On appeal the company argued (i) that the tie provisions were not severable and the transaction was wholly void; and (ii) alternatively, that the transaction ought to be set aside in equity because there was inequality of bargaining power between Total on the one hand and Mr and Mrs Lobb and the company on the other. Total cross-appealed, arguing that the lease-back was not a restraint of trade and that, even if it were it was reasonable and therefore valid.

DILLON L.J.: It is logical to consider the cross-appeal first and I can deal very shortly with the second of the above arguments: In *Esso Petroleum Co. Ltd v. Harper's Garage (Stourport) Ltd* (below, p. 690) it was held that the doctrine of restraint of trade had no applications to restraints imposed on persons who, before the transaction by which the restraints were imposed, had no right whatsoever to trade at all on the land in question. Their Lordships had in mind in particular the case where an owner of land grants a lease of the land to a person who had no previous right to occupy the land, and imposes by the lease restraints on the lessee's power to trade as he likes on the land. Such a lease would ordinarily not be regarded as an agreement in restraint of trade. In the present case however the granting of the lease-back to Mr and Mrs Lobb rather than to the company was a palpable device in an endeavour to evade the doctrine of restraint of trade. Mr and Mrs Lobb were only selected as lessees because they were the proprietors of the company previously in occupation. The court has ample power to pierce the corporate veil, recognise a continued identity of occupation and hold, as it should, that Total can be in no better position quoad restraints of trade by granting the lease-back to Mr and Mrs Lobb than if it had granted the lease-back to the company; see generally *Gilford Motor Co. Ltd v. Horne* [1933] Ch. 935, 961–962, and *D.H.N. Food Distributors Ltd v. Tower Hamlets London Borough Council* [1976] 1 W.L.R. 852.

As for the argument that the lease-back is not an agreement in restraint of trade because the restrictions in the lease-back derive from a disposal by the company of a large part of its interest in the property, I have had considerable difficulty in understanding the argument. It is of course clear that there is no agreement in restraint of trade where a person deprives himself of all right to trade as he wishes on land by selling all his interest in that land. In the present case, however, that is not what the company did and the whole object was that trade should continue in the property. The lease and lease-back have to be taken together as two essential parts of one transaction, and in my judgment it follows from the reasoning of their

Lordships in the *Esso* case that the agreement constituted by the lease and lease-back is an agreement in restraint of trade in as much as it subjects the company to a continuation for a longer period of the restraints on trading which had validly been imposed for a much shorter period before July 25, 1969 . . ."

[His Lordship went on to hold that the restraint was reasonable pointing out that the consideration for the restraint, the premium of £35,000, was arrived at by a professional valuation of the 51-year lease, subject to the lease-back: that the period of 51 years was chosen because, if the term had been less than 50 years, the premium would have been taxable as income in the company's hands; that the premium for a short term could not have been enough to recapitalise the company; and that the lessees were free to break the clause at the end of seven years. He went on:]

In the circumstances of this case, and not least because at the time of the grant of the lease and lease-back the company was subject to a valid tie for a term of three to four years, I can see no real significance in the difference between a tie for five years and the term of seven years to the first break under the lease-back.

In the light of these factors the restraints on trading in the lease-back were in my judgment reasonable. Accordingly I would allow the cross-appeal.

It follows that the question of severance which is sought to be raised by the appellants' first ground of appeal does not arise. None the less, in deference to the argument and in case this dispute goes further, it may be appropriate that I should express my view. . . . [Having quoted from Lord Selborne L.C. in *Earl of Aylesford v. Morris* (1873) L.R. 8 Ch.App. 484 at 490–491 his Lordship continued:]

The whole emphasis is on extortion, or undue advantage taken of weakness, an unconscientious use of the power arising out of the inequality of the parties' circumstances, and on unconscientious use of power which the court might in certain circumstances be entitled to infer from a particular—and in these days notorious—relationship unless the contract is proved to have been in fact fair, just and reasonable. Nothing leads me to suppose that the course of the development of the law over the last 100 years has been such that the emphasis on unconscionable conduct or unconscientious use of power has gone and relief will now be granted in equity in a case such as the present if there has been unequal bargaining power, even if the stronger has not used his strength unconscionably. I agree with the judgment of Browne-Wilkinson J., in *Multiservice Bookbinding Ltd v. Marden* [1979] Ch.84, which sets out that to establish that a term is unfair and unconscionable it is not enough to show that it is, objectively, unreasonable.

In the present case there are findings of fact by the deputy judge that the conduct of Total was not unconscionable, coercive or oppressive. There is ample evidence to support those findings and they are not challenged by the appellants. Their case is that the judge applied the wrong test; where there is unequal bargaining power, the test is, they say, whether its terms are fair, just and reasonable and it is unnecessary to consider whether the conduct of the stronger party was oppressive or unconscionable. I do not accept the appellants' proposition of law. In my judgment the findings of the judge conclude this ground of appeal against the appellants.

Inequality of bargaining power must anyhow be a relative concept. It is seldom in any negotiation that the bargaining powers of the parties are absolutely equal. Any individual wanting to borrow money from a bank, building society or other financial institution in order to pay his liabilities or buy some property he urgently wants to acquire will have virtually no bargaining power; he will have to take or leave the terms offered to him. So, with house property in a seller's market, the purchaser will not have equal bargaining power with the vendor. But Lord Denning M.R. did not envisage that any contract entered into in such circumstances would, without more, be reviewed by the courts by the objective criterion of what was reasonable: see *Lloyds Bank Ltd v. Bundy* [1975] Q.B. 326, 336. The courts would only interfere in exceptional cases where as a matter of common fairness it was not right that the strong should be allowed to push the weak to the wall. The concepts of unconscionable conduct and of the exercise by the stronger of coercive power are thus brought in and in the present case they are negatived by the deputy judge's findings.

Even if, contrary to my view just expressed, the company and Mr and Mrs Lobb had initially in 1969 a valid claim in equity to have the lease and lease-back set aside as a result of the inequality of bargaining power, that claim was, in my judgment, barred by laches well before the issue of the writ in this action.

DUNN and WALLER L.JJ. delivered judgment dismissing the appeal.

Appeal dismissed.

ATLAS EXPRESS LTD v. KAFKO LTD

Queen's Bench Division [1989] Q.B. 833; [1989] 3 W.L.R. 389;
[1989] 1 All E.R. 641

Kafko, a small company dealing in basketware, had secured a large contract from Woolworths and had obtained a large quantity of goods to fulfil it. They entered into a contract with Atlas, a national road carrier, to distribute the basketware to Woolworths' shops. Atlas's depot manager, Hope, had inspected a range of cartons used by Kafko and estimated that a trailer would carry a minimum of 400 and possibly as many as 600 cartons. It was on that basis that he quoted an agreed rate of £1.10 per carton. He had underestimated the size of the cartons and the first load contained only 200 which Hope said was not financially viable. After discussion but no agreement with Kafko, Hope sent an empty trailer to Kafko's premises on November 18, 1986. The driver carried a document, "Amended/Transferred Account Details," specifying a minimum charge of £440 per trailer. His instructions were that if the agreement was not signed, he was to take the trailer away unloaded. It was essential to Kafko's commercial survival that they should be able to meet delivery dates. It would have been difficult, if not impossible, to find alternative carriers to do so. A Kafko director, Armiger, signed the agreement and the deliveries were made.

TUCKER J.: I find that when Mr Armiger signed that agreement he did so unwillingly and under compulsion. He believed on reasonable grounds that it would be very difficult, if not impossible, to negotiate with another contractor. He did not regard the fact that he had signed the new agreement as binding the defendants to its terms. He had no bargaining power. He did not regard it as a genuine armslength renegotiation in which he had a free and equal say and, in my judgment, that view was fully justified.

In the words of the co-director, Mr Fox, he felt that he was "over a barrel." He tried in vain to contact Mr Hope but, as he said to Mr Armiger, they really had no option but to sign. I accept the evidence of the Woolworth manager, Mr Graham, that if the defendants had told them that they could not supply the goods Woolworth would have sued them for loss of profit and would have ceased trading with them. I find that this was well known to the defendants' directors. . . .

The issue which I have to determine is whether the defendants are bound by the agreement signed on their behalf on November 18, 1986. The defendants contend that they are not bound, for two reasons: first, because the agreement was signed under duress; second, because there was no consideration for it.

The first question raises an interesting point of law, that is, whether economic duress is a concept known to English law.

Economic duress must be distinguished from commercial pressure, which on any view is not sufficient to vitiate consent. The borderline between the two may in some cases be indistinct. But the authors of *Chitty on Contracts* (25th ed., 1983) and of *Goff and Jones on the Law of Restitution* (3rd ed., 1986) appear to recognise that in appropriate cases economic duress may afford a defence, and in my judgment it does. It is clear to me that in a number of English cases judges have acknowledged the existence of this concept.

Thus, in *D. & C. Builders Ltd v. Rees*, above, p. 267 Lord Denning M.R. said: "No person can insist on a settlement procured by intimidation." And in *The Siboen and the Sibotre* [1976] 1 Lloyd's Rep. 293 at 336 Kerr J. appeared to accept that economic duress could operate in appropriate circumstances. A similar conclusion was reached by Mocatta J. in *The Atlantic Baron*, above, p. 237.

In particular, there are passages in the judgment of Lord Scarman in *Pao On v. Lau Yiu*, above, p. 228, which clearly indicate recognition of the concept, where Lord Scarman said:

"Duress, whatever form it takes, is a coercion of the will so as to vitiate consent. Their Lordships agree with the observation of Kerr J. in *The Siboen and The Sibotre* [1976] 1 Lloyd's Rep. 293 at 336 that in a contractual situation commercial pressure is not enough. There must be present some factor 'which could in law be regarded as a coercion of his will so as to vitiate his consent.' This conception is in line with what was said in this Board's decision in *Barton* v. *Armstrong*, above, p. 640 by Lord Wilberforce and Lord Simon of Glaisdale, observations with which the majority judgment appears to be in agreement. In determining whether there was a coercion of will such that there was no true consent, it is material to enquire whether the person alleged to have been coerced did or did not protest; whether, at the time he was allegedly coerced into making the contract, he did or did not have an alternative course open to him such as an adequate legal remedy; whether he was independently advised; and whether after entering the contract he took steps to avoid it. All these matters are, as was recognised in *Maskell v. Horner* [1915] 3 K.B. 106, relevant in determining whether he acted voluntarily or not. In the present case there is unanimity amongst the judges below that there was no coercion of Lau's will. In the Court of Appeal the trial judge's finding (already quoted) that Lau considered the matter thoroughly, chose to avoid litigation, and formed the opinion that the risk in giving the guarantee was more apparent than real was upheld. In short, there was commercial pressure, but no coercion. Even if this Board was disposed, which it is not, to take a different view, it would not substitute its opinion for that of the judges below on this question of fact. It is, therefore, unnecessary for the Board to embark on an enquiry into the question whether English law recognises a category of duress known as 'economic duress.' But, since the question has been fully argued in this appeal, their Lordships will indicate very briefly the view which they have formed. At common law money paid under economic compulsion could be recovered in an action for money had and received: see *Astley v. Reynolds* (1731) 2 Stra. 915. The compulsion had to be such that the party was deprived of 'his freedom of exercising his will' (see 2 Stra. 915 at 916). It is doubtful, however, whether at common law any duress other than duress to the person sufficed to render a contract voidable; see Blackstone's Commentaries (12th ed. 1793), Vol. 1, pp. 130–131 and *Skeate v. Beale* (1841) 11 Ad. & El. 983. American law (Williston on Contracts (3rd ed., 1970), Chap. 47) now recognises that a contract may be avoided on the ground of economic duress. The commercial pressure alleged to constitute such duress must, however, be such that the victim must have entered the contract against his will, must have had no alternative course open to him, and must have been confronted with coercive acts by the party exerting the pressure: see Williston on Contracts, Chapter 47, s.1603. American judges pay great attention to such evidential matters as the effectiveness of the alternative remedy available, the fact or absence of protest, the availability of independent advice, the benefit received, and the speed with which the victim sought to avoid the contract. Recently two English judges have recognised that commercial pressure may constitute duress the presence of which can render a contract voidable [Lord Scarman then referred to the judgments of Kerr and Mocatta JJ. to which I have referred and continued:] Both stressed that the pressure must be such that the victim's consent to the contract was not a voluntary act on his part. In their Lordship's view, there is nothing contrary to principle in recognising economic duress as a factor which may render a contract voidable, provided always that the basis of such recognition is that it must amount to a coercion of will, which vitiates consent. It must be shown that the payment made or the contract entered into was not a voluntary act."

A further case which was not cited to me was *B & S Contracts and Design Ltd v. Victor Green Publications Ltd* [1984] I.C.R. 419 at 423, where Eveleigh L.J. referred to the speech of Lord Diplock in another uncited case, *Universe Tankships Inc. of Monrovia v. International Transport Workers' Federation* [1983] A.C. 366 at 384:

"The rationale is that his apparent consent was induced by pressure exercised on him by that other party which the law does not regard as legitimate, with the consequence that the consent is treated in law as revocable unless approbated either expressly or by implication after the illegitimate pressure has ceased to operate on his mind."

In commenting on this Eveleigh L.J. said of the word "legitimate" ([1984] I.C.R. 419 at 423):

"For the purpose of this case it is sufficient to say that if the claimant has been influenced against his will to pay money under the threat of unlawful damage to his economic interest he will be entitled to claim that money back . . ."

Reverting to the case before me, I find that the defendants' apparent consent to the agreement was induced by pressure which was illegitimate and I find that it was not approbated. In my judgment that pressure can properly be described as economic duress, which is a concept recognised by English law, and which in the circumstances of the present case vitiates the defendants' apparent consent to the agreement.

In any event, I find that there was no consideration for the new agreement. The plaintiffs were already obliged to deliver the defendants' goods at the rates agreed under the terms of the original agreement. There was no consideration for the increased minimum charge of £440 per trailer.

Action dismissed.

Question
What is the difference between this case and *Williams v. Roffey Bros.*, above, p. 231? Does it lie in the issue of consideration or that of economic duress? Both are cases of a party who has made a bad bargain seeking additional payment. Was not the "benefit" to Kafko of having the agreement performed at least as great as that to Roffey Bros? Does the court take the side of "the little company" (*Cf.* Lord Denning's opening words in *D. & C. Builders v. Rees*, above, p. 267)?

CTN CASH AND CARRY LTD v. GALLAGHER LTD

Court of Appeal [1994] 4 All E.R. 714.

The plaintiffs (C) bought cigarettes from the defendants (G) for resale in C's warehouses in six towns. G were not contractually bound to sell, each sale being a separate contract. G had arranged credit facilities for C but had an absolute discretion to withdraw these facilities. In November 1986, C ordered cigarettes to the value of £17,000 to be delivered to their Preston warehouse. By mistake, G delivered to the Burnley warehouse. C pointed out G's mistake and G agreed to arrange the carriage of the goods from Burnley to Preston but, the day before they were due to be collected, the goods were stolen. G believed, wrongly, that the goods were at C's risk and demanded payment of the price. C declined to pay until G made it clear that they would not, in future grant credit facilities unless the price was paid. C paid the price, as the lesser of the two evils. Their subsequent action to recover it on the ground of economic duress failed. They appealed.

STEYN L.J.: The present dispute does not concern a protected relationship. It also does not arise in the context of dealings between a supplier and a consumer. The dispute arises out of arm's length commercial dealings between two trading companies. It is true that the defendants were the sole distributors of the popular brands of cigarettes. In a sense the defendants were in a monopoly position. The control of monopolies is, however, a matter for Parliament. Moreover, the common law does not recognise the doctrine of inequality of bargaining power in commercial dealings (see *National Westminster Bank plc v. Morgan* [1985] 1 All E.R. 821, [1985] A.C. 686). The fact that the defendants were in a monopoly position cannot therefore by itself convert what is not otherwise duress into duress.

A second characteristic of the case is that the defendants were in law entitled to refuse to enter into any future contracts with the plaintiffs for any reason whatever or for no reason at all. Such a decision not to deal with the plaintiffs would have been financially damaging to the defendants, but it would have been lawful. A fortiori, it was lawful for the defendants, for any reason or for no reason, to insist that they would no longer grant credit to the plaintiffs. The defendants' demand for payment of the invoice, coupled with the threat to withdraw credit, was neither a breach of contract nor a tort.

A third, and critically important, characteristic of the case is the fact that the defendants bona fide thought that the goods were at the risk of the plaintiffs and that the plaintiffs owed the defendants the sum in question. The defendants exerted commercial pressure on the plaintiffs in order to obtain payment of a sum which they bona fide considered due to them. The defendants' motive in threatening withdrawal of credit facilities was commercial self-interest in obtaining a sum that they considered due to them.

I also readily accept that the fact that the defendants have used lawful means does not by itself remove the case from the scope of the doctrine of economic duress. Professor Birks, in *An Introduction to the Law of Restitution* (1989) p. 177, lucidly explains:

> "Can lawful pressures also count? This is a difficult question, because, if the answer is that they can, the only viable basis for discriminating between acceptable and unacceptable pressures is not positive law but social morality. In other words, the judges must say what pressures (though lawful outside the restitutionary context) are improper as contrary to prevailing standards. That makes the judges, not the law or the legislature, the arbiters of social evaluation. On the other hand, if the answer is that lawful pressures are always exempt, those who devise outrageous but technically lawful means of compulsion must always escape restitution until the legislature declares the abuse unlawful. It is tolerably clear that, at least where they can be confident of a general consensus in favour of their evaluation, the courts are willing to apply a standard of impropriety rather than technical unlawfulness."

And there are a number of cases where English courts have accepted that a threat may be illegitimate when coupled with a demand for payment even if the threat is one of lawful action (see *Thorne v. Motor Trade Association* [1937] 3 All E.R. 157 at 160–161, [1937] A.C. 797 at 806–807. *Mutual Finance Ltd v. John Wetton & Sons Ltd* [1937] 2 All E.R. 657, [1937] 2 K.B.

389 and *Universe Tankships Inc. of Monrovia v. International Transport Workers' Federation* [1982] 2 All E.R. 67 at 76, 89, [1983] 1 A.C. 366 at 384, 401). On the other hand, Goff and Jones *Law of Restitution* (3rd ed., 1986) p. 240 observed that English courts have wisely not accepted any general principle that a threat not to contract with another except on certain terms, may amount to duress.

We are being asked to extend the categories of duress of which the law will take cognisance. That is not necessarily objectionable, but it seems to me that an extension capable of covering the present case, involving "lawful act duress" in a commercial context in pursuit of a bona fide claim, would be a radical one with far-reaching implications. It would introduce a substantial and undesirable element of uncertainty in the commercial bargaining process. Moreover, it will often enable bona fide settled accounts to be reopened when parties to commercial dealings fall out. The aim of our commercial law ought to be to encourage fair dealing between parties. But it is a mistake for the law to set its sights too highly when the critical inquiry is not whether the conduct is lawful but whether it is morally or socially unacceptable. That is the inquiry in which we are engaged. In my view there are policy considerations which militate against ruling that the defendants obtained payment of the disputed invoice by duress.

Outside the field of protected relationships, and in a purely commercial context, it might be a relatively rare case in which "lawful act duress" can be established. And it might be particularly difficult to establish duress if the defendant bona fide considered that his demand was valid. In this complex and changing branch of the law I deliberately refrain from saying "never". But as the law stands, I am satisfied that the defendants' conduct in this case did not amount to duress.

It is an unattractive result, inasmuch as the defendants are allowed to retain a sum which at the trial they became aware was not in truth due to them. But in my view the law compels the result.

For these reasons, I would dismiss the appeal.

FARQUHARSON L.J. agreed and NICHOLLS V.C. delivered a concurring judgment.

Appeal dismissed.

Note

G, unlike Atlas Express (above, p. 653), were not threatening to break any contract, but they were demanding money to which they were not entitled and reinforcing their demand with a threat. Steyn L.J. thought the result "unattractive" and Nicholls V.C., who was a "little troubled" by it, noted that no claim for restitution based on wrongful retention of the money had been brought.

Cf. Cook v. Wright, above, p. 214. The withdrawal of the threat to withhold credit facilities was consideration for the payment in the present case, just as the withdrawal of the threat to sue was in *Cook v. Wright*.

What if the plaintiffs had paid because they shared the erroneous belief of the defendants that the goods were at the plaintiffs' risk? Might the plaintiffs then have recovered under the principle of *Solle v. Butcher*? The mistake was more fundamental than in *Solle*.

CHAPTER 19

VOID AND ILLEGAL CONTRACTS

A contract may be complete and perfect so far as offer, acceptance and consideration are concerned and yet still fail because its objects are contrary to the policy of the law. This may be because they directly infringe a rule of common law or a statutory provision or because they are regarded as "contrary to public policy." This last concept is inevitably vague and imprecise and accordingly the courts are careful to assert that no new heads of public policy may now be created; but for all that, opinions as to what is injurious to the public welfare must naturally vary with variations in social, moral and even political thought down the years. Again, the consequences of a contract's falling into one of the invalidated categories vary and, for this reason, it is thought fit to distinguish offending agreements as "void" simply or "illegal." The distinction is thought to be justified and important in three main directions:

(a) void provisions may, in appropriate cases, be "severed" from the contract, so leaving unoffending undertakings fully enforceable; this does not apply to void and illegal contracts;
(b) where a contract is void, money or property which has been transferred under it may be generally recovered in a quasi-contractual or other action. Ownership does not pass under a void contract but it may do so under a contract which is illegal. Where property has been transferred under a contract which is illegal but not void, recovery is possible only in cases where the parties are not equally at fault and only by the less guilty party;
(c) collateral transactions which would themselves be tainted by an illegal contract, will be unimpaired by connection with a merely void one.

The terminology used by the courts is unhappily not uniform and some contracts are commonly described as illegal when their effects are more properly consonant with mere voidness—agreements in restraint of trade are a conspicuous example. Terminology in this connection is very varied generally—*contra bonos mores,* "illegal," "void," "unenforceable," "immoral," etc., being used quite indiscriminately in the cases. In this chapter, accordingly, some of the principal causes of voidness and illegality and their effects are offered for consideration, with statutory cases discussed first and the others classified into separate groups of void and illegal contracts respectively.

Section 1. The Contracts Described

(a) CASES AFFECTED BY STATUTE

Where a contract offends against the provisions of a statute, much depends upon the object, purpose and interpretation of the particular provision. The one relatively coherent body of relevant doctrine on statutory invalidation of contracts is that dealing with gaming and wagering.

Wagering contracts are not illegal but void. The Gaming Act 1845, s.18, provides:

"All contracts or agreements, whether by parole or in writing, by way of gaming or wagering, shall be null and void; and no suit shall be brought or maintained in any court of law and equity for recovering any sum of money or valuable thing alleged to be won upon any wager, or which shall have been deposited in the hands of any person to abide the event on which any wager shall have been made. . . ."

The matters which fall to be considered are:

(a) the nature of a wagering contract;
(b) the effect of section 18
    (i) on proceedings in respect of the wager itself;
    (ii) on collateral transactions;
(c) agency and wagering.

A. The classical definition of a wagering contract is that of Hawkins J. at first instance in *Carlill*'s case (above, p. 31) who said:

"A wagering contract is one which two persons, professing to hold opposite views touching the issue of a future uncertain event, mutually agree that, dependent upon the determination of that event, one shall win from the other, and that other shall pay or hand over to him, a sum of money or other stake; neither of the contracting parties having any other interest in that contract than the sum or stake he will so win or lose, there being no other real consideration for the making of such contract by either of the parties."

The "uncertain event" may be a presently existing fact which is unknown to the parties. It is as much a wager when A bets B £5 that he is heavier than B as when A bets B £5 that the Conservatives will win the next General Election. Both parties must stand to gain or lose: if one may win but cannot lose, then the transaction is not a wager: see *Ellesmere v. Wallace* [1929] 2 Ch. 1. Again, it will be noted that Hawkins J. spoke of the parties not "having any other interest. . . ." It is the existence of such other interest which removes contracts of insurance from the realm of wagers. If A by a £50 premium insures for £1,000 against his wife having twins, this resembles a bet at 20 to 1 against twins; but A's interest in the size and maintenance of his household is insurable and the contract accordingly valid. It would be different if B, who had no liability for the maintenance of A's household, purported to effect a similar insurance.

It is the substance not the form of a transaction which determines whether it is a wager. In *Brogden v. Marriott* (1836) 3 Bing.N.C. 88 A agreed to sell, and B to buy, a horse for £200 if it trotted at 18 m.p.h. within the mouth, or a shilling if it did not attain this speed. This was held to be a bet on whether the horse would attain the speed. It is thought, however, that the result would be different if the difference in price represented a genuine attempt to assess the value of the horse with and without the capacity in issue. Suppose, for instance, that A agrees to make and sell to B a clay-pulverising machine—which both know to be commercially useless unless it produces six tons of clay-powder per hour; if they agree that the price shall be £1,000 if the machine attains this standard but only £100 if it does not, it is thought that the transaction would be valid.

Where the nature of transaction is ambiguous, regard must be had to the "interest and purpose" of both parties. If the interest and purpose of one of them is not wagering, it is not a wagering contract. In *Morgan Grenfell & Co. Ltd v. Welwyn Hatfield District Council* [1995] 1 All E.R. 1 Hobhouse J. held that an "interest rate swap contract" between a banker (the "fixed interest payer") and a local authority (the "floating rate payer") was not a wager because the interest and purpose of the local authority was not to wager but to achieve an accounting purpose. Hobhouse J. said:

"Certain contracts are by their very character gaming or wagering contracts, such as a bet upon what horse will win a particular race. Entering into such a contract inevitably has the purpose of wagering. Other contracts may on their face appear to have nothing to do with any wager but it may be possible to prove that the purported contract was a sham and that the true transaction was a wagering transaction. In between there are, as is visualised by the passages I have quoted, contracts which may or may not be wagering contracts, depending upon the interests of the parties and their purpose in entering into the particular contract. Interest rate swap contracts are such contracts. Since they provide for the payment of differences they are capable of being entered into by way of gaming or wagering. They have, at least potentially, a speculative character deriving from the fact that the obligations of the floating rate payer are to be ascertained by reference to a fluctuating market rate that may be higher or lower than the fixed rate at any given time. Such a contract is capable of being entered into by two parties with the purpose of wagering upon future interest rates."

Hobhouse J. added that even if the contract had been a wager, it would have been saved by s.63 of the Financial Sevices Act 1986, being entered into "by way of business" within the meaning of the Act. *Cf. City Index Ltd v. Leslie* [1991] 3 All E.R. 180, C.A.

B. The provision of section 18 that "no suit shall be brought for recovering" either the wager or a stake deposited with a stakeholder is directed at proceedings by the parties to the wager themselves in respect of it. Thus, if stakes have been deposited with a third person, either party to the wager could recover his own stake from the stakeholder, so long as it has not been appropriated to the other party: *Diggle v. Higgs* (1877) 2 Ex.D. 422. Similarly, if the loser had paid his wager to a person acting as agent for the winner, the latter would be able to recover the sum from the agent even though he would have been unable to proceed direct against the loser.[1]

(i) The effect of the provision in question is like that of non-compliance with the Statute of Frauds (above, p. 5), that is, it is procedural in operation, barring action to recover what is won on a wager. The significance of this became manifest in *Hill v. William Hill (Park Lane) Ltd* [1949] A.C. 530. As a wager is not illegal but void, it followed that an agreement to pay a sum won upon a wager, with a fresh consideration, would not be tainted. Thus, if a loser who had not paid his bet were, when pressed by the winner to promise to pay the amount, for example if the winner would refrain from, say, reporting him to his college tutor or his employer, there would be valid consideration for such promise by the loser and the winner could sue thereon. This was accepted in *Hyams v. Stuart King* [1908] 2 K.B. 696; but in *Hill v. William Hill* the House of Lords, while not denying that such a course produced a new and valid contract, emphasised the wording of section 18 and held that the sum so promised was "a sum . . . alleged to be won upon any wager" within the section and therefore irrecoverable by action. Problems might arise, however, if the subsequent agreement were not for the amount of the betting debt but for some other thing. Suppose that the loser promises that, if the winner does not report him to his father, he (the loser) will supply him with groceries for six months or will give him a motor-cycle: if he defaulted on this promise, would the winner be excluded from action to enforce it?

(ii) The problem of payment raises also the issue of collateral transactions, especially negotiable instruments—for settlement of bets will often be made by cheque—and loans. See Cheshire, Fifoot and Furmston, *Law of Contract* (12th ed.), pp. 334–339.

C. A special question of agency arises in connection with wagering. It is a general principle of agency that the principal must indemnify his agent for expenses

[1] *Cf. per* Scrutton L.J., *Cheshire & Co. v. Vaughan Bros. & Co.* [1920] 3 K.B. 240 at 255.

incurred in performance of the agency. It should therefore follow that, if a principal instructed his agent to place bets for him, the agent should be able to recover from the principal the sum so expended. This was indeed the position at common law, as is seen in the case of *Read v. Anderson* (1882) 10 Q.B.D. 100 and (1884) 13 Q.B.D. 779. This principle, however, offered an obvious loophole in the general fight of the law to make gambling debts irrecoverable and the gap was closed by the Gaming Act 1892, s.1:

> Any promise, express or implied, to pay any person any sum of money paid by him under or in respect of any contract or agreement rendered null and void by [the Gaming Act, 1845], or to pay any sum of money by way of commission, fee, reward, or otherwise in respect of any such contract, or of any services in relation thereto or in connection therewith, shall be null and void, and no action shall be brought or maintained to recover any such sum of money.

In summary, it can be seen that the general object of the policy of the law has been to make gambling a matter outside the province and protection of the courts, in which connection the concepts of illegality proper, voidness and unenforceability have all been employed.

Note

In *A.R. Dennis & Co. Ltd v. Campbell* [1978] 1 Q.B. 365, the defendant, the manager of one of the plaintiff's betting shops, allowed a customer, contrary to the plaintiff's instructions, to place bets on credit to the amount of £1,000. The customer never paid the sum. The plaintiff brought an action for £1,000 for the defendant's breach of his contract of employment: the defendant argued that the plaintiff had no cause of action because the contract with the customer was null and void under the Gaming Act 1845, s.18, and its performance could not be enforced in legal proceedings. Wien J. gave judgment for the plaintiff, holding that the action was on the defendant's breach of contract of employment which was not vitiated by any gaming transaction. The Court of Appeal (Lord Denning, M.R., Geoffrey Lane and Eveleigh, L.JJ.) allowed the defendant's appeal. Lord Denning, M.R. said: "The plaintiffs say that they are unable to recover (£1,000) from (the customer) because it is a void transaction, and so they claim it against Mr Campbell. The answer is that they simply cannot. Section 18 goes on to say as a second limb:

> 'no suit shall be brought or maintained in any court of law or equity for recovering any sum of money or valuable thing alleged to be won upon any wager . . .'

At one time that limb was thought to be mere procedure . . . but the House of Lords in *Hill v. William Hill (Park Lane) Ltd* (above, p. 661) held that that second limb was a perfectly good limb which operated separately from the first limb. It seems to me clear that this £1,000 here is caught by it. It is a sum of money alleged by the company to be won upon wagers. They say they won £1,000 on these bets. So by reason of the section they cannot recover the £1,000 at all."

(b) VOID CONTRACTS

There are three main groups of such contracts—those in restraint of trade, those to oust the jurisdiction of the courts and those to the prejudice of the married state.

(i) *Contracts in Restraint of Trade*

These agreements themselves may in turn be subdivided into three main types:

(a) agreements whereby a vendor of a business covenants with his purchaser that he will not carry on business in competition with him;
(b) agreements whereby a servant covenants with his master not to compete with the latter's business upon leaving his service;

(c) agreements whereby a group of traders contract to regulate their output, prices, etc.

Type (c) is now regulated by the Restrictive Trade Practices Act 1976. It is admittedly possible that a combination which is not invalidated by the Act could be held void at common law but that prospect is so remote as to make further consideration here of such contracts unnecessary and the reader is consequently referred to specialist works such as Albery and Fletcher-Cooke, *Monopolies and Restrictive Trade Practices*.

The general rules regarding the first two types of agreement are discussed and explained in the speeches, particularly, of Lord Macnaghten in *Nordenfelt's Case* [1894] A.C. 535 and Lord Parker in *Herbert Morris & Co. v. Saxelby* [1916] 1 A.C. 688 and may be summed up as follows:

(1) Every covenant in restraint of trade is contrary to public policy and prima facie void: but a covenant may be upheld if
   (a) the *covenantee* shows that it is reasonable as between the parties to it; *and*
   (b) the *covenantor* does not show that it is unreasonable in the interests of the public.
(2) Both (a) and (b) are matters of law for the decision of the judge.

While these have been hitherto the principal categories of offending agreements, it is important to note that they are not exclusive. In particular, the agreements known as "solus" agreements, whereby garages become tied to particular suppliers of motor fuels, have in recent years come before the courts: see *Alec Lobb (Garages) Ltd v. Total Oil*, (above, p. 650) and *Esso Petroleum v. Harper's Garage* (below, p. 690); it is also clear that the provisions of professional bodies for the conduct of their members may also constitute a restraint of trade which cannot be upheld as reasonable: see *Dickson v. Pharmaceutical Society of Great Britain* [1967] Ch. 708; [1967] 2 All E.R. 558, C.A.; [1970] A.C. 403, H.L.; and the provisions of the Football League and Football Association concerning the transfer and retention of players were found to offend against public policy in *Eastham v. Newcastle United Football Club* [1964] Ch. 413; in respect of cricket, see *Greig v. Insole* [1978] 1 W.L.R. 302. In respect of restraint provisions in partnership agreements between medical practitioners, see *Peyton v. Mindham* [1972] 1 W.L.R. 8; [1971] 3 All E.R. 1215 (Pennycuick V.-C.).

In view of their relative frequency of occurrence and their importance, contracts in restraint of trade will be used (below, p. 689) to illustrate void contracts.

(ii) *Agreements to Oust the Jurisdiction of the Courts*

That agreements to oust the jurisdiction of the courts are "illegal and void on grounds of public policy" has been already noted (above, p. 191) and a principle has been suggested to distinguish such ouster—which is ineffective—from an arrangement where there is a declared intention not to create legal relations, which is effective.

The application of that principle to a contract containing an arbitration clause is that recourse to the courts cannot be prevented. But it is possible effectively to provide that no action shall be brought *until* an arbitration award has been made. A clause so providing is called a *Scott v. Avery* clause, after the case in which it was upheld: *Scott v. Avery* (1856) 5 H.L.C. 811.

(iii) *Agreements Prejudicial to the Married State*

Once again three main kinds of transaction are invalidated by the legal policy which protects the status of marriage:

(a) A contract which purports to impose on one of the parties a restraint upon his liberty to marry whom he pleases. Thus, where A contracted under seal with B that he would not marry anyone other than B and would pay her £2,000 if he did so, it was held that the deed was void: *Lowe v. Peers* (1768) 4 Burr. 2225. It is to be noted that, in that case, neither A nor B directly promised to marry the other: an ordinary engagement to marry with the reciprocal promises of the parties was, of course, a perfectly valid contract at common law. The action for breach of promise of marriage was abolished by section 1(1) of the Law Reform (Miscellaneous Provisions) Act, 1970.

(b) A contract under which one party is to receive a remuneration for bringing about an engagement to marry. Such a contract is generally known as a "marriage brokage" contract and is void. The reader is referred to *Hermann v. Charlesworth* [1905] 2 K.B. 123 and to R. Powell, 6 *Current Legal Problems*, 254–273.

(c) A contract which tends to encourage immorality or infidelity in a party to an existing marriage.

An agreement entered into by H and W as to possible *future* separation is bad because it is potentially conducive to a weakening of marital bonds: *H. v. W.* (1857) 3 K. & J. 382. It would be a different matter in the case of an agreement for immediate separation which is, and long has been, valid. The distinction of course is that in the latter case the marriage has already broken down when the agreement is made.

(c) ILLEGAL CONTRACTS

Merely void contracts as just considered all bear their invalidating element, as it were, on the face of the agreement. In the illegal contracts proper, to which we now turn, the contract may be illegal *ex facie* or, while apparently good on its face, be vitiated by the purpose or motive behind it. This can be a matter of the greatest importance in considering the consequences and effects of an illegal contract, because the vitiating ulterior purpose may be shared by both parties or be in the contemplation of only one of them and, in this latter case, the innocent party may not always be precluded from relief (see below, Section 3). Another consequence of the possible invalidation of a contract because of a motive or object not apparent upon the face of the agreement, is that questions may arise as to the manner in which the illegality comes to the attention of the court: in this connection, the reader is referred to the principles enunciated by Devlin J. in *Edler v. Auerbach* [1950] 1 K.B. 359.

(i) *Agreements to Commit an Unlawful Act*

That the courts should refuse their aid in respect of contracts whose purpose is to commit an illegal act is common sense. Hence, an agreement to commit an assault or a burglary would be unenforceable, as also to publish a libel or to make a false representation. See *Brown, Jenkinson v. Percy Dalton* (below, p. 678). Instances of an arrangement seemingly valid but in substance designed to defraud will be found in *Alexander v. Rayson* [1936] 1 KB. 169 and *Miller v. Karlinski* (1945) 62 T.L.R. 85.

A contract which is perfectly lawful in its inception may become unlawful through the manner in which it is performed. If A contracts to sell fertilisers to B and, in pursuance of that perfectly valid contract, delivers the goods without also delivering an invoice stating the percentage of certain chemicals therein—an omission which is an offence punishable summarily with a fine—he cannot recover the price: *Anderson v. Daniel* [1924] 1 K.B. 138. This principle, however, should be considered in the light of *Marles v. Philip Trant Ltd* (below, p. 668) and *St. John Shipping Corpn. v. Joseph Rank Ltd* [1957] 1 Q.B. 267.

A contract is generally invalid in English law if performance of it is unlawful by the law of the country where it is to be performed. But in *Howard v. Shirlstar*

Container Transport Ltd [1990] 3 All E.R. 366, C.A., it was held that the plaintiff could recover an agreed fee for flying the defendant's aircraft out of Nigeria although he had taken off without permission from air traffic control which was a serious statutory offence under Nigerian law. He took off because he believed on reasonable grounds that his life and that of his wireless operator were in imminent danger so long as they remained in Nigeria. Although the Court said it would not be justified in departing from the judge's conclusion that the act was excusable under Nigerian criminal law, the principal ground of the decision appears to be that, even if the act was illegal, enforcement of the claim would not be an "affront to the public conscience" because it was not morally reprehensible. Staughton L.J. said that it would be the same if the offence had been committed in England. The decision was doubted in *Tinsley v. Milligan*, below, p. 685, where the "public conscience" ground was disapproved.

The English courts will not refuse to enforce a contract governed by foreign law which is not illegal but is contrary to the public policy of that country, unless the public policy is one which also applies in England: *Lemenda Trading Co. Ltd v. African Middle East Petroleum Company Ltd* [1988] 1 All E.R. 513 (Q.B.D.).

(ii) *Agreements Prejudicial to the Interest of the State*

This rather vague head covers four main types of offending agreement:

(a) *Agreements with enemy aliens*

An enemy alien is anyone who voluntarily resides in enemy or enemy-occupied territory in time of war, and any agreement made with such a person is bad. Again, a contract made in time of peace may be abrogated if, with the advent of war, one of the parties becomes an enemy alien. This, however, is not an absolute rule—a contract will escape abrogation if its performance involves no intercourse with the enemy and is not otherwise contrary to public policy—for instance, a separation agreement between a man and his wife, who has become an enemy alien. Again, though a contract be dissolved, rights which may have accrued to either party before the invalidating event remain valid and may be enforced upon the return of peace. The reader is referred to: *Ertel Bieber & Co. v. Rio Tinto Co.* [1918] A.C. 260, *Arab Bank Ltd v. Barclays Bank* [1954] A.C. 495 and *Bevan v. Bevan* [1955] 2 Q.B. 227.

(b) *Agreements hostile to a friendly foreign state*

A friendly state is, in effect, any state with which Britain is not in a state of war: any agreement which harms Britain's relations with such a state is bad and void. Examples include agreements to enable subjects of a foreign state to overthrow their government by force[1] or to smuggle liquor into a state whose constitution imposed a requirement of prohibition.[2] A striking instance of the possible width of the ban is to be seen in *Regazzoni v. K.C. Sethia (1944) Ltd* [1958] A.C. 301, where the House of Lords refused to give effect to a contract for the export of goods to South Africa from India which infringed an Indian statute forbidding such export; the implications of this decision are considered in a valuable note by Mann in 19 M.L.R. 523.

(c) *Agreements prejudicial to the administration of justice*

Agreements of this type are those which aim to interfere with the due course of law, for example to suppress a prosecution, to indemnify one who goes bail for an accuses person, not to appear at the public examination of a bankrupt, etc. With regard to stifling prosecutions, however, it must be noted that many wrongs give

[1] *De Wutz v. Hendricks* (1824) 2 Bing. 314.
[2] *Foster v. Driscoll* [1929] 1 K.B. 470.

rise to both civil and criminal remedies and, where the element of public wrong is subordinate to that of private injury, an agreement not to take or go on with criminal proceedings will be enforceable. Thus, for example, an agreement not to prosecute for libel or common assault would be valid; but not a similar agreement in respect of, say, a riot or obstruction of the police in the performance of their duty. The leading authority is *Keir v. Leeman* (1846) 9 Q.B. 371 and reference might profitably also be made to *Jones v. Merionethshire Permanent Benefit Building Society* [1892] 1 Ch. 173 and *Fisher & Co. v. Apollinaris Co.* (1875) 10 Ch.App. 297.

(d) *Agreements prejudicial to probity in public life*
Into this category fall such agreements as one to sell or procure a title of honour or public office (in which connection, see the Honours (Prevention of Abuses) Act 1925); also—and perhaps more probable in modern times—contracts for the assignment or mortgage of the salary of a holder of a public office, for the object of the salary is to enable the official to uphold the dignity of his office in a fitting manner. For the operation of this principle in relation to civil servants, see *Lucas v. Lucas* [1943] P. 68 and Logan, 61 L.Q.R. 240.

(iii) *Contracts to Promote Sexual Immorality*

Any agreement which has as its object future illicit sexual relations is bad under this head. Hence a promise to pay a monthly allowance to a mistress, even if made by deed under seal, would be void: so also a contract which, though seemingly innocent, has, to the knowledge of the parties, an immoral motive—see *Pearce v. Brooks, infra.* On the other hand, a promise of money, etc., in respect of past sexual immorality is not affected by the ban and consequently, if made under seal, would be enforceable: if not under seal, it would be ineffective simply on the ground that past consideration is no consideration; *Cf. Beaumont v. Reeve* (1846) 8 Q.B. 483.

Section 2. Effects of Illegality

(a) ON ACTIONS ON THE CONTRACT

PEARCE AND ANOTHER v. BROOKS

Exchequer (1866) L.R. 1 Ex. 213; 4 H. & C. 358; 35 L.J. Ex. 134; 14 L.T. 288;
20 J.P. 295; 14 W.R. 614

Declaration stating an agreement by which the plaintiffs agreed to supply the defendant with a new miniature brougham on hire, till the purchase-money should be paid by instalments in a period which was not to exceed 12 months; the defendant to have the option to purchase as aforesaid, and to pay £50 down; and in case the brougham should be returned before a second instalment was paid, a forfeiture of 15 guineas was to be paid in addition to the £50, and also any damage, except fair wear. Averment, that the defendant returned the brougham before a second instalment was paid, and that it was damaged. Breach, non-payment of 15 guineas, or the amount of the damage. Money counts.

Plea 3, to the first count, that at the time of making the supposed agreement, the defendant was to the knowledge of the plaintiffs a prostitute, and that the supposed agreement was made for the supply of a brougham to be used by her as such prostitute, and to assist her in carrying on her said immoral vocation, as the plaintiffs when they made the said agreement well knew, and in the expectation by the plaintiffs that the defendant would pay the plaintiffs the moneys to be paid by the said agreement out of her receipts as such prostitute. Issue.

The case was tried before Bramwell B. at Guildhall, at the sittings after Michaelmas Term 1865. It then appeared that the plaintiffs were coachbuilders in partnership, and evidence was given which satisfied the jury that one of the partners knew that the defendant was a prostitute; but there was no direct evidence that either of the plaintiffs knew that the brougham was intended to be used for the purpose of enabling the defendant to prosecute her trade of prostitution; and there was no evidence that the plaintiffs expected to be paid out of the wages of prostitution.

The learned judge ruled that the allegation in the plea as to the mode of payment was immaterial, and he put to the jury the following questions:
1. Did the defendant hire the brougham for the purpose of her prostitution?
2. If she did, did the plaintiffs know the purpose for which it was hired? The jury found that the carriage was used by the defendant as part of her display, to attract men; and that the plaintiffs knew it was supplied to be used for that purpose. They gave nothing for the alleged damage.

On this finding, the learned judge directed a verdict for the defendant, and gave the plaintiffs leave to move to enter a verdict for them for the 15 guineas penalty.

BRAMWELL B.: There is no doubt that the woman was a prostitute; no doubt to my mind that the plaintiffs knew it; there was cogent evidence of the fact, and the jury have so found. The only fact really in dispute is for what purpose was the brougham hired, and if for an immoral purpose, did the plaintiffs know it? At the trial I doubted whether there was evidence of this, but, for the reasons I have stated, I think the jury were entitled to infer, as they did, that it was hired for the purpose of display, that is, for the purpose of enabling the defendant to pursue her calling, and that the plaintiffs knew it.

That being made out, my difficulty was, whether, though the defendant hired the brougham for that purpose, it could be said that the plaintiffs let it for the same purpose. In one sense, it was not for the same purpose. If a man were to ask for duelling pistols, and to say: "I think I shall fight a duel tomorrow," might not the seller answer: "I do not want to know your purpose; I have nothing to do with it; that is your business: mine is to sell the pistols, and look only to the profit of trade." No doubt the act would be immoral, but I have felt a doubt whether it would be illegal; and I should still feel it, but that the authority of *Cannan v. Bryce* (3 B. & A. 179) *M'Kinnell v. Robinson*, (3 M. & W. 434), concludes the matter. In the latter case the plea does not say that the money was lent on the terms that the borrower should game with it; but only that it was borrowed by the defendant, and lent by the plaintiff "for the purpose of the defendant's illegally playing and gaming therewith." The case was argued by Crompton J. against the plea, and by Wightman J. in support of it; and the considered judgment of the court was delivered by Lord Abinger, who says (p. 441):

"As the plea states that the money for which the action is brought was lent for the purpose of illegally playing and gaming therewith, at the illegal game of 'Hazard,' this money cannot be recovered back, on the principle, not for the first time laid down, but fully settled in the case of *Cannan v. Bryce*. This principle is that the repayment of money, lent for the express purpose of accomplishing an illegal object, cannot be enforced." This court, then, following *Cannan v. Bryce*, decided that it need not be part of the bargain that the subject of the contract should be used unlawfully, but that it is enough if it is handed over for the purpose that the borrower shall so apply it. We are, then, concluded by authority on the point; and, as I have no doubt that the finding of the jury was right, the rule must be discharged.

With respect, however, to the allegation in the plea, which, as I have said, need not be proved, and which I refused to leave to the jury, I desire that it may not be supposed we are overruling anything that Lord Ellenborough has said. It is manifest that he could not have meant to lay down as a rule of law that there would be no illegality in a contract unless payment were to be made out of the proceeds of the illegal act, and that his observation was made with a different view. In the case of the hiring of a cab, which was mentioned in the argument, it would be absurd to suppose that, when both parties were doing the same thing, with the same object and purpose, it would be a lawful act in one, and unlawful in the other.

POLLOCK C.B., MARTIN and PIGOTT BB. delivered concurring judgments.

Rule discharged.

Questions

1. Could Bramwell B.'s seller of the pistol (above, p. 667) have recovered the price. See Glanville Williams, *The Criminal Law*, (2nd ed.). p. 366 *et seq.*, and *National Coal Board v. Gamble* [1959] 1 Q.B. 11 *per* Devlin J. at 23.

2. Do you agree that the plaintiffs could have brought trover for the carriage? See *Taylor v. Chester* (below, p. 650) and *Bowmakers Ltd v. Barnet Instruments Ltd* (below, p. 682).

Problem

Lawrence, a landlord, lets flats (a) to Ada whom he believes to be Ben's mistress; (b) to Poppy whom he believes to be a prostitute. He is correctly informed in both cases. Does this belief debar him from recovering rent in respect of the flats?

Cf. R. v. Thomas [1957] 1 W.L.R. 747; *Shaw v. D.P.P.* [1962] A.C. 220.

MARLES v. PHILIP TRANT & SONS LTD MACKINNON, THIRD PARTY

Court of Appeal [1954] 1 Q.B. 29; [1953] 2 W.L.R. 564; 97 S.J. 189; [1953] 1 All E.R. 651

The defendants, seed merchants, bought from the third party wheat under the description of spring wheat known as Fylgia and resold part of it to the plaintiff, a farmer, under the same description. The wheat was not spring wheat and was known as Vilmorin. The farmer sued the merchants claiming damages for breach of contract and warranty, recovering judgment for £418 5s. 10d. and costs. The merchants had added the person who supplied them with the wheat as a third party, claiming from him an indemnity for the loss of what they had had to pay to the farmer and also damages. The third party took the point that since the merchants had not, in conformity with section 1 of the Seeds Act, 1920, delivered to the plaintiff a statement in writing containing the prescribed particulars with respect to the seeds' variety, purity and germination, the contract of the merchants with the plaintiff was illegal and, therefore, the merchants could not recover their loss on it from the third party. The trial judge who, otherwise, would have given judgment against the third party, on the ground that it was their breach of warranty or of contract which had led to the damage, upheld the contention of the third party and gave judgment for him against the merchants. The merchants appealed and, before the Court of Appeal, the third party admitted that the merchants were entitled to recover nominal damages against the third party, but not an indemnity for their loss on their contract with the plaintiff.

SINGLETON L.J. delivered a judgment allowing the appeal.

DENNING L.J.: The first question which arises in this case is: what is the legal effect of the omission to supply the particulars prescribed under the Seeds Act? The trial judge has held that it turned the contract with the farmer, so far as the seed merchant was concerned, into an illegal contract. The judge so held on the authority of *Anderson Ltd v. Daniel* [1924] 1 K.B. 138 and *B. & B. Viennese Fashions v. Losane* [1952] 1 T.L.R. 750, and there are indeed some observations in those cases which warrant him taking that view. But I do not think that they are correct. There can be no doubt that the contract between the seed merchants and the farmer was not unlawful when it was made. If the farmer had repudiated it before the time for delivery arrived, the seed merchants could certainly have sued him for damages. Nor was the contract rendered unlawful simply because the seed was delivered without the prescribed particulars. If it were unlawful, the farmer himself could not have sued upon it as he has done. The truth is that it was not the contract itself which was unlawful, but only the performance of it. The seed merchants performed it in an illegal way in that they omitted to furnish the prescribed particulars. That renders the contract unenforceable by them, but it does not render the contract illegal. Atkin L.J. expressed the position with his usual accuracy in *Anderson Ltd v. Daniel* when he said simply that the contract was unenforceable. I do not think that the law has ever countenanced the idea that a transaction, lawful when done, can be rendered unlawful by the doctrine of relation back: see *Elliott v. Boynton* [1924] 1 Ch. 236. A transaction which is unlawful, when done, can be rendered lawful by relation back (see *Howell v. Falmouth Boat Construction Co. Ltd* [1951] A.C. 837) but not vice versa.

Once rid of the notion that the contract with the farmer was itself illegal, the question becomes: what is the effect of the admitted illegality in performance? It certainly prevents the seed merchants from suing the farmer for the price, but does it prevent them suing their supplier for damages? I think not. There was nothing unlawful in the contract between the seed merchants and their supplier, neither in the formation of it, nor in the performance of it. The seed merchants must therefore be entitled to damages for the breach of it. So far so good, but the difficulty comes when they seek to prove their damages. They want to be indemnified for the damages which they have been ordered to pay to the farmer. To prove those damages, they have to prove the contract with the farmer, and the circumstances under which the damages were awarded. It is said that once they begin to rely on their deliveries to the farmer, they seek aid from their own illegality; and that that is a thing which they are not allowed to do. The maxim is invoked: *Ex turpi causa non oritur actio.* That maxim must not, however, be carried too far. . . . The omission by the seed merchants to deliver the prescribed particulars was an act of inadvertence. It was not a deliberate breach of the law. I venture to assert that there is no moral justification for the court to apply the maxim in this case. But is there any legal justification? A distinction must be drawn, I think, between an illegality which destroys the cause of action and an illegality which affects only the damages recoverable.

So far as the cause of action itself is concerned, the principle is well settled that, if the plaintiff requires any aid from an illegal transaction to establish his cause of action, then he shall not have any aid from the court. That appears in all the books from *Simpson v. Bloss*, 7 Taunt. 246, down to *Berg v. Sadler and Moore* [1937] 2 K.B. 158 and *J. Dennis & Co. Ltd v. Munn* [1949] 2 K.B. 327. In my opinion, those cases have no application to this case, because the seed merchants here can make out their cause of action perfectly well without any recourse to the illegality at all. All they need to do is to prove the contract by which the supplier agreed to supply Fylgia seed, and then show that he in fact supplied Vilmorin. That is sufficient to entitle them, by way of damages, to the estimated loss directly and naturally resulting, in the ordinary course of events, from that breach of contract: see *Cory v. Thames Ironworks etc., Co.* (1868) L.R. 3 Q.B. 181 and section 53(2) of the Sale of Goods Act, 1893. There was no need for them to claim the particular loss arising from the sub-contract, and so long as they refrained from claiming that loss, there could be no possible objection to the claim: see *Gordon v. Chief Commissioner of Metropolitan Police* [1910] 2 K.B. 1080.

The difficulty only arises because the seed merchants claim the special loss resulting from the sub-contract. The supplier says, in effect, to the seed merchants: "I have discovered that you have been guilty of an illegality. You did not deliver the prescribed particulars to the farmers who bought from you. Therefore you cannot recover your loss." It is to be noticed that the omission to deliver the particulars does not make any practical difference in this case. Even if the seed merchants had delivered the prescribed particulars, the position would have been the same. The seed would have been described as Fylgia, and the plaintiff would have recovered his damages just the same. Nevertheless, the supplier says that he is entitled in law to be relieved of liability.

So far as this question of damages is concerned, the civil courts act on the principle that they will not lend their aid to a man so as to enable him to get a benefit from his own crime; nor will they help him to get reparation for the consequences of his own culpable criminal act. Thus, when a man committed suicide in order that the insurance moneys payable on his death might be obtained, his representatives were not allowed to recover the amount: *Beresford v. Royal Insurance Co. Ltd* [1937] 2 K.B. 197; [1938] A.C. 586. When a solicitor sought to be indemnified by his insurers against the consequences of his own champerty, his action failed: *Haseldine v. Hosken* [1933] 1 K.B. 822. When a wholesale wine merchant bought from a manufacturer liquor which he should have known was contaminated, and resold it, without lawful excuse, to his customers, he was not allowed to recover from the manufacturers the damages which he had to pay his customers: *Askey v. Golden Wine Co. Ltd*, 64 T.L.R. 379; [1948] 2 All E.R. 35. In those cases the plaintiff was undoubtedly seeking to get reparation for the consequences of his own culpable crime.

But there are cases nowadays where a man can be guilty of a crime without any moral culpability at all. Thus, a man who is induced by fraud to do a criminal act will have a cause of action against the deceiver, if he himself had no knowledge of the circumstances which rendered it criminal:

Burrows v. Rhodes [1899] 1 Q.B. 816, 831. And a provision merchant who relies on a warranty by his supplier, but subsequently is convicted for selling bad food, will be able to recover any damage he suffers by reason of reselling it to his customers (*Crage v. Fry* (1903) 67 J.P. 240; *Cointat v. Myham & Son* [1913] 2 K.B. 220; and *Weld-Blundell v. Stephens* [1919] 1 K.B. 520, 539) provided, of course, that the damages claimed are not too remote: *Simon v. Pawsons & Leafs Ltd*, 38 Com.Cas. 151, 157–158. It has been held that a motorist who had to pay damages for negligence could recover an indemnity from his insurers even though the negligence was so gross as to amount to manslaughter: *Tinline v. White Cross Insurance Association Ltd* [1921] 3 K.B. 327; and *James v. British and General Insurance Co. Ltd* [1927] 2 K.B. 311. I think that those cases were rightly decided. The right to indemnity for negligence should not depend on the chance whether a man is prosecuted, or the further chance whether he is convicted. Those cases were stronger than the present case. If public policy did not prevent recovery in those cases, it should not prevent recovery here . . .

In my opinion, therefore, the loss suffered by the seed merchants was due to the breach of contract by the supplier; and they are entitled to recover it notwithstanding their omission to deliver the particulars.

I agree with my Lord that the appeal should be allowed.

HODSON L.J. dissented, holding that there was no escape from the consequences of the decision in *Anderson v. Daniel.*

Appeal allowed.

STRONGMAN (1945) LTD v. SINCOCK

Court of Appeal [1955] 2 Q.B. 525; [1955] 3 W.L.R. 360; 99 S.J. 540;
[1955] 3 All E.R. 90

Sincock, an architect owner, contracted with Strongman (1945) Ltd, builders, to supply materials and to carry out work at his premises and promised orally that he would obtain all the licences necessary at that date under regulation 56a of the Defence (General) Regulations, 1939. Work considerably in excess of the licences granted was carried out. In an arbitration on a claim by the builders for the balance of the price over the licensed amount of work and materials, or alternatively damages for a similar amount for breach of a warranty that Sincock would obtain the licences, the official referee, the arbitrator, found that the warranty alleged was established and held that, though the plaintiffs were precluded from recovering under the contract, which was illegal, they were entitled to the same sums by way of damages for breach of the warranty. Sincock appealed.

DENNING L.J.: Let me say first that the builders cannot sue here on the contract to do the work, which was done in 1948 and 1949. At the time it was unlawful under Defence Regulation 56A for the work to be done without a proper licence. Licences were only in force to the amount of £2,150. When work was done to the value of over £6,000 the builders and the architect were all guilty of an offence for which they might have been prosecuted. Under many decisions in this court it has been held that a builder doing work without a licence cannot recover under the contract.

The builders seek to overcome this objection by saying that there was a warranty, or (putting it more accurately) a promise by the architect that he would get supplementary licences, or that if he failed to get them he would stop the work. The builders say that on the faith of that promise they did the work, and as the promise was broken they can recover damages in respect of it. . . . Applying the test which Lord Moulton laid down in *Heilbut, Symons & Co. v. Buckleton* (above, p. 363) the assurance given by the architect amounted to a collateral contract by which the architect promised that he would get any necessary supplementary licences or, if he could not get them, that he would stop the work.

The second question is whether the builders can recover in law on this collateral promise. The promise itself was not illegal, but it is said that damages cannot be recovered for the breach of it. It is said that, if damages could be recovered, it would be an easy way of getting round the law about illegality. This does not alarm me at all. It is, of course, a settled principle that a man cannot recover for the consequences of his own unlawful act, but this has always been confined to cases where the doer of the act knows it to be unlawful or is himself in some way morally culpable. It does not apply when he is an entirely innocent party. Take a case where a master sends out his servant to drive a lorry, and the servant has an accident and injures a third person on the road. It then turns out that the master had not taken out a proper insurance policy to cover them. Both master and servant are guilty of an offence under the Road Traffic Act, 1930, but, nevertheless, the servant, if sued for damages can claim an indemnity against the master. The reason is because the master impliedly promises that he will not ask the servant to do anything unlawful. The master having broken that promise, the servant can recover against him, although the servant was himself guilty of the criminal act of driving without being insured.

[Having considered *Gregory v. Ford* [1951] 1 All E.R 121, *Road Transport & General Insurance Co. Ltd v. Irwin & Adams* (unreported) and *Burrows v. Rhodes* [1899] 1 Q.B. 816, his Lordship proceeded:] I think the law is that, although a man may have been guilty of an offence which is absolutely prohibited so that he is answerable in a criminal court, nevertheless if he has been led to commit that offence by the representation or by the promise of another, then in those circumstances he can recover damages for fraud if there is fraud, or for breach of promise or warranty if he prove such to have been given, provided always that he himself has not been guilty of culpable negligence on his part disabling him from that remedy. . . . On the findings of the official referee, the plaintiffs were entirely innocent people who were led into this unfortunate illegality by the representation of the architect, amounting to a collateral contract, that he would get the licences. That contract not having been fulfilled, I see no objection in point of law to the plaintiffs recovering the damages, and I think that the appeal should be dismissed.

BIRKETT L.J.: Mr Dingle Foot suggested that if this method of suing on a warranty could be successfully raised the whole purpose of the regulation would be defeated. The position with regard to that is that, on the law as stated by Denning L.J., while it is perfectly plain that it is impossible to sue on a contract for the reasons given, where the particular facts of any one case do permit the finding that a collateral contract in fact existed, I can see no special reason on the special facts of that case why that particular cause of action should not succeed, even if it does mean that it puts one virtually in the same position as one would be in if one were able to sue on the contract.

ROMER L.J. delivered a concurring judgment.

Appeal dismissed.

Question

In *Re Mahmoud and Ispahani* [1921] 2 K.B. 716 a sale of linseed oil without a licence was prohibited by the Seed, Oils and Fats Order 1919. The plaintiff, who had a licence to sell linseed oil, asked the defendant whether he had a licence under the Order and the defendant replied that he did; in fact he did not. Relying on the representation, the plaintiff sold linseed oil to the defendant. The defendant subsequently refused to accept delivery of the oil and, in an action by the plaintiff for damages for non-acceptance, pleaded the illegality of the contract on the ground that he did not himself have a licence. The Court of Appeal, reversing Rowlatt J., held that the defence succeeded.

Do you think that, in similar circumstances now, *Strongman v. Sincock* would be of assistance to the plaintiff?

ARCHBOLDS (FREIGHTAGE) LTD v. S. SPANGLETT LTD

Court of Appeal [1961] 1 Q.B. 374; [1961] 2 W.L.R. 170; 105 S.J. 149;
[1961] 1 All E.R. 417

In March 1957 Archbolds employed the defendants for reward to carry a third party's goods, a load of whisky, by road from Leeds to London. The agreement was made through the defendants' lorry driver, Randall, and Field, the plaintiffs' traffic manager at their Leeds office. The Road and Rail Traffic Act, 1933, provides that no person shall use a vehicle for the carriage of goods unless he holds an "A" or a "C" licence; the former entitles him to carry the goods of others for reward; the latter allows him only to carry his own goods and not those of others. The vehicle in which the load of whisky was carried had only a "C" and not an "A" licence, a fact which the defendants knew but the plaintiffs neither knew nor ought to have known. During the journey from Leeds to London, the load was lost through the negligence of Randall. Archbolds claimed for the loss and the defendants contended that the contract was illegal, being prohibited under the Road and Rail Traffic Act 1933, since the vehicle used for carriage had only a "C" licence. Slade J. gave judgment for the plaintiffs; he held that the plaintiffs were deceived into letting the defendants carry the load to London and that they did not know that the lorry in which it was intended that the load should be carried only had a "C" licence. The defendants appealed.

PEARCE L.J.: It having been proved . . . that the plaintiffs were imposed on and believed that the goods could lawfully be carried on Randall's van, are they disentitled to sue? . . . Let us assume (although I am far from satisfied on this point) that the learned judge was in error in holding that the haulage contract could have been performed by the defendants in any way they liked (that is to say, lawfully as well as unlawfully). Let us assume first that it was a contract for carriage in Randall's van only and secondly that it was not by the nature of the contract one which could be performed vicariously. It must then inevitably be carried out unlawfully if (but only if) one adds the fact that Randall's van had a "C" licence and therefore could not lawfully carry the goods in question. But that fact, though known to the defendants, was unknown to the plaintiffs.

This is not a case where the plaintiffs can assert a cause of action without relying on the contract. Mr Leonard put forward an ingenious alternative argument based on the plaintiffs' rights against the defendants as voluntary bailees of the plaintiffs' property: see *Bowmakers Ltd v. Barnet Instruments Ltd* (below, p. 682), so that he might claim in negligence or conversion without having any recourse to the contract or exposing to the court as part of his cause of action its alleged illegality. But I do not think that he can make good that argument. His cause of action comes from the contract, and if the contract is such that the court must refuse its aid, the plaintiffs cannot recover their damages.

If a contract is expressly or by necessary implication forbidden by statute, or if it is *ex facie* illegal, or if both parties know that though *ex facie* legal it can only be performed by illegality or is intended to be performed illegally, the law will not help the plaintiffs in any way that is a direct or indirect enforcement of rights under the contract. And for this purpose both parties are presumed to know the law.

The first question therefore, is whether this contract of carriage was forbidden by statute. The two cases on which the defendants mainly rely are *Re an Arbitration between Mahmoud and Ispahani* (above, p. 673) and *J. Dennis & Co. Ltd v. Munn* ([1949] 2 K.B. 327). In both those cases the plaintiffs were unable to enforce their rights under contracts forbidden by statute. In the former case the statutory order said: "a person shall not . . . buy or sell . . . certain] articles . . . except under and in accordance with the terms of a licence." In the latter case the statutory regulation provided: "subject to the provisions of this regulation . . . the execution . . . of any operation specified . . . shall be unlawful except in so far as authorised." In neither case could the plaintiff bring his contract within the exception that alone would have made its subject-matter lawful, namely, by showing the existence of a licence. Therefore, the core of both contracts was the mischief expressly forbidden by the statutory order and the statutory regulation respectively.

In *Mahmoud*'s case the object of the order was to prevent (except under licence) a person buying and a person selling, and both parties were liable to penalties. A contract of sale between those persons was therefore expressly forbidden. In *Dennis*'s case the object of the regulation was to prevent (except under licence) owners from performing building operations, and builders from carrying out the work for them. Both parties were liable to penalties and a contract between these persons for carrying out an unlawful operation would be forbidden by implication.

The case before us is somewhat different. The carriage of the plaintiffs' whisky was not as such prohibited; the statute merely regulated the means by which carriers should carry goods. Therefore this contract was not expressly forbidden by the statute.

Was it then forbidden by implication? The Road and Rail Traffic Act, 1933, s.1, says: "no person shall use a goods vehicle on a road for the carriage of goods . . . except under licence," and provides that such use shall be an offence. Did the statute thereby intend to forbid by implication all contracts whose performance must on all the facts (whether known or not) result in a contravention of that section?

The plaintiffs' part of the contract could not constitute an illegal use of the vehicle by them since they were not "using" the vehicle. If they were aware of the true facts they would, of course, be guilty of aiding and abetting the defendants, but if they acted in good faith they would not be guilty of any offence under the statute: see *Davies, Turner & Co. Ltd v. Brodie* ([1954] 1 W.L.R. 1364; [1954] 3 All E.R. 283) and *Carter v. Mace* ([1949] 2 All E.R. 714). In this case, therefore, the plaintiffs were not committing any offence.

In *St. John Shipping Corporation v. Rank* ([1957] 1 Q.B. 267; [1956] 3 All E.R. 683) Devlin J. held that the plaintiffs were entitled to recover although there had been an infringement of a statute in the performance of a contract, but in that case the was legal when made. Though not directly applicable to the present case, it contains an observation (with which I entirely agree) on the point which arises here. He said: "For example, a person is forbidden by statute from using an unlicensed vehicle on the highway. If one asks oneself whether there is in such an enactment an implied prohibition of all contracts for the use of unlicensed vehicles, the answer may well be that there is, and that contracts of hire would be unenforceable. But if one asks oneself whether there is an implied prohibition of contracts for the carriage of goods by unlicensed vehicles or for the repairing of unlicensed vehicles or for the garaging of unlicensed vehicles, the answer may well be different. The answer might be that collateral contracts of this sort are not within the ambit of the statute." In my judgment that distinction is valid.

The object of the Road and Rail Traffic Act 1933, was not (in this connection) to interfere with the owner of goods or his facilities for transport, but to control those who provided the transport, with a view to promoting its efficiency. Transport of goods was not made illegal but the various licence holders were prohibited from encroaching on one another's territory, the intention of the Act being to provide an orderly and comprehensive service. Penalties were provided for those licence holders who went outside the bounds of their allotted spheres. These penalties apply to those using the vehicle but not to the goods owner. Though the latter could be convicted of aiding and abetting any breach, the restrictions were not aimed at him. Thus a contract of carriage was, in the sense used by Devlin J., "collateral," and it was not impliedly forbidden by the statute.

This view is supported by common sense and convenience. If the other view were held it would have far-reaching effects. For instance, if a carrier induces me (who am in fact ignorant of any illegality) to entrust goods to him and negligently destroys them, he would only have to show that (though unknown to me) his licence had expired, or did not properly cover the transportation, or that he was uninsured, and I should then be without a remedy against him. Or, again, if I ride in a taxicab and the driver leaves me stranded in some deserted spot, he would only have to show that he was (though unknown to me) unlicensed or uninsured, and I should be without remedy. This appears to me an undesirable extension of the implications of a statute. . . .

It is for the defendants to show that contracts by the owner for the carriage of goods are within the ambit of the implied prohibition of the Road and Rail Traffic Act, 1933. In my judgment they have not done so.

The next question is whether this contract, though not forbidden by statute was *ex facie* illegal. Must any reasonable person on hearing the terms of the contract (with presumed knowledge of the law) realise that it was illegal? There is nothing illegal in its terms. Further knowledge, namely, knowledge of the fact that Randall's van was not properly licensed, would show that it could only be performed by contravention of the statute, but that does not make the contract *ex facie* illegal.

However, if both parties had that knowledge the contract would be unenforceable as being a contract which to their knowledge could not be carried out without a violation of the law: see *per* Lord Blackburn in *Waugh v. Morris* (1873) L.R. 8 Q.B. 202). But where one party is ignorant of the fact that will make the performance illegal, is it established that the innocent party cannot obtain relief against the guilty party? The case has been argued with skill and care on both sides, and yet no case has been cited to us establishing the proposition that where a contract is on the face of it legal and is not forbidden by statute, but must in fact produce illegality by reason of a circumstance known to one party only, it should be held illegal so as to debar the innocent party from relief. In the absence of such a case I do not feel compelled to so unsatisfactory a conclusion, which would injure the innocent, benefit the guilty, and put a premium on deceit. I would dismiss the appeal.

DEVLIN L.J.: It is a familiar principle of law that if a contract can be performed in one of two ways, that is, legally or illegally, it is not an illegal contract, though it may be unenforceable at the suit of a party who chooses to perform it illegally. That statement of the law is meaningful if the contract is one which is by its terms open to two modes of performance; otherwise it is meaningless. Almost any contract—certainly any contract for the carriage of goods by road—can be performed illegally; any contract of carriage by road can be performed illegally simply by exceeding the appropriate speed limit. The error in the defendants' argument, I think, is that they are looking at the facts which determine their capacity to perform and not at the terms of the contract. Suppose that the contract were for a vehicle with an "A" licence, or—what is substantially the same thing—for a specified vehicle warranted as holding an "A" licence. That would not be an illegal contract for it would be a contract for the use of a licensed vehicle and not an unlicensed one. If those were the express terms of the contract, it would not be made illegal because all the carrier's vehicles, or the specified vehicle, as the case might be, had "C" licences. The most that that could show would be that the carrier might well be unable to perform his contract. . . .

I think there is much to be said for the argument that in a case of this sort there is, unless the circumstances exclude it, an implied warranty that the van is properly licensed for the service for which it is required. It would be unreasonable to expect a man when he is getting into a taxicab to ask for an express warranty from the driver that his cab was licensed; the answer, if it took any intelligible form at all, would be to the effect that it would not be on the streets if it were not. The same applies to a person who delivers goods for carriage by a particular vehicle; he cannot be expected to examine the road licence to see if it is in order. But the issue of warranty was not raised in the pleadings or at the trial and so I think it is preferable to decide this case on the broad ground which Pearce L.J. has adopted and with which, for the reasons I have given, I agree.

There are many pitfalls in this branch of the law. If, for example, Mr Field had observed that the van had a "C" licence and said nothing, he might be said to have accepted a mode of performance different from that contracted for and so varied the contract and turned it into an illegal one: see *St. John Shipping Corporation v. Joseph Rank Ltd* where that sort of point was considered. Or, to take another example, if a statute prohibits the sale of goods to an alien, a warranty by the buyer that he is not an alien will not save the contract. That is because the terms of the prohibition expressly forbid a sale to an alien; consequently, the question to be asked in order to see whether the contact comes within the prohibition is whether the buyer is in fact an alien, not whether he represented himself as one. *Re Mahmoud* (above, p. 673) is that sort of case. . . .

[Having considered *Re Mahmoud* and *Strongman v. Sincock* (above, p. 671), his Lordship concluded:]

Apart from the pleading point, it might not matter if the last two cases were not distinguishable, since the plaintiffs could obtain damages for breach of warranty as in *Strongman v. Sincock*.

SELLERS L.J. concurred in the decision.

Appeal dismissed

In *Ashmore, Benson, Pease & Co. Ltd v. A. V. Dawson Ltd* [1973] 2 All E.R. 856; [1973] 1 W.L.R. 828, the plaintiffs had manufactured a large piece of equipment known as a tube-bank, weighing 25 tons, and orally contracted with the defendants, a small road haulage company, for its transport from Stockton-on-Tees to Hull for £55. Nothing was said of the type of vehicle to be used but the defendants owned a small fleet of articulated lorries, the largest a "30-tonner." The plaintiffs' transport manager was present when the defendants' lorry came to take the load. When loaded, the lorry greatly exceeded the permitted weight so that the transport constituted an offence under section 64(2) of the Road Traffic Act, 1960; the tube-bank should have been carried on a "low-loader" of which the defendants had none. During the journey, the lorry toppled over through an error of judgment of the driver and the tube-bank was damaged to the amount of £2,225 which the plaintiffs claimed in this action for negligence and/or breach of contract. Waller J. held that the contract was lawful when made and that the defendants could not plead the illegality of their performance and gave judgment for the plaintiffs. Allowing the appeal, the Court of Appeal (Lord Denning M.R., Phillimore and Scarman L.JJ.) held that, on the evidence, the plaintiffs' transport manager must have realised that the loading was in breach of the Road Traffic Act 1960; accordingly, despite the legality of the contract at its inception, the plaintiffs, through the manager, participated in the illegality of its performance and were thus debarred from damages.

Question

A engages a builder to repair his roof: the builder uses a ladder to do the work in circumstances in which A knows the regulations to require scaffolding. When the work is complete can A refuse to pay, pleading illegality? If the work is badly done and causes damage, can A sue in contract? *Cf.* C.J. Hamson [1973] C.L.J. 199.

Note

In *Shaw v. Groom* [1970] 2 Q.B. 504; [1970] 1 All E.R. 702, C.A., to a claim by a landlord for arrears of rent, the defendant tenant pleaded, *inter alia*, that no rent was recoverable by the landlord in that the latter had not provided a rent book as required by the Landlord and Tenant Act 1962, s.4. Under section 4(1) of the Act, such failure on the part of a landlord constituted a criminal offence. The county court judge rejected the landlord's claim. On appeal, the Court of Appeal reversed the decision. Though failure to provide a rent book is an offence on the landlord's part, a rent book is not an essential of the contract of letting and the fact of the offence does not preclude the landlord from suing for his rent unless the relevant statute expressly or impliedly forbids it; which was not the case here. Sachs L.J. said (p. 526): "It seems to me appropriate, accordingly, to allow this appeal on the broad basis that, even if the provision of a rent book is an essential act as between landlords and weekly tenants, yet the legislature did not by section 4 of the 1962 Act intend to preclude the landlord from recovering any rent due or impose any forfeiture on him beyond the prescribed penalty."

BROWN JENKINSON & CO. LTD v. PERCY DALTON (LONDON) LTD

Court of Appeal [1957] 2 Q.B. 621; [1957] 3 W.L.R. 403; 101 S.J. 610; [1957] 2 All E.R. 846; [1957] 2 Lloyd's Rep. 1

The defendants had a quantity of orange juice which they wished to ship to Hamburg. The plaintiffs, as agents of the owners of the vessel on which the orange juice was to be shipped, informed the defendants that the barrels containing the orange juice were old and frail and that some were leaking and that a claused bill of lading should be granted. The defendants required a clean bill of lading, and the shipowners, at the defendants' request and on a promise that the defendants would give to them an indemnity, signed bills of lading stating that the barrels were "shipped in apparent good order and condition." The defendants, pursuant to their promise, entered into an indemnity whereby they undertook unconditionally to indemnify the master and the owners of the vessel against all losses which might arise from the issue of clean bills of lading in respect of the goods. The barrels, when delivered at Hamburg, were leaking and the shipowners had to make good the loss. The plaintiffs sued the defendants under the indemnity, the benefit of which had been assigned to them. The defendants refused to pay, alleging that the contract of indemnity was illegal, because it had as its object the making by the shipowners of a fraudulent misrepresentation. It was found that the shipowners did not desire or intend that anyone should be defrauded. It appeared from the evidence that the granting of clean bills of lading against indemnities was a common practice.

Judge Block gave judgment for the plaintiffs. The defendants appealed.

MORRIS L.J.: . . . On the facts as found, and indeed on the facts which are not in dispute, the position was therefore that, at the request of the defendants, the plaintiffs made a representation which they knew to be false and which they intended should be relied upon by persons who received the bill of lading, including any banker who might be concerned. In these circumstances, all the elements of the tort of deceit were present. Someone who could prove that he suffered damage by relying on the representation could sue for damages. I feel impelled to the conclusion that a promise to indemnify the plaintiffs against any loss resulting to them from making the representation is unenforceable. The claim cannot be put forward without basing it upon an unlawful transaction. The promise upon which the plaintiffs rely is in effect this: if you will make a false representation, which will deceive indorsees or bankers, we will indemnify you against any loss that may result to you. I cannot think that a court should lend its aid to enforce such a bargain.

The conclusion thus reached is one that may seem unfortunate for the plaintiffs, for I gain the impression that they did not pause to realise the significance and the implications of what they were asked to do. There was evidence that the practice of giving indemnities upon the issuing of clean bills of lading is not uncommon. That cannot in any way alter the analysis of the present transaction, but it may help to explain how the plaintiffs came to accede to the defendants' request. There may perhaps be some circumstances in which indemnities can properly be given. Thus if a shipowner thinks that he has detected some faulty condition in regard to goods to be taken on board, he may be assured by the shipper that he is entirely mistaken: if he is so persuaded by the shipper, it may be that he could honestly issue a clean bill of lading, while taking an indemnity in case it was later shown that there had in fact been some faulty condition. Each case must depend upon its circumstances. But even if it could be shown that there existed to any extent a practice of knowingly issuing clean bills when claused bills should have been issued, no validating effect for any particular transaction could in consequence result. . . .

I would allow the appeal.

PEARCE L.J. delivered a concurring judgment.

LORD EVERSHED M.R. dissenting: in *Alexander v. Rayson* [1936] 1 K.B. 169, 182, the principle was stated by this court in the passage already recited by my brother Pearce. "It is settled law that an agreement to do an act that is illegal or immoral or contrary to public policy, or to do any act for a consideration that is illegal or immoral or contrary to public policy, is unlawful and therefore void. But it often happens that an agreement which in itself is not unlawful is made with the intention of one or both parties to make use of the subject-matter for an unlawful purpose, that is to say, a purpose that is illegal, immoral or contrary to public policy. . . . In such a case any party to the agreement who had the unlawful intention is precluded from suing upon it. *Ex turpi causa non oritur act:.*"

The adjective *"turpis"* is thus expanded to cover the three characteristics: (1) illegal, (2) immoral and (3) contrary to public policy. The classic case of *Pearce v. Brooks* (above, p. 666) is the obvious instance of immorality; and when the purpose of the agreement, or the intended use of its subject-matter, is the commission of a crime or the doing of some prohibited act (for example, the infringement of the customs law), the principle is no less obviously invoked on grounds both of illegality and of public policy. The principle no doubt extends further. In *Alexander v. Rayson* itself, the proved purpose of the plaintiff was to use the instruments, which he entered into with the defendant, in order to deceive and cheat (as he did) the local rating authority: and in *Berg v. Sadler and Moore* [1937] 2 K.B. 158 (to take an example from the cases cited to us) the plaintiff was shown to have been engaged upon an enterprise of deliberate deception which amounted to a false pretence.

But how much further does it go? Does it cover every case in which the subject-matter of the action is shown to be part of a transaction which has involved the making by the plaintiff of a statement known to be untrue in a commercial document intended to be acted upon in the ordinary commercial course, even though it is not proved to have been acted on in fact by anyone, or (if it has been acted upon) not to have caused loss or damage to any person: and even though the plaintiff is not shown to have had at any stage in the transaction any intention that anyone should be damnified or to have been "dishonest" as that word is ordinarily understood? . . .

Thoughtless, misguided and irresponsible the plaintiffs may have been; but I am not satisfied for my part, on the evidence and what I take to have been the views of the judge, that it would be just for this court to condemn them as fraudulent and dishonest.

But even if we should conclude that the representation was made with such recklessness as to amount, in law, to the same thing as a representation made with the deliberate intention of deceiving, still I am not satisfied that it would be right to hold, or that any authority compels us to hold, that the proved circumstances were such that it would be contrary to public policy, *contra bonos mores*, to allow the plaintiffs to recover upon the contract of indemnity from the defendants. I have, I hope, sufficiently perused all the authorities, including those cited by my brother Morris. I have failed to find any case (apart from those involving immorality or public illegality) in which, upon the principle *ex turpi causa non oritur actio*, a plaintiff has been cast from the seat of judgment who has not been found personally dishonest. If there was a false statement deliberately made, it was made in accordance with a practice that was common and well known in the trade and with an intention that any consequences should be covered by their or their principals' liability to make compensation—in other words, in circumstances in which the plaintiffs, by reason of the current laxity in that respect, honestly believed would not damage anybody.

In my judgment, the result is not one which requires the court upon grounds of public policy to deny to the plaintiffs their right to sue.

Appeal allowed.

Questions
Is every contract induced by fraud thereby tainted with illegality?

(b) ON ACTIONS FOR THE RECOVERY OF PROPERTY

TAYLOR v. CHESTER

Queen's Bench (1869) L.R. 4 Q.B. 309; 10 B. & S. 237; 38 L.J.Q.B. 225; 21 L.T. 359; 33 J.P. 709

The judgment of the court (Mellor and Hannen JJ.) was delivered by

MELLOR J.: In this case the plaintiff declared on the bailment of the half of a £50 Bank of England note, to the defendant, to be redelivered on request, alleging a refusal by the defendant to redeliver such half-note. The second count was in detinue for the same half-note.

The defendant, after traversing the delivery and detention of the note, and to the second count denying that it was the property of the plaintiff, pleaded separately and specially to both counts, in effect, that the half-note in question had been deposited by the plaintiff with the defendant by way of pledge, to secure the repayment of money due and money then advanced by the defendant to the plaintiff and then due.

The plaintiff joined issue on the defendant's pleas, and also replied specially that the alleged debt or sum, in respect of which the defendant justified the non-delivery and detention of the half-note, was for wine and suppers, supplied by the defendant in a brothel and disorderly house kept by the defendant, for the purpose of being consumed there by the plaintiff and divers prostitutes in a debauch there, to incite them to riotous, disorderly, and immoral conduct, and for money knowingly lent for the purposes of being expended in riot and debauchery and immoral conduct.

The defendant rejoined, taking issue on the replication, and also demurred to its validity.

On the trial before me at Manchester, the case of the plaintiff was that the note had not been deposited at all with the defendant, but had been fraudulently taken and appropriated by her. The jury, however, did not adopt his view of the facts, but found that the note was deposited by way of security, as alleged by the defendant, and they further found upon the evidence that the debt was incurred and the money advanced as alleged in the plaintiff's replication to the special pleas. On these findings, the verdict was entered for the defendant, with liberty to the plaintiff to move to enter the verdict for him for £50 to be reduced to nominal damages in case the note should be returned to the plaintiff.

A rule was accordingly obtained to enter the verdict for the plaintiff, on the ground that the jury had found all the issues tendered by the plaintiff in his favour.

It was argued on the part of the defendant, in showing cause against the rule, and in support of the demurrer to the special replication of the plaintiff that, upon the finding of the jury and the facts as admitted by the demurrer, the plaintiff and defendant were *in pari delicto*, and that therefore upon the whole record judgment must be entered for the defendant. On the part of the plaintiff it was argued that it was the defendant who was relying on the illegal transaction as an answer to a claim of the plaintiff, founded on his ownership of the note, and his rights to recover back the same, and many startling consequences were pointed out to us as likely to result from a decision that the plaintiff could not recover. We have fully considered the case, and are satisfied that the plaintiff cannot recover under the circumstances found by the jury, and admitted on the record. The maxim that *in pari delicto potior est conditio possidentis*, is as thoroughly settled as any proposition of law can be. It is a maxim of law, established, not for the benefit of plaintiffs or defendants, but is founded on the principles of public policy, which will not assist a plaintiff who has paid over money or handed over property in pursuance of an illegal or immoral contract, to recover it back, "for the courts will not assist an illegal transaction in any respect": *per* Lord Ellenborough in *Edgar v. Fowler*, 3 East 222; *Collins v. Blantern*, 2 Wis. 341; Lord Mansfield in *Holman v. Johnson* Cowp. at p. 343.

The true test for determining whether or not the plaintiff and the defendant were *in pari delicto*, is by considering whether the plaintiff could make out his case otherwise than through the medium and by the aid of the illegal transaction to which he was himself a party: *Simpson v. Bloss* 7 Taunt. 246, *Fivaz v. Nicholls*, 2 C.B. 501. It is to be observed that in this case the illegality is not in a collateral matter, as in the case of *Feret v. Hill*, 15 C.B. 207; 23 L.J.C.P. 185, which was cited for the plaintiff; but is the direct result of the transaction upon which the deposit of the half-note took place.

Mr Herschell's argument was based upon the hypothesis that in spite of the finding of the jury, the plaintiff was entitled to recover by virtue of his property in the half-note, and that it was the defendant alone who set up an immoral transaction as the answer to the plaintiff's claim.

This argument appears to us to be founded upon an entirely erroneous view of the facts. The plaintiff, no doubt, was the owner of the note, but he pledged it by way of security for the price of meat and drink provided for, and money advanced to him by the defendant. Had the case rested there, and no pleading raised the question of illegality, a valid pledge would have been created, and a special property conferred upon the defendant in the half-note, and the plaintiff could only have recovered by showing payment or a tender of the amount due. In order to get rid of the defence arising from the plea, which set up an existing pledge on the half-note, the plaintiff had recourse to the special replication, in which he was obliged to set forth the immoral and illegal character of the contract upon which the half-note had been deposited. It was, therefore, impossible for him to recover except through the medium and by the aid of an illegal transaction to which he was himself a party. Under such circumstances, the maxim *in pari delicto potior est conditio possidentis*, clearly applies, and is decisive of the case.

It would appear from the case of *Scarfe v. Morgan*, 4 M. & W. at pp. 281, 282, *per* Parke B., in delivering the judgment of the court, that, notwithstanding the illegality of the transaction itself, out of which the deposit in this case arose, the lien would exist, because the contract was executed and the special property had passed by the delivery of the half-note to the defendant, and the maxim would apply *in pari delicto potior est conditio possidentis*.

It is, however, sufficient in the present case to determine it on the ground that the plaintiff could not recover without showing the true character of the deposit; and that being upon an illegal consideration, to which he was himself a party, he was precluded from obtaining "the assistance of the law" to recover it back. It is not necessary to consider what might have been the effect of a tender of the amount for which the note was pledged, and there is nothing to raise any such question in this case.

The result, therefore, will be that the verdict must stand for the defendant on the issues taken on the special pleas, and for the plaintiff on the issue taken on the replication; but as upon the whole record it is manifest that the plaintiff cannot recover, judgment will be entered for the defendant.

Judgment for the defendant.

Question

Cheshire, Fifoot and Furmston (*Law of contract* (12th ed.), p. 379) cite *Taylor v. Chester* for the proposition that "If . . . a seller sues for the recovery of goods sold and delivered under an illegal contract he will fail, for to justify his claim he must necessarily disclose his own iniquity." Did the plaintiff in *Taylor v. Chester*, fail because he disclosed his own iniquity? Or because there was a valid and unredeemed pledge? What would have been the situation if the plaintiff had tendered the amount for which the note was pledged?

BOWMAKERS LTD v. BARNET INSTRUMENTS LTD

Court of Appeal [1945] K.B. 65; 89 S.J. 22; 172 L.T. 1; 61 T.L.R. 62;
[1944] 2 All E.R.

Appeal from Croom-Johnson J.

The plaintiffs, Bowmakers, Ltd, sued the defendants, Barnet Instruments Ltd, to recover damages for the conversion of certain machine tools which they alleged were their property. The tools in question were the subject of three hiring agreements between the plaintiffs and the defendants, each containing an option to purchase, dated March 18, April 15 and June 16, 1944. They were described in the statement of claim as agreements Nos. 1, 2 and 3. In each case the machines were originally the property of a man named Smith, who was prepared to sell them to the defendants at prices which they were willing to pay, though not at once. The goods comprised in the first agreement were originally the subject of a contract of sale between Smith and the defendants, but this contract was rescinded. Eventually it was arranged in every case, for the convenience of the defendants, that the defendants should obtain possession of the machines, not by a direct purchase from Smith, but under a hire-purchase agreement from the plaintiffs. In pursuance of this arrangement Smith sold the goods to the plaintiffs, and the plaintiffs entered into the three agreements with the defendants. The contracts between the plaintiffs and the defendants were in a familiar form. Each of them contained a provision for the monthly payment of hire and further provided that "if the hirer shall duly make the said payments and strictly observe and perform all the terms and conditions on his part herein contained then the hirer shall thereupon have the option of purchasing the said chattels for the sum of ten shillings." The defendants after making some, but by no means all the agreed payments, sold for their own advantage, and so converted to their use, all the machines except that one which was the subject of agreement 2, and this latter they also converted to their own use by refusing to deliver it up to the plaintiffs on demand. They maintained, however, that the plaintiffs had no remedy against them.

The goods comprised in agreements 1 and 2 were new machine tools and the agreements may have infringed the provisions of S.R. & O. 1940, No.1784 S.R. & O. 1940, No. 1374 was infringed by agreement 3.

Croom-Johnson J. held that no illegality had been proved in respect of any of the hiring agreements and, accordingly, entered judgment for the plaintiffs against the defendants for damages for conversion. The defendants appealed. The judgment of the Court of Appeal (Scott and du Parcq L.JJ. and Uthwatt J.) was delivered by:

DU PARCQ L.J.: . . . we will assume in favour of the defendants that the three hiring agreements were all, as they allege, and for the reasons which they give, affected by illegality.

The question, then, is whether in the circumstances the plaintiffs are without a remedy. So far as their claim in conversion is concerned, they are not relying on the hiring agreements at all. On the contrary, they are willing to admit for this purpose that they cannot rely on them. They simply say that the machines were their property, and this, we think, cannot be denied. We understood Mr Gallop to concede that the property had passed from Smith to the plaintiffs, and still remained in the plaintiffs at the date of the conversion. At any rate, we have no doubt that this is the legal result of the transaction and we find support for this view in the dicta of Parke B. in *Scarfe v. Morgan* (1838) 4 M. & W. 270.

Why then should not the plaintiffs have what is their own? No question of the defendants' rights arises. They do not, and cannot, pretend to have had any legal right to possession of the goods at the date of the conversion. Their counsel has to rely, not on any alleged right of theirs, but on the requirements of public policy. He was entitled, and bound, to do so, although, as Lord Mansfield long ago observed, "The objection, that a contract is immoral or illegal as between plaintiff and defendant, sounds at all times very ill in the mouth of the defendant." "No court," Lord Mansfield added, "will lend its aid to a man who founds his cause of action upon an immoral or an illegal act": *Holman v. Johnson* (1775) 1 Cowp. 341,

343. This principle, long firmly established, has probably even been extended since Lord Mansfield's day. Mr Gallop is, we think, right in his submission that, if the sale by Smith to the plaintiffs was illegal, then the first and second hiring agreements were tainted with the illegality, since they were brought into being to make that illegal sale possible, but, as we have said, the plaintiffs are not now relying on these agreements or on the third hiring agreement. Prima facie, a man is entitled to his own property, and it is not a general principle of our law (as was suggested) that when one man's goods have got into another's possession in consequence of some unlawful dealings between them, the true owner can never be allowed to recover those goods by an action. The necessity of such a principle to the interests and advancement of public policy is certainly not obvious. The suggestion that it exists is not, in our opinion, supported by authority. It would, indeed, be astonishing if (to take one instance) a person in the position of the defendant in *Pearce v. Brooks* (above, p. 666), supposing that she had converted the plaintiff's brougham to her own use, were to be permitted, in the supposed interests of public policy, to keep it or the proceeds of its sale for her own benefit. The principle which is, in truth, followed by the courts is that stated by Lord Mansfield, that no claim founded on an illegal contract will be enforced, and for this purpose the words "illegal contract" must now be understood in the wide sense which we have already indicated and no technical meaning must be ascribed to the words "founded on an illegal contract." The form of the pleadings is by no means conclusive. More modern illustrations of the principle on which the courts act are *Scott v. Brown, Doering, McNab & Co.* [1892] 2 Q.B. 724 and *Alexander v. Rayson* [1936] 1 K.B. 169; but, as Lindley L.J. said in the former of the cases just cited: "Any rights which [a plaintiff] may have irrespective of his illegal contract will, of course, be recognised and enforced."

In our opinion, a man's right to possess his own chattels will as a general rule be enforced against one who, without any claim of right, is detaining them or has converted them to his own use, even though it may appear either from the pleadings, or in the course of the trial that the chattels in question came into the defendant's possession by reason of an illegal contract between himself and the plaintiff, provided that the plaintiff does not seek, and is not forced, either to found his claim on the illegal contract or to plead its illegality in order to support his claim.

Mr Gallop sought to derive assistance from the decision of the Court of Queen's Bench in *Taylor v. Chester* (above, p. 680). The decision there was, however, entirely consonant with the view which we have expressed. It differed from the present case in one essential respect, since in that case the defendant had prima facie a right to possession of the half-note which the plaintiff claimed. She was holding it as a pledge to secure the payment of money which remained due. The plaintiff could only defeat her plea by showing that the money due had been lent for an immoral purpose, and this could not avail him since he was *in pari delicto* with her. The judgment of the court, delivered by Mellor J., makes it plain that this was the *ratio* of the decision. "The plaintiff," said Mellor J., "no doubt, was the owner of the note, but he pledged it by way of security for the price of meat and drink provided for, and money advanced to, him by the defendant. Had the case rested there, and no pleading raised the question of illegality, a valid pledge would have been created, and a special property conferred upon the defendant in the half-note, and the plaintiff could only have recovered by showing payment or a tender of the amount due. In order to get rid of the defence arising from the plea, which set up an existing pledge of the half-note, the plaintiff had recourse to the special replication, in which he was obliged to set forth the inmoral and illegal character of the contract upon which he half-note had been deposited. It was, therefore, impossible for him to recover except through the medium and by the aid of an illegal transaction to which he was himself a party. Under such circumstances, the maxim *in pari delicto potior est conditio possidentis* clearly applies, and is decisive of the case." The Latin maxim which Mellor J. cited must not be understood as meaning that where a transaction is vitiated by illegality the person left in possession of goods after its completion is always and of necessity entitled to keep them. Its true meaning is that, where the circumstances are such that the court will refuse to assist either party, the consequence must, in fact, follow that the party in possession will not be disturbed. As Lord Mansfield said in the case already cited, the defendant then obtains an advantage "contrary to the real justice," and, so to say, "by accident."

It must not be supposed that the general rule which we have stated is subject to no exception. Indeed, there is one obvious exception, namely, that class of cases in which the goods claimed are of such a kind that it is unlawful to deal in them at all, as for example, obscene books. No doubt, there are others, but it is unnecessary, and would we think be unwise, to seek to name them all or to forecast the decisions which would be given in a variety of circumstances which may hereafter arise. We are satisfied that no rule of law, and no considerations of public policy, compel the court to dismiss the plaintiffs' claim in the case before us, and to do so would be, in our opinion, a manifest injustice. The appeal will be dismissed, with costs.

Appeal dismissed.

Note

C.J. Hamson, 10 C.L.J. at p. 251, says *re* the statement: "They (*sc.* the defendants) do not and cannot pretend to have had any legal right to possession of the goods at the date of the conversion": "This is remarkable. The court has held, and rightly, that the illegal sale by Smith to the plaintiffs vested the general property of the goods in the plaintiffs. But if the sale was, despite its illegality, effective to vest the general property in the plaintiffs, the bailment by the plaintiffs to the defendants under the illegal hire-purchase agreements was and must have been equally effective to vest the special property in the defendants."

Questions

1. Should the owner be able to give evidence of the terms of an unlawful bailment, in order to show that the defendant (the bailee) has, by transgressing those terms, committed an act of conversion?

2. Is a bailee who sets up the bailment able to prove the performance of his obligations under the bailment, even if it be illegal, to resist an action for conversion brought by the owner/bailor?

3. Burglar A lends burglar B his jemmy. B refuses to return it. Can A sue B in conversion? *Cf. N.C.B. v. Gamble* [1959] 1 Q.B. 11 at p. 20, *per* Devlin J.

TINSLEY v. MILLIGAN

House of Lords [1994] 1 A.C. 340; [1993] 3 W.L.R. 126; [1993] 3 All E.R. 65

Two women, T and M, described by the trial judge as lovers, jointly bought a house which was registered in the name of T as sole legal owner. They used the house as a lodging house in a joint business venture which provided most of their income. They agreed to register the house in the sole name of T so that M could make false claims to the Department of Social Security for benefit. After some years M told the Department what she had done and thereafter continued to draw benefit. T and M quarrelled. T moved out and brought an action, claiming possession and asserting ownership of the house. M counterclaimed that the house was held on trust for M and T in equal shares. T's defence to the counterclaim was based on (i) the maxim, *ex turpi causa* and (ii) the principle that she who comes to equity must come with clean hands. M obtained judgment on claim and counterclaim. T's appeal to the Court of Appeal was dismissed (Ralph Gibson L.J. dissenting) holding that it should adopt a "flexible and pragmatic" approach to the maxim and the "clean hands" principle, asking whether enforcement would be an affront to the public conscience. Here, where both claims were tainted with illegality and it would be a disproportionate penalty to deprive M of her share her house, it would not be an affront to the public conscience. T appealed to the House of Lords.

Lord Keith, agreeing with Lord Goff, said that he would allow the appeal.

Lord Goff said that the "public conscience" test developed in a series of cases in the Court of Appeal was little different, if at all, from stating that the court has discretion to grant or refuse relief. It was very difficult to reconcile the principle of policy stated by Lord Mansfield in *Holman v. Johnson* (1775) 1 Cowp. 341 at 343. Having examined the authorities, he continued:

It is sufficient for present purposes to say, with the greatest respect, that to apply the public conscience test as qualifying the principle established for nearly two hundred years as applicable in cases such as the present is, for reasons I have already stated, inconsistent with numerous authorities binding on the Court of Appeal. In expressing this opinion, I wish to stress that, as can so often happen, your Lordships have had the benefit of a far fuller citation of authority than was available to the Court of Appeal, which has revealed that (contrary to the view expressed by Nicholls L.J. [1992] Ch. 310 at 322)) the decision in *Curtis v. Perry* (1802) 6 Ves 739, 31 ER 1285 was not followed by "a surprising dearth of authority, for over a century". On the contrary, there were numerous cases decided during that period, many of which I have already cited, in which the principle was recognised or applied. Nor in my opinion can it be said (as stated by Nicholls L.J. [1992] Ch. 310 at 324)) that the authorities in this line in which equity refuses its assistance can properly be regarded as examples of cases in which, in particular circumstances, the court considered that to have granted relief would have been "an affront to the public conscience", or (as suggested by Lloyd L.J. ([1992] Ch. 310 at 341)) as cases "where the equitable balance came down against the plaintiff". There is no trace of any such principle forming part of the decisions in any of the cases in question. It follows that in my opinion, on the authorities, it was not open to the majority of the Court of Appeal to dismiss the appellant's claim on the basis of the public conscience test invoked by Nicholls L.J., or indeed on the basis of the flexible approach adopted by Lloyd L.J. . . .

I recognise, of course, the hardship which the application of the present law imposes upon the respondent in this case; and I do not disguise my own unhappiness at the result. But, bearing in mind the passage from the judgment of Ralph Gibson L.J. which I have just quoted, I have to say that it is by no means self-evident that the public conscience test is preferable to the present strict rules. Certainly, I do not feel able to say that it would be appropriate for your Lordships House, in the face of a long line of unbroken authority stretching back over two hundred years, now by judicial decision to replace the principles established in those authorities by a wholly different discretionary system.

LORD JAUNCEY and LORD LOWRY made speeches agreeing with LORD BROWNE-WILKINSON and dismissing the appeal.

LORD BROWNE-WILKINSON.: My Lords, I agree with the speech of my noble and learned friend Lord Goff of Chieveley that the consequences of being a party to an illegal transaction cannot depend, as the majority in the Court of Appeal held, on such an imponderable factor as the extent to which the public conscience would be affronted by recognising rights created by illegal transactions. However, I have the misfortune to disagree with him as to the correct principle to be applied in a case where equitable property rights are acquired as a result of an illegal transaction. [Having reviewed the cases, his Lordship continued.]

From these authorities the following propositions emerge.

(1) Property in chattels and land can pass under a contract which is illegal and therefore would have been unenforceable as a contract.

(2) A plaintiff can at law enforce property rights so acquired provided that he does not need to rely on the illegal contract for any purpose other than providing the basis of his claim to a property right.

(3) It is irrelevant that the illegality of the underlying agreement was either pleaded or emerged in evidence: if the plaintiff has acquired legal title under the illegal contract that is enough.

I have stressed the common law rules as to the impact of illegality on the acquisition and enforcement of property rights because it is the appellant's contention that different principles apply in equity. In particular it is said that equity will not aid the respondent to assert, establish or enforce an equitable, as opposed to a legal, proprietary interest since she was a party to the fraud on the Department of Social Security. The house was put in the name of the appellant alone (instead of joint names) to facilitate the fraud. Therefore, it is said, the respondent does not come to equity with clean hands: consequently, equity will not aid her. . . .

The presumption of a resulting trust is, in my view, crucial in considering the authorities. On that presumption (and on the contrary presumption of advancement) hinges the answer to the crucial question: does a plaintiff claiming under a resulting trust have to rely on the underlying illegality? Where the presumption of resulting trust applies, the plaintiff does not have to rely on the illegality. If he proves that the property is vested in the defendant alone but that the plaintiff provided part of the purchase money, or voluntarily transferred the property to the defendant, the plaintiff establishes his claim under a resulting trust unless either the contrary presumption of advancement displaces the presumption of resulting trust or the defendant leads evidence to rebut the presumption of resulting trust. Therefore, in cases where the presumption of advancement does not apply, a plaintiff can establish his equitable interest in the property without relying in any way on the underlying illegal transaction. In this case the respondent as defendant simply pleaded the common intention that the property should belong to both of them and that she contributed to the purchase price: she claimed that in consequence the property belonged to them equally. To the same effect was her evidence-in-chief. Therefore the respondent was not forced to rely on the illegality to prove her equitable interest. Only in the reply and the course of the respondent's cross-examination did such illegality emerge: it was the appellant who had to rely on that illegality.

Although the presumption of advancement does not directly arise for consideration in this case, it is important when considering the decided cases to understand its operation. On a transfer from a man to his wife, children or others to whom he stands in loco parentis, equity presumes an intention to make a gift. Therefore in such a case, unlike the case where the presumption of resulting trust applies, in order to establish any claim the plaintiff has himself to lead evidence sufficient to rebut the presumption of gift and in so doing will normally have to plead, and give evidence of, the underlying illegal purpose. . . .

In my judgment the time has come to decide clearly that the rule is the same whether a plaintiff founds himself on a legal or equitable title: he is entitled to recover if he is not forced to plead or rely on the illegality, even if it emerges that the title on which he relied was acquired in the course of carrying through an illegal transaction.

As applied in the present case, that principle would operate as follows. The respondent established a resulting trust by showing that she had contributed to the purchase price of the house and that there was a common understanding between her and the appellant that they owned the house equally. She had no need to allege or prove *why* the house was conveyed into the name of the appellant alone, since that fact was irrelevant to her claim: it was enough to show that the house was in fact vested in the appellant alone. The illegality only emerged at all because the appellant sought to raise it. Having proved these facts, the respondent had raised a presumption of resulting trust. There was no evidence to rebut that presumption. Therefore the respondent should succeed. This is exactly the process of reasoning adopted by the Ontario Court of Appeal in *Gorog v. Kiss* (1977) 78 DLR (3d) 690, which in my judgment was rightly decided.

Finally, I should mention a further point which was relied on by the appellant. It is said that, once the illegality of the transaction emerges, the court must refuse to enforce the transaction and all claims under it whether pleaded or not: see *Scott v. Brown Doering McNab & Co.* [1892] 2 Q.B. 724. Therefore, it is said, it does not matter whether a plaintiff relies on or gives evidence of the illegality: the court will not enforce the plaintiff's rights. In my judgment, this submission is plainly ill-founded. There are many cases where a plaintiff has succeeded, notwithstanding that the illegality of the transaction under which she acquired the property has emerged: see, for example, *Bowmakers Ltd v. Barnet Instruments Ltd* [1945] K.B. 65 and *Sajan Singh v. Sardara Ali* [1960] AC 167. In my judgment the court is only entitled and bound to dismiss a claim on the basis that it is founded on an illegality in those cases where the illegality is of a kind which would have provided a good defence if raised by the defendant. In a case where the plaintiff is not seeking to enforce an unlawful contract but founds his case on collateral rights acquired under the contract (such as a right of property) the court is neither bound nor entitled to reject the claim unless the illegality of necessity forms part of the plaintiff's case.

I would therefore dismiss the appeal.

Appeal dismissed.

Section 3. Void Contracts

(a) CONTRACTS IN RESTRAINT OF TRADE

KORES MANUFACTURING CO. LTD v. KOLOK MANUFACTURING CO. LTD

Court of Appeal [1959] Ch. 108; [1958] 2 W.L.R. 858; 102 S.J. 362; [1958] 2 All E.R. 65; [1958] R.P.C. 200

Two companies agreed by letter that neither would, without the written consent of the other, employ at any time any person who had been the servant of the other company during the period of five years previous to that time. Both companies were engaged in manufacturing similar products involving chemical processes, including exceedingly dirty work, in relation to which their respective technical employees might become possessed of confidential information and trade secrets. It was contemplated at the time of the agreement that their factories would be adjoining, though this had since ceased to be the case.

The action was brought by one company to restrain the other from employing a named former employee of the plaintiffs. Lloyd-Jacob J. held the contract void as in restraint of trade. On appeal, the judgment of the Court of Appeal (Jenkins, Pearce and Ormerod L.JJ.) was delivered by:

JENKINS L.J. having referred to and considered various authorities on restraints between master and servant): It is true that the agreement of 1934 was between two employers, and not between employer and employee. Nevertheless, it was wholly and solely directed to preventing the employees of either contracting party, on ceasing to be employed by them, from entering the employment of the other contracting party. Apart from the question of trade secrets and confidential information, we have described the matter requiring protection as being the adequacy and stability of the plaintiffs' and defendants' respective complements of employees. That, no doubt, is an interest which employers are entitled to protect by all legitimate means, as by paying good wages and making their employment attractive. We have further described the danger against which that interest required protection as being the unimpeded secession of employees of either of the parties to that of the other of them under the inducement of higher wages or better working conditions. But an employer has no legitimate interest in preventing an employee, after leaving his service, from entering the service of a competitor merely on the ground that the new employer is a competitor. The danger of the adequacy and stability of his complement of employees being impaired through employees leaving his service and entering that of a rival is not a danger against which he is entitled to protect himself by exacting from his employees covenants that they will not, after leaving his service enter the service of any competing concern. If in the present case the plaintiffs had taken a covenant from each of their employees that he would not enter the service of the defendants at any time during the five years next following the termination of his service with the plaintiffs, and the defendants had taken from their employees covenants restraining them in similar terms from entering the employment of the plaintiffs, we should have thought that (save possibly in very exceptional cases involving trade secrets, confidential information and the like) all such covenants would on the face of them be bad as involving a restraint of trade which was unreasonable as between the parties. Here the plaintiffs and the defendants have, as it seems to us, sought to do indirectly that which they could not do directly by reciprocal undertakings between themselves not to employ each other's former employees, entered into over the heads of their respective employees, and without their knowledge. It seems to us to be open to question whether an agreement such as that, directed to preventing employees of the parties from doing that which they could not by individual covenants with their respective employers validly bind themselves not to do, should be accorded any greater validity than individual covenants by the employees themselves would possess. We prefer, however, to leave that question open, and to found our conclusions as to the invalidity of the agreement of 1934 on the reasons given earlier in this judgment.

Appeal dismissed.

ESSO PETROLEUM CO. LTD v. HARPER'S GARAGE (STOURPORT) LTD

House of Lords [1968] A.C. 269; [1967] 2 W.L.R. 871; [1967] 1 All E.R. 699

H owned and operated two garages, Mustow Green and Corner, and had entered into solus agreements with E. The solus agreement in respect of Mustow Green garage was for a period of four years and five months from July 1, 1963, and contained clauses providing that H should buy exclusively E's motor fuel at their wholesale schedule prices; that sales should be made at E's retail prices (a price maintenance provision made unenforceable by the Resale Prices Act 1964); that the garage should be open at all reasonable hours; and that H should, if the garage were sold, get the purchaser to enter into a similar solus agreement. In relation to Corner, E had a mortgage dated October 6, 1962, over the premises to secure a principal sum of £7,000 lent to H and interest as well as a similar solus agreement; the duration of this agreement was 21 years from July 1, 1962, which was also the period over which the mortgage money was to be repayable by instalments. The mortgage contained provisions that H should buy exclusively E's motor fuels (as in the other agreement) and be open at all reasonable hours and also that the mortgage itself should not be redeemable other than in accordance with the covenant for repayment, *viz.*, by instalments over 21 years. From about the end of 1963 H had sold other fuels at Mustow Green and since August 1964 at Corner. E brought actions for injunctions in respect of each garage and the suits were consolidated in the present proceedings. Mocatta J. granted an injunction. On appeal, this decision was reversed by the Court of Appeal (Denning M.R., Harman and Diplock L.JJ.) on the ground that the ties in the agreements were in restraint of trade and unenforceable. E appealed to the House of Lords.

LORD REID: if a contract is within the class of contracts in restraint of trade the law which applies to it is quite different from the law which applies to contracts generally. In general unless a contract is vitiated by duress, fraud or mistake its terms will be enforced though unreasonable or even harsh and unconscionable, but here a term in restraint of trade will not be enforced unless it is reasonable. And in the ordinary case the court will not remake a contract: unless in the special case where the contract is severable, it will not strike out one provision as unenforceable and enforce the rest. But here the party who has been paid for agreeing to the restraint may be unjustly enriched if the court holds the restraint to be too wide to be enforceable and is unable to adjust the consideration given by the other party.

It is much too late now to say that this rather anomalous doctrine of restraint of trade can be confined to the two classes of case to which it was originally applied. But the cases outside these two classes afford little guidance as to the circumstances in which it should be applied. In some it has been assumed that the doctrine applies and the controversy has been whether the restraint was reasonable. And in others where one might have expected the point to be taken it was not taken, perhaps because counsel thought that there was no chance of the court holding that the restraint was too wide to be reasonable.

[Having referred to various authorities, his lordship continued:]

The main argument submitted for the appellant on this matter was that restraint of trade means a personal restraint and does not apply to a restraint on the use of a particular piece of land. Otherwise, it was said, every covenant running with the land which prevents its use for all or for some trading purposes would be a covenant in restraint of trade and therefore unenforceable unless it could be shown to be reasonable and for the protection of some legitimate interest. It was said that the present agreement only prevents the sale of petrol from other suppliers on the site of the Mustow Green garage. It leaves the respondents free to trade anywhere else in any way they choose. But in many cases a trader trading at a particular place does not have the resources to enable him to begin trading elsewhere as well, and if he did he might find it difficult to find another suitable garage for sale or to get planning permission to open a new filling station on another site. As the whole doctrine of restraint of trade is based on public policy its application ought to depend less on legal niceties or theoretical possibilities than on the practical effect of a restraint in hampering that freedom which it is the policy of the law to protect.

It is true that it would be an innovation to hold that ordinary negative covenants preventing the use of a particular site for trading of all kinds or of a particular kind are within the scope of the doctrine of restraint of trade. I do not think they are. Restraint of trade appears to me to imply that a man contracts to give up some freedom which otherwise he would have had. A person buying or leasing land had no previous right to be there at all, let alone to trade there, and when he takes possession of that land subject to a negative restrictive covenant he gives up no right or freedom which he previously had. I think that the "tied house" cases might be explained in this way, apart from *Biggs v. Hoddinott*,[1] where the owner of

[1] [1898] 2 Ch. 307; 14 T.L.R. 504, C.A.

a free house had agreed to a tie in favour of a brewer who had lent him money. Restraint of trade was not pleaded. If it had been, the restraint would probably have been held to be reasonable. But there is some difficulty if a restraint in a lease not merely prevents the person who takes possession of the land under the lease from doing certain things there, but also obliges him to act in a particular way. In the present case the respondents before they made this agreement were entitled to use this land in any lawful way they chose, and by making this agreement they agreed to restrict their right by giving up their right to sell there petrol not supplied by the appellants.

In my view this agreement is within the scope of the doctrine of restraint of trade as it had been developed in English law. Not only have the respondents agreed negatively not to sell other petrol but they have agreed positively to keep this garage open for the sale of the appellants' petrol at all reasonable hours throughout the period of the tie. It was argued that this was merely regulating the respondent's trading and rather promoting than restraining his trade. But regulating a person's existing trade may be a greater restraint than prohibiting him from engaging in a new trade. And a contract to take one's whole supply from one source may be much more hampering than a contract to sell one's whole output to one buyer. I would not attempt to define the dividing line between contracts which are and contracts which are not in restraint of trade, but in my view this contract must be held to be in restraint of trade. So it is necessary to consider whether its provisions can be justified.

But before considering this question I must deal briefly with the other agreement tying the corner garage for 21 years. The rebate and other advantages to the respondents were similar to those in the mustow green agreement but in addition the appellants made a loan of £7,000 to the respondents to enable them to improve their garage and this loan was to be repaid over the 21 years of the tie. In security they took a mortgage of this garage. The agreement provided that the loan should not be paid off earlier than at the dates stipulated. But the respondents now tender the unpaid balance of the loan and they say that the appellants have no interest to refuse to accept repayment now, except in order to maintain the tie for the full 21 years. . . .

The appellants argue that the fact that there is a mortgage excludes any application of the doctrine of restraint of trade. But I agree with your lordships in rejecting that argument. I am prepared to assume that, if the respondents had not offered to repay the loan so far as it is still outstanding, the appellants would have been entitled to retain the tie. But, as they have tendered repayment, I do not think that the existence of the loan and the mortgage puts the appellants in any stronger position to maintain the tie than they would have been in if the original agreements had permitted repayment at an earlier date. The appellants must show that in the circumstances when the agreement was made a tie for 21 years was justifiable. . . .

The Court of Appeal held that these ties were for unreasonably long periods. They thought that, if for any reason the respondents ceased to sell the appellants' petrol, the appellants could have found other suitable outlets in the neighbourhood within two or three years. I do not think that

that is the right test. In the first place there was no evidence about this and I do not think that it would be practicable to apply this test in practice. It might happen that when the respondents ceased to sell their petrol, the appellants would find such an alternative outlet in a very short time. But, looking to the fact that well over 90 per cent. Of existing filling station, are tied and that there may be great difficulty in opening a new filling station, it might take a very long time to find an alternative. Any estimate of how long it might take to find suitable alternatives for the respondents' filling stations could be little better than guesswork.

I do not think that the appellants' interest can be regarded so narrowly. They are not so much concerned with any particular outlet as with maintaining a stable system of distribution throughout the country so as to enable their business to be run efficiently and economically. In my view there is sufficient material to justify a decision that ties of less than five years were insufficient, in the circumstances of the trade when these agreements were made, to afford adequate protection to the appellants' legitimate interests. And if that is so I cannot find anything in the details of the Mustow Green agreement which would indicate that it is unreasonable. It is true that if some of the provisions were operated by the appellants in a manner which would be commercially unreasonable they might put the respondents in difficulties. But I think that a court must have regard to the fact that the appellants must act in such a way that they will be able to obtain renewals of the great majority of their very numerous ties, some of which will come to an end almost every week. If in such circumstances a garage owner chooses to rely on the commercial probity and good sense of the producer, I do not think that a court should hold his agreement unreasonable because it is legally capable of some misuse. I would therefore allow the appeal as regards the Mustow Green agreement.

But the Corner garage agreement involves much more difficulty. Taking first the legitimate interests of the appellants a new argument was submitted to your lordships that, apart from any question of security for their loan, it would be unfair to the appellants if the respondents, having used the appellants' money to build up their business, were entitled after a comparatively short time to be free to seek better terms from a competing producer. But there is no material on which I can assess the strength of this argument and I do not find myself in a position to determine whether it has any validity. A tie for 21 years stretches far beyond any period for which developments are reasonably foreseeable. Restrictions on the garage owner which might seem tolerable and reasonable in reasonably foreseeable conditions might come to have a very different effect in quite different conditions: the public interest comes in here more strongly. And, apart from a case where he gets a loan, a garage owner appears to get no greater advantage from a 21 tie than he gets from a five-year tie. So I would think that there must at least be some clearly established advantage to the producing company—something to show that a shorter period would not be adequate—before so long a period could be justified. But in this case there is no evidence to prove anything of the kind. And the other material which I have thought it right to consider does not appear to me to assist the appellant here. I would therefore dismiss the appeal as regards the Corner garage agreement.

LORDS MORRIS OF BORTH-Y-GEST, HODSON, PEARCE and WILBERFORCE delivered speeches to similar effect.

Appeal allowed in part and dismissed in part.
Order of Mocatta J. restored as to Mustow Green.

Note
In *Shell U.K. Ltd v. Lostock Garage Ltd* [1977] 1 All E.R. 481 the solus agreement, as varied in 1966, was reasonable. The parties did not foresee in 1966, that circumstances would arise in which Shell would subsidise neighbouring garages to such an extent as to force Lostock to trade at a loss. Because of the oil crisis, this happened in 1975. Lord Denning M.R. said that it is a mistake to say that a covenant in unreasonable restraint of trade is "invalid" or "void" *ab initio*. It is only unenforceable. He contrasted two situations: "First, when *at the time* of making the contract, it is seen that it may in the future operate unfairly or unreasonably, the courts will not enforce it. Secondly, when it is found *afterwards* to operate unreasonably or unfairly—in circumstances which were not envisaged beforehand—the courts will not enforce it." He therefore held that, so long as Shell continued to subsidise the neighbouring garages, the court should not enforce the covenant.
Ormrod and Bridge L.JJ. disagreed with this "novel principle." Ormrod L.J. said: "It would introduce into the law an unprecedented discretion in the court to suspend for a time a term in a contract; the repercussions of this are quite unforeseeable and unmanageable. For example, it would at once alter the approach of the courts to covenants in restraint of trade generally, because, if the restraint could be temporarily suspended when it was operating oppressively, many more covenants would pass the normal test at the time they were entered into. Moreover, neither party will be able to know when a covenant is or is not enforceable, or if temporarily unenforceable, when it becomes enforceable again."
Lord Denning M.R. and Ormrod L.J. held that it would not be just and equitable to grant Shell an injunction while they were supporting the neighbouring garages. Bridge L.J. agreed in the result because Shell's breach of the term which he found to be implied, amounted to a repudiation of the contract.
And see *Alec Lobb (Garages) Ltd v. Total Oil*, above, p. 650.

A. SCHROEDER MUSIC PUBLISHING CO. LTD v. MACAULAY

House of Lords [1974] 1 W.L.R. 1308; [1974] 3 All E.R. 616

The respondent, then young and unknown as a song-writer, entered into a contract with the appellant whereby the latter engaged his exclusive services for five years. The agreement, the appellants' standard form, provided that the respondent assigned to the appellants full copyright for the whole world in each original composition and lyric for which he, whether solely or in collaboration, was responsible at any time during the period of the agreement or at any time prior to it in so far as the respondent still owned and controlled them. The appellants agreed to pay the respondent £50 as an advance on royalties payable under the contract and to recoup the £50 therefrom. This procedure was to be repeated throughout the period of the agreement. If in that time the total of the respondent's royalties and advances equalled or exceeded £5,000, the agreement would automatically be extended for a further five years. The appellants could at any time terminate the agreement by one month's written notice but the respondent had no such reciprocal right: the appellants could further freely assign the agreement and copyright under it but the respondent could assign his rights only with the appellants' consent. The appellants were further under no obligation to publish any of the respondent's work. In the respondent's action for a declaration that the agreement was contrary to public policy, the appellants claimed that their standard form, common to agreements between song publishers and song-writers did not need justification on the ground of reasonableness. The House of Lords affirmed the decision of the Court of Appeal (Russell, Cairns L.JJ., Goulding J.) affirming the decision of

Plowman J. for the plaintiff. On the inference of the reasonableness of standard form contracts—

LORD DIPLOCK: Standard forms of contracts are of two kinds. The first, of very ancient origin, are those which set out the terms on which mercantile transactions of common occurrence are to be carried out. Examples are bills of lading, charter-parties, policies of insurance, contracts of sale in the commodity markets. The standard clauses in these contracts have been settled over the years by negotiation by representatives of the commercial interests involved and have been widely adopted because experience has shown that they facilitate the conduct of trade. Contracts of these kinds affect not only the actual parties to them but also others who may have a commercial interest in the transactions to which they relate, as buyers or sellers, charterers or shipowners, insurers or bankers. If fairness or reasonableness were relevant to their enforceability the fact that they are widely used by parties whose bargaining power is fairly matched would raise a strong presumption that their terms are fair and reasonable.

The same presumption, however, does not apply to the other kind of standard form of contract. This is of comparatively modern origin. It is the result of the concentration of particular kinds of business in relatively few hands. The ticket cases in the nineteenth century provide what are probably the first examples. The terms of this kind of standard form of contract have not been the subject of negotiation between the parties to it, or approved by any organisation representing the interests of the weaker party. They have been dictated by that party whose bargaining power, either exercised alone or in conjunction with others providing similar goods or services, enables him to say: "If you want these goods or services at all, these are the only terms on which they are obtainable. Take it or leave it."

To be in a position to adopt this attitude towards a party desirous of entering into a contract to obtain goods or services provides a classic instance of superior bargaining power. It is not without significance that on the evidence in the present case, music publishers in negotiating with song-writers whose success has been already established do not insist on adhering to a contract in the standard form they offered to the respondent. The fact that the appellants' bargaining power *vis-à-vis* the respondent was strong enough to enable them to adopt this take-it-or-leave-it attitude raises no presumption that they used it to drive an unconscionable bargain with him, but in the field of restraint of trade it calls for vigilance on the part of the court to see that they did not.

(b) SEVERANCE

In *Attwood v. Lamont* [1920] 3 K.B. 571 (C.A.) Younger L.J. said: "The doctrine of severance has not, I think gone further than to make it permissible in a case where the covenant is not really a single covenant but is in effect a combination of several distinct covenants. In that case and where severance can be carried out without the addition or alteration of a word, it is permissible. But in that case only."

RONBAR ENTERPRISES LTD v. GREEN

Court of Appeal [1954] 1 W.L.R. 815; 98 S.J. 369; [1954] 2 All E.R. 266

By an agreement of 1951, the plaintiff company and the defendant became partners in a weekly paper of sporting and entertainment news. A clause of the agreement provided that if one partner bought the other out, "the partner whose share is purchased shall not for five years from such date directly or indirectly carry on or be engaged or interested in any business similar to or competing with the business of the partnership." The partnership was in due course determined and the clause became operative. A company was formed to publish a periodical similar to that of the plaintiff company and the defendant wrote articles for this new publication. The plaintiff company sought an injunction against the defendant in pursuance of the clause cited. Roxburgh J. granted an interlocutory injunction. On appeal:

JENKINS L.J.: Mr Eastham, on behalf of the defendant, argued that there had been no breach of that restrictive provision because, on its true construction, it did not extend to the rendering of services for a salary or wages as distinct from being engaged in business on one's own account. I do not agree. In my opinion the words "carry on or be engaged or interested in any business similar to or competing with the business of the partnership" are apt, particularly in view of the word "engaged" to include a case where the party subject to the restriction takes employment in a business of either of the kinds mentioned at a salary or wages, as well as a case in which he embarks on such a business on his own account or in a partnership. In my view, therefore, assuming that the covenant is valid, what has been done does prima facie amount to a breach of it.

As to its validity, that was attacked by Mr Eastham on these grounds. First, he said that if, contrary to his primary submission, it did extend to prevent the defendant working as a salaried employee, it was on that account too wide. In my view, that is not so. I do not think that it can be said that this covenant is too wide, merely because it would extend to cases of salaried employment, or employment at a wage in a business of either of the kinds mentioned.

Mr Eastham next contends that the covenant is unreasonable as being unlimited in point of area. He says that a business similar to the business of the partnership might be carried on in any part of the world, and in whatever part of the world it was carried on it would be a breach of this covenant read in accordance with its terms. In my view, that argument must almost certainly prevail unless it is possible to sever the covenant, so as to segregate the words "similar to or," and make it read "shall not . . . carry on or be engaged or interested in any business similar to the business of the partnership or any business competing with the business of the partnership," the covenant being thus treated as imposing two distinct restrictions with respect to two distinct kinds of business—that is to say, a business competing with the business of the partnership, and a business similar to the business of the partnership. . . .

[Having discussed various authorities, his Lordship proceeded:] The explanation of the different conclusion reached in *Attwood v. Lamont* (above, p. 695) as compared with *Goldsoll v. Goldman* [1915] Ch. 292 and the *British Reinforced Concrete Case* [1921] 2 Ch. 563 appears to be that

Attwood v. Lamont was a case as between master and servant whereas the other two cases were cases as between vendor and purchaser, as is the present case. I think that it can be regarded as settled that the court takes a far stricter and less favourable view of covenants in restraint of trade entered into between master and servant than it does of similar covenants between vendor and purchaser. In the case of a covenant between vendor and purchaser, the court recognises that it is perfectly proper for the parties, in order to give efficacy to the transaction, to enter into such restrictive provisions as regards competition as are reasonably necessary to enable the purchaser to reap the benefit of that which he has bought; and restrictions of that kind are regarded as necessary, not only in the interests of the purchaser but in the interests of the vendor also, for they not only preserve the value to the purchaser of that which he buys but also enable the vendor to realise a satisfactory price. It is obvious that in many types of business the goodwill would be well-night unsaleable if it was unlawful for the vendor to enter into an adequate covenant against competition. . . . I find that what the defendant has been doing is plainly contrary to the terms of the restrictive covenant. I find further that prima facie the covenant, construed in the way that I have construed it, should not be held to be invalid.

HODSON L.J.: On the question whether the covenant was unreasonably wide, Mr Hesketh conceded that, as it stood, the covenant was unreasonably wide because the words "similar to or" preceding the word "competing" would be unnecessary for the protection of the plaintiff company's interest. Recognising that position, the judge has excised those words, and thereby severed the covenant; and the question principally argued on this appeal is whether it was legitimate so to do.

I have no doubt in my own mind that it is. It is quite clear that in a "vendor and purchaser case," in so far as matters of geography are concerned—as was pointed out by this court in *Goldsoll v. Goldman* which has already been cited—it is quite legitimate to deal with the area by severance.

HARMAN J. delivered a concurring judgment.

Appeal dismissed.

SCORER v. SEYMOUR-JOHNS

Court of Appeal [1966] 1 W.L.R. 1419; [1966] 3 All E.R. 347

The defendant had been employed by the plaintiff in sole charge at the Kingsbridge office of the plaintiff's estate agents' business, of which the main office was in Dartmouth. The written contract eventually concluded between them provided, *inter alia*, that, for three years after the termination of the contract, the defendant would not "undertake or carry on either alone or in partnership or be employed or interested directly or indirectly in any capacity whatsoever in the business of an auctioneer surveyor or estate agent or in any ancillary business carried on by (the plaintiff) at (the Kingsbridge and Dartmouth offices) within a five mile radius thereof. . . ." The defendant was dismissed by the plaintiff after a few months and thereafter practised on his own account in Salcombe within five miles of Kingsbridge but outside a five miles' radius of Dartmouth. In this action by the plaintiff to enforce the covenant, the county court judge held the covenant severable to be operative only in respect of Kingsbridge and granted the plaintiff an injunction. On appeal, Sellers and Danckwerts L.JJ. delivered judgments dismissing the appeal.

SALMON L.J.: I confess that my mind has fluctuated during the course of this appeal. It has been rightly pointed out to us on behalf of the plaintiff that this defendant behaved very badly when he was in the plaintiff's employ. Customers came to the office at Kingsbridge, of which the defendant was in charge, to sell their properties. It was his duty, at law and in common honesty, to sell those properties on behalf of his employer, the plaintiff. What he did, at any rate in one case, in breach of that duty, was to sell the property as a venture of his own and pocket the commission.

The fact, however, that he behaved improperly is really beside the point, because it cannot help to solve the only question in this case, which is: Was this covenant an unreasonable restraint of trade at the date it was written, namely, on June 2, 1964?

At one time it seemed to me that *Bowler v. Lovegrove* [1921] 1 Ch. 642 went a very long way, if not the whole of the way, to getting the defendant home. The county court judge in his judgment says (rightly, I now think) that the circumstances of the instant case are quite different from the circumstances of *Bowler v. Lovegrove*. He did not, however, state the respects in which the circumstances were different. Our attention has been drawn to these very important matters by Mr Crawford on behalf of the plaintiff. P.O. Lawrence J. said:

"It is true that the defendant came into personal contact with the plaintiffs' customers. But this fact loses its significance when the nature of the business carried on by the plaintiffs and the duties of the defendant in connection with such business are considered. The plaintiffs' customers with whom the defendant came into personal contact were not the ordinary recurring customers such as exist in most other businesses."

He was saying that the fact that a servant comes into personal contact with customers in the normal case might justify such a covenant but that it lost its significance in the case he was considering because the customers were not recurring customers. In the instant case, the judge has accepted the evidence which was called by the plaintiff; and there was cogent evidence on behalf of the plaintiff that he had many recurring customers. This is the fact which to my mind distinguishes the instant case from *Bowler v. Lovegrove*.

When the defendant was in the Kingsbridge office he *was* in effect the Kingsbridge office. Every customer who came into that office dealt with him. He was in a position in which he would have every opportunity of gaining knowledge of the customers' business and influence over the customers.

[Having considered *Morris v. Saxelby* [1916] 1 A.C. 688, his Lordship continued:]

Mr Crawford has argued (and in my judgment he is right) that in cases such as the present a covenant such as has been suggested would be too narrow from a practical point of view to be of any use. It might be very difficult indeed for the plaintiff to know whether or not, and perhaps almost impossible to prove that, the defendant was whittling away the plaintiff's trade connection. As far as this point is concerned, it is interesting to notice that a convenant in a form such as the present was approved in the House of Lords in *Fitch v. Dewes* [1921] 2 A.C. 158. That was a case of a covenant by a solicitor against his managing clerk. It was never suggested in that case by anyone, either in the Court of Appeal or the House of Lords, that the covenant was too wide because it would have been sufficient if it had merely restrained the clerk from dealing with any former client of his employers.

As far as the question as to whether this covenant is severable is concerned, I have no doubt but that it is. The defendant was restrained from carrying on the business or being engaged in the business of an estate agent or auctioneer within five miles of Kingsbridge and then, quite separately, within five miles of Dartmouth. The plaintiff does not seek to support the prohibition in respect of Dartmouth. The prohibition in respect of Kingsbridge stands quite separately and I have no difficulty in saying that the covenant is plainly severable. Equally plainly, in my view, it is not against public policy.

I agree that the appeal should be dismissed.

Appeal dismissed.

Note

In *M. & S. Drapers (A Firm) v. Reynolds* [1957] 1 W.L.R. 9; [1956] 3 All E.R. 814 R had been employed from March 1953 by M. & S., a firm of credit drapers, bringing with him a connection of customers acquired in previous employments. In August 1955 the parties entered into a written agreement determinable by two weeks' notice on either side and providing for R a weekly wage of £10. One clause of the agreement provided, "For a period of five years following the determination of this agreement the servant shall not . . . sell or canvass or solicit orders . . . by way of the business of a credit draper from any person whose name shall have been inscribed on the books of the firm as a customer during the three years immediately preceding such determination upon whom the servant has called in the course of his duties for the firm." In 1956, R left the employment of M. & S. and thereafter sold goods by way of credit draper's business to persons who were on the books of M. & S. during the three years before he left them. M. & S. sought to enforce the covenant against him. The county court judge held that, although M. & S. might have some proprietary rights in their list of customers a rescription of five years for a man of R's position, earning a modest wage, was unreasonable and gave judgment for R. On appeal, the Court of Appeal (Hodson, Morris and Denning L.JJ.) dismissed the appeal. Morris L.J. said, "as the judge pointed out in his judgment in his case, the customers of one credit draper can always be canvassed and are likely to be canvassed by other credit drapers. In a sphere where competition is normally free, since every householder is a potential purchaser, and where successful selling must to some extent depend upon the personal abilities of particular salesmen, and also to some extent on the quality of the goods which the salesman's employer can offer, a period of five years' banishment from particular doorsteps seems to me to be in any event of wholly unwarranted duration."

See also *T. Lucas & Co. Ltd v. Mitchell* [1972] 1 W.L.R. 938; *Home Countries Dairies Ltd v. Skilton* [1970] 1 W.L.R. 526; [1970] 1 All E.R. 1227, C.A.

GOODINSON v. GOODINSON

Court of Appeal [1954] 2 Q.B. 118; [1954] 2 W.L.R. 1121; 98 S.J. 369;
[1954] 2 All E.R. 255

Appeal from Judge Wrangham, sitting at Stamford County Court.

The husband and wife having separated, on July 21, 1950, the following agreement was entered into between them: "Whereas the husband without admitting any legal liability to maintain the wife has agreed to pay a weekly sum of £2 for the maintenance and support of the wife and child of the husband and wife. Now it is hereby agreed as follows: (1) The husband will pay to the wife for her support and maintenance the sum of £1 a week and for the support and maintenance of the child of the husband and wife, namely, David Goodinson . . . the sum of £1 a week until he shall attain the age of sixteen years. . . . (2) The said sum for the maintenance of the wife shall be paid by the husband during their joint lives so long as the wife shall lead a chaste life. (3) The wife will out of the said weekly sums or otherwise support and maintain herself and the said child and will indemnify the husband against all debts to be incurred by her and against all liability whatsoever in respect of the said child, and will not in any way at any time hereafter pledge the husband's credit. . . . (5) The wife shall not so long as the husband shall punctually make the weekly payments agreed to be made herein, commence or prosecute any matrimonial proceedings against the husband, but upon the failure of the husband to make the said payments as and when the said payments become due, the wife shall be at full liberty at her election to pursue all and every remedy in this regard, either by enforcement of the provisions hereof or as if this agreement had not been made."

The husband having fallen into arrears in the weekly payments the wife brought the present action in the county court, claiming £200 arrears of maintenance.

For the husband it was contended that by clause 5 of the agreement the wife undertook not to commence or prosecute a petition for divorce even if the husband was guilty of adultery; and that it was therefore an illegal covenant, *contra bonos mores*, and the whole agreement was invalidated and unenforceable.

The county court judge found for the wife. He held that clause 5 should be read as a covenant only against taking matrimonial proceedings in respect of maintenance; that the words "in this regard," coupled with other language used in the clause, indicated that the meaning of the covenant should be so restricted; and that, therefore, the covenant was not illegal. It was clearly not enforceable and the agreement must be read as if clause 5 did not exist.

The husband appealed.

Somervell L.J.: . . . In *Bennett v. Bennett* (below, p. 702) it was pointed out that there are two kinds of illegality of differing effect. The first is where the illegality is criminal, or *contra bonos mores*, and in those cases, which I will not attempt to enumerate or further classify, such a provision, if an ingredient in a contract, will invalidate the whole, although there may be many other provisions in it. There is a second kind of illegality which has no such taint; the other terms in the contract stand if the illegal portion can be severed, the illegal portion being a provision which the court, on ground of public policy, will not enforce. The simplest and most common example of the latter class of illegality is a contract for the sale of a business which contains a provision restricting the vendor from competing in or engaging in trade for a certain period or within a certain area. There are many cases in the books where, without in any way impugning the contract of sale, some provision restricting competition has been regarded as in restraint of trade and contrary to public policy. There are many cases where not only has the main contract to purchase been left standing but part of the clause restricting competition has been allowed to stand.

That being the position, it is argued in the first place that this agreement is based on the construction of clause 5, which, it is submitted, on its true construction, is an agreement not to take matrimonial proceedings of any

kind, whatever matrimonial offence may be committed by the husband. . . .
I think that when the clause is read as a whole the undertaking not to
prosecute any matrimonial proceedings so long as the sum is paid is
restricted, as the judge held, to matrimonial proceedings in respect of the
matters dealt with in the agreement. The judge put it in this way: "In my
judgment the clause should be read in a limited sense, as a covenant only
against taking matrimonial proceedings in respect of maintenance." He
relied, quite rightly, on the words "in this regard" in the latter part of the
clause. That point therefore goes. . . .

[Having discussed various authorities, his Lordship proceeded:] Of
course, as regards a clause of this kind in a separation deed, it may be plain
that the separation is an important ingredient which remains notwithstanding the disregard of an undertaking not to sue *quoad* the quantum of
maintenance. But in this case it is not a separation agreement. It is sought
on behalf of the husband to invoke this principle that, if the only
consideration moving from one side is a covenant which the law holds to
be unenforceable, then there is nothing to support the undertaking on the
other side in respect of which the unenforceable covenant purported to be a
consideration. Reliance is placed on the application of that principle in
Bennett v. *Bennett*. That was a special case in somewhat unusual circumstances and so far as this part of it is concerned it turned on the actual
provisions of the agreement and equally on the circumstances in which,
and the time at which, the agreement was entered into. . . .

The special circumstances, I think, are emphasised by an observation of
mine which is embodied in the headnote: "Any application to delete,
amend, or dismiss a claim for maintenance on the ground that the husband
has made provision for the wife should be left to be dealt with by the judge
at the hearing of the petition, and if made to a registrar before the hearing
should be adjourned." It was in those circumstances, and having regard to
the terms of the agreement in that case, that we held that the unenforceable
agreement was the main, though not the sole consideration for the
husband's agreement as to quantum. In the present case I think that there
is ample consideration to support this agreement apart from the covenant
not to sue, and to enable it to be enforced as against the husband in the
way in which the wife seeks to enforce it in these proceedings. First of all,
clause 3, under which she agreed to support and maintain herself and the
child and "indemnify the husband against all debts to be incurred by her
and against all liability whatsoever in respect of the said child and will not
in any way at any time hereafter pledge the husband's credit" is, of course,
coextensive with the sum to be paid, subject to the time for which the
agreement will subsist. Although, I think the point was not take a below, I
should have thought that the undertaking by the wife to have the custody
and control of the child and bring it up until it was 16 years old, in the
terms of clause 4 was also a consideration.

Then there is a matter which is more directly related to clause 5. This is
an agreement by the wife as to these sums as at that date and in the
circumstances then existing. If she had chosen to take proceedings, say, in
the following month it would not have been a complete shield but it would
have been of great importance (as the passages to which I have referred
point out) on the husband's side in asking the court to reject her
application. It would have been the strongest possible evidence unless

relevant circumstances had changed. For these reasons, therefore, I think that there is ample consideration to support this agreement. . . .

Birkett L.J. concurred.

Romer L.J. gave a judgment dismissing the appeal.

Appeal dismissed.

Note

In *Bennett v. Bennett* [1952] 1 K.B. 249; [1952] 1 T.L.R. 400; [1952] 1 All E.R. 413, C.A., after a wife had presented a petition for dissolution of marriage in which she asked for alimony pending suit and maintenance for herself and a son but before pronouncement of a decree nisi, her husband entered into a deed whereby he agreed *inter alia* to make financial provision for the wife and son in consideration of which a clause of the deed provided that she was to accept such provision in full satisfaction of any claims that she and the children might have against the husband and not to bring any proceedings for maintenance or the like. On hearing of the deed, the registrar struck out the prayer for maintenance. In due course, a decree nisi was granted to the wife and became absolute. The husband fell into arrears with his payments under the deed and the wife brought this action to recover the arrears. The Court of Appeal (Somervell, Denning and Romer L.JJ.), affirming the decision of Devlin J., held that the covenant provided the sole consideration for the husband's undertaking and was contary to public policy as seeking to oust the jurisdiction of the court and rejected the wife's claim.

The decision in *Bennett v. Bennett* was overruled by the Maintenance Agreements Act 1957 (above, pp. 220–221): see now Matrimonial Causes Act 1973, s.34.

MISREPRESENTATION ACT 1967

(As amended by the Unfair Contract Terms Act 1977)

Removal of certain bars to rescission for innocent misrepresentation
1. Where a person has entered into a contract after a misrepresentation has been made to him, and—

(a) the misrepresentation has become a term of the contract; or
(b) the contract has been performed;

or both, then, if otherwise he would be entitled to rescind the contract without alleging fraud, he shall be so entitled, subject to the provisions of this Act, notwithstanding the matters mentioned in paragraphs (a) and (b) of this section.

Damages for misrepresentation
2.—(1) Where a person has entered into a contract after a misrepresentation has been made to him by another party thereto and as a result thereof he has suffered loss, then, if the person making the misrepresentation would be liable to damages in respect thereof had the misrepresentation been made fraudulently, that person shall be so liable notwithstanding that the misrepresentation was not made fraudulently, unless he proves that he had reasonable ground to believe and did believe up to the time the contract was made that the facts represented were true.

(2) Where a person has entered into a contract after a misrepresentation has been made to him otherwise than fraudulently, and he would be entitled, by reason of the misrepresentation, to rescind the contract, then, if it is claimed, in any proceedings arising out of the contract, that the contract ought to be or has been rescinded, the court or arbitrator may declare the contract subsisting and award damages in lieu of rescission, if of opinion that it would be equitable to do so, having regard to the nature of the misrepresentation and the loss that would be caused by it if the contract were upheld, as well as to the loss that rescission would cause to the other party.

(3) Damages may be awarded against a person under subsection (2) of this section whether or not he is liable to damages under subsection (1) thereof, but where he is so liable any award under the said subsection (2) shall be taken into account in assessing his liability under the said subsection (1).

Avoidance of provision excluding liability for misrepresentation
3. If a contract contains a term which would exclude or restrict—

(a) any liability to which a party to a contract may be subject by reason of any misrepresentation made by him before the contract was made; or

703

(b) any remedy available to another party to the contract by reason of such a misrepresentation,

that term shall be of no effect except in so far as it satisfies the requirement of reasonableness as stated in section 11(1) of the Unfair Contract Terms Act 1977; and it is for those claiming that the term satisfies that requirement to show that it does.

Section 4 is *repealed*.

Saving for past transactions
5. Nothing in this Act shall apply in relation to any misrepresentation or contract of sale which is made before the commencement of this Act.

Short title, commencement and extent
6.—(1) This Act may be cited as the Misrepresentation Act 1967.
(2) This Act shall come into operation at the expiration of the period of one month beginning with the date on which it is passed.
(3) This Act does not extend to Scotland.
(4) This Act does not extend to Northern Ireland.

For discussion of the Act, see above, p. 352.

UNFAIR CONTRACT TERMS ACT 1977

(As amended by the Sale of Goods Act 1979, Supply of Goods and Services Act 1982 and Occupiers' Liability Act 1984)

PART I

AMENDMENT OF LAW FOR ENGLAND AND WALES AND NORTHERN IRELAND

Introductory

Scope of Part I
1.—(1) For the purposes of this Part of this Act, "negligence" means the breach—

(a) of any obligation, arising from the express or implied terms of a contract, to take reasonable care or exercise reasonable skill in the performance of the contract;
(b) of any common law duty to take reasonable care or exercise reasonable skill (but not any stricter duty);
(c) of the common duty of care imposed by the Occupiers' Liability Act 1957 or the Occupiers' Liability Act (Northern Ireland) 1957.

(2) This Part of this Act is subject to Part III; and in relation to contracts, the operation of sections 2 to 4 and 7 is subject to the exceptions made by Schedule 1.
(3) In the case of both contract and tort, sections 2 to 7 apply (except where the contrary is stated in section 6(4)) only to business liability, that is liability for breach of obligations or duties arising—

(a) from things done or to be done by a person in the course of a business (whether his own business or another's); or

(b) from the occupation of premises used for business purposes of the occupier; and references to liability are to be read accordingly but liability of an occupier of premises for breach of an obligation or duty towards a person obtaining access to the premises for recreational or educational purposes, being liability for loss or damage suffered by reason of the dangerous state of the premises, is not a business liability of the occupier unless granting that person such access for the purposes contained falls within the business purposes of the occupier.

(4) In relation to any breach of duty or obligation, it is immaterial for any purpose of this Part of this Act whether the breach was inadvertent or intentional, or whether liability for it arises directly or vicariously.

Avoidance of liability for negligence, breach of contract, etc.

Negligence liability

2.—(1) A person cannot by reference to any contract term or to a notice given to persons generally or to particular persons exclude or restrict his liability for death or personal injury resulting from negligence.

(2) In the case of other loss or damage, a person cannot so exclude or restrict his liability for negligence except in so far as the term or notice satisfies the requirement of reasonableness.

(3) Where a contract term or notice purports to exclude or restrict liability for negligence a person's agreement to or awareness of it is not of itself to be taken as indicating his voluntary acceptance of any risk.

Liability arising in contract

3.—(1) This section applies as between contracting parties where one of them deals as consumer or on the other's written standard terms of business.

(2) As against that party, the other cannot by reference to any contract term—

(a) when himself in breach of contract, exclude or restrict any liability of his in respect of the breach; or

(b) claim to be entitled—
   (i) to render a contractual performance substantially different from that which was reasonably expected of him, or
   (ii) in respect of the whole or any party of his contractual obligation, to render no performance at all,

except in so far as (in any of the cases mentioned above in this subsection) the contract term satisfies the requirement of reasonableness.

Unreasonable indemnity clauses

4.—(1) A person dealing as consumer cannot by reference to any contract term be made to indemnify another person (whether a party to the contract or not) in respect of liability that may be incurred by the other for negligence or breach of contract, except in so far as the contract term satisfies the requirement of reasonableness.

(2) This section applies whether the liability in question—

(a) is directly that of the person to be indemnified or is incurred by him vicariously;
(b) is to the person dealing as consumer or to someone else.

Liability arising from sale or supply of goods

"Guarantee" of consumer goods

5.—(1) In the case of goods of a type ordinarily supplied for private use or consumption, where loss or damage—

(a) arises from the goods proving defective while in consumer use; and
(b) results from the negligence of a person concerned in the manufacture or distribution of the goods,

liability for the loss or damage cannot be excluded or restricted by reference to any contract term or notice contained in or operating by reference to a guarantee of the goods.

(2) For these purposes—

(a) goods are to be regarded as "in consumer use" when a person is using them, or has them in his possession for use, otherwise than exclusively for the purposes of a business; and
(b) anything in writing is a guarantee if it contains or purports to contain some promise or assurance (however worded or presented) that defects will be made good by complete or partial replacement, or by repair, monetary compensation or otherwise.

(3) This section does not apply as between the parties to a contract under or in pursuance of which possession or ownership of the goods has passed.

Sale and hire-purchase

6.—(1) Liability for breach of the obligations arising from—

(a) section 12 of the Sale of Goods Act 1979 (seller's implied undertakings as to title, etc.);
(b) section 8 of the Supply of Goods (Implied Terms) Act 1973 (the corresponding thing in relation to hire-purchase),

cannot be excluded or restricted by reference to any contract term.

(2) As against a person dealing as consumer, liability for breach of the obligations arising from—

(a) section 13, 14 or 15 of the 1979 Act (seller's implied undertakings as to conformity of goods with description or sample, or as to their quality or fitness for a particular purpose);
(b) section 9, 10 or 11 of the 1973 Act (the corresponding things in relation to hire-purchase),

cannot be excluded or restricted by reference to any contract term.

(3) As against a person dealing otherwise than as consumer, the liability specified in subsection (2) above can be excluded or restricted by reference to a contract term, but only in so far as the term satisfies the requirement of reasonableness.

(4) The liabilities referred to in this section are not only the business liabilities defined by section 1(3), but include those arising under any contract of sale of goods or hire-purchase agreement.

Miscellaneous contracts under which goods pass

7.—(1) Where the possession or ownership of goods passes under or in pursuance of a contract not governed by the law of sale of goods or hire-purchase, subsections (2) to (4) below apply as regards the effect (if any) to be given to contract terms excludings or restricting liability for breach of obligation arising by implication of law from the nature of the contract.

(2) As against a person dealing as consumer, liability in respect of the goods' correspondence with description or sample, or their quality or fitness for any particular purpose, cannot be excluded or restricted by reference to any such term.

(3) As against a person dealing otherwise than as consumer, that liability can be excluded or restricted by reference to such a term, but only in so far as the term satisfies the requirement of reasonableness.

(3A) Liability for breach of the obligations arising under section 2 of the Supply of Goods and Services Act 1982 (implied terms about title etc. in certain contracts for the transfer of the property in goods) cannot be excluded or restricted by reference to any such term.

(4) Liability in respect of—

(a) the right to transfer ownership of the goods, or give possession; or
(b) the assurance of quiet possession to a person taking goods in pursuance of the contract,

cannot be excluded or restricted by reference to any such term except in so far as the term satisfies the requirement of reasonableness.

(5) This section does not apply in the case of goods passing on a redemption of trading stamps within the Trading Stamps Act 1964 or the Trading Stamps Act (Northern Ireland) 1965.

[Section 8, which amended the Misrepresentation Act 1967 (above, p. 703) is omitted.]

Effect of breach

9.—(1) Where for reliance upon it a contract term has to satisfy the requirement of reasonableness, it may be found to do so and be given effect accordingly notwithstanding that the contract has been terminated either by breach or by a party electing to treat it as repudiated.

(2) Where on a breach the contract is nevertheless affirmed by a party entitled to treat it as repudiated, this does not of itself exclude the requirement of reasonableness in relation to any contract term.

Evasion by means of secondary contract

10. A person is not bound by any contract term prejudicing or taking away rights of his which arise under, or in connection with the perfor-

mance of, another contract, so far as those rights extend to the enforcement of another's liability which this Part of this Act prevents that other from excluding or restricting.

Explanatory provisions

The "reasonableness" test

11.—(1) In relation to a contract term, the requirement of reasonableness for the purposes of this Part of this Act, section 3 of the Misrepresentation Act 1967 and section 3 of the Misrepresentation Act (Northern Ireland) 1967 is that the term shall have been a fair and reasonable one to be included having regard to the circumstances which were, or ought reasonably to have been, known to or in the contemplation of the parties when the contract was made.

(2) In determining for the purposes of section 6 or 7 above whether a contract term satisfies the requirement of reasonableness, regard shall be had in particular to the matters specified in Schedule 2 to this Act; but this subsection does not prevent the court or arbitrator from holding, in accordance with any rule of law, that a term which purports to exclude or restrict any relevant liability is not a term of the contract.

(3) In relation to a notice (not being a notice having contractual effect), the requirement of reasonableness under this Act is that it should be fair and reasonable to allow reliance on it, having regard to all the circumstances obtaining when the liability arose or (but for the notice) would have arisen.

(4) Where by reference to a contract term or notice a person seeks to restrict liability to a specified sum of money, and the question arises (under this or any other Act) whether the term or notice satisfies the requirement of reasonableness, regard shall be had in particular (but without prejudice to subsection (2) above in the case of contract terms) to—

(a) the resources which he could expect to be available to him for the purpose of meeting the liability should it arise; and
(b) how far it was open to him to cover himself by insurance.

(5) It is for those claiming that a contract term or notice satisfies the requirement of reasonableness to show that it does.

"Dealing as consumer"

12.—(1) A party to a contract "deals as consumer" in relation to another party if—

(a) he neither makes the contract in the course of a business nor holds himself out as doing so; and
(b) the other party does make the contract in the course of a business; and
(c) in the case of a contract governed by the law of sale of goods or hire-purchase, or by section 7 of this Act, the goods passing under or in pursuance of the contract are of a type ordinarily supplied for private use or consumption.

(2) But on a sale by auction or by competitive tender the buyer is not in any circumstances to be regarded as dealing as consumer.

(3) Subject to this, it is for those claiming that a party does not deal as consumer to show that he does not.

Varieties of exemption clause

13.—(1) To the extent that this Part of this Act prevents the exclusion or restriction of any liability it also prevents—

(a) making the liability or its enforcement subject to restrictive or onerous conditions;
(b) excluding or restricting any right or remedy in respect of the liability, or subjecting a person to any prejudice in consequence of his pursuing any such right or remedy;
(c) excluding or restricting rules of evidence or procedure;

and (to that extent) sections 2 and 5 to 7 also prevent excluding or restricting liability by reference to terms and notices which exclude or restrict the relevant obligation or duty.

(2) But an agreement in writing to submit present or future differences to arbitration is not to be treated under this Part of this Act as excluding or restricting any liability.

Interpretation of Part I

14. In this Part of this Act—

"business" includes a profession and the activities of any government department or local or public authority;
"goods" has the same meaning as in the Sale of Goods Act 1979;
"hire-purchase agreement" has the same meaning as in the Consumer Credit Act 1974;
"negligence" has the meaning given by section 1(1);
"notice" includes an announcement, whether or not in writing, and any other communication or pretended communication; and
"personal injury" includes any disease and any impairment of physical or mental condition.

PART II, which applies only to Scotland, is omitted.

PART III

PROVISIONS APPLYING TO WHOLE OF UNITED KINGDOM

Miscellaneous

International supply contracts

26.—(1) The limits imposed by this Act on the extent to which a person may exclude or restrict liability by reference to a contract term do not apply to liability arising under such a contract as is described in subsection (3) below.

(2) The terms of such a contract are not subject to any requirement of reasonableness under section 3 or 4: and nothing in Part II of this Act shall

require the incorporation of the terms of such a contract to be fair and reasonable for them to have effect.

(3) Subject to subsection (4), that description of contract is one whose characteristics are the following—

(a) either it is a contract of sale of goods or it is one under or in pursuance of which the possession or ownership of goods passes; and
(b) it is made by parties whose place of business (or, if they have none, habitual residences) are in the territories of different States (the Channel Islands and the Isle of Man being treated for this purpose as different States from the United Kingdom).

(4) A contract falls within subsection (3) above only if either—

(a) the goods in question are, at the time of the conclusion of the contract, in the course of carriage, or will be carried, from the territory of one State to the territory of another; or
(b) the acts constituting the offer and acceptance have been done in the territories of different States; or
(c) the contract provides for the goods to be delivered to the territory of a State other than that within whose territory those acts were done.

Choice of law clauses

27.—(1) Where the law applicable to a contract is the law of any part of the United Kingdom only by choice of the parties (and apart from that choice would be the law of some country outside the United Kingdom) sections 2 to 7 and 16 to 21 of this Act do not operate as part of the law applicable to the contract.

(2) This Act has effect notwithstanding any contract term which applies or purports to apply the law of some country outside the United Kingdom, where (either or both)—

(a) the term appears to the court, or arbitrator or arbiter to have been imposed wholly or mainly for the purpose of enabling the party imposing it to evade the operation of this Act; or
(b) in the making of the contract one of the parties dealt as consumer, and he was then habitually resident in the United Kingdom, and the essential steps necessary for the making of the contract were taken there, whether by him or by others on his behalf.

(3) [Applies to Scotland only.]

Temporary provision for sea carriage of passengers

28.—(1) This section applies to a contract for carriage by sea of a passenger or of a passenger and his luggage where the provisions of the Athens Convention (with or without modification) do not have, in relation to the contract, the force of law in the United Kingdom.

(2) In a case where—

(a) the contract is not made in the United Kingdom, and
(b) neither the place of departure nor the place of destination under it is in the United Kingdom,

a person is not precluded by this Act from excluding or restricting liability for loss or damage, being loss or damage for which the provisions of the Convention would, if they had the force of law in relation to the contract, impose liability on him.

(3) In any other case, the person is not precluded by this Act from excluding or restricting liability for that loss or damage—

(a) in so far as the exclusion or restriction would have been effective in that case had the provisions of the Convention had the force of law in relation to the contract; or
(b) in such circumstances and to such extent as may be prescribed, by reference to a prescribed term of the contract.

(4) For the purposes of subsection (3)(a), the values which shall be taken to be the official values in the United Kingdom of the amounts (expressed in gold francs) by reference to which liability under the provisions of the Convention is limited shall be such amounts in sterling as the Secretary of State may from time to time by order made by statutory instrument specify.

(5) In this section,—

(a) the references to excluding or restricting liability included doing any of those things in relation to the liability which are mentioned in section 13 or section 25(3) and (5); and
(b) "the Athens Convention" means the Athens Convention relating to the Carriage of Passengers and their Luggage by Sea, 1974; and
(c) "prescribed" means prescribed by the Secretary of State by regulations made by statutory instrument;

and a statutory instrument containing the regulations shall be subject to annulment in pursuance of a resolution of either House of Parliament.

Saving for other relevant legislation

29.—(1) Nothing in this Act removes or restricts the effect of, or prevents reliance upon, any contractual provision which—

(a) is authorised or required by the express terms or necessary implication of an enactment; or
(b) being made with a view to compliance with an international agreement to which the United Kingdom is a party, does not operate more restrictively than is contemplated by the agreement.

(2) A contract term is to be taken—

(a) for the purposes of Part I of this Act, as satisfying the requirement of reasonableness; and
(b) [applies to Scotland only].

(3) In this section—

"competent authority" means any court, arbitrator or arbiter, government department or public authority;

"enactment" means any legislation (including subordinate legislation) of the United Kingdom or Northern Ireland and any instrument having effect by virtue of such legislation; and

"statutory" means conferred by an enactment.

Section 30 is *repealed.*

General

Commencement; amendments; repeals

31.—(1) This Act comes into force on February 1, 1978.

(2) Nothing in this Act applies to contracts made before the date on which it comes into force; but subject to this, it applies to liability for any loss or damage which is suffered on or after that date.

(3) The enactments specified in Schedule 3 to this Act are amended as there shown.

(4) The enactments specified in Schedule 4 to this Act are repealed to the extent specified in column 3 of that Schedule.

Citation and extent

32.—(1) This Act may be cited as the Unfair Contract Terms Act 1977.

(2) Part I of this Act extends to England and Wales and to Northern Ireland; but it does not extend to Scotland.

(3) Part II of this Act extends to Scotland only.

(4) This Part of this Act extends to the whole of the United Kingdom.

SCHEDULE 1

SCOPE OF SECTIONS 2 TO 4 AND 7

Section 1(2)

1. Sections 2 to 4 of this Act do not extend to—

(a) any contract of insurance (including a contract to pay an annuity on human life);

(b) any contract so far as it relates to the creation or transfer of an interest in land, or to the termination of such an interest, whether by extinction, merger, surrender, forfeiture or otherwise;

(c) any contract so far as it relates to the creation or transfer of a right or interest in any patent, trade mark, copyright, registered design, technical or commercial information or other intellectual property, or relates to the termination of any such right or interest;

(d) any contract so far as it relates—

  (i) to the formation or dissolution of a company (which means any body corporate or unincorporated association and includes a partnership), or

  (ii) to its constitution or the rights or obligations of its corporators or members;

(e) any contract so far as it relates to the creation or transfer of securities or of any right or interest in securities.

2. Section 2(1) extends to—

(a) any contract of marine salvage or towage;

(b) any charterparty of a ship or hovercraft; and

(c) any contract for the carriage of goods by ship or hovercraft;

by subject to this sections 2 to 4 and 7 do not extend to any such contract except in favour of a person dealing as consumer.

3. Where goods are carried by ship or hovercraft in pursuance of a contract which either—

(a) specifies that as the means of carriage over part of the journey to be covered, or

(b) makes no provision as to the means of carriage and does not exclude that means, then sections 2(2), 3 and 4 do not, except in favour of a person dealing as a consumer, extend to the contract as it operates for and in relation to the carriage of the goods by that means.

4. Section 2(1) and (2) do not extend to a contract of employment, except in favour of the employee.

5. Section 2(1) does not affect the validity of any discharge and indemnity given by a person, on or in connection with an award to him of compensation for pneumoconiosis attributable to employment in the coal industry, in respect of any further claim arising from his contracting that disease.

SCHEDULE 2

"Guidelines" for Application of Reasonableness Test

Section 11(2) and 24(2)

The matters to which regard is to be had in particular for the purposes of sections 6(3), 7(3) and (4), 20 and 21 are any of the following which appear to be relevant—

  (a) the strength of the bargaining positions of the parties to each other, taking into account (among other things) alternative means by which the customer's requirements could have been met;

  (b) whether the customer received an inducement to agree to the term, or in accepting it had an opportunity of entering into a similar contract with other persons, but without having to accept a similar term;

  (c) whether the customer knew or ought reasonably to have known of the existence and extent of the term (having regard, among other things, to any custom of the trade and any previous course of dealing between the parties);

  (d) where the term excludes or restricts any relevant liability if some condition is not complied with, whether it was reasonable at the time of the contract to expect that compliance with that condition would be practicable;

  (e) whether the goods were manufactured, processed or adapted to the special order of the customer.

Schedules 3: (Amendment of Enactments) and 4 (Repeals) are omitted. For discussion of the Act, see above, p. 474.

THE UNFAIR TERMS IN CONSUMER CONTRACTS REGULATIONS 1994

Citation and commencement

1. These Regulations may be cited as the Unfair Terms in Consumer Contracts Regulations 1994 and shall come into force on 1st July 1995.

Interpretation

2.—(1) In these Regulations—

"business" includes a trade or profession and the activities of any government department or local or public authority;

"the Community" means the European Economic Community and the other States in the European Economic Area;

"consumer" means a natural person who, in making a contract to which these Regulations apply, is acting for purposes which are outside his business;

"court" in relation to England and Wales and Northern Ireland means the High Court, and in relation to Scotland, the Court of Session;

"Director" means the Director General of Fair Trading;

"EEA Agreement" means the Agreement on the European Economic Area signed at Oporto on 2 May 1992 as adjusted by the protocol signed at Brussels on 17 March 1993[1];

"member State" shall mean a State which is a contracting party to the EEA Agreement but until the EEA Agreement comes into force in relation to Liechtenstein does not include the State of Liechtenstein;

"seller" means a person who sells goods and who, in making a contract to which these Regulations apply, is acting for purposes relating to his business; and

"supplier" means a person who supplies goods or services and who, in making a contract to which these Regulations apply, is acting for purposes relating to his business.

(2) In the application of these Regulations to Scotland for references to an "injunction" or an "interlocutory injunction" there shall be substituted references to an "interdict" or "interim interdict" respectively.

Terms to which these Regulations apply

3.—(1) Subject to the provisions of Schedule 1, these Regulations apply to any term in a contract concluded between a seller or supplier and a consumer where the said term has not been individually negotiated.

(2) In so far as it is in plain, intelligible language, no assessment shall be made of the fairness of any term which—

(a) defines the main subject matter of the contract, or

---

[1] Protocol 47 and certain Annexes to the EEA Agreement were amended by Decision No. 7/94 of the EEA Joint Committee which came into force on 1 July 1994, (O.J. No. L160, 28.6.1994, p. 1). Council Directive 93/13/EEC was added to Annex XIX to the Agreement by Annex 17 to the said Decision No. 7/94.

(b) concerns the adequacy of the price or remuneration, as against the goods or services sold or supplied.

(3) For the purposes of these Regulations, a term shall always be regarded as not having been individually negotiated where it has been drafted in advance and the consumer has not been able to influence the substance of the term.

(4) Notwithstanding that a specific term or certain aspects of it in a contract has been individually negotiated, these Regulations shall apply to the rest of a contract if an overall assessment of the contract indicates that it is a pre-formulated standard contract.

(5) It shall be for any seller or supplier who claims that a term was individually negotiated to show that it was.

Unfair terms

4.—(1) In these Regulations, subject to paragraphs (2) and (3) below, "unfair term" means any term which contrary to the requirement of good faith causes a significant imbalance in the parties' rights and obligations under the contract to the detriment of the consumer.

(2) An assessment of the unfair nature of a term shall be made taking into account the nature of the goods or services for which the contract was concluded and referring, as at the time of the conclusion of the contract, to all circumstances attending the conclusion of the contract and to all the other terms of the contract or of another contract on which it is dependent.

(3) In determining whether a term satisfies the requirement of good faith, regard shall be had in particular to the matters specified in Schedule 2 to these Regulations.

(4) Schedule 3 to these Regulations contains an indicative and non-exhaustive list of the terms which may be regarded as unfair.

Consequence of inclusion of unfair terms in contracts

5.—(1) An unfair term in a contract concluded with a consumer by a seller of supplier shall not be binding on the consumer.

(2) The contract shall continue to bind the parties if it is capable of continuing in existence without the unfair term.

Construction of written contracts

6. A seller or supplier shall ensure that any written term of a contract is expressed in plain, intelligible language, and if there is doubt about the meaning of a written term, the interpretation most favourable to the consumer shall prevail.

Choice of law clauses

7. These Regulations shall apply notwithstanding any contract term which applies or purports to apply the law of a non member State, if the contract has a close connection with the territory of the member States.

Prevention of continued use of unfair terms

8.—(1) It shall be the duty of the Director to consider any complaint made to him that any contract term drawn up for general use is unfair, unless the complaint appears to the Director to be frivolous or vexatious.

(2) If having considered a complaint about any contract term pursuant to paragraph (1) above the Director considers that the contract term is unfair he may, if he considers it appropriate to do so, bring proceedings for an injunction (in which proceedings he may also apply for an interlocutory injunction) against any person appearing to him to be using or recommending use of such a term in contracts concluded with consumers.

(3) The Director may, if he considers it appropriate to do so, have regard to any undertakings given to him by or on behalf of any person as to the continued use of such a term in contracts concluded with consumers.

(4) The Director shall give reasons for his decision to apply or not to apply, as the case may be, for an injunction in relation to any complaint which these Regulations require him to consider.

(5) The court on an application by the Director may grant an injunction on such terms as it thinks fit.

(6) An injunction may relate not only to use of a particular contract term drawn up for general use but to any similar term, or a term having like effect, used or recommended for use by any party to the proceedings.

(7) The Director may arrange for the dissemination in such form and manner as he considers appropriate of such information and advice concerning the operation of these Regulations as may appear to him to be expedient to give to the public and to all persons likely to be affected by these Regulations.

SCHEDULE 1   Regulation 3(1)

CONTRACTS AND PARTICULAR TERMS EXCLUDED FROM THE SCOPE OF THESE REGULATIONS

These Regulations do not apply to—

    (a) any contract relating to employment;
    (b) any contract relating to succession rights;
    (c) any contract relating to rights under family law;
    (d) any contract relating to the incorporation and organisation of companies or partnerships; and
    (e) any term incorporated in order to comply with or which reflects—

        (i) statutory or regulatory provisions of the United Kingdom; or
        (ii) provisions or principles of international conventions to which the member States or the Community are party.

SCHEDULE 2   Regulation 4(3)

ASSESSMENT OF GOOD FAITH

In making an assessment of good faith, regard shall be had in particular to—

    (a) the strength of the bargaining positions of the parties;
    (b) whether the consumer had an inducement to agree to the term;

(c) whether the goods or services were sold or supplied to the special order of the consumer, and

(d) the extent to which the seller or supplier has dealt fairly and equitably with the consumer.

SCHEDULE 3 Regulation 4(4)

INDICATIVE AND ILLUSTRATIVE LIST OF TERMS WHICH MAY BE REGARDED AS UNFAIR

1. Terms which have the object or effect of—

(a) excluding or limiting the legal liability of a seller or supplier in the event of the death of a consumer or personal injury to the latter resulting from an act or omission of that seller or supplier;

(b) inappropriately excluding or limiting the legal rights of the consumer vis-à-vis the seller or supplier or another party in the event of total or partial non-performance or inadequate performance by the seller or supplier of any of the contractual obligations, including the option of offsetting a debt owed to the seller or supplier against any claim which the consumer may have against him;

(c) making an agreement binding on the consumer whereas provision of services by the seller or supplier is subject to a condition whose realisation depends on his own will alone;

(d) permitting the seller or supplier to retain sums paid by the consumer where the latter decides not to conclude or perform the contract, without providing for the consumer to receive compensation of an equivalent amount from the seller or supplier where the latter is the party cancelling the contract;

(e) requiring any consumer who fails to fulfil his obligation to pay a disproportionately high sum in compensation;

(f) authorising the seller or supplier to dissolve the contract on a discretionary basis where the same facility is not granted to the consumer, or permitting the seller or supplier to retain the sums paid for services not yet supplied by him where it is the seller or supplier himself who dissolves the contract;

(g) enabling the seller or supplier to terminate a contract of indeterminate duration without reasonable notice except where there are serious grounds for doing so;

(h) automatically extending a contract of fixed duration where the consumer does not indicate otherwise, when the deadline fixed for the consumer to express this desire not to extend the contract is unreasonably early;

(i) irrevocably binding the consumer to terms with which he had no real opportunity of becoming acquainted before the conclusion of the contract;

(j) enabling the seller or supplier to alter the terms of the contract unilaterally without a valid reason which is specified in the contract;

(k) enabling the seller or supplier to alter unilaterally without a valid reason any characteristics of the product or service to be provided;

(l) providing for the price of goods to be determined at the time of delivery or allowing a seller of goods or supplier of services to increase their price without in both cases giving the consumer the corresponding right to cancel the contract if the final price is too high in relation to the price agreed when the contract was concluded;

(m) giving the seller or supplier the right to determine whether the goods or services supplied are in conformity with the contract, or giving him the exclusive right to interpret any term of the contract;

(n) limiting the seller's or supplier's obligation to respect commitments undertaken by his agents or making his commitments subject to compliance with a particular formality;

(o) obliging the consumer to fulfil all his obligations where the seller or supplier does not perform his;

(p) giving the seller or supplier the possibility of transferring his rights and obligations under the contract, where this may serve to reduce the guarantees for the consumer, without the latter's agreement;

(q) excluding or hindering the consumer's right to take legal action or exercise any other legal remedy, particularly by requiring the consumer to take disputes exclusively to arbitration not covered by legal provisions, unduly restricting the evidence available to him or imposing on him a burden of proof which, according to the applicable law, should lie with another party to the contract.

2. Scope of subparagraphs 1(g), (j) and (l)

(a) Subparagraph 1(g) is without hindrance to terms by which a supplier of financial services reserves the right to terminate unilaterally a contract of indeterminate duration without notice where there is a valid reason, provided that the supplier is required to inform the other contracting party or parties thereof immediately.

(b) Subparagraph 1(j) is without hindrance to terms under which a supplier of financial services reserves the right to alter the rate of interest payable by the consumer or due to the latter, or the amount of other charges for financial services without notice where there is a valid reason, provided that the supplier is required to inform the other contracting party or parties thereof at the earliest opportunity and that the latter are free to dissolve the contract immediately. Subparagraph 1(j) is also without hindrance to terms under which a seller or supplier reserves the right to alter unilaterally the conditions of a contract of indeterminate duration, provided that he is required to inform the consumer with reasonable notice and that the consumer is free to dissolve the contract.

(c) Subparagraphs 1(g), (j) and (l) do not apply to:

— transactions in transferable securities, financial instruments and other products or services where the price is linked to fluctuations in a stock exchange quotation or index or a financial market rate that the seller or supplier does not control;

— contracts for the purchase or sale of foreign currency, traveller's cheques or international money orders denominated in foreign currency;

(d) Subparagraph 1(1) is without hindrance to price indexation clauses, where lawful, provided that the method by which prices vary is explicitly described.

INDEX

721